2018 NHL DRAFT BLACK BOOK
PROSPECT SCOUTING REPORTS & DRAFT RANKINGS

by HockeyProspect.com

The Hockey Press

ISBN-13: 978-0991677597

ISBN-10: 0991677595

© copyright 2018

2018 NHL DRAFT RANKINGS		10
2018 NHL DRAFT PROSPECTS		16
ADAMEK, JAKUB	17	
ADDISON, CADEN	17	
ALEXEYEV, ALEXANDER	18	
ALEXANDER, JETT	19	
ALMEIDA, JUSTIN	19	
ALMQUIST, BEN	20	
ANDERSSON, AXEL	20	
ANNUNEN, JUSTUS	21	
BABINTSEV, GLEB	21	
BACK, OSKAR	22	
BAHL, KEVIN	23	
BARTEAUX, DAWSON	24	
BARTON, SETH	24	
BEAUDIN, NICOLAS	25	
BEAUDOIN, TOMMY	26	
BENOIT, SIMON	27	
BERGERON, JUSTIN	27	
BERGGREN, JONATAN	28	
BERNARD-DOCKER, JACOB	28	
BERNARD, XAVIER	29	
BERNI, TIM	30	
BIBEAU, FELIX	31	
BINNER, ALEXIS	31	
BITTEN, SAMUEL	32	
BODAK, MARTIN	32	
BOKK, DOMINIK	33	
BOQVIST, ADAM	34	
BOUCHARD, EVAN	35	
BOUCHARD, XAVIER	36	
BOUDRIAS, SHAWN	37	
BOUTHILLIER, ZACHARY	38	
BRENNAN, TED	38	
BUCEK, SAMUEL	38	
BULYCH, KALEB	39	
BURZAN, LUKA	39	
BUSBY, DENNIS	40	
CALLAHAN, MICHAEL	40	
CHISHOLM, DECLAN	41	
CHYZOWSKI, RYAN	42	
CLARK, KODY	42	
COLINA, LLIJAH	43	
COPELAND, BEN	44	
CORCORAN, CONNOR	44	
COSKEY, COLE	45	
COTE-CAZENAVE, TRISTAN	45	
COTTER, PAUL	46	
COXHEAD, ANDREW	47	
DAHLIN, RASMUS	47	
DALEY, CAIDEN	48	
DAMIANI, RILEY	48	
DEL GAIZO, MARC	49	
DELLANDREA, TY	50	
DEMIN, STANISLAV	51	
DENISENKO, GRIGORI	52	
DER-ARGUCHINTSEV, SEMYON	54	
DERIDDER, DREW	54	
DESRUISSEAUX, CEDRIC	55	
DILIBERATORE, PETER	56	
DOBSON, NOAH	56	
DOSTAL, LUKAS	57	
DOUGLAS, CURTIS	58	
DUCHARME, JUSTIN	59	
DRURY, JACK	59	
DROZDOV, IVAN	60	
DUDAS, AIDAN	61	
DUNKLEY, NATHAN	61	
DURNY, ROMAN	62	
DURZI, SEAN	62	
DVORAK, DANIEL	63	
EGGENBERGER, NANDO	64	
ELEMENT, SHAWN	64	
ELIASSON, JESPER	65	
ELIIS, MAX	65	
EMBERSON, TY	66	
EMOND, ZACHARY	67	
ENNIS, WILLIAM	67	
ERIKSSON, ALBIN	68	
ERSSON, SAMUEL	69	
ETHIER, THOMAS	70	
EVERETT, CALEB	70	
FAGEMO, SAMUEL	71	
FARABEE, JOEL	71	
FEHERVARY, MARTIN	72	
FLORCHUK, ERIC	73	
FOCHT, CARSON	74	
FONSTAD, COLE	74	
FORTIER, GABRIEL	75	
FOUDY, LIAM	75	
GAJARSKY, ADAM	76	
GALENYUK, DANILA	77	
GIBSON, MITCHELL	78	
GILES, PATRICK	78	
GINNELL, BRAD	79	
GINNING, ADAM	80	
GIROUX, DAMIEN	81	
GOGOLEV, PAVEL	81	
GOLOD, MAXIM	82	
GOLDOWSKI, JAKE	83	
GORNIAK, JACK	84	
GRANBERG, FREDRIK	84	
GRAVEL, ALEXIS	85	
GREEN, ALEX	85	
GRONDIN, MAXIM	86	
GROSS, NICO	86	
GROULX, BENOIT-OLIVIER	87	
GRUDEN, JONATHAN	88	
GUAY, NICOLAS	89	
GUSTAFSSON, DAVID	89	
HAIN, GAVIN	90	
HAKKARAINEN, MIKAEL	90	
HALL, CURTIS	91	
HALLANDER, FILIP	91	
HALME, ALEKSI	92	
HALVERSON, JORDON	93	
HARRIS, JORDAN	93	
HARSCH, REECE	94	
HARTJE, CHASE	94	
HARVEY, SAMUEL	95	
HARVEY-PINARD, RAFAEL	95	
HAYTON, BARRETT	96	
HELGESON, BEN	97	
HENMAN, LUKE	97	
HILLIS, CAMERON	98	
HOELSCHER, MITCHELL	99	
HOFER, JOEL	99	
HOLLOWELL, MAC	100	
HOLMES, HUNTER	101	
HOUDE, SAMUEL	102	
HRABIK, KRYSTOF	102	
HRENAK, DAVID	103	
HREHORCAK, PATRIK	103	
HUGHES, QUINTIN	104	
HUGHES, RILEY	106	
HUTSKO, LOGAN	106	
INGHAM, JACOB	107	
ISAYEV, DANIIL	107	
ISKHAKOV, RUSLAN	108	
IVAN, MICHAL	109	
JAKOBSSON, CARL	109	
JANICKE, TREVOR	109	
JENIK, JAN	110	
JENKINS, BLADE	111	
JENSEN, JACK	112	
JOHANSSON, FILIP	113	
JOHNSON, ISAAC	113	
KAID, OLIVER	114	
KALINICHENKO, ROMAN	114	
KAMBEITZ, DINO	115	
KANNOK-LEIPERT, ALEX	115	
KARKI, KEEGAN	115	
KARLSSON, LINUS	116	
KAUT, MARTIN	117	
KEANE, JOEY	118	
KELLENBERGER, MATTHEW	119	
KEMP, BRETT	119	
KESSELRING, MICHAEL	120	
KETOLA, JUUSO	120	
KHODORENKO, PATRICK	120	
KHOVANOV, ALEXANDER	121	
KIEFIUK, CALEN	122	
KILLINEN, LENNI	122	
KINDREE, LIAM	122	

KIRK, LIAM	123	MCGOVERN, DUNCAN	160	REINHARDT, COLE	194
KIZIMOV, SEMYON	124	MCISAAC, JARED	160	RIPPON, MERRICK	194
KOEPKE, COLE	124	MCKENNA, JEREMY	161	ROBERTS, CONNOR	195
KONDELIK, JACHYM	125	MCLAUGHLIN, BLAKE	161	ROBERTSON, CARTER	196
KOOY, JORDAN	126	MCLEOD, RYAN	162	RODRIGUE, OLIVIER	196
KOTKANIEMI, JESPERI	126	MCLEOD, WYATT	163	ROMAN, MILOS	197
KOTKOV, VLADISLAV	127	MCMASTER< ADAM	164	ROMANOV, ALEXANDER	198
KOUMONTZIS, DEMETRIOS	128	MCSHANE, ALLAN	164	RTISHCHEV, NIKITA	198
KOVALENKO, NIKOLAI	129	MCQUAID, CHRIS	165	SAIGEON, BRANDON	199
KOWALCZYK, DANIEL	130	MERKLEY, RYAN	165	SALDA, RADIM	200
KRAL, FILIP	130	MIFTAKHOV, AMIR	166	SALMELA, SANTERI	200
KRAVTSOV, VITALI	131	MILLER, K'ANDRE	167	SAMUELSSON, ADAM	201
KRAWS, BEN	132	MINULIN, ARTYOM	169	SAMUELSSON, MATTIAS	202
KOPACEK, VOJTECH	132	MOE, JARED	169	SANDIN, RASMUS	202
KRYGIER, CHRISTIAN	133	MONCADA, LUKE	170	SAVAGE, RYAN	203
KRYGIER, COLE	134	MOROZOV, IVAN	170	SCHMID, AKIRA	204
KUCHARSKI, JACOB	135	MOSKAL, BILLY	171	SCHMIDT, COLIN	205
KUPARI, RASMUS	135	NASSEN, LINUS	172	SEMIK, JACOB	205
KURASHEV, PHILIPP	137	NELSON, JAXON	172	SEMYKIN, DMITRI	206
KUROVSKY, DANIEL	137	NEVASAARI, ARTTU	173	SEPPALA, PEETRO	206
KVASNICA, MICHAL	138	NIELSEN, TRISTEN	173	SHAFIGULLIN, BULAT	206
LAFERRIERE, MATHIAS	139	NIZHNIKOV, KIRILL	174	SHARANGOVICH, YEGOR	207
LALONDE, OWEN	139	NOEL, SERRON	174	SHEN, PAVEL	208
LAMASTER, LUKE	140	NORDGREN, NIKLAS	175	SKAREK, JAKUB	208
LAPOINTE, PHILIPPE	141	NOVAK, JAKOV	176	SMITH, NATHAN	210
LAUKO, JAKUB	141	NURSE, ISSAC	176	SMITH, NATHANSMITH, TY	210
LEBEDEFF, DANIEL	142	NYMAN, LINUS	176	SNELL, MASON	212
LEPPARD, JACKSON	142	O'BRIEN, JAY	177	SOKOLOV, EGOR	212
LEUFVENIUS, HUGO	143	O'REILLY, RYAN	178	ST. IVANY, JACK	213
LEVIN, DAVID	143	OKSANEN, EMIL	179	ST-LAURENT, EDOUARD	213
LEWANDOWSKI, MITCHELL	144	OKULIAR, OLIVER	179	STASTNEY, SPENCER	214
LILJA, DAVID	145	OLOFSSON, JACOB	179	STEEVES, ALEXANDER	214
LILLIBRIDGE, GRAHAM	145	ONYEBUCHI, MONTANA	181	STOTTS, RILEY	215
LINDBOM, OLOF	146	PATERSON, JOSH	181	STRATIS, PETER	215
LISKA, ADAM	146	PACHAL, BRAYDEN	181	STRUTHERS, MATTHEW	216
LOHEIT, LUKE	147	PADDOCK, MAX	182	STUART, BRODI	216
LUDVIG, JOHN	147	PECKFORD, RYAN	182	SUTTER, RILEY	217
LUNDESTROM, ISAC	148	PEKAR, MATEJ	182	SVECHNIKOV, ANDREI	218
LUNDKVIST, NILS	149	PERBIX, JACKSON	183	TANUS, KRISTIAN	219
MACDONALD, ANDERSON	150	PERUNOVICH, SCOTT	184	TEASDALE, JOEL	219
MACDOUGALL, MATTHEW	150	PETTERSEN, MATHIAS EMILIO	185	TENDECK, DAVID	219
MACPHERSON, JUSTIN	151	PIVONKA, JACOB	186	THOMAS, AKIL	220
MADDEN, TYLER	151	PLASEK, KAREL	186	TKACHUK, BRADY	221
MALIK, ZACK	152	POPOWICH, TYLER	187	TOPPING, KYLE	223
MALYSHEV, ANTON	153	PORTILLO, ERIK	187	TUCKER, TYLER	223
MANDERVILLE, ETHAN	153	POSPISIL, MARTIN	188	TYCHONICK, JONATHON	224
MANDOLESE, KEVIN	154	PROPP, CHRISTIAN	189	UTUNEN, TONI	225
MARCHENKO, KIRILL	154	PROSVETOV, IVAN	189	VALLATI, GIOVANNI	225
MCBAIN, JACK	156	PURPURA, VINCENT	190	VELENO, JOSEPH	226
MCCABE, DEVIN	157	RAGNARSSON, JACOB	191	VORLICKY, MICHAEL	227
MCCORMICK, ADAM	157	RANDL, JACK	191	WAHLSTROM, OLIVER	228
McCOURT, RILEY	158	RANDKLEY, CARTER	192	WALKER, ISAAC	229
MCDONALD, KODY	158	RANTA, SAMPO	192	WARNERT, BLAINE	229
MCDONOUGH, AIDAN	159	REGULA, ALEC	193	WASSERMAN, JACOB	230
MCFAUL, DUSTYN	159	REICHEL, KRISTIAN	194	WEISS, TYLER	230

WERNBLOM, LUKAS	231	DACH, KIRBY	260	MICHEL, JEREMY	280
WESTFALT, MARCUS	231	D'AMICO, DANIEL	260	MIRONOV, ILYA	281
WILDE, BODE	232	DAWS, NICOLAS	260	MISYUL, DANIIL	281
WISE, JAKE	233	DENIS, GABRIEL	261	MORGAN, CODY	282
WONG, AUSTIN	234	DESROCHES, OLIVIER	261	MRAZIK, MICHAL	282
WOO, JETT	235	DION, BENJAMIN	262	MURRAY, BLAKE	282
WOUTERS, CHASE	236	DONOVAN, RYDER	262	MUTALA, SASHA	283
WYLIE, WYATTE	236	DOROFEYEV, PAVEL	262	MYLLYLA, WILJAMI	283
YERYOMENKO, VLADISLAV	237	ELLIS, COLTEN	263	NAJMAN, ADAM	283
YLONEN, JESSE	237	FOOTE, NOLAN	263	NEWHOOK, ALEX	284
ZABRANSKY, LIBOR	238	GAUTHIER, TAYLOR	264	NIKKANEN, HENRI	284
ZADINA, FILIP	238	GUÉNETTE, MAXENCE	264	NIKOLAYEV, ILYA	284
ZAMULA, EGOR	239	GREWE, ALBIN	264	NUSSBAUMER, VALENTIN	285
ZAVGORODNY, DMITRI	240	GUSKOV, MATVEI	265	PAQUETTE, TYLER	285
ZHABREYEV, ALEXANDER	241	GUTIK, DANIIL	265	PARENT, XAVIER	286
ZHILYAKOV, BOGDAN	241	GUZDA, MACK	266	PEACH, BAILEY	286
ZHURAVLYOV, DANILA	242	HALE, JAKE	266	PELLETIER, JAKOB	287
ZUMMACK. ELI	243	HARLEY, THOMAS	266	PELLETIER, THOMAS	287
2019 NHL DRAFT RANKINGS	**244**	HEINOLA, VILLE	267	PENMAN, DUNCAN	287
2019 NHL DRAFT PROSPECTS	**246**	HOGLANDER, NILS	267	PERROTT, ANDREW	288
		HOLMSTROM, SIMON	267	PIIROINEN, KARI	288
AALTONEN, LEEVI	247	HONKA, ANTTONI	268	PODKOLZIN, VASILI	289
ABRAMOV, MIKHAIL	247	HUGHES, JACK	268	PORCO, NICHOLAS	289
AFANASYEV, YEGOR	247	HUGO-HAS, MARTIN	269	POULIN, SAMUEL	290
ALEXANDER, JACSON	248	INNIS, CHRISTOPHER	269	PRIKRYL, FILIP	290
ALEXANDROV, NIKITA	248	JONCAS, ALEXANDRE	270	PRIMEAU, MASON	290
ALLEPOT, ANTHONY	248	KAKKO, KAAPO	270	REES, JAMIESON	291
ANTROPOV, DANIL	249	KALMIKOV, BROOKLYN	271	RIZZO, MASSIMO	291
BARLAGE, LOGAN	249	KALIYEV, ARTHUR	271	ROBERTSON, MATTHEW	291
BEAUCAGE, ALEX	250	KEPPEN, ETHAN	271	ROBERTSON, NICK	292
BEECHER, JOHN	250	KNIGHT, SPENCER	272	ROSS, LIAM	292
BELLAMY, JAXON	251	KNYAZEV, ARTEMI	272	RUSSELL, MITCHELL	293
BERNARD, JACOB	251	KOKKONEN, MIKKO	272	SAARELA, ANTTI	293
BERTUZZI, TAG	251	KORCZAK, KAEDAN	273	SAFONOV, ILYA	293
BIZIER, MATHIEU	252	KOSTER, MIKE	273	SARTAKOV, VLADIMIR	294
BJERSELIUS, OSCAR	252	KREBS, PEYTON	274	SCHWINDT, COLE	294
BJORNFOT, TOBIAS	252	LADD, GRAYSON	274	SEIDER, MORITZ	294
BLAISDELL, HARRISON	253	LANG, MARTIN	274	SERDYUK, YEGOR	295
BOLDY, MATT	253	LAVELLE, SHANE	275	SHESHIN, DMITRI	295
BREWER, MITCHELL	254	LAVOIE, RAPHAEL	275	SIMONEAU, XAVIER	295
BRINK, BOBBY	254	LEGARÉ, NATHAN	276	SODERBLOM, ELMER	296
BRINKMAN, BEN	254	LEGUERRIER, JACOB	276	SODERSTROM, VICTOR	296
BROBERG, PHILIP	255	LEMIEUX, JONATHAN	276	SOJKA, DOMINIK	297
BROWNE, ETHAN	255	LIKHACHYOV, YAROSLAV	277	SPIRIDONOV, YEGOR	297
BUDGELL, BRETT	255	MAIER, NOLAN	277	SPROULE, EMMETT	297
BYRAM, BOWEN	256	MANCINELLI, MICHAEL	277	STAIOS, NATHAN	298
CAJKOVIC, MAXIM	256	MARCOTTY, FELIX-ANTOINE	278	STARIKOV, LEV	298
CAMPBELL, ISIAH	257	MARTIN, JEREMY	278	STEVENSON, KEEGAN	298
CARROLL, JOE	257	MASTROSIMONE, ROBERT	278	STRONDALA, VOJTECH	299
CAULFIELD, JUDD	257	MCCARTHY, CASE	279	SUZUKI, RYAN	299
CAUFIELD, COLE	258	MACKAY, COLE	279	SWANKLER, AUSTEN	299
CAVALLIN, LUKE	258	MCMICHAEL, CONNOR	279	TEPLY, MICHAL	300
CONSTANTINOU, BILLY	259	MERISIER-ORTIZ, CHRISTOPHER	280	THOMSON, LASSI	300
COSTMAR, ARVID	259			THRUN, HENRY	300
COZENS, DYLAN	259	MEYER, BRADY	280	TOMAN, MATEJ	301

Name	Page
TOMASINO, PHILLIP	301
TURAN, OLIVER	301
TURCOTTE, ALEX	302
TYUVILIN, DMITRI	302
VALENTI, YANNIK	302
VLASIC, ALEX	303
VUKOJEVIC, MICHAEL	303
VYLETELKA, SAMUEL	304
WARREN, MARSHALL	304
WASHKURAK, KEEAN	304
WILLIAMS, JOSH	305
YORK, CAM	305
ZEGRAS, TREVOR	305

2020 NHL DRAFT PROSPECTS 307

Name	Page
AUSTIN, TYE	308
BARRON, JUSTIN	308
BEAUDOIN, CHARLES	309
BELANGER, ALEC	309
BENIERS, MATT	309
BERARD, BRETT	310
JÉRÉMIE BIAKABUTUKA	310
BIONDI, BLAKE	310
BOLTMANN, JAKE	310
BORDELEAU, THOMAS	311
BOURQUE, MAVRIK	311
BUTLER, BLAKE	312
BUTLER, CAMERON	312
BYFIELD, QUINTON	312
CARDWELL, ETHAN	313
COE, BRANDON	313
COLLINS, TY	314
COMMESSO, DREW	314
CORMIER, LUKAS	314
COULOMBE, ANTOINE	315
CRANLEY, WILL	315
CUYLLE, WILLIAM	315
CZERNECKIANAIR, VICTOR	316
DAVID, ALEXANDRE	316
DESNOYERS, ELLIOT	316
DESROCHES, CHARLIE	317
DROVER, ALEX	317
DRYSDALE, JAMIE	317
DUFOUR, WILLIAM	318
EVANGELISTA, LUKE	318
FOUDY, JEAN-LUC	319
FOWLER, HAYDEN	319
FRANCIS, RYAN	320
GALLATIN, OWEN	320
GUAY, PATRICK	320
GUSHCHIN, DANIL	321
HALLIDAY, STEPHEN	321
HARDIE, JAMES	322
HOLTZ, ALEXANDER	322
KAMMERER, COLTON	323
KEANE, GERARD	323
KINGSBURY-FOURNIER, NICOLAS	323
KLEVEN, TYLER	324
LAFRENIÈRE, ALEXIS	324
LANGDON, ISAAC	325
LAPIERRE, HENDRIX	325
LAVALLÉE, CHARLES-ANTOINE	325
LAWRENCE, JOSH	326
LESSARD, MARSHALL	326
LUNDELL, ANTON	327
MALIK, NICK	327
MCDONALD, KYLE	327
MERCER, DAWSON	328
MERCURI, LUCAS	328
MOORE, LLEYTON	328
MORRISON, LOGAN	329
MURRAY, JAKE	329
O'ROURKE, RYAN	330
PANWAR, SAHIL	330
PERFETTI, COLE	331
PETERS, CAMERON	331
PETERSON, DYLAN	331
PIERCEY, RILEY	332
POIRIER, JÉRÉMIE	332
PORTOKALIS, WILLIAM	333
PROVOST, WILLIAM	333
PRUETER, AIDAN	333
RATZLAFF, JAKE	334
RAYMOND, LUCAS	334
RENWICK, MICHAEL	334
ROBINSON, DYLAN	335
ROBINSON, DYLAN	335
ROCHETTE, THÉO	336
ROODE, BENJAMIN	336
ROSSI, MARCO	336
ROY, PIER-OLIVIER	336
SCHLUETING, PACEY	337
SEBRANGO, DONOVAN	337
SEED, NOLAN	338
STRANGES, ANTONIO	338
TERRY, ZACK	339
THOMPSON, JACK	339
TOLNAI, CAMERON	339
TULLIO, TYLER	340
TUSSEY, NOAH	340
VALADE, REID	341
VIERLING, EVAN	341
VILLENEUVE, WILLIAM	342
WILLIAMS, JACK	342
WOOLLEY, MARK	342
WONG, NICK	343
YOUNG, DAVIS	343

GAME REPORTS 345

CREDITS 549

2018 NHL DRAFT RANKINGS

#	PLAYER	TEAM	LEAGUE	BIRTH	HEIGHT	WEIGHT	POS
1	DAHLIN, RASMUS	FROLUNDA	SWEDEN	13-Apr-2000	6' 2.8"	185 lbs *	D
2	SVECHNIKOV, ANDREI	BARRIE	OHL	26-Mar-2000	6' 2.0"	192 lbs *	RW
3	TKACHUK, BRADY	BOSTON UNIVERSITY	H-EAST	16-Sep-1999	6' 3.0"	192 lbs *	LW
4	ZADINA, FILIP	HALIFAX	QMJHL	27-Nov-1999	6' 0.3"	197 lbs *	RW
5	DOBSON, NOAH	ACADIE-BATHURST	QMJHL	07-Jan-2000	6' 3.0"	177 lbs *	D
6	KRAVTSOV, VITALI	CHELYABINSK	RUSSIA	23-Dec-1999	6' 2.8"	184 lbs *	RW
7	WAHLSTROM, OLIVER	USA U-18	NTDP	13-Jun-2000	6' 1.3"	208 lbs *	RW
8	KOTKANIEMI, JESPERI	ASSAT	FINLAND	06-Jul-2000	6' 2.3"	182 lbs *	C
9	HUGHES, QUINTIN	MICHIGAN	BIG10	14-Oct-1999	5' 9.8"	173 lbs *	D
10	BOUCHARD, EVAN	LONDON	OHL	20-Oct-1999	6' 2.0"	196 lbs *	D
11	BOQVIST, ADAM	BRYNAS JR.	SWEDEN-JR.	15-Aug-2000	5' 11.5"	165 lbs *	D
12	FARABEE, JOEL	USA U-18	NTDP	25-Feb-2000	6' 0.0"	162 lbs *	LW
13	BOKK, DOMINIK	VAXJO JR.	SWEDEN-JR.	03-Feb-2000	6' 1.0"	176 lbs *	LW
14	KAUT, MARTIN	PARDUBICE	CZREP	02-Oct-1999	6' 1.5"	176 lbs	RW
15	DENISENKO, GRIGORI	YAROSLAVL 2	RUSSIA-JR.	24-Jun-2000	5' 10.8"	172 lbs *	LW
16	LUNDKVIST, NILS	LULEA	SHL	27-Jul-2000	5' 11.3"	172 lbs *	D
17	SMITH, TY	SPOKANE	WHL	24-Mar-2000	5' 10.8"	176 lbs *	D
18	HAYTON, BARRETT	SAULT STE. MARIE	OHL	09-Jun-2000	6' 1.3"	190 lbs *	C
19	KUPARI, RASMUS	KARPAT	FINLAND	15-Mar-2000	6' 1.5"	189 lbs *	C
20	MILLER, K'ANDRE	USA U-18	NTDP	21-Jan-2000	6' 3.3"	199 lbs *	D
21	NOEL, SERRON	OSHAWA	OHL	08-Aug-2000	6' 5.0"	204 lbs *	RW
22	LUNDESTROM, ISAC	LULEA	SWEDEN	06-Nov-1999	6' 0.3"	183 lbs *	C
23	ALEXEYEV, ALEXANDER	RED DEER	WHL	15-Nov-1999	6' 3.8"	196 lbs *	D
24	O'BRIEN, JAY	THAYER ACADEMY	HIGH-MA	04-Nov-1999	5' 10.8"	176 lbs *	C
25	BEAUDIN, NICOLAS	DRUMMONDVILLE	QMJHL	09-Oct-1999	5' 10.8"	172 lbs *	D
26	MARCHENKO, KIRILL	KHANTY-MANSIYSK 2	RUSSIA-JR.	21-Jul-2000	6' 3.0"	187 lbs	RW
27	BERGGREN, JONATAN	SKELLEFTEA JR.	SWEDEN-JR.	16-Jul-2000	5' 10.0"	181 lbs	RW
28	ERIKSSON, ALBIN	SKELLEFTEA JR.	SWEDEN-JR.	20-Jul-2000	6' 4.25"	207 lbs	RW
29	DELLANDREA, TY	FLINT	OHL	21-Jul-2000	6' 0.3"	184 lbs *	C
30	SANDIN, RASMUS	SAULT STE. MARIE	OHL	07-Mar-2000	5' 11.0"	186 lbs *	D
31	WILDE, BODE	USA U-18	NTDP	24-Jan-2000	6' 2.5"	198 lbs *	D
32	THOMAS, AKIL	NIAGARA	OHL	02-Jan-2000	5' 11.3"	177 lbs *	C
33	HALLANDER, FILIP	TIMRA	SWEDEN-2	29-Jun-2000	6' 1.8"	188 lbs *	C
34	OLOFSSON, JACOB	TIMRA	SWEDEN-2	08-Feb-2000	6' 2.5"	189 lbs *	C
35	YLONEN, JESSE	ESPOO	FINLAND-2	03-Oct-1999	6' 0.0"	167 lbs	RW
36	TYCHONICK, JONATHON	PENTICTON	BCHL	03-Mar-2000	5' 11.5"	177 lbs *	D
37	VELENO, JOSEPH	DRUMMONDVILLE	QMJHL	13-Jan-2000	6' 1.3"	191 lbs *	C
38	BERNARD-DOCKER, JACOB	OKOTOKS	AJHL	30-Jun-2000	6' 0.3"	187 lbs *	D
39	SAMUELSSON, MATTIAS	USA U-18	NTDP	14-Mar-2000	6' 4.0"	218 lbs *	D
40	WISE, JAKE	USA U-18	NTDP	28-Feb-2000	5' 10.0"	195 lbs *	C
41	ADDISON, CALEN	LETHBRIDGE	WHL	11-Apr-2000	5' 10.0"	178 lbs *	D
42	BAHL, KEVIN	OTTAWA	OHL	27-Jun-2000	6' 6.3"	216 lbs *	D
43	WOO, JETT	MOOSE JAW	WHL	27-Jul-2000	6' 0.0"	200 lbs *	D
44	MOROZOV, IVAN	KHANTY-MANSIYSK 2	RUSSIA-JR.	05-May-2000	6' 1.0"	178 lbs	C
45	MCISAAC, JARED	HALIFAX	QMJHL	27-Mar-2000	6' 1.0"	189 lbs *	D
46	MCLEOD, RYAN	MISSISSAUGA	OHL	21-Sep-1999	6' 2.3"	206 lbs *	C
47	LAUKO, JAKUB	CHOMUTOV	CZREP	28-Mar-2000	6' 0.0"	179 lbs *	C
48	NORDGREN, NIKLAS	HIFK JR.	FINLAND-JR.	04-May-2000	5' 9.0"	169 lbs	RW
49	GINNING, ADAM	LINKOPING	SWEDEN	13-Jan-2000	6' 4.0"	206 lbs *	D
50	MCBAIN, JACK	TORONTO JC	OJHL	06-Jan-2000	6' 3.3"	201 lbs *	C
51	FOUDY, LIAM	LONDON	OHL	04-Feb-2000	6' 0.0"	174 lbs *	C
52	DRURY, JACK	WATERLOO	USHL	03-Feb-2000	5' 11.0"	174 lbs *	C
53	SKAREK, JAKUB	JIHLAVA	CZREP	10-Nov-1999	6' 3.0"	192 lbs *	G
54	RODRIGUE, OLIVIER	DRUMMONDVILLE	QMJHL	06-Jul-2000	6' 1.0"	156 lbs *	G

#	Name	Team	League	DOB	Height	Weight	Pos
55	JOHANSSON, FILIP	LEKSAND JR.	SWEDEN-JR.	23-Mar-2000	6' 0.8"	176 lbs *	D
56	SHAFIGULLIN, BULAT	REAKTOR	RUSSIA-JR.	29-Dec-99	6' 1.0"	163 lbs	C
57	ISKHAKOV, RUSLAN	CSKA 2	RUSSIA-JR.	22-Jul-2000	5' 8.0"	152 lbs	C
58	ANDERSSON, AXEL	DJURGARDEN JR.	SWEDEN-JR.	10-Feb-2000	5' 11.75"	178 lbs	D
59	BACK, OSKAR	FARJESTAD JR.	SWEDEN-JR.	12-Mar-2000	6' 3.0"	204 lbs *	C
60	FEHERVARY, MARTIN	OSKARSHAMN	SWEDEN-2	06-Oct-1999	6' 1.8"	194 lbs*	D
61	REGULA, ALEC	LONDON	OHL	06-Aug-2000	6' 3.5"	203 lbs *	D
62	CLARK, KODY	OTTAWA	OHL	13-Oct-1999	6' 1.0"	179 lbs *	RW
63	PROSVETOV, IVAN	YOUNGSTOWN	USHL	05-Mar-1999	6' 4.5"	175 lbs	G
64	JENIK, JAN	BENATKY N. J.	CZREP-2	15-Sep-2000	6' 1.3"	171 lbs *	RW
65	GROSS, NICO	OSHAWA	OHL	26-Jan-2000	6' 0.8"	185 lbs *	D
66	KOVALENKO, NIKOLAI	YAROSLAVL 2	RUSSIA-JR.	17-Oct-1999	5' 10.0"	174 lbs	RW
67	FORTIER, GABRIEL	BAIE-COMEAU	QMJHL	06-Feb-2000	5' 10.0"	170 lbs	LW
68	OKULIAR, OLIVER	TRENCIN JR.	SLOVAKIA-JR.	24-May-2000	6' 1.0"	191 lbs	LW
69	GROULX, BENOIT-OLIVIER	HALIFAX	QMJHL	06-Feb-2000	6' 1.0"	193 lbs *	C
70	MERKLEY, RYAN	GUELPH	OHL	14-Aug-2000	5' 11.3"	168 lbs *	D
71	ROMAN, MILOS	VANCOUVER	WHL	06-Nov-1999	5' 11.8"	196 lbs *	C
72	GRUDEN, JONATHAN	USA U-18	NTDP	04-May-2000	5' 11.8"	169 lbs *	C
73	STASTNEY, SPENCER	USA U-18	NTDP	04-Jan-2000	5' 10.0"	180 lbs	D
74	GREEN, ALEX	CORNELL	NCAA	18-Jun-1998	6' 2.0"	188 lbs	D
75	DEMIN, STANISLAV	WENATCHEE	BCHL	04-Apr-2000	6' 1.5"	190 lbs	D
76	RANTA, SAMPO	SIOUX CITY	USHL	31-May-2000	6' 1.5"	199 lbs *	RW
77	ZHURAVLYOV, DANILA	IRBIS KAZAN	RUSSIA-JR.	08-Apr-2000	6' 0.0"	163 lbs	D
78	SUTTER, RILEY	EVERETT	WHL	25-Oct-1999	6' 3.0"	203 lbs *	RW
79	KURASHEV, PHILIPP	QUEBEC	QMJHL	12-Oct-1999	5' 11.8"	190 lbs *	C
80	BOUCHARD, XAVIER	BAIE-COMEAU	QMJHL	28-Feb-2000	6' 3.5"	190 lbs *	D
81	HOELSCHER, MITCHELL	OTTAWA	OHL	27-Jan-2000	5' 11.0"	166 lbs *	C
82	MADDEN, TYLER	TRI-CITY	USHL	09-Nov-1999	5' 10.8"	150 lbs *	C
83	PERUNOVICH, SCOTT	MINNESOTA-DULUTH	NCHC	18-Aug-1998	5' 9.0"	164 lbs	D
84	EMOND, ZACHARY	ROUYN-NORANDA	QMJHL	20-Jun-2000	6' 3.0"	165 lbs	G
85	MASCHERIN, ADAM	KITCHENER	OHL	06-Jun-1998	5' 10.0"	205 lbs	LW
86	KHOVANOV, ALEXANDER	MONCTON	QMJHL	12-Apr-2000	5' 10.5"	198 lbs *	C
87	TOPPING, KYLE	KELOWNA	WHL	18-Nov-1999	5' 11.25"	185 lbs	C
88	MCLAUGHLIN, BLAKE	CHICAGO	USHL	14-Feb-2000	6' 0.0"	157 lbs *	LW
89	MCDONOUGH, AIDAN	THAYER ACADEMY	HIGH-MA	06-Nov-1999	6' 0.75"	174 lbs	LW
90	HENMAN, LUKE	BLAINVILLE-BOISBRIAND	QMJHL	29-Apr-2000	5' 11.5"	150 lbs *	C
91	STOTTS, RILEY	CALGARY	WHL	05-Jan-2000	6' 0.0"	172 lbs *	C
92	SMITH, NATHAN	CEDAR RAPIDS	USHL	18-Oct-98	6' 0.0"	177 lbs	C
93	INGHAM, JACOB	MISSISSAUGA	OHL	10-Jun-2000	6' 3.8"	191 lbs *	G
94	DOSTAL, LUKAS	BRNO JR.	CZREP-JR.	22-Jun-2000	6' 1.3"	166 lbs	G
95	VALLATI, GIOVANNI	KITCHENER	OHL	21-Feb-2000	6' 1.5"	184 lbs	D
96	CHISHOLM, DECLAN	PETERBOROUGH	OHL	12-Jan-2000	6' 0.75"	185 lbs	D
97	MOE, JARED	WATERLOO	USHL	22-Jul-1999	6' 3.25"	205 lbs	G
98	EMBERSON, TY	USA U-18	NTDP	23-May-2000	6' 0.5"	200 lbs *	D
99	DOUGLAS, CURTIS	WINDSOR	OHL	06-Mar-2000	6' 8.5"	248 lbs *	C
100	COTTER, PAUL	LINCOLN	USHL	16-Nov-1999	6' 0.0"	191 lbs	C
101	MCSHANE, ALLAN	OSHAWA	OHL	14-Feb-2000	5' 10.8"	185 lbs *	C
102	SHARANGOVICH, YEGOR	DYNAMO MINSK	RUSSIA	06-Jun-1998	6' 2.0"	196 lbs	C
103	PEKAR, MATEJ	MUSKEGON	USHL	10-Feb-2000	6' 0.0"	170 lbs	C
104	ALMEIDA, JUSTIN	MOOSE JAW	WHL	06-Feb-1999	5' 9.25"	158 lbs *	C
105	PIVONKA, JACOB	USA U-18	NTDP	28-Feb-2000	5' 11.8"	201 lbs *	C
106	GUSTAFSSON, DAVID	HV 71	SWEDEN	11-Apr-2000	6' 1.5"	196 lbs	C
107	KVASNICA, MICHAL	FRYDEK-MISTEK	CZREP-2	17-Apr-2000	6' 1.0"	187 lbs	RW
108	FONSTAD, COLE	PRINCE ALBERT	WHL	24-Apr-2000	5' 10.0"	159 lbs*	C
109	HRABIK, KRYSTOF	LIBEREC	CZREP	24-Sep-1999	6' 4.0"	209 lbs	C

#	Name	Team	League	DOB	Height	Weight	Pos
110	BURZAN, LUKA	BRANDON	WHL	07-Jan-2000	5' 11.75"	185 lbs	C
111	POSPISIL, MARTIN	SIOUX CITY	USHL	19-Nov-1999	6' 1.5"	173 lbs	C
112	PLASEK, KAREL	BRNO JR.	CZREP-JR.	28-Jul-2000	5' 10.5"	154 lbs	RW
113	KIRK, LIAM	SHEFFIELD	ENGLAND	03-Jan-2000	6' 0.3"	161 lbs*	LW
114	WOUTERS, CHASE	SASKATOON	WHL	08-Feb-2000	5' 11.5"	177 lbs	C
115	HUGHES, RILEY	ST. SEBASTIANS SCHOOL	HIGH-MA	27-Jun-2000	6' 1.0"	174 lbs	RW
116	KONDELIK, JACHYM	MUSKEGON	USHL	21-Dec-1999	6' 6.25"	226 lbs	C
117	KARKI, KEEGAN	MUSKEGON	USHL	25-Feb-2000	6' 4.0"	218 lbs	G
118	HRENAK, DAVID	ST. CLOUD STATE	NCHC	05-May-1998	6' 2.0"	192 lbs	G
119	HALL, CURTIS	YOUNGSTOWN	USHL	26-Apr-2000	6' 2.5"	200 lbs *	C
120	RAGNARSSON, JACOB	ALMTUNA	SWEDEN-2	23-Sep-1999	5' 11.0"	170 lbs	D
121	HUTSKO, LOGAN	BOSTON COLLEGE	H-EAST	11-Feb-1999	5' 9.75"	172 lbs	RW
122	WERNBLOM, LUKAS	MODO	SWEDEN-2	22-Jul-2000	5' 9.0"	165 lbs	C
123	WESTFALT, MARCUS	BRYNAS	SWEDEN	12-Mar-2000	6' 3.25"	203 lbs	C
124	MANDOLESE, KEVIN	CAPE BRETON	QMJHL	22-Aug-2000	6' 4.0"	177 lbs*	G
125	UTUNEN, TONI	LEKI	FINLAND-2	27-Apr-2000	5' 10.5"	169 lbs	D
126	SALMELA, SANTERI	KOOKOO	FINLAND	10-Jun-2000	6' 1.25"	194 lbs	D
127	FLORCHUK, ERIC	SASKATOON	WHL	10-Jan-2000	6' 1.5"	175 lbs *	C
128	MIFTAKHOV, AMIR	IRBIS KAZAN	RUSSIA-JR.	26-Apr-2000	6' 0.0"	158 lbs	G
129	KOTKOV, VLADISLAV	CHICOUTIMI	QMJHL	08-Jan-2000	6' 4.25"	202 lbs	LW
130	MALYSHEV, ANTON	YAROSLAVL 2	RUSSIA-JR.	27-Feb-00	6' 0.0"	181 lbs	RW
131	RTISHCHEV, NIKITA	CSKA 2	RUSSIA-JR.	23-May-2000	6' 1.0"	191 lbs	RW
132	ANNUNEN, JUSTUS	KARPAT JR.	FINLAND-JR.	11-Mar-2000	6' 4.0"	217 lbs	G
133	PORTILLO, ERIK	FROLUNDA JR.	SWEDEN-JR.	03-Sep-00	6' 6.0"	207 lbs	G
134	KARLSSON, LINUS	KARLSKRONA JR.	SWEDEN-JR.	16-Nov-1999	6' 1.0"	178 lbs	C
135	KUROVSKY, DANIEL	VITKOVICE	CZREP	04-Mar-1998	6' 3.75"	213 lbs	RW
136	BOUTHILLIER, ZACHARY	CHICOUTIMI	QMJHL	08-Nov-99	6' 2.0"	186 lbs	G
137	LINDBOM, OLOF	DJURGARDEN JR.	SWEDEN-JR.	23-Jul-2000	6' 0.5"	173 lbs	G
138	KRAL, FILIP	SPOKANE	WHL	20-Oct-1999	6' 1.0"	171 lbs	D
139	BERNARD, XAVIER	DRUMMONDVILLE	QMJHL	06-Jan-2000	6' 2.5"	202 lbs *	D
140	BERNI, TIM	GCK ZURICH	SWISS-2	11-Feb-2000	5' 11.25"	174 lbs	D
141	DVORAK, DANIEL	HR. KRALOVE JR.	CZREP-JR.	09-Jan-2000	6' 2.75"	156 lbs	G
142	BUSBY, DENNIS	FLINT	OHL	06-Jan-2000	5' 10.5"	188 lbs	D
143	BARTON, SETH	TRAIL	BCHL	18-Aug-1999	6' 2.8"	174 lbs *	D
144	HILLIS, CAMERON	GUELPH	OHL	24-Jun-2000	5' 9.8"	168 lbs *	C
145	LILJA, DAVID	KARLSKOGA	SWEDEN-2	23-Jan-2000	5' 11.25"	173 lbs	C
146	WEISS, TYLER	USA U-18	NTDP	03-Jan-2000	5' 10.5"	150 lbs *	LW
147	NASSEN, LINUS	FROLUNDA JR.	SWEDEN-JR.	17-May-2000	5' 11.25"	185 lbs	C
148	GILES, PATRICK	USA U-18	NTDP	03-Jan-2000	6' 4.3"	201 lbs *	RW
149	HOFER, JOEL	SWIFT CURRENT	WHL	30-Jul-2000	6' 3.25"	160 lbs	G
150	SCHMID, AKIRA	LANGNAU JR.	SWISS-JR.	12-May-2000	6' 4.0"	165 lbs	G
151	PETTERSEN, MATHIAS E	MUSKEGON	USHL	03-Apr-2000	5' 9.5"	170 lbs	C
152	ZAVGORODNY, DMITRI	RIMOUSKI	QMJHL	11-Aug-2000	5' 8.5"	175 lbs	LW
153	GOLOD, MAXIM	ERIE	OHL	18-Aug-2000	5' 10.75"	164 lbs	LW
154	BARTEAUX, DAWSON	RED DEER	WHL	12-Jan-2000	6' 0.5"	180 lbs	D
155	DER-ARGUCHINTSEV, S	PETERBOROUGH	OHL	15-Sep-2000	5' 9.75"	159 lbs	C
156	ROMANOV, ALEXANDER	CSKA 2	RUSSIA-JR.	06-Jan-2000	5' 11.0"	185 lbs	D
157	GALENYUK, DANILA	SKA ST. PBG 2	RUSSIA-JR.	11-Feb-2000	6' 1.0"	200 lbs	D
158	GOGOLEV, PAVEL	PETERBOROUGH	OHL	19-Feb-2000	6' 0.5"	175 lbs	RW
159	FAGEMO, SAMUEL	FROLUNDA JR.	SWEDEN-JR.	14-Mar-2000	5' 11.0"	190 lbs	RW
160	NEVASAARI, ARTTU	KARPAT JR.	FINLAND-JR.	23-Jan-2000	5' 11.0"	178 lbs	RW
161	KILLINEN, LENNI	BLUES JR.	FINLAND-JR.	15-Jun-2000	6' 1.5"	180 lbs	RW
162	DUDAS, AIDAN	OWEN SOUND	OHL	15-Jun-2000	5' 7.3"	164 lbs *	C
163	ZHILYAKOV, BOGDAN	DYNAMO ST. PBG 2	RUSSIA-JR.	06-Apr-2000	6' 0.0"	185 lbs	D
164	JENKINS, BLADE	SAGINAW	OHL	11-Aug-2000	6' 1.3"	201 lbs *	LW

165	GRAVEL, ALEXIS	HALIFAX	QMJHL	21-Mar-2000	6' 2.8"	222 lbs *	G
166	FOCHT, CARSON	CALGARY	WHL	04-Feb-2000	6' 0.0"	178 lbs	C
167	KESSELRING, MICHAEL	NEW HAMPTON SCHOOL	HIGH-NH	13-Jan-2000	6' 4.3"	191 lbs *	D
168	HARRIS, JORDAN	KIMBALL UNION	HIGH-NH	07-Jul-2000	5' 10.8"	179 lbs *	D
169	SNELL, MASON	WELLINGTON	OJHL	18-Jun-2000	6' 0.0"	191 lbs	D
170	MALIK, ZACK	SUDBURY	OHL	03-Aug-2000	6' 2.0"	165 lbs	D
171	KROPACEK, VOJTECH	SPARTA JR.	CZREP-JR.	22-May-2000	6' 1.0"	187 lbs	LW
172	SAMUELSSON, ADAM	USA U-18	NTDP	21-Jun-2000	6' 5.75"	240 lbs	D
173	NIZHNIKOV, KIRILL	SUDBURY	OHL	29-Mar-2000	6' 2.0"	190 lbs	RW
174	ERSSON, SAMUEL	BRYNAS JR.	SWEDEN-JR.	20-Oct-1999	6' 2.0"	176 lbs	G
175	WONG, AUSTIN	OKOTOKS	AJHL	26-Aug-2000	5' 10.75"	189 lbs	C
176	ROBERTSON, CARTER	OTTAWA	OHL	15-Jan-2000	6' 2.0"	181 lbs *	D
177	DUNKLEY, NATHAN	LONDON	OHL	05-Mar-2000	5' 10.75"	192 lbs	C
178	ZHABREYEV, ALEXANDER	DYNAMO ST. SPB 2	RUSSIA-JR.	24-Mar-2000	5' 7.0"	152 lbs	C
179	GORNIAK, JACK	WEST SALEM	HIGH-WI	15-Sep-1999	5' 10.8"	181 lbs *	LW
180	TUCKER, TYLER	BARRIE	OHL	01-Mar-2000	6' 1.0"	203 lbs	D
181	CORCORAN, CONNOR	WINDSOR	OHL	07-Aug-2000	6' 1.5"	185 lbs	D
182	CALLAHAN, MICHAEL	YOUNGSTOWN	USHL	23-Sep-1999	6' 2.0"	197 lbs	D
183	EGGENBERGER, NANDO	DAVOS	SWISS	07-Oct-1999	6' 2.0"	185 lbs	LW
184	RIPPON, MERRICK	OTTAWA	OHL	27-Apr-2000	6' 0.5"	191 lbs	D
185	PERBIX, JACKSON	ELK RIVER	HIGH-MN	13-Sep-2000	6' 1.0"	176 lbs *	RW
186	TENDECK, DAVID	VANCOUVER	WHL	25-Nov-1999	6' 1.25"	173 lbs	G
187	KRYGIER, CHRISTIAN	LINCOLN	USHL	05-May-2000	6' 2.25"	192 lbs	D
188	GIBSON, MITCHELL	LONE STAR	NAHL	25-Jun-1999	6' 0.5"	188 lbs	G
189	ST. IVANY, JACK	SIOUX FALLS	USHL	22-Jul-1999	6' 2.5"	198 lbs	D
190	SEPPALA, PEETRO	KOOKOO JR.	FINLAND-JR.	17-Aug-2000	6' 1.0"	178 lbs	D
191	MCFAUL, DUSTYN	PICKERING	OJHL	04-Aug-2000	6' 2.25"	185 lbs	D
192	BOUDRIAS, SHAWN	GATINEAU	QMJHL	14-Sep-1999	6' 3.75"	197 lbs	RW
193	HAIN, GAVIN	USA U-18	NTDP	03-Apr-2000	5' 11.0"	194 lbs	C
194	LOHEIT, LUKE	MINNETONKA	HIGH-MN	26-Jul-2000	6' 0.0"	183 lbs	RW
195	JOHNSON, ISAAC	TRI-CITY	WHL	24-Jan-1999	6' 2.0"	186 lbs	LW
196	O'REILLY, RYAN	MADISON	USHL	21-Mar-2000	6' 1.75"	201 lbs	RW
197	REICHEL, KRISTIAN	RED DEER	WHL	11-Jun-1998	6' 1.3"	177 lbs *	C
198	KOUMONTZIS, DEMETRIOS	EDINA	HIGH-MN	24-Mar-2000	5' 9.75"	183 lbs	LW
199	ZAMULA, EGOR	CALGARY	WHL	30-Mar-2000	6' 2.5"	160 lbs	D
200	STEEVES, ALEXANDER	DUBUQUE	USHL	10-Dec-1999	5' 11.0"	185 lbs	C
201	KRYGIER, COLE	LINCOLN	USHL	05-May-2000	6' 2.75"	192 lbs	D
202	ZABRANSKY, LIBOR	KELOWNA	WHL	26-May-2000	6' 0.75"	190 lbs	D
203	JAKOBSSON, CARL	FARJESTAD JR.	SWEDEN-JR.	13-Jul-2000	6' 1.5"	165 lbs	RW
204	TANUS, KRISTIAN	TAPPARA JR.	FINLAND-JR.	17-Aug-2000	5' 5.75"	158 lbs	C
205	MACDONALD, ANDERSON	MONCTON	QMJHL	16-May-2000	6' 1.8"	209 lbs *	LW
206	KUCHARSKI, JACOB	DES MOINES	USHL	25-Sep-1999	6' 3.75"	215 lbs	G
207	MCKENNA, JEREMY	MONCTON	QMJHL	20-Apr-1999	5' 9.75"	175 lbs	RW
208	MCCORMICK, ADAM	CAPE BRETON	QMJHL	25-Jun-2000	5' 10.75"	179 lbs	D
209	SAIGEON, BRANDON	HAMILTON	OHL	14-Jun-1998	6' 1.5"	194 lbs	C
210	BERGERON, JUSTIN	ROUYN-NORANDA	QMJHL	14-Sep-2000	6' 0.0"	180 lbs	D
211	KOOY, JORDAN	LONDON	OHL	30-Apr-2000	6' 1.75"	184 lbs	G
212	GRONDIN, MAXIM	SAGINAW	OHL	04-Jul-2000	6' 3.25"	206 lbs	C
213	SALDA, RADIM	SAINT JOHN	QMJHL	18-Feb-1999	6' 0.25"	185 lbs	D
214	DAMIANI, RILEY	KITCHENER	OHL	20-Mar-2000	5' 9.0"	164 lbs	C
215	DILIBERATORE, PETER	SALISBURY	HIGH-CT	31-Mar-2000	5' 11.0"	160 lbs	D
216	KOEPKE, COLE	SIOUX CITY	USHL	17-May-1998	6' 1.0"	196 lbs	LW
217	WASSERMANN, JACOB	HUMBOLDT	SJHL	09-Jan-2000	6' 5.0"	194 lbs	G

* Denotes that we have updated the players height and weight from the data taken at the NHL combine

2018 NHL DRAFT PROSPECTS

| NR | ADAMEK, JAKUB | TRINEC JR. | CZREP-JR. | 6' 6.25" | 200 lbs | LD |

Adamek is a huge defenseman from the Czech Republic, standing at 6'06" and over 200 pounds. He's easy to notice on the ice because of his size. This year, he played in the Czech U20 league with HC Trinec and also played internationally for the Czech U-18 team at the Ivan Hlinka tournament, November and February at the U-18 Five Nations' Tournaments and, most recently, the U-18 World Hockey Championships. There are not a lot of flashes with Adamek, who's at his best when playing a simple game in his own zone and protecting the front of his net. His play with the puck is average; when given the time, he can make a decent first pass, but his decision-making is not the best (or fastest). Under pressure, he's prone to turnovers. There's not a lot of upside with his offensive game. He has decent top speed; he's powerful and generates decent speed when rushing the puck. But there's a lot of work to do with his footwork and mobility. In today's NHL, where it's all about speed, it's not always easy for Adamek to defend against speedy forwards coming into his zone. In his zone, he has some value on the PK unit, he can clear the front of the net and has a good, long stick, which helps him knock pucks down and block passing lanes. He can play a physical game, using his size well, but we have not seen a real mean streak out of him. Adamek's skills set probably fit better in the 90s' NHL; he could get a look late in the draft.

| 41 | ADDISON, CADEN | LETHBRIDGE | WHL | 5' 10.0" | 178 lbs* | RD |

Calen Addison is an undersized, offensive minded defenseman who finished his second full season with the Lethbridge Hurricanes. The former 2nd overall pick in the 2015 WHL Bantam Draft had a productive season, recording 65 points in 68 regular season games and an additional 19 points in 16 playoff games as the Hurricanes reached the Eastern Conference Finals.

Addison is an explosive skater. He has a low centre of gravity, a powerful stride and is strong on his skates. His skating ability allows him to evade forecheckers with ease and get up and down the ice quickly, with and without the puck. He possesses excellent feet, with a great first step and the ability to move laterally quickly. These skills are the foundation for his offensive game, as he is able to buy extra time for himself because of his mobility.

Calen is a efficient puck mover, and has the ability to make any pass on the ice. He rounded out his offensive game this year, showing the ability to create space and offense both for himself and teammates on the powerplay and at even strength. Calen has quick hands and is creative when carrying the puck up ice and on the offensive point. He also has great instincts, consistently jumping deep into the offensive zone to receive a back-door pass. His shot is dangerous, as he has a heavy accurate one-timer and quick release in stride. Addison is a competitive player who has a strong will to score and make offensive plays. This is what makes him a unique offensive player, but his determination to make a difference offensively can hurt him defensively.

Addison has the skills to be effective without the puck, with excellent skating skills and a strong lower half. He has shown that he can be a physical presence, making big hits at times where he is emotionally involved. Calen can struggle in his own end, overcommitting to his man and has yet to show the ability to defend in one on one situations.

"If you draft him...you're not drafting him for his defense. He'll be a late first rounder." NHL Scout, October 2017

"I love his offense. He'll go high, I have him above (Ty) Smith and it's not that close for me." NHL Scout, December 2017

"Thought he was one of the best players at the Ivan Hlinka. I continued to really like his puck game and his offensive upside but he scared me on the defensive side of the puck. So my two knocks are size and defensive play." — HP Scout, Mark Edwards

| 23 | ALEXEYEV, ALEXANDER | RED DEER | WHL | 6' 3.8" | 196 lbs * | RD |

Alexander Alexeyev is a big Russian defender who finished his second full season in North America with the Red Deer Rebels. In the last two seasons, Alexeyev has dealt with significant injuries, including a season ending knee injury at the end of 2016-17. He is a late 99' who has developed into Red Deer's top defenseman, recording 7 goals and 37 points in 45 regular season games and another 5 points in 3 playoff games in 2017-18.

Alexeyev has a unique combination of strength and skill. His physical tools are strong, including a big frame and great strength on his skates. He has a powerful stride, and can move up ice with ease. In tight space, he is nimble and elusive and his feet have become quicker and more efficient over his two years in Red Deer. Alexander is extremely tough to knock off the puck and excels in puck battles because of his strong frame.

With the puck, Alexeyev has great skill and creativity. He has quick, creative hands and can make forecheckers miss when skating the puck, with rangy lateral dekes. This year, his confidence improved dramatically, and he was consistently jumping up into the rush, and stepping up from the offensive point. Alexeyev willed himself to the net on some occasions, and contributed offensively in variety of fashions, including scoring on breakaways and leading odd-man rushes. In addition to his individual skills, Alexeyev possesses very good hockey sense, and has the ability to scan the ice and find his teammates, both with first passes out of his own end and in the offensive zone. His production does not illustrate the impact Alexeyev had offensively.

Alexander is a competitive player, which makes him extremely difficult to handle offensively and hard to push off the puck in the defensive end. He made several big plays at big moments of the season, including having a terrific playoff. In a tough year, where he had to fly because of the passing of his mother, Alexeyev consistently had strong efforts at both ends of the ice. In his own end, Alexeyev can separate body from puck, has an active stick, and wins the majority of his battles. Alexander Alexeyev is a complete defenseman with size, skill and mobility and despite being injured for big chunks of the last two seasons, continues to improve and gain confidence with more time in North America.

"I need to see him more. I'm having trouble figuring out how high his upside can go." NHL Scout, December 2017

"He's got big upside. So much room to grow his game." — NHL Scout, May 2018

"Has range, grit and an intimidation factor - a player who grew on me quickly this year with his excellent offensive game which has has untapped potential for a big jump in production, plays well in all 3 zones and should dominate the WHL next year if he returns." — HP Scout, Andy Levangie

"A few teams gave me some very good reviews on their interviews with him. I like him too. He is mature and had a very tough year in his personal life. He arrived in Canada not speaking english and did his combine interviews in english." HP Scout, Mark Edwards

| NR | ALEXANDER, JETT | NORTH YORK | OJHL | 6' 4.5" | 187 lbs | G |

Alexander is a hybrid style goaltender with intriguing physical traits and maturity. Jett shows some rawness to his game as he continues to grow into his towering frame, however does possess intriguing athletic ability and developing technical tools. He does a good job utilizing his frame to his advantage as he cuts down his angles well and is often able to square up the shooter. Jett shows good reflexes and is able to move quickly from post-to-post while in the butterfly position. Alexander does need to improve his foot-work however as he can be limited in his initial shot positioning when moving side-to-side while standing. When opposing players get him moving side-to-side when attacking the offensive zone he can lose his positioning an over play to a post. Jett often uses his height so see around screens and track pucks from distance, however he does have a tendency to play deep in his net and rely on his frame to block the puck opposed to making a save. Pucks below his hip from depth cause him problems, while he would benefit from becoming more aggressive in battling to find pucks from the point. Jett shows average rebound control as he can do a good job to field pucks cleanly and swallow up pucks, however he can also show inconsistencies with his control as pucks tend to get way from him at times, forcing him to make secondary saves in unfavourable positions. Alexander will need to elevate his puck playing frequency and ability to have more of an impact at the next level.

"Visually He's not all that appealing but he seems to stop the puck. He's a big kid who just finds a way to get it done." - NHL Scout, May 2018

"I like him but my concern is his athleticism as far as projecting him to the next level." NHL Scout, May 2018

"There are things I like about him but I worry about about his overall mobility. Not a draftable player for me at this point." HP Scout, Mark Edwards

| 104 | ALMEIDA, JUSTIN | MOOSE JAW | WHL | 5' 9.25" | 158 lbs | LC |

Justin Almeida in his second year of eligibility had a massive breakout season with the Moose Jaw Warriors. Being a high bantam pick Justin had huge expectations going into his 17 year old season, but for whatever reason things didn't work out in Prince George. In his first full season with Warriors he scored 43 goals and 98 points in 72 games.

Justin possesses high-end speed and skill. He has the acceleration to beat defenders wide. His speed allowed him to draw penalties seemingly at will. We believe his release is NHL caliber. He has the ability to get the shot of in close quarters with speed and accuracy. Many of Justin's goals this season came from the high slot. The Warriors trusted Justin in all situations. First unit power play and penalty kill. He was relied on to win key face-offs as well.

The major knock on Justin's game has to be his size. In the new game he can get away with being the most undersized player on the ice because his high-end skill makes up for it. The playoffs were a different story he got pushed around and seemed to shy away from the dirty areas of the ice. Overall Justin had an increasable season that really opened some eyes. If he put in the work in the off-season and add size and strength that will round out his game.

"Justin has the ability to break a game wide open. One of the best wrist shots I have seen in a long time. If a team doesn't take a chance on him at the draft I'd be shocked" HP Scout Dan Markewich

| NR | ALMQUIST, BEN | HOLY FAMILY | HS- MINN | 5' 11.0" | 170lbs | LC |

Almquist was a dominate player all season for a Holy Family team that came within one goal of making it to the Minnesota State Tournament, falling to eventual state champion Minnetonka in overtime in the Sectional Final. Almquist is a consistent point producing two-way center that makes quick movements with the puck. Ben has average size but has quick feet and hands that make him dangerous with the puck, he is able to break containment and create space for himself in the offensive zone. Almquist good hockey smarts and work ethic all over the ice. Has an above average release and has shown the ability to shoot in stride and find the corners. Ben isn't a prospect that has got a lot of ink coming up through the Minnesota ranks but his all-around game has made considerable strides in the last year, resulting in an offer and commitment to the University of Wisconsin. Almquist will spend 18/19 in the USHL; Tri-City owns his rights before heading to Wisconsin in 19/20.

"I've seen a lot of this kid over the last two years, he's a hockey player." HP Scout, Dusten Braaksma

| 58 | ANDERSSON, AXEL | DJURGARDEN JR. | SWEDEN-JR. | 5' 11.75" | 178 lbs | RD |

Andersson had good success at the J20 level this year, amassing 31 points in 42 games and playing in all major international U-18 tournaments throughout the year. However, in those tournaments, he didn't get a ton of ice time and it was a bit harder to evaluate him in those events. He's a player whose toolset we like; he's an above-average skater with a good footwork. He can rush the puck out of his zone, he can escape pressure from the forecheck thanks to his good skating abilities, and he's quick to retrieve pucks in his own zone. He's good on the transition; he can make a good first pass out of his zone and also lead the rush. He's got some work to do with his defensive game, though. Nothing alarming, but just improving his positioning and using his stick more to block passing lanes would make him more efficient in his own zone. He does use his stick when he's defending one-on-one, though. He has a long stick and it helped him eliminate the space players had to work with. He also will need to get stronger physically, and engage in the physical game more, as he can get pushed over too often in the defensive zone. We would like to see him play a simpler and more efficient game in his own zone; he can take some risks with the puck or try low-percentage passing plays that result in turnovers and long shifts in his own end. There are some things to work on for Andersson in the next couple of years, but we like his puck-moving and power play abilities; we think he has a solid upside for the NHL.

"I had time for him last year. No clue why he's listed as the 7th defenseman here...he ends up not being number seven every game." - NHL Scout, February 2018

"A couple of our Euro scouts really like him." NHL Scout, March 2018

"His icetime was limited but I liked him in February at the Five Nations in Plymouth and he was good last year at the U17. He's a draft for me" - HP Scout, Mark Edwards

| 132 | ANNUNEN, JUSTUS | KARPAT JR. | FINLAND-JR. | 6' 4.0" | 217 lbs | G |

Justus Annunen was the starting goalie for the Karpat U20 squad, where he put up a 2.31 GAA and a .907 save percentage in 26 games, he followed that up with a 1.83GAA and .935 save percentage in 12 playoff games. Internationally, Annunen showed a good development curve, improving his play from the Hlinka to the Five-Nations and saving his best international performance at the end of the season where he helped Finland capture a gold medal at the U18's by putting up a 2.00 GAA and a .914 save percentage in 6 starts. He's slated to play for Karpat in Liiga next season.

Annunen's a massive goalie who takes up a considerable amount of space in the net but also has above average reflexes. He covers a tremendous amount of the net when in his butterfly or when he's attempting to cut down-angles by entering his V-H and reverse V-H, though all three techniques lack a level of fluidity. His lateral mobility is average but that's not unexpected given that he's one of the biggest goalies in this draft, he also doesn't transition into his butterfly at the same rate as some of the quicker goalies however he can make high-end reactionary saves to compensate for this. Additionally, he doesn't give up on a play if he's out of position, we have seen him make several difficult saves that require him to forget his technique and simply use his size and reactions to keep the puck out. His glove hand has good placement, specifically in his stance, he keeps it well positioned which has allowed him to make a consistent level of saves on that side. However, the same cannot be said for his blocker, specifically on certain post-up sequences where he's required to use it, there's a level of awkwardness that you can see in his movement and he looks uncomfortable when engaging shots on his blocker-side in some games. One of the more important areas he developed in throughout the season was his ability to evaluate the degree with which he needed to challenge a shooter in order to take away an angle despite his size. Earlier in the year he was relying too much on his frame and not enough on his reading of the play, however by the end of the season, he was aggressively cutting off angles more consistently and evaluating shot placement at a much higher rate.

There's some upside with Justus, however he doesn't come without some technical issues as well. He has difficulty absorbing rebounds during post-play sequences in some of our viewing's, he has limited flexibility and overall extension which makes it difficult for him to make certain secondary saves and the biggest limitation to his game currently is his overall mobility, which at this stage of his development is average. Regardless of his limitations, Annunen had a positive development curve this past season and has incredible size with the raw tools necessary to make himself an interesting goalie prospect in the 2018 draft.

| NR | BABINTSEV, GLEB | PETERBOROUGH | OHL | 6' 0.0" | 198 lbs | LD |

Babintsev is a cerebral defender with an intelligence to his game. Gleb shows developing two-way traits to his game, but was most effective in the defensive zone. He possesses a subtle physicality to his game, showing good timing on open-ice checks and willingness to be assertive with his physical traits in the dirty areas of the ice. He doesn't possess any one stand-out trait to his game, Babintsev plays a simple but effective, low maintenance type of game. He displays an ability to see the ice and advances the puck up ice well with a clean first pass. Gleb does show just average puck skills and would benefit from elevating his puck handling and willingness to carry the puck up ice. He shows good positioning in all three zones, allowing him to defend transition attacks well. Babintsev keeps strong gaps and angles opponents effectively, showing an ability to take away time and space and separate player from puck with contact or a quick stick. Gleb shows good awareness in the defensive zone and will combine a competitiveness and physical play with good positioning and an active stick to find an effectiveness. His simplicity can allow him to fly under the radar however he was an effective presence for the Petes. Babintsev will need to continue to elevate his game on the offensive side of the puck to increase his chances to play at the next level. While becoming quicker in his feet and with his puck retrievals would also be beneficial.

"Not a player that knocked my socks off this season." - HP Scout, Mark Edwards

59	BACK, OSKAR	FARJESTAD JR.	SWEDEN-JR.	6' 3.0"	204 lbs *	LC

Oscar Back put together a good development year while playing for Farjestad BK in the SuperElit, where he put up 32 points in 38 games including 22 assists. He followed that up with 2 points in three playoff games and also got called up to the SHL where he went pointless in 14 games. Oscar was also featured at international events where he looked stronger with each passing tournament, finishing the season with a good U18 performance where he posted 4 points in 7 games.

Back is a large, two-way, playmaking-center with a lot of tools at his disposal. He's got a broad frame and tremendous length which allows him to guard the puck at a high-level. This is an important attribute for Back since he doesn't generate a lot of power in his stride, there's a lack of explosiveness in his movement but he does have a fluidity to his skating, so although he's not very quick it's not a liability either. To compensate for his lack of separation speed, he's developed advanced puck protection skills using poise, patience and advanced reads. When under pressure from defense or getting aggressively back-checked, Back likes to turn and face away from his opponent while using his length to keep the puck at a safe distance, he then likes to use his soft-hands to make a play or use his high-end vision to thread a pass to his teammate. Arguably his best overall skill is his passing ability, he can make difficult passes look easy and there quick to come off his stick during give-and-go sequences; few centres in this draft can find the backdoor option at the rate he can. One of the reasons he is such a proficient passer is due to his hockey sense. He's a smart player who recognizes passing lanes, which allows him to make fast one-touch passes around the goal-mouth and during powerplay sequences. His intelligence can control the tempo of play when the puck is on his stick. Although he prefers the passing play, Back's shooting mechanics are good. His release point is a plus, he uses his length to change the angle while driving down the wings and it has a high level of accuracy, however the one area it needs work is in it's velocity.

His hockey smarts translate well on the defensive-side of the ice. He's a capable back-checker who used his reach to make some impressive stick-lifts in our viewing's. Furthermore, he's got good defensive positioning and uses an active-stick to deflect shots away which was notable this year when he was used on the penalty-kill. One of the areas of concern for Back at this time is that he's not always engaged on the ice and can look invisible for stretches at a time. However, when he's playing up to his abilities, he has shown an enticing tool-set packed into a large frame while also having a good understanding of the game at each end. He's the type of player who can make his teammate around him better with the combination of responsible play and passing ability that he's shown us this year.

"He's is better than Olofsson who did absolutely nothing in Plymouth (Five Nations) - NHL Scout, February 2018

"The Swedes don't have much skill up front this year and Back is in that group." NHL Scout, February 2018

"In general, the Swedes let me down this season. Back can't score." - NHL Scout, May 2018

"Back, Olofsson and Gustafsson all have their warts. None of them showed me they could score with any sort of consistency." – HP Scout, Mark Edwards

| 42 | BAHL, KEVIN | OTTAWA | OHL | 6' 6.3" | 216 lbs * | LD |

Kevin Bahl had a successful sophomore campaign for the 67's by stepping into the top defensive pairing at times which logged him heavy minutes, showing a high-level of consistency. He produced 18 points in 58 games, including 17 assists, before going pointless in the playoffs. Internationally, he was featured at the Hlinka where he had 2 points in 5 games and at the U18's, where he put up 3 points in 5 games. He also had a strong CHL prospects game this year, scoring a nice goal.

Bahl is a towering shut-down defenseman whose capable of making a quality first pass and carries a mean streak. He's got tremendous size, width and length, making him efficient at boxing his opponents out in-font of the net, counteracting attempts by opposing players who try to cut around him, and using his frame to drain opposing teams along the boards. His incredible reach allows him to make stick-on-puck plays at a high-rate and lets him recover even if a player does manage to get around him. Additionally, he's an aggressive and physical defenseman who punishes players in-front of the net or when a player is attempting to generate a transitional zone-entry against him. We have watched him send several players crashing side-ways into the boards, due to his ability to generate puck-separating hits with his powerful build. This aspect of his game should be highlighted since he's not allowed to be as physical in juniors but it should translate effectively to the pro's where a player of his mold is expected to punish the opposition. It's not just his size that creates his defensive-presence on the ice, it's also his surprising four-way mobility. He's a fluid and well coordinated skater for his size and this area of his game when combined with the rest of his defensive-attributes allowed him to be a force on the backend at times for the 67's. His physical attributes are impressive but his mental attributes aren't far behind, his positioning is a plus and he's capable of reading the play in advance in most sequences which allows him to get in the way of shooting and passing lanes to take away options.

Unlike his impressive defensive-game, his offensive-game is still a work in progress. He was put in all situations for the 67's, including the powerplay, however he's not overly skilled when walking the line and has trouble generating dangerous shots on most attempts. Bahl is at his best when he keeps his game simple when walking the line, using his accurate passes to distribute the puck to more skilled players that can execute at a higher rate than he can. Though, his offensive-attributes are not why a team will be interested in Bahl for the draft, it's his defensive-game and great physical attributes that will give him a shot to become a shut-down defender in the NHL who most teams would covet during a deep playoff run.

"He's was late first (rounder) for me in October and he still is." NHL Scout, January 2018

"I thin he's more of a long range guy...he'll need some development." – NHL Scout, February 2018

"Needs the skating to get better...footwork better...his reach allows him to recover right now when he gets beat skating wise, but t the next level those guys are gone...they're by him. – NHL Scout, April 2018

"Im lukewarm on him overall, I know he meaner than he shows but the OHL takes all the opportunity for toughness out of the game." – NHL Scout, April 2018

"He's a horse and you need guys like him in the playoffs." -NHL Scout, May 2018

"Big limited defensive defenseman. He'll be the defensive part of a good pairing...don't know if he's top four but he's a good enough player to find a spot. - NHL Scout, May 2018

"I like him...big guy, I like his composure with the puck. Skating is only going to get better. He has a mean streak and is a playoff type of player." - NHL Scout, May 2018

"Bahl had a few games where he struggled with some pressure, but overall I liked they way he moved pucks this year. His size and skating mixed with pretty solid puck moving ability keeps his stock up there for me." - HP Scout, Mark Edwards

"I got good feedback on his combine interviews with the exception of one scout. One scout was very impressed with a few of his answers to negative questions." - HP Scout, Mark Edwards

| 154 | BARTEAUX, DAWSON | RED DEER | WHL | 6' 0.5" | 180 lbs | RD |

Dawson Barteaux is a former first round pick by the Regina Pats, 14th overall in the 2015 WHL Bantam Draft. Dawson was traded at the deadline in 2016-17 to the Red Deer Rebels and finished his first full season with the team, recording 32 points in 64 games, mostly playing a top-4 role with presence on the powerplay.

Barteaux has very good puck skills and confidence skating the puck. He can move the puck laterally quickly and has shown some creativity when evading fore-checkers and turning away from pressure. His strong is long and methodical and he does not have trouble recovering on the back-check or skating past faced up defenders in the neutral zone. Although he has some strong skating skills, he appears to be casual with a lot of his game, lacking urgency with both his effort and decisions with the puck. His offensive skill is apparent, including a strong one timer that he does not use enough.

Dawson continued his struggles with his play in the defensive zone that saw him in and out of the lineup as a 16 year old. He is not a physical presence, and he creates turnovers because of his inability to get the puck off his stick quickly. Holding onto the puck often leads him into comprising situations where pucks are blatantly turned over or stripped from him. He does seem to bounce back with unwavering confidence after these mishaps, but his small flashes of offensive skill do not make up for his inability to defend dependably.

| 143 | BARTON, SETH | TRAIL | BCHL | 6' 2.8" | 174 lbs * | RD |

Seth Barton was passed over in last years draft playing for the Okanagan Rockets in the BCMML. This year he got an opportunity to have more exposure by playing in a more prominently scouted league, producing 33 points in 49 games, including 27 assists. In the playoffs, he scored 11 points in 16 games and played for Canada West at the WJAC-19 tournament, where he had 2 assists in 5 games.

Barton is a two-way defenseman who likes to join the rush yet is capable of playing a calm and composed style in his own-end. He's light for his frame but that didn't stop him from playing a physical brand of hockey when necessary and he showed good defensive-reads. Sometimes, he was too calm and would rely on his soft-hands to get him out of trouble but this occurred when he didn't like his passing options for the most part. He's capable of making a first-pass and has a fluid stride with plus edges which allow him to transition the puck effectively over the neutral zone. Barton looks to join the attack when he can, making timely pinches to generate chances while also showing good lateral crossovers to re-open his shooting lanes. His puck-skills are above-average and he can beat defenders while driving to the net, while also being able to use fakes at the line to set-up more dynamic scoring plays. His wrist-shot and slapshot aren't overly impressive as they lack some power but that should come in time considering he has a substantial amount of weight that he can put on his frame.

Seth had a notable year for the Smoke Eaters and showed enough offensive-upside, combined with his intelligence to put him into consideration to be drafted with a later pick.

25	BEAUDIN, NICOLAS	DRUMMONDVILLE	QMJHL	5' 10.8"	172 lbs *	LD

Beaudin had an amazing year with the Voltigeurs this season, with over a point per game, and finished 4th in scoring for defensemen across the QMJHL. He did some good work in the gym last summer, as he was able to defend better in his own zone and was able to compete better physically along the boards and in front of the net. Being physically stronger this year was a key in his development, as this always was a question mark with him in terms of whether or not he was going to be able to compete physically. The rest of his game has always been strong, as his vision and passing game are both excellent. He's very good at moving pucks quickly out of his zone with a quick first pass. If no passing option is available to him, he won't hesitate to rush the puck out of his zone, as his skating is above-average. On the power play, he's a pass-first player. He is very good at creating plays for his teammates and finding them in the offensive zone. He still has work to do with his shot; he doesn't have a powerful one, but does a good job getting it through and on net with a simple low wrister. He tends to use his wrist or snap shot, as they are more accurate; his slap shot lacks that same accuracy. His skating abilities are mixed, he has average top speed, but he makes up for it with his pure agility and his ability to change directions quickly to avoid the forecheck when rushing the puck. Beaudin is one the smartest defensemen in this draft class, and all year long, he was very consistent - we didn't see him have many average games. Defensively, he made some good progress under Dominque Ducharme this year, and he does a good job using his quick stick to defend. He became more and more dependable for his team as the year progressed,.

To conclude, Beaudin was a favourite of ours since the beginning of the season, and we feel that with his smarts and puck moving abilities, he could an asset for an NHL teams on the power play and for their transition game.

"He's smart, agile and can move the puck, NHL Central has his teammate but I prefer this kid. He looks like a top three rounds guy." - NHL Scout, November 2017

"I like (Rasmus) Sandin more but this guys pretty solid." - NHL Scout, November 2017

"Sandin is better, he's more physical." NHL Scout, December 2017

"I tweeted about him (praising him) prior to the Top Prospects game and then no less than seven scouts told me they saw the tweet and that they agreed with me." January 2018

"I liked him earlier in the season but he hasn't been good the last three times I've seen him. He needs to hit somebody once in a while. He has no shot, he's turned over pucks like crazy...what is he at the next level?" NHL Scout, April 2018

"I hadn't seen him for a while but just saw him a few times recently. He was really good. He's a first rounder for sure." NHL Scout, April 2018

"He's better (than Sandin) Sandin gets hit too much." NHL Scout, April 2018

"It's tight, that's a good comparison (on Beaudin vs Sandin) I would go Beaudin because I like him more on the powerplay." NHL Scout, April 2018

"He's possibly the player I have seen the most this year, and I don't think I had one bad viewing of him. Very consistent player from game to game." - HP Scout Jérôme Bérubé

"During my first trip to Drummondville this season, Jerome (Berube) told me to watch him. He was really good that game and I felt he could be a top 60 guy. The more I watched him as the season progressed, the more I was impressed with his game. He's one of the smarter players in this draft class." - HP Scout, Mark Edwards

"Very good on his assessment on his own game and the kid has a plan." NHL Scout, June 2018

"Rave reviews from several scouts about his combine interviews. One scout listed him as his top interview of the week." - HP Scout, Mark Edwards

NR	BEAUDOIN, TOMMY	ROUYN-NORANDA	QMJHL	6' 1.0"	215 lbs	RW

Beaudoin was one of the Huskies' biggest pleasant surprises this year. Recruited as a free agent out of Terrebonne in Junior AAA, Beaudoin found himself in the scoring column fairly regularly with almost 20 goals in his first year in the league, seemingly gaining more confidence in the second half of the year when he began to be used more frequently in key situations, such as the power play.

Beaudoin has a surprising set of hands for someone of his frame. Combined with his current average skating abilities, sometimes opposing defensive squads sometimes take him for granted, seeing him uniquely as a standard power-forward rather than one with pretty decent stickhandling abilities. He was able to show his quick hands during the season, particularly in shootout situations. He does well along the boards to protect the puck, allowing his linemates the time and space to generate scoring opportunities. He's still very raw and has not scratched the surface of his potential yet, he has good size and his offensive potential is there. Things to improve for him in the next two seasons: being quicker, skating-wise but also in terms of his decision-making. Conditioning will be another area to keep an eye on, as he never trained seriously until this year. With another strong summer, he could hit new highs next year. His play away from the puck could use work and enable him to become a more efficient player away from the puck. As we said, he's extremely raw as a player, but we like his potential. He should play a more prominent role next year in the top 6 of the Huskies and should see his offensive production improve.

Beaudoin really came out of nowhere this year, but made a big impression, even if he didn't play a prominent role on the Huskies. He has the size and scoring abilities to play pro hockey one day. There are still things to improve on in his game, but he's a great example of a late-bloomer and could surprise people a lot in the next two seasons.

NR	BENOIT, SIMON	SHAWINIGAN	QMJHL	6' 3.0"	192 lbs	LD

Benoit is in his 3rd year of eligibility for the NHL Entry Draft, and had his best season this season on one of the league's worst teams. Benoit is a big defenseman with surprising skating abilities. He's more of a stay-at-home defenseman in junior, with limited offensive upside for the next level. He's a smart defender, and with his reach and mobility, he covers a lot of ice in the defensive zone and makes good use of his stick. His physical game has improved ever since he started playing major junior hockey. He doesn't have a mean streak, though, but he's using his size more and more. Offensively, he's limited, and not overly creative with the puck. But with his skating abilities, he can skate the puck out of his zone and escape pressure from the forecheck. Benoit has the size and mobility to definitely play pro hockey down the road. Shawinigan didn't trade him this season, even if he was in high demand, and are hoping he's back next season as an overager.

210	BERGERON, JUSTIN	ROUYN-NORANDA	QMJHL	6' 0.0"	180 lbs	LD

Bergeron was in his rookie season with the Huskies and finished 3rd in rookie scoring for defensemen with 30 points. The Magog native was born September 14th, 2000 which makes him one of the youngest eligible players of this draft class. Originally drafted in the 4th round by Rouyn-Noranda in the 2016 QMJHL Draft, Bergeron was one of the top defensemen in midget AAA last year with Magog, where he averaged over a point per game.

Bergeron is a good skating defenseman; his top speed and mobility are above-average. He could be even more effective if he could improve his explosiveness, as that would help him create more separation and get away from pressure faster. He has good offensive potential; he started a bit slowly this year, but after the Christmas break he started playing with more confidence offensively and produced 19 of his 30 points. He's good on the power play; he's very poised with the puck and sees the ice well. He makes good decisions with the puck and likes to rush it out of his zone. He didn't do it as often this year as he did in midget, playing a more limited role, but with increased ice time, you'll see him play with more confidence and be more of a factor offensively. He's not afraid to put pucks on net, averaging over 2 shots per game, again, despite a limited role. His wrist shot is good, as he usually keeps it low, and it's accurate with a quick release. He reads the play well in the offensive zone to make smart pinches to provide other options to his forwards. Next season, he'll play on the Huskies' top 4 regularly, and will be on the first power play unit. Defensively is where there's some work to be done; he's not bad, but we would like to see him be more active in his coverage and play tougher along the boards and in front of the net.

Bergeron has flown under the radar this year, but as one of the youngest players available in this draft class, combined with his skill level, we like his long-term potential and feel he should get drafted somewhere between the mid to late rounds.

"Probably on an island on my own on this one, but I like this kid's skills, and I think that he should be drafted. I'm expecting a big year out of him next season with the Huskies." - HP Scout Jérôme Bérubé

| 27 | BERGGREN, JONATAN | SKELLEFTEA JR. | SWEDEN-JR. | 5' 10.0" | 181 lbs | RW |

Berggren started this hockey season with a solid performance at the Ivan Hlinka tournament in August. He was strong during the season in the J20, and finished the year with a great performance at the U-18s, with 10 points in 7 games, good for 4th overall in the tournament scoring race.

Berggren led the SuperElit league in scoring with 57 points in 38 games this season. He's a winger who plays the game at high tempo. He's not the biggest player, but he's not afraid to play in the tough areas in the offensive zone, whenever he has a chance, he will take the puck to the net. When rushing the puck, it is rare that he doesn't end up taking it to the net; he's willing to play in the tough areas to score goals, which is a good sign for him in the NHL. He has above average speed and is fearless on the ice. He has quick hands, a quick release on his shot and as the year progressed, he became Sweden's most dynamic forward, especially in the U-18s in April. He has decent top speed with nice acceleration; one thing we notice with him is his ability to change directions when rushing the puck, which makes it tougher for opponents to defend him. He has good poise with the puck, he's patient and has showed he can score, but his poise helps him create plays for his teammates, as he has good vision and creativity. Berggren has great potential; we think he has what it takes to be a top 6 forward in the NHL at some point. If not, he has enough smarts and good overall game to play on a 3rd line.

"I love his skill, first rounder for me as of today. I'm looking forward to seeing him again after Christmas." NHL Scout, September 2017

"The Swedes looked awful. Even the D were just average. Berggren was easily the best forward for Sweden (at the U18)" - NHL Scout, May 2018

"A fave of Jerome all season long. He was just ok early at the Five Nations but had a better finish there and that stronger play continued in April at the U18. High skill and he competes. Asking a few guys opinions they think he'll be a late first or early second rounder. Remember that if a team has a player at 27 on their list (as an example) it's highly unlikely they would reach his spot on their list if they were picking 27th." - HP Scout, Mark Edwards

"A few scouts mentioned they were quite surprised he wasn't at the combine." - HP Scout, Mark Edwards

| 38 | BERNARD-DOCKER, JACOB | OKOTOKS | AJHL | 6' 0.3" | 187 lbs * | RD |

Jacob Bernard-Docker has followed in the foot-steps of Cale Makar by becoming another impressive prospect from the AJHL who will get his name called on draft day. He became the main option on the backend for the Oilers this past season, producing 41 points in 49 games, including 20 goals. In the playoffs, he had 14 points in 15 games. Internationally, he played in the WJAC-19 where he produced 3 points in 5 games.

Barnard-Docker is a powerful two-way defenseman with an excellent wrist-shot. He's well-rounded, with a good combination of defensive smarts and physical play that make him difficult to deal with in his own-end. He can out-battle his opponents along the boards, use an active stick to disrupt plays and can use his powerful first-few steps to close gaps quickly. Furthermore, he processes information quickly on the ice, which allows him to play a smart and effective transition game. This makes him a versatile defender in the sense that if you need him to become the offensive-catalyst for plays on the backend, he can. He's capable of transitioning the puck through all three zones, while also pinching appropriately by using his strong skating ability, but this allows him to also be effective during recovery sequences. His ability to interpret the play and recover is where the other side of his versatility comes into play; he can play a shut-down role when tasked to do so but has a good amount of skill to compliment dynamic offensive-defenseman at the line. There's few defensemen who impressed us more in our viewings during sequences as far as supporting his partner. For instance, he's quick to recognize when his defensive partner is trapped and he reacts accordingly. He's quick to recognize his missed assignment when he does make a mistake, and he's able to communicate effectively to his defensive partners during odd-man situations. We saw good execution when attempting to keep the puck out of the net during high-percentage chances against.

Jacob's intelligence is notable in the offensive-end as well. He's good at timing when to join the rush and is able to find soft-ice at a high-rate to get off his wrist-shot. His wrist-shot is one of the better shots from the backend in a very deep class. It has an excellent release point, has a high-degree of accuracy, and generates a tremendous amount of power. Additionally, he's good at changing the angle by holding it for an extended period while laterally shifting positions or shooting it in one motion off the rush. His first pass allows him to make accurate outlet passes but he's also a capable puck distributor who can thread passes through high-traffic areas. His puck skills are a plus and he can fake out his opponents at the line though he's a safer player in this aspect compared to some of the more dynamic offensive-minded defenseman at the top of the class, rarely over-extending himself by trying to do too much with the puck on his stick.

Bernard-Docker is one of the more complete defenders heading into this draft. He lacks any glaring flaw. He's not the most offensively gifted defender, or the biggest defender, but he's versatile, smart, and well-rounded which should get his name called fairly early on day two of the draft.

"I liked him a lot more in Truro (WJAC). I didn't like his game tonight (CJHL Top Prospects Game)" – NHL Scout, January 2018

"Back in December I was with a group of scouts and they polled Bernard-Docker vs Tychonick. It ended up 5-2 with myself and one other scout choosing Tychonick. I like Bernard-Docker, but liked the upside for Tychonick a bit more." HP Scout Mark Edwards

"Good interview at the combine. He thinks he'll be a first rounder. To me he's a second rounder. BCHL is a factor." – NHL Scout, June 2018

139	BERNARD, XAVIER	DRUMMONDVILLE	QMJHL	6' 2.5"	202 lbs *	LD

Bernard was the 12th overall pick in the 2016 QMJHL Draft. After a tough rookie season, he bounced back nicely this year. He had a good season with the Voltigeurs, scoring 11 goals and collecting 35 points in 66 games during the season.

Bernard is a two-way defender with no major weaknesses in his game, but no outstanding skills either. He has good size and is still filling into his frame; adding some strength will help him be more efficient in his battles along the boards and in front of the net. He's not an overly physical guy, but made some progress in that area compared to his rookie year. He had some success offensively, getting plenty of ice time, and was used either on the first or second power play unit. He's also quite adept at paying on both the left and the right side. He's an average puck-distributor. He doesn't have high-end vision, but does a good job making the safe and smart passes in the offensive zone. He does have some issues moving pucks from his own zone; his decision-making when rushing the puck is not the best and this is where he gets into trouble. He can be victim to turnovers and the accuracy of his passes is average at best. What he was really good at was getting his shot through from the point; he does a good job finding shooting lanes. He doesn't have a great shot, but he has good accuracy and hits the net with regularity. He's not very flashy, but does a good job of keeping his game simple and making the high-percentage play well. He gets into trouble when he tries too much on the ice. His decision-making can be poor, and he needs to make these decisions quicker. Bernard has good size and decent mobility, which makes him interesting for NHL teams.

Bernard will continue to progress and become a solid two-way defender in the QMJHL, but in order to continue to progress with his offensive game, he'll need to make smarter plays while in possession of the puck and improve his play in the transition game. He's good when he plays within his limits, but this doesn't really translate to a big upside at the NHL level. At best, he'll likely end up becoming a 3rd-pairing defenseman if everything goes well (there is still a lot of work to do there, however).

"One NHL scout looked at our ranking and pointed at his name and just nodded his head sideways. I pointed at Beaudin who we had ranked much higher and he nodded his head up and down in approval."
HP Scout, Mark Edwards

140 BERNI, TIM — GCK ZURICH — SWISS-2 — 5' 11.25" — 174 lbs — LD

Tim Berni is a two-way defenseman who developed in both the NLB and NLA, gaining pro experience. He played 23 games for the ZSC Lions when including the playoffs, he put up zero points despite his team winning the NLA championship. In the NLB, he produced 15 points in 36 games, including 10 assists. He was featured at the U20's where he had some flashes, though he put up zero points in 5 games and at the Hlinka, where he had zero points in 4 games.

Berni is an undersized, yet aggressive transitional defenseman who looks to shoot the puck from the back-end. His acceleration isn't high-end considering his size but he's shown the ability to find soft-ice quickly and use his edges to weave in and out of traffic, giving him clean transitional zone entries in several of our viewings. If he can find an open skating lane, he's got a decent first-pass yet this skill wasn't always on point. His mindset is to attack both with and without the puck. He's not afraid to stand-up bigger players than himself in order to make a defensive-play, though his positioning can get thrown off by his aggression, causing improper spacing, leading to poor gaps. His decision making is his own end is average. We have seen him squeeze out players along the boards with correct timing, as well as see him make an accurate defensive-read even if it's a high paced play, but he's also prone to defensive errors due to a lack of decisiveness at times which puts him in-between the play.

His offensive-game is predicated around his ability to get his shot through traffic. He's got plus hands and uses them while in motion to breakdown opposing teams when rushing the puck, though he can be overzealous at times and force his shot through traffic. That being said, his wrist-shot and slapshot are heavy considering his size. The biggest drawback to his ability to walk the line is his lateral movement doesn't allow him to re-open shooting lanes at the rate you would want considering the shoot-first mentality that he had in our viewings.

Berni is an interesting defenseman with some raw offensive-upside but he needs to further refine his decision making in his own-end and continue to work on his four-way mobility in order to become an effective pro player.

| NR | BIBEAU, FELIX | ROUYN-NORANDA | QMJHL | 6' 0.0" | 189 lbs | LC |

Bibeau had a stellar preseason and first month of 2017-2018 before cooling off a bit, only to roar back in the second half of the season and surpass the 60-point mark, more than quadrupling his totals from last season. He was briefly slowed down by an injury in February, but remained one of the key offensive leaders on the Huskies.

Bibeau, in addition to being a key faceoffs' guy, likes to shoot the puck (he led the team in that department). He also found a unique chemistry with Huskies' leading scorer Rafaël Harvey-Pinard, as they complemented each other's strengths and weaknesses very well and were notably a force to be reckoned with on the man-advantage (nearly half of Bibeau's goals this year came on the power play). While his passing skills are not to be dismissed, he's slightly more eager to be the one to finish the play. Sometimes, however, his decision-making got in the way, leading to him overthinking and losing the puck as a result. He's excellent on the PK, more than willing to block shots and has great anticipation. Great work ethic; he shows up every game and his compete level is really good. He's a player who takes pride in doing all the little details well. He doesn't have a big upside offensively for the pro level, but his hockey IQ is excellent, and that could help him become a role player down the road.

| NR | BINNER, ALEXIS | MAINE | H-EAST | 6' 3.25" | 209 lbs | LD |

Alexis Binner is an athletic, shut-down defenseman who plays a physical style of hockey. After getting passed over in last years draft, Binner played for Maine where he produced 9 points in 36 games, including 8 assists.

Offense has never been a big part of Binner's game due to his lack of skill and inability to read the play in the offensive-end at a consistent rate. Instead, he plays a sound defensive game; he likes to play a punishing style in front of his own net and does a good job boxing guys out for his goalie. Against the rush, Alexis keeps a good gap and had good timing in being able to force players to the outside and finish his check along the wall. He doesn't have great explosiveness and needs to work on his foot speed in order to get separation from quicker fore-checkers. He isn't flashy with the puck and rarely skates it beyond centre ice. Though, he makes a solid exit pass to help transition the puck if the player is open. Where he gets into trouble is when his first read is not available, he tends to hang onto the puck too long which is where improving his explosiveness to gain separation becomes key for him going forward. In the offensive zone, Binner's game is very vanilla, relying on a big shot that he can put his size behind and has a really quick snap shot that he can get through traffic ok but he doesn't have a lot of creativity to open up lanes from the blue line or go D to D quick enough, where we have seen his cross-ice passes get telegraphed and taken in on breakaways. He tends to default to putting the puck back down the wall and into the corner. He doesn't take a lot of risks to keep pucks in the zone or pinch down the wall and will give up the blue line easily in most instances. Binner, right now projects as a depth defenseman or a support partner for a more offensive defenseman. He handles things in his own end and keeps pucks and players out of the middle of the ice well.

"He might be a late pick but I'm not convinced he's worthy yet. I question his hockey sense. - NHL Scout, March 2018

"Not really a skilled player.- NHL Scout, April 2018

"Powerful skater. I really like him." - NHL Scout, April 2018

| NR | BITTEN, SAMUEL | OTTAWA | OHL | 6' 1.25" | 192 lbs | LC |

Samuel had a bit of a slow start to the season with the 67's, which was his first full year in the OHL. Once he got to the 15-game mark for Ottawa, he became a very consistent player all year long. Samuel is a defensive center that showed a high IQ away from the puck and chipped in offensively throughout the year. He has a good shot coming down the wing and does a good job of using his large frame to protect the puck, helping extend play. He makes his biggest impact in the offensive zone by winning puck battles and applying pressure to the puck carrier. Bitten isn't a player who is going to beat you with high skill, though his puck skills steadily improved as the season went on. He seemed to have more confidence from game to game by showing his ability to rush the puck through the neutral zone, gain the offensive blue line and make a smart decision with the puck to set up a line-mate. Samuel's play away from the puck is his asset. He has good anticipation by positioning himself for outlet-passes when looking to exit his own-end. Despite his impressive play away from the puck, Bitten lacks top end speed and needs to work on his first couple of steps. Given his size, if he improves his speed, then he could be more effective offensively by taking pucks hard to the net. If Bitten can continue to develop over the coming years by increasing his speed and offensive-output, then he can contribute at both ends of the ice due to his high-compete level.

| NR | BODAK, MARTIN | KOOTENAY | WHL | 6' 0.0" | 189 lbs | RD |

Martin Bodak is entering his third year of draft eligibility. This past season was his first in North-America after getting drafted by the kootenay Ice in the CHL import draft in 2017. He had a successful rookie year in the WHL, putting up 31 points in 59 games, with 24 assists. Internationally, he captained the U20 Slovakian team, scoring 3 goals in 5 games.

Martin Bodak is a two-way transitional defenseman who has a well-rounded offensive-skill set. He's not the biggest defender but is capable in his own end. We have seen him deliver solid body-checks after reading plays in-tight to the net, as well as use his stick and a decent-amount of aggression to make life more difficult for opposing players when they attempt to park themselves in-front of the net area. His biggest defensive-drawback for us was that he wasn't consistent under pressure and sometimes was susceptible to the forecheck due to not being strong enough on the puck, allowing himself to get stick-lifted as a result. That being said, he's got plus four-way mobility and has a calmness to him in the neutral zone that wasn't as notable in the defensive-end at times. This when combined with his above-average hands, allowed him to weave in and out of traffic while avoiding active-sticks. His transitional zone entries while maintaining possession were a plus, which allowed him to be effective on the powerplay as well as at even-strength. When talking the line, he uses his crossover mechanics to create room where he released low, yet heavy slapshots that generated several rebounds in our viewings. His wrist-shot although lacking significant power, was accurate and he scored on a couple of well-placed shots in the slot area. Furthermore, he's capable of impressive shot-fakes using his wind-up to mask his intentions with the puck before dishing it off to create a more dynamic play.

Bodak was brought onto a rebuilding WHL team that lacked a promising defender, so he was tasked with becoming a go-to option on the backend and did an admirable job for his squad. Unfortunately, he doesn't stand out in any one area and lacks high-end upside or defensive qualities that would suggest his game can translate to the NHL at this time.

| 13 | BOKK, DOMINIK | VAXJO JR. | SWEDEN-JR. | 6' 1.0" | 176 lbs* | LW |

Dominik Bokk made the decision to move from Germany to Sweden in his draft year to continue his development after according to him, the Windsor Spitfires were unable to acquire him in the CHL import draft. He moved up and down between the SHL and J20 team throughout the season, dressing for 15 SHL games. From January to the end of the season, Bokk played for the J20 team and put together a successful junior season by producing 41 points in 35 regular season games, including 27 assists. In the playoffs he had 5 goals and 6 assists in 8 games which helped the team to the Gold Medal game where they were bested by HV71.

It was a year of adjustments for Bokk after lighting up the junior ranks in Germany, taking some time to adapt to the faster pace of the game in Sweden while playing against better competition. However, once he managed to adjust, he became one of the most dynamic offensive-threats in SuperElit and developed over the course of the season into one of the best offensive-talents the 2018 draft has to offer. There's very few players in this class that are as dangerous as Dominik in one-on-one situations. Whatever deke can be thought of, he can most likely do it. His hands are superb, he can pull pucks rapidly away and towards his body yet has a rare level of finesse that allows him to make subtle dekes that are no less effective; when combined with his tremendous balance and fluidity, he can do things with the puck that leave you in awe. We have seen him push his frame into a defender behind the net while simultaneously chipping the puck past him, then using the momentum of the defenders check attempt to rapidly spin-off while simultaneously pulling the puck back to his stick as one example. The main take away isn't necessarily the flair and flash of his skillset, even though it is impressive to look it, it's the rate of execution given the difficulty of the move he's attempting. There's arguably no forward better in this class at making a successful move that's got a high-degree of difficulty.

Once he's broken down his opponents using his skill-set, he's got a versatile attack at his disposal. His playmaking ability is exceptional, he can thread difficult passes at speed and has excellent offensive-awareness which allows him to recognize where his teammates are going to be positioned in advance of the play. He's not a pass first-winger though, as his offensive-instincts allow him to adapt to lanes on the fly and recognize when he's got an open shot. His wrist-shot has one of the top release points in the draft and he can use it in combination with his hands and body movement. He covers the release with his minimal body movement before spring loading into his shot. This made him dangerous off the rush where it was very difficult for goalies in the SHL, let alone junior to pick up on his mechanics. Contrastingly, he produces a lot of movement when generating power in his slapshot, this allows him to get the puck off his stick quicker on the powerplay.

Although Bokk has several dynamic offensive-qualities, his play away from the puck and his skating mechanics are a work in progress. That's not to say that he isn't fast, he can beat out players in races to pucks and can generate a decent amount of separation speed when in transition, he just has unrefined technique that needs some work, such as having an upright posture when in full-flight. His intelligence does allow him to recognize defensive-plays, where we have seen him intercept passes with his stick that are labelled to the opponent that he's covering and we have seen him make some aggressive backchecks that have resulted in takeaways. Mostly, it's his physical instincts and positioning at times that need to be refined. He looks to use his stick and not his body which doesn't allow him to compete effectively along the boards, which was even more noticeable in the SHL. Although he has areas he needs to work on, Bokk is an exceptional offensive-talent with one of the highest-ceilings in this draft which is why we have him ranked as highly as we do.

"He's skilled but he's a projection because he is so raw. It will be interesting to see what he does the rest of the season." NHL Scout, November 2017

"Not crazy about some of the body language I see from him." - NHL Scout, February 2018

"He's a euro version of (Mathew) Barzal" - NHL Scout, April 2018

"You can't deny this kids skill." - NHL Scout, May 2018

"I think he has very good offensive instincts, offensive hockey seems to come easy to him. He processes situations quickly. His hands are high end, very quick and shifty. The weakness is skating, he has a short choppy stride. That said, he has quick feet and seems to find a way to win races. He's a pure goal scorer and has skill to match some of the top players in this draft class. If the skating wasn't quite as ugly he might really go early on the Friday night. - HP Scout, Mark Edwards

"I got some mixed feedback on his combine interviews." - HP Scout, Mark Edwards June 2018

11	BOQVIST, ADAM	BRYNAS JR.	SWEDEN-JR.	5' 11.5"	165 lbs *	RD

Boqvist is one of the premier defensemen available in this year's NHL Entry Draft. This year, he played mostly in the SuperElit league, but also played 15 games in the SHL.

His offensive tools are high-end and his shot is really good, his release is elite and amongst the best in the draft. He loves shooting the puck; he has scored many times from the point with his wrist shot. His release is such a key component of his offensive skillset, but he's also good at finding shooting lanes and adept at faking shots and being patient with the puck to find a better angle to get it through. He thinks the game really well; his decision-making is excellent and he processes the game exceptionally well. On the power play, he moves the puck quickly to his teammates and has great vision to set them up for scoring chances. He's really like a 4th forward on the ice; he loves to rush the puck in the offensive zone and can make end-to-end rushes. His skating is above-average.. His mobility, agility and footwork are all above-average. He can be a bit risky with the puck, as he seemingly likes try to score on every shift; he wants to be a difference-maker on the ice for his team. His puck skills are excellent, he's dangerous one-on-one, as he can be unpredictable with his speed, shot or deke.

Defensively, he currently lacks the strength to compete against physically strong players, which is why he was not a full-time player in the SHL this season. He's a smart player and can defend well enough, but his lack of strength can hurt him when playing older stronger players. To improve his defensive game, we would like to see him compete a bit more in his own zone and be harder on the puck-carrier. Boqvist will probably need time in Sweden to gain some strength and mature physically, but has great potential and could be a premiere offensive defenseman in the NHL in a few years.

"He's already better than half the guys they (SWE) had in Plymouth (World Jr Summer Showcase in August)" NHL Scout, September 2017

"He's top 3 for me right now. He's more like Erik Karlsson than Rasmus is." NHL Scout, October 2017

"It's close between Hughes and Boqvist but I give the edge to Hughes because he's already closer to being great in the NHL. Boqvist is almost a year younger so he might end up being even better but he's farther away than Hughes is to being special." NHL Scout, May 2018

"I think he processes the game very quickly. He gets the puck and can move it quickly with a very smart decision. Offensively he is a weapon. He has a good shot and great offensive instincts. He's a work in progress in his own zone but largely due to lack of strength. I never like to hear the concussion word associated with any player, especially players I'd want to select high in the draft. The gap between Boqvist and Lundkvist shrunk quite a bit for me by seasons end." - HP Scout, Mark Edwards

"Good feedback on his combine interviews and I interviewed him myself and was also impressed. Good self evaluation of his game." - HP Scout, Mark Edwards

| 10 | BOUCHARD, EVAN | LONDON | OHL | 6' 2.0" | 196 lbs * | RD |

Evan Bouchard was selected 17th overall by the London Knights in the 2016 OHL draft. He captained London while putting up the most points out of any defender in the OHL, finishing with 87 points in 67 games, including 25 goals. In the playoffs, he scored 5 points in 4 games. He was a unique defender in the sense that London's offense ran through him. He was the leading scorer on the team despite being a defender, and generated the most shots on net out of any defender in the OHL.

Bouchard is a talented two-way defender who loves to join or literally be the rush. His offensive-instincts are excellent which allows him to make-well timed decisions when he jumps into the play, while also timing his pinches correctly at the blueline. He scored several high-end goals rushing down the wing before releasing his quick wrist-shot, which has both accuracy and power behind it. Although a transitional defenseman with good overall speed, his skating stride is awkward but he still generates power and manages to shift-gears quickly, allowing him to cut-wide on defenders and create additional offensive-chances. He doesn't need to join the rush to be dangerous though, as he can generate shots from the point at an extremely high-rate. He's aware of when his lanes are blocked and has a reduced wind-up on his slapshot which allows him to get it through traffic before his lanes fill up. If his lane does get blocked, he's capable of making shot fakes and head fakes to re-open his lanes. This made him extremely effective on the powerplay, where he could freeze opposing players at the blueline then distribute the puck quickly. His hockey sense in the offensive-end when carrying the puck allowed him to change the conditions on the ice to his liking, he forced his opponents to react to him as opposed to being reactive to them, and this made him consistently dangerous on a game to game basis.

Although Bouchard's offensive-game can't be understated, there's some cause for a bit of concern on the defensive-side. He does have a good-sized frame, and we have seen him use it effectively to block shots and weigh against opponents along the boards, however he can be very inconsistent in terms of his compete level. He does log heavy-minutes and seems to reserve himself for transitional zone-entries when attempting to gain the line, but it was an area of concern for us both last year and this year. Too many times we saw him lose puck battles that he should've won and he doesn't make life difficult enough for opposing players when he's attempting to box them out. Lastly, he has decent gap control but we have seen him get beat to the outside without much resistance more often than we would like. Despite this, he is capable of making a solid defensive-reads and has exceptional outlet passes that help reduce his defensive issues.

Bouchard is a very skilled defenseman but might not be quite as dynamic as a few of the other defenders at the top of this stacked class for high end defenseman. If he can improve his first few steps and compete more regularly on a shift-to-shift basis, that would go a long way towards fulfilling his potential of becoming a top-pairing defenseman who can quarterback a powerplay at the NHL level.

"He's a solid 2nd round pick" NHL Scout, October 2017

"Dale plays him 35 minutes a game, that's why he looks lazy." NHL Scout, December 2017

"He was really good in the Subway game, I feel better about him now than I did earlier this year. He wasn't good when I saw him my first few times this year." - NHL Scout, November 2017

"He reminds me of Jake Gardiner, there is no questioning his talent but he plays way too soft too often." NHL Scout, December 2017

"He picks his spots to rest because he plays so many minutes." NHL Scout, December 2017

"Skates the puck until he either turns it over or scores." - NHL Scout, December, 2017

"I see some of these rankings and can't believe it. Not in my first round but it looks like he's going top 10." - NHL Scout, January 2018

"He is a lot like Jake Gardiner to me and that's not too bad of a player. He adds tools to a teams back end." - Different NHL Scout than above, March 2018

"His skating reminds me of cough medicine, it leaves a really awful taste in your mouth but it works." - HP Scout, Brad Allen

"Has some qualities that remind me of a player I coached for a short time, Ryan Sproul. Obviously not in the skating department but rather that they both excelled inside the offensive blueline, but compete level was a big issue for both players in their own end." - HP Scout, Mark Edwards

"One of the early conversations with a scout regarding Bouchard was in October and the scout called him a solid 2nd round pick. I reminded that same scout of that conversation in February and he had moved him into the top 20. I got another update in March and he still said top 20 for him but predicted he would go in the top 10.." - HP Scout, Mark Edwards

"One scout singled him out as one of the better interviews of the week and feedback was positive overall. He did a good job with the media on the Friday of combine week." HP Scout, Mark Edwards

"Top 10 pick and won't shock me if it's Detroit or Ottawa either. I'd guess Detroit if I had to pick one." - NHL Scout, June 2018

"He'll be the 2nd defenseman off the board after Dobson." - NHL Scout, June 2018

| 80 | BOUCHARD, XAVIER | BAIE-COMEAU | QMJHL | 6' 3.5" | 190 lbs * | RD |

Bouchard, after a strong first season last year when he amassed 34 points, had a tougher 2nd season in the QMJHL, where his numbers were all down. He didn't take the next step in his development, as we had hoped for before the season.

He was a late cut in August for Team Canada's U-18 team for the Ivan Hlinka tournament. He didn't look as confident with the puck as he was last year, a lot of times this year he looked hesitant in his decision-making. His ability to join or lead the rush, something that made him successful the past two years, was not the same this year. He looked like a player who lost confidence and was scared to make plays. Bouchard remains a player with good size; he's tall and will keep getting stronger physically, as he continues to mature physically. He skates well; he could be more fluid with his lateral agility, but he has a long stride and generates some decent speed when he wants to join or lead the rush. He has a long stick, but doesn't use it efficiently in the defensive zone. He needs to be more active with it in the defensive zone to break passes or passing lanes. He's not a physical defenseman, despite his size. He prefers using his smarts to counter opposing forwards. He remains a smart hockey player, he's always been one, and it's a big reason to still believe in him after that tough season.

We wouldn't be surprised by a bounce-back season next year from Bouchard, who has the skills and smarts to do that. There are players in the QMJHL in the past who had really bad draft years for various reasons, and did bounce back the following year such as Maxime Comtois and Nicolas Roy, and we feel Bouchard might be a candidate to do the same thing.

"He had a disappointing season after a great rookie year in 2016-2017. I'm not quitting on him, though. He has good size and puck skills but needs to regain confidence, as he looked like he was afraid to make a play this year." - HP Scout Jérôme Bérubé

192	BOUDRIAS, SHAWN	GATINEAU	QMJHL	6' 3.75"	197 lbs	RW

Boudrias went undrafted last season, even though he had some interesting skills. When combined with his size and very late birthday (born September 14th, 1999), one must take into consideration that he was also the youngest player eligible for the 2017 NHL Entry Draft.

In his first full season with Gatineau, he had a good year, averaging close to a point per game on an offensively-challenged team. Oddly enough, he had his best moments offensively after his team traded Abramov and Balmas, their top two offensive players at the time. Boudrias can play both at center and on the wing; he plays a pretty complete game at both ends of the ice. He's a smart player; he understands the game well and can be an asset for a team's penalty-killing unit. He reads the play well with his good anticipation, and also uses his long stick well in the defensive zone to block passing lanes. He's a big kid and still growing it seems; he uses his body and long reach well along the boards to protect the puck and it's tough to take it away from him. His skating ability is still a work in progress. His offensive game has improved every year since he arrived in the QMJHL. He gets a lot of his points from hard work down low and in front of the net. One area that he has improved a lot since coming to Gatineau is his poise with the puck. He is calmer, and able to slow down the play and not rush his decision-making.

Boudrias doesn't project as an offensive star at the pro level, but with his size, defensive game and smarts, he may get a look late in the draft as a re-entry player.

"He went undrafted last year. This season was a big bounce-back year for him, and he's also still very young. I like his chances this year, as he had a big year offensively and produced a lot after Abramov was dealt." - HP Scout Jérôme Bérubé

136	BOUTHILLIER, ZACHARY	CHICOUTIMI	QMJHL	6' 2.5"	185 lbs	G

Bouthillier had an interesting draft year; he was traded from Shawinigan to Chicoutimi in late August after he was thought to be the goaltender of the future for the Cataractes. With Chicoutimi, he shared the workload with rookie netminder Alexis Shank. He played 38 games and won 13 of them, on one of the worst teams in the league.

Consistency has always been a big issue for Bouthillier, ever since his midget days with the Gaulois in Saint-Hyacinthe. In the first half of the season this continued to be the case: some decent performances mixed with some bad ones. His rebound-control was often poor, and this has also been a big issue with him in the past. After the Christmas break, he made some adjustments and looked more focused in his crease. He played some real good hockey in front of a bad team. Without a doubt, he had the best stretch of his career from January to March of this year. He has the ideal size for a goaltender, at over 6'02", and has good athletic abilities. He's a good athlete with good technique who is also very calm in his crease. He has great work ethic, doesn't quit on any pucks and can make 2nd and 3rd saves because of his athleticism. He had a great playoff series against Acadie-Bathurst in the first round, with some excellent performances despite facing (on average) 39 shots per game. He ended up winning two of those games for his team, which few people predicted. He had a great second half of the season and postseason; next year, it will be crucial for him to demonstrate that he can do this on a full season. His play after Christmas helped him a lot in terms of getting back into the draft rankings (as it didn't look like he was going to get picked after the first three months of the season). Now, he looks like he could potentially be a mid-to-late pick in the draft.

"He was outstanding in the last two months of the season, but we have seen a lot of inconsistencies out of him in the past few years, going back to his midget days." - HP Scout Jérôme Bérubé

NR	BRENNAN, TED	KELOWNA	WHL	6' 1.0"	202 lbs	LC

A true rookie who ended up bouncing around all 3 forward positions for Kelowna but ended up playing his most effective hockey on the left wing. An aggressive player with decent speed and lower body power, Brennan can win puck battles and does a good job forcing his body between his man and the puck doing his best work down low on a pure checking line. Most of the minimal offense he created was of the the chip and chase variety and rarely showed much in the way of offensive instinct, despite playing in the tight spaces he didn't exhibit much in the way of puck control to make plays and translate his ability to battle into scoring chances. Deserves credit for staying aggressive but keeping his penalty minutes down. Suffered a little from lack of ice-time as he buried low in the lineup on a top heavy team and couple injuries forced to play on higher lines but he looked over matched and couldn't use his toughness to agitate or free pucks up for more skilled players. Should benefit in year 2 from a larger role and could be utilized as more of checking centre if his footwork continues to improve as it did through the season – At this point we don't consider Brennan a viable draft prospect.

NR	BUCEK, SAMUEL	CHICAGO	USHL	6' 3.0"	192 lbs	LW

Bucek is a re-entry prospect that many scouts had high hopes for last season in his first draft eligible year. Moving from Chicago (USHL) to Shawinigan (QMJHL), Bucek struggled to find consistency with the Cataractes and eventually fell off scouts radars. Returning to Chicago (USHL) for the 17/18 season, Bucek has seen a bit of resurgence in his game. Bucek displayed much more sand paper and willingness to compete to win pucks. Where Bucek really showed strides was at the World Juniors in Buffalo this year where he carried a Slovakia team to a win over the United States and registering 3 goals and 4 assists in 5 Games in the tournament. Bucek has always had the size and physical tools to be a solid prospect and looks to be putting it together mentally by playing the right way and using the strengths to his advantage. Bucek's willingness to drive the net and use his big frame to gain position and create havoc in front is key to him being effective. His foot speed and agility has kept him from keeping pace with the game at times but that area of his game has made strides this season, as he has seemed to develop some extra jump with the puck on his stick. Bucek certainly still has some work to do before becoming a pro prospect, however his game has made some necessary strides this year to be considered as a later round draft pick.

"At this point I feel like I've been watching him for forever. I'll pass." NHL Scout, December 2017

"He's been an interesting prospect the last three years, two years ago in his underage year with Chicago in 15/16, I thought he was going to be a high end pick and then he had a very down year in the Q in his draft year, now he seems to be getting closer to the player many thought he could be. He can't go the NCAA route due to the one year in the QMJHL so whatever team drafts him will also have to decide a developmental path for him as well." HP Scout, Dusten Braaksma

NR	BULYCH, KALEB	VANCOUVER	WHL	6' 1.0"	165 lbs	RD

A speedy right shot defender Bulych is somewhat one dimensional with his skillset, he can skate well with good bursts of speed and the ability to side step and take the puck aggressively up ice, his shot leaves something to be desired which has led to his low point totals, he just doesn't get enough power behind his point shots to generate tips or beat a goalie clean. Makes a solid breakout pass when pushing the pace up ice can quickly grab a rebound and send a forward out of the zone. When Bulych holds the pucks too long his own zone trouble ensues, as he gets a pushed around easily and bumped off the puck; especially below the goal line and around the net. Has trouble boxing out players around his own net and doesn't do a great job clearing traffic. In a few viewings he was on the receiving end of some big hits knocking him clean off pucks and hitting the ground hard. Bulych has great feet and a good reach with strong offensive instinct and puck moving ability, but he needs to gets stronger and more aggressive defensively to become a prospect.

110	BURZAN, LUKA	BRANDON	WHL	6' 0.0"	180 lbs	LC

Luke Burzan was selected 6th overall in the 2015 WHL Bantam Draft by the Moose Jaw Warriors. After a productive 16-year-old season with the Warriors, Burzan was a major piece sent to Brandon for Kale Clague at the trade deadline. Burzan recorded 9 goals and 12 assists in the final 30 games of the season for the Wheat Kings in a top-6 role for the Club.

Burzan is an explosive skater with smooth edges and a powerful stride. He has the ability to create space with his feet and eat up defenseman on the forecheck with his straight-line speed. Under pressure, Luka is shifty and can turn away from pressure with ease. His smooth edges combined with his strong first few steps makes him tough to contain. Luka's overall offensive game is inconsistent. He is the type of player with excellent physical skills and talent but leaves you wondering why he does not produce more. His production comes in waves and he can disappear for periods at a time. When at his best, he shoots the puck often, displaying a quick heavy release. With the puck, Burzan can be creative and can make tough plays through bodies. Although he has the ability to find teammates, he does not make plays on a consistent basis.

This inconsistency is partly due to the fact Burzan can play casually a little too often. He can get caught floating and does not use his skating skills to the best of his ability. With the puck, Burzan has quick hands and can skate up ice with ease, but as with his play without the puck, he lacks the intensity to make the next step offensively. Burzan has the tools to be an excellent offensive player, and given his skating skills can play up a down the lineup. Do not be surprised if Burzan breaks out offensively, and is an intriguing prospect despite his average production in his second full season in the WHL.

142	BUSBY, DENNIS	FLINT	OHL	5' 10.5"	188 lbs	RD

Dennis Busby was selected in the second round, 23rd Overall at the 2016 OHL Draft by the Flint Firebirds. Dennis had a very difficult draft year due to injuries, finishing the 2018 season with zero points in 2 games. We have included our older profile of him.

Dennis is a smooth skating defenseman who likes to rush the puck up the ice. He gets a lot of power in his stride and can skate the puck out of his own zone. He has good puck skills and hits his targets in all three zones. He is capable of completing difficult passes or making the smart simple play up ice. Evidence of his puck moving ability comes from his 14 assists as a 16-year-old playing a third pairing role for the Firebirds for the majority of this season. He does a good job at the offensive blueline knowing when to pinch and keeps the play going. Dennis is decent in his own zone but needs to show some improvements in this part of his game. He also lacks strength at the moment and would benefit from improving his build. Next season should be a big year for Busby. It's disappointing that he suffered from the injuries that he did, but hopefully the kid can put his injuries behind him heading into next season.

"Just going on last year, he has good hockey sense. He's got good skill but undersized and not that hard to play against." - NHL Scout, May 2018

"There might be a team who will take him late (in the draft) his coach loves him." - NHL Scout, May 2018

"I actually got lucky and saw one of his games, it was the London game on October 27th. Flint got smoked 8-2 and Busby was minus two. Our evaluation is obviously based on older viewings and is somewhat incomplete." -HP Scout, Mark Edwards

182	CALLAHAN, MICHAEL	YOUNGSTOWN	USHL	6' 2.0"	197 lbs	LD

Callahan is coming off a successful rookie season in the USHL, which saw him get traded from Central Illinois to Youngstown in early February. Callahan has NHL size, has a strong frame for his age and can log a lot of minutes due to his ability to be efficient with his skating and physicality. Callahan is physical against opponents in front of his own net, in puck battles and wins his share of those battles. Callahan displays solid defensive positioning against the rush. Michael uses his efficient footwork and stick positioning to keep puck carriers to the outside and has good timing to finish his check along the boards. Callahan has good skating technique and explosiveness that allows him to escape pressure from fore-checkers and execute clean zone exits. His decision making and hockey IQ is high end, he takes good angles on puck retrievals and is able to make quick reads and find his forwards and stretch the ice consistently.

Callahan is a solid defensive defenseman but his game is not without some offensive tools despite limited offensive numbers this season (3 goals and 15 assists in 59 games). Callahan isn't going to dance around the offensive zone with the puck or make a lot of flashy plays but he is an accurate passer and his footwork allows him to successfully walk the blue line to open up passing and shooting lanes in order to move the puck around the zone. Callahan has a booming slap shot from the point that hasn't been utilized often in our viewings. Callahan has often been paired with an offensive defenseman due to his sound defensive game but has a raw skill set that may develop into more of an offensive threat in the coming years. Callahan plays a mature, low risk game and will fit in well at Providence where he will play in the fall.

"I think he's a bit underrated, he has a lot of tools, is a strong, athletic kid and has NHL size and high hockey IQ, plays a very mature game for his age." HP Scout, Dusten Braaksma (January, 2018)

"I don't think he's going to ever drive offense from the back end but he can be that stabilizing presence." HP Scout, Dusten Braaksma (April, 2018)

"Has a real mature personality and approach to the game" NHL Scout, March 2018

"He's a big kid and he's just ok. Not a guy on my list." - NHL Scout, March 2018

| 96 | CHISHOLM, DECLAN | PETERBOROUGH | OHL | 6' 0.75" | 185 lbs | LD |

Chisholm is an intelligent, two-way defender with strong mobility. Declan possesses above average skating abilities which he is able to utilize to elevate his game on both sides of the puck. Declan see's the ice very well, he shows an ability to make a hard and accurate first pass. He has shown added confidence in his skating abilities and puck skills, becoming more of a threat to carry the puck and push the pace in transition. While he would benefit from becoming more assertive in attacking the goal once gaining the offensive blue line, he shows strong decision making in his ability to move the puck to a teammate or simplify his game. Offensively Chisholm shows good decision making in his reads, jumping in from his blue line position appropriately. He also shows an ability to distribute the puck with effectiveness and open shooting/passing lanes with his quick feet. While defending transition Declan would benefit from tightening his gaps and creating more trouble for opponents looking to gain entry to the zone as he can passively allow zone entries. His quick stick and mobility does allow him to keep the play in front him and angle players away from the center of the ice. He shows good defensive zone awareness, as he is positionally sound and uses his stick and body positioning to defender. Chisholm will need to continue to improve his strength, but shows intriguing two-way upside.

"I saw him over six times this year and I still don't know what he is." NHL Scout, May 2018

"Tough year in Peterborough, bad team. Lost a year of development as a 16 year old ...thought his game started to progress this year but then he had some injuries." NHL Scout, May 2018

"Smart player, good skater...he has more than he's been able to show because of injuries." - NHL Scout, May 2018

"Struggled a to see him this year. He was out of the lineup in a many of my viewings. With that said, I liked Declan in his OHL Draft year and heading into this year" - HP Scout, Mark Edwards

NR	CHYZOWSKI, RYAN	MEDICINE HAT	WHL	6' 0.0"	183 lbs	LW

Ryan Chyzowski had a breakout year offensively for the Medicine Hat Tigers, recording 52 points and 21 goals in 72 regular season games. The former 1st round pick in the 2015 WHL Bantam Draft saw steady top-6 minutes with the Tigers, including on the team's first powerplay unit where he was usually posted on the half-wall.

Chyzowski has drastically improved his strength from his 16-year-old year, which allows him to excel at protecting pucks in the offensive zone. He is a strong cycle player, and has the skill to evade defenders and control pucks along the wall. Ryan has above average offensive instincts, and relies on his hockey sense and above average skill with the puck to make plays. His shot is strong, as he can score from distance with an accurate and deceptive release. He cannot be described as a dynamic as he does not have the explosive skating ability to be able to consistently create offense for himself as an individual. He can be described as doing a lot of things well offensively, but he is not dominant in any one category.

Ryan also shows a competitive side to his game. Having gained significant strength in his lower half, he can complete physically and land the occasional big open ice hit. As well he doesn't shy down from contact or a challenge, dropping the gloves when needed. His battle level is strong and he excelled in the playoffs, when the energy level picked up, recording 4 goals in 6 playoff games. Chyzowski is not dominant offensively, and his skating is only average, but he has some offensive upside and plays the right way without the puck.

62	CLARK, KODY	OTTAWA	OHL	6' 1.0"	179 lbs *	RW

Kody Clark played with more confidence this year then in his rookie season, which allowed him to utilize his talents more consistently. He had a solid year of production in his sophomore campaign for the 67's, producing 39 points in 56 games, including 18 goals before going pointless in the playoffs.

Clark is a skilled winger whose skating ability and hands compliment his possession game. He's a smart offensive player, that has good hockey IQ, this allowed him to be dangerous from the high-slot to the goal-line, where he would find soft-ice and receive passes in order to get off his dangerous shot. His release point is fast and deceptive, while also demonstrating a high-degree of accuracy. His shot is fine-tuned, giving him the ability to be dangerous both from a stand-still position and when in motion. We have seen him use his impressive edges and soft-hands to shift out of the way of a body check before wiring a puck bar-down over a netminder as an example. Despite Kody having a reduced wind-up on his slapshot to keep the accuracy consistent, we would like to see him work on his one-timer. There were times in our viewings, where he would receive a pass in a high scoring area and cradle the puck instead of shooting the puck right away. By taking that extra second or two, it gives the goalie time to get in position and get squared to the shooter. His playmaking skills are a plus and they helped translate to the powerplay, as he's good at finding the open man trailing or drawing defenders in and finding his teammates in the slot. If his passing lanes were taken from him, he showed impressive acceleration and has a fluid stride which allows him to get up to full-flight quickly. He used his speed and deceptive gear shifts to suddenly change his shooting angle when looking to generate off the rush.

Although Clarke has impressive offensive-skills, his mentality away from the puck doesn't translate well to a more physical and intense brand of hockey that occurs at the pro levels and especially in the playoffs. He's not always willing to engage aggressively with his opponents along the boards and tends to shy away from high-traffic areas, relying on a more perimeter style of play at this time. He needs to become more consistent at getting to the dirty areas of the ice and competing more regularly on a shift-to-shift basis. If he becomes more comfortable playing an up-tempo and competitive brand of hockey, then he could potentially become a point-producer at the pro levels.

"I question his willingness to go into the hard areas." NHL Scout, October 2017

"I'd like to see him be first on pucks more often. He's been a bit inconsistent for me as well." - NHL Scout, December 2018

"He can be invisible at times but he's got a lot up skill and compared to other guys in the OHL this year his upside is much higher." - NHL Scout, December 2017

"He's skilled and there is some upside but I'd like to see him win more pucks for himself...he pulls the chute at times too." - NHL Scout, February 2018

"I went back and forth on Clark this year. There were times I thought he disappeared and other times where he was their (67's) best player. One thing I noticed during a game in Peterborough was he took an extra half second to get the puck off his tape, it cost him. He needs to be harder on puck retrievals and win more pucks. He looked tentative at times when I saw him." - HP Scout, Mark Edwards

NR	COLINA, LLIJAH	PRINCE GEORGE	WHL	5' 9.0"	175 lbs	RC

A big scorer in Bantam Colina was a long shot as an 8th round draft pick of Portland in 2015 out of the Burnaby Winter Club, he was acquired by Prince George in Jan 2018 as one of the young roster players exchanged for top rental defenseman Dennis Cholowski. Speedy and small Colina is a typical undersize center, shows great ability to work on the parameter of the ice and zips pucks around the offensive zone with ease as his strength is in the set up game creating opportunities for his linemates. He a decent skater with good speed and strong edge work, but suffers from a lack of strength, so his elusiveness is his best asset with his feet. Can utilized some well placed shots but doesn't have much power behind that accuracy, would benefit greatly on a line with some pure shooters, but looked to be more of a possession driver once he was dealt to Prince George and got more opportunity among a less skilled forward group. Was tiny in his rookie year and it showed, we consistently knocked off pucks and bashed around by bigger defenders, show some bouts of toughness sneaking around the net, was never overly this consistent in that facet of the game but did look a little more powerful in his second season and showed a better ability to battle down low, however was still below average here. A long term project as a prospect who would have been ignored only a few years ago, he'll add organizational depth to a pro team but that's likely the ceiling.

NR	COPELAND, BEN	WATERLOO	USJHL	5' 10.5"	179 lbs	RC

Copeland has never been a big point producer so his 18 Goals and 44 assists in 60 games for Waterloo this season caught a lot of scout's attention. Copeland is a re-entry prospect as a 99' born. Copeland is an excellent skating centermen with NHL speed and explosiveness. He has another gear with the puck on his stick and forces defenseman to lose containment and turn early when he enters the offensive zone. Copeland has an ok shot release but it isn't overly powerful. Ben excels offensively when he uses his speed to create space for others and then uses his excellent passing ability and vision to get the puck to those areas. Copeland has developed more poise with the puck, where in the past he would just try to use his speed to blow past defenders with the puck or drive the net. He has developed more efficiency and less puck possessions are wasted as a result. Copeland competes for pucks at both ends and doesn't end up on the wrong side of battles very often. His skating allows him to cover a lot of ice and shows good effort on the back check. Copeland will join a pretty good recruiting class at Colorado College in the fall.

"I have seen him execute some really nice setups for goals in my viewings, his vision and passing ability is very good." HP Scout, Dusten Braaksma

181	CORCORAN, CONNOR	WINDSOR	OHL	6' 1.5"	185 lbs	RD

Corcoran is a simple, two-way defender with intriguing physical traits and good mobility. Connor shows an intelligence to his game in his consistency to make good reads both in possession and away from the puck. He shows an ability to make quick decisions which allows him to elude troubled situations. He has good foot-work and edges, Corcoran can often escape pressure with his feet, but would benefit from improving the quickness in his first few strides up ice. Connor does possess a long and fluid stride which allows him to generate good speed once he gets going. He shows a confidence in possession and will utilize his feet to carry transition up ice, gaining entry to the offensive zone. An average puck handler, Connor would benefit from becoming more assertive offensively once gaining the zone. Corcoran's first pass is also effective and he does a good job joining the attack up ice once he's moved the puck. He's simplistic in the offensive zone but can open lanes to get puck on goal and moves the puck effectively from his point position. Corcoran does show good velocity to his shot and can beat goaltenders from the point, however he isn't as assertive with his shot as you'd like to see.

Defensively Connor uses his feet to keep the play in front of him and contain effectively in transition. He often angles opponents wide and does a good job keeping the from cutting into the center of the ice. However he needs to tighten his gaps some as he can allow easy entry to the zone as he tends to stop moving his feet and wait for the play to come to him. Connor isn't shy physically, but with his size and strength it would benefit him to show more intensity and physical jam to his game.

"I like the way he plays the game. Good solid player who plays a pretty smart game. Scouts would like to see more offensive upside in his game but he does eat up minutes out there playing good defense." - HP Scout, Mark Edwards

| NR | COSKEY, COLE | SAGINAW | OHL | 6' 0.5" | 190 lbs | RW |

Cole was a highly skilled, high energy forward for the Chicago Mission U16 program when he was selected in the third round of the 2015 OHL Draft by the Saginaw Spirit. He was passed over in the 2017 draft. This year, he attended Toronto's development camp with his teammate Middleton, helping him in preparation for this season which translated on the ice where he scored a team leading 27 goals and 50 points in 68 games for Saginaw, he also scored 2 goals in 4 playoff games.

Coskey is a competitive, high-energy, physical winger who developed the ability to put the puck into the back of the net this past season. He's a very good forechecker, who's quick acceleration and plus top-gear compliments his tenacious style of play when battling hard along the boards for loose pucks or when attempting to get past a defender from a stand-still position. Despite his average size, he plays above his weight-class, throwing his weight around on a shift-to-shift basis which helped him get under the skin of opposing teams. He's not afraid of getting into altercations and plays with a chip on his shoulder at times. Although, not very tall, he is thick with a low centre of gravity and this allowed him to protect the puck when peeling off the boards or when guarding the puck off the cycle. Additionally, he does a good job of getting to the net even when taking a beating while making life difficult for opponents. Regardless of his physical play, what separates Cole from previous seasons in the OHL was his goal production. He was consistent at finding soft-ice around the goal-line and hashmarks, using a quick and accurate shot that he utilized through heavy screens and through give-and-go sequences that allowed him to take advantage of his release point before goalies could square up in time. Another area of his game that stood out this season was his puck-handling ability. He's got soft-hands despite playing an aggressive forechecking style, and this allowed him to beat opponents cleanly in one-on-one situations while also creating a more dynamic element to his overall game.

His increased production and improved development this season led to him becoming one of the most effective forwards for Saginaw. He's become a well-rounded player who can score which might make scouts more interested in him for the 2018 draft.

"Still not a draft for me but I think he is worth mentioning He was their best player in a couple of my viewings of Saginaw." - HP Scout, Mark Edwards

| NR | COTE-CAZENAVE, TRISTAN | VICTORIAVILLE | QMJHL | 6' 0.0" | 184 lbs | G |

Côté-Cazenave started the year as Victoriaville's number 1 goaltender, but eventually lost his starting role after the Tigres acquired Étienne Montpetit from Val-d'Or. Montpetit, in addition to being an overage goaltender, was considered to be one of the most in-demand acquisitions from the deadline period. However, Côté-Cazenave did see some quality ice time in the 2nd half of the season with Montpetit getting hurt; he won 25 games out of the 43 he was featured in.

He had an up-and-down year, similar to his team. Consistency is an area of his game we would like to see improve. His first half of the season was tougher, as Victoriaville (until December) had a lot more "downs" than "ups". He was originally drafted in the 4th round by the Tigres in the 2016 QMJHL Draft, after splitting that season with two Midget AAA clubs. The Longueuil native is a very vocal goaltender on the ice, communicating well with his defensemen, and it's something we noticed out of him right from midget. His size is okay; he's not a big goaltender, but not a small one either (for today's NHL). It can be difficult for him to track pucks when there's a lot of traffic in front of him. He has a great work ethic, competing hard for every puck thrown at him, and technically he's pretty sound. He has a good glove and does a good job handling the puck outside of his crease. There's no real strong part of his game, and at the same time, there's no real weakness either.

We don't expect Côté-Cazenave to be drafted, but we like his work ethic and there's a chance to see him get invitations over the summer for NHL rookie camps. Next season in Victoriaville, he should be once again the number one goalie on the team, with Montpetit either turning pro or playing at the USports' level.

100	COTTER, PAUL	LINCOLN	USHL	6' 0.0"	191 lbs	LC

Paul Cotter is a hard working power forward that likes to play an up tempo game. Cotter has good skating speed both with and without the puck and his agility allows him to find and create space in transition. While cotter doesn't possess elite offensive tools and isn't going to drive the offense very many nights, but there are not glaring weaknesses in his offensive game which allows him to adapt to each game and find a way to contribute on a nightly basis. Cotter is often first in on the fore-check; he is very strong on his skates and physical on the opposing defenseman. He creates a lot of energy for his time with his relentless physical play on the fore-check and can play on the edge with his physical play at times. With the puck on his stick, Cotter likes to drive the net and create havoc in front of the net; he uses his strength to out muscle defenseman for loose pucks and positioning. Cotter possesses an excellent release on his shot and is good at getting pucks on net off the rush and through traffic. Cotter is sound defensively and has developed into a good penalty killer and checker. He is able to have his stick in lanes, challenge plays and block shots when the situation calls for it. Cotter at this point projects as a bottom 6 forward at the next level but his high hockey IQ and work ethic will allow him to have the opportunity to move up a lineup.

" No weaknesses in his game, it's easy to imagine a team really liking this kid and moving up to take him." HP Scout, Dusten Braaksma

" Keep an eye on this guy...he's a riser." USHL Scout, January 2018

" He's been coming on in the second half but I'm still not sold on him." NHL Scout, February 2018

" If there is one USHL player climbing late it's probably him." NHL Scout, April 2018

" Hockey sense is a concern for me but he's a strong powerful straight line skater with a bit of skill."- NHL Scout, April 2018

" He didn't get as much icetime as some of his teammates but I thought he had some great shifts in Truro (WJAC) - HP Scout, Mark Edwards

NR	COXHEAD, ANDREW	QUEBEC	QMJHL	6' 4.0"	193 lbs	RC

Coxhead is a big centerman who the Quebec Remparts drafted in the first round of the 2016 QMJHL Draft with the 14th overall pick.

The Nova Scotia native is a smart hockey player who really understands how to play in all three zones, and has a great work ethic. He can play the role of a defensive forward really effectively; he does a good job coming back deep in his zone to help his defensemen out, and has a quick and smart stick to block passes. He's an asset to a team's penalty-killing unit; he's good on faceoffs and has good anticipation. He's very solid along the boards in all three zones. His puck-protection game is solid, as he does a very good job keeping possession of the puck with his big frame and ability to fight off players. He does a great job on the power play when it comes time to retrieve the pucks in the corner, and also he's tough to move from the front of the net. He doesn't have the best of hands; he's not a natural scorer and most of his goals will come from hard work down low and in front of the net. He lacks that quick release, as there's some hesitation when he's about to take shots on net. His skating is a big red flag, although he has made some improvements to it in the past couple of seasons (going back to his major midget season) but it is still not good enough at the moment. He doesn't have good top speed, his acceleration is lacking, and his feet are heavy. If he could improve those feet, he would improve his chance to get drafted and one day play in the NHL (although his upside remains low). With his size, work ethic, smarts, defensive awareness he could challenge for a 4th line role, but his speed is the big question mark.

With how the NHL is right now and going forward with the speed of the game, Coxhead's skating is a big downside, and with his low upside, he's a player we don't expect to get drafted. He could, however, get some invites for rookie camps.

1	DAHLIN, RASMUS	FROLUNDA	SWEDEN	6' 2.8"	185 lbs *	LD

We were very high on Dahlin heading into the season, ranking him 1st overall in our 2017 rankings in last years Black Book. Nothing has changed this year, as we have him ranked 1st overall for the 2018 draft class, he finished with impressive point totals while helping Frolunda finish top 3 in the SHL, putting up 20 points in 41 games while also being used in all situations. Furthermore, he had continued success in the playoffs, finishing with 3 points in 6 games before getting knocked out of the quarterfinals.

Rasmus is a well-built defenseman that has a propensity to make jaw-dropping offensive plays. He has a rare combination of high-end skating ability, dynamic puck-skills and the mentality needed to control a game from start to finish. At the World Jr Championship, he captured the most valuable defenseman award while showing the ability to adapt to having a target on his back throughout the tournament. Teams look to get under his skin and target him accordingly, however despite playing a finesse oriented offensive style, he has a mean streak and is willing to stand up for himself which we witnessed several times throughout the year.

Dahlin is both agile and elusive and this makes him very difficult to neutralize both when the opposition is attempting to forecheck and when he's getting pressured at the offensive blueline. He has an understanding of both body and stick feints, using his head to mask his passing options and his hands to breakdown opposing teams. His creativity with the puck allows him to make difficult plays look relatively easy and gives him the element of surprise in one-on-one situations or when teams are trying to overwhelm him. The weakest aspect of his offensive arsenal is his shot, although it's accurate and he can be patient before releasing it, it does lack power at this point in time. On the powerplay, he's a technician who can breakdown a defense better than any other defenseman in this class, using his skillset to control the tempo with the man-advantage.

Rasmus is also more than capable in his own end of the ice. He has an excellent first-pass and uses it to transition the puck quickly out of the zone. He doesn't mind taking a hit to make a play and takes his defensive responsibilities seriously. He will battle hard in the corners, support his defensive partner, and is willing to enter shooting lanes to block shots. When he does make mistakes, which are usually based around an errant pass or holding onto the puck too long which can result in turnovers, he's fast to recover showing the determination to make up for his mistakes.

We see Dahlin as a franchise #1 defenseman who will be utilized in every situation. His ability to adapt and take on an increased role with Frölunda, solidified himself as one of the most promising defensive prospects of the last decade.

"It's funny, he's the number one guy in the draft but because it's pretty much been a done deal all year long, scouts barely spoke about him this year. For the most part, the only thing the scouts said to me was he was clearly their top guy." HP Scout, Mark Edwards

"Not like he needed to, but he absolutely killed it at the combine." NHL Scout, June 2018

"His testing means nothing. He could've had a sleep during the pro agility test and then come up here and spit on a scouts shirt and he'd still go number one." (laughing) - NHL Scout, June 2018

NR	DALEY, CAIDEN	BRANDON	WHL	6' 0.0"	170 lbs	RC

Caiden Daley is a tall, lanky right shot centre for the Brandon Wheat Kings. He was a highly touted prospect, being selected 22nd overall in the 2015 WHL Bantam draft. However, things just haven't panned out for Caiden in his first two years in the WHL. He scored 7 goals and 19 points in 69 games this season, only 9 more points then his rookie year.

Daley is a smooth skater but is just lacking the size, which may still come, as he gets older. Playing on the Wheat Kings third or fourth line for most of the year he never found his stride. Decent shot when given the opportunity to get it off, just never found his scoring touch. In the faceoff circle Caiden was mediocre. He would get out muscled by the older stronger centre iceman. He primarily played a checking defensive role for the Wheat Kings. His compete level and intensity seemed to be there and he battled hard but had problems generating and offense. Turnovers were a major problem for Daley throughout the year. In the defensive zone struggled backing up he defense at times.

We don't feel Caiden will generate very much interest at the draft. After such a poor season his stock has really fallen in our eyes and it would be a surprise to see him drafted this season. 7 goals in 69 just wont cut it. He will need to work on being much more consistent if he wants to change peoples minds.

214	DAMIANI, RILEY	KITCHENER	OHL	5' 9.0"	164 lbs	RC

Riley Damiani was drafted 29th overall in the 2016 OHL draft. He had a decent rate of production before falling off in the final few weeks of the season, putting up 37 points in 64 games, including 19 goals. He picked up his production again in the playoffs, finishing with 12 points in 19 games, including 7 assists.

Damiani is a small center who plays with a ton of heart and is capable of going undetected behind defensive-coverage, this also allowed him to be effective away from the puck where he generated several take-aways in our viewings. He plays larger than his size, engaging on the forecheck, being involved in the dirty-areas of the ice, and cutting aggressively towards the front of the net if the play calls for it. He demonstrated plus offensive-positioning, finding soft-ice in the slot area and around the goal-line. His positioning applied to the defensive-zone as well, where he anticipated plays and would intercept passing attempts before rushing the puck up ice which allowed him to generate several successful short-handed opportunities. This made him an excellent penalty-killer, switching his gear and pressuring opponents while using an aggressive stick to generate takeaways. When he found himself in-tight to the net, he showed above-average puck skills which gave him the ability to deke around his opponents or get a goalie to bite early. Although not a burner for his size due to lacking power, he does have a deep-knee bend and good skating mechanics. However, his pivoting needs some work, he's not overly evasive given his build, but he was willing to take a hit to make a play and didn't back down against larger players which helped compensate for his edges to a degree.

Riley is the type of player that coaches love to have. He's a kid who's willing to do what it takes to help his team win, not by using high-end tools but instead by finding a way to be effective on the ice despite his build, relying on his high-compete level and ability to find soft-ice as opposed to using great puck skills or a great shot. He does generate shots at a pretty good rate but his shot isn't an attribute that stands-out too much, it's more his willingness to put himself in a position that gives him a higher-percentage chance that does.

In order for his game to translate to the pro levels, He's going to have to become more explosive out of the gate, continue to improve his puck-skills, and further develop his release point so that it can become more dangerous from the slot area and out.

"I want to like him because he's a worker. In the end he's just too small and I think he really struggles to get to the tough areas. He's willing...he just struggles to get there." NHL Scout, November 2017

"Good Junior player." NHL Scout, December 2017

"Like him a lot but probably not enough there to pull the trigger." NHL Scout, February 2018

"He's on my list but really late...in the area that we probably would take him." - NHL Scout, April 2018

"I know his minor midget coach and he raved about him to me in his OHL Draft year. Then my buddy coached him in Kitchener last season and he loved the kid too. That was a good starting point for me going into this season. As for the player on the ice, He's a heart and soul guy and will be a force for Kitchener going forward. I think his skill is limited and size/skating combo isn't ideal. I guess the hope is that he might be an outlier. Regardless, I'm a fan of the way he plays the game." HP scout, Mark Edwards

NR	DEL GAIZO, MARC	MUSKEGON	USHL	5' 9.0"	170 lbs	LD

Del Gaizo is an undersized but very mobile defenseman that is able to handle the puck and control the game from the back end. Del Gaizo is effective on the breakout due to his ability to use his skating to elude the fore-checker and make quick reads up the ice. He is an asset in the transition game due to his ability to stretch the ice and find forwards quickly in the neutral zone from deep in his own end. Del Gaizo doesn't give away a ton defensively despite his size due to his effective footwork and strong lower body. Del Gaizo has a stocky frame that allows him to hold position against bigger and stronger opponents.

Del Gaizo shows good poise on the point, he has good shooting ability and is able to make some slick moves to get to open space and create offense from the point. For having a lot of high end offensive skills, he plays a fairly risk free game and can play against other teams top players effectively. Del Gaizo will certainly need some seasoning at the NCAA level where he can learn to defend against bigger, more skilled opponents but with smaller skilled defenseman becoming more and more serviceable at the NHL level; it's not a stretch to see Del Gaizo being picked up by some team in June. Del Gaizo joins a very talented and mobile defense core at UMASS, joining NHL Draft picks Cale Makar (2017) and Mario Ferraro (2017) on the back end this fall.

"He moves the puck out of his own end well, both with his passing and with his feet, when he decides to skate it out there is no second guessing or tentativeness about it, he just goes" - NHL Scout (January, 2018)

29	DELLANDREA, TY	FLINT	OHL	6' 0.3"	184 lbs *	RC

Ty Dellandrea was selected 5th overall in the OHL draft by the Flint Firebirds. He was used in all situations and centered the top-line for Flint, producing 59 points in 67 games, including 27 goals. Internationally, he was featured both at the Hlinka Memorial where he had zero points in 5 games but was arguably one of Canada's best forwards at the U18's, saving his strongest performance for last by putting up 5 points in 5 games.

It was a difficult start for Dellandrea, after going through an adjustment period where not only did his team lose 9 games in a row early in the season but he also lost two of his better teammates after they were traded. This created an opportunity for Dellandrea to be the driving offensive-player for Flint, however he had some difficulties due to not having a lot of high-end talent with him. He also had opposing teams best defensive-units going up against him.

At the U18's in April, he showed what he could do with more talent around him. The most important aspect of his performance was that he didn't rely on his teammates for inflated production or was a passenger but instead he showed the ability to shut-down top offensive-talent on other teams while also driving his line in the offensive-zone.

Dellandrea has some good attributes that make him one of the more dangerous offensive-players in this class. One of his better attributes is his shot. He's got one of the best release points in this class, it comes off his stick extremely quickly while also generating a lot velocity. Furthermore, there's few tells in his body mechanics before his release which makes it difficult for goalies to pick up if he's attempting a blind-pass or firing the puck on net. His passing ability is just as refined as his shot. He's capable of making difficult passes at a high-rate; we have seen him cut around defenses while under heavy pressure, and despite being off-balance, still make a blind-pass from below the goal-line into the slot area for a scoring chance as an example. His vision compliments his passing ability, as he consistently tracks back-door options before passing the puck and is aware of where his teammates are attempting to position themselves in advance. He's one of the rarer centres in this class in terms of being able to be just as dangerous in the high-slot as he is behind the goal-line. If his shot or passing option has been taken-away, he's shown quick-hands and has a variety of dekes at his disposal. He re-opens lanes, beat goalies in tight to the net or beat an opponent one-on-one to create additional space before making a play.

He's not just offensively-gifted though. He shows defensive-awareness on the ice, giving him several high-quality defensive-plays in our viewings. Dellandrea's skating ability allows him to backcheck efficiently, help cover his defenseman when they get overwhelmed and he's got some length to disrupt passes. Furthermore, despite not being the largest center, he's got excellent balance and is difficult to handle along the boards, this was also noticeable when he would cut to the net, as he made several quality plays despite defenders physically engaging with him. The biggest drawback for Ty in our viewings, was that his motor and pacing was mixed. Some nights he just wasn't as engaged as he should be, though this was also a by-product of being on one of the worst teams in the OHL, where they would be down several goals early, and his teammates would fail to capitalize on his set-ups for them which would make it difficult to re-engage.

Dellandrea is one of the better centres in this class and he was in a difficult situation in Flint He certainly had some off nights and didn't produce at the rate his skill-set would indicate he could if given a better team to work with. That said, he was excellent at the end of the season and showed just how dangerous he can be when given high-end talent to work with.

"Not a smart player. He'll be long gone before he'd reach the spot on my list where I'd be willing to take him." NHL Scout, March 2018

"I really like his game, my only concern is his skating." - NHL Scout, March 2018

"Sometimes I get a bit concerned about the pace of his game." - NHL Scout, March 2018

"He was a riser on my list after Christmas and the way he played down the stretch and at the U18 solidified him as a first round prospect for me." NHL Scout, May 2018

"His U18 might get him into the late first round." -NHL Scout, May 2018

"Considering Flint's lack of firepower, it's impressive that he managed to generate the most shots on net in the OHL out of any first-year draft-eligible forward." HP Scout, Brad Allen

"Ty is a player I really liked coming out of his OHL Draft year. I thought he struggled a bit wearing the Team Canada jersey until this year's U18 in April. He was really good this year. Very few scouts I spoke to disliked him. The range of where the scouts who liked him would be willing to draft him varied from late first round to early in the third round." HP Scout, Mark Edwards

"Combine feedback was fine overall. Good far outweighed the bad." - HP Scout, Mark Edwards

"Didn't like his interview with us this week." NHL Scout, June 2018

"His interview was great...he's a great kid." NHL Scout, June 2018

| 75 | DEMIN, STANISLAV | WENATCHEE | BCHL | 6'1.5" | 190 lbs * | LD |

Slava Demin was drafted by the Portland Winterhawks in the WHL Bantam draft but chose to play in the BCHL. In his sophomore season, he produced 45 points in 57 games, including 36 assists. In the playoffs, he had 7 points in 20 games, with 5 assists. Demin also got a cup of coffee with the USNTDP, where he didn't look out of place. He is currently committed to the University of Denver for the 2018-2019 season.

Demin is a two-way defenseman with a tremendous tool-set. He's an excellent skater, who's four-way mobility runs through an efficient and fluid stride. He would use his effortless stride and anticipatory reads to transition the puck at an impressive rate. His lateral mobility and edges made it difficult to read his movement at the offensive-blueline, while showing plus feinting mechanics that allowed him to re-open his shooting and passing options. His playmaking skills compliment his excellent vision and this allowed him to move the puck at a fast rate through all three-zones. We have seen him use his skill-set to draw defenders to him, before making sharp-passes over to his open teammates for high-end scoring chance at a consistent rate. Demin's not just an adept passer though, having arguably one of the more refined wrist-shots from the backend in this class. The release point is both deceptive and comes off his tape very quickly, making it difficult for goalies to pick up. Although he can generate dangerous shots from a stationary position, it's his ability to shift gears which helps switch the angle of his shot when he's pinching, that gives him another offensive-element to his game.

His mobility allows him to play a calm and collected game when in the defensive-zone, rarely looking rattled when under pressure. His awareness away from the puck is a plus, and it allowed him to maintain consistent defensive-positioning in our viewings. Although he's capable of playing physically when he needs to, it's an aspect of his game that leaves us wanting more. He's not a tenacious defender, playing more of a finesse-oriented game by rarely showing grit or determination. This point can be highlighted during his transitional zone entries in the offensive-end and when walking the line as well. Despite having high-end puck skills and the mobility needed to enter the zone cleanly, he would look to pass it off to his teammates that were less skilled than himself, rarely driving offensive-play. This left us with a frustrating take on Demin, he's got a ton of talent but doesn't put himself in positions to use it nearly to the degree he could, especially when considering that he can both pass and shoot. He plays a passive and unselfish game to a fault. If Demin can learn to keep a higher pace and take advantage of his tools more than he currently does, then he can develop into a two-way defenseman at the pro levels.

"He's got tools but I don't like the hockey sense. He was a little all over the place out there." -NHL Scout, December 2017

"He looks like a first rounder in the warmup but he's looked like a mid rounder in a few games I've seen him." NHL Scout, May 2018

"He's a player I liked a bit less the more I saw him. He has too many shifts where he doesn't compete hard enough. He has great physical tools but I don't think he's maximizing his production out of his physical assets. He doesn't seem to get involved in the play unless he's forced to." - HP Scout, Mark Edwards

"Demin's body language isn't good. Looks like he'd rather be anyplace else right now." NHL Scout (During combine testing)

| 15 | DENISENKO, GRIGORI | YAROSLAVL 2 | RUSSIA-JR. | 5' 10.8" | 172 lbs* | LW |

Grigori Denisenko is a tenacious and skilled winger who put up 22 points in 31 games, including 13 assists while primarily being featured in a depth-role for Loko Yaroslavl. In the playoffs, he had 7 points in 12 games. He was also called up to Lokomotiv Yaroslavl of the KHL where he went pointless in 4 playoff games. He had a lot of success internationally while being featured in a more prominent role while creating chemistry with Andrei Svechnikov, however he missed the U18's regardless of being healthy.

Denisenko is a versatile winger who has a great mix of compete and high-end skill. He's the type of player who seems quick to adapt to any line he's put on, which allowed him to compliment a skill-line or be the driver of a depth-line.

Regardless of where he's playing in a line-up, it's rare for him not to make an impact on the ice. He's a deceptive player who can shift his speeds on a moments notice, effectively generating a high-percentage play from seemingly nothing. Grigori does this by switching his gears while using quick bursts of speed to find open-ice or to cut aggressively towards the net area, he's got good skating mechanics and can use his acceleration when coming off the half-wall or his straight-line speed when carrying the puck in open-ice. He's also excellent at interpreting when he should make a pass or use his shot. He doesn't hesitate when making a play, instead showing a high-degree of decisiveness with the puck on his stick. This ability compliments his motor, he's an excellent forechecker who plays far above his weight-class and comes away with the puck against much larger defenders in most of the games we viewed him in. Furthermore, he plays a 200-foot game, expending his energy to backcheck aggressively while using his acceleration to attack the blueline in order to takeaway the puck. The aforementioned skills allowed him to be an effective penalty-killer on most shifts. Though, he's also capable of distributing the puck efficiently along the half-wall on the powerplay. His passing skills are high-end, he can thread difficult passes through tight seams and can make technical give-and-go sequences with his teammates. Furthermore, he's dangerous both when in a stationary position looking to set up a play or when he's driving down a lane off the rush. He picks his spots to shoot, rarely forcing his play due to his offensive-awareness and anticipatory reads. The mechanics behind his wrist-shot are a plus, he doesn't have many tells before releasing the puck and he looks to use it at severe angles, catching goalies by surprise in some of our viewings.

He's not the bigger player and although he hasn't generated the production that most higher-end forwards in this draft have, he wasn't used as heavily by Loko Yaroslavl as we would have liked to have seen. Despite his production, Denisenko plays a fearless, North-American brand of hockey, not relying on perimeter play and instead showing an aggressive style that compliments his well-rounded game. Furthermore, he's got some of the highest adaptability and versatility offered in this year's draft that should make him a potential top-6 winger who can be used in all situations at the NHL level.

"He's easily the best player on the ice today." NHL Scout, December, 2017

"Looks like a lock for the top 10 to me." - NHL Scout, December 2017

"His quickness is ridiculous, he's pressuring all over the ice." NHL Scout, December 2017

"I can see why you have him high on your list now." NHL Scout, December 2017

"I assume you guys have him in the top 10? Seems like a lock to go there." NHL Scout, February 2018

"He's been really good this week. He teased a bit at Hlinka and in Truro and now we get an extended look at him showing some consistency." - NHL Scout, February 2018

"Few players in this draft play above their size like he does, yet have the skill that he possesses" - HP Scout, Brad Allen

"Saw him live several times and backed that up with quite a few games on tape. When he's on he can be a dominant player. He has a burst that is impressive. Apparently he has two years left on his contract in Russia but the kid told some scouts he wants to play over here." - HP Scout, Mark Edwards

"Didn't speak any english but his interview was good." - NHL Scout, June 2018

| 155 | DER-ARGUCHINTSEV, SEMYON | PETERBOROUGH | OHL | 5' 9.75" | 159 lbs | RC |

Der-Arguchintsev is an undersized, playmaking centre with good hockey sense. Semyon is at his best in possession where he is able utilize his puck handling abilities in combination with his above average vision and passing skills. He shows the ability to become somewhat elusive in possession, using his quick feet to create separation from a check and dart in and out of traffic, showing good change of pace and direction abilities. While Der-Arguchintsev does possess a quick first step, his skating does have room to improve. Semyon possesses a fluid, but short stride limiting the power behind his acceleration and ultimately his top speed. Continuing to improve his lower body strength should allow him skating to improve. He's limited because of his size at times. Der-Arguchintsev often utilizes his smarts and anticipation abilities to become effective while avoiding contact. He competes hard in the dirty areas and uses a quick stick to pull pucks out of traffic or strip opponents of possession. However, he can be simply pushed from possession or out worked in the dirty areas, adding strength is much needed. Semyon's quick hands, intelligence and playmaking traits are often elevated with added time and space, he looks his best on the man-advantage. He shows confidence and creativity in his game, elevating his skating and strength will be necessary for him to find any impact at the next level.

"I don't see enough. Not on my list." - NHL Scout, January 2018

"I've seen him a lot and I'm not sold." - NHL Scout, March 2018

"Too small to be effective in the NHL with his level of skating." - NHL Scout, March 2018

"Not on my list." - NHL Scout, April 2017

"No Petes on my list." - NHL Scout, May 2018

"He so tiny. He didn't get any bigger or stronger and he doesn't play with any pace. The positives are high-end skill and he can make plays but there isn't enough hard compete for me with him. For a little guy he just doesn't play hard enough. I like him as an OHL player but he's not for me in the NHL." - NHL Scout, May 2018

"Don't think one guy on our staff has him on their list so I'm guessing we won't be drafting him (laughs)." NHL Scout, May 2018

"Playing in the Ottawa area in his OHL Draft year I referred to him as being the Oates to Gogolev (Hull). I think his best days are still ahead as far as his OHL career goes, but when it comes to small players like him, I like to see high end skating, not average skating. Skilled player but a risk. when projecting to the NHL." - HP Scout, Mark Edwards

| NR | DERIDDER, DREW | USA U-18 | NTDP | 5' 10.0" | 168 lbs | G |

Drew DeRidder was the starting goaltender for the development program this past season and had a successful year, putting up a 2.76 GAA and .897 save percentage in 39 games. He also played well at international events with the exception of the U18's, showing a high-level of compete and consistency which lead to him helping the States win the U18 Five Nations Tournament. He's slated to play for Michigan State University next season.

DeRidder is an undersized goalie who lacks both width and height. It's very difficult for a goalie of his size to play at the pro level, however he does have attributes that allow him to counteract some of his physical limitations. With a goalie as undersized as he is, it's paramount that he can read the play and interpret the play correctly which he's been consistent at doing this season. He's always attempting to look through screens, is good at analyzing odd-man rushes and anticipating lateral passes in the slot area. Furthermore, he's made some interesting adjustments with his post play to compensate for his height, using a modified V-H. The standard V-H is when the goalies pad forms a vertical line away from the post and a horizontal line that hugs the post that effectively takes away the short-side option from the shooter; DeRidder doesn't sit down in his V-H like most goalies, instead standing more up-right to take the top part of the net away. Naturally, it creates more room down-low as well, however he's extremely flexible and transitions into his butterfly very quickly to counteract low-shots. We have seen him make some incredible split-saves on both breakaways and odd-man rushes; he's dextrous and can contort his frame which allows him to make some unorthodox and unexpected saves.

His glove hand is above-average in terms of his reflexes though he has shown inconsistencies in giving up rebound opportunities on that side. His shoulders have a high-degree of rotation and this allows him to get his blocker side up in a hurry which is important considering his height and the fact players target the top-areas of the net when facing him. His best attribute is his lateral mobility, he's incredibly efficient when moving post-to-post and this allow him to make some very impressive recovery saves, especially when combining his high-level of compete, he simply does not give up on shots regardless of how difficult the save might be. The biggest drawback in DeRidder's game as of now besides his height, is that he isn't as aggressive as he should be on certain sequences which allows high-end shooters to find openings on him.

It's an unfortunate situation for DeRidder, if he was 6'2 with a broader frame, he would be a potential draft candidate. Goalies with his stature are capable of playing in the NHL but it's extremely rare and requires a special talent. Although he is talented we don't think his skill-set is translatable to the NHL level as of writing this.

NR	DESRUISSEAUX, CEDRIC	DRUMMONDVILLE	QMJHL	5' 7.25"	159 lbs	LW

Desruisseaux was originally drafted in the 1st round in the 2016 QMJHL Draft (17th overall) by his hometown Victoriaville Tigres. He went back to Midget AAA last season with Trois-Rivières, and was eventually traded to Drummondville at the QMJHL Draft last June, in a big trade for veteran Mathieu Sevigny.

This season with the Voltigeurs, Desruisseaux enjoyed some success, scoring over 20 goals despite spending most of the year on a 3rd line. He's a tiny forward, listed at 5'08" and 153 pounds, but has the skating ability to be effective at the major junior level. He has good top speed with quick acceleration, also showing a good compete level without fear of bigger players. He has quick hands; he's got good creativity and vision in the offensive zone, and he will be an impact player offensively in the QMJHL. His offensive numbers will only increase when he adds physical maturity and receives increased ice time with the departure of some players. A key for Desruisseaux is to put him on a line with some bigger players, so that they can help him along the boards and give him some protection as well. He played for some of this year with overager Morgan Adams-Moisan as part of a very successful 3rd line along with 16 year old rookie Xavier Simoneau. He can be overmatched physically along the boards against bigger players, either in the offensive zone or when trying to clear the puck out of his zone.

Desruisseaux is not likely to get drafted in June but should receive invitation for NHL camps in the summer.

| 215 | DILIBERATORE, PETER | SALISBURY | HIGH-CT | 5' 11.0" | 160 lbs | LD |

Diliberatore, who's originally from Nova Scotia, elected to go the prep route and go to the NCAA instead of the QMJHL. He played his midget draft year with Dartmouth before playing for Salisbury the past two seasons. He committed to play college hockey at Quinnipiac University for the 2019-2020 season.

He has good mobility and footwork, and fits the bill for the new-age small, mobile and puck-moving defenseman. He's at his best when using his feet to make plays in the offensive zone and being active there. He has good puck skills, and can handle the puck very well while skating fast. That skill was on display right from midget, where he showed he was more advanced than most players in that area. He likes to rush the puck from his end zone, and with his speed and puck skills, this is really a strong part of his game. He's a good power play guy, good puck-distributor and we've seen make some good pinches to keep the puck alive in the offensive zone. Consistency is a big issue with his game; he needs to find more of a balance in his game. Size is also a concern with him, as he's still undersized and will need some extra time in the gym; he's still quite slim and will need to be stronger to play at higher levels. Diliberatore's USHL rights are owned by the Bloomington Thunder, and he could play there for one season before making the jump to the NCAA.

"Good skater with some skill and a pretty good puck mover." - NHL Scout, April 2018

| 5 | DOBSON, NOAH | ACADIE-BATHURST | QMJHL | 6' 3.0" | 177 lbs * | RD |

Dobson had an amazing season with the Titan, and was one of the top defensemen in the league. He was always known as a smart, strong defender, but his offensive game really exploded this year in his second season in the league. Dobson has an excellent hockey IQ. He is a very smart player who thinks the game really well both with and without the puck. He's an above-average skater; he'll join the rush when he sees an opportunity, but always does so in a smart way and will rarely get caught. His puck movement is excellent; he has a good first pass out of his zone and makes quick decisions with the puck. He really thinks the game well, and sees things happen in front of him faster than most players at this level. His on-ice vision is excellent in the offensive zone, and it's a great asset on the power play. He doesn't have an elite shot from the point, but made some strides there this year, as he was more effective in terms of scoring during the 2nd half of the season (scoring 12 of his 16 goals after the Christmas break). Defensively, he's tough to beat one-on-one; he has above-average footwork and lateral agility. He does some good work with his quick stick to pokecheck pucks away from opponents, and keeps a good gap. He's not yet physically mature yet; he could add another 15-20 pounds to his frame. His physical game is good enough for now, but with the added strength, he could be more assertive along the boards and in front of the net. His intensity and physical game are two parts of his game that will need to improve a bit, but with time and better competition, this shouldn't be a problem.

Overall, Dobson is a complete defenseman who can help a team many different ways. He's a guy who projects to play on both special teams' units.and is a potential number one defensman in the NHlL.

"He's high-end. Took me until now to get to see him and he was really good. He's up with the top D group for sure." - NHL Scout, October 2017

"He has it all., he's Poised and skilled,. He's the reason this team has a chance every night." - NHL Scout, November 2017

"He's the best D behind Dahlin and it isn't close." - NHL Scout, December 2017

"Dahlin, Dobson, Boqvist and Hughes are the top 4 defensemen." - NHL Scout, December 2017

"He's right behind Zadina. Easily the 4th best player in the draft." - NHL Scout, January 2018

"Between Dobson and Bouchard, it's Dobson by a wide margin. Dobson versus Boqvist is tighter. Bouchard is a tier down from those guys." - NHL Scout, January 2018

"Ottawa is going to have a pretty big need on their back-end. They have Chabot and who else? Where are they picking again?" NHL Scout, May 2018

"He really jumped out at me at the beginning of the season and made me realize how much I underrated his offensive upside last season. There's not many weaknesses to his game and so much to like. He's still improving, which is the scary part here." - HP Scout Jérôme Bérubé

"I only saw him play one game this season where he wasn't fantastic and it was the second to last game before the Christmas break. Only reason I was even there was because I was in Halifax for the WJAC anyway. That weekend before Christmas are bad games to scout in the CHL. - HP Scout, Mark Edwards

"When I compare the way Dobson plays defense to a guy like Bode Wilde, the difference is large, because Dobson plays everything so much tighter and smarter." - HP Scout, Mark Edwards

| 94 | DOSTAL, LUKAS | BRNO JR. | CZREP-JR. | 6'1.3" | 156 lbs * | G |

Lukas Dostal played for both HC Kometa Brno at the U20 level where he posted a 3.00 GAA and a .919 save percentage in 14 games as well as SK Horacka Slavia Trebic in the Czech2 league, where he posted a 2.43 GAA and a .921 save percentage in 20 games. Internationally, he was the starting goalie at every major tournament, where he saved his best performances at the end of the season by upsetting Canada at the U18's and put on another very impressive performance against a stacked U.S team.

Dostal is a reactionary butterfly goalie who has several note-worthy attributes, none more so than his split-second reflexes. He's got some of the best reflexes in this draft class and uses them to make highlight-reel saves. Additionally, he's capable of absorbing difficult shots at odd angles using his butterfly. This is in large part due to the speed at which he can enter and stand back up from his butterfly as well as due to having plus mobility while moving laterally and pushing off when attempting to cut down angles. He's a goalie who is at his best when he challenges the shooter and forces his opponents to react to his initial movement. This was evident at the U18's, where he was more aggressive in attempting to cut down angles when players were driving down the wings or cutting through traffic towards him than in previous international tournaments. Another one of his better attributes is his rebound control, his butterfly technique is sound and he's very good at absorbing the initial shot, his reflexes also allow him to make kick-saves quickly and take away the bottom part of the net consistently. Another plus attribute is his glove-hand, he's capable of making high-end glove saves from in-close and keeps it well positioned in his stance. There's a high-degree of technique in his mechanics when entering his V-H, reverse V-H and butterfly due to having good coordination.

Although he has some promising tools and decent size, he does have some areas he needs to improve. He was more competitive at the U18's but in some of our other viewing's when he lets in a soft goal or two, we have seen him look disengaged. Dostal has also demonstrated mixed reads when interpreting a shooting angle when a player changes their skating speed and this has led to him having difficulty picking up shots specifically off the rush, though this happens more-so on the blocker side than the glove side in our viewing's. He's good at tracking the puck across the slot area but has moderate difficulty tracking the puck through screens on occasion as well.

Dostal has some areas in his game that he needs to adjust in order to be successful at the next level however he does have some of the most important attributes a goaltender requires and has had a solid year developmentally, as he looked the most impressive in our viewings at the end of the season.

"Struggled at the Five Nations but played much better in April at the U18." - HP Scout, Mark Edwards

| 99 | DOUGLAS, CURTIS | WINDSOR | OHL | 6' 8.5" | 248 lbs * | LC |

Curtis Douglas is a towering center who split his season between two OHL clubs. He played the first half of the year with Barrie, producing 18 points in 28 games, including 11 assists. Once traded to the Spitfires, he produced 28 points in 38 games, including 15 goals. In the playoffs, he had 4 points in 6 games.

Douglas has a physical presence that compliments an untapped two-way game. Due to his height and age, he hasn't filled out his frame yet which causes him to have one of the weakest first couple of steps in this class. However, his skating technique is good and he has a ton of room for growth, which gives him an opportunity to correct his glaring weakness. In the offensive-end, Curtis uses his frame to move through traffic in-front of the net where he can be dangerous due to his length. He's also able to use his frame along the boards, where we have seen him correctly angle himself away from an opponent before generating scoring chances with his playmaking ability. His length gives him unique angles to both release his decent shot and pass. Lastly, his skill-level allows him to generate off the rush and below the goal-line, where we have watched him make no-look passes that are difficult for defensive units to track.

It's not just his offensive-potential when paired with his enormous stature that makes Douglas stand-out. He's a cerebral, yet competitive player who plays with an edge when needed and is willing to drop the gloves. He doesn't just rely on his physical presence, as he possesses a strong understanding of the game. This quality allows him to play in the defensive-end despite his acceleration, where he can his size and stick to disrupt the play. Furthermore, his ability to anticipate the play, lets him get into good position away from the puck to receive passes which helps further counteract his stride.

Once you look past Douglas's skating from a stand-still position, there's a rare and talented center who has the potential to develop into something more than a lot of previous draft selections that were based on their size could develop into.

"Huge kid. I started to hear the hype so I went back to see him a couple more times. I didn't change my mind. Maybe a late pick for me." - NHL Scout, April 2018

"Huge, borderline almost too big. Skating really needs to come a long way. More productive than I ever thought he'd be at this level." NHL Scout, May 2018

"Skating obviously isn't great, but his mechanics are ok. He's a big rig that looks fine after those first few ugly steps. He'll need more quickness to play though. Other than the skating I like a lot about his game." HP Scout, Mark Edwards

"Really like this kid, great interview with us this week." - NHL Scout, June 2018

| NR | DUCHARME, JUSTIN | ACADIE-BATHURST | QMJHL | 5' 10.5" | 178 lbs | LW |

Ducharme's best asset: his skating abilities. He has good top speed and a great acceleration. He's easy to notice because he can flat-out fly on the ice. He has gotten stronger over the last 2 years, and can be tough to contain now with his combination of speed and strength. In his first year in the QMJHL, he started off hot with a great first month, collecting 8 points in his first 13 games. However, he only put up 15 points in his last 40 games. With his speed, he can create a lot of chances, but lacks finish around the net. He's good on the PK with his work ethic and speed; he can be a threat to score shorthanded as well (as was often the case in midget). Ducharme's hockey IQ and smarts are average; this will hurt him in terms of his puck management and decision-making when trying to create offense. In the next 2-3 seasons in the QMJHL, he should be more of a scorer at this level, but will need to improve his decision-making and play a simpler game offensively to be successful at the pro level.

| 52 | DRURY, JACK | WATERLOO | USHL | 5' 11.0" | 174 lbs * | LC |

Drury is a strong power forward that has the ability to adjust to different styles of play and is at his best when he is physical, get under his opponents skin and draw penalties. Drury is a bit of a throwback as far as his style of play, he won't hesitate to mix things up with his opponent, has displayed the willingness to drop the gloves if the need arises and possesses good leadership qualities that can be a rare find at such a young age. For as hard-nosed as Drury likes to play, there is some skill in his game as well. Jack finished 4th in USHL scoring with 31 goals and 35 assists, with half of his point total coming on the Power Play. Drury likes to set up in front of the net for tips and rebounds and showed the willingness to pay the price in front and battle for position. Drury has shown decent range on his shot and can find the corners both using his wrist shot and one-timer on the Power Play. Despite his skating lacking some explosiveness, Drury has little issues in getting where he needs to be on the ice. He uses his anticipation and straight line approach to be quick to loose pucks. Jack displays good effort and attentiveness to the defensive end of the ice. He has shown the willingness and skill to block shots as well as being effective on the penalty penalty kill and on faceoffs. Drury lead the USHL Regular season with five shorthanded goals. The team that drafts Drury will get a player that can play in all situations and possesses the tools to play up or down in the lineup as well as bring mature leadership to the group. Drury will be off to Harvard University this fall.

"He first impressed me last season in the USHL in a game vs. Madison as a 16 year old when he had the entire Madison team trying to get a piece of him; eventually he fought a bigger, older player in the same game. Drury is one of those players that you're happy he's on your side, his play is infectious; he brings teammates into the battle with how he plays. He may not be an elite talent but he is a solid pick with everything he brings to the table" HP Scout, Dusten Braaksma

"I've get him in the 4th round but I could see him go higher. I like him more than both Hall and McLaughlin. I like his hockey sense and his compete. - NHL Scout, February 2018

"The USHL is different this year. A lot of the older players are not very good so younger guys like Drury are putting up some pretty good numbers. Just my opinion, but he's doing it with smoke and mirrors and he's not the only one" - NHL Scout, February 2018

"I need to go back and watch this Drury kid. I didn't see much but obviously there is something there. I can't believe the points." - NHL Scout, February 2018

"He's small, no skill and not a good skater and that's where it ends for me." - NHL Scout, March 2018

"That kid has one of the highest motors in the draft. He brings it every shift of every game. He purely gets results based on outworking and out thinking guys." NHL Scout, May 2018

"The player seems to think he'll go in the first round." - NHL Scout, June 2018

"He's smart hard working and is a really competitive player but he'll need to make it without having a whole lot of great tools in his toolbox. He might just do it." - HP Scout, Mark Edwards

"Easily one of the best interviews of the week." NHL Scout, June 2018

"Really impressive kid, one of the best interviews I've ever done." - NHL Scout, June 2018

"He put up good numbers. I think he'll go in the 2nd round." - NHL Scout, June 2018

"Rave reviews from scouts regarding his interviews at the combine." HP Scout, Mark Edwards

| NR | DROZDOV, IVAN | YUNOST, MINSK | BELERUS | 6' 0.0" | 174 lbs | RC |

Ivan Drozdov is a two-way energy winger who competed in the Belarus league for the Belarus U20 team, where he produced 8 points in 8 games and for Yunost Minsk, producing 6 points in 18 games, and zero points in 4 playoff games. Internationally, Drozdov showed that he can play with some of the top junior talent in the world at the U20's, producing 3 points in 6 games in a spirited effort.

Drozdov's game is based around his high-octane motor and tenacious effort at both ends of the ice. His skating ability is one of the most important aspects of his skillset, featuring an explosive and powerful stride, complimented by excellent edge-work and pivoting mechanics. Despite his stature, Ivan also features a strong base that makes him difficult to knock off balance. He used the attributes described above to compete effectively along the boards, backcheck at a consistent rate, and pressure opponents at the defensive-line. His ability to pressure opponents into causing turnovers in is own-end, his ability to intercept pucks in the neutral zone, and his ability to force the defense to react to him during forechecking sequences, allowed him to be an effective, yet versatile role-player for Belarus at the U20's. Furthermore, due to his speed and agility, Drozdov is good at making both defensive transitional zone-exits and offensive-zone entries. Once he breaks the line, he uses use an aggressive approach, looking to catch defenders on their heels or out of position and is capable of making difficult plays at high-speeds due to having a good-set of hands and the acumen needed to execute plays at an above-average rate. One example that impressed us at the World Juniors, was when he took advantage of a Russian defender who slipped in the corner while forechecking; he grabbed the puck and then used his hands and his escapability, darting around several Russian players with minimal space. He drew a penalty, passed the puck off before receiving it back and delivered a turn-around wrist-shot from his knees that got deflected over the net. Additionally, he can make blind-passes as well as deliver soft and heavy passes, though sometimes his execution rate with his passing can be mixed. Due to this motor, he has a tendency to rush options on occasion and has difficulty changing his pace which can make him less effective then his skill-set would indicate, depending on the sequence. Despite some inconsistencies, he's got a good release-point and is capable of catching goalies off guard using his deceptive shooting mechanics.

It's unlikely that Drozdov ever becomes a top-6 player at the NHL-level, however he wears his heart on his sleeve and showed a tremendous amount of hustle combined with some versatility and skill, that makes him an intriguing under the radar prospect.

162	DUDAS, AIDAN	OWEN SOUND	OHL	5' 7.3"	164 lbs *	RC

Dudas is an energetic, two-way centre with intelligence and skill to his game. He shows good puck handling abilities and has the ability to subtly raise the play of those around him with his vision and passing skills. Dudas possesses three zone effectiveness due to his work ethic and intelligence. He shows an effectiveness away from the puck as he is able to create space for his teammate by driving lanes and subtle pick plays to generate give-and-go opportunities. Aidan is a tenacious presence on the forecheck and combines an ability to quickly close on an opponent with a quick stick to create a turnover. His awareness and anticipation ability allow him to be an effective presence on the penalty kill were he consistently was able to create turnovers. A high energy player, Dudas doesn't let his size deter him from taking pucks to the goal in transition or getting his body into the high traffic areas to become a shooting threat. He shows a good release and accuracy to his shot, but would benefit from becoming more assertive with his shot. Dudas shows creativity in the offensive zone and consistently created opportunities with a combination of skill, speed and smarts. He will need to enhance his strength to have an effectiveness at the next level, while his skating for an undersized player is a concern. He is not an explosive skater which is a drawback given his size.

"Tiny. good skater but I think he'll need to add a step to have a chance at the next level, but good shot and offensive player. He plays a two way game. Size and strength are obviously the issue." NHL Scout, May 2018

"High motor but undersized guy...I love the kid, think he's a great Junior but not so sure about the NHL." - NHL Scout. May 2018

177	DUNKLEY, NATHAN	LONDON	OHL	5' 10.75"	192 lbs	LC

Nathan Dunkley was drafted in the first round 17th overall by the Kingston Frontenac's in the 2016 OHL draft. The playmaking center split time between the Kingston Frontenac's where he produced 33 points in 31 games, including 20 assists, and the London Knights where he had 24 points in 29 games, including 16 assists. In the playoffs, he produced an assist in 4 games.

Dunkley is a center with a pass-first-mentality, looking to set-up his teammates with accurate and crisp passes that he can execute at an above average clip. He has good hand-eye coordination and puck-tracking skills that make him dangerous near the goal-mouth. Furthermore, his playmaking ability gives him a plus cycle game below the goal-line and along the half-wall, showing plus hockey sense from the hash-marks down. Although he doesn't look to shoot the puck as much as pass it, his release is quick and he's shown the ability to find soft-ice in the slot on occasion, though it's not a shot that's going to scare opposing team's defenses.

Even with Dunkley showing plus passing skills and having a productive season, there's several areas of concern for Considering his slight lack of size as a center, his skating just isn't where it needs to be, his stride doesn't allow him to move efficiently and this decreases his straight-line speed. He's not as quick as he needs to be during transitional play.

This impacted his defensive-game, where we have seen him attempt to compete on the backcheck but not be able to keep up at the level he needed to. His skating works against him in the offensively as well, which diminishes his options when on the rush. There's also a lack of creativity when he holds the puck, he's a smart player but he's not going to dictate play too often when the puck is on his stick or throw a defender off with something unexpected..

There's some skill in Dunkley but he has to improve his skating ability and he doesn't have any dynamic offensive-trait to indicate that he can be a productive scorer at the pro levels. That being said, this is a weaker class for centres and he did show enough playmaking skills to get his name called later on in day two.

"His skating and pace of play is his biggest obstacle for me, but I like a lot about his game. He has skill." - NHL Scout, May 2018

"I think he's a draft..probably late but if he can fix the skating he's got a lot going for him." - NHL Scout, May 2018

"He has skill and good offensive instincts, I wish he was bigger and was a better skater." - NHL Scout, May 2018

| NR | DURNY, ROMAN | DES MOINES | USHL | 6' 2.0" | 201 lbs | G |

Durny came to the USHL in the middle of this season from HK 32 Liptovsky Mikulas program in Slovakia to join Des Moines after a successful World Junior tournament for the Slovakian Team where he notably stood on his head to defeat a powerful USA squad with a 43 save performance. Durny split time with fellow 2018 NHL Draft Prospect Jake Kucharski the 2nd half of the season for Des Moines. Despite not having a very good team in front of him, Durny put up very good numbers in 25 starts with a 2.39 GAA and a .920 save %. Durny doesn't have prototypical NHL goalie size but what he gives up in height he can make up for with a good combination of athleticism and poise. Durny is aggressive in challenging shooters, it can get himself out on an island at times but his athleticism allows him to recover relatively quickly. He is a right hand catching goalie with a good glove hand. Durny controls his rebounds well despite play a bit of an unstructured style and is effective in playing the puck.

"He's a fun goalie to watch, when you're his size you need to be very athletic and he certainly has the athleticism but I don't see an NHL goalie." HP Scout, Dusten Braaksma

| NR | DURZI, SEAN | OWEN SOUND | OHL | 5' 11.5" | 195 lbs | RD |

Durzi is a mobile, offensive-minded defender with competitiveness to his game. Sean shows fluid skating abilities, utilizing his edges and lateral quickness to elude contact and create space. While he does lack great straight line speed, Durzi is able to carry transition attack's pushing the pace in possession. A confident puck-handler, Sean shows good good awareness of his teammates. He is able to generate offensive opportunities from the back-end with his skating abilities and shows a willingness to inject from his point position at the appropriate times. In the offensive zone, Sean distributes the puck well, showing vision from the blue line. His quick feet allow him to walk the line effectively and open shooting lanes. Durzi has a quality point shot. Sean will recognize deflection opportunities and shoot for teammates sticks, as opposed to looking to beat goaltenders clean from the point. While defending Durzi does a good job keeping the play in front of him and angling opponents away from the centre of the ice. He uses sound body positioning and an active stick to defend. His edges and mobility allow him to contain well, while he quickly pressures puck carriers, taking away their time and space. Sean does rely mostly on his feet and stick to defend. Durzi has shown some durability issues over the past few seasons which is a minor concern moving forward.

"My opinion is the same as the last two years. Don't you have my quotes from the last two years? - NHL Scout, May 2018

"Really good offensive instincts ...competitive player but for me the skating needs to continue to improve...a bit of a wide tracker." - NHL Scout, May 2018

"Good skater but for the most part, that's all I see." - NHL Scout, May 2018

"He's like a 5'10" Vallati. Hockey sense just isn't there for me." - NHL Scout, May 2018

"I struggled to see him, he was injured for several games when I had Owen Sound on my schedule. I did see him late in the year. Maybe a late pick but that would be it for me." - HP Scout, Mark Edwards

| 141 | DVORAK, DANIEL | HR. KRALOVE JR. | CZREP-JR. | 6' 2.75" | 156 lbs | G |

Daniel Dvorak was the starting goaltender for HC Hradec Kralove in the Czech U20 league this past season, where he had a productive year, putting up a 2.14 GAA and .921 save percentage in 21 games. Furthermore, he had a standout performance at the Five Nations tournament against the U.S but wasn't as successful at the U18's, where he put up a 3.62 GAA and a .890 save percentage in 3 games with an uninspired performance in the bronze medal game against Sweden. He will be looking for an opportunity to play full-time with HK Hradec Kralove in the Czech league next season.

Dvorak is a pro sized goalie who plays a positionally sound game, and also relies on a combination of his reads and plus reflexes when stopping the puck. Despite having a large frame, he tends to fold both his blocker and glove in-tight to his body when in his stance. This leaves the shooter with more space than you would expect given his size both on his glove and blocker side. To compensate for this, he has displayed plus reflexes and is very good at absorbing rebounds on high-shot attempts, as well as aggressively cutting down angles and challenging the shooter. His blocker-side is arguably one of the best in this draft class; he's got an excellent range of motion and is very good at tracking the puck off of rebound attempts on that side when in his butterfly, which allows him to absorb the puck into his body after it comes off his blocker. Additionally, when in his butterfly, Dvorak has the ability to make reactive kick-saves off of primary and secondary scoring chances. We have seen him make some highlight-reel saves off rebound attempts by kicking out his pads to take away high-percentage scoring chances. Similarly, to his blocker and glove, he's got plus rebound control when attempting to absorb shots labeled for his five-hole. When a rebound is given up, he's good at reading the secondary shooting option and getting square in time to make the follow up save consistently.

Despite having notable strengths, he does have weaknesses which he needs to correct in order to develop properly at the pro level. He has a tendency to leave room when he enters his reverse V-H, he's sometimes late to transition into his butterfly as well, but his most glaring weakness is in regards to his ability to push off when moving laterally after misreading the play. Due to this, we have seen him scramble unsuccessfully when attempting to make recovery saves in some games. If Dvorak improves his weaknesses and continues to refine the technical aspects of his game, he does have the tools and the size necessary to potentially develop into a pro goalie.

183	EGGENBERGER, NANDO	DAVOS	SWISS	6' 2.0"	198lbs	LW

Eggenberger elected to go back to Davos this season, even though he had the opportunity to play in the Canadian Hockey League. He's a big two-way forward who, in limited ice time with Davos, had 3 goals and 5 points in 36 games.

He didn't take the next step offensively that we had anticipated this year. On the biggest stage of the season for him (the World Juniors in Buffalo), he didn't perform well. His offensive decision-making was lacking, as he made some bad passing plays and didn't use his size smartly. He has improved his skating since last year; he has decent top speed but still needs some work with his agility and ability to make quick changes in directions. He's a good defensive player, though; he's physical on the puck-carrier and can create some good momentum for his team with a good forecheck. He can get carried away at times and put himself out of the play by trying to go for the big hit on the forecheck. He has showed flashes offensively over the past two seasons; his best sequences happened at the November 2016 U-18 Five Nations' Tournament in Plymouth. Eggenberger was great in one game there, but in the past two World Junior Hockey Championships, he has encountered his share of struggles. He's a big body and he needs to simplify his game and use his size more to protect the puck and go to the net. We have question marks with his on-ice intelligence and offensive upside, and this is why he has dropped in our rankings since the beginning of the season. We like his tools, but we need to see more out of him than what we have seen this year.

"I always think back to his great game in Plymouth last year. Unfortunately it seems it was more of a one of than the norm." - HP Scout, Mark Edwards

NR	ELEMENT, SHAWN	BAIE COMEAU	QMJHL	6' 0.0"	182 lbs	LW

Element was the 9th overall selection in the 2016 QMJHL Draft, out of the Trois-Rivières' Midget AAA program. He's one of the most physical players in this draft class from the QMJHL, he likes to hit, and hits like a truck. He's good on the forecheck, and can set the tempo of a game with some good physical play. His skating is average; in order to continue to evolve his physical game, his speed will need to improve. This will help him be more effective in puck-pursuit situations, and keep up with fast-tempo hockey. In addition, improving his skating will help him create more offense, as his lack of speed hurts him when it comes time to create separation and give himself more room to manoeuvre. Most of his scoring chances come from hard work down low and going to the net with the puck. He's tough to handle physically; he's strong on the puck and has great lower-body strength, which helps him keep possession of the puck. He has a good shot, but has found it hard to take advantage of scoring chances, as his release could stand to be quicker. Element works hard every night, and can be valuable on the penalty-killing unit, as he is not afraid to block shots. With the puck on his stick, he's not overly creative, keeping things simple, but there's not a lot of high-end vision with him and he's offensively limited. We don't expect Element to get drafted, but his physical play and heart could lead him to get invitations for rookie camps this summer.

| NR | ELIASSON, JESPER | TROJA-LJUNGBY JR. | SWEDEN-JR. 2 | 6' 3.0" | 209 lbs | G |

Jesper Eliasson played for five separate teams in the IF Troja-Ljungby system. At the J18 Elit level he produced a 1.73 GAA and .946 save percentage in 18 games, and a 1.93 GAA with a .930 save percentage in 19 games for the J20 Elit team. At international tournaments, he was the back up to Lindbom, playing at both the Five-Nations and the U18's.

Eliasson is a pro-sized goalie with a high-level of composure and compete. He has a refined technical butterfly that he drops down into at an above-average speed, giving shooters little to work with when he's squared up and transitioned into the technique. Furthermore, his reverse V-H is also a plus, giving shooters very little room during off-angle or short-side shot attempts. Additionally, both his reverse-VH and butterfly are consistently sealed tight; it was rare for him to let in a soft goal during our viewings when he had entered these techniques. Jesper has several plus mental attributes, such as never giving up on a secondary shot despite showing average full extension and a lack of reflexive ability in his blocker and glove. We have seen him throw his technique out the window when trying to come away with two and sometimes even three impressive rebound saves in order to keep the puck out of the net. However, despite his ability to throw his technique at times to make a save, he's mostly calm and collected. On goals that sneak by him that he probably should have had, he doesn't shrink up in his net or display a lack of confidence, instead he continues to aggressively cut down angles at the top of his crease and challenge shooters when the play calls for it.

When we watched him, he didn't display an impressive glove-hand or blocker, relying more on his size and ability to cover the bottom part of the net. He can push off from his reverse-VH into his butterfly during shots where the opponent was moving laterally across his slot area or crease and he was good at absorbing shots, showing plus rebound control. Despite his height, he was average at best at tracking pucks from the point, showing difficulty readjusting his positioning when he was screened. Furthermore, Eliasson didn't display overly impressive athleticism in our viewings, relying more on his size and reads down-low around his net area. He possesses some interesting attributes and had a couple of solid performances but he has several areas he needs to improve before he becomes a consistent starter at the pro levels.

| NR | ELLIS, MAX | YOUNGSTOWN | USHL | 5' 9.0" | 141 lbs | RW |

Ellis is an undersized skilled winger out of the Detroit honeybaked program. Max was a 7th round pick of Peterborough in the 2016 OHL futures draft but decided to go the college route. Ellis is committed to Notre Dame for the 19/20 season and is finishing his 2nd season with Youngstown (USHL). Ellis is a hard working but skilled forward who brings consistent effort and skill on every shift. He has good edge work and uses it to be quick and relentless in puck pursuits. Ellis reads the play well at both ends of the ice, in our viewings he was often the one making the play in his own end to stop the cycle and clearing the zone if his team was getting pressured. Offensively, Ellis makes a lot of good plays off the rush, he has quick hands and is able to change the angle of his pass or shot and get the puck where he wants it to go. Ellis certainly has a ways to go physically and faces an uphill challenge to be a pro prospect, however he has the hockey smarts and skill to be a very effective college player and possibly extend his career beyond.

"I don't like writing kids like this off, especially at such a young age, the USHL is an older, bigger league now and he's acclimated himself well and improved over the last two years, he is probably a border line draft but a player that I wouldn't be shocked to see play pro hockey down the road. HP Scout, Dusten Braaksma (March, 2018)

"I don't know if he is dynamic enough to overcome his size but he has some good puck skills and motor" NHL Scout, (May, 2018)

| 98 | EMBERSON, TY | USA U-18 | NTDP | 6' 0.5" | 200 lbs * | RD |

Ty Emberson had a decent year for the USNTDP where he put up 24 points in 56 game, while also showing a solid defensive effort during international competition. He is expected to play for the University of Wisconsin next season.

Ty isn't a very noticeable player on the ice but this isn't a negative, it mostly implies that he plays a low-risk and largely mistake free game. He's a stream-lined defenseman who doesn't play with a lot of flash though he does have some substance, specifically in the defensive-end. He's well built and uses his frame to counter-act opposing players who attempt to drive around him or get into prime scoring positions. He can box-players out around his net and he's competitive along the boards, draining forecheckers with well-timed board pins and hits. He's got plus defensive-awareness which allows him to recognize when players are attempting to get behind his defensive-coverage, it allows him to play positionally sound and he rarely throws himself out of a play. His demeanour is one of his better attributes, he's calm and composed on the ice and this has a positive effect on the defensive-partner he's paired with. He's capable of a solid-first pass and prefers finding the open passing option as opposed to carrying the puck up the ice. He's not overly creative or skilled but is aware of his limitations which doesn't result in him over-extending himself and becoming a liability.

The biggest drawback with Emberson is that his offensive-ceiling is limited. He's capable of generating decent power in both his wrist-shot and slapshot which we have seen him get through traffic at a consistent rate in most games, however he's not dynamic when walking the line and isn't a defender who's going to be capable of running a powerplay. Though there is room for him to develop transitional breakout ability in the neutral zone due to having good skating mechanics; his top-speed is well above-average and he's a fluid skater who can hit an extra-gear when needed during recovery plays.

Emberson is a solid defensive-defenseman who can make a quality first-pass while playing a relatively mistake free game. In order for him to make it to the NHL, he will need to develop his offensive-skill set and continue to refine elements of his already well-developed defensive game.

"He's a simple player. He's vanilla. Not sure how high I'd rate his hockey sense and I have idea why he gets so much powerplay time. - NHL Scout, February 2017

"He really struggled in game 1 versus Canada (U18). I thought that he was a turnover machine in that game. The more I see of these guys (USNTDP defenseman) the more I think they are all overrated." - NHL Scout, April 2018

"He's not offensive...he's not great defensively. He's just a simple puck mover who stays out of trouble." NHL Scout, May 2018

"Zero sum player." - NHL Scout, May 2018

"He's average across the board for me except for the skating which is well above average and will give him a chance to improve his game." NHL Scout, May 2018

"I'm not a big fan, not that I don't think he's going to play (in the NHL) but those 6'1" guys don't do it for me...like are you going to win anything with those guys? No. Just my view on all of them" NHL Scout, May 2018

"Can have some defensive lapses in his own zone but seems to have worked on that part of his game this year. I think he flies under the radar a bit with the depth of that Defensive Core on the U18 team. I like his physicality and his ability to finish opponents without taking himself out of the play." HP Scout, Dusten Braaksma

84	EMOND, ZACHARY	ROUYN-NORANDA	QMJHL	6' 3.0"	165 lbs	G

Emond was a third-round selection in the 2016 QMJHL Draft and spent 2016-2017 with the Collège Notre-Dame Albatros, most notably as a key element in them winning the Dodge Cup.

In his QMJHL rookie campaign, Émond shared the Huskies' workload with experienced netminder Samuel Harvey. He won only 9 games out of the 24 he was featured in this season, but his is a case where the statistics don't tell the whole story. For the Huskies as a whole, the first half of the year featured a confident team who won games rather handily, whereas the second half saw its share of struggles. An injury to Harvey at the peak of the second half threw Émond in the spotlight, but one major quality to Émond's game that was tested during this time: his poise and ability to move on quickly after letting in goals. His strong mental game, as well as his size, helps him track pucks, and his rebound-control is good. He moves side-to-side really well for a 6'03" goaltender, and made numerous outstanding saves during the year. Like his goaltending partner, Émond is very calm in his crease and seems to have ice running through his veins.

Next season, Émond's role will depend largely on what happens with Harvey, as a Harvey departure will lead to Émond being the number 1 guy in Rouyn-Noranda. He's part of an interesting draft class of goalies for the 2000-born age group from the QMJHL, with the likes of Rodrigue, Gravel and Mandolese. He started the year behind this group, but slowly climbed the ranks throughout the year. We really love Émond's long-term potential, and we have liked him all year long.

"I struggled a lot in the first three months of the season to get viewings on him; he was either not playing or injured, like he was at the rookie tournament in Shawinigan. He flew under the radar this year, but had some remarkable performances, including a couple of games against the Remparts that really stood out for me as the top goaltending performance in the 2017-2018 season across the QMJHL." - HP Scout Jérôme Bérubé

"I didn't see him much but in a season where I wasn't crazy about many of the goaltenders I really liked him." HP Scout, Mark Edwards

NR	ENNIS, WILLIAM	OSHAWA	OHL	6' 2.25"	205 lbs	LD

Ennis is a defender with intriguing physical traits and a strong compete level. William shows an intelligence to his game that allows him to be impactful in a non-flashy way. He consistently makes strong reads and quick decisions with the puck on his stick, elevating his effectiveness, despite limited puck skills. Ennis can struggle when forced to skate the puck out of traffic as his choppy puck handling exposes the puck to opponents who can easily create a turnover. William's heaviness on the puck and ability to use his body to shield the puck from opponents often buys him added time to make a simplistic first pass. Ennis is limited with his flash and creativity however shows good vision from the back-end and can make a strong first pass. He's at his best in the defensive zone where he out-works opponents, uses his frame to push opposing player from possession and shows good positioning. While defending transition, his strong reads often allow him to take good routes to puck carriers and keep effective gaps. Ennis keeps the play in front of him and to the outside effectively. Limited offensively, William does make simple and smart decisions at the offensive end, putting pucks on net by changing the angle or velocity of his shot and distributing simply, but effectively. He will need to work on his lateral quickness and become smoother and quicker when pivoting from a backwards skating position to his forward stride, which would elevate his quickness on puck retrievals and recover ability.

"Not much in the way of flash with his game but he does his job and shows some smarts. I have time for him." - NHL Scout, May 2018

"I think he is what he is right now. You're pretty much looking at the finished product so that's an issue for me." - NHL Scout, May 2018

"He's effective at what he does. He's defensive defenseman who plays a simple game and makes simple plays with the puck. Not much in the way of flash to his game. I respect his game but he'd probably be sitting on the outside looking in as far as my list goes." - HP Scout, Mark Edwards

| 28 | ERIKSSON, ALBIN | SKELLEFTEA JR. | SWEDEN-JR. | 6' 4.25" | 207 lbs | RW |

Ericksson is a big raw project who has very interesting potential. He split this past season between the SuperElit league, where he averaged over a point per game with 40 points in 38 games, but also played in 17 SHL games. In the SHL, he had limited ice time and only had 1 assist in 17 games.

He's a big kid who's only scratching the surface of his potential. He's a natural right-winger, but can also play left wing. As a right-handed shot, he likes to play on the left side on the power play and be set up for one-timers. He likes to shoot the puck on net; he has a big heavy shot and also an excellent release. He's definitely a shoot-first type of winger. Ericksson will need some work with his skating, as his top speed is good for a player of his size, but he'll need to improve his agility and explosiveness. Improving his agility would be good for him to improve his quickness when he changes directions, and make sharper turns instead of making long, wide turns. Improving his explosiveness would only make him more dangerous, and with that, he could reach his top speed faster. His combination of speed and size can be impressive; if he can reach his top speed in the neutral zone while in possession of the puck, he can be very dangerous when entering the offensive zone. He likes to attack the offensive zone on his off-wing, often we see him rushing the puck from the left side. In addition, by coming from the left wing, he has a better angle to shoot the puck on net. He's a big guy, but could be even stronger, adding another 15-20 lbs to his frame to help him be more solid along the boards and tougher to counter down low and in front of the net. He's not a big physical player, but uses his size well to protect the puck and to go to the net. He works hard in general, showing a good effort on the backcheck and good support to his defensemen. He has a long reach, which helps him protect the puck and retrieve pucks along the boards. Ericksson is still very raw and has not played a lot on the international stage this season (Ivan Hlinka). We really like his upside and feel that he's still just scratching the surface of his potential.

"I haven't seen him as much as some of our guys but our guys really like him, especially our guy in Sweden. One of our guys has him ranked really high. Like first round high." NHL Scout, March 2018

"There are inconsistencies in his game and they come from thinking he's a skilled forward in a big man's body." NHL Scout, May 2018

"He doesn't play with an element of power or physicality but he uses his body properly to enhance his skill game. My best guess is that he's a high second round pick." NHL Scout, May 2018

"He's better than (Kirill) Marchenko." - NHL Scout, May 2018

"Great at protecting pucks and establishing space. Mid to late 2nd rounder would be my guess" - NHL Scout, May 2018

"This is an interesting player. I've pretty much given you everything I've heard from NHL Scouts on him. Pretty slim pickings." - HP Scout, Mark Edwards

"This was a fun player for me to scout. He's a 2000 birth but he was not given much exposure in tournaments. He barely got any icetime in the SHL but I liked him in every single viewing. He was smart and used his size to protect the puck. He did flash skill in SuperElit and that was key for our assessment of him. Do sleepers exist anymore? If so, this is probably one of mine." - HP Scout, Mark Edwards

174	ERSSON, SAMUEL	BRYNAS JR.	SWEDEN-JR.	6' 2.0"	176 lbs	G

Samuel Ersson is a goalie who played in Brynas's system this past season. He played the majority of his hockey with the J20 squad, where he posted impressive numbers, featuring a .253 GAA and a .920 Save Percentage in 40 starts. In the playoffs, he produced a 4.44 GAA and .857 save percentage in 5 games. At the U19's in Switzerland, he had a 2.69 GAA and a .910 save percentage in 3 starts.

Ersson is a modern-day butterfly goalie, who possesses a calm demeanour and fluid movement. His fluidity allowed him to come out of his reverse V-H or drop into it before most short-side shot attempts could get through. His ability to transition from a butterfly to a standing position and visa-versa is impressive. Furthermore, his butterfly is technically refined and this allows him to seal it shut on most shot attempts, as well as being able to absorb rebounds at a high-rate. It works in combination with his plus puck-tracking skills, giving him the ability to square up and stop the initial shot. It's rare to see Ersson have to scramble since he doesn't over-commit on most shot attempts and his rebound control reduces his need to make recovery saves. Another element of his game that helps him maintain position are his edges. He rarely takes away his own-angle on shots despite being an aggressive goalie, since he's able to reduce his movement quickly. Samuel has learned how to contain his movement when he's in the crease, giving him the appearance of a pro goalie, despite his age. Additionally, his reflexes are well above-average and he possess an excellent blocker, which took away several high-end scoring chances in our viewings. Although his blocker is sound, his glove isn't as impressive at this time, though it's still above-average relative to the other goalies in this class.

Ersson displayed a subtle confidence when he was on the ice, showing a lot of composure and net presence. He rarely looked disengaged or frustrated when he let in a soft-goal or when he was under siege. The more pressure that was applied to him, the better some of his performances became. Like all netminders, he still has some important development. He has a tendency to minimize his movement too much on certain secondary save attempts, and his athleticism doesn't allow him to make a lot of explosive movements when needed. Though the combination of his puck-tracking skills, composure, and refined mechanics help take away some of his concerns. We consider Ersson to have starting potential at the pro levels and is one of the sleeper goalies of this draft.

NR	ETHIER, THOMAS	BLAINVILLE	QMJHL	6' 4.0"	210 lbs	LW

Ethier made some good strides in his second season with the Armada, playing a more regular role. He became a solid contributor on the team's 3rd line. He posted respectable numbers this year, and also we saw some improvement with his skating. His speed looked a bit better than last year, and he was also more involved in the physical part of the game, playing more like a power-forward this year. His offensive upside is limited for the pro level. He's not super-talented, but will get his share of points by going to the net and has showed he can play with skilled linemates and not look out of place. Ethier does use his size well along the boards; he's always one of the bigger players on the ice in the QMJHL and will often play against much smaller defensemen, which makes his life easier down low and in front of the net. He does a lot of dirty work in front of the net, and was used on the 2nd power play unit in that role, as he scored 6 goals on the power play this season. He doesn't have goal-scoring hands; his hands are not quick enough to capitalize on all of his chances and he will miss some because he's too slow to release his shots. Ethier's upside for the next level remains low, and he doesn't bring value as a defensive forward or penalty-killer. We don't expect to see Ethier drafted in June, but there is a good chance he will get invited to a summer rookie camp.

NR	EVERETT, CALEB	SAGINAW	OHL	6' 1.25"	181 lbs	RD

Caleb Everett was drafted 106th overall by the Saginaw Spirit in the OHL Priority selection draft in 2016. He had a successful first season for Saginaw by establishing himself on the backend while being used in all situations. He had 20 points in 58 games, including 14 assists, while putting up zero points in 4 playoff games. He did not play internationally.

Caleb is a large, physical defender with a broad-frame that overwhelmed opposing teams in the defensive-end at times. His four-way mobility is a plus, highlighted by his two-step area quickness while showing a level of aggressiveness that gave him the ability to close his lanes quickly before his opponents could react, using his size to separate them from the puck, though his spacing was also inconsistent on some shifts. His man-to-man coverage was consistent in terms of tracking his opponent's movement and anticipating their attempts at eluding him. Furthermore, he was good at angling his frame away from aggressive forecheckers while remaining poised when assessing his passing options and was capable of distributing the puck efficiently while under pressure on most shifts. On the penalty-kill, he monitored back-door options and used his speed to recover when an opponent managed to breakdown his defensive-partner. Although he was impressive in spurts in his own-end, he wasn't as successful in our viewing's in the offensive-end. He's not a dynamic offensive player, lacking high-end puck skills and didn't demonstrate the ability to consistently threaten from the point. He's got a decent one-timer but his wrist-shot lacks velocity while having an average release. There's also a lack of offensive-instincts when he's walking the line. His shot had difficult getting through traffic on occasion and when it did get through, he had trouble identifying when a screen was set for him. Although, he did deal with pressure at the line properly, getting it off his stick and towards the net or finding an open teammate before turnovers could occur in most games we viewed him in. This allowed him to get some powerplay time, where he did have moderate success depending on the shift and the game. Lastly, he did demonstrate the ability to activate in the offensive-end at the right times depending on the shift.

Everett's best performances were in games where it was difficult to recognize his play unless you were seeking him out. This was largely due to solid, yet stream-lined defensive efforts, where he never took over a game or made flashy plays. Instead, he would quietly make the right play at the right time, which would help his team.

"Adds some offense but not overly physical or hard to play against. Just one of those tweener guys who doesn't have one defining element." - NHL Scout, May 2018

159	FAGEMO, SAMUEL	FROLUNDA JR.	SWEDEN-JR.	5' 11.0"	190 lbs	RW

Fagemo is a skilled winger from the Frolunda system. This season in the SuperElit league, he scored 19 goals in 37 games, and also played two games in the SHL. Fagemo is a shoot-first type of winger; he has a quick release and great velocity on his wrist shot. He likes to shoot the puck and is not shy to put pucks on net, even from bad angles at times. He has decent size; he's strong on the puck and does well along the boards thanks to his surprising strength. Fagemo has quick hands, good puck skills and good one-on-one abilities. He's not super tall, but his core strength is good, and that helps him along the boards in puck-protection situations. The Swedish winger will need to improve his skating, as he doesn't have great top speed and his acceleration lacks explosiveness. With improved skating abilities and his skillset, he would improve his chances to succeed at the NHL level. His vision and hockey IQ are question marks for us, as he doesn't always make the smartest plays on the ice. For example, with open teammates, he will try an extra deke or wait too long before making the passes. This could hurt him when it comes time to translate his game to North America and the NHL. His work ethic is inconsistent; in some games we saw he was working hard in all three zones, making good backchecks and in other games he was invisible out there. It's another area where we feel he'll need to improve upon. Fagemo has the potential to be a top 6 winger, but it's quite risky to project him achieving it, with some of the current flaws in his game.

12	FARABEE, JOEL	USA U-18	NTDP	6' 0.0"	162 lbs *	LW

Joel Farabee had an excellent season for the USNTDP, playing a key offensive role on the top-line, mostly with Hughes and Wahlstrom, while being deployed in all situations. He recorded 70 points in 57 games this past season and is slated to play for the University of Boston after next year.

He is a two-way winger that plays above his weight class and has a rare combination of skill paired with a relentless drive. His best attributes are his vision and his hockey-sense, he's also one of the best playmaking wingers in this draft class and is capable of making skilled passes that are difficult for opponents to gauge yet are easy for his teammates to handle. His passing ability is amplified when taking into account his hockey IQ which is very high; he reads developing plays quickly and is ahead of the play in most instances which allows him to make set ups with the puck on his stick that surprises defensive-units. His intelligence also allows him to control the tempo of the game in the offensive-end, he's excellent at changing the rhythm of a play to his liking and switching the conditions on the ice by re-opening lanes for his passing options. His shot is also an offensive weapon, similar to Wahlstrom, he's capable of hiding his intentions with his shooting mechanics and can release shots with surprising velocity given his build, he's also displayed great accuracy in our viewing's by finding small seems on goalies while shooting at severe angles. Furthermore, his puck skills are high-end and he's a creative player, who takes advantage of his ability to process the play at a fast rate, which lead to several well-executed give-and-go sequences with his teammates throughout the season.

Although slight of frame, Farabee has a powerful lower-body which he uses to push off into a fluid stride, his skating mechanics are a plus and he's capable of starting and stopping on a dime. His skating ability when combined with his surprising strength, makes him difficult to handle on the forecheck for opposing players. We have seen him physically out-muscle and out-battle against much larger players, even tossing them to the ice on some plays. His defensive game is also advanced for his age and his position, he's good at reading the play without the puck and was used in a penalty-killing role where he generated several short-handed chances. One criticism with his game, although it's a small one considering it's rare, is that occasionally he doesn't seem as engaged as he should be, for instance we watched him in games where he doesn't use his skill-set as much as could have for a period or two before becoming noticeable on the ice later in the game.

Farabee was not a passenger on his line, despite playing with excellent players, he was more than capable of driving possession without them and at times was the motor for them, showing a high-degree of versatility. We feel that Joel has untapped potential due to his style of play converting well if he grows a thicker frame which should develop in the coming years.

"He's smart and always effective, liked him last year. He and Wahlstrom are good together. His frame is too small for me to be as aggressive as you are on him though. I like him as a mid first." - NHL Scout, October 2017

"I think he's a complete player and maybe the most offensively creative forward in this draft." HP Scout, Dusten Braaksma

"Just solid across the board, a productive player who competes." - NHL Scout, May 2018

"Take it for what it's worth, but I had one scout single him out as an one of the combine interview that didn't impress him. The player impresses me on the ice and I didn't get other bad feedback. I have never interviewed him myself." - HP Scout, Mark Edwards

| 60 | FEHERVARY, MARTIN | OSKARSHAMN | SWEDEN-2 | 6' 1.8" | 194 lbs | LD |

Martin Fehervary is a two-way mobile defenseman who's willing to put his body on the line for his team. He had a solid development year while playing for IK Oskarshamn where he produced 7 points in 42 games. During the qualification round, he had 3 points in 8 games but his team failed to qualify for the SHL. He also got one game of pro experience in the SHL with HV71 where he went scoreless in his only game. Fehervary played for Slovakia at the U20 World Juniors where he was used on the top pairing and all situations while posting 2 points in 5 games.

Fehervary is a throwback defender in terms of his physical play. He's a tank on skates with a very powerful base and he plays an aggressive and punishing style that has generated momentum changing hits. He doesn't just play a tenacious brand of hockey though. He anticipates the play in most instances, and specifically when a player is attempting to drive wide on him. If he is beaten to the outside he's shown an active stick which he's used to takeaway the puck as well as have several well-timed stick-on-puck sequences in our viewings. He's shown that he can make plays behind the net and around the goal-line and has above-average defensive awareness. He's got the frame necessary to still make a first-pass after getting tangled up and taking hits, but it has also led to several turnovers when we have seen him. On the penalty-kill, he's good at keeping himself positioned to block shooting lanes but he can let his aggressive play get the best of him, which throws himself out of position sometimes. Arguably the best aspect of his defensive game is his pacing, he's relentless and is willing to put himself on the line in order to execute a play.

His powerful base applies to his skating ability as well, he's got solid mechanics and keeps a deep knee bend which allows him to skate low to the ice. This allows him to have plus four-way mobility and allows him to transition up the ice consistently. Unfortunately, he's not a very creative player at this time in his development. With the exception of the occasional head fake, he doesn't show any high-end skill at the line, instead relying on his shot. Both his wrist-shot and slapshot have solid technique and he can generate a lot of velocity, though his timing with his shot is mixed due to not waiting for the goalie to be screened or shooting it directly into a blocked lane. He also has displayed average vision which doesn't allow him to distribute the puck at the rate necessary to translate into a powerplay quarterback at the pro levels.

In order for Fehervary to become an effective pro, he needs to continue to develop the ability to process the play at a quicker rate, while not relying on his physical instincts as often so that he can execute better from behind the goal-line and out. Despite this, he's an ultra competitive defender who can transition the puck by using his skating ability.

"Steady-Eddie type defender who played smart positional hockey and competed hard. He won battles and used his size well. Not much in the way of offense but he did move pucks and he might be able to log some minutes as a shutdown guy in the NHL." - HP Scout, Mark Edwards

"He had a very good NHL Combine week." - NHL Scout, June 2018

"I had a few scouts comment to me that his interviews at the combine were very good. Several noted that he was honest about his game and knows what he is as a player." HP Scout, Mark Edwards

127	FLORCHUK, ERIC	SASKATOON	WHL	6' 1.5"	175 lbs *	LW

He was a trade piece in a move from contender to contender going from Victoria to Saskatoon at the deadline for draft picks. He was taken 13th over all in 2015 and grew quite a bit. In viewings it was more noticeable over time that he was growing more and more comfortable using his body. He skates with a decent top speed showing some strength in his legs through a stable stance and ability to drive the net. Where he needs to improved is with changes in gear; needs to develop some ability to separate from a defended, gain quickness in his opening strides and add some precision to his edgework. Florchuk is good puck carrier but doesn't over do it and shows some deception in his play and has good instincts to setup teammates, he makes effective plays on zone entries moving pucks quickly east and west to keep defenders moving causing breakdowns. He's not a great shooter and needs to work on his velocity and accuracy, would like to see him consistently drive the net and agitate more as his effort in this aspect of the game can come and go. Filling out his frame will help him be a more physical force for a full 60 minutes and further impose himself on the game and dictate play; should have defenders making note every time he's on the ice.

| 166 | FOCHT, CARSON | CALGARY | WHL | 6' 0.0" | 178 lbs | LC |

Carson Focht is a two-way centreman who split time with the Tri-City Americans and Calgary Hitmen in the WHL. He was a major piece sent to Calgary at the deadline for Jake Bean. Carson's icetime increased substantially after the trade, playing in all situations and on both special teams units, although his production was relatively similar with both teams. With Tri-City he had 16 points in 37 regular season games and with the Hitmen he finished the season with 17 points in 32 regular season games.

Carson's physical tools are solid, with no major weaknesses, although he is not an explosive player. His skating form is solid, with a strong stride and quick feet. He lacks some strength overall, seen by his slight stature, but given his strong fundamentals, when he gets stronger his skating should improve as well. His puck skills are strong, he can handle it well in tight areas and with speed. His shot is average, but he has shown the ability to tuck the puck under the bar in tight and has shown glimpses of skill. His hockey sense is strong, and he makes strong decisions with the puck, although these skills overall have not combined yet to make himself a major offensive threat in the WHL. Although a dependable player, he has not shown the skill level to be considered a top-6 NHL prospect. His skills would most likely translate better into a bottom 6 role at the NHL level.

The strength of Focht's game is his competitiveness and effort in all three zones. He is reliable in his own end, and wins puck battles despite his lack of weight. He was as strong penalty killer and wants to make a difference in all facets of the game. The upside to his offensive game is that he has shown the ability to make tough plays and passes through traffic to his teammates, although these plays have not been made consistently. If he can take a big step forward with his offensive game, he is an interesting prospect because of his other intangibles. He is considered a low end prospect for a team who is banking on him breaking out next year, but right now he projects as a solid but by no means dominant, two-way centre at the junior level.

| 108 | FONSTAD, COLE | PRINCE ALBERT | WHL | 5' 10.0" | 159 lbs* | C |

Cole Fonstad is an undersized playmaker in his second season with the Prince Albert Raiders. Cole was selected 5th overall in the WHL Bantam draft in 2015 and this season lived up to the hype. He scored 21 goals and 73 points in 72 games.

Cole's best quality is his vision and ability to find the open man. He quarterbacked the Raiders power play all season. He makes the passes that you don't expect him to make. Cole has the ability to seeming gain the offensive blue line at will. In the new NHL zone entries are a key stat and Cole is dominant at it. His hockey IQ is far ahead of his age. Whenever he carries the puck overt the blue line he can create a scoring chance. Cole is clam with the puck, he allows the play to develop and doesn't force things. He can finish if he needs to but his shot is still below average. His down fall is his defensive ability and aggressiveness. He got pushed around at times down low and had a tendency to lose puck battles. Skating is also average.

Cole played in the annual Top prospects game and was recently named to Canada's Under 18 team. Cole was Prince Albert's best player in their first round series against Moose Jaw. Cole's vision and playmaking abilities make him a joy to play with. With a high hockey IQ, if he can become a better-rounded player and add size he could make it in the new NHL.

| 67 | FORTIER, GABRIEL | BAIE COMEAU | QMJHL | 5' 10.0" | 170 lbs * | LW |

The first thing you notice with Fortier: his skating abilities. He has great top speed and acceleration. He's can absolutely fly on the ice, whether it be when he's rushing the puck down the wing or when he puts quick puck pressure on the puck-carrier on the forecheck. Fortier is not very tall, but has a thick frame and is very strong on the puck. His compete level is excellent and his motor never stops working. With his speed and anticipation, he can be an asset on a team's penalty-killing unit. He creates a lot of chances shorthanded, and can be a threat for players playing the point on the power play. A lot of his scoring chances come from his hard work down low and his speed off the rush. His vision and hockey IQ are fine, but if they were better, he'd be a more dominant player offensively. He had his best success offensively this year in the 2nd half of the season, averaging just under a point per game this season despite playing on an average Baie-Comeau team. Gabriel's older brother Maxime was signed by Columbus earlier this season after going undrafted for two straight years. There are some differences between the two brothers, as Gabriel has more tools in his game that could make him an NHLer one day. While Maxime projects as an offensive winger if he makes it, Gabriel has the chance of playing more of a bottom 6 and energy role if his offensive game doesn't translate (whereas Maxime doesn't have that same level of grit). Offensively, I would like to see him slow down the play a bit more in the offensive zone and use his linemates a bit more. In addition, improving his shot would also help him take more advantage of his scoring chances.

With his speed, intensity and two-way game, we feel that Fortier has a chance to be a mid-round pick in June.

"Not a huge upside offensively but I can see him making it, he has the speed and drive to play an energy role in the NHL.." - HP Scout Jérôme Bérubé

"Several scouts told me he was one of their best interviews during combine week. One answer from Fortier was so good I asked if I could use it even knowing I wouldn't get approval. It was worth a try.... I can say this much, it was one of the most impressive things I've been told a player said during a combine interview." HP Scout, Mark Edwards

| 51 | FOUDY, LIAM | LONDON | OHL | 6' 0.0" | 174 lbs * | RW |

Liam Foudy was selected in the first round, 18th overall by the London Knights in the 2016 OHL draft. He had a successful sophomore season, putting up 40 points in 65 games, including 24 goals. In the playoffs, he had 2 points in 4 games. Internationally, he produced 4 points in 5 games at the U18's. Although he didn't put up great overall numbers, he produced at a remarkable rate shortly after the Top Prospects Game, having a stretch where he scored 18 goals in 19 games.

Foudy generates a tremendous amount of power in his first few steps, exploding out of the gate which helps create one of the best top-gears in this year's class. His skating ability makes him very difficult to deal with when going North-South but he's also an agile player whose body-movement is difficult to read which allows him to open-up space when skating down aggressively on defenders or when stopping-up unexpectedly to make a pass. Due to his speed, he consistently gets breakaways and partial breakaways where he has shown a set of soft-hands when in-tight to a goalie. Arguably the most important attribute for Foudy is that he developed the ability to make plays while going at top-speeds. This made him very dangerous off the rush, where he showed plus vision and passing ability to feed his teammates. Despite being able to play at 100 miles-per-hour he's also able to change his pacing and rhythm, showing a good amount of poise and not rushing passing attempts. His passing is good but its his shot that makes defenders have to take notice of him. He's got an excellent release point, needing very little time to get it off his tape.

Although he has the tools necessary to be a defensive-force in theory, he didn't impress us as many times away from the puck as he did when carrying it in most of our viewings, so there's room for him to recognize when to use his tools in the defensive-end more than he currently does.

Liam took advantage of his increased ice-time after London decided to re-tool. In the second half of the season, he started to recognize how to use his excellent tools. He's a versatile player who is just starting to un-tap his upside.

"Well obviously he was much better after the Top prospects game, but he'll get over drafted because he's in London." NHL Scout, April 2018

"Reminds me of Formenton but he's not Formenton. You're readers will love that quote...like what the hell does that mean? (laughs)" NHL Scout, April 2018

"It was close but I have him over (Akil) Thomas." - NHL Scout, April 2018

"He's just behind (Akil) Thomas on my list." - NHL Scout, May 2018

"Love the speed but don't like the brain. I think he's a bit overrated." - NHL Scout, May 2018

"I'm not a fan." - NHL Scout, May 2018

"Great at the U18. I liked him before but he sold me in Russia." NHL Scout, May 2018

"Late bloomer...a lot of room to keep improving. He's got to get a lot stronger, got to add bulk...but good speed and has good skill and good hockey sense." - NHL Scout, May 2018

"Liked him a lot in his OHL Draft year but his stock has fallen with me since. Obviously played his best hockey after the Top prospects game but I still saw two stinkers after that game. At times I've mistaken him for Formenton during a shift because of their skating. My issue has been his strength and I'm still questioning his hockey sense." - HP Scout, Mark Edwards

"He was an impressive interview at the combine." - NHL Scout, June 2018

"Good feedback on combine and another player with a good combine interview story." HP Scout, Mark Edwards

NR	GAJARSKY, ADAM	BRNO JR.	CZREP-JR.	5' 10.0"	174 lbs	RW

Adam Gajarsky played for HC Kometa Burno U18 and U20 teams, as well as HC Kometa Brno in the Czech league and SK Horacka Slavia Trebic in the Czech2 league. He played the majority of his hockey for the U20 team, putting up 20 points in 25 games, including 11 assists. He was also used internationally by the Czechs in every major international tournament, finishing off the year with 2 points in 7 games at the U18's.

Gajarsky is a winger who makes up for his lack of high-end tools by playing a tenacious two-way brand of hockey. Adam's best attribute is his compete-level. He's not the biggest kid on the ice but he's got a ton of heart and plays much larger than his size. He's the first to go into the dirty areas of the ice and battle for pucks, as well as take punishment near the goal-line in order to try and make a play. He doesn't only play at a good pace in the offensive-end, showing a solid defensive-effort on the ice as well. We have seen him make several successful backchecking takeaway plays that have prevented breakaway opportunities and he's quick to take up a shooting lane and engage with bigger players at the defensive-blueline when the opportunity is there.

Despite not having a high-end skillset, he shows confidence when handling the puck and was successful at transitional offensive-zone entries when being deployed on the powerplay. This was in large part due to his edges and plus puck skills which allowed him to weave through traffic at a consistent rate. Although he plays a possession game, it can get him into trouble as he sometimes skates himself into corners and lacks the size to get out. Additionally, his motor works against him in terms of trying to do too much by himself. As an example, we have seen him go for a difficult-angled shot that have a low success rate even when he had an open teammate with a better shooting angle to pass to. That being said, his shot generates a lot of power and he's capable of dragging the puck to change the angle of his release, though he's only managed this in a couple of our viewings

Gajarsky is a versatile player who was used in all situations internationally. On the powerplay, he was deployed both in the slot area where he can use his shot and along the half-wall where he showed decent puck distribution, occasionally making high-level passes. In order for Adam to be a successful pro, he's going to need to continue to get stronger, develop quicker straight-line speed and learn when to pace himself since he plays the game quicker than he can process the play at times.

157	GALENYUK, DANILA	SKA ST. PETERSBURG 2	RUSSIA-JR.	6' 1.0"	200 lbs	LD

Danila Galenyuk is a physically mature defenseman who is capable of erasing his teammates mistakes in the defensive-end. He played his minor hockey with Mamonty Yugry and SKA-1946 St. Petersburg in the MHL before getting some pro hockey experience with SKA-Neva St. Petersburg of the VHL and got called up to the KHL where he played with SKA St. Petersburg. He played the most games with Mamonty Yugry where he put up 3 points in 13 games while going pointless in both the KHL and VHL. He also played at every major international event and was an anchor for his team, finishing the year off with a solid U18 tournament where he was an alternate captain and captured a top 3 player award for Russia.

Galenyuk is a calculated defenseman that plays a structured game in the defensive-end which compliments offensively minded teammates by delivering quick and accurate passes to help set them up, as well as help cover for their mistakes. He's a player whose more likely to make the safe play than he is to try and hit those high difficulty, low percentage ones. His skating has strong fundamentals and he has a deep knee bend, creating a smooth yet powerful stride with a good top-gear. He uses his skating ability to close gaps efficiently and take advantage of his physicality. Danila forces his opponents to respect his game. We have seen him deliver some heavy puck-separating hits all over the ice, and he's more capable of playing a physical brand of hockey down-below his goal-line, he's not an easy defenseman for opposing teams to play against. Additionally, he's good at reading the play without the puck and can thread the needle, making long stretch passes that land on the tape. During forechecking sequences, he stays composed and is still a capable puck distributor under heavy pressure.

He's never going to stand out too much on the ice and usually flies under the radar during a game even when he's playing well due to his style of play, though this usually indicates he's playing effective, mistake free hockey. Although defensively mature, his offensive-skill set is not overly developed at this point in time. He's got decent vision and doesn't panic with the puck on his stick while walking the line but he doesn't use any sort of fakes to breakdown opposing teams and although he's capable of getting his shot through traffic due to a reduced wind-up on his slapshot and having a decent release point on his wrist-shot, it's more of a shot meant to generate rebound opportunities and is not overly threatening. One of the more interesting aspects of his game to note, was that he was used in-front of the net on the powerplay during international play due to his size and his puck retrieval skills. On the one hand it's good that he was useful to his coach on the powerplay but on the other it speaks volumes to the offensive-limitations to his game while walking the blueline.

Due to his projectable frame, his solid skating mechanics, and relatively mistake free transitional game, he was called up to the KHL which is difficult for a draft eligible defenseman to accomplish. Galenyuk has already demonstrated that he has a lot of pro attributes and with added development to the offensive side of his game, he could turn into a workhorse at the pro-level.

188	GIBSON, MITCHELL	LONE STAR	NAHL	6' 0.5"	188 lbs	G

Gibson is a product of the Philadelphia Jr. Flyers and Team Comcast programs and is finishing a successful rookie campaign with the Lone Star Brahmas (NAHL) where he had an impressive 1.59 GAA and a .935 save % in 43 games. Gibson is a technically sound goaltender with excellent foot and edge work. His lateral movement is smooth and he makes side to side saves look effortless. Being only 6'1" Gibson needs to continue to work on strength and posture in the butterfly, as he can make himself look small in the net at times. When he is playing tall and on top of his crease he looks like a pro prospect in how he controls his crease. Gibson is committed to Harvard University but with a crowded crease situation in Cambridge, Gibson will likely spend one more season in junior hockey before heading to the Crimson.

"I don't have him as a draft but a lot of hockey people I know keep telling me he's going to get drafted." – NHL Scout, May 2018

"He's a good goalie. His height will obviously work against him but he's a kid with a lot of talent." – NHL Scout, May 2018

"I'm not drafting a 6'0" goalie out of tier 2. Some team will though." – NHL Scout, May 2018

148	GILES, PATRICK	USA U-18	NTDP	6' 4.3"	201 lbs *	RW

Patrick Giles is a prototypical power-forward who has had a mixed development year while putting up 20 points in 57 games in a depth-role for the USNTDP. Although his numbers are not impressive he does have plus tools and a high-level of compete to counteract some of his production. He's slated to play for Boston College next season.

Giles has tremendous size which he uses to generate power in his stride, he's an efficient and coordinated skater and this allows him to be very aggressive on the forecheck. He weigh's down the opposition while using his leverage and an actives-stick to turn the puck over. He plays a tenacious brand of hockey and is capable of engaging multiple players simultaneously while battling for loose pucks. His offensive-awareness is a plus, he's good at gauging the amount of time he has to make a play and can find soft-ice where he likes to power his way out of corners and drive towards the goal-line to create scoring opportunities. There's a high-level of composure when the puck is on his stick and he uses his length and size to keep opponents from knocking him off the puck while looking for passing options. He has above average vision and can make quick decisions with the puck on his stick which has created a couple of impressive primary assists in our viewings. In the defensive-end, he's good at taking up shooting lanes due to his size and is willing to help support his defenseman when the play calls for it.

Unfortunately, despite his skating ability, size, and offensive-awareness, his skill-set is average and his rate of execution when attempting to finish off passing plays or rebound attempts has been poor. He doesn't track the puck off of shots from the blueline well, which makes it difficult for him to get to rebounds before the defensive opposition does. His hands are a work in progress, and he's not capable of beating players one-on-one consistently. His shot is also average, his wrist-shot lacks any sort of high-end quality and it's rare for him to change the angle of his shot while in motion.

It's difficult to gauge Giles, on the one-hand he has some enticing tools and is willing to play a forechecking role which he's been consistently good at doing, however his execution in the offensive-end leads us to believe that his offensive-ceiling isn't very high at this point in time. Due to this we see Giles as a depth role-player who will need to learn how to execute with the puck on his stick at a higher rate in order to become successful at the NHL level.

"He's a simple player. He goes up and down his wing and on good days does some good work on the forecheck. Ceiling isn't high enough for me to look at him very high." - NHL Scout, November 2017

"I cannot believe he was ranked that high by NHL Central. That was my biggest shocker on that list." NHL Scout, February 2018

"Not done my final list but I'm not sure if he's even a draft for me, I noticed that NHL Central dropped him a bit." - NHL Scout, April 2018

"Some guys are probably a bit hard on him because of Central's ranking but I think if you forget about that and judge him on his merits he does some good things." - NHL Scout, April 2018

"I really like him as a player, I'm probably a bit higher on him than the masses, I see a lot of upside in his game." HP Scout, Dusten Braaksma

"The other scouts and myself don't like this player as much as Dusten does." - HP Scout, Mark Edwards

NR	GINNELL, BRAD	KOOTENAY	WHL	6' 0.5"	172 lbs	LC

Brad Ginnell is a tough center who was selected 105th overall by Portland in the WHL Bantam Draft. However, he was traded by Portland to Kootenay after putting up 11 points in 25 games, including 5 goals. On the Ice, he produced 8 points in 36 games, with 5 assists.

Ginnell is a two-way center who's capable of providing energy and bite to a line. He's got a decent set of hands that he looks to use in one-on-one situations or when under pressure. We have seen him quickly pull the puck around an opponent who was challenging him in the neutral zone before making a transitional zone entry. An additional attribute that he uses when rushing the puck up the ice are his edges. He's got above-average outside-edges that he uses to cut around his opponents and he's shown a degree of shiftiness in his play, where he's capable of side-stepping his opponent, effectively bypassing him while maintaining possession. Although we have seen him generate quality scoring chances on net with his shot in the slot on occasion, he's an instinctive playmaker when we watched him. He displays a decent cycle game, as well as the ability to fire a sharp pass over long distances or fake a shot and turn it into a pass in order to re-open his lanes. One of the best qualities to Ginnell's game is his willingness to stand up for his team. He's not a player that backs down from a fight and can take a big-hit before bouncing right back up before playing his next shift. This allowed him to be an effective role-player for the Ice this past season.

"Brad's father is a scout with the Vegas Golden Knights." - HP Scout, Mark Edwards

49	GINNING, ADAM	LINKOPING	SWEDEN	6' 4.0"	206 lbs *	LD

Adam Ginning had a solid development year for the Linkoping HC J20 team and their pro team where he put up 2 points in 28 games and had 1 assist in 7 playoff games. He was featured at the Hlinka, Five-Nations and U18's where he played top-pairing minutes primarily with Boqvist and showed that he was capable of shutting down the top opposition.

Ginning has excellent size, featuring a thick core and broad shoulders that gives him leverage when competing against opponents along the boards, as well as when he's attempting to block shooting lanes and when he's competing for space in the slot area by boxing-out the opposition. Furthermore, he's got above-average defensive awareness, consistently tracking backdoor passing options, playing positionally sound and evaluating passing lanes and shooting lanes in advance of certain plays. That being said, he does have a tendency to play overly physical at times which inadvertently throws him out of position. We have seen him fail to track the puck on some plays, which puts him into an instinctive mindset to throw his weight around even when the smarter play would have been to attempt to track the puck and use his stick to get the puck out of danger. Despite his physical instincts getting the better of him at times, he does play with confidence in his own-end, shows poise without the puck on his stick when dealing with odd-man situations and has a long reach which he uses during shot deflections and when attempting to disrupt plays. He's also good at handling in-coming forechecking sequences by using his frame to guard the puck and his first pass to move it out of the zone. We watched him consistently keep up against men in the SHL and against good offensive-oriented players at international tournaments. This was in large part due to the above-mentioned attributes and also due to his skating mechanics. Despite being a bigger kid, Ginning has good four-way mobility and is capable of using strong edges to pivot when necessary, this also allows him to prevent players from cutting around him most of the time and close his gaps quickly. He plays with a good pace is his own-end and he competes aggressively, not letting up or giving opponents much breathing room.

His overall offensive-game isn't nearly as advanced as his defensive game currently is but he does have some interesting tools. He's got enough confidence to handle the puck when driving down a wing and has the speed to cut aggressively using a well-timed pinch, however he's not as confident holding onto the puck while walking the line for extended periods of time. This is primarily due to playing a stream-lined game, he doesn't look to use his hands to create fakes and re-open lanes as much as he probably could since his puck skills are above average. He's shown the ability to use his hands to drag the puck away or towards his body or make a quick backhand to forehand deke and is good at executing his move-set while under pressure but doesn't use his hands often. However, he does show flashes of high-end passing ability, we have seen him make no-look reverse spinning passes from the point and have them land directly on the tape of his teammates but he doesn't do it with any sort of regularity at this point in time. His slapshot is hard and he's capable of getting it through traffic, he also is good at keeping the shots between the ankles and hip areas so that they are easily deflected, although he prefers finding an open teammate as opposed to attempting to generate shots from the point in most of our viewings. He's got a decent amount of offensive-awareness but prefers to play a more reserved style of game when in the offensive-zone.

Ginning has a solid foundation, showing a good first pass, a high-level of compete, and the physical tools to shut-down some of the better forwards featured in this draft class. He looks like a hybrid shut-down defender who can move the puck and has some untapped raw offensive-upside but hasn't found his comfort zone in that area of his game yet.

"Impressed me with my interview with him at the NHL Combine." HP Scout, Mark Edwards

NR	GIROUX, DAMIEN	SAGINAW	OHL	5' 8.75"	177 lbs	LC

Damien Giroux was selected 44th overall in the OHL by the Saginaw Spirit in 2016 priority selection. He improved on last years rookie season, by putting up 43 points in 68 games, including 24 assists and an additional assist in 4 playoff games, while establishing himself on a scoring line for much of the season.

Giroux is a two-way center who plays bigger than his size would suggest. He's not a great skater, lacking a level of elusiveness due to average edges and acceleration, though his top speed is adequate when attempting to create off the rush or when transitioning to the defensive-side. We tend to move a player down in our rankings when he lacks both size and high-end skating due to the difficulty of their games translating to the pro levels at a high-rate. However, Giroux does have some attributes to counteract his limitations on the ice. Arguably his best attribute is his hockey-sense, which gives him the ability to find soft-ice at a consistent rate and evaluate where he wants to pass the puck quickly. During odd-man rushes or when attempting to execute give-and-go sequences, Giroux has demonstrated the ability to recognize where his teammates want him to be before taking a pass and firing the puck. This allowed him to generate high-percentage chances not only in the high-slot but around the goal-line when managing to get behind defensive coverage. Damien doesn't need a lot of time to bury his chances, his release point is a plus which helps make up for a lack of power on most of his shots, though his slapshot does have velocity. The other attribute that helps him counteract his size and speed is his willingness to compete both with and without the puck. He does have a tendency to get overwhelmed down-low at times and has lost his share of board battles, however he's a determined player who's also had solid forechecking sequences and has established himself in the crease area despite larger defenseman weighing on him. When he's not offensively engaged, he's still a center who's shown a high-level of defensive responsibility by aggressively backchecking, putting his body on the line when blocking a shot, and using his stick to intercept passes, disrupting the opponents attack.

In order for Giroux to have a successful pro career, he's going to need to continue to refine his skating mechanics while increasing his strength to help compliment his 200-foot game and advanced positioning in the offensive-end.

158	GOGOLEV, PAVEL	PETERBOROUGH	OHL	6' 0.5"	175 lbs	RW

Gogolev is a dynamic, offensive minded winger with an intelligence and creativity to his game. Pavel shows a versatile offensive skill set that makes him unpredictable and difficult to contain. He shows the ability to handle the puck and make smart and skilled decisions at pace and oozes confidence in his willingness to become creative with the puck on his stick. Gogolev skates well, showing a fluid stride and generating a good top speed. He can be intimidating when moving with momentum and will expose a defenders who take poor routes to him or keep a poor gap. Pavel's most intriguing offensive trait is his shot. He displays a quick release and strong velocity and accuracy behind it. However he is a deceptively strong passer and shows impressive vision. Gogolev shows an intelligence in his ability to create space for himself and teammates. He consistently drives lanes in transition, circles scoring areas and provides strong puck support, allowing him to work give-and-go opportunities with teammates. While Pavel has improved his two-way play since his rookie season, he does need to become more consistently engaged away from the puck. He has the ability to win puck and position battles, showing a deceptive strength to his game, however his willingness to compete and be assertive with his physical traits are wildly inconsistent and effect his overall game.

"I thought he improved quite a bit this year. Good individual skill but he still needs to learn how to play the game." NHL Scout, April 2018

"Skating got better. Good shot, can score." - NHL Scout, May 2018

"Highly skilled but he's an under achieving winger for me. Should be able to more with the talent he has." - NHL Scout, May 2018

"I like the tools but don't like the production he's been getting out of the tools so far. I feel like there's a lot more there but we haven't seen it yet." - HP Scout, Mark Edwards

153	GOLOD, MAXIM	ERIE	OHL	5' 10.75"	164 lbs	LW

Max Golod was a late selection for Erie in the OHL draft yet has developed at an impressive rate. He had a solid rookie season with Erie, producing 33 points in 61 games, including 21 assists. Despite not having significant production, 71% of his assists were primary and Golod didn't have a lot to work with around him on a rebuilding Otters team.

Golod is a two-way winger with a high-degree of skill. Despite being one of the younger wingers available, he showed us a good 200-foot game that encompassed several tenacious and impressive backchecking efforts. Regardless of his size and weight, he does have length and showcased his ability to stick-press and stick-lift unsuspecting opponents. His active stick worked well with his surprising strength, using leverage to come away with the puck against significantly larger opponents when we viewed him. His power creates an impressive stride out of the gate, showing fluidity that generates into plus straight-line speed. His pivoting and edges when combined with his length and skating ability make him difficult to contain when he's taking the puck towards the net in traffic. Arguably Golod's best attribute is his puck-handling ability. Maxim's length, coordination and soft hands allow him to quickly pull the puck towards his body or drag the puck around defenders while in motion, which made him dangerous in one-on-one situations. We have seen him create impressive scoring opportunities while under pressure that lesser skilled players would have trouble executing. For instance, we watched him take the puck while going at full speed, spin-off pressure along the half-wall in the neutral zone and then fire a hard pass directly onto the tape of his teammate, before joining him on the attack which resulted in a goal. As the play just mentioned indicates, his passing ability is impressive and he rarely misinterpreted how much time he had to make a play before losing his passing lane or angle. His shot isn't as refined as his passing, yet he does have reach, a plus release point and showed the ability to change the angle while rushing down the wing.

Golod is talented but he does have areas he needs to improve. His shooting accuracy was mixed in our viewings and there were games where he didn't use his skill-set as much as he could have, there was a lack of assertiveness on the ice which led to some inconsistencies. Furthermore, although he processes plays quickly, his overall hockey sense wasn't as good as his other skills, sometimes he had trouble finding soft-ice or reading his teammates. That being said, he's an under the radar prospect whose skill-level superseded his production this past season.

"He's really productive considering he's on a really bad team." - NHL Scout, March 2018

"Who? Who is Maxime Golod?" NHL Scout, April 2018

"He's got a chance to be a late pick...him and about 8000 other guys. I like him though." - NHL Scout, May 2018

*"Skilled little f*****, he's a smallish guy...really weak but that kid has some skill. Where's he going to get to?" - NHL Scout, May 2018*

"I like Golod. I think he's a big projection but he has skill and can score. I know his minor midget coach and spoke to him about him. He had a lot of good things to say. He's a draft worthy player for me" - HP Scout, Mark Edwards

NR	GOLDOWSKI, JAKE	SAGINAW	OHL	6' 2.70"	192 lbs	RC

Jake Goldowski was selected 64th overall in the 2016 OHL draft by Saginaw. He didn't end up on the Spirit right away, instead playing for the U18 USNTDP team, where he had trouble establishing himself after posting 2 assists in 21 games in a depth-role. He had more success in the OHL, after putting up 21 points in 40 games, including 11 goals and had 2 assists in 4 playoff games while being used in all situations.

Goldowski is a tenacious two-way forward who makes up for his lack of coordination and fluidity in his movement by out-competing the opposition. His offensive-game is primarily developed through the forecheck by using his thick build and an advanced understanding of how to stick-press, body-check, and track the puck below the goal-line and around the net area. Jake compensates for his lack of high-end puck-skills and skating ability by creating pressure on defenses with his high-octane motor. That being said, he's also shown the ability to pace himself appropriately on the forecheck and when transitioning over the offensive-line, this allows him to create a degree of efficiency in his attack which makes up for his first couple of heavy steps out of the gate. He's aware of his limitations and adjusts, showing plus hockey sense in some of our viewings. We have seen him stop up at the line when dealing with a quicker defender while trying to find a teammate or dumping the puck deep, as opposed to attempting an aggressive cut towards the net. Although not an overly creative offensive player who's going to drive a line, he's more than capable of finding soft-ice both at even strength and on the powerplay. His wrist-shot and slapshot both generate a good amount of power and have decent placement in most viewings, this allowed him to score on the powerplay in multiple ways, either by finding soft-ice in the left-circle when deployed along the half-wall or using his puck-tracking skills to shoot in rebounds. Goldowski demonstrates the same level of commitment in the defensive-end that he does when on the forecheck. He's a relentless backchecker who puts in a maximum effort when attempting to break-up opposing teams offensive-plays in most sequences.

Despite not being a high-end offensive talent and most likely never filling a scoring role at the pro level due to being largely ineffective in the offensive-end when his forechecking presence isn't felt, he still filled in admirably as a role-player. With the proper development, added strength and improved acceleration, he could further enhance his already effective forechecking game when attempting to establish himself against better competition.

| 179 | GORNIAK, JACK | WEST SALEM | HIGH-WI | 5' 10.8" | 181 lbs * | LW |

Gorniak missed out on last year's draft by hours, being a 9/15/99 DOB but had he been eligible last year it's unlikely he would have been drafted. Gorniak got on many scouts radar this past fall playing for Team Wisconsin U18 in the Midwest Elite League against Minnesota HS competition where he was among the league leaders in goals and points in 21 games played. Gorniak is a speedy, opportunistic center that does a good job in harnessing his speed to use as a weapon. While his playmaking ability is not high end, he is able to create offensive chances by getting himself and the puck to key areas of the ice. Gorniak has a ways to go physically but shows good first and second effort for pucks and as he gets stronger he should become a serviceable fore-checker and someone that can win important battles at both ends of the ice. Gorniak is a good two-way center that executes his assignments in his own end efficiently and is good in the faceoff circle. Gorniak has signed a letter of intent to The University of Wisconsin where he will play this fall. With hardly any junior hockey experience, the jump Gorniak faces this fall, going from Wisconsin High School to NCAA hockey is a substantial one but he will be a long term prospect for any team that selects him.

"Opponents really keyed on him with his High School team, he was about the only offensive weapon they had and he still managed to put up good numbers. You could tell he was really pressing at times, he certainly makes better decisions with talent around him." HP Scout, Dusten Braaksma

"I don't see him as player that is ever going to drive or create offense at the NHL level." NHL Scout, February 2018

"That kid can really skate so he'll get drafted for that alone." - NHL Scout, February 2018

"A lot of buzz on him but I don't think he has any hockey sense." - NHL Scout, April 2018

"Had some impressive tests at the NHL Combine." - NHL Scout, June 2018

| NR | GRANBERG, FREDRIK | SKELLEFTEA JR. | SWEDEN-JR. | 6' 2.0" | 194 lbs | LD |

Granberg is good-sized defenseman who played this past season for Skelleftea in the SuperElit league, and also played in every major international U-18 tournament for Sweden this season. He's defensive defenseman with good physical attributes, including good size, and he doesn't mind playing a physical game in his own end and in front of the net. He's good on the PK; he shows a good compete level there and makes good use of his stick to block passing lanes in the slot. He's also a good shot-blocker in front of his net. Granberg does struggle with the puck on his stick; his decision-making is slow and he doesn't really help the transition game. He had some issues handling the puck and receiving passes, where he would fumble the puck on those occasions. He can be slow retrieving pucks in his zone because of his average footwork; in today's NHL, he will definitely need to improve his skating. He's not much of a threat in the offensive zone, and lacks puck skills and creativity. He's not a player with a big upside for the next level. In order to reach the NHL, he'll need a lot of work on his puck skills, skating and making quicker decisions with the puck.

| 165 | GRAVEL, ALEXIS | HALIFAX | QMJHL | 6' 2.8" | 222 lbs * | G |

After a good rookie season and impressive postseason against Rouyn-Noranda, there was a lot more ups and downs this season for Gravel.

He started the year in a backup role with Team Canada at the Ivan Hlinka tournament, losing the starting role to fellow Quebecer Olivier Rodrigue. Back in Halifax, Gravel had some tough moments in the 1st half of the season and did not play as often as anticipated. He found himself outplayed by Blade Mann-Dixon, an undrafted 5'07" goaltender in his 3rd season in the league. Gravel was better in the 2nd half of the season and was splitting games with Mann-Dixon. The Asbestos native has ideal size for today's NHL goaltenders, and moves well in his crease. He also has good agility and footwork in his crease. The biggest problems with Gravel that we noticed in the past two seasons have been his inconsistency and his rebound-control. This year, we really saw some struggles with his rebound-control; he had trouble keeping pucks close to him and gave up too many rebounds in the slot. He will need a lot of work there, as it's an important part of a goaltender's game and won't get better as he continues to play against better players at higher levels who have all better shots than players in the QMJHL. Gravel, with his size, covers a lot of room in his crease; when he challenges shooters at the top of his crease, this is where he excels. He can be out of position at times when he overcommits to shooters or when the puck goes behind his net, as he seems to have a hard time tracking pucks in that situation. Gravel has a good glove, and can make some great saves with it.

Gravel came into the season with a good chance of being the first goaltender picked in this draft; obviously, things didn't go as planned this year. Now we expect him to be a middle-round pick, probably between rounds 3 and 5, as NHL teams will bet on his size and a big comeback season next year.

"He was good today, much better than my last viewing. He was competing, looked quicker and more athletic. Still looks big though." - NHL Scout, November 2017

"One of the biggest disappointments this season in the QMJHL. It wouldn't surprise me if Halifax traded for another goalie next year for their Memorial Cup year." - HP Scout Jérôme Bérubé

"Same person I spoke to about Golod also coached Gravel. He's a big fan of the kid but I can't get passed what I saw in my viewings. Not a goaltender I'd personally have that much interest in after scouting him this season." - HP Scout, Mark Edwards

| 74 | GREEN, ALEX | CORNELL | NCAA | 6' 2.0" | 176 lbs | RD |

This is Green's third chance at draft eligibility, and he's almost certain to hear his name called in Dallas. He had a terrific freshman season at Cornell where he showed scouts he has the ability to skate with just about anyone.

Green has the size and he can retrieve pucks and quickly get the offense moving again. He has a great first pass and hockey IQ to know when to move it with his feet or when to just send a quick short pass to a forward supporting the puck, or move it more quickly up ice to a winger at the defensive blue line. with a stretch pass.

His two weaknesses are his lack of offensive upside and his compete level, he sometimes shies away from physical contact. Nonetheless, a 6-foot-2 defender who can skate and move pucks has some value.

| 212 | GRONDIN, MAXIM | SAGINAW | OHL | 6' 3.25" | 206 lbs | LC |

Maxime Grondin was selected 37th overall in the 2016 OHL draft. He built on his rookie year by producing 27 points in 66 games, including 16 assists, while also having a successful playoff, producing 3 points in 4 games despite being over-matched against the Greyhounds in the opening round. Although he produced more than double his point totals than the previous year, there was a still a lack of production you would expect to see considering his tools and physical gifts.

Grondin is a good-sized center with great tools an some skill to compliment his game. He's got length, height, and a broad frame which gave him a solid net-front presence where he scored several goals either off of rebounds or by deflecting shots. He wasn't just dangerous in-front of the net though, showing a strong skating skillset which allowed him to create scoring chances for himself and his team off the rush. He's got a wide-base and a long-stride which gives him the ability to accelerate quickly for his size and generate plus straight-line speed. His speed when combined with his shot gave him several high-quality looks when we watched him. His wrist-shot has a plus release point and he's capable of changing his shot by using his length to adjust the angle, there's also a lot of power generated, it's not easy for goalies to pick up. Unfortunately, he tends to over-commit on the amount of power he attempts to generate in his release, as opposed to focusing on the accuracy, which reduces how dangerous it could be. The most glaring aspect of his shooting game is the volume, he finished the year with the 158th ranking in shots on net in the OHL, so he simply doesn't generate enough shots given that it's one of his better offensive skills. This is further highlighted when taking into consideration that his vision hasn't been overly present on some shifts. He sometimes fails to recognize an open passing lane or a back-door option that would create a scoring chance. Despite this, he's capable of making quality passes occasionally and his play away from the puck has been a plus. His defensive-awareness was above-average in most of our viewing's, which allowed him to intercept pucks in both the defensive-end and the neutral-zone before transitioning back up the ice. He's also capable of using his length to disrupt the opposing teams attack.

Grondin's an interesting player in the sense that when he's playing a high-energy game and utilizing his tools effectively, you see glimpses of what could develop into a productive pro. However, at this time, he's shown inconsistent play, sometimes being difficult to spot on the ice depending on the shift and the game. If he can generate shots at a higher volume, expand his vision, and show a more consistent motor on a shit-to-shift basis, he could become more than his current production would suggest.

"There is something there. I have some time for him." – NHL Scout, December 2017

"He's big but his consistency is not very good. Wasn't a fan of his defensive play." NHL Scout, January 2018

"He doesn't do anything quick enough. He doesn't move quick enough and doesn't get his shot away quick enough." – NHL Scout, May 2018

| 65 | GROSS, NICO | OSHAWA | OHL | 6' 0.8" | 185 lbs * | LD |

Gross is a puck moving defender with good mobility. His game elevated as his confidence grew, Nico shows good poise in possession and is often able to lead transition attacks with his skating or smooth first pass. Gross shows good footwork as his edges and his quickness often allowed him to escape pressure and create space to make a play. He recognized open ice well and exploits it with his skating abilities, injecting offensively at the appropriate times. Nico shows good awareness and can simplify his game when needed but is able to push the pace of play and create. His decision making under pressure will need to improve as he tends to force plays to low percentage options, resulting in turnovers. Offensively Gross does a good job distributing the puck and will sneak in from his point position appropriately. He utilizes a quick and accurate snap shot to get pucks through, however enhancing his upper body strength would benefit the velocity of his shot. Nico shows an aggressiveness while defending, engaging physically and trying his best to be tough to play against. An active stick and positional play allow him to defend adequately, however he can chase the play at times when looking to play over aggressively. His transition defense had inconsistent results as his routes to puck carriers are inconsistent. When he takes appropriate routes and makes strong reads he's able to take away time and space and separate player from puck. Improving his neutral zone reads would elevate his defensive play.

"What is he at the next level? I see a player that tries to play a game he can't play. He's a later round guy for me." - NHL Scout, December 2017

"He's smart, I'm not sure he's all that self aware about what he is as a player going forward though. He's at his best when he keeps things simple but he's tried to do too much most of the times I've see him." - NHL Scout, December 2017

"He was good at World Jr, thought he played a lot smarter there and played more within his capabilities." NHL Scout, January 2018

"Highly competitive well rounded defensman but not an offensive guy. I love the way that guy competes...he doesn't take a back seat to anybody." - NHL Scout, May 2018

"Liked him right away in my very first viewing of him. Still needs to figure out who is as a player but I love how hard he competes. That will give him the chance to play in the NHL." HP Scout, Mark Edwards

| 69 | GROULX, BENOIT-OLIVIER | HALIFAX | QMJHL | 6' 1.0" | 193 lbs * | LC |

Groulx was the top pick in the 2016 QMJHL Draft out of the Gatineau midget program. His father coached in the QMJHL for 13 years with Gatineau, and is now coaching Syracuse in the AHL. The younger Groulx, as a coach's son, really understands the game well, taking pride in all the little details.

Groulx can play both at center and on the wing; he has good size and can play a gritty game in front of the net and along the boards. He's not a flashy offensive forward, but possesses a big heavy shot. In midget, he was the go-to guy for his team, whereas in junior, he has become the more all-around guy that does a bit of everything. His skating has limited him as far his offensive upside goes; he lacks that explosive stride to be a more effective offensive player who takes advantage of scoring opportunities. Groulx is the kind of player who can play different roles on a line, and this is what he did with Halifax this season. He can score, set up guys, play a physical game and make smart plays all over the ice. A very smart player who, if he makes it at the NHL level, would likely be featured as a role player. He doesn't have the offensive touch to be a top 6 forward at the NHL level, but he can be that role player who can play on the PK as well. Groulx lacks the necessary offensive dynamic qualities, which is why we project him more as a depth and role player at the NHL level.

Overall, we like his smarts, but have some concerns about upside and skating abilities.

"He plods along and I don't see skill. I know right now I'll have him ranked where we'd never get him." NHL Scout, October 2017

"He is so slow out there. He can't keep up to the pace now so how will he keep up in the NHL. Skating not as bad as Strome last year but that's what his situation reminds me of." NHL Scout, November 2017

"How many chances has he had tonight? He can't score so what is he? Skating is too weak to take him high given his lack of skill." - NHL Scout, November 21017

"No doubt about the fact that he is smart but when you start projecting him for the NHL I don't see much else in his game that would make me want to draft him before the 4th round." NHL Scout, November 2017

"A hard working coaches son. He does all the little things well." - NHL Scout, May 2018

"Smart player, but his skating and offensive upside are lacking. Not a first-round pick for me. He was invisible too many times when I saw Halifax this year" - HP Scout Jérôme Bérubé

"I like his smarts. He does a lot of little things right. I question his skill level and while some games I thought his skating might be passable, there were other games where he really struggled to have any pace in his game at all, especially when he was tired, it got really ugly." - HP Scout, Mark Edwards

72	GRUDEN, JONATHAN	USA U-18	NTDP	5' 11.8"	169 lbs *	LC

Gruden was drafted 100th overall in the 5th round of the 2016 OHL Priority selection but chose the college route. He had a successful year with the USNTDP by putting up 59 points in 56 games which was fourth amongst all players featured on the team. He is slated to play for Miami University next season.

Gruden is a unique player in the sense that arguably his best asset is a psychological one. Some players have the ability to play above their size, however this can't be emphasized enough in Gruden's game, he plays like a 6'4, 220-pound power-forward despite his frame. He's got a good first-step and is relentless on the forecheck, where he will throw his frame into whoever he can and compete consistently during puck battles along the boards. He also uses his speed off the rush and has a shooters mentality, he's also not afraid to aggressively cut through heavy traffic in an effort to improve his shooting angle. Below the hash-marks is where Gruden is usually most effective which doesn't add up on paper but he's tenacious as they come and plays with a degree of bravado when attempting to beat larger players then himself. He attacks the net in waves and has a solid release point on his shot which is matched by his accuracy, he's very good at getting the puck upstairs in a hurry even when in-tight to the net. His awareness around the net is also a plus and he's capable of recognizing when he can get behind defensive-coverage which allows him to score dirty goals around the net area before he gets boxed-out.

With his style of play comes potential injuries down the road but he's shown the ability this year to stay healthy and is good at tempering his play when he needs to. He's been a solid complimentary player and seems to develop chemistry with whoever he's been put on a line with throughout the season. The big concern with Gruden's game is if it's translatable to the pro levels. He's going to have to put on significant weight and although his play around the house area is impressive and he can score a lot of dirty goals, he will have to adapt his style to bigger and quicker defenseman.

"Goes completely under the radar on that U18 team but he is a heck of a hockey player." HP Scout, Dusten Braaksma

"This is a player who grew on me this season. I wasn't a huge fan in September but by April I started to appreciate his game more. - HP Scout, Mark Edwards

NR	GUAY, NICOLAS	DRUMMONDVILLE	QMJHL	5' 11.0"	174 lbs	RC

Guay went undrafted last season, but came back this year with a strong year, scoring close to 30 goals and playing a solid two-way game. Guay can play both down the middle and on the wing; he has good versatility and the necessary smarts to play an all-round game. In his first season as captain of the Voltigeurs, Guay established himself as one of the good two-way forwards in the league. He was used by his coaches in all situations; he's good on the penalty-killing unit with his smarts, anticipation and work ethic. He really does a lot of unsung work for his team, retrieving pucks along the boards and in front of the net. He's really unselfish on the ice, and will do a lot of small-detail plays that helps his team win hockey games. Offensively, he's not a flashy or high-end performer, but has a good shot and scores his share of goals. He has a good shot, a quick release, and will play in the tougher areas of the ice to score those ugly goals. His playmaking is fine, but this year it was his goal-scoring that was more on display compared to last season. Guay has grown quite a bit since his midget days, he was drafted out of midget listed at 5'09.5" and 163 pounds and now he's over 6'01" and weighs over 180 pounds.

We don't expect Guay to be drafted this year, but like last year when he was invited by New Jersey to their rookie camp, we fully expect the same thing to happen again this year with him.

106	GUSTAFSSON, DAVID	HV 71	SWEDEN	6' 1.5"	196 lbs	LC

Gustafsson has often played against older players in the past, due to his physical maturity and on-ice smarts. It was no different this year, as he was a regular in the SHL, playing 45 games with HV71. He's limited offensively, even though he had 12 points in the SHL this season playing against men. His skating is a big drawback and he lacks explosiveness and agility to his stride. He's very strong physically; his puck-protection along the boards is really good, as demonstrated in U-18 tournaments. He also won't be afraid to bring the puck to the net. He plays like a power-forward on the ice and he's at his best with the puck down low. His hockey IQ is good; he makes a lot of smart plays on the ice. His sees the ice well, making quick passes to open teammates in the slot. He works hard in all three zones, pays attention to the little details that not many players do at this age. He shows good support deep in his zone, helping out his defensemen when retrieving pucks and getting them out of his zone. He plays in all situations when we saw him on the international stage; he's good on the PK with his smarts and has a great stick. He has low upside for the NHL, but if his skating improves, he could find a way to make it as a role player at some point.

| 193 | HAIN, GAVIN | USA U-18 | NTDP | 5' 11.0" | 194 lbs | LC |

Gavin Hain had a decent year for the USNTDP where he put up 35 points in 61 games, including 15 goals. He was used primarily in a bottom-6 checking role for his team, however he did have spurts where he played with some of the more skilled players as well, such as at the Five-Nations tournament where he got some time on the top-line and on the 2nd powerplay. He is slated to play for the University of North Dakota next season.

Hain is a tenacious player with a thick frame that has a decent amount of skill who adapted well to his forechecking role. He's got a thick and powerful build which allows him to generate power in his stride which gives him a solid top-gear, though his stride is a bit short and his acceleration is below-average. His frame complimented a high-octane motor that he used to create havoc when he was on top of his game. He's consistent at aggressively tracking loose pucks and battling along the boards in an attempt to regain possession and is good at angling his body away from his opponents in order to protect the puck. Furthermore, he likes to enter high-traffic areas regularly where he cuts to the front of the net and look for soft-ice. We saw him use his frame to angle himself away from opponents in the slot area so that he could look for backdoor passing options or distribute it back to the point if his lane was cut-off. That being said, he's not a playmaker, his vision isn't below average but he has difficulty executing passes on occasion due to the speed at which he delivers them. Though, he does have a good release point and he generates a lot of velocity, however his shot isn't overly accurate. Hain was one of the more skilled depth-players featured on the team this past season, due to this, he was given powerplay time in spurts where he demonstrated the ability to use head and shot fakes to set up his teammates along the half-wall and recognized the time and space he had to make plays at a better rate when given more room to work with.

He's a player who competes hard at both ends of the ice and doesn't give up on a play, however the most concerning aspect of his game is his rate of execution. He plays the game at a high-pace but lacks the ability to slow the game down or change the tempo of a shift when he's carrying the puck most of the time. This lead to him creating unforced turnovers and he more often than not failed to bury his chances.

"I can't say anything bad about the kid except nothing comes across as high end to me, he'll give you max effort all the time, I think he's going to be a real good college player." HP Scout, Dusten Braaksma

| NR | HAKKARAINEN, MIKAEL | MUSKEGON | USHL | 6' 1.0" | 193 lbs | LC |

Hakkarainen is a 98' born, Finnish re-entry prospect for the NHL draft who just finished up his third season in North America. After a successful first season in North America playing for Brookings (NAHL) in 16/17, Mikael moved to the USHL where he struggled early in the year with Chicago and eventually was traded to Muskegon in the middle of last season. Mikael battled injuries this season but was able to register 15 goals and 31 Assists in 36 games for the Lumberjacks. Hakkarainen in a lanky forward that lacks skating explosiveness but makes up for it with good offensive instincts and getting himself into the correct areas of the ice. While his two-way game and awareness in his own end still need to improve, Mikael has made strides in this area of his game since he first came to North America. In some viewings he seems to show better compete than in other games. Hakkarainen is slated to attend Providence College this fall.

"I just haven't seen the consistency or all around development in the three seasons I have watched him play." HP Scout, Dusten Braaksma

| 119 | HALL, CURTIS | YOUNGSTOWN | USHL | 6' 2.5" | 200 lbs * | RC |

Tendered by Youngstown (USHL) in 2016, Hall just finished his 2nd full season with the phantoms after coming out of the Cleveland Barons AAA program. The Yale commit registered 13 Goals and 18 Assists in 54 Regular season games for Youngstown this season. Hall has NHL size, a centermen listed at 6'2" with good speed and athleticism that allows him to be quick on defenseman on the fore-check as well as patrolling the middle of the ice and attacking loose pucks. Hall is a two-way centermen that brings physicality and speed. Hall displays good work ethic and supports the play in all three zones. His commitment to playing a complete two-way game limits his offensive output a bit, however Hall possesses some offensive tools that make him effective in generating offensive chances for his team. He possesses an excellent wrist shot and release, however Hall can get too dialed in at shooting for corners at times which results in shots missing the net. Hall likes to play with speed, especially when entering the offensive zone but had been susceptible to taking unnecessary risks at the blue line that result in turnovers and the play going the other way. Hall is a strong kid that can gain middle ice, bull his way to the front of the net and does a good job out muscling defenders for position in front. Curtis will join the Yale Bulldogs this coming fall.

"Has impressive athleticism and balance, strong skater and high hockey IQ defensively, just not sure enough offensive thoughts are there to be a high end prospect." HP Scout, Dusten Braaksma

"It's a bad draft." - NHL Scout, December 2017

"Not a whole lot of offense there, he lacks skill. Not a physical guy either so someone else can have him, he's not on my list."- NHL Scout, April 2018

"His numbers dropped off a cliff in the second half. I saw him enough to know he just doesn't create that much offensively." NHL Scout, April 2018

"He's a mid to later rounder for me." - NHL Scout, May 2018

"He's another in a long list of players in the USHL I don't have high on my list. It's a bad crop in that league this year." -NHL Scout, May 2018

"Thought he was just ok in the WJAC, he played a simple game. I didn't cross him off my list but I certainly wouldn't take him before the middle of the draft at the earliest. Not enough in the way of skill, just a workmanlike player to me" - HP Scout, Mark Edwards

| 33 | HALLANDER, FILIP | TIMRA | SWEDEN-2 | 6' 1.8" | 188 lbs * | LC |

After beginning the season with a successful Hlinka tournament that includes a Bronze medal, where he scored 3 goals and had 1 assist in 5 games, Filip Hallander spent all but one game this season at the Allsvenskan level, helping Timra IK with a promotion to the SHL level for the 2018-19 season. Hallander had quite the season, scoring the 6th most points for an under-18 player in the league's 18-year history, right behind teammate Jacob Olofsson. Finishing the season with 20 points in 40 games and an additional 2 points in 9 qualification games.

Hallander is a versatile, two-way forward who looks to attack the net using a good amount of skill.

He currently has an average frame to work with but he is a quick skater with a great first step. This allowed him to catch up to players and cause some disruption on the forecheck and backcheck, as well as attack the defensive-line which made him dangerous on the penalty-kill. One of his best attributes is his mentality to take the puck into dangerous-area of the ice, regardless of the amount of traffic in-front of him. He made several high-end plays while dealing with pressure, such as wrapping the puck around the back of the net before attempting to jam it while dealing with a defender who's draped over him. He's not just dangerous in-front of the net area though, as he can create off the rush showing refined and deceptive passing ability. He can make plays while at top-speed and was very good at making sharp yet accurate backhand passes that he would saucer over sticks to his teammates. His shooting mechanics are just as good as his passing ability, using a snap-like release that was difficult for goalies to pick up on, especially when he would drive down the wings and look to change the angle. He had an uncanny ability of making plays happen when contorting his frame. This was primarily due to his balance, he's good at generating additional power in his snap-shot and slapshot when dropping to a knee and we have seen make high-level passes by re-balancing himself after physical pressure was applied.

He's a smart player in all three zones who does everything well. You can put him at center and have him drive a line since his motor and aggressiveness help compliment other skilled forwards; you can also put him on the wing where he can create technical give-and-go plays with a skilled playmaker. On the powerplay, he's capable of playing down near the goal-line and along the half-wall where he showed quick one-touch passes and no-look passes that resulted in some impressive primary assists. His willingness to play a 200-foot game makes him useful all over the ice.

The biggest knock on Hallander at this time is that although he's good everywhere, he's not exceptional anywhere either. He can continue to fill-out his frame so that he can develop a more powerful stride and further enhance his ability to guard the puck when cutting but overall there's no glaring weakness in his game. Due to his ability to play in all situations, we see Hallander as a potential third-line energy option who can compliment a top-6 when needed, while also getting some opportunities on both special-teams units.

"Had some flashes of greatness in my viewings but at times I also had to make sure he was still getting shifts." - HP Scout, Mark Edwards

"Didn't think he was that tall but that's what the combine measurement said." HP Scout, Mark Edwards

NR	HALME, ALEKSI	TUTO	FINLAND-2	6' 0.0"	194 lbs	LW

Halme is a native of Tampere, Finland that came to North America for the 16/17 season with aspirations of going the NCAA route after being drafted by Muskegon in the 11th round of the 2016 USHL Phase 2 Draft. Halme played parts of the 16/17 season with Muskegon, Cedar Rapids and Chicago. After struggling to adapt to the North American game Aleksi returned to the European ranks this year. Halme split the season between TUTO U20 Jr. A. and TUTO Mestis League. Halme has excellent natural skating ability. He displays crisp edge work and explosiveness and is strong on his skates. Aleksi has some good offensive tools and playmaking ability. What keeps Halme from being as dynamic offensively as he could be is his hockey sense. His awareness and ability to read and see plays develop is below average and as a result, often finds himself out of position and away from the play a lot. The bigger ice sheet in Europe has allowed him more time to make decisions and as a result has seen an uptick in his offensive production from last season in the USHL. Halme has the skill to make simple plays and can finish well around the net and beat goalies in one on one situations but his hockey sense limits his number of opportunities he gets. Halme will play with Jokerit of the KHL next season.

"I saw Aleksi a few times last season in the USHL with a couple different teams, I felt bad for him because I don't think he ever really got comfortable in a set role because he moved around so much. He looks to have settled in back in Europe, he isn't a draft for me but he might be a player that gets a look back in North America down the road." HP Scout Dusten Braaksma

"His hockey sense just isn't there but I've heard he looked much better over in Europe. His skating is high end." NHL Scout - May 2018

NR	HALVERSON, JORDON	HUDSON	HIGH-WI	6' 1.5"	191 lbs	LD

Halverson was a key piece to Hudson's Wisconsin State High School Title run this season. Halverson has good NHL size and strength. He is a physical defender that skates well and uses his clean footwork to stay in good defensive posture. He has good physicality along the boards, plays with some nastiness in the hard areas and will step up on plays in open ice when the situation arises. Jordon is technically sound in his puck retrievals, takes good angles to pucks and is a strong skater that allows him to elude or fend off the fore checker and turn the play out of his own end. Where Halverson can get into trouble is when he tries to do too much with the puck. There are times in our viewings where he will take unnecessary risks around the blue lines and try to reach beyond his skill set to try to create offense. When Halverson keeps his game simple, he executes plays from the back end efficiently. He is a head up player coming out of his own end and has the skills to buy time for things to open up for him. Jordon has a good arsenal of shots from the blue line but can take too much time to get them off and get shots blocked or get himself handcuffed at the top of the zone. Halverson is very raw at this stage but his size and skill set are good and his challenges going forward come down to judgement and hockey sense. Halverson will likely play for Janesville (NAHL) next season, however he will surely have some USHL suiters in this Springs Phase 2 Draft as well.

"Jordon is not without flaws but he's a real athletic kid and has a lot of snarl in his game, he defends his teammates and goaltender and makes opponents pay a price." HP Scout, Dusten Braaksma

"I need to see him play against better competition, but right now he looks to be a player that can certainly play in the NCAA and then we will see what happens from there." NHL Scout (April, 2018)

168	HARRIS, JORDAN	KIMBALL UNION	HIGH-NH	5' 10.8"	179 lbs *	LD

Harris is a smooth-skating, puck-moving defenseman with limited offensive upside. At the prep level, Harris was able to dominate puck possession. There were multiple games, even against good competition, where Harris seemed to have the puck on his stick for the majority of the game.

He does a terrific job retrieving pucks. What makes him so good is his long, fluid stride to get back to pucks quickly. He then has the hockey sense and footwork to make quick decisions and start the transition back to offense. He can side-step oncoming forecheckers to skate it out of trouble and he can also make a good pass up ice on the first touch.

He can walk the blue line, but he's not overly offensive. He looks frail, but he's heavier than he looks. However, his game isn't being physical. He can defend with his feet and stick, but there wasn't a lot of time for that at the prep level.

He did help his stock with a solid performance at the USA Hockey/CCM All-American Prospects Game in Buffalo in September. He showed there that his skating ability can help carry him, even against better competition. His father played college hockey at UMass Lowell and his brother, Elijah, is a goaltender committed to Division III Endicott College.

"I think he's overrated. He can skate but I question his smarts." NHL Scout, March 2018

"Someone is going to draft him because he can really skate...doubt it's us." NHL Scout, March 2017

"For me he's a no draft but I think someone will draft him." NHL Scout, March 2017

NR	HARSCH, REECE	SEATTLE	WHL	6' 3.0"	196 lbs	RD

Harsch is a two-way defender who passed over in last years draft class but managed to double his point totals, while playing 14 less games than in previous season. He finished the year with 25 points in 53 games, including 10 goals, and was used in all situations. In the playoffs, he produced an assist in 5 games.

Harsch is a large defenseman who relies on his defensive-awareness and size to keep the puck contained to the outside and away from the net area. He's a bigger kid who lacks both power and coordination which was evident in his push-offs, lateral-mobility, and pivoting mechanics. To counteract his skating limitations, he showed composure and awareness when dealing with faster opponents then himself who attempted to create plays around him. It was impressive watching him manage to stay in-front of his man in single-coverage, despite not having a quick turn-rate. One of his primary attributes that allowed him keep opposing teams to the outside was his stick-work. He has length and was good at timing when to try and knock the puck off a stick, knowing that if he failed at doing so, he could get burned. He was also above-average at dealing with pressure, though at times he had to rely on his size to counteract his lack of escapability. His first pass is above-average and he would use that as his main option to create clean transitional zone-exits when we watched him. At the offensive-line, Harsch keeps the game relatively simple, not showing the ability to make dynamic plays consistently. However, he did have well-timed pinches, and was good at recognizing when he needed to transition back to defense. Although Reece made progress this year in his development, it's difficult to see him translating at the pro levels at this time, due to his skating and lack of high-end offensive output.

NR	HARTJE, CHASE	BRANDON	WHL	5' 11.5"	190 lbs	LD

Chase Hartje is in his first season in the WHL. He started the season with the Moose Jaw Warriors then was traded to the Brandon Wheat Kings at the deadline. The Bemidji, MN product showed his offensive upside this season scoring 3 goals and finishing with 25 points in 58 games, which was second among defenseman on the Wheat Kings.

Being in a new country and starting the season with an injury didn't seem to affect Hartje when he joined Moose Jaw's lineup. He is a slightly undersized left shot defenseman who can move the puck and create chances offensively. He has the ability to slow the play down in his own end and make a good first pass out of the zone. Hartje's ability to handle the puck allows him to skate the puck to safety even under pressure.

Hartje saw his minutes increased in Moose Jaw when two of their top four defenseman went down with injured. Hartje quarterback a strong Moose Jaw power play when called upon and did a fine job moving the puck. His shot is the one thing lacking offensively. Often hesitating when the opportunity to shoot presented its self. Hartje is a great skater, he has the ability to jump up in the rush and still make it back defense if necessary. Defensively we feel Hartje still needs work. His size and body positioning made it difficult to win puck battles down low. He also needs to improve his positioning away from the puck. Throughout the season he was vulnerable to the back door pass. Overall Hartje had an impressive rookie season. He has the tools to play in the new style of hockey that the NHL requires, it is just a matter if he can put it all together.

"I feel Chase's offensive upside outweigh the holes in his game defensively. I believe he will continue to improve as he adapts to the WHL game." HP Scout Dan Markewich

| NR | HARVEY, SAMUEL | ROUYN-NORANDA | QMJHL | 6' 0.0" | 185 lbs | G |

This season was Harvey's coming-out party in the QMJHL. He was a major player in the Huskies' surprising first half, and his superior play led him to receive an invitation to the CIBC Canada/Russia Series in November. His excellent play in that series no doubt played a part in his invitation to Team Canada's World Junior selection camp less than a month later. While he didn't make it far in the process, his confidence wasn't swayed, as he continued to post great numbers until an injury slowed him down in late February. He was named the league's top goaltender (Jacques-Plante Trophy) and was nominated for the MVP award along with Alex Barré-Boulet and Vitalii Abramov.

This is the third season of eligibility for him, but he has vastly improved various facets of his play that will allow teams to get a longer look at him this season. He was very consistent all year long which was not in the case for him since he came into the league; in the past two seasons, he had more struggles in the 2nd half of the season. He's certainly increased in maturity; past seasons saw him as a bit of an overly-adventurous goaltender. He now calculates the risks he takes outside his crease a lot better. However, while he isn't a small goaltender, he's not a big one, so it should be interesting what happens with him at the draft as a 3rd-year eligible and average-sized goaltender. He can struggle with his rebound-control and puck tracking with heavy traffic in front of him. He's a battler in his crease; he doesn't quit on any pucks and was a leader for the Huskies this year. He's also very calm in his crease, and doesn't get rattled by much.

Harvey had a great season. By playing well in the Canada-Russia series and Canada World Juniors' camp, his chances only increased in terms of finally getting picked this year. We feel that he did enough this year to warrant a late selection, and there's possibility of him playing pro hockey as early as next season. If not, he'll be back in the QMJHL for a 5th and final season.

"Stood on his head in m=one game I saw this year, really impressive performance." – HP Scout, Mark Edwards

| NR | HARVEY-PINARD, RAFAEL | ROUYN-NORANDA | QMJHL | 5' 9.0" | 162 lbs | LW |

Tenacious is the word that best fits Harvey-Pinard, yet it only begins to describe what's made him a success in his QMJHL career thus far. The former 8th-round selection of the 2015 QMJHL Draft, formerly out of Midget Espoir, led his team in scoring in 2017-2018, just ahead of veteran leader Peter Abbandonato. It was rare to find his name absent from the scoresheet, a testament to his strong determination and gritty, hard-nosed play finding ways to get the job done.

Harvey-Pinard's stellar vision of the game contributed not only to his success, but also to that of his linemates. Whether it was at 5-on-5 or on the power play, his fast and effective play-selection led to a lot of offensive success. He has great hands and is a threat to score from in close, using his craftiness to find space that the average player wouldn't. He's also demonstrated above-average determination and skills when battling for loose pucks in high-traffic situations. His work ethic is unquestionable, although his size remains a factor. At just 162 pounds, he will need to add some muscle to his frame in order to better compete in situations where his smarts don't always get the job done. It's really hard for someone to dislike him as a player in junior, he's skilled and his work ethic is excellent.

Two things are hurting his case, his size and his speed. If he was a better skater he could have more of a chance to break through and possibly get drafted. Harvey-Pinard should be one of the league's top scorers next season, and if not drafted, there's a good chance of seeing him get an invitation to an NHL rookie camp.

18	HAYTON, BARRETT	SAULT STE. MARIE	OHL	6' 1.3"	190 lbs *	LC

Hayton is an intelligent, two-way centre with a good compete level and intriguing offensive tools. Barrett possesses a reliable 200-foot game that allows him to find success in various situations. He skates ok, he's more an elusive skater than an explosive skater. He generates a good top speed, however his first step could be more explosive. Hayton does a good job masking the issue by utilizing his anticipation abilities. He can quickly change direction and/or pace while remaining in-stride to create space from an opponent. Offensively Barrett shows a versatile skill set that allows him to find success as both a passer and shooter. His release is above average and he shows good velocity and accuracy to his shot. Hayton shows the ability to make quick, skilled and high percentage decisions while playing with pace, making him dynamic in the offensive zone. Hayton protects the puck well and can remain heavy on it in traffic, Hayton showed an ability to create off the cycle and an overall effectiveness along the boards. His play away from the puck both offensively and defensively was adequate as he does a good job at finding space, while supporting the puck offensively and strong positional awareness in the neutral and defensive zones. Barrett shows intriguing two-way tools, but does lack an elite offensive game which may limit his upside slightly the next level. A competitive centre, Hayton needs to elevate his consistency as he can become a passenger at times.

"He's a good player. Late first rounder for me." - NHL Scout, February 2018

"Don't have him as high as I see on some of those lists out there but I really like the player." NHL Scout, March 2018

"I love him. He's so smart, top 15 ish area on my list." - NHL Scout, April 2018

"In one viewing this year versus Mississauga he really stood out compared to Ryan McLeod. While Hayton competed all over the ice and went to the dirty areas seeking pucks, McLeod played on the outside and refused to bring a puck to the net. Hayton's shot impressed me going back to his AAA days with the Toronto Red Wings. Not sure he's a lock to play Centre in the NHL but he's a very smart player and looks to be a safe bet to suit up in an NHL uniform down the road." - HP Scout, Mark Edwards

"The Hayton kid was outstanding" (interview at combine) - NHL Scout, June 2018

| NR | HELGESON, BEN | HILL MURRAY | HS- MINN | 6' 0.0" | 187 lbs | LC |

Helgeson, a 2nd round draft pick in the 2016 USHL Futures draft by Waterloo, stayed in the Minnesota High School ranks. Helgeson is a smooth skating centermen that affects the game at both ends. His skating doesn't come across as explosive at first but his long strides allow him to cover a lot of ice in a short amount of time which makes him deceptively quick with the puck on his stick. His shot release might be his best offensive asset at this stage of his development, it is powerful and Helgeson does a good job disguising his shot by changing the angles of his release. While Helgeson doesn't have high end offensive skills, he is reliable at both ends of the ice and is good in the faceoff circle and on the penalty kill. He played in all situations for a young Hill Murray team that struggled throughout the year in a tough conference. His team saw the younger players develop late in the season and made a run to the Minnesota State Tournament, eventually being overmatched by eventual Champion Minnetonka in the Quarter Finals. Helgeson is committed to the University of Wisconsin for 19/20 so it looks like its possible Helgeson will return to Hill Murray for his senior season next or play for Waterloo (USHL) in 18/19.

"His stats look unimpressive when it comes to high school stats but Hill Murray was so young and struggled for most of the year, he was easily their best player for much of the year and good teams were really able to key in on him" HP Scout, Dusten Braaksma

| 90 | HENMAN, LUKE | BLAINVILLE- | QMJHL | 5' 11.25" | 150 lbs | LC |

Henman posted some good numbers offensively in the first half of the season, getting to play with the QMJHL's leading scorer, Alex Barré-Boulet, and getting power play time. Henman didn't enjoy the same success offensively after Drake Batherson came over at the QMJHL trade deadline, as he lost some ice time and opportunities on the power play. He did finish the season with 47 points, which was good for 9th overall among rookie scorers in the league.

Henman has a slight frame. He's tall enough, but lacks ideal strength, and his level of energy can be inconsistent due to this. There's no doubt that he'll need to get continue to get stronger to be a better junior player and have a chance to play in the pros. Listed at 148 pounds, Henman has a lot of work to do in the gym to reach the 175-180 mark, which would be ideal for him. Skating-wise, he has decent speed for major junior, but will definitely need to add some explosiveness to his skating stride, which would help him create more separation between himself and opposing players. By getting stronger, we could see his skating stride get better with having a stronger lower body. He currently is not strong enough just yet with the puck, and gets pushed over too easily along the boards. The Nova Scotia native is a pass-first type of player; he doesn't shoot a lot on net and his shot is just average. He's good at slowing down the play when he's rushing the puck into the offensive zone, and is able to make good passes to his teammates as a result, setting up the plays in the offensive zone. Henman also has good puck poise and makes good decisions with the puck.

Overall, there's a lot of growing that will need to be done with Henman physically, in order for him to be able to reach his full potential. The potential is there, however, and we could see him getting picked late in the draft by a team willing to bet that he'll be able to grow into in this body. In addition, with the Armada, he'll be a key player on the team next year, with the likes of Barré-Boulet, Batherson & Alain leaving for the pro level. Henman will get every opportunity to play on the top line and top power play unit.

"I think he's a sleeper and might be worth as high as a late 2nd round pick." - NHL Scout, Aril 2018

" Reminds me a lot of Francis Perron back in 2014 with his skillset and size. Perron was better, though." - HP Scout Jérôme Bérubé

" Liked him in one of my viewings, didn't get a ton of ice when I saw him which made my evaluation more difficult. Jérôme will be ranking this guy without my input." - HP Scout, Mark Edwards

144	HILLIS, CAMERON	GUELPH	OHL	5' 9.8"	168 lbs *	RC

Cam Hillis is a high-energy, pass-first center, who had a good first-season for Guelph, finishing with 59 points in 60 games, including 39 assists. In the playoffs he had 3 points in 6 games and was featured at the U18's where he didn't look out of place while finishing with 2 assists in 5 games. His production was the best among all rookie players in their first OHL season.

Cam's playmaking ability and hockey sense are his best assets. He uses a combination of technical fakes and a lethal level of precision when threading passes across the ice, while changing the tempo of a shift in the offensive-zone using his poise and awareness which allows him to play a heavy possession game. This made him an efficient distributor on the powerplay, where he was dangerous along the half-wall and in-front of the slot, making quick one touch passes to his teammates to force goalies to move laterally and open them up for scoring chances as an example. He can make sharp passes but he also demonstrated that he can make saucer passes and no-look passes consistently as well. He doesn't generate shots at a high-rate but he's an opportunistic scorer who uses his plus hockey sense to anticipate the play in advance which puts himself in a good position to receive passes near the hashmarks and track rebounds in our viewings. The most important aspect of Cam's game was that when he was on the ice his team seemed to be producing more offense as opposed to having to defend.

Although he's not the tallest center, his stride is long and provides fluidity in his movement, though we wish he still had an extra-gear when taking his size into consideration. He's also not great on the forecheck due to lacking strength at this time. Another area of improvement regarding his strength is in his release, he doesn't generate a lot of power on most attempts which makes him less dangerous from the top of the circles and the high-slot. Like most young centres, his play away from the puck could certainly improve as well.

Hillis is an interesting player to rank. He's had a successful year and has shown a good degree of skill and intelligence, but he's got an underdeveloped base, is undersized for a center and lacks any elite skill, so even with his impressive play, it's difficult to see him translating the success he's having in juniors to the NHL, though that could change if he becomes a more powerful and explosive player which are traits that can be developed.

" Smart and productive player but the skating needs to get a lot better. I like him though. Has a chance because of his smarts." NHL Scout, January 2018

" Smaller guy who did exceptionally well his first year in the league." - NHL Scout, April 2018

" I think his bad posture effects his balance. He has really good skill and has good vision. mid to late pick I'd guess." NHL Scout, May 2018

" He has a lot of offense in his game but his feet hurt his overall game." - NHL Scout, May 2018

"Cam is a tough one for me. I really like his game but trying to figure out if his skating will hold him back from being more than just a good Junior player is the challenge. He's a draft for me, it's just figuring out where to slot him." HP Scout, Mark Edwards

81	HOELSCHER, MITCHELL	OTTAWA	OHL	5' 11.0"	166 lbs *	LC

Mitchell is a strong two-way player for Ottawa with some offensive upside. He regularly plays a gritty style and consistently battles hard for loose pucks. He can accelerate quickly from the standing position, giving him the ability to separate himself from defenders on the rush. He handles the puck well with speed and is agile on his feet in the offensive zone. He gets himself to the dirty areas in the offensive zone to create scoring opportunities and force turnovers. He exhibited a noticeably high work ethic on the ice and showed good strength to defend the puck well against larger opponents. He flashes high offensive potential on occasion, deking multiple players at a time and utilizing a hard, accurate wrist shot. His offensive awareness is good, and he has the capability to make quick chip plays that allow his team to cross the blue line with speed or maintain possession of the puck effectively. Mitchell is a very strong penalty killer this year and could arguably be one the best in the whole OHL, he's good at pressuring the puck carrier and creating turnovers. He was a selfless player by blocking shots from the point and doing anything to keep the puck out of the net. Mitchell started quiet this year for Ottawa but half way through the year and until the end of the season was Ottawa's most consistent player every night. We think Mitchell strength at the next level will be away from the puck being reliable in his own zone, and chipping in the offense when needed.

"Another guy that didn't get opportunity early but got more opportunity midway though the season. He's weak, will need to get much stronger." NHL Scout, March 2018

"He's competitive, he's a smart player." - NHL Scout, April 2018

"He has a good brain but he's just really light and inexperienced right now. Looks to me like he's a smart player" - NHL Scout, May 2018

"He got more ice after Christmas and had a couple of good games when I saw him. Looked like a smart player. I wish I saw him a bit more." HP Scout, Mark Edwards

149	HOFER, JOEL	SWIFT CURRENT	WHL	6' 3.25"	160 lbs	G

Joel Hofer was the back up goaltender for the Swift Currant Broncos this past season. He faired well in his back-up role, flashing starting potential at the junior ranks by posting a 2.61 GAA and .914 save percentage in 19 games this past season. In the playoffs, he came in relief twice, posting a 2.60 GAA and .875 save percentage.

Hofer is a pro-sized netminder who displayed the ability to read the play in heavy traffic and react quickly. His dexterity and reflexes are impressive, and when combined with his frame, it allows him to cover a lot of ice when he's moving laterally and pushing out to cut down an angle. Both his glove and blocking mechanics are solid, and he can fully extend when kicking out his pads to take away secondary scoring chances off rebounds. Additionally, his butterfly is already above-average and he was at absorbing rebounds from hard shots. What makes Joel an exciting prospect isn't only his athletic attributes, it's that he's capable of tracking the puck at a high-rate in the games we viewed. This was notable during power-play sequences, where he would track-pucks through screens using his height and dexterity, which allowed him to square up to shooters and take away difficult cross-crease chances consistently. Despite having impressive movement and fluidity, he rarely threw himself out of position, with the exception of chances created behind his goal-line. In our viewings, he had difficult detecting a forward's movement and placement when trying a wrap-around or pass back into the slot area, which was due to not being able to anticipate the play as well from behind his net area. Like any young goalie, Hofer has to refine certain technical elements of his game and become more consistent, however there's a great base to work with.

NR	HOLLOWELL, MAC	SAULT STE. MARIE	OHL	5' 9.0"	170 lbs	RD

Hollowell is an undersized, offensive minded defender with good mobility. Mac is at his best in possession were he is able to utilize his quick feet to accelerate up ice and attack the offensive zone with pace and purpose. He shows a confidence with the puck and handles it well. Impressively Hollowell shows good vision and awareness when attacking. He will gain the offensive line and look to create hitting attacking and trailing options with a pass or will attack the goal himself. An aggressive player in the sense he loves to utilize his speed and skating to attack, Mac will jump into the offensive attack both in transition and from his blue line position. However his vision and puck distribution skills are his above average offensive traits. Hollowell makes a quality outlet pass and sees the ice well. Offensively his distribution skills allow the 5-on-5 and power play attack to the thrive. His mobility often allows him to keep the play in front of him while defending transition however he can be a bit of a neutral zone gambler looking to step up and pick off outlet passes, leaving him vulnerable without support when he's beat. Generally Mac angles the play to the outside and uses good stick and body position. Where he gets in trouble is dealing with a heavy forecheck. He can be exposed due to his lack of size and strength when the forecheck arrives an he is unable to use his feet to escape. Hollowell also does chase due to his aggressive nature and can be easily pulled out of ideal defensive positioning. Mac possesses intriguing offensive traits, but may be a player who is simply a strong junior hockey defenseman.

"If you draft him you need to know he can play in the AHL next season. You're not drafting him to play in the coast (ECHL) or go back to the Soo. He's not a draft for me." NHL Scout, February 2018

"I'm hearing guys say he'll go in the 3rd round! Look at him tonight...he can't get the puck now that they (the Soo) are playing a good team." - NHL Scout, May 2018

"Good skater and compete. He had a good year but the size and strength really concern me for a 19 year old. I think he's got a chance but it's a f***** small chance. I'm not sure he can play above the American League. - NHL Scout, May 2018

"He's like a right handed Perunovich. I like him but think he's an AHL player." - NHL Scout, May 2018

"You can't play at that size...like F*** it's impossible. I don't think his hockey sense is good enough either...he's a great skater...I don't get fooled by the Durzi's or these guys. They're good in the OHL because number 1: they can skate their way out of trouble ...and two: there's no hitting. I mean, I like him enough that I'd put him on our AHL team, but at the next level (NHL) I don't know how he plays." NHL Scout, May 2018

"Look at the playoffs. How does he play against Vegas or Winnipeg...like c'mon...it's not even close. I can't see it." - NHL Scout, May 2018

"I don't think he's high end (hockey) sense and I think that hurts him. I mean he can't defend Robert Thomas...he couldn't defend Caamano, I mean Caamano's not McDavid" NHL Scout, May 2018

"I like him, I'd like him for our AHL team but I can't see drafting him for that...I don't see any NHL in him." - NHL Scout, May 2018

"He loves to push the pace and use his skating to generate offensive opportunities." - HP Scout, Mike Mackley

"Had quite a few scouts give very similar opinions of him. I'm on board with their consensus. While I like really his game, I don't see NHL upside." - HP Scout, Mark Edwards

NR	HOLMES, HUNTER	FLINT	OHL	6' 0.75"	181 lbs	LC

Hunter Holmes was selected 22nd overall in the 2016 OHL draft, however he hasn't lived up to his draft position as of writing this. He did improve upon his rookie numbers however, posting 20 points in 40 games including 11 goals while being deployed in all situations for the Firebirds. He also missed some extended time this season.

Holmes is a good-sized center with good length and an above-average skill-set. He was at his best for Flint when on the powerplay, where he would primarily be stationed in-front of the net due to being able to take advantage of his frame and length around the goal-line during screen and rebound attempts. He has capable of finding soft-ice and has plus puck tracking ability which gave him several goals near the crease area which was also where he generated the majority of his high-percentage scoring chances. Furthermore, he did demonstrate patience with the puck on his stick in spurts, waiting for passing and shooting lanes to re-open. However, some of his passes were difficult to handle and he never displayed high-end vision when we watched him. Though, he did show decent hands, using his reach to pull the puck around players while making forehand to backhand dekes. Arguably the weakest aspects of Hunters game at this time is his lack of compete. He's not a player who likes to get physically engaged often despite having a build to absorb solid hits, and when Flint was getting overwhelmed it was rare to see him step up and push the pace to try and re-shift the momentum of the game in his team's favour. It was difficult to notice him consistently in several games we watched.

Despite showing the ability to play in-front of the net on the powerplay and having a decent frame, Holmes lack of competitiveness left us wanting more. For this reason, he's not a player we are high on.

"He's an intriguing player...size, skating, skill, he has it all. I just question if he wants to play badly enough." - NHL Scout, May 2018

"To me he doesn't compete hard enough, he won't go into the hard areas either. That's his weakness I can't get past." - NHL Scout, May 2018

"Had a lot of injuries so durability is a concern for me. Didn't make my list" - NHL Scout, May 2018

"There is talent there so he's a player to watch for sure but not a guy I'd have on my list. I didn't think he competed hard enough prior to entering OHL and still don't." - HP Scout, Mark Edwards

| NR | HOUDE, SAMUEL | CHICOUTIMI | QMJHL | 5' 11.5" | 160 lbs | LC |

Houde was Chicoutimi's 1st pick, 8th overall, in the 2016 QMJHL Draft after playing a year in Midget AAA with Collège Esther-Blondin. He took part in Hockey Canada's U-18 camp for the Ivan Hlinka tournament last summer, but was eventually cut. This season with the Saguenéens, he finished the season 4th on the team in points, with 31 in 51 games.

A reason why he went high in the QMJHL Draft was mainly his potential, but also his great hockey sense and vision. At a young age, he was already very comfortable playing the point on the power play. He was a great playmaker, with great puck poise and excellent vision. He was also a player who had slight frame; a lot of projection with him was once he would mature physically, he would even more dangerous on the ice. Now almost two years later, Houde has grown a bit, but he is still undersized and still has a slight frame, weighing around 160 pounds. Another issue with him two years ago was his skating abilities. Not much improvement has been made there, and playing on a big ice surface in Chicoutimi has not been helpful. He had a decent midget season in his QMJHL draft year, but not a dominant one, and was probably rushed to major junior last season. In a perfect world, he would have played at least half of last season back with his midget team. His shot is average; it lacks velocity, but adding strength to his frame would help it improve (but the same thing was said in his QMJHL draft year).

Some parts of his game have not developed as hoped, and this is why we think he won't get selected but he's a player who could blossom next season.

| 109 | HRABIK, KRYSTOF | LIBEREC | CZREP | 6' 4.0" | 209 lbs | LC |

Krystof Hrabik is a 1999 born center who possesses a rare combination of tools combined with a mature defensive game. He was one of the only 2018 draft eligible players who managed to play in the Czech league as a 16 year old last season. This year, he played with 4 teams but spent the majority of his time playing for HC Benatky nad Jizerou where he produced 15 points in 32 games, including 10 assists. In the top Czech league he produced zero points in 9 games for Bili Tygri Liberec. Internationally, he made the U20 World Junior Championship roster where he was featured in a depth-role and on the penalty-kill where he went pointless in 7 games.

Hrabik is an offensively raw center who has a fantastic developmental frame and a lot of tools at his disposal. He's got height, width, length and is a tenacious player who engages teams at both ends of the ice and knows how to use his frame to weigh heavy against opponents along the boards. Furthermore, he generates a lot of leverage which makes him difficult to deal with in the defensive-end, consistently creating turnovers in our viewings. His defensive awareness is a plus, showing solid positioning and anticipating shooting lanes in advance which allows him to make well-timed shot blocks. He's also coordinated for his size, transitioning fluidly from a block attempt into an upright position which allows him to make recovery plays quickly. Another interesting aspect of Hrabik is that with his mix of tenacity, length, coordination and size, he could develop into a center who dominates the draw.

Although he's defensively advanced for his age and was relied upon heavily during the U20 WJC during penalty-killing sequences, he's got a raw offensive-game. He's not the quickest kid out of the gate which should be expected given his frame however he does have decent straight line speed and we have seen him attempt to cut into the slot with the puck while driving down the wings. Arguably the best aspect of his offensive-game is his shot, he's got a good release point, uses his length effectively to change his angle and it generates a lot of velocity, which handcuffed goalies on occasion. Though, his passing ability isn't as at the same level that his shot currently is. He has trouble extending his vision to backdoor plays or making no-look passes sometimes and he can force his pass through traffic or extend it just past his teammates. Furthermore, his puck-skills are not overly refined but he does look to experiment on the ice occasionally which has led to flashes of what he could potentially develop into from an offensive stand-point. His biggest weakness in the offensive-end at this time is his ability to read the play without the puck, he struggles with his offensive-positioning and needs to learn where he needs to be on the ice to create effective cycle and give-and-go sequences with his teammates.

Hrabik is just beginning to un-tap his offensive-ceiling and overall potential. He's also shown an above average floor due to his defensive play so it will be interesting to see where he ends up on draft day.

118	HRENAK, DAVID	ST. CLOUD STATE	NCHC	6' 2.0"	192 lbs	G

Hrenak just finished a successful freshman season at St. Cloud State where he played 25 games, registering a 2.11 GAA and a .919 save % as St. Cloud went with a two goalie system for much of the year. While Hrenak didn't see much back to back action he was prepared for his starts putting up a 14-7-2 record. Hrenak was also represented Slovakia at the World Juniors in Buffalo, however only seeing one start due to the impressive play from Roman Durny. The red flag for Hrenak at this stage is he has never been in a starting role in his key developmental years. Last season was the most games he has played in a season when he played 33 games for Green Bay (USHL) while sharing the crease with Las Vegas Golden Knights draft pick Maxim Zhukov. So while he has looked impressive in a supporting role it remains to be seen if he can carry the load of games it takes to be a true starting goaltender. Hrenak is not without some high end skills in the net, he doesn't have the prototypical NHL size but he looks and plays big in the net. His lateral movement is above average and he doesn't lose his crease very often, using his strong edgework to change directions quickly. His is strong in traffic and controls the top of his crease well. Like almost all goaltenders, Hrenak is a long term prospect but is trending as a potential pro prospect down the road.

"I thought he was a draft prospect last year but many scouts would skip Green Bay's games if Zhukov wasn't in goal and he was every bit as good for Green Bay and had a solid freshman season this year, I think he's a pro prospect goaltender." HP Scout, Dusten Braaksma (April, 2018)

"He had a great year this season." - NHL Scout, May 2018

"Tracks the puck as well as any goalie in this draft." - NHL Scout, May 2018

NR	HREHORCAK, PATRIK	ROUYN-NORANDA	QMJHL	5' 10.0"	175 lbs	RW

The Slovak winger was the Huskies' first selection in the 2017 CHL Import Draft, 47th overall. With 48 points this season, Hrehorcak finished 7th overall in rookie scoring league-wide, adjusting rather quickly to the North-American game. His feistiness and willingness to play well above his listed size did not go unnoticed around the league (although it did sometimes get him into penalty trouble if he wasn't able to control it well enough).

If a team were to leave too much space open in the neutral zone, he often made them pay for it by using his speed to go on breakaways, which more often than not resulted in a goal. He created several shorthanded opportunities for himself in this way as well (3 shorthanded goals – tied for first in the league among rookies and 4th overall). His good vision, strong work ethic and craftiness enabled him to gain valuable ice time for a rookie, including on the power play where he was sometimes even granted opportunities on the first unit when key players were missing from the lineup. In the first half of the season he had trouble producing, but came back after the Christmas break and amassed 30 of his 48 points. He's a valuable player, as he can play any role in a lineup. He established himself as a physical player who likes to hit in the first half of the season, and in the 2nd half, he started scoring more and averaged a point per game.

While his size and at-times streaky offensive production may lead to NHL clubs passing on him this year, Hrehorcak should be primed to explode offensively next year in a bigger role with the Huskies. It was reported after the Huskies were eliminated that he would be back next season.

9 HUGHES, QUINTIN — MICHIGAN — NCAA — 5' 9.8" — 173 lbs * — LD

Hughes had a great year for the University of Michigan while being the go-to option on the backend, as he quarterbacked the powerplay and received quality minutes. He recorded 29 points in 37 games this past season while helping his team reach the frozen-four where they placed 3rd.

Quinn is a new-age, dynamic, offensive defenseman who drives possession. His most noticeable quality is his speed, simply put, Quinn is one of the best skaters, if not the best skater in this draft class. His four-way mobility allows him to penetrate defenses in creative ways with the puck on his stick, as well as close the gap efficiently in the defensive-end. His transitional ability is second to none due to his great top-gear, and he can take the puck from his own-goal line and go end-to-end as good as anyone in this class. Another important attribute of his game, is that he's capable of making plays while in motion and going at top-speeds, this helps him breakdown opposing team's defenses. Another reason he's effective at breaking down defenses is his composure with the puck on his stick, when under pressure he's rarely thrown off his game and seems to thrive with little time and space given to him. A major reason for this is due to his advanced feinting mechanics while walking the line. We have seen him use fake slap-shots, wrist-shots, spin-moves and exaggerated pivots using his elite edges that have toppled over players who are attempting to defend him.

Once he's used his speed and his fakes at the line, he likes to attempt to set-up his teammates using an excellent first-pass. He can deliver saucer passes, stretch passes, bank passes and thread them through multiple players when needed. His shot is also a weapon though he looks to pass the puck more than shoot it. His offensive awareness is high-end, he does recognize when a lane is open for him or if he has enough time and space to get his shot through traffic. His wrist-shot and slapshot are both a plus, he has a heavy wrist-shot and we have seen him go upstairs, while driving down a lane this season multiple times, so the accuracy is there as well. If there's one criticism with his shot, it's that he can rush his shot at the line on occasion but that doesn't happen often and especially when he's dialed in.

There's more confidence in his game in the offensive-end which leads to good decision making with the puck, he seems to always know what he wants to do with the puck on his stick, for instance he is aware of when he can pinch for the most part and does have the speed to recover after making an error. Without the puck in the defensive-end, he's prone to defensive-errors. This can be seen during odd-man rushes where he misinterprets the play on occasion and in one-on-one situations where he fails to close off his skating lane in time during certain sequences. His compete level in the defensive-end isn't what you want to see in a smaller defender on some shifts either. That being said, he can play bigger than his size occasionally, plays positionally sound on most shifts and can skate the puck out of dangerous areas. He's aware of his limitations defensively and uses an aggressive stick to deflect shot's away from the net and create turnovers as opposed to wearing himself out by getting overly engaged physically.

Although there's a lot of room for improvement on the defensive-side and he sometimes turns the puck over during offensive-zone entries, Hughes drives puck-possession better than most which should help counteract some of his shortcomings. The best attributes of his game are translatable at the pro level but we see his size as a liability. He's going to need solid development on the defensive side of the puck to log the minutes in the NHL necessary to justify his high pick.

"I had him ranked pretty much in the same spot all season, his talents are on display every night but the final 4-6 weeks of his season he was the best player in college hockey and is wasn't even close. The last few weeks really sealed the deal for me, having said that there will be an adjustment period for him into pro hockey, he will need to reign in some of his decisions around the blue lines." HP Scout, Dusten Braaksma

"He's a smaller version of Subban as for as his offensive game goes but he's got a ways to go defensively." - NHL Scout, November 2017

"He's pretty much a disaster defensively but here's the thing...he always has the puck when he's on the ice so...." NHL Scout, December 2017

"The creativity is really impressive. To say he plays with confidence is an understatement." NHL Scout, December 2017

"I saw him recently and it seemed like if he was on the ice he had the puck." NHL Scout, December 2017

"We won't be taking him, not a fit for us." - NHL Scout, January 2018

"A few Bode Wilde type needless turnovers that bug me but the kid has ridiculous talent." - NHL Scout, April 2018

"One of my fave players to watch over the past few years, I liked watching him in AAA with the Marlies and with the USNTDP as well. Last season was the first time I saw him have a subpar game, just too many high risk plays and poor decisions. He had a few of those this year as well but his good is high end stuff. He's so creative and the vision is unreal...he mixes in the use of the way he skates with those edges to get so much production out of his talent. I don't think he's ever seen a patch of open ice he didn't exploit. I love that he uses so much ice in the offensive zone to create offence. He'll jump into a play seemingly out of nowhere and either score, or at minimum create a great scoring chance. His play in his own end can be a big adventure but I think as he matures it will improve." - HP Scout, Mark Edwards

"I knew the kid wasn't going to blow the doors off in his testing. I just wanted to see him compete." NHL Scout, June 2018

"Had several scouts tell me they were not thrilled about him declining to test at the combine. I respect that everyone has their own opinions and it's the players personal decision on whether or not to test, but my personal thought is just go out there and do your best, it's all about willingness to compete. Regardless, he's a talented player and testing or not testing isn't going to make or break his season." - HP Scout, Mark Edwards

| 115 | HUGHES, RILEY | ST. SEBASTIANS | HIGH-MA | 6' 1.0" | 174 lbs | RW |

Hughes has the size, physical tools, and hockey sense in the offensive zone to intrigue anyone watching him for the first or second time. However, his unwillingness to play between or below the circles will surely put most observers off after multiple viewings.

He has a long, smooth stride that gets him to pucks, but he lacks that fight to win battles when he doesn't get there cleanly. He has a good release and can score some pretty goals under the bar or into corners from the high slot and around the circles. His vision allows him to make some pretty, highlight reel passes from time to time. What he lacks is the ability to score dirty goals or win battles near the net as he rarely visits that area of the ice..

"He can skate and he has some skill...smart player too." - NHL Scout, January 2018

"I like him. I think he'll probably be a 3rd or 4t round pick." NHL Scout, April 2018

"He might be the best high school kid not named Jay O'Brien." - NHL Scout, April 2018

| 121 | HUTSKO, LOGAN | BOSTON COLLEGE | H-EAST | 5' 9.75" | 172 lbs | RW |

Hutsko is coming off a very successful freshman season at Boston College where he registered 12 goals 19 assists in 37 Games which lead the eagles in points and finishing Tied for 12th in Hockey East Scoring which earned him Hockey East Rookie of the Year. Prior to attending B.C. Hutsko came from the USNTDP program where he entered the program as a highly touted prospect from Shattuck St. Mary's Prep but sustained a serious injury where he suffered a cervical spine fracture of his C6 Vertebrae, a terrifying injury for anyone but now has been given a clean bill of health going forward. Now healthy, Logan showed flashes this season why he was such a highly regarded prospect just a couple of years ago. While not many of Hutsko's skills can really be labelled as elite with exception of one, his work ethic on and off the ice. Off the ice Hutsko has displayed incredible character and work ethic to recover and return after such a serious injury. On the ice he is a hard worker at both ends and comes away with a lot of 50/50 pucks. Is effective on the fore-check in stripping pucks despite not being the most physically imposing player. Hutsko is a quick player with the puck on his stick and can create space with his speed in transition. He enters the offensive zone with control and is able to make plays with the puck high in the zone and create space. His shot release is a weapon but a lot of goals will come from driving to the net and out working his opponent.

"Not the biggest kid but I like his fearless style of play and that kind of production, in that league, being as young as he is, is hard to dismiss. He gets it done on every shift" - HP Scout, Dusten Braaksma

"I'm a fan. He missed last year with a neck injury." - NHL Scout, March 2018

"I thought he got better this year. He had a knee injury last year. Not a huge kid but he's skilled...he's a creative and slippery player." - NHL Scout, April 2018

"The forward version of Scott Perunovich." - NHL scout, May 2018

| 93 | INGHAM, JACOB | MISSISSAUGA | OHL | 6' 3.8" | 191 lbs * | G |

Ingham is a competitive, butter-fly style goaltender with impressive athletic ability and physical traits. Jacob shows impressive poise in the net and utilizes his frame to his advantage. A goaltender who shows good technical tools in combination with his athleticism, Ingham is also intelligent and shows an ability to anticipate the play allowing him to make acrobatic cross-crease saves. Jacob battles in the crease which often allows him to make secondary saves. He possesses good initial shot positioning and plays his angles well, challenging shooters all while making himself big in the net to deny the shooters eye. Ingham is able to use his height to see around screens fairly well, however he can show some inconsistencies in his ability to track pucks below the hip from far out. In the butter-fly Jacob shows good lower body strength in his ability to quickly push out from the goal line to the top of his crease, keeping his gloves and shoulders up to deny the upper half of the net. He moves well from post-to-post, however can lose his net when forced to make secondary movements back to the opposite post or to the centre of the net. Ingham displayed good rebound control at times but does have room to elevate this area. Consistency issues plagued Jacob throughout the season as he was often prone to a weak goal most games. His glove hand shows promise but was often beat glove side and would benefit from adding quickness in this area.

"Oh boy...F*** me. I was really big of him last year and then this year he just could not find his game." NHL Scout, March 2018

"He had no consistency this year. He'd play a good game and then two bad ones. That said, there are some good tools there." - NHL Scout, May 2018

"I wanted to see more production out of the sum of the parts. He has great size and excellent tools as a base point to build on. He's worth a pick in the draft just on the tools alone. This kid was very impressive heading into this season" - HP Scout, Mark Edwards

| NR | ISAYEV, DANIIL | YAROSLAVL 2 | RUSSIA-JR. | 6' 0.0" | 165 lbs | G |

Daniil Isayev split starts while playing for Loko Yaroslavl in the MHL this past season, where he had an excellent year, putting up a 1.56 GAA and a .936 save percentage in 19 games. Although he was involved with the Russian squad at international events, he was the back-up to Amir Miftakhov and as a result was used sparingly.

Isayev is an undersized yet reactionary goaltender who relies on his athleticism when attempting to stop the puck. He has several excellent attributes that help make his game stand-out. The most impressive being his glove hand, which is arguably the best in this draft class; we have seen him make some outstanding glove saves at point blank range throughout the year and he's very good at controlling rebounds on that side. Furthermore, his transitional butterfly is extremely fast, he can move in and out of his butterfly at a rapid rate and this allows him to make impressive recovery saves or get back to his stance quickly when needed. Another attribute of Daniil's that's a plus is his flexibility which allows him an impressive range-of-motion when making difficult saves that require full-extension. For instance, during passes that require him to move laterally across his crease, he's capable of entering the splits effortlessly. Additionally, he's an explosive goalie who is good at pushing off to cut-down angles or when needing to move across his crease to make a save. There's also refined technical aspects to his game, both his V-H and reverse V-H leave little room for the shooter and he transitions in and out of them fluidly. His impressive movement allows him to contort his positioning to look around screens from the point and make saves through traffic consistently.

Due to his powerful push-offs, he does have a tendency to throw himself out of position on certain sequences and needs to develop the ability to recognize when he should play more passively in the crease and minimize his movement. Although he does read the play well in most instances, due to his over-extension, he does tend to give up rebounds more than he should which forces him to rely on his reflexes when attempting to recover. His reaction-time is a plus, although given his size, it wouldn't hurt if it was slightly better than it currently is.

57	ISKHAKOV, RUSLAN	CSKA 2	RUSSIA-JR.	5' 8.0"	152 lbs	LC

Ruslan Iskhakov had a productive year for Krasnaya Armiya Moskva by putting up 30 points, including 24 assists in 33 games. Additionally, he was very consistent at international tournaments, putting up near point per game numbers through the Hlinka Memorial, WJAC-19, the Five Nations and the U18's.

Usually with a player of this stature, Iskhakov's diminutive size would be seen as a liability however he presents a dynamic skill-set that allows him to turn his glaring weakness into a strength when he steps onto the ice. The first area of his skill-set that allows him to overcome his physical disadvantages is his edge work, he's extremely shifty and elusive when driving down the wings with the puck and can contort his frame to evade incoming checks from larger players both in open-ice and along the boards. Furthermore, he's got elite puck-handling ability, he's capable of turning players inside-out in one-on-one situations or using his hands to set-up creative plays. His ability to process information on the ice rapidly is bordering on elite, we have seen him several times this year beat out multiple defenders simultaneously while under pressure before making a no-look spinning backhand pass to his teammates for a high quality-scoring chance as one example. He's capable of making plays like the one mentioned due to seemingly being ahead of the play, while most players are stuck thinking of the next move their opponent is making, he's two steps ahead in most instances. His vision and passing ability are exceptional, he can thread difficult passes through multiple players and identifies passing lanes before most defenders can react, there's a high level of finesse when he passes the puck, his passes are rarely difficult for his teammates to handle. Although he hasn't scored too many goals this year, that's more of a by-product of his pass-first mentality than it is a reflection on his shooting mechanics. His wrist-shot has a quick release point and he's shown the ability to change the angle quickly while in motion when driving down the wings, he just needs to be more selfish in certain sequences so that he can fully take advantage of his shot.

Although small and having a light-frame, Iskhakov is surprisingly strong. He's more difficult to knock off his base then you would expect based on his appearance, showing excellent balance and he's difficult to handle along the boards. We have seen him challenge and come away with the puck to our surprise against large and aggressive opponents by using an active stick. Although a small winger, he's also defensively responsible and we have seen him make high-end defensive reads without the puck resulting in several impressive turnovers throughout the season. Lastly, his motor is impressive and he usually stands out when he's on the ice.

While Iskhakov does have plus two-step area quickness and while he's certainly not slow, we would prefer seen better overall straight-line speed given his size. That being said, he has the mental approach necessary to overcome his limitations, he's a fearless player who has adapted a style that suits his build well which has helped him develop into one of the more interesting prospects in this year's draft.

| NR | IVAN, MICHAL | ACADIE-BATHURST | QMJHL | 6' 0.75" | 180 lbs | LD |

Ivan was drafted with the 38th overall pick in the CHL Import Draft last June, and finally joined the Titan in late October after playing 4 games with HKM Zloven in the Slovakia top men's league. With the Titan, he played in a top 4 role for most of the season, playing behind their big 3 of Galipeau, Dobson and Holwell.

Ivan finished the season with 17 points in 48 games. He saw limited ice time on the power play in the 2nd half of the season following the acquisition of Galipeau. The young player from Slovakia is more of a stay-at-home defenseman who takes cares of his own end instead of trying to be a flashy offensive defenseman. He plays a simple game and moves the puck safely. He's not very flashy, but takes care of the puck and plays well within his limits. He has improved the quickness at which he moves pucks in transition over the course of the season. He's not overly physical, but has good size. When needed, he can use his size to his advantage to win his one-on-one battles. His shot from the point will need some improvement; it's accurate but lacks velocity. With a stronger shot, he could be more of a threat offensively and on the power play. Ivan's upside for the next level is limited, and he projects more as a stay-at-home defenseman.

| 203 | JAKOBSSON, CARL | FARJESTAD | SUPER ELIT | 6' 1.5" | 165 lbs | RW |

Jakobsson is an intriguing prospect because of his size; he's tall but has some work to do in the gym to add some mass to his frame. This season, he played in the J20, and had 27 points in 41 games. He also played 11 games in the SHL, going pointless. He does some good work along the boards; he's not a great skater but has some surprising agility to win puck battles and avoid hits along the wall. But overall, his skating will need help; his acceleration and top speed are going to need to get better if he wants to play in the NHL one day. He lacks power in his stride, his strides are long and large, but he's not strong enough to generate the speed needed. He does some of his best work on the forecheck, as he's smart and uses his stick very well to knock or strip pucks from his opponents. He also plays with a long stick, which helps him in that part of the game. His long reach and size help him along the boards when protecting the puck and when bringing it to the net. Jakobsson is still raw, and he's not a high-end prospect, but has some qualities that could make him a valuable one down the road if his skating improves.

| NR | JANICKE, TREVOR | USA U-18 | NTDP | 5' 10.0" | 185 lbs | RW |

Trevor Janicke had a decent development year by managing to stay up the entire year with the USNTDP while putting up 17 points in 60 games. He played on a checking-line and looked more comfortable in his role as the year progressed, capping off his season with a rebound goal in the gold-medal final at the U18 tournament. He is slated to play for the University of Notre Dame next season.

Janicke had some difficulty keeping up with the pace of the game at earlier points of the year and looked lost on the ice during some shifts, however as the season progressed, he began to develop and become a solid forechecking presence on the ice while also being used on the penalty-kill. He had several tools that allowed him to be successful in his role. He's a quick kid out of the gate, has plus edges and has a powerful base that allows him to have some separation speed, which we have noticed during sequences on the penalty-kill when he managed to turn the puck over and rush up the ice while trying to generate scoring opportunities or when he's attempting to cut around a defender. His speed compliments his motor, he's a competitive player who isn't going to back-down against larger opponents and is willing to enter heavy traffic to make a play or battle aggressively along the boards in order come away with the puck. Furthermore, if he's knocked off the puck or disrupted while attempting to make a play, he's quick to attempt to re-engage and battle hard for possession. He's also capable of making an accurate pass but wouldn't be identified as a high-end playmaker or an overly creative player, playing a more streamlined game with an edge. The majority of his goals were around the net area due to his willingness to track down rebounds while paying a price in high traffic areas and although his wrist-shot has a quick release point, he's not proficient at changing the angle of his shot or hiding his intentions with the puck on his stick when driving down the wings or towards the front of the net. Simply put, his offensive-ceiling isn't very high as he lacks any high-end offensive attribute.

Trevor was a solid penalty-killer who used his skating ability to close down lanes quickly, disrupted play with an active-stick and was willing to pay the price by getting in the way of point shots when the play called for it. One area of improvement we noticed in his development was his ability to process the play with and without the puck improving to a small degree as the season progressed, though he's never going to dictate play with the puck on his stick or be the offensive catalyst for a line. His puck skills are adequate for the role that he was given on his team but at this point in time he lacks any attribute that has us believing he can become a regular NHL player.

64	JENIK, JAN	BENATKY N. J.	CZREP-2	6' 1.3"	171 lbs *	RW

Jan Jenik is the youngest player in this year's draft and played for multiple teams this past season. He played for Bili Tygri Liberec's junior team where he put up 7 points in 7 games as well as 5 points in 3 playoff games, with the pro club he went pointless in 6 games and was also loaned to HC Benatky nad Jizerou of the Czech2 league where he posted a respectable 11 points in 30 games. Internationally, he had a lot of success by having stand-out performances at both the Hlinka and the U18's where he posted over point-per-game numbers when combining the two events. Furthermore, he was named one of the top 3 players on his U18 team and had a stand-out performance against Canada.

Jan Jenik is a two-way center with a lot of raw upside who has the potential to develop into one of the top Czech forwards featured in this year's draft class. Since he missed the 2019 cut-off by one day, he's got extended time to continue to expand his ever-growing skillset. He's got a broad frame with a lot of room to still fill out, which is important for him considering the style of game he plays. He's a multi-faceted forward who likes to drive possession and he accomplishes this by using his excellent puck-protection skills, poise, and offensive awareness. When under pressure in the offensive-end, he likes to turn his back towards the opposition and use his plus edges to pivot and create different angles and looks for himself. He's got good vision and puck-skills which he uses to breakdown teams. Additionally, he likes to challenge defenseman one-on-one using his vast array of dekes before attempting to find his teammates or look for his shot. We have seen him drive down the wing and drag the puck across the high-slot before rotating towards the boards then making a no-look drop pass to his teammate as an example. He's an instinctive playmaker who likes to draw defensive-units to him so that it re-opens his passing lanes however he's also shown the ability to score. He's got length and is good at using it to drag the puck in-tight to his body which switches the angle of his release point while also being quick to come off his tape, the shots deceptive. Jan has also demonstrated the ability to use his length to generate dangerous scoring chances around the net area where he can wrap the puck around goalies when in-tight to the net, as well as attempt wrap-arounds behind the net.

Due to his lanky frame and being the youngest player in the draft, he's not developed a lot of power and this is apparent in his stride. Jan's got a wide base and has difficulty pushing off in his first few steps which slows down his momentum, though his stride is decently fluid and he does compensate for his average straight-line speed using his edges. However, he has also shown development in his skating as the season has progressed. Despite not having a lot of strength, he still battles and competes both with and without the puck and attempts to use his frame to regain possession during forechecking sequences. Additionally, he's got good defensive-instincts and uses them to play positionally sound in his own end as well as getting in shooting lanes to take away scoring chances, we have also seen him aggressively backcheck in some of our viewings.

Jenik already thrives at times in high-traffic areas while showing glimpses of what can develop into a power-center game. If he gains strength and continues to improve his skating mechanics, he has the potential to become a solid NHL contributor with a versatile skill-set.

164	JENKINS, BLADE	SAGINAW	OHL	6' 1.3"	201 lbs *	LW

Blade Jenkins was selected 4th overall by Saginaw in the 2016 OHL draft. He produced at a decent rate in his first year by putting up 44 points in 68 games, including 24 assists, while producing another 3 assists in 4 playoff games. However, his production is somewhat skewed, as he put up 14 points in 9 games, giving him the rookie of the month for November which helps demonstrate long stretches without much production.

Jenkins is a strong, multi-faceted power-forward whose got several high-end tools at his disposal. He's a well-built kid whose large upper frame creates some heaviness in his stride. Despite the mechanics being decent enough, when he pushes off, the power hasn't fully developed yet but it can develop and make a huge difference in the coming years for how he plays the game. Despite needing improvement in his overall speed, he does have plus edge-work and this makes him surprisingly nimble and elusive for his size. His pivoting mechanics need to be emphasized due to his aggressiveness when attacking near the net area and when cycling the puck, he can be very difficult to contain down-low for opposing teams. Furthermore, he's got an enticing package of soft-hands, plus hockey sense, and vision. We have seen Blade one-arm windmill the puck around an opposing player and then use his shiftiness to attempt to evade the incoming check while simultaneously surveying the ice to see if there's a passing option or an open skating lane for himself. Those skills when combined with his size, presents a lot of upside if he can begin developing a more explosive first couple of steps. His offensive-game is somewhat rare in the sense that despite having a plus release with a heavy shot, he's got refined passing ability and has shown plus playmaking skills. His passing allows him to become a multi-dimensional threat when he finds soft-ice because it's difficult for opposing teams to recognize where he's going to place the puck. This made him difficult to contain on the powerplay in spurts, where he's capable of recognizing the time and space he has to make a play, though this applies to even strength too, where he can make high-end plays in tight spaces. One of his other strengths, is that he can generate on his own and has shown flashes of being able to drive a line on some shifts.

Despite his offensive skill-set, Jenkins play away from the puck leaves you wanting more. One of the reasons he was transitioned from center to the wing earlier in the year was due to not recognizing the pace needed in the defensive-end at times and not knowing where he should be properly positioned. Furthermore, there's a lack of compete on some shifts and this makes him highly ineffective depending on the game. Lastly, although he was used in all situations and thrust into a scoring-role, there wasn't a lot of talent for him to play with which could explain some of his lack of production in spurts.

Jenkins is one of the more difficult power-forwards in this draft class to rank. Some tools are there, he's equipped with a solid frame, and he's got an aggressive yet varied attack when playing up to his talent, however he also goes invisible on the ice for long stretches. In order for Jenkins to develop into a regular NHL forward, he needs to continue to get faster and become a more consistent threat on a game to game basis.

"He's like Gogolev for me." - NHL Scout, March 2018

"I got nothing on Blade...I don't even know...he's not on our list." - NHL Scout, May 2018

"Good individual skill, good size but really needs to learn how to play the game the right way." - NHL Scout, May 2018

"I heard some good things from a few scouts when he got hot, but I never saw anything from him in my viewings. I chased him a bit at the end of the year to see if I could see what some guys saw, but I never did. I can only go with what I saw and that wasn't enough to make me want to bang the table for him if I was with an NHL team." HP Scout, Mark Edwards

"Not many scouts seemed to have him ranked very high. Very little chatter on him all year long to be honest. For myself I've didn't see him play a game this season where I left the rink thinking that I'd really want to draft him. Skating is just average for me and I'd like to see him play a heavier game." - HP Scout, Mark Edwards

"Didn't think he gave a great self assessment of his own game." - NHL Scout, June 2018

| NR | JENSEN, JACK | EDEN PRAIRIE | HIGH-MN | 6' 0.0" | 194 lbs | LC |

Jensen is a player many scouts expected to take a bigger step this season, having said that he was forced to do a lot of the heavy lifting on a young Eden Prairie team that saw a lot of turnover due to graduation and players moving on to Junior Hockey. Jensen's offensive numbers don't jump off the page, 20 goals and 18 assists in 26 games for Eden Prairie. Jensen isn't a player that is going to drive the offense but looked much better in the fall in the Midwest Elite league on Team Southwest where he had a bit more talent around him. Jensen is a fantastic all around skater, he possesses excellent explosiveness off the hop and is able to gain the edge on defenseman almost at will and take the puck to the net. Jensen brings good physicality all over the ice and plays with a lot of reckless abandon. His offensive skills are solid but not dynamic in any way. He isn't going to attempt a lot of highly skilled or fancy plays with the puck, but ha good enough hands to beat defenders one on one and is going to use his speed to gain his advantages. Jensen has a nice release on his shot but scores a lot of his goals in and around the crease where he shows a high compete level and willingness to pay the price in front. Jensen plays a solid two-way game down the middle of the ice; he picks up his man and supports the play all over the ice. In one viewing he was deep in the offensive zone on the fore-check and used his speed to come back into his own end and breakup a 2 on 1 scoring chance then took the puck back down into the offensive end to score a goal off the rush.

"He wasn't on a very good team but still managed to showcase his skillset well in most of my viewings." - HP Scout, Dusten Braaksma

"He's and excellent skater and brings a lot of pace and jam." - NHL Scout (December, 2017)

"He's a strong kid that can skate but I didn't think he showed much in the way of hockey sense. He's not on my list." - NHL scout, March 2018

"He can really shoot the puck. I like him." - NHL Scout, April 2018

"I think he's a scout tester... he's a player who gives you an idea if a scout knows what he's doing or not.." -NHL Scout, April 2018

| 55 | JOHANSSON, FILIP | LEKSAND JR. | SWEDEN-JR. | 6' 0.8" | 176 lbs * | RD |

Filip Johansson made his way through all levels of the Leksands system this season, spending time in the U18 and U20 leagues before his Allsvenskan debut. Johansson scored a single goal at the Allsvenskan level in 23 regular season games played. When it was time for SHL qualification, Johansson's stats improved dramatically. He scored twice and added three assists in 11 playoff games, including a game-winner in Leksands only win over SHL club Mora IK.

Johansson is blossoming into a two-way defender with untapped offensive potential. When watching Johansson at the Allsvenskan level, he played a quiet game trying to limit mistakes. He joined the rush when it was safe to do so, but always had defence on his mind in that he would drop out of the rush if there was a possibility the opposition would have numbers going back the other way. When the puck is in his own-end, he's shown a good amount of hockey sense and can read technical offensive-plays. This was shown through consistent gaps, taking away shooting lanes, and using an active stick at the correct times to disrupt passes or keep his man to the outside. He's a competitor in his own-end who has a good understanding of how to use his leverage and stick to press-down and weigh on his opponents along the boards, and he's displayed the ability to exit the defensive-end cleanly, using either a quality first-pass or his above-average straight-line speed. That being said, his acceleration is arguably the weakest aspect of his skating and this has caused him to get overwhelmed when attempting to race to pucks below the goal-line and on some recovery attempts.

At international events and when playing in SuperElit, he would pinch more regularly and look to utilize his offense. His most successful rush and pinch attempts came primarily from the left wing, where he would look to pass the puck off on his backhand or generate scoring chances. His hands are soft, yet he's still figuring out how to deceive players when the puck is on his stick, occasionally using them at the right time to pull into the middle of the ice to create a better shooting angle, but mostly opting for off-angle shots that are usually picked up by the goalie. His wrist-shot comes off his stick quickly but it doesn't generate overwhelming power, however his slapshot has a reduced wind-up on most attempts, which made it effective when he timed it with a screen or when attempting to use it while in motion. Although he can draw defenders to him using his hands which re-opened passing lanes, he sometimes demonstrates tunnel-vision, not using his impressive passing ability at the right times. This resulted in mixed decision making. Filip is still learning how to use his hands to create additional space and when he should pass and shoot appropriately but he's got impressive puck-skills, a precise shot, and an accurate pass that's capable of being threaded through multiple players. For Johansson, it's putting his attributes together and executing at a higher rate that will need to be further developed in his offensive-game, in order for him to take advantage of his offensive-ceiling.

| 195 | JOHNSON, ISAAC | TRI-CITY | WHL | 6' 2.0" | 186 lbs | RW |

After going undrafted in his first year of eligibility, Johnson transferred from Des Moines in the USHL to Tri City of the WHL, becoming a factor in their offense. His offense does go hot and cold but he certainly had some dominant stretches, especially in the playoffs against Kelowna. He is a player that works better playing with other skilled linemates, looking to work around the perimeter of the offensive-zone. He doesn't just create from the outside, showing no fear when darting in and out of traffic around the net area. He's good down-low because of his timing off rebounds and is active around the net area but doesn't like to stand stationary and battle along the boards. Instead, he prefers staying in motion, showing good skating ability with strong use of agility and balance on his edges. This allows him to work with an open-stance and be effective when moving from the outside to the inside areas of the zone. When he's found soft-ice, he is good at balancing his shot and pass. His shot has a quick release but he could stand to generate a higher shot volume, so that he can use his release more. Despite scoring 17 goals, he could have had more due to his minimal windup. Johnson displayed good physical tools with his size and reach but in our evaluation, there's aspects of Isaac's game that are lacking.

NR	KAID, OLIVER	VICTORIA	WHL	6' 0.25"	181 lbs	LW

A 3rd round draft pick of Victoria that was able to get a full WHL season in before his draft year and play a pivotal role on both contending teams. A true center who plays a strong defensive game and took a really high amount of faceoff offs in all viewings, plays positional hockey really well and is great at breaking up plays in the defensive zone with his active stick, works well along the wall both with his positional play and with that stick to break up cycles; shows strong battle efforts against bigger forwards and should continue to get better in this area as he's grown larger since his rookie season. Plays a lot in the defensive zone due his zone start percentage and has the ability to make a good pass out of his own end but needs a little more work carrying pucks out on a consistent basis, however did show some ability to transition up ice and start a dangerous breakout. Was hard up for offensive opportunities in viewing over the past 2 seasons, just never got any powerplay opportunity or much work starting in the offensive zone, mostly due to coaching staff sticking with older forwards on top lines. Needs faith from coaching staff and should a better opportunity with older players moving on.

NR	KALINICHENKO, ROMAN	TRI CITY	WHL	6' 2.0"	183 lbs	LD

The Russian import came to Try Cities for the first time in the 2017/18 season and suited up for only 44 games in his debut season. With a top-heavy defensive team, he lacked opportunity beyond 5 on 5 play but still made an impact, especially on the defensive side of the puck. He's rangy in defensive coverage and skates well with his top speed, quickness and 4-way mobility. He can cover a lot of area, does a good job of playing aggressively when defending, playing hard on the body and making screeners pay for their positioning. He uses his stick well to disrupt attacking forwards and in combination with his long reach creates strong zone coverage. His head is on a swivel on most shifts, he does a solid job of disrupting shooters and isn't afraid to get into lanes to block shots. Shows decent puck skills, can handle the puck with a bit of finesse and more often than not makes an accurate outlet pass, however usually turns most transition duties over to his partner and lays back as the safety net defensively while other players push up ice. Turn over in Tri City will give him a much bigger opportunity and if he utilizes his speed and big body, he will be a bigger asset in the WHL than he was this year. Look for Kalinichenko to take a step since his late birthday does nothing but help him as he played the entire season at 17.

| NR | KAMBEITZ, DINO | VICTORIA | WHL | 6' 0.25" | 185 lbs | RW |

A bruiser that played mostly bottom 6 minutes for Victoria a team that really implies a top 6 and bottom 6 mindset, so his opportunities weren't quite as plentiful as they could have been. Good awareness of his surroundings Kambeitz is a heads up player that shows solid reads and good timing which helps his ability to read and react to the play. Not afraid to finish a hit with authority and shows power driving through opponents despite his average sized frame. Displays a good release with minimal wind up and can really snap pucks in a deceptive way, would like to see him generate more shots but his results were good for the minimal opportunity he received in viewings. Uses his gritty nature well in front of the net makes an effective screen on the powerplay. His footwork is solid and agile and he skates with above average speed, never has much of an opportunity with highly skilled linemates so his transition game was pretty basic and when he doesn't have the puck he can get caught roaming into no-mans-land. Has some raw scoring potential but needs more opportunity to flourish

| NR | KANNOK-LEIPERT, ALEX | VANCOUVER | WHL | 5' 11.25" | 193 lbs | LW |

After a brief 8 game rookie season Kannok-Leipert suited up for 60 games in his draft year and faired quite well for being a 4th round pick of Vancouver in 2015. Often suiting up as the top pair right shot defenseman, playing big minutes and going against some high end forwards. He's a 3 zone player and his coaching staff trusted to start him in all 3 zones providing to be an effective option to defend or produce offence. As a defender Kannok-Leipert is a feisty competitor around the net, leans on bigger forwards and on several occasions prevented dangerous scoring chances by making smart stick checks and often showing more power than his 5'11 – 194 lbs frame would suggest. Has above average footwork allowed him to make some impressive end to end rushes in almost every viewing, he is elusive through the neutral zone making good side cuts to avoid defenders, his footwork helps him produce offense, knows how to make defenders bite on a fake, as well as he can shift to open shooting lanes and produce rebounds for players crashing the net, as he acts a powerplay QB when given the opportunity to run a unit. Wrist shot is good but needs to get quicker and more powerful to beat goalies cleanly, doesn't have much of one-timer or at least doesn't utilize it, makes quick decisions with the puck but would like to see him shoot more. Not excellent at anything but brings a little bit of everything to the game at an above average level, his point totals don't jump out at you but he really does have a strong IQ and a thinks at very quick tempo matching his foot speed, seems to have flown a little under that radar as he was inconsistent at times.

| 117 | KARKI, KEEGAN | MUSKEGON | USHL | 6' 4.5" | 216 lbs | G |

It has been a bit of a bumpy development path for Karki the last couple of seasons. After leaving the USNTDP after his U17 season, he was drafted by Omaha (USHL) and eventually traded to Muskegon (USHL) where he has seemed to settle in this year. Karki has pro upside and skill set. He has the prototypical size at 6'4" and possesses a great combination of size and athleticism. One of the more impressive aspects of Karki's game is his ability to recover and regain his crease when he gets out of position. Karki uses his height to see through screens and tracks pucks well coming through the slot laterally. Karki is the prototypical goalie teams are looking for in this era; however some off ice issues and questions about his mental makeup have drawn skepticism with some scouts. Karki is a highly athletic and talented goaltender with a high ceiling if he can put it all together off the ice.

"Fell out of favour at the USNDTP and then lost his offer from North Dakota, but he's a real talent, you notice it right away. I'm pulling for him to put it things together." HP Scout, Dusten Braaksma

"I think he has the talent to be an NHL number one someday, but he has a lot of growing up to do." NHL Scout (February 2018)

"Not sure as far as off ice as of now,...need to do my legwork but as far as just pure talent he's very good. He's my number one USA goalie." - NHL Scout, January 2018

"Big athletic kid...very good technically. Very talented ...up with the best goalies in this draft. Some other stuff might impact his draft stock though." - NHL Scout, May 2018

| 134 | KARLSSON, LINUS | KARLSKRONA JR. | SWEDEN JR | 6' 1.0" | 178 lbs | RC |

Linus Karlsson was one of the top point producers in the SuperElit, even though he was on a team that had the fewest wins in the regular season. He produced an impressive 52 points in 47 games, including 27 goals in the regular season. In the playoffs, he had 4 points in 6 games. Due to his impressive play, he was called up to Karlskrona's primary team, generating an assist in 13 games. He traveled to Switzerland to compete at the U19's, where he produced 6 points in 4 games.

Karlsson is a cerebral two-way center, who was used in all situations this past season. He's a natural thinker on the ice, tactically putting himself in position before the play unfolds, both with and away from the puck. His defensive-game and effort level are second-to-none. We watched him take away several high-end scoring chances from opposing teams, showing an advanced 200-foot game. Despite having a larger frame, Linus is able to stay undetected for the most part when attempting to strip players off pucks which is why he was so effective in our viewings of him. His maturity and understanding of where to be one the ice, allowed him to support his defenseman when they were engaged and set himself up for outlet passes routinely.

Karlsson is a capable offensive-threat as well. His bread and butter is his shot. Both his wrist-shot and snap-shot come off his tape in a hurry and he's capable of adjusting the angle while in motion. Arguably his best offensive-attribute is his composure and ability to find soft-ice. Just as he is in the defensive-zone, Karlsson has the unique ability of finding openings. If his shot is taken from him, he's good at interpreting his teammates and setting them up for quality chances. The last aspect of his offensive-game to note, is that he never seems rushed with the puck and can slow the game down. This should be highlighted, since he's not an explosive skater and lacks separation speed. Instead he relies on his edges and intelligence to remain elusive when carrying the puck.

Karlsson's not going to take a crowd's breath away with high-end puck skills or highlight-reel goals on most plays. Instead, using his intelligence on the ice to be a positive factor in all three-zones. Due to his intelligence and complete game, there's a chance that Karlsson can develop in a quality depth-option at the pro levels.

| 14 | KAUT, MARTIN | PARDUBICE | CZREP | 6' 1.5" | 176 lbs | RW |

Martin Kaut had a very good season for HC Dynamo Pardubice of the Czech league where he posted 16 points in 38 games, 9 of which were goals. Despite his age, he was also used in all situations and played on a scoring-line. He followed that up with 5 points in 7 playoff games and had a very good international tournament where he was the catalyst for several goals while playing for the Czech U20 squad at the World Juniors, finishing with 7 points in 7 games.

Kaut is a physically mature winger who can take advantage of defenseman who are either flat-footed or caught out of position by using his speed. He has the ability to change gears deceptively and throw his opponents off as he's capable of stopping-up or cutting directly to the net and mixing up his options with the puck on his stick. He's a smart player who's aware on the ice and recognizes how to shift the conditions to his liking in order to re-open passing lanes or stall long enough to wait for support in the offensive-end. He's a dangerous winger who features a high-degree of skill and can use his hands to force defenders to respect him, which usually allows him to play a heavy possession style game. His passing ability is some of the best in this class. He's got tremendous vision and at times appears to have eyes in the back of his head by consistently making difficult no-look passing plays to his teammates. This ability allowed him to become an architect on the ice when he was distributing the puck on the Czech's top power-play at the U20's. His vision should be highlighted when taking into account his ability to play below the goal-line and in-front of the crease, this also allows him to play an advanced cycle-game. He has arguably some of the best forechecking skills in this draft class, where he uses his mature and powerful frame and advanced angling to aggressively weigh heavy on the opposition to come away with the puck. We have seen him overwhelm his opponents with his size and an active stick to win a board battle and then execute an accurate pass that sets up his teammates for scoring chances all season. Furthermore, he's not a one-dimensional passing player. He's got a precise shot that's got a snap-like release meaning he doesn't always release the puck near the end of his blade in one motion, instead he likes to push the puck forward slightly before shooting it. He's also able to shoot the puck while skating down the wings or cutting across the slot and has a heavy slapshot which he likes to use in our viewings. Kaut's able to identify when to use his shot and when to use his pass to create the most effective scoring chance, never really relying on one over the other, showing good overall timing when he attempts either option.

Martin isn't only an offensive-minded player, he also plays an advanced defensive game for his position and age. His hockey-sense transfers to the defensive-end where he uses his stick to disrupt passes and he's an aggressive back-checker who is good at pressing his stick into his opponents, breaking down their attempted plays. Also, he plays with a good pace and has shown a consistent motor throughout our viewing's.

There really isn't any weakness in his skill-set. He could stand to improve the velocity on his wrist-shot and can continue to develop his all-around game but that's what makes him one of the most complete wingers in his draft, there's a lot of reward but little risk when assessing Kaut.

"He's raw but we need to dig deeper on him. He hasn't looked as good back home as he looked in Buffalo." NHL Scout, January 2018

"I went into Buffalo pretty blind on the Kaut kid, he was really good in both games I saw." – NHL Scout, January 2018

"He's a winger version of Bo Horvat." – NHL Scout, January 2018

"I'd guess he's a 15-20 range guy" – NHL Scout, May 2018

"Not elite at anything but elite at knowing what he is and getting elite production out of his tools." - NHL Scout, May 2018

"You know what you're getting from the time you draft him and that's not the case with some of these other first-rounders." - HP Scout, Brad Allen

"As the season progressed he kept moving up my list. He's smart, has a high compete level and some skill. Those are my big three components I look for in a player, he was consistent with all three and his skating is very good as well. Scouts were not really mentioning him to me until his performance during Christmas in Buffalo." HP Scout, Mark Edwards

"Not afraid to take pucks to the net and I thought he was really impressive down low. He forechecked effectively and was impressive along the walls. He showed the ability to both score and pass the puck. He showed vision with some good puck movement that led to goals. Defensively he was also solid. His work ethic didn't slide and he worked hard applying back pressure. He does all the little things and is one of the smarter players in the draft. Easily one of my favourite players in this draft class. - HP Scout, Mark Edwards

"The news is out there through various media sources that Kaut went home after his physical at the combine detected a heart ailment. I spoke to a few scouts about the situation and based on those conversations we are going to keep our pre-combine ranking for Kaut as is. Teams will be doing plenty of homework between now and the draft. I feel that I can say confidently that Kaut would've been a lock to be a top 20 pick. He very well may still be, but if he starts falling in the draft, you will know that it has nothing to do with his on ice performance. I'll reiterate again how big a fan I am of his game. Based on the info I've heard (I had it explained to me pretty well) since Saturday I'd still be inclined to grab him." HP Scout, Mark Edwards (June 4th)

"A couple of scouts told me today (June 6) that Kaut is planning to be at the draft. I think he'll have a few interviews ahead of him..." - HP Scout, Mark Edwards

| NR | KEANE, JOEY | BARRIE | OHL | 6' 0.0" | 180 lbs | RD |

Keane looked more comfortable during his 2nd OHL season playing big minutes on the matchup pairing. He is a fluid skater who gets around the ice rather effortlessly and never seems to tire. Even towards the end of long shifts, Keane didn't hesitate to take the puck the length of the ice and try to create offense. He was a one-man zone exit, and entry, machine all year long. He was always looking to rush the puck up ice and go on the attack. At times he did that to a fault, as he skated the puck deep into the offensive zone, ran himself out of real estate, and then had a long way to go to get back in the play. While he's an effective rusher, his outlets could still use some work. They were rather hit and miss in his rookie year and they were still erratic at times this past season.

Defensively he was mostly solid, particularly in the neutral zone, as his skating ability allowed him to keep tight gaps. He didn't need much of a head start to win races for loose pucks or get back if opposing forwards dumped pucks in and put it behind him.

Though he had a really strong year, we still think his NHL ceiling is limited.

"Had a few scouts mention he is a guy they might consider in the 7th round but they were busily doing some digging in on him." – HP Scout, Mark Edwards

NR	KELLENBERGER, MATTHEW	OAKVILLE	OJHL	6' 0.0"	183 lbs	RD

Kellenberger is an intelligent, offensive minded defenseman with good mobility and puck skills. Matthew is a talented skater who utilizes his effortless stride and quick feet to generate offensive opportunities. He shows good puck control and confidence in possession as he often carries transition attacks up ice and into the offensive zone. Matthew shows good decision making as he can simplify his game when need and make quick, high percentage decision when forced with pressure. His strong edges often allow him to elude pressure from a forecheck while his quick first stride allows him to create separation. Matthew see's the ice well and can make an accurate first pass, allowing him to push the pace up ice in transition. Offensively Kellenberger shows good puck distribution skills and vision from the blue line. He effectively quarter-backed a power play both in Oakville and with Team Canada East. Matthew uses his feet well to quickly open shooting and passing lanes and while an effective distributor he is assertive with his shot which boasts good velocity and accuracy behind it. Kellenberger's offensive instincts allow him to appropriately inject into the offensive both in transition and when stationed in the offensive zone. His foot-work and mobility allow him to keep the play in front of him while defending in transition, however he would benefit from closing gaps quicker and forcing a decision by the opponent at the defensive zone blue line. He can allow easy entries to the zone and while he does a good job angling the play to the outside and keeping his stick in lanes, heavier opponents willingly cut in an out power him to the net. He needs to become more assertive physically and win more puck/position battles. Adding strength is necessary.

"I had time for him last season but he kinda lost me this year in Truro. I thought he really had some struggles in that event.(WJAC)" – HP Scout, Mark Edwards

NR	KEMP, BRETT	EDMONTON	WHL	6' 0.0"	162 lbs	RC

Brett Kemp is a skilled centreman who finished his first full season with the Edmonton Oil Kings. The former second round WHL Bantam pick recorded 17 goals and 36 points in 69 regular season games for a very poor Edmonton team. Kemp played a top-6 role for the Oil Kings, seeing lots of time on the team's first powerplay unit.

Kemp plays a skilled and offensive minded game. He is smooth on his skates, an effortless skater with edges that allow him to turn quickly and skate up ice without losing much speed. Brett combines this skating ability with skill with the puck. He is creative and elusive and possesses good hockey sense. Unfortunately these skills were not shown consistently in 2017-18, mostly because Kemp did not show a strong compete level. He relies on his physical skills and did not illustrate the compete or effort level that is required to take his offensive skills to the next level. Kemp gets away with not working hard because of his ability to save ice and skate effortlessly, but he consistently gets caught floating. Without the puck, Kemp is a non-factor, as he lacks the will to retrieve pucks and make a difference on the defensive end of the ice. Overall, he has loads of talent, but his effort level and will to be a top player in WHL is in question.

| 167 | KESSELRING, MICHAEL | NEW HAMPTON | HIGH-NH | 6' 4.3" | 191 lbs * | RD |

Kesselring's size, skating ability, and offensive instincts has certainly intrigued some observers. His lack of attention to detail in the defensive zone and pension for making mistakes with the puck are areas of concern.

His compete level and overall hockey sense are both below average. He'll likely be selected due to his size and physical tools. He's the son of former Merrimack and minor pro star Casey Kesselring, who also is his coach at the prep school level. He'll be heading to Des Moines in the USHL for a season before college hockey.

"Skating is really weak but he's a smart player, uses his long reach well." NHL Scout, May 2018

"Not enough offense there for me to offset the feet." - NHL Scout, May 2018

"I think he gets drafted." - NHL Scout, May 2018

| NR | KETOLA, JUUSO | ASSAT | FINLAND JR | 5' 11.0" | 194 lbs | RD |

Ketola is not the biggest defenseman, but plays bigger than his listed size. He can be tough to play against, as he has good footwork and that helps him be physical and tough to play against in the neutral and defensive zones. He has good skating abilities; he's good at skating the puck out of his zone due to his quick acceleration and above-average speed. However, he gets into trouble after he has to make a decision with the puck. He has trouble making the right decisions, and his passing game is lacking. There's sometimes a lack of accuracy when he's moving the puck out of his zone. In the offensive zone, he has interesting skills, but these don't always result in offensive success. He doesn't stand still on the point, he likes to be active in the offensive zone and get open to receive passes from teammates. He lacks the creativity to be a power play quarterback. The best things about him are his skating abilities and compete level, and what he needs to work on is his decision-making. That will be important in regards to improving or simplifying his game, and crucial if he wants to one day reach the NHL.

| NR | KHODORENKO, PATRICK | MICHIGAN STATE | BIG10 | 6' 0.0" | 206 lbs | LC |

In his second year of draft eligibility, Khodorenko is coming off a successful sophomore season at Michigan State, putting up 13 goals and 19 Assists in 36 games for the Spartans. Khodorenko possesses a consistent down low and net front presents. He uses his strong frame to protect the puck below the dots and gain position on his defender in front of the net. Khodorenko has established a nose for the net and more of a willingness to go to the hard areas and compete for pucks. Khodorenko has quick and soft hands and is able to make some nice finesse plays in traffic. His shot has decent velocity and his quick hands help him get it off his tape quickly. Khodorenko doesn't have top end speed in regards to his skating and gets beat to puck races too often, however Patrick possesses good footwork in tight areas and has a strong base that makes him difficult to separate from pucks.

"I just don't see anything about his game that jumps out at me as an NHL'er but with some more growth in his all around game he could be a quality NCAA Free Agent option in a couple of years." - HP Scout, Dusten Braaksma

"I don't think he gets drafted." - NHL Scout, January 2018

"Not a player that's ever done much to get me to buy into his game." - HP Scout, Mark Edwards

86	KHOVANOV, ALEXANDER	MONCTON	QMJHL	5' 10.5"	198 lbs *	LC

Khovanov, after being drafted 2nd overall in the CHL Import Draft last June, had big health issues over the summer after contracting hepatitis A, eventually missing the entire first half of the season. He made his comeback in late December with the Moncton Wildcats. The young Russian did fairly well with them, averaging close to a point-per-game pace despite being behind the rest of his teammates (because of all of his inactivity), both physically and timing-wise.

He also played for Russia at the February U-18 Five Nations' Tournament in Plymouth, where he played on the top line with Andrei Svechnikov and Grigori Denisenko. These were the same two linemates he had last year at the U-17 Hockey Challenge. Unfortunately, he was not really a factor in this tournament, as his line was more of a two-player showing with Denisenko and Svechnikov doing all the work. Khovanov was more of a spectator on this line and looked a step behind his two skilled linemates. In Moncton, he was used often on the wing in order to not give him too many responsibilities at the beginning. After a month and a half, he was back full-time at center, where he's more comfortable. He plays a good two-way game, with good effort away from the puck, and showed good support down low to help his defensemen retrieve pucks. His puck skills are good; he has good poise and great on-ice vision. He's a pass-first type of forward; he has good scoring chances, but we would like to see him use his shot more. His shot is not bad; it's accurate and he can get it off quickly off his stick. Khovanov's on-ice vision remains his best asset, as he can find linemates quickly in the offensive zone and has good creativity. He's not overly big, and more importantly, his skating ability is average at best. He lacks that dynamic skating ability that you want in a smaller player. He plays often at the same speed; rarely will you see him use a quick burst of speed to beat a player wide. This is something we would like to see him improve; his skating ability will be the key for him to succeed at the pro level.

Khovanov will be a bit of wild card for this year, because there are still some unknowns with him and the question is how much better he will get once he's 100% healthy. He's definitely a skilled player, however, and there's part of his game that will definitely improve to reach the NHL one day, although there's a lot of work that needs to be done here. From watching him at last year's U-17, there were notably some flags in terms of the dynamism of his skating abilities.

"He's been good. He's solidly in my top two rounds." - NHL Scout, February 2018

"I wouldn't move on him until later in the draft and I'm guessing he'd be gone." NHL Scout, February 2018

"Don't get the hype with him, didn't see a lot of dynamic plays from him, and his skating is a red flag for me." - HP Scout Jérôme Bérubé

"I was looking forward to watching this year in the QMJHL. It took a while but eventually we got to see him. My biggest take away was I didn't see enough to get me excited about him given his size/skating combo." - HP Scout, Mark Edwards

| NR | KIEFIUK, CALEN | CENTRAL ILLINOIS | USHL | 5' 8.0" | 191 lbs | LW |

Kiefiuk is an elusive, undersized forward that plays a bigger style game than his physical size. He often initiates contact when he goes into puck battles and is relentless on his puck pursuits, both on the fore check and back check. Calen is a strong kid, especially in the lower body which allows him to get leverage against bigger opponents. Kiefiuk excels in the transition game and has good straight line speed and explosiveness in his skating. He is equally as fast with the puck on his stick and can make decisive plays with speed when entering the offensive zone. Kiefiuk has a quick shot release but needs to continue to work on his accuracy as he missed the net with some high end scoring chances we have seen. While none of his offensive skills can be categorized as high end at this stage, he was an effective point producer for a struggling Central Illinois team, registering 18 goals and 28 assists in 60 games. After finishing his 2nd full USHL season this year. Kiefiuk will be off to the University of Michigan this fall.

| 161 | KILLINEN, LENNI | BLUES JR. | FINLAND-JR. | 6' 1.5" | 180 lbs | RW |

Killinen has developed nicely physically since last season; he now has great size, and with his good speed, he can really be a threat on the forecheck. He's good on the puck pursuit; he can create turnovers by forcing opposing defensemen to rush their decisions. His skating is good, as he has quick feet and excellent acceleration to hit his top speed quickly. He's a threat to go around defenders wide with that great speed. Killinen has great work ethic, and works hard in all three zones, unafraid to get involved along the boards. Offensively, he works hard for his points, and will create scoring chances with his speed and tenacity. He's not very creative with the puck or in a playmaker role. His hockey IQ is average, and he has tunnel vision when in possession of the puck. We love the speed, size and work ethic, but we worry about his hockey IQ and being able to translate those to the NHL.

| NR | KINDREE, LIAM | KELOWNA | WHL | 5' 10.0" | 174 lbs | RW |

A fourth round Bantam pick of Kelowna, Kindree came in with some scoring prowess on his resume and exhibited a skill set that showed he could not only hang with skilled linemates but thrive in an offensive role due to his above average hockey sense. He showed great timing with good reads on offence and was often seen finding soft spots in and around the crease, driving the net hard and not backing down to stronger defenders in traffic. Skates quite well and while his end to end rushes weren't as frequent as one might have expected, he exhibited a better ability to use acceleration in bursts to create some open space to make a play. Showed a good balance of play making and scoring but as young players often do he did defer to his older more experienced linemates at times and looked much better complimenting highly skilled players but lacked ability to carry a line on his own when being the offensive catalyst. Racked up 13 points in November when he was given an opportunity on the top line complimenting his linemates speed and skill. Views during this time were where he peaked as they attacked dangerously as a unit with speed and skill and were difficult to contain and this is where Kindree shone, exhibiting his hockey sense where he can think at a high pace. Kindree wasn't ineffective on lower lines once returning players pushed him down the lineup but he was more dangerous with players who think at his pace. Unfortunately he lost over a month of the season due to a knee injury in early 2018 which seem to zap the momentum he had built up; he didn't quite look the same upon his return. To his benefit the Kelowna forward group looked a out of sync without him in the lineup taking away from a strong 3 line attack. .

| 113 | KIRK, LIAM | SHEFFIELD | ENGLAND | 6' 0.3" | 161 lbs* | LW |

Liam Kirk has taken one of the most unorthodox development paths, playing professional hockey in Great Britain. He had a successful sophomore year with the Steelers, producing 16 points in 52 games, including 9 goals. Internationally, he was featured at the division 2A U18s, where he produced 7 points in 5 games, the division 2A U20's, where he had 14 points in 5 games with 7 goals, and the D1A World Championships where he went pointless in 5 games. His performance at the U20's helped Great Britain capture a bronze medal.

Kirk is a creative and skilled player who uses his speed and fast reads to make plays happen around him. He's at his most dangerous on his off-wing, using his two-step area quickness, outsides edges and separating speed to drive down the right side of the ice. His off-wing is highlighted due to his impressive backhander, he gets it off his stick in a hurry and he's capable of lifting the shot in tight to the net. When Liam is attacking the net, he has a varied approach. He uses his puck-handling skills to make quick moves in traffic, his vision to look for a trailing option who he can pass the puck to, or his skating to cut towards the net area. His shot isn't heavy and lacks power but he's able to use it in motion, behind screens, and further enhance his angle by dragging it. His hockey sense compliments his skill-set well. He recognizes the time and space he has to make plays on most-shifts and chooses when to release his shot and when to pass it off at the right times, mixing up his options and remaining unpredictable. Furthermore, he's willing to use his skill-set to attack the net directly, not relying on an outside approach, he can make a highlight-reel play but can score a gritty goal too.

He continued to gain ice-time and powerplay time for the Steelers as he got more comfortable playing against men, showing an above-average ability to play away from the puck, as well as distribute the puck efficiently from the half-wall with the man-advantage. He's willing to support his defenseman, take up a shooting lane to make a block, and was aware of the positioning of the man he was tasked with covering. The drawbacks to Kirk's game at this time are mostly due to his physical immaturity and quality of competition. He's a slight kid who gets knocked off the puck easily in stride and has trouble during board battling sequences, though he does compete hard on most shifts and when he fills out there's a chance that a lot of his limitations at this time are addressed.

Liam has the opportunity to be the first-born and trained player from the United Kingdom to make it to the NHL. Look for him to get drafted in the upcoming CHL Import draft, where he can play in one of the top junior leagues in order to further develop his offensive-skill-set.

"I think he'll be a mid round guy. He has some skill and he can skate." - NHL Scout, April 2018

"He's very raw." - NHL Scout, May 2018

"Really enjoyed his interview at the combine." - NHL Scout, June 2018

"The player is receptive to playing in the CHL next season." NHL Scout, June 2018

"I only saw him on tape but I liked his talent. He competes, has skill and he can skate." HP Scout, Mark Edwards

"I know one thing, they are watching closely back home. I tweeted about him at the combine and it got the most interaction of any of my tweets that day." - HP Scout, Mark Edwards

| NR | KIZIMOV, SEMYON | TOGLIATTI 2 | RUSSIA JR | 6' 0.0" | 176 lbs | RW |

Semyon Kizimov put up decent point production on Ladia Togliatti in the MHL, finishing with 18 points in 30 games including 12 assists. He also played internationally for Russia by competing in the U19-World Junior A challenge, U18-Five-Nations and the U18 World Junior championships where he finished with 3 points in 3 games while playing in a depth-role.

Kizimov is a mid-sized, yet talented offensive-winger who has great puck skills, allowing him a high-degree of creativity which gives him a lot of flair when the puck is on his stick. He's a deceptive player whose difficult for defenses to read. His deception is created through his excellent set of hands which gives him a lot of moves. This makes him a dangerous player in one-on-one situations or off the rush. He also uses his move-set to compliment the fakes he uses, such as turning his head towards the net to fake a shot before chipping a backhand saucer pass over his opponents stick to his teammate. Another good attribute that Kizimov has is his vision. When he's using his hands to evade incoming sticks or checks he's usually assessing his passing options and processes the play quickly, which allows him to make some really difficult set-ups look relatively easy. Semyon possesses an above average release point and it has a good amount of accuracy, though he prefers the passing option if it's available to him from our viewings. Arguably the weakest aspect of his offensive-game is his positioning away from the puck, he rarely finds soft-ice so that he can be set-up by his teammates, though he does possess a skillset that allows him to create scoring chances for himself. What makes his mental-game unique, is that even though he lacks offensive-awareness without the puck on his stick, he actually has shown plus awareness when in possession of the puck. He's good at recognizing the time and space he has to make a play in most games and he's shown a good level of patience and poise under pressure due to his puck-skills. The last thing to mention about his offensive-game is that he's more than willing to take the puck directly to the net or cut across high-traffic areas to increase his scoring chances.

Although he comes across at first glance at a finesse oriented player, he can play physical as well. This is notable during board battles where he's capable of throwing his weight around. His defensive-game has developed throughout the season due to getting quality penalty-killing minutes against top competition while playing for Russia. He's got above-average defensive-reads and can intercept neutral zone passes before turning it back up ice.

Even with an impressive skillset he has some glaring issues that are holding him back in our rankings. His skating technique doesn't allow him to have much in the way of top-end speed, his stride is choppy and he doesn't have a deep knee bend resulting in a sluggish top-gear, though his edges are above average which helps him when he's cutting to the net. Also, his motor is average, he's not a tenacious player by any stretch and this has caused him to look invisible on the ice at times.

Kizimov is a prospect who needs to learn how to transform his flashes of high-end skill into more consistent play and continue to improve his skating mechanics in order to become a quality winger at the pro levels.

| 216 | KOEPKE, COLE | SIOUX CITY | USHL | 6' 1.0" | 196 lbs | LW |

Koepke was an excellent goal scorer for Hermantown High School in 15/16 but went undrafted and spent much of 16/17 injured. Koepke was drafted in the 2nd Round by Sioux City in the 2016 Phase 2 USHL draft, after being released by the Chicago Steel who drafted him in the 2014 Phase 1 Draft. Koepke is coming off a solid season for Sioux City (USHL) with 28 goals and 11 assists in 60 games. A native of Hermantown, Minnesota, Koepke is committed to Minnesota Duluth for this fall and is in his final year of NHL Draft eligibility as a 98' born. Koepke has excellent goal scoring instincts. His combination of shot versatility and ability to get himself into scoring position allows him to score in a number of different ways. Koepke is an explosive skater with high end top speed. His size along with his ability to play with speed with the puck is an asset offensively. Koepke works hard at both ends of the ice and plays with a good tenacity and physicality in battles. He has a strong frame and wide shoulders which he uses as an asset in winning pucks and position on the ice.

"He certainly can finish and has pro level skating but if you're a 98' born, in the USHL and committed to a top tier program like UMD you should put up the numbers he did this year." HP Scout, Dusten Braaksma (May, 2018)

| 116 | KONDELIK, JACHYM | MUSKEGON | USHL | 6' 6.25" | 226 lbs | LC |

Kondelik is a big, hulking centermen who despite his size of 6'6" and well over 220 lbs. gets around the ice fairly well. Jachym has good straight ahead speed and is difficult to handle with a head of steam given his size and stickhandling ability. His explosiveness in his first few strides is a red flag at this stage of his development. He can lose races to loose pucks and get chasing the puck carrier if he loses containment in the corners. When he is first on the puck, Jachym is able to dominate possession in the corners, using his frame and reach to shield the puck and displays some slick stick handling and decent footwork in tight areas. Has shown the ability to make plays from the half wall and below the dots to find teammates in the slot for scoring chances. Jachym has a quick powerful release to his shot that he can find the corners in traffic. Kondelik has a lot of tools that allow him to dominate for stretches at the USHL; however he will go for stretches of games where he blends into the game and miss opportunities to make an impact. His awareness away from the puck can be lacking at times and depending on the pace of the game, he can get chasing the play in transition due to lack of explosiveness in his skating. Kondelik is physical with his frame in puck battles and is able to separate players from pucks but needs to show more consistency in this area of his game going forward. Jachym is a U. of Connecticut commit and is slated to join the Huskies this coming fall.

"Jachym has a lot of tools aside from his size that make him an intriguing pro prospect but the lack of consistency at times is a real red flag and I question how his game translates to the NHL a few years down the road. If this is the 2010 draft I would be a lot higher on him" HP Scout, Dusten Braaksma

"This kid will test your scouting ability. He does a lot of things right, but those feet are not good. I don't know where he fits on my list right now." - NHL Scout, December 2017

"I just worry he's going to be too slow to keep up. He's got a brain and hands, but I don't see a lot of offense." - NHL Scout, December 2017

"He can't stop and start quick enough so that kills him for me. He makes big turns all over the place and that won't get it done." NHL Scout, December 2017

"He's actually good on the penalty kill but where do you go with that in your projection?" NHL Scout, December 2017

"Someone will over draft him because he's 6'6"." - NHL Scout, April 2018

"If he plays it will be as a 4th line Centre." NHL Scout, April 2018

| 211 | KOOY, JORDAN | LONDON | OHL | 6' 1.75" | 184 lbs | G |

Jordan Kooy established himself as a quality backup this past season and at times flashed starting potential at the junior level. He played in 24 games with London, which was more than double his previous year, producing a 3.11 GAA and .904 save percentage, including 1 shutout.

Kooy is an average-sized goalie whose puck tracking ability and reflexes consistently stood out. He's not the biggest goalie but compensates for his lack of size by displaying the ability to read the play at both a fast rate and in advance. There's a significant amount of poise in his game, rarely getting rattled when dangerous scoring chances presented themselves, this allowed him to come away with impressive secondary saves where he showed split-second reaction time. We have seen him drop into this butterfly and then kick out his pads very quickly which have taken away what look like sure goals. Furthermore, his reflexes apply to his butterfly which he can drop in and out of quickly, his technique is solid and he was good at absorbing heavy shots from the point. Additionally, his glove hand is positioned well which allows him to take away shots labelled for the top part of the net. Although, his blocker lags behind his glove-hand and butterfly technique at this time, where we have watched him let in some softer goals on that side. This doesn't apply to his reverse V-H technique though, he consistently sealed himself to the post and was fluid when exiting and going back to a standing position.

Arguably the biggest drawback to Jordan's game at this time is his range-of-motion, he's athletic in terms of being able to make a reactionary save, but he has trouble on saves that require extension. Furthermore, although his angles improved when we saw him over the course of the season, he's still not as aggressive at cutting down shots from certain areas of the ice as fast as he should have. Regardless of the skills he needs to improve, Kooy established himself as a decent goalie prospect who at the very least looks like he can become a quality starter as soon as next season for London.

"This kid is really good, he's going to be one of the better goalies this year." - NHL Scout, October 2017

"He really had some bad outings when I saw him early in the season but he finished with a strong one late in the season. I didn't happen to catch him much in his starts last season." HP Scout, Mark Edwards

| 8 | KOTKANIEMI, JESPERI | ASSAT | FINLAND | 6' 2.3" | 182 lbs * | LC |

Jesperi Kotkaniemi had an impressive year while playing for Assat by putting up 29 points in 57 games, he followed that up with 1 assist in 7 playoff games. Internationally, he had an underwhelming Hlinka Memorial but picked up the pace considerably at the Five-Nations and saved his best effort for Finland at the U18's where he was one of the more impressive players at the event, helping his team win gold.

Kotkaniemi is a large two-way center who has a high-level of intelligence and competitiveness that compliments a versatile game. There's not one specific attribute that stands-out above the rest for Jesperi, however he does have several good to great attributes that allowed him to become one of the most promising centres in this year's draft. Two of the most important factors when we assess a prospect is intelligence followed by skill, and that's what he brings to the table. He's a smart player who's capable of breaking down the opposition using patience, poise, and awareness of what his teammates are attempting to do, this allowed him to adapt to Finland's top pro league this past season as well as drive one of the most successful lines at the U18's. He's capable of accommodating and adjusting to conditions on the ice, for instance when playing along the half-wall on the powerplay, he can identify if the defense and adjust quickly, creating opportunities for himself and his teammates. Furthermore, he's a creative player who can set up unorthodox plays due to his soft-hands and excellent vision, for instance we have seen him bank a puck between a player's legs off the back of the net before using his length to re-collect the puck, effectively turning his opponent inside-out. He's also capable of threading accurate and crisp passes through heavy traffic but isn't a player who forces plays, this allows him to drive possession for his team without turning the puck over too often. It's challenging for defensive units to identify what he's attempting to do with the puck on his stick and this makes him difficult for goalies to read as well. Additionally, Kotkaniemi has a high-end release point. He has reach and generates a lot of velocity. Factor that with his ability to change the angle of his shot by dragging the puck in-tight to his body both at a stand-still position and while driving down a lane and it makes for a difficult shot for goalies to handle.

Although he has a fluid stride and likes to use his edges to manipulate his frame so that he can evade incoming checks and weave through heavy traffic, his acceleration is average and his base isn't fully developed yet, which puts him off balance when he attempts some of his more technical dekes. When he isn't offensively engaged or executing at the rate he's capable of given his skill-set, he still finds ways to be effective for his team. He's shown a high-level of compete without the puck and is willing to expend his motor in order to track-down the opposition during backchecking sequences, he's also willing to forecheck aggressively and finishes his checks along the boards.

Kotkaniemi demonstrated a mature, all-around game that gives him a high-floor with a lot of upside, his versatility allows him to move up and down a line-up and we see him as potentially developing into a solid two-way center at the NHL level.

"He's better than I thought." NHL Scout, February 2018

"I had Kupari ahead of him until now." - NHL Scout, February 2018

"Skilled 2nd line center and possibly even a number one center. He's a smart player." - NHL Scout, May 2018

"When I saw him in Plymouth (Five Nations Tournament) I knew instantly he was moving up our ranking. Those were the viewings that allowed me to see his playmaking ability and his skill. He went pointless in one game but easily could've had 4 assists if he got some help from his linemates. He's a smart, skilled responsible centreman. - HP Scout, Mark Edwards

"Good feedback from interviews at the NHL Combine." - HP Scout, Mark Edwards

| 129 | KOTKOV, VLADISLAV | CHICOUTIMI | QMJHL | 6' 4.25" | 206 lbs | LW |

Kotkov came to Chicoutimi after the Saguenéens drafted him last summer in the CHL Import Draft with the 32nd overall pick. Before joining the Saguenéens, Kotkov played last season in the MHL, where he had 3 points in 19 games with Krasnaya Armiya Moskva. But he made more of a mark internationally with Russia's U-17 team, mostly at the February U-17 tournament, making some high-skills' plays throughout the competition. This year with Chicoutimi, he scored 21 times and had 49 points overall in 68 games, playing on a weak team that finished 15th out of 18 teams in the league.

Kotkov is a huge kid, and the most impressive things about him are his soft hands. He's a very good stickhandler and makes some impressive dekes for a player of his size. Very good in tight, his quick hands are the best part of his offensive arsenal. He has a good, heavy shot, mixed with nice on ice-vision makes him a player that can be dangerous in the offensive zone. He's a player with great size, but he's not really a physical player and could be stronger on his skates when protecting the puck along the boards. Once he adds some mass to his frame, his puck-protection game down low will be better because this year he was losing too many battles there. In addition, his inconsistency and compete level were up and down all year. However, the number one thing Kotkov will need to improve on is his skating ability, as it is below-average and playing on a big ice surface in Chicoutimi didn't help. He's not strong on his skates, but he doesn't generate much speed out there. Top speed, acceleration and agility are all parts of his skating abilities that will need some serious work. His play away from the puck will need work too, as presently he's more of a one-dimensional player rather than a two-way player.

Kotkov can produce offensively and can make some highlight-reel plays out there, but in order to become an NHL player, he'll need to improve a lot of parts of his game. He'll be back next season with the Saguenéens, and with the Klima twins out of the picture, he'll be one of the most important players on that roster.

"You need to be patient with those big guys that can score." - NHL Scout (September 2017)

"I was patient with him due to his scoring potential and size, but there's not enough drive for me to really push for him in our rankings. Plus, his skating is scary." - HP Scout Jérôme Bérubé

198	KOUMONTZIS, DEMETRIOS	EDINA	HIGH-MN	5' 9.75"	183 lbs	LW

Demetrios played youth hockey in Minnesota through his Bantam seasons, which saw him get drafted by Everett in the 8th round of the 2015 WHL Bantam Draft. Koumontzis then moved to Phoenix AZ to play for the Jr. Coyotes U16 AAA program where he was a standout, eventually committing to nearby Arizona State and being drafted by Green Bay (USHL) in Round 2 of the 2016 Phase 1 Draft. Demetrios sustained a back injury in his 2nd season with the Jr. Coyotes and decided to return to Minnesota for 2017-2018 season to rehabilitate and further his development. Koumontzis played for Team Northeast in the Midwest Elite League this past fall where he led the league in scoring and for Edina High School where he registered 22 Goals and 25 assists in 29 games.

Koumontzis has a lot of offensive skill and he uses the space he creates well. He is confident with the puck on his tape. He doesn't have a lot of size but has a strong lower body and plays with a wide base which makes him difficult to separate from the puck. He doesn't shy away from contact and uses his body well in puck battles to gain leverage. While his skating stride is not very technically sound, he possesses good jump off the hop due to his lower body strength and has deceptive speed with the puck. Koumontzis won't score a lot of goals by using his shot to pick corners or beat goalies much one on one, but is good at using screens and quickly getting the puck off his tape. He possesses good instincts in knowing where to be in the offensive zone to have loose pucks find him. Defensively, he is a crafty player on the back check and displayed the ability to strip pucks and is on the right side of puck battles in his own end. Demetrios will be off to Arizona State in the fall.

"He certainly has the talent to go to a bigger NCAA program but he has stated he wants to be part of turning Arizona State into a prominent program, I like that kind of attitude in a young player. With later round prospects, their attitude and character are key to them eventually defying the odds." - HP Scout, Dusten Braaksma

"Probably the best of the bunch in a really weak Minnesota High School class this year." — NHL Scout, April 2018

"Pretty good hockey sense, strong skater. Built a bit like a fire hydrant. Not a player with a ton of skill but I like him...good hockey player." — NHL Scout, April 2018

66	KOVALENKO, NIKOLAI	YAROSLAVL 2	RUSSIA-JR.	5' 10.0"	174 lbs	RW

Nikolai Kovalenko is a dual American/Russian-forward who had a solid year for Loko Yaroslavl of the MHL, where he produced 31 points in 33 games, including 21 assists. He continued his production in the playoffs, putting up 12 points in 13 games while being used in all situations and helping his team win the Kharlamov cup. Additionally, he got pro experience with Lokomotiv Yaroslavl in the KHL where he had zero points in 6 combined games when factoring in the playoffs. He didn't play for Russia at any major international tournament this past year.

Kovalenko is a very skilled playmaking winger who has the potential to adapt to smaller ice-surfaces due to the speed which he processes the play. He's very good at predicting the movements of the defense in-front of him which allows him to be a step-ahead of the play, and this should be emphasized when discussing his play below the goal-line and around the net area. As an example, he's used his quickness to cut aggressively out from behind the net while using a body fake to cause the opponent defending him to inadvertently switch skating lanes, giving him a direct route to the net, resulting in a high-end scoring chance. Additionally, he doesn't just use body fakes, he also has very soft-hands and plays with a high-degree of fearlessness, which allows him to cut through defences' before finding his open-teammates when driving through heavy traffic. Despite not being very big, his compete level helps him counteract his physical limitations. When working the boards, he's always attempting to use his edges and smaller frame to become elusive, allowing him to evade incoming checks. He's the type of player who on certain plays just won't be denied, which is a very useful skill to have when attempting to deal with larger defenders. His hockey-sense allows him to be dangerous off the rush as well. We have seen him change his speeds to re-open and re-adjust his passing lanes while driving down the wing, then making accurate and crisp passes to his teammates. Furthermore, he's excellent at masking his intentions with the puck and can make difficult passes look relatively easy, such as making a no-look reverse forehand pass below the goal-line, which fools goalies who think he's attempting to wrap the puck around the net as opposed to setting up his teammate.

Nikolai is an instinctive passer. Even when given a high-percentage shot, he's still looking for his best passing option which at times gives his teammates open-net goals after he gets a goalie to bite however it also takes away some of his better scoring chances. This is largely due to not being as comfortable shooting the puck as he is passing it. He does have an above-average release point but it lacks velocity and he prefers his backhand at times, specifically when on breakaways. Additionally, he's got excellent two-step area quickness and good pivoting mechanics, but his straight-line speed isn't as good as the rest of his skating mechanics at this point in time. We've seen him strip opponents off the puck in the defensive-end and make some nice backchecking plays but it's not a prominent part of his game at this point, though it could help him translate to a center in the future if he continues to gain strength and improve his straight-line speed.

Kovalenko has flown a bit under the mainstream radar this year due to not having played internationally. Regardless, he's a talented and crafty forward whose game has the potential to translate to North-American ice.

"I feel that if he had international exposure this past season then he would be getting talked about a lot more. His game can translate to the NHL and he's talented." — HP Scout, Brad Allen

"Not a huge kid but he played bigger than his size. I was impressed with his shot, he has a quick release and something behind it. I also thought he flashed some impressive playmaking skills. Plenty of euros with skill in this draft. Skating is good but he looked slower compared to Denisenko who showed off his wheels on some shifts together." - HP Scout, Mark Edwards

NR	KOWALCZYK, DANIEL	HC KOMETA BRNO	CZECH JR	6' 2.75"	218 lbs	LD

Kowalczyk is a big defenseman with some good physical abilities. He likes to play physical in his own zone; he can surprise opponents with some good open-ice hits. His hits are solid along the wall. He has a bit of a mean streak in his own zone and in front of the net, and will clear the front of the net. He's strong physically. Kowalczyk will need to improve his mobility, as he can be in trouble versus quick forwards due to his poor footwork. He has strong and powerful legs, but his lateral agility is a big weakness. His puck skills are average at best; he's not an offensive defenseman and his decision-making can be too slow. He does have a good point shot from the point, but needs to release it quickly. Opposing teams have been successful in blocking it too often. He's more of a defensive, rugged defenseman, but his lack of puck skills and poor footwork are definitely big question marks for him if he wants to reach the NHL.

138	KRAL, FILIP	SPOKANE	WHL	6' 1.0"	171 lbs	LD

Filip Kral is a Czech born, two-way defenseman who was drafted by Spokane in the 2017 CHL import draft. He faired well in his first year in North America, producing 35 points in 54 games, including 26 assists, and had zero points in 5 playoff games. Internationally, he played at the U20's, where he was used in all situations and generated a goal in 7 games, while also having a stand-out performance against Russia.

Kral is an average-sized, responsible defenseman who uses fluid skating mechanics and an impressive first-pass to transition the puck up the ice. His best skating attribute is his pivoting ability and edges, which gives him both a primary or a back-up option when dealing with forecheckers. He's an elusive defenseman who relies on his shiftiness, vision and quick-decision making to move the puck out of danger. He can both spin off pressure or angle his frame away from an opponent and use his reach to effectively guard the puck while surveying his options up the ice. He's decent at transitioning up the ice while carrying the puck but is more efficient when he looks to use his sharp and accurate passing skills that consistently landed on the tape of his teammates in most of our views. Away from the puck in the defensive-end, he showed above-average positioning and impressive puck-tracking skills which allowed him to be effective when using his stick to disrupt the play. Furthermore, he would use his skating to block shooting lanes and was decent at keeping his opponents to the outside when they would attempt to cut. Kral's biggest drawback in his own-end at this time is his physical play. He can get overwhelmed and overmatched along the boards and at times showed a lack of engagement in-front of the net.

In the offensive-end, Kral demonstrated both poise and patience, gauging his passing lanes and shooting lanes consistently, which made him an efficient puck distributor. He possesses a quick wrist-shot that features both precision and timing, placing it behind screens effectively in some of the games we watched him in. Although his wrist-shot is more dangerous than his slapshot, he still was capable of delivering it through traffic and was good at setting it up for rebound opportunities. Despite his plus offensive-skills, Kral lacks any high-end offensive attribute and due to his average size and lack of physical play, it will be an up-hill battle for him to develop into a solid pro player at this time.

| 6 | KRAVTSOV, VITALI | CHELYABINSK | RUSSIA | 6' 2.8" | 184 lbs | RW |

Vitali Kravtsov had a tremendous development year while playing for three separate teams. He played for Belye Medvedi Chelyabinsk in the MHL where he put up 7 points in 3 combined games when including the playoffs. He also played pro hockey in the VHL with Chelmet Chelyabinsk while putting up 7 points in 9 games. Though, he played the majority of his season with Traktor Chelyabinsk in the KHL where he had 7 points in 35 games while being featured primarily in a depth-role. However, in the playoffs, he played his best hockey of the season while breaking the KHL single season record for points generated by a U20 player, finishing with 11 points in 16 games, including 6 goals.

Kravtsov is a highly-creative winger who has some of the most dynamic puck-skills featured out of any forward in this draft class. We have seen him make plays from his knees that most players can't make from a standing position to demonstrate his level of puck-handling ability. Factor in that he's got a rare combination of confidence when handling the puck and the compete level needed to utilize his impressive skill-set and it starts forming a picture of why he became the most successful player in the playoffs for his age-group in history. The kid plays with ice in his veins and rarely looked out of place in the KHL by showing the ability to read the play in advance and act quickly. Furthermore, he's got a high-level of hockey sense when handling the puck and this allows him to be experimental on the ice but at the same time not cause too many turnovers due to recognizing when opponents were attempting to use their frame against him or an active-stick. He's an adept playmaker, who can make high-level passes by setting them up using his hands which created an element of surprise. For instance, during rebound attempts where most players look to jam the puck in or get off a quick shot, we have seen him contort his frame to make it look like he's going to try and shoot around the goalie before making a spinning pass to his teammate who's got an open-shot as an example. His passing ability also allowed him to be an effective distributor of the puck along the half-wall while on the powerplay, where he made difficult passes look relatively easy. One of Kravtsov's more notable skills is his ability to manipulate his frame in order to re-open his shooting and passing lanes when they are closed off. He's a crafty player who has learned how to exaggerate his movements due to his high-degree of agility and dexterity, and this allows him to breakdown defenses at will. He's also got a deceptive-shot where he's capable of limiting his movement before using his snap-like release, where he doesn't always shoot the puck in one motion of his blade, but instead pushes it slightly forward before following through. His release also generated velocity and he was capable of shooting while in motion and through screens. Although he's capable of making highlight-reel finesse plays, he's not afraid to score an ugly goal or make a simple play when it calls for it either, which is an important aspect of why he's efficient on the ice in the offensive-end.

Although offensively gifted, he does have some room for improvement in terms of his physical development and play away from the puck. He was featured on the penalty-kill in spurts and was good at clogging his shooting lanes but occasionally was late to react to identifying where he needed to be in order to receive a pass from a defenseman when transitioning back up the ice. Additionally, he does play with a good pace which he varies intentionally to make it difficult to detect what play he's attempting to make but could stand to go into an extra gear during backchecking sequences occasionally. Furthermore, although he has size and length, he hasn't yet filled out his frame which has caused him to get knocked off the puck during board battling sequences, although this area of his game improved throughout the year after identifying how to angle himself better than he did earlier in the season. Even though his frame hasn't filled out, he still generates a good amount of straight-line speed due to having a deep-knee bend and a fluid stride which allows him to create off the rush while also recovering defensively. Lastly, his agility helped compensate for his lack of power, giving him plus edges which he used to weave through heavy traffic as well as spin-off pressure.

Kravtsov has one of the highest offensive-ceiling's in the draft and has an energetic demeanour on the ice where he's usually smiling, it's noticeable when he's having fun out there. His energy and poise when combined with his skill-level makes him one of the more exciting prospects in this class.

"He has star potential and is capable of elevating his play in high-pressure situations. There's very few players in any draft that have the combination of size, puck-skills and evasiveness that he brings to the table. If he becomes the third best player in this draft, I wouldn't be surprised." -HP Scout, Brad Allen

"He's a player who just kept getting better as the year progressed. There were little flashes when he showed some scoring skill that he reminded me of Elias Pettersson from last season. Skating, skilled and smart and his compete level was good as well. The playoff run was impressive. He still a bit raw on the defensive side of the puck but he's a high end player in this draft. One thing to note was that he got increased icetime and responsibility as the year progressed. He doesn't currently play a heavy game, he needs to a bit stronger on the walls but his skill is through the roof. Ceiling is really high for him." - HP Scout, Mark Edwards

"I felt much better about pushing him our rankings after I spoke to some scouts about his combine interviews." - HP Scout, Mark Edwards

"When asked about possible CHL next season he said that it all depends on what the team drafting him wants. I got great feedback on him from scouts. I was told he has a sister going to school in Toronto as well." - HP Scout, Mark Edwards

"Gave a very good self assessment of his game." - NHL Scout, June 2018

"I liked the kid when we interviewed him. There was a language barrier but he gave some very good answers to our questions." - NHL Scout, June 2018

NR	KRAWS, BEN	SIOUX CITY	USHL	6' 2.25"	165 lbs	G

Kraws is a tall lanky goaltender out of the Buffalo Jr. Sabres program. Kraws shared the crease in Sioux City in 17/18. Playing 20 games for Sioux City, Kraws had a 3.34 GAA and a .895 Sv %. While his numbers are unimpressive, they do not tell the whole story as Sioux City struggled defensively for much of the year. Kraws is slightly taller than his listed size and has grown to close to 6'4" this year. He has an extremely slight frame and as he gains more strength his side to side mobility will improve, as he has excellent mechanics but is not real explosive on his edges yet. He has a calming presence in the crease and has the ability to make a big save, control and cover the rebound at key times. Toward the end of the season Kraws was given the crease once Sioux City was eliminated from the playoffs and was impressive with his play, giving his team opportunities to win games. Kraws will likely spend another season with Sioux City before he heads to the NCAA. Ben is committed to Miami (OH).

171	KROPACEK, VOJTECH	SPARTA JR	CZECH JR	6' 1.0"	187 lbs	LC

Vojtech Kropacek made his way through the Sparta Praha system this past season. He played the majority of his games for the U20 squad, where he had 20 points in 30 games, including 11 assists. In the same system on the U18's, he had 11 points in 9 games, and 10 points in 9 playoff games. He got one game of experience with their pro team, scoring a goal in his only game. Internationally, he was featured at both the Five-Nations and at the U18's, where he had a lone assist in 7 games.

Kropacek is a high-energy, 200-foot center who uses his speed and anticipation to make plays. He's got sound skating mechanics and generates a good amount of straight-line speed, as well as showing impressive edges, giving him the ability to cut into high-danger areas of the ice and surprise opponents with impressive spins. Vojtech is good at assessing when he has a step-up on a player, exploiting additional soft-ice when it's given to him, though he doesn't always cut directly to the net as much as we would have liked depending on the game. That being said, his one goal in the Czech league was a direct result of cutting in-front of the net without the puck and burying a backhander after receiving a pass, which shows that he is capable of doing it. He likes to make plays at top speeds and has a pass-first mentality, looking to back-up defense who have to respect his ability to cut by them before dropping the puck back. His ability to track his teammates gives him good playmaking skills and he was consistent at using his vision to find his teammates in heavy traffic. We have seen him cut to the middle of the ice and spin off a check before making a nice backhand pass back to the circle as an example. Additionally, his shot comes off his tape at an above-average speed, though it's not as impressive as his puck-skills or passing ability. He does have soft-hands and can use them at top-speeds, looking to drag the puck around opponents or try technical moves that allow him to break through multiple players, such as one-arm wind-milling the puck past an opponent during a rush attempt.

Due to his speed, Kropacek was dangerous on the penalty-kill, closing his gaps effectively and creating short-handed scoring opportunities. Furthermore, his defensive-reads in the neutral zone were impressive, and this allowed him to create several transitional plays in our viewings. The areas Kropacek needs to improve, are to reduce his perimeter play at times and further develop the power he generates in his release so that he doesn't have to rely on this passing ability as much as he currently does.

187	KRYGIER, CHRISTIAN	LINCOLN	USHL	6' 2.25"	192 lbs	LD

Christian is finishing up his 2nd Full season in the USHL for Lincoln. The one time Wisconsin commit, along with twin brother Cole have switched their commitment to Michigan State where they will be playing this fall. Christian plays a physical, defense first style from the back end. Krygier rarely passes up opportunities to be physical against his opponent, sometimes to a fault as he is susceptible to taking himself out of the play or taking bad penalties. Krygier will need to show better judgment in this regard going forward. Krygier has NHL size and uses it to establish play in front of his own net as well as dominating opponents along the wall. While Christians skating and footwork are above average for his size, his defensive positioning against the rush have shown lapses in our viewings and is vulnerable to conceding the edge against speedy forwards as well as making some poor reads in his own end. Coming out of his own end Christian tries to play a simple, reliable game on breakouts, when he gets into trouble is when his first read isn't available he can panic and commit ill advised turnovers. In the offensive end, Krygier doesn't possess a lot of dynamic playmaking ability but has a big shot from the point and shows good coordination to hold plays in the zone.

"His hockey IQ is what holds him back. When he simplifies his game and picks his spots better with his physicality he can be an effective and fearful shutdown defender." HP Scout, Dusten Braaksma

"Christian struggles striking that balance between being hard to play against and taking dumb penalties and hurting his team. He just hasn't figured out that line you can't cross." NHL Scout, May 2018

" I get why they had to switch their commitment, they weren't going to play ahead of any of Wisconsin's returning defenseman or incoming defenseman, now they will have the opportunity for playing time at Michigan State, which is key for development right now." NHL Scout (May, 2018)

" I like him more than his brother because he's shown the ability to keep it simple. With his size he could be a good defender. I actually get the impression that I'm in the minority though and that more scouts like his brother better." - NHL Scout, May 2018

201	KRYGIER, COLE	LINCOLN	USHL	6' 2.75"	192 lbs	LD

Cole Krygier just finished his 2nd full season with the Lincoln Stars. Cole has flown a bit under the radar since his USHL/OHL draft year, with most of the attention going to his twin brother Christian as the most likely pro prospect. However Cole's complete game has made considerable strides in the last year. One key area of improvement this season is his decision making with the puck in all three zones. His poise and patients with the puck have led to more controlled break outs and less turnovers. Cole continues to be a physical presence on the back end and has shown improvement in regards to not taking bad penalties. He clears in front of the net well and is quick to protect his goaltender. Cole has good size and is strong on his skates and while his footspeed and edgework still need to improve, he is a powerful straight line skater and can get to the areas he needs to get to. Cole picks his spots well on when he wants to join the rush or move down from the point in the offensive zone. He is especially good at keeping pucks in the zone or pinching down the wall to hold the zone. He has a heavy shot from the point both with the slap shot as well as his wrist shot. Cole certainly projects as a long term prospect for any team that uses a pick on him but Cole is an athletic kid with a lot of raw tools. Cole and his brother Christian were committed to Wisconsin but have recently switched to Michigan State where they will play this coming fall.

" Not a fan of his puck game at all." - NHL Scout, September 2017

" He's made a lot of poor decisions with the puck this week." NHL Scout, September 2017

" I like this kid's game, personally I think he's got a bad rap due to misconceptions of the type of player he is and initial expectations. Wouldn't shock me at all to see him drafted, has shown considerable growth and maturity in recent months." HP Scout, Dusten Braaksma

" Probably never going to be a top 2 pairing guy at the next level but his athleticism and physicality will give him a shot if he continues to tend in the right direction" HP Scout, Dusten Braaksma

" He and his brother are the same...big kids who can skate. They are both physical but neither one has the hockey sense or skill to get me excited." - NHL Scout, March 2018

" Really struggled when I saw him in Pittsburgh to start the season. Nothing much changed in my viewings the rest of the way this year. - HP Scout, Mark Edwards

| 206 | KUCHARSKI, JACOB | DES MOINES | USHL | 6' 3.75" | 215 lbs | G |

Kucharski joined Des Moines in 17/18 after a very successful season with Austin (NAHL) the previous year. Kucharski played for Team USA at the World Junior A challenge this season where he was impressive in his showings. Kucharski struggled at times in 17/18, albeit on a struggling Des Moines team and lost the starting job to Roman Durny in the 2nd half of the season. Kucharski has a big frame that has a lot of strength and when he plays big, at the top of his crease, he doesn't give shooters a lot to shoot at. Kucharski is susceptible to letting in some soft goals through the body, especially when he moves laterally. Kucharski's skating and edgework is very good for a big kid and while he isn't really quick from side to side, he has smooth lateral movement and takes away the lower 1/3 of the ice very well with his long legs. Kucharski struggles in traffic where he tends to default to playing deep in his crease with screens in front which opens up the corners. Kucharski has the size and skill set to be an NHL goalie, like most young goalies, he needs to develop some consistency and structure in his game.

"I feel he relies on his size to make most of his saves, I haven't seen him make a lot of athletic or amazing saves, not saying that's a bad thing at all, if you have the size, use it and he does it pretty well." HP Scout, Dusten Braaksma

"Kucharski has been really good." NHL Scout, December 2017 (WJAC)

"I think this U.S kid has been really solid. this week (WJAC)" NHL Scout, December 2017

"He had a really poor second half. He's falling and might go undrafted now." NHL Scout, April 2018

"You saw his best, the good Jr 'A' Challenge was the best he played all year." NHL Scout, May 2018

"Like many NHL Scouts at the WJAC I thought he had some good games although a few rebounds were ugly. Unfortunately I didn't see him after that tournament. He was a big athletic kid though. Not a lot of goalies have impressed me this year." HP Scout, Mark Edwards

| 19 | KUPARI, RASMUS | KARPAT | FINLAND | 6' 1.5" | 189 lbs * | RC |

Rasmus Kupari started his draft eligible season with Karpat's U20 team before working his way up to a third line center role with the Liiga team. Kupari was loaned to Karpat's Mestis league affiliate, Hermes, for five games in December and racked up a goal and three assists. This opportunity afforded him with more ice time and special teams play. He made Finland's U20 World Junior roster as the youngest player, seeing limited ice-time in five games and recording no points. Upon returning to Karpat, Kupari's role expanded to include power play time on the second unit. With the addition of the power play time and increased confidence due to his skillset being further used from January onwards, his points started to show. In the 20-regular season Liiga games following the World Juniors, Kupari recorded 10 points, including 7 assists and by the end of year he finished with 14 points in 39 Liiga games. Following a first-round win over Assat, he was assigned to the U20 team for the remainder of the playoffs.

Kupari has one of the highest offensive ceilings' out of any forward in the 2018 draft. He's got high-end offensive-attributes which start with his skating ability. He's one of the best skaters in this class, his stride is explosive yet he's remarkably efficient and fluid. His skating allows him to have tremendous separation speed, generating breakaways at a high-rate as a result. If an opponent is caught off-balance, flat-footed or is out of position, there's few players in this class that can exploit them like Rasmus can, it's rare to find a player who has his mix of agility and straight-line speed. His speed helps compensate for his average-size and he's shown us that he can attack the net aggressively, not relying on perimeter play. Another great offensive-attribute is his shot. He has one of the best releases in this draft due to how fast it comes off his tape, yet how difficult it is for goalies to pick up. This is in large part due to his reduced movement in his body mechanics before shooting, he generates a lot of power despite not bearing down into his release. This attribute is enhanced when taking his speed into consideration, he's more than capable of shooting while rushing down the wing and we have seen him aggressively switch the angle of his skating lane to further manipulate the angle of his shot. The only drawback in his shot at this time is his accuracy can be mixed depending on the game. Although a better shooter than he is a passer, he's capable of making a crisp and accurate pass to his teammates, specifically during odd-man situations. However, he did show a lack of finesse on occasion in our viewings' by making passes too hard to handle for his teammates at times. Although he's capable of making difficult passes while in motion, he also has shown that he forces blind passes which resulted in turnovers. His vision is above-average which allows him to find his teammates in high-traffic areas but he also tends to rely on his excellent puck-skills and looks to beat defenders one-on-one even if there's a smarter and more efficient play to be made. There's a degree of tunnel vision depending on if he has developed chemistry or not with his line-mates. This was evident when Kupari played the bulk of his season with depth wingers before developing chemistry with Kristian Vesalainen.

Although he's a very skilled-player, he's still shown the ability to play physically when the play calls for it. He can protect the puck along the boards and uses his skating to keep himself active when attempting to peel off his opponents, this has forced slower players and defenders with poor gaps to take penalties against him. Although not an overly impressive defender, the biggest drawback to Kupari at this time is his decision making with the puck on his stick, his ability to process the play hasn't caught up to his skating ability yet.

Rasmus is a creative and dynamic offensive-talent. yet he lacks arguably the most important attribute when we rank our players. His decision making and processing speed isn't below-average, it's just not at the same level as some of the forwards who are ranked above him in this class, which is why he fell out of the top 10 as the season progressed.

"He slid for me a little bit because he was inconsistent." - NHL Scout, March 2018

"Just average smarts but has as much skill as the forwards in the top five." - NHL Scout, May 2018

"Ridiculous talent. He's a top 20 guy all day long because of that skill." - NHL Scout, May 2018

"I think he slides slightly because of the hockey sense. The more I watched him, the more it became a bit of a concern for me. Fantastic skill though." - HP Scout, Mark Edwards -

"Good feedback from his combine interviews. I'll note that in general, feedback from scouts was that it was a good year overall as far as interviews." - HP Scout, Mark Edwards

| 79 | KURASHEV, PHILIPP | QUEBEC | QMJHL | 5' 11.8" | 190 lbs * | LC |

Kurashev was in his second season with Quebec and averaged over a point per game this season and played for his country at the World Juniors in Buffalo. His highlight of the season was probably his performance at the Top Prospects' Game in Guelph, where he performed very well.

He has good versatility, as he is able to play on both the wing and down the middle. He's a smart player that can contribute at both ends of the ice. Defensively, he has shown good support deep in his zone when playing center, to help his defensemen retrieve pucks and start the transition game. He's a decent skater with good enough speed, and can surprise defenders off the rush with a quick burst of speed. He's inconsistent with it, though, and we would like to see him play more of a dynamic game out there on a more consistent basis. He also has a tendency to play too much on the perimeter; we would like to see him go to the net more often and score more "ugly" goals. Kurashev's skills are above-average, but in order for him to be more successful, he'll need to pay the price more in the tougher areas of the ice. As a 1999 late birthday and a talented 18-year-old in major junior, we definitely expected more than 19 goals this year (he scored 21 last year). He's got good vision, makes good passes, and can play with skilled players out there, as shown this year. However, he'll look good some games and disappear for long stretches of time. His work ethic will need to be better, and he will need to bring his A-game to the table more often. He's good in the faceoff circle, but took a lot less faceoffs this year compared to last year. He can play in different situations on the ice; he can play the point on the power play and also has value as a penalty killer.

Kurashev has flashed his skills over the last two years in the QMJHL, but has not been able to bring a consistent game to the table and this has some cause for concern. He's not a first-round talent, but has some skills that should enable him to be a potential pick in June in the top 3 rounds.

"I have waited for two years now to see him take his game to another level, and I'm still waiting. He always flashes his tools here and there, but there's not enough consistency from him." - HP Scout Jérôme Bérubé

| 135 | KUROVSKY, DANIEL | VITKOVICE | CZECH JR | 6' 3.75" | 213 lbs | LW |

Daniel Korovsky was passed over in last years draft, however he put on a considerable amount of weight which helped him compete against men in the Czech league, putting up 11 points in 43 games, including 7 goals, while being featured in depth-role. He was loaned to AZ Havirov in the Czech2 league where he had 9 points in 13 games, including 6 assists. Internationally, he played at the U20's where he was featured in a depth role and produced 3 points in 7 games.

Korovsky is an athletic power-forward who plays a 200-foot game and has a good-degree of hockey sense both with and without the puck. Like most larger forwards of Kurovky's mold, it took him time to grow into his body, however after improving his puck-skills this past season and developing the strength necessary to become a forechecking presence on a shift-to-shift basis, he managed to stand out against men in the Czech league. His skating progressed, using his more powerful base to push off into a fluid stride, he's surprisingly dextrous for his size and is capable of weaving in and out of traffic. This made him useful on the forecheck where he was able to play a heavy possession-oriented game instead of a dump and chase game while moving the puck below the goal-line. Once established along the boards, he would use his frame and length to drain smaller players, understanding how to use his leverage to strip players off pucks. This was notable in-front of the net area as well, he's got the right instincts for his player-type, assessing how to get to the front-of the net to set screens or look to create havoc when the opportunity presented itself. One area he needs to improve upon in order to become more dominant when establishing a net front presence is his balance, despite being a bigger player, there's being times where he's knocked down to the ice too easlly, given his size. Daniel doesn't just play a hard hitting and stream-lined style, he has skill with the puck on his stick, and was noted for having arguably the best deke at the U20's this past season, after receiving a pass in tight to his skates, he pulled the puck around his back to his outside leg, and kicked it ahead of himself between his legs, giving him a great look. He rarely showed plays of that calibre in the Czech league but he's still developing and demonstrated good tools.

Kurovsky has shown the ability to play in his own-end of the ice as well. Using good anticipation away from the puck to take away passing lanes and was able to support his defenseman along the boards on most shifts. Although he's a capable passer off the rush and showed that he can compliment a skilled line, his rate of execution wasn't consistent enough to be labelled as a future top-6 player. If Kurovsky makes it to the NHL, it will most likely be as a depth-player who can be difficult to handle around the net.

107	KVASNICA, MICHAL	FRYDEK-MISTEK	CZREP-2	6' 1.0"	187 lbs	RW

Michal Kvasnica had solid production this year while playing for three separate teams. They include, HC Trinec U20 where he put up 9 points in 8 games, HC Ocelari Trinec of the Czech league where he put up zero points in 8 games when combined with the playoffs, and he played the majority of his hockey in the Czech2 league with HC Frydek-Mistek where he had 16 points in 45 games played. He has an extensive international resume for the Czech-Republic as well.

Kvasnica is an all-around winger who can also play center with strong two-way skills and hockey sense. There's nothing flashy to his game but he's a fundamentally sound player, he's the type of player who coaches love to have in their line-up due to his responsible play both with and without the puck and his ability to prevent goals when he's out on the ice. Due to this attribute, he was used on the penalty-kill throughout the year at international events where he excelled, as he looked like a third defenseman at times when coming back to support his teammates while playing deep in his own end of the rink. He's got excellent defensive-awareness and positioning, seemingly ending up in the right place at the right time to move pucks out of high-danger areas or deliver a well-timed stick lift. We have seen him prevent several goals by back-checking aggressively and catching up to his opponent to takeaway the puck. He was able to accomplish this in our viewing's due to his powerful stride. He digs his heels into the ice and generates a lot of power out of the gate while keeping a deep knee-bend, which allows him to get up to impressive straight-line speeds. His speed and power aren't his only impressive tools, he's a bigger kid who's got a good developmental frame with room to grow into it and he knows how to use it by delivering heavy hits along the boards; he's also adept at using his frame to weigh down and overpower his opponents in the defensive-zone. He doesn't take shifts off in his own end very often, always trying to stay in motion while pushing the puck up along the boards during board battling sequences or when looking to take off during a transitional play. This aspect of his game is one of the reasons why he managed to get a call up to the top Czech league and be successful in the Czech2 league.

Despite having considerable defensive skills, Kvasnica's not the most dynamic forward. He's got average puck skills and isn't overly creative when handling the puck. However, he's got a shoot-first mentality and with good reason. His wrist-shot is quick to come off his stick and generates a lot of velocity which makes it difficult for goalies to absorb. Even though he's a shoot-first player, he does have the ability to find an open teammate and set them up for quality scoring chances, though this aspect of his game can be inconsistent at times. Due to his size, he's not afraid of high-traffic areas and is willing to track pucks around the net area and fight aggressively for space during rebound opportunities. His edge's aren't as impressive as the speed he generates but he's able to peel-off defenders along the boards and skate into the slot area to create high-percentage scoring chances for himself. He's not overly impressive when rushing with the puck due to his average puck-skills which prevents him from making a lot of high-end plays. Though he's good at finding soft-ice around the slot area and is at his most dangerous when paired with a teammate who can set him up so he can fire off his shot.

Kvasnica can shoot the puck, skate, and defend which is a good combination of skills to have however he's not a player who projects into a top-6 role for his team at the pro level as of writing this due to his lack of high-end offensive skills and inconsistent play in the offensive-zone. He's more likely going to develop into a versatile role-player who can play on the penalty-kill.

NR	LAFERRIERE, MATHIAS	CAPE BRETON	QMJHL	6' 1.0"	175 lbs	RC

Laferrière was acquired by Cape Breton last season in the big blockbuster deal that sent Pierre-Luc Dubois to Blainville-Boisbriand. He was was a big scorer in midget with Lac St-Louis, even winning MVP honours at the 2016 Telus Cup. In the QMJHL, he has not been able to translate those offensive successes just yet. This year, he played most of the first half of the year on a line with Sokolov and Batherson. Contrary to Sokolov, who struggled after the Batherson deal, Laferrière was better and increased his level of consistency in the 2nd half of the season. One key to his success in midget was his shot. So far, in the QMJHL, he has not been able to have the same type of success, and also has not shot enough on net. His skating is average; he lacks a dynamic and explosive stride. He often skates at the same speed, and doesn't use his burst of speed and change it up to beat defenders. He's a smart player at both ends of the ice, often coming back deep in his net to support his defensemen. This year, he played regularly on the PK unit. He will, however, need to get better in the faceoff circle. He lacks strength, he's not short but still not mature physically, and can be pushed too easily along the boards. He's not very intense on the ice either, and we would like to see more intensity out of him so that he can win more puck battles.

Laferrière improved his offensive game, if you look at the difference between him in the first half compared to the second half of season. He'll continue to evolve as a strong offensive producer in the QMJHL with time, but the key with him will rely on improving other facets of his game that we noted for improvement. We don't expect him to be drafted, but there's a chance to see him get picked late.

NR	LALONDE, OWEN	GUELPH	OHL	6' 1.0"	185 lbs	RD

Owen Lalonde is a shut-down defender who helped cover for his teammates mistakes. Although he hasn't lived up to his 2nd overall selection by the Sudbury Wolves in the 2016 OHL draft, he still has become a solid defender in his own-right, producing 22 points in 67 games, including 22 assists.

Lalonde is an average sized defender, who relies on his superior defensive-positioning, gap-control and accurate first-pass to help transition the puck up the ice. Although not the biggest defender given his shut-down, defense-first mentality, he's surprisingly strong. We have watched him keep some of the stronger and more physically gifted power-forwards in the OHL to the outside when they attempt to cut around him, as well as knock them off pucks resulting in takeaways. Furthermore, he's capable of dealing with large players in-front of the net and is more than willing to throw his weight around in order to box-out the opposition. One of his most important defensive-attributes is his ability to make quick decisions while under pressure around the goal-line. He's fast to find his open defensive-partner and can make long stretch passes that land on the tape when attempting to transition out of his own-end. When he does make mistakes he's active when attempting to recover but his knees bend slightly outward which doesn't allow him to push off and generate as much power considering his strength, when attempting to accelerate as we wanted to see. Instead he relies on his pivoting mechanics and composure during recovery sequences. He's good at picking when to increase his pacing and when to let up, which allows him to be very effective when choosing to engage physically in most of the games we saw him in. He's a smart defender who opts for the simple yet effective play as opposed to the more dynamic one. As an example, when walking the line when under heavy pressure, he will look to bank the pass off the glass as opposed to force a difficult pass through traffic, reducing the possibility of an odd-man rush against.

Even though he's defensively reliable and is a smart player, he's not a dynamic defenseman when walking the line. He rarely uses any sort of fakes and isn't overly creative when the puck is on his stick. Some of his assists came off of rebounds, where he would look to get off quick and low shots from the point.

His game might not stand out unless you go out of your way to look for him. He's the type of player that you root for due to his compete-level and the fact he plays the game the right way.

"Still can't believe he was taken so high. (OHL Draft)" NHL Scout, October 2017

"A solid Junior player but for me nothing in his game would make me want to draft him." - HP Scout, Mark Edwards

| NR | LAMASTER, LUKE | DULUTH EAST | HS -MIN | 6' 1.75" | 174 lbs | RD |

Lamaster is a puck moving defenseman that we have seen considerable growth in his game in the last year, particularly in his skating and footwork. Lamaster is a very strong kid with NHL size and strength already. Lamaster won the 2018 Reed Larson Award given to the Top Senior Defenseman in the State of Minnesota, racking up 4 goals and 39 Assists in 28 Games for Duluth East H.S.

Luke plays with great decisiveness with the puck. His outlet passes are firm and on his teammates tape, he doesn't float a lot of sauce passes or tentative backhand passes and has the ability to stretch the ice. When he decides to rush the puck up ice he does so with a lot of speed and power to advance through the neutral zone and gain the offensive zone with control. Lamaster has good hands at the offensive blueline; he is able to quickly change the angle of his shot to get it through traffic. Lamaster can take some risks offensively and will need to use better discretion with his decisions to join the rush or come down from the point in the offensive zone. On some viewings he had no support and chose to join the play. Defensively, Luke makes his presence known but plays with good efficiency in his physicality, doesn't take himself out of the play and preserves a lot of energy due to good positioning on his opponent. Lamaster can close on opponents, take the puck away and turn it up ice quickly. Lamaster has a raw skill set that needs time to refine. Lamaster finished up this season with Janesville (NAHL) where he was impressive before sustaining a knee injury. Lamaster is committed to the University of Wisconsin for the 19/20 season.

"There is so much to like about this kid both on and off the ice, I think he is worth a late pick flyer, I've seen less talented players taken in the later rounds." HP Scout, Dusten Braaksma

NR	LAPOINTE, PHILIPPE	LINCOLN	USHL	5' 11.0"	194 lbs	RW

Lapointe is a 3rd Round Draft pick of the Lincoln Stars (USHL) as well as 7th Round pick by the Guelph Storm (OHL) out of the Chicago Mission and Shattuck St. Mary's programs. Lapointe had a bit of an up and down season this season with Lincoln and saw 4 games for the USNTDP U18 squad. Lapointe has quick hands and playmaking ability with the puck on his tape but plays a largely pass first game on the perimeter in offensive situations, which limits his offensive upside at the stage. Lapointe has decent size and has developed physically the last couple years which has allowed him to add another physical dimension to his game but needs to show more willingness to take the puck to the hard areas of the ice. Philippe has a good motor and awareness in open space and is able to close on his opponents and pressure the puck carrier successfully. Lapointe will join a talented recruiting class at the University of Michigan this year.

"I don't think he'll get drafted. Limited skill, works hard....goes to the net. He'll be fine in college but too slow for NHL." - NHL Scout, March 2018

"His skating will be the thing that holds him back." - NHL Scout, April 2018

"I like his compete but like all the scouts I've spoken to, his skating is the problem." HP Scout, Mark Edwards

47	LAUKO, JAKUB	CHOMUTOV	CZREP	6' 0.0"	179 lbs *	LC

Jakub Lauko had an interesting development year while playing with Pirati Chomutov in the Czech league where he accumulated 9 points in 42 games, including 6 assists. His team was relegated but managed to avoid demotion, he contributed 3 points in 6 games to help avoid going to the Czech2 league. Internationally, he was featured at the Hlinka where he had a good performance in front of a home crowd while scoring 4 goals in five games. He was one of the few players to play at both the U18's and U20's, registering 6 points in 7 games at the U18's while being an assistant captain for his squad, and 1 point in 6 games where he was featured in a depth role at the U20's.

Lauko is one of the more dynamic, yet enigmatic players featured in this draft. He's got tremendous tools, featuring some of the best pure speed generated through an explosive first couple of steps. There's few players who can make highlight-reel level plays like he can. We have watched him carve through an entire team before scoring bar-down, unfortunately these are nothing more than inconsistent flashes to his game as opposed to being a consistent aspect of it. His rate of execution is poor considering the amount of high-end chances he can generate in a game by using his breakaway speed. This is largely due to his inability to hide his intentions with the puck on his stick when he's looking to shoot. He's got a solid release point and has both a heavy wrist-shot and slapshot but unfortunately his mechanics are noticeable to a goalie in most sequences which allows them to square up on time. That being said, this was a larger problem earlier in the year when he was displaying a high-degree of tunnel vision. He's a possession player who loves to drive play with the puck on his stick but this was a double-edged sword for him, where he would decide to shoot at severe-angles with better passing options in-front of the slot area or around the net, this also applied to breakouts, where he would look to use his speed after failing to recognize that he had a passing option that would create a more efficient breakout for his team. His decision making was poor in most games, but by the half-way point in the year, he started showing some adaptation in his game in the Czech-league. This applied when he was forced to rely less on his tools and more on his teammates at the U20 World Junior Championships as well. When he was dealing with older, stronger, and faster players, we started seeing him adapt and accommodate his skill-set. After getting shut-down in the offensive-end during the first-half of the U20's, he started using his vision and his plus passing ability to generate several chances for his team in the second-half, which helped him develop line chemistry with Kurovsky and led to his best games of the event.

One of the most surprising aspects of Lauko's development was how he went from an underdeveloped motor while showing little in the way of compete last season, to two of his best attributes becoming his compete level and high-octane motor this past year. Jakub is willing to play at a difficult pace for opposing teams to keep up with during forechecking sequences, he's also not afraid to put his body on the line in heavy traffic areas while searching for rebounds, and he's willing to take up shooting lanes so that he can block incoming point shots, which has caused him to suffer several injuries throughout the season. This adds to his enigmatic play, in the sense that we thought if he could develop the attributes described above, he would become one of the higher ranked forwards in this draft. That's not been the case due to his inability to make consistent reads on a shift-to-shift basis overall, calling into question his hockey sense.

We thought of Lauko heading into the year, as a player who had top-6 potential with a high-offensive ceiling given his toolkit, but now we think his development tracks more as a high-energy, third-line winger, who can specialize on the penalty-kill while being occasionally slotted into a top-6 role depending on the game.

"Interesting player. One of our biggest issues with him coming into the season was his consistency with work ethic. He did a fantastic job fixing this issue this season." - HP Scout, Mark Edwards

"Liked his interview. He was very good." - NHL Scout, June 2018

NR	LEBEDEFF, DANIEL	JANESVILLE	NAHL	6' 1.75"	194 lbs	G

After spending parts of the last two seasons with Madison (USHL), Lebedeff headed to nearby Janesville (NAHL) where he was given more of an opportunity to see ice time. While Lebedeff did see an increase in his games played compared to last season Daniel missed some games due to a concussion and despite some steady play coming back from injury he saw himself lose playing time in the playoffs due to some outstanding play by Janesville's other goalie Garrett Nieto.

Lebedeff is an athletic butterfly goalie with quick lateral movements. He can lose his crease laterally from time to time but his athleticism allows him to recover quickly. Lebedeff excels on making the first save but poor rebound control has lead to a lot of second chance goals against. He rebounds well from giving up early or bad goals and seems to get stronger as the game moves along. Daniel battles hard and doesn't give up on plays. Lebedeff is a goalie that seems to build off momentum and can go on a run when he is able to string together starts. That of which bodes well for him as he heads to the University of Wisconsin this fall as he should be given every opportunity to earn the starting job as a freshman.

"He had an up and down year and battled an injury but I'm not ready to throw in the towel on him yet, there is a lot of athleticism there." HP Scout, Dusten Braaksma (April, 2018)

NR	LEPPARD, JACKSON	PRINCE GEORGE	WHL	6' 1.25"	200 lbs	LW

A high pick in the 2015 bantam draft which showed some strong top end talent. Leppard fits among the higher end WHL player for the 2018 draft, he carried a big load for a poor Prince George team often lining up on the top line and managed decent numbers on one of the lowest scoring teams in the league (15G 21A). Good puck pursuer that attacks 50/50 battles with a good compete level based on his aggressive nature of play and ability to skate at a higher tempo; has the size and aggression to win battles with his body and digs puck our with a solid reach. Shows good north/south speed and will drive hard to the net to create chances for himself, or work hard on the forecheck to start the cycle and grind out in the difficult areas. In viewings saw him execute with his hands on good individual efforts protecting pucks, using toe drags to create scoring chances and working well on screen and in tight areas around the crease; likely the place he'll have to make a living at the pro level. A quick thinker that has a decent hockey IQ that helps with his timing around the net but his strength will be to utilize the power game, leaning on defenders and driving hard to the blue paint. The type of player that needed to be scouted closely in his situation and he can go unnoticed because he wasn't surrounded with skill, but Leppard could be a big asset to a highly skilled line helping open up space and compliment other finesse players. A team will like his work ethic if it gets a little more consistent but a good prospect asset for any organization.

NR	LEUFVENIUS, HUGO	SARNIA	OHL	6' 1.75"	224 lbs	LW

Leufvenius is a big bodied winger with competitiveness to his game. Hugo utilizes his size and strength well to enhance his offensive game. He shows a willingness to utilize his body for puck protection purposes and to will his body into the high percentage scoring areas. Leufvenius has shown a good shot and release but needs to become more assertive with his shot, often passing on quality opportunities to look pass. His vision and passing skills are good but not great. Hugo is a player who lacks one great talent, but one that does a number of little things well. He is at his best when using his frame to win puck and board battles and creating off the cycle. Leufvenius will need to elevate his skating to be effective at the next level as he lacks quickness in his first step and generates just an average speed. He does show a long stride with power behind it which can make him difficult in transition when he is able to generate momentum. Hugo has room to elevate his defensive zone play as he can make some questionable reads and decisions.

"Played good in the playoffs, big guy but doesn't play big. I worry a bit about his conditioning. He looked heavy in September and still looked heavy in the playoffs. He has underrated skill though." NHL Scout, May 2018

"Has skill and can make some plays but consistency is an issue with him." - NHL Scout, May 2018

"Probably not a player who would make my list if I was putting together my area list for a team." - HP Scout, Mark Edwards

NR	LEVIN, DAVID	SUDBURY	OHL	5' 10.25"	180 lbs	LC

Levin is a skilled winger with intriguing offensive. David is at his best in possession where he is able to utilize his puck handling skills and creative approach to generate offensive opportunities. He shows good awareness of his teammates and recognizes how to attack space effectively. David shows an ability to put himself in area where he can create for both himself and his teammates. Levin is at his best when he is able to make a quick decision and move the puck quickly. He can tend to over handle the puck and stick-handle himself out of idea positioning or turn the puck over. In possession Levin shows an elusiveness to his game, using his edges and quick feet in combination with his puck skills to slip checks and create space. David does need to become heavier on the puck however as when opponents do put a body on him he can easily cough up possession. David's compete level tends to waiver.

Levin is able to utilize his edges to make some impact on the forecheck but can be soft along the wall and in puck battles, limiting his ability to create a change of possession. Levin did begin to show more aggression to his game as the season progressed, however it tended to come out of frustration. Improving his play away from the puck and positional awareness in the defensive zone will be necessary to have any chance to progress to the next level. Levin shows great skill, but the tools surrounding his skill have been a work in progress since we began watching him.

"He's skilled, you better not sleep on him." - NHL Scout, November 2017

"He has tons of skill but he's another guy who struggles with the subtleties of the game." - NHL Scout, January 2018

"He's a pond hockey player to me...elite skill but doesn't play smart. Skating is an issue and he doesn't play with any pace. Not a guy who will be on my list." January 2018

"Not on my list." NHL Scout, May 2018

"Going back to his OHL Draft year I was never too excited about the style of game Levin played. I saw skill, but he never played a smart pro style game. It was always a game filled with too many dangle attempts, too many turnovers and not enough compete. I haven't seen anything since he started to play in Sudbury to change my mind. In short, he's just not my cup of tea and not a player who would make my final OHL area list if I was with a team." - HP Scout, Mark Edwards

NR	LEWANDOWSKI, MITCHELL	MICHIGAN ST	NCAA	5' 9.0"	184 lbs	LW

Lewandowski is coming off a decent freshman season for the Spartans that saw him put up 19 goals and 15 assists in 36 games plays which finished 2nd on his team in scoring. Lewandowski started his freshman season off of fire with 9 goals and 9 assists in its first 14 games but then only registered 4 goals and 2 assists after January 18th. Mitchell is an undersized winger but has a strong lower body that allows him to be strong on his skates and difficult to separate from the puck. Mitchell shows good work ethic to win puck races and battles and plays with a physical and fearless edge that allows him to overcome some of his lack of size. While none of his offensive attributes can be categorized as elite, his hockey sense in all areas of the ice is what will give him a chance to play pro hockey down the road.

"I have seen Mitchell play a lot of hockey the last three seasons both in the USHL and NCAA and one thing that always stands out is his work ethic both around and away from the puck, he's going to give you effort. His play to start this year certainly opened some eyes but as the season wore on you can see he really started to hit a wall, which is not uncommon among freshman in the NCAA where the competition is bigger and stronger across the board." HP Scout, Dusten Braaksma

| 145 | LILJA, DAVID | KARLSKOGA | SWEDEN-2 | 5' 11.25" | 173 lbs | LC |

Lilja played this past season in Allsvenskan, which is the second-best men's league in Sweden, and had 8 points in 37 games. He also played for Sweden in different U-18 tournaments this year, including the Ivan Hlinka Tournament in August and the World Under- 18s in April. Lilja has average size and lacks strength at the moment. Often, along the boards and in front of the net, he'll be easily handled by an opposing player who is stronger than him; opponents can take him out of the play or neutralize his stick. He will definitely need to get stronger physically to win more puck battles if he wants to play at a higher level. However, he has a strong hockey IQ and makes smart plays all over the ice. In the offensive zone (mostly on the power play) he does a good job keeping his feet moving and not standing still, making it tougher to counter him. He can surprise opponents with a quick burst of speed to beat them wide, but overall, his speed is just average. He makes smart plays in all three zones and also works hard on the backcheck. We saw him make great efforts this year to come back and eventually steal the puck from an opponent with his quick stick. Offensively, he showed nice vision and an ability to make some good passes. Overall, he didn't show a high upside offensively, but his smarts and vision make him an interesting player in the later rounds of the draft.

| NR | LILLIBRIDGE, GRAHAM | CHICAGO | USHL | 5' 9.0" | 156 lbs | LD |

Originally out of the Chicago Mission Program, Lillibridge is a re-entry prospect for this year's draft, is finishing up his 3rd USHL season after being tendered by Muskegon for the 15/16 season, eventually traded to Chicago where he has played the last two seasons. Graham is an undersized defenseman that moves pucks effectively in all 3 zones. There is no doubt Graham needs to get stronger, he can easily get dominated in front of his own net and in puck battles but his anticipation and ability to read situations give him a fighting chance in a lot of situations. His sound angles to pucks, clean footwork and stick handling allow him to escape an aggressive fore-check and he always seems to leave himself outs and his head is always up and surveying the ice on the breakout. Lillibridge is creative at the top of the power play, is active in the zone and doesn't limit himself to just playing at the top of the power play, he plays a rover style and is able to move around the zone and is hard for the opponents Penalty Killers to keep track of. Lillibridge can execute all types of shots from the point but they all lack velocity and he is better at puck distribution than goal scoring in the offensive end. After three successful USHL season's Lillibridge will join a really solid recruiting class for Yale University this fall. Defensively there is no doubt his size is a concern going forward but Graham relies on his skating to keep him good defensive position and is able to be more aggressive in certain situations because he is able to recover using his skating abilities. Like most undersized defenseman, Graham can get exposed when bigger stronger forwards drive the net against him.

"I like Graham's game but he's more of the wait and see as a possible NCAA Free Agent prospect for me, I certainly think he could make a successful AHL or European defenseman down the road, he's a smart and skilled player" HP Scout, Dusten Braaksma

| 137 | LINDBOM, OLOF | DJURGARDEN JR. | SWEDEN-JR. | 6' 0.5" | 173 lbs | G |

Olof Lindbom started for Djurgardens IF in the SuperElit where he put up a 3.10 GAA and an .897 save percentage in 20 games. In international play, he had a 2.50 GAA and .885 save percentage in 4 games at the Hlinka but was much more impressive at the U18's where he captured the best goaltender award at the tournament, by putting up a 1.66 GAA and a .949 save percentage in 6 games.

Lindbom is a highly technical goaltender with a mature skill-set for his age and a wide frame. His movement is fluid and he doesn't over extend himself or throw himself out of position on most save attempts. His technique is well developed which can be seen in his butterfly and he takes up a tremendous amount of the net in his reverse V-H which doesn't leave a lot of openings for shooters, especially once he gets squared up. This allows him to absorb rebounds at a high-rate. He's a composed goalie who reacts properly during most scramble sequences though he lacks explosive movement to get back into position if he's completely misread a play. He's got plus reflexes and is capable of extending when needed to for difficult saves during broken plays or screen shots, which was seen during several reactionary kick-saves during the season. His mobility for his size is a plus and he's fluid in his movement both when transitioning from his post-play and when moving laterally across the crease. His glove hand is above average but it's his blocker-side that stands out due to his ability to absorb rebounds off of high-shots that are difficult for most goalies to handle. He's also capable of tracking the puck through screens and on recovery save attempts, which was a major reason he was able to get himself squared up after the initial save on most plays. Another aspect of his game that was on display this year was that when his team needed a well-timed save most, he had a tendency to pull through, especially at the U18's.

One of the most appealing aspects of Lindbom is that he has no real deficiencies and from a developmental stand-point, there's a lot of refined ability already built into the fabric of his game, which is rare considering his age. That being said, there's no elite attribute that he has either, he might not have as high a ceiling compared to some of the other goalies in this draft class but he does have a solid foundation to build from.

| 162 | LISKA, ADAM | KITCHENER | OHL | 5' 10.25" | 184 lbs | LC |

Adam Liska is a Slovakian winger who was selected 34th overall in the CHL Import Draft by the Kitchener Rangers. He had some difficulty adjusted to the smaller ice surface in his first season in North America, while producing 31 points in 62 games, including 19 assists. In the playoffs, he produced 3 assists in 19 games. Internationally, he was featured at the U20 World Junior Championships, where he posted 1 goal in 5 games.

His hockey-sense is mixed.and his motor and pace can be hit or miss depending on the game. We have seen him make terrific defensive reads on the penalty-kill, take the puck away and then compete for extended periods of time along the boards, but we have also seen him go invisible on the ice where he doesn't skate hard enough or battle effectively. He's not the kind of shooter that can erase a poor game by wiring the puck into the back of the net with any regularly as well. His shot has average velocity and he didn't display the ability to change the angle very well in our viewings, though his release is above-average, it can come off his stick quickly. Another area of improvement for Liska, is his first few steps aren't developed enough given his build, though he does have solid straight-line speed when he hits open-ice.

We respect aspects of his game but there are some stoppers when projecting him for the NHL.

"Just ok skill but he plays hard. Skating is holding him back a bit. I have respect for his game...he was asked to play a role and he played it." - NHL Scout, May 2018

| 194 | LOHEIT, LUKE | MINNETONKA | HIGH-MN | 6' 0.0" | 183 lbs | RW |

It's rare to see a senior forward who is playing in the High School ranks finish 5th on his team in scoring with 15 goals and 20 assists in 30 games and be considered a solid NHL Draft prospect but that is the case in regards to Luke Loheit. Loheit played on a very deep roster and was called upon to play more of defensive roll for Minnetonka that eventually went on to win its first Minnesota Boys State Title. In many viewings Loheit was called upon to play against other teams top lines in a very tough conference. Loheit has good size and skating ability. He has a long powerful skating stride that allows him to cover a lot of ice quickly. He has good instincts in his positioning and ability to read the play when the other team has the puck. Loheit's game is not without some offensive skill, he has a quick and accurate wrist shot and has shown the ability to pick the corners and he can handle the puck effectively in order to buy time for players to get open. Loheit plays a mature two-way game for his age and displays quality leadership abilities and makes others around him better. Loheit is committed to Minnesota Duluth for 19/20 and USHL rights are owned by the Madison Capitols.

"He didn't put up a ton of points but Luke was easily one of the more mature players I saw in the Minnesota High School ranks this year, without him I don't think Minnetonka goes on the run they do. He really impressed me throughout the playoffs and at the State Tournament where he dominated." HP Scout, Dusten Braaksma

"I think he'll be a late pick. He's got size, a shot and a powerful skater." - NHL Scout, April 2018

"He's a mean, nasty rugged player who can skate." - NHL Scout, April 2018

"Hockey sense is his issue so I don't have him as a draft." - NHL Scout, April 2018

| NR | LUDVIG, JOHN | PORTLAND | WHL | 6' 0.5" | 186 lbs | LD |

John Ludvig played in a depth-role for the Winterhawks this year, while also getting some penalty-killing time. He produced 7 points in 51 games, including 5 assists. In the playoffs, he had 3 points in 11 games.

Ludvig is a mobile shut-down defenseman who competes without the puck and is willing to play a physical brand of hockey. He's a powerful kid who has a good first-step and impressive agility given his stocky frame. He used his four-way mobility to alleviate pressure in the defensive-end, as well as attempt to transition the puck out of dangerous areas. Although not an overly impressive puck-rusher when we viewed him, he did display an accurate first pass, and even hit a great stretch-pass for a primary assist in one of our viewings. Arguably his best asset is his compete level, he plays on the edge and is willing to punish players who attempt to drive towards the net area and causes his opponents to react to his presence on the ice. Furthermore, he's capable of dropping the gloves to shift the momentum of a game or stand-up for his teammates. Although he has some positive defensive abilities, John doesn't have a lot of high-end hockey skills or offensive-attributes in his game. This causes him to rely on his powerful slapshot and decent puck distribution skills to generate from the blueline. He plays at a good pace and has a good build for his shut-down playing style but lacks upside at this time.

| 22 | LUNDESTROM, ISAC | LULEA | SWEDEN | 6' 0.3" | 183 lbs* | LC |

Isac Lundestrom accomplished a rare feat by playing full-time in the SHL as a 16-year-old last season. In his sophomore year, he not only managed to stay up in the SHL full-time but developed to the point where he was featured in all situations while playing on a scoring line where he put up 15 points in 42 games, including 6 goals. He also made the U20 World Junior team which was an accomplishment in its own right due to the offensive-depth on Sweden where he put up 2 goals in 7 games, while having a standout performance against Slovakia despite getting limited minutes.

Lundestrom is a tactical two-way center who has advanced positioning in all three-zones. He's an efficient player who understands both where his teammates want him to end-up and where his opponents are attempting to go, he's capable of reading plays in advance. Due to his intelligence, he doesn't over-extend himself in certain sequences, instead opting to expend his tank when the play calls for it. This can make him appear to lack a high-end motor at times, or play at a slower pace, however he's good at recognizing the tempo and rhythm of a game and molding his play to what's needed on the ice. For instance, he might appear not to be too quick at first glance if the play doesn't require him to skate hard, however when skating to support his defense, or when transitioning the puck over the neutral zone during breakouts, or taking advantage of odd-man rushes, he's capable of entering another gear. His skating mechanics are refined and he can generate a good amount of straight-line speed, though he could use more explosiveness in his first couple of steps. Intelligent players usually can change their pacing to suit the situation and that's what Isac has demonstrated the ability to do throughout the season. Although his hockey IQ was one of the main reason's he was able to make the SHL at such a young age, it's also due to his physical maturity. Lundestrom is a well-built kid who's got a powerful base that makes him difficult to play against during forechecking sequences and in the defensive-end when he's supporting his teammates below the goal-line. Additionally, he's difficult to knock off the puck and is good at guarding the puck while peeling off of his opponents. Despite having a calm demeanour on the ice, he's got the ability to deliver a big hit when the play calls for it and can play a grinding style to force the defense to play heavy minutes.

Although a cerebral player, Lundestrom's offensive ceiling isn't as high as some of the other top-end forwards in this year's draft class. That being said, he does have plus puck-skills, where he can use his hands in tight to the net. His passing is precise and he has plus vision which allows him to make passes consistently, we have seen him make several nice give-and-go sequences throughout the season. Furthermore, his release point on his wrist-shot is above-average and he's demonstrated the ability to change the angle slightly while in motion. It generates a decent amount of power as well, though he's not great at masking his shooting movement before he releases it. When he's not effective offensively, he can still be a useful player due to having an advanced defensive game for his age. He's positioned well in the defensive-end which allows him to get in the way of shooting lanes and he's not a player who cheats on a shift.

Lundestrom's a mature player who plays a complete game and looks to have one of the higher-floors featured out of the top-end centres in the draft.

"He's a responsible player and it translates well when he plays down the middle. Skates well, good on is edges and a smart player. I'd like to see him shoot a bit more often and maybe drive the net a bit more as well." - HP Scout, Mark Edwards

| 16 | LUNDKVIST, NILS | LULEA | SHL | 5' 11.3" | 172 lbs* | RD |

Nils Lundkvist wasn't on anyone's first-round radar to begin the 2017-18 season. It took some time for him to adjust to the SHL after getting called up, but he began making noise around Christmas after worked his way into the starting lineup, playing 18-20 minutes per game. Lundkvist recorded two goals and three assists in 28 games and played in a pair of playoff games. Lulea were eliminated from the SHL playoffs in a best-of-three, and he was sent down to the J20 team for playoff help. He tallied five assists and Lulea lost the Bronze Medal game to Orebro.

Lundkvist a two-way, physical defender who is incredible at moving the puck out of his defensive zone, regularly escaping pressure and dishing out smart first passes. He's not very tall but he's got a solid frame which allows him to take a hit while still being able to make a play, which was one of the reasons he was good at dealing with the forecheck in our viewings. His frame allows him to generate a lot of power and when combined with his aggressiveness at the line, it resulted in some impressive hits when standing players up. Furthermore, his positioning improved throughout his SHL year as he became more comfortable with the pace of play, which in turn helped him run a good gap where he didn't let opponents get around him easily. What allowed him to adapt was his hockey-sense. He's a smart player that understood how to assert himself in all three-zones and this enhanced his ability to make decisive-plays. As an example, we have seen him react quickly to his teammates turn-over in the neutral zone, readjust his positioning while surveying his opponents passing option, before aggressively cutting off their pass attempt which has resulted in a lost scoring chance due to how quickly he gathered the information on the ice before executing

His transitional play once the puck is on his stick is very impressive. His main attribute that gives him the ability to rush the puck is his exceptional skating, characterized by four-way mobility and excellent pivoting mechanics. He used a combination of intelligence, confidence and speed to pinch appropriately which resulted in several scoring chances and a couple of goals when we watched him, after driving down the left-wing and finding soft-ice behind defensive coverage. Furthermore, his poise with the puck allowed him to generate several chances off the rush and he's an adept passer who threaded technical saucer passes as well as soft passes that landed on the tape. His shot's a laser, he's good at recognizing when his shooting lanes are open and doesn't hesitate before releasing powerful point shots that are difficult for goalies to handle. Additionally, he's got an array of fakes at the line and when combined with his skating ability, it makes it difficult for the opposition to pick up his movements and what he's attempting to do with the puck on his stick.

Lundkvist is a unique defender in the 2018 draft. In a class that has a lot of large defenders without a lot of high-end skill and a ton of smaller defenders that have skill but aren't as physically mature, Nils is an outlier in the sense that he's got a really impressive offensive skill-set to go along with a physical dimension to his game. He's arguably one of the most well-rounded defenseman in the draft which is why we think so highly of him.

"He's was as good as Boqvist if not better at Five Nations" - NHL Scout, April 2018

"There were a few times I mistook him for Boqvist" - NHL Scout, April 2018

"High end puck mover. He's smart and and a fantastic skater. He's a first rounder all day long." - NHL Scout, April 2018

"I loved him in Plymouth (Five Nations) and our euro scout is really high on him. He has him in the first round." - NHL Scout, April 2018

"He's a right handed Ty Smith." - NHL Scout, May 2018

"He popped on our radar late in the fall and was impressive. He's one of my personal favourites in this draft class. He's smart and has skill. He can really skate and he creates offence. He defends better than a lot of defenseman in this class. I thought he was fantastic at the Five Nations in Plymouth and I really liked him in league play back home." - HP Scout, Mark Edwards

"Several scouts mentioned him to me as one of their best interviews at the combine and one scout told me he was easily his top interview of the week. I wish I could share some of his answers to questions because they were excellent. He also tested well. As if I needed more reasons to have him ranked high." - HP Scout, Mark Edwards

205	MACDONALD, ANDERSON	MONCTON	QMJHL	6' 1.8"	209 lbs *	LW

MacDonald was acquired by Moncton over the summer from Sherbrooke, after things went south with the Phoenix organization. Back near his home, it was a new start for MacDonald, who started his season by playing for Canada at the Ivan Hlinka Tournament, winning the gold medal. With Moncton, the young power-forward had a slow start this year, but eventually found his game and started scoring his fair share of goals. MacDonald, first and foremost, is a goal-scorer; he's really good around the net. He has quick hands, and is quick to put his stick on loose pucks in the slot or jump on a rebound. He's also good at tipping pucks; he has good hand-eye coordination. Goal wise, he didn't improve on last year's totals, which explains a little why he slipped this year in our rankings. He made some strides with his overall game, though, and is less of a liability when he doesn't have the puck. He's still very far from becoming a good two-way forward that can play in all situations. His skating abilities have not improved a lot in the past 2-3 seasons. It is still a big question mark with him, when you see that the NHL is now a skating league. He has trouble keeping up with the pace when playing high-calibre game like the Ivan Hlinka Tournament, the Top Prospects' Game or against quicker teams in the QMJHL. He's a big body, but could be more assertive with his physical play. His lack of speed hurts him when on the forecheck.

Overall, MacDonald knows how to score, and that should get him drafted, but the rest of his game will hurt his draft stock.

"He's been too hard to find on the ice when I've seen him." - NHL Scout, December 2017

"Pro shot pro release." NHL Scout, May 2018

"Not a player that impressed me this year. His compete level is very low. Not sure I'd want to draft him at any point of the draft, just not my cup of tea." - HP Scout, Mark Edwards

NR	MACDOUGALL, MATTHEW	WINDSOR	OHL	5' 9.5"	170 lbs	LW

MacDougall is a competitive, undersized winger with an intelligence to his game. Matthew plays an effective two-way game, utilizing his combination of hockey sense and skill to excel. While MacDougall does lack an individual trait that he does at an elite level, he is able to do many things well and has a strong understanding of the game. He shows good skating abilities and slightly above average speed, Matthew is able to utilize his speed in various areas of the game. He's tenacious on the forecheck and uses his ability to anticipate to beat opponents to the puck or create turnovers. He shows his speed and tenacity on the back-check where he provides smart and quality back pressure allowing him to tie up his check or create a turnover. Despite his size, MacDougall shows a willingness to take the puck to high traffic areas and be assertive with his willingness to take a hit to make a high percentage play. He is well rounded offensively in his ability to move the puck, but also to finish plays, however neither is an elite stand-out trait. Matthew is able to create space for line mates with subtle pick plays and by driving lanes, while he often position's himself strategically following a net drive or pick play to receive a puck in space. An engaged and aware defensive presence, MacDougall gets his stick and body in lanes and does a good job forcing the play to the outside. A complimentary type player, Matthew would enhance his effectiveness in puck and position battles by adding strength. This would also enhance his effectiveness in possession when driving the goal or looking to become assertive by taking the puck to scoring areas.

NR	MACPHERSON, JUSTIN	NIAGARA	OHL	6' 0.5"	171 lbs	LD

MacPherson plays a solid game on both sides of the puck. He skates well so he covers ice and closes gaps quickly and has certainly improved in defensive positioning and reads from his rookie OHL season. His game is positive whereby he is steady in his own end, will make good outlet passes and will chip in offensively every now and then. He transitions the puck up to forwards fairly well. MacPherson is not overly physical. He fits the mold of KISS: Keep It Simple, Steady defenseman.

"Got better as the year went on..a little bit of a vanilla player for me. He defends ok but didn't generate a whole lot of offense. One of those doesn't really hurt you but doesn't really help you players." NHL Scout, May 2018

"I like him as a junior player but not for what I look for as far as an NHL prospect. goes - NHL Scout, May 2018

"Pretty simple but solid player, very vanilla. Not a guy that would be on my list if I was with a team though.- HP Scout, Mark Edwards

82	MADDEN, TYLER	TRI-CITY	USHL	5' 10.8"	150 lbs *	RC

It was a bit of an up and down season for Madden, which saw him get traded from Central Illinois to Tri- City near the midpoint of the season and there certainly was an adjustment period for him with his new team. Madden went to a much deeper team and didn't see the same opportunities he was getting with Central Illinois which contributed to a dip in his offensive production, however by the Spring, flashes of his offensive ability started to show itself again, finishing with 9 goals and 11 Assists in 32 Games with the Storm as well as being named MVP in the USHL/NHL Top Prospects game, scoring two goals for Team East. Madden also represented the USA at the World Junior A Challenge where he registered 3 goals and 1 assist for the American squad.

Madden is a highly skilled offensive player that is able to think and process situations quickly. He still has a ways to go physically, as his slender build lead to some struggles in what was his first season in the USHL, coming from Avon Old Farms Prep School last season. Tyler has quick hands and feet with puck on his stick, he has the ability to beat defenders one on one with his skill by assessing his opponents body positioning and exposing the time and space they give. Madden can play a little too much on the perimeter with the puck at times and needs to develop more of an urgency to getting himself and the puck into high scoring areas but he distributes the puck accurately and on time. Madden plays a responsible game at both ends of the ice, stays in solid defensive posture and supports the play in his own zone. Madden relies on his quick hands and stick work to win puck battles but will get muscled off of pucks along the wall. As Madden gets stronger his ability to win puck battles will improve given his skill set. Madden will be off the Northeastern University in the fall where the added gym time that NCAA provides will help his development considerably.

"Had some bumps in the road throughout the year but seemed to learn and get better from them, as most players with his hockey smarts tend to do. Has the mental makeup and skill to adapt to different situations." HP Scout, Dusten Braaksma

"He's easily one of the best players on USA" (WJAC) NHL Scout, December 2017

"I don't dislike him but I just like a lot of other guys more." - NHL Scout, December 2017

"He's skilled and smart but he doesn't skate all that well." - NHL Scout, April 2018

"One of those players I like but I'm not going to go to bat to draft him because his compete level wavered for me." - NHL Scout, April 2018

"I think he could go as high as the 3rd and as low as the 5th." NHL Scout, April 2018

"I liked him at the Fall Classic and in Truro. He has some skill and was one of the smarter players on the ice. I also interviewed him in Truro...nice kid who gave me thoughtful answers. He's got a very slight frame though and has a ways to go physically." - HP Scout Mark Edwards

"He good good reviews on his interviews at the NHL Combine." - HP Scout, Mark Edwards

| 170 | MALIK, ZACK | SUDBURY | OHL | 6' 2.0" | 165 lbs | LD |

Malik is a mobile, two-way defender with intriguing physical traits and good hockey sense. Zack possesses a rangy frame with a large wingspan that allows him to enhance his contain and elevate his defensive game. A good skater with some room to continue to improve his four-way quickness, Malik shows good gap control and is effective taking away time and space from opponents. He makes consistently strong reads in the neutral zone allowing him to create turnovers. In the defensive zone. While he has room to become stronger and more assertive with his size, his smarts in combination with his reach and compete allow him to remain fairly effective. Zack's offensive game is a work in progress. While Raw, Malik does show a willingness to get up ice, but could become more assertive in attacking the goal once gaining the offensive zone or more frequently sneaking in from his point position. He does show a good point shot and is able to create shooting lanes, however needs to get the puck on net more frequently. Malik possesses an intriguing amount of tools, however is still raw in some areas.

"First time I saw him this year was a game in Oshawa and he intrigued me with a solid game. It took me a while to see him again because he struggled with injuries this year. I chased him around late in the season when he returned from injury and he struggled in his own end." HP Scout, Mark Edwards

| 130 | MALYSHEV, ANTON | YAROSLAVL 2 | RUSSIA-JR. | 6' 0.0" | 185 lbs | RD |

Anton Malyshev is a two-way transitional puck moving defenseman with some bite. He played for Loko Yaroslavl in the MHL where he produced 10 points in 31 games and 1 point in 8 playoff games. Internationally, he was featured at every major tournament where he was used in all situations and saved his best performance for the U18's where he not only captained the team but was also named one of the top three Russian players, while getting an assist in 5 games.

Malyshev is an advanced player in the defensive-end with excellent defensive-awareness. He's got a wide-stance but generates very good four-way mobility which compliments his game since he's displayed aggressive defensive tendencies and plays at a high-pace. Despite being slightly undersized for a defender, he's got a powerful base which he uses to deliver well-timed hits against opponents who are attempting to drive wide on him. If he fails to knock them off the puck, he looks to use an active stick and his plus defensive positioning to keep them to the outside. He's adept at reading plays and watching them develop in-front of him when he doesn't have the puck, then reacting to the situations correctly in the majority of our viewings. For example, he's very quick to support his defensive-partner when they are overwhelmed and skates into shooting lanes consistently by interpreting where the shot is coming from in advance. Furthermore, he's very good at handling one-on-one defensive-coverage, keeping track of his opponent but rarely throwing himself out of position when he decides to engage along the boards. One of the other notable aspects of his game is the ability to close-gaps due to his acceleration. Forwards are rarely given a lot of time and space to make a play when he's on the ice. Perhaps his most important attribute in the defensive-zone is his ability to deal with pressure during forechecking sequences, it was rare to see him turn the puck over. This was due to his poise while holding the puck, his ability to process information on the ice fast, and his pivoting mechanics which allowed him to evade his opponents. After alleviating pressure from forecheckers, he displayed a sharp first-pass consistently.

He's efficient at walking the line using his lateral mobility which helps him change the angle of his passing and shooting lanes. This allowed him to get his hard wrist-shot and slapshot through traffic, yet he tends to sacrifice the accuracy of the shot in order to generate a lot of velocity. He's not a dynamic defenseman, but he can distribute the puck quickly and has the skating ability and the offensive-awareness needed to pinch at the appropriate times for the most part. He's also reliable at the defensive blueline since he's good at keeping pucks in and has the awareness needed to determine how much time he has to make a play before a potential turnover occurs.

Malyshev might not have a high-end offensive-ceiling compared to some of the other higher ranked defenders in the 2018 draft, but he's excellent in the defensive-zone and he's a kid who can skate the puck out of high-danger areas and transition the puck up the ice with his passing ability, which are skills that NHL teams covet.

| NR | MANDERVILLE, ETHAN | OTTAWA | CCHL | 6' 4.25" | 191 lbs | RC |

Ethan is a big Center that plays in the CCHL for the Ottawa Jr Sens after being drafted by the 67's in the 2016 OHL draft. He previously played in Kanata for the last 2 years and was traded to Ottawa. He's a big two-way center that understands the game well, is smart at reading plays, very reliable in his own zone, knows where to be and who to pick up in the defensive zone. Manderville is not a flashy player, he competes every night, he played on weak Kanata team last year and was able to put up some decent points, though he ended the year with not a lot of points for Ottawa when traded over. Ethan at the next level won't be a point producer, he will be more of a reliable center that is very smart in his own zone. Ethan's skating ability is what hurts him for the next level, he needs to work on his acceleration and quickness as it takes him a couple strides to get top speed, also with his size he needs to be more physical whether on the forecheck or just finishing checks as he tends to avoid those areas. We think with his size and strength, he could be that much more of a force on the ice and would create more offensive chances for himself. Ethan could be one of those kids that falls late in the draft; but could potentially down the road turn into a player if he works on the areas of his game that need improving. He has the size, smarts, and the pedigree but needs to fill into his body and figure out what kind if player he wants to be.

"I was in Ottawa on a Thursday after a Wednesday night game in Gatineau and asked our area guy if I needed to go see Ethan play that night. He said no so I chose another game. I ended up seeing him later in the year in the CJHL Top Prospects game in Mississauga and he had a solid night. One thing to note though, Port Credit arena is a very small barn and was very conducive to Ethan's weakness which is skating." - HP Scout, Mark Edwards

124 — MANDOLESE, KEVIN — CAPE BRETON — QMJHL — 6' 4.0" — 177 lbs * — G

Mandolese was the Screaming Eagles' number 1 pick in the 2016 Draft (13th overall) after playing his QMJHL draft year with the Collège Esther-Blondin in the Quebec Midget AAA league. For a second straight season he shared the workload in net with Kyle Jessiman. The Blainville native finished the season with 15 wins in 37 starts, a 3.46 goals-against average, and a .884 save-percentage, all numbers inferior to last year.

Mandolese has great size, standing over 6'03" already, although more often than not he's not aggressive enough in his crease and stays too deep. The positive with his size is that it doesn't hurt him as much as smaller goaltenders, but ideally, we would like him to be at the top of the crease, challenging shooters. With his size, if he's in a good position, he can even make saves when he doesn't see the puck from point shots. He still has a lanky frame, but he's slowly growing into it, and once he's ready to turn pro, he should be around 190-200 pounds. A key for Mandolese to reach the next level in his development will be his consistency from game to game. Since his midget days, he has had the capacity to win games by himself, only to struggle in the next one. His rebound-control is associated with his consistency. When he's on, he doesn't give up any rebounds and he's able to absorb all the shots. When he's not on his game, those rebounds come back in the slot too often. He made some improvements to his glove side since last year, but there's still work to be done with his athleticism, such as his movements from post to post and his footwork. His stats don't tell the whole story, however, as he played in front of a young and poor defense this year.

Mandolese is a bit of a project. He is still raw, but has some untapped potential to improve on in the next couple of years. He has the work ethic necessary to do so. He has the size that NHL teams covet, and if he can be more consistent, he could make a good goaltender at the pro level.

26 — MARCHENKO, KIRILL — KHANTY — RUSSIA-JR. — 6' 3.0" — 187 lbs — RW

Marchenko had an underwhelming sophomore year compared to his first season in the MHL by finishing with 16 points in 31 regular season games, including 8 goals. Though, he finished the year much stronger than when he started it, by putting up 7 points in 8 playoff games while also having success at both the Five-Nations and the U18's where he was featured on the top-line with his line-mate, Ivan Morozov.

Marchenko is a rare breed of power-forward with a lot of raw upside. He's got a broad frame, tremendous length and some of the best pure puck-skills in this year's draft which makes him very difficult to contain in the offensive-end. The skating mechanics are still a work in progress in terms of his base, he skates wide and is unorthodox with how he pushes off from a stand-still position, however he does generate surprising levels of speed in his first few steps regardless, due to having a natural athleticism which also gives him separation speed in full-flight, as well as plus edges which he uses to weave through traffic. He comes across as a kid who could turn into a great skater as he continues to grow into his body and when he further develops his base. His length, size and puck protection-skills make it very difficult to contain him when he's at his best and he uses them to drive wide while skating down the wings and doesn't mind a direct route to the net either. He's got an excellent array of dekes orchestrated through lightning quick hands and when combined with his reach, it's hard for opponents to interpret what he's' going to do with the puck on his stick. This point needs to be emphasized when taking into account that he can make a lot of his high-end moves while going at top speeds. Furthermore, he processes plays quickly, which is important with his skill-set since he does like to play at high speeds and attempt creative plays. This allows him to use his accurate and crisp passes to set up his teammates for scoring chances, and he's good at mixing up both his passing and shooting attempts. His length gives him a difficult shot for goalies to pick up and we have seen him generate a lot of power in his wrist-shot, the release point is very quick as well, as it comes off his stick in a whip like motion.

He's also engaged without the puck and has a good amount of defensive-awareness. He's got a solid motor and the ability to pick up his defensive assignments where he looks to take advantage of his reach while using an active-stick to disrupt plays. Karill uses his skating ability to backcheck effectively and he's also capable of recognizing shooting lanes where he uses his size to block incoming shots from the point.

Sometimes he's prone to turning the puck over while attempting a difficult deke or attempts the riskier play than the smarter or more effective play, but it seems like he's experimenting on the ice at times and trying to gauge what he's capable of doing. It's rare in any draft to find a 200-foot power-winger with dynamic puck-skills who's also got a high degree of hockey sense and we think Marchenko is just beginning to un tap his potential.

"A power winger who works and competes hard." - NHL Scout, May 2018

"He plays a simple game but he's very effective." - NHL Scout, May 2018

"I think he goes in the 2nd round but there are a lot of question marks. Anyone have any clue if he wants to come over here to play?" - NHL Scout, May 2018

"Need to be careful with guys like this. Is he coming to the combine?" NHL Scout, May 2018

"You gotta make sure he's coming right, but as a player I'd say he's a second rounder." - NHL Scout, May 2018

"There's some awkwardness to him but that just a physical maturity thing." -NHL Scout, May 2018

"If he develops properly, good luck stopping him off the rush. He's one of the more exciting players to watch when the puck is on his stick." - HP Scout, Brad Allen

"Powerful and skilled, he produces. He had some impressive games when I watched this season." HP Scout, Mark Edwards

| 50 | MCBAIN, JACK | TORONTO JC | OJHL | 6' 3.3" | 201 lbs * | LC |

Drafted by the Barrie Colts in the first round of the OHL Draft but opted to play Junior 'A' with the Toronto Jr Canadiens. He played with Team Canada East last season in the WJAC and had a solid showing. He was selected to the Team Canada Hlinka team back in August and got his draft season off to a strong start with a good showing. He was selected again this December to play for Canada East in the WJAC in Truro where we felt he had a mediocre showing. In January he competed in the CJHL Top Prospects game and in our opinion. missed another opportunity to impress a large number of scouts. He finished up his season playing for Canada at the U18 tournament in Russia and once gain left us wanting to see more from him.

Skating was a big issue coming out of his OHL Draft year and while it is still an area he'll really need to work on, we give him a lot of credit for how much it's improved since his Don Mills Flyers days. McBain has some skill but we question how much he'll be able to score at the NHL level. He competes hard and we feel he is a smart player. He wasn't helped by his situation this season. We saw a lot of smart plays leave his stick only to die on a teammates stick. He wasn't blessed with a ton of talent surrounding him on his Junior A team.

We were expecting a better season and were hoping to see him have better performances internationally to follow up his good Ivan Hlinka Tournament. We never saw him play a game post Hlinka that we felt warranted giving him a first round grade. We like him better on the wing and our ranking is projecting him as a winger. Based on the skill level we saw and the skating grade we have given him, he dropped significantly down our ranking from pre-season until our final list.

"He was good at the Hlinka." Several NHL Scouts

"He hasn't had a good week. (WJAC)" NHL Scout, December 2017

"I don't think he's a center. I've struggled with him all year because he hasn't played that great for me, but I love the size and he's not a dumb player." - NHL Scout, February 2018

"Needs to play with more pace...skating needs to get better. I don't think he has high end skill, I think he's good good skill. I love his energy, love his motor and his willingness to play a 200 hundred foot game but for me he's more of a 3rd line guy at this point." NHL Scout, March 2018

"He's not a centre for me. I thought his best games were on the wing." - NHL Scout, March 2018

"I think his abilities are underrated because he hasn't fully committed to being a hockey player until just recently. He's well rounded, he's smart and I think his skill is a bit undervalued. I see him as a 3rd line center or winger. Not sure of which yet because I'm not sure if he's a good enough playmaker to be center but I like the kid overall. I think he will find his way." - NHL Scout, May 2018

"I think we'll have him as a late first (rounder) if not, early in the second." - NHL Scout, May 2018

"Biggest feedback I got this year was in Truro. (WJAC) A lot of scouts were anxious to see what he could do there because they didn't like anything about scouting him on his Jr Canadiens team. The feedback was really poor. I didn't personally speak to one scout who saw him that week who raised his stock afterwards." - HP Scout, Mark Edwards

"I interviewed him after a game in Truro and I really liked the kid. He came across as honest and I thought he had a good sense of his own game. I used to coach with the Jr Canadiens and we spoke about a staffer who is still there. Jack was personable and enjoyable to talk to." - HP Scout, Mark Edwards

"If I were to make an estimate on where he gets drafted, the info I have is approximately 85% of scouts I spoke to had him as a 2nd rounder and 15% had him as a first rounder. Only takes one team though" - HP Scout, Mark Edwards

"Good feedback regarding interviews at the NHL Combine." - HP Scout, Mark Edwards

NR	MCCABE, DEVIN	LINCOLN	USHL	5' 10.0"	167 lbs	RW

McCabe came from to the USHL this season after playing for St. Paul Academy in the Minnesota High School ranks where he put up impressive offensive numbers. McCabe is a tad undersized, listed around 5'10" but possesses excellent offensive skills and playmaking ability. While he has a ways to go physically in order to get the most out of his skills, his hockey smarts allowed him to put up solid offensive numbers in his rookie season in the USHL, registering 16 goals and 17 assists for the Lincoln Stars. McCabe has a good motor and an excellent work ethic for pucks, often using 2nd and 3rd efforts to come away with pucks. While he isn't the most physical player in those situations, he uses his instincts and quick hands to win pucks away from bigger opponents. In the offensive zone, McCabe uses his vision and quick hands to make reads with the puck but isn't a player that is going to drive the offense. He has shown the willingness to take pucks to the net and pay the price in front and is an opportunistic player. McCabe has a quick, accurate shot and shows the potential to be a high end goal scorer as he continues to get stronger and add velocity to his shot. Defensively, McCabe holds up his end, he shows good effort away from the puck and has made some good defensive reads in his own end in our viewings. McCabe will play one more season in the USHL, which will give him some more time to develop physically before heading to Minnesota Duluth in 19/20.

"I like his offensive instincts and finishing ability around the net, certainly has the fearless element that is needed when you lack size and strength like he does." HP Scout, Dusten Braaksma

208	MCCORMICK, ADAM	CAPE BRETON	QMJHL	5' 10.75"	179 lbs	LD

McCormick is a very smart defenseman and we have liked him since his midget days with Fredericton in New Brunswick. He made a smooth transition to major junior thanks to his on-ice intelligence. He made good progress this year, and became a defenseman that Cape Breton coach Marc-Andre Dumont trusted in every situation this season. He has good puck-moving ability from the back end, and he can play on the power play, as he moves pucks quickly by making quick decisions with it. He's not a high-end power play guy, but he's very smart and effective with his puck decisions. At this level, he can defend pretty well. He's not the biggest player, but again, with his smarts, he understands how to stop guys off the rush with a good gap control and a quick stick. He's not a physical defenseman, but competes well in his zone and in front of his net. With his size, we would like to see him improve his footwork and skating abilities, as these are the biggest weaknesses in his game. He lacks explosiveness when skating with the puck to help him create distance between himself and his opponents. For a defenseman of his size, it's very important to have that added skating ability, and for now, McCormick doesn't have it - it's something he'll need to work hard with over the summer. Overall, he's a player we like. There are some "ifs" in his game, but he's smart, which is very important, and he works hard. We feel like there's a chance for him to get picked in the later rounds of the draft, and if not, he could get a NHL rookie camp invitation over the summer.

| NR | MCCOURT, RILEY | SAGINAW | OHL | 5' 11.25" | 170 lbs | LD |

Riley McCourt was selected 43rd overall by the Hamilton Bulldogs in the OHL priority selection. However, he split the year, playing 26 games for the Bulldogs where he recorded 9 points, before being traded to the Flint Firebirds where he increased his output, putting up 13 points in 30 games, including 9 assists.

McCourt is a two-way defenseman who relies on excellent pivots and strong edges to alleviate defensive pressure while also showing strong transitional play. His straight-line speed isn't great considering he's average-sized for a defender, however his acceleration and evasiveness allowed him to compensate for his build. This gave him the chance to recover when having poor gaps at times, and he plays with a good pace which helped compliment his initial gear when he would aggressively pursue opponents during man-to-man coverage, where he would use an active stick in an attempt to breakup plays. Furthermore, he's got a good level of poise when handling the puck and was capable of weaving in and out of heavy traffic in order to create a play after transitioning over the offensive-line. At the blueline, he was an adequate puck distributor who could thread passes, although at an inconsistent rate. That being said, he was capable of making smart and quick passes in his own-end under pressure, though his frame did get him knocked off the puck which led to a couple of goals against in our viewing's when he failed to find an open teammate in time. There's not a lot of dynamic or high-end skill in McCourts game, instead opting for quick shots at the point or using his initial steps to pinch and generate a scoring chance when activating in the offensive-end.

Despite being capable of transitioning the puck and showing an active motor, his size and tools are not overly enticing, which puts him on the outside looking-in on draft day on our list.

| NR | MCDONALD, KODY | PRINCE ALBERT | WHL | 6' 0.75" | 191 lbs | RW |

Kody McDonald is a big strong two-way center in his third year of eligibility. Kody stated the season in Prince George with the Cougars, and then was traded halfway through the year to the Prince Albert Raiders. Kody had a strong season offensively averaging almost a point a game with both clubs. He scored 34 goals and 66 points in 68 games this season.

Kody plays an extremely strong physical style of hockey. He hits everything that moves. He is very strong down low and able to cycle the puck above average. His compete level is 100% every game. Kody is willing to step up and drop the gloves when called up and can hold his own. This season Kody finished with 139 penalty minutes. Most of Kody's points were scored in the dirty areas. He isn't afraid to drive the net hard and bang in rebounds. Defensively Kody was relied on to win key face-offs and kill penalties. Kody is an average skater and lacks the high-end skill but has can finish in tight. Overall this season Kody showed he is one of the better 2 way players in league. If he wants to make at the next level he needs to work on his skating. McDonald could end up being a third or fourth line grinder that no one wants to play against if he can improve his skating.

| 89 | MCDONOUGH, AIDAN | THAYER ACADEMY | HIGH-MA | 6' 3.0" | 190 lbs | LW |

He's a high school player we like. Big strong kid who needs to improve the skating a bit. He will go to the dirty areas of the ice including going to the net. He suited up with Jay O'Brien at both Thayer Academy and the Cape Cod Whalers Under 18 team. He scored 25 goals in 29 games in Prep and added another 6 goals in 8 games with Cape Cod. He basically grew on us as we did our homework on Jay O'Brien. He needs to get better with his play without the puck but isn't a disaster in that area by any means. Liked his ability to read the play as far as offensive hockey goes. He was a good compliment to O'Brien. O'Brien would find him and he would score. Power Winger with some good scoring upside

"He's a draft for me. Probably the best high schooler after O'Brien." – NHL Scout, April 2018

"I thought he did some good things playing with O'Brien. Played a pretty simple but effective game." – HP Scout, Mark Edwards

| 191 | MCFAUL, DUSTYN | PICKERING | OJHL | 6' 2.25" | 185 lbs | LD |

Dustyn McFaul got better as the year progressed for the Panthers. He produced 19 points in 38 games, including 15 assists. In the playoffs, he had 2 points in 7 games. He has a good combination of size and skating ability. His two-step area quickness is impressive, using it to close his gaps smoothly in his own-end. He also used a combination of his pivoting ability, outside-edges, and a fluid stride to transition the puck through all three zones. Dustyn looked comfortable when handling the puck, which led to clean transitional zone entries and exits. His first pass was sharp, and he was capable of distributing the puck quickly on the powerplay. His lateral mobility allowed him to walk the line while driving possession, and he generates power on his slapshot. If his shooting lane was blocked, he used his skating to pinch, generating scoring chances by attacking the net while driving around traffic. One of his drawbacks is his physical play. He's over-matched along the boards and was knocked off the puck. Though, he did compete hard and was willing to engage despite having an underdeveloped base. There's some potential for McFaul to develop into a two-way transitional defenseman, but he needs additional time to develop since he's raw.

"Liked him the playoffs, he got better as the year went on. He's a big kid and he skates well. I thought his puck skills are better than I first gave him credit for. He's worth a late pick." – NHL Scout, May 2018

"I went to a playoff game and couldn't believe how many scouts were there. More interest than I expected." – NHL Scout, May 2018

"Not a really hard player but he competed and he plays a two way game. He's a guy who has kinda come out of nowhere..someone might take him late." – NHL Scout, May 2018

"Might be one of those guys that just needs time and then he starts to light it up in college. NHL Scout, May 2018

NR	MCGOVERN, DUNCAN	KOOTENAY	WHL	6' 1.75"	190 lbs	G

Duncan McGovern was traded from the Medicine Hat Tigers to the Kootenay Ice this past season, which allowed him to gain a starting role on one of the weaker teams in the WHL. Despite not having a great defensive-core in-front of him, McGovern did a decent job of keeping the puck out of the net, producing a 3.10 GAA and a .893 save percentage in 34 games.

McGovern is an athletic, hybrid butterfly goalie with good size. He's an aggressive netminder who can push off quickly to cut down angles, giving him plus lateral mobility and a solid transitional butterfly. Additionally, he's got plus reflexes and a good amount of extension in his legs which allowed him to make some high-end recovery saves. Arguably the most impressive aspect of Duncan's game is his compete level, he doesn't give up on shots no matter how difficult the save might be and has the speed necessary to make multiple saves in-tight to the net if needed. His ability to square up to shots labelled on his low glove-side was suspect in our viewings, despite having a pretty quick glove-hand overall. Additionally, his rebound control was mixed. When he's calm and composed, using his mobility and quickness when he needed as opposed to over-extending himself, his control was good, but there were games where he did have trouble corralling rebounds that led to several goals against as well. His reverse V-H technique is similar to his butterfly in the sense that he exits in and out of it fluidly and was capable of pushing laterally across the ice, forming back into his butterfly on cross crease attempts.

There's a good amount of tools in McGovern's skillset, he's great on recovery sequences and covers the bottom of the net at a high-rate. In order for him to continue to develop properly, he needs to become more consistent with his rebounds control, refine his movement so that he can look more composed in the net then he did at times, and further refine his puck tracking ability.

45	MCISAAC, JARED	HALIFAX	QMJHL	6' 1.0"	189 lbs *	LD

McIsaac was the 2nd overall pick in the 2016 QMJHL Draft, and has given the Mooseheads every reason to be happy about that pick. McIsaac had a slow start to the season, but eventually found his game offensively and started producing like the talented defenseman that he is. The Truro native finished the season among the defensive scoring leaders in the QMJHL. McIsaac has great combination of size and mobility, which is essential in today's NHL. He moves well, he has good footwork and a power stride that helps him create distance when rushing the puck. He can, at times, go end-to-end with the puck. He has the ability to do it, but over the last two seasons, he has learned to play a simpler game with the puck. When he came out of midget, he was trying too much and fell victim to some bad turnovers. Less is more with him. He has become a more effective two-way defenseman this year, compared to the offensive defenseman that he was coming out of midget. In the offensive zone, he sees the ice well and has a heavy shot from the point. There's still some improvement that could be done with his decision-making, which is a bit inconsistent as well, but if he improves those parts of his game he could be even better. McIsaac has good size and is not overly physical in his zone, but does just enough to keep opposing forwards honest when they come to his side of the ice. He's strong and has good impact when he hits players along the boards.

"Hasn't been overly impressive in my viewings." - NHL Scout, November 2017

"Never made a big impression on me to justify some of the high rankings I saw." - NHL Scout, December 2017

"Lacks the high-end skills and hockey IQ to be a premier offensive defenseman in this draft." - HP Scout Jérôme Bérubé

"He's a solid player but I thought he lacked the hockey sense and offensive tools of some of the players we have ranked ahead of him." - HP Scout, Mark Edwards

207	MCKENNA, JEREMY	MONCTON	QMJHL	5' 9.75"	175 lbs	RW

McKenna, who's in his second year of eligibility for the NHL Entry Draft after being passed over last season, just had a great year with the Wildcats and was one of the most-improved players in the league. His goal total went from 16 to 36 and his point total went from 26 to 77, and he also led the league in shots on goal with 313.

McKenna, who is originally from P.E.I., left his home province after his first bantam year to play for the Notre Dame Hounds hockey program in Saskatchewan for 2 seasons. After the Wildcats drafted him in round 5 of the 2015 QMJHL Draft, he went overseas to play for the Red Bull Academy in Salzburg, with fellow P.E.I. natives Noah Dobson and Chris McQuaid. Last season, he had limited success in his first year in the QMJHL, but Moncton was by far the worst team in the league. This year, with a better supporting cast and more confidence, McKenna was on fire at the beginning of the season, scoring at a torrid pace in the month of October. McKenna's number one weapon offensively is his wrist shot; he likes to shoot and has a quick release. He can play the point on the power play. His skating is a bit of a flaw in his game, however. At his size, we would like to see him improve his acceleration and quickness. He's a smart player and he's good at finding holes in the offensive zone. This year, he was consistently the most dangerous forward in Moncton. He works hard and has become a more valuable player away from the puck and on the PK. He doesn't have great speed, but his anticipation is good and helps him shorthanded.

McKenna will be back next season for his third season, and should be among the elite scorers in the QMJHL, as Moncton is expected to be among the top teams in the league. He could be a late pick in the draft, otherwise he will surely receive offers for rookie camps over the summer.

88	MCLAUGHLIN, BLAKE	CHICAGO	USHL	6' 0.0"	157 lbs *	LW

McLaughlin is a puck distributing winger that is able to create scoring chances with the puck on his tape in the offensive zone. While Blake can have the tendency to play a bit on the perimeter with the puck, it can be effective as he is able to draw defenders to him and open up space in the offensive zone for his teammates. He distributes the puck accurately and on time to set up scoring chances. At this stage of his development his shot doesn't have great range but he has a fairly quick release and has shown the ability to find the corners and beat goalies one on one. McLaughlin is opportunistic in the offensive zone and knows where to go on the ice find pucks quickly. His offensive instincts and skill is a dangerous combination in the offensive zone and provides high upside once he develops more of a nose for the net and willingness to take the puck to the middle of the ice.

McLaughlin isn't the most explosive skater; however he possesses a strong base, good footwork and mobility which makes him difficult to separate from the puck and allows him to be effective off the cycle and along the wall despite not having overwhelming size. Blake possesses decent straight line speed with the puck and has the skill to make plays off the rush and executes clean offensive zone entries using his hands and offensive instincts. McLaughlin displays good work ethic in puck battles and plays a well-rounded game at both ends of the ice. McLaughlin showed the willingness to block shots and take a hit to make a play. McLaughlin needs time to get stronger and gain more explosiveness, which he will have at the University of Minnesota this fall but his offensive skill and high hockey IQ will give some team a solid prospect in a couple years and give the Gophers some more offensive skill up front.

"Some nights it doesn't look like he does a whole lot special out there and then you look at the score sheet and he ended up with two or three points, Opportunistic player" HP Scout, Dusten Braaksma

"I don't see what all the chatter is about. Like a lot of the USA kids he hasn't been very good here." (WJAC) NHL Scout, December 2017

"I have some issues with is game." NHL Scout, December 2017

"He fell for me as I continued to watch him." NHL Scout, February 2018

"He has some skill and he's smart but his skating has a ways to go...mechanics are off. He plays kinda slow,...has a slight body and I didn't think his game progressed all that much." NHL Scout, April 2018

"Like many of the NHL guys I spoke to (about him) in Truro (WJAC) he didn't wow me as a guy I'd take too high. I interviewed him in Truro as well." HP Scout, Mark Edwards

"One scout mentioned to me he really liked the kid, another singled him out as one of his weaker interviews... I give you the NHL Combine.. I did hear a story involving Blake's family and a deer that was pretty much up there with the best things I've ever heard at the combine. I'm sure it will be told during draft coverage. It's pretty awesome." - HP Scout, Mark Edwards

| 46 | MCLEOD, RYAN | MISSISSAUGA | OHL | 6' 2.3" | 206 lbs * | LC |

McLeod is a playmaking centre with strong skating abilities. Ryan utilizes his fluid skating abilities and good speed to create offensively. He shows an ability to recognize open ice an exploit it. While McLeod is able to make controlled zone entries, way to often he refuses to take the puck to the net, instead he will stay wide and circle the net. He does need to become more assertive with his shot, often passing up shots in prime scoring areas to make a pass. Ryan does show good puck handling abilities and a creativity to his game that elevates his playmaking skills. With good vision and passing abilities McLeod can elevate the play of those around him, however he needs to recognize when to be selfish and utilize his shot. It is deceptively strong and comes off a good release. He's a player who shows intriguing offensive attributes.

McLeod will need to elevate his defensive zone play as he can chase defensively and loose contain of his check. Ryan played wing at times throughout the season and was often more effective in the defensive zone as a winger with limited defensive responsibilities. McLeod possesses good strength, but needs to be more assertive with his frame as he can lose board/puck battles or be pushed from possession despite possessing a 205 pound frame.

"Early second round for me." - NHL Scout, November 2017

"He has so much talent but I'm not sure he'll ever use it." NHL Scout, May 2018

"Third year in the league, I didn't think his game took the next step. He had a lot of perimeter play..." NHL Scout, May 2018

"Solid player who has a lot more to give competitively and getting to the hard areas of the ice. He's smarter than his brother but not even close to the same compete level...work ethics not even close." - NHL Scout, May 2018

"If we could combine him and his brother he'd be a star." NHL Scout, May 2018

"I could have listed the same basic quote from several scouts at least 8 times. In a nutshell it was this: Tons of talent but plays soft, makes big wide turns and just stays on the outside and he doesn't compete." HP Scout, Mark Edwards

"Majority of the scouts I spoke to had him in the 2nd round...some early 2nd, some mid 2nd. I still won't be one bit surprised if he goes in the first round though." - HP Scout, Mark Edwards

"One scout I know had him as a top 10 in November. He saw him a lot more after that and my last info from him (March area) was that he was barely hanging on as a late first." - HP Scout, Mark Edwards

"I wasn't a big fan of his brothers game and Mike didn't change my mind about him this season. Ryan has more skill but lacks in two important categories for me: Hockey sense and compete. Skating and skill are good and so is the size. obviously He can control much of his future himself if he chooses to compete harder, and if he does, he'll make our ranking look really bad." - HP Scout, Mark Edwards

"Pretty quiet on this player at the combine but two scouts mentioned him to me as one of their weaker interviews of the week. Nothing awful, just noted him as not being as good as many other players." - HP Scout, Mark Edwards

NR	MCLEOD, WYATT	EDMONTON	WHL	6' 2.0"	182 lbs	LD

Wyatt McLeod is an athletic defenseman with good size. He was picked late in the WHL Bantam Draft, 143rd overall by the Edmonton Oil Kings. After a decent 16 year old season where he earned some top-4 minutes towards the end of the season, he struggled to earn the confidence of his coaches as a 17 year old. In 49 regular season games in 2017-18, he recorded 2 goals and 8 points.

McLeod is a good-looking defenseman because of his strong physical skills. He has strong feet for a big body and can transition quickly and move laterally with ease. Wyatt is an active player and consistently has his feet moving and wants to make a difference on most shifts. His skating skills and size allows him to be involved most shifts.

Although Wyatt has some solid physical skills, he does not excel with or without the puck. He is average at both ends of the ice which is why he is yet to solidify himself as a top defenseman for the Oil Kings. McLeod can handle the puck, and shows some confidence skating up ice, but he is extremely inconsistent with his decision making in all three zones. The question about his game is his hockey sense, and his ability to be a dependable puck mover. He lacks the raw offensive skill to be an offensive standout and he must rely on his physical skills to be a dependable defenseman who occasionally contributes. He is the type of player who has one or two shifts a game that makes you ask why he cannot put it all together. Consider McLeod an interesting prospect, who has some good physical tools but will need to take big step forward to have a legitimate shot at the NHL.

NR	MCMASTER, ADAM	NORTH BAY	OHL	5' 10.0"	172 lbs	LW

McMaster is an undersized forward with above average skating abilities and playmaking traits to his game. Adam's skating dictates his game as he displays an explosive first step along with a fluid stride and strong straight line speed. His quick feet and strong edges often allow him to create separation from a check or space to make a play in tight areas. He can utilize his speed in transition well, exposing defenders who take poor angles to him by driving wide. However he also recognizes space well and will attack the center of the ice if opponents back off and allow him space. McMaster handles the puck well with speed and can be elusive at times due to his quick change of pace and direction abilities. He shows a deceptively good release with velocity and accuracy behind his shot, but does need to become more assertive with his shot as he can be too much of a pass first forward. Adam can also be a presence on the forecheck as his speed allows him to quickly close in on opponents, while his quick stick allows him to create a turnover. McMaster shows some creativity to his game but can struggle to produce offensively due to an unwillingness to go to the high traffic areas. He will needed to find more of a consistent compete level and improve his strength to enhance his effectiveness in position and puck battles. Adam's defensive game improved from his rookie OHL season but is still a work in progress as his engagement is lacking and inconsistent.

"Not a player I would draft this season if I was with a team." HP Scout, Mark Edwards

101	MCSHANE, ALLAN	OSHAWA	OHL	5' 10.8"	185 lbs *	LC

McShane is a slightly undersized, playmaking forward. Allan is at his best in possession were he is able to utilize his vision and passing skills to generate offensively. He's player who is able to find space and anticipate well. McShane possesses a versatility in the offensive zone with the ability to create with his playmaking and shooting abilities. Allan would however benefit from becoming more assertive with his shot, as he displays a quick release and good accuracy. Defensively his anticipation and quick stick help elevate his abilities, however his lack of size and strength can limit him when defending against bigger bodied opponents. Offensively McShane shows good skill to his game, a confident puck handler with the ability to create space with his creativity and puck skills. However he can be limited at times due to the combination of limited size and a short skating stride. While he moves his feet quickly and has good edges, McShane can struggle to generate speed and attack with pace. He shows a good skill set, but Allan needs to play with more urgency to his game and find a consistent compete level that will elevate his game.

"He's a top 20 pick." NHL Scout, October 2017

"Smart and can score and make plays but skating is weak." - NHL Scout, November 2017

"Mid round guy, probably one of my biggest fallers this year." - Same NHL Scout who said top 20 pick, April 2018

"I went into this season with McShane and Akil Thomas rated pretty closely together. By the end of the season it wasn't even close for me. I have Thomas way ahead. McShane scored some power play goals in my viewings but never played with enough compete or pace to get me on board. One of my biggest fallers this season. He slid way down my ranking." HP Scout, Mark Edwards

"Combine week followed the trend of the season. Pretty quiet on this player." - HP Scout, Mark Edwards

NR	MCQUAID, CHRIS	GATINEAU	QMJHL	6' 2.0"	179lbs	LD

McQuaid was traded from Rouyn-Noranda to Gatineau at the QMJHL trade deadline, and saw his ice time increase once he joined the Olympiques. Originally from P.E.I., McQuaid is a good-sized defenseman who didn't take the next step in his development this season and lost his spot on Rouyn-Noranda's defensive squad, being passed over by two other 2000-born defensemen in Justin Bergeron and Alexis Arsenault. McQuaid has a weird skating style. He gets around the ice and covers good ice with long strides and a long stick, but there's a ton of work that needs to be done with his skating strides: a lot of technical stuff that will help him become more fluid and waste less energy. Offensively, he didn't take the next step this year. He has a good high-velocity wrist shot, and can score with it as he showed this year, but he rarely uses his shot in games. He didn't get a lot of puck touches in the games we saw this year, and was rarely a factor in his team's transition game. In the offensive zone, with his long reach, he flashes some good puck skills and a good shot that could lead some to believe that there's some untapped offensive potential. In the next two years in major junior, there might be, but at the moment, he's still very raw and inconsistent. In his zone, he can get caught running around a bit too much instead of letting the play come to him. He has good size, but he's not really known as a physical guy just yet. Similar to a lot of his skillset, he showed flashes of a physical game as well, but there's a lack of consistency in that area of his game. Because of his inconsistency and lack of improvement, we don't see him as a draft this year.

70	MERKLEY, RYAN	GUELPH	OHL	5' 11.3"	168 lbs *	RD

Ryan Merkley is a dynamic offensive defenseman who generated the most primary assists out of any defender in the OHL. He was the first overall pick in the 2016 OHL draft and had a productive rookie season. This season he posted 67 points in 63 games, including 54 assists. In the playoffs, he produced 6 points in 6 games. Internationally, he produced 6 assists in 5 games at the Hlinka and had 3 assists in 5 games at the U18's in April.

Merkley a very polarizing player in this draft. On the one hand, he has fanttastic offensive-attributes that allow him to generate scoring chances both for himself and his team. On the other hand, his play away from the puck is a major cause for concern. He's got a fourth-forward mentality and uses the neutral zone as his launching pad to join the rush which he's exceptional at doing. His dynamic four-way skating ability allows him to separate quickly, where he loves to rush down the ice while surveying his options. Another dynamic quality that Ryan possess is his vision, he sees his teammates open before opposing teams do and can thread precise passes through heavy traffic. Additionally, he uses a variety of body and shooting fakes at the line to re-open his lanes and has one of the best slap-passes in this class. This made him especially dangerous on the powerplay, where he could take advantage of his full offensive-arsenal. He's poised under pressure, knowing that his crossovers and pivots are up to the task and he can spin to peel off pressure, while also showing a quick set of hands that allow him to avoid active sticks. Although more of a passer than a shooter, his shot has a surprising amount of power and his slapshot is accurate. He would time the release of his shot through screens at a high-rate. In the offensive-end, he's more than capable of drawing half a team to one-side in an effort to defend him, leaving him with several passing options at his disposal; time-after-time we have seen him magnetize an opposing team to him before executing a high-end pass, giving one of his teammates an open-net to shoot at. The last impressive element of his offensive-game is that his transitional zone-entries are advanced, it's rare for him not to gain the line when he attempts to enter a zone. There's very few forwards let alone defenders in this class that can weave through traffic and breakdown opposing team's defenses like he can.

He's a very talented player who unfortunately possesses a glaring flaw that could become the deciding factor in his career depending on if he chooses to fix it. Merkley's compete level away from the puck is very poor. It's one thing to misread a play, have an improper gap, fail to knock an opponent off the puck or have an opponent drive-around you, which are all defensive-lapses that Merkley has shown. It's another thing to totally give up on plays at the rate he does. We have seen him turn the puck over and not attempt to recover, stand stationary while letting slower players than himself easily cut around him while driving towards the front of the net. He rarely will engage along the boards despite if it's a player his size or even smaller. In one of our viewings in the final 40 seconds of a tied game, he tried to get off the ice after a failed rush which caused a partial breakaway due to not recognizing that no one else to coverd for him. In the same game, he was stripped off the puck behind the net area, and instead of attempting to recover or re-position himself, he swung his head back looking skyward while standing stationary. What makes his play away from the puck that much more puzzling is that he's capable of making high-quality defensive plays. We have seen him aggressively backcheck and dive at pucks which resulted in disrupted rush attempts. Unfortunately, for every good defensive play he executes, he makes several mediocre or bad plays, most of which could have been avoided if he played with an intensity and effort which he seems to reserve only for the offensive-zone.

There's several mental aspects to Merkley's game that need to be improved in order for his defensive-game to develop to the level necessary to play in the NHL.

"Despite his offensive-talents, he produced the worst defensive-sequence for me out of any player this year, it baffles me to this day when I think back on it" - HP Scout, Brad Allen

"I coached Junior A with Ryan's first year Minor Midget AAA coach, the late Tyler Cragg, so I've known about Merkley for a while. I'm not going to include all the scouts comments from this season. Suffice to say it wasn't very positive and numerous scouts told me they did not have him on their personal lists" - HP Scout, Mark Edwards

"Feedback I got from NHL scouts from their combine interviews matched feedback I got from NHL team scouts during the season. We will include Merkley somewhere on our list, but he's a player I'd suspect would be off the board long before I'd be willing to consider selecting him. if I was with an NHL team." - HP Scout, Mark Edwards

| 128 | MIFTAKHOV, AMIR | IRBIS KAZAN | RUSSIA-JR. | 6' 0.0" | 158 lbs | G |

Amir Miftakhov was the starting goalie for Irbis Kazan, putting up a 1.91 GAA and a .934 save percentage in 26 games. He also was the starter for Russia at international tournaments, posting an impressive 1.77 GAA and a .953 save percentage in 5 games at the Hlinka. At the U18's his numbers of a 3.31 GAA and a .883 save percentage in 5 games were considerably worse despite being named one of the top 3 players on his squad at the event.

Miftakhov is one of the more promising goalies in this year's draft class, showing a mental skill-set that's capable of compensating for his size. He's got an excellent combination of anticipatory reads and puck tracking ability. This allows him to get squared up for the initial shot and subsequent shots consistently in the majority of our viewings. His puck tracking allows him to recognize puck movement along the point and the high-slot which makes it difficult for shooters to generate rebound opportunities off of hard point-shots or make him over-extend himself on lateral passes due to already being in position. Furthermore, he's excellent at gauging the location of a release point and cutting down the angle using advanced skating mechanics when players are rushing down the wings. Even when he does let in goals, it's rarely due to Miftakhov's positioning as he tends to close off most openings before a shot is generated. In one-on-one situations where a player cut's in-front of the crease or gets a breakaway opportunity, he has shown the ability to gauge the movement of shooters at a high-level and make difficult saves look relatively easy while in close. He's also excellent at controlling rebounds by either deflecting them into the corners or absorbing them in his butterfly. His lateral mobility is a plus and he's more than capable of making impressive cross-crease saves. Although technically refined for his age, he's also demonstrated that he can break his technique when he does make the occasional misread or is dealing with a high-end play by lunging across the goal mouth which has resulted in some impressive reactionary saves. Specifically, he's made several remarkable glove-hand saves that have taken away what looked like sure goals. Lastly, his reflexes although not incredible for his size, are still very good and gives him another layer to his game when his technique isn't as sharp on certain plays.

There's no glaring weaknesses in Miftakhov's game with the exception of his physical limitations, he's prone to letting in a bad goal occasionally, though it is rare and he sometimes minimizes his movement too much which gives shooters room when he's moving laterally while attempting to cut down the angle, this also impedes him sometimes when attempting to make difficult saves off of rebounds or high-end passes that are difficult to read. That being said, he's one of the more promising goalies in this class and has arguably one of the strongest if not the strongest mental game, showing a high level of composure while under heavy pressure. It's for this reason and the attributes described that we think Miftakhov has a lot of upside.

20	MILLER, K'ANDRE	USA U-18	NTDP	6' 3.3"	199 lbs *	LD

K'Andre Miller has had an interesting development path after transitioning from forward to a defenseman over the past few years. This has resulted in Miller developing into a two-way defenseman who posted 27 points in 53 games and logged top-four minutes while playing in all situations for the USNTDP. He is slated to play for the University of Wisconsin in the 2018-19 season. The defender also had an impressive U18 Five Nations tournament, consistently shutting down top players at the event while showcasing a growing offensive toolset.

Miller dominates defensively in the defensive-end by arguably having the best athleticism of any defender in this draft class. This allowed him to make defensive plays and ridiculous recovery plays that not many other players can make. For Miller specifically, this was an important trait, considering he's only been playing the position for a handful of years; His physical gifts such as his wing-span and agility allow him to cover a lot of ground when attempting to recover. He also able to close gaps at a high rate and make defensive plays when off-balance or when transitioning from a blocked shot. His skating mechanics are explosive, he's got excellent two-step area quickness and he's fluid on his skates for his size which allows him to transition the puck up the ice consistently while also being able to skate the puck out of danger areas in the defensive-end. One area of improvement we noticed from the beginning of the year was his confidence levels increasing while holding onto the puck when moving over the neutral zone and moving over the offensive blueline.

Another strength of Miller is his stick-checking ability, he knows how to use his reach, using it to swipe at pucks both in-front of him and when he's attempting to backcheck after getting caught out of position. He's an unselfish defenseman in the sense that when paired with offensive-minded defenseman such as Wilde, he was able to adapt and allow Wilde an opportunity to play his game by playing back and making sure to recover positionally in case of a turnover. His defensive reads are a plus, he's able to identify turnovers in the neutral zone quickly and transition from offense to defense and vice versa. In his own-end, he's aware of his shooting lanes both at even strength and on the penalty-kill and plays positionally sound around his net area. He isn't afraid to use his frame to block a shot and plays with an intensity that allows him to get physically engaged when necessary, specifically, on zone-entries he can be aggressive at the line using his frame to lay a hit or his speed to close in on a pass attempt and intercept it before turning back up ice.

With the puck in the offensive-end, he's developed the ability to use his skating to re-open shooting lanes while moving laterally across the point and is willing to skate through traffic while looking to set up a play. Although he gets his shot through traffic for the most part, it lacks power at this point in time though the release point is above average. His passing ability is a plus, he can make stretch passes from end-to-end and hit his teammates with passes that require a high-degree of difficulty.

Along with his athletic traits, Miller competes hard at both ends of the ice and this allowed him to take over several games that we had seen throughout the year. K'Andre has a rare combination of tools and skill that give him a high-ceiling, that combined with his solid development year has us projecting him as a potential top-pairing defenseman who can be used in all situations at the NHL level.

"I've seen K'Andre play since his Bantam year when he was playing forward in Minnetonka, MN. His athleticism was apparent then, he probably could have switched to goalie then and figured out the position. He has that rare ability to absorb knowledge and apply it quickly. I think he's going to play a long time in the NHL." HP Scout, Dusten Braaksma

"I think he'll challenge for top 10 by the time June rolls around. He's already the best D on the team." NHL Scout, August, 2017

"I like him but not as high as you have him. I think he's a 20(th) to 30(th) guy. NHL Scout, November 2017

"I like him but not as much as you do..I question his hockey sense." NHL Scout, December 2017

"I'm with you on K'Andre now. He's my top D on the program." NHL Scout, December 2017

"I like him but still think he's a late first (rounder)" - NHL Scout, February 2018

"He makes some very questionable plays out there." NHL Scout, February 2018

"He's been so miscast, he has so much more to give." NHL Scout, February 2018

"Best physical tools of anyone in this draft." - NHL Scout, February 2018

"The first time I saw him was at the USNTDP U17 selection camp and he was really impressive. I was trying to focus on the OHL Draft eligible players but I couldn't help but notice him as he impressed me shift after shift." - HP Scout, Mark Edwards

"While Bode struggled in the neutral zone, I thought Miller was excellent. He used his physical tools so well to maximize his success. He had good gaps, used his huge wing span and his recovery ability was excellent if he happened to make a gaffe. He broke up plays before they could develop and was very good defending on entries to his own zone." – HP Scout, Mark Edwards

"He was already one of my personal favourites in this draft and that was before I had several scouts tell me that he was one of the best interviews they've ever had. One scout in particular couldn't rave enough about his mid year interview with K'Andre.. As far as on-ice goes, I feel like he's much better than the general consensus I hear out there. To me his ceiling is through the roof and although he's still a bit raw, he's made strides and his physical tools are high end. I don't think he's even scratched the surface of his offensive potential...I truly hope the team that drafts him helps him develop in that area. Some question his hockey sense and while I by no means thinks it's elite, I felt like it was more a case of him still being so new to the position." – HP Scout, Mark Edwards

"Predictably great feedback from scouts at the NHL Combine." – HP Scout, Mark Edwards

NR	MINULIN, ARTYOM	SWIFT CURRENT	WHL	6' 1.75"	201 lbs	RD

Artyom Minulin is in his second season of eligibility. This season with the Swift Current Broncos he scored 13 goals and 43 points in 64 games. Artyom suited up for Russia at the World Juniors in December and had a strong showing.

Artyom is a big two-way defenseman who can move the puck and create offensively while playing a sound defensive game as well. Offensively his biggest asset is his vision. He sees the ice well and is able to find the open man. He often found himself on the point for the Broncos top power play unit. Artyom has calmness to his game. He seems to never panic with the puck. Artyom isn't the smoothest skater so he uses his size and reach to control the puck when carrying it out of the defensive zone.

In the defensive zone his size and reach are his best asset as well. He uses his long stick to break up passes effectively. He is strong enough to battle down low and in front of the net. One knock on him is his mobility with and without the puck. He doesn't have the quickest feet so smaller faster forwards have had some success putting the puck in his feet and making the move.

Artyom has mad strides this season in improving his skating and mobility. He needs to continue working as the Broncos make their was to a possible WHL title, with Minulin being a strong reason why.

97	MOE, JARED	WATERLOO	USHL	6' 3.25"	205 lbs	G

Jared Moe was possibly one of the more consistent goaltenders all season long in the USHL. Coming from Holy Family catholic in Minnesota, Moe played 32 regular season games for Waterloo, putting up a 2.23 GAA% and a .919 save/%. Moe has a good combination of size and athleticism that makes him a solid pro prospect in the future. Jared has developed physically in the last year and added much needed lower body strength which has helped settle his game. His willingness to compete and not give up on saves has been impressive in our viewings. Moe is a right hand catching goalie with a quick glove and blocker. Jared still needs to learn to play his size in the net, he can tend to make himself small in the butterfly or when he is trying to look around screens in front but as a result also takes away the lower half of the net well in doing so. Due to a crowded crease situation at University of Minnesota, Moe will likely play one more season in the USHL before heading to Minneapolis to join the Gophers.

"His game has really grown in the last year, when I saw him last year in High School, I thought he was an athletic goalie that was all over the place, he seems to have made great strides in adding structure to his game." NHL Scout (April, 2018)

"Not pretty in the net but he can stop pucks. I'd draft him." - NHL Scout, March 2018

"I expect that he will be the first American goalie taken. He had a great year." - NHL Scout, May 2018

NR	MONCADA, LUKE	NORTH BAY	OHL	6' 0.0"	203 lbs	LC

Moncada is a big bodied, two-way centre with a competitiveness to his game. Luke shows an intriguing size and strength package that allows him to be effective off the cycle and along the half-wall. He can be assertive with his physical traits to earn ideal body position and win battles, however he does show an inconsistency with his willingness to play with a physical edge. Moncada shows complimentary skill to his game, as he can make simple decisions with the puck and complete opportunities that are created for him, however does struggle to generate offensively for himself. Luke displays a long and powerful stride, however lacks quick acceleration and generates just average speed. With generated momentum he can be difficult to push from possession when attacking the goal, however becoming more versatile will be necessary as he often tries to bull-doze his way to the goal opposed to putting his head up and utilizing other options. With a quality compete level and awareness defensively, Moncada was an effective presence on the penalty kill and showed an ability to clog shooting/passing lanes and block shots. He needs to become more assertive physically and begin to process the game quicker to take full advantage of his physical traits. Improving his foot-speed and adding elements offensively would also be beneficial.

44	MOROZOV, IVAN	KHANTY-MANSIYSK	RUSSIA-JR.	6' 1.0"	178 lbs	LW

Ivan Morozov is a versatile two-way pivot who had a productive year while playing for Mamonty Yugry, where he posted 23 points in 30 games. At international events, he was featured in a secondary offensive-role, giving way to other players such as Denisenko and Svechnikov, however they weren't available at the U18's, giving him first line minutes and top powerplay time where he excelled while posting 5 points in 5 games.

Morozov plays a detail-oriented game at both ends of the ice. Although a skilled and talented center, he's not a player who floats of takes shifts off in the defensive-end, instead he's a competitor who doesn't back down during physical altercations and is willing to support his defenseman when they need help down-low. His defensive awareness is advanced, he recognizes what the opposing forwards are attempting to do with the puck and takes away passing options consistently due to this. Furthermore, he's willing to expend his tank during backchecking sequences, and has a quick stick which he uses to intercept pucks. He's got excellent skating mechanics and a fluid stride that allows him to generate power quickly, giving him plus two-step area quickness and good straight-line speed. He used his speed without the puck to create pressure at the defensive-line, which lead to him creating short-handed chances throughout the season. The best attribute of his skating is his edge-work, he's able to rapidly change directions and this makes him very difficult to intercept when he's attempting to transition the puck in open-ice. Morozov does some of his best work during transitional play, where he can dictate the game using his advanced reads to turn pucks over or apply pressure, resulting in him making efficient plays with the puck before going north quickly.

In the offensive-end, Morozov has several high-end attributes that make him dangerous from all over the ice. He's not only an intelligent player in his own-end and the neutral zone, but he also has a high offensive IQ which makes him excellent at interpreting the time and space he has to make a play. Ivan is very good at finding soft-spots behind defensive coverage and reading the play in advance, which allows him to exploit defensive units before they know they have been exploited. He's aware of when his lanes are closed but has the tools necessary to re-open them, using patience, poise, and high-end vision to facilitate passing plays. Furthermore, he's elusive due to his edges and has soft-hands which make him dangerous in one-on-one situations or when attempting to carve through traffic. His combination of a plus motor, physicality, ability to guard the puck and shiftiness made it very difficult for defenses to handle him down-low, around the boards and in-front of the net. Arguably his most dangerous offensive weapon next to his hockey smarts is his shot. He's got a release that snaps off his stick in a hurry and generates a lot of power; despite it's speed, it's still accurate and he can pick corners even if there's little room presented, he's also capable of using his hands to change the angle and mask the release point. On the powerplay, he likes to have his one-timer set up at the left-circle due to being a right-shot center, and again he can generate a lot of power on the release. Morozov doesn't have any glaring weaknesses at this time which is one of the reasons we are high on him.

Morozov is a cerebral yet skilled center who became more dominant as the season progressed and took over games at times during his international play. We think his 200-foot game, hockey smarts, and skillset offers a lot of upside in the upcoming draft.

"There's very few centres in this draft who are as complete as he currently is"- HP Scout, Brad Allen

"Smart player who stood out for me at the Five Nations tourney in Plymouth." - HP Scout, Mark Edwards

NR	MOSKAL, BILLY	LONDON	OHL	5' 11.75"	185 lbs	LC

Billy Moskal was selected 40th overall by the London Knights in the 2016 OHL draft. After getting limited opportunities at the start of the year, he developed chemistry with Nathan Dunkley which helped him develop the offensive-side of his game. He finished the season with 26 points in 66 games, including 19 assists and zero points in 4 playoff games.

Moskal is an efficient and technical skating center who thinks the game pretty well. His skating mechanics allow him to generate excellent two-step area quickness, showing elusive edge work which allowed him to quickly shift skating lanes and drive through heavy traffic during rush attempts. He also has a low-centre of gravity and was able to come away with the puck against larger defenders, showing the ability to out-pace his opponents at times. Although he only generated 1.08 shots per game in a depth-role, he displayed a quick snap and wrist-shot that was difficult for goalies to pick up in some of our viewings. However, he's more of a playmaker than a shooter, and showed the ability to make difficult passes on occasion. When he was on his game, he was an excellent puck recovery option on a line due to solid puck retrieval skills. He's not a player who is overly physical, instead using his skating and stick to come away with the puck. Although not an overly skilled player, he was capable of making quick and smart decisions that made up for not having any game breaking offensive attributes. He showed a good level of compete and was willing to play at both ends of the ice, where he would take advantage of his skating ability during transitional breakouts.

| 147 | NASSEN, LINUS | FROLUNDA JR | SWEDEN JR | 5' 11.25" | 185 lbs | LC |

Linus Nassen played in Frolunda's system this past season. He produced 11 points in 28 games, with 8 assists, while been featured on the penalty-kill. In the playoffs, he had 2 assists in 5 games. At international events, he played at the Five-Nations, reserving his best game against the Czechs, producing a multi-point effort. He also was featured at the U18's, getting an assist in 7 games.

Nassen is a smart, 200-foot center, who competes hard at both ends of the ice. He's the type of center who doesn't cheat on his shifts, rarely floating when we watched him. He's willing to play deep in his own-end to support his teammates and had some great board battling efforts. He's not the fleetest of foot, since he lacks power out of the gate, but his straight-line speed is decent which helps with his pressure-oriented style. He plays bigger than his frame suggests and this allowed him to create some impressive forechecking moments. His vision complimented his forechecking efforts, since he was able to thread high-end passes towards the net area after winning puck battles along the wall. His hockey-sense is arguably his best attribute and helps compensate for an average skill-set. He can find soft-ice and positions himself to be an effective player in-front of the net area. Although he gave up good scoring chances to pass the puck off sometimes, he has a plus release point and showed a decent amount of accuracy. Nassen isn't going to end up on the highlight-reels, but he's the type of player that makes the subtle and smart play, that compliments higher-end players. There might be untapped potential in Nassen, if he can continue to become more powerful and develop his first-few steps.

| NR | NELSON, JAXON | SIOUX FALLS | USHL | 6' 4.25" | 206 lbs | RC |

Nelson just finished his 2nd season for Sioux Falls (USHL). After playing against weak competition in the Minnesota HS ranks, an adjustment period into the USHL was expected but there was not the jump in his development many expected this year. Nelson has a lot of size and gets around the ice well for a big kid. He plays a responsible two-way game as a center and is good in the faceoff circle in our viewings but doesn't play to his size much of the time. He tends to get pushed around in puck battles and in front of the oppositions net. Jensen has an excellent shot and release but doesn't get himself in enough situations where it can be utilized. At first glance of Jaxon on the ice, it's easy to vision him playing in the NHL, with his size and skating but he tends to just blend into the game once the puck hits the ice. Prospects like Nelson have panned out for teams down the road so we are not ready to write him off but he has some work ahead of him. Nelson was originally slated to join the University of Minnesota this fall but it's not hard to imagine the new staff in Minnesota wanting Nelson to play one more year of Junior Hockey to try to gain some more offensive confidence before joining a very difficult league.

"I don't see enough drive and compete in his game right now, he's just out there going through the motions a lot. Has a lot of athleticism and physical tools but the "want" isn't there enough for me and that rarely changes." HP Scout, Dusten Braaksma

"I don't think he'll get drafted. He skates ok but doesn't play hard enough." - NHL Scout, March 2018

| 160 | NEVASAARI, ARTTU | KARPAT JR. | FINLAND-JR. | 5' 11.0" | 178 lbs | RW |

Nevasaari scored 18 goals in 46 games in Finland's U20 league this season. Internationally, with Finland, he had some ups and downs playing in 3 major U-18 tournaments throughout the year. The best things about Nevasaari are his hands and shot. He's a shoot-first winger and has above-average hands. His shot is accurate and he gets it off pretty quickly. The rest of his game needs a lot of work; he's a good goal scorer, but his playmaking abilities are average and he doesn't make players around him better. His decision-making is lacking when playing in a playmaking role. He knows how to score (that's the dimension he's good at), but the rest of his game is lacking, making him a one-dimensional forward. He's not a speedster; at his size, he lacks the necessary speed. His top speed is average, and he lacks explosiveness and quickness. His play away from the puck is not really good; he's not very involved on the ice and often out of position. Even on the international team, despite with his goal-scoring potential, he would often end up playing on Finnish 3rd line due to being a defensive liability. Nevasaari's compete level is another area containing several question marks. He doesn't battle hard to win possession of the puck and usually stays on the outside, not getting involved in the tougher areas. Nevasaari has some good goal-scoring potential, but there are a lot of issues in the rest of his game which will make it tough for him to reach his full potential if not improved upon in the next couple of years.

| NR | NIELSEN, TRISTEN | CALGARY | WHL | 5' 10.0" | 181 lbs | LW |

Tristen is an undersized winger for the Hitmen who was originally drafted by the team 20th overall in the 2015 WHL Bantam Draft. He missed over 20 games in the middle of the 2017-18 due to an upper body injury but managed to finish the season with 35 points and 19 goals in 49 regular season games, with the bulk of his points coming in the second half of the season.

Nielsen lacks size but can compete in all areas of the rink because of his low centre of gravity and strong lower half. He has quick, powerful stride with his feet relatively wide apart, although he looks unconventional the puck follows him and he can win races. When he was playing with energy, he willed himself to loose pucks resulting in lots of individual opportunities including several breakaways throughout the year. In tight areas, Nielsen showed strength and finesse, combining good puck protection skills and strength on his skates which makes him able to participate well in cycle plays. In addition to his skating skills, Tristen shows some good skill around the net and can shoot the puck in stride.

Tristen's strengths are in his in physical skills. He can handle the puck, is strong on his skates and has some offensive skill, but the major reason why he hasn't taken the next step offensively is his lack of hockey sense and ability to make offensive plays quickly. Nielsen likes to hold onto the puck, rely on his physical skills and has not shown his ability to find teammates consistently. He can make the obvious play to a wide-open teammate, but when under pressure or in traffic, he tries to protect the puck or skate to open space.

Nielsen can be an asset without the puck, especially on the forecheck if he chooses to move his feet and play physical. This competitive edge is relatively inconsistent for Nielsen, and his effort in his own end can be questioned. Overall, Tristen has some physical talent but will need to take a big step offensively to be considered an NHL prospect with his stature.

| 173 | NIZHNIKOV, KIRILL | SUDBURY | OHL | 6' 2.0" | 190 lbs | RW |

Kirill was selected in the first round, 7th Overall by the Mississauga Steelheads at the 2016 OHL Draft. He refused to report and was traded to the Barrie Colts where he began his OHL career. This season he was traded to Sudbury where he attempted to rejuvenate his young career.

As we noted last season, Nizhnikov has high-end puck skills. He is a confident player with the puck, sees the ice well and can thread the needle with passes through tight spaces. Nizhnikov has an NHL-caliber shot and gets it off his stick quickly and with something on it. One big issue with his game is his play without the puck. He lacks the compete and desire to raise his game to a level that matches his skill. Turnovers are a big issue and it's an area that has not improved since he entered the OHL.

At the beginning of this season, Kirill had the potential to be one of the first players selected out of the OHL at the 2018 NHL Draft. That seems very unlikely to happen.

"He's borderline scared to me. Won't go to the hard areas, won't take a hit to make a play. Skill and skating is great but I question his willingness to compete on any sort of consistent basis." - NHL Scout, May 2018

"Absolutely loved his skill entering the OHL Draft and since that time his stock has fallen more with each one of my viewings. In one viewing this season I watched him turn over the puck three times in one shift. It led to a minus on his stat sheet." HP Scout, Mark Edwards

| 21 | NOEL, SERRON | OSHAWA | OHL | 6' 5.0" | 204 lbs * | RW |

Noel is a big bodied winger with intriguing raw abilities. He is at his best when assertive with his physical attributes, using his frame and reach to win battles and get himself into position to be a threat offensively. Serron shows a long and fluid stride and he generates a good top speed and covers ice quickly. He is very tough to contain once he's generated momentum as he barrels towards the goal. Serron shields the puck effectively with his frame and reach, however would benefit from improving his puck handling abilities along with the ability to make skilled plays off his back-hand. Serron shows competitiveness that allows him to play in various situations. He's reliable defensively, recognizing positional play and assignments, while using his reach an active stick to clog shooting and passing lanes. Noel has the ability to dominate games at times, but can struggle to add all of his intriguing elements together at the same time. Becoming more physical along the walls and assertive with his frame on a consistent basis would enhance his effectiveness. While Serron shows good speed and a rangy stride his agility and lateral mobility have room to improve and should as he becomes stronger and creates a more stable base. His ceiling is quite high and that will increase his draft stock when it comes time to select him on draft day.

"Inconsistent. needs to play power forward style all the time but I didn't see that regularly enough this year." NHL Scout, May 2018

"Good start but thought his production kind of fell off as the season went on." - NHL Scout, May 2018

"Struggled in the playoffs." NHL scout, May 2018

"Big power winger... he's not Tom Wilson because he's more skilled but he will create space like Wilson does. - NHL Scout, May 2018

"Some viewings he looked like he could easily be a top 15 pick but I did have a few viewings where he didn't show up. In the end, this is a player who is a huge physical specimen who also possesses speed and some skill. If he commits more to the power game he will be a productive NHL player down the road." HP Scout, Mark Edwards

48	NORDGREN, NIKLAS	HIFK JR.	FINLAND-JR.	5' 9.0"	169 lbs	RW

Nordgren is a player who made a smooth climb in our rankings all year long, but made his biggest impact at the last two big tournaments in February and April. Nordgren played this past season mostly in the U20 league, where he had great results, with 42 points in 28 games. He also played 15 games in the men's league, where he had 3 assists. He had his best success playing the Champions' league series, where he had 6 points in 2 games.

With Nordgren, the first thing you notice is his size. The second thing you notice: his skating. He lacks the ideal skating ability for a player of his stature. We thought he struggled with the speed in Plymouth in February, but his speed looked a bit better in April. Nevertheless, he will need to work on improving his quickness and explosiveness, as it is never easy for a small player to crack the NHL and even tougher when said player is not a good skater. We do, however, absolutely love his hockey IQ and smarts; he's one of the smartest players in the draft. He sees the ice extremely well, has great vision and also showed at the April U-18 World Championships that he can finish plays extremely well, scoring 8 times in 7 games. When he's in possession of the puck, he likes to slow down the play in the offensive zone. He's a thinker on the ice, and can be a threat for a team, whether it's with his playmaking or scoring prowess. On the power play, he likes to play on his off-wing, which is good for one-timers on the power play. Even at his size, he's not afraid to go in the slot and receive passes there. We have seen him score many goals from near the goaltender's crease. He's not a liability away from the puck; he works hard, has a good active stick, and good anticipation that can lead to scoring chances shorthanded. Physically, he gets outmuscled when battling for pucks along the boards and will get pushed over by stronger players. We noted that his compete level doesn't change, and that he keeps going hard. There's a lot to like about this player. If he was a better skater he'd be so much easier to rank.

"Skating is ugly but he seems to find a way to get around pretty good. A small player who has skating issues really needs to wow me in other areas to have me consider rating him as a draft, let alone rank him high. Nordgren does wow me in three other areas, compete, hockey sense and skill. He did a good job making me struggle with what to do with him on my list. Might be a sub par skating small guy outlier." - HP Scout, Mark Edwards

"Nordgren has skating issues. Ryan O'Reilly (not this years draft eligible Ryan O'Reilly) was far from a great skater in his draft year either. I still loved O'Reilly's game and ranked him 21st overall if memory serves, because Ryan had excellent hockey sense, skill and compete. He wasn't a huge player but wasn't 5'9" and a buck seventy either." - HP Scout, Mark Edwards

| NR | NOVAK, JAKOV | JANESVILLE | NAHL | 6' 2.25" | 202 lbs | LW |

Novak is a Riverside, Ontario native, out of the Windsor Jr. Spitfires AAA program and played his Prep hockey with New Hampton School in 15/16 before joining Janesville (NAHL) in 16/17. Jakov is a late 98' birth date who's game took a considerable jump this season with the Jets. Novak has NHL size, listed at close to 6'3" and showed the size and physical strength to dominate games for the Jets. Novak is a power forward that can play both wing and center due to explosive skating and agility. Novak has the tendency to get too involved after the whistle and can get to focused on trying to be that agitating presence instead of just playing his game and as a result can take some unnecessary penalties for his team. Earlier in the season, Novak struggled with consistency from period to period, however in the second half of the season he strung together a lot of consistent outings and this was less of an issue down the stretch. Novak excels offensively when he is able to play with speed and makes sound plays as he enters the offensive zone to create space. His shot has good range and can beat goalies one on one. Novak is committed to Bentley University for this fall.

| NR | NURSE, ISSAC | HAMILTON | OHL | 5' 10.75" | 174 lbs | RW |

Nurse is a competitive, two-way forward with smarts to his game. Issac brings a tremendous work ethic and competitiveness to the table, providing a consistent 200-foot game. Nurse found an effectiveness playing in a complimentary role were he utilized his speed to create havoc on the forecheck and his willingness to play physically to become agitating. While Issac lacks a singular great offensive talent, he uses his competitiveness to create turnovers and win battles, both puck and position, getting himself in ideal positions to be successful. A quality skater with good speed, Nurse will utilize his speed to create offensively, however does lack any real creativity to his game. He shows a good shot with velocity behind his release. He showed the versatility to play up and down the lineup, Nurse's ability to play in various situations makes him a toolsy player at the OHL level, however his upside is likely limited to a bottom six grinder at the pro level.

"Nurse is a player you watch and think, he must be a treat to coach. A competitive forward with an endless motor and great work ethic, you want him to succeed, but his offensive game just isn't what it needs to be for him to be consider a great talent" - HP Scout, Mike Mackley

"He's a player who makes you respect his game just based on work ethic alone. At bare minimum, he's a very effective junior player." - HP Scout, Mark Edwards

| NR | NYMAN, LINUS | KINGSTON | OHL | 5' 9.25" | 156 lbs | RW |

Nyman is an undersized winger with a versatile offensive skill set and good skating abilities. Linus thrives in possession were he displays strong puck handling abilities along with the skill to make a play while moving at top speed. He is versatile in possession as he shows good vision and playmaking skills that can elevate the play of those around him, however he also does a good job at utilizing his shot in the appropriate areas. Away from the puck Nyman shows a good understanding on how to create space. He drives lanes in transition, ultimately opening ice for a teammate and finding a spot to remain a threat in the play. While Nyman is small in stature his quick feet and shiftiness allows him to find an impact off the cycle and create give and go opportunities below the hash-marks. Linus shows good acceleration and can separate from a check. He can also change direction well and create space with his puck skills, however he is just a slightly above average skater which is a moderate concern due to his size limitations. Nyman would benefit from a more fluid and powerful stride, enhancing his lower body and core strength should enhance this area. Linus strength is a concern, he competes but is simply out muscled in the dirty areas, losing puck and position battles as well being easily pushed from possession.

24	O'BRIEN, JAY	THAYER ACADEMY	HIGH-MA	5' 10.8"	176 lbs *	RC

Jay O'Brien was selected in the 4th round, 96th overall by the Youngstown Phantoms in the 2015 USHL futures draft. However, he's primarily played with Thayer Academy, posting 80 points in 30 games. The Wise injury opened up a spot for him and although he was a late birthday, they selected him to join the team in the early pre-season games including the Fall-Classic and later against Michigan State on the USNTDP U18 team where he looked very impressive while putting up an additional 2 points in 7 games. What makes O'Brien's situation unique is that his late birthday makes him ineligible to play in international tournaments like the Four Nations and the U18 World Championships so there's a lack of international exposure there. He's also slated to play for Providence College next season.

His addition to the USNTDP line-up was so seamless was due to his hockey-sense. He has excellent anticipation both with and without the puck, this allows him to find soft-ice and get into position before receiving passes at a consistent rate around the slot area and allows him to identify openings for transitional plays. His decision making is also very good due to his ability to process information on the ice rapidly, this allows him to create and be apart of give-and-go sequences with a high degree of execution. Above all else, his intelligence that he's displayed has lead him to quickly adapting to a higher-level of competition. His hockey sense is also noticeable in the defensive-end where he's good at intercepting pass attempts, he backchecks aggressively when needed and is willing to support his defenseman when the play calls for it on most sequences.

O'Brien's a powerful kid whose developed an explosive first-step which he uses to surprise his opponents and beat them one-on-one when driving wide or when rushing the puck up the ice. His edges allow him to change directions quickly and create an element of surprise. His top-gear is good and he can use it to play a complete game by forechecking effectively and also being defensively responsible on the ice when the play is going the other way. His puck-skills are good, he's got soft-hands and can utilize a variety of dekes to beat defenders one-on-one or to bait an opponent into re-opening a shooting lane where he can use his wrist-shot. His shot has a high-end release, he generates power and he's good at shooting the puck in one motion, it's not an easy shot for goalies to pick up. His passes have a high-degree of precision, he's capable of threading soft-passes through tight seams on the ice and generates several quality set ups in our viewings. O'Brien is a well-rounded player with a level of versatility, his pacing can be difficult to keep up with and this makes him capable of making a forechecking play as well as a high-end play. One thing we really like about him is that there's no area in his game that stands out as a glaring weakness at this point in time.

When he stepped onto the ice for his first couple of shifts for the USNTDP, it was evident that he wasn't a player who looked lost on the ice or got caught trying to do too much, instead there was a lot of confidence in his game, with each passing play that he executed properly you began noticing his presence on a shift-to-shift basis. He's got a high compete level, plays a 200-foot game, and has a skill-set that we believe can translate to the pro level.

"The O'Brien kid looks like an 'A' player to me." NHL Scout, September 2017

"We have him as an early 2nd rounder." NHL Scout, February 2018

"I just saw him again and I'm back in the first round boat." - NHL Scout, April 2018

"A hard working skilled center." - NHL Scout, May 2018

"Starting at the All American Prospects Game I liked his game. I followed up with some viewings of him playing with the USNTDP and thought he was really good with limited ice. In his prep games he had more time and space and it allowed me to see his skill. He's smart and although not huge, he has skill and works hard. I'm a big fan." HP Scout, Mark Edwards

"He had a very productive combine for both interviews and on the testing floor. I spoke to him 1 on 1 after his testing and that conversation did nothing to change my draft ranking for him. He gave me a good self assessment of his game." HP Scout, Mark Edwards

| 196 | O'REILLY, RYAN | MADISON | USHL | 6' 1.75" | 201 lbs | RW |

O'Reilly led USHL rookies (Non-NDTP) in goals with 21 on the season despite missing some games with Mononucleosis. He has a NHL caliber shot and release. He is able to get the puck quickly off his tape no matter how he receives the pass. O'Reilly needs to work on his shot selection and accuracy, as he misses the net a lot when he tries picking the corners, especially when he shoots off the rush. Ryan shows flashes of some poise and playmaking ability in the offensive zone but still plays a shoot first; or drives the net style that limits the impact he can have on the game in the offensive zone. He protects the puck well using his body on his drives to the net. O'Reilly has developed some bite in his game away from the puck; he is physical along the wall and will deliver big hits if the situation arises. His effort away from the puck good but his lack of footspeed limits the effectiveness he has on the back check and winning loose pucks in his own end. He shows good skill in winning possession in battles but lacks the footspeed to get separation from the opponents. O'Reilly has a bit of an awkward and off balance looking skating stride, as he gets stronger in the lower body it could smoothen out but it holds him back in the transition game. His skating will need to improve before he can keep up with the pace of professional hockey. O'Reilly is likely heading to the University of Denver in the fall.

"I think he's going to score a lot of goals at the college level, I just don't see it translating to the NHL down the road but I'm pulling for him, from everything I've heard, he's a great kid that works hard" HP Scout, Dusten Braaksma

"He's 6'2" over 200 who can shoot it and can score but there is a lot wrong in his game. He'll probably be a later round guy."- NHL Scout, December 2017

"Opportunistic player who needs someone to get him pucks. He'll shoot it from just about anywhere." NHL Scout, April 2018

"Huge kid who scored over 20 goals so he could go in the 3rd round." NHL Scout, April 2018

"Late round guy for me because of his bad feet." NHL Scout, April 2018

"Big strong kid but he doesn't play big. he's a no draft for me." NHL Scout, May 2018

"I thought he struggled to make plays...skating is a big weakness and for a guy his size I'd like to see him get to the scoring areas more...he plays outside but he can shoot the puck." HP Scout, Mark Edwards

| NR | OKSANEN, EMIL | REGINA | WHL | 6' 0.5" | 185 lbs | LW |

Emil Oksanen is in his third year of draft eligibility. In his first season in the WHL with Regina Pats Emil had an up and down year. With the Pats hosting the Memorial Cup this season expectations for the team were high for the team and Emil. Emil scored 16 goals and 48 points in 58 games. After the trade deadline he saw his role reduced majorly with the acquisition of Cameron Hebig and Jesse Gabrielle.

Emil is a good-sized offensive minded forward. He has a very good shot and a knack for finishing up close. He uses his vision extremely well; he has the ability to find the open man and works great on the power play. Our concern with Emil his effort level and willingness to do what is needed in the defensive zone. After playing a season in the Finnish second league with men you'd think he would be able to use his size and dominate more down low. However, that isn't the case. Turnovers were a problem for Emil in the defensive and neutral zones.

Emil has great offensive talent but struggled with adapting to the North American game. He needs to put in more effort to become a more well rounded player if he wants to succeed at the NHL level or even the AHL for that matter.

| 68 | OKULIAR, OLIVER | HK DUKLA TRENCIN | SLOVAKIA JR | 6' 1.0" | 191 lbs | LW |

Okuliar is a two-way forward with a high compete level. His skating is average, but he gets around well enough. The key for him is that he keeps his feet moving all the time; he has an impact in all three zones. We were very impressed with his anticipation, as he reads the play well, and will often intercept a pass after making a good read. He's quick to put pressure on the puck-carrier all the time. He's very involved along the boards and plays a physical game, finishing all of his checks. He usually plays on the wing, but can also play down the middle if needed. On the power play, he likes to handle the puck from the half-wall position, showing good poise with the puck and good vision. He has a good shot and a decent release; he's not a high-end offensive player, though. However, he's a smart player who can play in all situations of the game and pays attention to the little details well. He's a player a coach can trust in any situation. It should be interesting to see where Okuliar plays in the next year or two; with his style of play, moving to the CHL could be a good option for him.

| 34 | OLOFSSON, JACOB | TIMRA | SWEDEN-2 | 6' 2.5" | 189 lbs * | LC |

Jacob Olofsson had a good season for Timra despite having some difficulties internationally this past season. He won the golden cage award for being the best junior player featured in the Allsvenskan, where he put up 21 points in 43 games for Timra IK, he also had success in the qualification round where he put up 4 points in 10 games including 3 goals which helped his team qualify for the SHL next season. During tournament play, it was a different story for Jacob, where he had inconsistent performances at every major event, including the Hlinka, the Five-Nations and the U18's where he put up 3 assists in 7 games. His performances left a lot to be desired when factoring in that he was primarily used on a scoring line and was deployed in all situations.

Olofsson is a physically mature, multi-faceted center, with a lot of tools at his disposal. He's got a pro-frame, soft-hands which he can use effortlessly to go around players in one-on-one situations and can skate. We have seen him keep up with some of the faster players in this draft class when aggressively backchecking and he's good at transitioning the puck from the neutral zone over the offensive-end. He does some of his best work when applying pressure on his opponents in the neutral zone, turning pucks over and then making efficient passing plays to move the puck back up the ice. He's got good hockey sense which allows him to read plays at a fast rate and he doesn't need a lot of time to make the smart and safe or the highly-skilled play. He's a swiss-army knife type of player in the sense that you can place him along the half-wall on the powerplay where he's a capable puck distributor, put him on the penalty-kill where he can recognize passing options and intercept the puck consistently, and you can also put him on a forechecking line or on a scoring line where he can compliment some higher-end players. Both his shot and pass have a level of precision and he's adept at masking his intentions with the puck on his stick by minimizing his movement and using advanced fakes to keep defenses guessing. His wrist and snapshot have a good release point and he can be dangerous when driving down a wing, however it's not the most powerful shot. He's a responsible player in all three zones and isn't a player who coughs up the puck or forces plays for the most part, though this can be a double-edged sword in regard to his style of play at times.

Despite having a wide array of skills, physical gifts, and hockey-sense, Olofsson has a couple of pressing issues he needs to address in order to become an effective NHL player. Specifically, in regards to his inability to be proactive instead of reactive in the offensive-end. He's a player who doesn't seem to understand just how good he can be if he was willing to be more selfish and recognize what he's capable of doing with the puck on his stick. We have seen him go completely invisible not just in stretches, but for entire games, and this should be emphasized when discussing his play at international events. We have seen him engage aggressively on the forecheck, use his frame to turn the puck over, then make a great pass into the slot to set up his teammate for a scoring chance, but then we have also seen him take the next 4 shifts off and frustrate us during our evaluations of him. He can play at a high-pace in spurts and has shown that he does have a decent motor but he needs to become more assertive both with and without the puck in order to become a regular center at the NHL level.

"Our guys seem a bit all over the place on this kid." "He's a player that has caused some heavy discussion." NHL Scout, February 2018

"The coach playing number eleven ahead of him (Five Nations) was a crime." - NHL Scout, February 2018

"Wasn't good in tournaments but our euros have liked him in league play." - NHL Scout, May 2018

"I love the kid, some of our guys think there is more skill there than I do, but I think he's a solid top 9 guy who sees the ice really well." NHL Scout, May 2018

"Accountable and responsible but not a great playmaker and that's going to be the difference between him being a solid 3rd line guy or potential 2nd line guy." - NHL Scout, May 2018

"I worry about his skill." NHL Scout, May 2018

"I compare him to Joel Eriksson Ek. Both solid 3rd line guys." - NHL Scout, May 2018

"No, Joel Eriksson Ek is more of a shooter, this guy is a playmaker, so you need players that can get open for him and get to the right spots." NHL Scout, May 2018 (same conversation)

"Smart player who showed very little offensive game when I saw him. He's a player who I keep thinking might have star type tools but I never seem to see the results." - HP Scout, Mark Edwards

| NR | ONYEBUCHI, MONTANA | KAMLOOPS | WHL | 6' 2.0" | 209 lbs | RD |

A bruiser of a defensemen that was dealt to Kamloops from Everett as part of the Garrett Pilon and Ondrej Vala deal as the US division leader was loading up for their playoff run. Onyebuchi is a right-shot defenseman who is as raw as they come but possesses a ton of size and reach which draw your eye to him both on the game sheet and on the ice. Raw is the key in the way you look at him, he's still a little sloppy and isn't the smoothest player, he looks awkward on the ice at times and unsure of his feet. However, his physical presence and battle level are strong, he plays decent defense and knows positioning well, enough so that he gets a fair number of defensive zone starts and his opponents feel his presence because he makes them pay when they're near the crease. He possesses a booming shot with really strong power behind it but his windup is a little on the slow side, not too many puck skills to speak of but managed the puck decently and makes an adequate breakout pass. If he harnesses his body by becoming more coordinated, then there is some future potential.

| NR | PATERSON, JOSH | SASKATOON | WHL | 6' 2.0" | 199 lbs | RW |

Josh Paterson is a big strong forward who played multiple positions this season for the Saskatoon Blades. In his second year of eligibility Josh scored 31 and 52 points in 72 games. The Blades trusted him in all situations and really stepped up for them after the trade deadline.

This season Josh proved he could score goals. He added size and strength, which help his game as a power forward. He used his body to create opportunities in front of the next. He does have great vision and his hands are coming along. He was able to work the cycle game and tire out defenders. He is still lacking the high-end skill however. His skating and acceleration are still below average. Josh tended to shy away from the physical play at times and could get lost out there. He wasn't always a difference maker. Being one of the biggest players on the ice he needs to assert more physical dominance offensively and defensively. Josh is much more suited for a slower paced game which isn't good if he wants to compete at the next level.

| NR | PACHAL, BRAYDEN | PRINCE ALBERT | WHL | 5' 11.75" | 198 lbs | RD |

Brayden Pachal is a strong mobile two-way defender. In his second year of eligibility Brayden scored 7 goals and 26 points in 68 games this season with the Prince Albert raiders. Pachal was relied up in all situations for the Raiders this season. He posses an above average shot that have good accuracy when taken from the point. Pachal has average hands but doesn't try to do too much with the puck. When he gets the puck he makes quick decisions. He has good vision and can find the open made leaving the zone. However, his first pass can be off at times. He has a tendency to force the pass if feeling the pressure. Defensively Pachal has good body position but his mobility got exploited at times. It was noticeable in the playoffs against the highly skilled forwards of Moose Jaw. He has good size but didn't use it all the time for win the battles down low. Overall Pachal has quite a few holes in his game and will need to put in a lot of work if he wants to achieve anything at the next level.

| NR | PADDOCK, MAX | REGINA | WHL | 6' 1.25"* | 150 lbs | G |

Max Paddock is a tall lanky kid. In his first full season with the Regina Pats Max saw lots of action due to trades and injuries. He has 19 wins and 7 losses in 33 games. With a GAA of 2.09 and Save% of 0.904 he had a solid first year. That being said he had a very strong team in front of him as they geared up the Memorial Cup.

Max covers the net very well but needs to add some muscle to fill it up a little better. He had good positioning and is always square to the shooter. Knows where he is in his net at all times. Rebound control is good. Early on in the season he looked indecisive at times on whether or not to go play the puck. One down fall for Max is that he seemed to get rattled when things didn't go his way at times. If that happens teams get a few quick ones past him. He just needs to control his emotions and trust in his defense. Going into next season Max will get the chance to be the full time starter and if he puts it all together can make a difference for the Pats in the future.

| NR | PECKFORD, RYAN | MOOSE JAW | WHL | 6' 0.5" | 191 lbs | LW |

Ryan Peckford is in his second year of eligibility. Peckford was acquired by the Warriors in a major deal but he never really round his stride in Moose Jaw. Inconsistency was a major factor. He was given the opportunity on Moose Jaw's second line with Brayden Burke and Justin Almeida but never really clicked. Most of the year he played a bottom six role. On the power play he struggled as well, trying to force shots and making poor passes.

Ryan is an effortless skater and makes thing look too easy at times. He often looks like he doesn't care and isn't putting in the effort. Some of the time we believe this to be the case. He has the skill but just doesn't seem willing to go that extra mile needed. Ryan does have a natural ability to put the puck in the net at times. He can finish when put in the right situations. His hands are one of his strongest qualities. Ryan has the ability to make guys miss when he has the puck. He can control down low with his edge work. Ryan was non-existent most of Moose Jaw's playoff run. Defensively turnovers in his own end were a problem.

Ryan does have that high-end potential but lacks the consistency and effort needed play at the next level. After being past over in last seasons draft and having an average year we don't see a team taking a chance on Ryan at the draft.

| 103 | PEKAR, MATEJ | MUSKEGON | USHL | 6' 0.0" | 170 lbs | LC |

Pekar is a hard working two-way forward that can provide quality minutes in all situations for his team and is a player that his contributions might not always show up on the scoresheet despite being close to a PPG player for Muskegon in 17/18. Matej has a good motor that he uses to be effective on the fore-check. He has the ability to read and anticipate the play and uses his crafty stick work and relentless puck pursuit to turn pucks over as well as win puck battles. Pekar isn't an explosive skater off the hop at this stage but has above average straight line speed, edges and good footwork in tight areas that allow him to be elusive with the puck on his tape. Pekar is able to drive possession in the offensive zone by using his body to protect the puck, has good vision of the zone and is able to distribute the puck to an open teammate and create a cycle game down low. Pekar likes to play more of a playmaking style and tries to set up his teammates for goals and will need to continue to develop his shot before he can become more of a scoring threat. Defensively Pekar is an asset for his team, his ability to win 50/50 pucks is an asset and he shows good effort on the back check as well as willingness to come back into his own end to provide support. Pekar isn't physical on guys in the sense he will deliver big hits but he is good an initiating contact enough to gain just a little bit of separation in order to win loose pucks and clear pucks out of his own end.

"I got higher on this kid as the season went along, brings a consistent effort every night and a really smart 200 foot player, is effective in executing the little things on the ice." HP Scout, Dusten Braaksma

"He'll go to the net but I don't like his skating mechanics." NHL Scout, December 2017

"Skating mechanics are bad but he gets around and he's got a shit load of points most of which I attribute to hard work." NHL Scout, January 2018

"Not that much skill there...4th or 5th rounder for me but I bet he goes higher." NHL Scout, January 2018

"I like the way he plays...he's a relentless player." – NHL Scout, March 2018

"He's one of the best in the USHL as far as forecheck and getting after pucks. He creates a lot of turnovers." – NHL Scout, March 2018

185	PERBIX, JACKSON	ELK RIVER	HIGH-MN	6' 1.0"	176 lbs *	RW

Perbix is one of the youngest players eligible for this year's NHL entry draft, born on Sept. 13th, 2000. Despite his age Perbix was able to dominate the Fall Midwest Elite League for Team Northwest, putting up 28 points in 17 Games as well as the Minnesota High School season where Jack registered 21 Goals and 47 assists in 27 Games. Perbix finished the season with Green Bay in the USHL where he acclimated himself well in a limited role in 19 games played.

Perbix has an NHL frame but has a ways to go physically before he has NHL size. Perbix has high end offensive skills with the puck on his tape, he has the ability to beat defenders one on one and deke around multiple players on his way to the net. He shows good poise with the puck in the offensive zone and is able to thread passes through narrow lanes and likes to play with a pass first mentality in the offensive zone. His skating stride needs development as he is not explosive in his first few strides and needs to get stronger with his edge work. As he matures physically these areas of his skating should improve. Perbix also needs to show more consistency in his drive and compete without the puck. Perbix is a highly skilled player with the puck but doesn't always work hard enough to get the puck back when he loses it and can look disinterested in his own end in some of our viewings. Too often he is waiting for the puck to come to him or is the second guy in on battles. With a talented Elk River team that can make a State Title run next year it wouldn't shock many if Jack played the fall and spring for Green Bay (USHL) but returned to Elk River for his Senior Season. Perbix is committed to the University of Notre Dame for the fall of 2019.

"There are some intriguing tools there for him to be a solid prospect but I don't think he is necessarily a player that is going to make others better." HP Scout, Dusten Braaksma

"He runs very hot and cold, sometimes not just from game to game but shift to shift" NHL Scout (December, 2017)

"He's a no draft for me but someone will probably take him." NHL Scout, January 2018

"Highly skilled and good compete but not a great skater." – NHL Scout, April 2018

"Skill level is just ok and his work ethic runs hot and cold, I think his games been exposed a bit in the USHL." NHL Scout, April 2018

| 83 | PERUNOVICH, SCOTT | MINNESOTA-DULUTH | NCHC | 5' 9.25" | 172 lbs | LD |

Scott Perunovich is a double over-ager who had tremendous success this past season after putting up 36 points in 40 games for Minnesota-Deluth, he also made the American team at the U20 world Junior Championships where he collected 3 points in 7 games in an impressive performance. Considered a late-bloomer, expect him to not get overlooked for a third straight year.

Perunovich lacks size, he's slight of build and not very tall, however he does have a skill-set that minimizes his physical deficiencies. Although his stride is short, he's a mobile player, with excellent edges and a quick first step and a fast-top gear that gives him separation speed. He uses his skating ability to carve in and out of traffic while rushing the puck and is capable of transitioning through all three-zones. His best qualities are his passing ability and vision. He's always got his head up and surveying the ice while looking for long stretch passes to his teammates. This was noticeable during the U20 WJC where he was one of the more proficient passers. His first-pass is sharp and lands on the tape of his teammates while in motion and he plays with confidence when he's setting up plays both from his own-end and in the offensive-end. This allows him to quarterback a powerplay where he uses his plus puck-skills and edge work to breakdown the opposing team before finding seems to thread his passes through. He's also a capable shooter though it's not his primary instinct, his wrist-shot has good mechanics and it's accurate, he's also good at getting it through traffic and using it as a fake to set-up slap-passes to his teammates around the net.

Due to his size constraints, the defensive-side of his game is based around his defensive-reads and his willingness to play bigger than his size when needed. He's not afraid to take on larger players along the boards and is willing to battle to attain a loose puck, although he recognizes his stature, preferring to use his stick to break up offensive plays. In our viewing's, his defensive positioning has been above average and his processing ability on the ice is high-end which allows him to evade incoming forecheckers by finding teammates with his passing ability before they can reach him most of the time. One aspect of his defensive game which could improve is his motor, sometimes he doesn't play at a pace that you would want to see, especially of a player his size, he seems to conserve some of his energy for his rushes.

"He had a good freshman year at UMD and a good World Juniors for Team USA, having said that I'm probably not as high on him as most. He was put in a lot of situations to be successful this year. Probably still worthy of a pick though." HP Scout, Dusten Braaksma

"I like him a lot, I think he's a late 2nd or early third rounder." NHL Scout, January 2018

"As dynamic as he is in the offensive zone, he's a very efficient puck mover as well." – NHL Scout, January 2018

"I have him as a 2nd rounder." – NHL Scout, January 2018

"He's a good skater but when paired with his size it downgrades him and that's what will keep him from being too high of a pick." - NHL Scout, January 2018

"Probably go top 60 but for sure a top 90 guy." NHL Scout, January 2018

"D-men like him are so valuable, great skill and has range all over the ice." NHL Scout, January 2018

"Better brain and skill than (Torey) Krug but not as good of a skater as Krug." NHL Scout, February 2018

"Not a burner out there but still a very good player. He's got some nasty in him and he doesn't back down" NHL Scout, April 2018

"Skilled, playmaking, free wheeling D-man but I'm not sure he's fast enough or has the hockey sense to play in the NHL. - NHL Scout, May 2018

"By the time I'd draft him I'm guessing he'd be gone." NHL Scout, May 2018

| 151 | PETTERSEN, MATHIAS EMILIO | MUSKEGON | USHL | 5' 9.5" | 170 lbs | LC |

Pettersen is a native of Manglerud, Norway, left for the United State at 14 to join Selects Academy in 2014 and then earning a tender offer from Omaha (USHL) in 2016 where he played the 16-17 season. Pettersen was then traded from Omaha to Muskegon in the spring of 2017. Mathias, once regarded as a potential first round pick, Pettersen's development has cause expectations to drop a bit in the last year but remains a solid Draft prospect. Pettersen is not the biggest player but has a strong base and protects the puck well on the perimeter. Pettersen has struggled with being too much of a perimeter player that would struggle against tougher competition. While much of that rang true early on in his USHL tenure, in recent viewings Mathias has shown he has adapted to the North American game and shown the ability to get to the net and gain middle ice. Mathias has displayed the ability to use his skill and determination to overcome the size disadvantage he may have on his defenders. Pettersen has deceptively quick release on his shot and can change the angle at the last second and beat goaltenders one on one. Has powerful, low center of gravity skating stride and a good motor on the fore-check. Shows good 200 foot effort but his defensive awareness has come into question at times. Pettersen may project better as a playmaking winger than a Center down the road and has played both positions this season. Pettersen will join the Denver Pioneers this fall, where a few departures have paved the way for him to have an opportunity to contribute right away.

"There is nothing really wrong with his game but nothing jumps out at you that screams NHL either." HP Scout, Dusten Braaksma

"Not really a guy that I had too much time for, but one of our guys banged the table a bit for him." - HP Scout, Mark Edwards

"I'd be surprised if he gets drafted. Not on my list." - NHL Scout, January 2018

"Good Junior Player." - NHL Scout, April 2018

| 105 | PIVONKA, JACOB | USA U-18 | NTDP | 5' 11.8" | 201 lbs * | LC |

Jacob Pivonka is an American born player of Czech decent who was drafted 53rd overall by the Hamilton Bulldogs in the OHL priority selection in 2016 but chose to stick with the U.S development program. Although his stat totals of 19 points in 54 games don't jump out at first glance, it's his complete 200-foot game that features a high-level of compete at both ends of the ice and the ability read the play with and without the puck that stands-out.

Featured as a depth player both at international events and on his USNTDP Junior team in the USHL, Pivonka excelled in a forechecking and penalty-killing role. When he was not involved in the game offensively, he managed to make an impact with his puck retrieval skills by being heavy on his opponents and using his frame as leverage to separate the puck from players on the forecheck and when battling along the boards in his own-end. One of his best assets is his defensive reads away from the puck, we watched him create turnovers at the defensive blueline by reading the play in advance and using his forecheck to pressure his opponents into making mistakes that led to generating short-handed scoring chances and puck possession. What makes him a capable forechecker is his thick frame which he's not afraid to throw around and his straight-line speed which is generated through a powerful lower-body. When he has the puck on his stick, Jacob plays a stream-lined game and doesn't have the high-end skills associated with some of his offensively gifted teammates, however he does think the game at a high level and is capable of finding soft-ice, as well as setting up his teammates for scoring chances. He likes to mix up his passing and shooting options, his shot is accurate and has power behind it though he's not someone who can consistently create scoring chances for himself in one-on-one situations or a player who looks to always drive-play. Instead, he is most effective when paired with someone who can find him behind coverage or off the rush where he can use his speed.

He's unselfish and knows the limitations of his game, rarely forcing play which makes him an effective and efficient player at both ends. Pivonka has had a solid year for the development program, showing a quality two-way game with some offensive-upside, though at this time he looks to be more of a depth player than a forward who will play regularly in a top-6 role.

"He's a Swiss army knife, I'd trust putting him over the boards in any situation, his hockey smarts are that good." HP Scout, Dusten Braaksma

"Liked him since my first viewing of him and I still do. Only difference is that with more viewings I started to downgrade his offensive upside a bit." HP Scout, Mark Edwards

| 112 | PLASEK, KAREL | BRNO JR. | CZREP-JR. | 5' 10.5" | 154 lbs | RW |

Karel Plasek is a talented winger who played for 4 teams this past season. They include the HC Kometa Brno U18 and U20 teams, as well as their pro team in the Czech league, and he played the most games with HC Prerov of the Czech2 league where he posted 11 points, including 9 goals in 18 games before going pointless in 2 playoff games. Like some of the other Czech forwards in this draft, he also has an extensive international resume, including captaining the Czech team at the U18 Five-Nations and put up 5 points in 7 games, including 4 goals at the U18's, while saving his best performance against Sweden.

Plasek is a skilled-winger with a slight frame who is dangerous off the rush. He's not the strongest kid so he doesn't generate too much power in his opening couple of steps but he's mechanically sound and this allows him to have plus acceleration regardless of his strength which helps him create an excellent top-gear that gives him good separation speed. We have seen him take advantage of his skating ability on the penalty-kill where he's capable of creating turnovers and then rushing the puck up ice, as well as generating quality chances during odd-man rushes. His puck-skills are good, he can make difficult toe-drags before releasing his shot while moving laterally across the slot and can use his hands to evade incoming sticks. This allows him to guard the puck well despite his stature and he's shown the ability to play at a high-pace in spurts. However, we found throughout the season that his energy levels were inconsistent and this reduced his overall effectiveness on the ice in some of his performances. He's a player who can go invisible in spurts and frustrate but he's also a player who flashes a lot of offensive-upside. His scoring ability is diverse, possessing a snap like release on his shot; he sweeps on the follow through and it generates some velocity. He can also beat goalies with quick stick movements, lifting the puck over them, as well as playing above his weight class in-front of the net which has allowed him to jam the puck in during rebounds. He has shown the ability to score from a variety of locations on the ice, and his one-timer has been threatening on the powerplay. He's got several ways to score on opposing goalies.

His offensive-upside is apparent and he's defensively responsible. However, there's been several times where we wished he would have used his offensive skill-set more than he does, his hockey-sense is above-average and we have seen him develop line chemistry and cycle effectively but there's too many shifts and too many games where he leaves you wanting more. That being said, Plasek is still a skilled winger who has a high-offensive ceiling, if he can learn to be more assertive and consistent on a shift-to-shift basis he could turn into a dangerous scorer at the pro levels.

NR	POPOWICH, TYLER	VANCOUVER	WHL	6' 4.0"	201 lbs	LC

Popowich has been given every chance to excel at the WHL level after being a the number 3 over all pick of Vancouver in the 2015 Bantam draft, he was able to get a full season in before his draft year but his decent bantam numbers haven't translated. In his rookies season he often looked out matched paying on the top 2 lines for a poor Vancouver team, despite his big frame he looked intimated at times, was pushed around and generally looked slow in most aspects of the game that required skating or agility; he has one gear and can't step his speed up to separate. Something clicked in his draft year, his numbers weren't much better but he became an integral part of a majorly improved Vancouver team. His compete level was far greater, he began to use his body and became a strong cycle player, learning his use his frame to box out opponents, he was being used to a lot in the defensive zone take a fair number of draws with decent success. Learned to stick up for his teammates and still only managed 31 penalty minutes. Left wanting more when viewing Popowich, as there are tools there but he would often make a couple good plays and vanish at times, when he can get into space his shot is strong and powerful, his lack of speed just cuts don't on his ability to generate shots. Will be an interesting player to track as a re-entry candidate over the next few years, but unless his clunky footwork improves, he won't see pro hockey.

133	PORTILLO, ERIK	FROLUNDA	SWEDEN JR	6' 6.0"	207 lbs	G

Erik Portillo played for three separate teams in Frolunda's system this past season, which caused him to remain under the radar compared to some other international netminders. He had a 2.41 GAA and a .931 save percentage in 10 games in the J18 Elite, and a 3.08 GAA with a .907 save percentage in the J18 Allsvenskan. He also played 2 games in the SuperElit, posting a 0.71 save percentage and a .974 save percentage.

Portillo is a very tall, yet coordinated and fluid goalie, giving him one of the better bases in this year's draft class. Despite his rangy build, Erik likes to cut off his angles aggressively. This allows him to take up a tremendous amount of the net when adjusting for shots off the rush or during lateral passes across the crease and high-slot. He can make saves that very few other goalies can make due to this length; for instance, when he has bitten on a fake short-side shot and his opponent attempts to wrap the puck far-side, he doesn't need to re-position himself to the same degree most other netminders would, having the flexibility and extension necessary to take away the entire bottom of the net when lying on the ice. Additionally, he can transition into his butterfly and his reverse-V-H at an impressive rate given his height, and when pressed up against the post, there's very little room for shooters to look at. Another one of Portillo's better attributes that separates him from other tall goalies in this class are his reflexes. After misreading initial shot attempts or having to respond to an impressive cross-ice pass that sets up a one-timer, we have seen him come away with high-end reactionary saves. Although, his glove-hand is kept-lower than most goalies in his stance due to his size, he's still capable of making impressive glove-saves.

Although he has great physical attributes and tools, Portillo does have trouble tracking the puck in heavy traffic at times and displayed average to below-average rebound control when we viewed him, as well as having a tendency to sit in his butterfly after the initial shot too long. Additionally, despite being mobile and fluid in net, his aggressiveness can get the best of him at times, throwing himself out of position on secondary saves. Despite his inconsistencies, Portillo is a dark-horse prospect due to being buried in a deep Frolunda system which didn't give him an opportunity to get noticed as much as some other goalies. Despite not getting as much opportunity, we think he has one of the highest raw-upsides in this class.

111	POSPISIL, MARTIN	SIOUX CITY	USHL	6' 1.5"	173 lbs	LC

Pospisil, a native of Zvolen, Slovakia who just finished his rookie season in the USHL, registering 8 goals and 29 Assists in 49 Games. Pospisil is a player that plays over the line a lot of the time. He gets under opponents skin but also takes a lot of bad penalties and his style of play has resulted in racking up 253 Penalty Minutes in 49 games as well as a number of suspensions this season. Martin is a gray area player that will deliver some vicious hits all over the ice and plays with a lot of disregard for his own or opponent's safety at times. As aggressive and physical as Martin's game is, it's not without offensive skills. Pospisil has good hands and vision and makes quick plays with the puck coming out of battles. Martin is a big strong kid and is able to take plays to the net and create havoc in front with his fearless style of play. His straight line skating is explosive and is able to get to a top speed quickly. His edgework and agility needs to develop before he can be offensively effective at the next level. Pospisil is heading to St. Lawrence University this fall where his style of play will need to be adjusted at the NCAA level. Pospisil misses opportunities to be more of an effective player because of his style of play; his offensive tools will give him a chance at the next level if he can reign in the rough neck style of play that tends to cost him and his team.

"He doesn't need to play the way he plays; he has enough skill to be effective without the stupid stuff, some of his actions, you just roll your eyes sometimes." HP Scout, Dusten Braaksma

"I think he gets too wrapped up in playing a role or putting on a show than being a hockey player and it comes across as selfish to me." NHL Scout (March, 2018)

"If this was 15-20 years ago he's probably be a first or second round draft pick." NHL Scout (December, 2017)

"I think he's over 200 penalty minutes. I struggled to see him because he was suspended all the time. This kid is prone to snapping the odd time. (laughing) - NHL Scout, April 2018

"If you look past the penalty minutes, He actually has a lot of skill and he's a smart player." - NHL Scout, May 2018

"No strength. He's kinda skin and bones and his skating is weak but he's draft worthy." - NHL Scout, May 2018

"If he gets stronger and improves his skating he's got a chance." NHL Scout, May 2018

"I like him. He's a nasty player with some skill. He makes plays." - NHL Scout, May 2018

NR	PROPP, CHRISTIAN	NORTH BAY	OHL	6' 2.0"	183 lbs	G

Propp is a good sized netminder with intriguing athletic ability and a maturity to his game. Christian shows raw, but improving technical skills, however does rely on his athletic ability often. Propp uses his physical traits to his advantage, Propp often challenges shooters, making himself big in the net to deny the shooters eye. He is able to use his height to battle through screens, enabling him to track pucks fairly well. Christian is able to play his angles effectively which elevates his ability to control his rebounds and cuts down the amount of net the shooter can see. Propp shows good lower body strength as he quickly can push out to the top of his crease from the butterfly position to square shooters. He moves well in the net, showing strong post-to-post movements, however there is room to become more fluid with his side-to-side pushes. Propp tends to rely to heavily on his athletic ability to recover when allowing rebounds and would benefit from anticipating the play more precisely as he can be slow to react and caught flat-footed. Christian is average in his puck playing ability, while his poise and maturity in the goal can allow him to be a calming presence.

"One of our guys liked him and wanted me to watch him. I don't personally see NHL upside." - NHL Scout, March 2018

63	PROSVETOV, IVAN	YOUNGSTOWN	USHL	6' 4.5"	175 lbs	G

Ivan Prosvetov is a 99' born re-entry goalie prospect. He played for the Minnesota Magicians (NAHL) last season in his first draft year and was impressive, putting up a 2.52 GAA and a .928 save percentage, but went undrafted in the 2017 NHL Draft. This year, he posted a 2.90 GAA and a .913 save percentage in 36 games for the Phantoms. In the playoffs, he led his team to the Clark Cup Finals, posting a 2.58 GAA and a .921 save percentage in 11 games.

Ivan Prosvetov is a raw netminder with one of the best combinations of size and athleticism in the draft. He showed progression sine last year, gaining considerable lower body strength which has allowed him to un-tap his athletic attributes. Considering his build, he's got exceptional coordination and reflexes, giving him the ability to make secondary saves and recovery saves that very few other netminders can make. His explosive push-offs and rapid east-west movement allowed him to cover a lot of the net in short-order. When he's playing with confidence and cutting down his angles aggressively, there's very little room to look it. Although raw in the sense that some of his mechanics aren't overly refined, his movement and reactions allow him to recover. His transitional butterfly is one of the best in this class, dropping in and out of his butterfly at an impressive level. Though, his rebound control isn't refined right now. This forces him to rely on his length and reactions more than on his technique. We have seen him get burned on goals that he would have stopped if he was looking to square up to the shooter and use his size, as opposed to his reflexes.

Additionally, Prosvetov has displayed a mixed glove-hand depending on the game. He's capable of making highlight-reel glove saves, but then occasionally loses his concentration or loses track of the puck and lets in a soft goal. Another interesting aspect of Ivan, is his stance when positioning himself for a draw, he tucks his glove next to the side of his calf due to his length, this might explain why he's late to certain glove-hand saves.

Prosvetov doesn't seem to be interested in going the NCAA route, so its undetermined where he will be playing next season. Ivan is at the stage of his development where he needs to continue to refine his technique so that it catches up to his tremendous base. There's few other netminders in this class with his ceiling and net presence when he steps onto the ice.

"He has a ton of pro potential, one of the top goalies out of the USHL this year in my opinion, I was surprised he wasn't drafted last year." HP Scout, Dusten Braaksma

"I'm not a big fan and I doubt he gets drafted." - NHL Scout, April 2018

"I need to go back to see him again, he's not bad." - NHL Scout, April 2018

"I saw him late in the year and he was very good. I liked his size and the kid is an athlete." - NHL Scout, May 2018

"Not a draft for me." - NHL Scout, May 2018

"There is a lot of upside to that kid." - NHL Scout, May 2018

"I watched him late in the year and liked his game. Not a ton of goalies I'm crazy about this year and he didn't exactly get much love from scouts I spoke to about him, but this kid is draft worthy in my opinion." - HP Scout, Mark Edwards

NR	PURPURA, VINCENT	OMAHA	USHL	6' 3.0"	174 lbs	G

Purpura is a 98' born goaltender out of the lesser known Chicago Fury youth Program. Vincent spent last season and that start of this season with the Johnstown Tomahawks (NAHL) but his steady play and an opening on the roster saw him get brought in by the Omaha Lancers in November. His steady play for Omaha in 23 games helped earn him an offer to Boston University where he has since given a verbal commitment for the 19/20 season. Purpura controls the top of crease well and challenges shooters aggressively in one on one situation without over committing himself or getting out of position. Purpura is aggressive in defending his turf in front of him and isn't shy about giving shots to screens in front of him. Vincent's lateral movement is not explosive but he displays a smooth technique that should improve as he gets stronger. Vincent does a good job in limiting rebounds that hit his body but can put pucks in dangerous areas on shots off his pads. Purpura will likely spend one more season in junior hockey before a spot opens up at Boston University.

120	RAGNARSSON, JACOB	ALMTUNA	SWEDEN-2	6' 0.0"	176 lbs	LD

Ragnarsson is the son of former NHLer defenseman Marcus Ragnarsson who played for 9 seasons in the NHL. Jacob who was born in California played this past season in the Allsvenskan league and as matter of fact he was coached by his father this season with Almtuna.

He's a solid two way defenseman, nothing flashy about his game but has good skating abilities and footwork. Over the course of the season as his game adapted to the Allsvenskan he was making quicker decision with the puck and moving his feet more efficiently. He doesn't do often but he can rush the puck into the offensive zone. He retrieves pucks well in his zone and he can avoid the pressure of the forecheck. He has not showed elite offensive upside, he's got a good first pass out of his zone but we didn't see any qualities other than skating that could translate to the NHL as an offensive defenseman. He has a good stick defensively and also has a good gap control. He's quick to put pressure on the puck carrier when defending one on one, giving less time to make plays on his side of the ice. He has average size and can be overpower physically in his own zone. He's not an aggressive player physically, he plays more with his smarts in his own zone but with added strength could compete a bit better and not get pushed over as much.

Ragnarsson upside offensively is quite limited for the NHL. We think of him as a potential late pick because of his smarts and footwork.

NR	RANDL, JACK	OMAHA	USHL	5' 10.5"	178 lbs	LW

Randl just finished his 2nd full season with the Omaha Lancers, registering 20 goals and 12 assists in 49 games. Randl is a hard working center with average size and above average skating ability. Randl shows a good motor all over the ice and is responsible at both ends. Randl doesn't have much in the way of dynamic offensive ability but through his work ethic he is able to score goals in close, around the net. Randl shows good anticipation without the puck, particularly on the penalty kills where he can be a shorthanded threat when challenging the points. Randl displays good straight ahead speed and is very strong on his skates. Randl doesn't project as a player that is going to drive a lot of the offense for his team but he has the hockey smarts and skating to do a lot of little things that when they add up, help his team win hockey games. Jack will likely be off to the University of Michigan this fall where he joins a team with a talented recruiting class that is coming off an impressive run to the Frozen Four.

"I don't think he has a ton of skill or anything but he is a player I will be interested in tracking as his college career progresses because of his high motor, work ethic and hockey IQ, he's just one of those players I think will find a way." HP Scout, Dusten Braaksma

"He's just a hard worker, I haven't seen him make any plays." - NHL Scout, September 2017

"He plays hard but he's 5'10" or something like that with no skill to speak of and no quickness." - NHL Scout, December 2017

"I respect his game. He's a meat and potatoes player...works his tail off but he's lacking in the skill department. I remember I was shocked the first time I saw him because when I first heard about him people were raving to me about how high end he was. When I watched him in Pittsburgh this fall I thought to myself that he's a late round pick if anything." - HP Scout, Mark Edwards

NR	RANDKLEV, CARTER	MOORHEAD	HS-MIN	5' 7.0"	150 lbs	LC

Randklev is a highly skilled but undersized winger that uses his quick feet and hands to create space and beat players one on one. There is some selfishness in his game from time to time; however he has shown strides in distributing the puck and using his teammates better in recent viewings. Randklev has a very slender build and not at lot of size at 5'7" so his creativity; hockey sense and quick skill are paramount in him being an impact player down the road. Randklev has showed the ability to be productive against bigger and older competition this year. Aside from his 47 points in 28 Games for Moorhead High School, Carter played 14 Regular season games for Fargo putting up 2 goals and 7 assists as well as being close to a PPG player for Fargo in the Clark Cup Playoffs. Carter needs time to develop physically, so the added gym time in the NCAA will go a long ways for him long term. Randklev was originally committed to Arizona State but opened back up him commitment this season and quickly committed to nearby North Dakota where he will play this fall.

"I think he has late round flier written all over him, his size is obviously an obstacle for him but he has too much skill and smarts to write off for me." HP Scout, Dusten Braaksma

76	RANTA, SAMPO	SIOUX CITY	USHL	6' 1.5"	199 lbs *	RW

Ranta is a native of Finland who just finished his second season with Sioux City after coming to North America from the Red Bull hockey Akademie. After struggling with injuries last season, Ranta enjoyed a healthy season for Sioux City, registering 23 Goals and 14 Assists in 53 games.

The first thing that stands out in Ranta's game is his dynamic skating ability and explosiveness. His skating is close to elite in all areas. He is able to get to top speed very quickly, which makes him dangerous in transition where he is able to quickly find gaps as well as gain the edge on his defender. While his speed and skating is his greatest weapon, on a lot of situations Ranta would simply skate himself out of scoring areas or beyond the play. When Ranta shows patients and poise and picks his spots to use his speed is when his offensive tools take over and can create offensive chances. Ranta possesses an excellent shot arsenal, especially off the rush where he likes to cut to the middle of the ice and use defenders as screens for shots on goal. Ranta possesses an accurate one-timer and does a good job getting in position; both off the rush and on the Power Play and can find the corners and get pucks on net with passes that are not set on a tee. Ranta doesn't have great playmaking ability but possesses a simple, effective skill set with the puck on his tape that includes accurate passing and good vision in all three zones. His compete level and work ethic both on and off the ice is an asset to any team he is on. Ranta possesses solid leadership attributes and played in all situations this season. Ranta competes hard and does a good job executing the small details in his game on a nightly basis. Ranta will be off to the University of Wisconsin this coming fall.

"Looks like a first rounder to me." NHL Scout, September 2017

"He's skilled but he's not a smart player." NHL Scout, September 2017

"He's all over the place...he's skating here, there and everywhere...shooting from anywhere. He's fast though so someone will take him higher than he should go." NHL Scout, February 2018

"People keep telling me he'll go early second but I don't see it...he just doesn't move the needle for me. I'll rank him where it's obvious I don't want him." - NHL Scout, February 2018

"His game hasn't evolved at all." —NHL Scout, May 2018

"I don't think he has fully figured out how to best use his speed and match it with his skill. That's his biggest challenge going forward because he has a lot of tools that show NHL talent." HP Scout, Dusten Braaksma

"I've been saying I'm not a fan of his game since the Fall Classic. I just don't see hockey sense. He skates fast and has skill but it gets wasted too often with poor decisions in all three zones. HP Scout, Mark Edwards

"Got some good feedback from one scout on his combine interview." – HP Scout, Mark Edwards

61	REGULA, ALEC	LONDON	OHL	6' 3.5"	203 lbs *	RD

Alec Regula is a defense-first defender but finished with 25 points in 67 games, including 18 assists, and he had zero points in 4 playoff games.

Alec was often tasked with covering for his defensive partners more offensive-minded style. He created chemistry while showing that he was capable of complimenting high-end defenseman, as opposed to disrupting them. The mental attributes that make him a complimentary defender were his defensive-awareness and positioning. This allowed him to aggressively close-gaps and disrupt both shooting and passing attempts. Alec likes to survey the ice and is a cerebral defender, who consistently surveyed back-door options and recognized passing lanes that his opponents were attempting to use. Additionally, he was good at recovering for both himself and his teammates by using an extra gear and out-competing opponents along the boards. He was was effective in man-to-man coverage due to his length and tracking ability. His mindset when carrying the puck was how to pass it off to his partner or another talented teammate as quickly as possible. He did this by making several smart and efficient passes in our viewings, and understood the limitations of his game, which allowed him to reduce the rate of turnovers he caused compared to several other defenders in this class.

He's never going to be an offensive-force, but his solid mobility and hockey sense allowed him to pinch at appropriate times and help generate some of his better scoring chances. His release point is average and he's not overly skilled which doesn't allow him to threaten too much when walking the line. He seemed aware that it wasn't an area of strength, opting to make simple plays that allowed his team to maintain possession. One area of strength we noticed was his ability to set Evan Bouchard up for his one-timer, so he showed that he can help compliment his defensive-partner not just in the defensive-end, but when also generating scoring chances.

Regula has an excellent defensive-base to develop from and we think if he can gain more muscle and continue to grow into his frame and further enhance his already impressive defensive-reads, he could become an NHL regular who may also be used on the penalty-kill down the road.

"I didn't see London in the first half of the season as much as I usually do but caught up a bit with them in the second half. Regula is a player that kept getting better as the season progressed." – HP Scout, Mark Edwards

| 197 | REICHEL, KRISTIAN | RED DEER | WHL | 6' 1.3" | 177 lbs * | RC |

Kristian is son of former long time NHLer Robert Reichel, and he established himself as a top-line centre in the WHL in 2017-18, his first season in North America. This is his second draft eligible season and he recorded 57 points and 34 goals in 63 regular season games for the Rebels.

Reichel is a competitive centre who loves to score goals. His best asset may very well be his explosive shot. He can shoot in stride and has a heavy one-timer. He played the point on the first powerplay unit consistently throughout the year. He releases the puck quickly and from anywhere in the offensive zone. In addition to his heavy shot he has skill with the puck and can make defenders miss. Kristian utilizes a long reach and can protect the puck well despite his slight weight. He has a strong, low centre of gravity he utilizes to win puck battles. Although he is a definite shooter, he has at times shown the ability to make plays for his teammates, but this is not an asset. He is most comfortable finding dead spots in the offensive zone and getting the puck off his stick quickly when he receives the puck. Overall, he was a consistent offensive threat because of his shot.

His skating ability looks a bit unconventional, as he generates most of his speed through cross overs where he appears to be "high stepping." His feet are sluggish and although he can get up and down the ice enough to be apart of the rush, he does not have an explosive stride or quickness to consistently create space for himself. He is at his best in the offensive slot or top of the circles where he is able to utilize his shot. At this point in time, Reichel appears to be a one-dimensional player. His ability to score may not be strong enough to overcome his lack of speed and explosiveness.

| NR | REINHARDT, COLE | BRANDON | WHL | 6' 0.5" | 203 lbs | LW |

ole Reinhardt was selected in the 9th round of the 2015 WHL Bantam draft. In his second season with the Wheat Kings he has defiantly proved many teams wrong. Scoring 19 goals and 34 points in 68 games, which was a major improvement from his rookie year.

Cole is a big strong grinding two-way player. He loves to play the physical style and be that pest on the ice that the other team hates to play against. Cole isn't afraid to drop the gloves and stick up for his teammates. He goes to the dirty areas on ice and often sacrifices the body to make the play. Played in all situations for the Wheat Kings this season with penalty killing being his strength. He would block shots when needed. Cole's skating needs some work. His mobility and acceleration seemed to be an issue some nights, which forced him into taking unnecessary penalties. Cole's compete level is never in question. Offensively may not be the most skilled but works hard every game and defensively Cole is extremely reliable. Overall Cole opened some eyes this season, however at best we see him being that role player on third or fourth line in the NHL.

| 184 | RIPPON, MERRICK | OTTAWA | OHL | 6' 0.5" | 191 lbs | LD |

Merrick is a defensive defensemen that had and up and down 1st season in the OHL. He started the year with Mississauga and struggled to get his feet under him coming from the JR. A ranks last year, he then got traded to Ottawa and slowly settled in.

He is a good-sized defenseman with good skating ability, whether it's skating forward with the puck or transitioning backwards. Merrick has a very good and hard first-pass coming out of the zone; he also has shown at times throughout the year to be smart with the puck. He wasn't given many chances to show his offensive side, either with Mississauga or Ottawa, but going into next year he might get more opportunity with Ottawa. He struggled this year in the defensive-zone versus big forwards working on the cycle, as he was getting pushed around a lot, he also was getting caught watching the play in front of him instead of staying with his man. He can play a physical game if needed and makes forwards pay when coming into his zone. He will sometimes tend to be overly aggressive in the defensive zone, which then leads to penalty's or missing his man and allowing them free access to the net

Merrick needs to work on slowing the game down when he has the puck and allow the play to develop in front of him; he also needs to work on getting stronger on his feet and to keep everything simple when in the defensive zone with or without the puck.

"To me he's like Chisholm. I saw flashes of ability there but not enough to say in our meetings that I really like this guy." - NHL Scout, February 2018

"There were times I thought he was a good skater, there were times I was like, this guy can't skate. Guys like him where I can't figure out what they are after a lot of viewings are guys I don't want on my list. He may play but I just don't like this type of player." NHL Scout, May 2018

He works really hard but I thought he was just too vanilla. He'd be a late pick for me if at all." - HP Scout, Mark Edwards

NR	ROBERTS, CONNOR	FLINT	OHL	6' 3.75"	210 lbs	RC

Connor Roberts was drafted 3rd overall by the Hamilton Bulldogs in the OHL draft. After having a relatively unsuccessful start to the season where he produced 8 points in 22 games with Hamilton, he was traded to Flint, where he was given top-line minutes and used in all situations, becoming one of Dellandrea's main passing options. His increased role came with greater success, posting 27 points in 44 games, including 15 goals.

Roberts is a center with pro-size who's also able to play on the wing and was mostly deployed on the right-wing for Flint. His offensive-output was primarily generated in-front of the slot area or directly at the top of the crease though he was also capable of generating points while rushing down the wing, while showing good skating mechanics, characterized by plus straight-line speed. Despite occasionally producing goals while shooting in motion, he was inconsistent in recognizing when he should change the angle of his release point and wasn't very good in the majority of our viewings at executing from the high-slot and out. That being said, from a stationary position, he can generate power in his shot and had a couple of well-placed goals when we viewed him. One of his biggest offensive-drawbacks was his inability to create for himself due to having average puck-skills, it was difficult for him to create space for himself or his team since he couldn't breakdown defenseman in heavy traffic or in one-on-one situations often. Furthermore, he showed mixed decision making with the puck at times, opting to make a low percentage-pass when he had a prime scoring chance in the slot as an example, though this was primarily from the hash-marks out, and he was capable of distributing the puck quickly around the goal-line while also having a couple of quality give-and-go sequences.

Despite having a pro-build, Connor's not overly aggressive and lacks a tenacious style of play. He's also not a highly competitive player and didn't take advantage of his physical gifts as much as we would have hoped to have seen this past year. Although he was capable of penalty-killing and making solid defensive-plays where he would use his reach and frame to disrupt passing attempts and block shots, he had difficult processing the play in some sequences by not recognizing the time and space he had to work with.

Roberts was very mixed in most of these aspects throughout our viewings, he would generate power on his release on one shot attempt, then shoot a soft shot on the next. He could make a quick pass around the goal-line, and then completely misfire on a delayed pass on the next attempt. It was hard for him to remain consistent with his skill-set. So, despite his pro-frame and above-average shooting mechanics, there's little in the way of high-end skill and when taking into account his consistency, it's unlikely he becomes a regular scorer at the pro levels.

The problem is hockey sense. I will say he was better in Flint but it's always been about his lack of hockey sense. He's big, he's ok once he gets rolling but quickness isn't there. He has skill but needs to be better thinking the game." - NHL Scout, May 2018

" In Minor Midget he had a few games where he flashed a great shot but in general he left me wanting more. He lacked some hockey sense and I feel that trend has continued so far in the OHL. Not a player I would draft if I was with an NHL team." - HP Scout, Mark Edwards

176	ROBERTSON, CARTER	OTTAWA	OHL	6' 2.0"	181 lbs *	LD

Carter is another good size defenseman that came into the league last year and struggled on a young blue line for Ottawa. He had some ups and downs which is usual for a younger player but showed some glimpse of what he can be as a player. This year he had a bit of a tough start trying to build off last year, because he was bothered with a lower body injury and missed a good amount of games at the beginning of the year. Carter is a puck moving defensemen, that has a decent first pass out of the zone, ok with his decision making with or without the puck, and he has good awareness around him. His skating lacks the acceleration or quick few steps coming out of the zone with the puck. Carter plays a reliable game in the defensive zone; he has good positioning and has a really good stick on the penalty kill. He has good gap control in the neutral zone and doesn't give defenders any room to move around him. He is good at identifying his man; he usually keeps his man in front of him and seldom loses one on one battle in the corners. Carter struggles with holding onto the puck too long sometimes rather then making the quick play to get the puck out of the zone, but has shown some offensive ability this year. He needs to work on his quickness both on the offensive and defensive side of the game.

" A faller for me this season. The more I watched the less I liked his overall puck game." - HP Scout, Mark Edwards

54	RODRIGUE, OLIVIER	DRUMMONDVILLE	QMJHL	6' 1.0"	156 lbs *	G

Rodrigue was the 3rd overall pick in the 2016 QMJHL Draft, the highest a goalie was chosen in 10 years at the annual midget selection. It didn't take long for Rodrigue to establish himself in the QMJHL last season, and he became the Voltigeurs' number 1 goaltender early in the season. He had a bit of a tough 2nd half, but bounced back big-time this season, starting the year by winning gold at the Ivan Hlinka Tournament for Canada as their starting goalie. This season, Rodrigue played over 50 games and won 31 games on a very good and young Drummondville team that surprised a lot of people. Rodrigue was a big part of their success. He was top 5 in the wins and goals-against average columns, and top 10 in save percentage.

Rodrigue is very technically sound; he's very quick and has great lateral agility in his crease. His footwork is excellent; he's very quick to adapt to shots changing direction in front of him. He has good rebound-control and has improved his puck-tracking with traffic in front of him, as last year he was getting beaten often with point shots while facing traffic. He's listed at 6'01", so in today's NHL, he's an average-sized goaltender. Physically, he's slight, and will need to get a bit stronger to improve his endurance. Rodrigue is very calm in his crease; he doesn't get rattled often and is pretty strong mentally, as he usually stayed pretty focused, even after allowing a bad goal. He has a great mental game; he grew up around goalies, as his dad is a goalie coach currently with the Edmonton Oilers.

Rodrigue is one of the top goaltenders available for the 2018 NHL Entry Draft.

"I started cold on him at the beginning of the season, but he won me over in the 2nd half. His size is an issue, and he will get drafted later because of it, but at least he can stop pucks, unlike some of those bigger goalies." -HP Scout Jérôme Bérubé

"One of the goalies who was good in my viewings this season. He may suffer from the NHL's 6'0 bias syndrome. One of the better goalies for me this season." HP Scout, Mark Edwards

"Six foot one at the combine..." NHL Scout, June 2018

71	ROMAN, MILOS	VANCOUVER	WHL	5' 11.8"	196 lbs *	LC

The 6th overall pick in the CHL import draft has made his presence known early in the year as a mainstay as Vancouver's top line centre, his presence added to their already solid forward group and he adapted quickly to the rougher style that is often seen in the WHL. Unfortunately he only managed to get into 39 games due to an ankle injury but still managed 32 points (10G 22A). He exhibits a strong top speed and a really good tempo of play with or without the puck, he's a heads up player with a strong cerebral aspect to his game, this combo gives him the ability to drive play and keep fluidity to the offense. Exhibits responsibility all over the ice and doesn't stray from strong defensive position unless he takes it upon himself to lead the rush up ice with other speedy Vancouver forwards. In viewings we appreciate his motor he uses it to attack loose pucks, its consistent and shows a good level of conditioning while despite missing almost 2 months he got back into a few games and look himself again by the playoffs contributing 3G – 3A in 7 games. He needs to improve on his faceoffs and his play below the goal line as he does compete well but can get out muscles, so despite his above average speed strength can be an issue. He isn't in the top end of this draft but as WHL players go he's one of the more intriguing offensive options and one of the few center with a really positive offensive upside, he will add some intriguing depth to a teams prospect pool expect his name to be called on day 2.

"He's a draftable player for me. Competes hard and has some skill." - NHL Scout, November 2017

"Probably a 3rd or 4th rounder for me but I like things in his game." - NHL Scout, December 2017

"A full season would have more people talking about Roman, he always looked to be in the right spot because his skating was sneaky good. More of passer than a shooter but would love to see him diversify his offence by shooting more." - HP Scout, Andy Levangie

| **156** | **ROMANOV, ALEXANDER** | **CSKA 2** | **RUSSIA-JR.** | **5' 11.0"** | **185 lbs** | **LD** |

Alexander Romanov played for Krasnaya Armiya Moskva in the MHL where he put up 14 points in 37 games including 7 goals. He also gathered an assist in 4 playoff games. He played for Russia at international events, putting up 4 goals in 4 games at the U19-World Junior A challenge and 3 points in 5 games at the U18 world Junior championships.

Romanov is a slightly undersized yet tenacious two-way defender who likes to shoot the puck. He's got plus puck-skills which he uses both at even-strength on the powerplay to alleviate pressure but doesn't use them consistently when we watched him. His offensive-instincts are a plus and he's good at recognizing how much time and space he has to make a play from the point. He's an instinctive shooter, always surveying the ice and looking for an open shooting lane to use his high-calibre slapshot. His slapshot is also difficult for goalies to absorb due to a reduced wind-up, which keeps them from always getting square to the shot in time and he's good at timing his shot with a screen to make it difficult to track through traffic. He's capable of shooting the puck in one-motion after receiving passes both during rushes and when stationary. Alexander is also fleet of foot, displaying good four-way mobility which allowed him to make some well-timed pinches. Although he has skill and a solid release, he's not overly creative and sometimes gets tunnel vision, opting to shoot even if there's a passing lane that would lead to a better scoring chance. However, he can be dangerous from the offensive-blueline and generates scoring chances at a decent clip.

He's not only involved in the offensive-side of the ice. He's a well-rounded defender who plays bigger than his size, showing a high-degree of fearlessness when engaging against larger players. We have seen him deliver some massive hits, sending much bigger player crashing to the ice. He has plus pivoting mechanics and this allowed him to alleviate the forecheck consistently when we watched him by either side-stepping his opponents or spinning off of them. His passing ability is sharp and he can make accurate stretch passes though he's also capable of rushing the puck up the ice where he usually makes a smart and simple play instead of attempting a creative play that might result in him losing his positioning. When he is caught, he's capable of backchecking aggressively, but he's also quick to recognize when he needs to transition from offense to defense which prevents this from happening too often. One of his best defensive qualities is his ability to hone in on his opponent during man-to-man coverage and he was aggressive with his stick when attempting to take the puck away.

Romanov has some untapped offensive potential and a well-rounded defensive game, however he's undersized, doesn't possess any dynamic qualities, and lacks the high-end puck distribution skills that you want to see out of an offensive-minded defenseman. He's a defender who's in a tough spot, he doesn't have a lot of physical tools and he's most likely not going to be a big time point contributor so he's going to need to continue to develop his defensive game and rely on his aggressive yet energetic style of play in order to be an effective pro.

| **131** | **RTISHCHEV, NIKITA** | **CSKA 2** | **RUSSIA-JR.** | **6' 1.0"** | **191 lbs** | **RW** |

Nikita Rtishchev is a high-tempo winger who excels on the forecheck. He played for Krasnaya Armiya Moskva in the MHL, where he put up 30 points in 45 games and an additional 2 points in 4 games in the playoffs. He also played in the Hlinka and U19-World Junior A challenge, where he was used in a checking role.

Rtishchev has a high-octane motor and impressive skating ability which allows him to apply overwhelming pressure to defensive-units. He's a large winger who has a strong base, and this allows him to generate a lot of power in his first couple of steps and then take off. He plays with a lot of confidence when rushing the puck which created several successful transitional zone-entries when we watched him play throughout the season. Additionally, he's strong on his skates and has plus edges which allows him to protect the puck. His puck skills are good and he can use his hands to beat defenders one-on-one or make them back up and respect him when he's coming over the line. Nikita is difficult to play against because he can adapt his skill-set on the fly due to thinking the game at a fast rate. As an example, when dealing with a large defender with length who can keep up with him off the rush, he would adapt and chip the puck into the zone, make the defender turn and use his skating ability and size to overwhelm down-low. His forechecking skill-set is tremendous, he's got an active stick, is adept at angling his large frame to protect the puck and is relentless during puck pursuit situations. His offensive-skill set is unique in the sense that despite his speed, he's usually at his most dangerous down near the goal-line as opposed to off the rush. His shot lacks velocity and he wasn't overly successful at using it through screens in our viewings. Despite some of his shooting mechanics, in-front of the net, he uses his size and puck tracking skills to look for rebound opportunities and has the hands in-tight to beat goalies upstairs. Additionally, he's got above average passing skills and can make high-end passing plays occasionally which gives him another element to his offensive game.

Nikita doesn't just compete hard in the offensive-end, he's willing to expend his energy to defend. He uses his speed to effectively backcheck and is an aggressive winger without the puck who closes gaps quickly at the blueline in an effort to turn the puck over and rush back up ice. Rtishchev doesn't have the highest offensive-ceiling compared to some of the other higher-ranked wingers but he's a competitive player who has the potential to excel in a depth-role at the pro levels.

| 209 | SAIGEON, BRANDON | HAMILTON | OHL | 6' 1.5" | 194 lbs | LC |

Saigeon is a two-way centre with an intriguing frame and skill to his game. Brandon has elevated his defensive game and play away from the puck throughout his OHL career allowing him to find success as a two-way forward. Brandon possesses an intriguing skill set, Saigeon handles the puck effective and shows and ability to make smart, skilled decisions with pace, showing good awareness of his surroundings. Offensively Brandon shows a versatility as he displays good vision and passing skills as well as a strong release and good accuracy behind his shot. Saigeon's playmaking skills are often elevated with added time and space, making him a player who's game elevates with the man advantage. There are consistency issues with Brandon's game as he can utilize his combination of size and skill to thrive throughout a game, but also can blend in and become a non-factor. For Saigeon to find an effectiveness at the pro level he will need to enhance his skating ability. He currently possesses a short stride that hinders his acceleration and overall top speed. While Brandon does show intensity to his game at times, he needs to become more aggressive and assertive with his frame in the dirty area and while competing for loose pucks or body position. He has taken time during his OHL career to begin to produce offensively, this trend might follow Saigeon to the pro level.

"A good junior hockey player with limited pro potential, unless he can significantly improve his skating and improve his consistency issues." - HP Scout, Mike Mackley

"I give him a lot of credit for the progress he's made in his game. Skating still an issue but he's worked hard to improve his game." - HP Scout, Mark Edwards

| 213 | SALDA, RADIM | SAINT JOHN | QMJHL | 6' 0.25" | 185 lbs | LD |

Salda was passed over in last year's NHL Entry Draft and made the decision this year to play in the Canadian Hockey League. He was drafted by Saint John in the CHL Import Draft. He was one of the most impressive rookies in the league this year, and a lone bright spot for the Sea Dogs, who were one of the worst teams in the QMJHL.

Salda has good athletic abilities on the ice; he skates well and has above-average mobility. He's active on the ice, has quick feet and gets involved offensively by supporting or leading the rush. He's also good on the power play by creating some scoring chances with his feet, and has a good point shot. He's a capable passer; he has a good first pass out of his zone and on the power play, he can move the puck pretty well. The biggest problem for Salda, and likely a good reason he went undrafted last season, is his decision-making. We had some viewings of him this season where he played quite poorly. The tools are there, but his decision-making was really questionable.. If he can improve that, he could be a player possibly down the road. He has decent size and can play a physical game as well; he's not shy to get involved and plays the game with passion. He plays a very North-American game along the boards.

Salda will be back next season for his 19 year old season in junior, and the Sea Dogs should be better next year and build a better supporting cast around him. After the Veleno trade, he was the key player of this team, and it should be the same thing next season.

"I don't mind him and think he could get picked late in the draft as a re-entry, but I can't forget a viewing that I had of him in Drummondville. If I were to judge him solely on that viewing, I wouldn't have picked him in a 15-round draft." - HP Scout Jérôme Bérubé, December 2017

"He lost me after a couple of viewings this season. Just too many mental errors, especially for a 2nd time eligible player. Jérôme has seen him more and likes him more than I do." - HP Scout, Mark Edwards

| 126 | SALMELA, SANTERI | KOOKOO | FINLAND | 6' 1.25" | 194 lbs | LD |

Salmela is one of the better defensive prospects from Finland for this year's draft, and this season he played most of the year in the top men's league in Finland (31 games with Kookoo). We like his smarts and skating abilities. He's not a flashy offensive defenseman, but he uses his skating abilities to quickly retrieve pucks in his own zone and can also adequately skate the puck out of his zone. He's plays a pretty smart and mature game on the ice, which did help him this year, as he was playing full-time in Liiga. He makes good decisions with the puck and plays a simple game without making a lot of turnovers on the ice. He manages the puck pretty well. He moves the puck decently, playing a safe and smart game with the puck on his stick. He lacks some upside offensively, and won't wow anyone with his creativity and play on the power play. He defends well, with good footwork to keep up with quick forwards, has a good gap control, and uses his stick efficiently. Salmela doesn't have the highest upside, but we like his smarts, defensive game and skating abilities.

| 172 | SAMUELSSON, ADAM | USA U-18 | NTDP | 6' 5.75" | 240 lbs | LD |

Adam Samuelsson is a physically developed shut-down defenseman, who can make a first-pass and chip in offensively. The defender finished with 24 points in 57 games while being used in all situations for the USNTDP. He is slated to play in the NCAA for Boston College next season.

Adam will likely never develop into an offensive powerhouse on the backend, he still has time for that area of his game to improve but it's other aspects to Samuelsson's game that allow him to have regular shifts. His most noticeable attribute is his size, he's an enormous kid who's physically well developed with a long reach. He likes to survey the neutral zone and deliver crushing hits that create turnovers, however, this can be to his detriment at times, overextending on transitional zone entries which inadvertently throws him out of position which creates odd-man rushes against. Despite this, he's more than capable of using his frame to weigh heavy against players along the boards and is good at anticipating when a player is attempting to drive wide on him where he uses his length to create turnovers and deflect pucks away from the net. His positioning in his own end is decent and he uses his thick frame to block shots in shooting lanes. His biggest drawback defensively is his inability to contain players who have a high degree of acceleration and at times he's unable to read the play at high speeds which puts him a step behind and forces him to cause turnovers when he doesn't have enough time to process where to place the puck for a passing option. Though he is capable of making a first pass.

While walking the line at even-strength and on the powerplay, he wasn't very efficient compared to some of his teammates. In certain sequences we have seen him get overwhelmed due to lacking the high-end skill or skating ability necessary to get himself out of trouble if his passing lanes were taken away. His shot isn't refined, despite his size, he doesn't generate a lot of power and his wrists don't seem to have the flexibility necessary to create leverage on his release at this point in time. His offensive-awareness is also mixed, he's capable of pinching appropriately but fails to recognize back-door options and when his shooting lanes are clogged depending on the shift and the game. We feel Adam didn't take advantage of his powerplay opportunities and selfishly, for our scouting purposes, we wish we could have seen some of the other defenseman get more of those opportunities instead.

If Adam doesn't make it to the NHL, it might be because of his skating deficiencies and some of his poor defensive reads causing him to get behind the play. A player of his size needs more time than the average kid when developing a first step and the edge-work necessary to make it at the pro level, so that needs to be factored in when assessing his development curve. He improved in that area to a limited degree as the season progressed. Samuelsson needs to continue to develop his skating ability to make it at the NHL level. If he is successful in doing so, he can become a potential bottom-pairing, shut-down defenseman who may be used on the penalty-kill.

"Everything is just a couple of beats too slow." – NHL Scout, November 2017

"His decision making just hasn't improved like I hoped it would, he has some tools and all the size you want but I think he projects as a shutdown defenseman and until his decision making improves he can't be trusted in that role." HP Scout, Dusten Braaksma

"Not a player that I'd personally have ranked more than a later round pick. Great size but he struggles to adapt in many facets of the game when the pace picks up." – HP Scout, Mark Edwards

39 SAMUELSSON, MATTIAS — USA U-18 — NTDP — 6' 4.0" — 218 lbs * — LD

Mattias Samuelsson was a defensive force for the USNTDP, who played top-four minutes and in all situations while putting up 31 points in 53 games. He's slated to play for Western Michigan University in the 2018-2019 season.

Samuelsson's a physical specimen who uses his frame and weight effectively to drain opposing forwards while also delivering big hits, which made him difficult to play against. He's a competitive player who tries not to give his opponents an inch. This made him effective in boxing-out players as well as weighing heavy against them along the boards. He's got a good blend of anticipation and bite to his game; the end result is a defenseman who has a high-degree of defensive presence when he steps onto the ice. He's an intelligent defender, who recognizes shooting lanes in advance and rarely throws himself out of position when looking for a big hit. It's probably expected for Samuelsson to be average with his first few steps considering his size, he's a young kid who's still developing into his frame. However, he does have a powerful base and has shown decent straight-line speed both with and without the puck. Another important aspect of his game defensively is his composure. Due to this, he's aware of his physical abilities and doesn't panic with the puck during aggressive forechecking sequences.

In the offensive-end, he doesn't play a high-tempo or dynamic game at the line, rarely using little more than a shot fake to re-adjust his shooting lanes and doesn't look overly comfortable when attempting to cut through traffic. That being said, his offensive awareness is good, making timely pinches to help support his teammates or generate a scoring chance for himself. Both his wrist-shot and slapshot generate power and he has an above average release. He also recognizes when goalies are screened at the point and when he has time to step-in and create a better scoring angle for himself. His first-pass allows him to transition the puck up the ice and he can make fast and accurate passes in the offensive zone, this allowed him to distribute the puck efficiently throughout the year on the powerplay.

Samuelsson's a cerebral, physically imposing, two-way defenseman who has a high-floor but not as high an offensive-ceiling as some of the other defenders expected to go in the first round. However, if he can continue to improve his first-few steps and round out his offensive-game. We see Samuelsson as a player who can develop into a defenseman who can log a lot of minutes for an NHL team.

"He's one of my favourites in this draft, very efficient in his style of play." HP Scout, Dusten Braaksma

"He dropped slightly for me as the year progressed because of my offensive projections for him but I'm a fan of his overall game. He'll eat minutes but he's not a player our whole staff is sold on as a potential high pick.. Not predicting nor did I hear anything, but it wouldn't shock me to see him in the OHL next season." - HP Scout, Mark Edwards

30 SANDIN, RASMUS — SAULT STE. MARIE — OHL — 5' 11.0" — 186 lbs * — LD

Sandin is a smart well rounded defender with good mobility. He shows good possession skills where he confidently handles the puck and makes strong decisions. He's a capable puck carrier with good foot-work, its his ability to see the ice and lead transition with an great first pass that allows him to thrive. Rasmus possesses excellent edge work and can effortlessly elude an opponent showing poise and strong foot-work. He does however need to improve his first step as it is one of the more average traits to his game.

Offensively Sandin acts as a distributor in the offensive zone, however he will often utilize his feet to walk the line and open shooting lanes, changing the velocity and angle of his shot appropriately to get pucks on net. He makes good reads away from the puck, showing aggressive pinches to extend zone time when needed and sneaking in from his point position to create offensive opportunities.

Defensively Sandin excels as a stick-on-puck defender, using his mobility and smarts to excel. He keeps strong gaps and is able to keep the play in front of him due to his skating. Rasmus angles the opponent to the outside well and shows deceptive strength in his ability to stand up an opponent and separate player from puck. In the defensive zone he shows an ability to contain.

Sandin is not a huge kid but he's not shy to battle and play a physical game. Our biggest concern is the amount of hits he sustains while playing the position. We noticed this even more down the stretch.

"He's one of the smartest draft eligibles in the OHL this year ...great puck mover too." NHL Scout, November 2017

"He's a tough one to evaluate, I think a team needs a plan for him if they are going to pull the trigger early in the draft." NHL Scout, May 2018

"One thing I like is he isn't afraid. He'll turnover pucks sometimes when he's pressured but he's not soft. The kid will go where he needs to go and he get's involved." - NHL Scout May 2018

"My biggest concern is injury. He isn't big and he really struggles to avoid contact. It's such an underrated facet for defenseman." - NHL Scout, May 2018

"Love his smarts and his puck moving ability, he's a great player. My only issue is one shared by several scouts I spoke to about Rasmus...he gets hit a lot and he's not a big player. The old saying...the biggest ability is availability. It's the only reason I dropped Robby Fabbri slightly back in his draft year, he got hit hard a lot in my viewings and so did Sandin." - HP Scout, Mark Edwards

"For development reasons, some NHL teams will be curious as to where he plans to play next season when factoring that into their draft day decision. Feedback I got from some scouts seemed to be a little bit all over the place." - HP Scout, Mark Edwards

NR	SAVAGE, RYAN	FARGO	USHL	5' 11.0"	187 lbs	RW

Ryan is former 1st Round draft pick of the Fargo Force who was well travelled in his minor hockey days. Ryan started in the Phoenix Jr. Coyotes youth system and then attended the Red Bull Akademie in Salzburg, Austria where his Father and former NHLer Brian Savage was an Instructor. Savage returned to North America and played for the Detroit Honeybaked program last season and this season played for Team USA at the Hlinka Memorial Tournament before joining Fargo of the USHL, eventually being traded to Omaha at the end of the season. Savage is a hardworking, smart forward that brings a physical element to his shifts. Savage is often first in on the fore-check, pressuring and being physical on the opposing defenseman. Savage does a good job staying below the pucks in his own zone and has shown willingness to block shots and make plays at key times in his own end. Offensively, Ryan doesn't have a lot of dynamic puck skills and plays a very straight ahead, power game with the puck on his tape. His skating is not explosive off the jump at this stage but possesses decent top end speed and can be difficult to handle when he drives the net and his shot is an asset off the rush. Savage projects as a checking line forward that possesses good intangibles and work ethic. Ryan will be off to Miami (OH) this fall.

"I wouldn't be shocked if a team grabbed him in the later rounds, having said that he a wait and see prospect for me, I don't think he skates well enough right now" HP Scout Dusten Braaksma

"I doubt he gets drafted. I don't really see any NHL projection for that kid" NHL Scout, April 2018

"I actually had time for him the first time I saw him, but the more I saw the more I couldn't ignore the lack of size and poor skating." - HP Scout, Mark Edwards

150	SCHMID, AKIRA	LANGNAU JR.	SWISS-JR.	6' 4.0"	165 lbs	G

Akira Schmid is a large and technically refined goalie who played for the Langnau U20 in the Elite Jr A, the SCL Tigers in the NLA and the EHC Thun in the recently formed league the SRL. Internationally, he was featured at several international tournaments, his best performance coming at the Hlinka where he put up a 1.96 GAA and a .930 save percentage in 3 games.

Schmid takes up a tremendous amount of the net due to having a broad frame and a wide-stance. This stance allows him to look around screen attempts easily which helped him track pucks through heavy traffic in most sequences. His frame allows him to take up a lot of net when he's in his reverse V-H, making it difficult for shooters to beat him upstairs. Unfortunately, due to his size and not having filled out his frame yet, he's not as agile or as athletic as some of the other top-rated goalies. We have still seen him make some great reactionary saves off deflections though and his ability to read the play when in-tight to the net is a plus, which has allowed him to recognize fakes in advance and not bite too early before sprawling out to make some high-level saves. His technical ability for his size and age is impressive. He has good mechanics when moving off posts and his butterfly leaves little room for the shooter to find a seam through, his glove is positioned high on most plays as well. Additionally, he rarely enters hit butterfly too early, and rarely looks panicked in the crease. He's a calm and composed goalie even when under heavy pressure, which occurred often due to the Swiss National teams having a lack of depth compared to some of the other squads at international events.

Akira's movement when pushing off laterally isn't as refined as other aspects of his game. Specifically, when pushing from left to right before attempting to square up on shots from his blocker-side. Although his lateral movement when in a standing position has room for development, his movement when pushing out to cut down angles is impressive. This has allowed him to make several high-quality saves by cutting down the angle aggressively during shots in the slot-area. Furthermore, when kicking out his pads on either side he does show a level of fluidity. That being said, arguably the weakest aspect of his game are his reflexes. He can still make saves off deflections and rebounds but it's not high-end, which makes it more difficult for him to make reaction saves and recovery saves compared to some of the other goalies in this class.

Schmid has a lot of plus attributes and the mental traits needed for a goalie. If he can continue to grow into his frame and develop quicker movement in net so that he doesn't need to rely on his reactions, he could develop into a solid pro.

NR	SCHMIDT, COLIN	WAYZATA	HS-MIN	6' 4.5"	228 lbs	RW

Colin Schmidt entered this season with high expectations among many NHL Draft Scouts. The 2016 1st Round Draft Pick of the Waterloo (USHL) and 2015, 11th Rd. Pick of Prince George (WHL) decided to return to Wayzata H.S. where many thought the 6'4" 220 lbs. Center would dominate his competition. While Schmidt wasn't bad for his team, his season didn't meet many scouts' expectations.

Schmidt possesses a wicked release on his shot and some good fundamentals in protecting the puck using his body along the wall but his effort shift in and shift out was inconsistent and looked uninterested for stretches of games. Schmidt carries around a lot of size but he gets around the ice pretty well for a big kid but in some viewings he would get caught out on the ice too long and become a liability for his team in his own end. For a player of Schmidt's size who could take the puck to the net at will against most competition at the High School level, he played a perimeter game in our viewings, electing to try to setup plays from the outside or take lower percentage shots from the outside that at the upper levels wouldn't result in the points like it does at the high school level. In the games that Schmidt used his size to gain middle ice he was as dominate as you'd expect him to be. Having said that, Schmidt looked like a much better player in his three games with Waterloo (USHL) at the end of the season and was able to dominate for stretches in a game against Madison in April.

" I started the season very high on this kid but after the first couple viewings he started to drop and never rebounded, he shows flashes but if some shifts you can't notice a 6'5" 220lb forward playing High School hockey, it's a big red flag. Having said that, when he makes himself noticeable, his size and skill is well on display!" HP Scout, Dusten Braaksma

" He always seemed to be out of energy when I watched him; I don't think his conditioning is where it needs to be or he was hurt." NHL Scout

NR	SEMIK, JACOB	DUBUQUE	USHL	6' 1.0"	174 lbs	LD

Semik is a former first round draft pick for Dubuque in 2016. Jacob finished is second full season with the Fighting Saints. Semik is out of the Detroit Honeybaked U16 program and a University of Michigan commit. While nothing about Jacob's game jumps out at you and screams an NHL prospect there are certain characteristics of his game that have seen tremendous growth in his two years in the USHL. Semik has tremendous poise with the puck, especially coming out of his own end where he is able to look past his first read and stretch the ice by hitting forwards with speed in the neutral zone and is good at recognizing his support and using it when he gets cornered. Semik possesses decent agility and footwork with the puck but needs to work on his footwork and leverage without the puck as he is susceptible to getting beat or outmuscled in one on one situations. While semik's offensive production isn't impressive points wise this year, 4 goals and 15 assists in 55 Reg. Season games, his game has some skill in the offensive zone. His footwork and poise with the puck allow him to open up lanes from the point and get pucks down to high traffic areas. The last we heard, Semik was slated to enter the University of Michigan this fall but with a lot of returning players it wouldn't surprise us if Semik played one more season in the USHL.

" I think he got written off a bit too soon, on too many nights he was his team's best defenseman, it's not all about points when you are a 17 year old defenseman in a tough league." HP Scout, Dusten Braaksma

| NR | SEMYKIN, DMITRI | STUPINO 2 | RUSSIA-JR. | 6' 3.0" | 201 lbs | RD |

Dmitri Semykin is a powerful, two-way defenseman who produced 15 points in 41 games, including 8 goals. Although his point production at first-glance doesn't stand out, he played on a vastly over-matched team, where they had 6 wins in 64 contests.

Despite his team's unfavourable circumstances, Semykin held his own in our viewings and was an option for Stupino on both special-teams units. He was dangerous at even-strength and on the powerplay due to his varied offensive skill-set. He had good anticipation at the offensive-blueline, which allowed him to jump into the play and use his size and plus straight-line speed to generate scoring chances when attacking the net. In one of our viewings, he intercepted a clear attempt and then aggressively cut down the left wing before lifting a backhander into the top of the net, as an example. Although he would hold his release point too long on occasion, Dmitri was good at bearing his weight into his shot and generated several rebounds. That being said, his puck-skills are not overly refined at this time and he had a tendency to over hold the puck when he didn't like his options.

Semykin's physical tools stood-out and complimented his aggressive game. We watched him deliver some big hits and he played with an edge. When put into a recovery sequence, he was mostly up to the task and would display a high-compete and effort level when trying to make up for his mistakes. Although defensively responsible, his gap-control was inconsistent and due to a lack of agility when pivoting, he was susceptible to players beating him wide when he was caught flat-footed. Despite some inconsistencies in his own-zone and not having a lot of help in the offensive-end, Semykin is a large right-shot defenseman, with impressive physical tools and an above-average ceiling.

| 190 | SEPPALA, PEETRO | KOOKOO JR. | FINLAND-JR. | 6' 1.0" | 178 lbs | LD |

Seppala is good two-way defenseman from Finland with decent skating abilities and above-average size. He can play on both sides. We often saw him play on the right side when playing for the national team. He has decent skating abilities, and can skate the puck out of his zone. He can either lead the rush or support it. He uses his good footwork to retrieve pucks in his own zone. In his own zone, he plays an efficient game, keeping things simple and playing relatively safe. He does a good job using his long stick to block passing or shooting lanes, and he's also good at knocking pucks down when defending one-on-one. He competes well along the boards and in front of the net. He's not a flashy defender (similar to Salmela, another defensive prospect from Finland). With the puck on his stick, we would like to see him make quicker decisions, mostly in the offensive zone, as his offensive upside is presently limited. However, he has made some improvements to his offensive game over the course of the past season. He can make a good, crisp, accurate pass, which speeds up the transition game. But overall, Seppala projects more as a defensive defenseman with some decent puck-moving abilities. If he can continue to work on his offensive game, he would only add to his value as a prospect.

| 56 | SHAFIGULLIN, BULAT | REAKTOR | RUSSIA-JR. | 6'1.0" | 165 lbs | LC |

Bulat Shafigullin had a very productive year for Reaktor Nizhnekamsk in the MHL, producing 36 points in 22 games, including 22 goals while being used in all situations. He also put up 15 points in 9 playoff games. Bulat got called up to the KHL where he had 2 assists with very limited icetime in 17 games before going pointless in 1 playoff game. He was never featured at any major international event despite his production.

Shafigullin is an athletic power-forward with a lot of high-end tools. He's got a broad frame which helps guard the puck, and a wide-stance when he skates, but he's an explosive player who can generate a lot of power in his stride, creating an excellent top-gear, despite having an inward knee-bend due to not having the strength developed in his legs yet. This causes him to get knocked off pucks and get overwhelmed when cutting around players occasionally, but he has a high-level of coordination and is agile, which allows him to weave through the opposition while avoiding contact. He's a possession player who likes to drive play with the puck on his stick and instinctively cuts to the net regardless of the traffic in-front of him. This has led to us watching some impressive individual efforts by him throughout the season. We have seen him fake his movement while skating down the wing before holding his release and aggressively cutting across the slot area, out-waiting the opposition, which allowed him to re-open his shooting lane. His goal-scoring output was prolific in the MHL and this was due to understanding how to find soft-ice without the puck, while also being able to generate a dangerous shot off the rush using his length and a quick release point. Although he has a take-over mentality with the puck on his stick and the hands to maintain possession, he's also capable of making some very difficult passes which we have seen him thread along the half-wall and around the goal-line, both at even strength and on the powerplay.

Unfortunately, despite his tools, he's prone to making notable lapses in judgement. For example, during a breakaway sequence where he had separation between himself and the defender, he inexplicably stopped up and made a no-look, between the legs pass to his teammate who was trailing him, this led to taking away any scoring chance. This type of decision making wasn't seen in every game we watched, but it was frequent enough where it became a discussion point when ranking him. Furthermore, he plays at an all-out pace, which is great on some sequences but makes him very inefficient in others. When driving down a lane he looks to get towards the net area as quickly as possible, which has given him success, but he would have an increased rate of success if he welcomed a change of pace and knew when to stop up and alter his attack more than he currently does. He plays the game one-way most of the time, which is to use his outside edges and his speed to cut aggressively while driving down the wing, if he can learn how to use his tools in multiple ways in the offensive-end more consistently on a shit-to-shift basis, then he can become a very productive pro player.

Regardless of his sometimes questionable decision making, his willingness to leave the defensive-zone too early on occasion, he can still make some of the more dynamic plays when compared to some of the other players in this draft class. Teams will need to decide when the upside wins out versus some safer, yet lower ceiling players.

"This is a strange year. As is the case with Kravtsov,, we have no live viewings of Shafigullin and were forced to rely solely on video. That said, the kid impressed me. There are parts of his game that remind me of Jonathan Huberdeau...he even looks to be about the same size at the same age. Shafigullin has a ton of skill and showed me the willingness to backcheck and take the puck to the net. Aside from a few brain farts, he showed some hockey smarts and his effort level was good in my viewings. The kid can score goals, has a quick release and shot is accurate. My issue is, as of now anyway, not knowing anything about him and no ability to interview etc.." - HP Scout, Mark Edwards

102	SHARANGOVICH, YEGOR	DYNAMO MINSK	RUSSIA	6' 2.0"	196 lbs	LC

Yegor Sharangovich is a double-overager entering his third year of draft eligibility, who can be considered a late-bloomer. This past season he had a solid year of production while playing regular shifts for Dinamo Minsk of the KHL where he posted 12 points in 47 games including 4 goals. He also played at the U20 World Junior's where he was featured on the top-line and used in all situations, collecting 5 points in 7 games.

Sharangovich is a rare type of player in this draft due to being a true power-center that can play a 200-foot game. He's a very strong kid who's got width, height and a powerful base to work with, this allows him to generate an impressive first couple of steps which allows him to take off, showing excellent straight-line speed. His speed combined with his strength and high-compete level made him a very difficult player to handle-down low both against men and at the world-juniors where he was dominant at times against less physically developed players who couldn't contain him. He plays at a high-pace while still being efficient and uses those attributes when bearing down on the opposition by engaging with his stick which gives him a lot of leverage when battling along the boards. This causes opposing defenses to play heavy-minutes against him where he then looks to use his solid pivoting mechanics to cut aggressively towards the front of the net or use his plus vision to set up one of his teammates. Arguably his best attribute isn't one of his physical tools, it's his hockey-sense. He's got good offensive-awareness and understands advanced positioning without the puck and where his teammates are attempting to position themselves when he is carrying the puck. This allowed him to be dangerous at even-strength and on the top powerplay at the U20's, where he had a lot of success by finding soft-ice towards the right-circle and getting his shot off. He's adept at placing his shot through screens and using his length to deceive the goalie while masking the angle that the shot is coming from. Due to his strength and shooting mechanics, he also generates a lot of velocity which gives him the ability to score from the high-slot. Although Yegor has several good offensive-attributes, his puck skills are not as good as the rest of his game at this time, he's still capable of making a quick backhand to forehand deke when cutting to the net as an example, but it's not one of the standout areas of his game.

Another impressive aspect of Sharangovich is his defensive-game. He's good at using his speed to backcheck aggressively in most of our viewing's and he's capable of supporting his defense down near the net, though he sometimes does lose his defensive assignments. Although a late developing center, he certainly didn't look out of place in the KHL and it will be interesting to see where he goes on draft day since he's already shown he can play in one of the top leagues in the world and plays a North-American brand of hockey.

"I think he's one of the more interesting players who's been passed on in previous drafts. It's tough to find true power-centres in any draft, let alone this one." - HP Scout, Brad Allen

NR	SHEN, PAVEL	KHANTY-MANSIYSK	RUSSIA	6' 1.0"	183 lbs	LC

Shen was undrafted last season after averaging just under a point per game in the MHL. He repeated that this year, but also played half of the year in the KHL, dressing for 29 games with Yugra Kanthy-Mansiyk and scoring 2 goals. Shen brings an interesting set of skills and size to the table. He generates good speed with his powerful stride. He has quick acceleration that he will use to go around defenders and go to the net. He has a good shot, a quick release and is good at finding dead spots in the offensive zone to receive passes in scoring areas. Once again, this year, he didn't get a lot of exposure in international play and that definitely will hurt his draft status. He has a good chance of becoming a regular in the KHL next season, as he was traded to Salavat Yulaev Ufa at the beginning of May.

53	SKAREK, JAKUB	JIHLAVA	CZREP	6' 3.0"	192 lbs*	G

Jakub Skarek split starts for HC Dukla Jihlava in the Czech league where he put up a 2.41 GAA and a .913 save percentage in 21 games, he was loaned to HC Litomerice in the Czech2 league where he put up a 1.90 GAA and a .942 save percentage in 10 games. Skarek also played for the Czech's internationally at the U20 World Junior Championships where he played poorly and lost his starting job, this continued a concerning trend of him playing below his capabilities at international events dating back to last years U18's.

Skarek is the most polarizing goalie of this draft class or any in recent memory for that matter. On the one hand, there is no goalie in this draft with the combination of physical tools and athletic gifts that he possesses, however on the other hand, there's few goalies who have mentally crumbled at the rate he's shown during international competition when a game is on the line. Jakub's physical gifts can't be understated, he's got modern-day size and tremendous width and length which allows him to take up a lot of the net, this combined with his explosiveness allows him to cover ground quicker than any other goalie in this class. He's capable of cutting off angles rapidly and has arguably the strongest transitional butterfly in this class, which allows him to absorb hard shots at a consistent rate. When he does allow rebounds, he has tremendous reflexes and flexibility, which gives him the opportunity to make some very good recovery saves that a lot of other goalies can't make. Due to his impressive coordination and fluidity, he's very good at transitioning from his stance into his reverse V-H, though on his blocker-side when in the reverse V-H he does leave some opening's which has been exposed occasionally in our viewing's, this applies less to his glove-hand side where he seals it shut more consistently. His glove hand is quick and he positions it well when in his stance, however when he's in his butterfly and specifically when he's coming off the post, he does have a tendency to keep it slightly low which has created opportunities for opponents to go upstairs on him. His blocker is not as refined as his glove-hand but he does use it effectively to control rebounds and have them fall into his chest off high-shots by rotating his elbow upwards after the puck hits his blocker. He's capable of tracking pucks in most instances and is good at reading cross-ice passes going either through his crease area or in the high-slot area.

For all of his technical and physical gifts, Skarek has some notable deficiencies. For starters, although he can track the puck without heavy traffic in-front of him, when there is heavy traffic he has a tendency to lose the puck during passes across the hash-marks and at the point, furthermore, he has difficulty tracking release points through screened shots. This point is emphasized when discussing players who change their speeds quickly before releasing the shot, he's shown an inability to adjust his angle to the shooters new angle when he's not on his game. The ability of a goalie to handle the puck isn't overly important at this stage of their development, that being said, Skarek is not a good puck-handler but likes to handle the puck regardless which has created some of the more bazaar goals against that we have seen this year. His most glaring issue at this time is a mental one, which is that when he lets in his first soft goal, his technique and fundamentals appear to breakdown, which subsequently creates opportunities for shooters to exploit him, resulting in periods where we have seen him give up multiple soft goals in a short period of time and essentially sink his team. This is further highlighted when discussing international play, where he's played his most uninspired hockey. He's a goalie who has shown an inability to regain his composure in high-pressure games at international events and this occurred at the U20 WJC.

Despite his flaws and needing to restructure aspects of his mental game, he's still a competitor who has tremendous upside and is one of the few goalies in this year's draft with the potential to become an NHL starter with the proper development.

"Watched him let in 10 goals (in London vs Team Canada in December) and didn't think he was that bad. Can't say i've said that before. No idea why the coach didn't give him a mercy pull." NHL Scout, December 2017

I think Skarek has all the tools to project to be a number one goaltender in the NHL. His season hasn't made it as easy to stay in his corner as he had some ups and downs. Goalies take time and he has a good base to build from." - HP Scout, Mark Edwards

"Got some very positive feedback from the combine." HP Scout, Mark Edwards

| 92 | SMITH, NATHAN | CEDAR RAPIDS | USHL | 6' 0.0" | 177 lbs | LC |

Nathan is a Hudson, FL native who dominated his competition in the very weak Florida High School ranks last season for Mitchell High School. Nathan was equally as dominate in his play with the Tampa Scorpions U18 AAA program, which is a Tier 2 program nationally. Smith saw four games with Aberdeen (NAHL) at the end of the 16/17 season where he showed the ability to acclimate himself to junior hockey quickly. Nathan saw another jump in competition this year by joining Cedar Rapids (USHL), where he made the team as a camp invitee and put together an impressive rookie campaign with 17 goals and 30 assists in 52 games, which was among the leaders of USHL rookies. Nathan is in his 2nd year of NHL draft eligibility as a late 98' birthdate.

Nathan has average size with explosive skating and quick feet mobility which allows him to cover a lot of ice and close on opponents in a short amount of time. Smith comes into the offensive zone carrying speed. Nathan doesn't display a lot of poise or willingness to slow the game down but can make plays off the rush using his vision and accurate passing skills. Nathan isn't a high end scoring threat with his shot at this stage. His shot often flutters off his tape and his release is a work in progress but Smith shows willingness to go to the hard areas to score dirty goals, however his slight frame keeps him from being as effective as he could be in those areas. Without the puck Nathan is susceptible to taking wide turns and getting out of position in a lot of instances and will need to add more North-South to his game to be effective at the next level. Smith is a very raw prospect at this stage and still getting acclimated to playing against better competition but his skating, quick strike playmaking and ability to learn and pick up things quickly will give him a chance going forward. Smith will be off to Minnesota State-Mankato this fall where he will have the opportunity to add some strength to his frame.

"I had time for him when I saw him in Truro.(WJAC) He flashed some skill, was a good skater and competed hard. Scored a nice goal versus Russia." HP Scout, Mark Edwards

| 17 | SMITH, TY | SPOKANE | WHL | 5' 10.8" | 176 lbs * | LD |

Ty Smith was the 1st overall pick in the 2015 WHL Bantam Draft. He had an excellent sophomore season for the Chiefs, producing 73 points in 69 games, including 59 assists. In the playoffs, he had 7 points in 7 games before being eliminated. Internationally, he played in the Hlinka, where he had 3 assists in 5 games and played well, however it was a different story at the U18's, where he went scoreless in 5 games.

Smith is a detail oriented, two-way, offensive-minded defenseman with arguably some of the best escapability and anticipatory reads from the backend in this year's draft. He's an impressive skater with excellent skating technique which helps compensate for a lack of power, yet it's his fantastic pivoting mechanics and edges that separate him. With the exception of a few defenders, there's arguably no other defender whose better at breaking down an opponent when walking the offensive-blueline. His intelligence and rate at which he processes the play are impressive and when you combine them with his ability to get an opposing player to commit, it allows him to seemingly open lanes at will. The reason he can get players to bite on his move-set, is due to having some of the best feinting mechanics available in the draft. He's adept at manipulating his frame and bearing his weight down into fake passes and shots, which makes it difficult for opposing players to be able to read him. We have watched him drive down a wing before suddenly pivoting, bearing down into a fake shot, then watching the player defending him buckle at the knees, allowing him to bypass the player before rushing the net area and passing it off for a scoring chance as an example. His consistent rate of execution given the dynamic skill-set he uses was impressive, as he was able to transition the puck through all three zones, as well as through heavy traffic in almost every game we watched this year. Once he's re-opened his skating and passing lanes, he's shown excellent vision which compliments his poise and awareness on the ice. This allows him to play a heavy possession style of hockey while dictating both the tempo and the pace, which should be emphasized when discussing the powerplay. The only real weakness to his offensive skill-set at this time is his shot. He's got an above-average release point and is consistent at getting his shots through traffic due to his ability to shift lanes, but it lacks the velocity you would want to see from a defenseman who is projected as a potential powerplay quarterback at the NHL level.

Ty's intelligence translates well to the defensive-side of the puck. He's good at interpreting the time and space he has to make a play under pressure, and this was especially true when evaluating loose puck races, where we have seen him pull up and re-assess his coverage just in time. Furthermore, he's good at handling the forecheck due to his first-pass, where he can make long stretch passes at a consistent rate. His spacing leads to good gap control and he's capable of reading pass attempts in advance which allows him to use an active stick to disrupt certain offensive sequences. The drawback to his defensive game is that he's not a big defender who relies on his intelligence and skating ability to recover when he does make errors, so there's a physical limitation that he's going to have to learn to overcome when going up against larger players at the pro levels. Due to his heavy possession style of game, he is prone to turnovers at times, which forces him to expend his motor at a high-rate while transitioning in both directions, which has caused him to ease up on some of his backchecking efforts. Lastly, his play at the U18's and in other stretches was concerning; he's the type of player who asserts a level of confidence when he's on the ice that seemingly wasn't there by the end of the year, so it's important that he doesn't let his confidence decrease to the point where it shuts down his game.

Smith is one of the most dynamic defenseman featured in the 2018 class, who possess a unique, yet balanced skill-set that should help him become a dominant defenseman in the NHL. In order for him to develop properly, he needs to gain strength so that he can generate more power which should improve his explosiveness. With a more explosive first-step, he can become more efficient when in transition and with added strength, he can improve the velocity of his shot.

"I threw out the this game (top prospects game) that wasn't him" – NHL Scout, February 2018

"I love him. Smart, skilled, great skater and he really moves the puck well." – NHL Scout, May 2018

"He's a really really good player and he's still not up with those big boys. There's a lot of good D in this draft." – NHL Scout, April 2018

"My only question is how close is he to his ceiling already?" – NHL Scout, May 2018

"Felt for the kid at the Top Prospects game. Not a night to remember...he's much better than he showed in that game." – HP Scout, Mark Edwards

"Very impressive kid." – NHL Scout, June 2018

"One of the few truly dynamic players from the WHL this year, his confidence with the puck is noticeable and mistakes don't seem to phase him, because he always bounces back with good plays. Truly commands the pace of play and when he's on the ice everything moves around his decisions." – HP Scout, Andy Levangie

"I got good feedback from his interviews at the combine. A few scouts noted that the player thinks he's going top 10." – HP Scout, Mark Edwards

| 169 | SNELL, MASON | WELLINGTON | OJHL | 6' 0.0" | 191 lbs | LD |

Mason Snell was drafted by the North Bay Battalion but opted to keep his options open and later accepted an offer from Penn State University. He played junior for Whitby in the OJHL before being traded to Wellington earlier this season. He was a member of Team Canada East but succumbed to older players eating up most of the minutes in the WJAC. Snell was also selected to the CJHL Top Prospects game in January. Lastly, he finished his season along with his Wellington Dukes teammates with a long successful playoff run, which carried them all they way to the RBC Cup.

Mason saved his best hockey for the playoffs. He played more within himself and made fewer high risk plays. He makes good offensive reads. In the offensive zone he is creative and has very good vision. We've also seen him flash a great one-timer more than once in our viewings, We've seen it going all the way back to minor midget. His skating is solid, he's good on his edges and shows good mobility. He's very strong defending 1 on 1 against the rush.

On some shifts in his own end we saw Mason make a poor read or lose his responsibility for a half second. It was far from a glaring issue, but something worth mentioning as an area we saw for improvement.

Overall Mason has good offensive tools and has the ability to buy himself some time with his feet. He plays much bigger than his size and does not shy away from any physical contact, if anything he initiates it. He makes a good first pass and we like the route he has chosen for his continued development. He has plenty of time to get stronger.

"Son of Winnipeg Jets Scout and former player Chris Snell. I interviewed Mason in Truro and he gave a good self evaluation of his game. Penn State route should be perfect for him. - HP Scout, Mark Edwards

"How about Snelly's kid...he finished up strong." NHL Scout, June 2018

| NR | SOKOLOV, EGOR | CAPE BRETON | QMJHL | 6' 3.75" | 223 lbs | LW |

Sokolov came to Cape Breton from Russia this season and was a nice surprise for the Screaming Eagles. He has great physical tools; he's a heavy and large kid who is tough to handle down low and in front of the net. His offensive output was the surprise this season, as he was not much of a factor offensively in 2016-2017 while playing for the Russia U-17 national team, but in the QMJHL, he showed good awareness in the offensive zone and a good shot. He's useful on the power play either by playing in the slot where he can take quick shots when set up for one-timers, or in front of the net. Due to his size, he's pretty much unmovable from there. His shot remains his #1 weapon offensively; it has good velocity and a good quick release. He's not a very creative player in the offensive zone. His playmaking abilities are average at best, and he needs to play with good players to produce offensively. Playing with Drake Batherson in the first half of the season was good for him, and this is where he had his best success. His drop in production was significant in the 2nd half of the season without Batherson. His skating will need a lot of work, as his feet are heavy and his top speed and acceleration are below-average. He's a bit of a one-dimensional player; he has good puck skills and can make plays offensively with quality linemates, but without the puck he's a bit lost and there's work to be done there too. Sokolov has some skills, and with his size, he's intriguing, but a lot of progress needs to be made with several areas of his game in order for him to one day reach the NHL. He is definitely a long-term project for an NHL team picking him in June. We believe he could either go in the mid-rounds or late in the draft.

| 189 | ST. IVANY, JACK | SIOUX FALLS | USHL | 6' 2.5" | 198 lbs | RD |

The Manhattan Beach, CA native just finished his 2nd season in the USHL and is a Re-Entry prospect for the 2018 NHL Draft after going unselected last year. St. Ivany saw a significant uptick in his offensive production from a year ago where he only registered 10 points in 52 games. This season St. Ivany registered 6 goals and 30 assists in 54 Regular Season games for Sioux Falls. (5th among USHL defenseman)

St. Ivany has good frame at close to 6'3", however he still has a ways to go strength wise as he lacks lower body strength and explosiveness in his footwork. Defensively St. Ivany uses his reach and active stick to take away time from his opponent and does a good job challenging plays at his own blue line and closing players off to the outside against the rush. Jack needs to add more grit and physicality and make things harder on opponents in front of his own net and in puck battles as he has been susceptive to losing battles. St. Ivany distributes the puck well on break outs and is able to stretch the ice using his vision and passing ability. He possesses good puck skills and is able to carry the puck up ice and through traffic when the situation calls for it. St. Ivany can run the Power Play at the point efficiently. While St. Ivany doesn't possess explosive footwork he has above average agility and east-west movement and is active on the offensive blue line in trying to open up lanes and will come down from the point, both with and without the puck and try to chip in on the offense. Much of St. Ivany's upside is contingent on him adding bulk to his frame and gaining lower body strength which he will have time to do going to college route. St. Ivany is expected to attend Yale in the fall.

"Has a high hockey IQ and plays an athletic game, needs to get stronger and improve his footwork before he is a pro prospect" HP Scout, Dusten Braaksma

"Big strong kid with good hockey sense." NHL Scout, March 2018

"Good size but not a physical player. I like his puck skills...he's a good puck mover. His feet are his biggest weakness." - NHL Scout, March 2018

"Smart player but the skating needs to get better." NHL Scout, April 2018

| NR | ST-LAURENT, EDOUARD | BAIE-COMEAU | QMJHL | 6' 0.0" | 171 lbs | LC |

St-Laurent was one of 4 first round picks by Baie-Comeau in the 2016 QMJHL Draft (16th overall). The speedy center has not been able to fully develop as an important offensive player for the Drakkar just yet, but showed some good progress in the 2nd half, scoring at a higher pace. He has done a fine job playing a more of a bottom-6 role thus far in his first two seasons in the QMJHL. With his speed and work ethic, he has had some nice sequences during those two seasons. He can make things happen with his speed off the rush, and he's quick to retrieve pucks in the corners. He has a lanky frame, and will need to keep getting stronger physically in order to handle playing against bigger and more physical players over the course of the season. With his speed, he can be an asset on the PK unit. St-Laurent does skate well, but lacks the vision and hockey IQ to be an impact playmaker at this level. He generates a lot of his scoring chances with his speed and off turnovers. His vision and puck-distribution is lacking, and is a big reason he has not been able to be an offensive contributor so far in the QMJHL. Due to this, we don't feel he'll get drafted this year.

| 73 | STASTNEY, SPENCER | USA U-18 | NTDP | 5' 10.0" | 180 lbs | LD |

Spencer is a transitional defenseman with good skating ability that's characterized by excellent two-step area quickness, as well as having an accurate and hard first pass. He put up 24 points in 52 games in a depth role on a very good USNTDP team.

Spencer is an undersized defenseman who uses a quick first couple of steps to evade the forecheck, this also allows him to maintain gap control and close it when the opportunity calls for it. His decision making in the defensive-end is a plus, he recognizes the time and space he has to make a play while under pressure and is consistent at recognizing when he has a step on an opposing player both when transitioning the puck out of the zone and when he's attempted to initiate a defensive-play. His size limitations hamper his ability to make separating hits or weigh heavy on opposing players along the boards. To compensate for this, he uses an active stick to deflect shots as well as disrupt opponents who are attempting to beat him one-on-one.

Spencer isn't the most dynamic player, opting for the simple yet effective play both in the offensive-end and defensive-end. When navigating the blueline, he looks to distribute the puck more than he looks for his shot, which is accurate however he doesn't generate a lot of power in both his slapshot and wrist-shot. His best traits are his passing ability and vision, he's calm under pressure and makes quick defensive-reads that allow him to distribute the puck effectively. Another aspect of his game that stands out is his ability to recover when his defensive partner makes a mistake. Several times during the year we have seen him identify a turnover from his teammates and use his skating ability to re-position himself which mitigates high-end scoring chances.

Spencer is a new-age transitional defenseman who has had success at the junior level, however he's going to need smooth development in order to be effective at the pro level due to having below average size while having an average offensive-ceiling.

"Give his ability to process situations quickly to some of the defenseman ranked near the top of this draft and you have a generational player, all he's lacking is size in my opinion. Spencer is one of my favourite players to watch in this draft class." HP Scout, Dusten Braaksma

"He's one of the least talked about good players in this draft." - HP Scout, Mark Edwards

| 200 | STEEVES, ALEXANDER | DUBUQUE | USHL | 5' 11.0" | 185 lbs | LC |

Steeves has just finished his 2nd full season with Dubuque and previously playing 39 games for Sioux City in 15/16. Alex is a late 99' birthdate whose game has taken a considerable jump offensively in his 3rd year in the USHL. Steeves does not have a lot of size, listed at 5'10" but possesses good offensive instincts and skill when given time and space. Steeves lacks explosiveness and agility in his skating and as a result struggles generating space to operate in the offensive zone. Steeves strong base makes him hard to knock off of pucks down low, but due to his lack of footspeed the longer he holds onto the puck the less likely he is able to generate a scoring chance. Steeves has decent finishing ability and with the puck on his stick in the slot and can be an offensive threat for his team. Alex possesses a good shot arsenal that includes a decent one-timer and a quick backhand that can beat goalies in close. Steeves has some crafty stick work along the walls and has shown the ability to pick the pockets of his opponents and generate turnovers in the neutral zone. After close to three seasons in the USHL, Steeves will be heading to University of Notre Dame this fall.

"There is some maturing left for him to do, both on and off the ice." HP Scout, Dusten Braaksma

"I think he'll get drafted but he's a bad skater and he can play some selfish hockey at times." NHL Scout, April 2018

"He's got really good hands and good on the power play. Skating is the issue." – NHL Scout, April 2018

91	STOTTS, RILEY	CALGARY	WHL	6' 0.0"	172 lbs *	LC

Stotts is a former top pick in the 2015 WHL Bantam Draft, selected 10th overall by the Swift Current Broncos. Riley struggled at the beginning of the 2017-18 with the Broncos, failing to establish himself as a top-6 forward on a top team, recording 3 points in 22 games. He was a major beneficiary when he was traded to the Calgary Hitmen after 22 games, immediately assuming top 6 minutes and a consistent role on the team's top powerplay unit. With the Hitmen he saw a major increase in production, recording 17 goals and 41 points in 47 regular season games.

Riley is an offensive minded centreman who plays a skilled game. His skating ability is effortless, with a long and exaggerated stride. His elusiveness and ability to make time for himself comes from his edgework. He eats up defenders because he doesn't lose speed when gliding, and can turn and transition effectively. He can change directions both in space and when in tight quarters, combining his skating skills with great ability to determine the presence and pressure of a defender when he has his back turned.

Stotts' strengths are with the puck, he is a playmaker and by time with his skating ability and soft hands in order to find teammates. His playmaking skills and vision make him a consistent offensive threat, he can make tough plays through traffic and consistently has his head up when puck-handling. In addition to his playmaking, he has also shown the ability to finish plays. He has a deceptive and accurate shot, which he could use more. Around the net he is patient, and has the ability to create his own chances, scoring a few highlight reel goals by making defenseman miss followed by a nice finish around the net. Although his production with the Hitmen was slightly below a point per game, he was the driving offensive force for a poor team. His linemates were average offensive players, and he seemed to create regardless of his wingers. Stotts' has the talent and skill to be a top scorer in the WHL and expect him to take more strides in terms of production in his third season in the league.

The hit on Stotts' game is his competitiveness. It is tough to determine his overall effort level because skating comes so easy to him. He saves ice very well and can stay engaged in the game with very few strides because of his efficient edge work. But, his game is not physical, he is prone to losing battles, especially in his own end. This also extends to consistency in his offensive game. Riley can disappear periods at a time and there is a question of his will to be a dominant offensive player. Stotts is a talented player, but his ability to develop into top-6 forward as a pro is in question because of his inconsistency.

NR	STRATIS, PETER	SUDBURY	OHL	6' 0.25"	190 lbs	RD

Peter started this year with Ottawa and was up and down for the first half of the season until he was traded to Sudbury at the deadline. He became more confident and played a simpler game for the Wolves.

Peter plays the point on their power play and is good at distributing the puck around in the offensive zone, he has good awareness with the puck. Stratis has shown a good low accurate shot on net. He has an inconsistent first pass, there will be games where he's moving the puck out on the breakout quick to teammate, but then there are also a lot of times where he gets the puck on his stick with time and space and he goes glass and out when his teammate is open. He holds onto the puck too long, effectively closing off his window which takes away opportunities to make a quick first-pass.

Peter's not a flashy player when he plays, he just keeps things simple. He plays a physical game in his own end, showing a great work ethic and ability to win battles in the corners against multiple forecheckers. He uses his frame to his advantage defensively, playing physical on the puck carrier when possible and tying up players in front of the net.

Peter needs to work on his skating and be more consistent with his breakout passes

" Just a productive junior player for me. Not a player I'd have on my list." - HP Scout, Mark Edwards

NR	STRUTHERS, MATTHEW	NORTH BAY	OHL	6' 2.0"	209 lbs	LC

Struthers is a rangy, two-way centre who elevated his game through the second half of the season, becoming more assertive with his physical traits while showing added confidence in possession. He makes himself an effective net presence. He shows deceptive puck skills in tight areas along with good hand-eye co-ordination which allows him to make plays in tight or deflect shots on goal. In possession

Struthers shows vision and passing skills to his game, however would benefit from becoming more assertive with his shot in the scoring areas. He effectively utilizes his frame along the wall and off the cycle, allowing him to show a strength below the hash-marks. While Matthew isn't overly physical he utilizes his reach and strong body position to win puck battles. Increasing his strength and aggressiveness would be beneficial. Struthers shows a long and rangy stride, but does lack first step and lateral quickness. His top speed is average and is a weakness. A positionally aware forward with a projectable frame and average skill level, Struthers will need to continue to work on adding strength along with his skating and becoming more assertive physically.

" I'd have him as a late guy at best because of his skating." - HP Scout, Mark Edwards

NR	STUART, BRODI	KAMLOOPS	WHL	5' 10.0"	167 lbs	LW

One of three 4th rounds pick for Kamloops in the 2015 draft and easily the most impactful and somewhat of a bright light in an otherwise disappointing season for both the teams record and their draft eligible players. Stuart is a somewhat undersize forward that plays with strong speed, both at his top gear and in his accelerations, knows how to carry pucks drive around defenders and through small spaces as an elusive player. Stuart doesn't avoid the dirty parts of the ice and isn't afraid to play feisty, he'll drive the net with or without the puck, grind in hard on the forecheck and take it upon himself to create scorings chances by leaning on defenders. He has show some truculence to stand up to opponents and protect teammates even if he ends up fighting bigger opponents, but doesn't end up crossing the line as he's more likely to as close as possible to it. He can generate shots and was often the good getting pucks to the net by utilizing his speed, the downfall to this was that his shots weren't always of the highest quality because it was an individual effort or a poor angle. A player we viewed that with no question would benefit from high tempo and high skilled linemates as he posses some really strong tools and could be a strong addition as the F1 on a line that plays with speed and a relentless forecheck.

At times his hockey sense did come into question, which may have contributed to his one-dimensional style of play, his development will be interesting to watch, he will need to keep his hard work style up to see pro success

| 78 | SUTTER, RILEY | EVERETT | WHL | 6' 3.0" | 203 lbs * | RW |

Sutter is the son of Ron Sutter (Calgary's Director of Player Development), so he obviously has hockey in his genes . He was selected in the bantam draft in the 6th round and has since grown into a solid force in the WHL. He uses his big frame and he's not afraid to play a rough and tumble game, consistently found in front of the net creating screens, battling defenders and generally making his physical presence felt. He plays a chippy game, stands up for his teammates and can finish hits with authority when his timing is right. As is true with a lot of players who line up for Everett, he is defensively responsible. Sutter was often found on the correct side of the puck playing in a good defensive position contributing to keeping attacking forwards out of the slot, he's usually supportive of his defenders and was a force in battles behind the net. He's a solid puck protector and uses his large frame well to shield off attackers to make plays. Sutter's shot is impressive and is likely his best attribute. He possesses a quick release with impressive velocity and shows a knack for getting his release off in a variety of body positions both set and off balance. Would like to see him shoot when in motion more often; the main aspect that holds him back from utilizing his shot is his lack of true separation gear. Sutter's skating can be suspect at times as he appears to do most things at one speed with very little change in tempo. Although his skating has improved since his rookie year it still has a way to go for him to see success at a pro level. Furthermore, his agility and edging both need work to truly unleash the peak potential of his physical attributes. His skating was a contributing factor to him only generating 171 shots, good enough for 84th in the entire league and not enough for a player who played top line minutes with his shooting ability. Most viewings over the course of 2 WHL seasons Sutter played center and although he's good on faceoffs he projects more as a winger down the road who could take draws on his strong side. He has potential to be a force along the boards and his body will be difficult to contain. If he gains a jump in his acceleration, he could be dominant at times but skating development will go hand in hand with is future success.

"He's a Sutter, he understands the game well and doesn't take any short cuts. He has a big body and he's just growing into it." - NHL Scout, January 2018

"He has a wide range to be a player at the next level. I think it might be as a winger...he's got a good shot and he plays the right way." NHL Scout, May 2018

"He'll get drafted for sure because he has impressive physical attributes, but in most views I was left wanting more out of his potential" - HP Scout, Andy Levangie

| 2 | SVECHNIKOV, ANDREI | BARRIE | OHL | 6' 2.0" | 192 lbs * | RW |

Andrei Svechnikov had a remarkable year in the OHL for the Barrie Colts by producing the highest goals-per-game average over the last two decades, beating out prominent scorers such as Steven Stamkos and John Tavares. He finished with 72 points in 44 games, including 40 goals. In the playoffs, he continued producing, putting up 11 points in 8 games with 5 goals. His production made him the first player to be named both the USHL rookie of the year and the OHL rookie of the year in back-to-back seasons. At international tournaments, he played at the U18 Five-Nations tournament, producing 8 points, including 4 goals and he was featured in a depth role at the U20 world Junior championships where he put up 5 points in 5 games.

Svechnikov is a power-forward and a cerebral player who picks his spots while showing a mature level of patience and poise when the puck is on his stick. This allows him to generate shots at a lower rate compared to some other elite-level shooters in previous drafts, but this may be due to getting the job done on the first attempt as opposed to the second. He's dangerous when driving down on his wing and finding a soft-spot to shoot the puck. His shot is impressive, his wrists allows him to change the angle of his release point before the goalie can square up on most attempts and he has a high-level of accuracy. This helps compliment his ability to mask his release point behind screens; in some of our viewing's he's put the puck in the back of the net before the goalie even recognizes which side the shot was released from. He's not just dangerous when driving down the wing and releasing his shot in one motion. He's also dangerous from a stationary position, where he uses a heavy one-timer with a reduced wind-up to beat goalies. This can be seen when generating shots on his off-wing as well, where even if he handles the puck when off-balance he can still go bar-down over a goalie. Additionally, he has a lethal backhand which allows him to mix up his shooting options and elevate pucks over netminders. His shooting proficiency due to his quick-release and the attributes already described makes him known more for his goal scoring ability but he is also an excellent passer and creator. Svechnikov whips the puck around with great force and can make any kind of pass. He has the finesse to make one-touch passes, the vision to see small openings, and the power to thread the needle through them or hit teammates in stride rink-wide. He's also a strong kid whose power is generated through a pro-frame which allows him to do a fantastic job of shielding the puck, power through contact, and get to the net whenever he wants.

Although not a flat-out burner, he skates well by generating good speed from powerful strides and is quick enough to take advantage of defenders if they're caught flat footed or out of position. He has deceptive gear-changes when the play calls for it. For instance, when driving to the net, it can look like the defender is keeping pace with him but then by using sharp cuts or spinning out of contact, he loses them.

Svechnikov's defensive game is also probably better than he gets credit for. He's often in good position and he has the size to push guys off the puck and win battles any time there's a puck up for grabs. This allows him to force opposing teams to play heavy minutes against him in the offensive-end below the goal-line but also allows him to weigh-down opponents in his own-end. He was frequently used on the penalty kill by Dale Hawerchuk. He's a point producer but there's a certain level of grit and bite to Andrei's game as well. A lot of times after taking a big hit, or slash, he'll give it right back to the opposing player and he doesn't necessarily hide it.

Svechnikov is arguably the most complete scorer in this draft class, but he does have room for improvement in his explosiveness in his first couple of steps. It could help him increase his acceleration and already solid straight-line speed. Beyond that, he's projected to become an elite first-line sniper who's very difficult to contain in the offensive-end.

"Much like Dahlin, not many conversations with scouts about this player this season. Locked and loaded into that two hole for us and many others all season long. - HP Scout, Mark Edwards"

| NR | TANUS, KRISTIAN | TAPPARA JR. | FINLAND-JR. | 5' 5.75" | 158 lbs | LC |

Tanus is a player we like because of his smarts in all three zones. He's involved in the play and competes well at both ends of the ice. He's shifty and keeps his feet moving all the time, making it tough to contain him. However, he lacks size and strength; he can be overpowered when battling for pucks along the boards or near the net. He's not a high-end talent or skater, which might make it harder for him to translate his game to the NHL. His skating is above-average, but at his size, you wish his speed was elite. His number one asset offensively is his vision; he's a talented playmaker who can make impressive passes in the offensive zone. He doesn't possess a heavy shot, but can surprise goaltenders with his quick release on his wrist shot. He has good puck skills; he's good at handling the puck in tight spaces and make plays near the net. He's a player who coaches can trust in any situation. On the PK, he's effective because of his speed, anticipation and he's also tenacious. Overall, we like a lot about his game, but worry about his size and how that would translate to the NHL. We also think that he would be a nice pickup for a CHL team in the Import Draft (if he's willing to report). His older brother played in for Peterborough for 2 years.

| NR | TEASDALE, JOEL | BLAINVILLE | QMJHL | 5'11.25" | 200 lbs | LW |

Teasdale went undrafted last season and came back strong this year with a better season, averaging a point per game and being a key player in the Armada's offense. He was very good on the power play, scoring 12 times on the man-advantage. He does a really good job in front of the net, creating havoc there. He's tough to move, and has good hands to tip in pucks and quickly jump on rebounds. His puck-protection has always been a strong part of his game; he makes good use of his size to protect the puck along the boards, and can create scoring chances for himself from there. He's very unselfish on the ice; he is a great team player that will take punishment in front of the net and might not always get the points he deserves, but does a good job doing the dirty work that doesn't always get recognition. This year he has improved his consistency, which was an issue last season. He brings a steadier game on a regular basis. He's not a natural goal scorer, but he possesses a good wrist shot (he will, however, need to improve his release). His skating abilities were a bit better this year, but remain a work-in-progress for him. With better speed, he probably would have been drafted last season. Teasdale is not a super-offensive player for the pro game, and he's not consistent enough with his physical game to play a grinding role in the NHL. His speed is average at best, and with the NHL being all about speed now, it will be a challenge for Teasdale to find a role.

| 186 | TENDECK, DAVID | VANCOUVER | WHL | 6' 1.25" | 173 lbs | G |

Late birthdays and Goaltenders are always a good combination as it gets them more reps and scouts more viewings over the course of their junior career this certainly benefited Tendeck as he came into his draft year with a solid hold on the Vancouver starting job and didn't relinquish it for the entire season. One of his most noticeable traits is ability to battle, he's aggressive with players around his crease and used his size to get a view around screens. When pucks do get through a crowd he shows quickness in his butterfly to cover the lower part of the net and track lose pucks around in tight. Tendeck is long a flexible; he's light but doesn't appear small in the net and has the type of broad frame that can add some needed bulk for a more rigorous schedule. Always tracks the first shot well and looks square to the shooter, at times has trouble containing rebounds as they rattle free from his gear but he rebounds nicely by making the 2nd and 3rd saves often. Gets side to side with impressive pushes, plays aggressive but fades back into the net quickly to cut down angles. Goes down early and often and needs to work a little on the quickness of his arms, however does keep his glove in a high position and made some impressive saves in viewings. Tendeck played a major role in the resurgence of Vancouver helping them challenge for the BC division until the final days of the regular season, he'll be a major part of them contending in 2018/19 and should only improve his number after the 2018 draft.

" Late birthday did Tendeck wonders, one of the best goalies I saw this year period. Gave his team identity while they felt the early part of the year out" - HP Scout, Andy Levangie

| 32 | THOMAS, AKIL | NIAGARA | OHL | 5' 11.3" | 177 lbs * | RC |

Thomas is an intriguing player as he has many quality skill sets that could potentially make him a first round selection in the 2018 NHL Draft. He has one of the better shots in the draft class as it is both accurate and quick in its release. He is also deceptive with the puck which handcuffs goalies when he shoots, as Thomas has good hands to either beat defenders or use as screens when shooting. Thomas will often choose the wrist shot and is good at changing the angle of release by dragging puck in or out to elude goalies. He shows good straight-line speed and handles the puck well when entering the offensive zone to get defenders back on their heels to create time & space that leads to offensive opportunities. Thomas can maneuver with the puck well as he can pivot, cut to escape defenders as solid skater with balance, agility, and uses his edges to create separation. Another good attribute to Thomas' game is his offensive awareness as he often finds the right spots to get the puck for high scoring chances and displays good vision to find open teammates off the rush or through the seams on the power-play. He can play hard on the forecheck to create positive turnovers and will use his body effectively. While he could use more strength for puck battles along the wall and corners, he will compete for possession and will make plays in possession not forcing pucks often. Thomas has certainly improved his play away from the puck this season and more concerted effort to position himself better, getting sticks in passing lanes, and not get caught puck gazing so much. Thomas was also used at center this past season and was decent at the face-off dot winning about 50% of draws. He was given more responsibility and shows versatility on the wing or center. Overall his game for the higher levels may be suited for the wing to utilize his speed, elusive puck skills, size, and more of a set-up and offensive mentality.

One of our biggest concerns on Thomas is his lack of consistency. There are times he is one of the best and most dangerous players offensively on the ice and yet there have been viewings whereby several shifts or half-period goes by until you take notice of his game. His compete level is up and down.

"He's had some good games for me but I don't see first round." NHL Scout, January 2018

"If I can take him somewhere in the 2nd round I'm feeling good about it, but first round is a reach for me." - NHL Scout, January 2018

"I think he's a hard working energy guy. I don't know that he'll be any more than a 3rd line guy though." - NHL Scout, May 2018

"Not in my first round." NHL Scout, May 2018

"I have him as an early 2nd rounder." NHL Scout, May 2018

"I like him but his compete was my issue. Very inconsistent. He's a second rounder for me." NHL Scout, May 2018

"My guess is I think he's a better competitor than he showed in the last part of the year, it's just that in Niagara they let him get away with stuff that wouldn't fly on other teams. He won't be able to do it at the next level...I think when he gets to the next level he'll get back to competing, working and providing energy every shift because that's the only way he's going to make it." - NHL Scout, May 2018

"Thomas possesses many good assets in skating, shooting accuracy, versatility, vision, and offensive awareness, so he's an intriguing prospect. Thomas is more of a playmaker than pure goal scorer for me. If he can put it altogether each night, he'll have success for the next level." - HP Scout, Russ Bitely

"My issue with Thomas is simply the fact that I never really saw him play a great game this season. I saw games where I thought he played ok, but not once all year did I leave the rink after seeing him and think to myself that he was a sure fire first rounder. I had a big issue with his compete level in too many games, but did see others where he worked reasonably hard. A frustrating season of Thomas viewings for me ." - HP Scout, Mark Edwards

"I got good feedback from scouts on his interviews at the combine." - HP Scout, Mark Edwards

3	TKACHUK, BRADY	BOSTON U	H-EAST	6'3.0"	192 lbs *	LW

Brady Tkachuk is a two-way, playmaking power-forward who posted 31 points in 40 games for Boston University this past season while playing in all situations. He had a successful U20 World Juniors where he put up 9 points in 7 games which was third on the team despite being one of the younger players, though he does have a late birthday and is one of the oldest players in this draft class.

Brady' game is rare, he possesses an excellent mix of skill that compliments a tenacious style of play that makes him very dangerous around the net-area. He's powerful, has length, and is a determined player which makes him very difficult to knock off the puck and forces opposing defence to play some longer shifts. He's arguably one of the best stick-checkers in this draft class and we have seen him cause turnovers and drive opposing teams into a frenzy trying to deal with his forechecking skillset which is also one of the best in this class. He has high-offensive awareness and is very good at recognizing small opening's that he can cut into in-front of the net, where he uses hands and reach to guard the puck while navigating through heavy traffic. He has a take-over mentality and doesn't shy away from getting physical along the boards, using his size to knock players off the puck and create screens in-front of the net. He has good hand-eye coordination and puck-tracking skills that makes him very dangerous near the goal-mouth during rebound opportunities.

He has a bit of pass-first mentality. That said, his shot is actually quite good, he uses his length to change the angle of his release point meaning he's capable of dragging the release in-tight to his body, though he doesn't use it as much as he should and is sometimes too unselfish with the puck, taking away scoring opportunities for himself. His vision and passing ability are both excellent, he consistently makes difficult and accurate passes while in motion and can find his teammates with blind passes, which he looks to set up while around the goal-mouth and from behind the net.

The biggest knock on his game at this time is his first-step, he's average out of the gate but his top-gear hasn't stopped him at all from getting up the ice during odd-man rushes.

Defensively, Tkachuk plays a complete 200-foot game and is willing to sacrifice his body to block a shot and gets physically engaged when attempting to support his defenseman. He's also the type of player who will stand up for his teammates and isn't afraid to get into altercations, if there's a pile up in-front of the net and some punches are being thrown, there's a good chance Brady is involved.

We see Tkachuk as a winger, who can dominate down-low and play a complete 200-foot game at the NHL level. He's one of our scouting staffs favourite players in this draft class.

"He makes guys around him better. Such a smart player." -NHL Scout, January 2018

"He's top 5 all day long. He's so much like his brother it's scary." - NHL Scout, January 2018

"People who don't think he has skill just aren't paying attention." NHL Scout, February 2018

"I haven't seen him for a while but I know our guys who saw him late really liked him." NHL Scout, April 2018

"I think Wahlstrom closed the gap but I'm still a Tkachuk guy all day." - NHL Scout, April 2018

"I've been leaning Tkachuk over Wahlstrom and Bogvist, especially after watching some playoffs...you just need guys like Brady Tkachuk." - NHL scout, April 2018

"He gives the phrase 'complimentary player' a good name." -NHL Scout, April, 2018

"I don't know if he's as high end as Corey Perry but I see a lot of Perry in him." NHL Scout, May 2018

"He's got heart, skill...a bitch to play against and he's smart. You saw it at World Jr's, when he played with guys like Casey Mittelstadt, he can create. I love that kid...I wouldn't hesitate to take him early. He's a gimme pick." - NHL Scout, May 2018

"Whatever team drafts him will have their top players asking to play with him." NHL Scout, May 2018

"If he was playing in the OHL this year he would've scored 40 goals." NHL Scout, May 2018

"One of those players you can plug into any line or situation and he will get the job done." HP Scout, Dusten Braaksma

"I think he's one of the smartest players in this draft class." HP Scout, Mark Edwards

"Much like i felt about his brother, I absolutely love Brady's game. He's so smart and in my opinion his skill is way underrated by some people I've spoken to about him. The kid can score and will score in the NHL. He's very creative and he just flat out gets it...he really understands offensive hockey concepts..He makes beautiful passes and sets up teammates for some tap in goals. He's often a step ahead of many of the players on the ice as far as the speed in which he processes the game in front of him. On top of all that, he's an absolute pain in the ass to play against. He's a beast all over the ice, he never passes up a chance to hit someone. He's a terror down low and owns the boards. Loved *his game last year and that didn't change this year. I can't say enough good things about him. I think he can follow in his brothers footsteps and play in the NHL right away. next year." HP Scout, Mark Edwards*

87	TOPPING, KYLE	KELOWNA	WHL	5' 11.25"	185 lbs	LC

Its been a slow and steady climb for Topping from 11th round pick to the BCHL to a his rookie WHL season to more than doubling his point total in his draft year (29 to 65). He's a great example of benefiting from a late birthday which has allowed him that extra time to develop, giving him an opportunity hear his name called on draft day. He showed a really solid level of consistency from wire to wire and anchored a really effective second line and second powerplay unit for Kelowna developing some great chemistry with Kole Lind.

When viewing Topping you'll notice his above average hockey sense and strong compete level, he has great knack for knowing where to be in the gap of seam or being able to find teammate when either receiving or giving a pass and quite often his passes lead to easy goals for teammates. He plays heads up hockey and knows what's going on around the ice, showing good use of puck control on zone entries, exits and when working pucks through the neutral zone in transition. Wont wow with end-to-end rushes but would rather put a speedy teammate in a great place to advance the puck. This brings us to his skating, which is an area he'll need to improve on, it got better from his rookie season and toward the end of 2017/18 but he still doesn't possess the high caliber gear changes and acceleration steps to make him a highly valuable draft choice. He shows good strength in his stocky frame and his mechanics are good but not great, his stride could use a straighter more elongated push, but by all accounts he is working on this and knows it's a weakness. More of a passer than a shooter (22G – 43A) he has an accurate but not over powering shot that will need to get heavier with a quicker release to beat goalies at the next level. However he is deceptive and can put it into all 4 corners of the net, makes smart plays with the puck and doesn't over handle it which helps cut down on his turnovers and exhibits more of that smart puck play. Knows how to position his body to keep defenders away from his stick giving him time and space, shows potentials to be a full time center and despite the occasional gaff is often found on the right side of the puck defensively. With true centres that have good IQ being at premium teams will have interest as Topping has long term pro potential if his slow steady development continues.

"One of the most consistent players I watched all season, found a niche with Kole Lind and allowed his creativity and intelligence with the puck to grow developing his scoring game, easily a sleeper pick and a true center." HP Scout, Andy Levangie

180	TUCKER, TYLER	BARRIE	OHL	6' 1.0"	203 lbs	LD

Tucker took on a larger role in his second OHL season playing primarily on the 2nd pairing for a Barrie team that won 42 games. He is a very physical defender who plays tough around the net and along the wall. He loves throwing open ice hits and is probably one of the more impactful hitters in the OHL. At times he takes himself out of position by chasing big hits, however, he did seem to improve in that area down the stretch and in the playoffs. Tucker is a pretty good neutral zone defender. He skates well enough that he can play most forwards tight without worrying about having his doors blown off. He has a good stick and does a good job of disrupting attackers and forcing dump-ins.

With the puck, Tucker is a mixed bag. He can be prone to launching pucks off the glass and out and throwing away possessions even when there is space available. He's much more of a rusher than a puck mover, which is probably a good thing given his passing ability. Tucker is far from trigger happy but he doesn't have a ton of power, or accuracy, in his shot and is not much of a scoring threat.

If Tucker is to carve out an NHL career, it will probably be as a physical depth defender.

"Big kid who plays hard. Hits really hard but crosses the line sometimes on what's acceptable and what isn't." - NHL Scout, May 2018

"His puck game is average at best for me and I worry about conditioning." - NHL Scout, May 2018

36	TYCHONICK, JONATHON	PENTICTON	BCHL	5' 11.5"	177 lbs *	LD

Jonny Tychonick had an excellent season for the Vees, producing 47 points in 48 games, including 38 assists. In the playoffs he had 17 points in 11 games, including 14 assists. Internationally, he had 2 points at the WJAC-19 and 2 assists in 5 games at the U18's.

Tychonick is a dynamic offensive defenseman who plays with some bite. What separates him in this draft from some of the other smaller defenseman, is that he's willing to play a physical brand of hockey. He's a tenacious and active player in his own-end at times, generating hits and showing a willingness to pin his opponents along the boards while competing for the puck. Although overmatched physically on occasion and not always reading the play properly in his own-end, he makes up for his deficiencies with exceptional passing ability and impressive four-way mobility. His first-pass is one of the better passes in this class, it takes him very little time to identify his passing lane and read how much time he has to move the puck under pressure before losing his angle. If his passing options have been taken from him, he's got impressive east-west movement, and a momentum shifting stride that allows him to generate a good amount of power. He's a kid who plays with a high-level of bravado, baiting his opponents at times to try and stop him from going end-to-end. This type of confidence when combined with his impressive tools have allowed us to see some incredible individual efforts from him this past season. None more so, than when we watched him weave through an entire team, before using his soft-hands to deke out the netminder for one of the best goals we watched this season. Unfortunately, his confidence can come with a price as well, as he does have a tendency to over-handle the puck in the neutral zone and has been prone to unforced turnovers in some of the games we viewed him in.

Despite his confidence being a double-edged sword at times, it does still allow him to make some of the cleaner transitional zone entries and exits out of the group on the backend when he's on top of his game. Once he's established himself at the line, he's shown advanced feinting mechanics, using his lateral mobility and shiftiness to readjust his lanes, before threading difficult passes with an impressive level of precision. Although an adept passer, he also has an effective shot from the point. This is due to his accuracy and placement more so than the velocity his shot generates. The majority of his wrist-shots and slapshots are aimed low, around the ankle area to increase the rate of deflections and rebounds. One of the areas he needs to improve with his shot is when to time it through screens, he does have a tendency to shoot without traffic at times, which generates a harmless attempt that is easily handled by netminders. That being said, we have also seen him use it to create fake-shot set-ups so that he can further take-advantage of his excellent passing. The biggest area of improvement for Tychonick in the offensive-zone, is in his pacing. Despite his offensive-gifts and ability to exploit defensive-units, he doesn't control the tempo of a game at the rate he theoretically should considering his skills. This is due to rushing his options at times or trying to do too much, which stems back to our earlier point about his mentality when he's on the ice.

Tychonick can leave you in awe with his transitional zone entries that are created through his quick hands and he can play a gritty game if he has to. So, despite his size, average defensive reads, and inability to dictate the rhythm of a game at a consistent rate, there's still a lot of upside that can be untapped with the right development.

125	UTUNEN, TONI	LEKI	FINLAND-2	5' 10.5"	169 lbs	LD

Utunen was Finland's captain at the recent U-18 World Hockey Championships, where Finland won the gold medal, upsetting the Americans in the final. After his play at the U-18s last year, there was a lot of hype surrounding him before this season. He had a solid campaign, but didn't live up to expectations, as he didn't take the next step in improving his offensive game. Nevertheless, Utunen is a solid two-way defenseman. He's solid one-on-one, and does a good job putting pressure on the puck-carrier to eliminate the time and space they have to make a play. He's not a big defenseman, but if the opportunity presents itself, he has good timing with his hits. He competes well in his own zone, and he's not an easy defenseman to play against. He's a smart defenseman; he reads the play nicely and usually plays a simple game so that he doesn't make a lot of mistakes on the ice. Offensively, he won't rush the puck end-to-end, but he can carry it out of his zone and join the rush. His smarts help him in that facet of the game. He lacks creativity with the puck in the offensive zone, though. He's been used often on the power play by Finland in international games, and he does a decent job, but didn't show any upside that makes us believe he'll be a big point-producer at the NHL level. Skatingwise, there is nothing wrong with his agility and footwork. He's not a high-end skater, but gets around the ice well enough. Overall, we like Utunen's competitiveness and defensive game. He projects more as a stay-at-home defenseman than an offensive one.

95	VALLATI, GIOVANNI	KITCHENER	OHL	6' 1.5"	184 lbs *	LD

Giovanni Vallati was drafted 16th overall in the OHL priority selection by the Kitchener Rangers. He had a successful rookie season and followed that up with a productive sophomore campaign, putting up 26 points in 65 games, including 23 assists. In the playoffs, Vallati posted 4 assists in 19 playoff games.

Vallati can play physical hockey when needed, he's capable of distributing the puck and was tasked with offsetting oncoming attacks by opposing teams and has several attributes that allowed him to be moderately successful at doing so throughout the season, specifically in the last quarter. The first attribute is his four-way mobility, showing a fluid stride and the ability to hit an extra-gear in recovery situations. He's got decent size, and is solid on his skates, showing good balance when getting physically engaged. Although he's capable of closing his gap quickly, we have seen him struggle in this area, sometimes misreading his distance which allows opponents to drive around him. Furthermore, despite being able to move the puck quickly, he sometimes gets overwhelmed by pressure and can struggle with his spacial awareness, causing him to turn the puck over. His compete level is high though; he's shown the willingness to block a point- blank- shot and attempt to make up for his mistakes during recovery sequences.

Although Vallati's primary game right now is focused on the defensive-side of the ice, he's capable of holding his own at the blueline as well, though his offensive-game is still slightly raw and untapped as of this writing. He's an instinctive playmaker who seems to prefer his passing option as opposed to the shooting option. Lastly, Giovanni was capable of feinting at the line, giving him the ability to make higher-end plays, although this was rare in the majority of the games we watched him in.

Vallati is a very competitive defenseman who was tasked with shutting down some of the more offensively gifted players in the OHL. He displayed the ability to defend and pass the puck. There's an above-average defensive-base to develop Vallati from, with the transitional tools needed to get drafted.

"I thought he was much better in the second half, that's when he was given more opportunity too. Excellent skater with good puck skills. Hockey sense is just ok." - NHL Scout, March 2018

"Decent two-way defenseman." - NHL Scout, May 2018

"Ranta, Foudy, Vallati... good skaters but just don't have the hockey sense." - NHL Scout, May 2018

"Slow start this season...struggled a bit with (forecheck) pressure but he played better in the second half of the year. He struggles with his spacial awareness and for me his hockey sense is still a bit of an issue." - HP Scout, Mark Edwards

37 VELENO, JOSEPH — DRUMMONDVILLE — QMJHL — 6'1.3" — 191 lbs * — LC

It was an interesting draft year for Veleno, who encountered a lot of ups and downs over the course of the year. It all started pretty well; he captained Team Canada to a gold medal at the Ivan Hlinka Tournament in August and was among the top-performing forwards on the team. The first half of the season was a tough one for Veleno, who was with Saint John at the time as part of the worst team in the league. He had a lot of difficulty scoring goals in those first three months of the season, but to his credit, still worked hard. However, his lack of goal-scoring was alarming. After his trade to Drummondville, he had more success offensively, piling up a lot of assists but also scored his share of goals. Drummondville was a team, unlike Saint John, with a lot of talent on their first three lines, which made it easier for Veleno to contribute.

Veleno is a good skater with decent top speed and acceleration although he does take some short choppy strides at times. He can be tough to handle when going wide on defensemen or down low when trying to create out of the corners. He amassed a lot of assists this year, showing some playmaking abilities. Despite all this, we would like to see him make quicker decisions with the puck. Sometimes, he forces plays when there's no option, rather than just being more poised and keeping the puck on his stick to slow down the play. He creates a lot of chances in the offensive zone with his forecheck rather than his hockey IQ. He's not a dumb player, but he's not a high-IQ player either. His work ethic is excellent, he's always been a hard worker since he played midget with the Lac St-Louis Lions. Defensively, his game has continued to improve, mostly positioning-wise. But he has always been known for his good backcheck, his ability to steal pucks from his opponents while on the backcheck, and for his quick stick. The biggest weakness in Veleno's game his is ability to score goals. His shot accuracy and velocity are average at best. He often ends up hitting in the goalie's chest. He scored more often in Drummondville, but if you break down his goals, not many of them are high-end skill plays that can translate to the NHL level.

His lack of goal scoring production at the QMJHL level is a bit of a concern. However, even without being a top goal-scorer, Veleno has good enough all-around tools to become a solid bottom six player at the NHL level. If he ever improves his goal-scoring touch around the net, then he could move up the lineup. He should be a dominant player in the QMJHL in the next two seasons, and Drummondville should be a dominant team in the QMJHL next season - one of the favourites to win the league next year.

"He worked hard and had a good tournament (Hlinka), it's summer hockey but it's better than starting poorly." - NHL Scout, September 2017

"If you forget about the exceptional status and put realistic expectations on him, he's not a bad player." - NHL Scout, September 2017

"The problem is people are expecting too much. He's a simple player who has some size, works hard and plays an honest game. If you are expecting more than a 3rd liner at the next level you will be disappointed." - NHL Scout, October 2017

"I don't get all the hype, he was invisible tonight." NHL Scout, November 2017

"He works hard and buzzes all over the ice but too many times he isn't accomplishing anything." - NHL Scout, November 2017

"To me he has no finish. I project him as a 3rd line winger and have him ranked in my second round." NHL Scout, May 2018

"I don't think he can play down the middle and I see him on a 3rd line...probably be a good penalty killer. He works as hard as anyone in the draft." - NHL Scout, May 2018

"He's going to put a lot of points on the board next season with the arrival of Maxime Comtois with Drummondville. The Voltigeurs will be a dominant team next season in the QMJHL." - HP Scout Jérôme Bérubé

"He reminds me of Mike McLeod at times and if you know me, you know that I wasn't as high on him as others were. Veleno and McLeod (Mike) work really hard, but in my opinion both have average hockey sense and lack the pure scoring ability to be able to score at the NHL level. I hear nothing but great things about Veleno's character and I wanted to like him more (he's even pretty much from my hometown) but I saw the same things in each viewing that bothered me. I also think he projects as a winger in the NHL because of the average hockey sense. Hope he proves me wrong." HP Scout, Mark Edwards

"His interview was excellent, I just wish he could score." - NHL Scout, June 2018

"I got very good feedback from scouts regarding his combine interviews. It didn't surprise me. Feedback I got from scouts who had interviewed him earlier in the year was also very positive. - HP Scout, Mark Edwards

NR	VORLICKY, MICHAEL	EDINA	HIGH-MN	6' 0.75"	162 lbs	RD

Vorlicky was part of a deep blue line for the Edina Hornets. Due to NHL prospects like Ben Brinkman (2019) and Jake Boltmann (2020), Vorlicky's role was more of a defensive one on the 2nd pairing. Despite lower offensive numbers, Vorlicky has good offensive skills with the puck on his stick and it starts in his own end. He is able to go through his reads quickly and stretch the ice. He skates well and has good edge work that allows him to rush the puck up ice and gain zones with control and distribute the puck as plays open up for him. In the offensive end, Vorlicky plays a simple game, he hold pucks in the zone but is quick to move the puck when under pressure. Michael has a heavy shot from the point that he gets off the stick quickly. Vorlicky has decent size but still needs to grow into his frame and add strength. Michael's straight line skating and footwork are smooth but but not explosive yet, he needs to add strength in his lower body. One area of Vorlicky's game that is very polished is his defensive positioning against the rush and shows good stick on puck capability. He keeps a solid gap against the rush and has an active stick that forces his opponent to make a skill play coming into the zone. He can take some risks at times to pinch down the wall or attack pucks in the neutral zone and will need to show better discretion in this regard. Sioux Falls (USHL) owns Vorlicky's USHL rights, however it's possible he returns to Edina HS for his senior year this fall. Michael is committed to the University of Wisconsin for 2019/2020.

"There are players with similar or less talents being considered as picks for this year's draft, take that for what it's worth. The offensive numbers are not impressive but he didn't play much on the Power Play due to the depth in front of him." HP Scout, Dusten Braaksma

7 WAHLSTROM, OLIVER — USA U-18 — NTDP — 6' 1.3" — 208 lbs * — RW

Wahlstrom is an American born forward of Swedish descent who is currently the youngest NCAA recruit after committing to the University of Maine at the age of 13 but has since changed his commitment. He had a tremendous season for the USNTDP program, putting up 89 points and 44 goals in 57 games. Wahlstrom is a dynamic power forward who's a technician on the ice, using superior hockey sense that allows him to anticipate defenses, then break them down with his high-level skill-set.

Oliver's most noticeable attribute is his fantastic shot, he's adept at masking his shot placement with his lack of tells in his body movement before his release, he fires pucks quickly off his stick and he can generate velocity behind his wrist, snap and slapshot. Another aspect that makes his shot dangerous is that he's not afraid to shoot at severe angles and is capable of shooting while going at top-speeds, as well as from stationary positions. Wahlstrom's not just a great shooter, he's also an architect with the puck on his stick, using superior vision to thread high-end passes to his teammates. This ability is magnified when taking into account that he can process the play at high-speeds and adapt to what the defense gives him. His creativity is apparent, he's capable of surprising his opponents by using advanced dekes and can create fake set ups then wait for his opponents to bite which develops additional plays.

He doesn't just rely on his skills, he has good physical traits and uses his frame effectively on the ice. During board battling sequences, he angles his body properly to come out of the corners and is consistent at maintaining possession during plays that require a high level of grit. As the year progressed he began to assert himself more consistently away from the puck, showing good puck retrieval ability and aggressively backchecking when the play called for it. Another aspect of his game that is a plus is his skating ability, he doesn't have high-end acceleration but he does have plus agility, has great balance and can take off when he hits open-ice, using a powerful base to generate good straight-line speed.

Wahlstrom can be more effective in the defensive-end and has room for improvement in his first couple of steps, however he's one of the most dangerous offensive players in this draft class. Due to the rarity of finding potential first-line multi-faceted power forwards, we expect Wahlstrom to be selected very early.

"What sealed it for me with him this year was his play away from the puck and his all around game. He has made a lot of strides in the last year in this regard." HP Scout, Dusten Braaksma

"Biggest thing I noticed right from the beginning of the season was an improvement in his compete level. The skill has always been there but it was nice to see the improvement in that compete area. He's a smart player and knows how to score. - HP Scout, Mark Edwards

NR	WALKER, ISAAC	MISSISSAUGA	OHL	6' 1.0"	192 lbs	LD

Walker is defender with intriguing physical traits who plays a simple game. He showed progression in his development throughout the season as he adjusted to the pace of play and his confidence improved. Walker doesn't possess any one great talent, but does a number of little things well, the simplicity in his game is what makes him effective.

Walker shows limited puck skills, however recognizes his limitations and limits his possession time by making quick and simple decisions with the puck. He is at his best on the defensive side of the puck were he utilizes a active stick and good reach to elevate his defensive tools. Isaac has the strength to out muscle opponents and separate player from puck. He showed an ability to contain 1-on-1 off the rush, keeping the play in front of him and to the outside. Walker does have room to improve his four-way mobility and quickness which would elevate his contain and allow him to more aggressively close gaps in the neutral zone. His ability to retrieve pucks is average due to his need to add quickness to his pivoting and first stride in a forward direction.

While Walker can make quick and simplistic decisions his reads before gaining possession need to improve as he can put himself in vulnerable positions and not have an outlet option. He is at his best using his strength and defensive tools, Walker projects as a stay-at-home/bottom pairing defender.

NR	WARNERT, BLAINE	CHASKA	HS-MIN	6' 5.0"	183lbs	LW

Warnert missed most of the 17/18 season due to injury, however had he played the entire season there is little doubt he would be on more scout's draft radar. Warnert is a big 6'5" centerman with above average skating ability and a lethal shot release. Warner played only 13 games for Chaska High School including playoffs but was able to register 13 goals and 8 assists in those games. Warnert was dominate in his showings this season and was able to dictate play all over the ice. Warnert does a good job using his size and reach to his advantage below the dots, he is able to gain just enough separation to get his shot off and uses his quick release to beat goalies. Warnert plays with a good mean streak in battles and was able to come away with the puck in most instances in our viewings. Its unlikely scouts were able to get enough viewings of him to use a draft pick on him in this draft but will be a player we will track next season as a possible re-entry prospect. Fargo owns Blaine's USHL rights and will likely be able to make that team next season if he chooses not to return to Chaska HS for his senior season. Blaine is a Nebraska- Omaha commit for the 19/20 season.

"I liked his game in the Fall Elite League but an injury cancelled out most of his High School season, haven't seen enough of him to be a draft this year." HP Scout, Dusten Braaksma

| 217 | WASSERMANN, JACOB | HUMBOLDT | SJHL | 6' 5.0" | 194 lbs | G |

Jacob Wassermann had an excellent season after being named the SJHL rookie of the year, by starting 28 games and producing a 2.69 GAA and .907 save percentage. He played 5 playoff games, producing a 2.94 GAA and a .909 save percentage. He also got a call up to the Regina Pats, where he played in 2 games, putting up a 3.88 GAA and .844 save percentage.

Wassermann is a rangy butterfly goalie who was adept at taking the bottom of the net away from his opponents. He had a good level of fluidity and coordination, which allowed him to have above-average speed when entering and exiting his butterfly, this applied to his reverse V-H as well. Due to his length, he covered up an incredible portion of the bottom of the net, this was notable during recovery save attempts. We have seen him take away what looked like sure goals by sprawling out on the ice, using his reach and extension to keep the puck out of the net. This skill should be emphasized when taking into consideration his compete-level, he did not give up on plays, knowing that he could take advantage of his length. His skating mechanics allowed him to push off laterally and take away one-timer options in the slot area and he was aggressive, cutting down his angles at a decent rate despite his size. Jacob's rebound control wasn't always consistent and his glove-hand was better at taking away the bottom half of the net then the top, though it was quick as well.

Sadly, Jacob Wassermann was involved in the Humboldt bus tragedy and is currently paralyzed from the waist down. We wish him well in his continued recovery from the accident.

"I was amongst over 100 scouts in attendance who saw Jacob play in Mississauga at the CJHL Top Prospects game. All of us at HockeyProspect.com wish him and his teammates all the best as they move forward with their lives following the tragic crash. My sticks are still on my doorstep today."
HP Scout, Mark Edwards

| 146 | WEISS, TYLER | USA U-18 | NTDP | 5' 10.5" | 150 lbs * | LW |

Weiss was selected 15th overall in the 2016 OHL Priority Selection by the Sarnia Sting but chose to play with the USNTDP. Due to playing behind several talented offensive players, he received a secondary offensive role on a very good USNTDP team where he contributed at a decent clip, finishing with 28 points in 53 games while having a stand-out performance at the U18 Five Nations tournament against Russia.

Weiss is an instinctive playmaker who plays a fast game and has plus tools which allows him to stand out on the ice. His acceleration allows him to launch himself out of the gate and catch the defensive opposition off guard, using a combination of edge work and plus straight-line speed to penetrate defensive units while looking to set up his teammates for scoring chances. He has a tendency to drive wide and cut behind the net while using his vision to set up players in the slot area and likes to make plays at top speeds, rarely slowing down the play, even if the play would be more effective if he did. One of the main reasons this occurs is due to his motor, when he's dialed in, Weiss plays at a high rate but doesn't turn it down on some plays when he needs to. His passing ability is a plus, he's capable of threading passes through multiple players and delivering them on the tape of his teammates at a consistent rate. His shot however, is inaccurate and he has trouble finding soft-ice for high percentage shots in some of the games we have watched. His defensive effort isn't below average but it's also not a stand-out area in his game at this point in time, although his puck skills are a plus and like the rest of his game, he can use his hands while going at top speeds.

His style of play can be a double-edged sword. On the one hand he can make high-end plays while in full motion but he also has a tendency to turn the puck over and make himself ineffective depending on the shift and the game. He's also unable to assess the tempo of a play at the rate you would want to see and his execution can be mixed. That being said, Weiss still had a decent year and showed some offensive upside, though at this time to us he's not looking like he can be a primary scorer at the pro level.

"He struggled at times this season but I thought he was really good at the U18's in the spring for Team USA." HP Scout, Dusten Braaksma

| 122 | WERNBLOM, LUKAS | MODO | SWEDEN-2 | 5' 9.0" | 165 lbs | LC |

Wernblom split this past season between Allsvenskan and the SuperElit league, and also played in various U-18 tournaments for Sweden throughout the year. He's a good skater with some quick, agile feet; he makes quick turns and has a low level of gravity, making it tough to defend against him one-on-one. He's not tall, but he's strong on his skates and has a stocky frame. His physical game really improved this year. He's often involved in scrums and he's way more effective along the boards compared to last year. We saw him throw some hard hits along the boards this season. He's a good playmaker; he sees the ice well and can find his teammates in scoring areas quickly. He's more effective on the power play than he is at even-strength, as he has a tendency of playing too much on the perimeter at five-on-five. On the power play, with more room to manoeuvre, he can display his playmaking skills and creativity. We would like to see more of this at even-strength. We love his smarts; they help him be a good player on the PK unit.

He's an interesting player, with his added physical game this year he can bring different things to the table but we are not sold if his offensive game will translate into a top 6 forward down the road in the NHL though.

| 123 | WESTFALT, MARCUS | BRYNAS | SWEDEN | 6' 3.25" | 203 lbs | LC |

Westfalt can play at centre and on the wing; he can be useful in different ways for a team due to his versatility and smarts. He can play on both special team units. On the PK, he's useful because of his smarts and effectiveness when killing time on the clock. He can hold onto the puck for a long time, and with his long stick, he's good at blocking passing lanes. On the power play, he's been used often by Sweden in international competition as the guy in front of the net. He's big and strong; he's tough to move from the front of the net and doesn't have bad hands to score some goals here and there. He's also able to take some punishment there, without feeling the need to reply. This year, he split the season between the SHL and the J20. In junior, he averaged over a point per game, and in the men's league, he didn't get much ice time (often the case with rookies in the SHL) finishing with 4 points in 31 games. Westfalt does a solid job down low, he's a good puck-retriever and his puck-protection is really good. He knows how to use his size to his advantage down low and in front of the net. However, skating is just average for him; he'll need to improve this over the next 2-3 seasons. Improving his quickness and acceleration will make him a better player offensively, as he will be able to take better advantage of the scoring chances he gets.

Overall, Westfalt has some good attributes that could make him a valuable player down the road. If he can improve his skating and continue to work on his overall game, he could become a bottom 6 player at some point. He's unselfish and smart, and can play down the middle or on the wing. His offensive ceiling is not high, but he could be a valuable player for an NHL team.

"He's a big kid, played smart hockey and a pretty good skater. He's responsible defensively, played a lot of PK minutes and his coach trusted him with key icetime. On the ice in the last minute with a one goal lead. Not a bad sign for a young kid. Didn't show me much in the way of skill when I saw him." – HP Scout, Mark Edwards

31	WILDE, BODE	USA U-18	NTDP	6' 2.5"	198 lbs *	RD

Bode Wilde is a powerful two-way defenseman who likes to rush the puck and is slated to play for the University of Michigan next season. He put up 41 points in 56 games, received top-four minutes and played in all situations for the USNTDP program.

Wilde is a physically gifted defenseman who is tenacious both with and without the puck. His skating is very good, relying on his edges to keep players on the outside when they attempt to drive wide and using his straight-line speed to transition the puck up the ice or penetrate defensive pairings in the offensive-end. Bode is somewhat of an enigma in the sense that one of his best attributes can be a detriment at times, that attribute being his take over-mentality. He loves to carry the puck up the ice and he loves to try and breakdown a team by himself. This has lead us to witnessing some of the more puzzling sequences out of any player in this draft class, both offensively and defensively. For instance, we have seen him make fantastic offensive-plays but we have also seen him throw the puck away in the offensive-end, regardless of pressure and regardless if there is a simple and more effective play to make instead. This is true defensively as well, again, he is capable of making some great defensive plays using his frame and his length to separate players from the puck and at times make high-end defensive reads, however depending on the shift and the game, he's more than capable of throwing himself directly out of the play as well. This was noticeable in several 2-on-1 sequences against, where he wouldn't remain patient and instead rushed the play which created unnecessary high-percentage shots. His love for skating the puck often gets him into trouble.. We lost count of the number of turnovers caused by him skating directly into multiple forecheckers, quite often directly up the middle of his own zone.

Bode is an interesting case for us, given our number one criteria we look at is hockey-sense. Despite his tremendous tools that allow him to look like a 4th forward on the ice at times, he has struggled to show us any consistency with his decision-making skills on the ice. He has a rare combination of strength and finesse which allows him to weave through traffic while rushing the puck and generate power behind an impressive wrist-shot. His release point is high-end and he can shoot the puck while going in full motion, which makes him dangerous when he's driving down the wings. In our viewing's, his wrist-shot was used more than his slapshot, though it isn't any less effective since he has a reduced wind-up which masks the release point and generates a lot of power behind it. That makes his shot difficult for goalies to pick-up. His passing ability is also a plus, he's capable of making stretch, chip and saucer passes all at a consistent rate while being effective at finding his teammates on the powerplay. However, his vision is average, as he sometimes has tunnel vision and looks to become a one-man army even with several passing options at his disposal.

Although Bode has not developed the ability to read the play at the level we want to see. He's still shown terrific offensive potential on the backend and if he cleans up the decision-making side of his game he could turn into a dominant, two-way, top-pairing defenseman who can be used on the powerplay at the NHL level.

"There is no questioning his upside but it all depends on his hockey sense coming around, he still can make some poor decisions in key situations." HP Scout, Dusten Braaksma

"No idea how anyone could see this kid as a top 10 pick. He's an accident waiting to happen out there. NHL Scout, August, 2017

"Bode has it clicking today...he's been unreal out there." - NHL Scout, September 2017

"He's an absolute turnover machine." - NHL Scout, September 2017

"He has his ugly moments but he has too much talent to drop past the middle of the first round. NHL Scout, November, 2017

"He's my number two overall in the draft. I love his game." - NHL Scout, February 2018

Decision making flip flops from bad to good from shift to shift...actually rush to rush." - NHL Scout, May 2018

"So much talent but frustrating to watch at times this season. Apart from the poor hockey sense which translated to numerous turnovers, my other issue was his play in the neutral zone. When I coached, I really stressed strong neutral zone play and it's still important to me now. I thought that Bode really struggled to be an effective player in the neutral zone. His gaps were big and he made it too easy for players to gain control between the blue lines and attack. He also gave up his own zone way too easily as well. I've coached some pretty high-end D-men and gap control tends to be all about confidence. Bode has a ton of talent but there is also a lot to clean up in his game. as he continues his development. He might be a boom or bust guy, there is no questioning his talent." - HP Scout, Mark Edwards

"A ridiculous number of discussions on Bode this season, both in house amongst our own scouts and on the road with NHL team scouts. One huge consistent was everyone questioning his hockey sense. I could have about 8 pages of quotes but 7 pages would just be repeating various scouts at various times of the year giving their opinions about his hockey sense" - HP Scout, Mark Edwards

"Interview was just ok and he's a bit of a high risk player for me."- NHL Scout, June 2018

40	WISE, JAKE	USA U-18	NTDP	5' 10.0"	195 lbs *	LC

He's had to overcome some adversity after landing on the IR with a broken collarbone but his game progressed at a high rate, finishing with 39 points in 33 games.

More of a playmaker than a shooter, one of his best attributes is his passing ability. His passes are both accurate and crisp and he can find players through heavy traffic or off the rush. His vision compliments his style of play well, considering he does instinctively look for the set-up play as opposed to taking a shot, even if it's a high-percentage shot at times. Though as the year progressed, he was finding soft-spots at a higher rate once his legs got underneath him which lead him to begin shooting the puck more often, while also executing at a higher clip. That being said, his shot is one of the weaker aspects of his game. There's times where he doesn't generate a lot of power and he has had difficulty changing the angle, specifically when off the rush. To compensate for this, he's developed a tendency to head to the front of the net for rebounds when he wasn't in control of the puck or working a give and go-sequence. He likes to use his slapshot even when in tight to the net, so he might have been making adjustments to counteract his wrist-shot deficiencies. Another trait of his that stands out is his hockey sense which he uses in many facets of his game and it shows up with his creative passes that he can make seemingly out of nowhere at times.

Although average-height for a center, Wise is stocky and well-built which allows him to protect the puck and he's not easily knocked off the puck. He's got a large upper frame and this may have been a factor in him generating less power than expected in his first few steps. However, he's got good straight-line speed once he gets going and is more than capable of rushing the puck up the ice. The biggest draw back with his skating for us is his agility. He's not as elusive for a player of his size as you would want to see, but he does have good puck-skills to compensate for this. He uses his soft-hands and strength to counter opposing defenses. Defensively, Wise plays a 200-foot game and we have seen some impressive backchecking plays from him throughout the year, although at times he could be more assertive away from the puck.

Wise is a two-way playmaking center with high-end passing ability and vision. We see him as a player who showed NHL potential with the proper development.

"I wish I had seen him more. I think he's a really good offensive player...good 1 on 1 player, good skill." - NHL Scout, May 2018

"He works hard, he plays hard...I think he's more of a solo offensive player than a playmaker...he likes to beat guys 1 on 1 and that opens up the game for him...I like him." NHL Scout, May 2018

"If I had a concern it's that he's 5'10" 190 pounds and he's fully grown. It's a valid concern" - NHL Scout, May 2018

"He didn't miss a beat when he came back from injury and was instantly one of the best players on that U18 squad. His vision of the ice is as good as anyone in the draft in my opinion." HP Scout Dusten Braaksma

"Really liked him going back to his OHL Draft year and I was looking forward to his return from injury. I thought he did a good job getting himself back on scouts radars with some strong performances shortly after his return." HP Scout, Mark Edwards

175	WONG, AUSTIN	OKOTOKS	AJHL	5' 10.75"	189 lbs	RC

Austin Wong produced near point per game numbers this past season, totalling 54 points in 55 games with 25 goals. In the playoffs, he produced 10 points in 15 games, including 7 assists and was a force in the CJHL Top Prospects game where he had 2 goals and got into several heated altercations.

Wong is a battering-ram on skates whose capable of delivering crushing hits. Despite not being the tallest player, he's got a stocky build with a thick frame and thrives when playing a tenacious, heavy hitting style of hockey. He's not one to back down from a bigger opponent during a confrontation and his mentality had him rack up 235 penalty-minutes. Additionally, his physical play translated into impressive board battling and puck retrieval skills, while also displaying the ability to take a direct route to the net. Although he plays a punishing style, Wong also showed us a decent set of hands, we wouldn't call them high-end but he's able to beat defenders one-on-one and change the angle of his release point by dragging the puck, though he's not overly coordinated or quick with his stick. Furthermore, like the rest of his game, his shot is heavy and displayed a good amount of accuracy when given the time to do so. He's not just a shooter though, showing the ability to make impressive give-and-go sequences between his teammates and himself, which led to several goals where he would receive a pass in the crease and jam it home.

Austin has an appealing blend of scoring instincts and an impressive physical base to work with, but his skating mechanics for his build don't allow him to have much in the way of an impressive top-gear, and he has trouble generating an efficient stride, due to its choppy nature at this time. Furthermore, although he can have games where he generates a lot of scoring chances and is willing to drop the gloves at a moments notice, he uses his best qualities inconsistently. In order for Wong's game to translate, he's going to have to increase his consistency on a game-to-game basis while further developing his puck skills and skating ability.

"The kid is a tank out there" - NHL Scout, January 2018

"The way he played in the Top Prospects game...in his league play he only plays like that once every four games.- NHL Scout, May 2018

"He really impressed me at the CJHL Top Prospects game in January. He worked his tail off, was tough as nails and hit everything that moved. - HP Scout, Mark Edwards

| 43 | WOO, JETT | MOOSE JAW | WHL | 6' 0.0" | 200 lbs | RD |

Jett Woo is a very strong old school defensive defenseman. Unfortunately Jett suffered two injuries which forced him to miss a significant amount of time this year. Jett scored 9 goals and 25 point in 44 games. When Jett was in the lineup he was one of Moose Jaw's best defenseman. Every night he would be tasked with shutting down the opposing teams best players.

Defensively Jett is one of the best in the league. He is always in the right spot to make the play. Going back to retrieve the puck his head is always up and on a swivel. Jett seldom loses a puck battle. His strength allows him to absorb and check and often times do more damage to the fore-checking player. Jett makes an excellent first pass out of his zone. Consistently on the tape to lead the player and never put them in harms way. Physical play is a major part of Jett's game. He will punish anyone entering the zone with his head down. Jett does not back down from any challenge. He will stick up for his teammates, but rarely takes undisciplined penalties. Jett's skating is surprisingly strong with and without the puck. With the puck has the ability to skate the puck to safety and slow the play down or turn in up and go end to end. Without the puck his acceleration is great.

The one knock on Jett is his offensive abilities. We don't feel he will ever be a high scoring defenseman at the NHL level. His shot is below average when he uses it, which is rare. He doesn't use the slap shot at all.

He does have the ability to make players miss at the blue line with his hands. However, if he does make the player miss he will often pass or use a bank off the boards to create a scoring chance.

Overall we feel Jett is one of the better defensive defenseman in the draft. He has the ability to make the great first pass. Jett is without a doubt one of the strongest players on the ice every night, rarely losing a puck battle. His offensive shortcomings can be improved. His injury riddled season may be a factor if he slides a bit in the upcoming draft.

"Jett was dominant when he was healthy. Watching him as a 16-year-old player looking like a man against boys, you knew he was going to be something special." HP Scout Dan Markewich

"Not enough there to be a first rounder for me but he's a solid player." - NHL Scout, May 2018

| 114 | WOUTERS, CHASE | SASKATOON | WHL | 5' 11.5" | 177 lbs | RC |

Chase Wouters is in his first year of eligibility and really had strong sophomore year in the WHL with the Saskatoon Blades. Being named an assistant captain part way through the year really encouraged Chase to preform. Chase scored 18 goals and 51 points in 72 games. Chase was rewarded by being selected to Canada's Under 18 Team.

Chase is the one of the more well-rounded players on the Blades this season. His willingness to do whatever it takes really proved he is a nature leader. Great in the faceoff circle, the Blades had faith-putting Chase out there in all situations whether it be to win a key draw in the defensive zone on the penalty kill or help run the power play. Chase has an extremely high hockey IQ. He always seems to make the right decision with the puck. On the forecheck he has relentless pressure and can create turnovers. Always has his head up and can find the open man. He is more so a playmaker then a natural goal scorer. Every time he steps on the ice it makes his teammates better.

Defensively Chase does an incredible job shutting down the other teams top players. On the back check he never gives up. His head is always up looking to find an open man to cover. Chase stock has risen immensely this season due to his durability being able to play in all 72 games this season and his willingness to do whatever it takes. Chase has the perfect attitude for a young up and coming player.

| NR | WYLIE, WYATTE | EVERETT | WHL | 6' 0.0" | 190 lbs | RD |

Wyatt Wylie had a productive campaign for Everett this past season while being used in all situations. He produced 21 more points than in his previous year, putting up 31 points in 72 games, with 26 assists. In the playoffs, he produced 8 points in 22 games with 6 assists.

Wylie is a transitional defenseman who has above-average decision making from the goal-line and out. Two of his better attributes are his hockey-sense and first-pass out of his own-end. These skills allowed him to quickly adjust to pressure, as well as assess his passing options to move the puck up the ice at a good-rate. He keeps his head-up and doesn't look rattled when getting physically engaged, showing poise, a solid base, and enough awareness to make subtle, yet important plays. Additionally, he uses his impressive-frame and fluid stride to control his gaps efficiently in most of our viewings and was excellent at blocking shots, sometimes showing an impressive effort level and taking away multiple scoring chances away in a single shift. His skillset in the defensive-end made him a standout penalty-killer when we watched him.

Although he doesn't have a high-end skill-set when walking the line, Wyatt displays a heavy shot from the point when given enough space and uses head-fakes and shot-fakes to readjust his angles and mitigate pressure from the blueline. He's never going to be an offensive-force at the pro levels or be used on the powerplay but there's elements of his game in the defensive-end that could entice some teams to consider him in the later rounds of the draft.

NR	YERYOMENKO, VLADISLAV	CALGARY	WHL	5' 11.75"	185 lbs	RD

Vladislav is a Belarussian defenseman who is in his second season with the Calgary Hitmen. The second year draft eligible player took a big step forward in his second season in North America, establishing himself as a top defenseman for the team, logging minutes in all situations and recording 41 points and 13 goals in 63 games in 2017-18. In addition, he represented Belarus at the World Junior Championships, in the first division. He logged big minutes for the team and recorded 4 points in 6 games. Yeryomenko can be classified as an offensive defenseman. To start the season, Vladislav played religiously with Jake Bean, and he excelled offensively, producing at a high level showing lots of confidence offensively. When Bean was traded, more load was put on the shoulders of Yeryomenko and his production declined.

Yeryomenko is mobile, with smooth edges and the ability to maintain speed when carrying the puck up ice. His edge work and transition game is strong, and he has no issues getting up and down the ice, maintaining a consistent presence on both sides of the ice. His stride is fundamentally sound, but could use more power and strength, as with the rest of his overall game. Vladislav uses his smooth edges and a wide base with the puck to carry the puck often, both on powerplay breakouts and even strength. He is often circling in the offensive end, and is able to protect the puck well and evade defenders because of his solid physical skills.

His puck moving ability is strong, and he can be considered a smart player who makes above average decisions. When the minutes rack up and he gets to the end of shifts, his decision making deteriorates and he is prone to holding onto the puck for too long. In moments like this, his lack of strength is magnified.When at his best, he is creative offensively and is deceptive both in open space and at the point. He has great ability to walk the offensive line and draw defenders before passing to a teammate. What stops him from being a next level offensive defenseman is his lack of shot. His shot lacks strength and a non-factor from the point, although he has shown the ability to finish plays in tight.

Without the puck, Yeryomenko does not play physical, and is an average defensive player. He has a decent stick but is prone to mental lapses in his own end and vulnerabilities when in one-on-one situations. If he is to excel at the next level, he will have to gain strength and rely on his puck-moving and offensive skills.

35	YLONEN, JESSE	ESPOO	FINLAND-2	6' 0.0"	167 lbs	RW

Ylonen made a big splash at last year's U-18 World Hockey Championships, where he finished with 9 points in 7 games, helping Finland win the silver medal. This year, he didn't make the World Junior team in December, and played in Finland's 2nd pro league with Espoo United and had 27 points in 48 games. Next year, he's expected to play in Liiga with the Pelicans.

His father Juha played in the NHL for Phoenix, Tampa Bay and Ottawa. Jesse was actually born in Phoenix. He's a very different player than his father, as Jesse is winger that likes to play the game with a lot of speed and pace. His top speed is good and his acceleration really helps him challenge defenders one-on-one. He's very agile, and his stickhandling skills are close to elite as well. He's a very fun player to watch with the puck on his stick. With his combination of speed and puck skills, he's really tough to defend against for opposing defensemen. He's a scorer and his vision and playmaking abilities are decent. There's some concern with his overall hockey sense and his play selection at times. He's a risky player who often tries to beat players one-on-one, and that can result in turning pucks over. He has grown a bit since last year, and is more physically strong, but still has a ways to go before being ready for the grind of the North American game. He'll need to become stronger to protect the puck and win more one-on-one battles but that is the case for many players in the draft each year.

Ylonen has proven that he can score and bring some good offense to the table. As far as the NHL goes, he has the talent to play an offensive role, but the rest of his game will need to improve in order for him to achieve it.

"Only saw him play once so..." - NHL Scout, May 2018

"Really hungry 200 foot game, not always the smartest but overcomes his average smarts with great work ethic and equally good hands." - NHL Scout, May 2018

"Mid second rounder." - NHL Scout, May 2018

"Our euros love him. Early second (rounder)" - NHL Scout, May 2018

"Easily one of the best players at the Under 20." - NHL Scout, May 2018

"I seem to be the one who is highest on him amongst our scouts." - HP Scout, Mark Edwards

202	ZABRANSKY, LIBOR	KELOWNA	WHL	6' 0.75"	190 lbs	RD

The right shot Czech defender came to Kelowna through the CHL import draft and had some strong showings at several different international tournaments including captaining the 2017 Ivan Hlinka where he put up 4 points in 4 games. Zabransky has had a difficult time translating his game to create success in the WHL as he was immediately thrown onto the top pair and into all situations and looked overmatched by bigger more physical forwards, he was getting outworked down low and in front of the net. It took quite a few viewings to start and see even flashes of his ability, which is unfortunate because he does have some they just didn't come out often. Shows some good skating ability with smooth mechanics and at times flashed his speed up ice but usually deferred his partner, however he does make a good breakout pass but it was often seen at him settling for that play. His strongest asset is his shot, especially off the one-timer, it smooth quick and powerful but it just wasn't utilized with traffic, on the powerplay, or assertively enough to become a scoring threat. If Kelowna is to relay more on Zabransky next season he will need to take responsibility, be more active driving play and far more assertive with his skills. Hard to see based on his WHL play that his efforts will translate into the pro game at this point in his career.

4	ZADINA, FILIP	HALIFAX	QMJHL	6' 0.3"	197 lbs *	RW

Zadina came to Halifax with a lot of hype after representing the Czech Republic many times in international play, including the 2017 World Under-18 Hockey Championships, where he had 3 goals in 5 games. He also played part of the 2016-2017 season against men in the Czech men's league, playing 25 games with Pardubice.

Zadina's reputation was as a goal scorer before he entered the QMJHL, and right from the start, he didn't disappoint. The Czech winger has an excellent shot, a deceptive release and great accuracy. While in possession of the puck, he likes to cut inside in the offensive zone to take his shot when coming down from the right wing. He's a much better passer and playmaker than he gets credit for; he has a good hockey sense and he's a smart player. One thing he improved this year was his play away from the puck; by December he was less of a liability away from the puck and was playing in all situations. During the year, he was sometimes a man playing against boys; he was strong on the puck and used his body well to protect it in the offensive zone. His skating is good; he has decent speed but also seems to find an extra gear that he uses when he sees an offensive opportunity or can beat a defender one-on-one. He's very passionate on the ice, demonstrating that he wants to be a difference-maker out there, and wants the puck on his stick in big moments in games.

Zadina was one of the top players in the QMJHL this season. With his late 1999 birthday and his level of physical maturity, we feel his chances of playing in the NHL are pretty high for next season.

"He's got a little soccer player in him as far as these injuries and miraculous returns go, but holy shit is he ever good. He can really shoot the puck" - NHL Scout, October 2017

"Crazy fast release on his shot." - NHL Scout, October 2017

"Well after that game, he's moving up some lists." - NHL Scout, October 2017

"You think he likes that cut to the middle and shoot move?" - NHL Scout, November 2017

"He's playing in the NHL next year." - NHL Scout, November 2017

"No doubt in my mind that he'll be in the NHL next year." NHL Scout, December 2017

"He's starting to challenge that number two overall spot for me." NHL Scout, December 2017

"He was really good in Buffalo, he's in the running to go second (overall)." - NHL Scout, January 2018

"Playing pro last year in the Czech Republic definitely helped him this season; he basically had zero trouble adjusting his game to the QMJHL from day 1." HP Scout Jérôme Bérubé

"I just kept hearing the same things from numerous NHL Scouts. They talked about his shot and talked about him being one of the best scorers in the draft. They also talked about him being in the NHL next year. His play in Buffalo seemed to win over any scout who wasn't previously sold on him in the top 5." - HP Scout, Mark Edwards

| 199 | ZAMULA, EGOR | CALGARY | WHL | 6' 2.5" | 165 lbs | LD |

Egor Zamula is a lanky, Russian defenseman who spent time with both the Regina Pats and the Calgary Hitmen in the WHL. He began the year with Regina, and was picked up off of import waivers at the trade deadline by Calgary. He finished the 2017-18 regular season with 2 goals and 18 points in 69 games.

Egor looks unconventional on the ice, because he is a tall defender that is yet to fill out his big frame. He is mobile for his side, as he utilizes a long stride that will become more powerful as he gets stronger. His ability to pivot and evade defenders in tight areas is average, and he is susceptible to outside speed. What helps him defend in these situations is a long active stick which is rangy and deceptive.

Zamula's offensive game is not flashy, but he has possesses good puck skills and can move the puck laterally effectively using his long reach. He can make a skilled play to avoid pressure and buy himself an extra second to make a play. At the offensive point, he has the ability to walk the line and drag the puck to change the angle of his shot. Although he has some skill with the puck, he plays a relatively conservative game. He does not take many chances to extend plays at the offensive point and picks and chooses his opportunities to skate the puck.

The strength of his game is his dependable puck moving skills. He tends not to panic with the puck, and is patient with is decisions. He can handle the puck and move his feet with his head up ice, and because of these dependable skills, he played a consistent top pairing role at the end of the season. Without the puck, Zamula does not tend to play physical, lacking the physical strength to be an aggressive defensive player. If Zamula can fill out his frame and increase his strength, he has the makings of a dependable puck mover as a pro.

152	ZAVGORODNIY, DMITRI	RIMOUSKI	QMJHL	5' 8.5"	173 lbs	LW

Zavgorodniy was the 8th overall pick in the CHL Import Draft last June, after he had a stellar U-17 tournament in Russia in the month of April that put him on the map. He had another great performance in August at the Ivan Hlinka Tournament, where he led the tournament in scoring with 10 points in 5 games.

After joining Rimouski at the end of August, Zavgorodniy had a hot start with the Océanic in the month of October. He averaged over a point per game then, but he hit a wall in November and was not the same player. He didn't look like the same player in November and December compared to what we saw earlier in the year. He played for Russia at the World Junior A tournament in December, but he was a non-factor in the tournament. After the Christmas break, he was much better and was producing at a much better rate than the previous two months. Zavgorodniy's size is a bit of a concern; his level of energy from game to game was not consistent and he went for long stretches during the year without being a factor for his team offensively. For a smaller player, his skating is not top-end. It's fine for junior, but we would like to see it add some more quickness and explosiveness. Although he's not big, his compete level was good when he was playing in tougher areas, and he worked hard without the puck in his own zone. By playing him at center, he showed a more complete game this season, but due to his limited size, when projecting him as a pro, we see him more as a winger down the road. He has good hands and can score; his shot is quite accurate but he could stand to improve his velocity in order to be more of a threat in the offensive zone. He showed good poise and vision with the puck; he came to the QMJHL with a reputation for his ability to score goals, but showed that he can make players around him better as well. That quality, with the lack of centres in Rimouski, was a factor in why he was switched to center.

Overall, we like his skill level. His lack of size, consistency and production in the QMJHL was a bit alarming for us. Nevertheless, we feel Zavgorodniy can be much better than what he showed this year, and could be up for a big year next season. His lack of size combined with his lack of explosiveness is a question mark when trying to project him for the NHL. We still feel he should be drafted in the mid-rounds come June.

"Started the year on fire with Rimouski, playing with Alexis Lafrenière, then was moved to centre on the 2nd line and his play cooled off the rest of the year. He's a winger for me, and on the international stage, he always played well on the wing for Russia at the U-17 Five Nations' Tournament in April 2017, Hlinka August 2017, and U-18s April 2018." - HP Scout Jérôme Bérubé

"Liked him more in the Russia jersey than I did in my viewings of him in the QMJHL." - HP Scout, Mark Edwards

| 178 | ZHABREYEV, ALEXANDER | DYNAMO ST.PTBRG2 | RUSSIA-JR. | 5' 7.0" | 152 lbs | LC |

Alexander Zhabreyev is one of the smallest centres featured in this years draft but he packs a lot of skill into the frame he has. He played for MHK Dynamo St. Petersburg in the MHL where he put up an impressive 30 points in 40 games, including 19 assists. He produced in the playoffs as well, putting up 7 points in 8 games. He also played for Russia at international events, producing the most points at the end of the season at the U18's where he finished with 4 points in 5 games.

Zhabreyev has a glaring drawback in his game, which is his size. He's extremely small however he's fearless around the net area and is at his most dangerous near the goal-line. Despite his frame, he can be difficult to knock off the puck due to his low centre of gravity and has excellent puck skills which he uses to evade defensive pressure. Furthermore, he's willing to enter heavy traffic areas and has great puck tracking skills which allows him to create additional scoring chances off rebounds. He likes to use his quick hands to lift pucks over goalies from in-tight and can make some dextrous drag moves that allow him to change the angle of his attack. He was used below the goal-line on the powerplay and has the vision necessary to find teammates regularly from behind the net. He generates a surprising amount of velocity on both his wrist-shot, snap-shot and slapshot and it's quick to come off his stick, though the accuracy has been mixed in some of our viewings. This allows him to threaten not just down-low but from the slot area and at the top of the circles as well. One of the best aspects of Alexanders game is that he's capable of setting up chances but he's also capable of creating for himself, he mixes up his options effectively and has good offensive-instincts.

Despite being a tenacious and dangerous player who competed hard at both-ends of the ice, its going to be difficult for his game to translate effectively to the pro levels. He's got plus two-step area quickness and great edges but his straight-line speed is underwhelming due to his short-stride, which needs to be highlighted considering his stature. Furthermore, it will be hard for him to continue to produce around the net area once he faces larger defenseman who can box him out at a higher rate and also defend against larger and faster forwards. That being said, he's a very talented player who has the mentality needed to potentially beat out his physical attributes when turning pro.

| 163 | ZHILYAKOV, BOGDAN | DYNAMO ST. PTBRG | RUSSIA-JR. | 6' 0.0" | 185 lbs | LD |

Zhilyakov has always played on the Russian national team over the past two years, with the U-18 and U-17 groups. Last season, he showed some potential to move the puck, but this year he had some struggles with his decision-making. He would often make bad decisions under pressure, and his puck movement didn't stand out. He has decent size and moves well on the ice, but he's not elite with his agility and footwork. He does a fine job utilizing his footwork to escape the pressure and rush the puck out of his zone. He can be used in all situations, but we didn't see his offensive game take the next step this season. There's some concern with his decision-making when he's pressed by the opposing team. He's not overly physical, but can throw some nice hits here and there when needed along the boards. He could stand to be tougher in front of the net. We expected a bit more out of him this year, after a good season last year with the U-17 group.

| 77 | ZHURAVLYOV, DANILA | IRBIS KAZAN | RUSSIA-JR. | 6' 0.0" | 163 lbs | LD |

Danila Zhuravlyov had an impressive year for Irbis Kazan in the MHL where he posted 18 points in 28 games including 9 goals, he then posted an assist in 5 playoff games. He was heavily involved in international competition by being featured in the Hlinka, WJAC-19, Five-Nations, and the U18's which is where he had his most successful output, posting 5 assists in 5 games. Danila was involved in all situations for his team while logging a lot of minutes at each event.

Zhuravlyov is a highly-mobile two-way defenseman who has shown to be a transitional puck-mover. He's a superb skater with excellent two-step area quickness that allows him to get up to one of the better top-gears in this draft class. Another great quality to his skating is his lateral movement, due to having advanced cross-over mechanics and he can pivot or cut on a dime which makes him excellent at weaving in and out of heavy traffic and gaining offensive-zone entries while transitioning the puck through all three-zones. Additionally, he can process and evaluate incoming pressure quickly which allows him to make smart and fast decisions when attempting to make an outlet pass to a teammate or when he's deciding to skate the puck out from behind his own-goal line. He doesn't just use his skating to move the puck up the ice, he also uses it to close his gaps efficiently, giving opposing teams limited time to react to him. He's a proactive defenseman rather than a reactive one, and he's willing to aggressively engage opponents using his length and an active stick in an attempt to disrupt offensive plays. This does cause him to throw himself out of position occasionally but he's got the skating ability to recover and he plays at a pretty high-pace which helps him get back into position. His overall positional awareness is a plus and he constantly keeps his head up and surveys passing options so that he can attempt to take away both passing and shooting lanes. One of the most impressive aspects of his recovery sequences is when he's transitioning from the offensive-line, when he or his defensive partner gets caught. We have seen him rapidly catch up to players on breakaways and disrupt their high-percentage attempts in some of our viewings.

There's a lot of untapped offensive-potential in Zhuravlyov's game. His lateral mobility allows him to change shooting lanes efficiently, he's got plus vision and demonstrated on the powerplay that he can distribute the puck at a consistent rate. Danila also has pretty decent puck-skills which gives him solid feinting mechanics but he doesn't use them as much as he should. We have seen him fake a pass when his lane is closed and then quickly change gears to re-open his lane before firing a wrist-shot but it's not as common as it could be. That being said, his shooting mechanics are solid, he's able to change angles when driving down a lane after a successful pinch and the puck is quick to come off his stick, though he does sacrifice some power in order to have a more precise shot. His slapshot does generate power however and he's good at keeping it low and on net, while also getting it through traffic at a decent rate. If Zhuravlyov continues to refine aspects of his positioning away from the puck in the offensive-end, including when trying to set-up his one-timer at the point after receiving a pass and he continues to gain more confidence in pinching at the appropriate times, he could potentially develop into a point producing defenseman at the pro-level.

The fact that he played the full season in the MHL gives him less familiarity amongst some scouts compared to most other players, but his recent U-18 performance and previous international exposure should help him on draft day, though his size might hold him back to some degree.

"I loved his transitional play, he's an impressive skater with untapped offensive potential." - HP Scout, Brad Allen

| NR | ZUMMACK, ELI | SPOKANE | WHL | 5' 9.0" | 177 lbs | RC |

Originally drafted by the Red Deer Rebels in the 2nd round of 2015, he never played a game for that franchise as he was dealt to Spokane in 2016 while he was still a member of the Minor Midget Okanagan Rockets. A small center that plays well above his 5'9 – 175lbs frame, he battles against bigger players in front of the net and below the goal line, he works hard on the forecheck and isn't afraid to throw hits against bigger forwards. His size does bite him a little as he gets pushed off pucks and knocked down a fair bit but not for lack of effort and he also shows resilience in his ability to bounce back and continue heading to those tough areas with determination. In viewings he was often seen providing strong backpressure through the neutral zone and making life difficult for puck carriers. He was a pretty consistent presence on the penalty kill and puts his body on the line to block shots. Zummack is shifty with the puck and shows really good control. His hands both when setting up plays and when carrying the puck at high speed and tight spaces allow him to easily navigate. His soft hands translate to his scoring ability because he can move goalies out of position and tuck pucks into the openings he creates. Although he doesn't have a blistering shot, its certainly accurate and more strength should build as he gets bigger and stronger. His quick pace and quick thinking help him overcome his size but he faces challenges as he continues to move up the lineup and face stiffer competition. As a right shot center with resilience, work ethic and a strong IQ Zummack has translatable skills for a pro game but it's a steep climb.

"Wasn't a game I saw that I didn't like, plays big but size holds him back even if he gets knocked around doesn't bother him, if he ever fills out he'll make a team really happy" - HP Scout, Andy Levangie

The * beside a players weight in this profile header indicates we updated his height and eight after the NHL Combine.

2019 NHL DRAFT RANKINGS

RANK	PLAYER	TEAM	LEAGUE	BIRTH	HEIGHT	WEIGHT	POS
1	Jack Hughes	U.S. National U17 Team	USDP	14-May-2001	5' 10.0"	161	C
2	Alex Turcotte	U.S. National U17 Team	USDP	26-Feb-2001	5' 11.0"	194	C
3	Alex Newhook	Victoria Grizzlies	BCHL	28-Jan-2001	5' 11.0"	183	C
4	Kaapo Kakko	TPS U20	Jr. A SM-liiga	13-Feb-2001	6' 4.0"	207	RW
5	Bowen Byram	Vancouver Giants	WHL	13-Jun-2001	6.' 0.0"	179	D
6	Maxim Cajkovic	Malmö Redhawks J20	SuperElit	03-Jan-2001	5' 11.0"	187	RW
7	Victor Söderström	Brynäs IF J18	J18 Elit	26-Feb-2001	5' 11.0"	176	D
8	Peyton Krebs	Kootenay Ice	WHL	26-Jan-2001	5' 11.0"	172	LW
9	Vasili Podkolzin	Vityaz Podolsk U17	Russia U17	24-Jun-2001	5' 11.0"	165	RW
10	Arthur Kaliyev	Hamilton Bulldogs	OHL	26-Jun-2001	6' 1.0"	165	LW
11	Matthew Boldy	U.S. National U17 Team	USDP	05-Apr-2001	6' 0.0"	174	RW
12	Kirby Dach	Saskatoon Blades	WHL	21-Jan-2001	6' 4.0"	185	C
13	Dylan Cozens	Lethbridge Hurricanes	WHL	09-Feb-2001	6' 3.0"	176	C
14	Daniil Gutik	Loko-Yunior Yaroslavl	NMHL	31-Aug-2001	6' 3.0"	179	LW
15	Raphaël Lavoie	Halifax Mooseheads	QMJHL	25-Sep-2000	6' 4.0"	192	C
16	Cole Caufield	U.S. National U17 Team	USDP	02-Jan-2001	5' 6.0"	154	C/RW
17	Cam York	U.S. National U17 Team	USDP	05-Jan-2001	5' 11.0"	165	D
18	Valentin Nussbaumer	Biel-Bienne	NLA	25-Sep-2000	5' 11.0"	159	C/W
19	Blake Murray	Sudbury Wolves	OHL	05-Jul-2001	6' 1.0"	179	C
20	Ryan Suzuki	Barrie Colts	OHL	28-May-2001	6' 0.0"	172	C
21	Michael Vukojevic	Kitchener Rangers	OHL	08-Jun-2001	6' 2.0"	201	D
22	Simon Holmström	HV71 J20	SuperElit	24-May-2001	5' 11.0"	172	RW
23	Anttoni Honka	JYP	Liiga	05-Oct-2000	5' 10.0"	170	D
24	Jakob Pelletier	Moncton Wildcats	QMJHL	07-Mar-2001	5' 9.0"	159	LW
25	Trevor Zegras	U.S. National U17 Team	USDP	20-Mar-2001	5' 11.0"	159	C
26	Matthew Robertson	Edmonton Oil Kings	WHL	09-Mar-2001	6' 3.0"	196	D
27	John Beecher	U.S. National U17 Team	USDP	05-Apr-2001	6' 2.0"	201	C
28	Tobias Björnfot	Djurgårdens IF J20	SuperElit	06-Apr-2001	6' 0.0"	187	D
29	Spencer Knight	U.S. National U17 Team	USDP	19-Apr-2001	6' 3.0"	194	G
30	Ryder Donovan	Duluth East High	USHS-MN	04-Oct-2000	6' 4.0"	185	D
31	Ben Brinkman	Edina High	USHS-MN	04-Oct-2000	6' 0.0"	174	D
HM	Alex Vlasic	U.S. National U17 Team	USDP	05-Jun-2001	6' 5.0"	190	D
HM	Lev Starikov	Windsor Spitfires	OHL	17-Sep-2000	6' 6.0"	187	D
HM	Samuel Poulin	Sherbrooke Phoenix	QMJHL	25-Feb-2001	6' 1.0"	207	LW

2019 NHL DRAFT PROSPECTS

AALTONEN, LEEVI
LW - KalPa U20 (Jr. A SM-Liiga) 5'09" 154

Leevi Aaltonen had a good year with Kalpa's U20 squad, where he produced 21 points in 34 games, including 13 assists. In the playoffs he scored 7 points in 13 games. Internationally, he was featured at both the U17's where he had 3 points in five games, and the U18's where he scored two goals in 7 games.

Aaltonen is a two-way skating winger with a tremendous motor that compliments a good amount of skill. He can take advantage of flat-footed or caught defenders, using an explosive first-step, great edges, and dynamic top speed to blow by his opponents. His speed compliments his style of play very well. He's relentless in puck pursuit situations and is willing to battle well above his weight class along the walls. This was notable in the defensive-end as well, where he would close his gaps before the opposition could react, stripped them off the puck and generating several shorthanded chances in our viewings. Furthermore, he can pass the puck and make skilled plays while going at top speeds. Though, his biggest flaw at this time is that his head doesn't always keep up with his skating. He doesn't always recognize the time and space he has to use his speed to attack the net, and he can get tunnel vision, choosing a lower-percentage play off the rush as a result. That being said, Aaltonen is a tenacious kid who was the catalyst for several impressive plays when we watched him throughout the year and looks to be someone who can be a good complimentary piece on a scoring line when heading into his draft year.

ABRAMOV, MIKHAIL
LC - CSKA Moskva U17 (Russia U17) - 5'10" 152

Abramov is a talented centre with good skating abilities. He likes to challenge players one-on-one and has the speed to go wide on defenders. He's quick to apply pressure on the forecheck and he's a good puck-retriever in both offensive and defensive zones. He showed a good wrist shot with a quick release. He also showed some good playmaking abilities, good vision and poise with the puck. He created a lot of his scoring chances with his speed; he did some good work down low and along the wall to protect the puck. His skating is his number one asset; it's dynamic and he uses it efficiently. Away from the puck, he showed good effort in his own zone and on the backcheck. He was one of the better players for Russia at the February U-17 Five Nations' Tournament.

AFANASYEV, YEGOR
LW - Muskegon Lumberjacks (USHL) 6'02" 190

Yegor is a strong, power forward winger out of the Detroit Little Caesars program. Yegor is playing only his second season in North America after coming over to the states from Russia. Afanasyev saw 45 games this season for Muskegon registering 6 goals and 8 Assists as well as represented Russia at the U17 in November where he was a point per game player for his team. Yegor is extremely strong on his skates and displayed the ability to dominate below the dots with the puck in some viewings. Yegor is not an explosive skater and needs to improve his footwork before he can be considered a legitimate pro prospect but Yegor does a good job compensating by using his frame and stick handling to get his defender off balance and gain his separation and beat defenders one on one. Yegor's best offensive weapon at this stage is his shot. He has the ability to quickly change the angle and get it off his tape quickly to catch goalies off guard. Like a lot of players his age, Yegor has the skills to be a dynamic playmaker but doesn't always use his teammates as well as he could. Afanasyev needs to continue to work on his defensive awareness and can lack compete to win or track down pucks but there is no doubting his size and offensive abilities will make him a prospect to track for the 2019 NHL Draft. Yegor will likely spend at least one more season in the USHL before heading to Michigan State.

ALEXANDER, JACSON
LD - Swift Current Broncos (WHL) 5'09" 174

Jacson Alexander is an undersized defenseman who split time with the Victoria Grizzlies in the BCHL and the Swift Current Broncos of the WHL. He recorded 5 points in 32 regular season games for the Broncos. On an exceptional Swift Current team, Alexander was a consistent member of the bottom pairing on the team.

Alexander has exceptional feet and quickness. He is very difficult to forecheck because of his ability to evade and turn away from pressure. Although he is undersized, he is difficult to check because of this creativity. His feet are consistently moving and he possesses a great motor. This mobility and skating ability made him a dominant player prior to Junior, but he has yet to translate this offensive talent as a Junior player. This tough transition is in part because he is forced to move pucks quicker and his lack of strength and sized is exposed when he tries to hold onto pucks and skate his way out of traffic. Given his aggressive offensive style, he can sometimes put himself into very vulnerable situations. But despite putting himself into these situations, he battles and competes with players outside his weight range. Jacson is a breakout candidate going into his second season in the WHL, but his size will continue to be a question.

ALEXANDROV, NIKITA
LC - Charlottetown Islanders (QMJHL) - 5'11"183

Alexandrov was the 50th overall selection in the CHL Import Draft last June by the Islanders. He's a dual citizen, growing up in Germany and playing most of his youth hockey there. His father, a former pro hockey player who played 1 year in North America with Springfield in the mid-90s, played most of his career in Russia and Germany. Now, he's a coach in the MHL in the Russian junior league.

With the Islanders this year, Alexandrov had some adjustments to make to his game, such as playing on a smaller ice surface, and didn't get a ton of ice time. He made some nice progress with his play away from the puck, and enjoyed some of his best success in the playoffs. He had 31 points in 66 regular season games, but averaged over a point per game in the playoffs with a surprising run by the Islanders. He played center all year long but can also play on the wing. He's a good skater and has good smarts. His puck skills are good, showing his Russian roots with the puck on his stick, and he can make plays in the offensive zone. He likes to shoot the puck; he had 175 shots on net this year despite not having regular ice time on the top 2 lines, or top power play ice time. Alexandrov missed the 2018 NHL Draft deadline by one day, as he was born September 16th. Next year, he will see regular top 6 and top power play unit ice time, and if his playoffs this year are any indication, he shouldn't be too far off from a point per game. Alexandrov is a smart player with some skills; his upside for the next level still remains to be seen.

ALLEPOT, ANTHONY
LD - Val-d'Or Foreurs (QMJHL) - 6'02" 182

Allepot made the big jump from the LHPS to the QMJHL at 16 years old, which has not been done before; the Foreurs drafted Allepot in the 2nd round, 37th overall last June.

The Trois-Rivières native is a big, raw, mobile defenseman who, in his first year, was brought in slowly and got his feet wet. His agility and mobility are impressive for that size; he can skate the puck out of his zone and be useful for his team's transition game when he uses his feet. He'll need to improve his decision-making with the puck, though; it's the biggest area that needs work in his game. He needs to play a simple game with the puck, and make better decisions.

Defensively, there's a lot of work to be done as well; he needs to play a meaner and more physical game in front of his net and along the boards. He has a great reach and a long stick, and that helps him protect the puck.

Next season, Allepot will see his role and ice time increase with the Foreurs, who have some good young talent in his age group that they can build with.

ANTROPOV, DANIL
LW - Oshawa Generals (OHL) 6'01" 192

Antropov is a big bodied winger with some skill to his game. Danil saw an elevated goal total in his sophomore OHL campaign as he became more confident in possession and more assertive with his shot. His improved lower body strength allowed him to slightly elevate his skating which was an area of concern in his rookie year. However, Danil does need to continue on enhancing his lower body strength to improve the power and quickness in his stride as he currently can struggle to accelerate and reach only an average top speed. Antropov is at his best in possession when utilizing his frame and momentum to get him where he wants to go. He handles the puck well and is able to protect it effectively through the high traffic areas. Danil shows an effectiveness off he cycle, using his frame to shield the puck and create space for his teammates. While there is intrigue to his game along he wall and below the hash-marks, he does need to become more aggressive and assertive with his frame. Danil to often is out-worked for lose pucks and positioning. Offensively his best tool is his shot. Antropov shows an ability to sneak behind opponents and find soft spots, releasing his shot quickly with good velocity behind it. Danil has raw, but intriguing traits to his game that could allow him to thrive if he can put them together and improve his skating.

BARLAGE, LOGAN
LC - Lethbridge Hurricanes (WHL) 6'04" 203

Logan Barlage is a big power forward who was drafted 4th overall in the 2016 Bantam Draft by the Swift Current Broncos. Barlage was traded at the trade deadline to the Lethbridge Hurricanes, a major piece in a package for Lethbridge's two top players. He recorded 20 points in 71 regular season games but had a strong post season, with an additional 8 points in 16 playoff games, as Lethbridge reached the Eastern Conference Finals.

Barlage is a huge kid, and with that his skating style is a little unconventional and awkward. His big body makes it difficult for him to achieve a deep knee bend and low centre of gravity, but he still manages to generate enough speed in stride to get up and down the ice with the play. Top speed and quickness is not an asset of his, but the question will be how much does his skating inhibit his ability to be an offensive threat at the next level.

Barlage is at his best below the dots in the offensive end. He utilizes his size and reach very well, protecting the puck and physically dominating the walls. This ability is what made him look like a man against boys against his peers, but as excepted, he did not show this ability to dominate the cycle game in his first season in the WHL. His puck protection skills are complemented with soft hands for a big man, as he can drag the puck laterally with ease and create space for himself in a variety of ways. Although he uses his size well to protect pucks, he likes to play a skilled game and does not play very physical without the puck. His puck skills combined with his size and strength make him an intriguing prospect for the 2019 NHL Draft. But he will need to take a major step offensively to overcome his skating woes.

BEAUCAGE, ALEX
RW - Rouyn-Noranda Huskies (QMJHL) - 6'01" 186

Beaucage had a good rookie season with the Huskies, scoring 37 points, also playing at the U-17 Hockey Challenge in November. Rouyn-Noranda drafted the Trois-Rivières' native with their first pick of the 2017 QMJHL Draft (20th overall, at the beginning of the 2nd round). Beaucage comes from a hockey family; his father was a very good player in the QMJHL and in Europe (playing 7 seasons in Germany).

Beaucage has a nice offensive toolset, his wrist shot is excellent and he can score from anywhere in the offensive zone with it. He's a sniper with that shot and that quick release; he's going to score a lot of goals using those. His skating is average; he could work on improving his acceleration and quickness. He has good scoring instincts, but his playmaking abilities are underrated. He sees the ice well and can find his linemates quickly on the ice. He has decent size; he's not a power forward per se, but he showed a good compete level this year, battling in front of the net and in the corners in some of our viewings. These were some good flashes of what we could see on a more regular basis in the seasons ahead. When asked to play the role of the guy in front of the net on the power play, he would do so. However, next year we feel that he's going to be the guy controlling the puck at the half-wall and become a big power play producer that way. His play away from the puck is good enough; he won't be a defensive or penalty-killing specialist, but he has good hockey smarts and won't be a liability on the ice for his team.

Beaucage's role and ice time will grow next season, and so will his production with the Huskies. He has good potential, and could be one of those players who has a breakthrough year next season and could climb the draft rankings as a result.

BEECHER, JOHN
LC - USA NTDP-17 (USHL) - 6'02" 198

Beecher has two-way potential with certain power-center elements to his game. He's got an excellent frame with a strong base. This is evident in his skating abilities; he's got a powerful stride and moves around the ice well. He's a center who doesn't stray from his defensive responsibilities and played a 200-foot game. He's a handful along the boards for the opposition, as he knows how to use his frame and reach effectively to maintain possession of the puck. Similar to the rest of his game, his shot is heavy and difficult to handle. He also has above-average puck skills; this, when combined with his acceleration and frame, allowed him to create chances for himself. Beecher didn't show the upside that could make him a first-round pick this year, but has good potential with his overall game.

He didn't get the chance to play on a top line until Hughes and Turcotte were promoted to the U-18 team, and he finished the season strong (23 points in his last 21 games). Before this hot streak, he only had 18 points in 39 games. Next season will be a big year for him to show that the last stretch of this season was not a fluke, and that he can be a key player offensively.

"I question the hockey sense a little bit." - NHL Scout, June 2018

BELLAMY, JAXON
LD - Sherbrooke Phoenix (QMJHL) - 6'03" 184

Bellamy was drafted by Moncton (16th overall) last June, but was traded this year mid-season to Sherbrooke after he requested a trade due to lack of ice time. Bellamy is originally from New Brunswick, which is why that trade request caught a lot of people off-guard.

Bellamy has a great mix of size and skating abilities. He skates really well for a player of his size at this young age. He can skate the puck out of his zone and quickly distance forecheckers. On the point, he has a booming shot with great velocity, although some work needs to be done with its accuracy. He's not shy on the ice; he can play a physical game in his own zone and has a bit of a mean streak in him. He'll need to improve his decision-making with the puck, as his passing game is one slated for improvement. As it stands, his passes are lacking accuracy and he can get himself into trouble with his poor decision-making. He has value as a power play guy because of his powerful shot from the point. It's one of the best shots from his age group, and he's not shy to use it. He will, however, need to pick his spots better and not just shoot for the sake of it. There are some question marks with him when we talk about hockey IQ, passing game and offensive creativity.

Bellamy has an interesting toolbox, with his size, physical play and skating abilities. He will draw some attention from NHL teams without a doubt. The key will remain the decision-making part of his game that, if improved upon, could take his game to another level.

BERNARD, JACOB
LD - Rimouski Océanic (QMJHL) - 6'00" 169

Bernard was drafted with the 38th overall pick last June by Rimouski in the QMJHL Draft. He split this season between his midget team in Lévis and the Océanic. He ended up playing 17 games with Rimouski, plus the playoffs, with them.

Bernard is a two-way defenseman with good skating abilities. He's efficient on the ice, but not very flashy. He's good at defending one-on-one, with the ability to play a physical game, and is tough to beat individually. He moves to the puck well from his zone; his passes are quick and accurate, which always helps his team's transition game. He's not an overly creative player in the offensive zone; he can help on the power play, but he won't be a top power play quarterback in major junior. He's more of a stay-at-home and penalty-killing type of defenseman for major junior. His decision-making is solid; he keeps his game simple and doesn't make a whole lot of mistakes on the ice.

Next year, Bernard should be a regular in the Rimouski lineup, and has a good chance of cracking their top 4 if they don't add anyone else to their D-corps.

BERTUZZI, TAG
LC - Guelph Storm (OHL) 6'0" 192

Tag was selected in the first round, second overall by the Guelph Storm at the 2017 OHL Draft. Bertuzzi finished his first season with Guelph by putting up 11 points in 41 games, including 8 assists. In the playoffs he had zero points in 1 game. Internationally, he was featured at the U17's where he had 4 points in 5 games for Canada Black.

Bertuzzi plays with a ton of energy and is constantly pushing the pace with his speed and puck skills. He can beat defenders one on one with his hands and his speed. He is an interesting combination of a dynamic skilled forward mixed with a high energy in your face forechecker who plays an emotional style of game and gets after his opponents when he doesn't have the puck. Furthermore, he used his frame to battle effectively which further complimented his style of play. His backcheck was a little inconsistent this year, sometimes he flew back to help his team out, other times he didn't show the same level of hustle going the other direction. The emotion he plays the game with works both ways for him as it can help him be successful, but it also can land him in the penalty box at times. Bertuzzi has plenty of upside and is already a player to watch for the 2019 NHL Draft, though he didn't put up the numbers some were expecting heading into the season, as he was being used primarily in a depth-role.

BIZIER, MATHIEU
LC - Rimouski Océanic (QMJHL) - 6'01" 176

Bizier was the 12th overall selection in the 2017 QMJHL Draft by Rimouski (their 3rd pick in the first round after drafting Lafrenière 1st and Christopher Innis 10th). Surprisingly, Bizier was left off the roster of the three Team Canada at the November U-17 tournament. Nevertheless, he had a good rookie season with Rimouski, scoring 10 times and finishing the season with 25 points. He also made his mark more in a defensive role and in PK situations.

Bizier is a very smart center who really understands how to play the game away from the puck and play more of a defensive role on a team. He has a smart active stick, is good at blocking passing lanes, good at poking pucks away and is not afraid to block shots on the PK. He's good in the faceoff circle and is always a strong presence down low in his zone to support his defensemen. He has a great work ethic; a lot of his offense comes from his hard work in the offensive zone. He's not a high-end skills' guy, but makes the players around him better. He has good vision, but his scoring potential is limited. His skating and footspeed are the 2 areas that will need some big improvements for the NHL.

He has defensive center upside, as a guy that can play that shutdown role. However, we want to see more offensive skills out of him that would translate better to the NHL. He should see more ice time next season with Rimouski, as they don't have the best depth at center for next year, and that should help him get more ice time and see his production improve.

BJERSELIUS, OSCAR
LC - Djurgardens IF (J20) - 5'11" 174

Bjerselius didn't show any high-end offensive abilities this year in our viewings, but did some good unsung work for his team. He worked really hard in the defensive zone, showing good awareness there, and often acted like a 3rd defenseman on the ice. He showed good support down low in the defensive zone and was quick to retrieve pucks deep in his own zone to start the transition game. He has decent size and speed; he drew some penalties with his speed and kept his feet moving. We like his smarts and attention to detail on the ice, but next year, we would like to see more offensive upside out of him. However, he has good on-ice vision and has some decent playmaking abilities. This year, Bjerselius played on three teams, including two at the J18 level, and finished at the J20 level, where he should play next year.

BJORNFOT, TOBIAS
LD - Djurgardens IF J20 (SuperElit) - 6'00" 187

Bjornfot is a complete defenseman from Sweden who plays a solid two-way game on the ice. He's solid in all areas. He has good size, skating abilities and can contribute at both ends of the ice. He's not a high-end offensive defenseman, but can contribute with his ability to rush the puck and possesses a good, hard, low point shot. His footwork is good. He is good at keeping up with quick forwards from opposing team; his gap control is solid and he makes good use of his stick in defensive situations. Often with Sweden's U-17 team, he was used as a shutdown defenseman, but was also able to bring some offense. He's active in his own end and was defensively aware, showing sound positioning around the net and using his thick frame to angle bodies away from the crease. He also played for Sweden's U-18 team at the U-18 World Hockey Championships, which was a good test for him and would help him get ready for next season as he will be a key player for Sweden's U-18 national team once again. The difference between Bjornfot and another Swedish defenseman, Victor Soderstrom, is that Bjornfot doesn't have the high-end offensive skills that Soderstrom has. His upside at the NHL level isn't that high. He doesn't have the high-end vision and skills that are required to be a point-producer like Soderstrom, but still has good potential as a two-way defender.

BLAISDELL, HARRISON
LW - Chilliwack Chiefs (BCHL) 5'10" 176

Harrison Blaisdell is a skilled forward who spent his 16-year-old season with the Chilliwack chiefs in the BCHL, recording 21 points in 49 regular season games. Blaisdell is committed to the University of North Dakota and his WHL rights lie with the Vancouver Giants.

Blaisdell is an extremely smart forward who thinks the game at a level beyond his opposition. He was dominant against his peers at the U17 Summer Camp but had a tougher transition to junior hockey. His best traits are his playmaking skills and ability to find his teammates in tight areas. He can generate open looks for teammates in the cycle game and plays through the opposition. His skating stride and fundamentals are strong, as he plays with a low centre of gravity and has above average top end speed. His puck skills are very good and he has soft, creative hands that he uses in tandem with his ability to change direction to create space. He also has great ability to strip pucks and forecheck. His strong will to retrieve pucks is what will take him to the next level offensively. In past seasons, he was a strong offensive player, but never dominant, and it is yet to be seen how much offensive upside he has at the Junior level.

BOLDY, MATT
LW - USA NTDP-17 (USHL) - 6'00" 174

Boldy is an interesting prospect out of the American U-17 team; he plays a strong power-forward game and he's at his best down low and in front of the net. He's still growing into his body; it doesn't seem like he's stopped growing and getting bigger and stronger. He was one of the top players on this team this year during the season and in international play; he had 76 points in 61 games combined.

The most underrated parts of his game involve his vision and playmaking abilities; he sees the ice very well and has excellent poise with the puck. His passes are crisp and accurate. He's very good down low; his puck-protection game is really good thanks to his size and long reach. He also keeps moving his feet, which helps him get away from his coverage. Offensively, he's also not afraid to shoot the puck; he has a quick release that helps him catch goaltenders off-guard. When he gets going, he can be tough to contain down low and when he goes to the net with the puck. His skating is improving; he has good top speed and a quick burst that he uses to create separation, although his footwork is a bit clumsy and his first three steps are still a work-in-progress. However, we have seen some nice progression in that area of his game since the beginning of the season.

Boldy is committed to play at Boston College for the 2019-2020 season, and will be one of the top players with the US program next year.

"One of my fave players on the team this past season. Skating isn't great but he's a very smart player."
- HP Scout, Mark Edwards

BREWER, MITCHELL
LD - Oshawa Generals (OHL) 6'00" 205

Brewer is a simplistic defender with good strength to his game. Mitchell played a poised and mature game for he Generals his season. He showed an intelligence and awareness to his game that allowed him to play in various situations throughout the season. Brewer possesses good strength to his game and was assertive physical in puck and position battles. His competitive edge often allowed him to emerge from puck battles with possession, while his continuous work ethic makes him tough to play against. In possession Mitchell keeps his game simplistic, opting for a quick first pass and trailing behind the play, keeping an effective gap, but rarely jumping into the offensive attack. Brewer does show a heavy point shot, but isn't overly assertive in using it. He would benefit offensively from getting more pucks on goal. Brewer is a slightly above average skater as he shows good but not great mobility. He can contain in transition by keeping the play in front of him and angling opponents wide. Brewer's maturity and effectiveness in the defensive zone makes him an appealing prospect.

BRINK, BOBBY
RC - Minnetonka Skippers (MNHS) 5'10" 165

Brink is coming off a breakout season for the Minnesota Class AA State Champion Minnetonka High School, where he led his team in assists and points. Brink finished the season with Sioux City of the USHL as well as being allowed to join the USNTDP U17 team for the USHL Clark Cup playoffs. In all those situations, Brink's skill was well on display. Brink has a great combination of speed and playmaking ability. His hands and footwork is a step above most of his opponents which allows him to beat his opponent's in one on one situations and make some highlight real plays. Where Brink really seemed to elevate his play was when the games meant the most. Throughout the Minnesota High School playoffs and the State Tournament, Brink registered 8 goals and 4 Assists in 6 games and scored many key goals for his team. Brink is not the biggest player at this stage, but plays a much larger game than his listed size. He is difficult to separate from pucks and has good strength to separate from defenders in front and win loose pucks. His hockey smarts and ability to read the play without the puck is an asset and was on display most on the penalty kill where he was a threat to score on a number of occasions and scored 7 Shorthanded goals in 31 games for Minnetonka. As of now it looks like Bobby will be off to Sioux City (USHL) full time next season but many scouts are not writing him off to return to Minnetonka High School in November. Brink was originally slated to attend University of Denver starting in 20/21 and much will depend on his academics but given Brinks development trajectory right now it's not hard to imagine him being ready for college hockey in the fall of 2019.

BRINKMAN, BEN
LD - Edina Hornets (MNHS) 6'01" 174

Brinkman is a former 1st Round, 5th Overall pick by Waterloo in the 2016 USHL Phase 1 Draft. Brinkman saw a considerable jump in his all-around game this season for a talented Edina squad. Ben showed the ability to control the game on most nights. Brinkman moves around the ice well, using his explosive footwork to escape pressure and showed the ability to quickly turn plays out of his own end. Brinkman comes out of his own end with his head up and can buy time by using his skating and puck skills to gain zones until his forwards get open. Defensively, Brinkman has good stick on puck capability and his footwork allows him to be more aggressive against the rush at his own blue line. Brinkman displayed good physicality against opponents but will need to learn to pick his spots better going forward, as he took himself out of the play on occasions when he didn't have to. In the offensive zone Brinkman can score from high in the zone with both his slap shot as well as his quick snap release that he can get through traffic and has displayed the skill to get around opponents that challenge the points and come down from the point position. Brinkman registered 10 Goals and 30 Assists in 25 Regular Season games for Edina and was equally impressive in the playoffs for his team. Brinkman has a good foundation and skill set to be a solid two-way defenseman at the next level. With Edina falling short of a State Title this past season, it's easy to imagine Ben starting and finishing the season with Waterloo (USHL) but returning to the Hornets for the High School season. Brinkman is scheduled to suit up for the University of Minnesota for the 2018/2019 season.

BROBERG, PHILIP
LD - AIK J20 (SuperElit) - 6'03" 192

Broberg is an interesting defenseman from Sweden; he already has great size and skates really well. He likes to use his feet often to skate the puck out of his zone and he's really successful at it. He's quick to retrieve pucks in his own zone thanks to his solid footwork. He skates well; he has good acceleration, good top speed and a powerful stride. He can rush the puck in the offensive zone as well; he can beat guys one-on-one by going wide on them. He'll need to improve his puck skills, as he was successful bringing the puck to the neutral zone from his own zone, but struggled when he had to beat a guy one-on-one with his stickhandling. He'll need to play a smarter game, too. He can take risks at times when rushing pucks and forcing plays, but if he can play a simpler game, he'll be more efficient on the ice. Defensively, he uses his size well to defend one-on-one and in front of the net, but could make better use of his stick to knock pucks down and block passing lanes.

BROWNE, ETHAN
LC - Prince George Cougars (WHL) 5'11" 181

Ethan Browne is skilled centre who was traded from the Everett Silvertips to the Prince George Cougars half-way through the season. He failed to be a regular on a good Silvertip team and even saw time in the AJHL with the Drayton Valley Thunder. Once traded he earned consistent icetime with the Cougars, finishing with 11 points in 30 games to finish out the season. Browne failed to make the World U17s roster despite having a solid summer camp and being a first round pick in the 2016 WHL Bantam Draft. Browne is a dynamic player who showed the ability to take over with his high end speed and puckhandling at the World U17 Summer Camp. Unfortunately, these skills have yet to translate into play in the WHL. Ethan does not play physical and is offensive minded, which is why he struggled in a bottom six role for a deep Everett group. Browne is a breakout candidate if he gains the necessary confidence and is put into offensive situations.

BUDGELL, BRETT
LW - Charlottetown Islanders (QMJHL) - 6'00" 180

Budgell started the year with Chicago in the USHL, and made the move to the QMJHL in January to join the Islanders, who had drafted him in the 2nd round of the QMJHL Draft last June (25th overall). He had an immediate impact with the Islanders and finished the season with 22 points in 32 games.

The Newfoundland native also played for Canada Red at the U-17 Hockey Challenge in November, but didn't register any points in 6 games. Budgell is a smart hockey player with a good hockey IQ. He played mostly on the wing, but can play at center as well. He has good two-way abilities; he's responsible away from the puck and he's not a liability in the defensive zone. Budgell does a good job in the offensive zone on a line because of his ability to retrieve pucks along the boards, and his work in front of the net. He can do a lot of dirty work for his line and his work ethic is great. His best asset offensively remains his shot, as he has a great release and great velocity to it, and he shoots the puck like a pro. There's still work to be done with his skating abilities; some improvement to his explosiveness would only make him a better and more dangerous player when it comes time to create offense.

Budgell is a pretty complete player and with no real weaknesses in his game. Next season, he should be a leader offensively for the Islanders, with a lot of players leaving the team. He should get plenty of ice time next season.

"He was great in the playoffs for the Islanders. He played a very pro and mature game, despite being just 16 years old." - HP Scout Jérôme Bérubé

BYRAM, BOWEN
LD - Vancouver Giants (WHL) 6'00" 179

Bowen Byram was selected 3rd overall in the 2016 WHL Bantam Draft by the Vancouver Giants, and played his first full season with the club in 2017-18, recording 27 points in 60 regular season games. He had a productive playoff, recording 7 points in 7 games including 3 goals, which earned him an invitation to the World U18s for Team Canada as an underage player. His confidence and production improved dramatically as the year wore on, and he developed into a top pairing defenseman and powerplay quarterback by the end of the WHL season.

Byram is an explosive skater. He sits back on his heels with a deep knee bend and has high end top speed and can reach it quickly. His ability to move laterally is exceptional, especially when walking the point and deking incoming forecheckers. His skating ability helps him excel in the offensive portion of his game. He is a true powerplay quarterback, wanting to take control of breakouts. Bowen makes skating with the puck up ice look easy and effortless. What makes him unique is he combines this speed with a high skill level. He is creative and elusive deking in all situations, whether it be at the point against a winger or on a rush against an opposing defenseman. In one on one situations he is dangerous, and he has a very good ability to score when left alone with a goalie.

On the powerplay, Byram's one timer is heavy and accurate, and later in the year he became an offensive force for the Giants. Early in the year, Byram struggled with confidence given his limited icetime. When he is not playing a ton, he seeks to make a difference and often fails to use his teammates. This was illustrated in the World U18s, where he was working hard to make things happen offensively which resulted in turnovers and running around in his own end. He will need to channel his competitiveness and will to make a difference. But his talent is legitimate and he should be a top prospect for the 2019 NHL Draft.

CAJKOVIC, MAXIM
LW/RW - Malmo Redhawks J20 (SuperElit) 5'11" 187

Maxim Cajkovic had a tremendous year after not only getting called up by Malmo's U20 team but sticking with them after tearing up the J18 team by scoring 14 goals and adding 3 assists in 10 games. He produced 21 points in 28 games, including 10 goals after his call up to the SuperElit. Internationally, he had a very impressive U18's performance, leading his team in points with 11 in 5 games, which was good for the second highest point total out of any player.

Cajkovic is a terrific talent whose one of the most skilled and dangerous forwards featured in the 2019 class. He has two-step area quickness, exceptional-pivots and explodes out of the gate which gets him up to his top gear fast, where he's shown separation speed. This made him very dangerous off the rush, where he displayed excellent hockey-sense and offensive-instincts. This ranges from subtle details of his game such as spacing himself properly to receive a pass, to more difficult and refined abilities such as anticipating defensive movements while going at full speeds and making a blind pass that lands directly on the tape of his teammates while under pressure. He's very difficult for opposing teams to read and can execute unpredictable plays at a consistent level. Furthermore, he's difficult to handle on the powerplay due to the puck coming off his stick in a hurry and having a laser of a slapshot. Away from the puck, he uses his speed and anticipation to hunt the puck along the boards and is a strong kid who can deliver puck separating hits, though his defensive game still has room for improvement. There's very few forwards who have a more dynamic skill-set heading into next years draft than Cajkovic.

CAMPBELL, ISIAH
LW- Cape Breton Screaming Eagles (QMJHL) - 6'03" 206

Campbell was traded mid-way into his rookie season in the QMJHL (from Saint John to Cape Breton) and played much better after the trade, amassing 17 of his 24 points with the Screaming Eagles (in 28 games).

Campbell is a forward with great size who is still raw in terms of his development. Over the years, he has slowly learned how to utilize his size more and more. He is not an overly physical player, but asserts himself into more and more space on the ice. His skating has improved as well, though there is still work to do with his agility and footwork. He has decent hands; he can finish plays at the net as well. He'll score most of his goals near the net, where he is tough to move from. This is where he can utilize his size well. He has a good shot, but in order for it to be more effective, he'll need to accelerate his release and his shot on net faster. He has good anticipation and a good stick on the PK, and can be a valuable player shorthanded if used in those situations.

If Campbell continues to play like he did in the 2nd half of the season with Cape Breton, he could become an important player for them in the next two or three seasons.

CARROLL, JOE
LW - Sault Ste. Marie Greyhounds (OHL) 6'02" 194

Carroll is a big bodied winger who combines a heavy game with a skilled game. Joe played limited minutes over the course of the season with a deep Sault Ste. Marie team, but was able to find ways to be productive and make an impact. Carroll showed complimentary skills as he was able to work the half-boards and corners to win loose pucks and quickly move them to teammates. He also showed some jam to his game, playing physically and becoming agitating at times. He has an intriguing frame that he was able to utilize to protect pucks and make an impact in transition and off the cycle. Carroll lacks high end skating abilities as he stride his somewhat clunky and awkward, limiting his overall speed, however there is power behind it and he can be difficult to handle when he generates momentum, showing a willingness to be assertive with his size. Joe is good on the forecheck and will play physically, however he shows intriguing skilled elements as well. He has quick hands in tight areas and can finish effectively. He may translate to a complimentary top six winger if his skating can elevate.

CAULFIELD, JUDD
LW/RW - USA NTDP-17 (USHL) - 6'02" 198

Caulfield is a power-forward with a heavy frame who likes to drive possession in the offensive end. He's capable of penetrating through defense using his above-average hands and excellent edges, which make him remarkably elusive despite his build, resulting in teams having difficulty containing him. This allows him to drain the opposition, causing them to play heavy minutes below the goal-line. There is an element of finesse to his game; he can drive through the slot and create havoc for opposing teams both along the boards and in front of the net, which he did successfully during tournament play. Although he was a capable shooter with an above-average release from the point, he preferred his passing options and was successful at finding openings in heavy traffic while displaying quick and accurate passes. He has some value on the PK unit; he looks to have good smarts, work ethic and anticipation. There's still some debate in regards to how much upside he has offensively, but he brings a solid package of skills and size to the table and will a player to keep an eye on next season.

CAUFIELD, COLE
RW - US National U-17 team (USNTDP) - 5'06" 154

Caufield was a scoring machine for Team USA this year, scoring 54 goals in 59 games while playing with the U-17 and U-18 teams over the course of the season.

He can really shoot the puck for a 5'06" forward; his shot has great velocity and an excellent release. He's agile and quick on his skates. He keeps his feet moving all the time in the offensive zone, and he's extremely strong on his skates for a player of his size. He can make plays down low or near the net because of his lower-body strength; he can fight off checks, which is usually not the case with players of his size. He's quick to apply pressure on the forecheck, and his puck pursuit is excellent. He can create turnovers with a great forecheck and force defensemen to make errant passes and turn the puck over. He's also a threat on the PK, as he's a hard worker and relentless on the puck. He has great anticipation and seems to know where the puck will go before anyone else. He's a very smart hockey player, and there is lots of talk about his goal-scoring prowess, but he distributes the puck well and has great vision, too.

There's literally no question Caufield will make a fantastic NCAA player down the road. He's committed to play college hockey at the University of Wisconsin. His NHL future will always be in question because of his size, but there are more and more smaller players in the NHL having success, and Caufield has the skills and drive to be one of them.

CAVALLIN, LUKE
G - Flint Firebirds (OHL) 6'00" 179

Luke Cavallin was thrown into 1B-role as a 16-year-old in his OHL rookie season due to the lack of depth that Flint had at the position. Despite his age he had some impressive performances with one of the weakest teams in the OHL in-front of him. He finished the season with a 4.20 GAA and .872 save percentage in 31 regular season games. Internationally, he was featured at the U17's, where he put up a .302 GAA and a .904 save percentage in 5 games.

Cavallin is an undersized goalie who flashes an above-average glove hand and can transition from his butterfly to standing position at a good speed. Due to his size, he focuses on anticipating the play properly which he's decent enough at doing, however he relies too heavily on his V-H technique which isn't refined at this time. That being said, his reverse V-H is better and he uses it in combination with above-average lateral mobility to take away the bottom of the net during cross-crease pass attempts. Another plus element to his game are his reflexes, they're not high-end but they are good enough to stop some difficult scoring chances directly in-front of him. One area of note, is that his reflexes in his upper-half seem quicker than the lower on most shot attempts. He's got a degree of aggressiveness in his style, and he's not afraid to cut down on his angles when the play calls for it. He needs to refine how he squares up on shots that are labelled for his low-glove side and learn when to use his V-H appropriately so that he doesn't put himself in compromising positions as often as he currently does.

CONSTANTINOU, BILLY
RD - Niagara IceDogs (OHL) 5'11" 173

Constantinou is average in size yet possesses strong mobility and agility on his skates with ability to handle the puck well. He plays an up-tempo style who likes to quickly lead the transition on offense by rushing the puck or following up on the play as the 4th forward. He also is active on the offensive blue line by finding shooting lanes as through using his mobile feet to walk around defenders. Constantinou will need to improve upon his defensive positioning and gap control as at times plays a bit undisciplined in his own zone and rover-like mentality. As soon as he learns to play more controlled he will be more effective for his team. Playing more physical sided game will be his advantage as well. Like fellow rookie teammate Tomasino he should earn more ice time next season and being used in various situations. A right-handed, offensive defenseman with energy, skating ability, and upside. Will be interesting to chart his progress on the blue line net season.

COSTMAR, ARVID
RC - Linkoping HC J20 (SuperElit) - 5'11" 181

Costmar is similar to fellow Swedish prospect Bjerselius, as an average-sized centre with good smarts who really takes pride in playing a solid game in his own zone. We like his involvement in the defensive zone. He can show good support for his defensemen to help them retrieve pucks deep in his own zone. He also works hard in the offensive zone, doing some good work along the boards and being tenacious on the forecheck. For a smaller player, he'll need to add some quickness. He's not slow, but he lacks explosiveness in his stride. In the offensive zone, he has good vision and can make some good passes, however, he lacks velocity on his shot. He projects more like a smart role player than an offensive player at this point.

COZENS, DYLAN
RW - Lethbridge Hurricanes (WHL) 6'03" 176

Dylan Cozens had a terrific first season in the WHL, winning the 2017-18 WHL Rookie of the Year. Cozens finished the 2017-18 season with 53 points in 57 games and added another 13 points in 16 playoff games. The winger was late in the first round of the 2016 WHL Bantam Draft at 19th overall, but has proved he is a legitimate prospect for the 2019 NHL Draft.

Cozens consistently improved as his first season in the WHL wore on. He was effective because he played a simple game on the wing where he played north-south and drove the net hard. He quickly gained confidence offensively, and began to find his scoring touch. With his size and decent feet and long stride, he is dangerous when driving the net. He has an excellent and accurate release, showing the ability to score in a variety of situations including in stride and with a one-timer. Many of his goals were impressive, picking tight corners under pressure. It is yet to be seen how complete of an offensive player Cozens can be. He was a beneficiary of an excellent powerplay unit and first line where he was a compliment player. Dylan likes to make simple plays and finish off his chances, allowing his teammates to create space for him, but with more confidence and responsibility, his playmaking skills and smarts should flourish.

As well, Cozens has a huge frame that will fill out. Given his strong skating fundamentals and quick feet, he is going to be tough to handle in the offensive zone when he gains some strengths. He already excels on the defensive walls given his ability to protect pucks and strong will to win battles. Overall, Cozens has the shot and physical tools to be an impact offensive player and his rookie season has made him a top prospect for the 2019 NHL Draft.

DACH, KIRBY
RC - Saskatoon Blades (WHL) 6'03" 185

Kirby Dach is a former 2nd overall pick in the 2016 WHL Bantam Draft, selected by the Saskatoon Blades. The big centre appeared in 19 WHL games as a 15 year old before becoming a mainstay in their top-6 in 2017-18, recording 46 points in 52 regular season games. He also represented Canada Black at the World U17s, recording 7 points in 5 tournament games.

Dach's physical tools are outstanding. He has outstanding size, reach and is an athletic player. He has an explosive first few steps and eats up defenders because of his deceptive edges. With the puck, he is extremely difficult to defend, showing creativity and utilization of his size and reach with the puck. His size, skill and ability to handle the puck with speed is dangerous on the rush. Dach can will himself to rush the puck from end to end, and can get to the net when he wants. If he learns to consistently drive the net show, he will be a force below the dots.

Kirby has great hockey sense and is easy to play with. He defers to his linemates, which is illustrated in his skewed goal to assist ratio. Dach has the release and ability to score goals, but can get caught trying to make the perfect play or passing up shooting lanes to try to find a better opportunity for a teammate. Without the puck, Dach can be a pain on the forecheck, as he has great takeaway instincts and can strip pucks when he keeps his feet moving. The key for Dach will be showing a consistent competitive drive to be a top offensive player. If he wills himself to retrieve pucks, he should have no issue being a top scorer and prospect in 2019.

D'AMICO, DANIEL
LC - Windsor Spitfires (OHL) 5'09" 178

D'Amico is an energetic, undersized forward with a competitiveness to his game. Daniel developed well throughout the season and grew noticeably more confident, becoming more assertive physically and with his skilled traits. He is a competitive forward who can be effective as both a centre and a winger. While Daniel acted more as a complimentary winger in his rookie season, he does possess an intriguing skill package of speed, goal scoring ability and passing skills. D'Amico shows a quick first step allowing him to separate from traffic and generates a good top speed. He is able to utilize his speed when attacking in possession and also to quickly put pressure on opponents on the forecheck. Daniel often finished his checks on the forecheck, creating turnovers while becoming agitating and tough to play against. He was strong up and down the wings and did a good job winning his puck and/or position battles. D'Amico plays aggressively and works the dirty areas well. He shows know hesitation taking pucks to traffic in transition, attacking the goal with purpose. However he shows the awareness and skill to utilize an opponent as a screen or to hit a trailing or attacking teammate.

DAWS, NICOLAS
G - Guelph Storm (OHL) 6'5" 223

Despite being a late pick by the Guelph storm in the 2016 OHL Priority Selection, Daws managed to solidify a backup position for Guelph in his rookie year, where he faired decently.

Daws is an enormous yet coordinated butterfly goalie, who's still raw in certain areas. He takes up a tremendous amount of the net yet manages to make himself look smaller in his butterfly on some shot attempts. Furthermore, his rebound control was inconsistent and he lacked flexibility when attempting secondary saves. Though, his ability to transition from a standing position into his butterfly and visa versa is very good for his age and size, which allows him to cover the bottom of the net rapidly. His glove-hand is above-average and we have seen him flash his glove on difficult shots that are labelled for the top-corner of the net. Although he's an aggressive netminder at times, he's still learning how to adjust his angles when under heavy pressure from the quicker skaters in the OHL. Lastly, he can track pucks at a decent rate, yet has trouble identifying some of the more skilled players intentions at times, which has left him susceptible in certain situations. Daws is massive and fluid, which in itself is a decent developmental base for him to work with, when heading into his draft year.

DENIS, GABRIEL
C/LW - Shawinigan Cataractes (QMJHL) - 6'02" 184

Denis played his first full season in the QMJHL this season after playing the past two seasons in midget AAA with the Collège Notre Dame in Rivière Du-Loup. Shawinigan was one of the worst team in the league this year but Denis was still able to establish himself as one of the better player this year scoring 11 goals and 32 points but it was mostly his play away from the puck and maturity that was impressive this year.

Denis plays a mature two-way game on the ice; he can play in all situations and earned his coaches trusts quickly in with the Cataractes this season. Denis is the kind of player that can play in all situations; he's good on the PK because of his smarts and work ethic. He anticipated the play well and he's willing to sacrifice his body to block shots as well. He's not a high end offensive player but does a lot of small details that makes him a useful player offensively. He's good on the forecheck and does a lot of dirty work in the corner and in front of the net. Skating is above average and has good size. He also can play a physical game along the boards and on the forecheck.

Denis will continue to be one of Shawinigan top two-way players next season and with a better supporting cast he should continue to improve his offensive numbers as his NHL draft value for the 2019 NHL draft will be determined on how much offense can he bring to the next level as he already has a pretty complete game.

DESROCHES, OLIVIER
RD - Shawinigan Cataractes (QMJHL) - 6'01" 185

Desroches was drafted by Acadie-Bathurst in the 2nd round of the 2017 QMJHL draft last June but was acquired by the Cataractes during the QMJHL trade deadline. The young defender saw his ice time and responsibility increase once he joined the Cataractes for the 2nd half of the season.

Desroches has good size and good skating ability which makes him an attractive defenseman for the next level. He's capable of rushing the puck out of his zone and to escape pressure from the opposing team forecheck. Decision making with the puck will need to continue to improves, he made some strides this year when you compared to his midget days with Laval-Montréal. The key for him will be to keep his game simple with the puck, make the quick outlet instead of trying too much with the puck and causing turnovers. In the offensive zone, same thing as he's more effective when he keep things simple rather than trying to be what he's not. He has a good point shot but lacks that high end vision and creativity to become quarterback on the power play at the next level. Desroches has good size and can play a physical game if needed, still not consistent from game to game with his physical implication. Defensively he needs to make better reads in the defensive zone and would like to see him being better defending one on one.

Desroches with one year under his belt should see more ice time next season and we should see some improvement in his game and become a more impact player for the Cataractes at both end of the ice. It's an important year for him in his development as we're waiting for his big breakthrough year which we have been waiting since his midget days to take the next step in his development.

DION, BENJAMIN
LW - Val D'Or Foreurs (QMJHL) - 6'01" 180

Dion was drafted in the 5th round by Val D'Or last June and surprised a lot of peoples by making the team out of training camp. He played 59 games this season with the Foreurs registering 6 points, playing on a weak team and getting limited ice time. Going back to midget AAA in the first half of the year wouldn't had been a bad idea to continue to work on his offensive game and continue to gain confidence with the puck on his stick.

Dion is a high energetic forward who loves to play a gritty physical game. He has the size and speed to play that agitator role and also he likes to talk a lot on the ice. During his midget draft year he made some nice progress with his offensive game and had an amazing tournament just before the QMJHL draft. He had long stretch this season where he didn't get any goals or points and that did hurt his confidence. He has a good heavy wrist shot, not many opportunities to use it this year in the role he played. Really easy to like his competitiveness and physical game but skill wise was probably not ready to play major junior this season. He was rushed to play major junior this year and should be interesting to see where he's at with his development next season as the Foreurs should be a better team next season.

DONOVAN, RYDER
RC - Duluth East Greyhounds (MNHS) 6'04" 185

Ryder turned down an Invite to join the USNTDP U18 team this past season to return to Duluth East High School where he lead his team all the way to the Minnesota class AA State Title game, where his team fell to an equally talented Minnetonka team. Donovan started his 17-18 season at the Hlinka tournament where he was one of the better players on an underperforming USA squad. Ryder is a late 00' born who has seen a considerable growth spirt since being drafted in the 8th Round by Dubuque in the 2016 phase 1 USHL draft. Donovan has a bit of an awkward skating stride but is able to get around the ice well enough and as he adds some physical strength and adapts to his big frame his skating stride should smooth out and improve. Donovan possesses average goal scoring ability and likes to play more of a playmaking and setup game with the puck on his tape. His technique, ability to protect the puck and display poise with the puck saw significant improvement as the season progressed and showed with his increase in production from the previous year. Donovan shows a mature approach to his two way game and has good defensive instincts in his own end. So much of Ryder's pro upside is contingent on his skating continuing to develop but his hockey sense and playmaking ability will make him a prospect to track for the 2019 NHL Draft. Donovan has stated he plans to return to Duluth East for his senior season but most expect him to start and finish the season with Dubuque as well. Donovan is committed to University of North Dakota for the 19/20 season.

DOROFEYEV, PAVEL
LW/RW - Stalnye Lisy Magnitogorsk (MHL) 6'00" 163

Pavel Dorofeyev had an excellent rookie season for Stalnye by producing 39 points in 48 games, including 20 goals. He scored 3 points in 5 playoff games before finishing his year by producing 4 points in 5 games at the U18's while looking dangerous against older and stronger competition.

Dorofeyev is a legitimate threat every time he's given open-ice in the slot. He has a dangerous shot with a great release and an advanced understanding of how to beat goalies before they set or wait them out if they go down too early. He's shown advanced shooting feints and a great backhander which help compliment a well rounded and versatile offensive-attack. Furthermore, his plus puck-skills and combination of straight-line speed and edges made him dangerous in one-on-one situations or when he was attempting to attack the net. He's not just a shooter, showing a good cycle-game in some of our viewings, though his shot is his most dangerous skill. His play away from the puck wasn't as impressive as his play with the puck, though that can be developed. Overall, Pavel's an instinctive sniper who had an impressive year and should be one to watch for next season.

ELLIS, COLTEN
Goaltender- Rimouski Oceanic (QMJHL) - 6'01" 190

Ellis has had quite the back to back season after leading his midget AAA team (Cape Breton West Islanders) to the Telus cup championship last year and this season he was stellar with Rimouski with his 33 wins and winning the QMJHL defensive rookie of the year award.

Ellis was acquired by Rimouski at the QMJHL draft last June for a 1st round pick as Cape Breton who originally drafted him in the 4th round of the 2016 QMJHL draft had already two young goaltenders on their roster. His transition to major junior was really smooth this year and won over the starting job pretty quickly in Rimouski. Ellis has okay size standing just over 6'01" but what stands out for him is his poise and calm in his crease. He's very composed and even when allowing a bad goal it doesn't affect him. He moves smoothly in his crease, has good footwork and his movements are very smooth. With his athletic ability, that helps him make tough saves look very easy for him. We like Ellis mental game and his athletic ability; he has average size if we look at today's NHL goaltenders though.

It was a great first year for Ellis this season, next year more pressure will be on him to prove that he's that good once again but this time in his draft year. Rimouski should be amongst the top team in the league again next season with him and Lafrenière leading the way.

"You could argue that he had the best season of any 2000-born goalie in the QMJHL this year. He's a very impressive goaltender, and along with Alexis Lafrenière, the Océanic will be a team to watch very closely in the next two seasons." - HP Scout Jérôme Bérubé

FOOTE, NOLAN
LW - Kelowna Rockets (WHL) 6'03" 187

Nolan Foote is a big power forward who finished his second season with the Kelowna Rockets, recording 40 points in 50 regular season games. He is a late 2000' birthday and his production stayed fairly consistent in comparison to his impressive 16-year-old season. Foote is the younger brother of Tampa Bay prospect Cal Foote, and son of long time NHLer Adam Foote.

Foote has a huge frame and utilizes his size to protect pucks and maintain possession of pucks along the wall in the offensive zone. He is a confident offensive player and has some strong puck skills for a player with his size. Foote has shown some offensive upside, but has not yet shown that these skills can translate for him to become an offensive player at the next level. Given his plateau production and overall offensive game, it may be likely that he will have to play a bottom six role in order to play in the NHL. The issue with Foote's game is his awkward skating ability. Given his size, he manages to get up and down the ice and be a presence off the rush, but he is no explosive or dynamic. This limits his ability to generate offensive chances and space for his teammates. As well, although he has a big frame, Foote does not play overly physical. He likes to drive the net and get to the dirty and busy areas of the ice but he does not utilize his size to the best of his ability, especially if he is to play at the next level in a bottom six role.

GAUTHIER, TAYLOR
G - Prince George Cougars (WHL) 6'01" 190

Taylor Gauthier is a talented goaltender who was drafted 10th overall in the 2016 WHL Bantam Draft by the Prince George Cougars. Taylor started the bulk of the games for the Cougars in the last half of the 2017-18 season as the Cougars shipped out their top players in a rebuilding season. His numbers suffered on a bad team, recording a 3.96 GAA and .885 SV%. He also represented Canada White at the World U17s, starting 5 games and recording a .915 SV%.

Gauthier is a confident goaltender, this is seen in his general poise and calmness when playing net. He stands tall and makes himself look big when both standing up and in the butterfly position. Although listed at just over six feet, he does look big in his net and does not have to overcommit to take up lots of net. His technical movements are strong and efficient and he shows off athletic ability and quickness in his net. He is able to handle traffic well, as he does fights to see pucks and anticipates plays well. Gauthier began making a difference in games later in the season, winning a few games for the team on occasion. He is a talented goaltender who has not yet been exposed to a full workload in the WHL, which is why 2018-19 will be a major test for the talented goalie.

GUÉNETTE, MAXENCE
RD - Val D'Or Foreurs (QMJHL) - 6'00" 171

Guénette was the Foreurs 1st pick in the 2017 QMJHL draft (5th overall) and saw some good ice time in his first year in the league as the Foreurs were one of the worst team in the league. Right from the start of the season he played regularly in the Foreurs top 4 on defense and played on both power play and penalty killing unit.

Guénette is a smart two way defensemen, he makes smart decisions with the puck and he's good on the transition with either his passing or skating ability. He didn't put a lot of points on the board this year playing on a bad team but next year he should be more productive offensively. He skates well to rushed puck out of his zone or away from the pressure but he's also has good mobility from side to side which helps him cover a lot of spaces on the ice. On the power play he's effective because of the quality of his passing game and vision. Defensively he can play against top players because of his smarts and good active stick.

Guénette remains underrated because he played in Val D'Or and the Foreurs were not a favourite team to watch amongst scouts this year because of their poor result and the lack of prospects. But with Guenette and others rookies the Foreurs are on their way up and should be more popular next season and should have better result. Guenette should be amongst the top draft eligible for the QMJHL draft next season and could be a candidate for team Canada at the Ivan Hlinka tournament in August.

"Val-d'Or was terrible to watch this year and I didn't see them many times, but Guenette is a kid who I liked a lot in midget and who has the talent to make some big noise next year." - HP Scout Jérôme Bérubé

GREWE, ALBIN
C/RW - Djurgardens IF J20 (SuperElit) - 6'00" 176

Grewe is a high-energy forward from Sweden who made his mark at the U-17s in November with his relentless physical play. He was a nightmare for opposing defense on the forecheck; he threw many big hits, has a good puck pursuit game and has a killer instinct when he finishes his hits. He didn't get much help at that tournament offensively, but he showed good shooting abilities and no quit in his game. He's a good skater, has good acceleration and uses it well on the forecheck and backcheck. He's a shoot-first type of player who likes to shoot on net from any angle on the ice. He's tough to handle when he decides to take the puck to the net, with his speed and strength combination, he's tough for defensemen to counter. We would like to see him make smarter plays with the puck. There is not a lot of creativity or playmaking when it comes to him. He goes 100% all the time, but could benefit by slowing down the play and using his teammates more on the ice. He has great physical gifts, and has had some good success this season playing for his national team at both the U-17 and U-18 level. He also enjoyed some success in the J20, with 27 points in 36 games. Lots to like here, but in order to continue progressing at a higher level, he'll need to play a simpler and smarter game.

GUSKOV, MATVEI
LC/LW - Krasnaya Armiya Moskva (MHL) - 6'01" 161

Guskov was a surprise add to Russia's Hlinka team in August, and made a good impression at this tournament as one of the youngest players there, scoring 2 goals in 5 games. He's a tall and lanky kid who can play on both wings and at centre as well. He has some interesting tools: he's a good skater and he's quite shifty on the ice, which helps him avoid hits along the boards. His top speed is good, with a nice, quick burst of speed that he uses when he need to beat a defenseman wide. At Hlinka, he was playing on the 3rd line and was working hard in all three zones. Fast-forward to November at the U-17s where he left us wanting more in terms of his work ethic and overall game. We like his potential; he can score (as he proved at the U-17s with 4 goals in 5 games) and he possesses a quick wrist shot. He likes to rush the puck into the offensive zone, although we would like to see him use his linemates more (mostly when he plays at centre). He can get caught trying too much with the puck sometimes, and this can result in turnovers going the other way. He lacks strength right now, but he's quite tall, and doesn't mind the physical game. He will get involved along the boards, but won't always win his one-on-one battles against bigger and physically stronger players. Overall, we would like to see Guskov improve some parts of his game, such as his consistency. We would also like to see him share the puck more, but his skill level is high-end and we're looking to see how him perform and progress next season.

GUTIK, DANIIL
RW - Loko-Yunior Yaroslavl (NMHL) - 6'03" 179

Gutik is one of the top prospects out of Russia for the 2019 NHL Entry Draft, and was a strong performer for Russia with the U-17 teams during the season. He was highly impressive in November at the U-17 Hockey Challenge in British Columbia.

He's got a good frame despite not having enough weight on him yet, and he used it to his advantage by protecting the puck against his opposition. His puck skills are a plus, and he showed throughout the year that he was capable of cutting through lanes and opening up

space for both himself and his teammates. His vision is one of his better attributes, and he can consistently find his teammates both at even-strength and on the power play. His offensive instincts are noticeable; he finds soft spots around the net and is able to recognize when his passing lanes are closed off and when they are open. He has an above-average wrist shot; he has a quick release to it. The quality he needs to improve upon the most is his skating; his stride lacks power and because of this, his acceleration is only average. Once he gets stronger we feel his speed will improve. He's still a bit raw as a prospect but we like his long-term potential.

GUZDA, MACK
G - Owen Sound Attack (OHL) 6'04" 202

Guzda is a big bodied goaltender with intriguing athletic abilities. Mack possesses an ideal frame for a pro goaltender and displays the athletic ability to match the physical traits. He shows confidence and poise in the crease for a young goaltender and combines his athletic ability with a good technical base. Mack shows a hybrid style of goaltending and utilizes his frame well to block pucks. He consistently challenges shooters and is able to play his angles well. Guzda does a good job with his foot-work to put himself in strong initial shot positioning which often allows him to field pucks cleanly. He uses his size to see around screens and can react and track pucks efficiently. Guzda moves well from post-to-post keeping his movements smooth and economical. Where Mack struggles is with his inconsistent rebound control. When unable to field pucks clean he can get in trouble and begin to swim in the goal. He tends to rely to much on his frame at times and becomes a puck blocker, not a stopper. Losing pucks in his feet was also an issue at times as he continues to grow into and learn how to utilize his frame.

HALE, JAKE
RF - Chicago Steel (USHL) 5'09" 168

Hale managed to make a deep and older Dubuque team out of camp but saw limited ice time in 33 games for the Fighting Saints. Hale has since been traded to Chicago in a post draft deal that sent multiple pieces to Chicago. Hale looked to struggle making the adjustment from a weaker Minnesota High School conference to a much older and faster opponent in the USHL but Jake's game is not without offensive skills. Hale is a dynamic skater in all areas, he is able to cover a lot of ice and be effective on the fore-check and his speed and agility with the puck can draw penalties. Hale has an above average release and an accurate shot and shows the willingness to go to the hard areas and compete despite not having a lot of size at this stage. Jake should come into the USHL much stronger and have more of an opportunity to showcase his skill with Chicago next season. Hale will likely spend the next couple of seasons in the USHL before heading the University of Minnesota-Duluth.

HARLEY, THOMAS
LD - Mississauga Steelheads (OHL) - 6'02" 170

Harley is an intelligent defender with developing two-way skills. Thomas shows impressive poise and plays a very composed and mature game. In possession he isn't easily rattled by an aggressive forecheck and shows the smarts to make a safe play or effective first pass under pressure. Harley recognizes pressure early for the most part and can use his feet to elude pressure. While Thomas shows good mobility, he does have room to improve his lateral quickness and continue to elevate his edge work to make quicker in tight areas. He shows a confidence with the puck and while his trademark is to make a clean outlet pass, Harley will utilize his long skating stride to carry the play up ice. Thomas isn't a threat in transition as he often gains the offensive zone and puts the puck deep; however he shows intriguing vision from the blue line in offensively. A player who has a good point shot, Harley isn't overly assertive with it, often looking pass first. He has the vision and passing skills to quarter back a power play next season. Defensively Harley showed more upside as an OHL rookie, using his mobility in combination with strong body and stick position to defend transition attacks. He kept good gaps and would deny easy entry to the offensive zone, taking away time and space appropriately. In the defensive zone he would benefit from being more assertive physically and showing more overall aggression along the boards and in the net front area. However, his body positioning, reach and smarts do allow him to defend with effectiveness.

HEINOLA, VILLE
LD - Assat U20 (Jr. A SM-liiga) - 5'11" 174

Heinola is a mobile defenseman from Finland who played on both his national U-17 and U-18 team throughout the season. In his home country, he split the season between the U18 and U20 league with Assat. With the U20 team, he amassed 17 points in 33 games.

He's a two-way defenseman with good four-way mobility, which allows him to put pressure quickly on the puck-carrier and close gaps quickly as well. With the puck on his stick, we like his calm and how he never seems to panic under pressure. He handles the forecheck well, and with his skating abilities, he can get away from the pressure in his own zone with just one or two strides. His skating is fluid; his top speed is not great but good enough at this point in his development. His poise with the puck is one of his best assets. He demonstrates good patience and can out wait opponents trying to block his shots. He's good at finding shooting lanes and putting pucks on net. He's a pretty smart defenseman, and a good puck-mover as well. He's not the biggest defenseman, but has the hockey IQ, and was one of the most impressive defensemen from Finland that we saw for the 2019 NHL Entry Draft.

HOGLANDER, NILS
LW - AIK (Allsvenskan) - 5'09" 183

Hoglander is a late birthday (born in December 2000) and this split the past season between the Allsvenskan men's league (where he amassed 7 points in 34 games) and the J20 league (where he had a point a game with 22 points in 22 games). He also played for Sweden at the U-18 level at various tournaments this season, including the recent U-18 World Championships in April.

Hoglander is a small, skilled winger with above-average skill level. In international play, he has battled with inconsistency issues and in many viewings we had, he was not too noticeable on the ice. He's a good skater with a good burst of speed that he likes to use to challenge defensemen wide to go around them. He's a good playmaker with a good vision; he likes to control the puck from the half-wall position on the power play. He has shown good finish playing in the J20 league this season, with 14 goals in 22 games. He possesses a quick shot, good puck poise and a quick release. He lacks size right now, but he can be tough to contain with his speed and is also quite shifty on the ice. He makes quick turns to avoid hits, and can be tough to pin down along the wall. He plays bigger than his size, and is not afraid to mix it up in front of the net. There's potential with Hoglander, but his consistency issues are a big flag right now. When he's on, he can be a valuable player, but too often this year we saw him not be a factor out there.

Next season, for his draft year, he should be a regular and full-time player in the Allsvenskan. Points are tough to come by in this league for young players, but we should see an improvement from this year.

HOLMSTROM, SIMON
LW/RW - HV71 J20 (SuperElit) - 5'11" 172

Holmstrom is one of the better prospects from Sweden for the 2019 NHL Entry Draft. This season, he recorded over a point per game with HV71 in the J20, and also played in one SHL game. He missed the first U-17 tournament in November, which hurt his exposure a bit, but played well in the 2nd tournament in February as one of the better Swedish players at this event.

Holmstrom is an average-sized winger who can play on both wings, playing much bigger than his listed size. He has a high compete level, and gets involved in the physical game along the boards and in front of the net. He's a good skater with good explosiveness in his stride; he's quick to jump on loose pucks and will often win puck races. He's tenacious on the puck and aggressive on the forecheck. At his best, he makes things happen on the ice with his speed and energy. Offensively, he demonstrates creativity in the offensive zone using his good vision and playmaking abilities. He's a complete player who shows good awareness in the defensive zone and has value as a penalty-killer with his speed, anticipation and work ethic.

Holmstrom should challenge for a roster spot in the SHL next season with HV71, and should be an impact player with Sweden's U-18 team throughout the year.

HONKA, ANTTONI
RD - JYP (Liiga) - 5'10" 170

Honka is the younger brother of Julius Honka, who plays for the Dallas Stars in the NHL. The younger Honka is a similar type of defenseman who lacks ideal size, but has good mobility and offensive upside. He had a nice impact already this season in the top men's league in Finland with 9 points in 20 games, and in the junior league he had 17 in 28 games. He was a regular in international competition for Finland throughout the year, playing in every major U-18 tournament from August to April.

He has good feet and moves well around the ice. Honka likes to rush the puck from his own zone, and his quick feet help him retrieve pucks quickly in his own zone. He moves pucks quickly to activate his team's transition game. He can be dynamic with the puck on his stick, as he has great puck skills and at his best can be a difference-maker on the ice. From our viewings of Honka this season, there were a lot of ups and downs with his play in terms of its consistency. He didn't have a good February U-18 Five Nations' Tournament in Plymouth, but bounced back with a good performance at the April U-18s. In February, he struggled with his adaptation to the smaller ice and didn't have the impact we had anticipated. His decision-making was poor in February, and this is an area of his game that will need to be better. He can be risky with the puck, electing to try low-percentage plays too often, but once he learns to simplify his game he'll be much better and his consistency will improve, too. He does a good job putting pucks on net, he has good puck poise and he can use slap or wrist shots quite efficiently. He has good vision and great creativity to create offense in the offensive zone. Defensively, his size is an obvious concern against bigger players when battling for pucks along the boards and in front of the net. He'll need to defend by playing smartly with his stick and use great defensive positioning.

Honka will be a regular in Liiga next season, and should be an impact player for Finland at the World Junior Hockey Championships.

HUGHES, JACK
LC - USA NTDP-18 (USHL) 5'10" 157

Hughes has had a record breaking year for the USNTDP U17 and U18 squads, putting up the most points out of any USNTDP player in history while having the highest PPG on the U18 team despite being the youngest forward, finishing with 61 points in 31 games. His game is electrifying and features several dynamic qualities that make him standout consistently on a shift-to-shift basis.

He's not the biggest Centre but uses his skating ability so carve through the defensive opposition, his first step has developed as he's continued to gain strength over the year. His edge work, agility and elusiveness are elite, managing to switch his stature from a disadvantage into an advantage and he generates surprising levels of speed that throw defensive-units off due to his fluidity and the ability to change directions suddenly. This alone isn't what separates Hughes from the rest of the 2019 draft class though, it's his processing ability on the ice which allows him to anticipate the play in advance that does. He's constantly analyzing his options and breaking down the next move he's going to be making dynamically, he feels off what his opponent is giving him and needs very little time or space to make the smart and safe play or the skilled play.

Hughes puck skills add another dynamic trait to his game, his hands are lightning quick, he can deke in-tight to his body and he can use them while going at top speeds. He also tends to use his move-set to not only beat players one-on-one but to also feel out the opposition and stall while looking for an additional play. His vision is also elite, he's capable of making blind passes that his opponents fail to pick up on and routinely finds players behind defensive coverage. He's an accurate passer and he can make difficult passes look easy while on the ice. His shot is arguably the weakest aspect of his offensive-arsenal, however when dealing with an elite talent it's relative in the sense that it's still well above average, his release is quick and he has an accurate shot, we have seen him score some highlight worthy goals while off balance due to his pinpoint accuracy.

Jack plays a fearless game, he's not a perimeter player in any sense of the word, opting instead to attack the net near the goal-line regardless of the size of the defenseman in-front of him and he's willing to take a hit to make a play or finish off a rebound. If there's any slight to his game at this point in time, it should come as no surprise given his size that he has some trouble defending against larger players off the rush and although he competes hard along the boards, we have seen him get knocked off the puck throughout the year. That being said, he's usually defensively aware and recognizes what his opponents are attempting to do with the puck consistently.

Hughes is a special talent that dictates play when he steps onto the ice and has tremendous potential as a franchise altering center at the NHL level. He's looking like the top pick in the 2019 draft and he's done his best to separate himself from the competition with his performance this year.

HUGO-HAS, MARTIN
RD - Tappara U20 (Jr. A SM-Liiga) 6'04" 187

Martin Hugo-Has is a Czech defender who put up good numbers in his rookie season in the Finnish junior circuit, producing 16 points in 47 games, including 7 goals. In the playoffs he went pointless in 8 games. He was featured Internationally at both the U17's and U18's.

Hugo-Has is a two-way defender who has good overall mobility for his size and age, though his backwards skating and pivoting mechanics need to be further developed. That being said, we have seen him side-step opponents at the offensive-blueline and skate aggressively when pinching while trying to generate scoring chances. His first pass is both accurate and sharp and his puck distribution earned him powerplay time against older players at the U18's. His slapshot showed accuracy, though his wind-up has a lot of extended movement which allowed goalies to get set. Additionally, this allows him to generate some power. He's not afraid to use his frame to press players into the boards and he has excellent reach which allows him to disrupt plays away from the puck. There's a lot of upside in Has's game, he will be an interesting defenseman to track given his tools and his aggressive style of play that he showed us in our viewings.

INNIS, CHRISTOPHER
RD - Rimouski Oceanic (QMJHL) - 5'11" 174

Innis was the 10th overall selection in the 2017 QMJHL draft after playing a year under Guillaume Latendresse with the College Charles-Lemoyne in the Quebec Midget AAA league. In his QMJHL draft year he made some very nice progress through the season and was a big riser going into the QMJHL draft.

Innis is not super tall but physically he's very strong with a strong lower body. He has good footwork and ability to use his feet to carry puck out of his zone and escape forechecker. His good skating ability also helps to retrieve pucks in his defensive zone. He's tough to beat one on one; he's aggressive on the puck carrier and quickly challenging players one on one. Over the last two years he has learned how to play a simpler and smarter game. He can play on the power play, he has a good hard low slapshot and his vision is good. This year in Rimouski is confidence grew as the season went on and by season's end he was playing some tough matchups against some good players from opposing team.

Next season, Innis will continue to establish himself and as a strong two-way defensemen through the QMJHL and will also see his ice time on the power play increase.

JONCAS, ALEXANDRE
RD - Sherbrooke Phoenix (QMJHL) - 5'10" 182

Joncas had a surprising good first year in the QMJHL playing a surprising important role for the Phoenix in all of the team game and amassed 15 points in the process. Sherbrooke drafted Joncas out of the Collège Esther-Blondin program in the 4th round (57th overall) of the 2017 QMJHL draft.

Joncas made a quick adjustment to the QMJHL because he doesn't really have any weakness in his game and physically he was more advance than a lot of players. He's not tall but plays a gritty game in his zone with a good competes level. He doesn't have any great or standout qualities though. He does however know how to play within his limit. He's capable of skating with the puck; with more experience next season he should rushed the puck out a bit more. His skating could use some improvement though (improving quickness and explosiveness) and that would make him more effective when rushing the puck. He's a decent puck mover with above average vision on the ice. Next season he should see more ice time on the power play and be a regular in Sherbrooke to four on defense. Physically he was mature and should be interesting to see how much he can improve next season as physically he's close to his peak.

KAKKO, KAAPO
RW - TPS U20 (Jr. A SM-Liiga) 6'04" 207

Kaapo Kakko had a very impressive year for TPS's junior team, producing 55 points in 38 games, including 25 goals. He was loaned back to the U18 team where he produced 9 points in 5 games during the playoffs. Internationally, he played at the U17's for 3 games where went pointless but at the U18's, he tied for the 3rd most points in the tournament, finishing with 10 in 7 games.

Kakko is large power-forward with high end tools and a ton of potential. He's got an excellent combination of size, skating ability, and a well-rounded offensive-arsenal that he used to breakdown opposing teams at will in the majority of our viewings. It's very rare to see a player of his skill-set who competes at the rate he's able to. He keeps an excellent pace which should be highlighted since he can physically dominate down-low and around the net area. Furthermore, he's got tremendous puck-skills which makes him dangerous when cutting through heavy traffic and during one-on-one situations. Furthermore, he got excellent hockey-sense which allows him to make plays at top speeds, it wasn't common to see a play die on his stick. Kaapo can both really wire the puck and change his release point while in motion, and his passing ability when combined with his vision, makes him a multi-faceted threat. When he's assertive and playing his game, he was the most dominant player on the ice even when contrasted with some of the higher-end Finnish forwards featured in the 2018 class. There's no offensive-weaknesses in his game and he's got arguably the best set of tools for the entire 2019 class when taking his size and wingspan into consideration. He's one of the only players who could be a direct threat to Hughes at the top of the draft board.

KALMIKOV, BROOKLYN
LW- Cape Breton Screaming Eagles (QMJHL) - 6'00" 153

Kalmikov had a successful rookie season, scoring 18 times and 36 points overall in the season. He was not picked for the U-17 hockey challenge in the month of November which is a bit surprising. The Screaming Eagles picked the young forward with the 15th overall pick in the 2017 QMJHL draft.

Kalmikov is good skater; he's very agile and quick acceleration. He can beat guys one on one with his speed wide but with good puck skills can use his good dekes to beat opposing defensemen. His hands are really good; he had one of the best pair of hands from the 2017 QMJHL draft class. He didn't get many opportunities in his QMJHL draft year playing on a stacked team with Collège Esther-Blondin with the likes of Samuel Poulin and Xavier Parent on his team. The fact that he made cape-Breton out of training camp was a pleasant surprise and proved them right by having a good rookie season. He can play all three position forwards having played a bit of center this season but with his skill set he projects better on the wing. Physically he lacks strength, there's a long way to go for him to reach his peak physically which gives hope that he's far from having reach his full potential yet. Kalmikov play away from the puck will need to continue to improve next season, right now he's a bit of one dimensional player but with a lot of talents in offensive situations.

Kalmikov should be a candidate for team Canada for the Ivan Hlinka tournament in August even though he was not invited to the U-17 hockey challenge last November. With the Eagles he should be playing on their top line and top power play unit as well next season with the likes of Sokolov and Laferriere who are key players in the Screaming Eagles youth movement.

KALIYEV, ARTHUR
RW - Hamilton Bulldogs (OHL) 6'02" 185

Kaliyev is a big bodied winger with impressive offensive instincts and skill to his game. Arthur possesses intriguing power forward traits to his game as he utilizes his frame very well, allowing him to get into the scoring areas and make an impact. He is good below the hash-marks, showing some aggression to his game, however is often more effective when simply using his size to create space. In possession Arthur shows strong puck control and can weave through traffic, showing confidence while creating shooting lanes. He willingly shoots from various angles and always looks to get pucks on net, enhancing his production. Kaliyev can be one dimensional offensively at times, however that dimension is his pure goal scoring talent. A player who displays an excellent release and shot, he can still be effective despite not being much of a threat to pass or create for a line mate. Kaliyev shows a good compete level in the offensive end and forecheck's instinctively, creating turnovers with his awareness and anticipation. He can be quiet away from the puck and will need to enhance his defensive zone play next season. Arthur is a bit of a deceptive skater, as he doesn't have the prettiest of strides and can be limited in his first few strides. However he does generate decent top speed and use his momentum while attacking the net down the wings.

KEPPEN, ETHAN
LW - Flint Firebirds (OHL) 6'02" 205

Ethan Keppen was drafted 10th overall by Flint in the 2017 OHL Priority Selection. He showed some promise in his first full-season with the Firebirds by producing 18 points in 63 games, including 10 goals. Internationally, he played for Canada White at the U17's, producing 4 points in 6 games.

Keppen is a large winger who knows how to generate chances by using his frame while off the rush and in-tight to the net. He's got a long and powerful stride which covers a lot of distance in a short amount of time, yet he stands up-right when attempting to reach his top-gear in open-ice, so the mechanics aren't overly refined. He uses his frame and power to cut on opponents or set himself around the crease area, where he showed decent hand-eye coordination while looking for deflections. He plays with a good pace on most shifts and also has a fair amount of bite. Like the rest of his game, his shot generates weight and he can fire the puck from far-out and still be dangerous. His size and energy allow him to be effective along the boards, where he comes out with the puck at a consistent rate. Keppen has good tools but needs to continue to develop the ability to execute at a higher rate. He's shown that he can play when there isn't much talent around him so he could be one to watch for the 2019 draft.

KNIGHT, SPENCER
G - USA NTDP-17 (USHL) - 6'03" 194

Knight is a Boston College recruit for 2020-2021, and this past year he split the season with stints with both the US U-17 and U-18 teams, finishing the year with a strong performance at the U-18 World Hockey Championships in Russia.

Knight is a big and athletic goaltender that NHL teams would covet. Not only is he big, but he's confident in his crease and challenges shooters at the top of his crease. By doing that and with his size, he covers a lot of net and doesn't give a lot of shooting room. His post-to-post movements are very good for a player of this size, his athleticism is fantastic and that helps him recover quickly on 2nd and 3rd shots. There still some consistency issues with him, which is normal at this age, but he has proven that he can bounce back strong after a poor performance. He did exactly that at the U-18 World Hockey Championships. After a tough game against Switzerland, he was excellent the rest of the way. There are not many things we don't like about Knight's game; he has the size, athletic ability, mental game and is also pretty good at playing the puck outside of his crease. He is, without a doubt, a favourite to be the top goalie picked in next year's draft.

KNYAZEV, ARTEMI
LD - Irbis Kazan (MHL) - 5'11" 176

Knyazev started the season with a lot of hype, after some great performances last year at the European Youth Olympic Festival. However, he didn't live up to said hype when we saw him playing internationally for Russia's U-17 team. He was still one of their better defensemen, though. He has some good skills, including good quickness and elusiveness to avoid the forecheck and get away from the pressure in his own zone. He can play on the power play; he has good puck skills and can rush the puck with some above-average skating abilities. He's active in the offensive zone, and is not afraid to come deep in the offensive zone to try to create some scoring chances. He's a risky player with the puck; when he rushes it, he can try to beat guys one-on-one which can then lead to turnovers. His passing abilities are above-average; we've seen him try many long passes from his end zone. His passes are crisp and usually on the tape. What he'll need to improve: his consistency and decision-making. He's also not a big defenseman, and that can give him some trouble defending down low and in front of his net. Knyazev may not be as good as what he showed us last year at the European Youth Olympic Festival, but has some good tools to work with.

KOKKONEN, MIKKO
LD - Kettera (Mestis) - 5'11" 190

Kokkonen is a physically-mature defenseman from Finland; he's the youngest player to ever play in the Liiga, as he played one game in 2016-2017 as a 15-year-old. This season, he spent the majority of the season in the Mestis league (the 2nd men's league in Finland) on a loan, and also played 12 games in Liiga. He was an international hockey regular for his country, playing as an underager for the U-18 team in various tournaments. He did the same thing last year because of how physically advanced he is; at 15, he was playing for the national U-17 team.

Kokkonen is a strong kid with good core strength but average height at 5'11", and likely won't grow much more. He's a two-way defenseman. In his zone, he uses his size well along the boards and in front of the net. He's not overly physical, but he is when he needs to be. His awareness in the defensive zone is sound, and he has good gap control and a good active stick that helps him to defend in his own zone. He has a good compete level in his zone and can be tough to beat one-on-one. He has decent puck skills and can make crisp quick pass out of his zone. In the offensive zone, he's a decent puck-distributor, we don't see high-end creativity or vision, but he does a decent job at moving pucks. One area that he will need to improve upon is the time it takes for him to make decisions with the puck. He can be victim to taking too much time and losing possession of the puck, or not making a smart play when under pressure from an opposing player.

Kokkonen is an interesting player because of his physical maturation and the fact that he always played with older players in the past, but there's a definite question with him in regards to how much better he will get in the next couple of years.

KORCZAK, KAEDAN
RD - Kelowna Rockets (WHL) 6'02" 183

Kaedan Korczak is a two-way defenseman who played steady minutes for the Kelowna Rockets in his rookie season. In 2017-18 he recorded 16 points in 67 regular season games and was solid in the playoffs, posting 4 points in 4 games as the Rockets were swept by the Tri-City Americans.

Korczak does not play a flashy offensive game, and he may not be a dominant threat on the powerplay but still is a major contributor at both ends of the ice. He is a dependable, smart puck mover, and has a terrific stick defensively. His skating fundamentals are sound, he has a long, powerful stride and good lateral movement for a lanky player. His puck skills are above average, but what makes him effective is that he does not over complicate the game, keeps his head up and is aware of where his teammates are on the ice. This smart, quick decision making extends to all 3 zones for Korczak. At the offensive point, he gets shots off quickly, often one-timing pucks. Without the puck, Korczak is not dominant physically, but uses his body effectively to separate players from pucks. He is smart and calculated in his own end positionally and with his gap control. Korczak plays the right way at both ends of the rink, and is a top prospect for the 2019 NHL Draft.

KOSTER, MIKE
LD - Chaska Hawks (MNHS) 5'08" 165

Koster split this past season with Tri-City (USHL) and Chaska High School in Minnesota where Koster lead his team in Points as a defenseman with 15 goals and 42 assists in 27 games. Koster also showed the ability to be productive from the back end for Tri-City, registering 2 goals and 9 Assists in 23 games with the Storm. Koster likes to play a rover style from the back end, often acting as a forth forward on the ice that joins or leads the rush out of his own end. Koster is an excellent skater with exceptional footwork and agility, both with and without the puck. Koster's skating allow him to defend effectively against the rush by having good gap control and good stick on puck ability but needs to show better discretion in his own end as he has looked too eager to jump into the offense, often leaving his defensive partner on an island. Koster has impressive offensive tools that will be an asset for any team he plays on going forward. The key for Koster is to not to also be a liability in regards to his decision making in his own end. Koster doesn't have a lot of size but is strong on his skates and plays a crafty, skilled game in battles that allows him to come away with the puck more often than not. Chaska returns much of their roster of a team that should contend for a State Tournament run, so it's easy to imagine Koster wanting to return and captain his High School team to their first ever State Tournament Appearance next season, however its likely he will see time in the USHL, much like he did this year. Koster is committed to the University of Minnesota for the 20/21 season.

KREBS, PEYTON
LW - Kootenay Ice (WHL) 5'11" 172

Peyton Krebs is a skilled winger who completed his first full season in the WHL with the Kootenay Ice. The former 1st overall Bantam pick, recorded 54 points and 17 goals in 67 regular season games with the Ice. He also represented Canada Red at the World U17s, recording 6 points in 5 tournament contests. Krebs played top line minutes for the Ice and was there offensive leader despite being a rookie.

Krebs is a skilled elusive forward, with unique creativity. He doesn't have great strength or size as of yet, but he avoids contact exceptionally well, consistently moving his quick feet, combining them with quick, soft hands. He uses a short stick which allows him to change directions and create space in very tight areas. He is fun to watch and is dynamic in one on one situations. Combined with his individual skill, his offensive game is dominant because of his hockey sense and ability to make his teammates around him better. He thinks the game a step ahead of the opposition and consistently finds teammates for high quality looks.

In addition to his exceptional playmaking skills, he showed a killer instinct in his first junior season. He scored big goals for his team and has the will to make a difference every single night. Peyton is one of the most talented offensive players in his age group, and he is ready to take a major step offensively in his next season. The only question about his game is whether his lack of strength will harm his ability to produce offensively at the next level.

LADD, GRAYSON
RD - Windsor Spitfires (OHL) 6'01" 162

Ladd is a simplistic defender with good mobility and physical traits. Grayson showed added confidence to his game following the trade to Windsor. He is at his best when keeping his game simple and using his mobility to his advantage. Ladd has the foot-work to elude a forecheck and create space to utilize his first pass ability. However, he would benefit from speeding up his decision making process to keep himself out of trouble. Grayson tends to turn pucks over when he overthinks the game, looking to make the complicated decision opposed to simply taking the first and most high percentage decision. He handles he puck well and does possess a maturity to his game as he is poised with the puck. Offensively Ladd will use his feet to open shooting and passing lanes, however acts more as a puck distributor and isn't overly assertive with his shot. He is developing two-way traits and there is potential upside as a two-way defender however a safe beat would be a strong and mobile puck-moving type.

LANG, MARTIN
LW - HC Plzen U18 (Czech U18) - 5'10" 165

Lang was a dominant player in the Czech U-18 league, scoring over a goal per game (37 goals in 35 games) and finishing 2nd overall in the league in that category despite being one of the youngest players. His shot is his best asset; he has a quick release and great velocity to it. He's really good at hiding his intentions, faking going the passing route and instead taking quick shots on net that can surprise opposing goaltenders. With the puck on his stick, he's involved in the play. But when he doesn't have the puck, he doesn't work as hard to get the puck back, and seemingly becomes disinterested. We would like to see him work harder to retrieve pucks and be more involved in his zone.

LAVELLE, SHANE
RW - Chaska Hawks (MNHS) 6'00" 165

Lavelle is a 5th Round pick of Madison (USHL) in the 2017 USHL Phase 1 Draft. Lavelle plays and up tempo game down the wing, using his skating and quick hands to be an effective fore-checker and a player that can create turnovers. Lavelle has a good sized frame that he still needs to grow into but he has an explosive first couple of strides and has developed high end agility to create and find holes in order to get to the net. Lavelle doesn't possess high end puck skills or playmaking ability at this stage but will drive the offense by out working his competition and knowing where to be on the ice for pucks to find him. His shot has developed into more of a scoring threat since his bantam years and looks to be an asset for him going forward. Lavelle is a smart two-way forward that makes a lot of subtle plays that help his team in a nightly basis. With the talent Chaska HS has returning, it's hard to imagine Lavelle playing full time for Madison in the USHL next season, however he is committed to the University of Wisconsin for 19/20 so it's not a stretch to imagine he will see some games in Madison at some point next season.

LAVOIE, RAPHAEL
RW/C - Halifax Mooseheads (QMJHL) - 6'04" 192

After splitting the 2016-2017 season between Halifax and his midget AAA team in Sainte-Hyacinthe, Lavoie established himself as key player for the Mooseheads this year scoring 30 goals including 10 game winners this year. He played both down the middle and on the wing this year and with his skating ability being sup par right now he probably project more as a winger right now.

Very impressive season for Lavoie this year, he made some real progress in his game and became an impact player offensively for the Mooseheads which was not really expected at the beginning of the season. He has great size and a long reach which helps him a ton to protect the puck along the board. Puck-handling ability is very impressive for a player of his size, can make players miss defensively with his hands and likes to attack defenders through the middle, or use his size and reach to drive wide. His offensive totals were impressive this year and one area where he made some good improvement from last year was his confidence with his shot. Now his shot is a weapon and can score from anywhere in the offensive zone, his shot has great velocity but could still work on his accuracy from long range. He has made some progress with his skating since his QMJHL draft year but there's still some work to do there for him. His top speed is fine but his acceleration and explosiveness need some improvement. He has good vision, really has great tools offensively as both in the scorer and playmaker role. When he plays center, he always does a fine job supporting his defense in his zone and coming back deep to help out. He understands his defensive assignments but sometimes lacks focus/hustle on the backcheck, can be caught cheating towards offence at times. He has good hockey IQ and if he continue to improve like he did this past season he could be a high pick in the 2019 NHL draft.

"Big improvement compared to last year. He can score from anywhere in the offensive zone with that big shot." -HP Scout Jérôme Bérubé

"To me he's a winger and not a centre at the NHL level." - HP Scout Jérôme Bérubé

LEGARÉ, NATHAN
RW - Baie-Comeau Drakkar (QMJHL) - 6'00" 197

Legaré is a strong two-way game who had a decent first season in the QMJHL finishing with 29 points in 62 games and also played well at the U-17 Challenge in November. The Drakkar drafted Legaré with the 6th overall pick in last June QMJHL midget draft.

Legaré has good versatility; he can play all three positions forward and has value on both power play and penalty killing unit. He has good size, he likes to play a physical game and he's very tenacious on the ice. He has a good compete level and he's tough to handle along the board and will win a lot of battles there. He uses his size well in the corners to retrieve pucks and not afraid to go the net. He not huge but does play like a power forward. On the PK he does some good work with his hustle and he's not shy to block shots. He's not overly skilled offensively and his offensive output for the next level might be limited as more of a grinding role. His skating ability is one area where he'll need the most work in the off season.

Legaré is part of a young Baie-Comeau team and should be part of the core of their resurgence in the next two or three seasons. This year he played more of depth role on the team but next year he should see more ice time on the top 2 line and on the power play.

LEGUERRIER, JACOB
RD - Sault Ste. Marie Greyhounds (OHL) 6'02" 195

LeGuerrier is a mobile defender with two-way abilities and intriguing size and strength. Jacob utilizes his skating on both sides of the puck, showing a confidence in possession that allows him to carry transition up ice and into the offensive zone. While he is effective carrying the puck, LeGuerrier does see the ice well and can lead transition with a strong outlet pass. Offensively Jacob shows good instincts and vision as he can utilize his feet to open shooting lanes and get pucks on net or distribute the puck effectively. He also shows the creativity to disguise his shot and utilize a hard slap-pass to create deflections. Jacob's skating allows him to contain defensively with effectiveness. However he is at his best when playing a simplistic game. To often he would get in trouble being overly aggressive through the neutral zone looking to step up and create a turnover or through a big hit, losing ideal body position. Improving his routes to puck carriers and simplifying his defensive game would be beneficial. Jacob also needs to show more patience with the puck he can play to aggressively and force passes through dangerous areas and have them picked off. To many high risk plays led to turnovers and hindered him at times.

LEMIEUX, JONATHAN
Goaltender- Val D'Or Foreurs (QMJHL) - 6'00" 174

Lemieux made the Foreurs out of training camp and was backup to Etienne Montpetit in the 1st half of the season before Montpetit was traded during the trade deadline. Lemieux saw more ice time in the 2nd half of the season and it was not pretty at time with the Foreurs having traded a lot of their good players they were outplayed badly on most nights.

He was the third goalie chosen in the 2017 QMJHL draft in the 3rd round with the 42nd overall pick. After being with the Foreurs all year long, he lost the starting job for the playoff to Mathieu Marquis who joined the team from junior AAA after the trade of Montpetit. Confidence wise, it was a tough season for him allowing a lot of goals, the second half of the season was really bad and he finished the season with 3 wins in 22 starts, with a 5,46 goals against average and a 867 save %. Lemieux has average size for the average NHL goaltender right now but could still grow a bit. He's an athletic goaltender with good flexibility; his post to post movements are good. Technically he's solid, he was the best technical goaltender from the 2017 QMJHL draft class. Lemieux is advanced at how he plays the puck outside of his crease and his rebound controls were solid in midget but a different story in junior.

It will be interesting to see him next year, where he's at mentally after a really tough rookie season and how he bounces back. Next season with the Foreurs he should be sharing the work load once again with Mathieu Marquis in net.

LIKHACHYOV, YAROSLAV
LW - Loko-Yunior Yaroslavl (NMHL) - 5'11" 168

Likhachyov is a super-talented winger from Russia. He possesses great puck skills and great one-on-one abilities. He's capable of scoring highlight-reel goals, In February he made some headlines by scoring a lacrosse-type goal from behind the net at the Five Nations' Tournament in Finland. He handles the puck really well in tight spaces, and can stickhandle in a phone booth. He's a right-handed shot, but likes to play on his off-wing, like many Russians tend to do. He has quick and soft hands; he has a quick release on wrist shot. He lacks speed right now, as his top speed is average and lacks the explosiveness that would help him take advantage of certain situations on the ice and create more separation. He sees the ice well, and likes to control the puck on the left side of the ice on the power play; he has showed us excellent playmaking abilities. He's not the biggest player, but has a low center of gravity with the puck on his stick which helps him protect it. Without the puck, he could stand to be more involved, and we would like to see more hard work from him both in his zone and away from the puck.

Likhachyov was Russia's leading scorer this season on their U-17 team, with 14 points in 10 games.

MAIER, NOLAN
G - Saskatoon Blades (WHL) 6'00" 170

Nolan Maier started 43 games for the Saskatoon Blades in his rookie season in the WHL, recording a 3.02 GAA and an impressive .917 SV%. Maier began to win over his coaches as the year wore on, starting crucial games down the stretch for a team that was in the playoff hunt. Maier is an athletic goalie, who is listed at below average height for a goalie, but makes up for this lack of size with his compete level and athleticism. Maier has great lateral movement and is not out of any play. His ability to read the play and quick lateral movements allows him to make tough cross-ice saves. Maier has the ability to take over games, but also has been victim of some tough outings where he was run out of the building, allowing weak goals in succession. Despite his inconsistency, his save percentage was impressive, and he is one of the top 2019 draft eligible goaltenders in the WHL.

MANCINELLI, MICHAEL
RC - Madison Capitols (USHL) 5'09" 166

Mancinelli is out of the Detroit Honeybaked and Compuware youth programs who was drafted in the 2nd Round by Madison in the 2017 USHL Draft. Mancinelli was often Madison's best forward in many of our viewings, he shows his excellent skating speed, agility and motor on most shifts. Michael registered 17 goals and 18 assists for a Madison team that struggled for much of the year. Mancinelli isn't a big player but works hard on every shift and uses his relentless approach and second and third efforts to make up for his lack of size. With the puck on his stick, he can be an offensive threat both in transition as well as in the possession game down low. His agility with the puck make him elusive and allows him to create time and space for himself. Off the rush, Mancinelli has a good skill set that he can execute at a high speed. Michael shows good compete in tracking back to the play and is sound in picking up his assignments on the back check. Mancinelli plays with a good physical edge and doesn't back down from opponents which has shown to get under his opponents skin in a lot of instances. In a game that seems to be transitioning more and more to an up tempo game, Mancinelli's fast skill seems to be taylor made for the transition period the NHL is currently in and he will be a prospect that will be closely tracked for the 2019 NHL Draft. Mancinelli is currently slated to head to the University of North Dakota for the 20/21 season, however if his development continues at its current pace, it's easy to imagine him in Grand Forks in 2019.

MARCOTTY, FELIX-ANTOINE
RW - Chicoutimi Saguenéens (QMJHL) - 5'11" 185

Marcotty had a decent rookie season with 28 points in 59 games with the Saguenéens. He was better in the first half of the season and had more difficulties later in the season. He had a long stretches late in the season with no point.

Consistency and intensity will be parts of his game that will need some improvement next season. He's a smart player with the puck, his on ice-vision is good and his on ice creativity is good as well. He's has good upside offensively, above average skating ability. He doesn't have any elite abilities but he's all around skills set is good. He's a good stickhandler and has the skills to put some good numbers in the QMJHL in the next 2-3 seasons. Next season with some key players leaving Chicoutimi he should see more ice time on the power play and see his production raises because of it.

MARTIN, JEREMY
LW - Shawinigan Cataractes (QMJHL) - 6'00" 175

Martin split the past season with Shawinigan and his midget team but became a regular with the Cataractes by the month of December. In midget he took the next step in his development averaging just under a point per game before getting called up.

Martin is a high motor energy winger who plays a fast pace physical game. He's easy to be noticed on the ice because of his speed and work ethic. He likes to finish his checks and he's quite effective on the forecheck with his speed and hustle. He's solid on his skate, not the biggest player but he's tough to knock down off his skates. With Shawinigan this year, in 34 games he had 7 points in 34 games in a tough situation as the Cataractes were one of the worst teams in the league. His offensive potential is still limited for the next level, he projects more as a grinder than a scorer. He's good on the PK with his speed and anticipation. He also won't be afraid to block shots on the PK as well.

Next season will be his first full year with the Cataractes and should establish himself as part of their top 9 forward, most likely on their 3rd line and being a useful player on their PK unit.

MASTROSIMONE, ROBERT
LC - Chicago Steel (USHL) 5'09" 159

Mastrosimone was a tender selection of the Chicago Steel last April out of Shattuck St. Mary's Prep School and was able to step right in and make an immediate impact for the Steel, registering 18 goals and 31 assists in 67 games. Mastrosimone is a up tempo winger that uses his speed to create a lot of his offensive opportunities. He is able to create separation from his back checkers and execute plays at a high speed coming into the offensive zone. Mastrosimone has high end individual skill and can beat his defender one on one and can make plays with his hands in traffic. Mastrosimone shows a good motor all over the ice but can be caught on the wrong side of the puck in battles and looks to stretch the ice and get behind defenders before his team has possession in his own end which has resulted in him costing his team at times. Mastrosimone doesn't have a lot of size but his skating and ability to make plays at a high speed will make him a pro prospect down the road. Mastrosimone is committed to Boston University and was also a 9th Round draft pick of Mississauga in the 2017 OHL Draft.

MCCARTHY, CASE
RD - USA NTDP-17 (USHL) 6'01" 194

McCarthy is a skilled two-way defenseman who played this past season his first of two seasons with the US Nationals program in Plymouth, Michigan. He's a smart defenseman who plays well at both end of the ice. We love his skating abilities, good puck rusher and also good at retrieving pucks quickly in his own zone. He's poised with the puck and doesn't make a lot of mistakes on the ice. He moves the puck smartly into the transition or distributes it in the offensive zone thanks to his good vision. His passes are crisp and accurate. He has value on the power play because of his good vision but also his big shot from the point. He can pinch at times in the offensive zone and does a nice job supporting the rush. However he'll have to watch to not get caught in the offensive zone, he used in lower level have enough skating abilities to come back defensively but now at this level and other levels coming up like NCAA or pro hockey he'll have to be more careful. He's solid defensively; he's tough to beat one on one with his size, mobility and good stick. He's a strong kid and he's strong along the wall and in front of the net. McCarthy has a lot of skills to translate to be an NHLer someday, he's currently committed to Boston University.

MACKAY, COLE
RW - Sault Ste. Marie Greyhounds (OHL) 5'10" 181

MacKay is an averaged size winger with good skill and smarts to his game. Cole played a limited role with the Greyhounds, but found ways to be productive despite limited ice. He shows impressive hockey sense as he always is seemingly on the right side of the puck, positionally sound and makes strong decisions in possession. Offensively MacKay showed an effectiveness off the cycle were he utilized his puck protection skills and quick first step to slip checks and recognize passing or shooting lanes. Cole shows an above average shot and release with good accuracy and velocity to his shot. He has pure goal scorer tendencies to his game and should see elevated production next season with top six minutes and speciality teams minutes. A player who plays up and down the wings and can create space for his teammates by effectively driving lanes, creating pick plays and drawing in opponents when in possession, MacKay's combination of skill and smarts creates intrigue to his game.

MCMICHAEL, CONNOR
LC - London Knights (OHL) 6'00" 170

McMichael is a two-way centre with an intelligence to his game. Connor received elevated ice-time following a mid-season trade to London and became more assertive with his play. He shows a confidence in possession and makes strong decisions with the puck. Connor handles the puck well but isn't a threat to beat a check in 1-on-1 situations. He displays a subtle creativity to his game and will take risks, however does so at the appropriate times, limiting his overall risk offensively. McMichael has an average shot, but is a pass first centre showing good vision and passing skills. He's often aware of trailing and attacking options and can disguise his intentions offensively. A competitive player, Connor is effective on the forecheck both aggressively and passively. He can quickly get in on an opponents stick to create a turnover or anticipate and get his body in front of an outlet pass. McMichael is competitive in the dirty areas but a lack of strength did limit his overall success. He will need to work on improving his skating if he hopes to enhance his offensive production. Lacking a quick first step and showing a short stride, Connor can be limited in his ability to generate speed and often only achieves and average top speed.

MERISIER-ORTIZ, CHRISTOPHER
LD - Baie-Comeau Drakkar (QMJHL) - 5'11" 165

Merisier-Ortiz was the 2nd defensemen drafted in the 2017 QMJHL draft and was Baie-Comeau 7th overall selection in this draft. This season with Baie-Comeau, he played more of a depth role and getting some power play ice time as the year progressed. He finished the season with 15 points in 62 games and also played in November at the U-17 hockey challenge.

The young defenseman has really good feet, can really skate and rushing the puck out of his zone is one of the best traits of his game. He excels where there's a lot of room on the ice, power play or 4 on 4 he can be really a threat in those situations. He has a good first pass out of his zone and in the offensive zone is where there's some inconsistency with his passing game. Decision making will be a part of Ortiz game that will need some improvement, he can really skate and play the game at high pace but sometime his brain doesn't think as fast as his feet and this cause trouble for him on the ice. Nevertheless, in the QMJHL with his skillset he should be able to make his mark as a power play quarterback in the next 3 seasons. He has good puck skills, he can beat guys one on one with his good stickhandling skills. He's not a tall defenseman but he has good lower body strength; defensively he's got some work to do and need to play a simple game out there and limited those errors and turnovers. As well he's not overly physical out there and he'll need to compete more in his zone along the board and in front of his net.

Next season Merisier-Ortiz should be more of an impact player offensively for the Drakkar and played more on the power play were he could excel.

MEYER, BRADY
LC - North Branch H.S. (MNHS) 6'05" 195

Meyer is another late 00' Birthdate out of Minnesota that also represented Team USA at the 2017 Hlinka Memorial Tournament. After dominating his competition in a weaker division of the Minnesota High School ranks for North Branch High School, registering 37 Goals and 34 Assists in 28 games, Meyer joined Central Illinois (USHL) in the spring where he was able to come in and contribute on a struggling team that was out of the playoff race. Brady has good size and uses it well to control the game down low with the puck, both at the High School and USHL levels. Meyer has quick hands and has good vision of the ice and is able to thread passes through sticks and setup teammates in the offensive zone. Meyer plays a power game and scores a lot of his goals around the net. Meyer competes for pucks and has a good nose for the net. His footspeed is not high end at this stage but Brady has decent agility and straight line speed when he gets going but will need to get stronger to improve his explosiveness off the hop. Meyer will likely start the 18/19 season with Central Illinois and is committed to Minnesota Duluth for the 19/20 season.

MICHEL, JEREMY
LW - Val D'Or Foreurs (QMJHL) - 5'11" 150

Michel is another one of those young prospects Val D'Or had on their team this year in which they are rebuilding with. He drafted late in the 1st round 17th overall out of the Lévis midget AAA program. This season on the rebuilding Foreurs he had 6 goals and 23 points in 65 games but was not selected to play at the U-17 hockey challenge.

Michel can play about anywhere in a lineup, he can play on the wing and down the middle. He has good two-way ability and has value as penalty killer as well. He's a good shooter but this year he was not put into situation to be successful as his shot is really good but only took 70 shots on net in 65 games. If he wants to score more often next season he'll need to use his shot more often than this. In the future he could be an option to play on the point on the power play as he did at the midget level. In possession of the puck he likes to slow down the play, he has good vision and likes to feed the puck to his teammates. He backchecks hard, he showed good work ethic away from the puck. The biggest knock on Michel even in midget has been is consistency and sometime can disappeared for long stretches during games.

Next season with a season under his belt, Michel should be a regular on the Foreurs top 3 lines and most likely top 2 lines if he's able to contribute more offensively than he did last year. He has good potential but we need to see him use his shot more and be more consistent from game to game.

MIRONOV, ILYA
LD - Loko-Yunior Yaroslavl (NMHL) - 6'03" 198

Mironov has great physical tools. He's strong on his skates, and in the defensive zone, he does a good job utilizing his long reach to block passing lanes and engaging quickly with the players in possession of the puck. He has not yet learned to fully utilize his size in front of the net, as he could be even more dominant physically due to the physical advantage he has right now. In the defensive zone, he can get caught puck-watching in the high slot and lose his man near the goal line. His skating is fine at this age and at this size, but with a better technique, he could produce more speed from his stride. His stride is fluid, but he doesn't bend his knees enough, so it loses power in his transitioning. He has a good first pass out of his zone and can be a good puck-distributor on the power play. He's not a flashy offensive defenseman, but can be efficient with some good puck-movement and his big, heavy shot from the point. He's not really a puck-rusher; he prefers to make a solid first pass to activate the transition game. Mironov was Russia's best defenseman at the U-17 Hockey Challenge in November, and he's intriguing because of his combination of skills and size.

MISYUL, DANIIL
LD - Loko Yaroslavl (MHL) - 6'03" 176

Misyul is an intriguing defenseman from Russia who played in the MHL this past season. He's intriguing because of his combination of size and skating abilities. He's a bit wild on the ice, and will need to learn to play his position better, but there's some upside there. He uses his skating well to rush the puck and he's quite active in the offensive zone. He's not afraid to pinch and go deep in the offensive zone in order to create some scoring chances and generate offensive zone pressure. On the power play, we often saw him play the forward position and be used in front of the net. He showed quick hands playing the forward role in front of the net. His puck skills are decent, as he can beat guys one-on-one with his skating abilities, quick hands and long reach. He can make good passes for the transition game, but he'll need to make better decisions with the puck. He can be victim to turnovers due to errant passes and trying too much with the puck. If Misyul can learn to play a simpler game, it would definitely make him a more efficient player on the ice. He doesn't mind the physical game and can be effective along the boards, although he can be caught out of position because he's too aggressive and his defensive awareness is only average. He's tall and lanky right now; he'll need to work in the summer to add strength to his frame to be more effective along the boards and in front of his net. Misyul's upside is intriguing; if he can improve his decision-making and get bigger, he could be an interesting prospect for the 2019 NHL Entry Draft.

MORGAN, CODY
LC - Windsor Spitfires (OHL) 5'11" 183

Morgan is a skilled centre with good hockey IQ and a competitiveness to his game. Cody is a confident forward with an ability to dictate the play around and was able to elevate his point production following a trade to Windsor from Kingston. He is at his best in possession were he shows sound decision making, strong puck handling abilities and quality playmaking skills. Morgan is versatile offensively as he does show a quality release and good accuracy and velocity to his shot, however he can tend to pass up shooting opportunities in favour of a pass. Cody already possesses good strength to his game as he is heavy on the puck and win battles. He's effective below the hash-marks and assertive with his frame. While not overly aggressive he combines a heavy style of play with good skill. Morgan is a somewhat deceptive skater as he has power to his stride and generates good speed but can be a little to upright in his stance as he moves around the ice. A player who has strong offensive instincts and hockey IQ, Morgan will need to elevate his competitiveness away from the puck showing the compete on and engaged play on a more consistent basis. Becoming more assertive off the rush and attacking the goal more frequently would also be an appealing addition to his game.

MRAZIK, MICHAL
LW - HK 32 Liptovsky Mikulas U20 (Slovakia U20) 6'04" 183

Michal Mrazik produced at a 0.5ppg rate after putting up 20 points in 40 games, including 12 assists. His team was relegated and during the relegation rounds he produced 7 points in 12 games. Internationally, he was featured at the U18's where he had a successful tournament after producing 4 points in 5 games.

Mrazik is big winger who has shoot-first mentality. He's got a plus release and uses his frame to weigh into his shot which generates a good amount of velocity on most attempts. This made him dangerous on the powerplay at the U18's. He had a decent amount of offensive-instincts, finding soft-ice with some regularity where he would look to get set up by his teammates for scoring chances. His puck-skills are a plus given his length and height, showing a range of moves including toe-drags that he attempts in motion. One of the more impressive elements of his skating ability is his agility and when he uses it properly when attacking the net, he can be a threat off the rush. He can also pass the puck but it's not his primary instinct in the offensive-end. Lastly, Michal is a two-way forward who's capable of using an active stick due to his length and had a couple of nice backchecks when we viewed him.

MURRAY, BLAKE
LC - Sudbury Wolves (OHL) 6'02" 180

Murray is a big bodied, modern day power forward with strong offensive instincts. Blake shows confidence and assertiveness to his game, utilizing his size and strength to get his body into the high percentage scoring areas. He possesses a pro-caliber shot and release that makes him a threat to score from all over the offensive zone. Murray does a good job keeping his feet moving and finding space away from the puck and shows quick strike ability. He willingly goes to the dirty areas and is an effective net presence showing a good hand-eye when deflecting shots and quick hands in the tight areas to finish. Murray shows a strength below the hash-marks were he remains heavy on the puck and creates off the cycle, showing deceptively good vision and passing skills. A deceptive skater, Murray possesses a long, powerful and smooth stride that allows him to cover large portions of the ice quickly. When he reaches top speed his ability control and protect the puck in combination with his size and strength and willingness to take the puck to traffic make him difficult to handle. Murray has pure goal scoring abilities however would elevate his game by adding more aggression and becoming a more physically dominating presence. While his skating is good, he would benefit from increasing the quickness in his first two steps. Murray like most rookie forwards will need to find better compete level in the neutral and defensive zone as his consistency in those areas can waiver at times.

MUTALA, SASHA
RW - Tri-City Americans (WHL) 6'00" 190

Sasha Mutala had a productive first season for the Tri-City Americans, scoring 11 goals and 26 points in 68 regular season games. The former 6th overall pick in the bantam draft also had a terrific World U18s for Canada Black, posting 5 goals and 8 points in 5 games, leading the team in scoring.

Mutala is an explosive player with a great motor. He has a strong lower half and that combined with his competitiveness makes him a nightmare on the forecheck. The puck seems to follow him and he has the ability to win the majority of puck races with his quick feet and explosive stride. His on ice work ethic makes him a leader on team's of his age group and he was relevant on an excellent Tri-City team with solid forward depth. Offensively, Mutala's combination of speed and a heavy, quick release is deadly. He can score from a variety of areas and doesn't hold onto the puck for long, making it very difficult for goalies to react. Sasha is captain material with high offensive upside and very good skating skills. Given his ability to play up and down the lineup, he is a valuable prospect eligible for the 2019 NHL Draft.

MYLLYLA, WILJAMI
RW - Hermes U20 (Jr. A Mestis) - 6'00" 157

Myllyla is not the most skilled player, but he brings something that few players can bring to the table. He brings a physical game every time he's on the ice. He's excellent on the forecheck; his puck-pursuit game is excellent and he creates a lot of havoc in the offensive zone with his relentless physical play. His motor never stops and he keeps his feet moving. He goes to the net hard, he's quick to jump on rebounds, and will play the Tomas Holmstrom role in front of the net if needed. His skating is not pretty, but he does generate some good power and his top speed is decent. He could generate more speed with a better technique and improve his agility and make quicker changes in directions. He works hard in all three zones, always demonstrating a good effort on the backcheck, and can create some turnovers there. He's not the most skilled player, his hands are average and the same goes for his puck skills. Overall, we like this player's energy and physical play, but in order to have a chance to play at a higher level, he'll need to improve his skills with the puck and make more plays offensively.

NAJMAN, ADAM
LC - HC Dukla Jihlava U20 (Czech U20) - 5'10" 165

Najman was one of the better forwards on the Czech U-17 team this year. He's not overly big, but has some skills and talent offensively. He skates well; he's not dynamic but he has above-average speed with good acceleration. He can play at centre and on the wing. He does a good job on the power play playing the half-wall, and likes to control the puck from there. He possesses good hands; we've seen some dynamic plays from him one-on-one and made some nice dekes to beat defensemen and goaltenders one-on-one. His hands are possibly his number 1 asset. He made some smart plays in the neutral zone with his good active stick, creating some turnovers and taking advantage of them. He comes from a hockey family: his grandfather was a long-time coach in the Czech Republic, his father played pro hockey in North America, the Czech Republic, and Germany. Now he's coaching in the Czech Republic, and his older brother played in the WHL for Spokane in 2016-2017.

NEWHOOK, ALEX
LC - Victoria Grizzlies (BCHL) 5'11" 183

Alex Newhook is a dynamic offensive-talent that put up excellent numbers for the Victoria Grizzlies this past season by producing 66 points in 45 games, including 44 assists. In the playoffs he scored 9 points in 12 games and played for Canada Black at the U17's where he continued his impressive output by putting up 4 points in 5 games. The Newfoundland native was named the top BCHL rookie and the CJHL rookie of the year after finishing 8th in league scoring while producing 14 more points than the next closest competitor.

Newhook is a highly-skilled two-way forward who continued to develop his offensive-arsenal this past season while also getting bigger. Newhook is dangerous offensively and can cut through opponents with great one-on-one skills, taking the puck to the net. He has scored some highlight-reel goals this season. In addition to his ability to put the puck in the net, Alex is a creative forward who sets up his linemates well and has good hockey sense and a good understanding of when to shoot and when to pass. Unlike a lot of high-end offensive players, Newhook is a good defensive forward who competes at a high-level. He is relentless on the backcheck, takes away passing lanes and is quick to get to the his responsibility in the defensive zone. Newhook is the type of player you want on the ice whether you're up a goal or down a goal in the final minute. He has as his ability to be a key player regardless of the situation. Newhook has a BCHL and QMJHL options available to him, but regardless what route he selects we think of him as a high-end prospect with possible top 5 upside projecting ahead to the 2019 draft in Vancouver.

"Really enjoyed watching him play in his OHL Draft season in Ontario and he was even more fun to watch this year in the BCHL. He should be a high pick. I would've liked him to play Halifax next year though. I'd love to see him in that lineup and compete in the Memorial Cup." - HP Scout, Mark Edwards

NIKKANEN, HENRI
LC - JYP U20 (Jr.A SM-liiga) - 6'02" 185

Nikkanen was a good performer for Finland at the U-17s this past November; the young centre finished the tournament with 5 goals and 9 points in 6 games. He was the captain of the team at this event. Despite having some success offensively, we thought he often played too much on the perimeter and was not involved enough in the play. There is not much of a physical game with him. He's a pretty complete player otherwise; good on the power play and penalty-killing units with good size. We like his smarts and how he has good defensive awareness away from the puck; he's a threat on the PK to score. In his zone, he does a good job of consistently supporting his defensemen deep in his zone to retrieve pucks and can quickly start the transition game. He's a good skater who lacks explosiveness, but his top speed is decent. He has some decent puck skills as well, including good one-on-one abilities and good vision.

Overall, he's a decent-sized centre with good hockey IQ, good smarts and decent offensive upside. We want to see him more involved in the play and for him to learn how to use his size more.

NIKOLAYEV, ILYA
LC - Loko-Yunior Yaroslavl (NMHL) - 6'00" 190

Nikolaev spent the majority of the past season in the NMHL; he also did play three games in the MHL, where he should play full time next season (unless he comes to play in the CHL). Nikolayev centered Russia's top line at the U-17s this past November, playing with Gutik and Podkolzin, two highly-skilled wingers. Nikolayev is a smart two-way centre who's not as high-end as his counterparts, but plays a sound game at both ends of the ice. He takes pride in the little details of the game, has a solid work ethic, and shows good awareness and reads the play well in his zone. He also can act like a 3rd defenseman on the ice, showing good support deep in his zone and helping his defensemen retrieve pucks down low. He has decent speed, though he lacks some explosiveness to his stride, but moves well enough on the ice. Overall, Nikolayev is not a flashy performer, but he does play a smart game in all three zones. Next year, we would like to see him add a bit more offense to his game, which would make him an even better prospect for the 2019 NHL Entry Draft.

NUSSBAUMER, VALENTIN
C/W - EHC Biel-Bienne (NLA) 5'11" 159

Valentin Nussbaumer had an excellent year in the NLA, producing 6 points in 26 games, including 5 goals. He also played for the U20 team where he produced 18 points in 20 games and had an additional 6 points in 8 playoff games. Internationally, he was featured at the Hlinka, where he had 4 points in 4 games, the U20's where he faired well for a player of his age while putting up a goal in 5 games, and the U18's where he produced 4 points in 6 games.

Nussbaumer is a two-way cerebral center with an incredible amount of talent. His speed is apparent, he has excellent acceleration which allows him to break into a fluid stride and he has separation speed despite having a slight build. His speed when combined with his great hockey-sense makes him dangerous when he's in motion. He's got the unique ability to anticipate plays two-steps ahead of most other players on the ice and this allows him to be an architect with the puck on his stick, forming plays that breakdown opposing teams using his vision, his poise and his awareness. He's a tempo-controller who can dictate play with the puck on his stick, who showed an advanced maturity for his age when under pressure. This stood out at the U20's where he rarely looked out of place, adapting to the pace remarkably well, and at times dominated against players who were 3 years older than himself. When finding soft-ice or getting behind defensive-coverage, he's demonstrated a quick release on his shot and has the ability to mask his intentions with the puck on his stick. Valentin isn't just an offensive-force though, his defensive-reads and willingness to support his defenseman in his own-end were noticeable. Despite his weight, he's surprisingly strong for his size, featuring good balance and doesn't play on the perimeter, instead showing the ability to attack the net with a good degree of fearlessness. He's one of the most promising centers heading into the 2019 draft.

PAQUETTE, TYLER
RW - Des Moines Buccaneers (USHL) 6'02" 205

Paquette saw 44 games for Des Moines after being drafted in the 2nd Round in the 2017 USHL Draft and making the team out of camp. Paquette has good size and can get up and down the ice well. His skating is explosive and edgework is crisp which gives him excellent agility and footwork for a big kid. Paquette showed a good physical presence, especially on the fore-check where he was able to pressure defenseman into committing turnovers with his speed. Paquette didn't display much offensive playmaking ability throughout his rookie season in the USHL and tends to rush plays and not take advantage of the space he was able to create. Paquette possesses a heavy and accurate shot but struggles to get himself into positions where it can be utilized. Paquette should get more of an opportunity to showcase his offensive game next season. Paquette is a Penn State commit and was also drafted by Peterborough in the 2017 OHL Draft.

PARENT, XAVIER
LW - Halifax Mooseheads (QMJHL) - 5'07" 165

Parent was the 4th overall selection in last year QMJHL draft and this year with the Mooseheads he did fairly well even if he didn't get first line & first power play unit ice time other top picks received this year. He finished the season with 13 goals & 29 points and had a great showing in November at the U-17 hockey challenge losing in the final with team Red.

Parent is great skater; he has good top speed and a great acceleration. He loves to attack players one on one when he's in possession of the puck. He has good edges and a low center of gravity which makes it tough to be knock down even though he's not a big player at all. He lacks size but can play a bit of agitating role on the ice and be pain for opposing defense to defend because of his good hustle and speed. He definitely has a good scoring touch around the net, his offensive totals will without a doubt improve by quite a lot next year as he gets more ice time in key offensive situations with Halifax losing a player like Maxime Fortier. He has a good shot with a quick release. One area of his game that will need some work is his passing game, he can make highlight reel passes and other sequences he will keep puck too long and will cause a turnovers for not moving the puck quickly enough. There's a lack of consistency there but not a lack of talent. No doubt Parent has all the talent in the world to be a major point producer in the QMJHL. Another area of his game that will need some adjustment will be his play away from the puck in his zone with his positioning, as is the case with any 16 years old playing major junior. He has good qualities to be one day a good player on the PK unit because of his speed and anticipation, a good example on his team is Maxime Fortier that he could have learn some tips this year. This season his minutes were carefully handled this season but he has proven himself ready for more responsibility. Began lining up at Centre regularly with a month left in the regular season and did performed well. He's likely to be a winger long term but if he can play center full time it gives him more value and more versatility.

Parent will be a player to keep an eye out next year as with increase ice time and role with Halifax he should produce a lot but the questions about his size will remain in the conversation without a doubt.

PEACH, BAILEY
RW - Sherbrooke Phoenix (QMJHL) - 5'10" 168

Peach was the 11th overall selection in last June QMJHL Draft by Sherbrooke and had a relatively though first season in major junior. He was a top scorer in midget with Cole Harbour but the adjustment to the QMJHL was tougher than anticipated and only scored 3 goals & 7 points in 49 games this year. He also played at the U-17 hockey challenge but went pointless in 5 games.

Peach number one asset is his skating ability, has really quick feet and a great acceleration. He has the speed to burn past defenders and likes to take the puck wide on defensemen one on one. He has quick hands and a good shot that he can release quickly. Part of his problems adapting to the QMJHL this season is lack of ice time & one dimensional game. Peach is first and foremost an offensive player, he won't help much a team by playing a defensive 4th line role. He will produce in the QMJHL when he plays with skilled linemates and get power play ice time. There's a lot of work for him to be done with his play away from the puck, intensity and consistency. Lots of times this year when we saw Sherbrooke there's was very few flashes from Peach. In midget he was successful playing with a excellent playmaker in Ryan Francis (Now with Cape Breton), if Sherbrooke can find him that kind of playmaker he could do some damage offensively for them in the future.

Peach should see his role expand next year and play more on the power play. Without a doubt his offensive production should improve with the increase ice time. Samuel Poulin and Peach are the center piece of Sherbrooke in the next three seasons.

PELLETIER, JAKOB
LW/C - Moncton Wildcats (QMJHL) - 5'09" 158

Pelletier was the 3rd overall pick in the QMJHL draft last June and right away he became an impact player for the Moncton Wildcats in his first season in the league. He finished the season with 61 points which is a new team record for points for a 16 years old player beating a record dating back to the 2001-2002 season hold by Steve Bernier.

Pelletier is an ultra-smart hockey player at both end of the ice, he can play in any situations that his coach will put him on and will succeed. His play away from the puck is pretty advance and already was one of his team best defensive forward. He's the type of player every coach love to have on their team. He can play at center but played majority of the year on the wing, it should be interesting to see if he does get more playing time down the middle next season. Pelletier sees the ice well and has a good on ice vision. His shot is decent but could work on improving his velocity which would make him a bigger threat to score from anywhere in the offensive zone. He does a knack for scoring big goals; he's definitely a gamer and won't get outworked on the ice. Already at 16, he was a big asset for the Wildcats on both special team units. He's a good skater and has a will to be a difference maker for his team. Last year he was a standout performer in midget AAA and scored many big goals in the Quebec Midget AAA playoff and Telus Cup in which he and his team lost in the final of the Telus Cup.

"Absolutely love this kid. He has a non-stop motor and plays his heart out every game. Not a huge kid, but has good skills, and he's smart." - HP Scout Jérôme Bérubé

PELLETIER, THOMAS
RD - Drummondville Voltigeurs (QMJHL) - 6'02" 190

Pelletier was Drummondville 3rd pick in the first round last June (19th overall) and this year played 48 games on a limited role with the Voltigeurs. He also played at the U-17 Hockey Challenge as a last minute injury replacement.

Pelletier has good size and a long reach that he uses well to defend one on one. He made some progress through the year with his play with the puck; he was moving puck more quickly than he did in midget or the beginning of the season. He has improve his footwork as well, still got some work to do with his fluidity and getting caught flat footed by speedy forward going wide on him but there's some improvement that was made through this season that we notice in the 2nd half of the season. Pelletier not known for his offensive upside but can be a power play defensemen because of his shot. He moves the puck well enough but doesn't have the quality with the puck to be a premier power play quarterback. He's more of a two way defensemen and if he can step up with his physical game next year that will add more value to his potential for the 2019 NHL draft.

Next season, he should get more ice time and possibly challenge for a top -4 role on the Voltigeurs defensive squad.

PENMAN, DUNCAN
LD - Saginaw Spirit (OHL) 6'0" 176

Duncan was selected in the second round, 25th overall by the Saginaw Spirit at the 2017 OHL Draft. He had a successful rookie campaign with Saginaw, putting up 10 points, including 6 assists in 55 games, while also getting playoff experience, where he registered zero points in 4 games.

Penman is a smart, two-way defender who plays with confidence when handling the puck in transition. His defensive awareness allows him to use impressive skating mechanics to elude the forecheck and carry the puck out of high-pressure situations. His base is wide but he possesses a strong stride and sharp edges which allows him to burst up ice and exploit skating lanes, as well as counter opposing players who are attempting to drive wide on him. In most of our viewings, he reacted to pressure quickly in all three-zones, showing the ability to process the play and adapt on the fly. This was the most prominent in the defensive-end, where he made several well-timed and well-executed passes to his teammates that helped move the puck up the ice. Furthermore, he showed above-average positioning for his age and was used on the penalty-kill where he didn't look out of place, controlling his gaps and was more than willing to battle in the corners. He's not a defender who forces the play and recognizes when he needs to switch gears in the neutral zone to gain an offensive zone-entry.

PERROTT, ANDREW
RD - London Knights (OHL) 6'00" 194

Andrew Perrot was selected by the London Knights in the second round, 34th Overall at the 2017 OHL Draft. He had a successful rookie season with London, amassing 9 points in 62 games, including 4 goals. He had an assist in 4 playoff games as well.

Andrew is a physical defenseman with impressive two-way upside. Andrew plays tough along the wall and is very difficult to match up with down low. Perrot handles pressure well, making decisive plays with the puck on his stick while relying on his edges to peel away from the forecheck. He's strong and wins the majority of his battles along the boards both with his frame and an active stick. He is also pretty physical in one on one situations and when the opportunity is there, he'll land the big open ice hit. Andrew has transitional defensive-zone exits and is capable of making consistently accurate passes up ice, while also protecting the puck and rushing up ice to advance the play. On the point he keeps his feet moving and opens himself up as an option. He has a powerful shot from the point and managed to get it through screens. His ability to assert himself in the defensive-end and play a composed game allowed him to get time with Bouchard, who he complimented well in some of our viewings. There's a good developmental frame in Perrott who should have increased responsibilities with London next season.

PIIROINEN, KARI
G - HIFK U18 (Jr.B SM-liiga) - 6'00" 161

Piiroinen is an average goaltender from Finland who was also the number one goaltender of the national U-17 team in international competition this past season. In Finland, he played the majority of the season in the U18 league, and also had a short stint in the U20 league. His size is obviously something that we will need to monitor next season, as NHL teams tend to shy away from average-sized goaltenders, unless they are dominant. He'll need to learn to make himself look bigger in net; currently he plays too deep in his net. We would like to see him challenge shooters more and therefore cover his angles better. There are some inconsistencies with his rebound-control; we would like to see more regularity in that area of his game. Some games he did really well keeping his rebounds close to him or redirecting them in the corners. For other games, his rebounds were all over the place. His compete level is good though, as he fights hard for every puck and there's no quit in his game. The key for Piiroinen will be to get bigger and find more consistency in his game.

PODKOLZIN, VASILI
LW/RW - Vityaz Podolsk U17 (Russia U17) - 5'11" 165

Podkolzin had quite the year on the international stage this season, playing the first half of the season with the U-17 team and in the 2nd half with the U-18 team.

He's a smart hockey player. At the U-17 level, he was the go-to guy offensively, and when he made the transition to the U-18 team, he adapted his game to become more of a role player that can contribute offensively. He has excellent puck poise; he's good at slowing down the play while in possession of the puck and can make high-quality passes to his teammates. He was great playing the half-wall role on the power play for Team Russia at the U-17s in November, where his passing abilities and vision were on full display. He has a good shot with a quick release; he's good at finding space on the ice and escaping his coverage. We saw him score a couple of goals like this at the U-18s, one-timing pucks from the slot after getting away from his coverage. He's also a very advanced defensive player; he's been very good on the PK in our viewings. For a skilled player, he was not afraid to sacrifice his body to block shots, and he's relentless on the puck-carrier. He's good at keeping possession of the puck and killing time in the offensive zone, holding onto the puck for a long time; it can also lead to the opposing team taking penalties on him. He's quick to apply pressure, and can be a threat to score on the PK as he can take advantage of turnovers. He has a good compete level; he can play a feisty game as well, getting involved in the rough stuff at times even if he's not the biggest player on the ice.

Overall, Podkolzin is an excellent prospect for the 2019 NHL Entry Draft, and one to keep an eye out for next season, as he should be the leader of the Russian U-18 team all year long.

PORCO, NICHOLAS
LW - Saginaw Spirit (OHL) 6'00" 168

Nicholas Porco was selected in the first round, fourth overall by the Saginaw Spirit at the 2017 OHL Draft. He produced at a decent rate in his rookie season, producing 14 points in 57 games, including 9 assists. In the playoffs, he produced 2 points in 4 games. Internationally, he was featured at the U17's, scoring once in 6 games for Canada White.

Porco is a skilled forward with game breaking abilities. A player who thrives in possession, he is at his best when playing with speed and confidence. Porco possesses puck handling abilities to beat a check in 1-on-1 scenarios and can generate offense for himself and his teammates. While Porco has a versatile offensive skill set as both a shooter and a playmaker he would benefit from better utilizing his teammates on a consistent basis. Porco possesses deceptively good passing skills however can be selfish at times and look to shoot or beat an opponent opposed to making the simple play. When Nicholas utilizes his teammates, he becomes extremely difficult to defend due to his versatile skill set. A player who likes to attack with speed, he is able to generate an above average top speed which when combined with his puck handling abilities make him shifty and elusive, however he will need to refine his stride though his acceleration looked improved in his first with the Spirit. He used his improved first few steps at the defensive-blueline to create pressure on opposing teams. He needs to add strength to his somewhat rangy frame would enhance his effectiveness along the boards and in the dirty areas. His strength issues can affect his shot to some degree, however it is still above average due to a quick release and good accuracy.

POULIN, SAMUEL
LW/RW - Sherbrooke Phoenix (QMJHL) - 6'01" 208

Poulin was the 2nd overall pick in the 2017 QMJHL Draft and with Sherbrooke this year he was playing with his older brother Nicolas an overager on the team. His father is former NHLer Patrick Poulin who played for 10 years in the NHL.

He had a tough start of his QMJHL career when he was hit hard in his first career game in Val D'Or and was concussed on the play. That slows down his adaptation to the league and didn't produce and perform as we had hoped for unlike others top rookie from this draft class. He started finding his game in December and from then he played like the number 2 overall pick and average a point per game from December to the end of the season. Poulin will need to keep working on his skating; keep improving his explosiveness will be a key for him going forward. He's a big kid, he uses his size well and wins his share of one on one battles and go to the net. Poulin can score; a lot of his goals come from his hard work. We would like to him improve his shot. He's a better playmaker than finisher; he sees the ice well and can set up his linemates well. He's a pretty smart hockey player, he has a two-way ability and can play on both PP and PK.

He was very impressive in the 2nd half of the season and next year he'll be without a doubt one of his team offensive leaders. Poulin will be a candidate for Canada U-18 Ivan Hlinka team this upcoming August.

He plays a heavy game and has good skills….skating is work in progress. He started slow but was one of Sherbrooke top player from Christmas to the playoff" - HP Scout Jérôme Bérubé

PRIKRYL, FILIP
LC/LW - HC Plzen U20 (Czech U20) - 6'01" 163

Prikryl was an important player for the Czech U-17 team this year, with 18 points in 15 games this season. He was called up to the U-18 team for the Five Nations' Tournament in February. In his league play, he had some great success playing in the U-18 league, averaging two points per game. In the U-20 league, he averaged just under a point per game. Prikryl is a centre with a good skill level, good size and quick hands. He's solid along the wall and near the net to protect the puck. He does a really good job protecting the puck with his body, and is technically good at putting his body in position so that opponents have a hard time taking pucks away from him. He keeps his feet moving along the boards; he has a good compete level. He had success offensively in the junior league in the Czech Republic, but was not as successful at the U-17s in November or the U-18s in February. Prikryl should challenge for a roster spot in the Czech top men's league next season, after his success in the U20 league this past year. He's also a candidate for the CHL to pick him up this summer.

PRIMEAU, MASON
LC - Guelph Storm (OHL) 6'05" 183

Mason was selected in the second round, 22nd overall by the Guelph Storm at the 2017 OHL Draft. In his first season with the Storm, he put up 13 points in 60 games, including 6 goals. In the playoffs he produced 2 assists in 6 games before being eliminated.

Primeau has impressive size and strength. There's versatility to his game that allows him to thrive in various roles. In the defensive-end, he helps support his defenseman and is willing to play deep in his own-end. However, he is arguably at his best in possession or off the cycle where he can utilize his combination of size and strength to dominate the play. Primeau isn't overly creative with the puck, however possesses intriguing vision and can create for his teammates with very subtle but effective playmaking skills. Primeau protects the puck very well and keeps his feet moving, which allows him to find success off the cycle, while showing the ability to recognizing when to attack the goal and open ice, his puck-tracking skills are a plus. Primeau's release is above average it can be inconsistent at times, showing power on one attempt and then not much on another. Primeau skates ok for a 6'4 player as he displays a fluid and powerful stride that allows him to generate a decent top speed. Primeau's strength over the puck and excellent awareness makes him a versatile threat in transition as he can beat defenders wide to the goal or create a play for a teammate at top in transition. He has shown an ability to shut-down opposing teams top centres in his own zone, showing quality defensive zone play and overall positional awareness. While he is effective without much of an edge, it would be intriguing to see him play with more aggression and physicality.

REES, JAMIESON
LC - Sarnia Sting (OHL) 5'09" 161

Rees is an energetic, two-way centre with skill. Jamieson shows intelligence and awareness to his game that allows him to find success in several areas of the game. He shows a confidence in possession as he utilizes his quick and powerful first step to create separation from a check and handles the puck well through traffic. He has the awareness and vision to makes skilled decisions with speed and is talented enough to make plays both on his forehand and back-hand. Jamieson possesses a strong motor and brings a consistent effort on a shift-by-shift basis. His energy and tenaciousness make him impactful on the forecheck. Rees isn't overly physical but does play with some aggressiveness in his compete level along the wall and in puck battles. With the puck on his stick he is able to shield the puck and shows a willingness to be assertive, taking the puck into the scoring areas. He is versatile offensively showing good finish and playmaking traits. Rees is also efficient away from the puck, finding space or creating space off the cycle or by driving lanes. Rees has the potential to drive the offensive attack for the Sting, however his size and durability will be a question mark moving forward. While not as high end as Travis Konecny their are similar traits and similar concerns.

RIZZO, MASSIMO
LC - Penticton Vees (BCHL) 5'10" 172

Massimo Rizzo is a flashy centre who had a productive first season with the Penticton Vees in 2017-18, recording 38 points in 50 regular season games and an additional 10 points in 11 playoff games. Rizzo appears to be taking the college route despite being selected by the Kamloops Blazers 15th overall in the 2016 WHL Bantam Draft.

Rizzo is a raw talent with exceptional skill. He has shown the ability to beat players in open space and is a player that loves scoring goals and making creative plays with the puck. Rizzo was an individual player that could dominate by going end to end at will at any level of minor hockey. His ability to deke and change directions with the puck is what made him dominant prior to junior. His top end speed is average and he has some sloppy feet, which did not hurt him at lower levels because his skill was enough to take over. In one on one situations, Rizzo is dangerous and has a way of beating defenseman with a deke through the stick or skates and finishing up high on the goalie. Rizzo can also facilitate for teammates when he wants to. He resorts too much to individual plays, but if he learns to use his teammates more, his offensive skills may be able to translate to the next level.

ROBERTSON, MATTHEW
LD - Edmonton Oil Kings (WHL) 6'03" 196

Matthew Robertson was selected 7th overall in the 2016 WHL Bantam Draft, and made an immediate impact for the Oil Kings in 2017-18, recording 7 goals and 24 points in 67 regular season games. He was excellent at the World U17s and earned himself a spot on Team Canada at the World U18s, posting 2 assists in 5 tournament games as an underage player.

Robertson is a big, mobile defenseman with offensive upside. He has good feet for his size, showing the ability to walk the line and cross-over quickly. Skating up ice, he has a long stride with good knee bend and his mobility allows him to win races in his own end and win loose pucks. He also utilizes his size well, not as much in a physical game but with a long active stick. This reach is also useful when he handles the puck as he can handle it on both sides of his body with ease. His offensive game is not necessarily creative but he makes himself active in the rush and makes sound, smart decisions in offensive situations. He was relied heavily on the powerplay, manning the point on the umbrella, and was decisive with his puck movement and shots. It is too early to tell his ceiling in terms of his offensive game but he has the tools to be a big, mobile puck-mover, and has already established himself as a top pairing defenseman in the WHL. He is a top defensive prospect for the 2019 NHL Draft.

ROBERTSON, NICK
LC - Peterborough Petes (OHL) 5'07" 143

Robertson is a competitive, undersized centre with good skating abilities. Nick had a strong second half to the season, as he received more playing time and showed more confidence. Robertson possesses above average skating abilities, displaying a quick first step and quality straight line speed. He attacks with pace and shows a confidence and creativity in possession. Nick can be tough to defend as he changes both pace and direction well and shows good puck handling abilities. His quick hands in combination with his speed allow him to create space. Versatile in the offensive zone, Robertson shows a quick release and accurate shot, however would benefit from adding strength to improve the velocity of his shot. Nick is highly competitive and shows know hesitation going to the dirty areas. A player who is tenacious on the forecheck and creates turnovers with his ability to anticipate and quick stick, Robertson possesses an intriguing offensive game. He will need to enhance his strength moving forward to excel more in puck and position battles, while like most young players he could stand to provide more consistent showings.

ROSS, LIAM
LD - Sudbury Wolves (OHL) 6'02" 188

Ross is an intelligent, two-way defender with intriguing physical traits. Liam was effective playing to his strengths and keeping his game simple and low risk. He showed a maturity to his game and played with poise and patience in possession. Ross often made good reads with the puck and was able to quickly move the puck to lead transition up ice. Liam rarely opted to utilize his feet and carry the puck up ice, but when presented with open ice he is capable of gaining the offensive side of centre. Ross would benefit from working on the quickness in his first step up ice, allowing him to better create separation from a check in the defensive zone. His short stride does limit his top speed, while his puck handling also has room to grow. Offensively Ross shows good instincts on when to jump into the attack from his point position and began to show more confidence doing so in the second half of the season. He can be somewhat reserved and cautious offensively but does show an ability to get pucks on net and a deceptively heavy point shot. Ross has room to improve his mobility with just average feet. He does a good job keeping his gaps tight and angling opponents to the outside, while utilizing his reach and length to defend. Ross would benefit from becoming more assertive with his size and adding more aggression to his game. Becoming quicker on puck retrievals is also necessary and should improve as he works on his four-way quickness.

RUSSELL, MITCHELL
RC - Owen Sound Attack (OHL) 5'11" 182

Russell is an average sized centre who plays a heavy style of game and displays a good compete level. Mitchell will need to enhance his strength to find success playing his style of game, however showed flashes of effectiveness throughout the season. He was arguably at his best below the hash-marks were he was able to use his puck protection skills and smarts to work the cycle and create space an offensive opportunity for his line mates. Mitchell was good along the wall as he positioned himself well to win loose pucks and remain in ideal defense position if the puck was to turnover. He keeps his feet moving offensively, circling the scoring areas and shows a willingness to get into the dirty areas to clean up rebound opportunities. Russell shows a deceptively good release and has velocity behind his shot. He will need to improve his skating to reach the next level as he displays a short stride, average speed and lacks any explosiveness in his first two strides. Enhancing his strength would be benefical to his style of play, while becoming more confident and assertive with his physical game and skill will likely elevate the space he can create and point production.

SAARELA, ANTTI
LC/LW - Lukko U20 (Jr A SM-liiga) - 5'10'' 176

Saarela is speedy forward who made a good impression on us this season, playing in various U-17 tournaments for Finland. The younger brother of Carolina draft pick Aleksi Saarela is a versatile forward with a good hockey IQ who plays a pretty complete game at both ends of the ice.

He's easy to notice on the ice because he works hard on every shift and has good skating abilities. His top speed and acceleration are good. His skating stride is effortless and he can reach his top speed quickly. He likes to generate speed through the neutral zone; if he can reach his top speed there, he can be tough for opposing defensemen to defend against when he enters the offensive zone quickly. He loves to rush the puck into the offensive zone and he's shifty with good footwork, which helps him avoid hits along the wall by quickly moving out of the way or rolling on a check. He has value on the PK unit because of his speed, anticipation and work ethic. On the power play, he's valuable because of his vision; he has good puck poise and likes to play from the half-wall to generate scoring chances on the man-advantage. He keeps his feet moving and is quite active in the offensive zone. He's not a big kid; he's not very tall, has a slight frame and will need to get stronger because he can get pushed and taken off the puck too easily. Saarela is a good two-way forward, but in order to improve his stock for next year, he'll need to get bigger and stronger physically to be able to compete better versus bigger players along the boards and in front of the net.

SAFONOV, ILYA
LC - Vityaz Podolsk U17 (Russia U17) - 6'02" 170

Safonov is a powerful center who has decent speed for a big man and good edges that allow him to cut into traffic and go hard to the net. He has good puck skills, which makes him a dangerous player one-on-one. He has a long stick that he uses well to protect the puck or in defensive situation to block passing lanes. He has good value as a two-way center; he only played on the 4th line at the U-17 Hockey Challenge in November and didn't have the chance to really shine offensively. He didn't show much in terms of playmaking and vision during the tournament, either. However, Safronov is intriguing at his size, and has nice hands to go with it. If he develops properly, he could be tough to contain down low and near the opposing net and bring a solid two-way game.

SARTAKOV, VLADIMIR
G - Spartakovets Yekaterinburg U17 (Russia U17) - 5'11" 165

Sartakov was one of the few players from Russia to play in both Five Nations' Tournaments this year (November and February). This average-sized goaltender is an early-September birthday (therefore one of the younger players eligible for the 2019 NHL Entry Draft). His size is obviously something that we will keep an eye on; at 5'11" he'll need to grow couple of inches in order to help his chances of getting drafted next season. As is the case with a lot of European goaltenders, Sartakov will need to learn to avoid playing too deep in his net, as he can get caught not covering his angles well enough. He was a victim of that in the two games he played in at the U-17s in November; he gave up some bad goals at that event. He also has a tendency to be on his knees early, which opens up the upper part of net for shooters. His rebound-control was not great either, and overall, he had two tough events in both November and February. In order for him to get drafted next season, he'll need to be better than what he showed us this year. He'll also need to get bigger, as at his current size, there's not a lot of hope for his chances of being drafted.

SCHWINDT, COLE
RW - Mississauga Steelheads (OHL) - 6'02" 165

Schwindt is an intelligent forward with intriguing size. Cole plays a simple and effective game and was a versatile presence for the Steelheads playing in various roles and succeeding due to his smart. He possesses a tall and lanky frame that adds to his appeal. Schwindt should become more of a factor as he fills out his frame and become more assertive with his size. He already shows the willingness to take pucks to the net in traffic and can protect the puck while remaining aware of his passing options. Cole's skating isn't explosive and he will need to improve his stride, however his skating is effected by a lack of strength as he begins to add to his lower body his skating should rapidly improve. He possesses a good top speed once he gets going and utilizes his momentum to attack. While his game is low risk, Schwindt does show some creativity and an intriguing skill set. He sees the ice well and can make quality passes to elevate his line mates. A competitive player who did show some aggression to his game, Cole is fairly reliable in all three zones.

SEIDER, MORITZ
RD - Jungadler Mannheim U19 (DNL) - 6'04" 183

Seider has already great size, and he's not hard to notice on the ice. He's a two-way defenseman who played in Germany this past season, and played internationally with Germany's U-18 team at various international tournaments. He was also in Ontario in January at the MacPherson Hockey Tournament. Not only is his size impressive, but with that, you get a long reach. He uses well in his zone to block passing lanes in front of his net during penalty-killing situations. He has decent feet and mobility for a kid his size and age. There's still work to do there to improve his explosiveness and overall quickness. Becoming quicker to react to certain plays and retrieving pucks faster would be beneficial for him. He loves to play a physical game in his own zone, competing hard near his net and hitting hard. He just needs to pick his spots better, and not take himself out of position after trying to go for a big hit. Another thing we like from him is his poise with the puck; even under pressure, he's able to make the smart outlet passes. However, he will need to learn to make quicker decisions with the puck. He's not nervous, but sometimes takes too much time moving it. We saw him rush it out of his zone and support the rush as well; with more confidence, he'll be more consistent in terms of making plays with his feet.

Seider has an interesting package with his size and raw skills. It will be interesting to see where he ends up playing next year. He could make the jump to the CHL in Canada, stay in Germany to play in the men's league, or possibly elsewhere in Europe, like fellow German Dominik Bokk (who made the move to Germany for his NHL draft year).

SERDYUK, YEGOR
LW/RW - Omskie Yastreby (MHL) - 5'11" 159

Serdyuk played as a 16-year-old in the MHL this season, and had modest offensive success with 13 points in 30 games. On the international stage with the U-17 team, he did well, with 9 points in 6 games.

Serdyuk is a complete player at both ends of the ice; we've seen him make some good reads in the defensive zone to try stopping the opposing team's rushes. He's strong on the puck, is good along the wall and makes it tough for the opposing team to take pucks away from him. He's got decent size, and uses it well to keep possession of the puck. He's good down low and in front of the net. He's not as flashy as other Russians, but plays an effective game. He's tough to handle one-on-one because of his physicality and strength to overpower opposing defensemen. He's always around the puck, has a good hockey IQ, and is also quite good at finding space in the offensive zone to go and receive passes from teammates for scoring chances. Overall, Serdyuk is a good all-around prospect, and we are looking forward to seeing how much he progresses next season.

SHESHIN, DMITRI
LW/RW - Stalnye Lisy Magnitogorsk (MHL) - 5'07" 143

Sheshin is tiny, but he's a very exciting prospect, and had quite a successful season for a 16-year-old in the MHL, with 38 points in 51 games. He led the MHL in scoring for U-17 players.

He usually plays on his off- wing (as a right-handed shot playing on the left side); his speed is average, but he's elusive on the ice. He plays with good energy and gets involved in the play along the wall. He plays much bigger than his listed size and doesn't back down on the ice. He plays in the tough areas of the ice in the offensive zone; he's often around the net. He'll get pushed over because he's small and lacks the necessary strength right now, but doesn't mind the rough stuff. In the offensive zone, he has good creativity with the puck. He possesses a quick wrist shot that he uses to beat goaltenders; he has a quick release on said shot. He works hard on the backcheck; we've seen him create turnovers with a big effort there.

Overall, Sheshin has a good skill level, but he'll need to improve his speed a lot if he doesn't grow much more than he is now.

SIMONEAU, XAVIER
LC - Drummondville Voltigeurs (QMJHL) - 5'07" 172

Simoneau was one of the top rookies in the QMJHL this year; he finished the year with 45 points in 61 games. The Voltigeurs drafted Simoneau with their 2nd pick in the first round (9th overall) last June after they picked Dawson Mercer one spot ahead of him.

This year Simoneau was very impressive on a very good Drummondville team, he usually centered the 3rd line but also played on both special team units. The Gatineau product is a highly smart player which made his transition smoother to the QMJHL, his on ice vision is second to none as he makes players around him better. He's good on the power play because of his vision and playmaking ability. He likes to play on the half wall and control the play from there. Very impressive puck poise and showed confidence through the year. Simoneau is not only an offensive forward, but his compete level and work ethic is off the chart as well. He can play an agitating role on the ice and doesn't hesitate challenging opposing players physically and is always involved in scrums after whistle. He's good on the PK because of his great hockey sense and anticipation. He's also not afraid to block shots. The biggest limitation for Simoneau remains his size, he's very undersize listed at 5'07"172 and with his style of play there's some injury concern. At his size we would like to see him continue improve his speed, his speed is fine for major junior but to play in NHL we would like to see more explosiveness with his skating stride.

Drummondville will be a dominant team in the league next season and Simoneau should be a big part of it once again, probably moving to the number 2 center spot behind Veleno on the team depth chart.

SODERBLOM, ELMER
LW - Frolunda HC J18 (Allsvenskan) - 6'06" 212

Soderblom is a huge kid already at this young age, at 6'06" and over 210 pounds. It looks like he's done growing. This year, he was not only a regular for Sweden's U-17 team, but also split his season back home between the J18 Elit and the J18 Allsvenskan league and averaged over a point per game.

His biggest plus is his coordination despite his size. He can handle the puck and display soft hands, making various dragging dekes throughout our viewings. He has fluid hands and his long reach helps him a lot when it comes time to beating guys one-on-one. One area that needs improvement should not come as a surprise given his frame: his skating. His stabilizer-muscles are underdeveloped, so he can get knocked off the puck easily. This also forces him to lean forward to counteract his shifting weight when attempting to skate North-South. Even at this size right now, he can lose puck battles, as he's not solid on his skates. That should come with time, however. He lacks power in his base, so his acceleration doesn't fare any better than his poor top gear. In a couple of years, if he can add muscle and begin generating power in his stride, he could develop into an intriguing forward given the rest of his tools in his toolbox. He's good at playing the role in front of the net; he's tough to handle there, and once again, his reach is useful as he can reach loose pucks quickly near the net. There's a lot of growing and development ahead for Soderblom, but there's some upside there, and he's definitely an intriguing talent for the 2019 NHL Entry Draft with that size.

SODERSTROM, VICTOR
RD - Brynas IF J20 (SuperElit) - 5'11" 176

Soderstrom is a premiere prospect out of Sweden for the 2019 NHL Entry Draft. This season, he was a key player for Sweden's U-17 team in international play, and back home he split the season between the J18 and J20 leagues.

He's an aggressive offensive defenseman; he's at his best when in possession of the puck and we like how quickly he moves it in the transition game. He's got good skating abilities, and can easily rush the puck into the offensive zone and use his feet to make offensive plays in the offensive zone. He makes quick decisions with the puck on the power play; he moves pucks quickly and has great on-ice vision. In his zone, he's excellent to move the puck out, either by making a quick pass or by skating it out. He reminds us a bit of Adam Boqvist in terms of how quickly he processes the game; the puck is never on his stick for a long time. There was some inconsistency with his decision-making this year, mostly at the U-17s in November, but it was much better in later viewings during the year. He has good footwork and good agility on his skates, which helps him a lot when defending one-on-one as he can keep a good gap and makes good use of his stick to knock pucks down. He's not overly big, but he doesn't mind the physical game. There is some good timing with his hits and they have good impact. However, he'll need to get stronger physically in order to be more efficient to defend deep in his own zone and in front of his net against bigger and stronger players. To conclude, Soderstrom will be a player to watch out for next year. It should be interesting to see if he's able to crack a roster in the Swedish Elite League or if he'll be back in the SuperElit league (J20).

"Really impressed with what I saw from him this season." - HP Scout, Mark Edwards

SOJKA, DOMINIK
LC - HC Branska Bystrica U20 (Slovakia U20) 6'05" 196

Dominik Sojka is a two-way center who produced 12 points, including 7 goals in 28 games in the junior Slovakian circuit. In the playoffs he had 1 goal in 2 games and at the U18's he produced an assist in 5 games.

Dominik Sojka is a towering center who's incredibly difficult to deal with down-low. His awareness around the net area is a plus and he uses his enormous frame to force defenseman to play heavy minutes against him. Additionally, his length and his compete, allowed him to be difficult to handle off rebound attempts where he would get to pucks before most other players due to his length and he was willing to put himself in the dirty-areas to make a play. He showed a quality two-way game in most of our viewings by using his leverage and frame effectively during board battling sequences. Despite being very large, his skating technique isn't poor and he pushes off into a fluid stride which he used to quickly transition. More of a north-south Center and not overly creative when we saw him but there's upside in a player of Sojka's mold.

SPIRIDONOV, YEGOR
LW - Stalnye Lisy Magnitogorsk (MHL) 6'02" 192

Yegor Spiridonov had a good first season in the MHL for Stalnye, putting up 19 points in 39 games, including 10 goals. In the playoffs, he had a goal in 4 games. At international events, he was featured in both the U17's and the U18's where he put up 2 points in 5 games at each event.

Spiridonov is a tenacious two-way winger with a good degree of skill to compliment his motor. Yegor plays hard and competes, giving up little room when he's away from the puck while also demonstrating the understanding of how to use his frame during forechecking sequences. His stride is powerful and he has a good degree of separation speed that compliments his aggressive style of play, overwhelming defenders at times. He's got good puck skills and has a nose for the net area where he showed us a good amount of agility that he uses to bypass defenders in one-on-one situations and in high-traffic areas. He can make plays at high speeds, showing plus vision where he's capable of threading difficult passes and finding his teammates quickly. Additionally, he's got a good move-set and soft-hands that allow him to play a possession game down-low. He's the type of player who compliments high-end forwards and can be moved around in a line up.

SPROULE, EMMETT
LC - Erie Otters (OHL) 5'10" 146

Emmett Sproule was drafted 21st overall in the OHL Priority Selection. He had a decent year of production in his rookie season on a rebuilding Erie squad, producing 13 points in 56 games, with 8 assists.

Sproule is an intelligent center who competed both with and without the puck. One of Sproule's most noticeable qualities based off our viewings, was his ability to anticipate the play in advance. He was quick to react to his defenseman needing support and was adept at reading where his opponents were trying to pass the puck, cutting off their lanes consistently as a result. Unfortunately, despite his plus hockey-sense, he features a choppy stride that doesn't allow him to take advantage of his reads at the level he could if his stride was more fluid and developed at this time. Furthermore, he's underdeveloped physically, lacking a degree of power which hurts his initial push-off and leaves his shot with an underwhelming amount of power. That being said, his skill level is above-average and he's capable of making impressive passing plays off the rush. Sproule needs to continue to grow into his frame and put on significant muscle in order to take advantage of his hockey smarts.

STAIOS, NATHAN
LD - Windsor Spitfires (OHL) 5'08" 168

Staios is an undersized defender with fluid mobility and a strong compete level. Nathan shows strong mobility that he utilizes well on both sides of the puck. He shows quick feet and strong edges that allow him to elude a forecheck and quickly create space for himself. Nathan does a good job recognizing open ice and quickly exploiting it, pushing the pace in possession. A confident puck handler, Staios knows when to simplify his game but will attack the offensive zone when he has support. Inside the offensive zone Nathan is at his best, quickly opening shooting and passing lanes with his feet and utilizing his vision to distribute the puck. He has a deceptively heavy point shot and will likely produce more goals as he become more assertive with his shot. Staios uses his mobility to keep the play in front of him when defending in transition. He angles opponents well but can look to step up for the home run type open ice check leaving him exposed. Taking consistent routes to puck carriers or picking his spots physically more appropriately would be benefical. Staios is ultra competitive and tries to not let his size deter him, however he can lose body position when defending out of the corners or in transition simply due to his lack of size. Staios needs to be spot on with his reads, body position and stick for him to have success defending below the hash.

STARIKOV, LEV
LD - Windsor Spitfires (OHL) 6'07" 190

Starikov is two-way defender with intriguing physical talent and he competes hard. Lev possesses a tall and rangy frame that still has room to add strength to, which will make him an even tougher player to play against. He has a large wingspan an utilize his reach effectively both in transition and in the defensive zone, enhancing his contain while allowing him to strip puck. Starikov gets around the ice well, showing a long stride with power behind it, however his lateral quickness and four-way mobility due have room to improve. He shows confidence in possession and will willingly carry transition attacks up ice showing average puck control. Offensively Lev has displayed a heavy and accurate point shot, however utilizing it more frequently and getting it on the net will benefit his production. Defensively Starikov is tough to play against, he utilizes his strength to win battles and can be difficult to earn ice against in tight space. He plays physically and uses his reach and size to provide suffocating 1-on-1 defense below the hash. His foot-work can elevate as his issues are with smaller, quicker opponents who can dart in and out of space. A player who provides and honest and consistent effort, Starikov is still raw in some areas only adding to his intrigue.

STEVENSON, KEEGAN
RC - Guelph Storm (OHL) 6'0" 174

Keegan Stevenson was selected 102nd overall in the OHL Priority Selection. He had a decent rookie year as a depth forward, finishing with 10 points in 61 games, including 5 goals. He increased his production in the playoffs, scoring 3 points in 6 games.

Keegan is a two-way center with a high-level of compete. He displays above-average two-step area quickness and a decent top-gear which allowed him to apply pressure on the forecheck. He has no problem throwing his weight around and can deliver puck-separating hits both along the boards and in open-ice. He has a good motor and stays active along the boards when fighting for loose pucks or when tracking his man in his own-end of the ice. His passing ability is okay when he's involved in cycling the puck but he didn't display above-average vision when we watched him. He's willing to attack the goal-line though and had an impressive spin-around goal in one of our viewings. In order for Stevenson to become more noticeable on the ice heading into his draft year, he needs to refine the mechanics in his skating, due to having a choppy stride at this time and learn how to generate scoring chances on a more consistent shit-by-shift basis.

STRONDALA, VOJTECH
LC - HC Kometa Brno U20 (Czech U20) - 5'07" 154

Strondala is a fun player to watch, because he's a tireless worker and has some good skills. He's a late 2000-born, making him eligible for the 2019 NHL Entry Draft. This season, he played in the U20 league in the Czech Republic, and had 27 points in 32 games. He was a key member of the Czech U-18 team at various tournaments.

He's more of a playmaker than a scorer, but he has good vision and he's a smart player with the puck on his stick. He's not big, either, but has a big heart and plays bigger than his size. He keeps his feet moving all the time, playing with a ton of energy, and he's tough to counter one-on-one because of his agility and shiftiness. He works hard in all three zones, and we love his effort on the forecheck and how he can be really annoying for opposing defensemen. He has a quick stick as well. He doesn't have the size to overpower opponents, but he's smart in how he plays with his stick. In the defensive zone, he has good awareness, and he's a good on the PK. Often, you'll see him deep in his own zone supporting his defensemen to help them retrieve pucks and try to start the transition game. There's a lot to like about this player, but his size is a big limitation for him as far as NHL potential goes. He's also not a high-end offensive player when we project him for the next level. He would make a good pick for a CHL team in the Import Draft.

SUZUKI, RYAN
LC- Barrie Colts - (OHL) 6'0" 172

Suzuki is a very effective player. He sees the ice very well and has the ability to lead teammates into open pockets of ice, which makes him a very effective puck distributor. He doesn't possess game breaking speed but he is quick enough to keep defenders on their toes., Skating is definitely not a concern. He is effective rushing the puck through the neutral zone and really seems to put a premium on gaining the line with possession. In the offensive zone, Suzuki is slippery,. one second a man is on him, and the next he's found a soft spot and is waiting for someone to feed him the puck in a dangerous area. He's very good at getting open, although his shot isn't good enough yet for him to take advantage of those opportunities as often as he should.

Defensively, effort is never a question with him. He backchecks hard and is smart enough to know where he has to be or who he should be covering.

All in all, he had a successful rookie season. He should play an even bigger role next season for what should once again be a strong Barrie team. He's poised to be picked in the 1st round in 2019.

SWANKLER, AUSTEN
LC - Oakland Jr. Grizzlies U16 (HPHL) 5'11" 157

Swankler was one of those underage prospect we thought could have played in the USHL this past season but a deep and older roster in Dubuque would have prevented him from getting much quality ice time. Swankler is out of the Pittsburgh Elite Penguins program but joined the Oakland Grizzlies program this season and switched his commitment from RPI to the University of Michigan in November. Austen has average size and strength but plays a much bigger game than he looks. Swankler takes the puck and himself to the net well. He shows good compete and strength in those areas and wins more than his fair share of those battles. He stays over top of the puck and shows good escapability from tight areas with the puck. He has high end skill and playmaking ability especially in tight areas, shown by his 38 goals and 63 Assists in 63 Games for the Grizzlies this year. Swankler's skating is above average and shows a good motor at both ends of the ice. Austen has good anticipation and a quick stick which allows him to read plays in the neutral zone and pick off passes and turn plays quickly in transition. Swankler was a 3rd Round draft pick of Ottawa (OHL) in the 2017 OHL Draft as well as Waterloo (USHL) in the 9th Round but looks to be committed to going the NCAA route at this stage.

TEPLY, MICHAL
RW/LW - Bili Tygri Liberec U20 (Czech U20) - 6'03" 176

Teply has great size already, and his puck-protection game is already good at this young age. He has a long reach and uses his body well to keep opponents away from the puck. He's good along the boards and down low to keep possession of the puck. This year, he played at both the U-17 and U-18 levels internationally for the Czech Republic. He lacks the speed required to be a better offensive contributor on the ice; he lacks acceleration and quickness and his top speed is only average. There's a lot of work that needs to be done with Teply's skating in the off-season. He's a good forechecker, he works hard and he's pretty smart out there. His skill level is average, as he does not have the best hands either, and he doesn't have big upside offensively. A lot of his scoring chances come from hard work down low and in front of the net instead of high-end skill plays. With his size and smarts, he has the chance to be a player down the road, but his skating will need to get better if he wants any chance to play in the NHL at some point.

THOMSON, LASSI
RD - Ilves U20 (Jr.A SM-liiga) - 6'00" 187

Thomson is a late-2000 who played in the U20 league this season in Finland, amassing 12 goals and 27 points in 49 games. He also played various tournaments for Finland's U-18 team (such as the Five Nations' in November, the Five Nations' in February and the U-18 World Hockey Championships in April).

Thomson is a good skater. He has a good and powerful stride that he uses well to skate the puck out of his zone often, and can rush it into the offensive zone on the power play. He uses his good footwork to quickly retrieve pucks in his own zone. He can contribute offensively, as he proved with his 12 goals this season; he possesses a heavy and accurate shot from the point. He likes to put the puck on net and won't hesitate to throw pucks there. He has decent size and can play physically along the boards. With his good footwork, he can defend well one-on-one; in February at the Five Nations' Tournament he did some good work versus the speedy Jakub Lauko, not giving him much room to manoeuvre offensively. This season was the first year Thomson played for the national team, having never played for the U-18 or U-17 team prior to the November Five Nations' Tournament. He could be considered as a bit of a late-bloomer, and next year, he could get his first action in the top men's league in Finland (Liiga).

THRUN, HENRY
LD - USA NTDP-17 (USHL) - 6'01" 183

Thrun was one of the good defensemen on the American U-17 team this past season, and was also called up to play in some games with the U-18 team over the course of the season because of his good performance.

Thrun is a smart two-way defenseman with good skating abilities. He has good size already, and covers a lot of ice with his mobility and active stick in the defensive zone. He has a good gap control and he's quick to pressure the puck-carrier into making decisions. His skating is good, and he also possesses quick acceleration that he can use when trying to get away from forechecking pressure in his own zone. With that separation speed, he's quite adept at rushing the puck out of his zone. Offensively, he's not very flashy; he makes simple plays with the puck in the offensive zone. He possesses a powerful shot from the point. We like his smarts, but we're unsure as to how much upside there is with him offensively. We feel that right now he's not at the same level as Cam York, but we're looking forward to watching him perform next season. Thrun is committed to Harvard for the 2019-2020 season.

TOMAN, MATEJ
RW - HC Ceske Budejovice (Czech2) - 5'10" 168

Toman is a good two-way forward who has shown flashes throughout the year of some good offensive skills. He showed an above-average shooting ability and scored some very nice goals that led us to believe that there's a good upside there. He can set up plays as well, with his above-average vision. He's a smart hockey player who is as good with the puck as he is without it. He's good on the forecheck; he works hard and has good anticipation to read the plays in front of him. He has good poise with the puck in the offensive zone. He keeps his feet moving in the offensive zone; we saw him score some goals where he kept his feet moving in front of the net, allowing him to be first on puck and get a goal.

TOMASINO, PHILLIP
RC - Niagara IceDogs (OHL) 5'11", 180

Tomasino is a player to watch for the 2019 NHL Draft. Although his production did not break any scoring records, as much of his TOI saw rookie minutes on the third or forth line, yet each game he displayed his hockey intelligence and high compete level. In his first season in the OHL, Tomasino did not shy away from the physical play and battled versus older players to establish puck possession. He has a very solid stride in which he can generate power and create separation. He handles the puck well in traffic and in transition. The offensive instincts shine around the net as he reads plays well, although he also is cognizant of his defensive responsibilities as again his awareness shines. With his offensive skill sets and high hockey IQ, it would not be unquestionable to see Tomasino double or even triple his scoring output next season as he sees more opportunity on the power play and consistent 5v5 ice time. As he gains more size, strength and confidence his game will grow. A two-way center to keep an eye upon next season.

"Obviously one of the higher picks in OHL Draft in 2017, yet the transition as true rookie is not the easiest with lack of opportunity and age difference. Tomasino handled himself well in each viewing. You can see the smarts and potential. Wouldn't be surprised if he starts making bigger name for 2019 NHL Draft next season." -HP Scout, Russ Bitely

TURAN, OLIVER
RD - Brookings Blizzard (NAHL) - 6'05" 218

Turan is a big Slovak defender who played in North America this season, but was a good performer as an underager for the Slovak team in August at the Ivan Hlinka Tournament and in April at the U-18 World Hockey Championships.

He's a towering presence who can skate relatively well given his enormous stature. He has impressive skating abilities for a kid of this size and age. He can surprise with his acceleration when rushing the puck, and he's good with his transitional play either with his feet or his passing abilities. He showed poise with the puck, and knows his limitations when carrying it. He rarely extends past his limits, which creates a relatively mistake-free game. Offensively, he's not the most creative player with the puck on his stick, which limits his upside, but he has a good slapshot and he's not shy to put pucks on net. He has good puck poise in both the offensive and defensive zones. He won't get rushed into making a decision, and his confidence is another plus to the impressive package that he offers. Turan has good potential as a two-way defenseman with that impressive size and skillset, and next season, he will be eligible to play in the CHL.

TURCOTTE, ALEX
LC - USA NTDP-17 (USHL) - 5'11" 183

Turcotte comes from a hockey family. His father (Alfie) was a first-round pick of the Montreal Canadiens, and his grandfather played at Michigan State from 1959 to 1962. Alex was a little bit overshadowed by Jack Hughes' in the first half of the season, but once Hughes left for the U18 team, he took over the number one center role and was the team's most complete player. He was a standout player at the U17's in November, and did great as an underager at the U18's in April. Overall this season, he amassed 63 points in 58 games playing with both the U17 and U18 teams this season.

He's a player with excellent skating abilities. He plays the game at a high tempo, has a solid work ethic and a great compete level. He's not tall, but he has a stocky frame and is strong on his skates, which helps him protect the puck along the boards. He really takes pride in the small details of the game away from the puck; he's an assertive player and recognizes the play on the defensive side of the puck, supporting his defense consistently. Offensively, the quality that stuck out the most was his ability to make highly-technical passes while in motion. He made several no-look tape-to-tape passes behind him while he was cutting through traffic, resulting in quality scoring chances for his teammates. His playmaking abilities are excellent and made everyone around him better. He has excellent puck skills, great vision, and he executed plays with a purpose. Turcotte is a high-end offensive prospect, and once you add his advanced defensive game, you get an excellent prospect for the 2019 NHL Entry Draft.

TYUVILIN, DMITRI
LD - Loko-Yunior Yaroslavl (NMHL) - 5'11" 170

Tyuvilin was one of the rare players to play in both the November and February U-17 Five Nations' Tournament this year for Russia. He's an average-sized defenseman who can contribute offensively with some good reads and a good wrist shot from the point. He has good footwork with good lateral agility, but he'll need to improve his top speed and explosiveness, which would make him more of a threat when he's rushing the puck from his own zone. He has good skills to be a power play guy right now; he was used often on the power play this year with the national U-17 team. He moves the puck well enough from his own zone, but his decision-making could be quicker. He does a good job getting his puck through to the net. He can also play a physical game in his own end, even if he doesn't have ideal size to play a high-impact physical game. He has a decent skill level, but he's not top shelf from what we've seen this year from him.

VALENTI, YANNIK
RW - Jungadler Mannheim U19 (DNL) - 5'10" 174

Valenti is a late-2000 birthday who missed the 2018 NHL Entry Draft by 9 days. This season, he played his second season with the Jungadler Mannheim U19 team, and averaged just under a goal per game (25 goals in 26 games). He also played 4 games in the top German men's league but was held pointless.

He has some dynamic qualities to his game; his hands are fluid and quick. He likes to have the puck on his stick, has good one-on-one abilities and challenges opposing defensemen one-on-one frequently. He skates well, and has quick feet plus good acceleration and good top speed. He's not big, and will need to get stronger for the next level to absorb the physical play better and be stronger on the puck. He'll also need to learn to be more consistent from game to game and work harder away from the puck. He's good on the power play because of his skill level, and has more room to manoeuvre than at even-strength. He's more of a scoring winger than a playmaker; he likes to shoot the puck on net and he has a good wrist shot with a quick release.

Valenti is expected to make the move to North America next season for his draft year, as it was reported that he'll report to the Vancouver Giants for the 2018-2019 season. The Giants drafted Valenti last summer 66th overall in the CHL Import Draft.

VLASIC, ALEX
LD - USA NTDP-17 (USHL) - 6'05"190

Vlasic has a very promising combination of size and tools. The first thing that stands out about this defender is his combination of size and mobility. He has a lot of room to grow into his frame, however, he's already powerful for his age and has surprising straight-line speed and moves laterally along the blueline pretty well. This allows him to move the puck up the ice efficiently and regain his positioning during recovery plays. His edges do need to improve, though, as he can get beaten occasionally in one-on-one situations where the opposition changes directions on him quickly. That being said, he plays with poise and has sound positioning in his own end, using his reach and an active stick to break up several offensive chances. Although raw offensively, he has good shooting mechanics and generates velocity in his point-shots. He was also aware of shooting lanes and timed his release well. His first pass is accurate, and he can make stretch passes to his teammates. Vlasic showed some good two-way potential and is an intriguing prospect for the 2019 NHL Entry Draft. Vlasic is committed to play college hockey at Boston University for the 2019-2020 season.

VUKOJEVIC, MICHAEL
LD - Kitchener Rangers (OHL) 6'02.25" 201

Michael was selected 33rd overall in the second round of the 2017 OHL Draft by the Kitchener Rangers. He was also selected in the first round, 8th Overall by the Green Bay Gamblers of the USHL Futures Draft. This past season he played for both teams, where he put up 2 assists in 12 games for the Gamblers and had 5 points in 24 games for the Rangers. In the playoffs, he produced 10 points in 19 games, further cementing himself as a potential first round pick in the 2019 NHL draft.

Vukojevic is a powerful, two-way defenseman with high-end mobility. He possesses intriguing physical tools along with a strong two-way skill set and above average hockey sense. Michael possesses the ability to dominate a game from his defensive position, showing a physicality to his game along with offensive upside. A powerful skater with a long and fluid stride, who has further developed his straight-line speed and utilizes it well. He see's the ice well and shows an ability to make a hard and accurate first pass. He will also exploit open skating lanes and carry the puck up ice, creating offense in transition, while becoming tough to contain as he enters the zone. Vukojevic can thrive offensively, utilizing his powerful and accurate point shot, while showing some vision from the back end, which allows him to distribute the puck with effectiveness. He keeps strong gaps and takes away the centre of the ice by subtly angling opponents to low percentage areas before separating his opponent from the puck with contact. This skill is further enhanced by his wingspan and aggressiveness. He learned how to react to offensively-gifted players in the OHL this past season and once he adapted to the pace, he began pinching at the appropriate times which generated several scoring chances.

VYLETELKA, SAMUEL
G - Little Caesars U18 (Midget) 6'02" 192

Samuel Vyletelka posted a 2.03 GAA in 30 games in Midget and produced a 3.67 GAA with a .902 save percentage in 4 games at the U18's where he showed a high-level of compete despite his team getting outmatched in some games.

Vyletelka is an aggressive and reflexive goalie with a good frame. There's a good mix of size, compete and lateral movement in Samuel, which allowed him to make several high-end saves at the U18's, none better than a blocker stop he made against Russia as he was caught going the wrong way but still came away with the desperation save. There's a lack of refinement in his butterfly and he let in leaky goals on occasion, plus due to having power when he pushes off, he can sometimes throw himself out of position which causes him to lose his technique during recovery plays. However, he's good at challenging most shot attempts, and his ability to transition from the ice to a standing position is good. Furthermore, he flashed a coordinated glove and blocker hand, had good rebound control and displayed a lot of confidence in the net. There was a certain level of net presence that he displayed and never appeared to look over-matched against top competition at the end of the year.

WARREN, MARSHALL
LD - USA NTDP-17 (USHL) 5'11" 161

Marshall is committed to Harvard University and just finished his first season with the US National program U-17 team. He's easy to notice on the ice because of his excellent skating ability; he's fluid on his skate and at his best when he's using his feet to make plays. He's excellent for his team transition game, whether if it's for retrieving pucks in his own end, moving the puck quickly out of his zone or to rush the puck from his own zone. He's not the biggest player physically, he doesn't mind the physical game but can get overpower deep in his zone or in front of his net by bigger forwards. He competes well and is work ethic is solid. His decision making is solid, he thinks the game quickly and has good anticipation which helps him defend.

WASHKURAK, KEEAN
LC - Mississauga Steelheads - 5'10" 174

Washkurak is an energetic forward with a competitiveness to his game. Keean possesses an excellent motor that allows him to wreak havoc on the forecheck and find an effectiveness on the penalty kill. He shows reliable three zone play and good positional awareness on both sides of the puck. Keean shows an intelligence to his game in his ability to put himself in strong positions to succeed both offensively and defensively by anticipating the play. Washkurak is a deceptive skater as he quickly moves his feet and has a fairly good first step. However a lack of power behind his stride makes it awkward and limits his ability to accelerate to an above average top speed. His energetic style of play makes him effective complimenting skill or playing in a check role, where he mostly saw ice time with the Steelheads this season. Offensively Keean shows limitations as his production came by working hard and getting to the right areas, and not so much on pure skill. Improving his strength will be important if he wishes to find more success as an energetic, two-way forward.

WILLIAMS, JOSH
RW - Medicine Hat Tigers (WHL) 6'01" 185

Josh Williams is a skilled winger and former 5th overall pick in the 2016 Bantam Draft. He struggled early on in his WHL career to earn ice time but gained confidence and began producing in the second half of the season, finishing with 11 goals and 20 points in 47 regular season games. Williams was a dominant player in the World U17 summer camp, showing explosiveness and great level skill against his peers. He was arguably the best offensive player at the camp, but failed to translate that early in the season for the Tigers. He failed to receive icetime consistently, but began to generate the confidence of his coaches later in the season, beginning to produce and be a presence in the slot on the team's top powerplay unit.

Williams is dynamic with the puck. He has explosive feet, both with his top end speed and in quick stops and starts. In the offensive zone he can change speeds and create space with both his feet and hands, and it makes him difficult to defend in space. Off the rush he make use of his ability to create space by getting pucks off quickly with his hard shot. His individual offensive skill is very high. The issue is that this skill level is not seen consistently, and his confidence level wavered as the season progressed. Although improvement was shown, he has much more to give offensively, and his own head is the only thing stopping him for reaching that next level.

YORK, CAM
LD - US National U-17 team (USNTDP) - 5'11" 165

York is originally from California, and was a standout performer this year with the American U-17 national program. He eventually finished the season playing at the U-18 World Hockey Championships, where he was one of the top defensemen for his team.

The first thing you notice with him: his skating abilities. He has great footwork, fluid strides and good agility. He's very poised with the puck, there is no panic with him on the ice and he makes sounds decision with the puck. He's good on the power play; his puck-moving distribution is excellent and he has above-average vision. He's also good at putting pucks on net and finding shooting lanes thanks to his patience with the puck and low level of panic. His shot is above-average and accurate, and with added strength could add more velocity, which would make him more of a threat to score from the point. He has made some good strides this season in his defensive game, his gap control is much better now and it's one of the reasons he was entrusted with the U-18s in April. He has learned to use his stick more in the defensive end. He has average size for a defenseman, but with his skating abilities and offensive upside, he fits better with the new kind of hockey we see these days in the NHL. He'll need to get bigger and stronger to compete more physically along the boards and in front of the net. York is a smart defender who doesn't make a lot of mistakes on the ice. His decision-making is quick and usually good. York will be back next season next season with the NTDP, and he's committed to play college hockey at Boston College.

ZEGRAS, TREVOR
LC - USA NTDP-17 (USHL) - 5'11" 159

Zegras is a New York state kid who had a great first year with the US program, amassing 59 points in 56 games this season.

We love his stickhandling abilities. He has an above-average speed to go with them, and this mix makes him a dangerous player one-on-one. He loves to have the puck on his stick and has the talent to make plays in the offensive zone. He loves to rush the puck from his own zone, and his puck skills are excellent. He can sometimes beat guys easily one-on-one. However, sometimes he does try too much with the puck and could be better served by sharing it more when rushing it. He's a good skater and has good agility while in possession of the puck to avoid hits along the boards. He has a quick shot with an excellent release and has proven to be a capable goal-scorer last season. He's not the biggest player, but didn't mind getting involved physically. However, he currently lacks the strength to win those one-on-one battles, despite his good compete level. Away from the puck, he showed that he's not only a skills' guy, but he also works hard on the backcheck and shows good support down low in his zone.

Zegras' bread-and-butter remain his offensive skills. As a centre, he's playing behind Alex Turcotte, and won't always have the toughest matchups. Still, look for him to put some good numbers on the table next season. His skill level is definitely above-average, and if he can get a bit bigger, he could be a great player down the road.

2020 NHL DRAFT PROSPECTS

AUSTIN, TYE
G - Kanata Lasers (HEO) 6'03.75" 171

Tye was selected in the 3rd Round, 43rd overall by the Peterborough Petes at the 2018 OHL Priority Selection Draft. Austin is a big goaltender who played for Kanata in the HEO U18 league this year. He split the games this year, but posted respectful numbers when he played with a 2.60 GAA, and a 910% save percentage while in the crease. Tye is a athletic goalie which is surprising with his size, he is good at cover his angles as he relies a lot on his size not giving shooter much room to shoot. Tye is good at challenging the shooter by being aggressive in the crease, he's good at getting to the top of crease on point shots and again not giving a lot of net for shooters to look at, the biggest issue is he will sometimes be over aggressive with coming out to challenge, and if the puck got by him and bounced off the boards there isn't enough time for him to get back in the net to make the 2nd or 3rd save. Tye is a butterfly goalie, and with his size covers the upper and lower parts of the net really well. He has quick feet and good lateral movement, and can recover quickly to make those 2nd or 3rd saves when he sets up properly. He has a competitive edge to him as well, verbal on the ice, he has good rebound control with high shots as he is able to suck the pucks into his chest and covering up and not giving up rebounds, he needs to work on his low shot rebound control as he tends to kick a lot of rebounds out into the slot and not into the corners. He was good at tracking pucks and battling to get around defenders looking for the point shots or shots high in the zone. Tye already has the size and athleticism for the next level, he just needs to get stronger overall and work on being a little bit more patient in the crease and allow the pucks to come to him instead chasing the pucks.

BARRON, JUSTIN
RD - Halifax Mooseheads (QMJHL) - 6'01" 188

Barron was the top defenseman from the 2017 QMJHL draft class and he didn't disappointed this year in his rookie season with the Mooseheads finishing with 21 points in 51 games. He also played at the U-17 in November but was hurt and couldn't played in the final vs team USA.

Barron has impressive poise and smarts on the ice, he only turned 16 in mid-November but he had the calmness of a veteran out there. Very cool and composed under pressure, never seems to panic on the ice. He makes the smart plays most of the time, he can skate the puck out with his good skating ability, he can make a good first pass as well and won't force a play as he preferred to keep making the simple plays and not make turnovers. Over the course of the season, he continued to earn the trust of the coaching staff along the way, used regularly in a top-4 role with special teams time and he is as trusted as any of the veterans already. As the season progressed he was more confident with the puck and was making more plays in the offensive zone and was trying to create more offense. He has good size, good mobility and reach. Has a solid frame to handle the size of junior forwards and the great skating ability to match any of the most dangerous players in the league, and has already shown some promise as a matchup, shutdown-style defender. Defensively he's tough to beat one on one and he's valuable on the PK unit with his long stick and shot blocking ability. Barron is more of a two-way defenseman than an offensive defenseman but his offensive abilities are still developing and he could have a big year next year as he could end up on the top pairing.

"He was often Halifax's top defenseman in the 2nd half. Really like his smarts and poise." - HP Scout Jérôme Bérubé

"It's very early, but he has the makings of a first rounder for 2020." - HP Scout Jérôme Bérubé

BEAUDOIN, CHARLES
RW - Cantonniers de Magog (LHMAAAQ) - 6'00" 168

Without a shadow of a doubt, the "sniper" label can be found next to this Cantonniers de Magog forward, Charles Beaudoin. In his first Midget AAA campaign, the right-hander recorded 24 regular-season goals, which was good for sixth overall in Midget AAA. He also added 14 assists in 38 games, ending his season with a point per game. This is without counting the seven goals he scored at the CCM Challenge held in Gatineau last December, where he performed very well, and was selected as a member of the All-Star Team at the end of the competition.

Beaudoin's talents as a natural goal scorer are eloquent: he has a powerful and constantly dangerous shot, and does not need a lot of space to let his quick release go and become a threat to the opposing team. Also, he is often in the right place at the right time, and rarely misses an opportunity to score. The Bromont native is a very good skater who has a powerful, wide, smooth and well-balanced stride, so he's hard to be destabilized while in control of the puck. He can make some nice passes in the offensive zone as well, but his decision-making was inconsistent this season. His acceleration is not one of his strengths, but he becomes threatening once his cruising speed is reached. However, the forward will have to work on his discipline, as on several occasions this season, he was on the receiving end of some bad penalties in the offensive zone. Beaudoin was drafted 11th overall by Shawinigan in the 2018 QMJHL draft.

BELANGER, ALEC
LD - Barrie Jr. Colts (OMHA-ETA) 5'11" 185

Alec was selected in the 3rd Round, 44th overall by the Ottawa 67's at the 2018 OHL Priority Selection Draft. Belanger is an offensive minded defender with good mobility. Alec possesses good skating abilities that allow him to thrive on both sides of the puck. A player who is at his best in possession, Belanger utilizes his foot-speed to push the pace in transition showing a confidence and creativity with the puck. Alec has an elusiveness to his game as he handles the puck well and can create space with his change of pace/direction abilities. A player who can gain the offensive zone with relative ease, Belanger looks to create once in the zone showing vision and creativity. Belanger does need to learn when to simplify his game however as to often he will look to create something when there are no options, resulting in turnovers and him caught up ice. Offensively Alec does a good job picking when to inject from his point position. He often is able to create shooting lanes and get his shots on goal, showing an ability to beat goalies clean from distance. Offensively Belanger possesses several intriguing tools that allow him to generate opportunities. While defending transition Alec uses his mobility to keep the play in front of him and his often able to force the play to the outside, using an active stick to increase his defensive effectiveness. Where he struggles is in the defensive zone. He can lose positional awareness and focus to frequently on the puck carrier and not his check. He inconsistently competes defensively and can be somewhat soft in puck/position battles. His decision making under pressure is inconsistent, however his quick feet and strong edges often allow him to elude pressure. However quicker decisions will be necessary at the next level.

BENIERS, MATT
LC - Milton Academy/Cape Cod Whalers U16 (NE Prep/MHSL U16) 5'10" 156

Beniers has grown physically over the last year, though still average in size, yet takes advantage of his skating ability with speed, ability, and balance. Beniers plays with pace, high compete level, good stick skills, and playmaking ability as he sees the ice well and possesses high hockey intelligence to read plays, especially with his offensive instincts. As a freshman and first season in the New England Prep School ranks, the left-handed pivot led his team in scoring with 11-16-27 in 23 GP. He was recently named to the USNTDP-17 roster and has NCAA offers from Boston College, Boston University, and Harvard. Beniers is one of the top players in the New England area for the '02 age level.

BERARD, BRETT
LW - Bishop Hendricken HS/Cape Cod Whalers U16 (RI HS/MHSL U16) 5'6" 135

Berard is a Rhode Island product that is already committed in-state to Providence and most recently was offered roster position on NTDP-17 for next season. He is not the biggest of players yet skates well and is shifty on his skates. Berard is a playmaker with offensive tools with good vision and possesses a powerful shot for undersized player. He's an athletic kid who will also play with some sandpaper.

JÉRÉMIE BIAKABUTUKA
RD - Riverains Collège Charles-Lemoyne - 6'03" 185

Biakabutuka is a defenseman with high-end tools and upside. The big right-handed defenseman skates well for his size, and particularly possesses good straight-line speed that makes him a valuable puck-carrier. His best attribute is his shot. He possesses a heavy release and is a really good shot generator, shooting 108 times this season. He'll need to improve the accuracy on his shot, and his shot-selection. His hockey sense is average, but his decision-making and readings improved throughout the season. Biakabutuka played huge minutes for his team this season in every situation. With the right development, he projects as an all-around defenseman with size and great athletic tools, who can be used as a shooter on the power play. He's a great athlete and has good genes, as his uncle Tim Biakabutuka was a star running-back with the University of Michigan and in the NFL with the Carolina Panthers. With his size, he's ready to play in the QMJHL next season was drafted 17th overall by the Val D'Or Foreurs in June.

BIONDI, BLAKE
RC - Hermantown Hawks (MNHS) 5'11" 174

Biondi, recently drafted in the 1st Round, 8th Overall in this year's USHL Futures Draft by the Sioux City Musketeers, is a highly intelligent and highly skilled forward who has displayed a second gear with the puck on his stick. After a very offensive productive final year for the Hermantown Bantam AA team, Biondi made the adjustment to older competition this year. First with his play for Team North in the Fall Midwest Elite League and eventually with Hermantown High School by scoring 30 Goals and 28 assists in 31 Games for the Hawks. After an impressive Elite League performance in the fall, Blake gave a verbal commitment to nearby Minnesota Duluth. Blake already has a good sized frame, and has time to grow into it before his first draft eligible year in 2020. Biondi displays great hands and stickhandling ability, especially in tight areas. Blake displays a high end hockey IQ at both ends of the ice and for all the offensive skill he can provide, he plays a hard 200 foot game for such a young player.

BOLTMANN, JAKE
RD - Edina Hornets (MNHS) 6'00" 154

Boltmann is a late 01' Birthdate and a 2nd Round selection of Central Illinois in the 2017 USHL Futures Draft. Boltmann plays a smart stay at home defensive game and uses his skating ability and hockey sense to make reliable plays with the puck coming out of his own end. Boltmann has displayed excellent patients and vision of the ice and is able to stretch the ice both North South and east West and finds his forwards in stride in the neutral zone. Boltmann supports his defensive partner well, stays in solid defensive position when defending one on one and makes the opposition pay the price in front of his own net. Jake doesn't have a lot of offensive creativity but can chip in on the offense by using his vision and crisp passing ability in the offensive zone. Boltmann saw 4 games for Central Illinois this past season and certainly will be in the running for a spot at camp but it remains to be seen where Boltmann will play next season. Jake is committed to the University of Minnesota.

BORDELEAU, THOMAS
LC - Phénix du Collège Esther-Blondin (LHMAAAQ) - 5'09" 163

Bordeleau was a noticeable player since the beginning of the season, and didn't disappoint anybody this year. In his second year in the LHMAAAQ, he finished second in the league with 64 points. Bordeleau was lethal on the man-advantage, as he got many points in these situations. He had more time to set up his plays and find his linemates. Bordeleau excels at passing the puck thanks to his great vision, one that allows him to make unbelievable passes. He's one of the few that are able to make plays at high speed with the puck. Despite having excellent accuracy with his shot, and despite his 26 goals, Bordeleau needs to improve the power in his wrist shot to become more dangerous around the net and make him more unpredictable. Like his father, Sébastien, Thomas is somehow a little undersized, and it is something that might slow him down at some point when he'll face bigger and stronger opponents. Nevertheless, Bordeleau has good tools, good skating abilities and an above-average hockey IQ that will help him to find ways to overcome his small stature. Bordeleau is committed to play for the NTDP program in Plymouth next season; he is a dual-citizen, as he was born in Houston when his dad played there. His QMJHL rights are owned by the Blainville-Boisbriand Armada who drafted him with the 86th overall pick but he would had been a top 10 pick if not of his commitment with the NTDP.

BOURQUE, MAVRIK
RC, Estacades de Trois-Rivières (LHMAAAQ) - 5'09" 154

Expectations were pretty high for this right-handed centre this season. After a few games adapting to the speed of Midget AAA, Bourque made sure to meet these expectations; we could even say surpass them. His skillset is very impressive, whether we're talking about his fluid skating strides while in possession of the puck, his great passing abilities or his wrist shot. He did take a few games before fully trusting his wrist shot, but once he did, we saw a mix of a quick release, precision and power that can surprise any goalie at this level. He's also deadly in tight spaces with his quick hands and decision-making skills. His hockey sense is among the best in this draft class, as he sees everything on the ice and anticipates every move defenders are about to make, while also being aware of his teammates' intentions. That makes him one of the top playmakers available. Even if he's not the biggest player, he uses his reach and can outsmart opponents to protect the puck effectively. However, his lack of size and strength is probably the area he could improve upon the most if he wants to continue to perform at the same level in the QMJHL. Even though he's not as spectacular in his own zone, he uses his smarts to be efficient. He's also good on the backcheck and on the forecheck thanks to his speed, quickness and anticipation. While he can close the gap with opponents quickly to apply pressure on them, he's really not a physical player and would rather keep his feet moving than complete his checks. That being said, he's not afraid to go in the corners or through traffic in the slot area. He has the ability to elevate his game when it matters the most (such as overtime and the playoffs). Bourque has everything it takes to be a top playmaker and first-line centre in the QMJHL. He was drafted third overall by Shawinigan in June.

BUTLER, BLAKE
RC - Lambton Jr. Sting (MHAO), 5'11.5" 190

Butler was selected in the 3rd Round, 46th overall by the Sudbury Wolves at the 2018 OHL Priority Selection Draft. Butler is a skilled centre who uses his near six foot frame to protect the puck and accelerate in the offensive zone ad has a strong puck possession game. He can be unpredictable in the offensive zone, sometimes looking to pass, while other times utilizing his shot, which is quite good. He is equally strong in his passing and shooting game, making him more difficult to defend. For a such a skilled player, he plays a physical brand of hockey and was the only draft eligible player in the Alliance to finish top 15 in points and PIM's. Butler can change speeds and catch defenders flat footed then has the puck skills to finish of plays. His first few steps need to improve, but Blake has all the offensive tools to be a top six forward in the OHL. He plays a physical style of game that will open more ice for his linemates, while also possessing the skill to finish or create offence. His defensive game has room for improvement.

BUTLER, CAMERON
RW - York-Simcoe Express (OMHA-ETA) 6'04" 190

Cameron was selected in the 2nd Round, 27th overall by the Peterborough Petes at the 2018 OHL Priority Selection Draft. Butler is a big bodied winger with skill to his game. Cameron possesses a combination of skill and physical gifts that make him an intriguing prospect. He is at best when utilizing his size and strength to engage physically while still utilizing the skilled elements of his game to generate offensive opportunities. To often throughout the season Butler was either using his size and strength to play physically or his skill to create. Rarely did we see Butler combine the two most intriguing elements of his game to dominate, however when he did he was able to take over the play. Butler possesses powerful and fluid stride that allows him to generate above average speed. He can be very difficult to contain when attacking the offensive zone with pace and he can simply lean on opponents and gain the lane towards the goal. Cameron does show good puck handling abilities and will efficiently create space by beating an opponent 1-on-1 with his puck skills. He does show a tendency to over-handle the puck at times and can be vulnerable to turnovers in the neutral zone. Offensively Butler possesses a strong release and velocity behind his shot, however his ability to finish plays in tight suffered towards the end of the year. Improving the quickness of his hands in tight areas would be beneficial. Cameron will need to improve the consistency in which he competes as he can begin to rely on his skill and size package an lack a real competitiveness. Improving his play defensively and away from the puck would also be beneficial. A player with imposing size and a great shot, Butler has all the tools to be an great player, however his lack of poise at times can be a detriment to his game.

BYFIELD, QUINTON
LC - York-Simcoe Express (OMHA-ETA) 6'03.75" 207

Quinton was selected first round, first overall by the Sudbury Wolves at the 2017 OHL Priority Selection Draft. Byfield is an elite talent with a combination of size, speed, skill and smarts that allows him to dominate. Quinton showed a consistency to his game throughout the season and remained our top prospect from start to finish. A player who possesses a strong compete level in combination with his great skill, Byfield can have a strong impact on both sides of the puck. Byfield possesses strong skating abilities, displaying an explosive first step and powerful stride that allows him to effortlessly generate speed and create separation for a check. His combination of size and speed often pushes back defenders and allows him time and space to make a skilled play. Quinton shows impressive awareness of his options when attacking in transition and shows an intriguing amount of versatility in his ability to create. Byfield will utilize his strength, skill and speed to beat opponents wide to the goal, utilize the opponent as screen for a shot or find a trailing or attacking teammate with a slick pass. Offensively Quinton does a good job recognizing and attacking space, exploiting any open lanes opponents give him. He does a good job utilizing his shot when in high percentage scoring areas, showing an above average release, good velocity and strong accuracy. A player who has all the ability to dictate the pace of play, he is confident and creative in possession. Byfield can dominate the play along the wall and below the hash-marks, utilizing his puck protection skills and physical attributes to simply drive where he wants to go at any given time. His ability to recognize passing and shooting options off the cycle is impressive. Quinton often makes quick, high percentage decisions with the puck and shows excellent awareness away from the puck, displaying a strong hockey IQ. Unlike most highly skilled forward, Byfield provides a strong effort on the back-check and engaged defensive zone play. He kills penalties and recognizes how to clog shooting lanes and force the play to the outside. If there is one small knock on Quinton its his puck control. Quinton projects to be one of the top players available for the 2020 NHL Draft and a potential candidate to play at the NHL level at 18 years old.

CARDWELL, ETHAN
RC - Clarington Toros (OMHA-ETA) 5'09.5" 157

Ethan was selected second round, 33rd overall by the Saginaw Spirit at the 2018 OHL Priority Selection Draft. Cardwell is an undersized, skilled forward with good speed and creativity to his game. Ethan possesses an explosive first step and strong skating abilities which is the foundation of his offensive game. He often is able to create space with his speed and will exploit the time and space given to him with skill. Cardwell however possesses the awareness and ability to dictate the pace of play, slowing transition when needed, often allowing teammates to join the rush while sucking in opposing players before making a play. Ethan is skilled in possession and displays a confidence and creativity in possession. He has the puck skills to beat a check in a 1-on-1 scenario and can make high skilled plays with pace. He does show awareness of his teammates in the offensive zone and has a versatile skill set that allows him to thrive as a playmaker or goal scorer. Where Cardwell gets in trouble is when he becomes overly individualistic, as he tries to create on his own leading to unforced turnovers in poor areas of the ice. Ethan does show good offensive awareness, putting himself in spots to finish plays, showing a strong release and accuracy to his shot. Away from the puck Cardwell has room to improve as he lacks a consistent effort and can become lazy when away from the play. He does however show an aggressiveness when on the forecheck, as he can hunt pucks and become physical on the forecheck, showing deceptive strength for an undersized forward.

COE, BRANDON
RW - North Bay Battalion (OHL) 6'03" 182

Coe is a big bodied winger with fluid skating abilities and intriguing upside to his game. Brandon possesses a long and fluid stride that allows him to effortlessly generate speed and maneuver around the ice. He consistently uses his speed while in possession to push the pace down the wings and gain a step on his opponent. Brandon shows the ability to beat an opposing player wide to the goal, however isn't overly assertive with his size and speed, often opting to stay to the perimeter and direct the puck towards the goal, opposed to attacking the net with authority. As he adds strength to his frame he should become more confident when attacking the goal and it will elevate his all-around offensive game. Despite staying to the outside more often than not, Coe shows good vision and passing skills with the ability to make plays with pace both off his back-hand and forehand. When Brandon recognized and attacked open space in transition he elevated his game as he opened shooting lanes and was able to utilize his slightly above average shot. Coe protects the puck well and can be effective off the cycle as he's tough to put a body on due to his foot-speed. However, when contained he can be easily bumped from possession. Brandon has some consistency issues as he can be a prominent contributor or blend in. Finding a more consistent physical edge would only elevate his game as has shown a willingness to play with jam at times, but when doing so he tends to lack on the offensive side. Improved play away from the puck and an elevated work ethic would also be beneficial.

COLLINS, TY
RW - York-Simcoe Express (OMHA-ETA) 6'00" 157

Ty was selected second round, 38th overall by the Guelph Storm at the 2018 OHL Priority Selection Draft. Collins is a skilled winger with good size. Ty has the ability to dominate at the offensive zone, utilizing a deceptively versatile offensive skill set. He possesses a great shot that shows strong velocity and accuracy off a lightning quick release. A player who possesses a shoot first mentality, Ty does possess subtle playmaking traits as he see's the ice well and shows quality touch on his passing skills. Collins does a good job keeping his feet moving and finding space offensively, allowing him to utilize his quick release when found with a pass. In possession Ty shows strong puck control and can create space and/or beat an opponent in a 1-on-1 situation with his puck handling abilities. Collins would benefit from improving his skating abilities however, as despite an ability to reach a good top speed and attack with pace, his first step does lack quickness and his stride would benefit from becoming longer and smoother. Away from the puck Ty can display inconsistencies to his game as his compete level away from the puck and in the defensive zone waivers. As the season progressed Collins began to rely on teammates to create more often then utilizing his pure skill to generate offensive for himself.

COMMESSO, DREW
G - St. Sebastian's School/Cape Cod Whalers U16 (NE Prep/MHSL U16) 6'1" 185

Commesso is considered by many to be one of the top '02-birthdate goalies in the USA. He originally verbally committed to UNH although last year changed his option to Boston University. He is decent size. He is strong on his skates in his crease as shows good movements and athleticism. He plays the butterfly style who reads plays well and solid in rebound control. He has already accepted roster position with NTDP-17 for next season.

CORMIER, LUKAS
LD - Moncton Flyers (NBPEIMMHL) - 5'08" 155

Quick, mobile and smart, Cormier was one of the premier defensemen available in this year QMJHL draft and was eventually picked 4th overall by Charlottetown Islanders. Though a bit undersized Cormier has adjusted to playing against bigger bodies, he has good edges and can escape pressure and protect the puck with his high end skating. He makes it hard for the opposition to retrieve pucks on his side of the ice, not only with his speed but he reads the play and gets to pucks first to send the play the other way. He's shown he can take over games with his ability to rush the puck, and he's a lethal quarterback on the point. Cormier is great when it comes to getting pucks to the net, he doesn't have a rocket of a shot but it leaves his stick fast and it's accurate. He recognizes when a goalie can't see the puck and can wire the puck to the back of the cage, if not he can get a puck into the goaltenders feet for a rebound. He's poised with the puck and patient. A bit more explosiveness in his skating could push him into the elite category, but Cormier has the smarts, speed and skill to jump into a Major Junior Lineup right away.

COULOMBE, ANTOINE
G - Chevaliers de Lévis (LHMAAAQ) - 5'11" 187

Coulombe was the first goalie off the board in the QMJHL draft, he was drafted by Shawinigan with the 35th overall pick. Coulombe, who already possesses an interesting size at 6'00" and 185 pounds, is an athletic goaltender that has quick lateral movements. He's really strong at covering the bottom of the net and has a steady position in his crease, which allows him to cover a lot of space. Most of the time, when he stops the puck, he's able to keep it close to him, but when he allows rebounds, he manage to redirect them into the corners of the ice. Coulombe had a fantastic year statistically, finishing almost first in both major goaltending stats for a 15-year-old goalie, a 2.34 goals-against average and a .913 save percentage. From what we've seen during the season, there aren't any big flaws in Coulombe's game, which suggests that Coulombe has an enormous potential to become a starting goaltender in the QMJHL in the near future.

CRANLEY, WILL
G - Peterborough Jr. Petes (OMHA-ETA) 6'02.25" 158

Will was selected second round, 35th overall by the Ottawa 67's at the 2018 OHL Priority Selection Draft. Cranley is a good sized goaltender with impressive athletic ability. Will displays quick and controlled movements in the net. A goaltender who moves smoothly from post-to-post, Cranley is economical in his movements and is able to stay square to the shooter as he tracks the puck carrier from side-to-side. Will often gets out to the top of his crease to challenge shooters and consistently makes himself big in the net my keeping his gloves high and playing his angles effectively. He uses his size effectively to help battle through traffic and is often able to field pucks cleanly. Cranley shows strong rebound control and does a good job staying on his feet. A goaltender who plays the puck fairly well, Will does have room to elevate that aspect of his game further. Will is strong down low and has the athletic ability to make reaction based saves. It would benefit Cranley to show better competitiveness on secondary shot opportunities.

CUYLLE, WILLIAM
LW - Toronto Marlboros (GTHL) 6'02" 193

William was selected in the first round, third overall by the Peterborough Petes at the 2018 OHL Priority Selection Draft. Cuylle is a powerful, physical winger with dangerous goal scoring ability. Will was able to utilize his combination of size, strength and skill to dominate the play offensively throughout the season. A player who uses his physical advantages to thrive along the wall and off the cycle, Cuylle protects the puck well by utilize his reach and body to shield pucks and becomes heavy on it when driving through traffic. Will shows a dynamic release and can utilize his shot in tight spaces. Will possesses good accuracy and velocity behind his shot that allows him to beat goaltenders clean. Strong along the wall, Cuylle will uses his strength to out muscle opponents for pucks and does a good job gaining ideal positioning in the offensive zone. Will would benefit from keeping his feet moving in the o-zone, however does a good job utilizing his size as a net presence. He shows an aggression to his game and will engage and finish with physical contact making him imposing and tough to play against. Cuylle handles the puck well and combines generate speed with puck skill and strength to drive through opponents and get himself where he wants to go. More of a shoot first winger, he does possess deceptive vision and passing skills, both traits are elevated in effectiveness with the added time and space of a man-advantage. Cuylle however would benefit from improving his skating. A player who lacks first step quickness, Will needs to rely on his strength over the puck while generating speed to elude a turnover. Will does generate a good top speed but his feet have room to improve.

CZERNECKIANAIR, VICTOR
LC - Selects Hockey Academy U15 (USHS) - 5'10" 165

Czerneckianair was his team Captain this year, and finished 3rd in team scoring with 75 points in 53 games. He's not as skilled as his teammate and linemate Jack Williams, but plays a pretty complete game in all three zones. He has decent size and uses his body well when it comes time to protecting the puck in the offensive zone and cycle it. He's good down low. He does a lot of dirty work in front of the net or in the corners. His skating is decent, but he could improve on his quickness and acceleration. He's a complete player and played in all situations this year with his team. He's not a high-end skills' player, but has a strong work ethic and has value as a complete player that can help in different facets of the game. He's good in the offensive zone in terms of how he finds space and gets open in the slot for scoring chances. He has a good one-timer and a quick release, which helps beat goaltenders with his shot. He's a smart player; he has good reads and anticipation. Czerneckianair is committed to play NCAA hockey at Quinnipiac University.

DAVID, ALEXANDRE
RW/RC - Newbridge U16 (PSHF) - 5'08" 163

An athletic skilled forward with with good skill and dynamic speed, David showcased his potential as a game-breaker who can dominate the play at times in the game. He's a strong skater who generates good power and every stride, is difficult for defenders to contain with his speed, keeps his feet moving, and can force defenders into taking a penalty to slow him down. He has a very good, hard, accurate wrist shot, which he can execute in motion or from a stationary position. He's a smart player who reads the ice really well, he can sometimes look, pass and make a quick shot to catch the goaltender off-guard, but he can also find his teammates in traffic to make a play. He's a versatile player who is good in the faceoff circle, and he uses his defensive skills to retrieve pucks in the corners. Despite being undersized, David has the skill to jump in and contribute right away to a junior lineup. David was drafted 26th overall by Acadie-Bathurst in June.

DESNOYERS, ELLIOT
LW/C - Gaulois de Saint-Hyacinthe (LHMAAAQ) - 5'11" 176

In his second season with the Gaulois de St-Hyacinthe, an even stronger offensive contribution should be expected in the case of centre Elliot Desnoyers. After putting up 18 points in 24 games in 2016-17 as a 14-year-old, the Gaulois forward finished his second campaign with 36 points (10 goals and 26 assists) in 40 games, increasing his average points-per-game ratio from .75 to .90. Nevertheless, this year, Desnoyers has matured as a player since his first game in the league.

Probably one of the best skaters among all players in his age group, his skating skills definitely place him in a class of his own. His wide and powerful strides, as well as his acceleration make him a very fast player, both with and without the puck. Used in every kind of situation all season by his coach, Desnoyers has confirmed with his play that he is certainly one of the most complete players in the league. He is effectively involved in both directions of the ice, and can play a 200-foot type of game. Whether it is to line up as a quarterback at the point on the power play, to kill penalties on the shorthanded unit or to take an important faceoff in the defensive zone to protect a tight lead, Desnoyers is able to fulfill his team's needs. Equipped with a high compete level, the centre does not hesitate to use his body to get involved physically or to block shots when he is in the defensive zone. While in control of the puck, the Gaulois forward is distinguished by his above-average stickhandling and by his wrist shot that he is able to release quickly. He's a complete player; one thing that we worry a bit about in regards to him is how much of a scorer he will be at the next level.

However, the rest of his game is solid. Good chance to see him in the QMJHL right away as he could play a role on a bottom 6 to start his career, he was drafted with the last pick of the first round by Moncton 18th overall.

DESROCHES, CHARLIE
RD - Selects Hockey Academy (USHS) - 5'09" 149

Desroches made the move to go play hockey south of the border this year, after playing as an underager last year in the NBPEIMMHL. He had 26 points in 33 games with Kensington. This year he had a good year, finishing with 42 points in 53 games, also committing to Northeastern University in December. He has good skating abilities, and can rush the puck out of his zone. His footwork is good as well. He likes to move around in the offensive zone to find better shooting angles, and his footwork helps him do that. His offensive upside is solid; he sees the ice well and has a good, hard, low shot from the point. On the power play, he moves the puck well, He's not elite, but could be a good power play quarterback in major junior. He'll need to simplify his game a bit, as he tends to try too much sometimes, and this is when he gets into trouble. Defensively, his lack of strength can be a problem for him along the boards and in front of the net where he gets overpowered. He has a good stick and footwork to keep up with speedy forwards and his gap control is solid. In his zone, he has some work to do with his positioning, but overall, his potential is solid and he can be a factor offensively. In June he was drafted by the Saint John Seadogs with the 32nd overall pick and was at the draft indicating strong chances to report to Saint-John next season.

DROVER, ALEX
RW/C - Halifax McDonalds (NSMMHL) - 5'09" 165

Drover was drafted with the 10th overall pick by the Cape Breton Screaming Eagles in the 2018 QMJHL Draft. From the start of this past season he was lighting up the NSMMHL, he started the year in mid-season form and never seemed to look back. Drover has great speed and plays the game at a high tempo, very rarely is in once place for long, especially with the puck, he gets to the net with speed, or will hand the puck off and try to sneak into an area for a one timer. He's primarily a sniper with great shot placement; he has a quick, accurate release and can really place the puck where he wants it. His penchant for scoring big goals in key games has been a theme throughout the season, and he's shown he can be a game breaker, capable taking a game into his own hands. There have been times where Drover would try to do too much on his own, and got frustrated when things didn't go his way, but he does seem to have an extra gear when it comes to big games. He's tremendously skilled, but primarily a north-south skater, He keeps his feet moving and plays with energy and can be very difficult to contain, there is a bit of wasted energy in his stride but very rarely during the season did Drover ever seem lethargic or out of gas. He's a player who will have a good impact in the QMJHL and rather sooner than later.

DRYSDALE, JAMIE
RD - Toronto Marlboros (GTHL) 5'10.25" 158

Jamie was selected in the first round, fourth overall by the Erie Otters at the 2018 OHL Priority Selection Draft. Drysdale is an elite, two-way defender with an intelligence to his game. Jamie possesses elite mobility that he utilizes to dictate his game. A player who oozes confidence in possession, Drysdale can dictate the pace of play with the puck on his stick. Jamie generates offense from the back-end by aggressively pushing the pace in transition. He is aware of his options when transitioning and has an elusiveness to his game due to his ability to handle the puck with pace and quickly change direction to elude contact. Jamie shows the smarts to simplify his game when needed. Offensively Drysdale utilizes his quick feet to open shooting and passing lanes and can be assertive with his shot, getting it on goal when lanes open. He shows vision and smarts in his ability to shoot for deflections or areas of the net, opposed to using pure velocity to power a shot on net. Jamie distributes the puck well from the back end and uses strong offensive instincts to insert from the blue line or make aggressive pinches to extend zone time. He is able to contain in transition with his feet, keeping the play in front of him. Drysdale's gap control and routes to puck carriers allow him to quickly take away time and space and force a low percentage decision. When Jamie is able to force the play to the outside he shows good stick-on-puck defensive tools and is able to match opponents stride for stride. A strong decision maker, Drysdale is effective in the defensive zone, using a combination of anticipation, positional awareness and quick feet. Jamie defends from an inside position and can quickly take away time and space, utilizing an active stick to create turnovers. A poised individual who possesses the foot speed to elude a forecheck and create space, Drysdale has the ability to dominate a game with his speed, skill and smarts.

DUFOUR, WILLIAM
RW- Blizzard du Séminaire St-François (LHMAAAQ) - 6'01'' 174

The Blizzard right winger showed great progress as this season progressed. Physically ready for the next level, Dufour distinguished himself by his skating abilities, quick hands and powerful, accurate shot that he can release quickly. His long reach helps him versus opposing defensemen and uses it well to protect the puck in the offensive zone. Also, his ability to change the angle of his shot when he's in motion gave a lot of goaltenders in the league some headaches this year. Not afraid of the physical game and a high level of involvement in front of the net, Dufour is tough to contain for opposing defensemen. He'll need to work on his consistency; he can dominate games at times and be quieter in other games. He was drafted 6th overall by the Rouyn-Noranda Huskies this past June.

EVANGELISTA, LUKE
RW - Oakville Rangers (OMHA-SCTA) 5'10" 146

Luke was selected in the first round, 14th overall by the London Knights at the 2018 OHL Priority Selection Draft. Evangelista possesses excellent puck skills and great hands. He is a pure source of offence due to his versatility as a playmaker and finisher. His high-end execution speed and agility complement his fantastic stickhandling to make him elusive to checkers and difficult to play against. When in possession he is most effective. He is difficult to knock off the puck as he separates himself with a quick first step and spins off attackers with good edgework. Evangelista manages to get to open ice to catch a pass effortlessly with excellent hand-eye. He then either exploits the space he is given with great speed or draws opponents to him before finding an open teammate with an accurate pass. His great vision allows him to be deceptive with his decision-making. He often will make a drive toward the net and either fake a shot or a pass to stun defenders and then beat them with speed and find a better lane. His creativity with the puck keeps defenders on their toes and makes him hard to contain. On the breakout, he provides a good passing outlet and stays mobile. Along the boards, he presses hard and uses a quick stick to win most battles. When provided a scoring opportunity, he picks his corners in high percentage shooting areas with a quick accurate release. He gets a stick on many point shots with great hand-eye and is often the first man on rebounds. He was consistently an offensive threat every game and should hear his name called early in the OHL Draft. He has above average power to his shot will be a serious scoring threat at the next level by further adding power to it.

FOUDY, JEAN-LUC
RC - Toronto Titans (GTHL) 5'10" 153

Jean-Luc was selected in the first round, 10th overall by the Windsor Spitfires at the 2018 OHL Priority Selection Draft. Foudy is an intelligent centre with high end skating abilities and above average skill. Jean-Luc consistently showed the ability to raise the level of those around him with his shrewd vision and playmaking skills. A high-end skater with an explosive first step, Foudy was able to exploit open ice by exploding through gaps and forcing defenders to defend, pushing the pace of play. His ability to dictate the pace of play made him to difficult to defend as he could utilize his skill package while playing with speed or he could slow the gap down and draw in defenders before making a play to a teammate. Jean-Luc has a versatility offensively that increases his difficulty to defend as he can beat opponents with pure speed or utilize his great puck skills and creativity to beat a check in a 1-on-1 scenario. Foudy also shows an awareness away from the puck as he can drive lanes and open space for teammates or quickly dish a pass to a teammate and drive open ice for a return pass, thriving when getting the puck with generated speed. A confident player, Jean-Luc shows the ability to make split second, high percentage decisions with the puck. While he was inconsistent with his effort on the forecheck, when he was competing at his highest level, Foudy was aggressive on the forecheck and utilized a combination of speed and smarts to close on puck carriers and create turnovers with his stick. Jean-Luc will need to improve his strength to become more assertive in puck and position battles. While raising his two-way effort and play away from the puck will also need to occur for him to receive ice-time at the next level. Utilizing his shot more frequently would make Foudy even more difficult to defend.

FOWLER, HAYDEN
LC - Erie Otters (OHL) 5'9" 174

Hayden Fowler was drafted 19 overall by the Sault Ste. Marie Greyhounds in the 2017 OHL draft. He played 33 games for them while producing 4 points due to being buried on a very deep team. He was traded to Erie, that involved sending Taylor Raddysh back the other way, which left a top-6 spot for Fowler. After receiving a more prominent role with Erie that included powerplay time, he produced 22 points in 28 games, including 10 goals. Internationally, he was featured on Canada Black at the U17's, producing an assist in 5 games.

Fowler is a deceptive sniper who plays with a lot of confidence. His best attribute is unsurprisingly his shot, which features a lightning quick release and mechanics that allow him to generate a lot of weight behind it. The best aspect of his wrist-shot is the accuracy, we have seen him score goals that goalies have very little chance on due to the precision. He displayed a good level of hockey-sense which allows him to find soft-ice and get behind defensive-coverage at times. When off the rush, he's good at minimizing his body movement which allowed him to create an element of surprise in his play-style. This aspect worked well with the rest of his skill-set, which features plus vision and an above-average set of hands. This made him dangerous when driving down on the left-wing due to having an excellent backhand pass, yet also having the ability to use his heavy shot depending on the sequence. The most important aspect of Fowler's game to improve is his skating ability, he doesn't have an explosive or powerful stride, as well as having average reach which made it difficult for him to pull off toe-drag moves when he attempted them. If he can continue to develop his skating and grow, he could become a very interesting scorer to keep an eye on for the 2020 draft.

FRANCIS, RYAN
RW - 5'08" 167 - Cape Breton Screaming Eagles (QMJHL)

Francis was a nice surprise with the Screaming Eagles this year scoring over 30 points in his rookie season after he was picked in the 2nd round of the 2017 QMJHL draft. He didn't turned 16 until earlier December but was still very effective in the first half of the season as the youngest player in the league.

Francis played most of the season on the wing but he was a center back in midget, should be interesting to see if he goes back to center next season. He's a highly intelligent player on the ice and he's top notch playmaker. He had great success in midget with Bailey Peach as the set up man and it's just a matter of time for him in junior to get paired with a scorer and do what he did so well in midget. The size and his average skating ability are a bit of a problem for Francis going forward when thinking NHL potential, the good news is that he has two full seasons to improve his speed and get stronger physically before he's NHL draft eligible. His play away from the puck will need to improve as well, defensively he can struggled when matchups versus bigger players and lose those battles. He's sneaky on the ice, you won't see him and out of nowhere he'll appear and score a goal. He's at his best on the power play, with more spaces on the ice he's able to make more plays on the ice.

Francis has some things to improve and if he can improve those traits of his game that could make the difference from him when evaluating him if he's a good NHL prospect or just a really good junior player. Cape Breton has a good young core and Francis is a big part of that core and will lead them offensively in the next 3 years.

GALLATIN, OWEN
LD - White Bear Lake Bears (MNHS) 5'08" 146

Owen is a highly skilled puck moving defenseman who is coming off an impressive freshman season for White Bear Lake High School. Despite his limited size at this stage, Gallatin is able to control the game with the puck on his stick. His all-around skating ability is close to elite and as he gets stronger will only become more of an asset for him. His hands work just as well as his feet which allow him to lead the rush up the ice. Gallatin has some development to go in his own end, as he can skip coverages and lose containment and position on his man. Owen will be off to the USNTDP for the next two years before heading to Minnesota Duluth.

GUAY, PATRICK
LC - Cantonniers de Magog (LHMAAAQ) - 5'08" 155

Brother of Nicolas Guay, captain of the Drummondville Voltigeurs in the QMJHL, Patrick is an extremely talented player who completed his first season with the Cantonniers de Magog as the second best scorer of the entire Midget AAA circuit with 64 points. His impressive total of 34 goals in 39 games places him at the top of the league, tied with veteran Justin Hryckowian of the Lions du Lac St-Louis. In June he was drafted 5th overall by the Sherbrooke Phoenix.

In addition to his obvious talent for scoring goals, the left-hander is recognized first and foremost as a great playmaker. He is a very creative player with the puck, and generated a lot of scoring opportunities for his team. He is the kind of player that is often referred to in the hockey world as one that knows how to make his linemates better. His offensive flair with the puck, his strengths in puck-control, and his high compete level make him a player of an elite class. Not necessarily the biggest player at 5'08" and 155 pounds, Guay amply compensates with his high intensity level and the presence he brings to each of his shifts on the ice. He is also very comfortable with getting involved physically during a game, as he has shown several times this season. He is able to distribute (as well as take) some solid bodychecks. Used in all kinds of situations by his coach, the centre can fulfill all kinds of missions, such as fuelling the power play with wise passes and accurate shots on goal, or killing penalties by thwarting passing attempts. He's a forward who has the gift of presenting himself at the right moment of a game and who manages to score goals that often make the difference. He had a great postseason that matched his talent, finishing first in scoring with eight goals and 20 assists in 17 games.

GUSHCHIN, DANIL
LW - CSKA Moskva U17 (Russia U17) - 5'08" 154

Gushchin was one of the better Russians at the U-17s this past November, even though he was the youngest player on the team. He's a decent skater in straight lines, but has great acceleration and agility. He's good at avoiding hits along the boards with his shiftiness. At his size and age, it's tough for him to compete physically at this stage, but his hockey IQ is high. He's a sniper; he scored 4 goals in 5 games at the U-17s and has a great nose for the net. He also possesses excellent vision; he is really adept at making those hard-looking cross-ice passes look easy. He's quick to retrieve pucks in the offensive zone, keeping his feet alive all the time and remaining quite active on the ice. One of the most impressive things about Gushchin is his compete level away from the puck, as well as his defensive game. He really stood out for his work ethic at the U-17s when he didn't have the puck, which was impressive for a 15-year-old. He has great one-on-one abilities, and can score highlight-reel goals like he did this past November. His hands are quick, fluid and possess a quick release that can surprise opposing goaltenders.

Gushchin should play full time in the MHL next season. He should work on improving his skating in order to become an even bigger threat on the ice, and tougher to defend against as he plays against better, bigger and stronger players. However, he was drafted in the 2nd round of the USHL draft by Muskegon (the same team Andrei Svechnikov played with in 2016-2017) which opens up the option for Gushchin to move to North America next season or the season after that, should he choose to.

HALLIDAY, STEPHEN
LW - Toronto Marlboros (GTHL) 6'03" 207

Stephen was selected in the third round, 41st overall by the Niagara Ice Dogs at the 2018 OHL Priority Selection Draft. He was also selected in the first round, first overall by the Central Illinois Flying Aces at the 2018 USHL Draft. Halliday is a big bodied winger with above average skill and hockey sense. Stephen possesses intriguing physical attributes and will utilize them to his advantage in various situations. A player who thrives in possession, Halliday possesses a versatility offensively that allows him to generate offense in multiple ways. Stephen handles the puck at an above average level and can beat an opponent in a 1-on-1 scenario to create space. While he would benefit from keeping his feet moving when looking to create with his hands or passing skills, his heaviness on the puck and ability to shield the puck from traffic with his size, gives him added time to make a play. Offensively Halliday see's the ice very well and shows a good awareness of his passing options, allowing him to elevate the effectiveness of those around him with his passing skills. He can dominate off the cycle due to his size and strength in combination with his puck handling and vision, however he will also exploit shooting lanes and become assertive with his shot. Halliday shows strong velocity behind his shot and a good release. Effective as a net front presence, Stephen shows good hand-eye co-ordination along with the ability to quickly find loose pucks and use his quick hands to finish in tight. A player who raises his level of effectiveness when physically engaged and assertive with his physical tools, Halliday can be strategic with his body positioning in puck battles to emerge with possession despite being overly physical. He lacks a consistent edge to his game, but possesses added intriguing when finishing his checks. Halliday's skating is deceptive, while his top speed has room to improve, he possesses a fluid and efficient stride, while the power and length to his first two steps allow him to beat opponents to pucks or create separation. Halliday's biggest flaw is his consistency and his play away from the puck. He needs to remain engaged on a night-by-night basis as he can be simply dominate or blend in with the crowd depending on his competitiveness.

HARDIE, JAMES
LW - Barrie Jr. Colts (OMHA-ETA) 5'10.5" 158

James was selected in the first round, eighth overall by the Mississauga Steelheads at the 2018 OHL Priority Selection Draft. Hardie is an offensive minded winger with good size and strength. James possesses goal scoring abilities, displaying a lightning quick release with strong accuracy and velocity behind his shot. A player with a nose for the net, Hardie shows a strong awareness for the high percentage scoring areas and does a good job finding space and putting himself in an area to utilize his shot. James can be a threat off the cycle were he peels off and releases his shot through a screen. He also does a good job working the half-wall in possession, were his deceptive vision and passing skills make him a dual threat and tough to defend. A player who possesses average skating abilities, Hardie will need to improve his first step quickness, however a randy and powerful stride does allow him to reach a good top speed. James attacks the net with speed and his aware of passing options. He will exploit time and space and be assertive with his shot when in the high percentage scoring areas, but shows a creativity that allows him to move the puck to a teammate once opponents are drawn in. Hardie has good strength to his game and utilizes is well when battling along the boards. He could become more assertive with his size and show a more consistent physical edge to add another element to his game. Defensively James has room to improve his positional play and become more engaged, however he defends his position on the wing adequately. Hardie's great shot is his most intriguing tool, however he can force his shot at times resulting in loss of possession, better creating shooting lanes on a consistent basis would elevate his effectiveness.

HOLTZ, ALEXANDER
LW/RW - Djurgardens IF J20 (SuperElit) - 6'00" 183

Holtz is a big-time prospect out of Sweden for the 2020 NHL Entry Draft. The 15-year-old has already made noise on the international stage with the U-17 group, scoring 8 goals in 8 games in 2 tournaments.

In the regular season, he split his time between 4 different clubs and levels in Sweden, scoring 59 goals in 46 games. He finished the season playing in the J20 league, with players up to 4 years older than him. In that league, he scored 4 goals and 8 points in 11 games, which is really impressive at such an age. He already has great size, and has proven to be physically able to compete with and be dominant against older players. He has great instincts in the offensive zone, reading the play very well, and he has a lethal shot. His shot is elite, has a quick release to it, and can pick corners up. He's a dynamic goal-scorer and also has good vision of the ice. He's strong on the puck and his puck-protection game is well-advanced. His skating is not bad, but there's some improvements that will need to happen in the next couple of years that should make him an even better hockey player. His first-step quickness is an area that he will need to improve upon. When he reaches his top speed, he's tough to contain, but he'll need to find a way to reach that top speed faster. He's still very young, and with the right training he should be more than fine. He's possibly the biggest challenge to Alexis Lafrenière for the top pick of the 2020 NHL Entry Draft at the moment. Next season, he should start in the J20 league. Depending on how he performs there, he could get some call-ups to the SHL during the season. He'll also be a regular on the Swedish U-18 national team, even as an underager, and should have a good impact like he did with the U-17 team this past season.

KAMMERER, COLTON
RD - Sarnia Sting (OHL) 6'00" 169

Kammerer is an intelligent, two-way defender with good mobility to his game. Colton plays a poised and mature game that allowed him to be impactful as an OHL rookie. He possesses a competitive edge to his game and brought a consistent level of play throughout the season. Colton handles the puck fairly well and shows good skating abilities that allow him to exploit open ice and carry transition attacks. He simplifies his game when need and will utilize his vision and first pass abilities when needed. Kammerer is smart and instinctive offensively, picking his spots appropriately when joining transition attacks or jumping in from his blue line position. He distributes the puck well in the offensive zone and will use his feet to create shooting and passing lanes. Colton is a quality decision maker and will play rather simplistic at times to avoid mistakes which can allow him to fly under the radar. While defending Kammerer does a good job keeping his gaps tight and angles opponents away from the centre of the ice. His mobility is good but will need to continue to improve and he would benefit from accelerating his four-way quickness. A stick-on-puck type defender, Kammerer is positionally aware an utilize his stick well. He can however be out battled in position and puck battles due to limited strength at this time.

KEANE, GERARD
RD - Chicago Mission U16 (HPHL) 5'10.25" 170

Gerard was selected in the third round, 42nd overall by the London Knights at the 2018 OHL Priority Selection Draft. Keane is an undersized, offensive minded defender with strong puck rushing abilities. While Gerard is undersized height wise, he possesses good strength to his game and utilizes it well to remain heavy on the puck when transitioning up ice. He also shows a physical edge to his game, as he willingly steps up in the neutral zone and at the line to deliver impressive open ice checks. While Keane has good defensive tools, he can run around at times in the defensive zone and rely on his skating abilities to allow him to recover. Gerard defends transition fairly well due to his mobility and the ability to stay in front of his checks, when he simplifies his defending and doesn't try to crush an opponent with a check he tends to show an ability to effectively take away time and space. Keane however is at his best offensively and with the puck on his stick as he can effortlessly elude a forecheck and quickly burst up ice, leading transition. He handles the puck well and shows an aggressiveness as he willingly pushes the play towards the goal. Gerard opens shooting lanes well but will also sneak down from his point position and make himself a threat.

KINGSBURY-FOURNIER, NICOLAS
LW - Phénix du Collège Esther-Blondin (LHMAAAQ) - 6'00" 173

Kingsbury-Fournier is an offense-first mentality player and his shot is his best asset, because when he has time and space with the puck in the offensive zone, he can be dangerous from anywhere. He has a good feel for the net and he knows how to position himself to receive the puck. On the other hand, Kingsbury-Fournier has the tendency to cheat a bit towards the offensive zone and leave his defensive responsibilities behind. He's also a player who had some ups and downs this season. Much like his season, from period to period, there were times where he was completely invisible on the ice. Otherwise, he already possesses a strong and powerful stride that allows him to be effective on the forecheck and to leave a mark when he finishes his hits. Kingsbury-Fournier has to become more consistent in his efforts, and bring the best of himself every night. He already has good size for the next level, so Kingsbury-Fournier is a player who should dominate offensively in the QMAAA next year. If he can improve his little flaws defensively and get consistent on a daily basis, Kingsbury-Fournier could have a stellar year and move up to the QMJHL afterwards. He was really good in late

April at the Gatorade Challenge, and this great performance should definitely help his draft stock. He was eventually drafted in the 2nd round by Moncton with the 27th overall selection in the 2018 QMJHL Draft.

KLEVEN, TYLER
LD - Fargo Davies High (USHS-ND) - 6'02" 183

Kleven was a standout performer at the NTDP in camp in March and eventually was offered a roster spot with the US U-17 team starting next season. He's a big raw kid from North Dakota who is committed to play college hockey at North Dakota University. He's a very physical game with the ability to throw big open ice hits and also along the boards. He can set the tempo of games with his physicality. Offensively he's still a bit raw but there's potential there, he moves puck well and has a hard shot from the point. For a kid of this size at this age his skating ability is impressive and he's a very intriguing package to watch for the 2020 NHL Draft.

LAFRENIÈRE, ALEXIS
LW - Rimouski Oceanic (QMJHL) - 6'01" 184

There was a lot of hype with Lafrenière in his QMJHL draft year season and after Rimouski selected him 1st overall he lived up to the hype and more in his first season in the league. He became the first 16 years old player since Sidney Crosby to score 40+ goals in a season and overall finished with 42 goals & 80 points which was good for 9th overall in scoring. Not surprisingly he was named the rookie of the year in the QMJHL.

One impressive thing about Lafrenière season was that he only scored 7 goals on the power play which meant he scored 35 goals at even strength which is extremely impressive for any players of any age but even more for a 16 years old. Lafreniere has good top speed when he gets going, he could still work on improving his explosiveness to obtain that top speed more quickly. That would make him even more dangerous in open ice. He's a player with a great hockey IQ and makes quick decision with the puck. He has superb vision and makes players around him better. He sees plays on the ice that not many players see, it's a sign of his elite hockey sense and smarts. He has a good accurate shot; he can pick corners easily and can also score his share of ugly goals in front of the net. He's not afraid to battles in the tough area of the ice, often near the net looking for rebounds. Along the board he's solid, he protects the puck well with his long reach but still lack some strength playing night after night against top defensemen , he'll get stronger eventually he's still very young and not mature physically yet. He made some progress with his play away from the puck this year, and next year we should see him play more regularly on the PK and becoming a better two way player. He's obviously highly skilled but he's a hard worker and plays hard every game.

Lafrenière will be one of the top or the best players in the QMJHL next season and should challenge for a spot on team Canada at the world junior as well.

"At the U18's in April, he showed the rest of the world what we already knew in Québec: he's a special player and he's still extremely young. I can't wait to see the numbers he's going to put up in his draft year in 2019-2020." - HP Scout Jérôme Bérubé

"It might be better for him to skip the Hlinka tournament this summer and go straight to Canada's U20 camp; he's already as good as most players who would end up on the invite list." - HP Scout Jérôme Bérubé

"Got to see him live for the first time this season. Looking forward to see more of him next year.". - HP Scout, Mark Edwards

LANGDON, ISAAC
LC - Quinte Red Devils (OMHA-ETA) 5'11.5" 170

Isaac was selected in the second round, 32nd overall by the Kitchener Rangers at the 2018 OHL Priority Selection Draft. Langdon is a powerful two-way forward with above average skill and hockey sense. A player who possesses intriguing size and strength to his game, Isaac recognizes his physical advantages and utilizes them to thrive on both sides of the puck. Langdon displays a fluid and powerful stride which allows him to generate a strong top speed, which he is able to utilize in various scenarios. A player who thrives in possession, Isaac handles the puck well and can create space with his speed and ability to back-off opponents. Langdon always attacks with awareness of his surroundings, while his versatile skill set makes him tough to defend. He has the ability to recognize time and space and will take the puck to the center of the ice and release a shot, however he will also impose his size and strength and drive wide past an opponent, displaying strong puck protection skills. Langdon also will utilize opposing players as a screen to release his shot that his both heavy and accurate or utilize his vision and passing skills to create for a teammate. Isaac has the uncanny ability to raise the level of players around him with is competitiveness and skill. In the offensive zone Langdon can dominate off the cycle and uses his physical attributes to excel in puck, position and board battles. A strong decision maker with great skill, Isaac possesses reliable two-way traits to his game. He is engaged defensively and always puts himself on the right side of the puck. Langdon will utilize his size and strength to separate player from puck effectively.

LAPIERRE, HENDRIX
LC - Intrépide de Gatineau (LHMAAAQ) - 5'11" 161

Lapierre was 1st overall selection in the 2018 QMJHL draft by the Chicoutimi Sagueneens. The center is an ultra-smart player who's able to read the play pretty well in front of him and reacts well to any situation. He uses his smartness in every situation, but particularly when he was used on the penalty kill. He was able to locate the area where he could go in the offensive zone and kill several seconds with the puck, or retreat and kill a lot of seconds there. Lapierre is a tremendous playmaker, he sets up a lot of plays for his teammates and he is able to complete all kind of passes in every situation, including in tight spots. He also got soft, quick hands that he uses to shift his opponents or score. He's got good skating abilities with good strides and speed that he uses well during the game. Lapierre is the kind of player that can be used in every situation during a game, and he did well in every situation. The centre could change a game within one shift alone, with his abilities. He finished the season with 17 goals and 40 assists in 35 games.

LAVALLÉE, CHARLES-ANTOINE
G - Gaulois de Saint-Hyacinthe (LHMAAAQ) - 6'02" 203

Lavallée was the 40th overall selection by the Moncton Wildcats in the 2018 QMJHL Draft. First of all, at 6'02" and 203 pounds, we must admit that he already has ideal size. In addition, his growth spurt is probably not even over, suggesting that these measurements are likely to increase in the coming months. For an athlete of his size, he remains a very agile goaltender in his crease. He has a good glove, grabs loose pucks well, and doesn't give up juicy rebounds in the slot. Adopting a style of play that could be described as a hybrid one, Lavallée also stands out with his quick pads and his good judgment to follow the puck through traffic while managing to control the rebounds. His lateral movements, flush with the ice, are perhaps the only downside element to his game that he will have to work on. Sometimes his leg thrusts are not sufficiently well-dosed to give him square enough positioning in front of the puck. The Gaulois' goaltender is very comfortable when playing the puck behind his net, and is effective to execute passes to his teammates to start the zone exit. Recognized for his calm and high level of confidence between the posts, Lavallée remains a competitive guy who offers consistent play and fights for every puck, regardless of the outcome of the game. He had a good first season in the Baillarge circuit, finishing with the sixth-highest save percentage (.914) and a 2.49 goals-against average.

LAWRENCE, JOSH
RC - Selects Hockey Academy 16U (USHS) - 5'09" 163

Lawrence has played for the past two seasons with the Selects Hockey Academy program after leaving New Brunswick after his first bantam season (where he scored 41 goals in 30 games). Lawrence had a lot of success offensively this year, leading his team in scoring with 83 points in 49 games and playing with older players as well. His best tools are his hands; he knows how to score goals and his hands are quick. He has a quick release and can beat guys one-on-one with his puck skills. He'll need to improve his skating; he has decent speed and can change speeds when rushing pucks, but he lacks some explosiveness. He's not overly big; improving his speed would only make him more dangerous on the ice. He could also stand to be more involved in the play and in the defensive zone. He tends to stay too much on the perimeter and we would like to see him work harder, showing a better compete level. He's good on the power play; he likes to handle the puck from his off-wing on the half-wall. He played on the point on the power play at times this year for his team. He also saw ice time shorthanded during the season. He's committed to Boston University for the 2020-2021 season. Lawrence was drafted 15th overall by Saint John in June, he was a top 10 talent in the draft but fell because of his NCAA commitment.

LESSARD, MARSHALL
RW - Cantonniers de Magog (LHMAAAQ) - 5'09" 180

A fiery player who shows up at every single game, Marshall Lessard is a hard worker who was a big part of the success the Cantonniers de Magog enjoyed this season. With a total of 18 goals and 22 assists in 34 games, the right-hander finished third in scoring for his team, 21st among all skaters in the Midget AAA circuit.

He is the type of player who plays a style similar to that of Brendan Gallagher, while making a contribution similar to what we are accustomed to seeing from the right-winger of the Montreal Canadiens. With an ability to play on both wings, Lessard is a player who hits hard and is very solid on his skates. Despite his 5'09" frame, he has a stature that is quite massive and well-developed. Not afraid of anything, he can easily overthrow an opponent who is much bigger and stronger than him with his bodychecks. Excellent on the forecheck, the Cantonniers' forward has demonstrated his efficiency in pursuit of the puck, completing his checks and managing to recover the puck more often than not, leaving the corners of the ice with the puck on his tape to install the attack. Not afraid to go play in places where traffic is heavy, Lessard is dangerous in front of the net to disturb the goaltender and to recover loose pucks. In addition to providing this contagious energy and high-level intensity shift after shift, the right-hander also has good assets while in possession of the puck, including a good wrist shot that he is able to release quickly. His skating is also another of his obvious strengths that ranks him above-average. His first three strides are explosive, allowing him to gain speed in the neutral zone and head to the net with speed by lowering his shoulder. Lessard was drafted with the 16th overall selection in the 2018 QMJHL draft by the Val D'Or Foreurs.

LUNDELL, ANTON
LC - HIFK U20 (Jr. A SM-liiga) - 6'00" 165

Lundell was an excellent player for Finland this season at the international level, at both U-17 and U-18 levels. What does stand out in Lundell's game is his poise and smarts. He is very calm with the puck on his stick and doesn't have any big flaws in his game. He has good size and his skating has improved from what we saw in November compared to what we saw in April at the U-18 World Hockey Championships. He's not a speedster; his top speed could still be better, but his agility and quickness was clearly better at the end of the season. He's not a flashy player that will go end-to-end with the puck, but he works hard in all three zones and always seems to make the smart play on the ice. He's the kind of player a coach can put in any situation, which is quite impressive at this young age. His hockey IQ is excellent. He has good vision, and on the power play, he likes to control the puck on the half-wall. He has a good frame; he should still get stronger with time, but already uses his size well in the offensive zone to protect the puck. His play along the wall is good as well. He's strong on the puck and plays quite a mature game. Defensively, he takes pride in all the little details, such as a good active stick in the defensive zone. He sometimes acts like a 3rd defenseman on the ice, showing excellent support down low to help his defensemen retrieve pucks.

Overall, after his performance at the April U-18 World Hockey Championships, Lundell is one of the top prospects from Finland in their U-18 group. He's not eligible for the NHL Draft until 2020. He's definitely one that we will keep an eye on in the next two seasons.

MALIK, NICK
G - HC Vitkovice U20 (Czech U20) - 6'0"161

Malik is the son of former NHL'er Marek Malik, and his older brother Zach is playing for Sudbury in the OHL (eligible for the 2018 NHL Entry Draft). The younger Malik was a star at the U-17 Hockey Challenge, playing as an underager there. He had some remarkable performances in the later part of the tournament. His best attribute is his compete level in the crease combined with his lateral movements; he doesn't give up on secondary rebounds, no matter how difficult the save might be. He used his reflexes and flexibility to make some high-end saves. He's really calm in his crease, we like his confidence. His puck-tracking with traffic is excellent as well. Right now, his size is average according to NHL standards, but he's such a young goaltender and his dad ended up being 6'04" (whereas his brother is 6'02"). There's a good chance that with time, he'll grow and have more than enough size for the NHL. He's still extremely young, but we love his potential and attitude in his crease.

MCDONALD, KYLE
RW - Ottawa Jr. Senators (HEO) 6'03" 176

Kyle was selected in the second round, 25th overall by the Windsor Spitfires at the 2018 OHL Priority Selection Draft. Kyle is a large, rangy forward with a lethal shot. He showed strong offensive awareness and a killer instinct to use his big frame to get the puck to high percentage scoring areas before releasing a hard, accurate wrist shot. His wrists hot is very mature and one of the best in the HEO, if not the best, and was a major contributor to him finishing 7th among all HEO players in goals scored. He doesn't play a particularly physical game given his size, but was using his size to his advantage in puck battles more often towards the end of the season. He played a responsible defensive game, back checking at full speed regularly. He demonstrated strong puck control, and uses his reach to his advantage to position himself effectively to avoid being checked off the puck. He shows an ability to make hard, accurate passes at high speed, and made quick plays in the offensive zone, often setting up his teammates for prime scoring chances. He was vocal on the ice on a few occasions and showed above average speed once in stride, but he would benefit from improving on his acceleration and ability to separate himself from defenders with his first few steps.

MERCER, DAWSON
RW - Drummondville Voltigeurs (QMJHL) - 6'00" 168

Mercer was the 8th overall pick of the 2017 QMJHL draft; he had a decent first season with the Voltigeurs finishing with 11 goals and 26 points in 61 games. The Newfoundland native is one of the most skilled player from the 2017 QMJHL draft class.

He had a good first half of the season, playing regularly on the top 3 line and getting some ice time on the power play. With any rookies there was some up and down with him but was showing some nice things on the ice. In the 2nd half his play slipped due to his ice time decreasing with new players added to the lineup that took his spot and end up playing most of the time on the 4th line with limited power play ice time. Mercer has great hands, he can stickhandle the puck in a phone booth, he likes to challenge players one on one and he's good at handling the puck in tight spaces. He has a good shot, quick release and his hands are soft. His decision making is not always on point, would like to see simplified his game a bit and use his linemates more on the ice. His play away from the puck is in need of work, a bit of one dimensional right now but he's still very young and as a 2020 eligible prospect has two full seasons ahead of him to improve. Drummondville is a really good young team, Mercer will need to find a way to crack the team top 6 forward next year and be a top power play guy. He has the talent skills to be a top point producer in the league.

MERCURI, LUCAS
RW/C - Grenadiers de Châteauguay (LHMAAAQ) - 6'03" 189

The 19th overall selection in the 2018 QMJHL Draft, Mercuri was in his second season in the Midget AAA after playing as an underager in 2016-2017. He managed to use his assets well and finished with a good season. He is a big size forward and uses his size in puck-protection situations. Aside from this, he is not the most physical player. He uses his reach well to cause turnovers in the defensive zone and he is a player who is also aware of his defensive game. He is a decent skater for a player of his size, but has room for improvement, especially for the next level. Mercuri has a good vision of the game and is an excellent playmaker, as his 27 assists in 40 games this season speak for themselves; he is able to put the puck in tight spaces with his accurate passes. Mercuri will have to work on his consistency and his level of involvement in games for the next level, as he may seem absent in certain sequences. He'll need a big summer to improve his speed in order to be ready for major junior next year. He finished the season with 41 points in 40 games.

MOORE, LLEYTON
LD - Toronto Marlboros (GTHL) 5'07.25" 160

Lleyton was selected in the first round, 12th overall by the Niagara Ice Dogs at the 2018 OHL Priority Selection Draft. Moore is an undersized, offensive minded defenseman with great skill. Lleyton possesses strong hockey sense and elite mobility that allows him to thrive despite his height. A player who can dictate the pace of play in possession, Moore utilizes his combination of skating, puck skills and smarts to generate offensive in various ways. Lleyton shows strong awareness of his surroundings and good poise to his game as he can recognize an aggressive forecheck and use his feet to elude a check. He handles the puck well, while carrying transition and has an elusiveness to his game as he utilizes his puck handling and skating abilities to maneuver through traffic. Moore can effortlessly gain the offensive zone in possession and shows an aggressiveness, attacking the net, looking to create an opportunity. Lleyton does a good job involving his teammates in transition attacks, showing good awareness, however he also shows the smarts to simplify his game to avoid a turnover. Offensively Moore uses his quick feet to walk the line and create shooting lanes. He displays a deceptively heavy point shot with good accuracy. His awareness from the point allows him to disguise his shot and change it into a pass or shoot for deflections. Moore can distribute well from the point and will look to sneak in from his point position. Lleyton shows an ability to defend transition well, keeping the play in front of him and/or to the outside, utilizing his foot-speed to match opposing players stride-for-stride, while utilizing stick-on-puck defensive tools. He does a good job keeping an effective gap and often takes strong routes to puck carriers. Defensively Moore has room to improve his game as he can puck chase and be out muscled in the dirty areas. However because more often is able to gain possession and quickly use a first pass or his feet to elude pressure, he rarely has to defend.

MORRISON, LOGAN
RC - Guelph Jr. Gryphons (OMHA-SCTA) 5'09.5" 142

Logan was selected in the first round, 18th overall by the Hamilton Bulldogs at the 2018 OHL Priority Selection Draft. Morrison is a second-year minor midget forward who has both skill and hockey sense. He is effective on both sides of the puck by reading the ice and acting upon his high-end skillset to make the play. Away from the puck he actively tracks down the open man and gets a quick stick in the lane to intercept or negate the pass to transition the other direction. When in possession, he is creative by utilizing his diverse arsenal of skills to either find the best passing outlet, rush the net on his own or generate a scoring chance by a well-placed shot. Morrison remains poised with the puck and does a good job protecting it by using his edges and quick hands to shelter the puck away from attackers. He refrains from forcing low percentage plays but regularly generates a scoring opportunity on solo efforts when given time and space. On the rush, he changes speeds to fool defenders. Morrison has terrific hand-eye as shown with his seamless puck receptions and deflections in front of the net. His playmaking ability is great due to vision and accurate passing. He uses a good stick in puck battles and when hounding down puck carriers to strip them of the puck. He has a great release to his shot as he manages to get it off timely and often on tough passes. Morrison's ability to execute quickly on his plays complement his game and make him a player who is usually a step ahead of his peers on the play. His stride is weak but it tends to get him where he needs to be in time. If he could add some speed to his skating to help him separate himself from players at the next level he could be an impactful player. The undersized forward needs to add some mass to withstand older and larger players to further be effective.

MURRAY, JAKE
LD - Oakville Rangers (OMHA-SCTA) 6'02.5" 190

Jake was selected in the first round, 13th overall by the Kingston Frontenacs at the 2018 OHL Priority Selection Draft. Murray is big two-way defenseman for the Oakville Rangers. He is an excellent skater who moves the puck well in all three zones. In the defensive zone, he executes a good first pass on the tape of an open forward. If no outlets are provided and space is provided he will rush the puck with good speed use his agility to avoid checkers. With no outlets or openings when carrying it through the neutral zone he will often put a hard wristshot on net. He has good vision with the puck with an ability to find teammates and lead them with a pass in the neutral zone. In the offensive zone, he moves the puck around well and with quick execution. Murray is an offensive threat when given any space in the offensive zone as he edges toward the slot to get a powerful wristshot or slapshot off. The release on his shot is very quick and is frequently used on the point on one-timers. The accuracy on his shots make it difficult for goalies to make a save and gives teammates an opportunity to redirect it. In the defensive zone, he ties players up in front of the net with his stick and closes the gap on open forwards quickly with a good first step and anticipation before passes. He does tend to jump up often but usually is successful at holding the play at the line. When he gets caught, he uses a strong effort on the backcheck to catch a man on the rush and get a stick in the lane. He tends to use his stick on most defensive plays but is not shy on using physicality to win battles along the boards. He could opt to use his size to his advantage more often to maximize his effectiveness. At times, he can get a bit ambitious on stretch passes and force a low percentage play resulting in a turnover. When faced with pressure from a heavy forecheck he tends to make plays too quickly and cough up the puck.

"He's a player that many scouts really liked that didn't do much for me. I didn't see first round talent when I watched him." - HP Scout, Mark Edwards

O'ROURKE, RYAN
LD - Vaughan Kings (GTHL) 6'00" 175

Ryan was selected in the first round, 20th overall by the Sault Ste. Marie Greyhounds at the 2018 OHL Priority Selection Draft. O'Rourke is a solid two-way defender with good strength to his game. Ryan's all-around game allows him to thrive in various situations. A player who possesses good hockey sense, O'Rourke can dictate the pace of play from the back-end. In possession Ryan shows a confidence in possession as he handles the puck well and utilizes his straight line speed to make his way up ice and effortlessly gain the offensive zone. He shows good awareness of his teammates and knows when to simplify his game to avoid turnovers. Ryan's ability to create in transition is most impressive, as he shows the offensive instincts to take the puck to the goal or peel back and hit a trailing/attacking teammate with a seeing eye pass. Offensively Ryan uses his quick feet to effectively open shooting/passing lanes. He possesses a heavy slap shot from the point, but will often utilize his snap shot to quickly release the puck. He makes good reads offensively, knowing when to sneak down from his point position and when to aggressively pinch to extend zone time. O'Rourke's skating ability allows him to stay in front of opponents when defending transition. He shows good gap control and often forces attacking opponents wide and away from the centre of the ice. His ability to deny easy entry to the zone and take away time and space, allows him to create turnovers. Defensively Ryan uses his size and strength to out muscle opponents to win battles or gain ideal body position. He makes smart reads, anticipating the play well to create turnovers and shows an active stick. O'Rourke has a physical edge to his game and will finish checks. He shows excellent poise under pressure and can use his feet to elude pressure and shows no panic. With an effective first pass, Ryan shows the ability to lead transition with his passing abilities.

PANWAR, SAHIL
LC - Detroit Honeybaked U16 (HPHL) 5'11.5" 177

Sahil was selected in the second round, 23rd overall by the London Knights at the 2018 OHL Priority Selection Draft. Panwar is a skilled forward with an impressive amount of creativity to his game. Sahil is at his best in possession where he utilizes his above average puck handling and skating abilities to create space and become elusive. He is able to quickly change pace and direction to slip checks and displays the puck skills to beat a check in a 1-on-1 scenario. Sahil skates well, showing good acceleration, a fluid stride and intriguing top speed. He has the ability to beat defenders wide in transition and shows an ability to recognize time and space, exploiting the centre of the ice when it is available. However Panwar can be individualistic to often and needs to utilize his teammates more effectively throughout. A player who oozes creativity and possesses good skill, he would benefit from simplifying his game at times as turnovers in the defensive and neutral zones can lead to direct scoring chances the other way. Panwar uses his speed to get back and engage defensively however he struggles with positional awareness and often is strictly in the zone chasing the puck.

PERFETTI, COLE
LC - Vaughan Kings (GTHL) 5'09.25" 170

Cole was selected in the first round, fifth overall by the Saginaw Spirit at the 2018 OHL Priority Selection Draft. He was also selected in the third Round, 46th overall by the Chicago Steel at the 2018 USHL Draft. He is currently committed to the University of Michigan. Perfetti is a highly intelligent, playmaking centre with excellent skill. Cole has the ability to raise the level of his line mates whenever he touches the ice, utilizing his above average vision and passing skills. A versatile offensive threat, Perfetti has shown the ability to generate offensive opportunities in 1-on-1 scenarios, away from the puck and by creating for his teammates. At his best in possession, Cole shows an ability to dictate the pace of play and displays excellent awareness of his options. He shows the puck handling ability to create space and beat an opponent in a 1-on-1 scenario, but will also utilize opponents as a screen, releasing a deceptive strong shot around them. Cole would however benefit from utilizing his shot more frequently, as he does possess impressive velocity and accuracy to his shot. A poised individual, Perfetti is just an average skater, however his ability to change pace and open ice with his edges in combination with his puck handling abilities make him difficult to contain at times. He does show good strength on the puck when he looks to beat defenders wide, remaining aware of passing options as he takes pucks to the net. Perfetti is a reliable two-way centre, showing good positional play and awareness in the defensive zone. While his strength is on the offensive side of the puck, his reliable play away from the puck allows him to thrive in various situations.

PETERS, CAMERON
LC - Toronto Marlboros (GTHL) 6'01" 177

Cameron was selected in the second round, 29th overall by the North Bay Battalion at the 2018 OHL Priority Selection Draft. Peters is a powerful centre with intriguing physical tools. Cameron utilizes his size and strength in combination with a versatile skill game to find an effectiveness. A player who displays a fluid and powerful stride, Peters is able to reach a good top speed and can be difficult to contain in transition when attacking the pace. He uses his size and reach to protect the puck when entering the offensive zone, but can also remain heavy over the puck when using his strength to drive his way through traffic. Cameron does a good job finding space in the offensive zone and his teammates are often able to find him in a high percentage scoring area were he utilizes his quick release and high velocity shot to generate offensively. Peters however would benefit from better creating shooting lanes or releasing his shot from better angles as he frequently tries to put pucks on net from poor angles or with traffic in front of him, leading to turnovers. Cameron has the ability to dominate the play below the hash-marks, combining his size, strength, skating abilities and skill to generate off the cycle and win various puck and position battles. A player who is at his best when physically engaged and assertive with his aggressive side, Peters would benefit from consistently utilizing his physical advantages. A shoot first centre, Cameron does show simple passing abilities and is able to make quick decisions avoiding the puck dying on his stick. Consistency issues did hinder Peters at times as he can dictate the play or simply blend in. His effort level away from the puck and defensive zone positioning/awareness will need to elevate for him to have an impact at the next level, next season.

PETERSON, DYLAN
RC - CIHA White (HEO), 6'3" 181

Dylan was selected in the 7th round, 126th overall by the Ottawa 67's at the 2018 OHL Priority Selection Draft. He is also committed to Boston University. Production wise it was a disappointing season registering 35 points in 29 regular season games but when viewing him live it's evident why he's held in such high regard. Dylan is a dynamic forward that possesses a tremendous amount of skill and can take over a game at will. Opposing teams need to be aware every time he steps on the ice as he is dangerous whenever he has possession of the puck. Peterson is the best skater in the league and is almost unstoppable when he gets the puck in stride or has time to regroup the play. When he reaches top speed, he will widen his stance and maintain a low centre of gravity which makes him extremely difficult to knock off the puck. He does an excellent job at keeping the puck to the outside of his body and will make subtle deceiving head fakes that allow him to freeze oncoming defenders and create more time and space for himself. At times Dylan can be guilty of trying to do too much on his own which can lead to poor decisions with the puck. Defensively he excels at anticipating and reading the play to intercept passes however there is still some room for improvement as he can occasionally lose track of his man in the defensive zone. Dylan was one of the top players eligible at the 2018 OHL Priority Selection Draft, however he has committed to the USA National Team Development Program for the next two seasons.

PIERCEY, RILEY
RW - Toronto Marlboros (GTHL) 6'02.5" 186

Riley was selected in the first round, 16th overall by the Barrie Colts at the 2018 OHL Priority Selection Draft. Piercey is a competitive winger with intriguing physical attributes. He played in a complimentary role throughout the season, however showed good individual skill to his game and was able to contribute despite the puck often being on a line mates stick. Riley creates space effectively for his line mates by driving lanes and using subtle pick plays below the hash-marks. A player who thrived off the cycle, using his length and reach in combination with his strength and puck skill, Piercey was effective driving off the cycle and releasing an accurate shot. However he showed the versatility and awareness to make a play off the cycle to a pinching defenseman or teammate who had found open ice. Riley has the ability to dominate down low and already does, however he projects to become even bigger and stronger. A player with average puck skills, Piercey utilizes his teammates to open space as he will quickly move pucks and burst through seams to receive a return pass in space showing the smarts need to open ice for himself. A reliable two-way presence, Piercey possesses a competitive edge to his game and will use his size and strength to become imposing with a physicality to his game.

POIRIER, JÉRÉMIE
LD - Grenadiers de Châteauguay (LHMAAAQ) - 6'00" 177

Poirier was drafted 8th overall by Saint John in the 2018 QMJHL Draft. He has very good mobility and great footwork, which helps him create space in the offensive zone as well as in the defensive zone in one-on-one situations. Poirier has a very good transition game with his smooth skating and good first pass, he reads the game very well in front of him and is able to identify the right player to pass the puck to on the rush (or choose not to). He is also calm while in possession of a puck, and does not cause a lot of turnovers under pressure. One thing that Poirier improved during the season was his decision-making, which further enhances the quality of player he is. However, he still needs to play a simpler kind of game with the puck, which should reduce the number of turnovers in his own zone. In the offensive zone, he can be the quarterback of a power play, as he distributes the puck very well to his teammates. His puck skills are high-end, as he can easily beat opponents one-on-one with his elite hands. He also has a powerful and accurate shot from the point. He finished the season with five goals and 26 assists in 40 games. For the next level, he will have to continue working on his decision-making (especially in the defensive zone) and also improve his physical strength.

PORTOKALIS, WILLIAM
LC Don Mills Flyers (GTHL) 5'10.25" 175

William was selected in the second round, 39th overall by the Mississauga Steelheads at the 2018 OHL Priority Selection Draft. Portokalis is a skilled forward with above average hockey sense and a strong competitiveness to his game. William possesses the versatility to play both centre and the wing and was effective in both areas, however he does project as a winger at the next level. A player who plays a highly structured, two-way game, Portokalis impresses with his ability to become a dynamic and highly skilled offensive threat, while remaining defensively strong. In possession William can be difficult to defend as he is unpredictable in the way he attacks the offensive zone. He shows the ability to create space with his puck handling and can beat opponents in 1-on-1 scenarios. However he also has the uncanny ability to release his shot, mid-stride with little time or space, utilizing an opponent as a screen. Portokalis displays an great release with excellent accuracy and velocity behind his shot. Despite his nose for the net, he possesses deceptively good vision and passing skills and can create for his teammates. William does a good job finding soft spots in defensive coverages and will exploit them with his quick release. A competitive forward, while tenacious on the forecheck, he is also controlled and will use his anticipation ability to create turnovers. In tight he displays a quick stick to separate player from puck. Defensively Portokalis is engaged and shows positional awareness. He utilizes his body/stick to clog shooting/passing lanes and will utilizes his strength to out muscled opponents in board and puck battles. William would benefit from adding a physical element to his game. He will also need to improve his first step quickness, while working on his skating as he provides just average skating abilities.

PROVOST, WILLIAM
LW/RW, Forestiers d'Amos (LHMAAAQ) - 5'10" 182

The young forward was drafted 13th overall by Val D'Or Foreurs in the 2018 QMJHL Draft. Provost is a left-handed winger who can play on both wings. He played as an underage player last season with the Forestiers, where he did well playing on a bad team. However, this season he exploded offensively, racking up 41 points in 38 games without much help around him once again. He's an offensive dynamo with great vision; his skating while in possession of the puck is off-the-charts. He has very quick hands and is tough to defend against, as he protects the puck well. He can really shoot the puck. This season, he's used on the point on power plays, where he distributes the puck effectively and also takes good one-timer shots. His wrist shot is excellent as well, with a quick release. Provost has one of the better shots of any players eligible in this year's QMJHL Draft. The biggest knock on his game is his lack of effort over 60 minutes and lack of grit. He's got one of the best offensive upsides in this draft class. It would have been interesting to see him with a better team around him, how much better he could have perform this past season.

PRUETER, AIDAN
LC - Saginaw Spirit (OHL) 5'9" 168

Aidan Prueter was selected 24th overall in the 2nd round of the 2017 OHL draft. He had a successful rookie year for Saginaw, producing 11 points in 63 games, including 8 assists. In the playoffs, he had an assist in 4 games and played for Canada Black at the U17's, where he had two points in 5 games

Prueter is a two-way center who was used in all situations for Saginaw despite his young age. This was a testament to his ability to elevate his line using his motor and energy. He's not the biggest kid and was playing against far stronger players on most nights but he would make up for his physical limitations by playing at a pace that allowed him to overwhelm defensive-units at times. His first-few steps caught defenders at the defensive-blueline and he was very good at predicting movement, which allowed him to cut off players and make them panic, allowing him to generate chances while short-handed in our viewings. He has plus playmaking skills and recognized when his angles were getting cut-off in advance, rarely turning the puck over while showing a good-level of adaptation to the OHL in his rookie season. His shot is surprisingly heavy for his size and he was good at putting himself in positions to set up his shot for scoring chances consistently. Prueter isn't available until the 2020 draft, so there's a lot of upside and opportunity for him to fill out before his draft year.

RATZLAFF, JAKE
RD - Rosemount High (MNHS) 6'02" 190

Jake is a University of Minnesota commit that was recently drafted by Green Bay in the 6th Round, 8th overall in the 2018 USHL Futures Draft. Ratzlaff is coming off an impressive freshman season for Rosemount High School where he was given additional responsibilities as the season progressed. Ratzlaff has developed physically earlier than a lot of his age group and it showed in his play as he was able to clear things in front of his net and win physical battles in the corners. Jake has a heavy shot from the point but needs to quicken up his delivery and use better judgement on when to use it, as his lanes can close on him on some occasions. Ratzlaff still needs to continue to work on his footwork, especially in his defending against the rush as he can lose containment against quicker forwards often. Ratzlaff is a raw prospect at this stage but his upside is high due to his two-way capability.

RAYMOND, LUCAS
RW/LW - Frolunda HC J18 (J18 Allsvenskan) - 5'10" 165

Raymond is the other top prospect out of Sweden for the 2020 NHL Entry Draft, along with Alexander Holtz. The young winger is a flashy winger with great puck skills and great shooting abilities.

This season, he played as an underager with the national U-17 team during two tournaments and scored 3 goals in 8 games. During the season, back in Sweden, he played at 5 different levels of hockey and combined for 37 goals and 83 points in 48 games. He finished the season playing 8 games with the J20 team, playing against player 4 years older than him. He went pointless in those 8 games. We really like Raymond's puck skills. He has the ability, with his hands and speed, to challenge opposing defensemen with his great arsenal of dekes. He's tough to defend against with that skill level, that speed and the fact that he can either beat you with his shot (which has an excellent release) or with his hands deking around you. His skating is more advanced than Holtz at this point, but Holtz gets the nod for his scoring abilities and size at this point. He's a good skater, has a good burst of speed and likes to challenge defenders wide with that great top speed. He's quite solid on his skates as well; he has good edges and is tough to knock down off his skates. Next season, he should be a regular in the J20 league as one of the youngest players in it (with Holtz) and it should be interesting to see the evolution of this player. He also will be a regular on the international scene with Sweden, either on the U-17 or U-18 team.

RENWICK, MICHAEL
RD - Mississauga Reps (GTHL) 5'11" 168

Michael was selected in the second round, 34th overall by the Hamilton Bulldogs at the 2018 OHL Priority Selection Draft. Renwick is a puck moving defender with good size and skill to his game. Michael possesses good mobility and utilizes his skating abilities to dictate his style of play. Renwick shows poise in possession and makes strong decisions with the puck. A player who is able to recognize pressure, Michael displays the quick feet and strong edges necessary to elude a forecheck and quickly bust up ice. An effective and confident puck carrier who recognizes when to simplify his decision making, Renwick also see's the ice well and makes a strong first pass. He will however need to learn to make better decisions when forecheck pressure is able to close on him as he can force plays looking to elude contact. In the offensive zone Michael does a good job walking the line and utilizing his quick feet to open shooting lanes. He often uses a quick and deceptively heavy snap shot from the point to get pucks on goal, but is most effective distributing the puck from his point position. Renwick makes good reads when injecting from his point position and is able to contribute offensively. While defending transition attacks he is able to keep the play in front of him and effectively take away the middle of the ice, using his footwork to angle opponents to the outside. Michael does lack strength and will rely on his positioning, gap control and stick to defend which can limit him in certain situations. In the defensive zone Renwick anticipates well and can beat opponents to loose pucks or use his smarts to gain ideal body position. However he does rely on his stick-on-puck defensive tools and the quickness in which he can take away time and space. Renwick can be limited in puck battles as he can be out muscled by opposing players despite a good compete level in the dirty areas.

ROBINSON, DYLAN
LD - Brantford 99ers (MHAO) 6'02.5" 164

Dylan was selected in the third round, 45th overall by the Windsor Spitfires at the 2018 OHL Priority Selection Draft. Dylan is an active defenseman on both sides of the puck with intriguing size and smarts. Robinson showed an excellent ability to beat the pressure of oncoming forecheckers by using his mobility to elude them creating time and space in the process. Dylan shows great confidence in possession, he has the ability to carry the puck up ice with his quickness and puck handling skills. Once he sets up in offensive zone Robinson becomes a dangerous threat, he can survey the ice from the blue line making strong accurate passes as well as firing hard accurate shots on net where they can be tipped. Dylan has a high hockey I.Q in all three zones, he can look off passes for a higher success rate, use his large wingspan to break up chances in the neutral zone and he displayed his ability to learn on the fly by trying new ways to break the puck out of his own end. With great size, mobility and the ability to box out players around the net its easy to see how Dylan brings so much defensively. The one area Dylan should look to improve is his first step.

ROBINSON, DYLAN
LC - Toronto Jr. Canadiens (GTHL) 6'01" 163

Dylan was selected in the second round, 28th overall by the Oshawa Generals at the 2018 OHL Priority Selection Draft. Robinson is an intelligence centre with good size and skill to is game. Dylan is at his best in possession where he has the ability to combine his physical attributes with good vision and playmaking skills. His combination of size, strength and puck skills can make him difficult to defend as he shields the puck well and utilizes his size to drive through congested areas. A player who is strong in transition, Robinson is able to generate a good top speed and will use his speed effectively to drive wide past an opponent, protect the puck effectively and create in transition, showing awareness of his lanes to the goal and passing options. Dylan can dominate the play down low with his size and skill, showing a strength off the cycle and ability to drive off the half-wall showing good recognition of time and space. His versatile offensive skill set in combination with his physical advantages make him difficult to contain. A player who shows above average passing skills, Robinson also possesses an above average shot with good accuracy behind it. His smarts show in his positional awareness and ability to anticipate the play with effectiveness. He can beat opponents to loose pucks by out thinking them, while his positional awareness shows in all three zones, providing reliable efforts away from the puck. Robinson would benefit from playing with a more consistent pace to his game as he can look disengaged at times due a slow pace of play. He would also benefit from using his physical gifts to become more assertive physically. Dylan flashes an aggressiveness to his game and is arguably at his best when combining his grit with his skill package, however his physical edge comes and goes.

ROCHETTE, THÉO
LC - Lausanne U20 (Elite Jr.A) - 5'10" 150

Rochette is a dual citizen with his father being from Quebec which made him eligible for the QMJHL Draft where he was drafted 7th overall by Chicoutimi. He had a huge year this season amassing 34 points in 43 games in the U20 league tying the record of Nik Ehlers for most points by an under -16 player in this league. He also played internationally for Switzerland with the U-16 & U-17 team through the year. He's not the biggest player currently but still has time to get bigger and stronger. He's really smart, great understanding of the game and his hockey sense is good as well. His play away from the puck at this age is pretty advance, he's good in the neutral zone at reading the plays and creating some turnovers with his anticipation and good stick. He has great hands and excellent vision. Skating is good and we like his complete game at both end of the ice. He'll need to keep working hard to get stronger and play with a bit more grit which he will learn by reporting to the QMJHL.

ROODE, BENJAMIN
RD - Dartmouth Subaru (NSMMHL) - 6'03" 196

Roode was drafted 14th overall by Acadie-Bathurst in the 2018 qMJHL Draft. The best defensive prospect out of Nova Scotia, Roode was one of the more intriguing players in this QMJHL Draft class. He's a big, rangy two-way defenseman who can skate. Roode has developed into a good and reliable shutdown player, using his size to win battles. He has a great set of hands, and is good at escaping pressure while protecting the puck to make plays. When he is at his best, he's reading the play at a high level, speed, and reach to get into passing lanes and intercept plays. However, he often plays a much simpler, safer game, which leaves you wanting more from him. We feel that his game is still pretty raw, and that Roode could get more out of his toolkit. He does however has the size and skating ability to play major junior.

ROSSI, MARCO
LC - GCK Lions U20 (Elite Jr.A) - 5'09" 154

Rossi is a late 2001 born player originally from Austria but has been playing in Switzerland since he was 10 years old. Rossi was very successful this season in the U20 league amassing 51 points in 34 games and also played 18 games in Switzerland 2nd men's league (NLB). He's a highly skilled forward with great puck skills and creativity. He's got good poise with the puck; he likes to have the puck on his stick and he's a threat one on one. His skating is good but at his size we would like to see him add a bit more explosiveness to hi stride. He's strong on his skate, makes quick change of directions which makes him tough to cover one on one. He sees the ice well, good passer and he's creative with the puck in the offensive zone. Rossi as a late 2001 birthday is eligible for the CHL import draft and would make a good candidate for a CHL team who would have him for two full seasons before his NHL draft year.

ROY, PIER-OLIVIER
LC/LW - Chevaliers de Lévis (LHMAAAQ) - 5'09" 156

The 9th overall selection in the 2018 QMJHL draft by the Gatineau Olympiques. Roy is one of the best two-way centers of this year's draft. He can do it all on the ice, as he's a great playmaker who's reliable defensively and will finish his hits. Even if he's not the biggest player, he's one of the most relentless, and will do everything he can in order to take pucks away from the puck-carrier. Roy demonstrated his leadership qualities throughout the year, as he showed he has character. He was used on both special teams by his coach. His shot-blocking abilities and ability to break up passes on the penalty kill was noticeable. Roy's playmaking abilities are great, as he can make passes from anywhere in the offensive zone to find his open teammates, and we've seen some tremendous saucer-passes from him during the season. The fact that he already plays a complete game on a 200-foot level makes him valuable for every team; because that shows that he has a hockey IQ and an understanding of the game that is above-average. The only question mark with him is how healthy will he be. He was injured twice at the end of the season. Roy was a favourite of our scouting staff this season, and will have a good impact in the QMJHL next season.

SCHLUETING, PACEY
LD - North Bay Trappers (GNML) 6'00.5" 170

Pacey was selected in the first round, ninth overall by the North Bay Battalion at the 2018 OHL Priority Selection Draft. Schlueting is a big bodied, two-way defender with above average skill to his game. An intelligent defender that possesses the ability to dictate the pace of play, Pacey possesses both the physical attributes and the skill to be a dominate defender at the next level. He displays a confidence to his game that allows him to be effective on both sides of the puck. A quality skater, Pacey possesses a long and powerful stride that allows him to generate good straight line speed. Schlueting will utilize his skating/speed to carry transition, were he confidently carriers the puck up ice, showing good puck control and an ability to create once gaining the offensive zone. Pacey is aware of passing options, however will also utilize defenders as a screen or take the puck to the goal. Where he gets in trouble is when he fails to simplify his game when an option isn't available to him, leading to turnovers with him caught up ice. In the offensive zone Schlueting distributes the puck well from his point position, however is more effective as a shooter, showing a heavy point shot. He recognizes traffic in front and will change the angle or velocity of his shot to utilize a deflection opportunity/to get a puck on goal. Pacey defenders well, keeping good gaps in the neutral zone and angling the opponent away from the center of the ice before finishing with contact. While his skating his slightly above average, his four-way mobility still has some stiffness to it, which can hinder his contain of explosive skating opponents, as well as his quickness on puck retrievals. Defensively Pacey has an aggressiveness and physicality to his game, using his size and strength to out muscle opponents in position or puck battles. He utilizes his reach to his advantage and can effectively take away time and space. He has room to improve his defensive zone awareness.

SEBRANGO, DONOVAN
LD - CIH White (HEO) 5'10.75" 162

Donovan was selected in the second round, 40th overall by the Kitchener Rangers at the 2018 OHL Priority Selection Draft. He was also selected in the second round, 32nd overall by the Waterloo Black Hawks at the 2018 USHL Draft. He is currently committed to Boston University. Donovan is a puck moving defensemen with very high offensive ability and very high hockey IQ. He is an excellent skater with or without the puck, and has outstanding mobility on the back end. Donovan really liked to go on the offense at the beginning of the year, and was getting caught too deep or pinching with no supports, but he made some adjustment at the midpoint of the season, and became more responsible both ends of the ice. He plays a very smart game and rarely makes mistake throughout the game, he is excellent with his first pass coming out of the zone, and he always makes the smart decision with the puck and rarely forces the puck into bad areas. He was there QB on the power play and everything started with him from the point, he distributes the puck really well to his teammates and knows when to pass the puck hard or show some touch on his passes. Donovan had a good an accurate shot, he seemed to always shot for the tip or rebound, has a very accurate shot. He has really good puck retrieval as it doesn't take him long to move the puck up the ice quick to get on the offence. Donovan has shown a physical presence on the backend and doesn't shy away from the contact; he was trying too much earlier in the season for the big hit, but quickly realized he needs to be smarter with his anticipation and knowing when to step up or when to stay back. Donovan compete level is excellent as he comes to play every night and sets an example for his teammates and you can see he leads by example. He has all the tools and intangibles to play at the next level, he just needs to work more on the little things of the game, and his play away from the puck, and getting stronger and faster.

SEED, NOLAN
LD - Smiths Falls Bears (HEO) 5'11.5" 152

Nolan is an effortless skating two-way defenseman that plays for the Smiths Falls Bears who was named top defensemen of the year for the HEO AAA league. He is a good size Defensemen with really good skating ability, his first couple strides are very strong, and there's time on the rush where he's able to break away from defenders with his speed. He also very strong on his skates and is hard to knock him off the puck. Nolan has really good puck skills; he has an above average shot from the point and would like to see him use it more often from the point. Nolan has a very good and hard first pass coming out of the zone, he very seldom misses and outlet pass, the one concern with Nolan when it comes to his outlet passes is he will try too many cross ice passes or stretch passes and gets lucky with no turnover, but at the next level he can't do that. Nolan is a very good puck moving defensemen and can create a lot of offense off the rush with his speed and skill. He is a smart Defensemen and has great anticipation on the ice, he is good at reading and reacting to plays in front of him, and is good at getting himself in position before the play develops, he is very good at making quick and accurate decisions in transition and is good at knowing when to jump into the play or sit back, he also has excellent puck retrieval skill as he gets back quick to get the puck and goes on the offense quick and effectively. Nolan loves to jump into the play a lot, he needs to some realize he can't jump up to much, and focus on the defensive side of game too. He is good in his defensive zone, very reliable defensemen that shows no panic in his game when faced with pressure. He has really good closing speed on defenders and closes the gap really quick not allowing much room for forwards to enter the zone. Nolan has a strong work ethic as he competes hard every night and very seldom takes nights off.

STRANGES, ANTONIO
LC - Detroit Little Caesars U16 (USA) 5'10" 165

Antonio was selected in the second round, 21st overall by the London Knights at the 2018 OHL Priority Selection Draft. Stranges is a highly skilled winger with high-end skating abilities. Antonio possesses an explosive first step and fantastic straight line speed that makes him difficult to contain. He shows strong edges and elite puck handling abilities that when in combination with his skating make him elusive and near impossible to contain. Stranges pushes the pace in transition and aggressively attacks the offensive zone, forcing opponents to defend. He possesses the uncanny ability to create space with his speed, edges and puck skills and can gain easy and controlled entry to the offensive zone. Antonio becomes increasingly more difficult to defend due to his versatility in possession. Stranges shows the confidence and puck handling abilities to beat and opponent 1-on-1 and create his own shot. However he will also utilize an opponent as a screen and release a shot mid-stride with little room needed and catch a goaltender flat-footed. While Stranges has elite individual skill, he is subtly an equally strong playmaker, showing excellent vision and touch on his passes, raising the level of his teammates. Antonio thinks the game at high level offensively and is dangerous away from the puck as he can find space, pounce on loose pucks and simply put himself in areas to generate offense. Stranges uses his speed effectively on the forecheck and has a quick stick to create turnovers, however also anticipates very well, allowing him to be first to pucks. His knock is his desire to over complicate things. Its hard to fault a player for utilizing his superior skill, however his over handling of the puck can lead to turnovers. Stranges is deceptively strong but fails to be overly assertive in the dirty areas.

TERRY, ZACK
RD - Oakville Rangers (OMHA-SCTA) 6'01" 180

Zack was selected in the second round, 36th overall by the Guelph Storm at the 2018 OHL Priority Selection Draft. Zack is a talented defenseman that showed great ability to skate and read the game. Terry plays an effective two-way style, defensively he uses his size and reach well to contain his opponents and to separate the player from the puck. His ability to read the game allows him that extra couple seconds to make a play which is all he needs to set up a breakout. Zack showed good mobility which allowed him to get up ice quickly while setting the pace for his team. Once he has possession he is hard to knock off the puck due to his excellent balance, strength and the ability to shield the puck with his body. He has the capability of quarterbacking the Oakville powerplay from the point using his above average vision to find team mates when paths free up. Terry can also open up shooting lanes for himself by effectively walking the line with his mobility before utilizing his heavy slap shot which he gets on net with regularity. At times Zack can rush plays in traffic which leads to turnovers but we feel he can learn from these mistakes and develop into a highly effective player at the next level.

THOMPSON, JACK
RD - Clarington Toros (OMHA-ETA) 5'11" 161

Jack was selected in the second round, 30th overall by the Sudbury Wolves at the 2018 OHL Priority Selection Draft. Thompson is an intelligent, two-way defender with good mobility. Jack thrived throughout the season playing hard minutes on a nightly basis against opposing teams top players and was very successful. A player who possesses power to his stride, Thompson is a good skater who shows confidence in possession and the ability to effortlessly gain the offensive zone in possession. Jack see's the ice well and often can lead transition with a clean outlet pass. Offensively Thompson does a good job recognizing when to inject himself into the attack, however is at his best along the blue line. He has the ability to distribute the puck well but his best trait is his point shot. Jack possesses a high velocity/strong accuracy point shot with the ability to open shooting lanes and get his shot through. He possesses the best one-time point shot in the draft class and has the ability to beat goaltenders clean from distance. On the defensive side of the puck, Thompson has the mobility to keep the play in front of him, however would benefit from improving his gap as he can sometimes sit back and wait for the play to come to him. He would benefit from challenging puck carriers more frequently. In the defensive zone, Jack shows good positional awareness and often utilizes his physical attributes to gain inside positioning while defending the net front area. He is quick to take away time and space and effectively uses his stick to poke pucks free and also clog shooting and passing lanes. Jack will show a physical edge, however doesn't chase contact, instead using it as a tool to separate player from puck. His strength and compete allows him to win battles in all areas of the ice. Thompson is a versatile defender however he can struggle with a heavy forecheck. While still able to avoid turnovers he can revert to simply rimming the puck opposed to make a quick decision/pass to a teammates.

TOLNAI, CAMERON
LC - Oakville Rangers (OMHA-SCTA) 6'00" 167

Cameron was selected in the first round, sixth overall by the Ottawa 67's at the 2018 OHL Priority Selection Draft. Tolnai is a dynamic centerman for the Oakville Rangers who dominated the SCTA this year and won SCTA player of the year honours. He has a good frame and uses his body and puck skill to protect the puck well. He uses his stick effectively on loose pucks and in puck battles to strip opponents of the puck with ease. He is a great skater with a powerful stride which gives him good four-way mobility, a good top speed and acceleration to separate himself from opponents. Tolnai is incredibly difficult to knock off the puck and when in possession he rarely makes a mistake. His playmaking and finishing ability are both excellent and he uses each interchangeably to remain unpredictable to opponents. His vision allows him to find teammates effortlessly and distribute the puck after attracting opponents to himself. When in possession in the offensive zone, he regularly skates the puck to create space for teammates or to force his way to the slot where he will fire a quick and accurate snapshot. Tolnai will also use a powerful slapshot when given time in the slot and picks his corners. All forms of his shot pack a lot of velocity and are very accurate. He tends to only use it when he works his way into a scoring position and will opt to hold the puck or pass it off until a better scoring chance is available. He is not limited to beating the goalie with just his shot as he will stun goaltenders with quick hands when in alone. Away from the puck he provides his teammates a solid outlet and supports teammates in board battles as a high man and scoops up the puck with a good stick. His hand-eye is excellent as he can knock pucks down on point shots and clearing opportunities. Tolnai is very complete player but adding some mass to fill out his frame to withstand stronger opponents next year would greatly benefit him. With some added strength and balance, he should continue to be a force at the next level.

TULLIO, TYLER
LC - Vaughan Kings (GTHL) 5'08.5" 150

Tyler was selected in the first round, 11th Overall by the Oshawa Generals at the 2018 OHL Priority Selection Draft. Tullio is a skilled forward with good speed and aggression to his game. A versatile offensive threat, Tyler has shown the ability to play both the centre and wing with two-way effectiveness. Tullio displays an intelligence to his game that allows him to thrive both in possession and away from the puck. He has the uncanny ability to find space offensively and burst to open ice to make a play, showing strong play away from the puck. Tyler however possesses the above average skill set necessary to also carry a line offensively, combining his speed with strong puck handling and awareness of his options. He can beat a check in a 1-on-1 scenario with his puck skills, but can also slow or speed the pace of play to create with his skating. Tyler is versatile in the offensive zone as both a playmaker and shooter, displaying a dynamic shot off a quick release. While Tullio is skilled, he provides a physicality that adds to his intrigue. A player who is aggressive on the forecheck, Tyler is often first to pucks and shows the quick thinking to make a play upon gaining possession. When he arrives second he does a good job angling the puck carrier into oncoming traffic or will finish with contact to create a turnover. A quality skater with quick acceleration, Tullio utilizes his speed on both sides of the puck effectively and has an ability to be elusive in possession. Tullio shows engaged defensive zone play and can take away shooting lanes by effectively forcing the play to the outside, however will sacrifice the body to block shots, making him an effective presence on the penalty kill. Tyler does have some size limitations which can limit him in battles against bigger/stronger opponents, however his determination in position/puck battles can allow him to find an effectiveness. Tullio will however need to begin to stop on pucks more frequently as he shows a tendency to circle back to pucks which can have him a step behind the play.

TUSSEY, NOAH
LW - Stillwater Ponies (MNHS) 5'10" 161

Coming into the past season, Tussey was regarded as one of the top players in his age group in the State of Minnesota, resulting in a commitment to the University of Minnesota in November. Tussey is a dynamic skater with excellent explosiveness in his first couple of strides. Just a freshman this season for Stillwater, Tussey registered 11 goals and 6 assists for the Ponies. Tussey has decent size for his age and is extremely strong on his skates. Tussey is a smart player with high end offensive skills and good finishing ability with the puck on his tape Noah should see more key minutes and have more of an opportunity to showcase his skill this coming season for the Ponies and will be a prospect to track the next couple years to see if he can put the entire package together. Tussey was recently drafted in the 6th Round and 84th Overall by Sioux City in the 2018 USHL Futures Draft.

VALADE, REID
RW - Toronto Marlboros (GTHL) 5'10" 160

Reid was selected in the first round, 17th Overall by the Kitchener Rangers at the 2018 OHL Priority Selection Draft. Valade is an energetic winger with good skill. Reid displays a versatile skill set, combining speed, skill and a physical edge that can make him tough to play against. A strong skater, Valade shows a quick first step along with a fluid and powerful stride that allows him to create separation from a check and dictate the pace of play. Reid shows the ability to make quick and high percentage decisions while playing with speed and shows an ability to play with skill while moving at a high pace. He often utilizes his speed in transition to back off opponents, creating space for himself to utilize his shot. However Reid will exploit opponents who keep tight gaps and utilize his speed to drive wide before attacking the goal. Valade will however need to learn to become less predictable off the rush and utilize his teammates more frequently while attacking the offensive zone. Reid does a good job using his speed away from the puck to make himself an effective presence on the forecheck. While he has the ability and willingness to arrive first, when he doesn't, Valade does a good job pressuring puck carriers into low percentage decisions and often finishes with contact. His work ethic along the wall and in the dirty areas of the ice can allow him to become an agitating, but effective presence. In the offensive zone, Valade benefit's from keeping his feet moving and finding space, to utilize his quick release and strong shot. Defensively Reid needs to improve his awareness and find a more consistent compete level as it can waiver in effectiveness.

VIERLING, EVAN
LC - York-Simcoe Express (OMHA-ETA) 6'00" 145

Evan was selected in the first round, second overall by the Flint Firebirds at the 2018 OHL Priority Selection Draft. Vierling is a skilled centre with intelligence to his game. Evan displays a strong two-way effort that allows him to thrive in various scenarios. He's a player who is arguably at his best in possession, Vierling shows impressive poise and awareness when generating offensive opportunities. Evan has the ability to raise the play of those around him with his high end hockey sense and playmaking abilities. A versatile offensive threat that shows the ability to dictate the pace of play, Vierling shows the skill necessary to be effective creating his own opportunities, as well as using his vision and shooting skills to contribute. Evan handles the puck at a high level and consistently showed the ability to create space and beat an opponent in a 1-on-1 scenario with his puck skills. He often exploits time and space and will take the puck to the middle of the ice frequently, enhancing his options, before making a strong decision with the puck. Vierling shows a deceptively high end shot, coming off a quick release while showing excellent accuracy. He has the ability to carry a line and is able to generate a good top speed and make skilled decisions with pace. Vierling does have room to improve the efficiency of his stride and allow it to become more fluid, however continuing to add strength to his lower body should allow this to develop. A competitive player with a two-way presence, Evan uses his intelligence to anticipate well in the defensive zone, slipping in front of passing attempts or getting his stick in a lane to negate opportunities. He shows an effectiveness on the penalty kill, clogging lanes and keeping the play to the outside. On the forecheck Vierling also anticipates well and can intercept passing attempts or utilize a quick stick to separate player from puck. While Evan is effective defensively, enhancing his strength would benefit him at the next level.

"He was my second favourite player in his OHL Draft class. Kid is very smart and skilled and has a burst when he's skating that reminded me of Kyle Connor's burst at that age." - HP Scout, Mark Edwards

VILLENEUVE, WILLIAM
RD - Cantonniers de Magog (LHMAAAQ) - 6'01" 154

The 2nd overall selection in the 2018 QMJHL Draft, William Villeneuve is a very intelligent player who offers reliable and effective play in all three zones. A right-handed offensive defenseman, he is able to get involved regularly on the attack when an opportunity arises, not hesitating to carry the puck from his own zone and support his forwards by offering options to them during counter-attacks. Excellent from the opposite blueline, he is particularly effective on the power play, where he is very active with the puck. Ensuring a continuous movement of the puck, he circulates it well with his teammates and moves his feet well by making intelligent moves that force opponents to compromise themselves. In addition to having mobility that puts him in a class of his own, Villeneuve also generates very good shots on net (either wrist shots or hard, low slapshots). The right-hander stands out by his ease in finding passing lanes as few others know how to do; he is actually very effective to start the zone exit by executing smart first passes out of his zone. In addition to having undeniable offensive skills that make him a unique player, Villeneuve also offers very solid play in his own zone, making him quite complete at both ends of the ice. Used very often by his coach to kill penalties or in critical defensive situations, the young defender manages to control his opponents by using an active stick and making good use of his big size. Moreover, despite being still relatively small for a player of a 6'01" frame, there is no doubt that this Cantonniers' player is far from being physically mature, which suggests good things when it comes time to project the kind of size he could display in a few years.

Stats-wise, Villeneuve has done very well in his first season at Midget AAA level, scoring nine goals and 25 assists for 34 points in 40 games, good for first place among all defensemen in the league. Considering his potential that is more than interesting, we see him become a first-pairing defender and a quarterback on the power play in the QMJHL.

WILLIAMS, JACK
LW - Selects Hockey Academy 15U (USHS) - 5'10" 146

Williams had a great year with the Select Hockey Academy program, finishing 2nd in points and goals with 37 goals and 79 points. Williams, originally from Maine, is a shoot-first type of winger. He likes to put pucks on net, and doesn't mind holding onto the puck for an extra second to find better angles. He's really good at finding space on the ice and getting himself open in the offensive zone to receive passes in scoring areas. He usually plays on his off-wing, and likes to set up on the left side on the power play and use his one-timer. He's a sniper, but has above-average vision. He can find his linemates in the offensive zone with ease. His vision is good, but his bread-and-butter remains his goal-scoring instincts. He has a good wrist shot with a quick release and has excellent hands as well. He has a slight frame, and will need to get stronger to compete better along the boards and win more battles. He has decent speed and is good at escaping pressure, but for the next level, he will need to improve his explosiveness. Away from the puck, he will need some work with his effort and consistency, along with his compete level in his own zone. Overall, Williams has the shot and scoring instincts to be a sniper at the NCAA or major junior level. He's not elite, but he could be a good player for a QMJHL team that can get him to report to them. He's committed to play NCAA hockey with Northeastern University.

WOOLLEY, MARK
LD - Guelph Storm (OHL) 6'2" 203

Mark Woolley was drafted in the 3rd round, 54th overall in the 2017 OHL draft. He managed to play a significant amount of games on the backend for Guelph despite being eligible for the 2020 draft. He finished the year with 9 points in 66 games, including 7 assists. In the playoffs, he had one assist in 6 playoff games.

Woolley is a large two-way defenseman who's got an accurate and crisp first-pass. His vision and passing ability are arguably his two best qualities, he's capable of making long stretch-passes, soft bank passes, and sharp passes that can land on the tape of his teammates in motion. Furthermore, he can make passes under pressure in his own-end. This is especially important for Woolley due to having poor skating mechanics at this time. He's a big kid who's still developing his lower-base and this is apparent when viewing his movement on the ice, since he's not coordinated. He has an awkward and upright stride, with a lot of unnecessary extra moment when attempting to shift-gears. Due to this, he relies on his ability to process information before using his playmaking ability in order to execute plays. At the offensive-blueline, although his shooting mechanics need some work, he has shown plus puck-skills and generated some scoring chances while pinching. It's important for Woolley to continue to develop his skating mechanics in order to continue developing into a promising up and coming prospect.

WONG, NICK
RW - Oshawa Generals (OHL) 5'09" 172

Wong is an undersized, skilled winger with a quality hockey IQ. Nick displays a strong work ethic and intelligence to his game which allowed to play up and down the line for the Generals this season. He shows confidence in possession along with good puck control and an ability to make good decisions under pressure. Wong however does need to clean up his neutral zone turnovers and do a better job recognize when to utilize his creativity with the puck. Nick is a player who complimented whatever line he played on well, showing an uncanny ability to find space in the offensive zone and instinctive play that allowed him to pounce on loose pucks in tight and finish. He shows a quick release and accurate shot, improving his upper body strength would only benefit his shot's velocity. Wong showed an effectiveness on the forecheck were he used a quick stick to create turnovers. While he does possess deceptive strength it still is an area that needs to be enhanced to better suite his abilities along the wall and in the dirty areas. Wong will need to elevate his skating for an undersized player as he shows a short stride and somewhat heavy feet. Improving his quickness would go along way in elevating his skill and production.

YOUNG, DAVIS
LC - Mississauga Reps (GTHL) 5'10.75" 175

Davis was selected in the second round, 37th Overall by the Hamilton Bulldogs at the 2018 OHL Priority Selection Draft. Young is an intelligent, two-way centre with a competitiveness to his game. Davis shows strong playmaking traits to his game that allow him to elevate those around him while generating offensive opportunities. A player who possesses strong hockey sense, Davis is often aware of his surroundings both in possession and away from the puck, allowing him to play in various situations successfully. Young displays a fluid stride and ability to generate a good top speed. He plays with good pace to his game and shows the ability to dictate the pace when in possession. When in transition Young shows excellent awareness of his surroundings and can be difficult to defend off the rush due to an unpredictability in the way he attacks the zone. Davis will utilize his speed to burn opponents wide, however will also slow the play and look to make a pass off his forehand or attack with pace and hit an attacking teammate with a disguised pass off his back-hand. A player who shows good puck control, Young often was able to make space in tight areas with his puck handling and foot speed, showing an ability to shield the puck in traffic. Davis shows good play away from the puck as he will drive lanes in transition to create space for attacking teammates and also does a fine job keeping his feet moving in the offensive zone to find space in scoring areas. His two-way abilities are appealing as he shows strong positional awareness and engaged defensive zone play. Young will need to improve his strength to better defend from the centre position, however an active stick along with his ability to anticipate the play, allows him to use a combination of smarts and pressure to defend adequately.

GAME REPORTS

Unites States (blue) vs Sweden, World Junior Summer Showcase, July 29, 2017

Team Blue –

BL #7 C/LW Tkachuk, Brady (2018) – Brady stands at 6'2, 200 pounds and has a broad frame which he used to gain leverage on his opponent resulting in a turnover in the offensive zone. Shows tenacious forechecking and a high-octane motor, especially for someone his size. Like his brother, he's no fun to play against down-low in the offensive zone which is highlighted by his presence directly in-front of the net where he uses his hand-eye to redirect shots. Speaking of shots, I wish he would shoot more often, he's a selfless player but he has reach and uses it to mask the angle that he's going to release his shot on, it's difficult for a goalie to remain square to him. He was arguably the best American forward in this game even though he didn't show his passing ability as much as he normally does.

BL #14 C/RW Wahlstrom, Oliver (2018) – Transitioned a toe drag into a seamless pass for a high-end scoring chance off the rush that was misjudged by the defence. Puck skills are evident. Has good cross-over technique in his skating. Has a fluid stride and good acceleration which gets him up to his quick top-gear. He plays a very efficient game but I wish he would dictate with the puck a bit more based off todays viewing. Considering he's one of the youngest kids on the ice he looked excellent, his technical ability is very high. There's an attentional to detail to the way he plays.

BL #18 C Khodorenko, Patrick (2018*) – Shows ability to drive to the net while guarding the puck well. Demonstrated poor acceleration during a sequence that showed an inability to adjust to sudden changes in speed where he should have had a good short-handed scoring chance on a 2 on 1, instead It resulted in nothing. Once he get's up to top speed though he showed a sequence where he can puck rush when the opportunity arises, he likes to shoot and isn't afraid to let his decent release go at anytime, unfortunately this lead to having several of his shots blocked in traffic. He looks like a kid who should have been drafted late based off todays viewing.

BL #24 C Dhooghe, Sean (2018*) – Plays a high tempo game which results from his skating ability. His skating is remarkable considering how short his stride is, relies on pure power in his lower body to compensate for the lack of range of motion in his legs. Showed high end defensive awareness along the blueline by being in the right place at the right time, resulting in a turnover. His shot is lethal, I don't know how he gets the leverage he does on it but there's no denying the power and his release point, it's all there. I feel so bad for the kid, if he was even 3 inches taller he would have been drafted and I think would have had a real shot of doing damage in the pro's, but he's already getting thrown off the puck relatively easily and was pinned along the boards without much effort regardless of his attempts to escape. I hope a growth spurt hits him so we can get excited about his future.

BL #27 D Anderson, Mikey (2017) – Active in his own end, constantly using his feet to put himself in shot blocking positions, there's a lot of hustle in his defensive play. He was excellent on the penalty kill, constantly monitoring where players were on the ice and getting into shot blocking lanes when needed. He Isn't very dynamic but he moves the puck out of his zone efficiently. Likes to hit the opposition whenever possible. His offensive ability is limited, he's not patient and his vision isn't great, he treats the offensive zone similarly to the defensive zone where his mentality is usually to get the puck off his stick as quickly as possible regardless of traffic or if there's a better play to be made, the couple of pinches he had were ineffective. He's a prototypical shutdown D-men who hits everything in sight and can make the first outlet pass when needed.

Team Sweden -

SWE #15 C/RW Gustafsson, Glenn (2018+) – Has a very thick frame which he uses to deliver some hard hits along the boards, unfortunately these led to multiple penalties. Stations himself effectively in-front of the net on rebounds. Had a nice chip play to clear the puck out of the D-zone. Offensively speaking, he offered very little, his vision didn't seem particularly good and he doesn't seem to read his teammates well on rushes. He didn't play like a kid who should be drafted as an over-ager.

SWE #8 D Dhalin, Rasmus (2018) – shows good composure with the puck in his own zone under high pressure. Uses his skating ability and his edge work to box out opponents attempting to drive past him. During a sequence behind his net he evaluated multiple threats quickly while simultaneously guarding the puck with his body, his processing speed is very high end. Unfortunately, sometimes he tries to do too much with the puck which was emphasized when he caused a turnover that lead to a scoring chance in the slot after he was pushed to the ice. Showed some physicality when necessary, not afraid to take a hit or give one. Demonstrated some snarl by not backing down against a larger player after the whistle and initiated some contact. Offensively, he had a quite game although he did generate an assist. His shots were inaccurate but they had some velocity on them. His ability to transition the puck from his end to the offensive end was only matched by Timothy. Overall, I thought he didn't play like a first overall pick but he still displayed why he is so highly touted for the 2018 draft. He has all the tools and the processor necessary to make those tools effective.

SWE #23 D Sellgren, Jesper (2018++) - Had an excellent sequence where he kept Wahlstrom to the outside in a 1-on-1 before physically overpowering him and knocking him to the ice. He plays a poised game but not one fans are going to notice, which isn't necessarily bad. He was mistake free most of the time in his own zone and reads dump sequences well. His game was average, he never stood out but didn't hurt his team either.

SWE #28 F Lundestrom, Isac (2018) – Shows good puck moving ability which was displayed on a neutral zone rush. Was hit very hard early but bounced back up quickly while attempting to shake the cob webs. Had a nice rush at the end of the second where he beat his man and created a scoring chance. He's good at getting under the skin of his opponents and demonstrated some tenacity with hits before and after the whistle. He was very noticeable in certain sequences and then somewhat invisible in others. Looks like a potential first round pick in this year's draft.

Final Score 4-3 Sweden

Canada vs Russia, Hlinka Memorial, August 7, 2017

Canada –

CAN #9 C Joe Veleno (2018) – The first Quebec born player to ever be granted exceptional status. Veleno started this game relatively slow and didn't really start to use his tools until the third period. His skating is excellent, his first steps are explosive and it allows him to gain a step on opposing defenseman. He's considered more of a playmaker than a shooter but he really stepped up in the third and started using both his slap shot and wrist shot. The mechanics behind his wrist shot are good, he spends a bit too much time thinking about his placement but gets it off quickly enough where it can be a weapon. Regardless of his overthinking, he still displays a quick processor on the ice which is emphasized given his speed. He can make difficult plays at high speed and this is where he shines. He had several sequences demonstrating his ability to dash in and out of a lane before feeding a teammate for a scoring chance and used his positioning to anticipate plays defensively, causing a turnover in the third that lead to a scoring chance. He wasn't dominant but he went from having a poor game through the first two periods, to an average one given his body of work in the third.

CAN #22 RW Serron Noel (2018) – Has excellent size, standing at 6'3, with a large wingspan, yet is surprisingly shifty and good at avoiding checks. Had a nice pull up resulting in a high percentage scoring chance in-front of the net that he failed to capitalize on, the release was average, too much wind up not quick enough off his stick, especially in tight, a lot of wasted movement. Another sequence had a defender coming down on him from the side and shifted his body very quickly to avoid the hit and then delivered a nice back-hand pass into the slot for a scoring chance. He's got good acceleration and uses it to forecheck affectively and recover. On one sequence, he inadvertently tripped but managed to get right back up, deke under pressure and pass the puck off, it showed his versatility during a recovery play. Had an excellent defensive sequence where he aggressively stick-checked a Russian forward and rushed the puck back up ice for a scoring chance. Noel had a great game, he was consistent both offensively and defensively and stood out among more talented players than himself.

CAN #7 D Ryan Merkley (2018) – The first overall pick in the 2016 OHL priority selection, He's a modern day, undersized puck moving defenceman who relies on his agility and a fluid stride to transition the puck. He's not an explosive skater but a technically sound one who always looks in control with the puck on his stick. He's exceptional on the power play, using his agility to change directions along the blueline, it's difficult for the opposition to gauge what he's going to do because he's always using his edges to change the angles at which he attacks. One sequence demonstrated this ability on Canada's first power play where he left the puck and then drew his stick back to his right while still skating and picked the puck back up, the forward defending him was caught tracking the puck which allowed Merkley to penetrate below the slot. He's not only capable of subtle, yet effective plays, he's also skilled with the puck. If a player is coming at an angle, no problem, he'll spin off-of him effortlessly, if he's pressured by multiple guys he will use head feints and stick feints to freeze them and then either pass the puck off or deke through them. He's multi-faceted and very poised. He was Canada's best player today.

CAN #5 D Calen Addison (2018) – Another undersized puck moving defenceman who plays with some jump. He's got a good first step and gets up to his top gear quickly which allows him to transition the puck up the ice in all three zones. He had an outstanding offensive sequence in the second where he drove down on the right side of the slot and hesitated just long enough to bait Miftakhof into committing and then delivered a perfect pass for a goal. Addison looked good with Merkley on the power play; showcasing puck moving ability and showing patience, he doesn't force his passes through lanes when nothing's available, he's more methodical in his approach but is capable of dynamic plays when there available. An example of this was during the third period when Calen threw a spin pass into the slot to Thomas resulting in the game tying goal. He showed good puck tracking ability on that specific power play as well, keeping the puck in along the blueline on clearing attempt, which allowed an additional set up. He's a smart player, who knows how to compensate for his 5'9 frame.

Russia –

RUS #14 LW Grigori Denisenko (2018) – A highly skilled forward who's already had success at the MHL level as a 16-year-old. The first thing that stands out about his game are his hands and he can use them at high speeds. Displayed some tenacity in the early second during a puck pursuit race where he showcased a good top gear and then used body positioning plus a quick deke to come away with the puck against two players, additionally he had to contend with another defender and came away with the puck, it took support to finally strip him of the puck, he was a one-man army on the sequence. Defensively speaking, there's an attention to detail that's surprising considering his age and his offensive skill. He stepped up at the blueline and knocked players off pucks, he also had an alert stick tip early in the third where he recognized the passing lane and disrupted it. I was hoping for more offense from Denisenko but he played a decent game.

RUS #22 F Ruslan Iskhakov (2018) – A diminutive winger who tore up the Slovakian U18 league. He's quick out of the gate which is very important considering his size though I would prefer seen additional gear that he lacks. His skill level is high end and he used it to create an unorthodox drop pass by contorting his body and throwing a blind pass that lead to a good scoring chance. On another sequence midway through the third he dangled around several players and drove to the net, drawing a penalty on the play. Defensively speaking, he showed a smart defensive anticipatory read during a dump in sequence, he tracked the play before it occurred and skated towards where the puck was going to drop and got there first. He's not afraid to battle larger players for pucks, showing an effort to stick check and try to come away with the puck, which he surprisingly did in several instances. He plays bigger than his size and had two shoot-out goals that displayed excellent puck skills.

RUS #17 F Dmitri Zavgorodny (2018) – Had a nice goal in the second where he recognized his passing lane was blocked and capitalized on Gravel over committing to the pass, giving him space on the short side. The release point was good and there wasn't wasted movement, it was difficult for Gravel to pick up. During a power play sequence, he showed good breakaway speed and an ability to carry the puck under heavy traffic. Had a play late in the second that showcased he can beat players one on one by turning McIsaac inside out. Showed in the third that he can score in multiple ways and not just off the rush by burying a rebound, the release point was excellent on this goal as well. He was the most dangerous Russian today.

RUS #28 D Nikita Okhotyuk (2019) – A player who put up near point per game numbers in the U17 Russian league. He's got excellent skating technique which was demonstrated on a play along the blueline where he used forward crossovers to gain just enough space to release a point shot, the release point was good and he shoots with a whip like motion which helped the shot gain some velocity. His acceleration allows him to stay composed under pressure in his own end and if he loses the puck he's willing to deliver a solid hit, he also gets up to another gear during puck pursuit situations. His passing ability is very good, he made several out-let passes that were tape to tape regardless of the distance. I can't emphasize enough this kids poise, considering his age and level of competition he's facing. There's a ton to like here.

RUS #16 D Nikita Solopanov (2018) – Average in height but thick in build, Nikita demonstrated an excellent sequence midway through the first which lead to the first goal. He was pressured by a fore-checker behind his own net but managed to outbattle Dudas before dropping the puck back to his teammate; he then received the puck in the neutral zone, carried it into the offensive end and froze the opposition with a subtle yet effective feint by pretending to drive into the lane before passing it off, giving him a primary assist. The play demonstrated his poise under high pressure and a fast processor for transitioning the puck and distributing it effectively. He also uses that processor in the defensive end by making fast and quick passes under pressure as well as reading his opponents at the blueline and acting accordingly. One sequence in the second showed his ability to adapt to sudden shifts in speed quickly when he realized Veleno was going to drive around him, he quickly turned and skated cutting off Veleno's lane to the net and effectively pinning him, resulting in a turnover. Except for one neutral zone turnover caused by Veleno, he had a solid game defensively while showing he can rush the puck up the ice when needed.

Final Score: Russia 4 – Canada 3 (SO)

Scouts Notes:

Canada vs Russia – There was a couple of lines that were switched throughout the game to find chemistry. The line that stood out the most in having little chemistry involved two of the most talented Russian players in Denisenko and Iskhakov, who both like to control play. Due to this it was difficult to gauge either in the offensive zone.

Canada vs Finland, Hlinka Memorial, August 8, 2017

Canada –

CAN #16 C Akil Thomas (2018) – A potential first round pick. Thomas didn't impress me yesterday despite his goal but he came out of the gate looking more engaged today. Specifically, in the second period he had a sequence where he created havoc in the offensive zone. He recovered a botched deke attempt from his teammate and passed it back to the point, then he positioned himself properly along the goal mouth almost getting to the rebound. The puck went past him but he ended up back checking effectively to create a turnover, then he passed the puck off before taking a big hit, bounced right back up and made another additional play to another teammate. We're not finished with this shift yet, after Canada lost the puck, he showed his two-way game by intercepting a pass that was heading into the slot and then transitioned the puck right back into the Finish zone. Arguably the best shift in the entire tournament with nothing to show for it on the score sheet. Defensively he was good, he was communicating effectively with his teammates and wasn't afraid to get physical when necessary. He was the best Canadian forward today.

CAN #19 C Benoit–Olivier Groulx (2018) – A teammate of McIsaac and a promising prospect in own right. Groulx showed his acceleration early by spinning out of pressure and racing up the ice with the puck. He again demonstrated his speed when he rushed to the net and tipped in McIsaac's pass. On a sequence in the third, he flew through the neutral zone and split the defenceman, managing to get the puck deep into the zone on the play. He's been assigned a fore-checking role and he's bought into it, been effective and consistent on the forecheck.

CAN #14 D Jared McIsaac (2018) – A two-way defenceman who's lacing up for a stacked Halifax Mooseheads squad this year. He looked engaged early, establishing his presence along the blueline by having a nice defensive read where he used his hand eye to tip a puck out of the zone, which stopped Finland's attack. Moments later, he intercepted a neutral zone pass from Maccelli, fought off a check and delivered a beautiful pass resulting in a tip in goal. In the second period, he showed his defensive ability on the penalty kill, displayed good gap control and then stick checked a Finish player resulting in a cleared puck. He's physical when he needs to be in his own end and was very solid today for Canada.

CAN #2 D Kevin Bahl (2018) – An enormous defenceman, standing at 6'5, 230. He used his size in the first period, measuring Petman up and cutting across the slot, delivering a devastating, yet clean hit. It was the best hit of the tournament so far, a tempo altering hit. His skating is surprisingly technical considering his size, usually bigger kids who haven't grown into their bodies have an unorthodox push off or awkward stride; this isn't the case with Bahl, he's fluid. This fluidness combined with his reach allowed him to close the gap quickly on Kotkaniemi, poking the puck off his stick then getting to the lose puck and clearing it along the boards. He's got a lot of upside.\

CAN #31 G Olivier Rodrigue (2018) – An average sized goalie playing out of Drummondville. His best attribute is his lateral movement. He can push off explosively in any direction and this allows him to square up quickly, as well as cut down angles on aggressive shooters. In the first period during Finland's first power play sequence, he demonstrated good puck tracking skills and then used his lateral push offs to make a couple of saves along the point. His glove hand was quick and he didn't allow too many rebounds except for the late goal. He wasn't busy but made the save when he was called upon to do so. It will be interesting to see if Canada goes back to Gravel.

Finland –

FIN #28 C Jesperi Kotkaniemi (2018) – Had a quite first period but had a nice play in the second where he intercepted a pass into the neutral zone, broke over the line using his hands and delivered a turning shot onto the net. In the third period, he had a nice defensive block in-front of the net on a point shot and managed to clear the puck. On the power play late in the third he showed his sharp passing ability, setting up his teammate in the slot. He was better than Kupari today but neither were very effective.

FIN #37 D Toni Utunen (2018) – An undersized defenceman coming out of Tappara's system. He had an excellent sequence early in the second by reacting immediately to a rebound that landed on Veleno's stick that would have been a high scoring chance if it wasn't for Utunen's awareness and timing with his own stick. He then tracked Veleno in the corner and kept up with him just enough to get him off the puck. The play demonstrated high end defensive awareness around the goal line as well as keeping up with one of the faster players in the tournament. His breakout ability was mixed on the power play. He had miscommunication with his line-mates behind his own net and when he attempted to transition the puck into the neutral zone, he looked uncomfortable, on another power play, he transitioned the puck up the ice but didn't use any passing options resulting in a turnover down below the goal line. He looked far more comfortable on the penalty kill, assessing where passes were coming from and positioning himself effectively. He was the only noticeable player on Finland today, showing a good defensive presence, making solid outlet passes when needed and transitioning the puck occasionally.

Final Score: Canada 5 – Finland 1

Scouts notes:

Canada vs Finland – Finland looked flat from the opening drop of the puck, this was highlighted as Annunen aggressively slammed his stick into the ice to try and wake the team up. Unfortunately, it did little to help and you could count on one hand the number of high end scoring chances for Finland, very poor showing overall.

Sweden vs. Czech Republic, Ivan Hlinka Memorial Tournament, August 8th, 2017

CZE #13 Lauko, Jakub - Really good speed. Broke free in the offensive zone in the middle of the first period and created a good chance but couldn't get control of the puck in time and subsequently crashed into the swedish goalie. Was fairly quiet in the first period however. Really smooth skater with good balance. Generates a good amount of power with each stride. Wasn't really able to make his impact felt in this particular game. Made a great defensive play on the power play when Zabransky bobbled the puck in the neutral zone and was about to give the swedes an odd man rush when Lauko came rushing back and recovered the puck.

CZE #18 Zabransky, Libor - Has a really hard slap- and wristshot that is a real weapon. Good passer. Puck skills are a bit lacking however.

CZE #1 Dvorak, Daniel - Really poor rebound control. Made a nice play where he ventured far out of the crease to play a puck, effectively preventing a breakaway. Seems confident with the puck on his stick. Hasn't really made any big saves whatsoever in this game, but he alone can't be blamed for the goals he let in as the czech defense was rather spotty at times.

CZE #3 Malik, Zack - Good mobility for a bigger guy. Demonstrated good passing abilities, but can sometimes get stressed under pressure and turn the puck over.

CZE #15 Plasek, Karel - Took advantage of Rasmus Sandin's mistake on the blueline and created a breakaway for himself on which he made no mistake and gave the czechs a 1-0 lead. Showed off his speed and skill when he made a couple of quick moves before lifting the puck up into the roof of the net. Clean finish. His soft hands were on display in the second period where he smoothly toe-dragged around a swedish defender but got body checked before he could get a shot off. Scored his second goal of the game early in the third on the man advantage when he picked up a loose puck in the chaos in front of the net, moved it to the side and found an open shooting lane.

SWE #1 Lindbom, Olof - Stays square and moves out to the top of the crease to challenge shooters. Can struggle with lateral movement and does not seem like the most athletic goaltender. Prone to start scrambling once he gets down on his knees. Gets caught out of position too easily and fails to recover. Has trouble staying calm and in position when there's a lot of traffic in front of him.

SWE #3 Boqvist, Adam - Added an assist on a shot from between the left faceoff circle and the blue line which created a rebound for Fagemo to score on. Again showed off his stickhandling and elusiveness in the first period as he danced through multiple czech players all the way down to the extended goal-line. Incredibly creative and dynamic player who rarely gets stripped off the puck despite his high-risk style of play. Really calm under pressure and knows what his options are in every situation. Consistently makes good reads. Looks very much like a top10 talent in this draft and based off what I've seen from him so far this year I believe he should be a prime candidate to make the World Juniors team.

SWE #6 Andersson, Axel - Drew in instead of William Fransson in this game. Had a quiet evening. Andersson plays a low-event and smart game which revolves around making high percentage decisions in all three zones. His best attribute is his passing ability and vision as he can find forwards in stride with clean breakout- and stretch passes. Would like to see him activate offensively a little more as I know he has an accurate shot with a good release.

SWE #9 Sandin, Rasmus - Was on his toes and had an excellent start to the game. Moved his feet and made quick decisions with the puck, moving the play in the right direction before he could be pressured. Had a hard slapshot from the point on the PP in the first period which created a rebound but there was no swede in sight to take advantage. His strong first period performance all came undone when he bobbled a puck on the offensive blue line and gave the czechs a breakaway on which they scored 1-0.

SWE #13 Gustafsson, David - Made a nifty play on a faceoff in the middle of the second period where he won it and went straight forward, then dishing the puck in front of the goal where Jonatan Berggren had positioned himself and potted the 4-2 goal. Scored the 7-3 goal after a quick series of events where first Berggren had a great opportunity in one end, then a czech player came free in the other, and then the play turned again and Gustafsson hurried up the ice and found himself all alone with the czech goalie and put it five hole.

SWE #15 Hållander, Filip - Scored the 5-2 goal on a broken play which saw both Boqvist and Wernblom being unable to get their shots through before the puck bounced out to Hållander who pounced on it and put it into the back of the net. He hasn't stood out as much as I was expecting him to do. He seems to be struggling to produce those really high-quality scoring chances. From a potential 1st round pick I would expect more than what he has shown so far.

SWE #16 Fagemo, Samuel - Beat out three czech players to a rebound on a shot from Adam Boqvist to score the equalizer for 1-1. Scored his second goal of the game late in the second period. You really don't see much of him on the ice as he's rarely involved in the build-up of plays, but he is a deadly finisher when he gets the chance. Scored this one from the slot after a nice individual effort from Carl Jakobsson.

SWE #17 Berggren, Jonatan - Makes lots of nifty plays to set up teammates for scoring opportunities. Likes to enter the zone with speed, drawing defenders in, then put the brakes on and find an open teammate. Headed straight for the net on a faceoff play where David Gustafsson won the draw, skated forward and passed Berggren in front of the net. Berggren had a lot of open net and made no mistake. Had a another great play in the third when he picked up the puck in the neutral zone with his jersey-flapping speed, dangled through one czech player and got a good scoring opportunity, albeit from a slightly awkward angle, but flubbed the puck and it went low and wide. Worked really hard on the backcheck immediately after as the play turned the other way. Berggren has been a major positive over the last week and is someone that should be sneaking into talks for a top92 draft selection.

SWE #21 Olofsson, Jacob - Scored the 2-1 goal after linemate Carl Jakobsson forced a turnover. Came in from the wing with speed, shielded the puck from the czech defender and tucked a backhand with plenty of velocity just over the right pad of the goalie. Really needs to become a more consistent player as he always seem to leave you wanting more. It is however impressive that he is able to find his way onto the scoresheet even when he is quiet for the vast majority of the game. He has the ability to turn 'nothing plays' into scoring chances.

SWE #27 Jakobsson, Carl - Had an assist on the 2-1 goal after he got in a czech defender's grill and did a good job of forcing a turnover which Olofsson picked up and scored on. Picked up another assist late in the second period when he walked around a czech defender deep into the offensive zone then threaded a backhand from just below the goal-line back into the slot where he found an open Samuel Fagemo. A beautiful play. Consistency is the key with Jakobsson moving forward.

Slovakia vs Canada, Hlinka Memorial, August 9, 2017

Slovakia –

SVK #8 LW Oliver Okuliar (2018) – He was one of the better Slovakian forwards out of the gate today. After coming out of the box as his penalty expired, he received a pass and then held up quickly which fooled the Canadian defender, resulting in a prime scoring chance which he missed. Later in the first he displayed good penalty killing instincts behind his own net and then transitioned the puck into the neutral zone out of danger. He showed an ability to battle against larger defenders as well. Smith pushed him to the ice but he got up quickly and managed to retrieve the puck below the goal line. In the second, he showed his skating ability by rushing the puck over all three zones before attempting to set up the power play. He was stripped on the play and slammed his stick into the side boards. The last thing you want to do, is showcase to the opposition that their frustrating you, especially when the game is only 3-0. After getting into the face of McIsaac, he seemed rejuvenated and ended up with the primary assist on Slovakia's first goal of the game off a nice pass to the high slot.

SVK #19 RW Robert Dzugen (2018) – Despite been vastly overmatched in todays contest. I felt Dzugen was one of the more energetic forwards today. He showed an ability to battle for pucks, barreling Woo down to the ice while attempting to get to a lose puck in the second. During one sequence, he stripped the puck off a Canadian player, used a nice feint and then delivered a backhand pass into the slot for a scoring chance. He also displayed a willingness to block shots in his own end.

Canada –

CAN #9 C Joe Veleno (2018) – He had a nice sequence off a pass from Woo, where he skated back up the blueline and turned the corner, using his acceleration to explode into the slot and shot the puck over the net. His shooting has been mixed for me, and here again I found myself not been overly satisfied with his release point, the mechanics are good, but it's coming off his stick too slowly, allowing goalies to get set resulting in his shots going over the net or hitting nothing but chest. Unlike his shot, his passing was on point again tonight, showing off a nice no look back-hand pass and threaded several passes into the slot for scoring opportunities. He had a power play goal in the third but overall, he wasn't very effective. He's been very mixed this tournament so far.

CAN #21 C Barrett Hayton (2018) – A center developing in the Greyhounds program. He had a great sequence in the first where he drove down toward the goal line and delivered a tape to tape pass in the slot to Addison for the first goal. In the second he demonstrated an ability to transition the puck from his own end to the neutral zone, before delivering a clean pass. Had a beautiful goal midway through the second. He hesitated, dragging the puck, before pulling it back and changing the angle of his shot. It had velocity and the placement was perfect. Later in the second, he utilized his toe drag again to walk around a defender, making space for his shot to get through. Midway through the third, he positioned himself in the crease and tipped home a slapshot from smith, resulting in a power play goal.

CAN #20 C Jack McBain (2018) – A large center, standing at 6'3 and weighing 200 pounds. His skating is excellent for his size. He has a long stride and a powerful base which allows him to get up to top gear with relative ease. He was good early as well, showcasing an ability to separate himself and create scoring opportunities by driving through lanes. Early in the second, he had a great sequence where he out hustled his opponent to a puck at the offensive blueline, then under high pressure, made a no look spin pass off the boards which was tape to tape. He then demonstrated high offensive awareness after assessing where the puck would end up, after a board battle involving Veleno resulting in him retrieving the puck. At the end of the sequence, he skated up to the top of the slot and released a low wrist shot which missed its target. On a penalty kill in the second, he managed to strip the puck in the offensive zone and wire a wrister that missed the net. He was active today and played well.

CAN #3 D Ty Smith (2018) – A teammate of Kailer Yamamoto coming out of Spokane. Smith's game is based around his superb skating ability. He has an explosive first step and a very fast top gear. It allowed him to transition seamlessly from his own end to his opponents before the opposition could set, allowing him multiple options on several plays. In the first, during a sequence on the power play, he showcased his feinting technique by faking a wrist shot that he really bared down on, this completely fooled the defense. He then used his lateral skating ability, giving him space to shoot a wrist shot through traffic. During several other sequences, he showcased his deceptive hands, making space for himself in the process. Defensively, he was active, pursuing opposition with relative easy behind his own net, and knocking opponents to the ice. He's short but he's powerful for his size. On a very stacked Canadian blueline, he might be the most dangerous of the group when walking the line due to his unpredictable skill-set which is highlighted by his advanced feinting mechanics. He used exaggerated posture and movement to throw his opponents off and he was very good at picking up when they misjudged his movement, burning them accordingly. He has so many tools at his disposal, from his explosiveness, to his hands and his passing ability, which allow him to create plays at will. If he doesn't see a pass or want to create a play for his teammates, his wrist shot has few tells and the release point is quick. His slapshot is a cannon from the point when he gets leverage on it, which he did on a power play tip goal, midway through the third. He was a force tonight and showed tremendous upside.

CAN #14 D Jared McIsaac (2018) – McIsaac has been consistent all tournament and that occurred here today as well. He plays a pro style game compared to some others on the back end, so that might make him less flashy, but he's just as effective. He stood out early, cloaking himself behind the Slovakian defence which allowed him to receive a pass which he rung off the post. Later in the first, he showed his defensive prowess, using his size and physicality to drain the Slovakian forwards. He makes players work in the defensive zone. In the second, he showed his one on one defensive ability, skating backwards as effortlessly as he skates forwards, while poke checking the puck off the Slovakian's stick, then winning the board battle. He also bailed out Woo on a poor passing attempt; grabbing the puck and managing to transition from his defensive end to the neutral zone. Offensively speaking, he also can use feinting mechanics which he demonstrated throughout the contest in spurts. He doesn't angle his body like Smith and Merkley to catch his opponents with edge work and he doesn't like to walk the line to the same degree as them, instead using head feints and stick feints to create options. He can be dynamic but he plays a more reserved style.

CAN #8 D Jet Woo (2018) – A defender coming out of the Hitman program. He was having a relatively quite tournament but showcased well here today. He displayed his transitional ability early, where he had a sequence demonstrating not only his speed but his ability to weave through multiple defenders, splitting through them. On the same sequence, he regained control of the puck, used his frame to keep his opponents at bay and then passed the puck off resulting in puck possession. The sequence was especially impressive considering it was a four on one against him when he came over the line with the puck. He faked a slap shot along the blueline and managed a good hard pass to the corner in the first as well. Later in the third, he showcased his physical play, standing up a Slovakian player and dropping him to the ice with a hard body check. He then made a nice move in the neutral zone and delivered a tape to tape pass resulting in an offensive entry.

CAN #17 LW Gabriel Fortier (2018) – A player who's already shown an ability to score in the QMJHL. Like Smith, he also has an explosive first step but it's less busy and more fluid. He used it to weave his way into the slot for a scoring chance early. Later in the first period, he displayed high defensive awareness, intercepting a pass along the blueline and then using his top speed to back up the Slovakian netminder, before shooting the puck, bar down over him. In the second, he showed off his speed game again, almost catching a puck that was ruled an icing. He was chirping the Slovakian player after the whistle, knowing if he had another half second, he would have caught up to him. He was utilized on the penalty kill, where he was good at getting into shooting lanes and again using his speed to disrupt plays.

CAN #7 D Ryan Merkley (2018) – Had an uncharacteristic start to this game. He turned the puck over in the offensive zone after misreading a passing option; he then sloppily played a puck that hit a stick behind his own net, resulting in a second effort to clear the puck. However, he settled down after those opening moments and again showed his effortless stride, his intelligence and his puck transitioning ability. In the second, he stopped a potential two on one sequence for Slovakia, when he stick-checked his opponent, just as the puck was about to be cleared and managed to keep it in. He was excellent on the power play, using a combination of body feints and edge work to create traps for the opposition, when they bit, his lanes would open. On a sequence in the third, he forced half the Slovakian team to one side leaving Veleno all alone resulting in a primary assist. He has the ability to get shots through traffic as was demonstrated in the third, where he had a low, hard wrist shot find it's way through multiple players, resulting in a difficult kick save. I would like to see him mix up his shots and passing more often but overall, he was still very effective.

Final Score: Canada 6 – Slovakia 1

Rouyn-Noranda Huskies vs Drummondville Voltigeurs, August 18th, 2017

RN #7 LD Arsenault, Alexis (2018): Arsenault was solid at defending one-on-one in this game, because of his quick stick and good body positioning. He also had one excellent hit in this game against a much bigger player in front of his net. He played a relatively smart game, outside of one sequence in the first period where he tried too much at the offensive blueline, losing the puck. However, he showed a good effort skating hard coming back, and stopped Desruisseaux on his breakaway.

RN #4 RD Gagné, Jean-Christophe (2018): Gagné was active in the transition game of his team, often joining the rush and trying to create some offense in the offensive zone. He was physical in his own end, using his size along the boards and in front of the net. It showed in this game that Gagné had already played in the QMJHL, compared to many in this game.

RN #16 RW Beaucage, Alex (2019): It was a bit of a quiet game from the Huskies' top QMJHL Draft pick last June. He still scored the game-winning goal with 0.1 seconds left in the game, using a great wrist shot after entering the offensive zone. He showed great velocity and a quick release on his shot through the game. He showed a good ability to handle the puck in tight spaces along the boards. He didn't create or receive many scoring chances outside of his game-winning goal in this game.

RN #15 C Rouleau, William (2019): Rouleau flashed some good speed and puck skills throughout the game. He showed good creativity in the offensive zone, but also showed some immaturity while trying to do too much with the puck and was victim to some turnovers. Physically, another year of midget would be beneficial for him, as he lost too many puck battles tonight.

RN #28 RW Ianniciello, Samuel (2018): The 17-year-old forward was often around the net in the game today, and this is where he scored the game's opening goal following a rebound from a Diotte shot from the point. He didn't hesitate in getting his nose dirty in front of the net. Skating was okay, but he could stand to add more explosiveness to it.

RN #19 C Haché, Luc-Olivier (2019): A three-point game for the New Brunswick native, he showed a good combination of speed and skills today. He had some good moments with the puck, beating Drummondville's defensemen one-on-one. He was always around the puck, and found ways to get open in the offensive zone with his good hockey sense. He was one of the better players in this game.

RN #51 C Tourigny, Félix-Antoine (2018): Tourigny was good today, playing a very smart two-way game. He was excellent on the PK, where he showed his good anticipation to make things happen there. He also showed a good active stick, blocking passes and stripping pucks from Drummondville players. He showed good poise with the puck and an ability to find his linemates in the offensive zone. He protects the puck well in the offensive zone and uses his low center of gravity well, too.

DRU #33 G Paradis, Mathieu (2018): Played half of the game and did well, stopping 17 of 18 shots. He started the game a bit nervously and fumbled a couple of rebounds, but bounced back and played well the rest of the way. His rebound-control was much better after his shaky start, and he made himself look big in net.

DRU #16 C Simoneau, Xavier (2019): Simoneau was Drummondville's top player today; he showed good speed and vision throughout the game. Even at his size, he did well handling the puck along the boards and in the offensive zone; his low center of gravity and lower-body strength helped him protect the puck. He did a good job at this on Drummondville's first goal of the game, coming from the corner with the puck and feeding David on the point. You could see his skill level and speed was on another level compared to most players in this game. He used his speed well to put pressure on the puck-carrier and win puck races.

DRU #17 LW Desruisseaux, Cedric (2018): He didn't get many chances today at even-strength; he had his best moment on the power play while operating from the half-wall. He showed good quality shots and vision from there. At even-strength, he didn't create a lot of offensive chances, and stayed a bit too much on the perimeter, not getting involved in the play. His skating was good, but it lacked an explosive stride that could have allowed him to distance himself faster from the opposing player covering him.

DRU #55 LW Girouard, Nicholas (2019): He was bit nervous with the puck early on in the game, not handling it smoothly. He's a big kid, but was a bit shy along the boards, not using his size like he should. He lost some puck battles against some smaller players. He looked nervous most of the game and didn't generate many scoring chances or much speed today.

Victoriaville Tigres vs Shawinigan Cataractes, game, August 18th, 2017

VIC #21 RW Paré, Felix (2018): Strong game from Paré, who finished the game with 3 points (2 goals) and was Victoriaville's top player tonight. He used his size well in the offensive zone and was involved physically along the boards. He won his fair share of one-on-one battles. He didn't hesitate to shoot the puck on net when he had the chance to do it. He showed some good velocity on his wrist shot.

VIC #24 LW Reid, Alec (2019): Reid worked hard during the game. He may not be the biggest player, but showed good hustle and grit throughout. He kept his feet moving and made some good backchecks, where he could steal pucks away from Shawinigan forwards. He was quick to put pressure on the puck-carrier.

VIC #6 RD Larochelle, Sean (2019): Victoriaville's first pick (20th overall) in last June's QMJHL Draft was solid today, playing in all situations and playing with a lot of confidence. His good footwork allowed him to retrieve pucks quickly in his zone, and he made accurate passes out of his zone to start the transition game for his team. He was poised on the power play, making smart decisions on the point.

VIC #2 LD Sevigny, Vincent (2019): Not very flashy today, Sevigny played a smart and effective game in his own zone. He made some good plays in his own zone with a good active stick and blocked shots, including a key block at the end of the 2nd period which could have resulted in a Shawinigan goal. Not many plays in the offensive zone from him, but he showed on a couple of occasions that he has a heavy slap shot from the point.

SHA #5 LD Belley-Pelletier, Gabriel (2019): The young defenseman played in every situation tonight and ended up playing a decent game overall. He didn't flash his great skating abilities as much as he's capable of, but remained solid and didn't make any mistakes on the ice. He played more of a stay-at-home type of game. He showed some good strength on his skates, as he was able to keep possession of the puck after taking some good hits along the boards. Defensively, he did a good job defending, and did it smartly with a good active stick. His footwork and overall skating abilities helped him counter opposing forwards coming down his side of the ice with speed.

SHA #6 LD Horvath, Jason (2018): Horvath showed a good arsenal of shots from the point. His slapshot is powerful, and he can utilize his wrist shot as well. He usually kept his shot low, which was good for tips or rebounds. He's a strong kid, and did well along the boards in physical confrontations. His decision-making was usually good, but we would like to see him make quicker ones. It's when he takes too much time that he gets into trouble in his zone, which happened a couple of times tonight.

SHA #74 LD Lafond, Jerome (2018): Undrafted, Lafond was invited to the Cataractes' training camp and did well tonight. He was very physical along the boards and showed good timing with his hits. He moved well on the ice, with good footwork and an ability to rush the puck out of his zone, and was also quick to retrieve pucks deep in his zone. He made some decent first passes out of his zone too, including some high-risk passes that worked in his favour. We would still like to see him make smarter decisions with the puck.

USA vs. Czech Republic, U17 Five Nations' Final, August 27th, 2017

USA #30 G Haider, Ethan (2019): Loved his competitiveness in net; he battled hard and never quit on any pucks. He bounced back well after allowing a bad goal, coming back the sequence right after and made some key stops. He would have liked to have the 2nd goal back; it was a weak wrist shot that beat him glove side. In the first half of the game, he did a good job playing with the puck outside of his crease; he did, however, take a penalty for throwing the puck in the stands. He has decent size, and he's calm in his crease. He was named USA's top player in this game.

USA #7 RD Miller, Mitch (2020): Not the biggest defenseman, but he showed good wheels and an ability to move the puck quickly in the offensive zone. He was successful at carrying the puck into the offensive zone. He has a good top speed and a good burst of speed to distance himself from the forecheck.

USA #3 LD Johnson, Ryan (2019): The California kid showed glimpses of his good skating abilities in a couple of rushes today. His best sequence came on USA's winning goal after making a great zone entry and great cross-ice pass that led to a great scoring chance for Silianoff at the side of the net, in which he scored seconds later on another chance. Lacks size, but his skating abilities are making him noticeable out there.

USA #5 RD McWard, Cole (2019): Arguably USA's best defenseman today. He showed good footwork and good potential as a puck-mover. He was agile, moving laterally with the puck on the point, showing good poise to make the opposing team move and open lanes for him to pass the puck. In addition, on the power play, he was active on the ice, not standing still and giving different options to his teammates. He made a nice feed on USA's 3rd goal with a perfect pass at the side of the net. He got caught by surprise on the Czechs' 3rd goal, as he couldn't keep up with the speed of #17 (Najman), who beat him wide pretty easily.

USA #6 LD Webber, Cade (2019): Really interesting package on the blueline, with his size and mobility. Still very raw, but has enough mobility at his size that he could be a player down the road. He had some iffy moments with the puck; no major mistakes, but he missed some passes on the transition and fumbled the puck a couple of times too.

USA #19 F Kaliyev, Arthur (2019): Didn't notice him a ton in the game, but he showed quick hands on his goal, scoring in front of the net on a one-timer where he showed a quick release. Showed some good anticipation, decent speed and went into the dirty areas.

USA # 18 F, Svejkovsky, Lukas (2020): Smooth skating, versatile, and started to be more noticeable mid-game. Took the puck from his own faceoff spot area, rushed it with speed over the bluelines from east to west, and released a backhand shot. Nice hands. Crisp passes.

USA #16 F Groll, Josh (2019): Another California kid, Groll was noticeable because of his blazing speed. He created some good things offensively with his speed, and brought some good energy to his team because of his hustle and physical play. He scored USA's 1st goal of the game, and it was a highlight-reel goal. He exploded after taking possession of the puck, beating the Czech defenseman easily one-on-one, then beat the goaltender on the backhand. He didn't have a consistent game offensively, but brought different things to the table.

USA #21 F Silianoff, Grant (2019): Good skater. Created a turnover with his good speed and good anticipation. He did a good job putting pressure on the puck-carrier and created some chances off turnovers. He scored the game-winning goal after jamming the puck in, after two solid scoring chances near the goaltender's crease.

USA # 20 F, Nodler, Josh (2019): Nice assist to Kaliyev during the power play, when the Czechs were out of position in the defensive zone. Nodler positioned himself excellently for a redirect from McWard, leading to a goal. He ended the game with one goal and an assist.

USA # 17 C, Mastrosimone, Robert (2019): His top speed is good, he plays sound positional hockey, has mobile, smooth skating, and created an odd-man situation with #21 (Silianoff). Quick release on a wrist shot in the 3rd period.

USA # 12 F, Hale, Jake (2019): Good anticipation, good forecheck and is good at retrieving pucks. Good skating with good top speed. He worked hard with a good backcheck straight after an attack in the offensive zone.

CZE #5 RD Kubicek, Simon (2020): Took some good shots on net, did a good job keeping his shots low. One of his shot got tipped by #21 Psenicka for the Czechs' first goal of the game. Skating and footwork seems to be average; he was a bit slow retrieving pucks in his own zone.

CZE #4 LD Klikorka, Karel (2020): Started noticing him more in the 3rd period, where he started being more involved in the play in the offensive zone and moving pucks better. Good footwork and nice first pass. He needs to be more physical in front of his own net to keep the forwards outside, or to poke or lift their stick better.

CZE #11 LD Kucerik, Radek (2020): Often played on the point on the power play, and he showed a decent offensive potential in this game. He was moving pucks quickly on the transition and taking some good shots on net. Skating and footwork was average, similar skillset to Rubicek.

CZE #13 LW Teply, Michal (2019): The tall and lanky-framed winger lacks strength right now to be more effective along the boards, but has an interesting long-term upside. He lost control of the puck because of that lack of strength a couple of times. He has a long reach and once he gets stronger, he could become tough to handle down low. He lacks explosiveness with his skating, but again, due to his current lack of strength, that could improve over time. His decision-making was inconsistent.

CZE #20 F Vitouch, David (2019): The first thing we noticed with Vitouch was his speed; a good top-end speed with a great burst of speed. He put some good pressure on the forecheck with it. He often rushed the puck into the offensive zone, but often the play ended up going nowhere with no scoring chances.

CZE #29 F Muzik, Radek (2019): He was a front-of-the-net presence during this game, playing in the tough areas of the ice. He was annoying to the other team and goaltender, especially with his net presence. He showed a quick release from the point on the power play, where he played a bit during the game.

CZE #14 F Barinka, Marcel (2019): Barinka used his size well to protect the puck in the offensive zone; he had some excellent sequences keeping possession of the puck down low in this game. He's tall with a good reach. He showed a good and heavy shot. He was quiet in the first, but played much better in periods two and three, where he showed some interesting things. He worked hard at both ends of the ice; he made a very nice backcheck in the game to save a dangerous scoring chance for Team USA. Skating lacks an extra gear, though.

CZE #21 LW Psenicka, Ondrej (2019): Tall guy with lot of frame to fill. Good speed, made some good reads. We liked his poise with the puck, and he made some nice passes for his teammates. Good along the boards, and finished the game with a goal and an assist.

CZE #17 F, Najman, Ondrej (2019): He made some good plays offensively. I liked his speed and acceleration. He showed the ability to beat defensemen wide with his speed. His speed created the 3-3 goal from Jouza. He was named the Czechs' best player.

CZE # 12 F, Raska, Adam (2020): Looked weak and out of energy, and didn't use his skills and vision like in previous viewings. Didn't have any poise or confidence with the puck in this game. Was a big disappointment, and Raska usually lacks consistency from game to game.

Team Czech Republic vs. Team USA, U17 5 Nations, August 28th, 2017

CZE #21 LW Psenicka, Ondrej (2019) - Tal guy with lot of frame to fill. Speed and very good reading on the ice, Poise, finding team mates with assists, smooth skating and quick passes difficult to read for opponent. Strong by the board.

CZE # 4 D Klikorka, Karel (2020) -Showed some few occasions when brining the puck on a rush and going to center ice passing 2-3 Blue, needs to be more physical in front of own net to keep the F outside or to poke or lift check better. Nice first pass.

CZE # 13 LW Teply, Michal (2019) -Nice read in middle, sog in beginning, good hands but seems to take the wrong decisions when to use it, risky uncontrolled moves in middle zone as last guy, passes was not the best, took bad decisions/stopped to skate while backchecking that resulted in penalties,

CZE # 27 F Jouza, Daniel (2019) -Haven't noticed him during the seasons and didn't saw him much at all in beginning of the game. Nice received pass from Psenicka and he covered the puck nice and went on the goal scoring 3-3.

CZE #15 F Najman, Ondrej (2019) -Didn't noticed him much in the game. Najman had a second assist where he read the game quick and gave a pass to a player in open ice. Was named as the Best Czech player.

CZE # 15 F Toman, Matej (2019) - Visualized from time to time, quick release on wrist shot,

CZE # 8 D Rasin , Patrick (2019) - As a D going backwards and stopping to move the feet's and the stick never leads to good result.

CZE # 17 F Najman, Adam (2019) - Bit to slow reading on two on one advantage. Received nice redirection from Psenicka in mid zone, took the puck nice in offensive zone covered the puck good and went on goal, ended on rebound and 3-3.

CZE # 13 C Barinka, Michal (2019) - Was not a good game, this kid was bombing in goals last season and although I only seen him in 1 junior game and 2 games with CZE U16 before, this was not a game where he used his tools. A couple of shot and one was a decent nice toe in. Strong on the board. Didn't snowed poise.

CZE #29 F Muzik, Radek (2019) - Managed to get one shot on goal. Was having some shift to give energy with speed and a bit irritating the goalie.

CZE # 12 F Raska, Adam (2020) -Looked week and out of energy, didn't used his skills and vision at all. Looked to be without poise and confident. Was a big disappointment but Raska usually do do excellent games mixed with invisible games.

CZE # 20 C Vitouch, David (2019) -Good reading and rush, decent speed with puck, decent positioning.

USA # 17 C Mastrosimone, Robert (2019) -Top speed, positioning, mobile smooth skating, created a 3 to 1 situation with 21 Sillianoff I believe. Quick release on a hipshot in the 3rd period.

USA # 21 C Sillianoff, Grant (2019) -Very good reading, poised, worked good with stick and mobility during boxplay, created a chance with 2 men less on the ice, visualized as one that created, mobile smooth skating. In front of goal for rebounds.

USA # 5 RD Mcward, Cole (2019) -Nice mobility and quick release on accurate wrist shot.

USA # 20 F Nodler, Josh (2019) -Nice assist to Kaliyev during pp when Czechs where miscalculating and misplacing themselves. Nodler positioned himself excellent for a redirecting the shot from Mcward leading to 1-3. Ended the game on.

USA # 16 F Groll, Josh (2019) - Visualized, good reading, speedy legs, good quick checking's on opponents while in BP, good puck rush in boxplay passing a frozen opponent, good hands,

USA # 1 LW Kaliyev, Arthur (2019) - Showed some good reading, decent speed, went in to dirty area. Sneeked in to the slot and released a quick shot (game winning assist). Ended the game on.

USA # 14 C Farinacci, John (2019) - Wasn't noticing him so much but had some good reading and positioning. Went in to the net for rebounds.

USA # 2 D Boltmann, Jake (2020) - Wasn't visualized much, nice slick first pass.

USA # 30 G Haider, Ethan (2019) - Wasn't following the goalies super much but Haider had a super great couple of saves especially at 3-3 with 6 minutes with 14.20 left. Was picked as best player for USA with 44 of 47 shots saved.

USA # 18 F Svejkovsky, Lukas (2020) - Smooth skating, versatile, started to be visualized in mid game. Took the puck from own faceoff spot area, rushed the puck with speed over the blue lines from east to west and released a backhand shot. Nice hands. Crisp pass.

USA # 3 D Johnson, Ryan (2019) - Wasn't visualized much but showed offensive skills, poise and good hands in the end bringing the puck from midzone to offensive red where he found Sillianoff at the farther pillar.

USA # 12 F Hale, Jake (2019) - Good reading, good forecheck retrieving the puck, mobile skating with good top speed. Worked hard with backchecking straight after an attack in offensive zone.

Vaxjo Lakers HC at Rogle BK, August 30th, 2017

VÄX #26 LW Bokk, Dominik (2018) - The recent German arrival from Cologne seems to have quickly adapted to Sweden and its hockey. Looked fairly uninterested in warmups but was dialed in as soon as the puck dropped. The first thing that stands out is his intensity and the speed he plays at. He's an explosive player who only need a few strides to reach top gear. His skating as a whole is superb and he can stop on a dime or fool defenders with sharp lateral cuts. He showcased an ability to chase pucks down and worked hard in both directions. He came back hard on the backcheck and was at times able to strip players of pucks who wasn't paying attention. He seemed unwilling to use his shot and passed up a few good scoring opportunities to set up his teammates instead. He registered his first shot with a minute left in the 2nd period, and had another one in the 3rd. Bokk was the focal point on his line and was the center of most of the action. On one occasion he flipped a nice backhand pass over the defender's stick on a 2on2 rush that his teammate was unable to convert on. The next shift he stickhandled through two opponents from a standstill just inside the offensive zone and set up a glorious scoring chance after some beautiful tic-tac-toe play by him and his linemates. Bokk plays at a very high pace, almost constantly. This can sometimes get him into trouble as he prefers to take the most direct route to goal, even if there are better options available. His errant pass on his own blueline led to a turnover and Rögle's equalizing 2-2 goal. He's like a sports car driver who prefer to drive his Ferrari from point A to point B at full speed on the highway rather than taking the scenic route out in the landscape. Which is not necessarily a bad thing, just something he needs to adress and improve upon. Overall an exciting player who keeps you on the edge of the seat and someone who could be in contention to be selected in the 1st round come June.

VÄX #11 C Seger, Gabriel (2018) - Seger is a late '99 birthday blessed with size. At near 6'4, 220 lbs he has a long reach and is able to protect the puck nicely. His skating has improved from last year. He is balanced on his skates and has solid edgework. His top end speed is not too bad but what is really lacking is his acceleration. He's got a very ugly and inefficient stride that will need significant work to reach NHL level skating. Seger is at his best on the man advantage where he positions himself behind the net. There he uses his size, reach and puck-protection to his advantage and combined with his vision and playmaking skills he is a threat. That is also really where he excels and he had a sweet cross-crease pass from behind the net to set up his teammate on the Power Play for a goal. The next shift he came flying through the neutral zone and created a great scoring opportunity for himself and tried to put the puck over the shoulder of the goaltender but was robbed. The downside of Seger's game, outside of his limited skating abilities, is his passive play off the puck. Does not seem to like traffic or to get his hands dirty, rather he prefers for the play to come to him. It is disappointing to see his unwillingness to use his large frame to impose his will on the game, being physical and winning puck battles, as he'd be a much more effective and dangerous player if he added that physical presence to his game. Overall I see Seger as a potential late round pick.

RÖG #4 D Kjellberg, Simon (2018) - Simon is the son of former NHLer Patric Kjellberg. Like his dad he has plenty of size, being listed at 6'3, 190 lbs. Through the two pre-season games I've seen him in so far, he has been disappointing relative to my expectations. He had a promising 16/17 season and I was hoping he'd take that next step, but so far it looks like he took a step back instead. Kjellberg is a smart player with good size and a good first pass, but that's about it. He is mobile at a basic level and thanks to his smarts he is rarely caught out of position even though he is not the fleetest of foot. He is however a very soft player and does not seem to have a mean bone in his body. He is also more of a stay-at-home D than a two-way guy as he does not get involved a lot offensively and does not seem to have the tools to be successful in that regard. He is someone to keep an eye on throughout the season but right now I see him as a late round pick at best, but perhaps more likely to go undrafted.

Owen Sound Attack at Oshawa Generals, September 13th, 2017

OSH #5 LD Ennis, William - Ennis played a simplistic game which allowed him to stay out of trouble. William would benefit from improving his puck handling abilities as they do hinder his ability to elude pressure and make a first pass. Ennis displayed an intelligence to his game, was able to make an effective first pass and showed an ability to contain transition attacks by taking strong routes to puck carriers and angling effectively.

OSH #8 RW Noel, Serron - Noel's combination of size and compete made him an appealing skater throughout the game. However, inconsistencies throughout left you wanting more. Serron's skating has taken another step forward since last season as he looks to have improved his lower body strength making his stride more fluid and powerful, directly enhancing his top speed. Noel is rangy and can utilize his size well, however will need to improve his puck handling abilities which are still fairly choppy and unrefined. Serron will also have to learn to better stop on pucks as he consistently circled back to the puck following turnovers.

OSH #20 LD Rupoli, Joseph - Rupoli possesses good size and strength to his game and was able to be effective in a simplistic bottom pairing role. Joseph is a bit stiff in is skating movements and will need to continue to enhance his mobility, however did a fine job defending in his own zone. Rupoli closed his gaps in the defensive zone well and utilized his strength to win puck and position battles. Joseph will need to move the puck at a quicker rate during the OHL regular season, however was able to make an effective first pass.

OSH #28 LW Hewitson, Mitchell - Hewitson wasn't overly impactful but did display some intriguing attributes to his game. Mitchell has a pro-style frame and was able to utilize his size and strength in transition as he leaned on opposing defenders protecting the puck well as he drove through traffic. Hewitson does need to improve his foot speed, as his first step is heavy and limits his ability to create separation. With that being said when Mitchell got going he did reach an average top speed.

OSH #42 LD Brewer, Mitchell - Oshawa's first round pick in the 2017 OHL Priority Selection, Brewer seems to have made a fairly seamless transition and was arguably Oshawa's top defender throughout the game. Mitchell wasn't flashy but was effective. Brewer has grown and added strength and was tough to play against in his own zone, often engaging physically and using his strength to win puck and position battles. Brewer's feet are fairly good and he was able to exploit open ice and transition the puck. However more impressive was Brewer's ability to make quick and high percentage decisions, often showing an ability to make a strong first pass. Mitchell wasn't perfect and did have a few hiccups, however was impressive.

OSH #61 LC McShane, Allan - McShane had moments where he showed elite skill which allowed him score Oshawa's lone goal in the game. While Allan had some average shifts and would be quiet for extended periods as far as creating offense goes, he did display an abundance of intelligence throughout. McShane's ability to anticipate allowed him to be first to pucks, put himself in strong position to be successful and was fairly reliable in the defensive zone. Allan displayed elite vision and playmaking skills on multiple occasions, creating in transition for his teammates and was even more of a threat on the power play.

OS #6 LD Beamish, Luke - Luke looks to have added some strength to his frame since last year's Dudley Hewitt Championship where he skated with the Georgetown Raiders. Beamish possesses strong feet, showing impressive edge work and four-way mobility along with a fluid stride that allows him to generate good straight-line speed. Luke utilizes his feet and an active stick to defend and can angle opponents away from high percentage scoring areas in transition. However, he will need to continue to add muscle to his frame as he struggled handling opponents below the hash-mark and lost to many puck battles.

OS #11 RW Groulx, Daylon - Groulx made a impression in a limited amount of time. Daylon displayed a lethal shot that came off a lightning quick release and boasted both velocity and accuracy. Despite his prowess as a shooter, Groulx set up Owen Sound's first goal with an impressive pass to Mitchell Russell. Early into the second period, Groulx engaged Mason Kohn and was ejected for instigating a fight. Important to note Daylon handled himself well in the fight and showed an edge to his game.

OS #15 LC Struthers, Matthew - Struthers possesses intriguing size and flashed confidence in possession. Matthew was inconsistent in his ability to make an impact however did attack the offensive zone with purpose and utilized his puck handling ability to create space. Struthers is able to generate average speed but will need to work on his first step and stride as it did hinder his ability to create at times.

OS #22 RC Russell, Mitchell - Russell scored three goals in the Attack's 3-1 win. While it's hard to ignore Russell's production he did have a limited impact during the majority of 5-on-5 play. Mitchell did show intriguing offensive instincts, finding soft spots in the Generals defensive zone coverage, putting himself in ideal position to find success, which he was able to. Russell's skating looks to have taken a minor step forward since his minor midget season.

OS #23 LC Filyaev, Vasili - Filyaev was good for Owen Sound, utilizing his size and strength over the puck to work below the hash-marks and off the cycle effectively. Filyaev protects the puck well and shows and ability to create off the cycle, recognizing time and space, while subtly showing deceptive vision and playmaking traits to his game. Vasili does need to work on his skating, while not poor, he does lack first step quickness and his stride is fairly choppy and lacks fluidity, which effects his speed.

OS #27 RC Dudas, Aidan - Dudas had a quiet first period but was very good through the second and third. Dudas showed outstanding speed along with the ability to make high skilled plays with pace. Aidan's ability to attack the offensive zone with pace allowed him to earn space to create. Dudas showed above average puck handling abilities and made a high skill play beating an overage defenseman in transition 1-on-1 with speed and puck skills before cutting sharply into the goal and showing quick hands in tight to put an opportunity on goal. Dudas was undoubtedly Owen Sounds top performer on the night.

Linkoping HC at Rogle BK, September 17th, 2017

LIN #38 C Södergran, Johan (2018) - Södergran is an energetic forward who works hard all over the ice and plays at a high tempo. Has a good frame and protects the puck well. Has a creative streak to his game but will likely never be mistaken for an elite offensive forward. Södergran is not a flashy stickhandler but he displayed strong puck-handling abilities. A fundamentally solid skater, very good on his edges and has good balance. Fast but lacks the seperation gear to switch tempo and blow by guys. Has an accurate shot that lacks power to be a real threat. Not afraid to take the puck to the net. A strong transitional forward with a high compete level, Södergran lead the attack for much of the game and he looks to have taken on a leading offensive role with Linköping this year.

LIN #3 LD Worge Kreü, William (2018) - Tall and very lanky defenseman listed at 6'4, 163 lbs. Generates fairly decent speed in a straight line but his backwards skating, agility and balance needs significant work. Had a strong first period and showcased some passing-ability but his performance as a whole faded as the game went on. Has a very long reach and was able to break up a dangerous chance off the rush with his stick.

LIN #25 RW Pasic, Nikola (2019) - Somewhat undersized at 5'10, 181 lbs. Pasic is a skilled player who loves to have the puck on his stick. Displayed some creativity and good vision. Was a mainstay on the first powerplay unit and scored the 3-1 goal on the PP with a shot in the top corner from the right faceoff-circle.

LIN #45 RD Lundmark, Simon (2019) - A late '00 birthday, Lundmark is an intriguing player with a lot of upside. At 6'1, 190 lbs he has good size but needs to get stronger still as his strength on the puck is somewhat lacking. His defensive game as a whole is very raw and he can, at times, be a little careless with the puck. On one occassion he got stripped of the puck just as he was trying to transition it up the ice from his own end, which led to a dangerous scoring opportunity for Rögle. Later on he also lost the puck on his own blue line after failing to control the puck when receiving a pass. However, he was able to make a good recovery by skating back and blocking the forechecking forward with his body, allowing his teammate to collect the puck. On the upside, Lundmark has fantastic vision and is very adept at moving the puck. His stretch-pass from deep in his own zone straight through the middle and to the offensive blue line gave teammate Nikola Pasic a clean breakaway that really deserved a better fate. Lundmark is a very solid skater but could benefit from added lower-body strength.

LIN #40 LW Lindberg, Gustav (2018) - Late '99 birthday who scored 19 goals and 30 points in SuperElit last year and made his Allsvenskan debut. Lindberg is a small but stocky player with a low center of gravity. Has good speed but is not a dynamic skater. Showed off good anticipation in the offensive zone when he snuck into the slot on the power play, got his hands on a loose puck and buried it.

LIN #41 C Costmar, Arvid (2019) - The youngest player on the ice have some maturing to do. Did not like his body language when he frantically banged his stick on the ice for a pass, did not receive one and got visibly upset. Has a choppy and inefficient stride which makes it look like he is skating in mud when he is trying to accelerate quickly. Had some good touches in the offensive zone and is clearly talented but will likely need some time to adjust to the level of play in SuperElit.

LIN #43 RW Rapp, Christoffer (2018) - A slightly undersized forward, Rapp showed off great hustle combined with good speed and some skill. Had a nice backhand sauce on a 2on1-rush which his teammate did not bury. Finished his checks. Scored the 4-1 goal in an empty net. Overall, Rapp had a strong performance in the limited 4th line minutes he played.

RÖG #20 Wennström, Kevin (2018) - Another smallish guy, Wennström is a skilled player and is likely to be one of Rögles most productive forwards this year. Has good hustle and instincts in the offensive zone. Can both set up and finish plays. Is however limited by his subpar skating which will likely prevent him from getting drafted by an NHL team.

Team Leetch vs Team Chelios, American Top Prospect game, September 21st, 2017

LET #1 G Mor, Jonathan (2018) – He does not possess the best techniques yet he is the battling type of goalie. Will need to continue to work on rebound control.

LET #3 LD Samuelsson, Adam (2018) – His mobility and positioning was lacking on the night. He still looks steps behind from competition from knee injury last season. The BC commit has not yet gained back game shape and processing. On one play in 2nd period he was almost on his Dman partner's side of ice in the NZ to give opposition scoring opportunity down the lane. Not only was the positioning poor he couldn't pivot and catch the forwards from neutral zone into the defensive zone. He took bad slashing penalty in 2nd period too for his lack of mobility and/or quickness. He did manage secondary assist end of 2nd period off face-off win in defsnive zone, simply threw puck high off glass to NZ and #11 Randl picked up and created 2-on-1 goal with #18 Savage.

LET #6 LD Statsney, Spencer (2018) – He did not factor on the scoresheet yet liked his handle, puck retrieval, and mobility with the puck along with his puck moving ability and thoughts. He is not overly big in size yet played solid game.

LET #8 LD Hughes, Quinn (2018): A dynamic skater on the blueline, Hughes was dangerous while in possession of the puck in the offensive zone. There are no weaknesses in his skating abilities: his top speed is excellent, he has great acceleration, and can turn on a dime. He fell in the corner in his defensive zone, and that led to Team Chelios' first goal of the game, a rare bad play from Hughes. He's small, but has game- breaking abilities every time he touches the puck.

LET #10 LW McLaughlin, Blake (2018) – He played fairly well showing some glimpses of offensive knowledge and made good offensive zone entry on in 2nd period on 3rd goal as possessed crossing blue line then dished to #14 Wise and then went to net to then receive back-door set-up from #9 Tkachuk to score. He will be a player to keep close eye upon in the USHL this season.

LET #11 LW Randl, Jack (2018) – Randl showed well here at the AAPG. Although did not earn MVP honors (#9 Tkachuk) he nicely chipped in with one goal and two assists. On the 1st goal of the game he went hard on the forecheck gained possession and then fed #22 Pivonka in slot going to net. He also picked 2nd assist in 2nd period as read play to release out of zone to gain puck on a clear to create 2-on-1 and fed #18 Savage on the tape for goal. Randl then scored in his own fashion was he bolted to net in 3rd period off #5 Harris rush and popped rebound home out front beating back checker for position and possession. He isn't high-end skilled player, yet plays smart and reliable at both ends.

LET #12 Costello, Braden (2018) – Costello was quite but showed glimpses where he had some offensive opportunities. He made nice move and fake around Dman in late 1st period then simply failed to finish in tight on the goalie when going forehand to backhand cutting across crease. Would have liked to seen more consistency yet will have opportunity in USHL to showcase.

LET #2 LD Demin, Slava (2018): He showed decent skating abilities to skate the puck out of his zone when under pressure. He was cool and calm with the puck, showing good poise when rushing it. He made a nice cross-ice feed to Savage on the 2-1 goal, showing good vision from the blueline.

LET #4 RD Wilde, Bode (2018): Decision-making was poor at times. He often tried to rush the puck, but got into trouble when trying to do too much and ended up turning the puck over. He showed great stickhandling skills and an ability to shoot the puck, but always found a way to get himself into trouble with his decision-making.

LET #7 LD Krygier, Christian (2018): Played a sound game in his own end without being flashy. Good size, and his skating abilities make him an intriguing prospect. His twin brother Cole was the most noticeable player tonight, however.

LET #9 LW Tkachuk, Brady (2018): Tough to play against. Played hard all game long and was tough to handle down low and in front of the net. He didn't hesitate to go to the net, even crashing into the opposing goaltender. He made a nice pass to McLaughlin for the 3-2 goal, showing good passing skills and vision.

LET #14 C Wise, Jake (2018): Wise showed his speed throughout this game, and was at his best when he gained speed through the neutral zone and attacked the offensive zone in full stride. He's good with the puck on his stick, showing good stickhandling skills and beating guys one-on-one. He tried too much at times with the puck, turning it over. He would be more efficient on the ice if he simplified his game.

LET #15 RC Hall, Curtis (2018) – Hall was a bit quite on the night yet has some skills sets although each viewing has yet to really establish himself as a top prospect for the draft. Uses his reach well with the puck and made nice play in 2nd period below the dots in the offensive to takeaway puck and then set-up scoring chance. Would like to see more consistency and increase in impactful plays.

LET #18 RW Savage, Ryan (2018): Scored 2 goals today, showing his great shooting ability and scoring potential. Not the biggest or fastest player, but knows where to go in the offensive zone and it showed today. Liked his release on his wrist shot, which is similar to his father Brian's.

LET #5 LD Harris, Jordan (2018): Harris was a factor in this game with his great speed. After Hughes, he was the best skating defenseman in this game. He showed good top speed with nice acceleration, he had some excellent rushes from his own zone and was often looking to create some offense. He was moving the puck quickly on the transition and in the offensive zone. A bit on the small side, Harris will need to make adjustments to his physical and defensive game, but has great tools to work with.

LET #19 RW Prokop, Noah (2018) – He was a little silent in the game. Liked his game at Select 17s in the summer.

LET #20 RW Gricius, Jake (2018) – He is big body winger that possesses average skill sets and thoughts. He tried getting involved on a few shifts using his body yet wasn't overly impressed with effort on the night.

LET #21 RW Schmidt, Colin (2018) – Schmidt was a player hoping to see continue his steady play from Select 17s in the summer yet his stride and speed looked noticeably behind. He never really got his game going just a bystander.

LET #22 LC Pivonka, Jake (2018) – The NTDP centerman plays a solid 2-way game that is reliable to make plays offensively and defensively as well. He scored the first goal of the game as he came into the play received #11 Randl pass at the dot off the forecheck cut in slot and fired far-side blocker for the goal.

LET #23 RC Nelson, Jaxon (2018) – Still looking to find when Nelson will show up and utilize his big frame, reach, and shot. He has the pro frame yet lacks the quickness and edge to make plays or be effective. He looked to be strolling around ice. Will be interesting how much he contributes in the USHL in his 2nd season after dominating lower-level Minnesota HS.

LET #30 G Kucharski, Jake (2018) – He is good size, moves well. Played as steady as you could in prospect style game with positioning. He might just be the best goalie prospect in the game.

CHE #7 RD Regula, Alec (2018): When used on the power play, he was moving the puck well enough, but didn't show potential as a true power play guy. His puck skills looked average. Most of the game he made smart plays and didn't get into trouble, with the exception of the 2-1 goal after he made a brutal turnover.

CHE #4 LD Kryger, Cole (2018): Cole was better than his more touted twin brother Christian today. He showed that he's a good skater and that he moves pretty well for his size. He showed a good quick wrister that hit the net on a regular basis. He showed great speed coming back to stop a breakaway with great closing speed.

CHE #3 LD Miller, K'Andre (2018): He had some impressive rushes with the puck from his end zone. He's all power; his strides are powerful and he possesses a heavy shot from the point. His decision-making was good, except for a couple of turnovers in the 3rd period. He showed good vision on certain sequences of the game, including on the 5-5 goal where he made a very nice pass to O'Reilly for the goal.

CHE #2 RD Samuelsson, Mathias (2018): Steady game from Samuelsson, who was physical along the boards and didn't make any mistakes. He's big, strong and moves fairly well for someone his size at this age. He didn't show much with the puck in this game, however.

CHE #8 LD Semik, Jacob (2018) – Semik is an average Dman and was never huge even before he committed to Michigan during his HoneyBaked days. He did not do anything that really impressed and question whether his speed defensively in reading plays and pivoting is keeping pace.

CHE #9 RW Wahlstrom, Oliver (2018): Inconsistent in this game, but showed high-end skills. He's really good with the puck, and has quick and soft hands. Already possesses good size, and with his ability to score, he makes for one intriguing talent in this draft class. He showed good finish on his goal; he and Farabee seemed to have good chemistry on the ice tonight.

CHE #10 RW O'Reilly, Ryan (2018) – His game is in his shot. He scored team's 5th goal in the 2nd period as all defenders drew to #3 Miller and then he received pass down low at bottom of circle and quickly fired short-side, high to beat the goalie. The foot speed needs improvement and the stick skills are average. Decent skills around the net, yet wouldn't categorize as high end. The power forward that relies on others offensively with asset in his shot.

CHE #11 RW LaPointe, Philippe (2018) – LaPointe did not make much noise in this game as normally will battle around the rink to gain possession and make plays below the dots.

CHE #12 RW Perbix, Jack (2018) – Perbix started to make some offensive plays in the 2nd period as his line scored two goals less than minute apart. He scored team's 4th goal as he went to the net and nicely re-directed #23 Jensen pass from the outside on his backhand up top. Previously missed golden chance on 2-on-0 with #21 O'Brien setup.

CHE #14 LW Weiss, Tyler (2018) – Weiss has slippery skills yet in the early going he was trying to impress to much making odd passes and turning over puck. Then in the 2nd period he showed his offensive awareness as he created scoring chances on a breakaway and then nifty move in tight by goal – he did everything but the finish. He's a skilled player that will garner attention this draft year.

CHE #15 LW Farabee, Joel (2018): He showed some quick hands, great poise with the puck and a high hockey IQ. He was good at finding available spots on the ice to get open and receive passes in the offensive zone. Did a good job when making zone entries; did well to slow down the play and leaving his linemates the time to get open.

CHE #18 LC Gruden, John (2018) – Normally solid two-way player and not that Gruden looked out of place yet did not really make any significant plays. He made couple good plays away from the puck. Still believe Gruden goes a little under the radar and will gain more attention as season progresses.

CHE #19 LC Hain, Gavin (2018) – Hain always gives a solid effort and competes on both sides of the puck. He should develop into solid NCAA player and with his smarts and skills looks to be mid-round selection.

CHE #20 LC Drury, Jack (2018) – He made a nice rush up the ice down the wall gaining the offensive zone, then making simply pass to trailing #3 Miller after putting on the breaks for team's 5th goal in the 2nd period. He is an all-around versatile player that will block shots, play defensive responsible, and will chip in offensively.

CHE #21 C O'Brien, Jay (2018): He had an impressive game, showing good skating abilities and elusivity to beat guys one-on-one. He showed good speed and stickhandling abilities throughout this game, including two highlight-reel plays that had *wow* factor: his goal and another chance that he missed earlier in the game.

CHE #23 LW Jensen, Jack (2018) – Jensen showed off his speed on a few shifts as well as his hands and offensive awareness. He was the force behind two quick Team Chelios goals in the 3rd period to bring team back with two primary assist. On the 1st goal he eluded check in the NZ then speed down wing while feeling pressure dropped puck to #21 O'Brien for the goal. Less than minute later made nice walk-around Dman down the off-wing and fed #12 Perbix going to the net for redirect goal. He will be one of the Minnesota HS players that will receive looks throughout the year.

CHE #30 G Kraws, Ben (2018) – He made some decent saves as read the play yet was also kind off hung out on 3 of 4 goals allowed off off-man rushes or defensive lapses. He certainly had the most work seeing 19 shots on goal.

Toronto Jr. Canadiens vs. Stouffville Spirit, September 21st, 2017

TJC #19 LC McBain, Jack (2018) – McBain looks to have added some muscle weight since last season as frame looked bigger. On his second shift in created nice scoring opportunity as he wheeled with puck through NZ and made quick move around defender at offensive blue line and released solid shot on net that the goalie needed to make good save. Looked improved with puck possession and stick skills in tight areas and along the wall that led to bigger plays. He played a very controlled and smart game that dictates the pace. Would still like to see quicker initial steps, yet the skating stride was stronger in speed in comparison to last season. The face-off percentage was still average as was not winning a lot of draws early in the game. He picked up three assists on the night. He made nice play to start the 2nd period, as right off the face-off took puck down the slot, ripped shot off the post with rebound goal to his line mate #9 Joffe to tie game at 2-2. He then again made nice rush in 2nd period with nice cut back buying time and space with a little east-west cut back in offensive zone, which drew hooking penalty. Then on the pursuing PP his team scored to take 3-2 lead. MacBain then factored in on another goal late in 2nd period off face-off win, then ran scissor play eventually and sets-up 4th goal to #7 Paveglio showing nice vision. McBain is an intelligent, 2-way player that plays a variety of situations from PK, PP, to 5v5. The foot speed is better yet still do not see as pure goal scoring type, although certainly a player to monitor closely this season.

Final Score: Toronto Jr. Canadiens: 5 – Stouffville Spirit: 4

Ottawa 67s at Barrie Colts, September 21st, 2017

BAR #14 RW Svechnikov, Andrei (2018) – Svechnikov was dominant in this game from start to finish. He was very decisive with the puck and consistently made crisp, firm passes to his teammates. He showed incredible power blasting home a one-time goal from a bad angle and scored another just seconds after bouncing out of a big hit attempt by Kevin Bahl. Svechnikov seemed to have the puck on a string throughout and he was very good using his size to shield it, especially on the penalty kill when he was able to kill off a lot of time along the wall. The only complaint about Svechnikov is that on a couple occasions he retaliatory slashed players after taking a hit, which could lead to some bad penalties in the future.

BAR #61 LW Suzuki, Ryan (2019) – Suzuki was very good in his OHL debut. He made quick, smart decisions with the puck and played with good pace. He was positionally sound on the penalty kill and did a nice job of keeping his stick moving and taking away shooting and passing lanes. He scored on a perfect shot over the shoulder and under the bar and also picked up an assist on a 2-on-0 play with Lucas Chiodo. Suzuki did get muscled off the puck a couple times, including once in the defensive zone that led directly to a quality scoring chance.

BAR #71 LW Nizhnikov, Kirill (2018) – Nizhnikov was very good through the neutral zone as he was able to regularly gain the line with possession and side step, or deke around, defenders who challenged him. He displayed good speed while slipping past his man on the rush. Nizhnikov did fire off a few shots with some zip but it was his passing that was particularly good in this game. He put it on tape with regularity and picked up four assists, which included involvement on a beautiful tic-tac-toe play and a perfect one-time pass to Svechnikov.

OTT #10 LW True, Oliver (2018) – During his first couple shifts he was darting all over the ice and Ottawa was able to sustain pressure in the offensive zone. That didn't amount to anything, though, and was very quiet after. He struggled to create space for himself and forced a couple shots into shin pads as a result.

OTT #13 C Bitten, Sam (2018) – Bitten was one of Ottawa's better players in this game. He worked really hard, was very engaged in battles even after the score was out of hand, and his effort and grittiness seemed to bother some Barrie players (he drew a penalty after Justin Murray decided he was tired of Bitten breathing down his neck while carrying the puck). While his defense and effort were what stood out, he did chip in offensively with a primary assist on Ottawa's lone even-strength goal.

OTT #28 D Okhotyuk, Nikita (2018) – Okhotyuk had a tough night. He made some mistakes early and it seemed like he was trying to do too much to compensate, which only made things worse. He was caught pinching several times and that led directly to at least two goals. He also tried to force some passes that simply weren't there. You can see he has a good skill set (he moved around the ice effortlessly and can really rush the puck) but he made some bad decisions that proved to be costly. The highlight of his night came when he blocked an Andrei Svechnikov shot while down eight goals in the 3rd, then got back up and flattened Svechnikov along the wall.

OTT #88 D Bahl, Kevin (2018) – Bahl's night was hit and miss. He seemed to defend well in one-on-one situations and when the play was directly in front of him, but he also made some questionable decisions that made life harder than it needed to be. For example, he pinched up the boards in the offensive zone to try and land a big hit, which he did, but it took him completely out of position and went the other way for a quality scoring chance. In general he was too aggressive at times.

Final Score: Barrie Colts: 11 – Ottawa 67's: 2

Kamloops Blazers vs Kelowna Rockets, September 22nd, 2017

KEL #26 LW Kindree, Liam (2018) – A quick strike player who had a role on the top line, moved well showing strong foot mechanics and was a good contributor to his line driving the pace of play. Didn't handle the puck a lot in this contest but when he did he looked effective making simple plays to keep cycles alive. Showed a good use of timing attacking the open areas around the net looking for rebounds and passes in tight; attacked the posts well and did a good job of frustrating defenders in and around the crease. His best drive to the net resulted in an excellent re-direct goal tipping a hot pass from the corner right through the goalies five-hole, picked up a primary assist as a linemates cleaned up one of his shots that missed the net.

KEL #24 C Topping, Kyle (2018) – Part of the best line of the night picking up opening the scoring gathering a bounce off the back boards and making one quick move out front to chip it over the goaltender. Pick up his second of two goals on the rush capping off a 3 on 2 drifting in as the last man, it took Topping a little extra to get up to top speed but the passing play was quick and finished at a high tempo with quick hands on the far side. There is a strong improvement in Topping's skating and a noticeable up tick in his top end speed, and although his footwork and acceleration looks better there is still room for improvement. His possession game was strong, his line had the puck a lot, he made good use of his body to keep defenders away from his stick and add some time and space to his game, played intelligent, read attackers better than last year.

KEL #7 RD Zabransky, Libor (2018) –Had some opportunity as the lone point man on the 1st powerplay unit, he looks a little nervous throughout this game as it was his first in the WHL regular season. Flashed a couple rushes showing off some of his speed and helping turn the play into the other direction. Looked strong reading the flow of offensive play and fired a couple powerful shots on net including and really quick one-time with impressive velocity using his entire body behind the shot. As the game went on his role and ice-time faded a little, it would be expected that he takes a little more time to adjust to the league until his game is heavily critiqued

KEL #14 LW Kushniryk, Wil (2018) – Took a little while to get involved into the game for a few reasons, one would be a lack of ice-time in the first period and the possession dominance of the top 3 lines. He's a massive player and rattled some pucks free on the forecheck playing well along the boards, also started the 3 on 2 rush picking up an assist that lead to a goal. Intriguing mix of size and showed a bit of puck ability to make plays.

KEL #29 C Foote, Nolan (2019) – With a few players missing at NHL camps Foote shifted from last years position at left wing over to center while still putting some havoc on the goaltender and the defense around the net. Foote looks stronger and more powerful around the net looking virtually impossible to move at times. Picked up toe assists on the night, one of which he took a cross ice pass and fed it softly back to the front of the net for a tip-in. Worked hard along the boards and held positive possession throughout the evening, looks to have taken positive steps over the summer with his skating, power stride looked cleaner and quicker that last years viewings.

KAM #7 LD Zazula, Luke (2018) - A dynamic skater with great footwork and acceleration he has a great knack for pushing the play up ice and making great use of that footwork to pick his lanes and drop back reorganize the rush and maintain possession for his team. His coughed up the puck a few times when looking to make a breakout pass trying to force the pass, this was a lot of his game tonight and looked as if he was trying to do too much and not trusting his teammates to help him with the play, it allowed forwards to key in him and rush him into decisions.

KAM #17 RW Stuart, Brodi (2018) - Didn't get much ice-time until the game was out of hand for Kamloops but once Stuart had some more frequent touches with puck he made a couple of nice passing plays and used some good puck movement to deke out attackers and gained a little extra time and space. Stakes with great speed and acceleration and as the game went on he looked more confident carrying the puck and kept up his top speed while doing so.

Final Score: Kelowna Rockets: 6 – Kamloops Blazers: 2

MHK Dynamo St-Petersburg vs. Loko Yaroslavl, September 26th, 2017

MHK #9 C Zhabreev, Alexander (2018): Looked like one of the smaller players on the ice today, but he does skate well and he's quite shifty spinning off checks. He has good acceleration when skating with the puck. His lack of size hurt him, as he lost one-on-one battles and could be pushed off the puck easily. He didn't generate a lot of offense during this game.

MHK #2 LD Zhilyakov, Bogdan (2018): Zhilyakov scored from a nice slapper in the 3rd period, and also added an assist late in the 3rd period. He threw some hits in his zone, with a good sense of timing, and was good defending the rush. Down low in his zone, he took the wrong angle when pursuing players, and even after throwing a hit, the opposing players were able to get away from him. Even if he finished with 2 points, he was not a big factor in the game offensively, and I didn't see a lot of play with the puck with him in this game.

Loko #93 LD Misyul, Daniil (2019): Misyul was involved in the play, and didn't shy away from supporting the rush and creating some odd-man rushes a couple of times in this game. His play with the puck got better as the game went on, and he was more active in the 2nd and 3rd periods. He started moving the puck faster in those two periods. He scored the 3-1 goal with a nice slapshot from the faceoff circle. There was some physicality from him, and he has good size. His skating is decent; he's not the smoothest or most agile skater, but generates enough speed for this level.

Loko #92 RW Slepets, Kiriil (2018): Undrafted last season, Slepets showed an ability to avoid hits in this game. He lacks the strength to compete physically, but did a good job avoiding those hits along the boards. He had some good scoring chances in this game; including one where he was robbed with a great glove save by the opposing goaltender. He has a good shot with a quick release.

Loko #14 C Denisenko, Grigori (2018): Denisenko made some excellent passing plays in this game; his passing game was at an elite level for this viewing. He showed good vision and passing abilities. He had some issues with his shot, however; on the power play, he had trouble hitting the net with his one-timer from the point. He loved to have the puck on his stick, liked to rush the puck and challenge defensemen one-on-one. His effort on the backcheck was inconsistent during the game. He played in all situations in this game and at center (we have always seen him on the wing on the international stage).

Loko #51 RW Kovalenko, Nikolai (2018): Son of former NHLer Andrei Kovalenko, Nikolai looks a lot like his father on the ice. He has a stocky frame like his dad, and used his size well to win battles and protect the puck in this game. He was very efficient in terms of puck-protection. He played in all situations in this game, including some good work on the PK, and made a nice pass on the power play for the 1st goal. Kovalenko played a very North-American game today, and flashed good shooting skills with his quick release.

Loko #86 LW Dyadenkin, Danila (2018): A good-sized winger, I liked his work along the boards and how he protected the puck well. Not an explosive skater, though. He made a nice pass on the power play to #24 for the 4-1 goal.

Loko #44 LD Lukichyov, Anton (2019): Not a lot of ice time for this late 2000-born defenseman, but he showed decent puck and passing skills. He made some nice passes to speed up the transition game. In the 2nd period, he had one or two bad shifts where his decision-making was too slow and led him to get caught in his own zone for long shifts.

Sioux Falls Stampede vs Green Bay Gamblers, USHL fall Classic, Sept 27 2017

Green Bay Gamblers –

Gamblers #16 D Tyler Spott (2018) - Had a nice outlet pass from behind the goal line to his teammate in the neutral zone. In the second he displayed some confidence by making a no look back-hand pass to his teammate in his own end. He had a tenacious back checking sequence in the second, unfortunately he cross-checked Acosta directly into his own goalie but it did off set the breakaway. Had a heads up play in the second where he realized his winger was out muscled, he quickly skated over and recovered the puck leading to further puck possession.

Gamblers #25 D Michael Vukojevic (2019) - Made a nice defensive read in the first period. His opponent attempted to cut around him, he read the play and made an aggressive poke check which caused a turnover. When players cut across him on the blueline, he's not afraid to step up and knock them off the puck. He has a defensive presence which should be highlighted considering he's a 2019 draft eligible. Didn't get an opportunity to showcase his offensive abilities but showed promise on the back end.

Gamblers #9 C Noah Prokop (2018) - His physical tools combined with his motor stood out on the ice. He showed good defensive awareness by monitoring where his opponents were located around the top of the slot and made several aggressive back checks. He demonstrated a willingness to block a shot along the point towards the end of the first. He intercepted a pass in the slot but didn't show plus hands to take advantage of it, instead making a very readable back hand move that was stopped. In the second he was physical, standing up a player on one play as they crossed the Gambler blueline. In the third, he showcased plus speed for his size, and used it to go wide on a defender. Although he was offensively stagnant, he did demonstrate a willingness to play sound defensively.

Gamblers #14 C Mckade Webster (2018) Plays with a lot of energy. Demonstrated offensive awareness and a good forecheck by intercepting a couple of passes along the boards. Had a tape to tape cross crease saucer pass in the first, that set up his teammate for a scoring chance. Was holding onto the puck in certain sequences for too long when he couldn't find passing options, this lead to turnovers.

Sioux Falls Stampede –

Stampede #4 D Brandon Tabakin (2018) - He's aware of his physical limitations and compensates by using positioning and an active stick to try and strip players off pucks, which lead him to winning puck battles against larger opponents. Had a nice sequence in the second under pressure, where he spun off a forechecker and made a spinning back-hand pass that resulted in a puck clear. His straight-line skating isn't as good as you would like to see considering his 5'8, 160 pounds frame, however his edge work got him out of some dangerous situations in the corners. During a power-play sequence he showed good lateral mobility while walking the line. Tabakin demonstrated an ability to defend in this game despite his small stature, as well as make a first pass out of the zone.

Stampede #7 C Jaxon Nelson (2018) - A kid with size, standing at 6'4 and weighing 210. He plays big, using his frame and length to keep the puck away from his opponents. He plays heavy and intelligently along the boards, using leverage to weigh on the opposition, this allowed him to come away with the puck along the boards on several plays. Although he had limited scoring opportunities, he buried one in the third. It was a quick, low, far-side snap shot that had good placement and surprised the goalie.

Final Score 5-3 Stampede

Malmo Redhawks at Rogle BK, September 27th, 2017

RBK #15 LD Bondesson, Jakob (2018) - Bondesson is a strong and efficient skater with good size who needs a lot of work in all three zones. Displayed poor gap control on a few occasions and had a tendency to run around in his own zone. Relies on his skating too much and does not play a smart defensive game, getting into, and staying in, proper positions. Also does not use his body to seperate players from pucks. Does however have a fairly active and effective stick. Loves to jump into the play and transport the puck up ice but when he gets there he does not seem to know what to do with it. Often skates himself into trouble and subsequently loses the puck. Is a bit of a gambler and takes too many risks in all three zones. Bondesson plays a very immature game that way and will need a lot of maturing to be considered a legit NHL prospect. He is at his best when he plays an up-tempo game and lets go of the puck quickly and supports the play. If he simplified his game and improved his decision-making he has the tools to be a good defenseman, but that is currently a long ways away.

MIF #6 LW Schmid, Sandro (2018) - Had a good sequence early where he demonstrated strong puck-protecting abilities along the wall against two opponents, came out with a puck and served a sweet dish to a teammate. Very undersized at 5'10, 157 lbs but he is stronger than those numbers would indicate. Skating needs improvement, especially his first few steps. He has a good feel for the game and is very effective at finding open space around the net. Finished the game with a goal and an assist.

MIF #96 RW Cajkovic, Maxim (2019) - Cajkovic is a 16 year old slovak who made his debut in J20 SuperElit on this evening. Despite his youth and inexperience you could not tell he was the youngest player on the ice. He was very active and involved in the play and played with a rare zest for a player at this level. Displayed great anticipation in all three zones and was able to intercept a D-to-D pass in his own zone and create a semi-breakaway for himself but was hooked and couldn't get a good shot off. He has good speed for a young player but could become more explosive. Very agile and shifty which makes him hard to contain. Had one sequence where he pounced on a loose puck near the goal and with a quick couple of strides made sure he was the first guy there and got away a quick shot that was saved. On a few occasions he displayed good vision and passing ability. Faded as the game wore on and was not much of a factor in the last 20-30 minutes of the game.

MIF #12 RD Lindstrand-Cronholm, Linus (2018) - Incredibly smooth and mobile skater with good balance. Generates a lot of power with his crossovers and crossunders. Quick to retrieve pucks but seems unsure of what to do once he gets it. Does not seem to process the game at a very high level and his slow decision-making gave him trouble in situations that should have been fairly routine. Had a tendency to just throw pucks away without really knowing if there was a teammate there or not, seemingly stressed from forechecking pressure. Other than that he does a fairly good job in the defensive zone. Strong physically and really likes to finish checks and plaster guys to the boards. Had one really noticeable and heavy shoulder-to-shoulder hit behind his own net. Offensively Lindstrand-Cronholm was passive and never really tried to involve himself in that part of the game. A longshot-prospect right now but if decision-making improves he could have a future at a higher level as he does possess some intriguing tools.

MIF #23 RW Rosdahl, Jesper (2018) - A late '99 birthday, Jesper Rosdahl is a big, strong and athletic player who is a surprisingly good skater for his size. Generates great speed with long, fluid strides, although his startups could use some work. Has a long reach with his stick and showcased good anticipation in the defensive zone and was able to intercept several passes on the penalty kill. The PK was where he did his best work in this game as he was always a threat with his ability to break up plays and his speed to generate something in the other direction. Rosdahl played limited minutes in a 4th line role and did not have much opportunity to make something happen in the offensive zone.

Cedar Rapids RoughRiders vs. Sioux Falls Stampede, September 29th, 2017

CR #6 LD Jubenvill, Tyler (2018) – He is average size Dman although showed some offensive side in 2nd period as rang shot off post on a broken 2-on-1 chance with #12 Timmons. He is a late '99 from Canada, so will need to monitor this season.

CR #8 RC Roy, Harrison (2018) – He looked average in the game not making real lasting impression. He speed was average as well. He took incorrect side of player on the back check and actually hit opposition into his own goalie causing confusion for his team and luckily for him the Fgoal against was waived off.

SFS #7 RC Nelson, Jaxon (2018) – He certainly has the pro frame as listed 6'4" 205lbs and has the long reach for centerman. Although his foot speed is very average and lateral steps could certainly use work. He did not do a whole lot to attract your attention and not sure his game is anything significant. He is committed to Minnesota and has had past success at the lower level Minnesota HS ranks, so will be interesting if Nelson can adjust to USHL pace and skill sets.

Final Score: Sioux Falls Stampede: 5 – Cedar Rapids RoughRiders: 4

U.S National Team Development Program vs Central Illinois Flying Aces, USHL Fall Classic, Sept 29, 2017

U.S.A –

USA #18 RW Oliver Wahlstrom (2018) – Wahlstrom looked physically engaged early, using his frame to push his opponent off the puck on a back-checking sequence. Moments later he displayed excellent balance by staying upright on one leg with his face positioned towards the ice, after a defenceman slid into him while trying to block his cross-crease pass; he then delivered a pass from behind the net into the slot for a scoring chance. Had an excellent sequence later in the first where he forced the Aces to play heavy minutes. After getting behind the Aces defence, he chipped the puck behind the net, out muscled his opponent and then showed tenacious fore-checking by battling against three different players while waiting for help. It was good to see him assert himself physically. He was the best player in the first period and started the second with a high-level rush. He skated over the neutral zone, side stepping his opponent, then went outside-inside very quickly, allowing him to split the defence, setting himself up for a prime scoring chance. In the third, he had the primary assist on Farabee's goal. He anticipating a pass that was exiting the zone, then used his edge work to stop and side step his opponent, then under pressure, used his hands to make enough space for himself to pass it off to Farabee down at the bottom of the right circle. Scored a shorthanded goal off the rush after Farabee's excellent pass and buried it over Gordon's glove hand. Wahlstrom was physically engaged, asserted himself on the ice consistently and was the best player overall on either team.

USA #30 G Jonathen Mor (2018) – Plays a conservative butterfly and has a pro frame, standing 6'2, 200 pounds. He was very good for the U.S today, stopping several high-quality scoring chances. None were more impressive than his save in the second, where he read a quick passing play, pushed off to the top of his crease, cutting off the far side and absorbed the puck with his blocker, resulting in no rebound. Mor is a highly technical goalie who has little wasted movement, it's some of the best control I've seen out of a goalie thus far in this year's draft class. It allows him to push off laterally fluidly and doesn't get him caught over-committing on plays. He's also good at reading plays, on one sequence he slowed down his lateral movement while tracking the puck, realizing it was going to take additional time before reaching the opponent on the right side of his slot. He assesses where players are attempting to position themselves in-front of his crease, which allowed him to see plays through traffic. His technical skating was on display and it allowed him to square up for the first shot and additional shots, absorbing rebounds throughout the game. Overall, Mor displayed excellent movement while tracking the puck effectively.

USA #7 RW Trevor Janicke (2018) – Due to the talent on this squad, Janicke is assigned 4th line duties. He embraced the role early by showing tenacious board battling skills against multiple opponents. He knew how to angle his body, demonstrated good balance while getting cross checked, and stick-checked effectively, resulting in puck possession. In the second, he managed to get a pretty quick wrist shot off, and knew where to be at the right time to collect a lose puck for the scoring chance.

USA #28 LW Joel Farabee (2018) – Had an ineffective start to the game, he did deliver a quick pass into the slot for a redirect but was quite otherwise in the first. He had multiple turnovers to start the second, losing the puck off the rush on one play while trying to skate over the line and then passed the puck directly to the opposition along the half wall moments later, he was visibly frustrated on the play. During a penalty kill sequence, he came alive, managing to set up his teammate in the slot for a scoring chance after transitioning the puck out of his end, then later in the same shift ended up with a breakaway which he failed to capitalize on. In the third, he showed his shooting ability by scoring a beautiful off-angle wrist shot. There was little movement, no knee bend and both his core and shoulders were not completely turned towards the net, so Gordon didn't expect the shot. The placement was also perfect, there was no chance for Gordon to stop it. Wahlstrom and Farabee's chemistry continued after the play. During a 2 on 1, Farabee came down the left side, held up, gauged Gordon's reaction to the potential shot, before making a saucer pass over the defenceman's stick to Wahlstom who buried it. Although he started off slowly, he dominated the third, showing his high-end puck skills, his intelligence, and his shot.

USA #14 C Jack Deboer (2018) – Deboer was playing between Wahlstrom and Farabee on the 'second line' and had some moments with them. He had several high-end passing plays, none more impressive than a tape to tape saucer pass that was threaded through multiple Aces players, setting up Wahlstrom for a scoring chance. However, given his line mates I would have liked to have seen a bit more from him today. Skating is a weakness.

USA #9 LW/C Tyler Weiss (2018) – Had one of the best plays in the third. He dove for a lose puck that went behind the net, he then used his frame to strip the smaller Raith off the puck and swung a pass into the slot, while falling, this lead to O'Brian's first goal on the national team. He showed a lot of energy, playing at a high pace that overwhelmed the Aces defence at times. He posted three points today.

USA #11 C Jay O'Brien (2018) – Centered a very effective 4th line today in his first game of action. He showed a good motor, going after lose pucks and battling along the boards all night. His play was rewarded in the third, he took a pass from Weiss and waited out the goalie before pulling it back-hand for his first goal with the U.S.

USA #15 D Bode Wilde (2018) – A defenceman with excellent physical tools. His base is powerful, which allows him to explode out of the gate, getting up to his top gear quickly. He had a sequence in the first where this was demonstrated off a turnover, where he received a pass and drove wide, separating himself, this created a breakaway scoring chance. Had a bazaar play early in the second where he transitioned the puck up the ice and instead of wrapping it around the boards or trying to set up his team, he tried to do a hard back-hand pass off the glass which went into the netting. The play would have made more sense if he was under a lot of pressure but he had already driven around the Aces player who was attempting to stop him. His decision making in the offensive end was mixed, in the third, he had multiple passing options but opted to shoot the puck into heavy traffic which resulted in a block and turnover. He was average today, failing to assert himself offensively with the exception of a breakaway sequence.

USA #5 D Adam Samuelsson (2018) – An enormous defenceman standing at 6'5, 240. He established himself in the defensive zone through out the first period with a couple of blocks, one from the point which he then cleared and another during a sharp angle shot. His stride is short and he has trouble pushing off from his first step. This makes his acceleration below average even for his size, which makes it very difficult for him to generate any speed coming into the neutral zone. During a sequence on the power-play, he was forced to pass the puck back to his teammate's while under pressure since he can't separate himself. Defensively, he was a presence all night, using his frame to take away lanes and box players out of the slot area.

USA #27 D, D.J. King (2018) – Had a good defensive read in the first. Madden used a feint to open up space on the right side of the slot, but King read where Madden wanted to place the puck, so he aggressively cut off the lane and blocked the shot. Showed hustle when skating after a lose puck that he needed to get to quickly after missing a pass from his defensive partner. In the second, he had a mental lapse, where he got tunnel vision and stepped up to hit a player, completely throwing him out of the play. It led to the Aces second goal of the game and showed a lack of defensive awareness in the neutral zone by King. Ended up taking an unnecessary penalty by spearing Kiufiuk on the side of his net after a whistle, resulting in a 5-minute major. Showed some ability in this game but his defensive reads were mixed, leading to a goal against.

USA #10 D Ty Emberson (2018) – Got engaged physically early by standing up a player coming over the blue-line, with a clean yet powerful hit that knocked his opponent to the ice. Shortly after, he had a well-timed pin along the boards leading to a turnover. In the second, he continued using his physical abilities, unfortunately his timing was off, instead of been patient and staying in position, he forced a hit that left him vulnerable, almost leading to an odd man rush. When King threw himself out of a play in the second, Emberson did a good job defending a three on one sequence. He stayed in-front of his man, used his stick to cut off the passing lane and gave Mor the shooting option, the puck still found the back of the net but it wasn't Emberson's fault.

Central Illinois Flying Aces –

CIL #7 D Michael Callahan (2018) – Was effective at transitioning the puck out of his own zone and using his defensive partner to alleviate an aggressive fore-check for most of the night. Had a nice goal, he scored off a hard slap-shot that beat Mor, far-side in the second.

CIL #8 D Brady Smith (2018) – During the first Aces power play, Smith showed that he was quick out of the gate, which allowed him to drive down the left lane, before pulling up and passing it into the slot which lead to a high-quality scoring chance. In the second, he didn't get too many chances to carry the puck, but when he did, he showed an ability to walk the line, using feints combined with his skating to open up lanes and options for himself. In the defensive end, he's aware that he can't get caught physically against bigger players. On one sequence he spun off a fore-checker, then pulled up so quickly that he sent another player crashing into the boards. He's 5'8 with a small frame, so it's good to see that he has the total skating package. He can accelerate from a stand still position quickly and his straight-line speed allows him to transition the puck up the ice, while his edge work gives him options defensively to avoid danger and create offence from the back end. He looks like a modern day, undersized, offensive defenceman who can skate.

CIL #10 C Tyler Madden (2018) – He was the best forward for the Aces today. He has a combination of speed and feinting mechanics that allowed him to be the most successful out of any Aces player at breaking down the U.S's very large and mobile defense. During one sequence, he used his acceleration to go wide then used a wrist shot feint to create a scoring chance that was blocked by King. He has technical dekes as well. During one play, he made a well timed, between the legs toe drag which created space for himself while driving down the left side of the slot. He's good as assessing his opponents body positioning, which allowed him to time when he could use his acceleration and hands effectively. On another sequence, he got off a quick wrist shot in the slot and managed to corral the rebound for an additional scoring chance. He continued to show his offensive instincts in the second by pulling a bad pass from behind him while skating over the blue-line leading to a partial breakaway. It was subtle but was difficult to execute. In the third, it looked like he ran out of gas, making unforced turnovers while attempting to enter the opposing zone and started missing his passing options. Although, he stayed composed along the half-wall on the power play and was decent at distributing the puck.

CIL #28 LW Drew Elser (2018) – Played high tempo hockey in the first, utilizing excellent speed to drive into scoring lanes and fore-check effectively behind the net in the offensive zone. Took too much time setting up his wrist shot which was stopped after receiving a great cross crease pass from his teammate.

CIL #13 LW Calen Kiefiuk (2018) – Attempted a saucer pass that just missed his man and would have led to a breakaway scoring chance as he recognized that Adam Samuelsson was caught out of position. Due to the size of the U. S's defenceman, Kiefiuk found himself driving wide to try and create passing options for himself, which he was successful at doing throughout the first frame. Helped set up a nice tic-tac-toe passing sequence by making a subtle backhand pass after driving down the right wing, he then received a pass from below the goal line before quickly passing it in the slot for the scoring chance.

Final Score: Team USA 5 – Central Illinois Flying Aces 2

Scouts Notes:

Mattias Samuelsson was tossed from the game after getting a boarding penalty behind his own net

Jay O'Brien was added to the roster. Seth Appert told us he won't be full time because he's a 99 birth but was a good fill in because of an injury.

Waterloo Black Hawks vs. Green Bay Gamblers, September 29th, 2017

WAT #48 RD Szmagaj, Ethan (2020) – The '01 Dman did double duty on the day as played 9am morning game with U16 Little Caesars and then upped the ante at 5pm game with Waterloo. He plays a steady game on the blue line even though bit undersized. He moves puck, kept it simple and played physical when needed. Faired pretty well holding his own for not only rookie, yet playing game earlier in day. Michigan commit goes a little under radar and will have next three seasons to garner draft talk as late 2001.

WAT #44 LW Guzzo, Patrick (2020) – A power forward like his teammate Szmagaj also played U16 Little Caesars in the morning before taking his game to the USHL in the evening. Oddly enough also is committed to Michigan and late '01 birthdate. He managed to use his long reach, and stick skills to fire a few shots on net. He shoots the puck with authority. Will play another year of U16 and then two seasons of USHL before becomes draft eligible.

DUB #7 LD Semik, Jacob (2018) – He is decent size defenseman that moves well and simply plays a steady, puck moving style. Scouts and coaches have been raving about the blue liner since Honeybaked days and when he committed early to Michigan. Although not sure his game has continued to develop offensively. He played defensive style adequate with gaps and positioning. He can get pucks on net from the point, yet nothing dynamic in creating scoring threats consistently.

DUB #13 LW Pietila, Logan (2018) – Pietila is smaller in size that needs size and strength to make the next level. He plays a smart game and showcased some skill as made nice set-up out of the corner for scoring opportunity. Will need to round defensive game away from puck and gain strength. Will project as good NCAA player.

DUB #12 RD Fulp, Aidan (2018) – Fulp started to make some headway with scouts at Select 17s this summer although here he played an average game. He will need to improve upon his foot quickness as exposed a few times against forwards that were fast. Also, his defensive positioning was odd at times giving up some SOG. There will be a little bit of learning curve as adjusts from Tier 1 U16 level to juniors.

DUB #21 LC Steeves, Alex (2018) – He's a late '99 entering his second year in the USHL whereby he has some slippery offensive skills. He does not wow you right away but he's a playmaker that sees the ice and made a couple good plays in tight around the net. In one sequence he made good takeaway in offensive zone after face-off that lead to possession and opportunity.

Final Score: Waterloo Black Hawks: 6 – Dubuque Fighting Saints: 2

Sioux City Musketeers vs. Muskegon Lumberjacks, September 29th, 2017

SC #8 LW Ranta, Sampo (2018) – The Finnish product showed his scoring touch in this one as he netted the hat trick. His first goal in the 1st period displayed his quick, hard, accurate release at the dot off broken play as he labeled far-side over the glove. The second goal in the 2nd period came off offensive face-off when as Ranta simply walked into the shot at top of circle as again quickly, snapped shot far-side over the glove. He finished off the hat trick in the 2nd period on a 2-on-1 rush with #22 Ford as he quickly showed his hands in tight to crease going backhand/forehand for the goal. He will get looks this season from scouts with size and scoring abilities. Committed to Wisconsin.

SC #23 RW Salonen, Samuel (2018) – Salonen is the other Finnish player on Sioux City roster and interesting enough scored the other goal as well along with three goals previous night at USHL Showcase. His tally came in 2nd period on the power play as took cross ice pass as left alone in slot as beat goal blocker side with a little mustard in getting it past the goalie. His shot release technique is bit odd as will drag back leg each time. His skating stride is weaker and will be interesting if he keeps pace with the scoring and speed in the USHL.

SC #24 LC Pospisil, Martin (2018) – He has some good size at center. The stick skills are not exceptional, decent but not high end. He did show good puck decisions and was given point duty on the power play to distribute the puck. Will be interesting how he adapts as rookie to North American game in draft year. Not sure he will develop into high offensive player.

SC #65 LD Babbage, Jack (2018) – Babbage is uncommitted Dman that has decent size, mobility, and handle. Sometimes his defensive zone positioning was questionable and that's is probably why some NCAA coaches and scouts have time to keep watching his progress. More of a steady Dman with offensive thoughts limited.

MUSK #3 LD Del Gaizo, Marc (2018) – The late '99 Dman is bit undersized. He handles and moves the puck well, yet in this game he really did not impress too much. UMass commit that might be worthy of late round pick.

MUSK 12 LW Pekar, Matej (2018) – Pekar played Tier 1 last season gaining some attention as Czech Republic native. He is decent size and scored goal in 3rd period to start the Muskegon comeback. He has some offensive qualities with the puck, yet will need to learn the 200-foot game.

MUSK #20 LC Pettersen, Emilio (2018) – Pettersen lacks the size yet he was one of the more impressionable players on the day as he plays with pace and showed offensive skills creating scoring chances with the puck or going to the net in reading the play to tip a shot. He was finally rewarded in the 3rd period on the scoresheet as he tallied a goal while setting up the game tying and game winning goal in OT. On the OT GWG he made nice read in the neutral zone to pick off the pass the center ice and then quickly move puck to #5 Bongiovanni that created 2-on-1. The Denver commit will be one to watch after producing respectable numbers last season with Omaha in the USHL.

MUSK #23 LW Afanasyev, Egor (2019) – He has the size and stick skills are decent. He was given third line duties and had a couple shots on net although rookie trying to find his way. Plays with energy and likes to drive the net. A power forward style.

MUSK #22 LD Staudacher, Matt (2018) – He was steady on the blue line. He did not offer high end offense, yet he will find shooting lanes from the point and will block shots in the defensive end. He is good size, has mobility, and makes outlets.

MUSK #25 LC Kondelik, Jachym (2018) – Kondelik is a huge body that is now in second USHL season. He showed glimpses of offensive thoughts and plays. He made nice seam pass in 2nd period in offensive zone that led to scoring chances and later set-up goal in 3rd period. He possesses long reach and stick skills are decent for big body. The skating is adequate as well, as not fast yet decent enough north-south game. The late '99 birthdate will get plenty of looks to see if worth of mid-round pick.

MUSK #30 G Borgiel, Zach (2018) – Borgiel came in relief to start the 3rd period and played steady game as rookie after playing U16 Honeybaked last season as made all nine saves. He is good size over 6-foot mark. He moves fairly well and shows decent athleticism.

Final Score: Muskegon Lumberhacks: 5 – Sioux City Musketeers: 4

Trinec J20 at Kometa Brno J20, September 29th, 2017

BRN # 13 LW Gajarsky, Adam (2018) - Gajarsky shows as usual on team level a good hockey sense, good skating, good reading, playmaking ability. He uses speed to create gap and opportunities. Gajarsky works active with his stick and skates all game and he is the one that lifts himself when the team stands on the heels. He can deliver passes that is very difficult to predict for the opponent and goalie. He didn't use his shot to much today as he should. One very nice flip from the board was by the first pillar before no one even reacted. Gajarsky looks very thin on the board and needs to gain hockey muscles and weight. Gajarsky had a fully ok game and ended on 0+1. Gajarsky is one that I think is better in U20 then in national team but hopefully will develop and be more consistent during the year, with a bigger role in U20, and some games in top and 2nd Mans league.

BRN # 11 LW Svoboda, Matej (2018) - Svoboda was quit quick, had decent compete level, read the game good from time to time. Searching the referees to blow a penalty instead of just continuing to play. Showing a lower reading level when 2-3 m (6-9 feet) away from the opponent and he just gives away the puck behind his back believing that the Trinec Forward where closer. Looks like he needs to build a lot of leg muscles. Ended on 0 points and +-0

BRN # 11 C Strondala, Vojtech (2019) - Strondala is a late born 2000 player that had an excellent Hlinka and got 3 not to notable shifts in the Extraliga game. He is a very small C that has excellent FO% and speed. He has good competitive level. He has good hands but when he don't use his speed added on it, sometimes it can be a bit too complicated. I feel that Strondala is better in the national team then in J20 team. With more weight he will be a very interesting player. Today Strondala had an average game and he ended on 0p and +-0

BRN # 24 RW Plasek, Karel (2018) - Plasek had a good game where he used his speed and read the game good. He has good speed both with and without puck. Creates gap and with more weight and maturity he will be very interesting. He was good in penalty killing and very active with high forechecking and stick checking. A couple of time Plasek was waiting some half second to much before he shot. His game was better than the points says 0 P and -1. Consistency in producing points needed, although he is consistent in the work on league level. Good attitude.

TRI # 31 LW RW Peterek, Jonas (2019) - Good with puck, good on skates with nice mobility one second and the next it looks unbalanced. Looks like the edges on the skates where un sharp. Showed excellent reading and good skills with the stick. He delivered a super nice pass to Papaj that indicated he reads the game excellent. He has very nice stickhandling and puck receiving. He used his skill and brought the puck from own red over the ice and delivered a decent shot. With some more weight and a bit more grit Peterek is one of my favourites born 2001. Peterek can show some inconsistency (especially in national team) but today he had a good game in a weak team and was one of the better even if O p and -1.

TRI # 32 RW Raska, Adam (2020) - Late September 2001 born wing with nice long stride. He plays his usual game and finishing hits, competitive, drives with puck to net. It's not a very aggressive league but Raska delivered a nice clean open ice on Karel Plasek. Raska also played with grit and can sometimes be a bit ugly but still on the right side to not get penalties. He has a decent hard and accurate shot, good reading and positioning. Even though very thin and easy he plays himself in front of the net ready to do dirty work. He was perfect in the penalty kill and very aggressive with high forechecking. Adam ended on 1 goal and +-1. He worked good in both zones and joins home all the time. He lifts himself in the end when its required, showed confident.

Chicoutimi Saguenéens vs. Drummondville Voltigeurs, September 29th, 2017

CHI #77 LD Groleau, Jeremy (2018): He played a lot of minutes today, and with Galipeau was the team's most trusted defenseman, to counter Drummondville forwards. He played a lot on the PK and blocked quite a few shots. He was solid one-on-one, and was tough to play against in one-on-one and corner situations. He showed a good compete level throughout the night while in his zone. Not much in terms of puck-moving, or plays in the offensive zone, as Chicoutimi didn't have the puck a whole lot in this game.

CHI #23 LW Kotkov, Vladislav (2018): The big Russian winger had a slow first half, where there was not much offense to talk about from him until late in period 2. He showed that he's effective around the net, he has good hands, and is willing to stand in front of the net. He's a big body and is tough to move from there. He scored on the power play in front of the net, and had 2-3 more scoring chances the rest of the game from that area. His skating is a work-in-progress, as he will need some work with his top speed, acceleration and agility.

CHI #35 G Bouthillier, Zachary (2018): Gave up 5 goals on 38 shots tonight, as his defense had all kind of difficulties handling the Voltigeurs' speed. He looked nervous and did not look confident early in the game, as he was having trouble handling rebounds, and was out of position on rebounds. He also made some questionable plays while trying to play the puck outside of his crease. He didn't challenge shooters enough in this game, playing too deep in his crease.

CHI #88 C Houde, Samuel (2018): Houde centered Chicoutimi's top line, but was not much of a factor in this game offensively. He showed, at times, some good vision when passing the puck, but few of these occasions resulted in scoring chances out there. Houde lacks good acceleration. He likes to rush the puck, but lacks that separation speed. He got into a fight in the 2nd period, but quickly lost against Baker.

CHI #91 RW Marcotty, Felix-Antoine (2019): Marcotty finished the game with 2 assists; showing good playmaking abilities in this game (mostly in the 3rd period). He made a great cross-ice pass to Kevin Klima for Chicoutimi's 2nd goal of the game. He played on the top line, paired with Houde tonight.

DRU #33 G Rodrigue, Olivier (2018): Quiet night for Rodrigue, who only faced 19 shots. Eight of them came in the 3rd period, with the game already out of hand. He was calm in his crease, and didn't give up any rebounds. He made one key save in the first period, stopping a breakaway after not facing any shots for a long time, demonstrating good focus. He gave up two late goals in the 3rd period, but the game was already too far gone for Chicoutimi.

DRU #92 LD Beaudin, Nicolas (2018): Smart puck moving from Beaudin tonight. Excellent passing game and he was a key player for the Voltigeurs' transition game. On the power play, I noticed he was taking more shots on net that he did last year. He does not have the most powerful shot, but he was still hitting the net on a regular basis with his point shot. Very poised with the puck, never panicking with it, and always seems to make the smart play with it. Good decision-making, good offensive flair to know when to lead and support the rush.

DRU #55 LD Bernard, Xavier (2018): The left-handed defenseman was playing on the right side with Duquette tonight, but was back playing on the left side on the power play (2nd unit). He was efficient one-on-one, using his size and mobility well to defend. His decision-making with the puck could stand to improve.

DRU #6 LD Baker, Jared (2019): Another left-handed defenseman that was playing on the right side for the Voltigeurs tonight. He won a quick fight in the 2nd period and was physical tonight, throwing some good hits along the boards. He did a good job putting pucks on net, showing a quick release and no hesitation to get pucks on net from the right point.

DRU #19 RW Mercer, Dawson (2020): Drummondville's top pick in last year's QMJHL Draft, he showed good flashes of his elite puck skills on the power play. He was shifty with the puck and demonstrated a good ability to avoid hits while in possession of the puck. He will need to get stronger over time. He was mostly noticeable on the power play.

DRU #81 C Simoneau, Xavier (2019): Simoneau was one of the top Voltigeurs today. He was very quick to get to loose pucks, and used his speed very well tonight. He scored his first QMJHL goal shorthanded on a breakaway. He's small, but his compete level was excellent tonight. He plays much bigger than his size. He showed great passing skills and vision on the power play. Simoneau played in all situations tonight, and finished the game with two points. He was the game's 2nd star.

Everett Silvertips at Kelowna Rockets, September 29th, 2017

KEL #24 LW Topping, Kyle (2018) - Looked good carrying puck in traffic showed a greater confidence in his all around command of controlling the play and being more of a catalyst for offence and less of complimentary player. Got some time on both the penalty kill and 1st unit powerplay. Finished with no points but certainly had a couple chances on net that were foiled by a really solid goaltending performance, looked good creating space for his hands to work while boxing out around the net.

KEL #16 LW Kindree, Liam (2018) - Pulled off a couple nice give and go moves to attack the net and showed a strong ability to dart in and out of seams looking for rebounds and generally showing a pretty solid ability to cause a some nascence type play around the crease. Made a couple good plays to shield off defenders and muscle pucks out of the defensive zone, which in turn lead to a couple good neutral zone rushes exhibiting good use of his skating ability, which is not high-end but certainly is a positive asset.

KEL #7 RD Zabransky, Libor (2018) – Showed some confidence in sending a quick wrist shot to the net, release is a fast but his shot could use a more power to become dangerous. Scored a goal off a snap shot that was a good display of his quick release, didn't look like the goalie expected him to shoot; caught him off guard. Had a few issues using his feet in both transition and in to effectively get pucks out of the zone, slows a lot when trying to carry it.

KEL #29 C Foote, Nolan (2019) – Lining up as center due to a thinner lineup with players away at NHL training camps. Obviously his usual effectiveness along the wall was not felt, he was having trouble staying on the correct side of the puck when playing defense loosing position to some of the quick players attacking his net. Isn't a rather quick puck carrier and looked to get a little tired and frustrated by the end of the game not lending much to the transition game or getting too involved in the offense.

EVE #14 C Sutter, Riley (2018) – Made a couple plays that showed his poise to create offense including a cross ice pass on a 2 on 1 that was a great play by the goaltender for a save but the offense that he did create was mostly from a standing position, really looked slow when moving with the puck and rarely showed any type of deception with his footwork – Played at a steady pace with little in terms of changes in gear. Did show some good hands in and around the net on the powerplay, tipped a few pucks while screening and showed his strength being difficult to move.

EVE #29 LD Wylie, Wyatte (2018) – Was an all situation guy playing both the powerplay and the penalty kill, looked really safe all game, stayed back made simple D to D passes and rarely tried to push it up the ice with either a pass or his footwork; something he was capable of in previous viewings. Wylie's skilled looked a little handcuffed in this game while his partner took the chances

EVE #5 LD Onyebuchi, Montana (2018) – Not a major factor in this game but looked solid and strong with some sound positional play in his defensive zone, he's strong on the wall and can finish a check. Didn't get it off that often but has a booming slap shot from the point.

EVE #9 RW Butt, Dawson (2018) – Showed some good ability to battle and was persistent working hard along the board, constantly going at it. Unfortunately was on the losing end of most of the battles getting boxed out or bumped off pucks, grinding along the wall but not to the fault of his effort, has the size for success just needs a better technique.

Final Score: Everett Silvertips: 4 – Kelowna Rockets: 3 – OT/SO

Vitkovice J20 at Kometa Brno J20, September 30th, 2017

BRN # 13 LW Gajarsky, Adam (2018) - Gajarsky had a OK game but without any points. He had a good cooperation with #4 Matej Novak and they created some nice opportunities by quickly moving the puck between them. All the regular attributes that Gajarsky use, such as good skating, good reading positioning and communication was used. He received a nice pass from behind the goal by # nr 4 Novak but under some duress Gajarsky only managed to release a hard shot with bad accuracy from the slot. When he uses the speed Gajarsky is difficult to stop but once stocked by the board he is very light. I where lacking some of the grittiness Gajarsky usually do. Needs to bulk up and shoot more. Gajarsky is one of my favorites although based on reading, skills and potential.

BRN # 11 LW Svoboda, Matej (2018) - I found Svoboda invisible or on 70-80% gas the first period. Strondala and Plasek produced but he wasn't there. In second period it was like the gage was released and after 1-0, at minute 25, Svobodas started to be visualized and the line clicking. The 5-2 goal was a delicacy where Svoboda, Plasek and Strondala really where playing with the Vitkovice U20. Svoboda and his lines mate was using their skills, their speed and their reading and created a 3 on 1 situation and the 5-2 goal. Svoboda was big part of it with good positioning and high puck receiving and delivery skills. Svoboda ended on 1+2 and +-2. I would say the numbers where better than his game but he had some nice shifts.

BRN # 14 C Strondala, Vojtech (2019) - Strondala had a very successful game, especially with Plasek but in later part of the game the full line with Svoboda was good. Strondala wins the Faceoffs so that the line can continue to work directly, no time spoiled on chasing the pucks. Once he does miss a faceoff he chases with lot of energy and creativity to win the puck back. If he would be more consistent with that speed and energy Strondala would be one of the best in the league. He has great tool box and use most of them. I find him to be on good competitive level. Strondala took sometimes to long shifts and when he ended having a rush to the goal his shot was on the level as a pass to the goalie. Strondala ended on 0+3 and +-2.

BRN # 24 RW Plasek, Karel (2018) - Plasek again had a good game but this time with good productivity in points. 2+1 +- 2. He looked very confident and active on the ice. He used his speed and read the game good. Maybe Vitkovice is not a top team but it's still a U20 team and Plasek managed to close and create gap. He was good in penalty killing and very active with high forechecking and stick checking. A couple of time. Plasek had good work ethic.

BRN # 15 Cejka, Jakub (2018) - Cefka was visualized from time to time and had a OK game with some small nicer things. He got a nice quick puck rush creating a 2 on 1 situation, but Cejka didn't manage to flip the puck over a good defending Vitkovice stick. Cejka was good in penalty killing with active forechecks, and he did 1 goal -1.

BRN # 4 Novak, Matej (2018) - Novak was having one of his better games and it was visualized why he got so many GWG last years. If he could lift himself to a more consistent level I think the guy has a great toolbox. He was reading the game very good and was very competitive. He had 2 situations during the game where he was lying on the ice winning the puck back

BRN # 23 Krejci, Petr (2018) - Krejci showed some of his skills with the skating and mobility. Had a couple of very nice opening first passes.

VIT # 24 LW Balaz, Jozef (2018) - Balaz was one that was better in Vitkovice. Balaz had quickness and skilled hands and ended on 1+1.

VIT # 91 Toman, Radim (2018) - Good hands, reads ok, aggressive in front of the net. He leads the offense in Vitkovice U20 being 17 and put up assist to the both goals.

Baie-Comeau Drakkar vs. Drummondville Voltigeurs, September 30th, 2017

BAC #9 C Fortier, Gabriel (2018): Fortier was solid for the Drakkar today, playing his usual strong two-way game, and finished the game with 3 points. He scored a nice goal on a two-on-one chance, following a good puck exchange with Jordan Martel. He was tenacious on the forecheck and used his speed to pressure opposing defensemen in their decision-making. He also used that great speed to come back hard on the backcheck; he made one excellent backcheck to break up a two-on-one chance the other way. His great forecheck eventually led to Baie-Comeau's 3rd goal of the game. As usual, Fortier was really fast, and was one of the hardest workers on the ice. He had a tough night in the faceoff circle, though.

BAC #20 RD Bouchard, Xavier (2018): Bouchard had some up-and-down moments in this game. He had a good scoring chance early-on, taking advantage of a bad Drummondville line change, taking a long pass from his goaltender before coming down the right wing, but couldn't beat Rodrigue with a low shot blocker-side. He made some good passes in the offensive zone, showing some nice vision, and he played mostly on the 2nd power play unit tonight. He did a fine job putting pucks on net. He does not possess a hard shot, but his shots were still getting through. He got beaten wide a couple of times in this game, and had a hard time (much like the rest of his team) adjusting to the speed of the Drummondville forwards. He looked tired in the 3rd period and had some long shifts in his zone; making two bad passes behind his own net on the same shift that almost led to a Drummondville goal.

BAC #34 G Blanchette, Justin (2018): Tough night for Blanchette, who gave up 7 goals on 27 shots in 40 minutes of play. He was not back on the ice in the 3rd period. Simply put, he didn't give his team a chance to win the game; he gave up two goals immediately after Baie-Comeau had scored to try and get back in the game. He was either too deep in his net, out of position or just outside of his crease. There was some back luck involved as well, with bad bounces from the boards, but in the 2nd period, he didn't have much confidence stopping any pucks. It was a game to forget for him. He had some hit-and-misses with his puck-handling, as he absolutely loves to play the puck outside of his crease, but sometimes tries too much. That was definitely the case tonight. He made a great long pass to Xavier Bouchard early in the game that almost resulted in a goal for the Drakkar, but on other occasions, he turned the puck over trying too much with it.

BAC #25 C St-Laurent, Edouard (2018): St-Laurent has great speed; he's quick to put pressure on the puck-carrier on the forecheck. He's also quick to retrieve pucks in the offensive zone, but didn't make smart plays with it. He needs to show more poise while in possession of the puck, and make smarter decisions in the role of playmaker. Skating is his number 1 asset; he has good top speed and acceleration.

BAC #27 RW Martel, Jordan (2018): Martel was the best player on Baie-Comeau today, finishing the game with 4 points. The '98-born forward was playing on the top line with Fortier and Chekhovich. He was dangerous playing on his off-wing because of a good, quick shot, and good speed. He possesses a quick wrist shot that he used to score his goal, and has a quick release. He showed nice vision throughout the game and made an excellent play on the Chekhovich goal in the 3rd period. He made things happen with his speed on most of his shifts. He will be a player to keep an eye on this season, as a possible late-bloomer.

DRU #33 G Rodrigue, Olivier (2018): Left the game after 20 minutes. He didn't look hurt out there, and was sitting on the bench in the 2nd and 3rd periods. He gave up two goals in the first period; he had no chance on the Fortier goal, as they did a good job making moves east-to-west and Fortier had an open net to shoot at. On the 2nd goal by Girard, even with a bit of traffic in front of him, he probably would want that goal back. He made 7 saves on 9 shots in that period.

DRU #55 LD Bernard, Xavier (2018): Again playing on the right side with Duquette, Bernard was solid defending one-on-one and playing his man well. He played on both sides during the game, and was featured on the left side on the 2nd power play unit. He struggled with the accuracy on his breakout passes, and was not a factor in the transition or offensive game of his team.

DRU #92 LD Beaudin, Nicolas (2018): Beaudin showed good anticipation in the neutral zone, cutting some passes and creating some turnovers. He made good passes to speed up his team's transition game. His passes are very accurate, and most of the time go from tape-to-tape. Skating is smooth, and he picks good spots to join or lead the rush. Another smart game from Beaudin.

DRU #90 RD Pelletier, Thomas (2019): Rookie blueliner saw some ice time on the 2nd power play unit. He didn't get a ton of ice time at even-strength, but was solid when on the ice. He kept things simple and didn't make any major mistakes out there. He was solid defending one-on-one and used his stick well to pokecheck the puck away. He kept his play with the puck simple, making short passes instead of difficult ones.

DRU #6 LD Baker, Jarrett (2019): Baker was solid again tonight, playing an efficient two-way game. He was moving pucks quickly and smartly out of danger. He's a left-handed defenseman but was playing on the right side once again; he seems very comfortable playing on his wrong side, as he has done a lot since last year.

DRU #9 C Guay, Nicolas (2018): Guay scored the game-winning goal by going to the net and pushing the puck past the red line after a shot by Desmarais went through Blanchette. Guay worked hard at both ends of the ice. He did a good job in his own zone, supporting his defensemen and starting the transition game from there. He flashed some fancy puck skills in the first period during some sequences, beating guys one-on-one. He showed a quick release on his shot.

DRU #19 RW Mercer, Dawson (2020): He scored the 3rd Drummondville goal; he created a turnover in front of the Baie-Comeau net and finished it by beating Blanchette. He had also scored early in the game, but his goal was waved off after the net was displaced. He showed his puck skills on the power play once again tonight. He is still only 15 years old, but showed great passing skills throughout this game.

DRU #81 C Simoneau, Xavier (2019): Good D-support deep in the defensive zone, he worked hard all game at both ends of the ice. Even at his size, he's not shy to go to the net, although he'll need to ease up on the physical play a bit as he'll become a target on the ice pretty quickly otherwise. Controlling his physical play will help him stay away from injuries, and save some energy in the long term. He showed good acceleration while in possession of the puck, or when rushing the puck through the neutral zone. He has the ability to surprise opposing defensemen with that good burst of speed.

DRU #37 RW Desmarais, Guillaume (2019): Nothing fancy about his game. Desmarais gets pucks deep and gets on the forecheck. Not the most creative player with the puck, but did a good job on the forecheck and going to net. He did just that on his team's 6th goal of the game, by bringing the puck to the net and taking a backhand shot that went through Blanchette. Meanwhile, Guay made sure that the puck crossed the red line.

USA Hockey's National Team Development Program vs Omaha Lancers, USHL Fall Classic, Sept 30, 2017

USA Hockey's National Team Development Program –

USA #1 G Drew Deridder (2018) – A small, yet mobile goalie standing at 5'10, 168. His skating is excellent, which allows him to push off laterally and to the top of his crease fluidly, which is necessary considering his small stature. His edges allow him to stop quickly so that he doesn't over commit on a player based off today's game. He's aware of his limitations and compensates for them with some unorthodox post ups. For instance, in his V-H during one sequence in the first, he assessed the shot and came up off one pad to lean into the top part of the net that would have been available if he didn't contort himself. In the second, he made his best save, pushing across laterally and kicking out his left pad to take away a high-end chance. He didn't have a lot of work in the net today but took away some high percentage shots.

USA #21 C/RW Jake Goldowski (2018) – While attempting to transition the puck from the neutral zone to the offensive end, you could see that his stride is wide and he looks awkward when attempting to push off. There seems be a lack of power in his base which doesn't allow him to have any North-South speed. Late in the third he rung a puck off the crossbar, the shot was hard and well placed.

USA #28 LW Joel Farabee (2018) – Had a relatively quiet first period again by only having one scoring chance off a rebound around the crease, however he did display a combination of vision, puck skills and poise by coming over the blueline laterally while waiting for his passing option to open, which it did, a common theme for Farabee. Continued to display chemistry with Wahlstrom by stopping up and delivering a pass directly on his stick that lead to a good scoring chance. Drove down the right side, used a spin to angle himself away from his opponent and held up while waiting for his defenceman to set, delivering a pass for another scoring chance. His passing accuracy is exceptional. I wish he was more involved in today's game, he wasn't taking shifts over like he was against the Flying Aces.

USA #11 C Jay O'Brien (2018) – Did most of the work for the opening goal at the end of the first. He rushed the puck down the right wing, held up, assessed his options as he skated into the slot where he then delivered a pass to the right side of the goal line, leading to a tic-tac-toe goal. Grabbed a rebound off Millers shot from the point, skated laterally while been patient which gave him an open net but he was robbed by Driscoll. Driscoll stopped him again after releasing a hard, low wrist shot far side that was kicked away. Late in the second, he continued to put himself in scoring positions, receiving a pass in the slot that was turned away, it was his third high-end scoring chance of the second alone. Got physical behind his own net, pressing a Lancer into the boards and knocking him to the ice which caused a takeaway. O'Brien made the most of his call up by playing a tenacious two-way game, while consistently been in the right place at the right time in the offensive end. Took some shifts with Farabee and Wahlstrom in DeBoer's spot. Didn't look his listed height to the naked eye. We shall find out at some point.

USA #18 RW Oliver Wahlstrom (2018) – Wasn't as dominant early as he was last game but he still managed to get his shot through traffic on a couple of plays. Had a great sequence early in the second during a power play, where he anticipated Wilde turning over the puck along the boards in the neutral zone, collected it and then fed it back to Stastney. Directly after that play, he put himself in position to receive a pass and transitioned the puck over the Lancers blueline, where he backed up the defence using his hands and passed it off to Hain who hit the crossbar. He hit the post on an attempt around the goal crease, displayed good hesitation with the puck. Made a beautiful technical pass late in the second. He skated down the left wing, spun off his defender before rotating his core back towards the blue-line and made a no look pass in the slot that gave Pivonka a prime scoring chance. Showed some defensive game in the third by using his stick to block a shot on the penalty kill, then cleared the puck from the slot. Wahlstrom had another great game today and was the driving force of his line.

USA #7 RW Trevor Janicke (2018) – Showed poor defensive awareness early by not picking up his man on the back-check who had a great scoring chance in the slot because of the misread. Was willing to get physical after the whistle with a bigger lancer player. Generated speed quickly while driving on a defender wide.

USA #9 LW/C Tyler Weiss (2018) – Showed good fore-checking instincts by noticing that a Lancers defender didn't have his head up while trying to move the puck, he then stripped it off him and set up O'Brien in the slot with a tape to tape pass. Displayed good vision on another passing play through the slot, he identifies teammates for passing options quickly in the offensive end. Picked up that the defence was starting to react to his pass first mentality, so he shifted to walking in the slot and fired a hard wrist shot on net when the passing lane was blocked. Showed quick hands that allowed him to evade pressure and deliver a no-look saucer backhand pass to the left side of the slot. Had a good defensive read at the blue-line where he poke-checked a puck and transitioned up the ice. Weiss showed a combination of vision and intelligence on the ice today.

USA #16 LW Erik Middendorf (2018) – Managed to walk the line effectively on one play, this gave him an opportunity to set up from the slot but his pass was blocked. Had the primary assist off a backhand pass that he directed towards the slot for the opening goal. I thought he was somewhat invisible against the Flying Aces and was not much better here.

USA #17 LW Johnny Gruden (2018) – Rushed the power play on the half-wall by forcing an unnecessary pass through traffic just as his teammates were getting set, which lead to the puck been cleared.

USA #8 C/LW Gavin Hain (2018) – Demonstrated that he can make plays in heavy traffic after he received a pass at the blue-line. He spun around multiple players, and then patiently distributed the puck to Miller on his back-hand, understood the time and space he had to make a play in the offensive end with the puck. In the second, he received a backhand pass from Wahlstrom and shot it off the crossbar. Had a good fore-check where he hit his man off the puck leading to the first empty net goal. Played well on the 4th line.

USA #20 C Jacob Pivonka (2018) – Took a pass from Wilde and slapped a puck past Driscoll for a short-handed goal. He didn't take any time to settle the puck and showed good hand-eye coordination on the play. He was good on the penalty kill.

USA #10 D Ty Emberson (2018) – Looked somewhat uncomfortable while transitioning the puck over the neutral zone, there were options but his decision making wasn't fast enough and he ended up skating into traffic and turning it over. Looked good walking the line, his cross-over mechanics are good and he can cover a lot of ice quickly which allowed him to shoot through traffic and get his shot on net. In the third, he showed his ability to deal with fore-checking pressure by spinning off a Lancer player, then used decent hands to deke around another player before passing it off.

USA #5 D Adam Samuelsson (2018) – Was quarterbacking today on the power-play. He kept his game simple, making passes to open players but didn't try and hold onto the puck too long which was nice to see, he recognizes his limitations when walking the line. Had a poor defensive play in the first, where he retrieved the puck below the goal line and had multiple passing options but then panicked when he was pressured and turned the puck over. It didn't seem like he knew where his defensive partner was or that he had support. Was rewarded for parking himself in the crease as he scored on a nice passing play by O'Brien and Middendorf. Had a terrific open ice hit in the neutral zone which knocked the wind out of his opponent. Continued to show his physical game in the third by dropping the gloves. Used his size effectively and ended up with a goal off a good pinch. My concerns are he's slow footed and slow thinking at times as well.

USA #19 D K'Andre Miller (2018) – Had a nice zone entry towards the end of the first. He went end-to-end with the puck and used a feint as he stepped over the blueline before drop passing it off to his open teammate, showed poise with the puck on his stick on the play. Had a good passing option on a power play early in the second but didn't show the vision to see the open man on his left. Recognized a shooting lane opened and shot a hard-low wrist shot from the right side of the point, which created a rebound that lead to an excellent scoring chance. Held the line in the third with multiple Lancers pressuring him, showed poise. He was better today than he was against the Aces.

USA #25 D Spencer Stastney (2018) – Had a good sequence midway through the first where he retrieved a puck from behind his net, then under pressure delivered a hard pass that landed on Goldowski's stick. Had a great poke-check as the puck was entering his defensive zone, he then used open ice to rush the puck into the offensive end before passing it off along the half wall. Only needs a couple of strides to get up to top speed, displayed good edges while protecting the puck on the play. I would like to see him engage offensively more than he does, he has the speed necessary to pinch on certain sequences.

USA #15 D Bode Wilde (2018) – Had a good sequence, where he dealt with a forechecker by spinning off a hit attempt and then transitioning the puck up the ice with a tape to tape pass. Had a shot on net midway through the first where he pulled it back so that the defender couldn't knock it off of him, it was hard and low but he didn't have time to change the angle. Had support behind him while attempting to transition the puck up the ice on a power play but instead of using it, he attempted to carry the puck and got caught by a fore-checker resulting in an unnecessary turnover. Had a great feinting sequence while walking the line, he bared down on his stick to fake a wrist shot, then used a head fake to fake which direction he was taking the puck and skated around his opponent. He recognized that when he beat his man that a lane would be left open and passed it off quickly which was good to see. Drew a penalty while transitioning the puck out of his zone, but still not utilizing his teammates who are there waiting for the passing option, he's trying to be a one-man army when he doesn't need to be. After drawing the penalty, he received a pass and recognized that he had both time and space to walk in and he used a quick wrist shot to beat Driscoll far side. The release point was high-end, he masked the shot well, and it was a hard shot, difficult to pick up. Transitioned the puck up the ice from end-to-end, didn't stay patient and ended up throwing the pass into heavy traffic which resulted in a cleared puck. During a 2 on 1 sequence in the third, he came flying down the left wing but didn't look towards Wahlstrom, or angle his body to throw off the goalie, resulting in an easy stop. However, shortly after, he had another 2 on 1 sequence where he hesitated and used a nice backhand saucer pass to set up his teammate Pivonka, for a goal. Although Wilde showed mixed offensive reads, he was dominant in stretches, using his speed, his size and his shot to create quality chances all over the ice. He's got to simplify his transitional breakouts and use his teammates more but he was good today.

Omaha Lancers –

OMA #18 LW/C Tyler Carpenter (2018) – He had a play where he cleared the puck in the second during a penalty kill and had one shot on net but couldn't really get going. Tough to gauge him out there today with limited minutes.

OMA #28 C/LW Jack Randl (2018) – Showed straight line speed while crossing over the neutral zone, displayed agility by side stepping a defender as well, though he did lose the puck on the play. Had a scoring chance at the end of the second, he fired a slap shot but the angle wasn't great. He had limited opportunities offensively. Showed some limitations in his game.

Final Score: USA Hockey's National Team Development Program 5 – Omaha Lancers 1

Scouts Notes: Mattias Samuelsson was not in the lineup due to a suspension

Quebec Remparts vs Halifax Mooseheads, October 6th 2017

HFX #11 RW Zadina, Filip (2018): Johnny on the spot PP goal in the 2nd, again showing his ability to get lost in coverage & make defenders forget about him in the offensive zone while sliding into good position to score... has great edges, can turn on a dime... hustled back after a change in possession in the offensive zone to be in good position to pick off the breakout attempt... great physical puck protection in the neutral zone leading to a rush, a few nice moves and a good shot on goal.

HFX #14 LD McIsaac, Jared (2018): Some good stretch passes... nice pinch deep into attacking zone early in the 2nd to break up a rush... jumped into the play well... took a couple of aggressive penalties along the defensive wall... nice read on a neutral zone pass to pick it off and quickly transition for a chance... uses his stick well to defend his own blueline and break up rushes.

HFX #19 C Groulx, Benoit-Olivier (2018): Great physical play... big hit on PP in 2nd.... doesn't take shortcuts anywhere on the ice... consistently Halifax's most trusted faceoff man... got beat wide on the OT winner.

HFX #67 LW Parent, Xavier (2019): Lots of jump for Parent in this one... feet are always moving and he always seems to be picking up speed... good backcheck to strip his man after a chance on the PP... gaining confidence with the puck rapidly... put on a stickhandling clinic in overtime, some nice moves to exploit the extra open ice including a few spin moves while covering the point in the offensive zone... blew a tire at the end of this sequence and almost gave up an OT breakaway, but swatted the puck deep while on his tummy.

QUE #96 C Kurashev, Philipp (2018): Makes good decisions with the puck... trusted to run the PP/breakout, good at finding lanes and distributing to teammates... smart offensive player with clear puck skills.

QUE #20 C Coxhead, Andrew (2018): Great on draws tonight, winning 10 of 12... a big, rangy centerman who is defensively responsible... can get around the ice well enough for a big man but will need to improve footspeed to take the next step... positions himself well on the ice, staying in the middle and finding lanes.

University of Michigan vs. St. Lawrence University, October 6th, 2017

MICH #43 LD Hughes, Quinn (2018) – Hughes is a smooth skating offensively minded defenseman. His mobility is exceptional as he can move laterally well and in all directions. He likes to have the puck on his stick and make plays. On his 2nd shift in the offensive zone he walked in, made nice fake to get defender to bite, had a shooting lane when moving in yet made drop pass and play was going the other way. He will need to learn to simplify at times as what he could do at juniors is not forgiving in the NCAA or certainly the NHL. On the defensive side, he could hone his game yet for his first collegiate game he had a good outing. Sometimes his positioning is questionable as leaves opponent underneath in defensive zone or just circles around instead of putting on brakes to defend. Also, when he does gain possession as uses smarts and stick to read plays, he is quick to jump to offensive although sometimes high risk-reward with moves. Like cutting in front of own net, trying to dip around player in own slot, or turning puck over 6-ft inside blue line off rush. Although he has great abilities and skills, thus teaching the defensive side at Michigan and beyond can be done over time. Will need to be quicker as well wheeling puck up ice at times with 1-hand on stick for higher levels, although very elusive nonetheless with the puck as sees ice well with head up. He scored a nice power-play goal in 2nd period as he saw the shooting lane and quickly snapped off shot from point in motion with screen set. He also later in 2nd period wheeled puck around in offensive zone, got to the top of the circle and made a little stutter-step move to elude defender for scoring opportunity down slot. He took a couple of minor penalties in the 3rd period (hooking & holding), nothing too bad. Lots of talent in skating, puck skills, and smarts. His game will translate to the pros in the near future. He has been a 1st round talent for some time now.

Final Score: Michigan: 3 – St. Lawrence: 1

Peterborough Petes at Ottawa 67's, October 6th, 2017

OTT #25 RD Stratis, Peter (2018) - Peter had a real up and down game for Ottawa, he made a great play early to step up for the huge hit during a 1 on 1 but had an early giveaway which lead to two great scoring chances against. Peter worked hard to get back in the play from a couple bad pinches in the neutral zone. Peter struggled with speed tonight, there was 2-3 times where Peterborough forwards beat him wide and took the puck to the net, luckily Peter was able to recover quick with an active stick breaking up the chance. I would like to see him make better passes out of his own zone in the future if he were to take the next step. He played on the power play and was able to move the puck well; he struggled to hit the net with any shot from the point.

OTT #71 F Clark, Kody (2018) - Clark's offensive skills stood out in this game. He made a great deke at one point in the first period showing patience to pull two defenders toward him and make a clean pass behind the net to his open linemate. He plays top minutes and sees time on both the Powerplay and the Penalty Kill. He did a good job using his body to protect the puck and has very good instincts in the offensive zone. In the first period, he dodged a hit and held onto the puck with one hand to maintain possession and set up his teammate in front for a prime scoring opportunity. He made a great move on the Powerplay to bully his way to the front of the net with his body. In the third period, he had a strong forecheck on the Powerplay to pressure Chisholm and steal the puck. He was able to accelerate to high speeds on the rush and would skate back hard on the backcheck, one time breaking up the play. He flashed a hard wristshot in the third period.

OTT #88 D Bahl, Kevin (2018) - Bahl had a quiet, defensively sound first period. He demonstrated more offensive skill as the game went on. He has a good first pass on the breakout and made multiple outlet passes to create quick transitions for Ottawa's offence. He can hit teammates at high speed with his passing and at one point made a nice, accurate saucer pass in front of the net on Powerplay. The opposition had a difficult time knocking him off the puck at times and he made good decisions with the puck to avoid giveaways and alleviate pressure in his own end. His defensive game and hockey IQ are where he shines. Bahl uses his size to his advantage in front of his own net and makes safe clearing plays off the glass in tight defensive situations. On a 4-on-4 in the second period, he made a no-look pass to the open winger from the blueline for the second Ottawa goal. He made good, quick decisions at high tempo throughout the game and plays top defensive minutes in important situations for his team at the OHL level.

OTT #28 D Okhotyuk, Nikita (2019) - Okhotyuk plays a strong stay at home game and likes to play physical. At one point he wheeled with the puck in the offensive zone and picked up lots of speed to get a clear shot on net, although he probably had better offensive options with the space he created. He played a rough style throughout the game, and likes to hit and go to the dirty areas. In the second period, he made a great defensive play to knock the puck into the corner on the Penalty Kill and then throw a big hit on the incoming forward.

PBO #7 LD Babintsev, Gleb (2018) – Played a strong simple game on the backend tonight, had a good first pass tonight, didn't show any panic in his game moving the puck, he didn't force pucks into bad spots if he didn't have an outlet he would go glass and out. Couple good pinches in the neutral zone breaking up passes, he was good positional in the defensive zone, stayed with his man, he always kept his man in front of him and had his head on a swivel. Gleb isn't an overly physical defenseman but played the body well, he didn't lose a lot of 1 on 1 battle in the corner. He was able to get a few shots on net from the point, he was good at keeping shots low and looking for tips in front or rebounds.

PBO #17 F Gogolev, Pavel (2018) - Ripped hard wrist shot 4-on-4. Nice hard, accurate slap-pass far side to his linemate for a tap in goal. Plays the penalty kill. Average skating. Break away opporunity, nice deke and big save in overtime

PBO #19 F Der-Arguchintsev, Semyon (2018) - Played a lot of powerplay minutes. Quick on the forecheck. fast skater. Good vision in front of the net, lucky goal, deflected in off own player. Nice wrap around opportunity, good offensive awareness. Nice wrap around opportunity and good offensive awareness. Nice through the legs deke in overtime.

PBO #20 D Chisholm, Declan (2018) - Chisholm received top minutes for Peterborough and played a solid two-way game. Chisholm has a strong stride and demonstrated impeccable vision of the ice. He made good decisions under pressure and rarely gave the puck away. He's not afraid to jump into the play when an opportunity presents itself, and his speed allows him to get back into possession defensively He demonstrates very high hockey IQ. Consistently made tape-to-tape passes in the offensive zone, making good decisions. Flashed some speed on the rush and was able to pull off a deke at high speed to get around the defender and stay with the puck Was weak in the second period battling for the puck in his own end. Plays the point on the powerplay and demonstrates his vision quarterbacking Peterborough's top powerplay unit on the league's then 7th-ranked powerplay. Good box out skating back on the rush and made a strong outlet pass to transition his team up the ice.

Des Moines Buccaneers at Madison Capitols, October 6th, 2017

DM #16 LW Costello, Braden (2018) – Despite scoring midway through the 2nd period on a rebound put back in front of the net, it was a fairly quiet game for Costello. Costello didn't display a lot of physicality but has good hands and a quick stick to win puck battles, and showed good explosiveness in his first couple strides. Costello registered 3 shots on goal on the night.

DM #33 G Kucharski, Jake (2018) – Kucharski didn't see a lot of action in the first couple periods but his combination of size and mobility will make him a highly scouted goalie prospect for the upcoming draft. Kucharski plays on the top of his crease, challenges shooters and did a good job holding his ground in traffic. Kucharski controlled his rebounds and was quick to cover loose pucks.

DM #19 RD Ugbekile, Colin (2018) – Moves pucks quickly out of his own end, didn't make a lot of flashy or highly skilled plays but was effective at getting the puck up to his forwards and executing the correct reads on the breakout. He communicates well with his goalie and defensive partner and supports the play well. Ugbekile scored late in the game on the Power Play as well.

MAD #18 C Mancinelli, Michael (2019) – This year's 2nd Round pick in the USHL Futures Draft out of the Detroit Honeybaked Program showed speed and his skating is definitely his biggest asset. The North Dakota commit has quick change of direction and can make plays with speed. Thought he rushed some plays on some zone entries when he didn't have to, there will certainly be an adjustment period for a player his age and size at the USHL.

MAD #29 RW O'Reilly, Ryan (2018) – Skating still has a ways to go as he isn't real explosive off the jump, but has good hockey IQ and is skilled enough to create offense despite his skating setbacks. O'Reilly found himself on two 2 on 1's and passed the puck in both instances, neither instance resulted in a Shot on Goal. O'Reilly has an NHL caliber shot and needed to use it more tonight, he did however Display some crafty stick work with the puck in tight areas.

Kootenay Ice at Moose Jaw Warriors, October 6th, 2017

KTN #3 D Schaufler, Loeden (2018) – Good size stay at home d-man. Was caught flat-footed on a couple of occasions. Worked hard down low. Was in tough against a very strong talented Moose Jaw offence. Second power play unit.

KTN #5 D Patrick, Zachary (2019) – Undersized, but showed good work ethic. Never shied away from physical play. Beat wide one multiple occasions. Needs to work on skating. Didn't see much ice, but when he did effort level was there.

KTN #11 D Russell, Bobby (2018) – Played a good strong physical game. Speed was not there to keep up with Moose Jaw. Bad first passes out of the zone. Second power play and penalty kill units.

KTN #17 LW/RW Kohler, Gilian (2018) – Kohler played on a line with Krebs, displaying decent chemistry, although he wasn't able to generate much in the way of scoring chances for himself or his team, while showing below average tools. Kohler is listed at 5'11, 160 but looked smaller than that on the ice, his stature combined with his below average top-gear made it difficult for him to engage off the rush. The Swiss winger did however display an accurate pass which he utilized in spurts with Krebs, setting up his talented teammate for some scoring chances. Another plus element that he showed against the Warriors was his willingness to defend, his positioning was sound and he attacked the point. Kohler finished with 1 assist and 2 shots on goal.

KTN #19 LW Krebs, Peyton (2019) – Was the best player on the ice for Kootenay. Tough game for the entire team but he showed in spurts why he was the first overall pick in the bantam draft. Definitely not the biggest player on the ice. Great vision. Playmaker with a pass first mentality. Nice pass on a two-on-one to set up the second Kootenay goal. First power play unit.

MJW #4 Woo, Jett (2018) – He was extremely composed and calm on defense. Held the line well. Showed impressive strength every time he was on the ice. Great speed on the back check. Carried the puck out of the defensive zone multiple times with ease. Was a plus 2 with 4 shots on goal. Took a bad interference penalty. Played big minutes with no signs for fatigue. One of the best players on the ice. First power play and penalty kill.

MJ #14 LW Smithies, Tyler (2018) – Smithies played on a line with Popple and managed to generate offense early, although he was inconsistent. His most dangerous scoring opportunity came after he found soft-ice to the left side of the slot and fired an accurate wrist-shot behind a screen that rung off the post. His play away from the puck was effective in the neutral zone. On one play, he threw all of his frame into his opponent along the boards for a big hit, which created a forced pass by the Ice player. On another play, he read a passing option and broke up the attempt which resulted in a turnover. Smithies was inconsistent for the Warriors but had an offensive chance and generated positive plays away from the puck. He finished with 2 shots on net.

MJW #26 Benson, Matthew (2018) – Big body, played the physical game. Good body position in the corners. Bad pinch lead to a goal. Needs to work on his puck handling.

MJW #6 Hunt, Daemon (2020) – Made his WHL debut and did not look out of place. Never panicked. Great chip high and off the glass leading to a goal. Assist for first career point. Was given lots of ice time with second D unit. Second power play and penalty kill unit.

MJW #27 Burzan, Luka (2018) – Undersized but showed flashes of greatness tonight. His speed and skill were on display creating multiple scoring chances. Had four shots on goal but nothing to show for it. Playing along side two veterans Gregor and Halbgewachs, they dominated all night. Lacking the physical aspect of the game. Second power play unit.

Final Score: Moose Jaw Warriors: 5 – Kootenay Ice: 2

Red Bull Salzburg Academy at Olomouc J18, October 7th, 2017

SAL # 15 RW Barinka, Marcel (2019) - Excellent reading and positioning. Barinka was found several times in front of net, in slot and with stick ready for rebounds. Good with the right-shooting stick. Barinka don't have a super smooth skating but very mobile and ends on right places due to hockey sense. Barinka had plenty of opportunities with scoring chances and set up team mates with opportunities. The 5'11" body looks thin but still has leg muscles to create gap and speed, when and if he wants. Looked like the competitive level was low and energy on 85-90%. Looks like Salzburg reorganized the line ups and Barinka showed bad body language and disappointment towards team mate when not receiving the puck, being free by the pillar. Barinka didn't communicate with the team mate. With some better speed and communication Barinka could have ended this game with 2-3 points. Now he ended on 0 points and -1.

SAL # 10 F Schutz, Justin (2018) - Clearly the best player on ice. Very good hands and stickhandling, good confidence on the ice, quickness and speed, Good skating all directions. Strong with puck on the board, got 3 Olomouc players attacking but still managed to get the puck delivered to Dube for 1-1. High competitive level. Ended on 1+1 +- 3.

SAL #19 D Zundel, Kilian (2019) - Right shooting offensive D that was mobile and positioned himself very good for being active part of the attacks. Zundel shot a nice quick accurate wrist shot for re-direction. Created a quick turnover with Alanov and set Jentzsch up for an odd man rush. 0+2 +-4

SAL #21 D Alanov, Yegor (2019) - Looked calm and confident. Read the players and the ice good. Offensive minded D. Nice turnover with Zundel ending in 3-1. Ended on 0+1 +- 3

SAL # 28 F Jentzsch, Taro (2018) - Right shooting quit big F. Did a good offensive tackling by the board to keep the puck in offensive zone. Not looking the puck when handling and shooting. Read the goalie and took advantage of a slightly misplaced goalie leaving some inches by the pillar. Jentzsch shoot the puck hard, high and accurate very difficult to catch. Mobile and good control on the skates. Decent quick. Showed Playmaking skills. 1+0. -1

SAL # 13 LD Hadamczik, Filip (2018) - Stay at home defender that read the game decent and positioned himself mostly good to stop the Olomouc forwards. Still, far from the best game. 0+0, -1

SAL # 29 Huber, Paul (2018) - Intimidating size (6'3, 203 lbs) that could be used more (probably would have resulted in penalties today due to very sensitive referees). Decent mobility considering the size but legs looks slow. Competitive, good stick checking, 1+1 +-2

SAL #34 Dube, Samuel (2020) - Small Canadian/German player, born 2002, with good eyes, Read the game good, picks down a puck on volley behind net and delivers a quick backhand to Schutz for 1-1. 0+1 +- 3

SAL # 18 LW Schitz, Edwin, 2018 - Big LW that reads the game and positions himself good for shots, Acted as playmaker from the right side. Very nice smooth skating and good edges, created good gap on a puck rush ending with scoring a goal with an accurate hard high shot on left side. 2+0, +- 1

SAL # 14 RW Lobach, Dennis (2018) - Small skilled confident player that did a lot of good things with the stick and puck. Went in from board with puck between two players and got a nice backhand on the net. Based on the game he contributed a lot more than the numbers shows. 0+0, -1

OLO # 17 Indrak, Daniel (2019) - Small with good reading and usually ended up where the puck arrived. Legs moves but so far lacking strength to become quick. Went on net a few times and place himself in front of the goalie during powerplay. Visualized that he Played U16 since he was 12,5. Very active and competitive and level probably would be 1,5 PPG in J18 in a better team. 1+0 +-1

Linkoping HC at Rogle BK, October 7th, 2017

LHC #37 LD Ginning, Adam (2018) - Looked disinterested in warmups and that attitude seemed to carry over into the game as he started off really poorly in the first period. Was not alert and did not move his feet early which made him look slow. Got into trouble already on the second shift as he lost the puck to a forechecker as he was trying to skate it up ice. Later on he took a penalty while his team was already down a man, leading to a 5on3. His bad woes in the first period continued with an ill-advised outlet pass that went straight to the blade of an opponent in the neutral zone. Also had a moment of hestiation behind the net as he rang a puck around the boards but did not commit to it fully, leading to a half-assed pass that could have been intercepted by a Rögle forward and lead to a dangerous scoring chance had they been paying attention. Instead a teammate took care of it and move it out of the zone. His gap control was poor and he got beat to the outside a number of times as he was just not moving his feet in time or enough. However, after his weak start Ginning got better as the game went on. He displayed a willingness to join the rush on multiple occasions, sometimes acting as a forward and driving to the net, both with and without the puck. Found himself on a breakaway as he exited the penalty box and received a pass on the offensive blue line but was not able to convert as he hit the top of the crossbar with a quick shot. His completed pass percentage this game was uncharacteristically bad. While he had moments where he did not move his feet enough, he does possess good speed and a powerful stride once he puts his head down. Acceleration and overall mobility, including edgework and backwards skating, could improve. Demonstrated strong offensive instincts and good hands on two great rushes along the right side where he picked up speed in the neutral zone and used it to beat defenders wide and drive the net. His lone goal in this game was scored in exactly that manner. Ginning finished the game off on a strong note and looked more himself the longer the game went on, although worth to note is that Rögle got increasingly deflated as Linköping ran up the scoreboard.

LHC #45 RD Lundmark, Simon (2019) - Lundmark played on a pairing with Adam Ginning and was clearly the better player of the two in the opening moments of the game. Showed off his skill at moving the puck out of danger in high-pressure situations multiple times. His vision and passing is excellent. Defensive play needs work; was beat to the outside close to the net which gave Rögle a high-danger scoring chance. Lundmark received a lot of ice time on the man advantage but does not look natural in the role of a power-play quarter-back. While he has the playmaking down pat he is currently lacking the shot and overall puck skills to be a threat from the point. Overall he is not a very willing shooter. A raw player with intriguing upside. Finished the game with two assists to his name.

LHC #31 G Myrenberg, Jesper (2018) - Myrenberg is an average-sized goalie at 6'1, 180 lbs. He makes up for his lack of pro size with strong reflexes and athleticism. Very active in net but not very economic in his movement. Exerts more energy than necessary. Not a necessarily calm goaltender. Myrenberg reads the play and tracks the puck well. He displayed solid rebound control in either being able to re-direct shots out of danger or corral the puck before any opponent had a chance to get to it. Myrenberg had a strong game and kept Rögle to a single goal, one which he had no chance saving.

LHC #25 LW Pasic, Nikola (2019) - Pasic had a strong game and his creativity, high level hockey IQ and good motor was on display. Works hard defensively and plays a high tempo game. Strong skater who can turn on a dime and shake defenders. Had an assist on the 4-1 goal where he showed patience with the puck, waiting for the trailer to come in instead of rushing a lateral pass that would have been tricky to pull off. Despite not being blessed with size he is strong on his skates and protects the puck well against bigger adversaries. Has good acceleration and is adept at gaining the offensive zone. Demonstrated good anticipation skills when he found an open space around the net and scored the 5-1 goal.

LHC #40 LW Lindberg,Gustav (2018) - Lindberg was fairly anonymous in the first half of the game but increasingly made his presence felt. Had a strong shift late in the second period where he circled around the offensive zone and fired a hard slap shot on net. Later that same shift he took the puck behind the net and just as he was passing by he made a backhand pass behind his back into the slot that deserved a better fate. Scored the 7-1 goal on the man advantage with a shot that he almost caressed into the left top corner from the right face-off circle. It looked as if the puck was almost travelling in slow motion and I guess the goaltender must have been screened because it was not a very hard shot although highly accurate. Overall Lindberg plays a smart game and is very balanced in his decision-making.

LHC #41 C Costmar, Arvid (2019) - Costmar had a better game than last I saw him. Played a good 200 foot game and was trusted to take key faceoffs in the defensive zone on the penalty kill. Had an absolutely incredible Peter-Forsberg-to-Rob-Blake-type lob pass to Flyers prospect Olle Lycksell that led to the 2-1 goal. Works hard and gets in on the forecheck. His stride is inefficient and needs work. It looks like he is almost sprinting on the ice when he is trying to accelerate quickly. Overall a good performance for Costmar in 4th line minutes.

RBK #15 LD Bondesson, Jakob (2018) - Found himself on a breakaway but did not protect the puck well enough and lost it to a minor slashing play. Has good tools but does not seem to know how to use them. Unlikely to be drafted unless he picks up his play and finds that next level.

Pirati Chomutov at HC Ocelari Trinec, October 8th, 2017

CHO # 4 LD Buchtela, Ondrej (2018) - Found him disoriented in the few shift he got and pushed a bit to hard instead of just keeping the F on the outside. Joined the rush, Got the puck on the red line and brought it on outside and released a not dangerous wrist shot above the goal. To easy and to slow on this level. Was pushing to high and to far out a couple of time ending up giving free ice.

CHO #17 LD reg as RD Grman, Mario (2018) - Not the most smooth skating, reads decent, stick checking succesfull, keeps the forward on rush out,
In order to keep the player on the outside I think he went to far out at occasions,opening up for the F when he passed him. Used in PP without any further notices.

CHO # 13 C Lauko, Jakub (2018) - I really liked Laukos performance today, he used most of his tools, he was competitive, played easy, used his speed and took mature decisions. Lauko had good reading, positioned himself good and showed some quick first strides. More weight and maturity will do good on him but Lauko got some gap on rushes both with and without puck. Quicknes mixed with his hockey sense made him off 5-7 feets before the Trencin D:s even reacted. Lauko was blocking the puck 2 times, one time by throwing himself (or falling) infront of David Musils shot. Lauko is competitive by the board and infront of both nets. He is surely not going to win any fistfights against any big guys but I liked that it didn't stopped him from going in to the net battling for puck (vs 209 lbs V. Roth) or to mark protection of goalie by putting a glove on Marcinko 212 lbs. Blocks a forward good . Long rush to forecheck (looks wasting of energy but decent high speed). Fights at the board. Looks little. Competitive, . Poletin # 33 stickchecks on blue, rush to the right corner to catch the puck, and with 3 Trinec players around him in corner close to the board, Poletin turns around and and reach Lauko has sneeked in to the slot, Lauko skates a meter and lifts it up in left corner with confidence. Lauko some nice edges on own blue, turns quick and rush the puck to offensive blue by the board, turns with puck and delivers it to team mate. Reads and positioned himself good, looks junior but played it easy and used speed. Creates gap without the puck on a rush towards net. Unfortunately Koblasa shot a straight shot instead easy to catch for the goalie. I did not see all his Faceoffs, stats says he won 4 of 7 but the one I saw was quick and controlled. Throwed himself (or Fell) to stop a puck by David Musil. Some tendency to use the stick and to be a bit aggressive by the board but its for improvement. After whistle he puts the hands on Marcinko 6'4" 212 lbs to make sure he don't go closer to the goalie. Got a nice rush over the whole ice vs undrafted 97 player, wasn't able to create gap. (had a longer line) Works good and hard all over the ice in both zones. Moves head a lot to scan the ice. Had a situation with 3 Trinec player where some Trinec mistakes made Lauko ending up with the puck on the stick due to high competivness. Lauko gets a shot on the net and rush to the goalie before he catch it . Not hesitating or stopping by having some gloves and arms from 209 lbs Vladimir Roth. For me Lauko has been a 3rd rounder but I think he slammed on the door to enter 2nd round. Not an aggressive player but I liked that he finished the hits when he had the chance. As acting as a D infront of own net Lauko could have looked for the red players, now he focused on the puck and it turned to be a chance. Nice reading and quick leg created some chance and without having the nicest hands he showed some skill passing them. Founds some nice passes

Cape-Breton Screaming Eagles vs Drummondville Voltigeurs, October 8th, 2017

CAP #81 RW Laferrière, Mathias (2018): Made some good passes on the power play in this game, showing good vision. On his 1st goal, he made a nifty no-look backhand pass to Sokolov in the slot. On his team's 2nd goal, he made a nice touch pass to nearly send Batherson on a breakaway, leading to Sokolov's 2nd goal of the period. On the 3rd power play goal by the Screaming Eagles, he made a great cross-ice pass to Batherson from the top of the faceoff circle. He was rather quiet the rest of the night outside of those three plays. He was not much of an impact at 5-on-5.

CAP #26 LW Sokolov, Egor (2018): Sokolov showed a quick release on his shot in the two power play goals that he scored in the 1st period. On both goals, the puck was off his stick quickly, and both times he was going to the net when he received the puck, which is always a good sign. However, his skating is rough; there's a lot of work to be done in terms of speed and agility. He's big and large, but was not a real physical presence out there today.

CAP #31 G Mandolese, Kevin (2018): His rebound control was decent overall, and he didn't give up ugly rebounds in the slot. He uses his big frame to cover the net well out there. He has long legs, and did a good job covering the lower part of the net, making a highlight-reel save in the first period because of those long pads. He showed a willingness to play the puck outside of his crease, but his play with the puck was a bit off, as his passes were iffy and lacking accuracy. He's a big goaltender, but his post-to-post lateral movements were not on point a couple of times, and that cost him on one goal. He also would like to have the game-winning goal back, after the puck went through him following a Xavier Simoneau shot using one hand on his stick.

CAP #7 LD McCormick, Adam (2018): Very good with his stick today. He pokechecked pucks away from forwards rushing the puck on his side of the ice. In the defensive zone, he did a good job blocking passes with his stick. Very effective in the defensive zone and on the PK. His play with the puck was kept simple, and was not a factor on the transition game. He had some issues dealing with the speed of some of the Drummondville forwards in the 2nd half of the game.

CAP #23 LW Kalmikov, Brooklyn (2019): The rookie winger showed good speed throughout this game, using good, quick feet and a nice burst of speed. He currently lacks the strength to battle along the boards, and lost too many battles there today. He did a good job putting some good pressure on the forecheck, which led to Jordan Ty Fournier's goal in the 3rd period (which tied the game at 4).

CAP #17 LW Bourret, Olivier (2018): He played a physical game down low and worked hard there. He's a big kid who uses his size well to protect the puck, but didn't show a lot of vision or creativity with the puck today.

DRU #19 RW Mercer, Dawson (2020): Showed flashes of his quick hands on a couple of rushes today, but didn't generate much offense. On the power play, he likes to control the puck from the faceoff circle and make plays from that position. He drew a penalty after a nice move to get around a Cape Breton defenseman.

DRU #29 LW Eckl, Bastian (2018): He scored a nice goal at the end of the first period, when he got behind two Cape Breton defensemen and beat Mandolese with a great accurate shot, high-glove. He didn't show me a lot of smarts or creativity out there today, and his skating is a work in progress, but his shot is excellent. However, he made some bad passes that made me question his vision and hockey sense.

DRU #55 LD Bernard, Xavier (2018): Bernard was a regular on the 2nd power play unit and struggled with the puck when under pressure. He fumbled it at the offensive blueline too many times, seeming calmer in the 3rd period. There, he was under less pressure and he kept his game simpler with the puck. He was caught flat-footed on Cape Breton's 2nd goal by Batherson, who blew past him. However, he showed some good effort, diving to pokecheck the puck away from Batherson. Unfortunately, the puck went right onto Sokolov's stick, and he scored immediately.

DRU #81 C Simoneau, Xavier (2019): Once again, Simoneau was excellent today for the Voltigeurs, playing a complete game in all three zones. He showed great anticipation and always seemed to know where the puck will go on the ice. He was seemingly always near the puck today, on the 3rd line with Morgan Adams-Moisan (who acted like his bodyguard on the ice). Together, they have developed good chemistry on the ice. He scored the game-winning goal on a great effort to get around #5 MacLellan, and then beat Mandolese with one hand on his stick. He was named first star of the game in the arena.

DRU #9 C Guay, Nicolas (2018): Guay was a tireless worker today, working hard in all three zones. With some good smarts, he has become a complete player. He scored his team's first goal on the power play off a good one timer from the faceoff circle; I could tell he was active and wanted to make a difference on the power play. His skating has improved in the last 3 seasons (since his QMJHL Draft year) but still could use more explosiveness.

DRU #90 RD Pelletier, Thomas (2019): Pelletier's ice time was limited with all the power plays both teams had in this game, but when he did play, he kept his game simple and made the plays he needed to make. Simple passes out of his zone; in the offensive zone, on one occasion, he had the chance to create some offense, but was too slow to get his shot off at the point and his shot was eventually blocked in front of the net by McCormick.

DRU #92 LD Beaudin, Nicolas (2018): Another smart puck-moving game from Beaudin today, whose passes are always on target. He showed good vision and poise on the power play. He made good outlets to get the puck out of his zone. He made sure to hit the net with his shots tonight; there may not be a lot of velocity behind his shots, but they hit the net.

DRU #35 G Moody, Daniel (2018): He fought the puck all night long; he didn't look too good out there despite a winning effort. He was lucky to get a win in this game. His rebound-control was not good, he made some saves but he was unsure where the puck was at times. He didn't look confident in his crease.

Frolunda HC at Rogle BK, October 12th, 2017

FHC #33 RW Raymond, Lucas (2020) - Despite his young age, Lucas Raymond was one of the most consistent offensive threats on the ice in this game. He is a quick and smooth skater with good balance on his edges. His speed combined with his soft hands made him a threat every time he touched the puck and he was dangerous in transition all night. While he has good acceleration he currently does not have a seperation gear and because of that struggled at times to get past defensemen off the rush. His vison and hockey sense gives him many options however and he showcased his passing ability with hard and crisp passes on the tape. Raymond was a consistent presence in all three zones, both forechecking and backchecking hard. He is the type of player that can drive the play and there always seemed to be something happening when the puck was on his stick. He finished the game with an assist to his name (on a nice cross-ice pass in the offensive zone) but could have had more points to his name as he failed to convert on a clean breakaway and also set up his teammates for a couple of good chances throughout the game.

FHC #36 RD Lerebäck, Leon (2018) - A fairly average defender, Lerebäck does most things well but nothing at an exceptional level and certainly did not stand out in this game in J18 Elit. He does his best work offensively and really likes to jump into the play, sometimes being a little too eager. He showcased some decent hands and offensive instincts when he rushed up the right side and then stickhandled himself from the corner and in front of the net but was not able to steer the puck around the goaltenders right pad. Defensively he can maintain a good gap but too often takes himself out of position by stepping up on guys and going for the hit rather than just keeping the gap, driving opponents wide and using his stick. This led to him being walked on a number of occasions.

FHC #45 C/W Andersson, Isac (2019) - Had a quiet game, in large part due to receiving very little ice time despite scoring the 1-0 goal. Decent skater but needs to work on his first few steps as well as top speed.

FHC #37 LW Söderblom, Elmer (2019) - The brother of undrafted goalie prospect Arvid Söderblom. A huge unit at 6'3, 190 lbs, Elmer Söderblom is a lumbering but not necessarily awkward skater with surprisingly good lateral movement. Decent agility and edgework. I could see him becoming an overall good skater once he becomes more comfortable with his own body. His best assets are his hands and he was able to create havoc in the offensive zone when he came down the wing with speed and used some nifty mittens to get past his opponents. Could use his size better. Had an assist on the 1-0 goal.

FHC #1 Portillo, Erik (2018) - A very tall goaltender listed at 6'6, 198 lbs. Aside from his size, Portillo does not have that much going for him. His technique is lacking and he had trouble with shots that should have been routine saves. Does not appear to be tracking the puck very well and his rebound control needs improvement. Looked very scrambly and reactive in net. The good news is that he covers a lot of net and at this level is able to stop a lot of shots because of it. Finished the game with only one goal allowed and a save percentage of 97.9%.

Edmonton Oil Kings at Moose Jaw Warriors, October 12th, 2017

EDM #6 McLeod, Wyatt (2018) – Good-sized d-man, seemed to struggle with the speed of the Moose Jaw forwards. Panicked under pressure and had bad communication with his partner. Bad clearing attempts, soft ring around the boards put forwards in bad position. Made a great sliding play on three on one.

EDM #8 Cap, Ethan (2018) – Ethan was Edmonton's top defenseman. Showed his strength and composure every shift. He was very calm when under pressure. Never mad a bad decision with the puck. Very impressive game all around. First power play unit and second penalty kill unit.

EDM #15 Atkinson, Scott (2018) – Solid 2 way forward. Good on the face-offs and sacrificed his body multiple times to block shots. Played physical and did not take any chances, made smart plays. Did not show the high end offensive talent. Great penalty killer on the first unit.

EDM #24 Kemp, Brett (2018) – Decent sized forward with a good work ethic. Battled hard behind the net to draw a holding penalty. Showed offensive upside with a good shot and nice assist on the second Edmonton goal. Second power play and penalty kill units.

MJW #4 Woo, Jett (2018) – Once again another very strong game from Jett. Never forced the puck on net, made multiple nice plays off the end boards to create scoring chances. Used his speed to draw a tripping penalty. Quarterbacked the MJ power play, he slowed things down and always made the right play. Strongest player on the ice. First power play and penalty kill units.

MJW #8 Almeida, Justin (2018) – Justin seemed to by trying too hard out there. Tried to make the fancy plays, which lead to turnovers in the offensive zone. He's highly skilled but shies away from the physical play. He did have a couple good scoring chances. Second power play unit.

MJW #26 Benson, Matthew (2018) – Played a strong physical game. Had the hit of the game standing the Edmonton forward up and his own blue line. Fanned on a scoring opportunity, which led to a scoring chance for Edmonton. Great defensively. Needs to work on the offensive side.

MJW #27 Burzan, Luka (2018) – Was trying to do too much out there. Used his speed effectively to get to good areas but didn't look for his teammates. Drove wide and set up the Warriors first goal. Second power play unit.

MJW #39 Evanoff, Adam (2018) – This was Adam's first career start in goal. The first few minutes he looked nervous but that is understakable. Settled down very nicely and looked great. Allowed a goal from a bad angle. Made 40 saves and picked up the 4-2 win.

Hamilton Bulldogs at Oshawa Generals, October 13th, 2017

HAM #10 RC Roberts, Connor (2018) - Connor possesses intriguing physical attributes but failed to make much of an impact throughout the game despite good opportunity. Roberts did score a goal, going to the net hard and depositing a rebound opportunity. Connor displayed heavy feet and struggled to accelerate leading to many of his pass attempts to come from a flat-footed position, while also limiting his ability to separate from a check.

HAM #27 LD McCourt, Riley (2018) - McCourt is slightly undersized, however does utilize his foot-work and edges to elude check's well. Riley displayed good mobility and overall skating attributes as he often got up ice aggressively and showed a willingness to make himself an option offensively. Riley relied heavily on stick-on-puck type defense and while effective at times, showed an inability to contain bigger & stronger opponents both in transition and below the hash marks. To his credit McCourt did show the willingness to eat pucks, taking hits to make high percentage plays.

HAM #34 RW Kaliyev, Arthur (2019) - Kaliyev was at his best in possession where he displayed impressive confidence and skill with the puck. Arthur looked to create in the offensive zone as he pushed towards the high percentage scoring areas and avoided being a perimeter player. Kaliyev was able to reach an average top speed but his stride has room to improve, while his first step quickness would only enhance his game.

HAM #77 LC Murray, Jake (2018) - Murray played limited fourth line minutes for Hamilton, however was noteworthy for his work ethic and willingness to play aggressively despite his undersized frame. Jake was first to pucks and finished checks; however, his lack of strength hindered his effectiveness in a checking role.

HAM #91 LC McMichael, Connor (2019) - McMichael played in all situations for Hamilton and showed an effectiveness in various roles. Connor displayed a two-way effectiveness and reliable defensive zone play, however would become more effective while defending below the hash-marks with added strength. Connor utilized his intelligence/anticipation skills to find space and create space for himself effectively. In possession McMichael showed good awareness, moved the puck well but also showed the willingness to look to create on his own when limited options presented themselves. Connor does need to work on enhancing his skating as it is currently average at best.

OSH #5 LD Ennis, William (2018) - Ennis flew under the radar due to the simplicity of his game. However, he was very good on both sides of the puck. Offensively Ennis could stand to improve his puck handling abilities and make quicker decisions however he often thrived making simple plays, opening lanes to get pucks on net or avoiding turnovers by simply chipping pucks deep. Defensively Ennis makes good read and shows good positional awareness. His 1-on-1 defense was most noteworthy as he contained well in transition and separated player from puck well.

OSH #8 RW Noel, Serron (2018) - Noel battled inconsistency throughout the game as many Generals did, however was able to find the net. Serron picked up a loose puck and utilized his opponent as a screen, releasing a shot quickly on net that beat the goaltender.

OSH #15 LC MacLean, Kyle (2018) - A re-entry candidate, MacLean didn't show a whole lot of upside offensively, however his competitiveness and smarts make him a very capable bottom six presence. Kyle was consistently first to pucks, created turnovers on the forecheck and was a presence on the penalty kill. MacLean makes simple decisions with the puck but it's usually the right, high percentage choice.

OSH #61 LC McShane, Allan (2018) - McShane had a quiet night offensively but showed his high-end vision and skill in small spurts. Allan makes quick reads with the puck, allowing him to thrive on the power play as his puck movement creates seams and dysfunction within the penalty kill unit as the begin to chase. During 5-on-5 play McShane's time and space was taken away fairly well, however when he did have space he was able to utilize his vision and playmaking ability to create chances for his line mates.

OSH #66 LD Gross, Nico (2018) - Gross didn't have a great showing in this one. While he continues to show good puck distribution skills at the offensive end of the rink, excelling on the man advantage, his reads both in possession and away from the puck were less than stellar in the loss. Nico was slow to make decisions resulting in limited options and turnovers, while his desire to aggressively get up ice had him caught up ice. Consistency has been an issue with Nico early on this season.

Calgary Hittmen at Kelowna Rockets, October 13th 2017

CAL #15 RW Nielsen, Tristen (2018) – Has a tendency to play a bit above his size in somewhat of a fearless way, he started a 2 on 1 with a great shot block in the defensive zone. Buzzed around a lot and was trying to cause some havoc but in the end his play didn't have a big impact on the game, attack the net for one unsuccessful scoring chance. Had trouble connecting his effort to results.

CAL #4 LD Toder, Layne (2018) – Displayed some of his good puck skills by sticking handling well to create some space and showing some good confidence. Had a role throughout the entire game playing both the powerplay and penalty kill and despite being in his own zone a lot was a good defensive presence around the crease clearing the net and boxing out, was a good asset on the breakout and made some strong first passes out of his zone. An all around a solid game for Toder.

CAL #5 LD Van De Leest, Jackson (2019) – Not a great game as for the most part his footwork holds him back from being a real strong factor in the game, looks clunky in his reverse stride and on his crossover. Was a factor on the PK despite his lack of mobility standing in shooting lanes and using his reach to disrupt the play.

CAL #17 RW Campbell, Hunter (2019) - Didn't get a lot of icetime throughout this game but exhibited a great release as he scored Calgary's second goal of the game unassisted. His release was a great snap shot from the right circle cleanly beating the goal who was in position.

KEL #24 C Topping, Kyle (2018) – Had a strong game putting up 1cgoal 2 assists on this evening, for his first set up he gathered the puck in the defensive zone and fired a quick up for a zone entry sending 2 players in for a 2 on 1 and the second coming off a zone entry and finding a streaking Cowell with a nice pass at high speed. Scored one on one against the goalie as he took a pass while breaking down the slot. Overall has a dangerous game and took advantage of a couple defensive zone break downs showing good use of his hockey sense and ability to think quickly around a developing play.

KEL #26 LW Kindree, Liam (2018) – After several views being give an opportunity on scoring lines Kindree was slotted on the bottom line and didn't get much icetime throughout this game and in-turn wasn't create or much of a factor

KEL #7 RD Zabransky, Libour (2018) – Looked a little complacent throughout this game, played really safe giving Cal Foote the opportunity to do most of the significant things for their pair differing all puck carrying, breakouts and transition play to him and generally sitting back. Did pick up an secondary assist on a zone entry after his team regrouped in the neutral zone but ultimately was left wanting more from his effort.

KEL #29 C Foote, Nolan (2019) – Appeared more as a passenger on his line tonight really doesn't handle the puck enough to be considered the center of this line and his puck touches don't last very long, tis role keeps him away from the walls a little too much, the place where his skills are best suited, didn't get that tonight. He did score a goal that was a bit of missed shot ending up bouncing off a defenders skate and in.

KEL #6 Korzack, Kaeden (2019) – Real simple but strong game made a lot of zone entries difficult along his side of the closing a quick gap and looking efficient driving guys into the wall. Was confident standing up against attackers and showed good use of his stick to pop pucks free and create turnover or start plays moving in the other direction. Looked the most confortable of any game we've viewed.

Final Score: Calgary Hitmen: 4 – Kelowna Rockets: 3

Northeastern University at RIT, October 14th, 2017

NU #28 RC Solow, Zach (2018*) – Solow was bypassed in 2017 NHL Draft after leading the USHL in scoring. The reasoning is because Solow is bit undersized and does not have the speed to differentiate himself. What Solow does well is that he goes to the right places and sees the ice extremely well. He plays smart and his vision with and without the puck allows he to create scoring chances. He made nice wrap-around attempt in the 1st period. He got on the scoresheet in the 2nd period on Northeastern's first goal on the power play as he quickly made touch pass off the goal line to #19 Griffin after receiving pass from point. He also made two nice back-door passes on the power play to #15 Jozefek in the 3rd period that led to great scoring chances. He plays in all situations from PP, PK, and 5v5. He was smart on the PK as well with good stick position and gaining body position to clear the puck smartly. He also made great offensive opportunity in the 2nd period on the penalty kill with pressure as forced turnover at the wall and fed #8 Gaudette in the slot for golden chance. If he can gain strides in his initial steps and keep the point/game pace in the NCAA in his frosh season, Solow will most likely hear his name in June.

Final Score: Northeastern: 3 – RIT: 3

Sherbrooke Phoenix at Drummondville Voltigeurs, October 14th, 2017

SHE #29 RW Poulin, Samuel (2019): He showed great strength along the boards for a 16-year-old, and was protecting the puck well there. At even-strength, he did not produce a lot of chances with his line in the first two periods, but had 3-4 good scoring chances on the PP, coming close to scoring his first career QMJHL goal. He was often around the net was and tough to move from there. His skating is decent, but he didn't show his good burst of speed down the wing that he showed us in midget last year. He is still adjusting to the QMJHL, playing in only his 5th game this season.

SHE #9 LW Peach, Bailey (2019): Not very noticeable offensively today, playing on Sherbrooke's 3rd line. He had some mishaps in the defensive zone in terms of his coverage.

SHE #27 LD Senken, Connor (2018): Skating abilities and footwork are good strengths of his, and he did a good job of skating pucks out of his zone and away from the pressure. He played on the power play; his decision-making and play with the puck overall were just okay. Didn't always make the smartest plays with the puck.

SHE #23 RW Alexeyev, Yaroslav (2018) Alexeyev is in his 2nd year of eligibility for the NHL Draft. He was quiet in period one, but was great the rest of the game, finishing with 2 points. He showed great vision with some excellent passes. He scored on the power play after finishing off at the side of the net, following up on a nice feed from Marek Zachar. He showed some good puck skills in one-on-one confrontations, beating guys one-on-one, and also a good ability to quickly change directions when rushing the puck, making him tougher to defend one-on-one. He struggled in the first period, playing on the perimeter, and was afraid of getting hit on 2-3 sequences.

SHE #93 C Tardif, Benjamin (2018): Tardif played on the 4th line today. Did some good work down low, working really hard to retrieve pucks. While in possession, he didn't hesitate to put pucks on net. Liked his effort away from the puck, how he provided good support to his defense on the backcheck, and down low deep in the defensive zone.

SHE #44 LD Crête-Belzile, Olivier (2018): The rookie blueliner was calm in his zone, kept the game simple and didn't do anything extra with the puck. Made sure to get pucks out of his zone and stay out of trouble. He did a good job handling one-on-one confrontations. However, in the offensive zone or neutral zone, when rushing the puck, he was a bit hesitant to make plays offensively.

DRU #92 LD Beaudin, Nicolas (2018): Very active in the offensive zone and liked to make things happen out there by refusing to stand still at the blueline. Struggled a bit in the first period with his passing game (it's worth noting that overall, the Drummondville power play was not good in that period). He was much better in terms of his passing game in periods 2 and 3, including on a highlight-reel play involving Morgan Adams-Moisan's goal in the 3rd period, where he used a nice deke to beat his man, then made a sweet backhand pass to Moisan in the slot for the PP goal.

DRU #10 LW Desruisseaux, Cedric (2018): The best QMJHL game that I have seen out of him this season. He was very involved in the play, using his speed and hustle to put pressure on the forecheck. He had an excellent shift that led to Drummondville's 2nd goal, where his good forecheck was a key factor. He showed quick hands in some sequences, dangling the puck and beating defensemen one-on-one. Even at his size, he didn't shy away from taking the puck to the net and playing in traffic.

DRU #19 RW Mercer, Dawson (2020): A bit of a quiet game from Mercer, even if he played on the 2nd line and got some good ice time on the power play. He took some good shots on net on the power play, where he played on the point, but none of them were really dangerous. He was not too noticeable on the ice and didn't create much offense; Mercer will only turn 16 years old in two weeks and is still adjusting to major junior.

DRU #55 LD Bernard, Xavier (2018): Scored two goals today: the first came from the point on the first shift of the game, and the 2nd one came in the 2nd period, a nice top-corner shot where he showed a quick release. He did a good job on his shots to get them through to the net. Overall, he played a simple game; he was good at defending one-on-one and cleared the front of the net. He made simple outlets to get puck out of his zone. He played in all situations tonight, including on the power play and penalty-killing units.

Olomouc vs. Chomutov, October 17th, 2017

CHO # 13 C Lauko, Jakub (2018) - Jakub Lauko had a good game, played mature and used most of his toolbox. His team didn't have a good game and some frustration was seen, Lauko however lifted himself and the team by competing. Lauko use his speed and hockey sense. Lot of time standing still on his skate, reading and position himself and starting with explosive skating instead of constant skate. From time to time it looks like Lauko plays a quicker game than his team mates and in a higher line or a quicker league I believe his potential will be more useful. By using his speed, he creates penalties and Powerplays so I definitely think he should skate more. His head is constant moving to see opportunities and read the game. Plays easy when in defense under high pressure, puck out. In first period Lauko gets the puck at own blue, flips it under the stick of Red #23, rush the puck to offensive blue and with head up delivers an accurate pass to captain Vondrka in the slot for 1-1. Receives the puck on red, tries to rush puck with 4 red players within 4-9 feet's away. With more leg muscles the quick legs will create more gaps. In third period he takes the puck on the right FO zone up to offensive right FO zone, he did a good rush but when the power is not enough to create gap or he is not using his body enough to cover the puck, instead Lauko turned the breaks on and turned towards the right board and fell. Coach Ruzicka told Lauko with big arrows on the coachboard of direction towards net but clearly liked that Lauko was trying to create. Lauko was selected as Player of the game. Lauko is constant communicating and seems to get good guidance on the bench mainly by Poletin, Koblasa and captain Vondrka, once in a while about to tie the skates or a hand pulling Laukos jersey to jump on the ice. I like that he goes back to protect the goalie after whistles, and once someone attacks the goalie a bit he tries to mark it with gloves. He is not big and most likely won't win any fist fights but he stands up consistently no matter if a 212 lbs guy or as in this case with Kevin Sundher. He finishes his hits. For me he is a third rounder knocking on the door to second round.

OLO #79 RD Galvas, Jakub (CHI) - Galvas is usually not much visualized since not a flashy type of game. More a stay at home D. Galvas had a good game and was placed good, reads the game good and sometimes has very nice opening first passes. Doesn't look like he gained a lot of weight since I saw him before the draft but he wins battles on the board and gets out with the puck, holds his opponents away. Chomutov opened up a lot on the left side and the LD and LW where following the puck on the right side, opening the left side free. Father L Galvas put puck over to left side, Jakub Galvas did quick reading and sneaked behind the D and got a quick accurate pass from Mraz that he scored 3-1 on (GWG)

CHO #17 LD Grman, Mario (2018) - Mario Grman is a right handed 97 born Slovak that already tried 2 seasons in WHL. Since he is draft eligible I kept an eye on him but I didn't change my mind. His vision mainly and skills are limited but might be enough for a career in Czech or Slovak league. Used some speed and some body power to hold his opponent away.

Acadie-Bathurst Titan vs. Gatineau Olympiques, October 18th, 2017

BAT #15 LW Theede, Dawson (FA) - Dawson played to his strengths against the Gatineau tonight. Dawson used his strong balance and size to win battles along the boards, and retrieve possession while attacking. He ended the night with 2 goals both his goals came from a strong forecheck and driving hard to the net, one was a tip in goal and the other he came out of the corner and fire the puck top corner over goalies shoulder. Dawson showed good poise in his own zone, often reversing the play to alleviate pressure; he didn't force pucks up the wall with no support. He is a tough, physical player.

BAT #53 RD Dawson, Noah (2018) - Noah is a fluid two-way defenseman that uses his excellent mobility to move freely around the ice. His effortless stride and high I.Q allows him to retrieve pucks quickly and transition the play up ice fast with quality hard passes that are easy to receive. Noah vision was evident tonight as he was able to make a couple nice stretch passes to forwards behind defense, he was good to not forcing pucks in bad spots, he would slow the play down in front on him and wait for a teammate to get open and make the simple play. His reads are very good as he pinched twice on the same shift to keep the puck in the zone and extend the attack. He shows no panic with the puck on his stick at the offensive blue line; not panicking with pressuring forwards and is still able to make a play in the offensive zone without turning the puck over. On the defensive side of things Noah is trusted to kill penalties and is very aggressive when pucks are available. He did struggle with pressure from the forechecker, he was getting knocked around a lot early in the game, but he adjusted throughout the game and he wasn't putting himself in those bad spots. He was fun to watch tonight.

BAT #71 C Ducharme, Justin (2018) - Justin was relentless on the forecheck tonight for Bathurst. He uses his quick feet to get to pucks before others and has the strength and determination to win a high percentage of battles. Justin generated a lot of his chances off turnovers by using his speed and forecheck ability. Justin engaged in battles in front of net proving he's not afraid of those high traffic areas; he was able to strip the puck off the Gatineau's defender and unleash a rocket shot top shelf from the side of the ice. Justin did an excellent job of keeping possession showing off his ability to play a strong cycle game.

GAT #4 RD Thompson, Will (FA) - Will played a safe game from the backend, providing a good first pass, and keeping Bathurst attackers to the perimeter. He showed the ability to effectively control the gap against a aggressive Bathurst forecheck, with possession Will turned to indirect passes off the boards to counter the forcheck. He slowed the game down, and displayed great patience from the backend. Will played a very consistent game and stayed within his game, and trusted his defensive partner's abilities, often deferring the play to Breton when tasked with leading the rush up the ice on the attack.

GAT #8 RD Lacombe, Pierre-Olivier (FA) - Pierre kept his game fairly simple in this game showing quick and effective decisions making both in possession and away from the puck. Pierre displayed slightly above average feet and overall mobility that allowed him to elude fore-checker's and make his way up ice when open ice presented itself. He was able to make a clean outlet pass throughout the game, he has a strong hard shot from the point which he used tonight from the point on the power play scoring Gatineau first goal.

Final Score: Acadie-Bathurst Titan: 5 – Gatineau Olympiques: 3

Jihlava U20 at Kometa Brno U20, October 19th, 2017

BRN # 24 C Plasek, Karel (2018) - Plays and finishing with poise, looks very confident, Good control of the stick. Good chemistry with Strondala. Brings the puck along the left board and manage to get through all way but makes an error pass. He uses his speed and excellent reading and Plasek is quick putting pressure in both zones. Plasek got 1G+1A but created plenty more opportunities.

BRN # 14 RW Strondala, Vojtech (2019) - Strondala had a very good game looking very mature considering he is still 16. Compensates his small size with excellent reading, speed and quick turns by the board and on open ice. Created a lot of opportunities with Plasek. Guides his team mates. Talented with the stick and with more weight and hockey muscles he will be outstanding. Good on FOs but holds his hands high on the stick. 3 Assists, 1 shot in the post and plenty more opportunities.

BRN # 11 LW Svoboda, Matej (2018) - First to puck, constructive and good reading. Competitive. Svobodas is not a player that makes me wowed, skating is average (or below) and not quick. But he is very useful in front of the net, disturbing the goalie, ready for re-directions and rebounds. Quick crispy passes. Today I would say he had a game under his regular level but still he produced 2 A and his 3rd GWG this season (11GP), a rebound perfect positioned. Lined up with speedy Plasek and Strondala (or Novak) he completes them good and he gives an impression of having more weight than the 181 lbs. Nice receiving of the puck with the back towards the Jihlavas left post, turns around when the D attacks and gives a nice pass on the opened ice to Plasek in the slot.

BRN # 2 G Dostal, Lukas (2018) - Solid game, wasn't tested too much although its registered 39 SOG. Looks calm, prepared and focused on the attacks. Good reactions with the picking glove, quick moving sideways. Working a lot down in butterfly but with good coverage of the posts upper and lower parts. I didn't see much communication between him and his Ds.

BRN # 13 C/LW Gajarsky, Adam (2018) - Finished hits, has the toolbox but looks like he is missing the confidence and speed from the past. Use his legs to little. Created a one-man rush but no one joined the rush. Joined the rush nice with Mlynar a couple of times, received the pass on the left side post but would have had better result if arriving with more speed and with turned body prepared to take the shot. Now he had to stop the puck with the skate and gave the goalie time to move over sideways. Next time Gajarsky got the pass in the slot but finished it without confidence and creativity.

BRN # 22 RD Kowalczyk, Daniel (2018) - Big RD 6'3" 212 Lbs that doesn't play very aggressive. Nice hard low direct shot in powerplay from Offensive FO zone, Havlat tips it down for 1-0.

BRN # 4 RW Novak, Matej (2019) - Visualized as one using speed in today's game, creates all though not on high end. Good rush with puck from red with speed, tick tack puck with Strondala, fools the goalie to go left and Novak finish with a high backhand on goalie's right side.

BRN #23 Krejci, Peter RW (2018) -Krejci had a game above his usual level and was visualized from time to time with speed, creating turnovers, always moving the legs carrying while slaloming with the puck, seek himself in front of the net. Nice assist to 2-0 doing just that.

BRN # 17 C Mlynar, Tomas (2018) - 98 born far from top player but showed some nice stick control and passes

BRN # 8 Suss, Jan (2018) - Showed some nice hands with good stickhandling with the puck by the board

Kitchener Rangers at Oshawa Generals, October 21st, 2017

KIT #11 LD Vallati, Giovanni (2018) - Vallati got off to a very strong start but was ejected towards the end of the first period for checking to the head. In the time Giovanni did play, he utilized his feet and mobility very well, eluding pressure on the forecheck and quickly bursting up ice to lead transition. Away from the puck Vallati got up ice well and consistently made himself option. Giovanni also utilized his feet offensively to open shooting lanes.

KIT #13 RC Damiani, Riley (2018) - Damiani battled inconsistency throughout the game as he had moments where he was able to display intriguing skill to his game, while there were also moments where he was largely unnoticeable. In possession Riley displayed quality puck handling abilities and creativity to his game, however he does need to add strength as he was often easily bumped from possession. Damiani's ability to keep his feet moving in the offensive zone allowed him to find space and when he was found with a pass he displayed a quick release. Riley had an enhanced impact offensively on the power play with added time and space.

KIT #88 RW Meireles, Greg (2018) - Meireles played with good energy throughout the game as his competitive edge allowed him to be effective in multiple scenarios. Greg showed excellent defensive awareness as he was positionally sound, engaged and able to create turnover. Meireles was very good on the penalty kill as he kept his feet moving and clog shooting lanes well, leading to turnovers on multiple occasions. Greg forecheck hard and was able to create offensive chances with his hard work.

KIT #89 LC Guest, Eric (2018) - Guest played in a fourth line role but did show some intrigue to his game. Eric was at is best in possession, showing impressive awareness along with vision and playmaking traits. Where he struggled was defensively. Despite good positional awareness, Eric's size limitations effected his ability to defend bigger and stronger opponents below the hash-marks.

OSH #5 LD Ennis, William (2018) - Ennis continue to be effective while playing a simplistic style of defense. William looks to have more confidence in possession however does realize his limitations with the puck and often makes a quick and quality first pass. When forced to transition the puck, Ennis can struggle some, however enhancing his puck skills would quickly enhance his versatility as he does display strong instincts. William made good reads throughout, most notably with his neutral zone reads. Ennis showed good gap control and was often able to neutralize attacks.

OSH #17 LW Krastenbergs, Renars (2018) - Krastenbergs was arguably Oshawa's best forward throughout the game. Renars competed hard on a shift-to-shift basis and was rewarded finishing a play after creating a turnover. Krastenbergs showed a high motor and his willingness to compete in the dirty areas was noteworthy. His play on the penalty kill allowed him to create multiple turnovers and turn them into offensive chances. Renars won a number of puck and position battles and shows improved strength to his game.

OSH #42 LD Brewer, Mitchell (2019) - Brewer showed impressive poise for a sixteen-year-old defender. A player who makes simplistic, but effective decisions throughout the game, Mitchell handles pressure well and rarely panics in possession. Brewer showed good strength to his game in his ability to push opponents from possession, while he is also heavy over the puck when exiting the defensive zone in possession. Mitchell also displayed an ability to make a quality first pass.

OSH #61 LC McShane, Allan (2018) - Allan has battled inconsistency and that continued in this game. In possession McShane can thrive showing strong awareness of his surrounding along with above average vision and playmaking skills. However, Allan seems to rush his decision making lately resulting in more turnovers that opportunities. McShane did however show enhanced abilities on the power play with the added time and space afforded to him, allowing his skill and creativity to take over.

OSH #66 LD Gross, Nico (2018) - Nico had an iffy first period as he made some poor neutral zone reads and telegraphed outlet passes. However, he did begin to raise his level of play and two-way effectiveness through the second and third period. Offensively Nico utilized his feet well to walk the line opening shooting/passing lanes. Gross used his vision and passing skills to distribute effectively, an attribute that was enhanced on the power play. Nico's gap control and ability to angle opponents away from the centre of the ice was fairly good, however when he looks to engage physically and separate player from puck, a lack of strength can hinder his overall effectiveness.

OSH #90 LW Antropov, Danil (2019) - Antropov still battles with inconsistencies on a shift-to-shift basis, however he was most effective when utilizing his frame to his advantage. Danil was good off the cycle as he protected the puck well and possesses the skill necessary to make a play off the cycle, recognizing time and space well. Antropov possesses a good shot, with accuracy and velocity to it, however he needs to make the decision to shoot quicker as he seems to hesitate.

Vaxjo Lakers HC at Rogle BK, October 22nd, 2017

RBK #15 LD Bondesson, Jakob (2018) - Had a relatively strong game and scored the 1-0 goal from the top of the right faceoff circle on a shot he did not hit cleanly. Showcased his terrific skating as well as some skill and was dangerous offensively at times throughout the game. Did not get tested too much defensively as the Växjö forward group was rather bleak this noon.

VÄX #45 LD Bäckman, Jakob (2018) - Bäckman is a defender with decent size and above-average hockey sense. Showed a willingness to join the rush and participate in both ends of the rink. Displayed good vision and made some creative passes. Skating is fairly average and acceleration needs to get better.

VÄX #26 RW Bokk, Dominik (2018) - Was active early and created havoc with his powerful speed and quick feet. Showcased his explosive offensive game when he beat a Rögle player to the outside and before going behind the cage feathered a forehand pass to a teammate in front of the net. Later he had a glorious opportunity right in the blue paint but was unable to elevate the puck above the goaltenders leg pad. Bokk displayed a repeated willingness to backcheck hard. However, he is quite poor in his own zone and resorts mostly to waving his stick around, sometimes rather carelessly, instead of engaging the puck-carrier directly. Bokk can also be prone to cherry-picking and flying the zone early. A bit too eager offensively at times and could benefit from switching it up and playing the game at a slower pace now and then. Would like to see him shoot more and also to use his speed to carry the puck up ice and gain the zone. His shot needs work in terms of accuracy and power. He can struggle to play in traffic and is too easily muscled off pucks.

VÄX #11 C Seger, Gabriel (2018) - Seger had an underwhelming game. Hockey IQ is a question mark, he is constantly behind the play and has a tough time making himself available to teammates. Combined with his subpar skating it is not a great look. Added an assist on Växjö's lone goal with a simple pass from the corner on the PP. Created a breakaway for himself when pouncing on a loose puck on the penalty kill and got away a good shot but Rögle goalie Joel Svensson made a nice blocker save.

London Knights at Mississauga Steelheads, October 22nd, 2017

LDN #2 RD Bouchard, Evan (2018) - Evan had a strong offensive showing for the Knights in the win, utilizing his strong offensive instincts to inject into the attack on multiple occasions. Bouchard showed good poise with the puck throughout the game and often carried transition, exploiting open ice. On the occasion space was taken away, Evan did show an ability to make a good first pass. Where he struggled was when limited options presented themselves, opposed to re-grouping or eating the puck, he would simply force a play, leading to a turnover. Bouchard distributed well on the power play and was able to score on a one-timer attempt. Defensively Evan needs to show more urgency and use his body more effectively as he relies far too much on his stick.

LDN #18 LC Foudy, Liam (2018) - Foudy displayed a fluid and rangy stride that allowed him to generate good speed throughout the game. Liam utilized this speed to create space in transition, where he had arguably his biggest effect on the game. Foudy effectively created space while attacking the offensive zone and used the defender as a screen, quickly releasing an accurate snap shot that beat the goaltender high. Liam will need to improve his strength as he was largely ineffective in puck battles, simply being pushed from possession.

LDN #24 RD Perrott, Andrew (2019) - Perrott played a simplistic but effective defensive game. Andrew showed good strength to his game and was fairly tough to play against in the defensive zone, as he was able to close gaps quickly, contain and finish with contact. Perrott also showed impressive character coming to the aid of a teammate in a post whistle scrum, despite being the youngest player on the ice.

LDN #72 RD Regula, Alec (2018) - Regula had a strong game despite a non-flashy style of play. Alec displayed developing two-way traits to his game as he has begun to inject himself into the offensive attack more than in previous views. Regula was at his best however on the defensive side of the puck where he was able to utilize his combination of strong positional play, above average awareness and good mobility. He often closed gaps well in the neutral zone and effectively took away the middle of the ice. When he was unable to close a gap quickly he effectively forced attacking forwards wide to low percentage areas of the ice. In possession Regula made strong reads and while he rarely used his feet to get up ice, he did show an ability to make a quality outlet pass.

LDN #92 RW Cottam, Harrison (2018) - Cottam played sparingly in 5-on-5 situations, skating on the Knights fourth line. However, he was able to become impactful skating on the Knights second power play unit. Harrison showed an uncanny ability to find space and place himself in ideal positioning to release his above average shot. Cottam displayed a pro style release with impressive velocity and accuracy.

MISS #4 LD Walker, Isaac (2018) - Walker is a simplistic type of defender who was at his best on the defensive side of the puck. Isaac limited his possession time by quickly moving the puck to the high percentage outlet, which allowed him to remain effective despite limited puck handling skills. Walker showed good size and strength to his game as he was able to work over opponents along the boards and in front of the goal. He also showed a willingness to engage physically when opportunities presented themselves. Walker will need to continue to adjust to the pace of the OHL as he looked frantic at times.

MISS #10 LD Rippon, Merrick (2018) - Rippon had a quiet game, however his skating was continually a noteworthy attribute. Merrick often utilized his feet to elude a forecheck and would quickly get up ice to make himself an option transition. Rippon was limited on the offensive side of the puck; however, he does handle the puck well and shows an ability to distribute the puck effectively. Merrick's skating allows him to stay in front of attacking opponents, however he would benefit from closing gaps quicker and taking better routes to puck carriers. Rippon did flash an intriguing amount of toughness as he was aggressive in the defensive zone.

MISS #11 RW Schwindt, Cole (2019) - Schwindt had a strong game for the Steelheads, showing a strong compete level, smarts and deceptive skill to his game. While Cole needs to work on improving his first step quickness and refining his stride, he was able to reach an average top speed. Schwindt consistently went to traffic and used his size to become an effective net front presence. While Cole was unable to produce in this particular game, he was able to generate chances with his work ethic opposed to pure skill. He was also a reliable three zone player, displaying good positional awareness.

MISS #91 LC McLeod, Ryan (2018) - McLeod battled with inconsistent play throughout the game. When he was most intriguing was when he utilized his fluid skating and speed to attack the offensive zone. Ryan attacked with his head up aware of his options but still shy's from attacking the goal, option to peel back and make a pass. Which in this game often led to turnovers opposed to successful passes to a trailing/attacking teammate. McLeod does do a good job of eluding opponents with his quick feet and strong edges; however, he needs to show more desire to attack high traffic areas. Ryan did score a nice goal when he took the puck to the middle of the ice and released a quick snap shot.

MISS #92 LC Washkurak, Keean (2019) - Washkurak had a noteworthy performance, showing an impressive amount of energy to his game and a tireless compete level. Keean made an impact creating turnovers on the forecheck, showing relentless puck pursuit and a willingness to finish checks. He played with a physical edge throughout the game, that will only become more impactful as he adds strength. Keean was able to generate chances with his work ethic, however showed limited creativity on the offensive side of the puck. Often going to the net hard looking for loose pucks in the crease, opposed to making skilled plays.

Pardubice U20 at Kometa Brno U20, October 27th, 2017

BRN # 24 C Plasek, Karel (2018) – Plasek had a good game although he wasn't his usual self. It looked like him and the team had a game or a hard training before. Last 20 min he was one that lifted the speed and where more competitive. I like that he shows good character stepping up in the end of the games if needed. Skating looks smooth and very good with the stick. Plasek had one nice one-man rush ending on a backhand while he was pulled down without any penalties. Some nice actions in Overtime. Nice shootout fooling the goalie by quick left and right turn and then with a quick hidden wrist dropped the puck between the goalie's legs.

BRN # 14 RW Strondala, Vojtech (2019) – Strondala was one with similar speed as usual in a Brno team. Created a lot with Plasek but had difficulties to get the puck to the net. Got a one-man rush after a good reading and released a hard wrist shot but outside the net. Played with poise in Overtime. Had a very quick backcheck in 3 on 3 play during Overtime, catching up the Pardubice F with puck. Strondala probably saved the game for Brno. Excellent shootout going straight to the goalie and then a super quick left move and finishing the puck in net high by the left post.

BRN # 11 LW Svoboda, Matej (2018) Mature good game, a couple of good skate rushes and good leg muscles. Svoboda has decent speed once he gets up there and today he used it a bit more. Battled and got the puck at offensive blue, brought the puck and scored 1-0 with a backhand.

BRN # 13 C/LW Gajarsky, Adam (2018) – Some of Gajarskys speed and confidence had returned from the beginning of the game and constantly grew during the game. Gajarsky was on the ice while shorthanded. Gajarsky scored the 2-2 goal with a accurate wrist shot after a very nice action from own goal line via tick tack play between Kowalczyk, Novak and himself. It looked like it was a big relief for Gajarsky and the whole game for him looked like a big step back to confidence. Showed confident in the last period and Overtime. Had a couple of good chances in Overtime created by speed and reading. Gajarsky had poise on the Shot out after overtime, Nice shoot out that almost looked like he had to slow speed but very confident finishing with a hard low accurate wrist shot, the Game winning goal. 2 Goals for Gajarsky. Gajarsky was set as an extra player for the CZE U18 team that goes to Finland but more games like this and he will be back in the team soon.

BRN # 4 RW Novak, Matej (2019) – Quick legs, creating, gives energy and today also got points. Created some chances with Kucer and Strondala. The 2-2 goal was a nice action from red goal line by Kowalczyk and all over the ice via Gajarsky and Novak. 1A for Novak.

PAR # 19 LD Bucko, Martin (2018) Tall Slovak born 2000, wasn't visualized much and was not getting all shifts. Bucko had a good chance with a decent hard shot in overtime but Brno Goalie managed to hold the puck. Played easy and was usually on the right spot.

PAR # 1 G Vlk, Tomas (2018) – The usual goalkeeper and the extra goalie for CZE U18 was not even on the bench today. .

Toronto Jr. Canadiens at Whitby Fury, October 27th, 2017

JRC #9 RW Joffe, Jake (2018) - An averaged sized winger, Joffe excelled in possession where he was able to utilize his vision and playmaking skills to create for his line mates. Jake was able to generate good speed and often attacked the offensive zone, changing his pace which made him difficult to contain. Joffe often drew in defenders before sliding pucks over to trailing/attacking line mates.

JRC #12 RD Smith, Jeremy (2018) - Smith is an undersized two-way defender who displayed intriguing offensive instincts throughout the game. Jeremy often utilized his quick feet and strong edge work to elude a forecheck before quickly bursting up ice and leading the transition attack. Away from the puck Smith would inject into the play and look to make himself an option. Smith distributed the puck well on the power play and showed a deceptively heavy point shot. Jeremy often relied on positional play and a quick stick on the defensive side of the puck.

JRC #16 RW O'Brien, Matthew (2018) - O'Brien was good in a complimentary role for the JRC, utilizing his strength to win battles along the boards and make himself an effective net front presence. Matthew fore-checked well and was often a physical presence throughout the game. O'Brien's strength over the puck allowed him to make some impact off the cycle.

JRC #19 LC McBain, Jack (2018) - McBain displayed fluid skating abilities and a good top speed which he often used to attack the offensive zone and create space. Jack showed an above average intelligence to his game and thrived in possession, using his vision and passing skills to generate opportunities for his line mates. McBain's defensive zone game was also noteworthy as he was consistently engaged and positionally aware. While his ability to anticipate with effectiveness allowed him to get his stick in lanes and create turnovers. Jack flashed elite ability to dictate the game, however seemingly played down to the level of play and simply only did enough to get by, turning up his compete only on occasion.

WBY #44 LD O'Rourke, Ryan (2020) - Despite being OHL Draft eligible, O'Rourke played in all situations for the Fury and was effective doing so. In the early stages of the game Ryan's gap control was a little spotty however as he adjusted to the pace of play he began to improve his gap and became highly effective. O'Rourke showed good strength to his game as he was able to out battle opponents below the hash-marks and was able to separate player from puck. In possession

Ryan was able to carry transition at times but looked to keep it simple and made a quality first pass. O'Rourke also displayed a heavy point shot on the power play.

WBY #91 LC Perfetti, Cole (2020) - Perfetti was the second OHL Draft Eligible player to skate for the Fury in this game. Cole was able to translate his elite hockey sense and playmaking abilities to the tier two junior A level. Perfetti showed impressive poise and patience in possession and was able to make quality decisions, simplifying his game when needed. While Cole's inability to chip a puck out in the defensive zone did lead to a JRC goal, it was the lone blemish on an otherwise strong showing. Perfetti played on the power play and excelled with added time and space showing strong playmaking skills and creativity.

WBY #92 RC Robertson, Liam (2018) - Robertson displayed a fluid and powerful stride that allowed him to generate a quality top speed. Liam often used his speed on the forecheck and was able to make an impact along the wall and off the cycle. Robertson used his strength over the puck when taking the puck to high traffic areas. Liam kept his game simple in possession however did flash deceptive skill at times.

WBY #98 LW McCutcheon, Riley (2018) - McCutcheon possesses intriguing size and strength to his game and showed good skating abilities for a player of his size. Riley showed a rangy but clunky stride however was able to reach a good top speed and often used his speed to his advantage on both the forecheck and back-check. McCutcheon displayed a strong work ethic and was a reliable three zone presence, however in possession his simplistic style of play limited his ability to generate offense. Riley would benefit from utilizing his size more and becoming more of a physical presence.

Spokane chiefs at Red Deer Rebels, October 27, 2017

Red Deer Rebels -

RED #31 G Anders, Ethan (2019) - Anders had a solid night in net for the Rebels. The attribute that stood out the most was his glove hand. On one sequence he made a nice wind-mill glove save on a breakaway where a Chiefs player cut across the slot before shooting it backhand. On another sequence, he pushed across his net too aggressively, throwing him out of position, however he flashed the glove and caught it despite it looking like a sure goal, it was one of the better saves for either goalie. He's a battler too, as he had to deal with a lot of pressure around his net but was effective at using his blocker to push away opponents and find the puck through heavy traffic.

RED #5 RD Barteaux, Dawson (2018) - Barteaux was mixed today, he was decent offensively but left a lot to be desired in his own zone. Barteaux's pivoting and gap control need a lot of work as he was beaten cleanly several times on players driving wide on him, this caused him to take a blatant holding penalty behind his own net, on another sequence he held a player who was going through the slot, he knew it was holding as he looked back at the ref, but wasn't called for it. He wasn't great at supporting his teammates in board play sequences behind his own net either, preferring to park himself in the crease and watch. Offensively, he was better, getting his slap-shot through traffic on a couple of occasions. One of his shots was deflected late which tied the game with less than a minute left.

RED #4 LD Alexeyev, Alexander (2018) - Alexeyev showed a high level of composure under pressure in today's game. His skating was fluid however he doesn't generate much power in his stride, which makes both his acceleration and top gear average at best. Despite his lack of foot speed, he was more than capable of transitioning the puck through the neutral zone and into the offensive zone. This was due to his ability to assess pressure correctly and find open space; he was also capable of dealing with forecheckers that were attempting to strip him off the puck. On one sequence he had two Rebel players trying to stick-check him, due to a lack of support he opted to use his hands to drag the puck back and pass it up the ice to his teammate. HIs passing was good tonight both at even strength and on the power-play, making tape to tape passes out of the zone as well as moving the puck around the high circles in the offensive zone. One sequence on the powerplay which he was quarterbacking, showed his offensive skill set. He received a pass on the left side of the point, then used a wrist shot feint by dragging the puck to his side before making a pass into the slot for a quality scoring chance. He prefers using his wrist shot over his slap-shot, although it wasn't overly threatening, the release point is average, he was delayed in picking his spots, although he did get it through traffic occasionally and recognized when his lane was closed off.

RED #3 LD Donohoe, Hunter (2018) - Donohoe is a big kid, standing at 6'4 with a wide frame. He used all of it in the middle of the first period, lining up a Chiefs player and delivering a hard body check in the neutral zone, the check sent the player crashing to the ice. Defensively, he used his frame against the boards to box out the opposition but during a penalty kill, he lost his position on a smaller player in front of the net that resulted in a tap in goal against. I would have liked to have seen him use his leverage more when stick-checking on the play as well. His passing ability was mixed while trying to come out of his own end. He had one really poor defensive play, he had no pressure, however he softly passed the puck into the middle of the ice leading to an unforced turnover despite multiple options been available. He was responsible for the first goal that his team scored, as he delivered a low slap-shot that was redirected into the back of the net, so he did manage to contribute offensively.

RED #12 RW Douglas, Chris (2018) - Douglas had a couple of moments that stood out in the defensive end and on the penalty kill. He showed good back-checking ability, skating hard after his opponent gained separation from him, then catching up and cutting off a pass that was intended for the high-slot. On the penalty kill he had a tremendous sequence where he took away a shot from the point before diving aggressively to move the puck out of the zone while under heavy pressure. Offensively speaking, he wasn't dangerous in today's game.

Spokane Chiefs -

SPK #24 LD Smith, Ty (2018) - Smith displayed his transitional skills, controlling the tempo of the game offensively, while also showing two-way ability. It starts with his skating, he's got great acceleration, a top-gear that allows him to separate from his opponents and elite edge work. There were several plays where he would start from behind his own net, find open ice and get the puck deep into the offensive end without turning it over. He displayed a high level of intelligence on one subtle play. The puck was flipped up into the air along the boards and as he skated to retrieve it before the opposition, he recognized that he was going to be caught if he didn't let up just before getting to the puck, this allowed him to regain defensive position and not allow a potential two on one sequence from developing. On another sequence in the offensive zone, he recognized poor spacing by the Rebels defender then exploded wide, driving around him and pulling to his backhand in the slot before making a beautiful yet subtle no-look pass to his teammate for the Chiefs second goal. These two sequences demonstrated his ability to make the subtle play as well as make the dynamic play. Defensively, he had an excellent block on the penalty kill which stung him after it went off his hip, he was also tracking players well that were attempting to get behind his defensive coverage. That been said, he was late coming back on the overtime goal and he wasn't playing physical hockey. I also wish he would be more selfish offensively depending on the play, he had a tendency to pass the puck too much when he was in a good position to shoot the puck.

SPK #12 LW Chenier, Cedric (2018) - Chenier showed off decent vision today. He was playing on the half-wall on the powerplay and was consistent at distributing the puck to his teammates, giving them different looks. On two sequences he threaded passes to the slot area resulting in high quality scoring chances, one of them turned into Anders best glove save of the night, robbing him of an assist that he deserved. He processes plays quickly as well, when driving wide down the right wing, he released a backhand pass into the slot but it went off a defenseman's skate, going directly to him, he immediately passed it off into the slot again to the surprise of the Rebels. Despite been undersized he was defensively responsible, making sure to hustle back when the puck was going the other way and pressuring players from behind on more than one shift.

Final Score 4-3 Rebels (OT)

Mississauga Steelheads at Kingston Frontenacs, October 27th, 2017

Mississauga Steelheads –

MISS #1 G Ingham, Jacob (2018) – Ingham stopped 21 of 22 shots. He show-cased his lateral movement, stopping several cross-crease one timers both in the high slot and around his goal crease. In overtime he made his two most impressive saves by cutting across the net and stopping not only the first shot but the rebound by kicking out his right pad. Both his ability to anticipate the play and react accordingly to secondary scoring chances were excellent tonight. On a sequence in the first period, Dunkley had both time and space to walk in alone and shoot, however Ingham read the pass based off Dunkley's pa high percentage scoring chance, although I think he would have stopped it had the play occurred later in the game when he was playing with bravado.

MISS #4 LD Walker, Isaac (2018) – Walker was effective defensively today. He showed good composure, spinning off an aggressive fore-checker before passing the puck up into the neutral zone. He also demonstrated hustle in getting to lose pucks in the corners. His most impressive play came on the penalty kill, he anticipated a pass behind the net and reacted by skated aggressively to the player who received the pass and poked the puck off his stick leading to a turnover. His acceleration and positioning allowed him to stand out on several defensive plays throughout the game.

MISS #91 LC McLeod, Ryan (2018) – Mcleod showed both his tremendous tool kit as well as why he can be frustrating at times. His acceleration allows him to change gears quickly and enter a top gear that most defenceman simply can't keep up with when he drives wide. This is a double edge sword however, it does allow him to create chances for himself but it also makes him fairly predictable at times. I wish he would demonstrate more creativity when he steps over the offensive blueline, he didn't stop up, and he didn't attempt to change his pace to throw the defenceman off in today's match up. That been said, he still created multiple scoring chances for himself when he did drive towards the slot area, although his passing was off, he had an unforced pass that missed everyone resulting in a zone clear for the Frontenac's. On another passing sequence, he delivered a pass that was too hard for his teammate to handle, on what could have been a quality scoring chance. He played at 100 miles an hour, he needs to settle his game down and realize that he has more time then he thinks he does.

MISS #92 LC Washkurak, Keean (2019) – Washkurak was very effective at fore-checking and creating havoc along the boards. He's got explosive skating ability and this allowed him to dump the puck in and retrieve it down in the corners. He never stops moving his feet and he's got a ton of energy which resulted in several drawn penalties and a fatigued Frontenac's squad, he forced them to play heavy minutes below the goal line and you could see the frustration mount on his opposition. That been said, he didn't have to many offensive chances, however he was the catalyst in breaking down the defense when he was on the ice. He's got a motor and he plays bigger than his size, which is a good combination to have.

Kingston Frontenacs –

KIN #2 LD Brand, Evan (2019) – He played limited minutes for the Frontenac's today, however similar to the last time I saw him, I thought he was effective in a minor role. He's a towering presence on the ice and knows what he has to do to be a factor. He was winning board battles, using his excellent reach to deflect shots and making quick first passes along the boards to get the puck moved up the ice. His defensive reads combined with his physical gifts make him intriguing.

KIN #9 LC Dunkley, Nathan (2018) – Dunkley showed off impressive vision. During the first period, he had a beautiful no look backhand pass just over the offensive blueline that resulted in a quality scoring chance. He also demonstrated the ability to carry the puck over the neutral zone. He was stagnant offensively, as was the majority of the Frontenac's today.

KIN #47 LW Popov, Sergei (2018) – Showed some tenacity during board battles on several plays. He's got a wide skating base but he still manages to generate decent speed when fore-checking. There was a couple of plays where he put himself in bad spots along the boards in the offensive zone which forced him to do more work to maintain puck possession. He wasn't offensively a factor today.

KIN #75 LW/RW Nyman, Linus (2018) – Nyman was a stand out offensively for the Frontenac's. He was all over the ice, showing a willingness to retrieve lose pucks, take big hits to make plays to his teammates, and finish his own checks despite his small stature. He had several quality cross-crease passes that led to high-end scoring chances. He plays at a high pace, unfortunately this got him in trouble by been overzealous on a back-check, leading to a power-play while trying to protect the lead.

Final score: Steelheads 2-1 (OT)

Tri City Americans at Kelowna Rockets, October 27th 2017

KEL #7 RD Zabransky, Libor (2018) – Early in the game was getting a lot of defensive zone starts and it ended up inhibiting his ability to contribute to offence, he was passive when looking to clear his own zone and was settling on playing way to much defense. He looked slow to lose pucks and really had zero urgency to his game, has show better efforts in prior viewings, not much positive play tonight.

KEL #24 C Topping, Kyle (2018) – Lined up as the slot presence on the powerplay, a new position for him, showed good use of his hockey sense by timing his net drives really well to create screen, receive passes and attack rebounds. Skating has always needed to improve but it was noticeably ridged tonight just didn't look to comfortable with high speed plays, took a poor hooking call getting beat to the crease by his man. Despite looking a little poor at high speed did flash some good edge work and stick handling to create some space for himself and make some plays on offence, too all his strong side faceoffs (left) and fair pretty well winning most.

KEL #1 G Porter, James (2018) – A small goalie but quick, he tracked puts well tonight and uses good side to side movement to get square to the shooters. None of his goals screamed that he should have them, but he did roam out of his net once and played the puck on the powerplay causing a bad turnover which ended up in his net.

KEL #6 RD Korczak, Kaeden (2019) – Starting to show more confidence with each passing game, noticing this game he was more and more comfortable being the lead defenseman up the ice utilizing his solid speed to push and strong reverse to recover that includes a good gap and edging. Slowly but surely he is looking to push more and help drive play up ice, he's not overly involved in the offence but there is a strong feeling its beginning to come.

KEL #29 LW Foote, Nolan (2019) – Foote was back on the wing after several games in the center spot. Showed a better ability to work the puck up the boards carrying better on zone exits and through the neutral zone and helping far more in the team transition game than in previous viewings; Foote looks far more natural on the LW side. Played a good role on the penalty kill and got in front of a few shots. Showed off his great one-timer from the right circle but hit the post just missing after a clean beat of the goalie

TC #4 LD Kalinichenko, Roman (2018) – Solid defensive defender really plays tight without crossing the line, especially around the crease, showed perfect timing to break up a 2 on 1 with an impressive shot block. Was getting zone starts all over the ice and ended up sliding up to the top pair with Valimaki getting a lot of ice-time and looking impressive while playing with a bit of an edge, doesn't defer to his partner, makes plays and uses shifty stick handling and strong outlet passes to catch the eye.

TC #17 C Focht, Carson (2018) – His chippy nature was shining through today and he threw a greasy crosscheck from behind that crossed the line a little. Its always Focht's skating that you notice in his game he's quick and has the ability play quick in so many aspects of his game, left wishing he attacked this net more with that speed, but did pick up a secondary assist on solid pass into the slot that was eventually banged in off a rebound.

TC# 19 LW Bouchard, Connor (2019) – Small but speedy he exhibited some really strong puck control and shifty play in this game, showed a good effort and was throwing his body around while going after some bigger players. Ended up with an assist but didn't look overly dangerous on this night.

TC# 34 RW Mutala, Sasha (2019) – Plays a quick game and its easy to appreciate his tempo, makes accurate passes and overall with his limited icetime he left Intrigue for future viewings.

Final Score: Kelowna Rockets: 4 – Tri-City Americans: 3

Farjestad BK at Rogle BK, October 28th, 2017

FBK #28 LW Carl Jakobsson (2018) - Jakobsson put on a strong performance and was likely Färjestads best forward in this game. Showed his willingness to go to the rough areas when he drove the net and tapped in a rebound on his first goal of the night. Demonstrated a quick and powerful release on his second goal of the game on a snap shot from the slot on the man advantage. Was feisty on the forecheck all night long.

FBK #31 C Oscar Bäck (2018) - Had a bleak performance this evening. Worked hard all over the ice but was often behind the play. Had trouble creating any real dangerous scoring chances. His lack of natural skill was evident. Bäck plays a fast and simple game that leaves little room for creativity.

Chicoutimi Saguenéens vs Blainville-Boisbriand Armada, October 28th, 2017

CHI #23 LW Kotkov, Vladislav (2018): Kotkov flashed some good puck skills throughout the game, including on a couple of one-on-one confrontations. He made good use of his long reach to get around defenders. He's a big player, but had trouble staying on his feet, losing too many one-on-one battles. Chicoutimi was outmatched all game long, but Kotkov didn't show a lot of drive or willingness to make a difference on the ice.

CHI #77 LD Groleau, Jeremy (2018): This was not the best game to judge Groleau, as Chicoutimi didn't spend too much time with the puck. The Armada outplayed the Saguenéens for most of the game. His feet are slow, which gave him issues when facing speedy forwards off the rush. Overall, he kept his game simple with the puck, as he usually does.

CHI #17 C Rubtsov, German (PHI): He was Chicoutimi's top player in the game by a large margin, scoring twice in a losing effort. He created his scoring chances by skating well and being strong on the puck. He didn't get much help from his linemates, and he didn't create many chances for his teammates, either. His individual talent was the reason for his success tonight. I liked the release he had on his shot; one of the best in the QMJHL.

BLB #6 LD Crête-Belzile, Antoine (2018): He kept his play with the puck simple, he tried rushing pucks out of his zone, and had some difficulty getting away from the forecheck, as he lacks that separation speed. He played a smart game; I didn't see him get into trouble in his zone too often.

BLB #4 LD Anttalainen, Aleksi (2018): Loved his compete level. He plays an intense game and plays much bigger than his listed size. He didn't hesitate to clear the front of the net when he had to. He showed decent mobility on the back end and showed a powerful slapper from the point. Good first pass out of his zone, and overall, this was the best game I've seen out of him this year.

BLB #24 LW Teasdale, Joel (2018): He was strong on the puck in the offensive zone and didn't hesitate to take the puck to the net. He's strong on his skates, and was tough to handle down low and in front of the net. He was in front of the net on the PP, and didn't stop going there, even if he took some punishment. He created a penalty by taking advantage of a forward playing on the point, beating him wide with a good burst of speed.

BLB #16 C Henman, Luke (2018): Scored in the first period on the backhand from the slot. He played in all situations and showed some good smarts at both ends of the ice. He looked like an average skater when rushing the puck; I would like to see him add some speed to his game, which would make him more of a threat offensively. He lacks strength as well; if he added some more, it would help him win some more one-on-one battles.

Prince George Cougars at Kelowna Rockets, October 28th, 2017

PG #22 RW Mosher, Matthew (2018) – Plays with a good tempo and shows some flashes of speed, started a few rushes from his own end exhibiting a good ability to help clear the zone using his feet. He was a little lost after that after his rushes he really just tossed the puck away and didn't create offence or even much of a forecheck

PG #2 LD Moberg, Cole (2019) – Played his offside and looked solid doing it not having much trouble on his backhand along the wall, made good use of his feet in this situation and it helped contribute to his strong outlet passes using the middle of the ice as more of an option. Was solid in his own end using and active stick to chip away pucks to corners and break up plays around the crease. He played tight in transition keeping close to attackers and made a couple good reads to pick off passes and turn the play in the other direction.

PG #6 RD Harkins, Jonas (2019) – A player that appears to move well for size, skates in an efficient manner with a long stride. Tried to throw a couple of hits and really came up empty, had a few misses and didn't look very powerful or punishing, lacked some power for his size.

KEL #24 C Topping, Kyle (2018) – Great example of his timing and hockey sense as he passed the puck to a teammate on the far side and used a stutter step to create space and drive the far post scoring a goal. Looked quick tonight almost like he made an adjustment to his skating style, quick with pucks and really controlled the tempo of the play. Was the catalyst for his lines transition game and played really well and looks to have some strong chemistry with Kole Lind.

KEL #7 Zabransky, Libor (2018) – Questionable compete level at some points throughout this game, to often was picking and choosing when to be active in the play, needed to find some level of consistency and it wasn't there. Allowed a bad zone entry against on the powerplay and ended up not wanting to out work his opponent and just took a poor penalty instead, then shortly after took another penalty considered lazy as he grabbed an opponents stick after he was beaten on the play.

KEL #1 G Porter, James (2018) – Really looks calm in the net and showed a good ability to stay still until a skater makes the first move. Kept his team in the game on a couple occasions saving a penalty shot and a breakaway in the third period, he's not a very big goaltender but he always looks big and made a point of bieng in front of shooters consistently.

KEL #29 LW Foote, Nolan (2019) - Had a relatively quiet night but showed one particular move that was something not seen often in other viewings, as he was in his sweet spot on the circle and instead of shooting as would quite often be his first choice he first a really accurate pass to the opposite side of the net for a nice tap in goal for Topping.

Final Score: Kelowna Rockets: 4 – Prince George Cougars: 2

Zilina at Slovan Bratislava, October 29th, 2017

BRA # 1 G Vojvoda, Michal (2018) - I like his calm and mature play, he reads the game good, he showed good stick control, and looked confident and focused. Good reaction and he made sure rebounds went directed to corners or out of danger. Good awareness of moving the puck to teammates. Didn't saw much communication and the post to post moving could be quicker. Slovan gave Zilina the possibility to play with 2-man advantage from minute 58.14 – 59,53 and pp in Overtime resulting in Vojvoda giving 3 goals away where at least 2 of the goals was with very little help from his teammates.

BRA # 12 RD Vitalos, Martin (2018) – With Boldziar away Vitalos got more ice time and stepped up a bit. Was shooting a lot. Skating doesn't look very smooth or balanced but average for Slovak U20 level. Positioned himself good and played easy.

ZIL # 25 C Hryzak, Ivan C (2018) – Tall guy 6'3" Got a lot of ice time, was almost on ice all the time In the end. Good 1faceoffs. Had 1 shot on goal during the whole game and had a negative +-. Scored 3-3 during a 2-man advantage with 7 seconds left that took them overtime.

ZIL # 4 RD Dlugos, Marcel (2018) – This guy is 6'4" and with 205 lbs but was not using his body size much or at all. Reading looked average. Considering he is one of the more producing Ds in Zilina and the trust from trainer with plenty of ice time I think he was missing confidence. Was the most shooting in Zilina and scored 1 goal.

Halifax Mooseheads at Gatineau Olympiques, November 3rd, 2017

HAL #11 LW Zadina, Filip (2018) – Filip was outstanding tonight for Halifax and showed why he could be a top pick in this year's draft. He had excellent speed and great acceleration; he was good tonight at creating offense or scoring chances at top speed. Filip ended the night with 3goals 1assists; on all 3 of his goal he showed his quick and deadly accurate shot not giving the goal anytime to react to the shot. He scored 2 goals coming off the rush along the boards and then cutting into the slot and shooting top corner again no chance for goalie. He showed high hockey IQ and smart decisions all night for Halifax, it showed on Halifax 1st goal as he drew 2 defensemen towards him and made a really nice touch pass to his winger trailing back door. He was smart defensively as well, he was back to support his defense in the defensive zone and didn't leave the zone early and gave them an easy outlet pass on the breakout. Filip showed high-end skill tonight and smarts and was fun to watch tonight, as you sometimes sat back and said did that just happen.

HAL #14 LD McIssac, Jared (2018) - Jared was most effective in possession where he was able to utilize his foot speed and mobility to elude a forecheck and quickly start up ice with the puck. Ben showed the smarts to simplify his game at times and make a quality first pass while moving up ice. While Loreto does have room to improve his play in the defensive zone, he does use his skating ability to contain fairly well in transition and would simply benefit from taking away time and space quicker. Jared also showed good puck distribution skills on the power play. They were too many times he forced pucks up the wall to his wingers that were covered, he needs to slow the game down in front of him and make more précised passes. He had a good stick in the defensive zone breaking up a good amount of passes in the defensive zone.

GAT #13 RW Shestopalov, Mikhail (2018) – Mikhail displayed impressive skill to his game as he thrived in possession showing above average puck skills and creativity to his game. Mikhail showed intriguing vision and passing skills to his game, which allowed him to effectively raise the level of his line mates. He scored a nice onetime goal in the slot; he was good at getting the puck of quick and not stopping it then shooting. Mikhail quick feet and strong edges allowed him to create space for himself. With the addition of his puck skills he became very elusive and tough to contain down low on the cycle.

GAT #26 C Balmas, Mitchell (FA) – Mitchell showed good fluid skating abilities, including a quick first step and strong straight-line speed. He was one of Gatineau more consistent threats throughout the game, using his speed both when attacking in possession and on the forecheck. Mitchell ended the night with 1 goal 1 assists, and his line was clicking on cylinders tonight and seemed to create chances every time they were on the ice. He would benefit from becoming more assertive when in possession and utilize his speed to push the pace more aggressively at times.

Final Score: Halifax Mooseheads: 7 – Gatineau Olympiques: 5

Barrie Colts at Ottawa 67's, November 3rd, 2017

OTT #25 D Stratis, Peter (2018) - Stratis was moving the puck well in this game. He saw some time on the Powerplay and demonstrated good vision and quick decision making to consistently make clean, accurate passes both on the breakout and in the offensive zone. He has a very smooth stride, which makes him effective carrying the puck up through the neutral zone, as he can maintain and adjust his speed quickly. He seems to always know where his teammates are on the ice, consistently making accurate no-look passes, which make them difficult to intercept for the defenders.

OTT #27 D Robertson, Carter (2018) - Robertson showed a high hockey IQ, strong skating and good offensive upside in this game. He is a strong, agile skater with a smooth stride who can move quickly in the lateral direction. His agility allows him to maintain strong gap control when defending on the rush. He made perfect, crisp passes throughout the game on a consistent basis. For the most part, he exhibited sound and quick decision making, although he held onto the puck too long in the third period at one pint, which led to a poor giveaway in his own zone.

OTT #88 D Bahl, Kevin (2018) - Bahl played top minutes again in this game for Ottawa and had multiple scoring opportunities throughout the game on the Powerplay, but finished the game without a point and only one shot on net. He saw time on both the penalty kill and Powerplay, and occasionally jumped down low on the powerplay, using his massive frame to act as a screen in front of the net . He was set up with a one-timer at one point in the second period on the Powerplay, but his shot was blocked. In the third period, he had a great opportunity to score on a nice pass but missed the net with his shot. He has a noticably strong slapshot, but could work on getting his wristshot off more quickly, which would make him a more dynamic offensive threat at the OHL level. He moves deceptively well around the ice, but it's tough to see in his stride. He does a good job of using his long legs to push off, giving him a very long stride but his feet don't seem to be moving quickly when you watch him skate. He can play physical when needed, but isn't known for stepping up to make the big open ice hit. At the end of the game, he took a player out in the corner with a hard hit that led to a scrum between Ottawa and Barrie, but was given a game misconduct for a check to the head.

BAR #71 F Nizhnikov, Kirill (2018) - Nizhnikov possesses a high skillset and was an offensive force for Barrie in this game despite not cracking the scoresheet. In the first period on the Powerplay, he made a hard, accurate cross-ice pass in the offensive zone to his open linemate for a scoring opportunity. He possesses strong puck handling abilities, in the second period making a nice loose puck deke to get around multiple defenders with very little space. He showed an ability to anticipate the play before it evolved, which enabled him to track down loose pucks very quickly. His vision and no-look passing was also on-point, at one point in the third period, he made a perfect, no-look pass across the blueline to his linemate on the rush as Barrie entered the offensive zone.

BAR #21 F Douglas, Curtis (2018) - Douglas is a big body forward who played top minutes for Barrie tonight. He was effective offensively throughout the game, creating scoring opportunities and picking up the second assist on Barrie's first goal of the game. He started the game for Barrie and saw quite a bit of time on the Powerplay. He was occasionally matched up against Kevin Bahl in Powerplay situations and exhibited a high compete level to get physical and battle for ice in front of the net with one of the league's largest defencemen. He moves noticably well for his size. Although he isn't the fastest skater, his acceleration was quick on the rush.

Minnesota Magicians at Janesville Jets, November 3rd, 2017

MIN #31 G Saville, Isaiah (2019) – Saville is out of the Colorado Thunderbirds program, he just misses out on the 2018 NHL Draft by a few days. Saville has acclimated himself well to junior hockey this season. Saville was a little bit erratic at times tonight but showed good athleticism and ability to recover from being out a position. Saville is aggressive in challenging shooters and likes to play on top of his crease. Saville did an excellent job in limiting 2nd hand chances for most of the night. His one goal against was a shot from the point that was deflected in front, through a screen.

MIN #4 RD Schultheis, Ben (2018) – Schultheis didn't show a lot in the way of dynamic puck skills or offensive impact tonight but showed excellent defensive awareness and fundamentals in his own end. He gapped up well against rushes and displayed a good stick and reach to disrupt plays entering the zone. Schultheis was physical against players coming into the zone but was sure to get his stick on the puck first and didn't risk taking himself out of the play. Schultheis has sound footwork and his straight line skating is above average but it looks like there is some room for improvement in his first couple stride where he got beat to loose pucks in his own end.

JVL #19 RW Renlund, Sam (2018) – Renlund made his debut for Janesville tonight after starting the season with Muskegon (USHL) for the first 5 games. The Colorado College commit didn't find his way onto the score sheet tonight but generated some offensive chances using his speed and ability to get to the middle of the ice. Renlund played with a lot of pace through the neutral zone and showed good poise with the puck in the offensive zone, he worked hard all over the ice and had some good plays on the back check.

JVL #30 G Lebedeff, Daniel (2018+) – His team was on their heels for much of the night, Lebedeff did a good job in keeping his team in it to the end. Lebedeff plays big in the night and challenged shooters 1 on 1. The Wisconsin commit make a couple really good saves moving from his left to right to make some pad saves. Lebedeff didn't lose his crease as much tonight as he has in past viewings, he played a much more positional sound game and didn't have to rely on his athleticism and scrambling to make saves.

Frolunda HC at Rogle BK, November 4th, 2017

FHC #44 LW Fagemo, Samuel (2018) - Has a quick first step but his edges and top speed has room for improvement. Was active and pounced on loose pucks. Is smart when it comes to shot selection and uses defenders as screens to mask his release. His hard one-timer was on display. Was energetic to start the game but became less of a factor as the game progressed. Was featured both on the PP and PK. Fagemo is a decisive passer and they are often crisp and tape-to-tape. Was seen cherry-picking on more than a few ocassions. Fagemo is a fairly one-dimensional player who only seem to have one gear in his gearbox.

FHC #52 LD Hasa, Filip (2018) - Hasa is a tiny blueliner who does his best work from inside the offensive zone. Creative and an able skater, uses headfakes and smooth hands to fool defenders. Good lateral mobility. Weak defensively and is prone to make errors in judgement in all three zones. Was a liability on the ice at times and was the main culprit for giving Rögle a short-handed breakaway.

FHC #7 LD Persson, Filip (2018) - Played on the top pairing with Filip Westerlund. Persson is a smooth skater and demonstrated an ability to read the play when he stepped up on his own blueline to intercept a dangerous cross-ice pass. Did not show a whole lot offensively but had a couple shots on goal.

FHC #5 Westerlund, Filip (ARI) - The best player by a large margin for Frölunda in a 3-1 loss. Repeatedly displayed his smarts and poise on the ice. Very calm with the puck on his stick. Made some risky plays at times but was successful in doing so. Had a good rush up the ice and fired a hard wrist shot which snuck just outside the post. Showed soft hands and made a nice backcheck recovery to prevent a dangerous scoring chance on one sequence where he lost the puck in the offensive zone.

Halifax Mooseheads vs Drummondville Voltigeurs, November 4th, 2017

HFX #14 LD McIsaac, Jared (2018): McIsaac had a couple of scoring chances in this game by supporting the rush, but couldn't capitalize on them. He showed a good and heavy wrist shot, but lacked some accuracy with it. Defensively, he played a physical game in his own zone, using his size well and making good use of his stick to block shots. He has good skating abilities. A couple of times during the game, he skated himself out of trouble with his powerful stride.

HFX #19 C Groulx, Benoit-Olivier (2018): He showed some improvements to his skating, showing better separation speed to get away from defenders. However, in his shifts in the 2nd half of the game, his speed was not as good. He was possibly feeling tired from back-to-back games. He showed a good level of commitment to the defensive game in his own zone, showing good support down low in his zone. Offensively, he had a couple of chances in the game and showed a good shot with a quick release. While he was in possession of the puck, he had trouble handling it when making zone entries, and didn't show much creativity out there.

HFX #50 C Lavoie, Raphaël (2019): His skating was rough, and he didn't generate a lot of speed on the ice. I liked his work along the wall, as he does a good job using his body and reach to protect the puck and making quick turns to get away from defenders. He didn't work as hard as I've seen in previous viewings, when not in possession of the puck.

HFX #11 RW Zadina, Filip (2018): It was a bit of a quiet game for Zadina tonight, but he still found a way to score a nice goal in the 2nd period, easily beating Jarrett Baker one-on-one by cutting inside and scoring on his rebound. He showed a quick release on his shot, and good vision, making good passes in the offensive zone. He played on the PK, but made a couple of bad plays there, including a bad pass in his zone that led to Drummondville's 1st goal of the game.

DRU #6 LD Baker, Jarrett (2019): Baker had one tough shift in the 2nd period, where he got beaten by Zadina one-on-one for Halifax's lone goal of the game. The rest of his game was solid. He made some simple passes to move the puck out of his zone and made smart pinches in the offensive zone. He also showed some physicality in his own zone and didn't back down from confrontations with Lavoie a couple of times during the game.

DRU #92 LD Beaudin, Nicolas (2018): Beaudin scored the overtime winner, making a good read coming from the weak side on a 4-on-3 power play, which left no chance for Halifax's goalie to go from post to post to make the save. Beaudin, all game long, was making smart plays with the puck, was good on the transition and showed good vision. He did a good job putting pucks on the net in the first period. Beaudin played another strong game today; he has showed good consistency this season, as he had not had many bad viewings this year.

DRU #33 G Rodrigue, Olivier (2018): Not tested a lot today, but did a fine job with his rebound-control throughout the game. He looked calm and confident in his crease. On the goal he gave up to Zadina, he made the first save but couldn't get back in position in time to stop the 2nd Zadina shot.

DRU #55 LD Bernard, Xavier (2018): Bernard was solid defending; he was aggressive on the puck-carrier and was quick to put pressure on them. He played on the right side, paired often with Beaudin at even-strength. He moved the puck well enough during the game, but he didn't show any superior offensive skills. He did a good job a couple times while controlling the puck on the blueline and bringing it down low and/or to the net, rushing it along the boards.

DRU #20 LW Desruisseaux, Cedric (2018): A bit quiet in the first period (much like the rest of his teammates), but Desruisseaux started using his speed well in the 2nd period. He showed he has the speed to beat defensemen wide, and did it 2-3 times for quality scoring chances. He had some good scoring chances during this game, but couldn't finish them. Liked his work ethic and how he played in the tougher areas of the ice, even if he's very undersized.

University of North Dakota at University of Wisconsin, November 4th, 2017

ND #16 RW Mismash, Grant (NSH) – Mismash was engaged in the game physically, was hard on pucks and showed good patients with the puck in the offensive zone. Used his body well to shield defenders and buy time to find guys coming into the zone late. Registered 1 assist on the game tying goal in the 3rd period by keeping a puck alive along the boards in the offensive zone.

ND #6 RD Poolman, Colton (Free Agent) – Poolman played a solid all-around game in all three zones tonight. He made some key plays and shot blocks on the Penalty Kill. Had very clean exits out of his own end, moved the puck quickly which made it hard for Wisconsin to establish a fore check. Made it difficult for Wisconsin forwards in front of his own net.

ND #19 LW Gersich, Shane (WSH) – Scored the tying goal late in the 3rd by jamming home a rebound off the end boards at the side of the net. Gersich was a pest all night, was engaged in the game physically all and his line of Rhett Gardner (DAL) and Grant Mismash (NSH) were able to generate a lot of offensive zone time. Gersich did a lot of the heavy lifting for this line in terms of winning puck battles and creating turnovers with back pressure.

ND #24 LD Wolanen, Christian (OTT) – Showed the ability to control the game from the back end at times tonight, his D-Pairing with Colton Poolman was very good at executing their breakouts quickly and efficiently. Wolanen Walked the offensive blue line effectively on the Power Play and was able to open up some shooting lanes but passed the puck a few times where he had an opportunity to get the puck down low to the net.

ND #1 G Thome, Peter (CMB) – For Making just his 2nd NCAA Start in front of a large and loud crowd, Thome acclimated himself well and showed a lot of poise early when Wisconsin came out flying. Made an excellent blocker save early in the 3rd period on a 2 on 1 that kept the game tied. Thome is a big goalie that played a very sound game positionaly. When Wisconsin was able to get him moving laterally, both on the penalty shot, on their goal in the 3rd and during the shootout is when they were able to find success, but anything Thome saw he stopped and controlled rebounds for the most part.

UW #18 LC Malone, Seamus (Free Agent) – Was a physical presence on the ice all night and seemed to get under the opponents skin for much of the night. Missed the net on some good scoring chances both 5 on 5 and on the Power Play.

UW #17 RW Johnson, Will (Free Agent) – Johnson was at a PPG clip coming into this game and was one of Wisconsin's best forwards tonight as far as winning puck battles and being able to keep pucks alive and generate sustained offensive zone time. Johnson showed good speed and won a lot of races to loose pucks.

UW #24 RW Dhooghe, Sean (2018+) – It has been a bit of an adjustment to College hockey for the 5'3" tall forward, which was somewhat expected. Tonight Sean got his first NCAA goal on a penalty shot after being held on a breakaway after coming out of the penalty box. Was able to create some space for himself with the puck in the offensive zone and developed a couple high end scoring chances.

UW #24 LC Frederic, Trent (BOS) – Not the best game from the big centerman tonight. He was able to be in on some odd man chances with the puck on his stick but the play fizzled without a scoring chance developing. Frederic had the tendency to try to slow things down and try to let the play develop and didn't drive the net as much as he typically does in those situations. Aside from a couple odd man rushes, Frederic was a non-factor in the offensive zone but had a strong 2-way game and made some plays in his own end.

UW #5 RD Inamoto, Tyler (FLA) – Ejected late in the 1st period for Contact to the head after stepping up on a North Dakota player in the Neutral Zone.

UW #20 Ess, Josh (CHI) – Stepped up and played a solid all-around game while playing extended minutes for the final 2 periods as Wisconsin was down to 5 defenseman.

UW #2 LD Kalynuk, Wyatt (PHI) – Calming presence with the puck on his stick for most the night, was able to slow things down when his team was pinned in their own end for stretches of the game. Showed good poise with the puck at the top of the power play and was able to cover a lot of ice to keep plays in the offensive zone.

UW #33 G Hayton, Kyle (Free Agent) – Hayton displayed some technical flaws in his game tonight, but made some high end saves at key times of the game, notably on a 5 minute penalty kill on the Inamoto Major Penalty. Hayton is an athletic goal who moved east west very well. Failed to hold to right post on the game tying goal on a shot off the end boards that was jammed past his pad at the side of the net.

Team Finland vs Canada Red, World Under-17 Hockey Challenge, Nov 5, 2017

Canada Red -

CAR #8 D Ortiz, Christopher (2019) - Ortiz was solid defensively for Canada today. He's listed at 5'11, 165 but he played bigger than his size and was good at repositioning himself when the opposition was skating wide on him. On several different plays, he used a powerful base to drive Finnish players into the boards and came away with the puck. He did most of the dirty work for Byram but was effective both at getting the puck out of his own end and finishing his checks.

CAR #4 D Byram, Bowen (2019) - Byram displayed a two-way game against Finland. Defensively, his gap control was good and it allowed him to use his reach effectively to deflect several shots away from the Canadian net. His effort levels along the boards were noticeable as well, there was one play where he was simultaneously fighting off two forecheckers, yet he managed to still hold them off long enough before getting support. He also showed some highly technical feints while transitioning the puck into the offensive end. On one sequence, he drove wide down the left wing, then angled his body to pass the puck into the slot, before repositioning his hips to drive past the defender and getting a scoring chance. He was quarterbacking the powerplay for Canada, however he wasn't utilizing his shot very often, preferring to pass at the top of the circles and creating different looks for Krebs along the half-wall.

CAR #11 LW Lafreniere, Alexis (2020) - Lafreniere was the best forward for Canada Red in the first period but slowly trailed off and wasn't as effective for the rest of the night. During today's game, he down the right wing and used his puck skills to beat Finnish defenders 1-on-1. His most effective sequence on the rush was the result of making a deke where he pulled the puck back and moved laterally to the left side of the right circle, releasing a quick wrist shot that was difficult for Piiroinen to handle. Lafreniere had Canada's first goal on the powerplay. He stationed himself down at the top of the crease, corralled a rebound and then roofed a shot off balance, it was impressive how accurate the shot was considering the difficult angle he had to shoot from. His passing was more mixed than the last time I watched him, he made some uncharacteristic turnovers along the half-wall but was still relatively effective at distributing the puck at even strength and on the powerplay.

CAR #24 LW Parent, Xavier (2020) - Parent showed his motor and created some scoring opportunities for himself. He had a couple of sequences where he got some open ice and took off down the wings, firing several shots on net. His most impressive play came off a board battle behind Piiroinen's net. He beat out a larger defender for the puck yet he lost his balance, on his way down to the ice, he threw a backhand pass in the slot which landed on the tape of one of his teammates leading to a great scoring chance. In today's game he had some tunnel vision. There were several plays where he had a passing lane but inadvertently cut it off by holding onto the puck too long and running out of space. It was frustrating since as the above play shows, he's capable of making a strong first pass. He's only 5'7 so when he was in these situations he caused a couple of unnecessary turnovers after getting physically overpowered along the boards.

CAR #17 LW/RW Krebs, Peyton (2019) - Krebs who is the captain of Canada Red was the best forward today. His skating was excellent, he had a fluid stride and his top speed allowed him to separate himself against the opposition on several plays. On one sequence, he drove wide on a defender, realized his lane was cut off so he used his edges and cut past the Finnish defenceman; this allowed his passing lane to open back up and he delivered a tape-to-tape pass through the slot for one of the better scoring chances. His goal demonstrated that he has a hard and accurate shot, as he picked his spot near the face-off circle. He also showed a lot of poise while under pressure. He was carrying the puck along the blueline and was running out of space but didn't panic and waited to turn the corner, he then tapped the puck ahead of himself, knowing he could collect it before the defenseman in-front of him. Most other players wouldn't have been able to keep the puck in but he not only kept it in, he created an offensive play out of the situation.

Finland -

FIN #29 LW Myllyla, Wiljami (2019) - Myllyla stood out despite playing on the 4th line. His skating mechanics need some refinement, he's got a wide base and pushes off awkwardly, however he still generates power in his stride giving him both good acceleration and a surprising top gear. His speed combined with his hands allowed him to penetrate the Canadian defense leading to some significant plays. On one sequence he darted through traffic, deked from his forehand to backhand at the top of the crease and then passed it off to his teammate on the right side of the slot for a great scoring chance. He stripped the puck off a Canadian just over the blueline on another sequence, then skated up the ice and got the puck in deep using his hands to weave through the defense. His wrist shot was heavy and he changed the angle on his only shot that he got on net.

FIN #36 LW Puistola, Patrik (2019) - Puistola had a good offensive game. He had a couple of scoring chances by getting a couple of shots on net on his off-wing. His wrist shot had velocity and it resulted in some rebounds. His best sequence came as he undressed the larger Brand by pulling the puck and using his edges to cut around him, this lead to his best scoring chance of the game. He also recognized Brand's reach advantage on the play and reacted properly when gauging the 1-on-1 situation. There was an attention to detail to his offensive game today.

FIN #19 LW Miettinen, Veeti (2020) - A smaller forward, standing at 5'8, 150, who used the most of his powerplay time while generating two goals. He wasn't consistent, so his stat line was somewhat misleading, that been said he did find some offense. His first goal was a result of receiving a beautiful pass that Saarela threaded across the high-slot, which he buried. His second goal was a byproduct of Cavallin cheating off his post and Saarela recognizing his opening while been parked on the right side of the net, this resulted in his powerplay tally. He didn't get many opportunities offensively but he took advantage of the ones he did have.

FIN #20 C Lundell, Anton (2020) - Lundell showed highly technical passing ability resulting in three points. On several sequences he made tape to tape passes under pressure, one specifically, was arguably the best pass of the night, where he avoided a check and made a blind pass to his teammate who was rushing up the ice on his wing. He had good offensive awareness and this combined with his accuracy led to very few turnovers while distributing the puck to his teammates at a consistent rate.

Final Score 4 - 2 Finland

CIBC Canada Russia Series Game #1 – Russia at WHL, November 6th, 2017

RUS#32 Alexeyev, Alexander (2018) – The Red Deer Rebel defencemen played a strong physical game. Being one of the biggest players on the ice he was a very imposing figure. However, Alexander was in tough against the WHL All-Stars. His speed and skating were tested every shift. Had a bad turnover that lead to a scoring chance early in the game. Took two bad penalties. Showed signs of his offensive game. Did not look out of place playing against the best in the league. Second penalty kill unit.

Russia vs Finland, World Under-17 Hockey Challenge, Nov 6, 2017

Finland –

FIN #4 LD Rasanen, Livari (2019) – Rasanen was used on the top pairing while showcasing a two-way game. His gap control and reads were good in the neutral zone. On one play, he anticipated a Russian forward's attempt at a breakout and countered by closing in and using his stick to separate the puck. He showed awareness in the defensive end, using his wide frame to keep players on the outside, this allowed Keinanen to see the ice from the point. Although Russia scored 6 goals, none of them were a result of a screened shot and part of that was due to Rasanen's consistent defensive effort. Offensively, he didn't have too many opportunities, however on one sequence he showed the ability to feint his point shot, which gave him room to cut around his opponent and get a good-looking wrist shot off. He was solid but wasn't dynamic or offensively threatening with the exception of the play mentioned.

FIN #3 RD Loponen, Kalle (2019) – Loponen played on the top defensive pairing with Rasanen but struggled for much of the game. His difficulties were primarily in the neutral zone, where his gap control and inability to read transitional play got him in trouble. Two specific sequences demonstrated this, as Gushchin was rushing the puck, he failed to assess the Russians speed and due to his short gap distance, he was exposed, leading to a breakaway goal against. The other play was similar, his spacing didn't allow him an opportunity to recover defensively, leading to an odd-man rush. His poor play continued in the third when he took a hooking penalty just over his defensive blueline. The plus for him, was that he executed several first passes. He was caught behind the play for much of the game but was better yesterday against Canada Red.

FIN #5 LD Holtinkoski, Aapo (2019) – Holtinkoski was effective at rushing the puck while playing on the third unit. His best sequences started from behind his net, he was good at assessing his breakout options and then using plus acceleration and a good top gear to move the puck up the ice. He was frustrating the Russian players by alleviating pressure using his speed, drawing a hooking penalty on one sequence and collecting loose pucks below the goal-line before Russia could establish an effective forecheck. He was also good at finding teammates with tape to tape passes in the neutral zone and read the play well today. He was noticeable out there as a puck-mover.

FIN #10 LW Aaltonen, Leevi (2019) – Aaltonen was used on the top line, the powerplay and the penalty-kill. His best attribute was his speed, he's got an explosive first step, needing only a couple of strides to get to his top gear which the Russian defense had trouble keeping up with. He was tenacious on the puck, this allowed him to play aggressively along the point during the penalty-kill and at even strength. On one penalty-kill sequence, he anticipated the pass and used his acceleration to close the distance on a surprised Russian defenseman who was stripped off the puck by Aaltonen. Although his defensive awareness was on display, his offensive awareness was mixed. After gaining a step on MIronov by driving wide down the left side of the slot, he failed to realize that he had caught Tiuvilin flat-footed; what should have been a breakaway opportunity turned into a shot from the high-slot, which resulted in a routine stop. On the powerplay, he wasn't utilizing his teammates enough, opting for ineffective wrist shots from the point without heavy traffic. That been said, he still used his speed to create chances for himself. He has plus tools and stood out but he was trying to do too much by himself.

FIN #15 LC Saarela, Antti (2019) – Saarela showed two-way ability, while also been inconsistent. He had a tremendous backcheck, where he realized his Finnish teammate had lost a step on his man, so he rushed the player down and stick-checked the puck, causing a turnover. He also was awarded a penalty-shot which he capitalized on. He came down the right side of the slot and buried a quick wrister short-side on Sartakov. He was looking for Sartakov to move when he started drifting laterally slightly and this gave him the room he needed. Similar to yesterday, he showed some highly technical plays but hasn't been making them on a shift-to-shift basis.

Russia –

RUS #23 LD Mironov, Ilia (2019) – Mironov was on the top defensive pairing and top powerplay unit. Mironov was more engaged physically in the defensive zone today than he was against Sweden. He was good at defending 1-on-1 and pressured Finland by using his reach and weight. During one sequence, he lost his stick, but took over the play with his frame and strength by aggressively checking three different opponents around the goal-line. His skating could use some technical improvements as his knee bend didn't allow him to push off with as much power as I feel he could have, however he still gets around the ice well enough for his size and this allowed him to make transition plays up the ice. Although he got his shot through traffic at the blueline, nothing was very threatening.

RUS #7 LD Shaposhnikov, Aleksandr (2019) – Aleksandr was featured on the bottom defensive pairing for Russia while doing an excellent job of shutting down the offense of Finland. His ability to read the play in his own end was a plus and he demonstrated this with multiple puck-on-stick deflections. During one sequence, Aaltonen rushed into the slot off a turnover and had a high-percentage shot that Sartakov had little time to square up on, however Shaposhnikov reacted quickly and reached into the lane, causing what should have been a scoring chance into a puck-deflection. Despite his 5'10 height, he's broad and used his frame to keep Finnish players from driving wide or getting many rebound opportunities. He was offensively disengaged, simply shooting the puck deep along the boards when he had possession, however he stood out defensively.

RUS #19 RW Podkolzin, Vasily (2019) – Podkolzin was one of the more dynamic forwards yesterday, and again today he displayed dynamic qualities. Podkolzin showed plus skating against Finland, his mechanics are good and his edges allowed him to come over the neutral zone while cutting through traffic. His lateral skating is fluid as well, and on the first goal, he skated over the slot, used a subtle feint before moving laterally, changing the angle of his shot, which he sniped on the far post. It was highly technical and he generated power behind it. On the powerplay, he wasn't using his passing ability as much as he was in the previous game, however he was taking the puck to the net and generated a couple of high-percentage shots from the top of the slot. He had a great defensive sequence. A Finnish defenseman used a feint and Podkolzin bit by dropping to a knee, however he recovered quickly and threw his body back into the shooting lane which gave him the block. He was a step ahead of the play out there.

RUS #15 RW Gushchin, Danil (2020) – Guschin played on the 2nd line, the top powerplay unit and the penalty-kill. He's a small player, standing 5'8, 154 but his acceleration allows him to separate himself from larger players. His top gear is good, taking off on a breakaway where the very mobile Aaltonen couldn't catch up on the backcheck. I thought he was ineffective against Sweden on the powerplay, but today he was better at mixing up his passing by skating across the right circle and delivering wrist-shots through traffic. His first goal of the game, while not on the powerplay, was a quick snap-shot through a screen at the right circle. His second goal of the game came short-handed and was impressive. He separated himself from the Finnish defense and scored off a wrist-shot far side, he didn't give Piiroinen any tells on the play. He was dominant tonight, scoring three goals while adding an assist which should be emphasized since he was one of the younger players.

RUS #24 LC Safonov, Ilya (2019) – Although Ilya was the 4th line center, he had two excellent sequences leaving me wanting to see him out there more often. The first play demonstrated that he knows how to use his big 6'2 frame, as he angled himself into the side of a Finnish defenseman, cutting hard to the net and delivering a backhand shot far-side that rung off the post. The second play was high-end, he transitioned the puck from the neutral zone and aggressively cut through heavy traffic by using an inside-outside move, giving him a dangerous scoring chance near the crease. He attacked the net and showed skill

Final Score 6-4 Russia

Czech Republic vs Canada White, World Under-17 Hockey Challenge, November 7, 2017

Canada -

CAN #1 G Gauthier, Taylor (2019) - Gauthier was consistent between the pipes today for Canada white, as he stopped 25 of 27 shots. He's not the tallest goalie, standing at 6'0, however his frame is broad and he was good at cutting down angles and reading shots that were directed towards the net. He had a couple of nice recovery saves in-tight around his crease and was good at smothering loose pucks. His best save came from a high-slot slapshot off Lang's stick which he caught. His blocker side wasn't as effective as his glove side and his reflexes looked average but his frame combined with his ability to cut down angles and absorb rebounds compensated for this.

CAN #6 LD Lee, Jake (2019) - Lee displayed a solid two-way game in today's match up against the Czech's. Despite having a misplay at his own blueline where he threw an errant pass directly on the tape of a Czech forwards stick, he consistently moved the puck around the boards both on the penalty kill and at even strength. Another aspect of his game was his physicality, he finished his checks consistently. In the offensive zone, he scored after recognizing that the short-side was open on Malik and used a quick wrist shot to beat him. He didn't display any dynamic qualities but he stood out.

CAN #4 LD Bellamy, Jaxon (2019) - Bellamy played a great defensive game for Canada white. His instincts were good, he was aware when forecheckers were pressuring him and handled that pressure well, delivering several quality passes to his defensive partner and teammates without panicking. He's a big kid, standing 6'3, and this allowed him to angle the Czech's away from the slot area, his speed is average though, he doesn't generate much power out of the gate, however his defensive reads allowed him to maintain position and not get caught behind the play. His offensive game didn't stand out, but he did get an assist after his shot from the point created a rebound goal, his celebration was great too.

CAN #22 LC Pelletier, Jakob (2019) - Pelletier showed a high-level of awareness and anticipated the play around the crease against the Czech's. He centered the top line for Canada today, however he wasn't the driver of his line or the main puck distributor. What he did display was the ability to find loose pucks off rebounds. Both his goals came in heavy traffic where he anticipated where the puck would be after rebounds, resulting in two goals. The second goal was a wrist-shot that was well placed above Malik's blocker. Considering his slight stature at 5'8, it's impressive to see him do well against larger defenders around the crease. Despite his goals, there was inconsistencies on a shift-to-shift basis.

CAN #16 RW Clarke, Graeme (2019) - Clarke was the most effective player today for Canada White, while been the primary driver of the top-line. Clarke had several high end transitional plays where he demonstrated poise and patience with the puck. One specific sequence stood out more than the others, he weaved through heavy traffic after coming over the offensive-blueline, slowed the play down, and delivered a perfect backhand no-look pass under pressure. His vision and offensive zone reads were excellent, resulting in 4 assists.

CAN #11 RW McMichael, Connor (2019) - McMichael played with energy today on the 2nd line. He skates hard and his top speed was above average, which allowed him to aggressively forecheck effectively. He was also capable of making high-end plays, one that stood out occurred behind the net, where he made a no-look spinning backhand pass into the slot for a quality scoring chance. His goal displayed good hand-eye coordination as he tipped the puck out of mid-air off a missed shot that went off the backboards.

Czech Republic -

CZE #30 G Malik, Nick (2020) - Malik allowed 5 goals on 25 shots which caused him to be pulled, however he demonstrated potential on the ice. He's not the biggest goalie, standing at 6 feet but his lateral movement and reflexes were impressive, on one play he pushed across the slot and got his blocker up in time to stop what looked like a sure goal. His defense in-front of him had several breakdowns and the majority of goals he did let in were off rebounds. He didn't look technically refined and he did allow several rebounds that he should have absorbed but you can't teach the kind of explosiveness he showed out there.

CZE #22 LW Lang, Martin (2019) - Lang was the most dangerous offensive threat for the Czech's today, displaying a high-level skill set. His first goal was the most impressive goal of the game. He skated over the left face-off circle, used a head feint to fake a pass and then wired a hard wrist-shot short side, Gauthier had little chance on the goal. The shot was highly technical, he masked his placement and there was no tells for Gauthier to pick up. His second goal of the game was very different than his first, as he found space between the Canadian defense and used quick hands to get Gauthier to bite early, giving him room along the ice to tuck it in. He almost scored on two other offensive sequences, one along the goal-line when he was planted at the side of the crease and another after getting time to deliver a hard slapshot at the top of the slot. He scored two goals on the powerplay while also playing on the top line for the Czech's.

CZE #15 RW Toman, Matej (2019) - Although Toman didn't get any points today, he was noticeable while playing on the 2nd line. His vision was good and he was capable of slowing the play down in the offensive zone, this allowed him to find his passing options, resulting in some quality passes to his teammates.

Final Score 7 - 2 Canada White

Canada Black vs Unites States, World Under-17 Hockey Challenge, November 7, 2017

Canada -

CAN #30 G Maier, Nolan (2019) - Maier stood on his head for Canada Black and kept his team in the game after getting out-shot 48 to 18. He's not the biggest goalie but his ability to transition from his butterfly to a standing position combined with his ability to track rebounds allowed him to make a couple of excellent saves off high-danger shots. His best save occurred after he did a lunging split after giving up a rebound near the crease, he showed flexibility and quick reflexes on the play. He started to fatigue in the third period, which resulted in four goals by the U.S, however there wasn't a goal he let in that could classify as a soft goal, they were all redirection, breakaway and rebound goals. Although he let in 5 goals, he was one of Canada Blacks best players.

CAN #2 LD Robertson, Matthew (2019) - Robertson had a mixed game today for Canada Black while playing on the top defensive pairing and the powerplay. He's got size, standing at 6'3, weighing 194 and used all of it to level Judd Caulfield as he attempted a move over the Canadian blueline. This play stood out due to Matthews physical strength and his ability to read Caulfields deceiving movement, which the rest of his blueline was unable to deal with. Unfortunately, despite a sold physical effort, the majority of the U.S team was able to cut wide on him while driving down lanes and he didn't' clear as many loose pucks from the front of the net as he could have given his size. He had one glaring turnover at the offensive blueline, which was unforced and allowed a breakaway chance against, otherwise his passing ability was okay. He did manage to collect a secondary assist with the man advantage but overall he had defensive lapses and wasn't effective offensively.

CAN #14 C Dach, Kirby (2019) - Dach was very good at distributing the puck on the powerplay and transitioning into the offensive zone. He's got size and can skate, he used this to his advantage to cut through traffic and distribute to his teammates. On the powerplay, he was very effective while playing on the half-wall. On one sequence he cut across the offensive blueline, then made a great pass through traffic in the slot that landed on the tape of Mutala's stick for the opening goal. His goal on the powerplay resulted from a redirection off a skate after attempting a pass near the crease. He was the driver of his line, showing good playmaking ability, leading to a three-point night.

CAN #17 RW Mutala, Sasha (2019) - Mutala wasn't as offensively dangerous as I've seen him in past games but still had a powerplay goal and some quality scoring chances. His goal came off a beautiful feed from Dach on the powerplay. He was positioned well and didn't need any time to settle the puck down before putting it in the back of the net, the release was good. He had a tremendous sequence late while Canada Black was trying to tie the game, by driving down the left wing and using quick hands in-tight to bypass multiple defenders, giving him a high-end scoring chance in-front of the net. He had his moments but wasn't consistent on a shift-to-shift basis.

CAN #20 RW Mercer, Dawson (2020) - Mercer played with his heart on his sleeve and was rewarded for his efforts with a late goal. His defensive reads were excellent and he needed to use them consistently as Canada was out-paced by the U.S today. His most noticeable defensive sequence involved him making a lunging block and then following that up with a solid hit. He was aggressive and relentless at the blueline and this allowed him to capitalize on a turnover by the U.S, getting a partial breakaway. Although he was limited to 4th line minutes, he still had some offensive chances, one resulting in a goal, where he found a soft spot in the slot and buried his chance. He was used on the penalty-kill and stood out despite limited minutes on the 4th line.

Unites States -

U.S #32 LD York, Cam (2019) - Despite going pointless, York had a good two-way game today while playing on the top pairing and top powerplay unit. Defensively, his positioning was mixed, he was good at tracking the play along the boards, although he had a tendency to place himself too high, leaving his opponents open around the slot area and around the net on a couple of plays. His best defensive sequence came on the powerplay after Mercer skated up the ice for what should have been a great breakaway chance. York had other ideas though by using explosive skating to backcheck and dive in-front of Mercer's shot, resulting in a deflection out of play. The recovery was impressive. Offensively, he wasn't overly mobile along the blueline and he didn't feint a lot but he didn't have to and that's because his release point on his wrist shot was exceptional. His shot came off his stick before the Canadian defense could get into position and this made him dangerous. He rung one of his shots off the crossbar and the shots that were stopped were not easily absorbed, allowing his team additional scoring opportunities. It's one of the better wrist-shots I've seen this tournament.

U.S #38 LD Fensore, Domenick (2019) - Fensore stood out due to his excellent mobility. He's extremely small for a defenseman, standing 5'6, however his four-directional skating makes up for it, he was able to transition from offense to defense and visa-versa effortlessly. This resulted in him transitioning the puck up the ice on several sequences. Although he's small, he wasn't afraid to finish checks, but I wouldn't classify him as someone who plays bigger than his size based off today's viewing. Offensively, he didn't have too many opportunities, however he did have one of the best primary assists of the night. He skated down the left wing and used a wrist-shot feint before threading a pass to Caufield for a redirection goal.

U.S #43 LC Hughes, Jack (2019) - Hughes wasn't dominant in today's game but he set up his teammates consistently, resulting in a primary powerplay assist. He's got poise while carrying the puck and he used it to navigate through Canada's defense both at even strength and on the powerplay. He had several tape-to-tape passes along the goal-line and in the slot. His vision and offensive awareness were both extremely good, this allowed him to cycle effectively which resulted in the Canadian defense getting worn down over time. I wish he used his shot more than he did, there was a couple of times that he had room in the slot but decided to look for his passing options. He seemed to lack confidence with it after fanning on an attempt in the slot. He was still noticeable and the tools are top-end.

U.S #59 RW Caufield, Cole (2019) - Caufield's a diminutive winger, standing 5'6, additionally he's not the fastest skater for his size, however his ability to read the play in the offensive zone made him a threat when he was on the ice. He played on the top powerplay and was very effective while playing the left side of the half-wall. He had several high-end passing plays in the slot and was dangerous along the goal-line. Despite his size, he was aggressive at the sides of the net, continuously looking for rebound opportunities. His first goal came as a result of his positioning. He was stationed on the left side of the slot and received a beautiful pass that he one-timed into the back of the net. His second goal was a redirection off another great pass by his defenseman. On both goals, his awareness of what his teammate were going to do with the puck and his positioning were on point. He finished with two goals and an assist today.

U.S #41 RW Caulfield, Judd (2019) - Caulfield was dominant on the puck, while driving the best line in today's game. He's a big winger, standing 6'2, 200 pounds and this needs to be emphasized because he has the agility of a player who's 5'8 due to his edgework. One of the sequences that highlighted this occurred early in the game. He had the puck at the blueline, calmly spun off a check and then feinted going counter-clockwise, when the defenseman bit, he swung back to his forehand and skated down the right face-off circle, he then made an additional move by swinging his body past another player. It took three different players to try and knock him off the puck. His passing was good as well, and this combined with his size and elusive skating made him a nightmare to match up against. He scored a breakaway goal, showing a soft set of hands and angling his body to defend the puck from the backchecker. Caulfield's tools combined with his frame make him an intriguing prospect.

U.S #49 LW Boldy, Matthew (2019) - Boldy showed good chemistry while playing with Caulfield and Turcotte on the 2nd line. He wasn't having much success early, as he was relying too heavily on his shot, which he was having difficulty getting on net. However, in the second period, he started using his vision. On one sequence, he drove past a defenseman along the boards near the goal-line and then delivered a perfect tape-to-tape pass, resulting in Caufield's first goal of the game. He scored a goal off a rebound to the right side of the net while parked in-front early in the third, which turned out to be the catalyst for the U.S's offense. He showed the ability to adapt when things weren't going his way out there and turned it around.

Finals score 5-4 United States

Finland vs. Czech Republic, U-18 Five Nations, November 8th, 2017

FIN #37 D Utunen, Toni (2018) - Utunen who Captains Finland, demonstrated solid defensive reads while playing on the top PowerPlay unit. The two-way defenseman's defensive awareness was good today. He plays a safe game by not pinching often and looking to get the puck off his stick quickly if he's dealing with a scenario where he could potentially turn the puck over along the blueline. This lead to him shooting the puck on net as opposed to looking for his open teammates occasionally but it also made sure he had a relatively mistake free game. His most impressive sequence occurred when Kropacek came flying over his blueline, the puck was bouncing and Utunen recognized that if he waited for it to settle, he could potentially get burned as Kropacek could tap it past him; to counteract this he used his hand-eye to hit the puck down to the ice out of mid-air giving him more time to get a pass to his teammate. This play was subtle but it showed the level of awareness Utunen possesses when gauging his time and space to make a play under pressure in his own zone. He transitioned the puck out of his zone effectively, using his thick frame to protect the puck and made some good first passes to move the puck up the ice.

FIN #36 RW Siikanen, Patrik (2018) - Opened the game with a huge hit along the boards that caused a turnover leading to the opening goal, showed good acceleration heading up the ice with Kivenmaki on the play. He missed a couple of quality scoring chances when receiving passes across the slot by rushing the release when he had time to settle it down. He had physical moments but was otherwise pretty quiet.

FIN #32 C Kivenmaki, Otto (2018) - Had separational speed on his breakaway goal after an errant pinch by Kleiner, went forehand to backhand and roofed it over Dostal's glove. Later in the first he had another explosive play where he flew over the neutral zone and into the offensive zone, his pass to his teammate was a bit off on the play but the speed is impressive. Showed good offensive instincts where he anticipated a board battle sequence, then used his skating to come away with the puck before passing it off to the point. His entries are effortless considering his speed, his passing ability was mixed however. some of his passes weren't clean and led to turnovers. He was noticeable due to his transitional ability.

FIN #7 D Ketola, Juuso (2018) - Ketola had a difficult time getting his shot through traffic today but showed the ability to make high-end plays. He attempted several slapshots through traffic but wasn't recognizing when his lane was open or closed and wasn't using feints to force the opposition to re-open his shooting lanes. He did have a terrific play at the offensive blueline where he recognized that the puck was going back out of the zone, he reached out in full speed, managed to control it then spun back into position and delivered a hard pass into the slot for a scoring chance in-front of the net. He was aggressive at closing his gaps on some sequences and was active in his own end.

FIN #23 C Petman, Ville (2018) - He wasn't consistent on a shift-to-shift and his line didn't get much done offensively. That been said, he did have a fantastic sequence that showed his puck skills and elusive skating while playing in-tight along the boards. As he was involved in the board battle, he tapped the puck ahead of the defender, then jumped to the side, grabbed the puck, spun off the check from the defender, then got tripped but still managed to maintain puck possession before passing it back up to the half-wall.

FIN #18 RW Maki, Eetu (2018) - Wasn't consistent but had some moments. His best play came down below the Czech goal-line where he spun-off a check, then passed the puck into the slot and directly on the tape of his teammate for a scoring chance, he had very little time but the execution was on point. On another play, he drove down the right-wing and made an aggressive move to the net resulting in a scoring chance.

FIN #25 D Seppala, Peetro (2018) - Seppala demonstrated excellent transitional ability. His skating is superb, he skates in four directions effortlessly, he's got a fluid, yet powerful stride and was capable of assessing open space to take advantage of it. On several plays, he would start in his own end, evade forechecking pressure and rush the puck up the ice before passing it off to his teammates. He had the cleanest entries out of any player on the ice. Another element to his game is the ability to make plays at top speeds and under pressure, he was excellent at evading pressure below his goal line while making crisp and accurate passes.

CZE #2 G Dostal, Lukas (2018) - Dostal came up with some big saves at critical times while standing on his head in the third period and making a breakaway save in overtime. He let in a goal early that went high-glove, I would have liked to have seen him be more aggressive on the breakaway sequence but he plays a more conservative, reactionary style. That style lead to him making several excellent saves off cross-crease passes, where he had to push across and use his dexterity to kick away scoring chances. Throughout the game he was able to track the puck off rebounds around his goal-line, one one sequence after giving up a rebound, a shot was fired to his right side along the ice, he let go of his conservative style and lunged back with his glove, making one of his better stops. In overtime, he stopped a breakaway blocker side, he was fairly deep but his reflexes were up to the task. Not too long after that stop, Jenik scored the overtime winner. He was a big reason why the Czechs came away with a victory and also showed the ability to make break his own style when the play calls for it.

CZE #3 D Kleiner, Jakub (2019) - Had a bad read at the blueline, where he made an aggressive stick-check but the puck ended up out of the zone, putting him out of position and giving Kivenmaki a breakaway goal. He did make up for this shorty after by standing a player up and using his reach to steal the puck, then transitioning it back up the ice. His defensive reads were mixed overall though and he didn't offer any solid offensive plays today.

CZE #12 D Seemann, Vit (2018) - Had a good transitional sequence. He received a pass with multiple Finnish players coming in on him, eluded the pressure by making a subtle shoulder feint, then took off down the left side of the ice before getting the puck in deep and making a spinning backhand pass to his teammate. He transitioned the puck in stretches and had a nice blocking sequence down in-front of the net during a critical 5-on-3 penalty kill sequence.

CZE #13 LW Lauko, Jakub (2018) - He struggled throughout the game, showing a lack of awareness in both the offensive and defensive zone which contributed to his line been offensively stagnant. He had a poor sequence after failing to recognize where he should be in the offensive zone after his teammate pinched down the half-wall to keep the puck in, he then got the puck in the neutral zone, turned it over and fell while trying to backcheck. Late in the first he had a better sequence where he caused a turnover at his blueline and rushed the puck up ice, giving him a shot on net, although I would have preferred him going around the net and waiting for support. Defensively, he's aggressive at the blueline, which gave him his two best plays of the night. The first been a tremendous block where he put his body on the line and paid the price as he was hurt on the play, however he did return. The second sequence involved him seperating the puck from a Finnish forward at the blueline and then passing it up the ice for a breakaway. His ability to read the play is very inconsistent. He recognized passing options occasionally when the play wasn't at even strength, however when his lanes were clogged, he had tunnel vision and would try and do everything by himself, causing him to turn the puck over. He's got excellent tools but his lack of intelligence on both sides of the ice overshadowed them.

CZE #14 LW Jenik, Jan (2018) - Jenik was one the best Czech forward today while also been the youngest 2018 draft eligible player. The attributes that stood out the most tonight were his ability to make high-level plays while protecting the puck under pressure. This was demonstrated during a sequence at the end of the first where he showed poise with the puck while walking the line, he had limited time and space but delivered a clean pass. Shortly after that play, he displayed good hustle in getting to a loose puck and shot it back in towards the right faceoff circle. Later in the game he was able to cut to the net by guarding the puck on his backhand and using his edges to drive into the slot for a scoring chance. He scored the overtime winner by collecting his own rebound after his wrist shot hit a skate which changed the angle, he capitalized on this by shooting the puck five hole through Annunen.

CZE #11 LW Kropacek, Voltech (2018) - Kropacek showed good speed while playing on the third line. His best sequence involved him picking up the puck from Lauko's chip pass and then exploding down the wing, where he wind-milled past an opponent with one arm and used strong edges to create a partial breakaway for himself, he was too close to the net to really get a quality shot off though. Had a great backchecking play where he cleanly stripped the puck and transitioned it back into the offensive zone. Showed good defensive awareness in the neutral zone after recognizing a drop pass and taking it away from Finland. His defensive awareness was impressive and he can skate.

CZE #15 RW Plasek, Karel (2018) - Scored a powerplay goal around the crease by jamming at the puck, it was a gritty goal that he worked hard for. Almost had his second of the night after trailing the play and positioning himself behind defensive coverage, setting up a one timer that was stopped. He has a lanky frame so he's unable to generate too much power in his legs but once he gets going his top speed allows him to move the puck. He showed good chemistry out there with Jenik on the 2nd line today and helped set up the overtime winner after spinning off an aggressive Finnish player and passing to the high slot, resulting in the goal. He's got to gain some strength but it will come.

Final Score: Czech Republic: 3 – Finland: 2 – OT

USA vs Switzerland, U-18 Five Nations, November 8th, 2017

USA #25 LD Stastney, Spencer (2018): He showed good skating abilities throughout the game rushing the puck, and quick footwork on the power play, moving his feet well and giving his teammates different options on the point. He was active on the power play; he was always in movement and did not stand still at the point. He showed good anticipation to break up passes in the neutral zone.

USA #28 LW Farabee, Joel (2018): He worked hard throughout the game and showed excellent speed and hustle. He may not be the biggest player, but Farabee played with grit and got involved in front of the net. He showed good chemistry with Wahlstrom; both of them are super creative with the puck in the offensive zone. He's a good skater and was also good today at making quick changes in directions to avoid defenders in the offensive zone.

USA #23 LD Samuelsson, Mattias (2018): It was a rough game for Samuelsson in the puck-moving department; he had some struggles moving the puck quickly and accurately in the offensive zone and on the power play. A lot of his passes were not on target, and he was not moving the puck smartly. He has a good, hard shot, but had trouble getting it through on net as the Swiss team did a good job blocking many shots today. He was physical when he needed to be, and for a big and strong defenseman, he's very strong on his skates as well.

USA #18 RW Wahlstrom, Oliver (2018): Today, Wahlstrom showed that he has a dynamic skillset. One underrated part of his game remains his play along the boards, where he's very strong, and more often than not he came back from the corner with the puck. He possesses an excellent wrist shot, as he showed by scoring USA 2nd goal of the game, and later on in the shootout. His shot is accurate, and he gets it off very quickly. He is very dangerous with the puck on his stick, has elite puck skills, and more often than not he tried to challenge players one-on-one today.

USA #5 LD Samuelsson, Adam (2018): Samuelsson is huge, but for a player of that size, he moves well enough on the ice. He likes to play a physical game when he can, but didn't go out of his way today for big hits. He had some issues with his decision-making in the first period, but was good enough the rest of the game. He didn't excel at moving the puck on the power play, but made simple passes. He had problems on one shift, where he was beaten wide easily by a Swiss forward because he couldn't handle the speed of said forward, who blew right past him.

USA #17 C Gruden, John (2018): Gruden was doing some of the dirty work on his line; retrieving pucks in the corners and acting defensively responsible, which allowed Farabee and Wahlstrom to have more offensive freedom. He skated well and provided his line with some good puck pursuit and energy in this game. He was a good complimentary player with his two ultra-skilled linemates.

USA #15 RD Wilde, Bode (2018): There was some good and some bad from Wilde today, which has become a recurrent theme this season. In the first period, he had some bad turnovers including one on the Swiss first goal of the game where he threw the puck away for no good reason, then lost a battle behind the net which eventually led to the goal. In the 2nd period, he played a more simple game on the back end and was moving the puck well on the power play. He also showed some dynamic qualities, beating guys one-on-one to create himself a scoring chance from the point. He was rushing the puck a bit more in the 2nd half of the game, and playing a smarter game. Although on the power play he had trouble getting his shot through to the net, a lot of USA defensemen had this issue in this game, as the Swiss forwards really did well blocking point shots. Late in the 3rd period, he made a great feed to Wahlstrom to send him on a breakaway, which gave USA a 2-1 lead.

USA #19 LD Miller, K'Andre (2018): A bit of a sluggish first period (much like the rest of team USA), but Miller started showing off his tools in the 2nd period. He has good speed and showed it in his attempt to rush the puck; he has good acceleration and good enough speed to beat defenders wide. Defending one-on-one, he was aggressive and quick to put pressure on the puck-carrier. He created a couple of turnovers by stripping the puck-carrier of the puck. In his zone, he was a bit wild in the first period, but played a more poised and calm game in the 2nd and 3rd periods. He didn't hesitate to take shots on net in the game; he has a quick and hard shot.

USA #10 RD Emberson, Ty (2018): Early on in the game, he had some tough moments when he had to play on the left side for a bit. He had trouble handling the puck when receiving passes along the boards and moving pucks out. He showed good skating abilities and footwork during the game, playing physical along the boards when need be, and showed a good compete level in his zone.

USA #20 C Pivonka, Jake (2018): Pivonka was quite good at escaping defenders by using his quickness and making quick turns to get away from his coverage. He showed some good smarts all over the ice, making simple plays such as taking a defenseman's spot after one had pinched in deep in the offensive zone. In addition, he showed good support deep in the defensive zone, acting like a 3rd defenseman out there. He liked to distribute the puck from the half-wall position on the power play, showing good vision. He didn't show the good shot of a goal scorer though, as it was not a hard shot and often found itself in the chest area of the goaltender.

USA #24 RW Giles, Patrick (2018): Giles used his size in front of the net and along the boards. He showed some good smarts and vision, making good passes in the offensive zone. I liked how patient he was with the puck, which gave his linemates time to get open. He was used on the power play in front of the net, where he was willing to take some punishment and was tough to move from. He's big and strong, although his skating will need to get better, as he doesn't generate a ton of speed.

Baie-Comeau Drakkar vs Halifax Mooseheads, November 9th 2017

HFX 11 RW Zadina, Filip (2018): one of the weaker games Zadina has had in the Q thus far... didn't seem to be clicking for him as he fanned on a couple of great chances to score near the goal... a tough night defensively as he whiffed on a breakout pass in his own end leading to a bad giveaway that ended up in his net for the 1st goal... seemed a bit hesitant to do the work on the defensive side of the puck, at one point staying deep in the offensive zone when he should have covered a pinching defender... that said, his consistency is impressive as even on a "bad" night he found ways to affect the play... his positioning, skating ability, and nose for the net create opportunities for him to score every night... has great on-ice awareness and seems to know who's going where and how quickly at all times... on one play, he was first to a loose puck around the attacking blueline on a rush, but quickly read that he'd have a man on him fast, so he poked it to an open linemate, keeping the play alive and leading to a couple of Halifax chances... plays a very refined game, he reads the play well and is proactive rather than reactive, always seeming to take as few strides as possible to reach his destination; not in a lazy way, just good anticipation

HFX 14 LD McIsaac, Jared (2018): McIsaac continues his strong play in recent weeks in this one... with seven defenders in the lineup, McIsaac was arguably the most effective... made some great outlet passes and saw the ice well... possesses a quick, accurate wrist shot that can find its way through traffic... fired one wrist shot that was much harder than I'm used to seeing from him... doesn't use his slapshot often... has great anticipation and frequently uses it while defending in the neutral zone, stepping up to intercept passes... used that anticipation to deliver a thundering open ice check in the neutral zone in this one... showed a real control over his part of the ice all night, using his great skating and stickchecking to force turnovers and break up plays

HFX 19 LC Groulx, Benoit-Olivier (2018): didn't have a particularly notable night in a game where the Mooseheads struggled to find their feet a bit... skated well and got involved physically... was hesistant moving the puck out of his zone on 3rd BC goal and got stripped... a responsible player in his own zone with the anticipation and skill to make a quick transition to the attack... always seems to have purpose on the ice, knows where to be both offensively and defensively and keeps his feet moving... scored on the PP, finished with 2 pts and named 2nd star

HFX 1 G Gravel, Alexis (2018): turned in a solid outing in his first action in 2 1/2 weeks after injury... bailed out his team on a number of occassions when turnovers led to chances against... strong lateral movement in this game in particular, getting across the crease and tracking the puck well to make some important stops... Mooseheads were sloppy with the puck on all three goals leading to odd man rushes and quick chances for BC... Gravel made some key saves late in the game as the Mooseheads were pressing for an equalizer... a big blocking-style goalie with good athleticism

BAC 9 LC Fortier, Gabriel (2018): showed off his speed and skill at various points in this game... can really generate some speed on the rush, though it doesn't stand out as much as I might have expected when he was in junior... a good passer who can make some difficult plays... landed a nice backhand saucer pass on a teammate's stick through a defender's legs on the rush... also showed off the saucer pass to spring a linemate through the neutral zone... a tenacious skater, showed good hustle on the backcheck after creating an offensive chance to get physical and force a turnover in the netural zone, then leading the rush back on the attack and creating a chance.

Oshawa Generals at Ottawa 67's, November 10th, 2017

OTT #71 F Clark, Kody (2018) - Clark was effective in the offensive zone again tonight, putting up 3 primary assists. In the first period, he wheeled up the sideboards in the offensive zone and set up Travis Barron in front of the net with a perfect tape-to-tape pass for Ottawa's first goal of the game. He demonstrated quick feet entering the offensive zone with the puck and showed a willingness to go to the dirty areas in the offensive zone in order to battle for the puck. In the second period on the Powerplay, he faked a shot forcing the goalie to come out to cut down the angle and made a pass backdoor for Ottawa's second goal of the game. In the first period, his puck handling skills were on display, as he made a nice move to pull the puck back to change the angle of a pass and make a clean pass off to Travis Barron for his third assist of the game.

OTT #88 D Bahl, Kevin (2018) - Bahl played an aggressive style and was tough to play against in his own end throughout the game. In the first period he showed tremendous strength behind his own net to fend off a check and make the pass cleanly and accurately to his defence partner. He was consistently difficult to play against in front of his own net, battling hard against some of Oshawa's large forwards and boxing out players like Serron Noel effectively on most occasions. He doesn't seem to have that explosive acceleration to separate from the play but he moves quickly around the ice once in stride. He was very physical in his own end down low on the penalty kill and played aggressively on the defensive side of the puck throughout the game.

OSH #61 F McShane, Allan (2018) - Allan McShane was dominant offensively in Oshawa's losing effort tonight. In the first period, he exhibited a high skillset to drop to his knee and put the rebound goal in the back of the net up high on a quick play on the powerplay. He consistently does a good job of finding the open space on the Powerplay by moving his feet and remaining engaged, anticipating where the puck will be and finding the open passing lanes to remain open. He saw some time killing penalties on a 5-on-3 for Ottawa, where he dropped down to the ice to block a shot from the point. In the second period, he had his second goal of the game, showing off his quick release by snapping the puck over the goalie far side, hitting the post and in with a perfectly placed shot. Later in the period, he was set up on a beautiful give-and-go play to score his second goal in the period. He was dynamic offensively with his speed and shooting ability throughout the game, and easily could have scored a few more goals if he got the right bounces. He is quick on his feet once he's in stride and did a good job of leading the rush up the middle at one point in the third period. At one point in the third period, he showed strong hand-eye coordination by knocking down a clearing attempt with his stick oon the Powerplay to maintain Oshawa's offensive zone time. Later on the Powerplay, he led another quick rush up the ice and was dominant with the puck, stick handling through multiple defenders and getting another shot off with a quick release, missing the net by a small margin far-side.

OSH #8 F Noel, Serron (2018) - Noel is a big body forward who battles hard and likes to plant himself in front of the net in the offensive zone. He does a good job of screening the goalie while following the play and battled hard against Ottawa's defencemen to maintain his positioning in front of the net. In the second period, he showed some offensive skill by setting up his linemate on the backdoor with a hard, accurate pass, but the goalie made a big stop to keep him off the scoresheet.

OSH #90 F Antropov, Danil (2018) - Antropov had a strong game for Oshawa, playing a consistently physical style and contributing with some offensive opportunities. He is a large player at the OHL level and uses his body to his advantage in terms of his physical playing style. He skates well for a player of his size, and has a smooth stride which makes him effective on the forecheck. He was consistently making hard, accurate passes on the rush and demonstrated quick, smart decision making. For example, at one point in the first period, he received a pass by immediately one-timing it up the ice tape-to-tape to his teammate, showing strong awareness of where his linemates were on the ice. He finished the game with a second assist on McShane's third goal of the game.

Sweden vs USA, U-18 Five Nations' Tournament, November 10th, 2017

SWE #1 G Lindbom,Olaf (2018): Was named the player of the game for Sweden with the win and shutout. He was calm and confident in his crease, making every save look easy with his good positioning. He has a good mix of size and athletic abilities. He did a good job tracking pucks with traffic in front of him, including a couple of nice saves off deflections right in front of him.

SWE #10 LD Ginning, Adam (2018): He showed some good skating abilities when skating with the puck, including a good, powerful stride that generated some good speed. Agility and footwork are still a work in progress for Ginning, and those elements would help him be more efficient in his own zone. He was physical at times in his own zone as well. With the puck, his decision-making was a bit slow, and that got him into trouble when he was under pressure. He'll need to address that facet of his game.

SWE #5 RD Johansson, Filip (2018): It was a solid but not spectacular game for Johansson today, who showed a good, low, hard shot from the point which resulted in Sweden's 2nd goal of the game. He was moving pucks well in the transition game, with a simple first pass out of his zone. He played in all situations today: even-strength, power play and penalty kill.

SWE #7 RD Lundkvist, Nils (2018): Solid game from Lundkvist today, who was moving his feet well and making quick passes out of his zone. He showed good things when rushing the puck out of his zone; he has good speed and agility to avoid opponents in the neutral zone. A bit on the small side; in his zone versus bigger players, he can encounter some difficulties, but he was Sweden's best puck-mover today on the back end.

SWE #15 LW Hallander, Filip (2018): Hallander played a simple North American game today. He was playing hard along the boards and went to the net as often as he could to finish his plays. A good-sized winger, he used his size well to win puck battles and to protect the puck along the boards. He was skating well while he was in possession of the puck today; he may not be a high-end skater, but his speed was above-average today.

SWE #11 C Back, Oskar (2018): He showed some good smarts throughout this game at both ends of the ice. Early in the game, while killing a penalty, he stripped Mattias Samuelsson of the puck at the blueline with his quick stick to create a breakaway chance for himself while shorthanded. He's a good player along the boards; his puck-protection is good because he uses his size well to shield opponents away. He also made good use of his long reach in those situations. His speed was good today, much better than what we saw in August at the Hlinka tournament. He showed decent cruising speed, as well as a quick burst to distance himself from the man covering him.

SWE #14 RW Johansson, Wilson (2019): Loved his energy and work ethic. He played on the top line with Back and Hallander. He was effective along the boards and on the forecheck. His feet are quick, and he never stops moving them. However, he didn't create much offense on his line and we didn't see a lot of high-IQ plays from him. He played on an offensive line, but played more like an energy winger.

SWE #19 RW Hoglander, Nils (2019): The youngest player on the team, Hoglander showed some feistiness during this game while battling versus much bigger defensemen in front of the USA net, and didn't back down, often coming back for more. He didn't show a lot of his talent offensively in this game, and his skating looked fine, but there was no top speed from him. His speed was just okay, and he didn't show any 2nd gear.

SWE #17 RW Berggren, Jonatan (2018): Berggren showed good skating abilities today. He has quick feet and a good burst of speed. He showed that he was capable of going wide on defensemen, and even at his size, he didn't hesitate driving the puck to the net.

USA #15 RD Wilde, Bode (2018): Player of the game honours were attributed to Wilde today. He was excellent in this game, showing his great offensive tools, but also that he can play a smart game (which has been an issue this season). He tends to overthink the game, and will make high-risk plays only to get burned by them. Today he had a chance to make those high-risk plays, but elected to be more poised with the puck and go for the simpler, safer play. He showed great puck skills on the power play, including good stickhandling prowess, and distributed the puck well on the power play. He's a smooth skater, looking effortless in a couple of rushes in the 2nd half of the game. In that second half, he was also more active rushing the puck, as USA were down by 2 goals and looking to get back in the game.

USA #10 RD Emberson, Ty (2018): Solid game for Emberson. Nothing flashy, but he was effective in more of a stay-at-home role on this team. He was tough to beat one-on-one; he has good footwork and could keep up with the speedy forwards from Sweden. He has good anticipation and timing, delivering some good hits during the game.

USA #19 LD Miller, K'Andre (2018): Miller made some good plays with the puck, had a good first pass, and was active in the offensive zone from the point. He showed good anticipation and an ability to create offensive chances by acting like a 4th forward at times in the offensive zone, not standing still on the point. He's big and strong, covering a lot of space on the ice with his reach and skating ability.

USA #23 LD Samuelsson, Mattias (2018): Samuelsson had some iffy moments with the puck, fumbling it a couple of times. One of these moments led to a breakaway chance for Sweden. However, after losing the puck, he showed a great level of commitment, coming back hard to disturb the player on the breakaway in order to stop him from taking a clean shot, also not taking a penalty on the play. When it came to defending one-on-one, Samuelsson was intimidating for the smaller Swedish forwards attempting to make their way to his side of the ice. He's powerful, and didn't lose many battles today. Outside of those few bad plays with the puck, Samuelsson made some good, hard, crisp outlet passes today.

USA #28 LW Farabee, Joel (2018): Farabee had a good showing in different facets of the game today. He had some good scoring chances, was good on the PK and was also involved in the physical game, playing a feisty game in front of the Swedish net. He showed excellent patience with the puck; often when he would rush it, he would slow down the play to give himself more options in his play-selection, as well as extra time for his linemates to get open. On the PK, we saw him block a shot and also get a breakaway chance, showing a strong, complete game.

USA #18 RW Wahlstrom, Olivier (2018): The young winger showed excellent puck skills today, including the ability to beat guys one-on-one. He was able to hold onto the puck for a long time in the offensive zone. Not only does he have great puck skills, but he can also fight off checks with his great strength. He played a bit on the point on the power play; his shot lacked some accuracy, however (mostly when he used his one-timer).

Vancouver Giants at Kelowna Rockets, November 10th, 2017

VAN #13 C Popwich, Tyler (2018) – Popwich's footwork just wasn't up to snuff tonight, he looked slow getting to loose pucks and routinely lost 50/50 foot races, he enjoys going to the net to look for rebounds and cause traffic but often during this game was late to the play. Overall laboring in his footwork he really just looked over matched in this game, when he does get the puck he can handle it with decent skill but just does everything at one slower speed. Not a factor tonight despite lining up on a scoring line.

VAN #41 RD Kannok-Leipert, Alex (2018) – An all situation player he was the top right defensemen for his team playing a pivotal role throughout this game. Stood up to anyone willing to attack the net and did a strong job of tying up sticks when opponents planted themselves around the crease, certainly made thing difficult. Made a great play by driving a check at someone who was hunting him, protected the puck and completed an entry pass. Agile through the neutral zone, showed good changes of speed and stick handled around checkers with no fear to jump into the rush; really showed a good ability to stick handle to create his own passing lanes. Feathered am excellent cross-ice pass through the slot landing in perfect position for a primary assist, all around an excellent game.

VAN #40 C Roman, Miles (2018) – Flashed his strong top speed and good acceleration throughout this game, lined up as the top center in this game and hand a variety of zone starts in all areas and situations fairing pretty well on both sides on the ice. Played at a high tempo the entire game with an impressive amount of energy and used this to attack pucks and puck carriers. Pick up 3 assists in this game 2 on the powerplay, one came off a shot he put on net and the other 2 were the result of starting out solid puck movement on 3 way passing plays. Garners attention while on the ice and easily the most noticeable player on the ice.

VAN #1 G Scott, Todd (2018) – Showed a good ability to read and react stopping Kole Lind on a breakaway after he made 2 nice moves, did a great job to stay with him. Let in a goal off a band angle that came from the corner of the ice as he wasn't tight to the post and allowed it to get pass him short side high.

KEL #24 C Topping, Kyle (2018) – Looked quicker tonight that usual (his speed seems to vary game to game) and hockey sense shined on zone entries looking elusive and knowing when to drive the puck deep or pull up and wait for teammates with speed. Coughed up a few pucks on the cycle tonight but showed good hustle on the backcheck, overall his line struggled to create tonight and lacked a little chemistry but individually his stickhandling was good and showed good effort despite staying off the score sheet.

KEL #7 RD Zabransky, Libor (2018) – During a moments when he's decisive he looked good creating offense snapping quick shots from the blueline to the net, even displaying a solid one-timer; something that hasn't been frequent in many earlier viewings. Played tight on defense and stuck close to attackers using his feet to keep pace. Made an excellent breakout pass to his Lind for breakaway. Consistency of confidence is a common theme for Zabransky, tonight he looked poised and put up one the of the better efforts in recent viewings.

KEL #1 G Porter, James (2018) – Appeared slow going side to side, couldn't get his skate planted quick enough to really explode over and cover one-times. Was showing good effort to be square to shooters and helping look big by playing out toward the top of the crease. Did let some big rebounds bounce off him into some more dangerous areas making more work for himself and his defense.

Final Score: Kelowna Rockets: 5 – Vancouver Giants: 4

Acadie-Bathurst Titan vs Blainville-Boisbriand Armada, November 11th, 2017

AB #71 C Ducharme, Justin (2018): He showed good speed down the wing, and has the ability to go wide on defensemen with great acceleration. He played at center today, which is not the best for him, as he's more useful on the wing with his speed. His decision-making when playing down the middle will need to be quicker, as he would be the puck distributor on his line.

AB #29 LD Ivan, Michal (2018): Had some struggles in the defensive zone with his reads and ability to defend one-on-one. He played a bit on the power play and penalty-killing units during the game. He didn't do a whole lot for his team's transition game, as he didn't have the puck a lot during the game. Skating and mobility looked average from what we saw today; this was our first viewing of Ivan since he joined the Titan

AB #53 RD Dobson, Noah (2018): Excellent game from Dobson, who was very poised with the puck and made smart plays all game long. He moved the puck well in the offensive zone from the point or from deep in the offensive zone, when he adventured himself deep in the Armada zone. He took some good point shots, always keeping his shot low which facilitated deflections or rebounds for teammates. His shot is hard, accurate and has good velocity behind it. He is a very smart player who always lets the plays come to him instead of trying too much on the ice. Showed a good ability to beat guys one-on-one with strong stickhandling skills.

AB #31 G Pickard, Reilly (2018): Pickard was pretty good in the first two periods; he was making some quality saves and keeping his rebounds close to him. He had a tough 3rd period, however, giving up goals he would like to have back - which gave the win to the Armada.

BLB #4 LD Anttallainen, Aleksi (2018): Good compete level in his own zone, including on some good battles along the walls. He showed a good ability to skate the puck out of his zone and get away from the pressure of the forecheck.

BLB #17 LW Ethier, Thomas (2018): Ethier is a big kid who played in front of the net on the power play. He was tough to move from there, and did a good job playing this role. He got himself in position for scoring chances, but lacks the hands to finish some plays. He was playing and skating better in the 2nd half of the game, playing more physical and bringing more energy to his team.

Finland vs USA, U-18 Five Nations Tournament, November 11th, 2017

FIN #31 G Annunen, Justus (2018): Big and calm in net today, Annunen was really good for Finland in their shootout win over Team USA. He made tough shots look like easy saves, and his rebound-control was good today. It took some perfect shots, like the one by Farabee, to beat him. He covered a lot of space and was able to track pucks well, even with traffic in front of him. In the shootout, he was once again confident and made some big saves to help his team win the game. He is not the most athletic goaltender, though. He has great size, but could stand to be quicker with his lateral movements.

FIN #9 RD Honka, Anttoni (2019): Honka was not as good as he was in the previous game against the Swiss. However, he still found way to make an impact in this game. He made a great backhand saucer pass to his teammate Nousianen for Finland's 3rd goal of the game. He made some good plays to speed up the transition game for his team, such as quick passes out of his zone and puck-rushes. He has impressive lateral agility, his footwork is excellent, and this makes him a threat in the offensive zone. He did encounter problems in the defensive zone, however; his lack of size became more of an issue today as he faced some big forwards on Team USA in his zone.

FIN #20 LD Kokkonen, Mikko (2020): Played on the left side today after spending the majority of the tournament on the right side. He had played on the right side in most viewings we had since he played at the U-17 level last season. He showed good skating abilities and footwork. He was a bit more fluid when playing on the left side. He has good physical maturation for a 2001-born player, but doesn't look intimidating along the wall and played a simple and smart game with the puck. He scored a nice shootout goal, showing good patience and shooting five-hole to beat the American goaltender.

FIN #34 RW Maccelli, Matias (2019): He showed good skating abilities, some quick bursts and an ability to change directions quickly off the rush. He made a nice play on the game's opening goal, winning a puck race and feeding Nevasaari the puck on a 2-on-1 rush. He didn't have a huge impact offensively in this game outside of this play, as the American defensemen did a good job containing him and skating with him.

FIN #27 C Tanus, Kristian (2018): Showed a good effort in all three zones today, and good support in the defensive zone. He helped his defense out by retrieving pucks deep in their zone. He has quick feet and was quick on the puck; he created the first goal by chipping the puck away from a USA defender which led to Maccelli feeding Nevasaari for Finland's 1st goal of the game. Strong effort all game long, but lost some battles because of his size limitations and the fact that he was playing against a big USA team. He showed some good puck skills while handling the puck in the neutral and offensive zones.

FIN #34 LW Nevasaari, Arttu (2018): He showed great hands today, including good stickhandling skills, and scored two goals during the game. He scored his first goal by finishing the pass from Maccelli on a 2-on-1 rush, and for the 2nd goal, he made a nice deke in front of the goalie before beating him on the backhand. He showed a nice burst of speed on some of his chances tonight, but I would have liked to see him use that speed more often during the game. He scored another goal in the shootout, thanks to his soft hands.

USA #23 LD Samuelsson, Mattias (2018): He made a bad pinch on Finland's 2nd goal of the game, as the lone defenseman on the power play. Nevasaari took advantage of this in order to put his team up 2-0. He scored twice in the game, both similar goals, shots from the point. Nothing fancy, just simple shots on net that went through with heavy traffic in front of the Finland goaltender. He played in all situations once again today.

USA #15 RD Wilde, Bode (2018): Another solid performance from Wilde today, who showed great abilities one-on-one, beating guys easily with his good puck skills and strong skating abilities. He was playing with confidence and was rushing the puck often into the offensive zone. His skating looked effortless out there, as he has good top speed and good acceleration. He has good stickhandling skills, including soft hands and a long reach that he used well to get around defenders in one-on-one confrontations.

USA #28 LW Farabee, Joel (2018): He scored a beauty where he showed very nice acceleration after a Finland turnover, and then beat Annunen with a perfect shot over his left shoulder. He was not dominant offensively, as he didn't get a ton of chances, but he worked hard and played a smart game with and without the puck.

USA #24 RW Giles, Patrick (2018): Giles was very good along the wall today; he used his big frame well and used his long reach well, too. His puck-protection game down low in the offensive zone was excellent. He was often seen around the net, and Finland had a tough time moving him out of there.

USA #8 LW Hain, Gavin (2018): He brought some good energy to his team in the first half of the game, using his speed and hustle to bother Finnish defensemen with a strong forecheck game. He struggled a bit with the puck on his stick, losing control of it because of poor stickhandling in one-on-one confrontations.

USA #18 RW Wahlstrom, Oliver (2018): Wahlstrom showed good top speed and acceleration while in possession of the puck, when rushing it into the offensive zone. He also used his speed to beat defenders, going wide on them. He possesses a strong shot and used it well in the offensive zone when coming down his off-wing, and also in the shootout.

Red Deer Rebels at Kelowna Rockets, November 11th, 2017

KEL #24 C Topping, Kyle (2018) – Made a couple nifty plays with his feet tonight kicking pucks to his stick or deflecting pucks to teammates, usually more of a player that drives to the post he played a lot in the slot tonight and got a few tips on pucks. Showed some good puck patients, protected pucks with his body and controlled the pace of play using, was able to slow things down or push the pace with his linemates. Ended up with secondary 2 assist on the night after some longer zone time cycling the puck.

KEL #26 RW Kindree, Liam (2018) – Got an opportunity on the topline tonight and did a really good job fitting in and looking dangerous. Finished the night with 2 points setting up a nice primary assist on a one-timer on the powerplay and scored a powerplay goal with a snap shot off the right circle that cleanly beat a goalie with no traffic; impressive release. Strong tempo throughout the night, playing with speed and making crisp passes, really liked him with this line and contributions were impressive.

KEL #7 RD Zabransky, Libor (2018) – Was held off the powerplay tonight and really didn't get much ice-time as it looked to dwindle as the night went on. Got in front of a couple shots when defending and did make some solid stick plays in the defensive zone.

RD #4 LD Alexeyev, Alexander (2018) – A bug minute defender that was playing a pivotal role throughout the night, was able to use his feet and his passing to create effective and impressive zone exits and transition play. Showed real confidence with the puck on his stick and was the offensive catalyst from the blueline, especially as a powerplay quarterback. Shows a calm demeanor throughout his play, but would have liked to see a little more hustle to loose pucks where he could take advantage of his skating ability to win battles. Played with pretty much every right handed defender in the lineup and looked unfazed, did spend a fair amount of time defending in his own zone but looked good clearing the net and keeping pucks to the outside; knows how to clear the zone in a variety of ways.

RD #8 RD Herauf, Jacob (2018) – His stick work was the highlight of his play, closed his gap well, made good use of his stick to poke pucks away and create turnovers, especially down the wall. Played a lot of minutes with Alexeyev and allow him to push the pace while Herauf stayed back and played safer. He was calm and didn't look at all looked panic really showed maturity in game and handled most everything that came down on his side of the ice.

RD #3 LD Donohoe, Hunter (2018) – A long and rangy defender that was covering a lot of space and using his reach effectively. Got tangled up a few times when being taken wide off the rush as his pivots look clumsy. Was sloppy with the puck and didn't really show much on the breakout, deferring to his partner or landing passes into skates.

Final Score: Kelowna Rockets: 5 – Red Deer Rebels: 2

Regina Pats at Moose Jaw Warriors November 12th, 2017

REG#2 Zamula, Egor (2018) – Egor was non-existent tonight. Did not show me anything. Bad game for the entire Pats team. A short handed Moose Jaw team dominated the game. Egor played second unit power play and penalty kill and ended a minus one.

REG#18 Lockner, Bryan (2018) – Showed good speed at times tonight. Crashed the net hard and banged in the Pats first goal. Forced the play at times which lead to turnovers. Second penalty kill unit.

MJW#4 Woo, Jett (2018) – Jett suffered an injury minutes into the game and never returned.

MJW#16 Hartje, Chase (2018) – Chase had to step up early when Moose Jaw lost Woo and Benson. Moose Jaw was forced to play with four d-men for most of the game. Chase showed great speed and vision making great first passes. Rushed the puck on multiple occasions and jumped into the rush. Best game I have seen Chase play. Ended the game plus three and was named first star. First unit power play and penalty kill.

MJW#26 Benson, Matthew (2018) – Matthew suffered and apparent upper body injury early in the second period and did not return.

MJW#27 Burzan, Luka (2018) – Speed was on full display once again. Drove wide to the net and created a great scoring chance. Great pressure forcing turnovers. Played third line tonight. Needs to get stronger. Second power play unit.

Edmonton Oil Kings at Kelowna Rockets, November 14th, 2017

KEL #24 C Topping, Kyle (2018) – Took an opportunity to drive the net with his stick down, first attempt was save but grabbed a rebound and tucked it in. Wasn't forcing things showed good patients off the half wall to create, was letting plays develop and attacking when he saw opportunity. Slightly more passive game for Topping and his line didn't look bad just weren't creating with speed quite as well as usual.

KEL #26 RW Kindree, Liam (2018) – Right off the drop of the puck he created a passing zone entry and worked a quick 3 way passing play for an assist. Pick up a second assist as he sent Dube in for a breakaway as he gathered a puck off the wall and went hard up ice seeing his linemate get behind the defense; accurate stretch pass. Good use of his speed to break up a scoring chance as he drove hard to create back pressure and strip the puck. Straight away speed is strong and he knows how to push the pace, Kindree tries to go east west he loses some of that speed, it showed tonight as he had a little trouble taking guys wide on the attack.

KEL #7 RD Zabransky, Libor (2018) – The trend of his low ice-time with no powerplay has continued and it looked to be effecting his confidence with some mistakes, miss handled the puck at his offensive blueline and loses the zone and sees and odd man rush go in the other direction; not much east west movement along the blueline. Did receive a few penalty kill shifts, had some trouble below the goal line just getting out muscled and didn't look great defending zone entries off the rush.

KEL #29 LW Foote, Nolan (2019) – Worked his game mostly around the outside and at the dots tonight, did look to interesting in fight for space around the crease while looking to settle for wide angled shots mostly. The defense did a good job of taking away his shot making sure to play him tighter tonight, trying to go through them instead of around them.

KEL #6 RD Korczak, Kaeden (2019) – Mostly safer play tonight for him, laying back and letting his partner take the rush up ice. A real low event night for him taking him time to get up ice and deferring most of the night.

EDM #8 LD Cap, Ethan (2018) – Showed off his solid skating ability tonight looked going forward and reverse while being able to close his gaps quickly and keep pace with changing speeds. Was holding back on the rush and making sure he was the last player up ice really focusing on not letting the quick counter attack happen. Did flash his speed for one end-to-end rush setting up a nice scoring chance, likes to utilized the give and go at the attacking blueline. Was having a little trouble against the forecheck getting bumped around and boxed out, especially down low behind the net.

EDM #24 C Kemp, Brett (2018) – Was using a solid skating ability to attack pucks and push hard against to win his 50/50 battles, produces a hard aggressive forecheck. His speed helped him draw penalty and he was consistently splitting defenders. Liked his stops and starts and use of his edges, it was helping him gain space and stutter around checkers.

EDM #5 RD Platz, Jayden (2018) – Decent physical presence in this game, finished his checks with some authority. Showed no fear to pinch in when needing to create offence has some skill to open up some options and loop back to the blueline quickly. Played a big role on the penalty kill, was active with his stick and didn't allow anything across the slot during his shifts.

EDM #25 LW Pavlenko, Andrei (2018) – One great noticeable rush early in the game, burst toward the net with a good head of speed and pulled a toe drag to take a defender out of the play, got a solid scoring chance but couldn't beat the goalie. Left the game in the mid second and didn't return.

Final Score: Kelowna Rockets: 5 – Edmonton Oil Kings: 2

Calgary Hitmen at Moose Jaw Warriors, November 17th, 2017

CGY#5 Van De Leest, Jackson (2019) – At 16 years old he was the biggest player on the ice. Big strong kid with good defensive awareness. Skating needs improvement, but that is understandable for such a big body. Saw lots of ice time 5 on 5 and shorthanded.

CGY#15 Nielsen, Tristen (2018) – Tristen impressed me with his vision and passing ability. Made some passes I did not think he could make. Not the biggest guy but played physical. Overall good game with one assist. Second power play unit.

CGY# 8 Yeryomenko, Vladislav (2018) – Paired with Jake Bean on the Hitmen top pairing Vladislav held his own nicely. More of a stay at home dman who liked to shoot the puck. Good first passes, but some bad decisions on the power play that lead to turnovers. One in particular that gave Moose Jaw a 2 on 1. First power play and penalty kill units.

MJW#6 Hunt, Daemon (2020) - After getting the call up from Midget AAA due to the injury to Jett Woo Daemon was thrust into a big roll Friday night. Playing in all situations the 15 year old had his up and downs. Quarterbacked the first power play unit. Made some great defensive plays to keep the puck out of his net. If he weren't wearing the full cage there is no way you would know how young he was. Held his own in Moose Jaws top 4.

MJW#16 Hartje, Chase (2018) – Once again playing big minutes due to Moose Jaw's injury problems Chase showed he could play that roll. Showed good speed and vision with the puck. Body position down low I felt was an issue at times. Not the biggest player on the ice and it showed tonight. Looked good offensively jumping up on the rush. Had a nice assist on the power play. I feel Chase should be on a lot of team's radar so far this season. Second power play and first penalty kill units.

MJW#27 Burzan, Luka (2018) – Luka played one of his better defensive games tonight. Never took a shift off. Hockey I.Q. was on full display always in the right spot. Luka had 2 assists. Second power play unit.

MJW#39 Evanoff, Adam (2018) – Kept the Warriors in the game at times making key saves on multiple breakaways. Handled the puck well under pressure. Let in a weak goal early in the second period but settled down nicely. Overall steady performance from Adam stopping 38 of 40 shots.

University of Michigan at University of Wisconsin, November 17th, 2017

UM #17 RW Calderone, Tony (Free Agent) – Michigan's leading goal scorer going into the game added 2 more goals tonight and just missed on a couple of other opportunities with some great saves by the Wisconsin goalie. Showed the ability to find open ice and get separation from his defender and bury his chances. Played a heavy game in front of the opponents net. Played with a lot of passion and energy and was involved in scrums at both ends of the ice.

UM #10 RW Lockwood, Will (VAN) – A rare quiet game from Lockwood tonight until the 3rd period where he was able to get it going and play with his usual pace and energy. Assisted on a 3rd period tally by creating space and a passing lane and finding #33 Joseph Cecconi (D) in the high slot.

UM #43 LD Hughes, Quinn (2018) – It wasn't the strongest of nights for Hughes, but even then, his skating and overall skill set were on display on almost every shift. Hughes took some aggressive lanes coming out of his own end and committed some turnovers in his own zone that were ill advised but his ability to escape pressure and move the puck quickly and hit his teammates tape was on display. Most of his issues tonight came from decision making not skill. Hughes showed good physicality against opponent trying to drive wide to the net and Hughes finished the player along the boards behind the net. His excellent skating allows him to defend and keep a good gap on players. No points tonight but according to the final stat sheet, Hughes registered 7 Shot Attempts with 4 being blocked or going wide of the net and SOG being saved by the goalie.

UW #34 LC Frederic, Trent (BOS) – Had 1 Goal and 1 Assist on the night. Scored when a shot from the point was blocked in front and ended up on his tape in the left faceoff circle and Frederic quickly put a shot on net that was able to get through the goalie. Frederic continues to struggle with his space awareness at times, when he has lots of time to make a play he tends to rush things and when he doesn't have a lot of time he doesn't make a play fast enough. Frederic continues to be impressive down low and along the wall in protecting the puck and maintaining possession but didn't create a lot from it tonight.

UW #19 LW Hughes, Cameron (BOS) – Hughes did a lot of the heavy lifting on his line tonight, scored a beautiful Power Play goal on the zone entry as he fell off to a one-timer position near the left faceoff dot and beat the Michigan goalie over the shoulder with a powerful one-timer. Not the most physical player in puck battles but came away with the puck more times than not tonight.

Hamilton Bulldogs at Ottawa 67's, November 18th, 2017

HAM #7 LD Landry, Kade (2018) - Kade displayed intriguing two-way tools to his game as he utilized his skating to show effectiveness on both sides of the puck. Kade showed a strength utilizing his feet to carry transition up ice and did a good job recognizing pressure and when to simplify his game. While Landry was able to elude pressure at times, he did over handle the puck in his own zone and it led to a turnover and goal against. Making quicker decisions with the puck would benefit his game. He has good size and showed some puck moving ability tonight, really good first pass and didn't force pucks.

HAM #14 C Bitten, Will (MTL) – Great game for Will tonight, he was all over the ice, he created a lot of scoring chances by using his speed and acceleration beating defensemen, and fore checking hard down low creating turnovers. Will showed off his quick release in the slot on the first goal of the game, he found the open ice in the slot took the pass and didn't waste any time getting the puck off his stick. He competed hard all game and every shift tonight and showed good leadership qualities on the ice. Defensively he was good too, he supported his defense well giving them an easy outlet pass, but he also was good at indentifying his man and staying with them.

HAM #34 F Kaliyev, Arthur (2019) - Kaliyev demonstrated high offensive skill and was effective for Hamilton throughout the game. In the first period, he led an offensive rush with the puck, showing strong puck control to race around multiple defenders and enter the zone. His strength could use some improvement, as he appeared to struggle in puck battles and was boxed out in front of the net effectively by some of Ottawa's larger players. However, at one point in the first period, he fought off the defensive coverage and released a quick shot on net from close range on the backhand. He saw some time on the Powerplay for Hamilton throughout the game, and skated hard on the forecheck, stealing the puck from Ottawa's defencemen on at least one occasion and maintaining possession for sustained offensive pressure. Midway through the third period, he showed off his skill, making a nice move around a defenceman to get to the front of the net and scoring low five-hole for Hamilton's fifth goal of the game.

HAM #29 G Donofrio, Nick (2018) - Nick is a athletic goalie that stays square with shooters, he demonstrated great lateral movement throughout the game but most impressively he was able to stop a 3 on 1 by stretching out and making the save with a quick side to side transition. His flexibility and excellent compete level kept his team in the game despite being peppered with lots of high quality scoring chances. Nick was very competative tonight in the crease for Hamilton, challenging shooters, being aggressive on odd man rushes. He was good at tracking pucks from point shots and either kicking the rebound to the corner or freezing the puck.

OTT #27 D Robertson, Carter (2018) - Robertson was arguably Ottawa's best defenceman in this game and wasn't on the ice for any of Hamilton's five goals despite playing top minutes in the game. In the second period, he flashed his speed, showing a quick and agile skating ability, to pivot and skate backwards, maintaining a close gap while defending on the rush to keep his defensive assignment to the perimeter in the offensive zone. His stick placement was effectively while on defence, occasionally out in front of him and in the passing lane while forcing his opponents wide. He is willing to take a hit to make the play when necessary, absorbing one behind his own net to make a clean outlet pass to his defensive partner for a quick transition. He was demonstrating good vision throughout the game, often anticipating the play and responsibly ensuring he was in position to defend on his team's turnovers. He also saw some Powerplay time in this game, and used his vision to make quick, accurate passes along the sideboards and across the blueline cleanly. In the third period, he led a rush with the puck, and showed off very quick hands to deke around the defencemen and hit the blueline with speed.

OTT #88 D Bahl, Kevin (2018) - Bahl played top minutes for Ottawa in this game and although he was on the ice for multiple goals against, he found the scoresheet with a beautiful wristshot from the point in the first period, releasing the puck quickly to hit the cross-bar and in. He demonstrated above average speed and agility for his size at the OHL level and his strength was on display in this game, effectively boxing out Hamilton's skilled forwards, and pinning forwards in the corner in the defensive end with ease. Ottawa took a lot of penalties in this game, and Bahl saw a ton of time on the Penalty kill, where his aggressiveness and work ethic was on display to pressure the puck carriers and defend effectively on his own assignments.

OTT #71 F Clark, Kody (2018) - Clark has taken a step forward offensively for Ottawa, and is arguably one of the club's best offensive forwards right now. In the first period, he did a good job of finding the open ice in the offensive zone when he didn't have the puck, moving his feet when necessary to remain in the open passing lanes. He produced multiple offensive opportunities in this game. At one point on a 2-on-0, he made a hard, accurate pass across the crease for a one-timer five-hole that was stopped by Hamilton's goaltender. He was consistently hard on the puck carrier when defending, and at one point in the neutral zone, he anticipated the play unfolding and jumped up into the passing lane to pick off a long pass and skate the puck into the offensive end for an opportunity. He found the scoresheet on Ottawa's second goal, putting home a one-timer on the backdoor of the net by staying open, moving his legs and skating hard to the net.

University of Michigan at University of Wisconsin, November 18th, 2017

UM #9 LC Norris, Josh (SJS) – No Points tonight but Norris was much better in this game than Friday night. Tonight he took more shot attempts and created a lot in the offensive end with his patients and vision of the ice sheet and was able to penetrate the middle of the ice and get to the net. Was solid defensively, tracks back into the play hard and provided good back pressure for his defenseman to be aggressive.

UM #43 LD Quinn Hughes (2018) – Hughes got better as the game went along tonight and really stepped it up in the 3rd period and was the best player on the ice in the 3rd. Hughes took back to back penalties in the 2nd period, one was a cross checking penalty while his team was on a power play, Hughes mishandled the puck with no pressure on the breakout, Wisconsin was able to pin the play along the boards and kill the remaining bit of the power play in the offensive zone and Hughes took a Cross Checking penalty out of frustration on the play with his team with a 2-1 lead. A few minutes later Hughes took a slashing penalty that resulted in Wisconsin tying the game on the ensuing Power Play. His vision coming out of his own end was very good and was able to stretch the ice and find forwards in the neutral zone with relative ease. Hughes assisted on the game's opening goal as well as the tying goal in the 3rd period with an end to end rush where he lost control of the puck in the offensive end but was able to chip it over to Jake Slaker who beat the Wisconsin goalie. His skating gives him a lot of time to find open players but his quick thinking and vision allowed him to move the puck a lot quicker tonight than last night.

UM #21 LW Pastujov, Michael (2018+) – Pastujov did not dress in either game this weekend and has only played in 1 game this season for Michigan.

UM #33 RD Cecconi, Joseph (DAL) – Cecconi was good all weekend. Played with a lot of physicality in his own zone and punished the opposition in front of his own net. He took care of the puck coming out of his own end and made a lot of clean outlets. Logged a lot of minutes in a tight game and was used in all situations for Michigan. His explosiveness in his first couple strides resulted in some lost puck races in his own end.

UM #30 G Lavigne, Hayden (Free Agent) – Positioning was not very good on some of the goals against, got beat both over the blocker and over the glove on the short side on the game tying goal, both from the same area of the ice due to being too deep in the crease. Didn't see a lot of high quality chances outside of the 2nd period where his team was on their heels for much of the period but controlled his rebounds well for the most part and limited second chances.

UW #17 RW Johnson, Will (Free Agent) – Johnson is starting to garner some attention as a potential Free Agent Signee. He's not ready yet but he's a Quick player on the fore check with a good stick and hands did a good job creating some turnovers on the back check and get the play going the other direction quickly. Keeps pucks alive along the walls and plays with some physicality despite his size. Got some scoring chances by going to the front of the net but wasn't able to convert tonight.

UW #33 G Hayton, Kyle (Free Agent) – Lateral movement is very good, was able to get his left pad over and make a huge save on a one-timer late in the game. Takes away the lower half of the net really well with his athleticism and tracks pucks in traffic but can be beaten up high. Let a bad goal through the body on Michigan's first shootout attempt and got beat badly on their 2nd attempt.

UW #2 LD Kalynuk, Wyatt (FLA) – 3 assists on the evening, 2 coming on the Power Play and the 3rd on the game tying goal late in the 3rd with the goalie pulled. Runs the point effectively on the Power Play, did a good job getting pucks through traffic. Doesn't force a lot of plays and takes what is given.

UW #19 LW Hughes, Cameron (BOS) – Tied the game with the goalie pulled late with a shot from the face-off circle over the goalies glove on the short side, under the bar.

Spisska Nova Ves U20 at Trencin U20, November 19th, 2017

TRN #22 CE Ferenyi, Nicolas (2019) –Not any quick legs but decent top speed. Tall legs and stick, good positioned. Joined home in full speed when needed. On one rush he managed to pass by a couple of players by the board and had vision for the other players. Similar happened on 8-3 goal where he did a quick turnover from own zone and passing it back to the D for a quick shot. Lot of time standing in front of net for rebounds and redirections. Protecting the puck good with his body by the board.

TRN #28 RW/CE Kukuca, Andrej (2018) –For Slovak U20 he is quick but comparing on international top level its under average. Good hands. Brought the puck from own defensive FO and slide in to the net with some nice hand moves, finishing with 7-3 goal. Creates a lot with Okuliar.

TRN #59 RW Luhovy, Michal (2018) –Super small 99 born player that has never played in any of the Slovak national teams. Very hungry, moves good on the ice and always on the right spot. Act good as playmaker. Nice redirections in front of net. Quick efficient passes sideways to move the SNV team. 5-2 goal was such but it touched on each and everyone so Luhovy was not getting the A-points for that.

TRN #81 LW Okuliar, Oliver (2018) For Slovak league this guy has good tools. Skates quick, creating and closing gap, moves his head to screen the ice. Nice edges. Joins back in the defense. Creates a lot, especially with Kucera. Quick shot and shoots a lot.

TRN #89 CE Kovacik, Kristian (2018) – With 1,63 PPG in U20 and at least 1 game with Trencin in Slovak Extraliga, Kovacik was the main reason for my visit in Trencin. Didn't play and haven't been on ice since 22nd October.

SNV #20 Tyczynski, Damian LW/CE (2018) - Good positioned, Played almost all the time in the end.

SNV #19 Dzugan, Robert RW/LW (2018) – Up straight skating with lot of gliding. Positioned good and lifted himself in the third.

SNV #15 Zekucia, Alexander, RD (2018) – Neutral game, some risky passes in the end. Not visualized much but got very much icetime in the end period. At ones from the left defensive FO area side he gets the puck and with a lot of fighting manage to get the puck trhough Trencin players for an odd man rush after leaving Trencin Defender Sagat some 6-9 ft behind.

Final Score: Trencin U20: 9 – Spisska Nova Ves U20: 5

Saskatoon Blades at Moose Jaw Warriors, November 21st, 2017

SAS#27 Farren, Michael (2018) – Farren didn't stand out tonight. Worked hard every shift but did not contribute to the score sheet in a high scoring 7-6 loss. Took a bad-hooking penalty. Second power play unit.

SAS#44 Wouters, Chase (2018) – Passed up a great scoring chance in the slot, would have liked to see him soot the puck. Once again good in the faceoff circle. Ended the game a minus one. Second power play unit.

SAS#77 Dach, Kirby (2019) – One of Saskatoon's best players all game. Demonstrated high-end speed and skill with the puck. Created multiple scoring chances. Confidence in key situations, such as playing on the point on the first power play unit. Saw minutes in overtime as well. Out muscled at times. One assist on the night. Expect big things from Dach in the future.

MJW#6 Hunt, Daemon (2020) – Not a strong game again for Hunt. Struggled defensively all night. Poor decisions with the puck. However, playing big minutes as a fifteen year old would be tough for anyone player in the WHL.

MJW#16 Hartje, Chase (2018) – Quarterbacked the first power play unit great all game. Chase continues to put up points adding 2 assists. Got caught flat footed and beat wide which lead to a Saskatoon goal. The entire team had a third period let down allowing Saskatoon to come back from a 6-2 deficit to tie the game and force overtime. Chase looked good in O.T. controlling the play.

St. Thomas Academy Cadets vs Minnetonka Skippers, November 24th, 2017

MIN #2 LD Docter, Grant (2019) – Grant is a tad undersized but has elusive skating and showed the ability to control the game with the puck on his stick. Docter made some good plays from the point in the offensive zone, showed a decent one-timer and has a low, hard shot that gets through to the net. Has some quick hands and footwork allows him to elude pressure. Committed a couple turnovers when attempting some cross ice stretch passes coming out of his own end. Docter is a late 00' birthdate and has flown a bit under the radar up to this point but it starting to garner some USHL and NCAA interest.

MIN #3 RD Luedke, Josh (2019) – Luedke scored the Overtime winner with a quick wrist shot from the top of the faceoff circle, other than the game winner the Northern Michigan commit was fairly quiet in this one.

MIN#9 RC Brink, Bobby (2019) – Brink will be a force in the Minnesota High School ranks all season long and his skills were well on display in this game. Brink had a beautiful end to end rush in the 1st, where he showed a smooth pivot along the half wall in the offensive zone to elude the defender, circled behind the net and zipped a pass across the slot to the far side defenseman for a scoring chance. Had 2 assists tonight, one off the faceoff where Brink gets the puck and position off the faceoff and makes a backhand feed from the goal line to #34 Teddy Lagerback in front. Brink is a University of Denver Commit and a 2017 Phase 1 USHL 1st Rd. Draft Pick of the Sioux City Musketeers.

MIN #8 RC Loheit, Luke (2018) – Loheit is a Minnesota Duluth commit with decent size that uses it well along the wall. Scored a beautiful Unassisted Power Play goal off a face off at center ice where he split the defense, poked the puck past the defender and beat the Minnetonka goalie over the glove on a shot from about 20 feet out.

MIN #29 LC Bayless, Jack (2018) – Scored a Power Play goal when he got the puck high in the offensive zone and was able to skate in unapproached and fire a wrist shot that beat the goalie up high.

MIN #34 RW Lagerback, Teddy (2020) – Lagerback is a big kid with a strong base. His skating looked sluggish at times and struggled to keep up with the pace in transition at times but was effective in front of the net on the Power Play. Registered a goal and an assist in this game. Goes to the paint which is how he scored, finding a loose puck on the back door and finding the back of the net.

STA #9 R/LW Vega, Nico (2019) – Vega is a smaller forward that relies on his skating a quick puck skills to be effective. Despite not registering any points in this game, Vega was all over the puck for stretches of the game; he was a pest on the fore check and won a lot of puck battles against much older and bigger opponents. It was just one viewing but was impressive in this game.

STA #11 RC Christy, Rob (2019) – Without a doubt Rob Christy was the best player on the ice for St. Thomas for much of the game tonight. Rob scored a shorthanded goal by getting the puck in the neutral zone, gaining position on defender and beating the goalie with a low wrister. Rob Christy is a Colorado College commit and a 2017 2nd Round Phase 1 draft pick of Des Moines (USHL).

STA #21 RC McFadden, Brendan (2019) – Tied the game early in the 3rd by putting in a loose puck in traffic. McFadden was a physical presence all game long, won a lot of puck battles for his team. Did a good job disturbing things in front of the opponents net which helped open the scoring early in the game.

Moorehead Spuds at Lakeville North Panthers, November 24th, 2017

MD #5 RD Frisch, Ethan (2019) – Frisch is a North Dakota Commit and a 2nd Round pick Futures Pick of Green Bay (USHL) in 2016. Solid all-around game tonight, finished with 1 goal and 1 assist, scoring the eventual game winner late in the 2nd period with a quick pivot and shot from the point just above the faceoff circle that the goalie would like to have back. Frisch's skating agility and skill with the puck was on display tonight and made reliable low risk plays for much of the night but his play in the defensive zone was equally as impressive. Despite being a tad undersized by today's standards, Frisch was physical and at times nasty against players in his own zone, he made players pay a price in the hard area's and did so in a fashion that he didn't get himself out of position or take himself out of the play.

MD #6 LW Randklev, Carter (2018) – Showed the ability to create space using his quick hands and feet and had a couple scoring opportunities set ups that just missed connecting for goals. Had a couple lazy shifts where he didn't move his feet without the puck and took 2 stick infraction penalties in the 1st period. Tried a high risk toe drag at the offensive blue line that resulted in a turnover, luckily Lakeville North wasn't able to convert on the mistake. No points for Randklev tonight but his line generated some good chances in the offensive zone, the Lakeville North Goalie made some outstanding saves.

Frolunda HC at Malmo Redhawks, November 25th, 2017

FHC #27 RW Engstrand, Eric (2018) - Big man at 6'4, 198 lbs. Solid skater for his size, very agile and athletic on his skates. Gets in on the forecheck and is responsible defensively. Had a neat sticklift on a backcheck in the neutral zone. Good anticipation and makes sure to be the first guy to a puck. Like his motor. Displayed decent hands and a good eye for the game. Created a couple of scoring chances and added an assist to his name. Puck skills can improve and he could also improve his first few steps. Potential late round pick.

FHC #44 LW Fagemo, Samuel (2018) - Fagemo had a disappointing performance. He really does not contribute much to the game when the puck is not on his stick. Very one-dimensional. Had a great scoring chance on a clear breakaway but Malmö goalie Linus Gidbark made a superb glove hand save. Was penalized for hooking later in that same shift. Looked frustrated in this game and was seen doing his usual cherry-picking. Do not like his body-language, he has a selfish look to him and appears to be very much an individualist.

FHC #20 C Miketinac, Kalle (2018) - Undrafted last year, Miketinac recently returned from an injury which had kept him out of action for the entire season so far. Despite the long absence he looked good. His skating looks improved compared to last year and mainly his first few steps look quicker. Still, he is not an elite skater and not as fast as you would ideally want a smaller guy to be. His smarts was however very visible in this game and he was the architect behind a couple of quality scoring opportunities. Finished the game with an assist to his name.

FHC #18 LD Roos, Filip (2018) - Another undrafted '99 born player, Roos is making his first season with the Frölunda program after transferring from the IF Troja-Ljungby organization. Roos has good size and displayed smarts, calmness and an ability to rush the puck. Played on the first pairing with Arizona Coyotes prospect Filip Westerlund and had a strong game. Does not appear to have a lot of offensive upside however and is probably not an NHL prospect at this point in time.

Rouyn-Noranda Huskies vs Drummondville Voltigeurs, November 25th, 2017

RN #19 LW Hrehorcak, Patrik (2018): Playing on the 3rd line, the young Slovak played a feisty game with a strong compete level. He has good, agile feet, generating some decent speed down his wing. He had some good net drives in the 3rd period as well, not shying away from going to the net with the puck. He played and hustled hard in tonight's game.

RN #4 LD Bergeron, Justin (2018): Played on the right side, and paired with McQuaid once again tonight. He was quick to move the puck by making short passes, speeding up the transition game. He was also quick to retrieve pucks, and did a fine job of putting them on net. He had his regular shift on the power play.

RN #11 LW Harvey-Pinard, Rafaël (2018): Harvey-Pinard worked hard throughout this game. His compete level was good, and he was playing in the tougher areas of the ice as usual, even as a smaller player. He had some scoring chances in the game, including on a 2-on-1, but couldn't finish the play. Overall, the Huskies were quiet offensively tonight.

RN #6 LD McQuaid, Chris (2018): He supported the rush more and had more chances to touch the puck than we saw from him this season in our previous viewings. His skating stride is not pretty, but he generates decent speed with it anyway. He was able to escape pressure from the forecheck, skating the puck out of his zone on some sequences in tonight's game.

DRU #33 G Rodrigue, Olivier (2018): He was calm in tonight's game, not often tested in period 1 but stayed focused when he faced shots. He was a little busier in period 2, but did not face a whole lot of high-quality shots. His rebound-control was good, and he did a good job re-directing them into the corners.

DRU #92 LD Beaudin, Nicolas (2018): Played on the right side at even-strength while being paired with Duquette, but was on the left side on the first power play unit. Beaudin was not a real factor in his team's win tonight, which has not been the case often this year. He didn't play bad, but was not a key player for his team. He was a bit more active in the 3rd period, coming close to scoring early In the 3rd period after jumping into the rush and taking a quick shot on net that almost beat Harvey. Beaudin has good puck poise, with the ability to slow down the play on the ice.

DRU #55 LD Bernard, Xavier (2018): He played a smart puck-moving game tonight, nothing flashy, but made short and simple passes from the point on the power play. He finished the game with 2 assists, both on the power play. His skating is decent; enough to keep up with the Huskies' players tonight, and he made good use of his long reach.

DRU #90 RD Pelletier, Thomas (2019): While he was in possession of the puck, he kept his game simple. He didn't try too many fancy plays, and made sure to get the puck deep in the Huskies' zone. He did a fine job of using his feet to skate the puck out of his zone, at least until the neutral zone. Despite his young age, he didn't back down from physical confrontation after whistles, getting involved in couple of scrums.

DRU #9 C Guay, Nicolas (2018): He showed a good burst of speed down the wing in this game, including on the first shift, where he easily beat one of the Rouyn defensemen and took the puck to the net. As always with Guay, he worked hard at both ends of the rink. He had another good scoring chance in the slot after some good work by Dawson Mercer down low. Guay was denied by Harvey, but took a quick wrist shot after receiving the pass.

DRU #19 RW Mercer, Dawson (2020): The youngest player in this game was playing on the 2nd line and saw regular ice time on the power play. He did some really good work down low controlling and protecting the puck, which led to a great scoring chance by Guay. He showed an excellent release on his shot during the game. When he gains more confidence and becomes physically stronger, he'll be an excellent player in this league. Skating looked fine as well.

DRU #20 LW Desruisseaux, Cedric (2018): He scored a nice goal at the end of the first period with a quick wrister, but the goal was eventually waved off due to being offside at the offensive blueline. He showed throughout the game that he has a good, quick release when taking shots on net. However, he's undersized and his size was not helping him in some of battles along the boards against the bigger players from Rouyn-Noranda.

DRU #81 C Simoneau, Xavier (2019): Simoneau did it all tonight for the Voltigeurs, scoring two goals, playing an agitating game and playing on both the PP and PK units. His goals both came on the power play, and featured two good shots on net. He has great hockey sense and controls the puck and play very well on the power play. He's very impressive despite his size, and he's very successful for someone of this young age. His compete level was excellent, he doesn't back down from anyone on the ice. At his size, this could be worrisome, but his courage is admirable. Good work on the PK, he has excellent anticipation and works really hard when he was used shorthanded.

Victoria Royals at Moose Jaw Warriors, November 28th, 2017

VIC#10 Peckford, Ryan (2018) – Impressed me right from puck drop. On the first shift of the game laid a big hit on one of Moose Jaw's strongest players. Showed good speed and control with the puck, had one assist on the night. Second power play unit.

VIC#14 Florchuk, Eric (2018) – Eric was strong in the faceoff dot going 6/10. Fair sized but did not stand out very much all game.

MJW#16 Hartje, Chase (2018) – Saw his minutes reduce a bit due to the fact that Josh Brook returned to the lineup. Had another assist, which gives him 13 on the season so far. Made multiple good first passes. Used his speed to get out of trouble. Second penalty kill unit.

MJW#8 Almeida, Justin (2018) - Justin was the first star of the game. Recorded his first career hat trick in the win. Justin played a great game using his speed and skill. Having a breakout season with the Warriors he is over a point a game. Ended the game with 4 points. Second power play unit.

MJW#27 Burzan, Luka (2018) – Got an opportunity on Moose Jaw's second line and did not look out of place. Generated chances of the rush with his speed. Luka had 5 shots on goal, 3 of which were inside home plate. Second line power play.

Prince George Cougars at Kelowna Rockets, November 29th, 2017

PG #8 LW Leppard, Jackson (2018) – Really high-end compete level was consistently pursuing pucks and playing an intimidating, worked hard to win his 50/50 battles and did a good job of finishing some hard and rather jarring checks. His compete level helped him create some offensive chances, was constantly playing in the tough areas of the ice and despite not capitalizing he was dangerous and good around the net including pulling off a toe drag around a defender but was stopped by an impressive save.

PG #29 RW Mikhalchuk, Vladislav (2018) – Game was on tonight, really looked like one of the better forwards from the beginning of the night and his ice-time increased as the game went on getting moved up a line at 5 on 5. Was skating well and was one of the faster players on the ice at top speed, edging, directional changes and stop are starts stood out but could. Also utilized his skating to put good pressure on puck carriers and force some quicker plays to be made. Good instincts on the powerplay as a slot presence presented his stick well and used his reach to get to shots. Picked up a primary assist on the powerplay centering an accurate pass to Bathune

PG #3 RD Moberg, Cole (2019) – Showed off solid skating ability that was more noticeable in reverse, didn't often get beat wide and played with a tight gap, liked his ability to put pressure on attackers and make them lose the puck when coming down his side. Moberg was also aggressive with his back pressure and did a good job targeting sticks when coming from behind. Looked poised for a first year player and despite not getting the top attackers, defended well. Did have one tough shift that stood out where he was hemmed in with the 4th line and was puck chasing a little.

KEL #24 C Topping, Kyle (2018) – Another multi point night for Topping, really looks comfortable playing at home, especially on the powerplay. Edged hard a shook off a defender behind the net sending a perfect pass out into the slot for a primary powerplay assist. His second powerplay assist he sent a pass into the slot for a streaking Twarynski, both passes really are great examples of his vision and ability to distribute the puck using a high IQ. Struggle tonight getting around defenders off the rush, just couldn't get to that extra gear to turn the corner and drive the net.

KEL #26 RW Kindree, Liam (2018) – Showed a bit of physical edge tonight and banging bodies and absorbing checks to buy some time for him to make a play. Picked up an assist by finding a defender sneaking in from the point, put it right on the tape with accuracy. Really seems to enjoy driving the net and was showing good timing chasing point shots that were coming off the goaltender.

KEL #7 RD Zabransky, Libor (2018) – Showed a little more urgency and confidence in game tonight especially at the offensive blueline. Had a few really good pinches down the wall to keep plays alive and sustain zonetime, but still needed to see more hustle plays in his game to fight for lose pucks. Looked solid defending his own blueline, denied a few zone entries by tightening his gap and closing off quickly.

KEL #1 Porter, James (2018) – He's not a large goalie but usually does a good job at covering the lower part of the net but tonight looked a little small, lots of saves tucking his feet back. Was scrambling around in traffic a little bit and gave up a goal on a short handed breakaway, where he just faded backwards and gave up too much of the net. He did keep his team in the game and beside the SHG he only gave up powerplay scores nothing 5 on 5.

KEL #29 LW Foote, Nolan (2019) – First game returning from injury after a short absence and he looked a little rusty, legs weren't with him for most of the night but wasn't much of a contributor to the offense. Did throw a couple powerful hits to get himself into the game but he was eased back into the lineup and his chances were limited.

KEL #6 RD Korczak, Kaeden (2019) – Displayed some lateral movement along the offensive blueline keeping his head up and looking to open up some options, this was new for him and would really benefit his game if he gained more confidence controlling the flow of the attacking zone like this. Quick decision to snap pucks at the net leads to him picking up an assist. Really like his footwork all around tonight, pushed the pace up the defensive zone to open outlet options and made strong passes.

Final Score: Kelowna Rockets: 5 – Prince George Cougars: 3

Sault Ste. Marie Greyhounds at Peterborough Petes, Nov 30

Peterborough Petes -

PBO #20 LD Chisholm, Declan (2018) – Chisholm was efficient at both ends of the ice while been one of the better Petes Defenseman. His skating stride is powerful and he gets up the ice quickly, on one sequence he took the puck from behind his own net and went over all three zones, using his agility to weave around a forechecker and his straight line-speed to enter the offensive end. He showed awareness in his own end regarding the amount of time and space he had to make a play. During another rush attempt, he recognized that the forechecker was about to stick-check him, he made a nice backhand pass to his support before it occurred. Below the goal-line in his own end, he had two Greyhounds players pressuring him, he feinted a pass and remained poised with the puck, assessing his options quickly, making a nice pass to his teammate before he got pinned along the boards. He wasn't overly engaged offensively but he did make tape to tape passes to his teammates and shot a couple of wrist shots that weren't dangerous. He showed puck moving ability out there while playing on the 2nd defensive pairing.

PBO #16 LC Robertson, Nick (2020) – Robertson is a diminutive forward, standing at 5'7, 143 but his combination of plus puck skills and speed allowed him to make plays, although he was inconsistent. His acceleration allowed him to be aggressive on the forecheck and he didn't mind going to the dirty areas despite his size. His release point on his shot was good and he showed plus vision, threading a couple of passes to his teammates around the high slot area. He played on the third line and had powerplay time.

PBO #17 RW Gogolev, Pavel (2018) – Gogolev showed a versatile game while been offensively threatening. He's not overly coordinated and as a result his skating mechanics appearing awkward but he still gets up the ice well enough. His offensive awareness was good today, there were several plays where he assessed where he needed to be or where his teammate would be. On two different sequences he had excellent scoring chances in the slot that he missed on, he wasn't accurate but the release was quick. He showed plus passing ability, as he hit his teammates around the net on several different plays. He stood out while playing on the third line.

PBO #19 RC Der-Arguchintsev, Semyon (2018) – Der-Arguchintsev made plays at top speed while displaying high-end vision, consistently feeding his teammates for quality scoring chances. His acceleration is explosive and he can stop quickly, this allowed him to open passing lanes and breakdown the defense in the offensive end. On one of his primary assists, he jetted down the left wing, stopped quickly at the goal-line and delivered a beautiful pass at the left circle to Korostelev for a goal. Although he's skilled he also showed responsible two-way play. On one sequence, he hustled down the left wing and used an aggressive stick-check at the defensive blueline, turning the puck over. He was also physically engaged in the corners, fighting for puck possession on the forecheck. Der-Arguchintsev played on the top line, had powerplay time and finished with two assists while been an offensive catalyst for his team.

Sault Ste. Marie Greyhounds -

SSM #9 LD Sandin, Rasmus (2018) - Sandin had an excellent game for the Greyhounds, showing the ability to process the play quickly in both the offensive and defensive zone. Sandin's skating was fluid and efficient, he's not an explosive skater but he's quick, this allowed him to transition the puck effectively today. His passing ability was on point, he made quality passes in both ends of the ice consistently. His best pass came during the powerplay, he used a head feint at the right circle before threading a pass across the slot to the surprise of the Petes penalty kill unit, landing on the stick of Kopacka for an easy goal. His defensive reads stood out, he recognized how much time he had to move the puck out of the zone during forechecking sequences and had several stretch passes. His frame is slight and at times he was easily knocked to the ice, however he was willing to take a big hit if it resulted in the right play for his team. Sandin finished with 2 assists while playing on the first pairing with Timmins and getting both powerplay and penalty kill time.

SSM #27 LC Hayton, Barrett (2018) - Hayton was largely invisible against the Petes. His best sequence came after he stick-lifted the puck from a player on the offensive zone, then skated down the wing and delivered a quality pass to his teammate for a scoring chance. He was used on the top powerplay unit and had some success at screening Wells in-front of the net while distributing the puck. He finished with an empty net goal but with the exception of a few plays he didn't assert himself in today's game or stand out.

Final Score 7-5 Greyhounds

Rimouski Océanic vs Drummondville Voltigeurs, December 1st, 2017

RIM #11 LW Lafrenère, Alexis (2020): It was a tough night offensively for the Océanic. They didn't create a lot of offense, generating only 5 shots on net after 40 minutes. Lafrenière didn't get a lot of puck touches, however, he did show flashes of his talent in some sequences including one on Rimouski's first goal of the game where skated hard to win a puck race and made a perfect pass on the backhand in front of the net to Dove-McFalls. He also showed quick puck decisions; he thinks the game quickly and at another level compared to most players on the ice. He's a skilled player, but did well battling in the corners and in front of the net. He did a good job in front of the net on Rimouski's 2nd goal, disturbing Rodrigue on Charles-Édouard D'Astous' point shot. His skating is fine, but he could use some more explosiveness to his skating stride.

RIM #24 C Bizier, Mathieu (2019): Bizier might have been one of Rimouski's top forwards in this game. He centered the 3rd line and was also a regular on the PK unit. He showed great smarts throughout this game, including an excellent positional game. He was always on the right side of the puck. His skating was a bit rough, as he lacks some explosiveness and agility. Not a speedster, either, but he has good anticipation and smarts. He did a good job on the PK, showing that he is a good puck-retriever and puck-protector along the boards. He made a great feed on a 2-on-1 to Carson MacKinnon at the side of the net for what would eventually become the winning goal of the game.

RIM #17 C Zavgorodniy, Dmitry (2018): The young Russian had a tough game offensively today, not producing many scoring chances for his line, nor did he generate a lot of energy or speed. He did, however, show a good game away from the puck. He worked hard and showed good support in his zone. He was responsible in his zone and was not a liability on the ice. He centered the 2nd line and was used on the 1st power play unit, and regularly on the PK unit. His lack of size showed along the boards, as he was outmuscled couple of times in the game.

DRU #33 G Rodrigue, Olivier (2018): Tough game for Rodrigue, as he only faced 5 shots in the first 40 minutes and gave up 3 goals in the 3rd period to take the loss. Couldn't blame him on the first or third goal, as they were really nice plays and he had no chance to stop them. On the 2nd goal, he had traffic in front of him and couldn't track the puck well enough. He didn't make the big saves that were necessary in the 3rd period to help his team keep their lead. He was calm in his crease until Rimouski started crashing the net a bit more; he lost his patience with Lafrenière a couple of times when he was in his crease.

DRU #92 LD Beaudin, Nicolas (2018): Beaudin did a good job of skating the puck out of his zone or out of trouble. He made some good PP breakouts. On the power play during some sequences, he had a hard time getting his shot through; Rimouski did a good job blocking his point shots. His passing game was good, but not as great as we've seen from him this season. He had a couple of errant passes in his zone.

DRU #55 LD Bernard, Xavier (2018): Lots of ice time for him today. He was often used on the PP and PK, in addition to his regular ES shift. He kept his game simple, as he has done for most of the season. Nothing flashy, but he made easy outlets and took good shots on net from the point on the power play. Not very creative with the puck, though.

DRU #20 LW Desruisseaux, Cedric (2018): Desruisseaux lacks size, but played a feisty game, not backing down from the bigger players on some sequences during the game. He showed good speed and quickness during the game; he was moving his feet well and played with good energy throughout the contest. He often rushed the puck into the offensive zone thanks to his good speed. He played on the power play, but most of the time he was playing on the half wall.

DRU #81 C Simoneau, Xavier (2019): The young rookie center was not a standout offensively tonight, but was effective at both ends of the ice. He was a regular on the PK, showing good anticipation and compete level, battling for pucks against much bigger players on the ice. His speed is decent, but he has quick and agile feet. This makes it tough to defend against, as he can make quick turns to get away from defenders. He showed good vision on the power play, not generating a ton of chances, but still demonstrating that he sees the ice very well.

Swift Current Broncos at Moose Jaw Warriors, December 1st, 2017

SC#23 Patterson, Max (2018) – Big, strong 2 way forward. Battled hard and worked the cycle well down low. Needed to be better in the faceoff dot. Swift utilized his size on the second power play unit by putting him in front of the net. No points for Max on the night.

SC#37 Barlage, Logan (2019) – Great size for a 16 year old. Used his strength to get to the dirty areas of the ice. Worked hard every time he was on the ice. Saw some time on the second power play unit. Finished minus 1 on the night.

MJW#8 Almeida, Justin (2018) – Justin seemed a bit off tonight. Made some poor decisions with the puck. His size seemed to be factor at times getting pushed off the puck. Had 1 assist, going 50% in the faceoff dot and finished the game a minus 1. Missed the second period after taking a high stick. First power play unit.

MJW#16 Hartje, Chase (2018) – Chase played another solid game, adding an assist to move his point steak to eight games. When he gets the puck in the defensive zone, he slows it down and alleviates the pressure with his speed and ability to make a good first pass. Finished the game a plus two. Second penalty kill unit.

MJW#26 Benson, Matthew (2019) – Benson played a much more physical game then I am used to seeing. After laying a massive hit along the wall, he stood up for himself and dropped the gloves. Made a few mental errors, held his own playing in Moose Jaw's top four. Ended the game a minus one.

MJW#27 Burzan, Luka (2018) – Burzan stepped up for Moose Jaw in the absence of Brett Howden in a big way. He moved up to the second line and fit in nicely. Used his high-end speed to make played and created scoring chances. Tried to do too much a couple times which resulted in turnovers. One assist and played second line power play.

Vancouver Giants at Prince George Cougars, December 1st, 2017

PG #8 LW Leppard, Jackson (2018) – Leppard was utilized on the top powerplay-unit and played with Mikhalchuk on a line that had some decent scoring chances. The winger has good size, standing 6'2, 200 and utilized it in-front of the net, screening Tendeck effectively. This lead to his best scoring chance of the game, after he was the first to a rebound, using his range to collect the puck and attempted to jam it in far-side. His skill level is above average, and he can handle the puck while in motion, this allowed him to penetrate the slot area on one sequence, it didn't lead to a scoring opportunity, but it demonstrated his willingness to drive to the net and showed plus agility. One aspect of his game against the Giant's that showed a need for improvement was his decision making with his shot. He didn't shoot off the rush, instead opting for severe-angle, low percentage shots without traffic, which lead to routine saves. There was also a lack of power generated in his release and he didn't attempt to utilize screens. His best quality he displayed today was his motor, he plays at a high-pace given his size and this made him consistently stand-out when he was on the ice. Leppard finished with 2 shots on net while showing above average tools.

PG #29 RW Mikhalchuk, Vladislav (2018) – Mikhalchuk wasn't as effective as Leppard was against the giants. Although he's like Leppard in size, standing 6'3, 187, he wasn't as powerful and this lead to average acceleration, although his stride is long and fluid. This allowed him to cut across the neutral zone and go wide on an opponent during a sequence, however he was toppled over behind the net, showing a need for an improved base. His execution was mixed today, he was having difficulty handling passes while transitioning up the ice, and made some errant plays himself, holding onto the puck too long, resulting in turnovers. He never threatened offensively, finishing with zero shots on net in a poor performance.

VAN #25 RD Bulych, Kaleb (2018) – Due to several injuries on the Giants blueline, Bulych was given an increased role, getting top pairing minutes while been used on the penalty-kill. He didn't display much in the way of creativity while walking the offensive blueline, but he did show an accurate shot that generated enough velocity to create rebound opportunities. In the defensive end, he was mixed. On one play, he used his large frame to pin a Cougars player effectively behind his own-net and was willing to sacrifice his body on the penalty-kill, however his positioning was poor one some plays. Specifically, on one sequence, Bulych was caught out of position while attempting to check an opponent behind the goal-line instead of recognizing that he needed to remain near the side of the net which would have allowed him an opportunity to cut off the pass that lead to the goal. Bulych doesn't look like a defender who can quarterback a powerplay based on today's viewing but showed some shut-down qualities and has a wide frame with room to grow into it.

VAN #41 RD Kannok-Leipert, Alex (2018) – Kannok-leipert had an effective performance for the Giants while displaying two-way qualities. He's an aggressive defenseman which was a double-edged sword. On some plays, he used his aggression and plus acceleration to close gaps quickly and create pressure against the Cougars, however one other plays, he would inadvertently throw himself out of position. Under pressure, he was good at recognizing how much time and space he had to make a play. On one sequence he made a quick bank-pass off the boards to himself while getting forechecked, on another, he made an accurate and smart bank-pass to his teammate in the neutral zone. In the offensive-end, the defender didn't get too many opportunities, however on one sequence, he took a pass at the point and processed the play quickly, showing soft-hands that he used to deke around an aggressive winger and then cut down the left wing before passing the puck into the slot, resulting in a difficult play for Grant to handle. His execution was consistent for the Giants, while finishing with 1 assist and 2 shots on net.

VAN #40 LC Roman, Milos (2018) – Roman was dangerous against the Cougars, playing at a relentless pace that was difficult for the opposing team to handle. He's got excellent skating mechanics and only needs a couple of steps to get into full flight. This made him effective at pressuring the Cougars on the forecheck and creating turnovers. In some past viewing's, he's tended to play the perimeter too frequently, however in today's game, he was aggressive in-front of the net and drove into the slot. This lead to a great scoring opportunity off a tip on one play, and on another he scored off a rebound at the top of the crease, where he used an accurate wrist-shot that went far-side. His playmaking ability was on full display, making consistent and accurate passes throughout the contest. Specifically, on one play, he made his most technical pass, driving down the right wing behind the net and faked going to his backhand while rotating his core, he flipped to his forehand and made a beautiful pass into the slot that resulted in a goal for Ronning. He wasn't only offensive engaged today, playing a solid, two-hundred-foot game. He supported his defense and played at a high-pace in the defensive-end as well. Roman scored 1 goal and had 1 primary assist while been used on the top-line and all situations.

Final Score: Vancouver Giants: 5 – Prince George Cougars: 3

HMHK Nitra U20 at HC Slovan Bratislava U20, December 2nd, 2017

BRA # 56 RD Ledenev, Roman (2018) - Good reading for Slovak league but against quicker and better Nitra he wasn't paid for his offensive game. Not too much super dangerous happened for Nitra when he was on the ice and at Nitras 1-0 goal they were a quick puck moving team and it wasn't much Ledenev could have done. Couple of good shots and good first p as s and good reading. Skill-vised he is one of the better 2000 born player on the ice.

BRA # 12 LD Vitalos, Martin (2018) - Vitalos had decent flow in his game and where showing will. Delivered hits and well prepared when receiving hits. Some nice first pass.

BRA #72 CE Adamovic, Juraj (2018) – Decent skating, decent shot. Redirected the shot good in front of net. Delivered a tough hit openice. Good faceoffs.

BRA # 1 G Vojvoda, Michal (2010) – Good positioned, good reading, quick moving sideways, covered his pillars good. Looked a bit nonenergetic and slowly to get out his left foot on the Nitra GWG. Saved 23 of 25 shots.

BRA # 14 CE Vcelka, Kristian (2019) – Played aggressive, sometimes on the border. Decent skating. Was winning back the puck after catching up Nitra player, delivering an aggressive hit midzone on the board and bringing the puck back to Nitra slot.

NIT # 15 RW Stefanka, Tomas (2018) – Tall but thin RW that had good impact in the midzone game considering starting in 3rd line. Quit ok level for playing Slovak U20. Some nice passes and good moving and reading. Offensive minded attitude. Falls easy but looks to have some tools that will do when more weight eventually. Competitive, good positioned and covers shot in defensive zone.

NIT # 7 CE Hvizdos, Alexander (2018) – Not to tall but 194 lbs that he used with plenty of hits. Lot of times in front of net to catch rebounds or irritate a bit. Not super visualized but made some nice reading in good speed, finding his CE with a pass behind back.

HMHK Nitra U20: 2 – HC Slovan Bratislava U20: 1

Cretin-Derham Hall at Eden Prairie, December 2nd, 2017

EP #9 RW Mittelstadt, John (2020) – For his first ever High School game, Mittelstadt was impressive in his confidence with the puck. Showed good speed through the neutral zone and explosiveness on the game's opening goal by getting around the edge against a bigger defender and taking the puck to the net where his teammate cleaned up the rebound. Good vision and playmaking ability on the Power Play received the puck in the high slot and fed a nice pass down to teammate at the goal line through traffic for a scoring chance. Finished the evening with 2 assists. Mittelstadt is a 16th Round Phase 2 Draft Pick of Green Bay (USHL) and is a late 01 Birthdate and will be an interesting prospect to follow in the next couple years.

EP #18 LC Jensen, Jack (2018) – Tonight wasn't a real effective night offensively when it comes to points for Jensen but some of his notable skills were on display. Had excellent speed with the puck entering the offensive zone and showed quick hands and the ability to shoot in stride off the rush. Was physical on opponents and was good at digging pucks off the wall and make a quick play to get the things going in the right direction. Showed good vision while executing a beautiful one-touch pass across the slot to the far point from the half wall on the Power Play. While Jensen only was able to register 1 Assist tonight it was evident he is able to think the game at a higher level than his opponents at the high school level and generated a lot of the chances for his line.

CD #15 F Gleason, Matt (2020) – Showed quick feet and hands and can be elusive with the puck in tight areas. Scored from the hash marks on a quick shot, reaching across his body to his off side on a centering feed from the near corner. Showed good defensive awareness late in the 3rd by poke checking a D to D pass that resulted in an Empty Net goal to seal the victory. Was around the puck a lot in this game. Gleason is a late 01' DOB and was a 4th Round Draft Pick of the Chicago Steel in the 2017 USHL Futures Draft and still remains uncommitted to an NCAA Program.

Dulka Trencin U20 at Slovan Bratislava U20, December 3rd, 2017

BRA # 56 RD Ledenev, Roman (2018) – Good game. Very visualized and together with Baranov Ledenev was a big impact on the game with quick first passes or when joining in the rushes. Stick skills on top level for Slovak league by the small Russian player. Almost impossible to see who he will pass and the pass comes very quick. Two assists and 2 SOG

BRA # 12 LD Vitalos, Martin (2018) – Usually shoots more. 1 hard quick wrist shot from blue but not to accurate. Some good reading in third but overall not to much visualized in the game. 1 A and 1 SOG today.

BRA #72 CE Adamovic, Juraj (2018) – Had a quit invisible game for 2 periods although very good from points. Shot two times and one went in. Got another goal, setup by Baranov and Ledenev, when standing in front of the goal bouncing the puck. 1 strong hit. 2G 2 SOG.

BRA # 14 CE Vcelka, Kristian (2019) – Had a decent game and was involved in some of the chanses with Baranov and Ledenev. 1 A and 2 SOG.

BRA # 33 CE Egor, Baranov (2018) – Late 98 born player as usual the main reason of Slovan victory. Controls the puck, moves excellent on Slovak U20 level. 5-3 goal Baranov just took speed with the puck from offensive right FO area and brought it to the net splitting 3 Trencin player and passing the goalie, tipping the puck up high by the most far away pillar. I seen him in Slovak league since 2014/15 and at least he would do average to ok in Swedish U20 league. 1G 1A, 5 SOG.

TRN # 28 RW/CE Kukuca, Andrej (2018) – 6'2 right shooting late 99 born player with good tools that probably would have been in most of Slovak junior teams unless 99 version is the best in long time. Kukuca shoots the most in Slovak U20 league. Good hands, reading and speed. 2-2 he was during box play doing a high forechecking on Vitalis. 2-3 was a speedy rush with Okuliar, Kukuca finishing a pass from Okuliar up in the net corner. Kukuca was behind a lot today, especially together with Okuliar. 2G and 7 SOG.

TRN # 81 LW Okuliar, Oliver (2018) Was one of the better player on the ice and was one Trencin player that didn't slow down in third period, but stepped up. Competitive. This guy wanted to win. Very good in Box play and creating several turnarounds. Okuliar was throwing himself to block shots, goes full speed the whole shifts, removes Bratislava players efficient from net. Was having big impact on the game but didn't manage to get super many dangerous scoring chances. Nice rush together with Kukuca in box play resulted in 1A. 3 SOG

TRN # 59 RW Luhovy, Michal (2018) –Super small 5'5 99 born player that came in with good confidence after a 3-point game yesterday. Uses all his tools and on Slovak U20 level the size is not giving him any disadvantages since he plays with speed and pass players low by the board. No one seems to have told him that he is little because he plays aggressive, competitive and delivers hits and wins pucks with body checks. Extremely competitive and skates full speed until he is back on the bench. 1G, 6SOG.

TRN # 22 CE Ferenyi, Nicolas (2019) –Tall guy with some decent tools for Slovak U20 level. Decent reading but looks to think some half second too much. Not quick but once in a while he has ok speed and reach good. Good faceoffs. Looks thin but finish hits on the tougher Slovan guys a couple of times. Prepared with offensive hits by the board. Contributes in all zones. 2 SOG

TRN # 14 LD Chatrnuch, Michal (2018) – Defender that, if considering it's a 17-year-old kid playing in Slovak U20, has good eyes for the ice and can deliver nice passes. Shoots quit much regularly. Today wasn't so much visualized but finished some hits and had 1A to Luhovy. 3 SOG and +- 1

TRN # 89 CE Kovacik, Kristian (2018) – With 1,63 PPG in U20 and at least 1 game with Trencin in Slovak Extraliga, Didn't play and haven't been on ice since 22nd October.

Final Score: Slovan Bratislava U20: 5 – Dulka Trencin U20: 3

Medicine Hat Tigers at Moose Jaw Warriors, December 5th, 2017

MED#12 Rybinski, Henry (2019) – Rybinski was on the starting line for the Tigers, but other then that he did not show me very much. Decent size, but I did not notice him for most of the game. Playing on a line with two of Medicine Hat's top players he did not rise to their standards.

MED#29 Chyzowski, Ryan (2018) – Solid faceoff man, going 10/18. Took a bed hooking penalty. Had a costly turnover at the offensive blue line that led to a scoring chance for Moose Jaw. Second power play unit.

MJW#8 Almeida, Justin (2018) – Scored a goal and added an assist as part of Moose Jaw's top line. Took a majority of the face-offs for the Warriors. Took a tripping penalty. First power play and penalty kill unit.

MJW#16 Hartje, Chase (2018) – Chase had a terrible turnover behind his own goal which led to a Medicine Hat goal. Continued his point streak adding an assist. Second line power play, which scored a goal while he was on the ice.

MJW#18 Popple, Tate (2018) – Best game Tate has played all season. He has really stepped up in the past two weeks in the absence of Brett Howden moving up to the second line center spot. Worked hard every shit. Battled for pucks on the fore check. Coach Hunter showed major confidence in Tate putting him out on the 5 on 3-penalty kill. Tate added another assist tonight. Second power play and penalty kill units.

MJW#26 Benson, Matthew (2019) – Matthew's strongest game offensively this season with 2 assist. He put the puck on net nice and jumped up in the rush. Defensively however, ended the game a minus 3. That aside I felt he played a strong overall game. Second power play and penalty kill units.

MJW#27 Burzan, Luka (2018) – Showed his willingness to go the extra mile blocking a shot with little time left in the game to keep the game time. He did not register any points but his speed was a problem for the Medicine Hat D all game. Second power play unit.

London Knights at Niagara Ice Dogs, December 7th, 2017

LDN #2 RD Bouchard, Evan (2018) – Bouchard is the making of NHL defenseman down the road with size, strength physically and the ability to make plays. He made good, smart pinch early in the game from the blue line to keep offensive possession and was making good puck decisions from the back-end knowing when to rush, head-man puck, or join the play. He did mismanage on the first goal against as he did not tie up the goal scorer #23 Corneil stick out front on the crease. He also took unnecessary cross-check penalty in the 1st period in the corner when player really was not threatening. In the 2nd period he again was lacking on DZ coverage as partner #72 Regula took puck carrier up wall, but he let #15 Castleman the rebound, goal scorer through as he stood beside him. Also had concern on his desire to score on the power play from top of circle. He logs plenty of quality minutes and on PP it seemed his shot release was delayed and when he did shoot he was not really bearing down to put puck in back of net. He seemed a bit too relaxed and not utilizing his powerful shot or shot high/wide creating no rebound. You almost wonder being his 3rd year in the OHL he is getting a little bored. He has skill sets with physical play, puck mover, shot, good mobility and handle. Yet you would like for Bouchard to be a little more influencing at both ends of the ice for possible 1st round selection.

LDN #18 RW Foudy, Liam (2018) – He is decent size with overall solid skill sets and smarts, yet nothing high end. He played a steady up-n-down game on RW with good backcheck in 1st period to negate play. He missed breakaway opportunity early in the game. He did not show much for offensive game but effective in 2-way role. At this point he looks mid-later round pick.

LDN #24 RD Perrott, Andrew (2019) – For a rookie '01 OHLer, Perrott played a steady game as he worked he way into TOI as rostered as 7th Dman with Knights. He has a solid frame yet not overly tall. His skating stride is a bit choppy and will need to improve on initial steps to elude pressure although he did a good job at the offensive blue line with poise. He would side step and be active with puck to find shooting lanes or distribute puck. He made good puck decisions on outlets as well from the back end. Was pleasantly surprised with his game in making jump to juniors after watching last season with Honeybaked.

LDN #74 RD Regula, Alec (2018) – Regula was partnered with #2 Bouchard most of the night and actually played the off-side as a rookie. He did good job picking pucks on the left side as being RH off the wall. He made nice stretch pass early in game up the middle from own goal line to #18 Foudy for breakaway. He played with good poise to knowing where pressure was coming from and making a good 1st pass. At times he could have kept it a bit more simple in opting for quick pass, instead got pinned back in own zone. On the 1st goal against in the 1st period, he got caught up a bit on the crossing, weave play by Niagara forwards that exposed open ice and passing lane that lead to goal. He played solid minutes and good puck mover that has good potential with decision making, skating, handle and jumped up on the play at the right times to try and create more offense.

LDN #76 LC Moskal, Billy (2018) – He was lined up as 3rd line center and really did not think much of his play then early in 2nd period in went toe-to-toe in the OZ against #7 Langdon. He certainly threw some good punches. Later on in the period he showed a glimpse of some offensive sense as he skated behind net in OZ and threw pass back out front against his direction on #26 Nelson stick for great scoring opportunity.

LDN #31 G Kooy, Jordan (2018) – Kooy came in relief of starter #32 Raaymakers about 4 minutes into the 2nd period after an apparent 4th goal was scored, yet was then disallowed. Still Kooy played the rest of the way allowing no goals against. He is average size and height might be bit inflated as listed. He played steady while showing good positioning and made handful of saves in 3rd period to keep his team in the game.

NIA #4 LD MacPherson, Justin (2018) – He played an average game and did not really make impression one way or another. Keeps game simple with outlets and does not offer much offensive game.

NIA #26 RC Tomasino, Philip (2019) – At first did not really take notice to the '01 forward yet as the game went on you could see his hockey sense, ability to make plays with the puck in the offensive zone, and he versatilely. He was not afraid to battle along the walls for pucks and would find open man to create offense after gaining possession. He showed good signs for OHL rookie and will be a player to monitor over the next 18 months to track his progression.

NIA #28 LW Bruder, Andrew (2018) – He received limited TOI as 4th line LW. Did not see whole lot in skill sets as played limited role.

NIA #44 RC Thomas, Akil (2018) – Thomas was playing center on the night and did a decent job at the face-off dot as mostly played on the wing in viewings last season, probably went 50/50 on draws. He received secondary assist on the first Niagara goal as he and #16 Singer weaved upon zone entry getting Dman #72 Regula back on his heels which opened up time and space, leading to eventually #23 Corneil goal at the net. He then scored PPG in 1st period after London failed to clear puck, Thomas had lots of time in the high slot, while he could have opted to pass, he shot the puck beating the goalie high blocker side, looked like it muscled through a bit as well. He has offensive sense with good speed, yet not sure he is a 1st round pick. Thomas does not impact the game enough with possession and plays. He needs more consistent offensive pressure as only SOG came on his goal.

NIA #72 RW Johnson, Bradey (2018) – Watched Johnson a few times last season and was given limited TOI and hardly worthy of any notes. Although he still does not get top PP minutes and only 3rd line RW duties he plays smart as gets into position in the offensive zone for scoring opportunities and shows some decent stick skills, along with speed. Johnson shows some good instincts around the puck. Will be worthy to continually monitor in the second half of the season.

Mlada Boleslav U20 at Kometa Brno U20, December 8th, 2017

BRN # 14 RW Strondala, Vojtech (2019) – Short small Strondala was hungry and had a quit good game and with very energetic quick moving legs. He showed quick first steps although he is not yet so powerful in the legs. He reads the game good and was extra competitive today. Strondala was one that had a consistent level on the speed today. He showed a couple of quick released shots, quick wrists and some nice offensive puck moving in high speed. He looks mature and with confident. I constantly need to remind myself that this guy is still 16 years and do these things in U20 team. He has very efficient FO% and more or less cuts the puck to get it where he wants. Lack of weight and hockey-leg-muscles makes the balance, quick starts and turns possible to develop. At some times Strondala continues to focus on referees and Boleslav players after game started, lead to mistakes and Boleslav opportunities. 1G (GWG) and +-2

BRN # 11 LW Svoboda, Matej (2018) – I liked Svoboda today, very good attitude, competitive and he played with more speed than usual. Two times nice rush from own blue, did some quick direction changes, used toe ins. Noticed some good shots, first time a hard shot from slot slightly above the bar and second time resulting in a goal (5-1) with a quick wrist on goalies top corner. Looks to have good communication with Kowalczyk and Strondala. Today Svoboda used his tools good. Not sure if the higher speed was a coaching request due to quick Plasek away from the Strondala-Svoboda - Plasek line. 1G + 1A +-2

BRN # 13 C/LW Gajarsky, Adam (2018) – Has his stick down good, prepared for shots and redirections. Quick released accurate direct shots. During 5-10 minutes in second period he used his skills and most of his speed. Gajarsky and #23 Krejci had a nice puck rush and it was not too far away from Gajarsky to redirect the shot into the net. Gajarsky also had some nice combinations with #9. The 2-0 goal was a very quick accurate pass to the right side when Gajarsky was acting as LD in PP. Kowalczyk scored before the team and goalie managed to change side. Over the whole game Gajarsky did not used all his tools and Gajarsky was on ice both at 58.59 and 59.25, when Boleslav scored 2 quick goals against a Brno team that went on half gas. Gajarsky was covering his guys but the team cooperation was low on the line. I miss the attitude and the willingness to go flat out even if it will result in mistakes. Gajarsky has the tools to be one of the top Czech player. Today he had 1A and gets registered on -2.

BRN # 22 RD Kowalczyk, Daniel (2018) - Big RD that from time to time did really good stuff. Had some nice first passes, one to # 11 that was brilliant. He had a couple of quick shots from blue, one was really a bomb resulting in 2-1 goal. Had some unnecessary penalties and he could play more aggressive considering the big frame. Good positioned and gives a big impression size.

BRN # 25 LD Mlcak, Jan (2019) – The 01 born Mlcak was playing very mature, read the game good, he kept calm when under pressure. Played easy puck out but always with direction to Brno player. Mlcak did not hide himself, he took the opportunities to be in the game. He was on ice +1.

MLB # 15 Grim, Jan (2019) – 00 born. Didn't saw him much in the game. Big guy, did what expected. Had very good forecheck against Brno # 14 resulting in a turning and a scoring chance. 1+0, +-0

MLB # 5 Sipek, Jakub (2019) – Sipek did his 2nd game in U20, I didn't see much of him during the first 55 minutes. Sipek had ok skating and was visualized with high energy in the end, won the puck in the corner and put it in front of the net, then joined to the battle, against a week Brno line, in front of net resulting in a 5-3 goal.

Final Score: Kometa Brno U20: 5 – Mlada Boleslav: 3

Canada East vs Russia, U19 WJAC, Dec 10 2017

Canada East –

CAE #19 LC McBain, Jack (2018) – McBain had an average game for Canada East while centering the top line. He wasn't generating sufficient power in his stride, causing his acceleration to put him at a disadvantage while attempting to transition the puck up the ice in the neutral zone. The Russian defense and back-check was aggressive and targeted him for much of the night. Despite this, he did manage a primary assist after absorbing a cross-check before peeling back near the left circle, making a nice pass to Campoli for Canada's only goal. Along the boards he used his large frame and reach effectively to maintain puck possession and showed good vision, consistently setting up his teammates, including a nice passing sequence in the slot resulting in a great scoring chance late in the game. His best offensive moment came after he cut across the slot and wristed a heavy shot that barely missed the top corner, otherwise, like the rest of his team, he wasn't very dangerous.

CAE #9 LC Campoli, Nick (Golden Knights) – Campoli was drafted in the 6th round by Vegas in the 2017 draft and showed offensive flashes while centering the second line. He had a nice sequence in the first period, setting up his teammate at the top of the left circle and then rotating into position in-front of Miftakhof, where he tipped a shot which almost fooled the Russian netminder. He was in good position to receive a pass from McBain at the left circle, then delivered a quick wrist shot that was tipped off a Russian stick, leading to Canada's only goal. He had a couple of clean passes in the slot resulting in scoring chances however on a couple of plays he wasn't as patient with the puck as he could have been which resulted in turnovers.

CAE #5 LD Snell, Mason (2018) – Snell was playing on the third pairing for Canada while only getting a couple of shifts. During one sequence in the defensive end, he spun off Denisenko who was forechecking but got caught, he then attempted to recover and move the puck up the ice but was stripped of the puck leading to a quality scoring chance against. This play might have been one of the reasons his minutes were limited.

Russia –

RUS #1 G Miftakhof, Amir (2018) – Miftakhof anticipated the play consistently at the Hlinka and that continued here today. He's a small goaltender, standing 5'11 and although his reflexes are above average they're not his standout skill. What is his standout skill is processing a technical offensive play quickly, resulting in several quality reads that made difficult saves look relatively easy. His best save came off a read during a beautiful passing sequence that McBain had set up, however Miftakhof had anticipated the extra pass and moved into position, taking away the far side of the net. He rarely was caught out of position and remained square consistently throughout the game, this resulted in excellent rebound control and a minimal amount of secondary scoring chances against. He's got poise in the crease and has attributes that help him compensate for his size. He stopped 27-28 shots in a great performance.

RUS #28 RD Okhotyuk, Nikita (2019) – Okhotyuk showed a two-way physical brand of hockey while playing in all situations and receiving top pairing minutes. It took only 30 seconds for Okhotyuk to make a statement after delivering a massive yet clean body check on his opponent at the defensive blueline. That physical play continued for much of the night as he looked to use his size and aggression against any Canadian who was willing to drive into the slot or hack at Miftakhof while looking for rebounds. He transitioned the puck up the ice effectively from his own-end and was well positioned in-front of the net. His offensive game showed continued improvement, in some previous outing's I found it was streamlined, opting for routine plays that didn't use his tools enough, however in today's game he cut wide, driving towards the net on a couple of sequences and he also cut across the slot, making a nice feint that opened up his shooting lane, giving him a quality scoring chance. He was good on both sides of the ice.

RUS #3 LD Galeniuk, Danila (2018) – Galenuik was Okhotyuk's defensive partner and played in all situations. His defensive play was also physical and he used it along the boards, effectively pinning players and hitting the Canadians in open-ice. He made consistent defensive reads on the penalty-kill, effectively getting into shooting lanes and boxing out players around the crease. Offensively he wasn't overly threatening but he did distribute the puck on the powerplay, recognizing that the best plays for him were to deliver quick passes to his dynamic teammates who controlled the pace of the play along the dhalf-wall.

RUS #14 LW Denisenko, Grigori (2018) – Denisenko was the most dangerous player on either team today, showing good chemistry with Kotkov on the third-line while playing on the top powerplay. His skating isn't explosive but he's got a fluid stride and terrific edges, making him elusive. During one sequence, he cut across the slot, slipping past two Canadian defenders and wiring a wrist shot off the far post. On another sequence, Denisenko used plus acceleration to cut wide on a defender and then hesitated which created a reaction by Alexander to think a pass was coming across the slot just as he shot it far-side. Denisenko displayed high-end vision which resulted in a beautiful three-way passing play, giving him a primary assist on Romonov's goal. His puck skills and poise are excellent and this allowed him to control the tempo of the game on the half-wall during the powerplay and at even-strength. His defensive game was good as well, he had a couple of aggressive back-checks, but he did get ejected with 10 minutes left after checking a player in the head. It felt like Denisenko was capable of generating any offensive play he chose in today's game, he finished with three points including two assists.

RUS #7 RW Kotkov, Vladislav (2018) – Kotkov showed a finesse element to his game while displaying chemistry with Denisenko on the third-line. He's a towering winger, standing 6'4, 200 pounds, unfortunately he doesn't generate much power in his base despite his build, giving him average top speed. He used his plus puck skills and vision to compensate for his lack of foot speed giving him several nice sequences. He was responsible for the first goal even though he registered the secondary assist; as the puck was about to exit the offensive blueline, he used quick hands to keep it in and then passed it off to his teammate before using his frame to screen Alexander, resulting in the goal from the point. He had several quality passing plays with Denisenko, leading to scoring chances. He finished with two assists.

RUS #22 RW Iskhakov, Ruslan (2018) – Iskhakov is a diminutive winger who played bigger than his size on the top-line and powerplay unit. On several shifts, larger players would attempt to knock Iskhakov off the puck unsuccessfully, as he used superior balance to stay up-right and make plays under pressure. During Denisenko's powerplay goal, Iskhakov out-competed a larger player along the boards before making a quick pass which resulted in the goal. On another play, he stripped a bigger defenseman off the puck from behind the net and then delivered a nice pass into the slot giving him a primary assist. He's not intimidated and showed skill with the puck on his stick.

RUS #17 LW Zavgorodny, Dmitri (2018) – Although Zavgorodny caught fire during the Hlinka, that didn't happen against Canada East today. His offensive game wasn't consistent, as he was largely invisible for the first half of the game. His play did pick up after Denisenko's 5-minute major, which resulted in a quality scoring chance using his elite release that came close to beating Alexander far-side. He showed some physicality out there, back-checking effectively on one play and delivering a hit on another.

Final Score 5 – 1 Russia

Canada West vs Czech Republic, U19 WJAC, Dec 10 2017

Canada West -

CAW #6 LD Tychonick, Jonny (2018) – Tychonick showed dynamic offensive ability while playing in all situations for Canada West, including top pairing minutes. He displayed the ability to rush the puck by using his speed. His skating mechanics are excellent and his stride looked effortless, this allowed him to walk the line effectively, creating space, as well as carry the puck from the defensive end to the offensive end consistently. He scored a beautiful goal off an end-to-end rush by weaving around multiple defenders and cutting across the crease, firing a wrist-shot over Kloucek's pad. He wasn't only aggressive in the offensive end, as he took away space quickly against the Czech's in the defensive end as well, using an active stick for puck retrieval along the boards and finishing his checks. His first pass was hard and he needed little time to assess his options effectively when breaking out of the zone. On the powerplay, he used feints such as angled slap passes to create looks for his teammates and got his shot through traffic. He was the most noticeable player on either team.

CAW #4 RD Bernard-Docker, Jacob (2018) – Bernard-Docker was utilized on the top defensive pairing, displaying a solid two-way game. He understood his role, playing more passively than Tychonick, which allowed Tychonick more opportunities to use his gifts in the offensive end, however he still showed the ability to carry the puck over the offensive blueline, making several effective rushes. Defensively, he displayed a good first pass and supported his teammates along the boards. He finished with a primary assist.

CAW #3 LD Gourley, Jarrod (2018) – Used on the third defensive pairing, Gourley showed some shut-down qualities on the ice. His skating needs work as he has a slow first step, this caused him to get burned by Rousek leading to the first goal against, however he did keep the Czechs to the outside for most of the night. His best attribute was his physical play and when combined with his 6'2, 200-pound frame, he delivered some big hits, none bigger than a solid body check on the much larger Kondelik, which sent the centre crashing to the ice. His first pass was mixed, he took too much time identifying his options on some plays in the defensive end, this caused him to send telegraphed passes that lead to turnovers, however he did make a heads-up play in the neutral zone by delivering a quick backhand pass to his teammate under pressure, preventing a turnover as well. His size and physicality stood out.

CAW #9 LW Crookshank, Angus (2018) – Crookshank played with good pace and was the driver of his 2nd line. He's an aggressive player on the forecheck and took direct-routes to the net despite his smaller stature. His acceleration was above average and he was tenacious when pursuing the puck, there were several shifts where it seemed like the puck was following him around the ice. He showed plus puck skills and this allowed him to breakdown the Czech defense, leading to quality scoring chances. He picked up a secondary assist off De Jong's goal.

CAW #23 RC Johnson, Kyle (2018) – Johnson had an effective two-way game today for Canada, showing good penalty killing instincts while centering the third line. He made several good defensive reads at the blueline on the penalty-kill and had a tenacious backchecking effort on one sequence, stripping a player off the puck, resulting in a clear. Offensively, he showed plus hands as he attempted to pull the puck between his legs and drive wide on a Czech defender. He was also an effective puck distributer, making tape-to-tape passes to his teammates quickly as he entered the offensive end.

Czech Republic –

CZE #3 LD Zelingr, Matyas (2018) – Zelingr has excellent size for a defenseman, standing 6'3, 200-pounds with a broad frame, using it to effectively shut-down Canada's more dynamic forwards. Logging first-pairing minutes put him up against Canada's top-line and he was very good at shutting this line down for much of the game. He used his strength to overpower Canada down-low in the corners, causing turnovers, he also was effective at angling aggressive players who were attempting to drive wide on him. His first pass out of his own end was accurate but he didn't look comfortable when carrying the puck over the neutral zone. Offensively, he played a relatively simple game but did recognize when a lane was open to get his shot through traffic, his slapshot had weight behind it. He was good out there today.

CZE #29 LC Kondelik, Jachym (2018) – A towering center who used his size to his advantage while centering the Czechs top-line and been deployed on the powerplay. Despite his 6'6 build, Kondelik has impressive coordination, giving him plus skating mechanics. His acceleration is well above average for his size and he can generate surprising speed which he used on the forecheck. On one sequence, he knocked a defender off the puck in the corner during a foot-race, this play was the catalyst for the Czechs second goal. On the powerplay, he was an immovable object in-front of the net and ended up scoring a quick backhand goal. His passing ability was better than his shooting ability in today's match up, I found his shot was soft and the release clumsy. Overall, Kondelik finished with a goal and an assist while showing plus tools.

CZE #20 LC Rousek, Lukas (2018) – Rousek was one of the more dangerous forwards for either team while centering the third line and been utilized on the powerplay. His acceleration and edge work are both high-end, this combined with his ability to change his pace made it difficult for the Canadian defense to predict his movement. On one sequence, he used soft hands to skate over the offensive blueline and then cut wide on Gourley before firing a quick wrist shot five-hole for the opening goal. He continued to show plus offensive instincts as he recognized the defense was too high, poking the puck past them to his teammate, resulting in a quality scoring chance. On a two-on-one sequence, he delivered a quick saucer-backhand pass to his teammate resulting in an excellent scoring chance. Although his play trailed off towards the end of the game, he generated several quality scoring chances.

Final Score 5-2 Czech Republic

JYP Jyväskylä at Kometa Brno, Champions League QF, December 12th, 2017

BRN # 25 LW Plasek, Karel (2018) – Plasek was given 5,45 minutes in the earlier part of the game. He was using his speed and created quick pressure on the JYP puck mover. Plasek had some very active shifts, was creating opportunities. Once he was breaking the puck on own blue and the next he was reading and keeping the puck in offensive zone. Did some Ok passes to Necas at one shift when they were lined up. On game playing 4 on 4 he joined on a rush with #90 but let #90 go all way instead of joining to take rebounds, receive passes or confuse he goalie. I saw Plasek stopping up later in a similar position, not sure if it was done based on coaching. More visualized during the 5,45 minutes given then the points and stats where telling. 0 SOG, 0p.

BRN # 13 LW Gajarsky, Adam (2018) – Gajarsky was only given 2 shifts and had 0.36 TOI. His legs where moving more than they do in U20 team and he looks more relaxed and confident. He had good speed and was competitive, was positioning himself in front of the net with stick down, got a puck from behind net but got the upper body turned too little to get a good angle and a good hit. Gajarsky wasn't seen more on ice after that. 1 SOG.

BRN # 88C/ RW Necas, Martin (CAR) – Necas will always be entertaining to view with his skills and talents. Regular quick reading and nice skating. Excellent quick turns, quick passes opening for scoring opportunities. Not sure if Necas put too much pressure on himself or was thinking slightly too much to win the game; over the whole game he wasn't looking as his regular game although at occasions he is the same brilliant player, especially in the end when more pressure to act. He looks to have added weight. On the 0-1 goal Necas is acting as a defender when 3 Brno players went a bit to high, looks like Necas has good control of the #26 coming in but potentially tries to catch the puck instead of removing the other player or his stick. At 0-2 Necas in very short millisecond looked to slightly misread and went on one player a bit too hard instead of staying in the middle using a long stick. Necas was joining a good rush with RW Svoboda but he either miss to shoot or lets the puck pass through him to LW# 16. Necas and # 16 had a good rush and Necas is always ready with the stick, receives a good backwards pass and directs the puck in net before the D or the Goalie can do anything. Very hidden nice passes camouflaged and in the middle of a dribbles. Necas adds extra energy in the end and really tries to catch up, creating chances and win the game.

BRN # 17 RW Mlynar, Tomas (2018) – 98 born Mlynar gives me the impression that he accepts his role better in the CHL and TELH team. Mlynar had 5,21 TOI and during some shifts he was having speed, being competitive. Other shifts he looks like he pushes a little bit too much. Had a nice rush receiving a long pass from own D, but didn't reached the net. 0 SOG. 0P

BRN # 22 LW/C Suss, Jan (2018) – 99 born Suss had 3 SOG in the last weeks CHL game and scored 3 goals while just 8,46 TOI. Today Suss had less impact. Suss won 3 of his 6 Faceoffs, had good reading but I didn't saw so much of his regular speed with puck or competing for his own rebounds. Only 5,23TOI, 2 SOG.

Final Score: JYP Jyväskylä: 5 – Kometa Brno: 3

Owen Sound Attack at Barrie Colts, December 14th, 2017

BAR #2 D Tucker, Tyler (2018) – Tucker had an up and down game. He did a nice job keeping gaps tight as a whole but on a couple occasions quicker players used that to their advantage and turned on the jets to get by him and create chances (and in one case, draw a penalty). For the most part, though, he was able to stay close to attackers, steer them wide, and seal them off. He landed a few big hits, including a massive bone crunching hip check after forcing a player wide at the blue line. With the puck, he was pretty quiet. He made a surprisingly accurate two-zone outlet to send teammates on an odd-man rush but he didn't carry the puck often and was not overly involved when play was set up in the offensive zone.

BAR #14 RW Svechnikov, Andrei (2018) – Svechnikov was the best player on the ice from start to finish. He got into some pretty feisty battles early on and that really seemed to get him going. He was a force along the wall, as well as in the cycle game, and did a great job of using his powerful frame to protect the puck. He routinely skated through contact and stick checks and had no problem driving to the net to create Grade A opportunities any time he wanted to. His best sequence of the game came on a play where he skated circles around the entire Attack team in the offensive zone before dishing the puck off to an open teammate, driving the net, and banging in the rebound. He scored a hat trick (one goal came with an empty-net) but he probably should have had another goal or two. He was that dominant.

BAR #61 LW Suzuki, Ryan (2019) – Suzuki didn't get on the scoresheet but I thought he had a pretty good game. He was effective on the forecheck and was able to pressure Owen Sound's defense into a couple turnovers that led to chances. His puck movement in general was good but the highlight definitely came when he accepted a pass in stride with a defender on him and made a beautiful pass on his backhand to a trailing player to send him on a mini-breakaway.

OS #15 C Struthers, Matthew (2018) – Struthers wasn't able to generate much offense for himself, especially in one-on-one situations, but he did a nice job in front of the net screening Lazarev and that led directly to one of the Attack's goals. He struggled in the faceoff circle and spent a lot of his time in the defensive zone.

OS #27 C Dudas, Aidan (2018) – Dudas was definitely Owen Sound's biggest offensive threat. He was dynamic with the puck on his stick and his plus playmaking skills were on full display as he was distributing the puck all over the ice to create chances for teammates. He did a good job of not only hitting teammates with passes, but leading them into open ice where they'd have a better opportunity to make something happen. He used sharp cuts on a couple occasions to lose defenders and buy himself more time to make a play. He was tough to pin and contain along the wall as well. While he was excellent with the puck, there were a few occasions where he was hemmed into the defensive zone and caught running around.

OS #11 RW Groulx, Daylon (2018) – Groulx only played a minute or so but it was certainly eventful. He started his game off with a nice play luring a defender to him and moving the puck to a teammate to attack the open space and create a chance. He was drilled over the middle right after that and was clearly frustrated as shortly after he took a five minute penalty for checking to the head.

Final Score: Barrie Colts: 6 – Owen Sound Attack: 4

Unites States vs Russia, U19 World Junior A Challenge, December 14 2017

Unites States –

U.S #9 LC Drury, Jack (2018) – Drury continued to show a dangerous game on the powerplay against Russia but wasn't overly effective at even strength. He has an above average top gear, using it to carry the puck over the offensive blueline and set up a couple of scoring chances. On one shift he made an accurate bank-pass off the boards to his teammate in the neutral zone, he made the play under pressure and it was well executed. His most dangerous moment was when he made a nice reverse spin along the goal-line, coming out in-front of the net and firing a wrist-shot that he put over the bar, he showed some creativity and he recognized the space he had.

U.S #10 RC Madden, Tyler (2018) – Madden was dangerous against Russia, scoring twice while also been an effective penalty killer, showing two-way qualities. He could have had a hattrick, as he had a dangerous scoring chance after receiving a pass in the slot where he was robbed by Miftakhof's blocker. He ended up tucking in a puck to the side of the net off a missed shot and his second goal was a result of been in the right place at the right time in-front of the net, where he scored off a quick wrist shot that went under Miftakhof's pad. He had a beautiful sequence in the 2nd showing his puck skills and ability to think quickly under pressure as he made a pass to himself off the boards, eluding one Russian forechecker in the neutral zone before peeling back and using his hands to beat an aggressive defender one-on-one. Defensively, he was engaged again today and he made some great plays on the penalty kill resulting in quick clears and transitioning the puck up the ice to eat the clock.

U.S #16 LW McLaughlin, Blake (2018) – McLaughlin showed strong skating mechanics and continued to find his teammates in the offensive end. He had a good sequence where he carried the puck to the top of the right circle and then used a wrist-shot feint before passing it off to his teammate for a scoring chance. His shot wasn't dangerous, he received a pass from his teammate but took to long to settle into the shot, he had trouble changing the angle on a couple of different attempts. His top speed was above average as he went around a Russian player on the powerplay, he was under heavy pressure but was strong on the puck, out powering his opponent leading to continued possession for his team. He made a strong defensive play using his speed again, stick-checking a surprised Russian along the boards and stripping him off the puck. His vision and passing ability are high-end and he played well along the half-wall on the powerplay.

U.S #17 LC Cotter, Paul (2018) – Cotter had some good sequences while getting limited minutes. He scored the first goal of the game after recognizing an opening in the slot, he received a pass and took little time getting his shot off for the first goal of the game, the release was quick and the shot was accurate, beating MIftakhof far-side. He showed a physical presence both on the forecheck and backcheck, delivering multiple hits in the first that caused turnovers, he knows how to use his frame and his timing was excellent, he caught his opponents off balance.

U.S #21 LW Steeves, Alex (2018) – Steeves was more noticeable against Russia, finishing with two assists. He fired a low wrist shot in the slot that resulted in an assist after the rebound was collected and tucked in the net from behind the goal-line. Had a good sequence midway through the second where he set up his teammate for a scoring chance before gliding into the slot and deflecting the puck on net through a screen. He showed defensive awareness as he made a nice deflection off a Russian pass attempt in the neutral zone, disrupting the play.

U.S #24 LW Randl, Jack (2018) – Randl was arguably the most effective bottom six player on either team. Had a good keep in at the blueline, delivering a nice pass to his teammate on one shift, had a wrist-shot that went far-side that was difficult for Miftakhof to handle. On another play, he made a nice drop-pass as he cut across the slot leading to a quality scoring chance. His best sequence occurred when he absorbed a hit in the neutral zone and then skated hard over the offensive blueline where he made a saucer pass that landed on the tape of Hall who missed the net, he regathered the puck and delivered another quality pass in the slot under pressure with his back turned before the net was knocked off. He showed that he can pass the puck and played with good pace.

Russia –

RUS #28 RD Okhotyuk, Nikita (2019) – Okhotyuk had a difficult game for Russia as he didn't seem to have any energy out there. His decision making was mixed, choosing to dump the puck in several times while transitioning into the offensive end, both times resulted in the puck getting turned over, one of them was on the powerplay, so would have preferred him attempting to hold onto the puck on the sequence. He still displayed a physical brand of hockey, taking a huge hit after the whistle but bounced right back up, had two big hits himself in the first. Had an unforced penalty by flipping the puck over the glass, again the decision making just wasn't there in either zone. Was slow getting to a lose puck in the corner, he had no business getting out-competed considering the American forechecker started his pursuit at the blueline and Okhotyuk was only a few feet away from the puck. His first pass which has been accurate in previous viewings wasn't there against the States, he had an uncharacteristic game but still put his body on the line and has upside.

RUS #14 LW Denisenko, Grigori (2018) – Denisenko wasn't utilized enough against the States but still had some dangerous sequences and showing excellent forechecking skills. Denisenko had a breakaway attempt where he telegraphed the shot location, however on the same shift he fired a quick one-timer on net resulting in a difficult save, he was the best Russian in the first. Took a bad high-sticking penalty in the second right after his team got a powerplay opportunity, this might be why his ice-time was reduced. Had a quality sequence on the powerplay where he carried the puck around the U.S goal-line and came back out in the high-slot releasing a quick wrist-shot that missed the top corner, shortly after, he received a pass from the half-wall and delivered a one-timer on net. Had a tremendous forechecking sequence early in the second where he aggressively checked one American off the puck and then pulled back to his forehand which evaded the pressure from the other defenseman before making a tape-to-tape pass to his teammate at the top of the blueline. Again, on a penalty-kill, he beat his man to a loose puck and created havoc below the goal-line. He plays bigger than his size along the boards and showed off his skill, though he was more inconsistent today.

RUS #22 RW Iskhakov, Ruslan (2018) – Iskhakov was one of the more effective forwards for Russia, playing at a high pace while utilizing his skating ability. Had an end-to-end rush where he showed plus agility and edge work, weaving his way through traffic before losing the puck off a check. Showed quick hand on a breakaway, pulling to his backhand at the last second but failed to capitalize as he was aggressively backchecked on the play. His decision making is quick, as he had a heads-up sequence where he anticipated a clearing attempt on the powerplay, got into the lane and used his stick to knock down the puck before it exited the zone, he then spun off pressure and delivered a pass to Denisenko at the right point to maintain puck possession. Had a great scoring chance after rushing down the wing, pulling the puck while drifting which opened up the U.S goalie, he missed short-side but the release was quick and there was velocity behind the shot. Used his speed throughout the game, drew one penalty off a backchecker and should have drawn two but the refs missed a call when he was tripped after going around an American player. He had more energy and determination than most of his teammates against the States, he was competitive and was noticeable.

Final Score: 5-0 United States

Elk River Elks vs Edina Hornets, December 15th, 2017

ED #20 RD Vorlicky, Mike (2018) – Vorlicky has decent size and displayed above average footwork and decent straight line skating. Showed the ability to walk the offensive blue line and change the angle for his shots from the point. Vorlicky executed some nice rushes up the ice with the puck, using his size and stickhandling on one play up the wall and then finding a teammate in the slot as he entered the offensive zone for a good scoring chance. Vorlicky did have one play at his own blue line where he blew a tire, allowing the opposition to go in on a 2 on 1 in the first period, luckily the opposition wasn't able to convert on but for the most part was very solid in his one on one defending and defensive zone coverages. Vorlicky is part of a very talented D-core for the Edina Hornets but saw a decent amount of time on the Power Play tonight where he didn't make a lot of dynamic plays but was able to distribute the puck around the offensive zone and get pucks through traffic. Vorlicky was a 6th Round futures pick in 2016 of the Sioux Falls Stampede (USHL).

ED #17 LD Brinkman, Ben (2019) – Brinkman displayed some of the high end skills tonight that show why he is one of the higher end defensive prospects for next year's NHL entry draft out of the State of Minnesota. The University of Minnesota commit showed excellent poise with the puck in all 3 zones. Scored on a nice low hard wrist shot coming down from the left point, as well as registering an assist on another goal. Displayed a lot of clean outlet passes and did an excellent job in finding his forwards quickly with speed in the neutral zone which allows his team to play with a lot of pace. Brinkman did try a couple high risk plays at each blue line in this game that could have cost his team, on one play he tried jumping up the grab a puck with his hand at his own blue line that he missed on that results in a 2 on 1 against and tried to stickhandle through at the offensive blue line that also resulted in a chance going the other way, however in this game the good far outweighed the bad in regards to his overall play. Showed sound 1 on 1 defending against Jack Perbix of Elk River on one play who tried an outside-in move coming into the offensive zone, Brinkman effectively playing the body.

ED #23 LW/C Koumontzis, Demetrios (2018) – Koumontzis isn't a big player but showed a strong skating base and has above average footwork that allowed him to create space for himself. Displayed some slick hands in traffic and was able to find the open man in the offensive zone effectively. Koumontzis scored off a center ice faceoff by being first into the offensive zone and pressuring the Elk River defenseman which resulted in the Defense getting crossed over and he found the puck on his stick in the slot and beat the goalie with a quick shot. Koumontzis effort in all three zones was consistent in this game, he doesn't possess impressive size or explosive straight line skating but his all-around effort, hockey IQ and puck skills were all on display in this game, resulting in 1 goal and 1 assist.

ED #2 RD Boltmann, Jake (2019) – Quietly registered 3 assists in this game. Boltmann is a late 01' DOB and also a University of Minnesota commit and it's easy to imagine both Boltmann and Brinkman being Defensive partners at Minnesota in the future. They work well together as a pair, Boltmann played more of a stay at home game tonight and supported his partner in situations and defended some odd man rushes well. Boltmann displayed excellent passing in the offensive zone, threading some cross slot feeds on the tape as well as creating lanes for himself by making quick moves with his feet. Couple of his assists came from good point shots that were able to get through traffic and to the net area.

ED #22 LW Jungels, Jett (2018) – Plays a very similar game to his teammate and line mate Sammy Walker (2017 Rd. 7 TBL). Displayed explosive skating and an up tempo game that gave Elk River fits in transition. Jungles had 5 Assists in this game and created scoring chances with most of his zone entries with the puck. Can make plays at a high speed and makes crisp tape to tape passes. Showed the ability to come out of the corners with the puck against bigger, stronger opponents and despite not having a lot of size, shields and protects the puck well. Shot isn't overly powerful so his scoring ability doesn't stretch too far out in the offensive zone at the stage, but can get it off quickly and through screens. Played a little bit too much on the perimeter, which he can get away with at this level but may not translate as well at the Junior or college levels.

ED #10 RC Walker, Samuel (TB) – Walker showed in this game why he really shouldn't be playing High School hockey this year. Walker registered 5 goals and an Assist in this game and that is probably the least he could have scored in this one. Walker scored in a number of different ways, he was opportunistic, finding some rebounds in traffic that he was able to put home. He also beat a defender 1 on 1 going through the stick and feet and beating the goalie while falling down going to the net on his off side. He showed he is able to make plays at a speed that is very hard to stop at the high school level.

ER #12 RC Perbix, Jack (2018) – Appeared to score off a cycle play on the half wall where he cut to the middle, did a good job creating space for himself and beating the Edina goalie over the shoulder but the shot might have been deflected. Perbix has impressive size and displayed good physicality along the walls and in front of the net. Hey was keyed in on for most of the night and showed the ability to still create despite not be given a lot of space once he got the puck in the offensive end. Perbix lack of explosiveness is his skating continues to be a work in progress as he lost some puck races and was able to get caught with back pressure at times. Perbix has high end offensive instincts and is good creating offense out of nothing but his skating will need to continue to improve in order for him to be more of a threat in transition.

ER #9 LC Michaelis, Zach (2020) – Showed a high motor and work ethic all over the ice, even late with the game out of reach. Scored on a quick shot from the faceoff circle, coming off the boards that caught the goaltender by surprise. Played with a fearless approach in driving middle ice and going to the net. Will likely be a fairly high pick in this coming USHL Phase 1 Draft.

Kamloops Blazers at Moose Jaw Warriors, December 15th, 2017

KAM#7 Zazula, Luke (2018) – Played the game on a fine line between a pest and a dirty player. Got under the other teams skin, but at times made some plays that I felt were dirty. Moved the puck well, and used his speed. Undersized but did not back down. Second power play unit.

KAM#18 Zary, Connor (2019) – Had 2 assists, showed off good skill and hands through out the game. Made some great passes. High hockey IQ.
First power play unit.

MJW#16 Hartje, Chase (2018) – Chase saw his minutes increase tonight due to injuries to Josh Brook and Jett Woo. Chase stepped up on the second power play unit moving the puck vey well. Struggled in his own end defensively. In a 5-2 he finished the game even.

MJW#26 Benson, Matthew (2019) – Terrible turnover in front of his own net lead to the fourth Blazers goal. Struggled with the pressure that Kamloops showed all night. Second power play unit.

MJW#27 Burzan, Luka (2018) – Luka didn't show me anything tonight. Speed was good. All of Moose Jaw struggled to get anything going offensively. Second power play unit.

MJW#39 Evanoff, Adam (2018) – The first loss of the season for Adam. Let in a few weak goals early, which put MJ under the eight ball. I didn't like some of his decisions playing the puck. Finished the game strong.

Czech Republic U17 at Kometa Brno U20, December 19th, 2017

CZE #27 F Rychlovsky, Jakub (2019) - Rychlovsky is a small guy I have not noticed before, have never seen him in national team and this year he has played 4 games in U20 Liberec and managed 5 points. Managed to score a quick 1st goal with a quick finishing assisted by Peterek and Berenek. Came in with speed in second period and released a shot not too difficult to catch by the goalie. Was putting high pressure on the Brno puck mover. Decent skating and agility.

CZE # 24 F Berenek, Martin (2019) - Was behind the 1-0 with Peterek ending with a goal by Rychlovsky. Put good pressure on puck mover and goalie. Berenek had quit good skating and agility. Tall. Went quick on a puck from Peterek and gave a quick very hidden pass to a free Peterek for scoring chance.

CZE # 16 F Peterek, Jonas (2019) - Was behind 1-0 goal 1 A, Had some few chances in second but not too much visualized. Peterek has excellent puck checks and reading but I would like him to use his speed more. More visualized in the end. Was winning a loose puck behind in defensive right corner, brought the puck, lifted the puck for a quick moving Berenek by the right board while skating to mid ice, receiving the puck back and tried a backhand shot. Lying on the ice behind offensive net he was managed to get a pass indicating that has very strong wrists.

CZE # 17 F, Najman, Adam (2019) - Did not saw much of him although had good points in National team earlier. Good shot in end of 3rd Had good moving of the legs especially in some shifts in the end of the game bringing the puck south north with speed.

CZE # 22 F, Lang, Martin (2019) Very nice quick combination between Lang, Morong and Muzik resulted in 2-1 by Muzik. Very alert and visualized. Almost involved in every chance in the last 15 minutes. Active with Muzik and Koffer.Not the highest full speed but quick first strides.

CZE # 5 D, Kubicek, Simon (2020) Tall right shooting defender had a nice shot in third.

CZE # 23 C, Koffer, Filip (2019) - Small quick player that had a good day. Had a backhand shot in second. Was later in 2nd shooting the puck on net and Zeman scored on the rebound to 3-1. Read the good game and was first on pucks. Tipped a very quick invisible pass from behind the net but no one including in the other U17 player managed to read it and score what would have been a free puck in the empty right side of the goal. Good skating and went for an open ice hit in 3rd although backed from it. Good chance with Mlcak at 56.44 but goalie moved quick. Good chemistry with Muzik and Lang. Clever with body by the board to win puck.

CZE # 19 F, Morong, Matej (2019) - Very nice quick combination between Lang, Morong and Muzik resulted in 2-1 by Muzik. Put good quick pressure in boxplay resulting in turnarounds.

CZE #29 F, Muzik, Radek (2019) - Very nice quick combination between Lang, Morong and Muzik resulted in 2-1 by Muzik. Nice reading of Brno mistakes led to a rush in 2nd period but no one joined him on the rush and the released shot was blocked by Goalie. Muzik and Koffer had good chemistry with accurate perfect timed passes. Muzik used a mistake during powerplay and brought the puck, Muzik released the shot that Koffer got a stick on for redirection.

CZE # 10 F, Zeman, Tomas (2019) - Small right shooter that had a nice shot from the board in second. Was moving stick good when in offensive zone on forecheck, managed to keep the puck and create a scoring chance.

CZE # 13 F, Pistek, Theodor (2019) - Didn't see much of him during the game. Very active in the end with competitive game and going on the net for rebounds and irritation. 0+0

CZE # 18 C, Pytlik, Jaromir (2020) - Tall playmaker that was not as visualized. Joined Najman on a rush in the end and went quick on net to get rebounds.

CZE # 6 LD/RD, Mlcak, Jan - Good playmaking skills resulted in a hard-accurate shot from Mlcak from right side.

CZE # 26 C, Kremen, Adam (2019) - Did not see much of him but he was very active and competitive in the end, was blocking shot and killed time. Had 1 goal.

BRN # 14 RW/ C, Strondala, Vojtech had quick legs and nice puck moving skills, quick changes of directions, some successful toe ins and when CZE U17 set up a very defensive strategy, Strondala managed to get through a couple of times. Very competitive and one of the biggest challenges for CZE U17 today. Playmaking skills setup some quick puck moving shifts that created chances to pass a defensively very talented CZE U17 team.

BRN # 22 RD, Kowalczyk, Daniel - Big RD had some nice shots and showed good reading and playmaking. Not getting stressed.

Final Score: Czech Republic U17: 4 – Kometa Brno: 2

WJC U20 - Team Russia vs. Team Czech Republic, December 26th, 2017

RUS #14 RW Svechnikov, Andrei (2018) – He is LH shot that plays the right wing and also sees time on the PP on the off side and on the PK as well. He was on the ice for first goal against on the PK, as play made out of the corner with pass in the slot. Svechnikov makes smart puck decisions with puck in breakout, transition, or puck movement on the power-play. He rarely forces the play as has good awareness. He made nice play in 2nd period off rush to set-up #11 Abramov with nice seam pass for beauty scoring chance at net. He snapped a shot on net on the PP in 3rd period, yet he did not show any dynamic play. His skating is adequate with no high-end speed or superior agility or edge work and stick skills are above average. He succeeds because of his smarts and when he does find that opportunity he strikes.

CZE #11 LD Kral, Filip (2018) – Kral played a steady. Smart game. He takes care of business in his own zone with good stick placement and gap control. He is a puck moving Dman who competes in all three zones. He scored the eventual GWG on point shot in 3rd period on 1-timer that beat the goalie blocker-side that seemed to waffle a bit past the goalie.

CZE #16 RC Kaut, Martin (2018) – Kaut was the draft eligible player that made the most impression in Game 1 of WJC. He made play early on the PP out of corner as he fed #8 Necas in the slot with nice saucer pass over Dman stick on 1st Czech goal from the goal line. He then again showed patience and vision on the PP on the 3rd Czech goal in the 2nd period as he took pass down low off the side of net on FH, and had option of shooting yet found better option in back-door pass to #18 Zadina for the goal. He then set-up #11 Kral for 5th goal simply by showing good puck decision and laying pass right in wheelhouse for 1-timer. He played a steady 2-way game at center that competes at both ends. He has long reach and good puck skills and awareness. He seems to fall into early-mid round selection for 2018 NHL Draft.

CZE #18 LW Zadina, Filip (2018) – Zadina is a good skater as he is shifty, agile on edges and shows good bursts to create separation. He also handles the puck quite well on his stick in small areas or off the rush with speed. He won puck battle in corner on 1st goal on the PP that led to secondary assist. He showed good hands in tight and he is one of those players that is dangerous around the puck. He scored PPG in 2nd period off back-door #16 Kaut pass that he made no mistake and stuck up top making sure goalie had no chance coming back across. He is a player that shows good offensive instincts and high 1st round pick for June's NHL Draft.

CZE #20 LW Lauko, Jakub (2018) – Lauko is average size and skill sets were average here too. He skates adequately with no high-end speed or great lateral footwork. He was given limited time on ice. He is a player that worked hard on the forecheck and tried competing for pucks. He actually looked a bit nervous as fell a few times. At this point, not sure he is worthy of NHL pick.

WJC U20 - Team Sweden vs. Team Czech Belarus, December 26th, 2017

SWE #8 LD Dahlin, Rasmus (2018) – The first aspect you see in Dahlin is the skating ability. He is very good skater with his edge work, agility, lateral mobility. He has the ability to cut on a dime and likes to take puck down wall on off-side and quickly change direction to set himself up on his forehand for a shot to the net or play to teammate in offensive zone. He has good puck handling skills from the back end and has good vision as sees the ice well ahead. He thinks smart and quickly as transitions puck up ice with stretch pass or will wheel himself. He does a good job as puck distribution on the PP at the point as he thinks pass first, yet did snap a couple SOG from point that goalie had to be aware. He shoots effectively and quick with good placement rather than bombing shot. He picked PPA on dish to #14 Pettersson at the top of circle in the 1st period and then picked up PPA as made nice reception of pass on the move at the top of blue line and slid pass back to #24 Andersson after attracting the two defenders. Just a smart, little play that opened up space for his teammate for the goal. He also played the body well as will check effectively to separate opponent from puck. Defensively overall he did good job in controlling gaps and reading plays 1-on-1. He did slip and catch edge in 2nd period that gave Belarus forward some daylight, yet he recovered fairly well and angled player out in corner to nullify opportunity. He is still just 17-years old so he can add more muscle to frame for the highest level. Dahlin has lots of tools and high ceiling of potential as will most likely go first overall in the NHL Draft in June.

SWE #20 LC Lundestrom, Isac (2018) – He is a late '99 birthdate and another draft eligible that was given 3rd line center for line-up. He was limited for TOI and any true PP opportunity with Sweden top two lines and first power-play unit receiving majority of ice time. He is average in size who can handle the puck with slick puck skills and offensive thoughts. Will need to bulk up for the future. He skates well with smooth stride. Honestly will need more viewings as this game did not exactly give him opportunity to show his thoughts and skills.

USA vs Slovakia, U20 WJC, December 28 2017

United States –

USA #6 LD Hughes, Quinn (2018) – Hughes is a dynamic offensive defenseman, currently developing with the University of Michigan. He didn't get many shifts to start the game but capitalized on them when he did get some ice-time. He had a rush with the puck midway through the first, using his superb skating to enter the offensive end before dropping the puck back to the top of the right circle, resulting in a scoring chance for his team. Had a great keep in at the line, using a soft backhander to chip the puck to his teammate, which eventually resulted in an additional scoring chance for his team. Showed poise and strength in the defensive end, using his body to angle a Slovak forechecker away from the puck along the boards and later in the same shift, with a man draped on him, managed to get the puck out of danger. Had more opportunities to showcase his talents in the second period, he alleviated pressure from a forechecker by using his edges and cutting back towards the neutral zone and finding Mittelstadt for a quality scoring chance. Sometimes his puck rushes do cost him though, as he had an inadvertent pinch that lead directly to the 2-on-1 sequence that Slovakia scored on. He delivered a big hit at the top of his crease, barreling smolka into Woll, again showing that he's got a powerful base despite his height. His skating ability was on full display again as he made several end-to-end rushes showing excellent separational speed. He did have trouble getting his shot through traffic though, not utilizing his feints as often as he normally does.

USA #15 LD Perunovich, Scott (2018++) – Perunovich was paired with Lindgren in today's match up against the Slovaks. He's quick out of the gate which is important considering his 5'9, 160-pound frame, though his stride is short. Showed hard and accurate passing ability to start the game, skating down to the half-wall and delivering a pass back to the blueline on one play and on another, delivering a pass through the high-slot. Didn't get a lot of ice-time in the second or third but he did make a couple of quick passes moving the puck up the ice and delivered a hard, low wrist-shot at the right point that found it's way through traffic. His best attribute so far has been his passing accuracy, he's very good at making tape-to-tape passes, including stretch passes from his end to the neutral zone.

USA #7 C/LW Tkachuk, Brady (2018) – Tkachuk is currently developing in the NCAA, playing for Boston University. He played on a forechecking line with Poehling and Anderson, which proved to be the most consistent line against the Slovaks. He started with a good drive, going around the back of the Slovak net and delivered a pass to his teammate at the blueline. Midway though the first, he had a tremendous sequence. He came out with the puck in the corner and fired a shot just below the right faceoff circle, ringing the puck off the crossbar, he didn't watch his own shot though and instead, went right back to work, out-competing the Slovakian defense for the puck by using an aggressive stick-lift; he then made a power-move below the goal-line, wrapping the puck in-front of the net for another scoring chance. He's got excellent reach, making it a difficult shot for goalies to pick up since he can change the angle quickly by pulling the puck closer to his body before releasing the shot, which was demonstrated on this attempt. Had another great opportunity at the top of the slot after receiving a pass and delivering a hard one-timer snap-shot, that proved to be a difficult save. Had a beautiful forechecking sequence where he kept a puck alive below the goal-line and delivered a quick pass resulting in a scoring chance for his line-mate. Although not known for his skating, since he doesn't generate as much power in his stride as his frame suggests he could, giving him average acceleration; he did show enough straight-line speed to create a breakaway scoring chance for himself, which he capitalized on by using his soft hands, pulling forehand-to-backhand and tucking it five-hole. We mentioned that Tkachuk should have been more offensively assertive against Denmark, he listened, having a dominant game that showcased his excellent tools, finishing with a goal and four shots.

Slovakia –

SVK #30 G Durny, Roman (2018) – Durny is a goalie developing in the Slovakia league while playing on the U20 team. Slovakia has seen remarkable performances in recent years at this tournament from their goalies, and here again, Durny channeled his inner Godla and put on a spectacular performance. He's got a broad frame, standing 6'1, 210 and covers a lot of net when he's in his butterfly. Although heavier than you normally see in a goalie at his height, he's surprisingly athletic and needed to be while under siege from the Americans in the third period. He made several high-light real saves that kept Slovakia in the game when America was pressing. On one play, he made a reactionary right pad save on Yamamoto and then sprawled on the ice, using his arm to stop the rebound chance on Mittelstadt. He made another important save showing refined lateral movement, as he cut across his crease after tracking a pass across the slot and robbing a U.S forward with his glove while diving forward. His team rewarded him, as Bucek scored a brilliant goal, giving Slovakia the win. Durny was by far the best Slovak on the ice today, making 43 saves on 45 shots while showing interesting tools and good size.

SVK #6 LD Fehervary, Martin (2018) – Fehervary is currently developing with IK Oskarshamm in the Allvenskan. He's got a solid, 6'1, 190 pounds frame and he likes to line up his opposition and deliver devastating hits. He delivered several against Canada, and again here, he was physically engaged against the large U.S squad, showing an excellent base. He's difficult to play against and tracked highly skilled players well. On one sequence, he allowed enough space for an American to drag the puck but he anticipated the play, quickly cutting off the lane to the net, forcing his opponent to the outside. He quarterbacked the top powerplay, delivering a hard and low wrist-shot that went through heavy traffic, targeted the knee to ankle area, looking for tips from his teammates. Had a great stick-on-puck play against Tufte who was releasing his wrist-shot at the right circle while driving down the wing late in the game. Fehervary continued to show a punishing brand of hockey while logging heavy minutes on the backend.

SVK #12 LD Ivan, Michal (2018) – Ivan is a well sized defenseman currently playing in the QMJHL for Acadie-Bathurst Titan. He had some good moments against Canada and here again, had some quality plays for the Slovaks. He had a wrist-shot from the point that deflected off of Roman and came close to finding the back of the net. Ivan had a tremendous blocking sequence on an American powerplay, where he read Fox's placement of his shot from the point, getting in-front of it, before quickly turning around and blocking an additional hard shot from Poehling. Showed good defensive awareness and positioning on the play. He made an errant stretch pass resulting in an unforced icing, he was visibly disappointed with his execution, which wasn't as consistent as it was against Canada.

SVK #26 LC Roman, Milos (2018) – Roman had a good performance at the U18's last year, showing the ability to play on the world stage. He displayed great skating mechanics after rushing the puck over the neutral zone and making a clean offensive entry, before making a subtle backhand pass to his teammate and then looked for the redirect tip in-front of the net. Delivered a big, clean, body check on Poehling, hurting the forward on the hit. Had a subtle but effective backchecking sequence, catching up to Lockwood and stick-checking him just before he got a chance at the top of the crease. Had a good scoring opportunity in the slot, chipping a shot that required Wall to make a reactionary glove save. His bread and butter is his passing ability, making a great outlet-pass to Ruzicka from the defensive blueline to the offensive blueline. His shooting mechanics were average, his wrist-shot lacked power and he didn't use any feints or look to change the angle, also opted for a low-percentage shot selection. However, he displayed two-way qualities, using speed and a solid first pass, although he wasn't overly threatening in the offensive end.

SVK #18 LW Liska, Adam (2018) – Liska is developing in the OHL with the Kitchener rangers. He had a tough game against Canada and was inconsistent again today, however he had a couple of high-end passing plays. On one play, he had a quick snap-shot that was aimed for the five-hole but didn't have enough mustard behind it for it to be dangerous, however he did retrieve the puck at the side of the net and made a quick no-look backhand pass that allowed for a jam attempt at the side of the net by his teammate. Had the best sequence out of any Slovak in the second, driving down the left wing while handling pressure, he then made a beautiful no-look backhand pass below the goal-line to his teammate in the slot for one of the best scoring chances of the game. He then recollected the puck and made a nice pass while showing poise in the slot. He showed that he can be deceptive when carrying the puck, masking his passing plays well but needs to be more engaged in the offensive end.

Final Score 3-2 Slovakia

Czech Republic vs Sweden, U20 WJC, December 28 2017

Sweden –

SWE #8 LD Dahlin, Rasmus (2018) – Dahlin is currently developing in Frolunda's program and having a remarkable year for a 17-year-old defenseman playing in the SHL, which is why he's the consensus 1st overall pick in the 2018 draft. He played on the top defensive pairing while also quarter-backing the powerplay. Made his defensive presence felt early, using an active stick, knocking the puck into the corner as Zachar attempted to carry the puck into the slot. Nice pass in his own end under pressure with two Czech forecheckers cutting him off, leading to a breakout. Great pinch along the boards against Kurovsky who can be a handful below the goal-line, shows the power that Dahlin has when using his frame. He's got an effortless stride and showed his transitional breakouts through-out the game. He was exceptional on the powerplay, showing excellent poise and advanced feinting mechanics, while effectively distributing the puck to his teammates. He uses his head feints to hide what he's going to do when carrying the puck, this allowed him to re-open lanes on the powerplay, he has elite pivoting ability, which allows him to contort his body movement, and when paired with his head feints makes him extremely difficult to gauge for the opposition when he's distributing the puck or attacking the net. On one sequence, he looked at his passing option at the top of the right circle, this fooled the Czech pressing him into over-committing when taking away his lane; this allowed Dahlin to stutter step to his left side, bypassing the player and creating a shooting opportunity for himself where he showed quick hands, dragging the puck and changing the angle of his shot in motion. It was an advanced play that very few defenseman of his age could execute. He showed an advanced two-way game, covering lanes, playing physical, showing defensive awareness while executing high-end offensive plays with speed. Dahlin finished with 1 assist on 4 shots.

SWE #20 C/LW Lundestrom, Isac (2018) – Lundestrom has an interesting development background, having transitioned from a defenseman to a center, while showing first round potential, playing for Lulea HF in the SHL. He used his speed to draw a penalty on Safin in the neutral zone, leading to a powerplay goal. Had a nice pass to Soderlund in the slot for a scoring chance, he was decisive and made the pass quickly. Lundestrom continues to get very limited ice-time but did display flashes of his speed and skill against the Czech's.

Czech Republic –

CZE #1 G Skarek, Jakub (2018) – Skarek is considered the top goaltender in the 2018 draft class and is currently developing with HC Dukla Jihlava of the Czech league. He has modern day size, standing 6'3, 200 with plus mobility. He looked engaged early, specifically on Sweden's first powerplay where he tracked the puck well when Sweden was distributing it around his crease and across the high-slot. He made several saves, none better than a high-redirect in-front of the slot that he picked up quickly, pushing laterally and squaring up on Anderson's pass, making a difficult save look routine. Excellent reactionary kick-save of Andersson in the slot during a powerplay sequence. Late in the third he made another reflexive save, tracking a tip placed in-front of him and blocking it short-side. His reflexes are quick for his size and it gives him a secondary saving option when he's not square to a shooter. Skarek in previous viewings, has a tendency to let in a soft goal or two while also showing the ability to make a spectacular save, however he was consistent today, stopping 32 of 35 shots. I don't blame him on any of the goals, as all of them were well placed shots.

CZE #11 LD Kral, Filip (2018) – Played on the third defensive pairing with Jakub Galvis against Sweden while getting second unit-time both on the penalty-kill and powerplay. He had a good defensive sequence to start out the game as he positioned himself in the slot, blocking a scoring chance against Pettersson, then used his body and angled himself away from the pressure, making an accurate pass over to Galvas. Had a good stretch pass at the end of the first Czech powerplay giving his team a scoring chance. Had another good defensive block against Pettersson, anticipating the angle change and getting on a knee to take away the chance. He did a good job of swarming Pettersson and other skilled Swedish forwards when they had the puck, he tried to limit their time and space, and played positionally sound, although he wasn't as dangerous offensively or as noticeable today as he was against Russia.

CZE #7 LD Salda, Radim (2018+) – Salda was a defensive force against Russia and continued his solid-play against Sweden, showing a more developed offensive game then last year, when he went undrafted. In the defensive end he continued to be both active and engaged, winning a foot race against Nylander for a puck going into the corner, then quickly distributing it to his partner. Great defensive sequence on the penalty-kill, blocking multiple shots to the right side of the net, unfortunately on his third block attempt he was out-waited by Nylander. Got in the face of Soderland after a whistle, he never backs down against his opponent. In the offensive end, he hit the crossbar on a seeing eye shot at the point. Showed offensive awareness, pinching and rushing into the slot while getting a wrist-shot off, it wasn't overly dangerous but his timing was good. Salda demonstrated a two-way game today for the Czech's, finishing with 4 shots on goal. He won't be overlooked by scouts if this play continues.

CZE #17 LC Hrabik, Krystof (2018) – Krystof is a center currently developing with Bili Tygri Liberec of the Czech league. He received limited minutes today but continued to have a defensive presence on the penalty-kill. He had a couple of nice defensive reads, quickly closing lanes and making a nice block in the high-slot that prevented a scoring chance. Offensively, he was rushed, on one sequence he had time at the blueline to stop-up and assess his options but chose to spin and fire a slapshot that was easily blocked, leading to a cleared puck. His best offensive moment came after driving down the right wing and delivering a pass that was intended for Kurovsky but just missed him. He wasn't very noticeable against Sweden.

CZE #15 LW Kurovsky, Daniel (2018++) – Kurovsky demonstrated a two-way game today while receiving 2nd unit powerplay time. In the defensive end, he had a block late in the first at the top of the slot, using his size. Aggressively attempted to stick-check a player shortly after the above play, but didn't get under the Swedish forward enough, would have like to have seen him use his leverage more on the attempt. Was in good position on the penalty kill while attempting to block Pettersson's goal, avoided screening Skarek but the shot was perfect. Offensively, he had a good sequence, getting his wrist-shot off on the short-side. Great spin-move just outside the offensive blueline, showed his evasiveness despite his size. Had a nice offensive zone entry, side-stepping his opponent and setting up the powerplay.

CZE #18 LW Zadina, Filip (2018) – Zadina is developing in the QMJHL with the Halifax Mooseheads and is considered one of the best prospects in this year's draft class. He continues to show chemistry with Necas and was dangerous on the powerplay for the Czech's. Zadina showcased his skill in the later part of the first, dragging the puck in-tight to his body then going around another Swedish player with his quick-hands, before running out of room. He can make technical plays under pressure, with little space or time. Used his hands to change the angle of his shot while rushing down the left wing, he fanned on the attempt but the skill was apparent. Scored a powerplay goal at the right faceoff-dot after receiving a feed from Necas and delivering a quick slapshot from his knee that snuck under the glove of Gustavsson; he get's leverage on his shots using his momentum generated from his body mechanics, making his one-timer very effective. He was dangerous offensively, although he was having difficulty getting his shot through traffic, he needed to show more patience and utilize his teammates better, he's very talented, so he attempts the more difficult one-on-one play at times, instead of the simple yet more effective play. Defensively he was engaged today. Great backcheck along the half-wall, using a stick-check to press down on a Swedish forward and creating a turnover, on the same shift in the offensive end, he showed a willingness to battle along the boards, showing strength as he pushed the Swedish defenseman off the puck and passed it to his teammate, creating possession for his team. It's very rare to find someone of Zadina's talent level combined with his motor, he's a tenacious and hard-working player who's offensively gifted. He finished with a powerplay goal and 6 shots on net in a better effort against Sweden.

CZE #16 RW Kaut, Martin (2018) – Kaut is currently developing with HC Dynamo Pardubice in the Czech league. He had a great sequence midway through the first, battling in a one-on-one situation and eventually coming away with the puck in the corner and then delivered a hard pass directly onto the tape of his teammate. He was excellent on the top powerplay unit, where he played in-front of the net and near the goal-line, displaying good offensive awareness while executing crisp passes. On one offensive sequence, he attempted to set up his teammate on a 2-on-1, after recollecting the puck in the corner, he skated around the net and distributed the puck back to the line. Kaut is superb at tracking the puck and the play in general when he doesn't have the puck on his stick, he's the first to rebounds and loose pucks consistently because he can breakdown plays happening in real-time very quickly, making smart and quick decisions. He finished with 2 shots on net but wasn't as effective today against Sweden as he was against Russia.

Final Score 3-1 Sweden

Drummondville Voltigeurs at Gatineau Olympiques, December 28th, 2017

DRU #9 C Veleno, Joseph (2018) – Joe struggled tonight for Drummondville, he was up and down a lot tonight, showed goof burst of acceleration with the puck tonight carrying the puck up the ice and beating defensemen easily wide for chances. He was trying to do too much at blue line too much stickhandling and being fancy, which led to too many turnovers. I think he was trying to do too much tonight because he just got traded over from Saint John and was looking to make an impression. He had a strong game on the penalty kill tonight. Showed flashes of his high hockey skill with he puck and vision moving the puck as well, needed to be simpler tonight.

DRU #92 LD Beaudin, Nicholas (2018) –Nicholas was good tonight, he was Drummondville more consistent player tonight, he very seldom made any mistake. He is a strong skater, quarter back on the power play, moves puck well on it, easy transition forward to backwards or vice versa, good first pass. Nicholas had a good stick at dzone blueline, broke up the play created an offside, strong pinch in the neutral zone created a turnover in neutral zone; and he brought it back on a 2 on 1 for a chance, simple plays but always makes the right pass and its always tape to tape, strong postionally in defensive zone, able to take body then puck,

DRU #33 G Rodrigue, Olivier (2018) - He looked shaky all night long for Drummondville, he looks bad on the 2nd and 3rd goals for Gatineau, he was deep in net and was late reacting to the shot, he showed quick lateral movement, rebound control was good, was good at sucking the puck into his chest, look liked he struggled tracking the puck tonight. Olivier fought the puck tonight, wasn't tested much but didn't look good, bad rebounds in the 3rd couple soft goals, didn't make the key save when needed in the end.

DRU #55 LD Bernard, Xavier- Xavier was good 1 on 1 at blue line, good long stick, good at angling them to the boards, they had him on power play tonight not sure he should be there, he moves the puck well and has a good first pass, he just holds onto the puck to long before needs to make quicker decisions with the puck. Xavier gave too much room at start on 2nd for entry and gave to much room for the forward to make a move and score, needs to step up and take the body, good active stick at his blueline with forwards trying to enter and a good stick on the penalty kill getting in lanes and breaking up passes very effortlessly

GAT #37 G Berube, Tristan (2018) – Tristian was good in nets tonight for Gatineau, there wasn't a lot of movement in crease, tracking puck well in the 1st period, was down to early on 1st goal against got beat high glove side, bad 3rd goal given up, should of froze the puck, left it there miscommunication with his d led to Drummondville putting puck past him. He made a couple huge save in the 3 to keep team in it; he showed quick feet and quick lateral movements post to post. Tristian tracked puck well also.

GAT #22 C Boubrias, Shawn (FA) – He skated well tonight, puck was on his stick a lot in the first period, he had couple strong rushes in the neutral zone up the ice, strong play on his 2nd goal turn defence inside out then went wide forward back hand beating goalie short side. When he is skating he is dominant, scored 3rd goal in slot on power play quick release no time for goalie to react, excellent 3rd period, strong play from the corner passing puck cross ice to onetime goal. Shawn competed hard all night tonight for Gatineau and led by example.

Swift Current Broncos at Moose Jaw Warriors, December 28th, 2017

SC#23 Patterson, Max (2018) – He is a big strong body, battled hard every shift. Made a couple solid hits. Strong in front of the net on the power play. Lacking the high-end skill.

SC#37 Barlage, Logan (2019) – Great size for a 16 year old. Played a high pace strong power game. Worked the cycle well. 7/11 on face-offs. Saw some penalty kill time.

MJW#4 Woo, Jett (2018) – Jett returned to his old self in his second game back from injury. Started the game a little slow, made a couple poor choices with the puck, but quickly turned it around. Made multiple people miss at the offensive blue line. Great first passes. Moose Jaw's best D-man all game. Had one assist and was a plus two. First penalty kill and second power play unit.

MJW#16 Hartje, Chase (2018) – Chase had one assist and finished a plus two. One of the stronger games he has played. Started on the third pair but by the third period he worked his way into the top four. Great skating and vision. Second penalty kill unit.

MJW#27 Burzan, (2018) – Scored an incredible goal. Beat the defender wide with his speed then drove the net and tucked it far side. Added an assist as well, finished a plus three. Second power play unit.

Belarus vs Russia, U20 WJC, Dec 29 2017

Belarus –

BLR #8 RD Yeryomenko, Vladislav (2018+) – Yeryomenko paired with Deryabin to start todays match up against Russia and showed well again, displaying a mobile, two-way game. He had several well-timed checks and pins along the boards, he thinks the game fast and assesses his opponents, adapting to their capabilities. On one play, he chipped the puck directly over a Russian forechecker coming in with a ton of speed, knowing the Russian couldn't stop up in time, he then side-stepped him and recollected the puck before moving it to his teammate. He's constantly assessing opening's around the slot in the defensive end when he doesn't have the puck and is aware, closing back-door lanes at the appropriate time on most plays. Had good positioning in-front of the net and a well-timed stick-check on Abramov as he attempted to cut into the crease. I didn't like one defensive play, as Yeryomenko's positioning on Kayumov's goal in the slot was too low, since the net already had been covered by his teammates, if he was higher in the slot he could have prevented the tally. Yeryomenko was consistent in the offensive end. He had a good end-to-end rush, showing fluid skating, making a controlled zone entry. Had a hard point-shot on the powerplay that created havoc in-front of the net and made a nice lateral slot pass while skating down the right circle on the same shift. Great wrist-shot from the blueline, it was hard and was dangerous, he was consistent at getting his shots through traffic. Collected a drop pass from Sushko and found open-ice, releasing a quick and low wrist shot at the right faceoff dot, hitting the post, he utilized a screen properly on the shot attempt. He finished on a low note, as he had a poor read during a 5-on-3 after his scoring chance; he passed the puck back to the point with no one there, causing a critical clear for the Russians, it was a tough play.

BLR #5 LD Deryabin, Dmitri (2018) – Deryabin was strong on the puck in the defensive-end and showed good gap control. When Abramov made a between the legs deke, pulling from backhand to forehand, Deryabin had great spacing and kept him to the outside so he couldn't cut towards the net. On another play in the first, he showed strength handling a Russian player along the boards and coming out with the puck before skating behind the net and making a first pass, alleviating the pressure. He was on the ice for the goal against in the first but it wasn't his miscommunication the lead to the opening for Rubstov, he played his man correctly. Had an end-to-end goal, upon entering the offensive zone he released a harmless wrist-shot at the top of the left circle that Sukhachyov missed, displayed above-average speed on the play. His shot doesn't appear threatening but he was solid defensively again for Belarus and showed mobility, finishing with a goal on 4 shots.

BLR #19 LW Drozdov, Ivan (2018) – Drozdov showed dynamic two-way qualities and played the half-wall on the second powerplay unit. He showed his defensive prowess, making an excellent defensive play, using his acceleration to close his gap quicker than the Russian forward could react to, resulting in a take-away. Continued to showcase his tenacious board-battling skills in the second period; he's not the biggest kid but he's relentless and doesn't back down against larger players or if he's fighting off multiple opponents simultaneously. Showed a willingness to backcheck hard, using his straight-line speed to aggressively cover the slot and take-away the passing option. On the powerplay and at even strength, he made quick passes to his teammates to give Belarus different looks, on one specific pass, he rushed down the half-wall and delivered a pass into the slot for a one-timer to his teammate which was blocked. His skating is dynamic and is allowed him to have an incredible sequence in the third. After taking advantage of a Russian defender who slipped in the corner while forechecking, he grabbed the puck and then displayed his hands and his elusiveness, darting around several Russian players with minimal space: he drew a penalty, passed the puck off before receiving it back and delivered a turn-around wrist-shot from his knees that got deflected over the net. His offensive reads without the puck were mixed and he tries to do too much with the puck on his stick occasionally, but he's a proactive offensive player who competes consistently with and without the puck.

BLR #17 LC Sharangovich, Yegor (2018++) – Sharongovich played on the top-line and powerplay unit, while showing that he reads the game well in the offensive end. He had a great keep in at the left point in the offensive end, using his power and stick to out-battle two Russian players, he then passed the puck up and drove directly to the net but the puck never got to him. However, that was his only threatening sequence in the first, his game picked up as the game progressed. Showed his awareness, skating around the back of the net and distributed the puck, then came back around the high-slot and found a soft spot, he received the pass from below the goal-line and shot-far side trying to pick the corner. He missed the shot but it was dangerous and heavy, it was Belarus's best scoring chance in the second. Had a nice play while rushing up to the half-wall in the offensive end, stopping up and finding Sushko for a scoring chance. Showed excellent offensive awareness around the slot area, this was demonstrated on the 5-on-3 powerplay in the third after Yeryomenko hit the post. He was the first to collect the puck after been in perfect position to collect it, showing patience, out-waiting several Russian players before delivering a wrist shot, short-side that required a difficult save from Sukhachyov. Throughout the powerplay opportunities that Belarus had, Sharangovich displayed accurate and well-timed passes, consistently distributing the puck below the goal-line and along the boards when Russian defenders took away his shooting lanes. He's been Belarus's most consistent forward through the first three games.

Russia –

RUS #5 RD Minulin, Artyom (2018+) – Minulin displayed two-way qualities today with better mobility then last season. He aggressively cut off a Belarusian forward who had caught the Russians out of position using his improved straight-line speed. He delivered a hard board check, which resulted in a turnover. Showed composure and poise under pressure, making a nice backhand pass up the boards to his teammate in the defensive end, mitigating the forechecker. Continued to show his improved skating as he beat a Belarusian forechecker to a lose puck before feeding it across the slot to get the puck out of danger. Had a great defensive play, diving down and blocking the far-side for Sukhachyov during a scramble on the penalty-kill. On the powerplay he had a great fake slapshot pass that landed on the stick of his teammate on the left side of the goal-line. He had additional slapshot-feint at the line, using it to re-open his shooting lane. He was offensively engaged and wasn't a liability in the defensive end, making quality defensive plays.

RUS #14 RW Svechnikov, Andrei (2018) – Svechnikov played on a line with Kostin, while getting limited minutes again. Continued to display his passing ability and use his frame effectively below the goal-line in the first period. Had a great sequence where he out-battled a Belarusian defenseman and passed the puck into the slot creating a quality scoring opportunity. Continued to display chemistry with Kostin in the second period, as he had a primary assist off a beautiful give-and-go sequence with him below the goal-line. He's got a heavy shot but he's showing accurate and technical passing ability out there as well. He's got a rare combination of size, power, puck skills, vision and shooting ability, there's not much that Svechnikov can't do at a high-level. Didn't get a lot of playing time in the third since the Russians were on the penalty-kill for much of the period but he finished with two assists, while making it increasingly difficult for Bragin to keep him off the ice.

Final Score 5-2 Russia

Unites States vs Canada, U20 WJC (outdoor game), Dec 29 2017

U.S –

USA #6 LD Hughes, Quinn (2018) – Hughes played on a pairing with Perunovich while getting 1st unit powerplay time. The poor ice conditions didn't slow Hughes down, as he continued to demonstrate his dynamic skating ability combined with poise to spin off a forechecker from behind the net, peel off an additional Canadian forward in the neutral zone, and move laterally across the blueline, finding several openings to get his hard shot through traffic. Took a penalty after losing the puck while skating up the half-wall and then turned around and slashed the stick out of a Canadian defender's hands, it was poorly timed considering it happened directly after the U.S tied the game. He was calm and composed a the blueline for much of the game, and adapted to the weather conditions by attempting less dynamic plays, and making simplified passes. He wasn't as good today as he was in his previous viewing, but it was a difficult game to assess in general.

USA #15 LD Perunovich, Scott (2018++) – Perunovich played on a defensive pairing with Hughes while also getting powerplay time. His passing ability has been noticeable so far in the tournament, and that continued. He had a beautiful give-and-go powerplay goal in the third period; he found open space in the high-slot, received a pass from Tkachuk and then delivered a pass down to the left of the goal-line, then fired home a quick one-timer after receiving it back in the slot area. Delivered a hard-wrist shot that he was looking to have deflected in-front of the net. Excellent defensive read on a 2-on-1 in overtime, he knew the ice was poor, so he chose to aggressively defend the shooter, forcing the passing option which immediately skipped over the Canadian forwards stick, resulting in no scoring chance, it was a heads-up play. We have said it once, but again, he can really pass the puck. He scored a powerplay goal while finishing with 3 shots.

USA #7 C/LW Tkachuk, Brady (2018) – Tkachuk's offensive game stood out again today, showing chemistry on a line with Yamamoto and Mittelstadt. He found an opening in-front of the crease and quickly buried a sharp pass by Yamamoto for a goal, he was in the right place at the right time to receive the pass. Later, Mittelstadt had a give and go sequence with Tkachuk, again Tkachuk showed his deceptive release, putting the puck just over the cross-bar on the far-side. Made a mistake in the defensive end, turning the puck over causing a dangerous scoring opportunity for Canada. Made up for it though with a shoot-out goal, the release point is lightning quick and the shot was very accurate, Hart had little chance on it. He continued to show against Canada how difficult he can be to contain when he's on his game. One area of improvement is he needs to stay more composed in his own end when the game is on the line, this is back-to-back games now where he's made a poor defensive play late in the third period and overtime, leading to a goal and a prime scoring chance against.

Canada –

CAN #31 G Hart, Carter (PHI 2016) – Hart was drafted 48th overall by the Flyers and has been the focus of Canada in the media so far, and with good reason, as he's had a dominant year for the Everett Silvertips in the WHL. This was an interesting test for Hart, as the weather conditions created several broken plays while the sun was capable of obscuring his vision depending on the angle the puck came into his zone. However, these conditions didn't phase him in the least, as he played a composed and reserved game, showing a minimalist style of movement, rarely over-committing on a play. Only Lockwood managed to catch Hart out of position but the post bailed him out. Otherwise he tracked the puck consistently, had excellent rebound control, and was quick to react to rebound situations, squaring up to secondary attempts and making some excellent saves. He allowed 3 goals in the game but two of them were off beautiful feeds in-tight to the net that Hart didn't have time to react to, while the other was a blast from Bellows on the powerplay, as he had time and space to walk in, slightly changing the angle that Hart had challenged initially. He finished with 33 saves on 36 shots while been named Canada's best player, which he was.

CAN #7 RD Makar, Cale (COL 2017) – Makar is a dynamic offensive defenseman who was drafted by Colorado with the 4th overall pick in the 2017 draft. Although he had limited minutes, he made the most of them. Was utilized on the powerplay and displayed his offensive skill-set early, scoring a powerplay goal with a low-wrist shot that went through Oettinger. At first glance, it looked like a weak goal but Makar utilized a screen in-front of him to mask his shot well. Had an offensive anticipatory read in the neutral zone, using his skating to stop-up quickly and attempt a wrist-shot that was blocked. He had a good defensive read in the neutral zone, closing the gap quickly and using an active stick to whack the puck back over the U.S blueline, ending the rush attempt. Makar had an excellent defensive sequence late in the third, winning a board-battle in the corner and then rushing the puck up the ice, he then transitioned from offense to defense swiftly as the puck was turned over in the neutral zone, been the first defenseman back and deflecting a puck out of play. Makar finished the game with a powerplay goal and 2 shots.

Final Score 4-3 US

Victoria Royals at Kelowna Rockets, December 30th, 2017

KEL #24 C Topping, Kyle (2018) – Crashed the crease hard and banged in a goal tonight, showed a good ability to battle tonight and match the physical play of defenders to get his space around the net. Chipped a puck out of the zone to Lind which started a 2 on 1 with good use of speed getting up the ice, ended up at the shooter but couldn't capitalized, overall a strong play minus the finish.

KEL #26 RW Kindree, Liam (2018) – Showed good jump on his first couple shifts, took a hard hit and looked to be favoring a leg, was carried off the ice by teammates and did not return to the game.

KEL #10 LW Brennan, Ted (2018) – Looked like he got a little more ice-time due to the Kindree injury. Played quick and wasn't afraid to park himself in the tough areas and button down to be difficult to play against. Has some good power behind his wrist shot but missed the net on a couple occasions, could have a been a product of nerves but still created some of his own chances.

KEL #29 C Foote, Nolan (2019) – Back filling in at the center position with teammates away at the World Juniors, was running around a little this game chasing hits early on; especially on the penalty kill where he was supposed to be in the middle of the ice. Usually carries a shoot first mentality that was hurting his lines ability to create sustained offense, didn't do much to get them involved or let them feed of him, head down and shoot. Picked up an assist on Topping banging in a rebound of one of his shots.

KEL #30 G Basran, Roman (2019) – Allowed a goal from the far corner of the goal line into the top of the net, was a good shot but he wasn't tight to the post and wasn't standing up, a goal that shouldn't go in and he would likely want back. That was really his only gaff of the evening, faced 38 shots and allowed 2 goals. Continues to impress in his starts we've viewed, so composed and square to shooters despite the poor angled goal tonight nothing looks easy against him. Was dynamic tonight especially against some of the high skilled forwards from Victoria.

VIC #14 LW Florchuk, Eric (2018) – Tipped a pass off a zone entry to pick up a secondary assist. Was a big factor on the penalty kill tonight plays a disruptive style and makes sure he's attacking puck carries forcing them into quick decisions and taking away their time and space. Has see some improvement in his puck carrying ability since last season, looks more confidant carrying in transition and is playing at a higher tempo but still lacks a true separation gear, some teammates are out skating him on rushes.

VIC #34 C Oliver, Kaid (2018) – Limited role in this game but when given the chance he was paying well against bigger forward getting inside body position and not backing down in scrums and board battles. Not creating much or starting often in the offensive zone.

VIC #5 LD Prowse, Mitchell (2018) – Playing it safe tonight and really staying back in the defensive zone and not doing much to push the pace of play. Snapped a few accurate passes out of his zone to his forward group, did a good job leading speedy forwards, but was differing to his partner or to forwards for any rushes. Had a good net front presence and doesn't let anything easy happen around his goaltender.

VIC #25 LW Kambeitz, Dino (2018) – Showed some tenacity to his game, throwing some strong hits with authority. Makes good use of his body in front of the net especially on the powerplay, not an easy player to move. Was a solid skater with decent footwork, didn't carry the puck to too often but when he did he looked good doing so, would have liked to see him use this skill a little more. Often knew what his play was before receiving the puck, quick on and off of his stick, including his ability to release the puck making good use of his snap shot.

Final Score: Kelowna Rockets: 3 – Victoria Royals: 2 – OT/SO

WJC U20 – Team Switzerland vs. Team Czech Republic, December 31st, 2017

SUI #16 LD Gross, Nico (2018) – Gross was decent on the PP as plays the point and distributes the puck. He shows good mobility and handle. He moves the puck up ice. Played situation well defensively in the 2nd period on #6 Zachar as opposing forward had speed, yet Gross positioned well and stopped the pass with good anticipation. He certainly has some potential in his game with skating, handle, and IQ.

SUI #23 RW Nussbaumer, Valentin (2019) – He's not big in size/weight yet then again he is a late '00 birthdate so he will have time to develop physically. What you like is his stick skills and offensive instincts. He showed deceptive speed and handles the puck well through traffic. He also showed some good vision as set-up teammates for a few chances going to the net. He will be a player to monitor for the next 18 months.

SUI #22 LC Eggenberger, Nando (2018) – He showed some good puck skills in the offensive zone and thoughts with the puck to create chances. Liked his hustle in the 1st period on the break check to break up play. He also made nice to drag move on defender off the rush to send quality shot on net. In this tourney on team outpowered, it is not always easy to consistently show talent, though Eggenberger displayed qualities to make worthy of continuously watching for the draft.

SUI #23 RW Kurachev, Philip (2018) – He has some good offensive thoughts along with speed and puck skills to create offense. He made nice rush to the outside by Czech Dman #11 Kral down his off-wing for backhand shot on goal. The skating and puck skills were evident on shifts.

CZE #7 LD Salda, Radim (2018*) – Salda is that steady, sturdy Dman that can log minutes and kill penalties. He will play physical and makes it difficult on opposing forwards. He moves fairly well and can handle the puck sufficiently for initial outlets. He shows good defensive positioning and stick to break plays up.

CZE #11 LD Kral, Filip (2018) – In a second viewing of Kral within the week, he has some potential yet skill sets and mind are not high end. There were a couple times whereby his feet were behind the pace of the play and his processing lacked as well. He got beat in the 2nd period wide by #23 Kurashev. He will move the puck up with outlets, yet skill sets in skating and offensive skills and hockey IQ appear average. Just too many little things like fanning on 1-timer in 3rd period from the point with no defender and losing some puck battles or being on the incorrect side of the puck.

CZE #16 RC Kaut, Martin (2018) – Kaut is catching scouts' eyes or at least this one. Right away he made nice dish to line mate #21 Chytil with speed entering the offensive zone for high scoring chance. Kaut sees the ice very well and his puck pursuit was very good in this game, as has great knack for using long reach and picking opposing player's pockets from the back side to create the turnover. He picked up PP assist in 1st period as his backhand shot went off post and out to #8 Necas in the slot who then buried. Kaut shows good puck support in all areas and forechecking to gain possession. He made nifty lob pass in air to send #21 Chytil on breakaway in 2nd period too. He then got on scoresheet himself on PP in 2nd period as he turned to face play off rush on off-side and slipped shot 5-hole on goalie from slot. He shows rounded game as plays the body effectively and good defensive stick in re-loads and DZ coverage. Kaut stock is rising after solid performance at WJC. He has been one of the better draft-eligible players showing his 200-foot game.

CZE #18 LW Zadina, Filip (2018) – Zadina showed off his slick hands and offensive thoughts again in this game. He is a shoot first mentality and although he did not score in this game his was certainly firing the puck. He wired a shot off the post in the 1st period, displayed his quick shot release throughout the game, yet made the goalie look good a few times. Although the goalie #30 Wuthrich did made some solid saves on Zadina. He is creative with puck, finds open lanes or teammates, using his quick hands to maneuver around offensive zone and create scoring opportunities. He made nice rush out of nothing in 3rd period toe dragging around defender 1-v-1 with solid backhand shot on net. Zadina does good job as well away from puck to find the open ice to shoot and receive the puck.

CZE #20 LW Lauko, Jakub (2018) – Lauko scored his 1st goal of the tourney off a rebound as he cut across the crease with goalie down holding on backhand and then finding open net. He showed a little more jump in step and confidence from earlier in the week. He made nice move late 1st period to set-up #15 Kurovsky at the net for scoring opportunity. One aspect noticed in his game is that he tends to fan on his shots. Overall, does not appear to think the game fast enough and have skill sets that allow him to thrive.

CZE #22 RC Reichel, Kristian (2018*) – Reichel made more of an impression this game vs Swiss. Normally you see the value as a utility type player on PK or used to take important face-offs, yet he also found the scoresheet twice. He scored the Czechs third goal early in the 2nd period as he went to the net on 2-on-1 and received #25 Pavlik pass across the crease and finished in tight. He then also scored in 3rd period showing his north-south speed as blew in from offensive blue line beating goalie with nice forehand/backhand deke. There looks to be some value as re-entry pick, especially with some NHL bloodline from father.

WJC U20 – Team USA vs. Team Finland, December 31st, 2017

USA #6 LD Hughes, Quinn (2018) – The best asset is his smooth skating ability which you cannot teach that natural ability. Yet have noticed more and more each viewing as the skill levels rise over the years and strength in opponents increases that Hughes loses his edges and falls more often, ate least this season at Michigan, AAPG, and WJC. He is a risk-reward player that can break game open or give up costly turnover. Against the Finns he easily played the least amount of the seven defensemen. On the first goal against in the 2nd period he got caught out of position as he as outside the dots a bit and did not close gap quick enough in the NZ along the Finns to come through with speed and lanes. He is talented no question will need to learn the smaller details of the game and gain core strength.

USA #7 LW Tkachuk, Brady (2018) – Tkachuk is always doing his thing each night and shift not only playing high compete game below the dots, in the corners, and around the net yet also loves to intimidate away from the puck on opponents with on-ice gestures. He looks to be just a younger version of his older brother – Matthew v2.0. He made play on 2nd goal in 1st period as easily could have shot puck down low off side of net after receiving #15 Pernunovich pass from the point, yet wisely slid puck back-door to #11 Mittlestadt breaking to the net for open net goal. Again, he was in on USA 3rd goal in 2nd period as he established net front presence and his rebound shot on PP was finished by line mate #13 Anderson. He then was in on the game winning goal late in the game as he simply made the play on the breakout as he chipped the puck of the wall to #11 Mittlestadt coming through into the NZ and eventually leading to #8 Fox goal. Tkachuk has a great combination of grit, finish, smarts, and ability to simply make plays. He will be high 1st round pick like his brother back in 2016.

USA #15 LD Perunovich, Scott (2018*) – The 2nd year draft eligible skates well and handles the puck from the back end. He makes good outlets and will join the rush as well as show his mobility, offensive thoughts from the blue line in the offensive zone. He made nice play in 1st period on second USA goal as he held the blue on a failed Finnish clear, then quickly sent a cross slot pass low to #7 Tkachuk off the side of the net that lead to goal. Good vision and heads-up play. Yet on the flip side in the 3rd period while on the PP, he broke down the wall in OZ and forced pass into slot that was quickly transitioned other way leading to short-handed, 3rd goal against. He is not overly physical or big in stature, yet finds success in skating and puck moving abilities. He is having success as freshman at UMD, might be worthy of mid-round selection.

FIN #34 RC Kupari, Rasmus (2018) – This game was really a tough one to judge as Kupari as very limited ice time as given 13th forward in line-up. Finally received some shifts in 2nd period where he showed good defensive positioning in own zone to eventually gain possession. Another shift did display bit of offensive tools and shiftiness on skates in corner as couple stops/starts moves to gain space that led to penalty being drawn. WJC in general not the greatest evaluation platform for Kupari.

North Bay Battalion at Oshawa Generals, January 1st, 2018

NB #6 RD Mailhot, Travis (2018) - Mailhot played a simplistic style of defense and was at his best in the defensive zone utilizing his size, strength and reach. Travis played physically, however wouldn't chase contact. He showed good timing on an open ice check at the blue-line separating player from puck. Mailhot has room to improve his puck skills, however limits his puck possession time by making simplistic decisions. Travis will need to improve his foot speed and four-way mobility as well as the quickness in which he retrieves pucks.

NB #21 RW Coe, Brandon (2020) - Coe possesses good size and displayed fluid skating abilities, generating above average speed. Brandon also showed a willingness to play with an edge as he delivered two noteworthy checks and several other smaller ones. Coe does however need to improve his play away from the puck. Despite a good back-check to negate a chance in the first, Brandon was disengaged defensively and played with no urgency away from the puck. Coe also showed a laziness to his game as he often took large circles back to the play and lacked an effort if he felt he was to far out of the play.

NB #27 LC McMaster, Adam (2018) - Adam displayed elite skating abilities including an explosive first step and above average speed. He routinely utilized his speed to create space and gain easy entry to the offensive zone. However, despite showing a quick release with good velocity behind his shot, he was unable to generate much offensively.

NB #28 LW Moncada, Luke (2018) - Moncada possesses an intriguing frame and good strength to his game, which he was able to utilize along the half-boards and off the cycle. Luke protected the puck well and showed an ability to make simplistic decisions in possession. Moncada displays a long and fairly smooth stride however he lacks quickness and failed to generate much more than average speed. Luke will also need to improve the quickness of his hands as he shows the awareness to make a play just needs to speed up the process.

OSH #5 LD Ennis, William (2018) - Ennis subtly had another strong and effective game for the Generals. William kept his game simplistic but defender very well and was able to make good, high percentage decisions in possession. Ennis was strong defending 1-on-1 as he quickly took away time and space, closing gaps effectively and finishing with contact.

OSH #8 RW Noel, Serron (2018) - Noel was the top player on the ice from either side, utilizing his size, speed and a strong compete level to impact the game on both sides of the puck. Serron was physical on the forecheck and showed a relentlessness in puck pursuit allowing him to force turnovers and quickly turn them into offensive opportunities. Serron utilized his size well to get where he wanted to go rather effortlessly and showed some elusiveness to his game as his change of direction while moving at top speed has significantly improved. While Noel was showing no hesitance taking pucks to the goal and using his size to get into ideal position, his hands in tight need to improve further.

OSH #61 LC McShane, Allan (2018) - McShane had a quiet first and second period, essentially blending into the play. However, he had a strong third period as the Generals as a team found a second gear and poured on the offense. Allan showed impressive vision and awareness of his teammates while making plays in transition. He also displayed touch on his passes which seemingly found their way through numerous bodies and onto the tape of teammates. His defensive zone play was good as he was aware positionally and reliable down low.

OSH #96 RC Wong, Nick (2020) - Wong contributed two goals in the Generals win. While he was effective through the first two periods, he did little to stand out, blending in while skating on Oshawa's fourth line. Nick excelled in the third as his nose for the net showed. Wong did an excellent job at anticipating the play and finding space offensively which allowed him to become a target for his teammates. Nick displayed quick hands and good finish in tight, along with a deceptive release that is only getting better as he continues to get stronger.

Finland vs Czech Republic, U20 WJC Quarter-Final, Jan 2 2018

Finland –

FIN #34 RC Kupari, Rasmus (2018) – Kupari got his first shift of the game in the third period, but made the most of his opportunities, having his strongest play of the tournament. On his opening shift, he displayed his high-end straight-line speed to drive down the right-wing, receiving a hard saucer-pass on the odd-man rush but it was ahead of him. On another sequence he showed his soft-hands, pulling up on a Czech forward while deking from his backhand to forehand, then used his hands again to evade an additional Czech player who pressed him before making a nice pass into the slot. The talented center had a great forechecking sequence late in the third, using his speed and a strong stick-lift to take the puck away from Salda below the goal-line, he competed hard and made an additional pass to his teammate before pressing on the backcheck, stripping the puck off another player in the neutral zone. He wasn't utilized in overtime despite his performance. He finished the tournament with 0 points in 5 games while receiving limited ice-time.

FIN #3 LW/RW Jaaska, Juha (2018++) – Jaaska had a strong game for Finland, using his speed to press in the offensive end. He had a good shift late in the first, screening Korenar in-front of the slot and using his acceleration to grab a lose puck before passing it off to his teammate. Showed a plus top-gear, making a solid pass to the offensive blueline, resulting in a scoring chance for Finland. His line wasn't used much in the third but he did have another strong shift, making two passing plays, one subtle pass behind the net and an additional one to the point, he also received a pass at the left circle giving him a scoring chance but the shot missed. Late in the third, he stripped the puck off Zadina in the neutral zone giving him a breakaway chance, releasing a quick and hard wrist shot that went over the net. Jaaska finished the game with two shots and finished the tournament with 1 assist in 5 games.

FIN #33 LW Innala, Jere (2018++) – Innala had a good game for Finland, threating offensively. The Finnish winger had one of the better scoring chances in the first, receiving a pass in the slot and firing it wide, he had room. He showed a good motor in the first frame and was one of the more active Finnish players, battling for the puck despite his frame. He side-stepped an incoming hit by Hajek which drew a penalty. Had a scoring chance at the left circle, getting his shot through traffic, though it wasn't as dangerous as his previous attempt. Showed good acceleration again but his top gear is still lacking, as he was unable to catch the speedy Reichal on a breakaway. Had a tremendous scoring chance in the slot shortly after Finland's third goal but was robbed by Korenar with a sprawling glove save. Innala finished the tournament with 0 points in 5 games.

Czech Republic –

CZE #11 LD Kral, Filip (2018) – Kral had an average game for the Czech's, making defensive lapses, he also didn't receive any ice-time in overtime which was reflective of his performance. In the opening frame, Kral made several good passes up the boards in his own end and was alert at the offensive blueline, keeping the puck in by chipping it up the half-wall on one play. He had a poor pass in the neutral zone that resulted in a quality scoring chance for Finland, he did attempt to recover though and used his stick to stop a deflection opportunity. Had a tough sequence in the second period, he used his reach to knock the puck away on two separate occasions from Finland, unfortunately the puck went right to Juolevi who buried a wrist shot. The reargaurd didn't display his two-way game today.

CZE #7 LD Salda, Radim (2018+) – Salda had a mixed defensive game for the Czech's but it wasn't for a lack of effort. The defenseman had a couple of nice blocks in the slot area in the opening frame, he's usually well positioned and aware of his shooting lanes. However, on a penalty-kill in the first, this wasn't the case, he was too high on the right circle which allowed a great scoring opportunity for Finland, Salda did pick up on the play and rushed back but was a step-behind though it didn't result in a goal against. Had a nice block on the penalty kill that broke his stick before trying to make an additional block in the slot, his positioning was sound. Although Finland scored on the play the goal wasn't on him. He got caught in the neutral zone, not recognizing the Finnish transition up the ice, resulting in a 2-on-1 for Finland, he skated aggressively to attempt to get back into position. Had poor defensive positioning on Finland's third goal. He was keeping an opponent to the outside near the left point, then rotated back into the high-slot which was already covered, leaving Tolvanen soft-ice near the slot area, this resulted in a rebound goal. He needed to cover the open-side, which he usually does and attempted to do on this goal but he was behind the play. Had miscommunication with Galvas in the slot area leading to poor defensive positioning, resulting in another prime scoring chance for Finland in the last minute of the third with the game on the line, he was visibly frustrated with Galvas after the whistle, as they discussed what had happened. He finished on a good note, getting back on track in the extra frame by tracking Juolevi and wall-papering him along the boards while playing better positionally.

CZE #15 LW Kurovsky, Daniel (2018++) – Kurovsky was moved up to the third line after an excellent showing against the Swiss, while also receiving penalty-killing time. The power-winger had two great chances in the slot early. On the first, he took a pass and made a spinning backhand move that missed the top corner, it was unexpected, he continues to move well for his size. On the second attempt he got it off his stick quickly, shooting a low snap shot far-side, it was a difficult save for Luukkonen. Drove hard down the left wing and cut across the net but was disrupted by a good stick, he was offensively involved in the first. Defensively, he used his size to overpower Heponiemi along the boards and showed his agility, transitioning from a blocking position at the right point to an upright stance effortlessly, allowing him to defend aggressively and keep the Finnish players to the outside as they attempted to drive down the wings on him. Had a good keep in at the offensive blueline from his knees, using his length and his strength to get the puck in deep. Battled in the neutral zone for a puck which deflected to Reichal resulting in a goal, it was a strange bounce but wouldn't have happened without Kurovsky engaging physically. Kurovsky was solid today for the Czech's, showing two-way ability while using his size.

CZE #20 C/LW Lauko, Jakub (2018) – Lauko didn't threaten offensively but had some good moments without the puck. The quick forward had a good defensive play, using his speed to rush into a shooting lane in the high-slot, forcing the Finnish defender to forego his shot attempt and pass it off. Lauko looked engaged defensively again, he used his speed to try and apply pressure when he could. Had a heads up defensive read in the neutral zone, where he used his explosive acceleration to beat a Finnish player to a loose puck and chip it into the offensive end, resulting in possession for the Czech's. He had limited playing time again this evening but wasn't a liability out there, finishing with 1 shot on net.

CZE #18 LW Zadina, Filip (2018) – Zadina had difficulties on a shit-to-shift basis but still managed to contribute offensively. The winger scored a powerplay goal in the first period. He's been used on his off-wing, so that playmakers like Kaut can take advantage of his left handed-shot, however he showed that he can score on either side, as he fired a beautiful wrist-shot from the left circle that went in the top corner over Luukkonen who read the shot and was in good position. He continues to show that he can shoot with velocity without needing a lot of momentum. Scored the game tying goal by tipping a point shot in traffic in the slot, the goal highlighted how he can score in multiple ways. Had a good defensive stick-check below the goal-line resulting in a turnover, later, he had a block at the left circle, kicking out his skate, showed a willingness to put his body on the line. After making several solid defensive plays, he had a mental lapse in the neutral zone, holding onto the puck too long, resulting in a turnover and a dangerous scoring opportunity for Jaaska. Zadina had a high-skill play in overtime, after receiving a drop pass at the right circle, he tried to release a quick shot that was stick-checked, as he fell to his knee while in motion, he still managed to pull off a secondary wrist-shot that just missed far-side, he generated a surprising amount of velocity on the shot considering he was on his knees. The dynamic forward had his issues against Finland, the Finnish defense was good at engaging him, keeping him to the outside for much of the game. Despite this, he finished with 2 goals and had 7 shots on net.

CZE #16 RW Kaut, Martin (2018) – Kaut wasn't as effective in the offensive end today but continues to show his intelligence on the ice. The playmaking winger had a quiet first period but started distributing the puck more in the second, setting up his teammate while driving down the slot, passing it off to the right circle. Had a heads-up play, the Czech's were making a line-change just as Finland was about to gain possession of the puck, which would have allowed them to make a quick transition up the ice; to counteract this, Kaut used his acceleration to beat the Finnish defender to the puck and knocking it below the goal-line, resulting in a clean line-change. Good anticipation along the half-wall on the defensive end, intercepting a pass back to the point, resulting in a transitional breakout for the Czech's where he was hard on the forecheck. Kaut was the catalyst for the Czech's game tying goal, winning an important puck battle along the boards which gave his team possession just before the point-shot that was redirected by Zadina took place. His energy levels weren't the same today, as they had been in previous viewings.

Final Score 4-3 (SO) Czech Republic

Tri-City Americans at Kelowna Rockets, Jan 3rd 2018

TC #17 C Focht, Carson (2018) – an inconsistent game overall for Focht looked like he was giving his all on some shifts and looked a little lazy and indifferent on others. Pulled up a couple times to avoid hits and generally shied away from the hard battle areas while picking his spots and not doing very much to engaged with a physical Kelowna defense around the net. His ice-time in the third period showed as he only ended up with a couple shifts in what was a close game.

TC #4 LD Kalinichenko, Roman (2018) - Tended to make noise on all is shifts both good and bad through this game, noticeable on his first shift as he missed a clean breakout pass and turned over the puck which ended up leading to goal against certainly his biggest gaff of the game. Always playing aggressive and making sure to finish his hits, wasn't quitting on any plays and didn't back down from anyone. Was assigned to check the top line for Kelowna and ended the night even as he was on the ice for 2 goals for and 2 goals against all at even strength in on one goal he gave far to large of gap allowing the for the forward to shoot around him and beat the goalie clean. Took a massive hit to try and make a breakout pass and didn't get it off in time. Had a serviceable game but made way to many mistakes for a coaches liking.

TC #34 RW Mutala, Sasha (2019) – Played a pesky game in and around the net looked hard to move and created a couple good screens. Can move his feet well and put his speed with the puck on display on a couple of strong individual efforts from the defending zone to the attack, ended up with a good drives to the net both with or with out the puck. Makes good moves but lacked a bit of killer instinct to finish off the play for scoring chances but did take advantage of his opportunity to help two of TC's top forward enjoy some extra room on the ice.

KEL #21 C Topping, Kyle (2018) – Was really strong on his zone entries tonight knew when to change speeds and delay to gear up and streak to an opening for a teammate to catch him with a pass defenders were having trouble keeping pace with his line. Snapped a quick shot on goal leading to a primary assist for him on the opening goal of the game; started the game with good jump and a high tempo making it difficult to contain his line. Stick was solid tonight both defending and showed his eye hand off by knocking a waist high zone exit pass out of the air and keeping the play alive. Was solid on faceoffs and won the final one of the game to kill the last 15 seconds when down 6 on 5. Finished with 2 assists after starting the breakout on the game winner.

KEL #7 RD Zabransky, Libor (2018) – Not a great game from Zabransky on a couple levels, his body language was poor and he lacked hustle throughout the game which was evident on one particular icing play where he just game up. Having trouble connecting plays can often start a good play and ends up not knowing his next best move, wrecking the momentum of the play, seems to have trouble reading the movement of his teammates.

KEL #1 G Porter, James (2018) – Compact and calm throughout the game, didn't appear to have lots of holes around his body and did well absorbing pucks. Played aggressive and made sure to consistently look big by aggressively pushing out to the top of his crease. Cut down the angles tonight well on most shots from the outside, with the exception of one from just above the goal line in the corner, he was down on the ice and should have been standing up hugging the post to cover the top of the net. Still has those starts where he seems to let in a softer goal that needs to be saved, that bad goal was one tonight.

KEL #6 RD - Korczak, Kaedan (2019) – Could have been a little more quick in his decisions tonight, when to pinch when to attack a puck carrier looked like he was second guessing his instincts, he just looked a little tentative at times and was then making the easy play to defer to his partner for breakouts. Broke out this tentative mindset on one single rush he gathered the puck and kick his skating into a higher gear went clean through the neutral zone and had a solo scoring chance, he continues to improve and this viewings negative aspects seemed like a one off based on his play of late.

KEL #29 C – Foote, Nolan (2019) – Not usually a center and looks little forced playing the position, awkward carrying pucks with any amount of speed and just doesn't look comfortable or in the correct position most of the night. Did end up with 2 points on the night picking up an assist on a one touch pass entering the zone, solid play to get it to the trailing forward coming with speed. Showed off his powerful one time shot scoring on a knee drop goal from a big angle, displayed his impressive ability to raise the puck quickly and in tight from a short distance, this shot is difficult for any goalie to stop; perfect spot.

Final Score: Kelowna Rockets: 5 – Tri-City Americans: 4

White Bear Lake Bears at Edina Hornets, January 4th 2018

WBL #3 LD Gallatin, Owen (2020) – Gallatin doesn't have impressive size yet, but what he gives up in size he made up for with excellent vision, high end hockey smarts and dynamic skating ability in this game. Gallatin displayed the ability to think the game quickly and make some hard plays look relatively simple. His breakouts where clean and on the tape, often using his slick footwork to escape the pressure and turn the puck up ice. Made a beautiful one-touch pass from his own blueline to his forward at the far blue line to hit him in stride. Had a good defensive play on Sammy Walker (TBL 17') in transition to keep walker from going in on a breakaway. Gallatin was confident in running the top of the Power play for the Bears and displayed a calm demeanor under pressure, which was impressive for being just a freshman and playing the top team in the state that challenges the points on the PK. Owen used head fakes and his footwork to create plays through the middle of the ice and showed he has a plan with the puck on his stick in all 3 zones. Gallatin did get beat by Sammy Walker on one instance where walker was able to spin out of the corner with Gallatin in close on him and take it to the net for a goal. All together it was an impressive game for the freshman defenseman. Expect Gallatin who is a Minnesota Duluth Commit to go fairly high in this Springs USHL Phase 1 Draft as well as get considerable consideration for the USNTDP.

ED #20 RD Vorlicky, Michael (2018) – Vorlicky showed a long powerful stride that allows him to gain separation from forecheckers with ease at this level. He was proficient in running the top of the power play, displaying some quick hands to get around pressure at the point and move the puck to teammates down low. Vorlicky had an impressive end to end rush coming out from behind his own net where he displayed good stick handling abilities getting through opponents in the neutral zone and entering the offensive zone with control where he made an excellent cross ice feed to #22 (Jungles) for a scoring chance. His defensive positioning was ok in the sense he was able to keep rushes to the outside for most of the night but on a few instances he collapsed down toward his net a bit too far, giving players some time and space to get their shots off unchallenged.

ED #23 LW Koumontzis, Demetrios (2018) – Displayed a strong skating base which allowed him to protect the puck well, one on instance guarded the puck from defender around the top of the faceoff circles to buy time until a play opened up and made a nice cross ice feed on the opposite side that his teammate wasn't ready for. Has quick hands and makes crisp, confident passes all over the ice. Koumontzis didn't make a lot of soft or tentative feeds with the puck. Didn't show much defensive effort on a few plays coming back into the zone and seemed to get lost or out of position when his team was pinned in their own end. For having a strong base, Koumontzis wasn't good along the wall and lost some puck battles due to poor body position along the boards.

Sault Ste. Marie Greyhounds at Oshawa Generals, January 5th, 2018

SSM #3 LD Wale, Holden (2018) - Wale displayed quick feet and good four-way mobility which often allowed him to elude pressure and skate the puck out of traffic. Holden's strong edge work also allowed him to create space by quickly changing direction, while handling the puck effectively. Wale needs to add strength as he relies too much on his stick to defend below the hash marks and can be simply out powered by stronger opponents. A poor neutral zone read, looking to step up and finish a check, led to a Generals break-away and ultimately a goal.

SSM #8 LD LeGuerrier, Jacob (2019) - LeGuerrier had an effective two-way game for the Greyhounds, simplifying his play when needed, while showing deceptive two-way traits. Jacob showed vision from the back-end as he disguised a slap shot from the point before dishing it to a teammate off to the side of the goal for a scoring opportunity. LeGuerrier jumped into the rush on occasion, however picked his spots appropriately and remained aware of his defensive responsibilities. When carrying the puck in transition, Jacob was able to effectively gain the offensive side of centre and made simple decisions to avoid turnovers.

SSM #9 LD Sandin, Rasmus (2018) - An undersized defender, Sandin displayed above average foot-work and mobility along with strong decision making and overall hockey sense to his game. His ability to effortlessly elude pressure and create space with his feet was apparent throughout the game. Rasmus also utilized his feet well in the offensive zone, creating shooting lanes and injecting from his point position to make himself an option offensively. While Sandin showed an effectiveness carrying the puck, he consistently made a quality first pass and showed poise under an aggressive forecheck. Defensively his size was a concern, however it mainly became an issue in board battles and not while defending. His anticipation abilities along with strong positional play, skating and quick stick allowed him to defend transition attacks effectively.

SSM #19 LW Carroll, Joe (2019) - Carroll possesses a projectable frame and good skill to his game but is still raw in some areas. Joe consistently went to the dirty areas of the ice and made an impact winning battles along the wall, while also creating off the cycle, using his size to shield the puck and quick hands to make plays in tight spaces. Carroll wasn't rattled by veteran opponents playing physically with him and pushed back equally as much. His skating is his area of concern as his stride and first step need improvements.

SSM #24 RW MacKay, Cole (2019) - MacKay flashed intrigue throughout the game as he would burst through seams and make smart reads to open ice for his line mates, while also making himself an option to receive a pass in strong positioning. Cole used his speed well to play up and down the wings and was reliable in the defensive zone. MacKay was unable to muster much offense however he did display a dynamic shot, off a quick release.

SSM #27 LC Hayton, Barrett (2018) - Hayton was the Greyhounds top performer throughout the game, displaying a combination of skill and intelligence that allowed him to thrive on both sides of the puck. Barrett showed excellent positional awareness and was always on the right side of the puck. His anticipation skills often allowed him to be first to pucks or put himself in ideal positioning to succeed. In possession Hayton displayed poise and awareness of his options, while disguising his intentions well, making him a versatile threat. Hayton showed quick bursts of speed, allowing him to accelerate past defenders and create separation from a flat-footed position. He showed an above average release and velocity to his shot and effectively used opponents as screens at various times.

SSM #37 RW Roth, Ryan (2018) - Roth had an inconsistent performance as he flashed skill and strong decision making, however his skating hindered his game. Ryan was unable to quickly accelerate and create separation from checks, which often limited him due to his size as he was bumped from possession. In flight Roth handled the puck well and recognized his options and was able to make quick, high percentage decisions with the puck. He found space effectively in the offensive zone but failed to make a real impact offensively.

SSM #39 RW Jacklin, Brett (2018) - Jacklin possesses a tall and projectable frame, however will need to add muscle if he hopes to find success in a bottom six role. Brett played sparingly but competed well and showed positional awareness in all three zones. His skating will need to improve as he lacks any explosiveness to his first step or stride.

OSH #5 LD Ennis, William (2018) - Ennis was good again, limiting his time of possession and doing a number of little things well. He played a "vanilla" style of game and didn't stand out negatively anyway, just kept his game simplistic. William continues to look stronger which has enhanced his ability to win battles in the corners and in front of the net. While his puck skills are still improving he does show vision from the back-end and can make a capable first pass.

OSH #8 RW Noel, Serron (2018) - Noel performed well for the Generals in the narrow loss, as he consistently utilized his combination of size and speed to create offensively. While Serron's first step is average, his long and powerful stride allows him to generate speed quickly. He showed this when picking up the puck flat-footed along the half-wall before exploding up the ice and driving wide past the Soo defender. On the play Noel showed good puck protection skills and a willingness to go to traffic. His hands in tight continue to get better however there is room to improve. Serron competed well on the back-check and was able to clog lanes defensively, while utilizing his reach at times to create turnovers.

OSH #61 LC McShane, Allan (2018) - McShane had an inconsistent performance as he struggled to make much of an impact during 5-on-5 play, however was strong on the power play with added time and space. Allan see's the ice well and can anticipate the play with effectiveness, however his compete level came and went throughout the game. On the power play McShane showed excellent passing skills and creativity to generate multiple scoring opportunities. Finding a way to create consistently during 5-on-5 play the same way he does on the man advantage would significantly increase his draft stock.

OSH #66 LD Gross, Nico (2018) - Playing in his first OHL game after his performance at the World Junior Championships, Nico had one of his strongest games as a General. He confidently injected himself into the offensive attack, while remaining aware of his defensive responsibilities. Gross scored the second Generals goal as he got up ice and into the play and was hit with a pass as a trailer and showed an impressive release on his snap shot, beating the goalie high glove. Nico kept his game simpler in the defensive zone, but showed aggression throughout. In possession he was able to create space with his feet but relied more on a first pass then skating the puck up ice.

Seattle Thunderbird at Kelowna Rockets, January 5th 2018

KEL #24 C – Topping, Kyle (2018) – Was relentless tonight and played like he had something to prove a little bit, attacked loose pucks and put on impressive back pressure on a couple occasions and picked some pucks off players to turn the play onto the attack quickly. Scored goal in the dirty area in front of the net off a screen he was creating, grabbed a rebound and beat the goalie to the far post to tuck it past him exhibiting great use of his shifty hands. Took draws all over the ice and was easily the most effective center to gain possession and in the defensive end for Kelowna tonight.

KEL #1 G – Porter, James (2018) – Score doesn't properly reflect his game tonight as his team left him out to dry on a few goalies and was alone against a couple forwards. He was his usual compact self a looked sounds in his positioning. Made a coupe good reactionary saves off skaters moves but ultimately missed a few tips and couldn't quite keep his team in the game in the third period.

KEL #29 C – Foote, Nolan (2019) – Lineup again at center due to Kelowna missing players and didn't look confortable holding the puck for long periods of time and being the driving force behind offense. He couldn't take defensemen wide on plays and had trouble breaking check when he was defended tightly. He's cast in the wrong spot here in this viewings and has been for a few games and his struggles take away from his strengths. Things should change but it should solidify where he belongs in the lineup

SEA #24 LD - Lee, Jake (2019) - Was a little easy for opponents to enter the zone against him, he was backing off a little to early instead on playing a forward tight, but skates well enough to close gaps quickly and ended up rubbing a few guys out along the boards to stop rushes just wasn't fully utilizing it tonight. Showed a good offensive move or two to move pucks through the neutral zone but didn't end up with enough ice-time to make a siginificant impact on the game.

SEA #22 LW – Hamaliuk, Dillon (2019) – Scored a goal by being in the right place at the right time, drove the net and stopped on the crease and end up tapping in goal that popped free from the far side; right place right time. Pucks seemed to be difficult to handle for him tonight and he looked off on his control nothing could stay on his blade and it lead to some turnovers. Was better as the F1 on the fore check helping start the cycle that was the strength of his game tonight, he has some trouble carrying pucks at top speed through the neutral zone he was coughing things up.

Final Score: Seattle Thunderbirds: 6 – Kelowna Rockets: 4

Sweden vs Canada, U20 WJC Gold Medal Game, January 5 2018

Sweden –

SWE #8 LD Dahlin, Rasmus (2018) – Dahlin played the majority of the game with Liljegren, showing poise under an aggressive Canadian forecheck that was targeting him throughout the final. Had a good recovery play early behind his goal line, as he made a poor drop-pass that ended up on a Canadians stick but closed on the puck quickly, using his stick to disrupt the play and move it up along the boards. Had a rush into the offensive zone, showing his straight-line speed, before passing it off to Steen who got an excellent scoring chance on a wrap-around. Dahlin was pressured by Timmins who hit him as he passed it off, but there's finesse to his game, resulting in a soft pass regardless of getting pushed forward. Dahlin handled the quick Canadian forecheck well, he had several quick passing plays, displaying the ability to process the play and make the right decision with the puck while not getting caught. On his best sequence in the first, he cut around his own net under pressure then banked a pass off the boards to his teammate, stayed in proper position along the boards giving him repossession of the puck after it was knocked back to him, he then made an additional outlet-pass that was accurate to the neutral zone and finished the play by quickly reacting to a turnover, making his final pass on the sequence up to his teammate which gave them an offensive zone entry. The sequence won't end up on the highlight-reel but it's just as important as one that would. Had an excellent sequence midway through the second, he rushed the puck into the slot and released a wrist-shot that went over the net, then supported Pettersson as he lost the puck with good positioning at the blueline, regained possession and fed a pass into the slot resulting in a quality scoring chance. Took a bad penalty at the end of the second, it was a senseless play at a critical time. In the third period, he was active on the penalty-kill, using his skating to pressure his opponents and was physical when he needed to be. Dahlin came as advertised at the WJC, finishing with 6 assists in 7 games.

SWE #20 C/LW Lundestrom, Isac (2018) – Lundestrom continued to display chemistry with Soderlund and steen on the third line, while getting 2nd-unit powerplay time. The center had a redirect chance in the slot area, he was well positioned on the play. He's got plus skating mechanics and used them to drive up the ice and weave through the opposition, before releasing a wrist-shot through a screen that was absorbed by Hart. Made a nice pass into the slot to Soderlund resulting in a scoring chance late in the first. Had a great chance early in the slot on a feed from Steen, however he was delayed getting the puck off his stick, which allowed Hart to regain position. Showed good defensive awareness, supporting his defenseman below the goal-line in the corner, resulting in possession. Lundestrom finished the tournament with 2 goals in 7 games.

Canada –

CAN #31 G Hart, Carter (2016 PHI) – Hart's composure is an attribute that stands out in his game and you could see early, that he was dialed in, playing with ice in his veins, there was no perceived pressure coming from him in the biggest game of his life. His positioning and ability to square up in the opening frame was apparent, as he absorbed the majority of shots that were shot towards him. When he couldn't use his butterfly to swallow the puck, he showed excellent rebound control, using his pads to deflect the puck into the corners so secondary chances wouldn't occur. On one sequence in the first, he stopped an initial shot in the slot with his butterfly and had already assessed the follow up shot before it was off the Swede's stick, making a difficult save look harmless, which is one of Hart's better traits. Had a great skate save on Lundestrom, he wasn't completely square but got just enough of it. He was scored on in the second frame while Sweden was short-handed. Soderlund flew down the right wing and used a head feint and was patient, freezing Hart before wiring a wrist-shot off the post and into the net, Hart had very little chance on it. In the third period, Hart didn't need to be as good as he was in the first two, as Canada started taking over the game, leading to powerplay time. That been said, his calm approach and timely saves gave him another excellent performance after making 34 saves on 35 shots. Hart finished the tournament with a 1.81GAA and a .930 save percentage in 6 games.

CAN #23 LC Steel, Sam (2016 ANA) – Steel was drafted 30th overall by Anaheim in the 2016 draft, while playing for the Regina Pats in the WHL. The talented center had two well-timed defensive plays in the first period. The first was along the half-wall, as he quickly skated towards his opponent, closing the gap and deflecting a pass attempt into the slot out of harms way. The second saved a possible goal, as he was in excellent position to support Hart on Steen's wrap around attempt, using a stick-check to disrupt the play. Distributed the puck quickly along the half-wall on the powerplay in the opening frame, on one play, he was pressured into the boards but still made a sharp and accurate pass before having the puck taken from him. Displayed soft hands while gauging his lane before passing it up into the neutral zone from the defensive end, the play led to Canada's opening goal, giving him the secondary assist. Continued to show excellent passing ability in the third period on the powerplay, threading a hard pass through traffic across the slot, resulting in a tic-tac-toe passing play that went off the post. Steel finished the tournament with 4 goals and 5 assists in 7 games.

CAN #19 RC Batherson, Drake (2017 OTT) – Batherson was selected as an overaged player 121st overall in the 2017 draft class by Ottawa. He had a nice give and go sequence with a teammate in the neutral zone while rushing the puck up the left wing, he attempted a backhand pass into the slot with speed. Showed power after delivering a tremendous hit in the corner of his own end, knocking Liljegren flat to the ice. Showed a high compete level against multiple Swedish forecheckers along the boards, he's got a good build and used his stick aggressively to fight for possession. Had a good backhand pass into the slot area, resulting in a quality scoring chance for his team in the second. In the third period, he had the most important sequence he's ever had, winning a board battle in the corner and using his base to maintain balance as he passed the puck back to the point, which lead to the game winning goal. Batherson finished the tournament with 7 goals in 7 games.

Final Score 3-1 Canada

Northwood Prep School vs Nichols Prep School, January 6th, 2017

NWP #16 LW Leal, Cole (2019) - Leal had a strong performance for Northwood displaying good skill to his game along with fluid skating abilities. Cole shows a wide skating base and a powerful stride that allowed him to quickly accelerate and generate good speed. Leal was confident in possession and showed quick hands and an elusiveness in possession as he beat opposing player in 1-on-1 situations. Cole found open ice away from the puck and displayed a quick release as he scored the first goal of the game. Leal also showed quick hands in tight, on his second goal of the game.

NWP #7 LD Gilbert, Andrew (2018) - Gilbert is a big bodied defender who kept his game simplistic but highly effective throughout. While Andrew played a stay-at-home style of defense he did show an ability to move the puck and was poise under pressure. Gilbert's four-way mobility has room to become more fluid and quicker, which would enhance his ability to retrieve pucks and control quicker attacking opponents. Despite room to improve his feet, Andrew played a smoother style of defense and combined his size and strength with his reach and active stick to defend with effectiveness. He quickly took away time and space and took good routes to opposing puck carriers.

NWP #20 RC Hartikainen, Santeri (2018) - Hartikainen showed an effectiveness below the hash-marks and off the cycle as he utilized his puck protection skills, strength over the puck and quick hands to create space and opportunity. Santeri would recognize space and drive off the cycle, showing a quick release with impressive velocity behind his shot.

NWP #6 LW Panico, Stephen (2018) - Panico possesses a tall and lanky frame and competed hard throughout. Stephen displayed good skill to his game and was able to generate a good top speed, which made him difficult to defend off the rush due to his reach and ability to place the puck in areas were opponents simply couldn't not dislodge it from him. Panico was aggressive on the forecheck an often utilized his reach to poke free the puck before finishing with contact. He showed smarts to his game in his ability to anticipate the play, while he also always seemed to be on the right side of the puck and positionally sound on both sides of the puck.

NPS #9 LW Morrison, Chris (2018) - Chris is an undersized, but energetic and physical winger who was effective in a complimentary role. Morrison displayed a fluid stride and generated good speed, which he often utilized on both the forecheck and back-check. In possession his quick feet allowed him to maneuver in tight spaces, as well as quickly accelerate and separate from a check. Morrison's physical edge and aggression throughout made him an agitating presence.

NPS #16 Lugris, Dylan (2019) - Lugris had a strong performance for Nichols as displays an intriguing combination of size, strength and above average skill. Dylan was also a strong two-way presence as he was engaged defensively, showed good positional awareness and competed hard. While Lugris has room to improve his feet, more specifically his first step, he can reach a good top speed and wasn't hindered by his feet. Dylan showed the ability to quickly make high percentage decisions and didn't panic under pressure. He protected the puck well in traffic and showed quick hands allowing him to create space and/or beat a check. Lugris showed a versatile skill set offensive as both an aware playmaker and a shooter.

NPS #35 G Nuchereno, Robbie (2019) - Nuchereno was strong despite his team losing as without his effort the score could have been much more lopsided. Robbie shows good anticipation abilities which allowed him to make dynamic cross-crease saves. His post-to-post movements where fluid and under control always remaining square to the shooters. As an undersized goaltender Nuchereno recognizes when to challenge shooters even greater than simply being at the top of his crease, showing an awareness of his angles and cutting down the shooters eye. His ability to square shooters and face them at strong angle allowed him to coral pucks and/or effectively control his rebounds.

Duluth East Hounds at Minnetonka Skippers, January 6th, 2018

DE #22 RC Donovan, Ryder (2019) – Donovan has good size, listed at close to 6'4" and showed good explosiveness and speed in this game. It didn't take him long to get to top speed in transition. Showed a higher gear with the puck than anyone else on the ice which allowed him to create hole for himself and drive the net. Donovan had 2 secondary assists in this game; showed good compete on the 2nd assist, keeping the puck alive in the corner by being physical on the Minnetonka player and poking the puck up the wall to the point. Showed a hard, quick release from the high slot on a shot on the power play that the goalie made a great glove save on. Donovan is a late 00' Birth date and turned down an NDTP invite this year to take a run at a State title with the Hounds. The University of North Dakota commit showed the makings of being a high end prospect for the 2019 NHL Draft. Donovan will likely finish the year with Dubuque (USHL) once his High School season finishes and should be a key piece for that team next year.

DE #25 RD Lamaster, Luke (2018) –Lamaster showed good vision and passing ability all over the ice, he was able to find teammates in stride and create some decent scoring chances by stretching out the opposition. One example where Lamaster got the puck in his own end and sent a beautiful stretch-bank pass off the near side boards to the far blue line to send his team in on a 2 on 1. Showed good vision and ability to read the play in the 1st period where he stepped up and picked off a pass up the middle of the ice by a Minnetonka player and was able to come down the middle of the slot for a good scoring chance that Lamaster couldn't convert on. Lamaster showed strong footwork and was difficult to separate from the puck on the fore-check, however Lamaster lacks explosiveness in his skating which may prevent him from being a Draft pick at this stage but has enough talent and Hockey smarts to be a player to track as he goes through Junior and college hockey.

MN #8 RC Loheit, Luke (2018) –Loheit has displayed excellent finishing ability this season and in this game did it again on the Power Play early in the 3rd where he received a pass below the faceoff dot on his off side, and rifled a quick release over the goalies shoulder on the short side. Loheit was also responsible for his team getting the power play when he blocked a play at his own blue line, got past the defender and drove hard to the net where he drew a hooking penalty. Loheit made a number of sound defensive plays coming back into his own end, tying up his man going to the net. Made a careless blind pass up the middle early in the game that sent a player in for a scoring chance

MN #9 RW Brink, Bobby (2019) – Brink isn't the biggest player but worked hard all over the ice, his skating allowed him to close on defenders quickly on the fore-check and force turnovers and errant passes. Brink was impressive on puck retrievals, especially on the Power Play. Brink showed the ability to make quick decisions with the puck in setting up his team's first goal early in the game by coming into the zone with speed and hitting his defenseman joining the rush on the far side of the ice.

Kanata Lasers vs. Ottawa Jr. Senators, January 10th, 2018

KAN #33 G Carriere, Gabriel (2019) – Gabriel was outstanding tonight for Kanata and was the only reason Kanata came away with a point in OT tonight. He was very quick post to post tonight; he must of stopped 3-4 cross crease back door passes tonight with good anticipation and excellent lateral movement. He competed hard tonight, challenging shooters not giving much room to shoot, his rebound control was good as he was able to either redirect shots to the corners or covering them up for the whistle. He made a bad play coming out to play the puck and turned it over for Ottawa first goal. After that goal he showed good composure and work ethic, as it didn't bother him. He showed athleticism in the crease tonight but I think he is more or a positional goalie, he plays his angles really well.

OTT #25 C Manderville, Ethan (2018) - Ethan flashed an intelligence to his game with his ability to anticipate the play with effectiveness and overall sound positional play on both sides of the puck. Ethan utilized his ability to read the play to forecheck under control but still create turnovers. Manderville found space in the offensive by using his big frame and excellent reach; he just needs to continue to do that in the offensive zone to be more effective. Ethan line was effective tonight on the cycle creating some chances. Ethan needs to work on be more consistent with his shifts; there were too many times where you would even notice him on the ice. He was strong tonight in the faceoff circle winning more than 60% of his draws.

Final Score: Ottawa Jr. Senators: 2 – Kanata Lasers: 1

Spokane Chiefs at Kelowna Rockets, January 10th 2018

SPK #24 RD – Smith, Ty (2018) – an all situation defender as usual this game, playing power play, penalty kill and staring in all 3 zones. Had a rough start to the game because was standing still and tried a breakout pass from his own goal line that lacked any power and landed right on an opponents stick leading to extended zone time. He also whiffed on a pass in his own end that was immediately turned over and shot right into his net for the opening goal of the game. Was his regular mobile self along the blue line, his east/west play with the puck was quick and causes defenders to miss his shot; has a knack for getting open looks. On most Spokane zone entries Smith ended up looping at least half way into the zone and was often pinching deeper looking to create, his speed helps him get back quickly on defense. He was kept off the score sheet but everything on offense flows through him and he was doing a great job of helping sustain pressure along the blue line. His defensive play in this game wasn't great as he get chasing players around a lot and was getting lost in coverage below his own goal line.

SPK #29 C – Zummack, Eli (2018) – Was really proactive in the neutral zone throughout this game, plays attackers tight in transition and doesn't give up easy plays. Was really aggressive on his back checks and attacked puck carries with solid back pressure leading to some obviously impressive takeaways and making his work ethic noticeable. Played well with the puck throughout this game showing off his shifty stick handling to avoid giving up pucks but when a defender focused on his body he became easy to knock down or off the puck. Still was relentless and didn't back down from playing in the harder areas along the boards or around the crease. Started an impressive 3 way passing play for a secondary assist but it was obvious he knew the end play would lead to a goal.

SPK #3 LD – Leduc, Matt (2018) – Looked poised along the blue line, made a quick move to snap a point shot through and pick up an assist. Uses his long reach well around the net and does a strong job of keep guys away from the net and keeping players who drive the goalie honest. Picked up a fight with Hilsendager and won easily after landing a few blows. Not a high event game but stead and smart staying in position and is effective.

KEL #24 C – Topping, Kyle (2018) - Solid game with 2 goal and 1 assist on the night and played a lot as easily the most effective attacking line, picked up a turnover off Smith and quickly drove the net to snap his first goal. On his second goal he made a nice move to put a defender on his back and fended him off with on hand on the stick flipping a little back hand over the goalie for an impressive goal. For his assist he stopped quickly and button hooked to feed the point for a quick one-time from a defender. Looked fluid and fast tonight with that effective line, zone entries we clean and his chemistry with Lind was on display tonight, continually kept his feet moving and was difficult to contain, one of his better viewings recently.

KEL #30 G – Basran, Roman (2019) – Started this game and made a couple impressive saves looked quick and was getting post to post with serious reactionary speed. Made an excellent full splits save and came up laboring on the play, he would later leave the game and not return (this would end up his last game of the season as he suffered a torn ACL)

KEL #6 RD – Korczak, Kaeden (2019) – His first period might have been the best in any viewing this season. Making a lot of simple and short plays to relieve pressure and give his teammates time to break out, nothing was rushed and his confidence with the puck was very noticeable. Pinched in and snapped a shot from the low corner that found the top corner of the net for his first of the year, poor angle but nice location for his shot. Really steading defending along his side of the ice nothing easy getting past him, pushing attackers hard to boards and staying in front of anyone going down the middle, just very steady all around including denying entries. Was heads up with his breakout passes, looked casual and calm but was accurate and read the neutral zone very well.

KEL #29 C – Foote, Nolan – Didn't look good at all on faceoffs tonight and had very little impact on most of the game despite showing up on the score sheet with a 2 point evening. Drove the far post and ended up with a tap in on a puck that squirted free, grabbed the puck from the goaltender and dished to a defender who ended up end to end. In recent viewings where Foote was playing center he tried to handle the puck a lot in this viewing he looked a little more confortable because he skates with the puck less and relied more on his line mates to create transition. It looked more like he knew what he wasn't capable of and didn't try and force things as much.

Final Score: Kelowna Rockets: 7 – Spokane Chiefs: 4

Waterloo Black Hawks at Madison Capitols, January 12th, 2018

WTL #4 LD Tabor, Peter (2018) – Tabor showed good backwards skating and agility both with and without the puck but his forward explosiveness and stride caused him to lose some puck races and keep him from getting separation from fore-checkers on breakouts. Tabor made a good play coming off the bench just inside the offensive blueline where he intercepted a pass up the middle and threaded a nice feed down low to a teammate for a high end scoring chance. Tabor made reliable plays with the puck at both ends and executed some excellent breakout passes, hitting his man in stride up the ice but will need to continue to develop his straight line skating in order to develop into a pro prospect down the road.

WTL #9 RD Ferrandino, Michael (2018) – Ferrandino is slightly undersized defenseman that relied on his good skating technique to make plays and move the puck. He ran the top of the umbrella on the Power Play where his footwork and quick feet allow him to cover a lot of ground at the point, chase down pucks to keep them in the offensive zone and open up lanes. Michael didn't show a big physical presence in this game, however showed good gap and stick and body position in defensive situations and showed he is able to be effective in defending against bigger forwards.

WTL #18 LC Drury, Jack (2018) – Drury scored a goal late in the 3rd period on the Power Play in a 6 on 4 situation by one-timing an excellent cross slot feed. Drury did an excellent job in backing away from the slot to get separation and positioning himself in a lane for a one-time opportunity and was able to beat the goalie, what looked to be just inside the near side post. Aside from his goal late Drury didn't do a lot of drive the offense with the puck on his stick tonight. Drury continued his game of battling hard in front of the net and does a good job getting in position for tips and passes in traffic and worked hard along the walls to win possession for his team.

WTL #35 G Moe, Jared (2018) – This being night one of a 3 game weekend for Waterloo, Moe did not play in goal tonight.

MAD #29 RW/C O'Reilly, Ryan (2018) – It was a pretty quiet night for O'Reilly. He didn't threaten in the offensive zone aside from a couple shots off the rush that missed the net or were blocked by the defender and plays seemed to fizzle out with the puck on his stick on the Power Play. O'Reilly did finish some hits on the fore-check and showed good compete for pucks but all in all was not a big factor in Madison's Win tonight.

Chicago Steel at Madison Capitols, January 13th, 2018

CHI #4 RD Bucheler, Jeremie (2018) – Buchelar has NHL size and showed good straight line and lateral skating abilities for having such a big, lanky frame. While Bucheler's reputation is having good passing abilities, that trait wasn't on display in this game. Bucheler made some questionable reads with the puck, either passing into danger in the middle of the ice or to a teammate that wasn't open and seemed like he wasn't able to look beyond his first read out of the zone. Bucheler has smooth footwork and was able to escape pressure and buy time for himself both coming out of his own end and at the offensive blue line. Didn't display much in the way of dynamic playmaking ability in the offensive zone but played a reliable game in the offensive end and got some pucks on the net from the point.

CHI #21 LW McLaughlin, Blake (2018) – McLaughlin registered 1 Assist on the night by executing a slick cross ice feed on the Power Play to Dugan who made a play to the point where the defenseman scored with a slap shot to the top corner. McLaughlin made a couple uncharacteristic soft plays in the neutral zone with the puck resulting in turnovers and was visibly upset with himself with a couple of them going back to the bench. His puck retrievals on the power play allowed his team to sustain offensive pressure and McLaughlin used his quick hands and playmaking ability to make a couple nice setup's in the offensive zone that his teammates weren't able to capitalize on. On a couple of those instances McLaughlin passed the puck on some good scoring opportunities. The compete was there all game long, however McLaughlin seemed a little off and battled the puck a bit in this one.

CHI #11 LD Gurney, Xan (2018) – Was a physical presence in this game, supported and communicated with his Defensive partner (Jeremie Bucheler) well. Stepped up on some players at his own blue line and created some turnovers because of it. Gurney made reliable breakouts for much of the night but missed some opportunities to stretch the ice and find his forwards up the ice.

CHI #24 RW Mastrosimone, Robert (2019) – Showed excellent skating, both straight line and east-west. Was quick on defenders on the fore-check and battled for pucks. Didn't threaten a lot in the offensive zone but moved the puck quickly and accurately in transition in the neutral zone.

MAD #29 RW O'Reilly, Ryan (2018) – O'Reilly tended to force some passes to the middle of the ice when he pulled up with in the offensive zone, some passes he connected on and some plays were telegraphed by the defense and the play went the other way. Attempted to beat defender with an outside in toe drag move but lost control of the puck on one instance. O'Reilly scored on a quick release off the rush where he entered the zone in the middle of the ice, slightly changed the angle to get the shot through the defender, using him as a screen and beating him on the glove side.

Rouyn-Noranda Huskies at Drummondville Voltigeurs, January 14th, 2018

RN #11 LW Harvey-Pinard, Rafaël (2018): Harvey-Pinard scored the lone Huskies' goal tonight, and was one of their better players in a 5-1 loss to the Voltigeurs. He scored late in the game by jumping on a loose puck in front of the net. Not much went right for the Huskies tonight, but Harvey-Pinard showed great work ethic. His compete level was good, and he played with an edge. I liked his work on the PK unit with Bibeau.

RN #31 G Émond, Zachary (2018): Émond gave up five goals in the first period, but with Harvey still sick on the bench, the team kept him in goal for the rest of the game. Émond was playing his 3rd game in 3 days, and it showed in some of the bad rebounds he gave up in the first period. It has to be said that the team in front of him didn't help much, in addition to being down two veteran defensemen (Lauzon and Ford). He bounced back in periods 2 and 3 with some solid saves and showed a good level of commitment to stay focused in the game, despite the score. Overall, he worked hard to track the puck with traffic in front of him, showing good quickness moving side to side and covering the lower part of the net.

RN #4 LD Bergeron, Justin (2018): This was the most ice time I've seen Bergeron get this season with the Huskies. He played his regular shift on the power play that he usually gets, but this time he was on the first PP unit. He also saw action on the PK unit. He made some aggressive reads in the neutral and defensive zones, showing good confidence and putting pressure on the puck-carrier. However, this also came off as a bit risky, as he got caught being too aggressive in the neutral zone. He still has some things to work on in the defensive zone, as he has decent feet and mobility, but currently lacks the strength to separate players from the puck. He showed good confidence with the puck, either by skating it out or making a good first pass out of his zone.

RN #16 RW Beaucage, Alex (2018): Beaucage had a couple of solid scoring chances in the game; his favourite weapon remains his shot (and its release). On the power play, he likes to play on his off-wing, putting himself in a position to receive passes around the faceoff circle that he can one-time on net. He has a very impressive release on his shot; one of the best out of all the 2001-born players in the QMJHL. He played a regular shift on the 3rd line and saw ice time on the power play as well.

DRU #33 G Rodrigue, Olivier (2018): Rodrigue was great today. He was close to getting a shutout before giving up a late goal to Harvey-Pinard. His positional stance in net was good. He was always in the correct position to make the save, making it look easy on most shots. He did a good job tracking pucks; his reaction time was really good on shots that got redirected. He has excellent quickness and footwork in his crease. He was very calm in net and played with confidence.

DRU #55 LD Bernard, Xavier (2018): Nothing fancy out of Bernard, who logged a lot of ice time for Drummondville once again. He played in all situations and finished the game with 2 assists (two secondary assists though). He played a safe and smart game with the puck while being not overly creative with it. He was very efficient out there, with no turnovers. On the point on the power play, he makes the simple pass well, and does a really good job getting his shot through to the net. One aspect of his game that has really improved this year is his physical play, and today he had some good hits in his zone, including a good open-ice hit.

DRU #92 LD Beaudin, Nicolas (2018): Beaudin was solid tonight. He was really good at skating the puck out of his zone and into the offensive zone. His skating ability is good; he has good top speed and acceleration. He also has very good agility to change directions when rushing the puck to avoid opponents. He made good decisions with the puck, showing good vision. He also showed some character in the 3rd period, after one of his teammates got hurt by a knee-on-knee hit. He immediately went after and got into a fight with the much bigger opponent (it was not much of a fight, but it was still good to see).

DRU #90 C Veleno, Joseph (2018): Veleno was really good today, and did everything well in this game – except for scoring. He came close at least 4-5 times, but couldn't get the puck past Émond. He also got one goal waved off. He showed good on-ice vision during the game; in the first period, he made 2 great cross-ice passes to set up goals for his team. He also showed good patience with the puck and an ability to hold onto it for a long time in order to allow his teammates to get open in the offensive zone. He used his good speed well tonight; he was flying and playing with a lot of confidence. He was also a key player on the PK unit, with some good hustle and working hard while shorthanded.

DRU #81 C Simoneau, Xavier (2019): Simoneau was pain in the butt for the Huskies today. Despite being the smallest player on the ice, his compete level was excellent as always, and he was involved in a lot of scrums. He showed good work ethic on the backcheck; I saw him steal the puck from a Rouyn-Noranda player a number of times when backchecking. On the forecheck, he used his speed well to put pressure on the puck-carrier. In the offensive zone (but mostly on the power play), he's always in movement on the ice, and always gets open to receive a pass from a teammate.

Saskatoon Blades at Kootenay Ice, January 14, 2018

Blades –

SAS #17 LC Florchuk, Eric (2018) – nice pass from the boards to the high-slot resulting in a scoring chance, was active on the forecheck but missed his man with the hit, showed above average hands combined with poise while under pressure in the offensive-end, his puck movement was the catalyst for the Blades opening goal, had a rush down the left-wing but lost his shooting angle after taking too long to decide to shoot after recognizing his passing option was closed off, didn't get anything on the shot. Had his best scoring chance late as he found soft-ice in the slot area and lifted a backhander that required a difficult glove save, had a nice shot-fake before passing the puck to his teammate that put it top shelf over McGovern, arguably the most impressive forward for the Blades

SAS #44 RC/LW Wouters, Chase (2018) – got the first real scoring chance for the Blades, dropped to a knee to generate more power on his shot but didn't get enough on it, plus board battling work using his frame effectively, his hits generate a lot force and he's active when helping support his defense, looked for a sharp-angles shot that he fired wide, big open-ice hit which sent a player crashing into the ice, was used on the penalty-kill and made the other team work to maintain possession, his motor stood out and he competed as he usually does

Ice –

#30 G Duncan McGovern (2018) – didn't have a lot of work in the opening frame since Kootenay were all over the Blades, scoring 4 unanswered goals before he let in his first of the night off a nice pass down-low on his glove-side, he fully extended to try and take the bottom of the net away but was late. His best save came off a quick backhand from in-tight where he flashed his glove while showing plus reactions, he was good at absorbing rebounds, had a good level of composure and was consistent at cutting down his angles properly today

#15 RD Martin Bodak (2018++) – had a nice defensive sequence where he was a bit late to his assignment in-front of the net but overpowered his opponent and effectively boxed him out. Demonstrated his ability to take his man-off the puck with a big hit, he angled himself properly and the execution was clean, had a well-timed pinch that allowed him to carry the puck deep, showed poise in the neutral zone while under pressure, showed decent hands on a penalty-shot despite the puck rolling off his stick

#27 LC Bradley Ginnell (2018) – applied pressure in the neutral zone and the offensive-zone, shifted his lane to escape a check and had his stick get knocked down the entire length of the ice, nice evasive move though, on the same shift he had an accurate and sharp pass that set Taphorn up for a scoring chance from the right-circle, dropped his gloves at the horn so he's willing to fight if he feels provoked

#12 LC Cole Muir (2018) – good support in the defensive-zone during a sequence which helped transition the puck up the ice, had a great scoring chance at the top of the crease on the powerplay after he was given some time due to the blowout

#14 RW Keenan Taphorn (2018) – scored a powerplay goal during a 5-on-3 after receiving a pass in the slot and firing it far-side, the shot was more accurate than powerful, took his time with it so would have liked to have seen it come off his stick quicker, had a scoring chance late from the right-circle but it was absorbed, the shot wasn't overly impressive, didn't change the angle and lacked power

#19 LW Payton Krebs (2019) – had a good scoring chance in the slot early, hesitated in the slot with the puck before passing the puck to his teammate who buried is short-side, had a nice rush down the right wing and made a backhand pass that led to another chance in-front of the net, pivoting ability was apparent when he would stop-up or peel off an opponent, on the powerplay he showed that he was capable of running it from the half-wall and made several quality passes to his teammates that set them up for prime scoring opportunities throughout the game

Final score 7-2 Kootenay

Lethbridge Hurricanes at Kelowna Rockets, January 17th 2018

LET #2 RD – Addison, Calen (2018) – Overall a really strong game from Addison, especially on the offensive side of the ice, there were a few mistakes on defense however he wasn't tasked with a lot of defensive zone starts or and penalty kill time so he was a bit sheltered. His skating and edge work were elite and his displayed the ability to make players miss on their checks, especially when he had the puck. His ability to pinch and recover was the best of any skater tonight and his timing is great on this. Showed great quickness with his instincts to get out of the zone either with a pass or his feet and was turning the play in the offensive direction at a really impressive pace. His 4-way mobility was obvious throughout this game but it appears he chooses to skate forward more often than reverse. Got in trouble when he stopped moving his feet, tried to make a stick play at the offensive blue line and coughed the puck up leading to a short handed goal. At times in the defending zone he looked a little easy to play against as he was pushed around easily, was allowing entries on his side of the ice to softly and didn't cut guys off at the boards often enough.

LET #27 C – Barlage, Logan (2019) – second line pivot in this viewing and a mainstay on the Lethbridge penalty kill and showed good use of his stick in that role and in the defensive zone, clearing the net and creating some takeaways. His upper body moves a lot when he skates which seems to hurt his opening strides but his top speed was decent throughout the game. His hands were also quick what stickhandling with the puck, easy to tell that he likes to handle the puck but at times he coughed it up in traffic. He battles and was making good use of his size to get position while defending and to cause a little trouble around the opposing goalie.

LET #24 RW – Cozens, Dylan (2019) - A 2 assist night for Cozens as he had a solid game all around, his most impressive play was a quick back check creating a clean takeaway and showing off his hockey IQ by immediately flipping it to a teammate on the open side of the net, it was an instinct play and he looked good. Showed off his knack for the net and does use his size to get there however he showed his finesse by stick handling to the crease a couple times. Took up the slot position on the powerplay and took all the punishment that was given to him, he looked fearless battling in there against anyone and works his positioning around the crease quite well. Got stuck out for a few long shifts and looked gassed while scrambling around his defensive zone, but a rather impressive viewing from a rookie forward.

KEL #24 C – Topping, Kyle (2018) – Wasn't at his best through this game but especially in the first couple periods, had difficultly creating any sustained pressure and his line was just generally quite because their normal chemistry wasn't connecting. Usually plays around the puck a little more, has some touches in transition and on zone entries just didn't engage enough until the 3rd period. More assertive in the 3rd worked a few plays off the half wall and created a few chances but his teammates couldn't cash them in, more handling of the puck as well in the 3rd and trying to attack the net but at this point it was a little too late for him to contribute. Was quite strong on faceoff during this game.

KEL #7 RD – Zabransky, Libor (2018) – Was settling for a zone exits off the boards and out after fumbling a few puck in his feet, he's been shifted down to the 3rd pair and appears to have lost some of his confidence and the confidence of his coaching staff.

KEL #6 RD – Korczak, Kaeden (2019) – Given an opportunity to work on the second powerplay and getting and quite a few shifts on the top pair with Cal Foote, looks as though his solid play of late is dictating a better opportunity for him. His shot didn't look overly powerful on a couple attempts but he managed to get most of the them past blockers and to the net leading to a couple scoring chances, picked up a secondary assist this was. Was much better around the offensive blue line making just simple but smart plays to keep pucks in and help the offense extend shits, its telling that his hockey IQ knows when not to just fire it, he makes a lot of smart plays. Made a great hustle play after a turnover to knock the puck off a rushing forwards stick; impressive effort.

Final Score: Kelowna Rockets: 4 – Lethbridge Hurricanes: 3 - OT

Saginaw Spirit at Barrie Colts, January 18th, 2017

BAR #2 D Tucker, Tyler (2018) – Tucker had several rushes up ice and looked really confident carrying the puck. On one play, he skated the length of the ice, gained a step on the defender, and drove the net for a good chance. He didn't convert but the puck bounced back to him. Rather than trying to throw it on net while off balanced from a bad angle, he smartly played it down low and got back into position. His most impressive play came when he accepted a pass at the attacking blue line, side-stepped around the forward and then walked into a good shot in the slot. Defensively, his gap control was pretty solid. He forced several dump ins and he made forwards pay with heavy open ice checks when they did try and carry it in on him, though one of his checks was completely unnecessary and it turned a Saginaw 3-on-2 into a 2-on-1.

BAR #14 RW Svechnikov, Andrei (2018) – As usual, Svechnikov was one of the best players on the ice. He showed his high-skill level early on by getting off a one-touch shot in tight and also by deflecting a pass behind his back to a teammate open on the wing. Whether he drove the net himself or hit teammates attacking the crease, he was routinely able to get the puck into high-danger areas for chances. He put his NHL shot on display by firing a puck through a small window short-side shelf to beat Evan Cormier from a tough angle to the side of the net. He also played with some bite by landing heavy checks, including one on Katic, and picking up a post-whistle penalty for mixing it up with another Spirit player.

BAR #61 LW Suzuki, Ryan (2019) – Suzuki poked one in on the goal-line late but otherwise had a disappointing game offensively. He was able to continually find soft spots in the defense and get open but he just couldn't make anything happen once his teammates got him the puck. Several of his shots went right into the shin pads and he also missed the net on a few occasions, including one he was found wide open for a backdoor tap-in that he somehow failed to convert. It was just one of those nights where the touch wasn't right.

SAG #8 D Everett, Caleb (2018) – Everett was a mixed bag in this game. He showed good power on a couple shot attempts but wasn't able to get them on target. He also took two minor penalties, although one was offsetting, and his neutral zone gaps were too big, That resulted in Barrie forwards gaining the line with relative ease when they targeted him. His passing was crisp, and accurate, and he did a nice job of eluding forecheckers when under pressure. He also showed good instincts knowing when to activate and when to back off in the offensive zone.

SAG #27 Katic, Danny (2018) – Katic played a really heavy game. He finished his checks, was effective cycling the puck, and did a nice job of getting to the net and causing havoc in front. He managed to pick up an assist on a scramble play after some sustained pressure in the offensive zone.

SAG #19 Jenkins, Blade (2018) – Jenkins had a strong offensive game. He showed good vision and patience skating the puck into the offensive zone and then looking for trailing players once he set up shop. He created several chances for teammates by doing so, including one where he hit Damian Giroux all alone driving to the net. In general, Jenkins did a nice job of threading pucks through open seams and finding the open man. He also showed good hands in tight on his power play goal. His skating and first few steps were a little choppy and that hurt him in races for loose pucks.

SAG #96 C Giroux, Damien (2018) – Giroux was in the middle of everything. He was relentless on the forecheck, he was physical, and he caused several turnovers with his pressure and attacking mentality. He brought that to the table at both ends of the rink as he back-checked hard and was able to prevent potential odd-man rushes from coming to fruition. While killing penalties, Giroux used his stick to disrupt Barrie's puck movement and he also showed no fear sprawling to block a one-timer with his upper-body. He had a couple good chances around the net, including one where Jenkins hit him all alone, but he was unable to finish.

Final Score: Saginaw Spirit: 6 – Barrie Colts: 4

Victoria Royals at Kelowna Rockets, January 20th 2018

VIC #5 RD - Prowse, Mitchell (2018) – A defensive mainstay in this game starting quite often in the defensive zone in all game situations both 5 on 5 and on the penalty kill. Was punishing presence in front of the net where he gets physical with his size and his stick while making sure to punish forwards that are planted for a screen and making his presence felt throughout the game; his energy and compete levels were consistent throughout this game. Unfortunately was on the ice for 2 goals against, one where he was screening his goalie and one where he left the front of the net to roam for a hit. He plants himself in front of the net quite often and had a tendency to get in the goalies sightline when trying to block shots. Always plays physical but was getting tunnel vision chasing hits this game.

VIC #34 RW – Oliver, Kaid (2018) – Not much opportunity for Oliver throughout this game, less ice time that he would usually receive due to the high amount of special teams where he doesn't get any chance to play. Oddly enough he was pushed over to the right wing from his usual center position, although he did take quite a few faceoff's on his strong side. Looked good carrying the puck on a couple rushes through the neutral zone but didn't get into much of rhythm due to long gaps in shifts.

KEL #24 C – Topping, Kyle (2018) - Slide down to the third line in this game from his usually second like spot with his usual linemates and didn't get a minute of powerplay time in the first period which was a first in the multiple viewing this year. However it only last one period as he made 2 great individual plays in the first to spit the defense off the rush and get scoring chances he just couldn't cash in, positive to see him take the puck to the net aggressively as he usually prefers to pass it around the net or find the open ice in weak coverage. Hi new line didn't generate much much in the way of scoring chances but they did cycle the puck well and maintain possession for long periods. Was moved back onto the powerplay and rewarded his coaches decision by walking in from the circle and snapping a quick wrist shot through a screen.

KEL #6 RD – Korczak, Kaeden (2019) - As has been the trend in viewing lately his game and gotten stronger and stronger and his confidence to make plays is more noticeable. Was more involved in the play post zone exit, where in previous games he would make and outlet pass and hang far back entering the zone last, he was more often making an exit pass and joining the rush becoming and option to assist on the entry; looks far less afraid to make a mistake. Started an impressive give and go play that lead to him picking up an assist, did take a poor hooking penalty because he got beat to puck but he did prevent a breakaway.

KEL #29 RW – Foote, Nolan (2019) – Got an opportunity on the penalty kill this game, which hasn't happened to many previous viewings but also lined up on the wing and looked more comfortable and was in turn more effective throughout with a 3 assist effort. Foote is strong on the boards and bruised his way through a defender closing on him by powering through a check and centering a pass to a streaking linemate. Picked off a pass shorthanded and took it through the neutral zone hitting a speedy linemate for a nice 2 on 1 set up. For a player who usually likes to shoot it was positive to see some diversity in his offensive game tonight.

Final Score: Kelowna Rockets: 8 – Victoria Royals: 4

Trail Smoke Eaters at Penticton Vees, January 20th, 2018

PEN #8 RD Reid, Luke (2020) – Reid was utilized on the top powerplay unit and played on the second pairing. Had an exaggerated body feint which changed his shooting lane before delivering a quick and hard wrist-shot towards the net. Made a quick pass behind his own-line while under pressure, it initiated the eventual goal by Rizzo. Displayed explosive acceleration late in the first as he drove through the neutral zone and down the right wing, the separation speed is there. Throughout the match up he was making accurate and quick first passes while under pressure, showing an awareness of the time and space he had to make a play. Despite been the youngest player on his team, he was noticeable for the Vees.

PEN #20 LD Tychonick, Jonny (2018) – Tychonick had a strong two-way effort for the Vees. He had an effective defensive pin along the boards early and skated quickly towards his net to get a stick-check on a Smoke Eaters player looking for the puck. Quarterbacked the powerplay, distributed the puck effectively in the first. His wrist-shot has a quick release but he wasn't waiting for traffic, opting to shoot several low-percentage shots that didn't cause any issues for the Smoke Eaters. Had a good anticipatory defensive read just outside his blueline where he grabbed the puck and delivered a sharp pass to his teammate in the neutral zone. Had a good defensive sequence early in the second by communicating well with his defensive partner during a 2-on-1 against. As the Smoke Eaters player rushed down the right wing, Tychonick timed his partner getting back into the passing lane well, then used his edges and acceleration to close the gap quicker than the Smoke Eaters player could react to, using in an active stick to separate him from the puck, he then transitioned the puck up through all three zones from behind his own goal-line on the next play. Made a beautiful spin to peel off pressure at the blueline, then used a head feint before passing it to his teammate who hit the crossbar, it was a high-end play. In the third period he had a tremendous hustle sequence, identifying a loose puck along the right half-wall in the offensive zone and aggressively skating before diving towards it, knocking the puck down into the corner which allowed for continued offensive possession. The talented rearguard capped off a good performance by scoring the overtime winner by delivering a hard and low slapshot that found the back of the net during a powerplay. Overall, Tychonick played defensively sound, transitioned the puck effectively using both his passing and skating ability, while also playing a composed game on the blueline, resulting in few turnovers. I would like to see him use his feinting mechanics more at the offensive end to penetrate the defense as he was a bit too predictable at the blueline on occasion in today's contest. He finished with a powerplay goal while playing top pairing minutes.

PEN #13 C/LW Rizzo, Massimo (2019) – Rizzo played the half-wall on the powerplay and centered the second line. Showed his puck-skills early, utilizing them to beat his opponents and carry the puck effectively below the goal-line. Had a fortuitous goal, as he drove down the right wing, he kept his head positioned towards his teammate during a 2-on-1 and delivered a pass that banked off a Smoke Eaters stick and into the back of the net. Would have preferred seen Rizzo shoot with the head feint since he telegraphed his passing option by not looking back at the goaltender before delivering the puck through the hashmarks. Rizzo has good acceleration which he used to penetrate the neutral zone and showed plus edges. He used them in the third by pivoting and changing his trajectory, bypassing a Smoke Eater player which allowed him space to walk into the slot and use a low wrist-shot which created a rebound scoring chance. Overall, Rizzo displayed soft hands and elusive skating ability which allowed him to set up his teammates and make plays consistently, although one aspect of his game that was weak today was his wrist-shot, he doesn't generate velocity well and he didn't show the ability to change the angle.

PEN #34 C/RW Barnes, Jack (2018) – Barnes played a limited role offensively although he received penalty-killing work. He showed plus acceleration as he attempted to forecheck midway through the first. Had an excellent forechecking sequence midway through the second. He pushed his opponent which knocked him off the puck, then quickly angled his body into the space he created, giving him leverage on the inside with his larger defensive opponent, he then displayed a strong base as he pushed the puck along the boards, the play resulted in an offensive scoring chance due to his tenacious effort. There's effort in his game at both ends of the ice, after his forechecking effort, he was exhausted but skated hard in an attempt to recover on the backcheck. Had a good stand-up hit in the defensive end in the third period, and followed that up with a great defensive effort on the penalty-kill, showing the ability to recognize where the Smoke Eaters were trying to distribute the puck and intercepted a pass, resulting in a cleared puck. Although Barnes didn't display offensive upside today, he was hard on the forecheck, played with effort in the defensive-end and was a positive contributor for his team.

Final Score: Penticton Vees: 3 – Trail Smoke Eaters: 2

Team East vs Team West, CJHL Top Prospects Game, Jan 23, 2018

East –

TE #9 C Angus Crookshank (2018) – great play down-low on the cycle, using his edges and shiftiness to evade pressure and finding his teammates, excellent backchecking sequence where he used a strong stick to take away the puck and negate a scoring chance, had a partial breakaway where he angled himself to protect the puck properly but it didn't result in a good scoring chance, made a nice pass fake while rushing down the right wing before releasing his wrist-shot that was partially deflected, had a good burst of speed showing plus acceleration before making an inside-outside move around his opponent, he was engaged and used his skill and motor to stand out for Team East

TE #10 RW Austin Wong (2018) – threw some heavy punches at Snell, wasn't backing down even during an all-star game so the compete doesn't turn off, massive hit on Snell after he got out of the box, seems to hold a grudge, had a heavy wrist-shot attempt that was labelled for the top corner from the right-circle that required an aggressive save, showed hustle as he had a nice rush before attempting to stop up and get his shot off though the play was disrupted, scored on the powerplay after firing a quick wrist-shot far-side that was both low and hard, destroyed his opponent behind the net and then had another altercation with Snell after the whistle, scored his 2nd goal of the game after skating through heavy traffic and tucking it in under Purboo, he was a force out there by using his thick frame to deliver crushing hits and scored 2 big goals

TE #24 RD Jacob Bernard Docker (2018) – shot a couple of hard wrist-shots from the line and delivered a massive hit along the boards that sent his opponent crashing to the ice, kept proper gaps in the opening frame, well-timed spin at the point which protected the puck and kept it in to open the third, had a great stretch pass from his own-end that sent Crookshank in on an odd-man rush that resulted in a scoring chance, Bernard was effective and continues to show what we have seen from him in previous viewings, in a complete two-way performance

TE #20 LD Jonathon Tychonik (2018) – played with speed in the opening period, he used his skating and his hands to breakdown the defense on the powerplay and got a quality scoring chance in the right circle where he let go a threatening wrist-shot, dangerous shot near the end of the 2nd period and delivered a good hit in his own end which separated his man from the puck, great shot fake, head fake and soft hands to re-open his lanes before making a soft-backhand pass to Prokop who put shot bar-down, impressive high-skilled play, Tychonik was getting the puck out of his own-end quickly all game and flashed his high-offensive ceiling throughout the game

TE #17 LD Stanislav Demin (2018) – made a difficult pass from behind his own-net under pressure, he fell down while getting the puck off his stick but showed strength as he was dealing with a stick-check but didn't turn it over, had a good active stick which disrupted an attempt during the penalty-kill, Demin didn't do anything overly flashy but he played a composed and effective game, he created a calming influence for Team East

TW #4 RD Seth Barton (2018+) – turned the puck over early after getting caught at the half-wall and running out of room, showed strength on his skates though as he was under heavy pressure below the goal-line, had a sharp transitional pass on the penalty-kill, played the body during a transitional zone exit by a team west player, used the same behind the back drop-pass to move to himself along the half-wall in the offensive-end as he did in the defensive-end, yet this time he had more success with it, was pretty ineffective at the offensive-blueline today, he missed 4-5 quality shooting opportunities but he was composed under pressure even if he turned the puck over once or twice

West –

TW #19 LC Jack McBain (2018) – delivered a sharp pass that went back to the point before skating hard into the slot area to look for the tip while setting the screen, had a well-timed defensive clearing in-front of the net followed by an accurate pass on the tape of his teammate out of the zone, McBain got tossed for a backcheck after the whistle when he took exception to Wong's hit behind the net in the third

TW #7 LC Zachary Tupker (2018) – throws his weight around despite his size, had a nice strip on Tychonik before making a subtle no-look backhand pass across the slot resulting in a scoring chance, great defensive play midway through the 2nd where he read the shooting lane in advance and blocked a shot, the shot block was unorthodox but he got the job done, great scoring chance in the left circle after having a give and go sequence before releasing a quick wrist-shot labelled far side that required a big glove save by Wasserman, Tupker competed and stood out in spurts for Team West

TW #25 RC Ethan Manderville (2018) – helped support his defenseman down-low early by using his size to weigh heavy, showed a set of soft-hands while weaving through traffic before going behind the net and attempting a wrap-around, plus tools were flashed on the play, had a great backcheck where he entered another gear and used his reach to stick-lift a surprised Team East player, he then created two scoring opportunities for his teammates, his best pass on the sequence was a no-look pass below the goal-line, had a terrific chance in-front of the net but put it over the bar, coordinated for his size with a smooth stride, scored off a rebound that initially hit the crossbar on the powerplay, his positioning was good and he got it up in a hurry, Manderville was arguably the best player on the ice for Team West today, showing an impressive combination of size and tools

TW #2 LD Declan Carlile (2018) – had a well-timed pinch and buried a short wrist-shot near the bottom of the right circle, had a transitional zone rush that was a clean entry unfortunately his teammate went offside, took advantage of his late replacement spot by getting a goal though wasn't overly noticeable otherwise

TW #20 LD Mason Snell (2018) – played on the penalty-kill and was very active, went into an extra gear to compete for a loose puck, beating out his man and clearing it, although somewhat overwhelmed against larger opponents he was competing out there and got some important pucks cleared out in-front of the net in the first period, Snell and Wong got into it and then Wong buried him in the corner with a check after getting out of the box, great defensive sequence late in the second where he took his man into the glass and turned the puck back up ice out of danger, although over-matched at times, he was willing to battle and compete

Final Score 5-2 West

Sherbrooke Phoenix vs Blainville-Boisbriand Armada, January 26th, 2018

SHE #9 RW Peach, Bailey (2019): He had his best scoring chance came when he took a quick shot from the slot, but outside of this, he didn't create a ton of offensive chances. Defensively, he was late in his coverage on the Alexandre Alain goal, and later in the game, he made a nice backcheck on the puck-carrier only to lose the one-on-one battle. This led to a great scoring chance for the Armada.

SHE #14 C MacKinnon, Evan (2018): MacKinnon had a good night in the faceoff circle tonight; he didn't lose many, from my count. Early in the game, he made a really bad pass in the offensive zone that led to one of Alex Katerinakis' goals. MacKinnon was on the point, and made a blind cross-ice pass. He didn't have many offensive moments during the game, and his speed looked just okay.

SHE #23 RW Alexeyev, Yaroslav (2018): Not a standout offensively, Alexeyev still showed some good flashes in the game when he had the puck on his stick. He showed good skating abilities, nice acceleration in the neutral zone, and a good ability to avoid opponents with his elusivity. Often, he rushed the puck up the ice and showed good stickhandling work while maneuvering through opponents. His best moment came when he was rushing the puck into the offensive zone, but once there, not much came of it in terms of an actual scoring chance.

SHE #2 RD Grégoire, Thomas (2018): He was poised on the power play, showing good decision-making on the point, and scored the 3rd Sherbrooke goal from the point with a nice, low slapshot. He almost got another one later on after making a great read to jump into the play at the side of the Armada net, but couldn't get much on his shot. His skating and mobility are decent, but for a defenseman of his size, you would like to see these attributes being quicker out there.

SHE #29 RW Poulin, Samuel (2019): Poulin did the little things well out there. I liked his forecheck and how he uses his size down low to protect the puck. He saw regular ice time on the power play, mainly in front of the net to obstruct the goaltender's view. His skating abilities will need some improvement, as he lacks a top gear and the necessary acceleration to create more separation between himself and his opponents. He also worked hard away from the puck, and on the backcheck.

SHE #72 LD Bellamy, Jaxon (2019): Bellamy got good ice time on the power play tonight, and his passing game was fine. He made hard passes, but still needs to make quicker decisions with the puck, as there was some hesitation from him. He didn't use his big shot from the point, and in the offensive zone, he rarely had possession of the puck. He was battling hard in his own zone and showed some physical play along the boards.

SHE #69 C Zachar, Marek (2018): The 19-year-old Czech played on the point on the power play tonight. He showed good speed throughout the game and was at his best when he could hit his top speed in the neutral zone, and could attack the offensive zone. He used his speed well going wide on the opposing defensemen. With his speed, he often tried to challenge opposing defensemen one-on-one. His work ethic was good, and he was always giving his all on every shift and working very hard away from the puck as well. He was the most noticeable forward for Sherbrooke tonight, and he did a good job at getting pucks on net.

SHE #44 LD Crête-Belzile, Olivier (2018): Not a flashy performance from Crête-Belzile, who was not really a factor in the offensive part of the game. However, he was solid defensively. He played with Grégoire, and was used to play against the top line of the Armada. Good gap control, and he was quick to put pressure on the puck-carrier in his zone. Good active stick too.

BLB #16 C Henman, Luke (2018): His lack of strength was showing tonight, as he was having some tough shifts while holding onto the puck along the boards and not much room to maneuver on the ice. He played the half-wall on the 2nd power play unit. He lost too many puck battles and was easily taken off the puck. He had difficulty creating separation while in possession of the puck, and his skating was lacking an extra gear.

BLB #24 LW Teasdale, Joël (2018): Teasdale made a nice play on the Armada's 3rd goal by being quick to retrieve a puck behind the opposing team's net, then making a quick feed to Alex Barré-Boulet for the goal. He played his typical heavy game down low and along the boards. He used his size well to protect the puck and win battles there. He played in all situations, even almost scoring on the PK in the 3rd period. He did score a nice goal with his stick between his legs in front of the net, late in the game. He was often used as the "in front of the net guy" role on the power play, playing it well.

BLB #4 LD Anttalainen, Aleksi (2018): He started the game with a very intense shift in his zone playing very physically. He played the rest of the period with some good intensity. His puck moving was okay, and with some time and space he was able to make decent first passes. However, under pressure, he rushed his plays and this is where he got into some trouble with his passing game.

Kelowna Rockets at Medicine Hat Tigers, January 26th, 2018

MH #20 LD Longo, Trevor (2018) – Although inexperienced on the backend for Medicine Hat, Longo wasn't looking out of place while playing a shut-down role for his team. The defender has prototypical size standing 6'2, 200 pounds but wasn't overly engaged physically today. He does however play with poise and can make a first pass. One aspect of his game he needs to work on is recognizing when his opponents are getting behind coverage, several times he lost his man, and this led to a breakaway on one sequence. On another sequence Lind rushed the puck down the wing and cut around Longo's defensive partner, he was late recognizing that he needed to support his teammate on the play which lead to a goal against.

MH #29 LW Chyzowski, Ryan (2018) – Chyzowski is the most talented 2000 born forward featured on Medicine Hat, showing a dangerous release and a two-way game, although he was inconsistent offensively. Based off today's viewing, he's not going to drive a line, however he showed the ability to rush the puck down the wings and create scoring chances. His best sequence was when he rushed down the right wing and used a quick release that generated a lot of velocity on his shot, it went over the top of the bar, but it was dangerous. After the shot, he recollected the rebound in the slot and passed it back to the point, he then anticipated the rebound and directed the puck towards the front-of the net, before making an additional pass back to the point on his knees. The play showed he was willing to compete under heavy defensive pressure and make quick decisions with the puck on his stick. His release point is unorthodox, he rotates his core explosively while whipping his stick in one motion, it allows him to create a lot of power and made it difficult for Salmond to pick up. The winger was engaged defensively, his best defensive play came near his own-net under pressure, he turned his body away from an opponent and made an accurate flip pass that created a transitional breakout. He finished with 2 shots on goal and almost scored the game winning goal with just seconds left in the third.

MH #12 LW Rybinski, Henry (2019) – Rybinski played on a line with Chyzowski but wasn't consistently engaged in today's game. His best sequence came early, where he was tenacious on the forecheck, using a quick stick-lift resulting in a turnover and then showing plus puck skills while distributing the puck across the hash-marks, resulting in a quality scoring chance. With that exception he was quiet while finishing with 1 shot on goal.

KEL #6 RD Korczak, Kaedan (2019) – Korczak is the youngest defender on Kelowna's back-end but didn't look out of place and showed two-way ability. He's got good size, standing 6'2, 180 with room to grow into his frame and generates above average power from his first step. He used his acceleration when recognizing opportunities to pinch and support his forwards when gathering loose pucks. He looked to shoot the puck and showed that he can get it through traffic. Defensively, he was engaged and used his frame to box the opposition to the outside and he was willing to block shots and compete along the boards.

KEL #29 LW Foote, Nolan (2019) – Foote showed an interesting combination of tools and size while playing on a consistent line with Topping and Twarynski. The wingers similar to his brother in stature, he's got a big frame and has plus short area quickness due to the length of his stride. He utilized it on several plays, specifically, to cut to the slot after driving down the wing and near the net when looking for rebounds. His best scoring chance came directly off a rebounds in-front of the net which he shot through the crease and out the other side. In today's game he was using his passing ability to set up his teammates consistently. He's capable of making a skilled play and following it up with a physical play, he demonstrated this several times by delivering heavy checks that separated the puck from his opponents. Foote finished with 2 shots on net while generating scoring chances for his team.

KEL #24 RC Topping, Kyle (2018) – Topping displayed a willingness to drive his line while displaying plus playmaking ability. He likes to control play with the puck on his stick, angling his frame to the outside and finding his teammates with short passes. He set up his defenseman several times and looked to find opportunities to thread passes through the slot. Unfortunately, due to his size limitations, standing 5'11, 180, he tended to hang onto the puck too long at times, this resulted in him getting knocked off the puck by stronger players and leading to turnovers on some shifts. He's not an explosive skater and lacks power but his mechanics are decent, and he can cut with his edges, this allowed him to stop up and change the angle of his wrist-shot on one play. Similar to his stride, his shot also lacks power, he doesn't generate a lot on it, however he did look to utilize it at the right times. Topping finished with 4 shots on goal.

Final Score: Kelowna Rockets: 4 – Medicine Hat Tigers: 3 – OT

Everett Silvertips at Seattle Thunderbirds, January 27th, 2018

EVT #29 RD Wylie, Wyatte (2018) – Wyatte displayed two-way qualities in today's contest against the Thunderbirds. He's not the tallest defender but he's got some bulk to him, so he can keep his opponents to the outside consistently and he was physically engaged out there. He showed the ability to transition the puck through the neutral zone and find his teammates. His ability to make an accurate pass under pressure was excellent today, there were several sequences where he delivered sharp passes behind his own goal-line, on one specifically, he was getting aggressively forechecked but managed to make a no-look backhand pass to his teammate which alleviated the pressure. The defender was used on the powerplay and showed plus tools, displaying a heavy wrist-shot that got through traffic as well as making well-timed head fakes that re-opened passing options. Wyatte was solid for the Silvertips and finished with 3 shots on goal.

EVT #14 RW Sutter, Riley (2018) – Sutter showed two-way qualities while playing on the most effective line for the Silvertips. He's got substance but very little flash, staying within the boundaries of what he's capable of doing with the puck. This allows him to be effective at both ends while not creating too many turnovers. That been said, his lack of edge work and creativity does occasionally handcuff him. During one sequence, he ran out of space while skating back towards the blueline and was stripped, leading to an odd-man rush. His skating mechanics are awkward, this doesn't allow him to accelerate quickly but his straight-line speed is adequate, and he used it to backcheck and play deep in his own-end. He looks like a third defenseman at times, staying well positioned, using his frame to block shots and to battle along the boards. Offensively, he wasn't overly threatening today but did manage to get an assist. I would like to see Sutter attempt to go outside his comfort levels more and show a willingness to be more creative with the puck given his soft hands and accurate passing.

SEA #24 LD Lee, Jake (2019) – Lee showed below average defensive IQ in today's match up against the Silvertips while playing a top four role. His frame is solid, he's got a thick build and he's tenacious in-front of the crease as he displayed throughout the game by fighting for every inch of positioning he could attain. Unfortunately, despite his efforts, he made several plays that showed his lack of positional awareness as well as an inability to make decisions quickly under pressure. During one sequence where Bajkov was rushing down the left wing, Lee didn't engage him and instead covered a Silvertip player near the left side of the goal-line, this allowed Bajkov to skate directly into a dangerous scoring area. Later, he was aggressively checked while carrying the puck, which forced a pass directly to his opponent at the blueline. His first pass was also mixed, although it was accurate in spurts, he did throw a very dangerous pass directly through his own hash-marks instead of opting to make the safer play. In the offensive end, he recognized that his shooting lane was blocked at the left point and side-stepped the player, resulting in his shot getting through traffic, otherwise he wasn't involved. Lee wasn't offensively engaged and had several defensive lapses, although he plays with heart and has good size.

SEA #22 LW Hamaliuk, Dillon (2019) – Hamaliuk showed a combination of creativity and physicality against the Silvertips. The winger was attacking the net with the puck consistently throughout the game by using a powerful stride and superior edges. This allowed him to drive down the wing and towards the net on one sequence and on another, he stopped up quickly and cut across the high-slot looking for a shooting opportunity. He was good at switching his momentum while using his 6'1, 200-pound frame, he's coordinated. There was a physical element to his game, he delivered some hard hits along the boards and during one sequence at the face-off dot, he got into an altercation and toppled over his opponent, he's a strong kid. The winger also showed soft hands, as he attempted several drag-moves and was relatively effective in his execution. He has some promising tools and finished with three shots.

Final Score: Seattle Thunderbirds: 3 – Everett Silvertips: 2 – OT/SO

Medicine Hat Tigers at Kelowna Rockets, January 30th 2018

MH #29 C – Chyzowski, Ryan (2018) – Good speed and good pace to his game, got a ahead of the puck a couple times and rattled it though his feet instead of keeping it on his stick. Played the center position well and was supportive of his defense, stayed back on breakouts as a safety blanket while the defense moved up with the puck, puts good pressure on puck carriers making attacking difficult for them. Was decent on faceoffs and took quite a few in the defensive zone. Had a few difficult times with his assignments of Kelowna's top line, couldn't break their cycle. Made a dangerous hit to the head and was tossed out of the game.

MH #15 C – Brown, Elijah (2018) – Threw his body around a fair amount through this game and looked as though he was comfortable playing up in size because he's not a very payer; solid forechecker. Was constantly winning foot races and in most one on one situations it was difficult not to notice his compete level in a good way. Played in all situations and earned his ice time through effort, however blew an obvious assignment ok the penalty kill leaving Lind wide open for a goal.

MH #12 RW – Rybinski, Henry (2019) – Fair number of defensive zone starts in his assignment tonight played with good speed and acceleration and his footwork to stood out as one of his strengths as he's great on his edges and tracks other players well with good directional changes. Had a couple glairing lazy back checks what stood out as plays where his compete level needs a serious boots. Was shifted to the top line and to play center when Chyzowski was kick out of the game. Displayed good offensive instincts and looked comfortable keeping an attack going, didn't utilized his speed with the puck well enough thought, passed up pucks too soon.

KEL #24 C – Topping, Kyle (2018) – Looked a little static in the offensive zone tonight waiting for the puck to come to him and not presenting him as an option and losing his time to make a play. Was moved to a new powerplay unit and position on the left half boards, looked out of sync for most of the night there with his new unit. Looked a little slow in general throughout the whole game never picked up his pace much. Did make a few impressive stick plays to wins battles and takeaway pucks.

KEL #29 RW – Foote, Nolan (2019) – Played with good jump tonight but was kept off the scoresheet, was wide open one on one with the goaltender and couldn't get it past him, looked like he had too much time. Imposed his physical will on a smaller team and really was difficult for anyone to contain. Foot speed looked better that recent viewing, especially without the puck and allowed him to attack the crease and get behind defenders, caused some net havoc one goal that came from the point.

KEL #6 RD – Korczak, Kaeden (2019) – Looked as thought the opponents game plan was to drive toward him and try and pressure him when he had the puck as much as possible, he came out on top of this played with very little panic in his game. His decision making was solid and he stuck to his game of varying the force he puts on a pass to relieve pressure around him chipping pucks to safety or finding and open teammate. Used his feet more than usual and on several occasions made a few impressive rushes through the neutral zone to lead the rush and throw off forechecker; a newer element to his game that is starting to grow.

Final Score: Kelowna Rockets: 4 – Medicine Hat Tigers: 2

Drummondville Voltigeurs vs Blainville-Boisbriand Armada, , February 2nd, 2018

DRU #90 C Veleno, Joseph (2018): It was a really quiet game for Veleno until the last 10 minutes of the game, where he recorded 3 assists during Drummondville's attempted comeback. The Voltigeurs didn't generate a lot of things offensively in the first 50 minutes of this game, and Veleno was rushing things a bit too much with the puck. When he did take shots on net, they were not dangerous shots, or they were getting blocked. He played like his usual self in other parts of the game; he did well on the PK with his anticipation and quick stick. His speed was not a big factor tonight, or at least not as much as in past games.

DRU #81 C Simoneau, Xavier (2019): Did a good job of slowing things down while in possession of the puck in the offensive zone. Liked his smarts and vision in the offensive zone as well. His compete level was good, and he was always working hard with some good backcheck efforts, also playing a bit of an agitation role. He was the smallest player on the ice, but got his nose dirty in front of the net.

DRU #33 G Rodrigue, Olivier (2018): Gave up 4 goals in the first two periods, but none were the result of bad goaltending on his part. He did his best to keep his team in the game, and they eventually responded by almost coming back in the game, late in the 3rd period. The Armada scored some very nice goals on him, like one of Batherson's, which was a highlight-reel goal. Rodrigue's rebound-control was good, and with traffic in front of him, he did a good job of tracking pucks.

DRU #92 LD Beaudin, Nicolas (2018): Like the rest of his teammates, he was quiet in the first two periods, but had a strong 3rd period. He started being more active in terms of rushing the puck out of his zone with his good skating abilities. He also showed nice creativity in the offensive zone, making quick decisions. Very smooth and poised while in possession of the puck.

DRU #55 LD Bernard, Xavier (2018): Quiet game for Bernard, who didn't do anything major in the offensive part of the game. His puck movement was not efficient, and he took too long to make plays in the transition game. He failed to advance the puck for his forwards efficiently. Defensively, he was sound, but I would have liked to see him use his size more when battling for pucks along the boards and in front of the net.

DRU #9 RW Guay, Nicolas (2018): Guay worked hard all game long; he eventually finished the game with 2 goals because of his hard work. When things were going badly for his team, he attempted to start a fight to get them back on track. He showed good leadership and character qualities. He made some good, smart plays, and did some dirty work for his line in the corners.

BLB #24 LW Teasdale, Joel (2018): Solid game for Teasdale, who played on the 2nd line, but was once again on the first power play unit playing his role well in front of the net. He took the puck to the net often, using his strength to bring it there. He did some good work down low and in front of the net, playing a heavy game. He scored the first goal of the game with a very good wrist shot that beat Rodrigue high glove.

BLB #17 LW Ethier, Thomas (2018): Big kid who did some nice work along the boards and in front of the net. His skating was not the best, but he still managed to get around a Drummondville defenseman one-on-one for his best scoring chance of the night.

BLB #6 LD Crête-Belzile, Antoine (2018): Solid game in his zone, good gap control and good stick, which helped him defend well one-on-one. He finished some checks during the game, mostly in the first period where I saw a more physical game out of him than usual. Smart defenseman, whose footspeed and overall skating abilities will need to get better.

USNTDP U18 VS Madison Capitols, February 2nd, 2018

MAD #18 RC Mancinelli, Michael (2019) – Displayed elite skating, anticipation and ability to read the play and be an asset for his team on the fore-check. Mancinelli was able to pressure defenseman and disrupt the breakout on a number of shifts. Displayed quick hands and feet with the puck on his stick and was able to get the puck to the middle of ice in the offensive zone. Mancinelli was easily Madison best forward in this game, playing with a lot of pace and showed good compete along the walls for pucks, often against much larger defenseman on the USA squad.

USA #8 LW Hain, Gavin (2018) – Hain showed a high motor and compete level all over the ice. Was often the first player on his line in on the fore-check and was physical on the opposition defenseman and gained possession for his line. Hain didn't show great skill with the puck, making some errant plays on some zone entries and often skating the puck into pressure and not generating time and space very well and as a result some plays in the offensive end would fizzle out with the puck on his stick.

USA #12 LC Wise, Jake (2018) – Wise displayed high end hockey sense and passing ability in this game. Consistently finding open teammates and getting them the puck in scoring areas. Made a beautiful setup in the 3rd period by entering the offensive zone cleanly, pulling up at the half wall and finding his defenseman Emberson driving the net with a slick sauce pass. Wise also just missed setting up a goal from behind the goal line when he was able to thread a pass to a driving Gruden in the slot that the goalie made a point blank save on. Wise showed a solid 2-way game, keeping is feet moving and showing good skating edges in all three zones and was able to pressure plays in the neutral zone as well as applying back pressure to create turnovers. Wise played much of a pass first game with the puck but did register some shot attempts, his shot didn't look overly powerful but he gets it off his tape quickly.

USA #24 RW Giles, Patrick (2018) – Giles is a big bodied winger and showed long stretches of being able to dictate the play down low in the offensive zone. Giles and Jake Pivonka worked well off the cycle together and were able to pin Madison in their own zone on multiple shifts. Giles didn't display explosive skating but can be difficult to handle when he gets a head of steam. His agility and footwork in tight areas was a plus and Giles was still able to win races to loose pucks by using his body positioning and leverage on the opponent, showed he has a good understanding of his game and how to be successful. Giles showed the ability to drive the net and be available for passes and tips in front. Showed good hockey sense in front on one instance where he got himself just enough separation from the defenseman for a split second to receive a pass from Pivonka for a point blank scoring opportunity.

USA #9 RW Weiss, Tyler (2018) – Was around and on the puck a lot in this game. Weiss made some nice quick passes, either coming out of his own end or in the neutral zone to find teammates with speed and keep plays going north. Showed solid fundamentals in his stick positioning on the back check as well as in his own zone. Weiss was relentless in puck battles and showed good 2nd and 3rd efforts to win battles and keep pucks alive. Weiss didn't see a lot in the way of high end scoring opportunities himself but his hard work in the zone lead to a lot of offensive zone possession and opportunities for others on the ice.

USA #28 LW Farabee, Joel (2018) – Playing on a line with Jack Hughes (2019) and Oliver Wahlstrom, Farabee likes to enter the zone with speed and pullup at the half wall with the puck and feed his line mates either coming down the slot or execute a give and go down low. Showed his excellent vision on one play by threading a pass through traffic to the far side of the offensive zone. Farabee showed excellent hockey sense, he was not only able to create space for himself but he showed the ability to open things up for his teammates at times, by drawing defenders to him and using his quick hands to feed a pass into the vacant space he just created. Farabee was held pointless in this game but was a dynamic playmaker and created a lot of scoring chances for his team.

USA #43 LC Hughes, Jack (2019) – Hughes was clearly the best and most offensively skilled player on the ice for either team and showed it on nearly every shift. Despite not having overwhelming size, Hughes was hard on pucks and on a couple instances was out numbered in puck battles and still came away with the puck. Hughes displayed excellent edgework which allowed him to avoid hits in the open ice or being pinned along the boards. Like a lot of skilled players, Hughes got caught hanging onto the puck too long at times and missed opportunities to feed the puck to open teammates and as a result turned the puck over, however the good far outweighed the bad in this game. Hughes scored the eventual game winning goal early in the 2nd period, where he got the puck off the wall, high in the offensive zone, skated toward the slot area where he used his quick hands to make a slight move around the defenders stick and fire a shot, beating the goalie on the blocker side.

USA #17 LW Gruden, Jonathan (2018) – Gruden wasn't real noticeable in this game despite registering 2 assists. Gruden showed good hockey sense on the Goal by Jack Hughes in the 2nd by coming out of the corner and driving the net, providing a partial screen on the goalie for Hughes shot from the slot.

USA #18 RW Wahlstrom, Oliver (2018) – Was kept off the score sheet tonight but was far from going unnoticed and had his share of scoring opportunities. Wahlstrom showed the ability to process situations quickly; his line with Jack Hughes and Joel Farabee played a quick transition game and moved the puck quickly in all 3 zones. Showed high end puck skills and skating on one instance where he changed the angle with his feet and hands and threaded a beautiful pass back against the Grain through a couple of sticks to Farabee who was driving the net from the half wall. Wahlstrom also showed the ability to shield the puck, gain the edge on the defenseman and drive hard to the net. Wahlstrom was quick to turn pucks north coming out of his own end, both with his feet or hitting teammates with speed.

USA #20 LC Pivonka, Jake (2018) – Pivonka played in all situations for his team, was good on face-offs and out worked the opposition all over the ice. Pivonka was good in the cycle game and his play along the boards. He wasn't a flashy player in this game but the details in his game were on and he brought a lot of pace and physicality to his line.

USA #19 LD Miller, K'Andre (2018) – Showed good backwards skating agility that allowed him to keep good defensive posture against the rush. Miller used his long reach to poke check pucks, challenge plays and keep a lot of plays to the outside. He was physical in front of his own net, often mixing things up after the whistle and protecting his goaltender. Miller struggled coming out of his own end and made some errant passes that missed the intended target and would go for icings or turnover possession. In the offensive end, K'Andre was a tad stagnant at the point and had some shots get blocked as a result, later in the game Miller was better at using his feet and hands to change the angle and was able to get some pucks through to the net.

USA #15 RD Wilde, Bode (2018) – Tonight wasn't the best showing for Wilde this season. Bode committed a couple errant turnovers at the offensive blue line and made some poor decisions in pinching in the neutral zone without support that he was lucky to get away with. On the positive side, Wilde showed good vision coming out of his own end and executed some solid breakouts and was able to stretch the ice on a couple occasions.

USA #23 LD Samuelsson, Mattias (2018) –One of USA's best players tonight. Samuelsson was excellent at the offensive blue line in keeping pucks in the zone and didn't waste time getting the puck off his stick and towards the net area. Showed a quick and heavy snap release from the point. Mattias's skating coming out of his own end was a plus, he showed an explosive stride that left some fore-checkers in the dust and would rush the puck through the neutral zone effectively. Showed good defensive awareness and communicated with his D-partner in key situations, showed a mean streak in front of his own net and in the corners where he was able to win puck battles and move the puck to his D-Partner to relieve pressure.

USA #10 RD Emberson, Ty (2018) – Aside from losing track of a Madison player behind him in the neutral zone on his first shift of the game after a poor neutral zone pinch by Adam Samuelsson that resulted in Madison only goal, Emberson was solid in most areas in this game. His smooth edges and skating stride allowed him to be effective in both moving pucks out of his own end as his defensive positioning. Emberson made a nice play behind his own goal line, looking off his d-partner and quickly firing a long stretch pass to find a teammate in the neutral zone. Emberson challenged plays the defensive blue-line and showed the ability to force a player outside and finish his check along the boards. Emberson was active in the offensive end, picking his spots to jump into or lead the rush which lead to his goal in the 3rd period where he drove down the middle of the slot and received a pass from Wise for a deflection goal in front of the net.

USA #25 LD Stastney, Spencer (2018) – Stastney was listed as the 7th defenseman on the line chart but played a large portion of this game with multiple d-partners. Stastney was trusted in all situations and showed the ability to control the game. Spencer's dynamic skating allow him to cover a lot of ice in a short period of time, this was on display in multiple situations in racing down pucks in order to keep them in the offensive zone. Stastney consistently was able to buy time for himself with the puck and find the open players all over the ice. He can walk the blue line effectively and displayed great hands, elusiveness and poise with the puck when under pressure. Stastney used his plus skating effectively in defending and showed the ability to challenge plays all over the ice and the ability to recover and breakup plays that get behind him.

USA #30 G Mor, Jonathan (2018) – More wasn't challenged much in this game, despite being scored on early on an excellent placed shot over the glove hand off the rush, Mor settled into the game and was sound positional. His skating and edge work allowed him to be square to oncoming shooters and he controlled his rebounds and limited second chance opportunities.

Red Deer Rebels at Moose Jaw Warriors February 2nd, 2018

RD#5 Barteaux, Dawson (2018) – In tough against the top offense in the league, Dawson had a strong defensive game. He kept the Warrior forwards on the outside all night. Body position was good. Played high-end minutes with Alexeyev out. Made good decisions all night moving the puck

RD#21 Reichel, Kristian (2018) – Kristian was Red Deer's top forward tonight. Showed off his skill with the puck on multiple occasions with great hands. His complete level impressed me the most. Battled every time he was on the ice. Had one goal and finished a plus 3. First power play unit.

MJW#8 Almeida, Justin (2018) – One of the weaker games I have seen Justin play. He had one good scoring chance from the middle of the slot where she showed his quick release, other then that he wasn't much of a factor tonight. However, as a whole this was on of the worst games the Warriors have played as a team. Justin saw second power play and penalty kill minutes.

MJW#15 Peckford, Ryan (2018) – Ryan seemed uninterested at times on the ice. He was beaten to loose pucks multiple times. The effort level just wasn't there tonight. Made some poor passes in the defensive and neutral zones that lead to turnovers. Finished the game minus one. Second power play unit.

Everett Silvertips at Kelowna Rockets, February 2nd, 2018

KEL #24 C - Topping, Kyle (2018) – Like recent viewings he has been on the half board on the left side on the powerplay, looks a little lost as to what to do, not really playing as a catalyst for offense and seems a little undecided when he does have the puck, looks more effective in the slot or beside the net. Appears a little slow tonight as he has in a few games recently (possible something is bothering him) and a strongly defensive team seems to be stifling his play. Did make one stand out play tonight pressure the puck carrier at the blueline and started the odd man rush down ice, dished the puck off and drove the net for a well executed 2 on 1 goal.

EVE #14 C – Sutter, Riley (2018) – Played his typical rough and tumble game he was doing a good job of driving the net and causing a little chaos in and around the crease, he's a strong player and can be difficult to contain that at times was noticeable tonight. Picked up a second assist on the powerplay tonight, wasn't a noticeable play, just part of his team moving the puck. Did pull off a nice power move to protect the puck and drive to the net from the corner just shooting the puck over the bar. Got caught admiring a breakout pass and took a pretty big hit in the defensive zone knocking him over and he was clearly a bit of target tonight because he plays a pesky game and likes to agitate but took it to far when he got a undisciplined roughing penalty for a sucker punching someone in a scrum. Was on for a goal against tonight gets caught out of position sometimes and doesn't have the foot speed to correct his mistakes.

EVE #20 LD – Walker, Kyle (2018) – Played a really solid defensive game this evening, lays hard clean and effective body checks that separate man from puck and was making it really difficult for attacking players to end the zone on his side of the ice, closed his gaps quickly along the wall and moved well for a player of his size. Strong net front play protects his goalie and did a good job of allowing him to see shots coming in, didn't roam to much out of position boxed out in front of the net well keeping shots to a difficult angle.

Final Score: Everett Silvertips: 3 – Kelowna Rockets: 2

Prince George Cougars at Moose Jaw Warriors, February 3rd, 2018

PG#3 Rhinehart, Rhett (2019) – I was Impressed with his size and strength against the speed of Moose Jaw. Skating and decision-making were an issue at times, which is understandable for a first year player. He panicked with the puck a few times and threw into bad areas. I could see that he wanted to bring a physical presence to the game. Finished a minus one with a bit of penalty kill time.

PG#8 Leppard, Jackson (2018) – It was a tough night defensively for Jackson. Finished a minus three. Had problems exiting his own zone, he turnover the puck at this own blue line. I really liked his competiveness. Being one of the bigger players on the ice he really tried to impose his physical play on Moose Jaw. 100% Effort every time he was on the ice. One assist and first power play and penalty kill time.

PG#35 Gauthier, Taylor (2019) – Taylor was a standout tonight in net against the top team in the WHL. Named the third star, he stopped 44 of 48 shots. He kept Prince George in the game with some incredible saves in which he has no business making. 3 of the 4 goals he had no chance of stopping.

MJW#8 Almeida, Justin (2018) – Strong bounce back game for Justin. Named the first star, he had a goal and two assists. Showing off his skill with a very quick release from the top of the slot. Justin's speed has been improving over the past few games. He has been consistently beating people wide and driving to the net even though he is undersized. First power play and second penalty kill units.

MJW#15 Peckford, Ryan (2018) – Peckford had a bounce back game as well. Looked motivated and alive out there tonight. Showed a great cycle game down low. Peckford and his line mates constantly held the puck in the offensive zone. One assist on the night and played second line power play.

MJW#39 Evanoff, Adam (2018) – Solid all around game from Adam. He was never really tested but made every save look easy. Played the puck very well and limited the second chance opportunities. It helps having one of the best D cores in the WHL in front of you but Adam held his own. Stopped 22 of 23 shots.

Rouyn-Noranda Huskies vs Drummondville Voltigeurs, February 6th, 2018

RN #19 LW Hrehorcak, Patrik (2018): The rookie Slovak winger was good, playing on the 3rd line and getting some ice time while shorthanded as well. I really liked his physicality during this game; he set the tempo on his first shift with some good hits on the forecheck and had another big one later on against Pavel Koltygin, which eventually drew a penalty. With barely any power play time, he didn't generate a lot of scoring chances, but worked hard all night long.

RN #11 LW Harvey-Pinard, Rafaël (2018): He worked hard away from the puck, and was one of Rouyn-Noranda's best defensive forwards tonight. He was tenacious on the backcheck, and showed good anticipation to intercept some passes in the defensive zone. He lacks explosiveness in his stride, but his overall game was solid. He made a great play on the forecheck to create the turnover that led to his team's only goal of the game.

RN #16 RW Beaucage, Alex (2019): Beaucage had a good amount of ice time tonight and had a regular shift on the power play. He had some good scoring chances in the game, where he was able to use his best weapon, his wrist shot. He also showed nice vision with some passes during the game, including one to Justin Bergeron in the first period that came close to putting the Huskies on the board. He also got involved in the physical game; he was intense in front of the net in the 3rd period, not backing down, and threw some hits on the forecheck.

RN #2 LD Regis, Samuel (2019): Regis was called up for this game from Midget AAA, and this was, in fact, his first career QMJHL game. He played with a lot of confidence and didn't look scared on the ice. He was confident with the puck, showing good poise and moving the puck smartly to his forwards. He was using his stick well to pokecheck pucks away from opponents, and physically handled himself well.

RN #4 LD Bergeron, Justin (2018): Bergeron was playing on the right side tonight, and saw regular ice time on the power play. He was active in the offensive zone, more than in previous viewings, trying to create more things offensively. He made some good offensive reads to get open and receive passes from his teammates in scoring positions. He joined the rush often, acting more like a 4th forward on the ice and giving his teammates an extra option. Defensively, he'll need to be more aggressive on the puck-carrier and tougher to play against, as he can easily be pushed over.

RN #7 LD Arsenault, Alexis (2018): Arsenault has showed good improvement this season, and with all the injuries on the Huskies' back end, he has seen his role and ice time increase in the last few weeks. He played a good physical game early on. He is not the biggest defenseman, but showed a good compete level in his own zone. He moved the puck nicely into the transition game for his team, and his puck confidence is much higher than earlier in the year.

RN #1 G Harvey, Samuel (2018): Harvey fought the puck a lot in the first half of the game, but his compete level is always very strong, and he was able to keep his team in the game even if he didn't look comfortable on some shots he faced. He was beaten twice by Joseph Veleno. One goal came off of a rebound on a 2-on-1 rush, and the other one was from a weak backhand shot that touched a defenseman's stick in front of the net before going behind him. He showed good agility going from post to post to rob Nicolas Guay of a sure goal at some point. He also showed good quickness to adapt, when he made a couple of nice saves following quick deflections in front of the net.

DRU #90 C Veleno, Joseph (2018): Veleno scored 3 goals tonight, including one into an empty net to seal the 3-1 victory for his team. His speed was a real factor tonight; the young Huskies defensive corps had a lot of difficulty handling it. As usual, he worked hard all night long at both ends of the ice. He played in all situations, and his speed was a great asset while shorthanded. On his first goal, after making the pass on a 2-on-1 rush, he went hard to the net and jumped on the rebound. On the 2nd goal, it was a bit of lucky goal, on a weak backhand that also touched a Rouyn-Noranda defender's stick before going through Harvey.

DRU #33 G Rodrigue, Olivier (2018): Very calm in his crease, Rodrigue made a lot of saves look easy out there today. His rebound control was good, and he did a good job re-directing pucks to the corners. He made a great save in the first period, stopping Mathieu Boucher on a penalty shot where he showed great athletic ability - he looked like beaten, but was still able to block the shot with a last effort. Even with a lot of action in front of his net in the 3rd period (Rouyn-Noranda was crashing the net a lot more) he remained calm out there, showing good poise in his crease.

DRU #55 LD Bernard, Xavier (2018): Quiet game from Bernard, who played a simple game with the puck and made high-percentage short passes, electing not to take any risks out there. Defensively he was good (no big mistakes on his part) and he was involved in some scrums in the 3rd period, showing some jam in his game that we don't often see out of him.

DRU #92 LD Beaudin, Nicolas (2018): It was also a quiet game for Beaudin, who still did a lot of nice things out there, but was not as much of a difference-maker. He was moving the puck nicely in the offensive zone, putting some on net. He wasn't using a powerful shot, but an accurate shot that was easy to tip in front of the net or get a rebound from. He rushed the puck out of his zone a couple of times during the game. His skating is good (not great) but I loved his agility and ability to change directions quickly in order to avoid opponents.

DRU #4 RD Pelletier, Thomas (2019): Pelletier was not used often in the 2nd half of the game, but had a regular shift in the first two periods. His confidence with the puck is much better than it was earlier in the year. I saw him make some quick passes to accelerate the transition game on his team. His footspeed and overall skating abilities looked better as well, and he was defending well against forwards coming into the offensive zone on his side. Good stick work to defend.

DRU #9 RW Guay, Nicolas (2018): He had one great offensive scoring chance in the game but was robbed by Harvey. Overall, it was a more quiet game for him tonight. However, he does a lot of unsung work on his line, like retrieving pucks in both the offensive and defensive zones. He works hard in the defensive zone, and formed a nice shorthanded duo with Veleno. He played RW on the 2nd line (instead of center) and also played on both the PP and PK units.

DRU #81 C Simoneau, Xavier (2019): The diminutive center was an agitating force tonight, playing much bigger than his size. He got hit hard a couple of times along the boards, losing some physical battles as well, but always came back for more. He was playing on the 2nd power play unit, mostly from the half wall. He had one big scoring chance coming untouched from the faceoff circle, but couldn't beat Harvey with a quick wrist shot. His skating, combined with his small frame, was lacking a bit tonight. For a player of his size, he'll need to get faster and more explosive in the summer in order to compete better.

DRU #19 LW Mercer, Dawson (2020): Mercer was playing on the left side, on the Voltigeurs' 3rd line with Simoneau and Adams-Moisan. He also saw ice time on the 2nd power play unit. He showed nice poise with the puck, making zone entries in the offensive zone. Good puck confidence for a young player, and he has quick hands to handle the puck. His decision-making was poor, though. He'll need to pass the puck to his teammates faster. A lot of plays in the offensive zone ended up going nowhere, as he ended up in the corners and lost the puck there.

Vancouver Giants at Kelowna Rockets, February 7th, 2018

KEL #24 C – Topping, Kyle (2018) – A 2 assist game for Topping he had good jump and was really involved in the game tonight was attack the net and trying to shoot around screens liked to work the puck toward the net and try and pass off for the open man. Playing a little more physically that usual tonight and getting bumped around a little bit but doesn't seem fazed by it. Attacked with some back pressure and ended up creating a takeaway and snapping a pass in the opposite direction for a well deserved secondary assist. Toppings other assist was a play where he took it quickly to the net and a teammate banged the rebound in.

KEL #6 RD – Korczak, Kaeden (2018) – Tonight Korczak was really good with the short game around him, making excellent short passes and reliving pressure with a calm demeanor, knows when to softly move a puck or quickly move a puck especially around his defensive zone. His decision making was quick and he is now being trusted with some top assignments and quite often taking shifts on the top pair, looks really confident and poised and this is leading to him handling the puck more. Had quite a few moments in this game where he his calmed play down in his own zone and his team fed off that.

VAN #41 RD – Kannok-Leipert, Alex (2018) – Played a shifty game tonight and agitated his opponents throughout the game often standing up to bigger player and or throwing his body around. Plays with confidence and likes to make plays even if he makes a mistake. Had a few nice shifty plays around the offensive blue line making fakes or walking the line to get shots past blockers, was a strong powerplay quarterback but his shot isn't overly hard and the unit was kept off the scoresheet. Likes to take the offensive rush himself and has the ability to dart around the neutral zone, was making players miss and dodging stick with ease throughout the game.

VAN #25 RD – Bulych, Kaleb (2018) – Skated and moved the puck well tonight, when he can avoid traffic made a couple impressive breakout passes to break pressure, he's really accurate and showed tonight can relieve pressure with both his passes and his skating. Getting knocked down really easily throughout the game and had a tough time leaning on guys around the net, looks a little tentative to engage physically while it was pretty obvious that he wasn't too interested in contact tonight, especially after taking a really big hit that landed him into the back of the net.

VAN #30 G – Tendeck, David (2018) – Tracked pucks well throughout the game and battled around the crease did a good job of cutting down secondary chances around the net when the play is scrambling in front of him. Fights through screens and uses his head well to track the play often position himself at the top of the crease to protect his space. As usual his legs are quick, he's flexible doing a excellent job of covering up the bottom of the net. Got deked out pretty badly on a goal by Lind, it was a nice inside outside move and he over committed and left his net wide open. He was quick from side to side but tonight but noticing that when he makes that move he opens up a lot almost flailing his arms and leaving a lot of open area for the puck to go. He saw a lot of shots tonight and looked energetic until the game ended, did a good job of cutting down rebounds and kept his team in the game early as he faced a barrage of shots.

VAN #44 LD - Byram, Bowen (2019) – He was a driver of play through all 3 zones for the entire game and easily the best Vancouver defender on the ice tonight. Often taking it upon himself to start the rush with his feet and open up options through the neutral zone, makes his decisions quickly in every facet of the game and did a really good job or varying the weigh in which he passes the puck with based on the situation he was faced with or where he was on the ice. When defending he was consistently pressuring the puck carrier making it difficult for them to make plays around him. Stepped up a couple times and pick off Kelowna passes in the neutral zone showing off his good timing assertive nature and his IQ for reading the game. Difficult to tell that he's a rookie the way he plays and defends.

Final Score: Kelowna Rockets: 4 – Vancouver Giants: 1

Sault Ste. Marie Greyhounds at Niagara Ice Dogs, February 8th, 2018

SSM #7 LD DeMeo, Anthony (2018*) – He has the size although the foot speed, lateral ability, and overall mobility are average. There are at times he struggled to break away from pressure and would fan on pass or clear attempt.

SSM #8 LD LeGuerrier, Jacob (2019) – Being a late '00 LeGuerrier will have another season for scouts to view. He is good sized Dman that moves well and keeps his game simple. He made solid plays of the defensive side stepping up at the blue line to negate attacks using active stick and positioned himself well on 1-on-1s to break plays up. He made good play at offensive blue line in 1st period as well keeping the puck in the zone off a bad pass that could have led to breakaway. He plays steady, simple game and moves puck up to start transition.

SSM #9 LD Sandin, Rasmus (2018) – He showcased his smooth mobility and puck handling abilities from the start. He displayed how he can get the puck at the offensive blue line with the skating ability to move around defenders to create plays and shots on net. He is poised with the puck in his own end, showing little panic in his game and makes good puck decisions on outlets. In the first period, he made smart puck retrieval using the net to elude forechecker and then effortlessly wheeled puck up ice through NZ and around defenders then feeding teammate #16 Frost going to the net as he set backhand pass on his tape for the 1st SSM goal. He exemplified good vision and distribution skills on the power play. He is not overly big, yet uses his smarts, skating, and awareness to succeed. He made good play on PP in the 3rd period as he quickly fired puck on net 1-timer that created rebound #27 Hayton goal and eventual GWG. He is good prospect for the 2018 NHL Draft and one to track closely for the remainder of the season.

SSM #11 RD Hollowell, Mac (2018*) – Hollowell is a 2nd year draft eligible that in the beginning in all honesty was not paying a lot of attention to until continuously watched the undersized Damn show his mobility, puck handling, and passing skills. He made solid puck decisions at both ends of the ice. He showed good vision on the PP and outlet passes. For lacking size, he read plays well, had active stick at defensive BL to break plays up and then would transition up ice quickly to start the offense. Although he did not register a point, wonder why he is not gaining more draft attention. He was -1 although on the play he did good job riding his man up the wall, just a breakdown defensively with other teammates. In remembering from last season's viewing, his puck decisions have improved. Scouts should not dismiss based on size and being bypassed original draft year. He is a player that needs more live viewings to fully evaluate to see if his hockey IQ and skill sets will translate into the pros or is he just a solid junior level player.

SSM #18 LW Trott, Zack (2018) – He is OHL rookie in draft season that saw 4th line ice time and limited opportunity. He did have good hit in 1st period in the defensive zone.

SSM #19 RC Carroll, Joe (2019) – Carroll was relegated to 4th line center duties with limited TOI. He has good size and decent stride and who showed some offensive skill sets and thoughts. He went about 50% at the face-off dot. He will be a player to watch next season for the 2019 draft and monitor the progression.

SSM #27 LC Hayton, Barrett (2018) – He plays 3rd line center although gets opportunity to show talents as plays PK and PP. in the 1st period he had a good shift by winning the defensive zone face-off and then killing time along the wall with compete level and gain puck possession. He made a nice play with patience on the 2nd period off broke play on the PP, as puck popped out to #12 Katchouk he fed Hayton on the crease. Instead of just shooting in tight, he recognized pressure coming at him and saw teammate #16 Frost on his back-side and laid backhand pass while facing opposite way for 3rd goal of the game. He then showed his offensive awareness again in the 3rd period on the PP, as he went to the net and quickly gathered rebound on the crease stuffing it home for the eventual GW goal. He does not show a lot of "wow' factor, yet more of a playmaker than pure goal scorer using his smarts and offensive instincts to make plays and factor on the scoresheet.

SSM #37 RW Roth, Ryan (2018) – American-born player in rookie OHL season that is undersized yet finds the right lanes and spaces in the offensive zone. His speed is decent, although will need to improve for the higher levels along with strength. He made good play on his 1st shift with awareness in the DZ to quickly get to the point to block point shot. Roth fired a couple shots on net as shows some offensive thoughts. His skill sets with the puck and shot are good, although nothing of high-end caliber.

SSM #39 RW Jacklin, Brett (2018) – He is bigger winger playing 4th line. His stride and speed are a bit awkward. He did not do a whole lot to make impression either way with limited ice time.

NIA #4 LD MacPherson, Justin (2018) – He played an average game and did not really make impression one way or another. Keeps game simple with outlets and does not offer much offensive game.

NIA #15 LW Castleman, Oliver (2018*) – He made pass on the 1st Niagara goal to #17 Lochead and shows some offensive awareness yet not enough to really garner any 2nd year draft talk.

NIA #16 RW Singer Daniel (2018*) – Singer is another 2nd year draft eligible players on the Niagara team that shows spurts of skill sets. He is undersized although he shows some good offensive instincts around the net and in the OZ. He was given 1st unit PP time, yet then makes odd pass like in 1st period in the offensive zone on the PP with no look pass that led to turnover. Right now, even though he has doubled his goal production from previous season, not sure he's the caliber player for the next level as lacks consistent play with and without the puck.

NIA #18 LC Philip, Matthew (2108*) – He is average size, yet the best asset is his shot. There were a couple of times whereby he quickly released shot once down the wing on odd-man rush that made the quickly react.

NIA #26 RC Tomasino, Philip (2019) – He is OHL rookie that showed glimpses of his skill set and a player to keep on the radar for 2019 NHL Draft. Looked to get his 1st shift with 6 minutes left in first period and showed good speed down the wing to get SOG. He does not back away from the wall and corners as tries to possess the puck, yet at times you could tell was over powered. Although he showed good hands in traffic, solid at the face-off dot, and made nice take-a-way in 3rd period on #9 Sandin in the offensive zone that led to possession and point shot. You see the potential in puck skills and awareness on both sides of the puck.

NIA #28 LW Bruder, Andrew (2018) – Lined-up 4th line left wing and did not show much as given limited opportunity yet showed some power forward instincts late in the 2nd period as he drove the puck to the net for scoring chances.

NIA #44 RC Thomas, Akil (2018) – Not sure if Thomas is a pure center man and maybe more of winger to utilize speed and offensive skills rather than player that needs to be responsible for playing 200-ft game. He was little quite through first half of the game until he made nice cross slot pass from high to low on the diagonal to #23 Corneil for golden scoring chance that should have been a goal. He was also robbed himself point blank in the slot in the 3rd period off huge glove save. He was in on the 3rd Niagara goal late in 3rd period as got puck to the net that eventually popped to #13 Maksimov off the side of the net. Thomas has some offensive tools and thoughts as finds himself around the puck yet needs to find more consistency. He looks to be more of 2nd round selection at this point.

NIA #72 RW Johnson, Bradey (2018) – He did not really factor in the game as seemed with limited ice. Last viewing he had more opportunity.

NIA #98 LD Roberts, Elijah (2018*) – He is undersized yet moves well from the back end. He is in 2nd year draft eligibility as can wheel and handle the puck. Roberts at times plays a bit erratic and can get running around of lack the defensive awareness, as on the 1st goal against he got caught puck watching and failed to pick up player #16 Frost coming to the net while his Dman partner played the puck carrier. Although there are assets in his game with skating and puck handling as he logged plenty of ice time 5v5 and on the PP. He made nice play on the 2nd goal in the 3rd period keeping the alive in OZ and found #23 Corneil at top of circle leading to goal. He managed the puck well in making good puck decisions on outlets and distribution on the PP and you like how he competes on both sides of the puck.

Eden Prairie Eagles at Wayzata Trojans, February 8th, 2018

WZA #3 RC Schmidt, Colin (2018) –Schmidt displayed his plus shot release on his goal when a loose puck found his tape in the slot and Schmidt quickly fired and snap shot over the goalies blocker. Schmidt registered 1 Goal and 2 Assists in this game and was a threat with the puck on his stick in the offensive zone. Showed the ability to use his size to drive the net on one sequence that just missed short side. Where Schmidt struggled in this game was his play without the puck, on too many occasions he was caught coasting and looking uninterested in his own zone, on a few occasions pucks went by him because his stick was up at waist height in his own end. Schmidt displayed average straight line speed and showed flashes of playing a power forward style and able to use his size effectively but was not consistent in the regard and his foot speed and agility looked like they have a ways to go in order to be effective at the pro level.

EP #18 LC Jensen, Jack (2018) – Jensen's strong 2-way game was on display in this game and attributed to his goal to start the 2nd period. Jensen disrupted plays in his own end, showed a good motor to come from deep in his own zone to deliver a strong hit on the end boards on the fore-check in the offensive zone and then displayed a good stick and awareness to intercept an errant pass in the offensive zone around the hash marks and go in alone on the goal tender and score on a back hand fore hand move between the goalies legs. Jensen was physical in all areas of the ice and his quick feet and edges allowed him to be quick on pucks and jump into lanes with and without the puck in the offensive zone. Jensen added another tally late in the 2nd period when the puck found his tape, open on the back door and scored on a partially fanned on shot that found the net.

Karpat vs. Jukurit, February 9th, 2018

KAR #8 RW Maenalanen, Saku (NSH 2013) - Maenalanen showed off a long, powerful stride and was quick for his size. He is willing to battle in front of the net to provide a screen. Flashed some skill on a successful zone entry with a very nice toe drag. He is effective at creating space for his teammates on the power play. His speed and some physical play caused a disruption on the forecheck during a penalty kill, taking roughly 15 seconds away from Jukurit. While up 3-1, Saku had some fun and attempted a lacrosse-style goal from behind the net in the third period. Finished his checks when necessary. He had trouble receiving more than a few passes, but was able to recover the puck. Got a little too aggressive on a late penalty kill trying to cut off a pass across the blue line that gave the defenceman space to set up a goal. Karpat were confident enough in his speed to ice the puck late with an empty net and have him beat out the icing call. Maenalanen is trusted in all situations, playing both PP and PK.

KAR #19 C Kupari, Rasmus (2018) - Kupari immediately showed an ability to protect the puck along the boards and in open ice with body position, as well as the skill to pull the puck toward dangerous areas of the ice. Displayed extremely smooth skating and edgework. Good puck retrieval on the power play as he stopped a clearing attempt by stripping the puck off Vahatalo. His stickhandling appears to be well above average, as he was able to make space for himself and get the puck from the boards to the middle of the ice at multiple points in the game. While playing 4-on-4, he dangled his way to the net with ease and drew a penalty; Karpat scored on the power play to go up 4-2. Kupari was utilized at even strength and on the power play. The bulk of Kupari's year was played primarily at even strength, but has found himself on the power play since returning from Karpat's Mestis affiliate Hermes.

KAR #35 G Vehvilainen, Veini (2015) - Vehvilainen has a very compact stance and mostly sticks to the blue paint. He is quick moving laterally and post to post. He was able to make himself big while in butterfly to stop higher shot attempts. Seems to read the play well as he is always in position. His head is always moving to look around screens and follow the puck. He used his stick to block plays in front when the opportunity presented itself. Vehvilainen is aggressive in tracking and covering rebounds. He did not handle the puck a whole lot, but did give the puck away once when his own players were nearby. He got aggressive with a Jukurit player who continued to poke at his glove after the whistle. Veini was beaten twice on the power play, once high blocker on a 5-on-3 and high glove on a 5-on-4.

JUK #88 C Vahatalo, Julius (DET 2014) - Decent skater but found himself lying on the ice more than a few times throughout the game. Attempted to protect the puck with his backside and was pushed forward onto his stomach somewhat easily. His first few steps are poor. Was able to use an active stick to break up a few plays on the penalty kill. Vahatalo was used in all situations.

Skelleftea AIK vs. Vaxjo Lakers HC, February 10th, 2018

SKE #6 RD Berglund, Filip (EDM 2016) - Jumped in offensively for scoring chance down the wing in the 1st period. Nice active stick to deflect passes. Got walked around somewhat easily to set up Vaxjo's second goal. Made a somewhat questionable passing decision in the 2nd period while playing 4-on-4; passed backward to his defensive partner who had no time to play the puck, resulting in a good scoring chance. A quiet game for Berglund otherwise.

SKE #8 RW Berggren, Jonatan (2018) - Limited minutes on the 4th line. No plays he made had a negative effect on the game. Received a puck in the slot and directed it on net, almost got his 1st SHL point on an assist. Showed a glimpse of his vision with a fantastic cross-ice pass at the blue line following a zone entry and stop up.

SKE #9 RW Soderlund, Tim (CHI 2017) - Defensive awareness on display early as Soderlund noticed a defenceman joining the play and got into the passing lane; would have resulted in a 2-on-1. In another defensive play, this time on the forecheck, Soderlund barged through a couple Vaxjo players and stole the puck preventing a break-out. For a smaller guy, Soderlund has a powerful stride that helps him get up to a great top speed. He threw a big hit that turned the puck over and found a teammate across the ice for a grade A scoring chance. Beautiful forecheck in the 3rd allowed him to get in close one-on-one with the goalie where he drew a hooking penalty.

SKE #16 C Lindstrom, Linus (CGY 2016) - Lindstrom is a middling skater, his first few steps and top speed look closer to average. He is not afraid to engage physically or play a little rough. Lindstrom used his offensive awareness to spot an opening between defencemen and called for a pass, but the pass was airborne and he could not knock it down. Smart passes out of the defensive zone. Sprawled out in front of his goalie and saved a go-ahead goal halfway through the 3rd period.

SKE #38 LW Eriksson, Albin (2018) - Albin did not see the ice at all as the extra forward, but had a great seat to watch the game.

VLH #6 LHD Hogberg, Linus (PHI 2016) - Strong passer again and again through the defensive and neutral zone. He was able to spring Reddox for a breakaway with a very nice, crisp pass from the defensive zone up the middle. Hogberg was reliable down low and made smart plays when pressured.

VLH #40 LW Pettersson, Elias (VAN 2017) - The skills are evident, but he seemed vulnerable to Skelleftea's physical play in this game at times. Pettersson showed his ability to recover as well as his top speed with great back checking after a teammate was picked off on the powerplay, breaking up a potential shorthanded scoring play with his stick. Used his speed again to hunt down a Skelleftea defenceman and steal the puck, finding the late man for a scoring chance. The seam across to Pettersson on the power play was covered most of the game. Vaxjo tried to force passes over early in the game on the power play but were blocked or picked off. One pass did make it across the ice for a very powerful one-timer.

Sweden vs. USA, U18 Five Nations, February 13th, 2018

SWE #26 LW Westfalt, Marcus (2018) – Westfalt was quiet for the majority of the game despite starting on the first-line. The winger drove down the right wing and shot a soft backhand that was easily handled, this play turned into his only real scoring opportunity in the match up. He did have a nice forechecking sequence where he out paced a U.S defenseman, recollected the puck and then poked it back to the point while under pressure which resulted in prolonged offensive zone time for his team. Westfalt finished with 1 shot on goal in an uninspiring performance.

SWE #13 LC Gustafsson, David (2018) – Gustafsson centered the third line and had a decent two-way performance. He played on the penalty-kill and was effective at clogging shooting lanes near the point on a powerplay in the opening frame. Had one of Sweden's best scoring chances in the first after receiving a pass from Back in the slot, didn't get everything on the shot but it still required a reflexive save by DeRidder. Great backcheck on the powerplay on Farabee which mitigated a prime scoring opportunity in-front of the net, he didn't get a penalty-call and was smart with his stick positioning while disrupting the play. However, he did take a poorly timed penalty midway through the third which sparked the U.S after Wahlstrom scored on it. He finished the game with a solid defensive backcheck where he parked himself in the slot and supported his defenseman. Gustafsson was defensively responsible and showed attention to detail in his own end but never really got going offensively like the rest of his team, as he finished with 2 shots on net and had only one quality scoring chance.

SWE #17 RW Berggren, Jonatan (2018) – Berggren was largely ineffective for Sweden while playing on the third line with Gustafsson and Westfalt. The winger was quiet to start the game while taking a penalty, but towards the end of the first he had a scoring opportunity after driving down the right wing, switching from his forehand to backhand, putting the shot just wide. He failed to generate much in the way of offense at any other point in the game while finishing with 1 shot on net.

SWE #23 LW Wernblom, Lukas (2018) – Wernblom was physically out-matched for much of the game and ended up taking out his frustrations on Miller, getting him ejected for an illegal head-shot. The small winger showed finesse elements with fluid skating mechanics, he was getting overwhelmed by the larger U.S defense in the first but settled down and made some plays in the middle frame. He had a good defensive read on the penalty-kill near the blueline which resulted in a turnover, he then skated up the ice and made a beautiful backhand pass that landed on the tape of his teammate in the slot for a high-end scoring chance. On the powerplay he continued to show his vision along the half-wall, making a highly technical saucer pass across the high-slot. Despite his physical limitations and getting ejected he did show a degree of skill to his game, finishing with 1 shot on net.

SWE #11 LC Back, Oscar (2018) – Back was offensively stagnant but did display defensive elements to his game while centering the top-line. A large center standing 6'2, 200 who penetrated the U.S defense late in the first and fed a nice backhand pass to Gustafsson for a scoring chance across the slot. He had a great backcheck which prevented a scoring opportunity in the high-slot by stick-checking Hain, he then collected the puck and distributed to his defenseman which alleviated the forecheck. Late during a penalty-kill sequence, he was effective during a board battle and created pressure which ate him time on the U. S's powerplay. He never got offensively engaged, finishing with 1 shot on net.

SWE #19 RW Hoglander, Nils (2019) – Hoglander had an average game while getting time on the top-line and playing on the penalty-kill. The winger rushed down the right wing and fired a quick wrist-shot far side that was absorbed by DeRidder, would have liked to have seen him take another step or two towards the net and gauge how much time he had as opposed to getting the shot off as quickly as he did. Defensively, on the penalty-kill he played with purpose and was part of the late sequence with Back where they created sustained forechecking pressure after battling hard against the U.S defense.

SWE #21 LC Olofsson, Jacob (2018) – Oloffson centered the second line with his teammate Hallander while only having one threatening chance on net but did show hustle in his own end of the ice. The center played hard below his own goal-line and used his size to effectively battle along the boards, he supported his defense with some transitional passes in the opening frame. Had a beautiful individual move, turning a U.S defender inside-out which gave him a prime scoring chance, the release on his shot is high-end and he generated power on the shot that he attempted to go upstairs with. He was engaged on the penalty-kill, using his stick to disrupt plays in the slot area and one play he managed to chip the puck past Wahlstrom which sent Hallander in on a breakaway. I would have liked to have seen him more involved in certain sequences given his plus tools and his size, he was disappointing relative to his abilities. Oloffson finished with 1 primary assist and 1 shot on net.

SWE #15 RW Hallander, Filip (2018) – Hallander was one of the better Swedish players in today's game, using his speed on the penalty-kill to generate chances. The winger had an in-effective first period, although he did display his motor on the forecheck and made a nice side-step which took away an incoming hit from a large U.S opponent. Showcased his speed in the second period on the penalty-kill, generating a scoring chance off the rush where he fired a dangerous wrist-shot far side that just missed the net, moments later he got a partial breakaway but was disrupted on an aggressive backcheck by Wise, he did however compete in the corner and showed plus puck skills by putting it between the U.S players legs and then attempted to redirect it off the back of DeRidder. Took advantage of a mistake by Wahlstrom at the defensive blueline where he missed the puck, giving the winger a breakaway where he hesitated and waited for DeRidder to drop before roofing it over him, the play showed Hallander's patience and technical shot. He finished with Sweden's only goal of the game.

SWE #24 RW Grewe, Albin (2019) – Grewe wasn't consistent today but he did flash a lot of potential while playing on the 4th line. The winger made a beautiful backcheck on Wise during the penalty-kill, using his superior speed to catch up to him and strip him off the puck resulting in a turnover. He showed a combination of tenacious board work along the half-wall in the offensive-end and then showed plus agility as he cut out in-front of the slot area and delivered a dangerous wrist-shot on net that was difficult for DeRidder to handle. He finished with 2 shots on net.

SWE #16 LW Fagemo, Samuel (2018) – Like the majority of his team, Fagemo had difficulties generating chances in the offensive-end while playing on the 4th line. He showed some evasive skills on a number of occasions while transitioning over the offensive blueline despite not been able to generate much in the way of speed but did show plus agility leading to a drawn powerplay after he stopped up quickly and got tripped. His only scoring chance came in the second frame at the bottom of the left-circle where he released a quick wrist-shot on net. He finished with 1 shot on goal.

SWE #3 LD Boqvist, Adam (2018) – Boqvist was an offensive catalyst for Sweden, although he was over-matched in the defensive-end around the goal-line on certain sequences. The defender was aggressive defensively, using his two-step area quickness to close gaps and attack with an active stick, this lead to multiple turnovers and on one play while defending around the goal-line, he drew a penalty after moving his feet and getting tripped by Gruden. However, on other plays, he had difficulty keeping up with the U.S forecheck and lost his defensive position at times. His offensive instincts were on display through the game. On one play, he made a timely pinch and cut towards the net while driving down the right-wing where he received a pass through heavy traffic and released a hard wrist-shot that required DeRidder to make his best save of the period. He had an additional high-end chance after driving down the right-wing later in the third but was stopped short-side by DeRidder again. He was also getting his shot through traffic at the point and did try a couple of highly technical drags to compensate for his size against the U.S squad but was disrupted on both attempts. Boqvist flashed his excellent offensive tools while playing in all situations and finishing with 4 shots on net.

SWE #6 RD Andersson, Axel (2018) - Andersson was the 7th defenseman but took advantage of the time he did have on the ice, finishing with a team-high 5 shots. The defender was poised in his own-end and showed transitional skills by carrying the puck from the defensive-end and intro the neutral zone on one sequence. He had a crisp and accurate first pass to his teammates for the majority of the game and managed to get his shot through traffic consistently, although only one of his shots generated enough power to be a threat.

SWE #10 RD Ginning, Adam (2018) – Ginning was one of the better defenders for Sweden while showing plus vision. The defender has excellent size, standing 6'3, 196 while having broad shoulders. This allowed him to board battle effectively, on one sequence the defender used his size to deliver a well-timed squeeze along the boards which forced Wahlstrom to turn the puck over. He was physical and showed high-end defensive awareness, constantly monitoring backdoor options and using his frame to overwhelm the U.S down-low in the corners. In the offensive end he displayed a highly technical first-pass, as he had a tremendous seeing-eye pass through traffic that landed on the tape of Boqvist for one of Sweden's best scoring chances in the game, on the same play he rushed back and broke up a scoring chance for the States. On another play he showed the ability to defensively read the play during a 3-on-1 against, where he anticipated the pass and used his body to deflect the puck, on the same sequence he deflected another puck in-front of the net while showcasing his strength. Ginning didn't finish with any shots on net but passed the puck effectively and was one of the few Swedish players who could match the U.S's physicality.

SWE #30 G Eliasson, Jesper (2018) – Eliasson played better than his stat line suggests and kept the Swede's within striking distance for the majority of the game despite been badly outplayed. He's got pro size, standing 6'3, 200 pounds and used it to take away the bottom of the net on several high-end scoring chances. The Swedish goalie was good at assessing plays that were developing in-front of his net which allowed him to read several cut attempts by the States which were stopped by Eliasson's positioning. Although not overly athletic based on today's viewing, he didn't give up on any shot and was willing to break his technique in order to try and make a desperation save. There's room for improvement in his lateral mobility but that comes with having a big frame at a young age. Eliasson stopped 28 of 33 shots and the majority of goals that were scored on him were on the powerplay where he had little chance of stopping the high-quality shots.

USA #43 LC Hughes, Jack (2019) – Hughes showed his outstanding skillset while playing on a line with Farabee and Wahlstrom and receiving top powerplay time. The center was executing along the half-wall on the powerplay, using excellent four-way mobility and superior edges to breakdown the Swedish defense before finding his teammates with regularity. He's a natural playmaker but he was looking to fire the puck early as well and was effective at doing so, on one shot specifically in the right circle, he got a lot of leverage and the release was quick, requiring an excellent save by the Swedish netminder, the shot generated enough velocity to create a rebound opportunity as well. Showed dynamic skating ability in the second period during a breakaway sequence but it didn't result in a scoring chance. Hughes scored an even-strength goal after receiving a beautiful pass by Wahlstrom and tucking it in. His offensive reads combined with his puck-skills and skating mechanics make him incredibly dangerous, he finished with 1 goal, 1 primary assist, 1 secondary assist in a dominant effort.

USA #12 LC Wise, Jake (2018) – Wise displayed high-end vision and passing ability while centering the second line between Weiss and Gruden which had chemistry. He had a difficult opening frame. His base isn't very powerful and that made it hard for him to generate power in his stride which allowed the Swedes to contain him and cut him off in the offensive zone rather quickly. Specifically, on the powerplay, he was stripped from behind by Grewe and didn't seem to handle the checking pressure well on the play. On another sequence in the opening frame while under pressure in the offensive-end, he tried to make a highly technical pass between his legs which ended up causing a turnover, the simple play would have been preferred as he had passing options along the boards. He did have a chip-pass in the neutral zone which was the catalyst for the U. S's opening goal though. As the game progressed, Wise became much more dangerous where he generated high-end plays. On one of them he made a one-touch passing set-up to Weiss at the right side of the net, and received two different passes from Weiss that generated high-end scoring chances. He showed offensive creativity by attempting to spin to his backhand and surprise the Swedish goalie during one of those attempts. Despite his excellent vision and the ability to make technical passes consistently, he didn't show a lot of poise when put in high-danger scoring areas, rushing his opportunities. That been said he was effective along the half-wall on the powerplay when given time and space. Wise finished with 1 primary assist, 1 secondary assist and 2 shots on net.

USA #18 RW Wahlstrom, Oliver (2018) – Wahlstrom played on the top line with Farabee and Hughes while also manning the point on the powerplay. He was effective in his board battles, using his skilled hands and his size to come away with the puck and set up his teammates efficiently. He has shown chemistry with Farabee throughout the year, and in the second period, it was noticeable again after making a beautiful give-and-go sequence that resulted in a redirect scoring chance in the slot. Showed his two-way game in the third after making a terrific and well-timed stick-check on Gustafsson which took away a good scoring opportunity since DeRidder was out of position. Later in the third he scored from the point on the powerplay after firing an accurate wrist-shot that went through traffic from the point. On another sequence he showed his vision and passing ability, making a technical pass below the goal-line to Hughes for a goal. Wahlstrom played with a lot of poise in all three zones and continues to show versatility in his game while finishing with 1 goal, 1 primary assist, 1 secondary assist and 3 shots.

USA #28 LW Farabee, Joel (2018) – Farabee had an effective offensive game, using a tenacious forecheck combined with plus offensive awareness to continuously threaten. The winger was offensively engaged early, as he had multiple scoring chances off a Hughes wrist-shot in-front of the net. He was battling in the corners and out-hustled his opponents while using an active stick; he's slight of build but he makes up for it with his combination of tenacity and skill. He had a nice drive down the left wing where he cut around a Swedish defender and attacked the net by shooting a quick backhander low. Displayed his two-way game, where he had a solid penalty-killing sequence by skating aggressively in-front of a Swedish defender and driving towards the net where his stick was shattered before he could get his backhander off. He's not as big as Wahlstrom and not as dynamic as Hughes but he plays bigger than his size and continues to show his intelligence on the ice. Farabee was all over the puck today, finishing with 5 shots on net and picking up a secondary assist.

USA #16 LW Middendorf, Erik (2018) – Middendorf showed two-way qualities while playing on the 4th line and getting penalty-killing time. He showcased his speed as he rushed down the left wing and made a move to the net on his backhand which was stopped. Had a tremendous penalty-killing sequence in the offensive-zone along the boards. As the U.S were changing, he was tasked with keeping the puck in deep and he did more than enough by fighting against 4 Swedish players simultaneously and taking 15 seconds off the clock, he out competed the Swedes on the shift. Middendorf finished with 1 shot on net but was effective.

USA #8 C/LW Hain, Gavin (2018) – Hain played on the 3rd line and second powerplay unit. He had a good scoring chance in the first after he recognized that he had a shooting lane on the powerplay, where he delivered a hard wrist-shot which was absorbed by Eliasson. Throughout the game, he continued to try and get his shot off in the high-slot; there was a number of sequences where he found soft-ice behind defensive coverage which put himself in position for quality scoring chances. The winger also showed decent puck distribution skills on the powerplay and wasn't afraid to battle for loose pucks in the corners. Hain finished with 2 shots on net.

USA #9 LW/C Weiss, Tyler (2018) – Weiss had a solid game for the U.S, showing speed and generating chances for both himself and his linemates. He was effective in the opening frame and set up the first goal of the game. He drove down the right wing after the Swedish defense was caught and made a nice head fake towards the net that made him look like he was going to shoot just before passing it to Gruden who had an open net after the Swedish goalie bit on the initial fake. Made a sharp pass across the slot to Wise for a scoring chance and later in the same shift he received a pass from Wise, firing a quick shot short-side. He continued to find soft-ice, after receiving a pass from Stastney in the left circle, he generated a lot of velocity as he wired a puck over the crossbar. On the powerplay, he used his speed to transition over the offensive line and made simple, yet smart passes that allowed his teammates time to set up the man-advantage. At other points this season, he's been offensively unengaged in some viewing's, however today he played at a high-pace and was threatening through-out the game. Weiss finished with 1 primary assist and 3 shots on net.

USA #17 LW Gruden, Johnny (2018) – Gruden displayed chemistry with Weiss and Wise while getting penalty-kill and powerplay time. The winger showcased good top-end speed and was effective on the forecheck in the opening frame. He opened the scoring after rushing down the slot and receiving a pass from Weiss where he buried it. He had a great redirection opportunity in-front of the slot after receiving a pass from Wise which missed the net. The Swedish defense had difficulties containing Gruden for the majority of the game, he finished with 1 goal and 3 shots on net.

USA #15 RD Wilde, Bode (2018) – Wilde played on the second pairing with Miller and had an effective two-way performance. He was deployed on the top powerplay unit and used on the half-wall where he looked like a 4th forward, generating chances for himself with his wrist-shot which he successfully got through traffic for the majority of the game. This was showcased when he used his speed as he weaved through the Swedish opposition on the powerplay and fired a hard-wrist shot that missed the net on the far-side. He scored a powerplay goal after firing a blistering one-timer from the point on the powerplay that went through heavy traffic. His decision making in the offensive-end was relatively good today, however during one sequence, he used soft hands and his mobility to create space for himself for a prime scoring chance in the high-slot but opted to pass the puck back to Wahlstrom at the left circle who wasn't ready to receive the pass and with good reason, as it would have been a great scoring opportunity that Wilde dismissed. Defensively his decision making was consistent for the most part, making quick transitional passes up the boards and not holding onto the puck for extended periods unnecessarily. Wilde finished with 1 powerplay goal, 1 primary assist, 1 secondary assist and 3 shots on net in a dominant offensive effort.

USA #5 LD Samuelsson, Adam (2018) – Samuelsson had a solid two-way effort for the U.S today while playing on the third pairing and getting 2nd powerplay time. He made a great stretch pass to Samuelsson from the defensive-end that gave his teammate a prime scoring chance. Along the offensive blueline, eh managed to get a couple of low shots through traffic, though he wasn't generating power on his shots. He also mishandled the puck at the offensive blueline during a powerplay sequence, showing below average puck skills on the play. One area that Samuelsson looked slightly improved was his backwards skating ability. At times throughout the year I've seen him lose his man and get beaten on the outside, however today he was quicker to recover during defensive transitional plays. Samuelsson finished with 2 shots on net and played a relatively mistake free game in his own-end.

USA #10 RD Emberson, Ty (2018) – Emberson played on the top pairing with Samuelsson and got some powerplay time. He fired a quick wrist-shot that generated good velocity from the blueline and had a good defensive play in the first where he showed a powerful base despite his 5'10 stature, pressing his opponent along the boards and forcing a turnover. One aspect of his game that remains inconsistent is his decision making along the point, there's time where he seems to be caught thinking if he should pass the puck or shoot which causes hesitation in his play, that again was on display in spurts. That been said, in the defensive-end, he was quick to pass the puck to counter-act the Swedish forecheck.

USA #19 LD Miller, K'Andre (2018) – Miller was outstanding for the U.S in today's game, making several high-end defensive plays and effectively transitioning the puck. He had a dominant opening frame, utilizing his excellent skating mechanics at both ends of the ice. On one play demonstrating this, he transitioned up the ice effortlessly from his own end, before making a soft backhand pass into the slot. On a sequence in the third, he rushed down the left wing and delivered an accurate backhand pass into the high-slot that landed on the tape of his teammate, resulting in a high-quality scoring chance. In the defensive-zone, he cut across the high-slot to the surprise of an overwhelmed Swedish forward and used his length to knock the puck off the Swedes stick, he then transitioned the puck up the ice with an accurate pass. His speed and length allow him to close gaps at a very quick rate and when combined with his size and his pacing in his own-end, he can be very difficult to play against. No play emphasizes Miller's rare skill set and highlights his athleticism better than a recovery play he made in the third period. After Hollander attempted to drive down the left wing, Miller who was caught out of position at the blueline, aggressively skated back towards the Swede before making a diving stick-check which disrupted the play, he didn't take a penalty on the defensive effort as well. Later in the third, he continued to impress defensively, using his hands to freeze the forecheck before making a simple and safe backhand pass to his teammate which allowed for a breakout. Earlier in the season, I had seen him attempt unnecessary stretch passes from his own-zone that resulted in turnovers occasionally, so it was nice to see him make the more mature and smarter pass on this sequence. Miller didn't finish with anything on the score-sheet but was arguably the best defender on the ice.

USA #23 LD Samuelsson, Mattias (2018) – Samuelsson played with Emberson on the first pairing and got some powerplay time, while having a dominant two-way game. The defender showed offensive awareness as the Swede's were changing lines, he took advantage and rushed up ice and down the left wing, firing a hard wrist-shot over the net. He had another sequence showing plus offensive instincts by making a timely pinch where he battled on the forecheck and had a tremendous hit before attempting to distribute the puck out in-front of the net, although he was unsuccessful in doing so. Later in the third period, he received a pass along the blueline and then fired a hard and accurate wrist-shot that went bar-down for a powerplay goal, the Swedish netminder had no chance on the shot. Defensively, Samuelsson was a force, showing a tremendous defensive effort where he used his frame to weigh heavy on his opponent which caused him to topple over in the corner, creating a turnover during the penalty-kill. He was defensively engaged consistently and was very difficult for Sweden to play against, using his size to counteract the skilled Swedish players attempts at penetrating the slot area or generating high-quality chances. Samuelsson finished with 1 powerplay goal and 1 shot on net.

Final Score: Team USA: 5 – Team Sweden: 1

Finland vs Czech Republic, U17 Five Nations, February 14th, 2018

FIN #31 G Piiroinen, Kari (2019): Good game for him, even though Finland lost the game. His rebound control was solid for most of the time, except on the Czechs' 1st goal of the game. He was calm, poised, and made himself look big in his crease.

FIN #4 LD Rasanen, Iivari (2019): Rasanen was strong on the puck, often rushing it deep into the offensive zone, and it was tough to take the puck away from him. He moved it quickly on the point on the power play. His skating looked fine, but it was not dynamic. He often used his feet to carry the puck into the offensive zone or to skate the puck out of danger in his zone.

FIN #6 LD Hatakka, Santeri (2019): Liked his physical game in his own zone. He played more of a stay-at-home game today. His play with the puck was average at best, as he made bad passes and was lacking some accuracy. Footwork was average; doesn't move terribly out there, but was lacking some fluidity. He was also a bit slow at retrieving pucks in his own zone.

FIN #18 RD Puutio, Kasper (2020): He was not afraid of putting pucks on net, but he does take a long time to get his shot off, with a long wind-up with his slapshot. Thought he was moving pucks well in the transition game.

FIN #3 RD Loponen, Kalle (2019): He was used often on the power play during this game, he was noticeable when he used his big slapshot from the point. His shot is very accurate and also very heavy. Defensively, he made a good first pass out of his zone to help the transition game of his team.

FIN #34 RW Intonen, Aarne (2019): Didn't create a lot of offense today, but showed good skating abilities throughout the game. His top speed was above-average, and he made quick turns while in possession of the puck in order to avoid opponents. He also showed good, quick acceleration through the neutral zone, where he showed a nice burst of speed to attack the offensive zone.

FIN #36 LW Puistola, Patrik (2019): Puistola had some nice sequences in the offensive zone in this game. On those sequences, he showed good skills while handling the puck in traffic and in tight spaces. He also showed a quick release on his shot.

FIN #15 C Saarela, Antti (2019): Very noticeable because of his speed and acceleration. Not a big player, Saarela was very impressive with his speed and play at both ends of the ice. Not only was he fast with his feet, but he was also a quick thinker on the ice. He was making quick decisions with the puck in the playmaker role, and was used on the half-wall on the power play. He has a slight frame, but was good at rolling on hits or avoiding most of the impact of the hits he received.

FIN #24 RW Tuomaala, Arttu (2020): He was quiet most of the game, until the 3rd period, where he started showing some good things on the power play. Good hands in tight spaces where he handled the puck well down low and near the net. He showed soft hands while handling the puck and while beating guys one-on-one in the offensive zone. He has a nice mix of size and skills.

FIN #19 LW Miettinen, Veeti (2020): Solid game for Miettinen, who was on the 3rd line, but also saw ice time on the power play. He's easily noticeable because of his good speed and acceleration. Not a huge kid though, and this showed when he was pushed off the puck a couple of times by bigger players along the boards. But he does work hard, and gets involved in the offensive zone. He scored with about a minute left; the 2nd Finland goal off Nick Malik's back.

FIN #20 C Lundell, Anton (2020): Smart in all three zones today, Lundell played a complete game. Appreciated his play in the neutral zone, where he showed all of his smarts by creating turnovers and blocking some passing plays from the Czech team. However, his skating looked average at best out there today.

CZE #30 G Malik, Nick (2020): Malik was strong in net for the Czechs today; he was confident and was tracking the puck well with traffic in front of him. His rebound-control was good as well today. He is not a huge goaltender at the moment, but he was fighting for every puck and showing impressive cool for a 2002-born goaltender.

CZE #6 LD Mlcak, Jan (2019): An undersized defenseman, Mlcak was effective in this game when he used his feet to make things happen offensively. He was good for the Czech transition game, either by rushing the puck himself or by making quick passes out of his zone. He did exactly this on the Czechs' first goal of the game, using his feet to rush the puck on the right side of the ice and putting the puck on net, which resulted in the goal.

CZE #9 RD Has, Hugo (2019): Steady at both end of the ice, Has possesses a good point shot and used it a bit today, as he was used on the first power play unit. He has good size and moves around the ice just well enough, he could stand to be more agile and fluid in his movements. He didn't show good puck skills today, but did show that he was effective, playing a simple game with the puck.

CZE #17 C Najman, Adam (2019): Najman centered the top line for the Czechs and scored 2 goals in the game. He showed quick hands around the net, scoring his first goal on a breakaway and the second with a quick shot from the slot. Skating looked decent, and he gets around well enough on the ice but didn't look very dynamic or show any bursts of speed. He was solid along the boards and created some plays from the half-boards, or behind the net after winning some puck battles.

CZE #5 RD Kubicek, Simon (2020): The big defender showed decent abilities on the ice, but lacked some fluidity in his movements. He took some good shots on net from the point, and has a good, hard, low point shot. Liked his physical game and reach in the defensive zone.

CZE #11 LD Kucerik, Radek (2020): Physical game from Kucerik, who was paired with Kubicek today. Similar to his defensive partner, Kucerik has a good reach and physical game in his own zone. He didn't show much in the offensive zone today, as there were not a lot of puck touches from him. He elected to play a safer, simpler game in his own zone.

CZE #15 RW Toman, Matej (2019): He showed good, quick feet and some energy today. He scored the first goal for his team by going to the net and jumping all over a bad rebound from the Finnish goaltender. Good effort at both ends of the ice; he had a couple of nice sequences on the backcheck too, working really hard to put pressure on the puck-carrier.

CZE #14 C Barinka, Marcel (2019): Good-sized centerman. His speed looked decent on some sequences rushing the puck into the offensive zone. He was involved at both ends of the ice, and he did good work deep in his own zone to support his defensemen.

CZE #18 RW Pytli, Jaromir (2020): He showed a quick release in this game with his wrist shot. He had some good sequences on the power play, showing a good mix of speed and skills. Liked his creativity with the puck as well, and some of his good passing plays in the offensive zone.

Czech Republic at USA, U18 Five Nations, February 14th, 2018

CZE #13 LW Lauko, Jakub (2018) – Lauko generated scoring chances with his speed throughout the game while continuing to play on the top-line. On one sequence, he used his mobility to cut across the slot and get a low wrist-shot through heavy traffic, on another, he cut hard to the net after driving down the right-wing and despite getting hit to the ground, made a second effort by shooting a one-handed backhander wide. He's got a strong base, this allowed him to generate power in his slapshot from the point, as well as hit a larger opponent off their skates, which he did against Samuelsson along the wall in the neutral zone who's significantly bigger than he is. The check he made occurred directly after he was hit by Emberson, which speaks to his competitiveness. He was defensively active, using his skating ability to catch up to Wahlstrom and diving behind him to knock the puck off his stick, he then tracked him to the corner and engaged along the boards with him. Lauko played hard again today while finishing with 1 primary assist and 1 shot on net.

CZE #10 LC Pekar, Matej (2018) – Pekar showed his vision and passing ability against the U.S, consistently setting up his teammates for dangerous scoring chances. The center showed his forecheck early by out-battling Deboer below the goal-line and angled his opponent away from the puck which gave Lauko the opportunity to pass to Plasek in the slot for a primary assist. Later in the first he continued to display an accurate pass by going cross ice in the neutral zone during a transitional entry. Later, he made a beautiful pass to Lauko from the neutral zone that he threaded through multiple players, the pass tuned into a penalty-shot attempt. He generated the most shots out of any Czech forward against Finland while against the U.S he was the architect for several high-end passing plays.

CZE #15 RW Plasek, Karel (2018) – Plasek didn't generate much in the way of offense yesterday and here again today he was inactive despite scoring the opening goal of the game. The winger scored off a one-timing shot in the slot area that went through DeRidder, the shot was low and hard with solid placement. On another play, he backhanded a pass across the slot on a 2-on-1 giving Plasek a good scoring chance, the speed he has stands out, he can get up the ice quickly and in previous viewing's he's shown plus puck skills but hasn't been able to utilize them so far at this tournament.

CZE #23 LW Gajarsky, Adam (2018) – Gajarsky wasn't offensively threatening like he was yesterday, while playing on the third line. The winger continues to show the ability to execute properly on offensive zone entries during powerplays as he had a couple of clean entries while showing plus straight-line speed and poise with the puck. He had an unnecessary penalty in the second period by slashing Mor's stick out of his hand, it was a bazaar lapse in judgement and allowed the U.S continued momentum at the wrong time. He wasn't much of a factor after taking the penalty.

CZE #21 LC Cajka, Petr (2019) – Cajka displayed two-way qualities while centering the second line and getting powerplay-time. The center had the primary assist on the Czech's first powerplay marker after penetrating the high-slot from the boards which forced the U.S defense to respond, this created the opening needed to feed Blumel the puck. Had a great stick-lift on Miller in the offensive-zone as he attempted to transition the puck up the ice, got off a wrist-shot during the play but it wasn't threatening. Near the end of the game he had a great defensive block on Wilde at the left-circle.

CZE #19 LW Kvasnica, Michal (2018) – Kvasnica had a difficult opening game where he didn't play well before getting ejected in the 2nd frame, however against the U.S he showed good defensive awareness on the penalty-kill while capitalizing on a poor defensive play. He found soft-ice and after receiving a pass from the half-wall and buried a beautiful wrist-shot that was well placed far-side, the shot had a plus release. On the penalty-kill he was actively engaged at the line during certain sequences, however he still wasn't able to generate too many opportunities offensively. Kvasnica played on the 4th line and scored a short-handed goal.

CZE #11 LC Kropacek, Vojtech (2018) – Kropacek had a great defensive effort for the Czech's, making several quality defensive plays while centering the third-line. The center had a great forecheck on the penalty-kill where he took advantage of a mistake by Miller who held the puck too long, used his stick to pull the puck from the defender and found Kvasnica in the slot area for a shorthanded assist. Showed good defensive positioning which allowed him to intercept a pass from Farabee that would have resulted in a good scoring chance if it wasn't for Kropacek's stick. Capitalized on a slip from Hughes at the defensive-line which gave him a breakaway opportunity but he failed to show any skill on the attempt, instead opting for a shot on the blocker side that wasn't overly threatening. He had a postional block off a one-timer attempt by a U.S player at the right circle. Although kropacek didn't display much in the way of offensive skills today he was defensively engaged away from the puck.

CZE #16 RW Blumel, Matej (2018) – Blumel had a game to remember, scoring 4 goals in a variety of ways while playing on the third-line. The right-winger buried a one-timer from the right circle on the powerplay after receiving a nice pass from Cajka. He displayed plus edges as he cut around Emberson and fired a quick and accurate wrist-shot far-side on

Mor. He scored his third goal of the game on a partial breakaway, he stopped up and flicked a backhander that went over the top of Mor, the play demonstrated poise though his top-speed appeared average due to a wide-stance. His last goal was an empty-netter. Although on paper Blumel appeared dominant, he didn't control play, drive his line or dictate the tempo of the game, however he did execute at a high-rate with the chances he was given.

CZE #22 LD Dajcar, Tomas (2018) – Dajcar had good reads and made smart decisions with the puck in the defensive-end while also showing the ability to transition the puck. On one defensive sequence he recognizing that he needed to tie-up Weiss in the slot area just before the pass was made to him for the one-timer. The defender had a low and hard wrist-shot from the point that got through traffic. Had a good block on Wilde in the slot by positioning himself well. Used his length along the boards to counter a passing attempt, then made a quick bank-pass to his teammate, the play was the catalyst for Blumel's third goal. The defender's got a big 6'4 frame and used it to block shots effectively, keep opponents to the outside and showed plus mobility for his size.

CZE #8 RD Dluhos, Jan (2018) – Dluhos had a couple of noteworthy defensive sequences against the U.S squad while playing on a second-pairing with Dajcar. The defender had a great defensive effort on the penalty-kill along the boards which resulted in him obtaining the puck and transitioning it up the ice where he made a nice pass to Blumel for a shorthanded goal. Great defensive sequence in the third where he used an active stick and solid defensive positioning to stay in-front of Hughes before knocking the puck off him, as it went into the corner he aggressively pinned Wahlstrom, causing an additional turnover and then transitioned the puck out of the zone with a short pass to his teammate. He was the only defender who finished with a +3 rating and had a primary assist on the penalty-kill.

CZE #4 RD Doktor, Vojtech (2018) – Doktor showed plus mobility for his size as he demonstrated after transitioning over the neutral zone with a fluid stride and made an accurate pass to his teammate. He closed his gap and made a puck-on-stick play that ramped the puck over the glass which took away a shot late in the game. Despite been somewhat undersized at 6'0, 170, he was aggressive in his own-end and around the goal-line and competed hard against the U.S squad.

CZE #1 G Dvorak, Daniel (2018) – Dvorak had a sensational game against the U.S, stopping 44 of 46 shots. The Czech goalie looked calm and composed from the opening whistle, displaying the ability to read the puck through heavy traffic. The States used Wilde and Wahlstrom on the powerplay who generated heavy shots, yet he managed to absorb their shots consistently and find the puck during scrambles in-front of him after allowing rebounds, he also tracked the velocity of the shot attempts well. There were several sequences where he squared up not just on the initial shot but the secondary shot as well, on the shots he couldn't square up to, he showed fast reflexes in his legs. Specifically, on one sequence he stopped an initial shot with his chest from the slot and on the rebound, which landed right on the tape of a U.S player at the top of the crease who shot quickly, he managed to kick out his right leg, taking away what looked like a sure goal. On the two goals he allowed, one was well placed on the short-side while the other he had no chance on after it deflected off a leg and into the net while he was moving laterally.

USA #18 RW Wahlstrom, Oliver (2018) – Wahlstrom controlled the tempo of the game when the puck was on his stick, while also making high-skilled plays off the rush that generated scoring chances. He had a beautiful primary assist after freezing the Czech defense from behind the offensive goal-line while using a head fake to mask his pass to Farabee at the bottom of the right circle. The power-forward made high-skilled moves while going at top-speeds on several sequences. One specifically in the first was impressive, where he made an inside-outside move before shooting a dangerous backhander on net. He played defensively responsible, having two separate backchecking sequences that stood out, one of them been an impressive recovery play after initially losing the puck, he's at his best when engaged with and without the puck, which occurred here today. Wahlstrom finished with a primary assist and had multiple scoring chances.

USA #43 LC Hughes, Jack (2019) – Hughes was a chance generating machine on the ice for the U.S today, using his elite skill set while at top speeds. The center was in full-flight in the opening frame, generating scoring chances off the rush and cutting through the Czech defense with relative ease. He had an end-to-end rush where he went through the majority of the Czech team before firing a quick wrist-shot on net. On another rush he displayed his high-end vision, making a sharp backhand pass through the slot that landed on the tape of Farabee for a quality scoring chance. He has the rare ability of knowing when he should handle the puck and when he should give it up, this allowed him to be very dangerous with Farabee and Wahlstrom down-low during cycling sequences. One negative was that he wasn't as engaged away from the puck in the defensive end but he controlled the play on the majority of his shifts, so it didn't affect the U.S squad. His processor is elite, his skating is effortless, and he's got tremendous upside.

USA #12 LC Wise, Jake, (2018) – Wise wasn't as noticeable in the offensive-end today as he was against Sweden. I commented on Wise's base lacking power against Sweden and here today he was getting moved off the puck along the boards against small opponents, however his skating ability isn't as affected, as his play down-low in the corners is by his base. On one sequence, he showed a fluid stride while moving through the neutral zone resulting in plus straight-line speed. He displayed vision in the offensive-end today but didn't drive possession nearly to the same extent as yesterday.

USA #28 LW Farabee, Joel (2018) – Farabee was dangerous, generating scoring chances all over the ice for both himself and his teammates. He had a rebound attempt at the top of the crease which was consistent with yesterday, showing he's not afraid to play in heavy traffic areas despite his size. He scored the opening goal for the U.S by taking a pass from Wahlstrom and then skated above the goal-line while using a head fake to make it look like he intended to pass the puck which caused Dvorak to move slightly off the post; he recognized the opening quickly and wired a sharp-angled wrist-shot over the glove of the Czech netminder. He was very good at finding soft-spots in the offensive-end and continues to display excellent vision, making several quality passes off the cycle and around the net.

USA #16 LW Middendorf, Erik (2018) – Middendorf drove to the net and was hard on the forecheck while playing on the 4th line. The winger was the benefactor off a deflection pass that bounced off him and into the net for the U. S's second goal of the game and he started a tic-tac-toe sequence on the powerplay, after making an accurate pass to the left point while skating down the left-wing. He's got a big 6'1 frame and was the first in the corners on a couple of shifts where he used his size properly to weigh heavy on the Czech defense.

USA #8 C/LW Hain, Gavin (2018) – Hain played on the top-line and in all situations for the U.S squad, getting several scoring chances in-front of the net. He had a prime scoring chance to the right of the goal crease after receiving a seeing-eye pass, on another scoring chance he was shut down by the Czech goalie again after getting behind the defensive coverage in-front of the net and releasing a quick wrist-shot.

USA #20 LC Pivonka, Jake (2018) – Pivonka displayed a 200-foot game highlighted by plus defensive awareness. He was defensively engaged early, supporting his defenseman by using good positioning and anticipating where pucks would end up out of board battles, there were multiple plays where he would grab a loose puck while his defenseman battled against the Czechs. He was making smart and simple passes to his teammates in the offensive-end, on one of them, he rushing down the right wing before turning his body and making a subtle drop pass to Miller for a scoring chance. He had a great opportunity late in the game but fanned on his shot in the slot while attempting a one-timer from his knee. On one forechecking sequence, he forced a turnover using his frame to battle effectively against a larger defensive opponent. Pivonka didn't show up on the scoreboard but had solid play away from the puck and was engaged at both-ends.

USA #15 RD Bode Wilde (2018) – Wilde showed his offensive abilities on the backend, while generating several high-end scoring chances from the left-circle on the powerplay. In some previous viewing's he would have tunnel vision or not find the simple yet more effective passing option but against the Czech's he was consistent in making accurate and well timed transitional passes from his own-end and looked for his teammates when his lanes were closed in the offensive-zone. He was very dangerous on the powerplay, ringing a hard wrist-shot off the post on one attempt and on another he showed plus lateral mobility and soft-hands before releasing a seeing-eye wrist-shot through heavy traffic, resulting in a difficult save for Dvorak.

USA #25 RD Spencer Stastney (2018) – Stastney executed several excellent passes while playing on the 3rd pairing with Samuelsson and on the penalty-kill. He's one of the smaller defenseman on the U.S squad but he makes up for it with his quick decision making under pressure and with his vision. There were several sequences both in the defensive and offensive-end where he delivered sharp tape-to-tape passes to his teammates. The defender's quick on his skates and although overmatched physically, he uses an active stick. On one play he aggressively closed his gap at the defensive-blueline, used an active stick to turn the puck over and then found his teammate in the neutral zone. He wasn't dangerous on the point in the offensive-end but his transitional play allowed the U.S to attack more efficiently.

USA #5 LD Adam Samuelsson (2018) – Samuelsson was composed in his own-end under pressure making smart and effective defensive plays, however he struggled holding the puck at the offensive blueline. The defenseman had a great defensive shift in the opening period. He peeled off pressure below the goal-line and made a couple of accurate passes while attempting to transition the puck out of the zone, however it was kept in at the line and resulted in an odd-man rush for the Czech's where Samuelsson showed a combination of proper defensive positioning and a well-placed stick that disrupted the pass across the slot and broke up the play. At the offensive blueline, he showed good anticipation as well, after successfully pinching into the high-slot from the point in an effort to knock the puck back into the corner so that the Czech's didn't get possession. During the powerplay and at even-strength he mishandled the puck along the line which caused unforced turnovers and hurt the U. S's momentum, although he did overhandle the puck he was still effective overall.

USA #19 LD K'Andre Miller (2018) – After having a great defensive effort yesterday, Miller got off to a poor start against the Czech's. The defender held the puck too long while on the powerplay at the half-wall in his own-end and despite having several options and time to make a play, he over-handled the puck before getting stripped which led to a short-handed goal against. On a transitional breakout in the defensive-end, he was aggressively backchecked while not recognizing that he was under heavy pressure which caused a turnover and scoring chance for the Czech's. Despite those defensive lapses, he still had several excellent defensive reads while competing hard and using his tools effectively as well. An example of this was when he had good anticipation at the defensive blueline, using his combination of size and skating to close in and disrupt a Czech transitional attempt on a sequence. His best defensive sequence came midway through the third as he used a combination of his skating ability and length with his active stick to disrupt the Czech's attempts at gaining control of the puck multiple times. At the point he displayed the ability to make a highly-technical pass off a shot fake that landed on the tape of Hain for a high-end scoring chance and was distributing the puck quickly to his teammates, while also getting his shot through traffic.

USA #10 RD Emberson, Ty (2018) – Emberson had a decent game for the U.S while playing on the top-pairing with Samuelsson. The defender had a well-timed, yet unorthodox hit as he closed his gap quickly and leveled Lauko with a partial hip-check, sending the winger flying into the air and turning a potential scoring chance into a none threatening shot. He had poor gap control in the neutral zone which allowed Blumel to cut wide on him and score a short-handed goal, that been said, he still played positionally sound and showed a solid first-pass from the goal-line. He was engaged offensively today, and on one sequence had a successful pinch on the powerplay which gave him a high-end scoring chance in the left circle, he took a hard wrist-shot that was labelled for the top corner but Dvorak aggressively cut down the angle.

USA #23 LD Samuelsson, Mattias (2018) – Samuelsson displayed intelligence at both ends of the ice while playing on the top-pairing. He had several successful pinches, none better than a pinch along the right half-wall, where he used his frame and his stick to turn over the puck, he then made two different passes to his teammates under pressure which continued offensive possession. He's poised in his own-end and today didn't over-think his play when carrying the puck, making effective and well-timed outlet passes to his teammates that allowed for transitional breakouts. He's been very impressive through the first two games of the tournament.

Final Score: Team Czech Republic: 6 – Team USA: 2

Red Deer Rebels at Kelowna Rockets, February 14th, 2018

RD #4 LD – Alexeyev, Alex (2018) – A rangy all situation defender that was easily trusted by his coach to do most things throughout this game and do them very well. He played with a calm demeanor and has a knack for commanding the ice I really controlling the flow of play, especially when he transitions the puck or worked the offensive blueline. Picked up a nice assist where he pinched in from the point hit the goalie and pick up his own rebound then quickly he looked off his defender and centered it for a easy goal, it was a quick play and a good example of hockey IQ. He's not a bad skater but there is not a ton of urgency in his feet he wasn't having issues as he efficient with good mechanics and puts his body in really smart positions; his ability to use his reach to protect puck was on display the entire game, its one of his best traits. Displayed his snap shot from the point a couple times, he's got a quick release and made the decision to shoot quite often. Likes to be involved in the rush more often than not and was a big asset to his teams zone entries. His gap was great and he was disruptive to players entering the zone against him. Great overall viewing

RD #5 RD – Barteaux, Dawson (2018) – Trusted with quite a few defensive zone starts in this game and rightfully so, he was defending well plays a strong positional game made several good plays with his to pop puck away from attacker, defends the middle ice with good range and keeps players away from dangerous scoring areas and cleaned rebounds away reducing secondary chances. Seem ok letting guys enter the zone along the wall and was more concerned with defending the middle ice, could have balanced that a little better. Had a few breakout passes go astray just blatantly missing his target causing icings or turnovers. Had a 2 assist night both of which were primary, picked up one a zone clearing play on the empty net goal and the second was a product of some good puck movement while working the point on the powerplay. Quick and efficient on the powerplay while quarterbacking the second unit.

RD #19 LW – Tarzwell, Josh (2018) – A feisty left winger that didn't miss an opportunity to get in on the forecheck and finish his hits with some power. He was a continual physical presence for a full 60 minutes in the game. Tasked with quite a few defensive zone starts trough this game he plays and agitating game when defending by consistently getting into the face of opponents, attacking puck carries and never passing up that opportunity to lay a hit; for all his physical play he doesn't cross the line, simple played hard all game. Likes to drive the net in the offensive zone and as he did while defending he was pesky around the goaltender. He timed a goal nicely by following a point shot to the net and banging in a rebound.

KEL #24 C – Topping, Kyle (2018) – Cycle game was on point for parts of this game, his line did a good job of keeping possession in the offensive zone, worked his way into the slot for a couple scoring chances but didn't create as much as they usually do; had some difficulty getting to the middle of the ice. Topping looked satisfied with giving up the puck to his line mates tonight instead of helping create, he is more effective when he touches the puck often and drives play. Did score a powerplay goal in this game, drove to the near post and finished on a one-timer short side, quality accurate finish.

KEL #7 RD – Zabransky, Libor (2018) – Back on the power play after an extended absence not getting an opportunity there didn't do anything wrong but felt more like a place holder just helping work the puck from one wall to the other and wasn't taking shot attempts. Looks a little hesitant to move to far away from the blue line, could have pinched a couple times to keep offensive zone time alive, instead just stayed at the point or retreated; doesn't want to make a mistake. Made a few nice breakout passes from his own zone to start the rush, was satisfied with letting his teammates do most of the work after that.

KEL #6 RD – Korczak, Kaeden (2018) - Made a really impressive end to end rush for a scoring chance, something that has been few and far between in other viewings shows a good example of his growing confidence. Worked the blue line offensively to create shooting lanes utilizing his skating more often that he has in the past, got a few chances past blockers. Showed some mature play to maintain possession for his team, even if he had to back out of the offensive zone to re-collect, this was a smart play. Got into a fight standing up for a teammate that ended up pretty even in the end, something not seen in any previous viewings.

Final Score: Red Deer Rebels: 4 – Kelowna Rockets: 1

Finland vs Russia, U17 Five Nations, February 15th, 2018

FIN #4 LD Rasanen, Iivari (2019): He used his feet often tonight to carry the puck into the offensive zone or outside of his own zone. He was the best puck-rushing defenseman on Team Finland tonight. On many occasions, he was leading the rush into the offensive zone. He doesn't have great top speed, but it's above-average. He's also strong on the puck, and it's tough to take it away from him. He also used his feet well to retrieve pucks quickly in his own zone.

FIN #6 LD Hatakka, Santeri (2019): Good-sized defenseman who played a more physical game in the 2nd half, and was more assertive out there. He has good feet, and moves around well on the ice. He didn't show much in terms of being a puck-moving offensive defenseman, but with his size, skating abilities and physical play, there's some potential there.

FIN #18 RD Puutio, Kasper (2020): The youngest player in this game, Puutio showed a good wrist shot during this showing. He already has nice size at this young age, and used his body well in his own zone in order to play a physical game and separate opposing forwards from the puck.

FIN #15 C Saarela, Antti (2019): Saarela showed good skating abilities in this game, including good top speed and good acceleration that he used well to go wide on opposing defensemen. He has a slight frame, and lost the control of the puck when he was getting pushed over. He's very smooth on the ice, and has good puck poise. He was at his best when playing at top speed, and he liked generating speed through the neutral zone while in possession of the puck.

FIN #19 LW Miettinen, Veeti (2020): Miettinen showed some good creativity with the puck in the offensive zone, he showed good vision and an ability to make hard passes to his teammates. He also showed good speed, and an ability to make quick turns, which made him difficult to counter in one-on-one matchups. On a couple of occasions, he showed quick hands, making nice dekes in those same one-on-one matchups.

FIN #20 C Lundell, Anton (2020): He generated some good speed in tonight's game, with a smooth and effortless skating stride. Overall, he played a solid game in his own end, showing good support by helping his defensemen deep in Team Finland's zone. Offensively, it was quieter. He did have a couple of nice sequences offensively, rushing the puck into the offensive zone. Pretty complete player at both ends of the rink.

FIN #29 RW Myllyla, Wiljami (2019): Always gave an honest effort every time he was on the ice. Great work ethic. He played on the 4th line, showing that he has a nice size-and-speed combination going for him in that role. He liked hitting defensemen with a good forecheck. He generated good speed with his skating stride, but he'll need to work on improving his agility. Not a lot of offensive chances, if any, from him tonight, but he played hard and was noticeable.

RUS #3 LD Tiuvilin, Dmitrii (2019): Tiuviļin, the captain of his team, scored one of Russia's goals today with a good wrister from the faceoff circle after some good work by Abramov down low. He did a bit of everything for them today, including helping the transition game by either making nice passes or rushing the puck in the offensive zone. He also had some physical shifts in his own zone. He has good feet, his skating is fine (as he doesn't have great top speed) but it gets the job done for now. He didn't show elite skills today, but was his team's top defenseman in this game.

RUS #6 LD Christyakov, Semen (2019): He was very physical in the first period, with two big open-ice hits that set the tempo of this game. He was not as physical the rest of the game, but players knew when he was on the ice and had the awareness to make sure their heads were up. His footwork was good; there were a couple of nice sequences where he showed elusive footwork to get away from the forecheck. His play with the puck was average at best; I thought he struggled to make passes to his teammates in the transition game.

RUS #9 C Abramov, Mikhail (2019): The best player on team Russia today, Abramov played a complete game at both ends of the ice and scored a nice goal late in the 3rd period. He also did a great job down low protecting the puck, which led to Russia's 2nd goal of the game by Tiuvilin. He showed strong skating abilities, his top speed is good, and his acceleration is really good as well. He played with some good jump and energy today. Thanks to that great speed, he was also a quick puck-retriever in all three zones.

RUS #10 RW Likhachyov, Yaroslav (2019): He showed some quick and soft hands, handling the puck in tight spaces, and good one-on-one skills with some nice dekes. He created a penalty after a nice deke versus a Finnish defenseman who had to hook him up after. He made a nice backhand pass on Russia's first goal, showing some good vision on that play. Later on, he scored a lucky goal when his pass hit a Finland stick in front of the net.

RUS #14 LW Garaev, Amir (2019): He generated some good speed with his long skating strides. His puck-protection was good along the boards. He had one sequence where he created a scoring chance after a strong forechecking shift. Not the strongest game out of him, but he flashed some good potential.

RUS #25 RW Seshin, Dmitrii (2019): The smallest player on Team Russia, Seshin played a good first period, but his play slipped in the 2nd and 3rd periods. He showed good playmaking abilities, making some really nice passes and showing above-average vision. He created one turnover by making a nice read in the neutral zone, intercepting a long pass from a defenseman from Finland. He has decent speed, but at his size, you would like to see him add an extra gear. He was getting pushed over in this game along the boards. He didn't back down, but had some limitations in his play due to his lack of size.

RUS #19 LW Berezkin, Maksim (2020): Berezkin found his legs in the 3rd period and started skating better. Beforehand, his speed was just okay. It was in the 3rd period that he found that extra gear. He's got some good puck skills, and was good around the net and in tight spaces. In the 3rd period, he was at his best when he could generate his speed from the neutral zone and attack the offensive zone at full speed.

RUS #20 C Ovechkin, Ilja (2019): Liked his compete level; he worked hard at both ends of the rink. Not a highly-skilled player, but he showed good work ethic and was involved in all three zones. He played some physical hockey along the boards and did a good job on the PK unit. He also did a fine job coming back deep in his own zone to support his defensemen, retrieving and moving the puck out of their zone.

Finland at Sweden, U18 Five Nations, February 15th, 2018

FIN #15 LW Nordgren, Niklas (2018) – Nordgren had a consistent offensive-effort, using his plus vision and poise to set up his teammates regularly while playing on the top-line. The winger showed patience with the puck near the goal-mouth after faking a shot, pulling the puck to this backhand and delivering a soft-pass in the slot for a scoring chance. He's been consistent with faking his shot and finding his teammates from the left-circle and around the net since the start of the tournament. Scored in the first period after been in the right place at the right time around the net, he's not the biggest player, standing 5'8 but he's not afraid of high-traffic areas. Had a nice pass into the slot area that set up kotkaniemi for Finland's last goal. On the defensive-side he competes, however from a stationary position his below average acceleration can get him into trouble, this allowed Swedish players to dance around him occasionally. Norgren finished with 1 goal and 2 primary assists.

FIN #28 LC Kotkaniemi, Jesperi (2018) – Kotkaniemi was the most dangerous Finnish forward and had his best game of the tournament so far while centering the top-line. The center had a dominant opening frame where he controlled play using his puck skills and vision. He had the primary assist after masking his intentions with the puck, changing his passing angle by shifting his body position, this slowed down Johansson who was looking for an initial pass, he then cut down near the goal-line and delivered a hard pass to Nevasaari in the slot for the goal. Scored a goal in the first after finding soft-ice in the slot area where he collected a rebound and fired a quick wrist-shot over Lindbom. He was driving to the net at multiple angles and was making the right decisions quickly when analyzing if he should pass the puck off or look for his shot. He was aggressive around the net, on one play he skated from behind the goal-line and attempted a shot short-side which deflected to Nordgren at the bottom of the left-circle who put home the rebound. He scored Finland's last goal from the slot after firing a well-placed shot into the top corner of the net. He displayed defensive skills as well. On the penalty-kill he aggressively skated to cut off a shooting lane and made a nice block that took away scoring chance for Boqvist. Kotkaniemi was having an average tournament up to this point but he really showed a combination of agility, intelligence, plus puck skills and both the ability to mix-up his passing and shooting options while finishing with 2 goals and 2 assists.

FIN #24 RW Kakko, Kaapo (2019) – Kakko had another excellent game for Finland while been the catalyst in the offensive zone from the half-wall on the powerplay. He displayed soft-hands that he used while transitioning up the ice with the man-advantage, he's good at changing his speeds to disrupt the flow of the play with the puck on his stick, which allowed him to transition over the offensive-line and begin orchestrating the set-up on the powerplay along the half-wall. The winger picked up a primary assist on the powerplay by threading a pass-through traffic that landed on the stick of Nevasaari in the slot area, he showed patience with the puck on his stick and the pass was both accurate and sharp. Kakko has asserted himself well at this tournament, he's got a good blend of skill and speed however it's his tenacity and decisiveness that really makes you notice him.

FIN #34 LW Nevasaari, Arttu (2018) – Nevesaari showed that he's comfortable going to high-traffic areas and generated multiple scoring chances in today's game. In the previous games he was more on the perimeter however against Sweden he found soft-ice in-front of the net which gave him two different redirection goals. On both goals, he showed excellent stick positioning and displayed good offensive-instincts by assessing and reading what his teammates were attempting to do with the puck. He continues to display a shoot-first mentality however he did manage to make a couple of accurate passes to his teammates as well. Nevesaari has shown speed, puck skills and a willingness to shoot the puck.

FIN #37 LD Utunen, Toni (2018) – Utunen had an excellent defensive-effort while playing on the top-pairing and been used in all situations. Although he's undersized, it doesn't seem to impair most aspects of his defensive play and one of the main reasons why is due to his awareness away from the puck in his own-end. In some previous viewing's he's shown the ability to make defensive-reads and execute quickly both with and without pressure, and he accomplished that today against Sweden. On one play that demonstrated this, he tracked a rebound and realized he was out of range due to his reach limitations however he dove and knocked the puck out of danger which took away a scoring threat, he can compensate for his physical limitations. He does have a thick frame and this allowed him to keep players from cutting to the net on him for the most part, though his size does hinder his ability to keep players boxed-out on the powerplay, which allowed several rebound scoring chances for Sweden. There wasn't much creativity from the point today but he did distribute the puck efficiently and got his wrist-shot through traffic.

FIN #4 LD Heinola, Ville (2019) – Heinola was firing wrist-shots that were getting through traffic and looked to set his shot through screens, which proved effective after he picked up a primary assist from a rebound, which he generated from a shot from the left-point. The defender had an aggressive checking play at the defensive blueline that cut off Berggren's attempt at driving down the boards, he doesn't mind playing physical despite his size. Got caught by Berggren shortly after the above play due to not angling his body properly causing him to be flat-footed, his recovery effort was a check while going off balance that put him in the box but the main takeaway was he did attempt to make up for his initial mistake. Heinola had an effective game overall while finishing with a primary assist.

FIN #31 G Annunen, Justus (2018) – Earlier in the year, Annunen appeared to lack mobility due to his size, however he looks to have lost significant weight which has allowed him to make several noticeable improvements based off today's viewing. His improved movement allowed him to cut off his angle aggressively during a breakaway before making a shoulder save, he then tracked the puck and showed above-average reflexes as he kicked out his right-pad and took away the rebound scoring chance. He was under heavy pressure for most of the third period but looked calm and in control while stopping several high-quality scoring chances. His best save of the night came off a rebound where he used his length to stretch out and glove what looked like a sure goal from Olofsson who was in disbelief after it was stopped. The goalie also displayed the ability to track the puck through heavy traffic despite giving up the first goal from the point while screened and was consistent at squaring up on secondary scoring chances. Annunen displayed plus tools while finishing with 21 saves on 24 shots.

SWE #13 LC Gustafsson, David (2018) – Gustafsson displayed a mature two-way game while centering the first line and played well on the penalty-kill. In the offensive-end he had his best scoring chance early off a rebound where he drove hard to the net and shot a quick wrist-shot that was absorbed. The center had a solid defensive effort on the five-minute penalty-kill, aggressively skating and creating pressure at the blueline. On one play he was rewarded for his effort, as he tipped the puck out allowing for an important line-change. Shortly after, he helped support at the boards and deflected the puck out again. He was engaged in the defensive-zone and made quality passes to his teammates for scoring chances despite not showing up on the score-sheet.

SWE #17 RW Berggren, Jonatan (2018) – Berggren was more offensively engaged today than he was in his last game, using his speed and puck skills to penetrate the Finnish defense. The winger showed good straight-line speed which gave him a breakaway scoring chance, he attempted to fire a shot over Annunen's glove but couldn't raise it over the large goalie, despite the save, the release point was high-end and he generated a lot of velocity on the shot. Showed his quick hands while skating down the right-wing, going from his forehand to his backhand and evading an active stick, giving him continued possession. Used his poise and plus agility in the neutral zone to spin off a check and bypass another Finnish player before transitioning the puck over the line and driving down the right-wing that drew a penalty due to side-stepping at the right time which caught the Finnish defender off guard and put him behind the play which forced the hook. Berggren was the catalyst for several dangerous offensive plays while playing on the top-line and along the half-wall on the powerplay.

SWE #22 LW Nikola, Pasic (2019) – Although Plasic wasn't noticeable in either the offensive or defensive zone consistently, he did spin away from pressure in the slot and found Lundmark, who scored from the point giving him a primary assist on one sequence in the opening period.

SWE #11 LC Back, Oscar (2018) – Back had a strong two-way effort for Sweden, executing at a high-rate at both ends of the ice while centering the 2nd line. He was the catalyst for Sweden's opening goal by intercepting a pass on the backcheck in his own end, before making an accurate pass that transitioned the puck up the ice. He then scored the opening goal for Sweden after finding soft-ice in the slot while showing soft hands before tucking it upstairs on Lindbom. His vision and passing ability were apparent today, on one sequence, he used soft hands before spinning off a check and making a no-look backhand pass to his teammate. On another, he got a primary assist after making a quick pass to Fagemo across the crease for a goal that Annunen had no chance on thanks to the speed at which Back moved the puck. He was arguably the most impressive forward for Sweden today and displayed a rare combination of size, high-end tools and two-way intelligence.

SWE #21 LC Olofsson, Jacob (2018) – Olofsson had a solid two-way game for Sweden though he's had trouble asserting himself consistently. The center showed his defensive backchecking after using his skating ability to catch up to a Finnish forward while using his size to knock him down to the ice. He had another terrific backcheck in the 2nd, his shot was blocked but he tracked the puck well and used his skating ability and his stick to disrupt a Swedish forward in the right circle which resulted in a turnover. He had an odd-man rush that demonstrated that he's too unselfish with the puck at times, as he had open-ice to cut directly across the goal-mouth or fire his plus wrist-shot, however he opted to hold up and flick a backhand pass across the slot which negated a scoring chance. He had a dangerous shot attempt showing his quick release off the draw, the shot handcuffed Annunen who had to reach back and make a solid recovery save on the play. Closed out the game with a great scoring chance in the final minute by parking himself to the right of the goal-crease where he snapped a rebound opportunity but was robbed by the glove of Annunen. Olofsson was better today than he was in his last performance and the tools are there.

SWE #15 RW Hallander, Filip (2018) – Hallander wasn't consistently dangerous but he still showed a solid two-way effort while been centered by Olofsson on the third-line. The winger displayed his defensive acumen without the puck by intercepting a pass in the neutral zone and rushed back up ice before releasing a dangerous shot that went far-side, just missing the post. Had a good shift on the 5-minute penalty-kill, using his speed to put pressure on the Finnish defense during a forecheck, where he showed good defensive awareness by intercepting a pass attempt and then had the option of dumping it in but made the intelligent play, passing it back in the neutral zone for extended possession. He had a scoring chance in the high-slot that showed his ability to generate velocity on his wrist-shot from far-out although he missed the net on every shooting attempt he had today.

SWE #24 RW Grewe, Albin (2019) – Grewe was mixed defensively but still flashed his high-offensive ceiling. The winger had a dangerous defensive sequence where he over-handled the puck and made a poor decision by cutting directly into his own-slot area under heavy traffic which came close to resulting in a turnover. In the offensive-end he did use his speed to grab a loose puck and had a quick passing play while under pressure. He showed his plus puck-skills as he drove into the high-slot and released a quick wrist-shot that found it's way through traffic, he can use his hands while going at high-speeds.

SWE #16 LW Fagemo, Samuel (2018) – Fagemo had a good two-way performance against Finland while playing on the 4th line and getting powerplay time. He had a solid effort along the boards which helped his team move the puck up the ice. Displayed above average hands while playing on the left half-wall during the powerplay, on one sequence he toppled over a Fin using his hands, passed it back to the point and then put himself in good position for a one-timer after recognizing that his lane was open due to the player who fell over putting himself out of position. He showed plus defensive awareness after supporting his defenseman down-low during a board battling sequence during a powerplay. Found soft-ice in the slot area during a powerplay in the third but fanned on the shot however he made up for his earlier misfire after slapping home a one-timer off a cross crease pass with a few seconds left in the game.

SWE #7 LD Lundkvist, Nils (2018) – Lundkvist showed great offensive tools and excellent four-way mobility while playing on the third-pairing and receiving powerplay time. Despite his 5'11, 174-pound frame, he was tenacious down-low in-front of his own net, refusing to give space to larger Finnish forwards and making sure they didn't box-him out. He displayed a strong base for his size, as he tracked Kotkaniemi's attempt at driving down the right-wing and delivered a cross-check to the chest that sent the Finnish center crashing to the ice which resulted in a turnover. Displayed good gap-control before using his stick to disrupt a shot attempt at the right-circle, he then transitioned the puck up the ice with an accurate first pass. Showed a good level of patience and poise with the puck on his stick during a powerplay sequence, as he skated down the left-wing, he angled his body towards the slot to mask his passing attempt back to the point, which set up Boqvist for a point-shot. His skating was fluid and he needed only a few steps to take off which resulted in a great top-gear, as he drove down the slot area on an odd-man rush and fired a quick snap-shot that went off the cross-bar, he got a lot of leverage under the puck and didn't require anytime to settle the puck down on the play. He also showed the ability to generate velocity on his wrist-shot from the point while getting it through traffic and had a variety of feinting mechanics while walking the line. Lundqvist was very impressive today and played well with Boqvist on the powerplay.

SWE #3 LD Boqvist, Adam (2018) – Boqvist was an offensive catalyst, generating several scoring chances from the back-end while playing on the top-pairing with Ginning. The defender drew a penalty early in the game by using his agility to cut wide which forced Nordgren to hold him. He had a cut to the net where he showed good offensive awareness by dropping a pass back to his teammate at the goal-line before getting hit. Displayed his skill with the puck as he was tripped, he still managed to make a nice pass to his teammate below the goal-line. Had a solid pass behind his own goal-line while under heavy pressure and made several first-passes to initiate transitional breakouts. His skating is very fluid but during a transitional zone entry he showed that he has another gear that he can get up to when the play calls for it. On the same shift he displayed his excellent offensive-instincts during a give-and-go sequence with Back at the right circle where he displayed the ability to use a screen and change the angle of his shot quickly, which just missed short-side. Boqvist was dangerous in the offensive-end today, quarterbacking the powerplay efficiently and driving possession.

SWE #5 LD Johansson, Filip (2018) – Johansson was effective for Sweden while playing in all situations. The defender skated hard to a loose puck below his own goal-line, then under pressure, made a nice move followed by a quick pass that took away the forecheck; on the same sequence he made an accurate pass that resulted in a transitional breakout. He displayed unorthodox stick positioning on lateral passing attempts. On Kotkaniemi's primary assist he didn't keep the stick in-front of him and instead angled it behind him which didn't give him a chance to deflect it, and on a penalty-kill sequence he angled himself with one arm on his stick while bent over at the waist which would have allowed quicker opponents an opportunity to cut wide and re-open passing lanes. He showed fluid skating mechanics and plus top-end speed as he rushed down the left-wing before delivering a difficult wrist-shot for Annunen to handle from the short-side, the release was quick and it was well placed. He battled hard in the right circle on the penalty-kill, pressing his stick into his opponent to move him off the puck and then used an active stick to knock the puck free which resulted in a turnover and a puck clear for Sweden. Johansson was solid at both-ends of the ice and displayed offensive-upside.

SWE #8 RD Lundmark, Simon (2019) – Lundmark showed the ability to play physical and shot the puck at a consistent rate from the blueline. The defender opened the scoring for Sweden after putting a seeing-eye wrist-shot on net at the right-point that went through heavy traffic for Sweden's opening goal. Had another dangerous slapshot from the point that found it's way through traffic, creating a rebound and a scoring chance. Showed flashes of physical play as he used his frame to drive a Finnish forward who was attempting to cut around him in the corner and on another sequence, he stayed in-front of his man and used his body to separate the puck during an attempt to cut to the net. He showed plus offensive instincts as he recognized when he needed to pinch along the boards in the offensive-end on another play in the third period. Lundmark didn't look out of place on the back-end for Sweden today.

Final Score: Team Finland: 5 – Team Sweden: 3

Sweden vs USA, U17 Five Nations, February 16th, 2018

SWE #1 G Rheyneuclaudes, Lucas (2019): Tough game for Rheyneuclaudes, who gave up 10 goals to the Americans, including 7 in the 3rd period. He has good size and had some success in the game by making himself look big in his crease. He looked bad on some shots he faced and didn't look too confident. Because of this, his defense was playing more and more nervously in front of him. He has good size, but he didn't show a lot of athletic abilities in this game. Once the USA started making him move side to side, they had great success scoring on him.

SWE #7 LD Bjornfot, Tobias (2019): He was steady in his own zone, and it was a solid all-around game for the Swedish captain. He showed good competitiveness in his own zone, and won his share of battles along the boards. He's not overly physical, but did a good job bringing his man to the wall and out of the play. He showed enough skating abilities to rush the puck out of his zone, and made some good puck rushes into the offensive zone. He didn't display any elite plays with the puck on his stick.

SWE #5 LD Lundqvist, Alexander (2019): Lundqvist played a simple game with and without the puck. He scored the opening goal for the Swedes, with a simple wrist shot from the point that the Amercian goaltender never saw because of the traffic in front of him. In his zone, he kept a good gap, and a good stick-check to pokecheck pucks away from USA forwards. He has decent size, and his skating abilities seem decent, but he could stand to improve his agility and fluidity.

SWE #4 LD Brodberg, Philip (2019): He showed good skating abilities during this game. Often, he would rush the puck into the offensive zone. He didn't hesitate to jump in the play and attempt to create some offense. His puck skills are average, he beat players one-on-one with his speed, not necessarily his puck skills. Defensively, he showed some courage in blocking shots on the PK unit.

SWE #6 RD Soderstrom, Viktor (2019): Liked his game in possession of the puck, he showed good quick puck movement on the back end and was one of the better Swedish defensemen for the transition game. He rushed the puck often out of his zone, he showed an ability to beat players one-on-one with his good skating abilities and agility. Defensively, in the first two periods of this game, he did some good defending one-on-one with a good gap control.

SWE #27 RW Holtz, Alexander (2020): Not many good offensive sequences for him today; his skating needs some work (mostly with his first two-three step quickness). Once he gets going, his speed is fine, and with his power, he can be tough to handle for defensemen. He had 1 or 2 decent scoring chances in the game; he's pretty advanced for a 2002-born player in terms of how he can shoot the puck.

SWE #15 LW Holmstrom, Simon (2019): He showed good creativity with the puck; his vision and passing game shone today in a losing effort. He showed a good compete level along the boards, he was not shying away from contact and didn't back down from the physical game. His speed was good, with a good burst of speed down his wing.

SWE #26 RW Raymond, Lucas (2020): Raymond scored a nice goal with a very quick release to beat the USA goaltender in the first period. On his goal, he made the entire play happen with a nice stick-check in his own zone to create the turnover. He showed impressive stickhandling abilities, and also showed he's capable of beating guys wide with his quick acceleration. His shot is very impressive too; he doesn't shoot the puck like a 15 year old at all.

SWE #18 C Bjerselius, Oscar (2019): Did a lot of dirty work in the corners for his team, nothing fancy with him offensively, but he played his role well. He often showed good work ethic away from the puck and showed good support to his defensemen deep in his own zone.

SWE #28 C Sundsvik, Albin (2019): Good awareness away from the puck. He was very involved in the defensive zone. Seems like every shift he was back deep in his own zone, acting like a 3rd defenseman. He didn't create much offense, centering Sweden's 3rd line.

USA #35 G Knight, Spencer (2019): Like his size. He is a tall goaltender who has good projectable size down the road. He was not tested much in this game after that first period, he couldn't track the puck on Sweden's first goal of the game from the Lundqvist point shot, and on the 2nd goal, he couldn't do much after that great shot by Raymond.

USA #32 LD York, Cam (2019): York showed good footwork and skating abilities while rushing the puck out of his zone and into the offensive zone. His skating abilities are good, he has good top speed, acceleration and he's very fluid on his skates. He was moving the puck well on the power play and played a smart game.

USA #33 LD Thrun, Henry (2019): Similar to his D-partner Cam York, Thrun was effective with his feet. He showed good acceleration when rushing the puck and was used in all situations today.

USA #36 LD Vlasic, Alex (2019): Not a lot of puck touches for the tall defenseman today, but when he did have the opportunity, he showed some good puck poise. His skating and agility are very impressive for a defenseman of this age and size.

USA #37 LD Warren, Marshall (2019): Another mobile defenseman on the USA back end, Warren has quick feet and he's in the same mold as York and Thrun. He was very much involved in the transition game with his feet and passing game.

USA #48 C Turcotte, Alex (2019): Turcotte was one of the better USA forwards today. He had an amazing shift in the first period where he showed good puck strength, fighting off Swedish players. He then demonstrated good speed, creating space for himself, and then great vision when he found an open teammate at the side of the net. Unfortunately, his teammate couldn't finish the play. Numerous times in the game, Turcotte showed great passing abilities and vision. Good skater with a nice burst of speed. He's also strong on the puck, as he skated with a low center of gravity that helped him protect the puck.

USA #59 RW Caufield, Cole (2019): A very impressive shooter, Caufield is tiny, but has a heck of a shot and can really skate. His compete level was excellent; on the PK unit, he's excellent at putting pressure on the puck-carrier. He has great speed, but makes quick turns, which make him tough to defend against, as he can be unpredictable. Overall, Caufield is an impressive little player.

USA #49 LW Boldy, Matthew (2019): Boldy was a horse down low, and was very tough to handle when using his size and long reach down low. He showed good vision in today's game, his passes are hard and accurate. He sees the ice well, and showed he's a good playmaker. He showed some high-end plays in the 3rd period, including a strong power-forward game with a real good skill level.

USA #53 C Zegras, Trevor (2019): Zegras skates well, generating some good speed, and was also good at changing directions quickly. He showed good puck skills throughout this game, and soft hands while handling the puck in traffic. He has a good shot, and a good, quick release as well. He had good chemistry with Matthew Boldy on USA's 2nd line today.

USA #52 C Beecher, Johnny (2019): Beecher centered the 3rd line, playing with Farrell and Caulfield. Liked his work along the boards and down low, he used his big frame well and played like a power-forward out there. He created some good pressure on the forecheck, which led to him scoring USA's 1st goal of the game.

USA #41 RW Caulfield, Judd (2019): Didn't show high-end talent like a lot of his teammates in this game, but I liked his work ethic at both ends of the ice. He was good on the forecheck, he created some turnovers with his puck pressure. He also was one of the better USA players in terms of his commitment to the defensive game and backchecking. He played a key role for them on the PK unit.

USA #46 RW Moynihan, Patrick (2019): Moynihan played on RW on the 4th line. He had a couple of chances in the offensive zone, and took some good shots on net. He had a couple of nice hits on the forecheck as well.

USA vs. Russia, U18 Five Nations, February 16th, 2018

RUS #14 LW Denisenko, Grigory (2018) – Denisenko's skill level stood out today as he made highly technical plays consistently with the puck on his stick. The winger scored a goal for Russia that showed hesitation and the ability to adapt to what DeRidder was giving him. He froze the U.S netminder, holding his release and when he bit on the fake, Denisenko used his hands to tuck it around him, it was a high-skill goal. Played the half-wall on the powerplay as he's been doing all tournament and showed his skill along the boards; on one sequence while under pressure he spun and faked a pass to the point before passing the puck on his backhand towards the goal-line. He's had better performances at this event but he still had quality game while competing at both ends of the ice.

RUS #13 LC Khovanov, Alexander (2018) – Khovanov continued to show his technical passing ability however he continued to be a passenger on the top-line. The center had a highly technical primary assist on Denisenko's goal, he reacted quickly to Wilde's attempt at closing distance on him during a 2-on-1 by flipping a high saucer-pass that required a high level of finesse to make. He's been on the perimeter too much at times during this event, but in the first period he made a fast-lateral cut across the high-slot while looking for a scoring chance. When the game was on the line, Khovanov didn't step up and lacked the necessary pace to keep up with the U.S's top players.

RUS #7 RW Svechnikov, Andrei (2018) – Svechnikov was using his passing ability to transition the puck up to his teammates that created odd-man rushes which lead to two secondary assists in the opening period. At the beginning of the second, he had a good defensive read, cutting off Samuelsson's passing lane and using his powerful stride to create a breakaway where he also froze DeRidder before pulling to his backhand and putting it past him. Had a nice drag move during a penalty-killing sequence while rushing down the left wing, the drag changed the angle and made it difficult for the U.S goalie to pick up on the dangerous shot that just missed far-side. He had another high-end chance in the third period which he shot wide as well. He started the game by turning the U.S defense inside out and dominated play, however as the game progressed he took a bad penalty and wasn't as effective in the third period.

RUS #21 LW Marchenko, Karill (2018) – Showed the ability to change pace quickly with his skating after driving through the left circle and then pulled up while finding Morozov at the side of the net which gave him a primary assist. He was shooting the puck often in his last effort so it was good to see that he can mix it up when the play calls for it. While on the powerplay he continued to show the ability to make high-skill plays while in motion, as he cut across the high-slot and made a no look backhand pass to his teammate. Marchenko's tools were on display today although he wasn't consistently dangerous against the States.

RUS #8 RC Morozov, Ivan (2018) – Morozov was solid at both ends of the ice. The center positioned his stick properly while driving down towards the goal-mouth which resulted in an easy tap in goal during an odd man rush with Marchenko. He battled hard below the goal-line on a defensive sequence where he used his stick and his frame to aggressively fight for the puck, although on one sequence this led to a penalty against. Had a good scoring chance in the slot but an active stick from Wilde took it away, however the play demonstrated that he has no problem going into high traffic areas with the puck on his stick.

RUS #22 RW Iskhakov, Ruslan (2018) – He's been displaying elite balance for his size all tournament and against the U.S that was on display again. Specifically, on one play below the goal-line, he absorbed a huge hit from Miller and guarded the puck with one arm, it took support from Miller's defensive partner to knock him off the puck. It speaks volumes to his base when an athletic defender who's 8 inches taller and roughly 50 pounds heavier needs help containing him. Despite showing flashes of his excellent puck skills and using his skating to attack the U.S on some shifts, overall this wasn't one of his better efforts.

RUS #17 RW Kizimov, Semyon (2018) – Kizimov had a solid two-way performance for Russia. The winger had a highly technical pass while in motion in the high-slot where he angled his body towards the right circle before using his stick to flick it back which through the U.S defender off guard and resulted in a set up for his teammate. He was used on the penalty-kill and had an effective sequence while the U.S had the man advantage in the second frame by coming away with the puck during a battle along the defensive blueline, he then drove wide and cut around the net before passing it back to his teammate in the neutral zone which took time off the clock. He took two hits on the play and had to kick it back to his skate yet he remained in control and showed poise. Found soft-ice in the high-slot and delivered a hard snapshot that missed short-side. He's shown flashes of high-end skill at this event.

RUS #23 RD Zhuravlev, Daniil (2018) – Zhuravlev was aggressive along the blueline in the offensive end. The defender was in charge of quarterbacking the powerplay where he had a nice head fake by looking back towards the left circle before delivering a hard wrist-shot that was gloved down, the shot got through traffic but he didn't have a body in-front of DeRidder for a screen. Scored the 4th goal for Russia after firing a quick wrist-shot from the top of the right-circle that redirected off DeRidder and into the back of the net, used a screen again to mask the shot. His defensive game wasn't as good today, he was in position on most sequences however he wasn't transitioning the puck out of the zone as efficiently as he had in previous games and the U.S was using their speed and forechecking ability which hampered him occasionally.

RUS #25 LD Misyul, Daniil (2019) – Misyul had an excellent shut-down performance against the States. The defender reacted quickly to the U.S forecheck while displaying an accurate first pass that lead to multiple transitional breakouts. He's got a big frame, standing 6'3, 180 with room to grow and he used it to effectively counter incoming hits, absorbing the forecheck and remaining calm while keeping the puck closely guarded to his body and waiting for support. He had a heads-up play on Hughes at the start of the second period that showed good defensive awareness, as he closed his gap and used his frame to knock Hughes off his skating lane towards the net as the U.S center was attempting an aggressive cut. Had a good read in the neutral zone where he cut off a stretch pass attempt and delivered it back down the ice during a penalty-killing sequence. He was consistent at taking away skating lanes and defended well against the U.S's best forwards.

RUS #28 RD Okhotyuk, Nikita (2019) – Okhotyuk had a decent two-way performance against the U.S. The defender had a great stick play near the circle after Miftakhof gave up a rebound, Wahlstrom was streaking towards the net and would have gotten to the rebound if it wasn't for his heads-up play. Had a good defensive read and communicated effectively with his defensive partner as he took away a shot from Pivonka using his stick, he then turned the puck over and rushed it over the neutral zone creating a transitional breakout for his team, he displayed composure on the sequence. Showed his offensive game on one play where he cut across the high-slot and fired a hard wrist-shot which DeRidder gloved down, he sometimes has a tendency to fire his shot without re-opening his lane however that wasn't the case on this play.

USA #43 LC Hughes, Jack (2019) – Hughes attacked the net tonight, showing the ability to play bigger than his size when needed. He's been using his skating to create havoc and here again he was using his acceleration to penetrate through the Russian defenses at will. He scored the 2nd goal of the game by been in the right place at the right time in-front of the slot, reading the play well and recognizing where the pass was coming from in advance. Had a beautiful passing play to Farabee after cutting through the slot and finding him on the backhand, the split-second decision making needed to execute the play properly was there. He was one of the primary reasons the U.S managed to mount the comeback that he did, he's had a very impressive tournament.

USA #12 LC Wise, Jake (2018) – Wise showed his two-way game today, having a consistent effort at both ends of the ice. On a play near the blueline he was stripped off the puck but made a night recovery stick-lift of his own which he used to take away the puck before skating over the high-slot and releasing his wrist-shot that went wide. His shooting mechanics aren't poor but there's an inability to generate mustard on most of his shots. Generated good top-end speed after making a transitional breakout play by rushing the puck up the ice and finding his teammate. Rang a puck off the post after taking a pass from Farabee, the release point was quick and he was decisive with his placement, he was good at finding open-ice against Russia. Wise helped generate several high-end scoring chances and had a high rate of execution with the puck on his stick.

USA #18 RW Oliver Wahlstrom (2018) – Wahlstrom wasn't able to generate chances at the pace he normally does in the first two periods but that changed in the third, where he took the game over. The winger made a dynamic passing play where he cut through the slot and then made a no look forehand-to-backhand pass that found Farabee in the right circle for a quality scoring chance. Later, he made a nice cut to the net through traffic resulting in a difficult backhand stop for Mitakhof, he showed his physicality on the sequence as well, delivering a hard hit along the boards after the failed shot attempt. Scored the game-tying goal after firing a hard and quick wrist-shot at a tough angle off the draw, the shot surprised Miftakhof. Wahlstrom had half a dozen scoring chances in the third period alone and was competing at a high rate; when he's dialed in, it's difficult for teams to stop him.

USA #28 LW Joel Farabee (2018) – Farabee had excellent puck distribution against Russia, reading the defense and anticipating when lanes were opening and closing. He made several one-touch passes both to Wahlstrom at the point and to Wilde who was playing on the other half-wall on the powerplay and was dangerous throughout the game. He delivered a dynamic pass near the goal-line where he made a reverse no-look spin pass that he threaded through several players in-front of the slot. Had a beautiful saucer pass that landed on the tape of Wise who rang it off the post, it was technical and well-timed. Scored a goal in the slot after receiving a pass from Hughes, the shot was hard and accurate. Farabee continues to show that he can compliment the top-line with Hughes and Wahlstrom, he's not a passenger in any sense of the word and makes the players he plays with better.

USA #8 C/LW Gavin Hain (2018) – Hain had an effective performance against Russia while getting some time on the 2nd powerplay unit. He had a prime scoring chance on the powerplay in the slot area after receiving a pass from the half-wall then quickly shot far-side, resulting in one of Miftakhof's best saves of the game. Had a nice fake with the man advantage where he skated into the slot area and used his head to bait Russia into thinking he was going to shoot before making a deceptive pass to the right side of the net which created a quality scoring opportunity. Demonstrated that he wasn't afraid to attack the goal-line after receiving a pass before quickly cutting directly to the net. Showed a solid top-gear while rushing the puck through the neutral zone, his stride is a bit short but it doesn't really hold him back with his skating. Had a good hustle play late as he dove for a loose puck which created possession and a scoring chance for his team, he was tenacious in the offensive-end for most of the game.

USA #14 C Jack DeBoer (2018) – Used his frame effectively to angle himself and take a hit which negated a potential turnover along the boards. Had a deflection in-front of the crease, finding soft-ice and positioning himself well. Had a solid keep-in along the point and wasn't afraid to take a hit to make the play happen. DeBoer did a lot of little things right out there although he wasn't too noticeable in the offensive-end.

USA #9 LW/C Tyler Weiss (2018) – Weiss was dangerous in the offensive-end against Russia. He was skating hard today and used it to both with and without the puck. On one sequence early in the first, he closed in on an opponent who didn't detect him, used a stick-lift and then found his teammate towards the side of the crease which was directed just wide of the net. On the powerplay he was using his skating ability to move across the ice laterally which allowed him to re-open lanes and set up his passing options. There were multiple plays where he would explode down the wings and cut to the net, on one of them he managed to cut right into the crease which almost resulted in a goal. Late in the third, he l used his speed to cut around the net and threw a backhand pass that banked in off Miftakhof for the game winner. This was Weiss's best performance of the tournament so far.

USA #17 LW Johnny Gruden (2018) – Gruden demonstrated his net front presence against Russia, using his tenacity and lack of fear near the goal-line to create scoring chances for himself. The winger plays bigger than his 5'11 listing suggests and had several scoring opportunities around the net area. He had an accurate and well-timed transitional pass from the neutral zone which allowed the U.S to set up their powerplay and on the same powerplay, he showed composure under pressure at the right half-wall by maintaining his balance and readjusting himself after receiving a difficult pass, it was impressive that he didn't turn the puck over on the sequence. Had a similar play to Hain where he used a head fake which froze the defense who were thinking shot, before he passed it off. Attacked the net late, spinning into heavy traffic while looking for an opportunity to shoot.

USA #15 D Bode Wilde (2018) – He's shown the tendency to use his two-step area quickness to close his gap and surprise players during 2-on-1 sequences against, and here again he attempted to cut off Khovanov's lane aggressively, however his aggression cost him as the puck was flipped into the air which left DeRidder out to dry, he's got to learn that the safer defensive play can be better than the more tenacious play at times. Despite that defensive play, he had an effective poke-check behind his net and then took off down the ice while putting himself in good position for a scoring opportunity and on a play where he was caught, he showed hustle while cutting off the passing attempt by a Russian forward while on the powerplay. Wilde wasn't as effective offensively today and made a couple of defensive errors, however, overall, he still competed and made some well timed defensive plays.

USA #19 D K'Andre Miller (2018) – Miller was the catalyst for the U.S comeback against Russia. He recognized that a Russian forward who was attempting to hold the puck in at the blueline had his head turned away from him, so he used his quickness to close the gap and separate the puck before the Russian player could react, which lead to a transitional breakout. The defender took a shot from the high-slot and scored on an accurate seeing-eye wrist-shot that went far-side on Miftakhof, this goal rallied the U.S and shifted the momentum, it was a timely goal. Had a terrific play at the start of the third period, using his speed to cut wide before making a no-look backhand pass into the slot area for a primary assist on Hughes goal. He made a mistake under pressure by firing a pass up the middle that was picked off, however he used his skating ability to recover by aggressively closing the gap on the Russian forward who had to force the shot. Miller had a strong two-way performance against Russia.

Final Score: Team USA: 5 – Team Russia: 4

Regina Pats at Moose Jaw Warriors, February 16th, 2018

REG#20 Oksanen, Emil (2018) – Oksanen was a non-factor until the third period when he scored the go ahead goal on the power play. Great one timer from the circle. It gave the Pats the spark they needed to close out the game. Second power play unit.

REG#33 Paddock, Max (2018) – Strong bounce back performance for Max coming off the loss to Moose Jaw just two days prior. Showed off his flexibility making two unbelievable saves in the first period to keep his team within striking distance. Stopped 25 of 28 shots.

MJW#4 Woo, Jett (2018) – In his first game back after being injured for the second time this season, Woo was eased into the lineup. He did not get any time on the power play or penalty kill minutes. You could definitely see the rust in his game, which was understandable. Passes just weren't crisp and decisions weren't made as fast as he is capable off. One thing that was impressive and much needed in the Warrior lineup was his physical play and grit. Woo did not back down from anyone in the Pats lineup. Used his body very well to create separation and maintain the puck.

MJW#8 Almeida, Justin (2018) – Almeida continues to impress. Scored the final goal for the Warriors on the power play with only seconds left in the game. However, the goal was a non- factor because it was 5-2 Regina at that point. Justin may have been the fastest player on the ice tonight. He gave the Pats defense problems down low all night. He makes one spin move and he was gone. Needed to be better in the faceoff circle. First power play and second penalty kill unit.

MJW#15 Peckford, Ryan (2018) – Tough night for Ryan, It was a struggle for himself and the entire second line for Moose Jaw to create offense with Brayden Burke out of the lineup. Ryan did demonstrate some great stick handling on the rush putting the puck in the feet of the Pats defender and making multiple moves to create a scoring chance. Would have like to see him shoot the puck more. Second power play unit.

Kootenay Ice at Lethbridge Hurricanes, February 18th, 2018

LET #2 RD Calen Addison (2018) – Confident passes in his own end, threaded a nice backhander that allowed for a clean transitional zone exit, got overwhelmed down-low on back to back plays resulting in turnovers, improper gap spacing during a couple of rush attempt by the ICE, good neutral zone rush where he showed poise and skill before entering the offensive-blueline, ejected from the game after delivering what looked to be a clean and solid hit.

LET #10 LW Yegor Zudilov (2018) – Didn't compete hard enough to strip the puck off an opponent who was unable to detect him in his own end, opportunistic rush that almost resulted in a scoring chance, decent speed on the play, demonstrated the ability to change his angle on his release as he cut across the high-slot, the shot lacked accuracy and power though, showed he can generate a chance by himself though.

LET #18 RC Keltie Jeri-Leon (2018) – Got an off-angle shot on net, it was relatively harmless, had some energy out there and was notable in spurts on the forecheck.

LET #24 RC Dylan Cozens (2019) - Used his frame to angle himself properly to absorb a hit while moving the puck behind the goal-line, showed awareness without the puck after attempting to intercept a pass that he recognized in advance of the play, used on the penalty-kill where he had two solid defensive-plays that helped minimized two high-percentage attempts, played with good pace away from the puck, showed plus hand-eye coordination by batting a puck down out of mid air resulting in an important clear, on the same shift had impressive edge work as he spun off pressure to maintain possession at the line.

KTN #30 G Duncan McGovern (2018) – Didn't show enough patience and bit on a fake which dropped him into his butterfly too quickly, though the butterfly transition was a plus, active communicator with his defenseman, looked to handle the puck often though this led to an unforced turnover and rush attempt on him, great positional save that showed patience after a Lethbridge forward was left alone in-front of the net, had good rebound control in the opening frame, had some difficulties with screened shots today which led to two lack lustre goals, however he displayed good rebound control and competed in the net, stopping a couple of difficult point-blank attempts.

KTN #27 LC Bradley Ginnell (2018) – Good positioning while going towards the net, was looking to tip it but the pass never got through, got caught with his head down while cutting across the high-slot, he returned to the game showing some toughness but wasn't overly involved in the play.

KTN #17 LW/RW Gillian Kohler (2018) – Used on the powerplay, had a nice interception in his own-end, had a decent chance at the side of the net but reach wasn't there to receive the pass.

KTN #12 LC Cole Muir (2018) – Slow in recognizing transitional play after a turn over, nice pass from behind the net leading to a scoring chance in the first, good disruptive hit on the forecheck and had a quick backhand pass which allowed a clean exit, attacked the net area when looking for a rebound.

KTN #19 LW Peyton Krebs (2019) – Helped support his defenseman down below the net after they got hemmed in their own end for an extended period of time, used along the half-wall on the powerplay where he showed quick-puck distribution, was the driver of the powerplay, despite another solid effort he missed an assignment in-front of the net on the penalty-kill and his team paid the price, didn't recognize that his defenseman was looking for him to open himself for a back-door pass on a couple of occasions, good controlled offensive-blueline entries using his skill and skating ability.

Final Score: Lethbridge Hurricanes: 4 – Kootenay Ice: 1

Mississauga Steelheads at Barrie Colts, February 22nd, 2018

BAR #2 D Tucker, Tyler (2018) – Tucker's decision making was questionable in this game. He seemed a little too focused on landing a big hit and took himself out of the play on a couple occasions to try and land one while defending off the rush. This resulted in 3-on-2's turning into 2-on-1's and some easier opportunities for Mississauga. He did skate well and that helped him maintain good gaps in the neutral zone and force dump-ins. He was also quick to jump into the rush and provide an extra layer of offense while trailing.

BAR #21 RW Svechnikov, Andrei (2018) – Svechnikov was a man amongst boys in this game. He fought through contact and stick checks all night and they didn't seem to slow him down in the slightest. He showed good vision coming from behind the net and hitting activating defensemen on the tape. He was effective in the cycle game using his size to protect the puck and sharp cuts to lose defenders that were draped on him. He also was fully engaged physically and routinely buried opposing puck carriers with ease. Svechnikov was a handful around the net and showed the ability to make plays in tight with limited space. He showed off his NHL release on numerous occasions getting off a powerful one-timers while also beating a challenging goaltender with a perfectly placed snapshot off the post and in. Svechnikov was also responsible without the puck. He caused turnovers with powerful stick checks and forced a bad pass on an odd-man rush by hustling back and applying pressure.

BAR #61 LW Suzuki, Ryan (2019) – Suzuki consistently made smart decisions with the puck on his stick. He showed good patience waiting an extra second for lanes to open up and he also used the boards to his advantage to get the puck to teammates. Despite his small stature, he did a nice job of winning puck battles by staying on the outside and reaching in from a distance. He showed his finishing ability still needs work as he missed the net entirely on some excellent opportunities from in the slot area.

BAR #72 Allensen, Nathan (2019) – Allensen played a really solid two-way game. He was aggressive attacking puck carriers at the line. He liked to challenge, force turnovers, and immediately rush the puck up ice with numbers. He made a good first pass and sprung Jason Willms on a breakaway with an excellent multi-zone outlet right on the tape.

MISS #7 LW Little, Michael (2018) – Little had a great opportunity playing alongside Tippett and Foget on the top line and he took advantage of it. He played a simple, north-south game. He got in on the forecheck and won battles to recover pucks for the skill guys. He lived around the net and showed good effort battling to create space for himself. He was rewarded with a couple garbage goals on the doorstep. While he had three points, you could see his offensive game is limited. He missed a few pretty easy passes in the neutral zone and also bobbled the puck, and lost it entirely, unforced while carrying it up ice.

MISS #91 C McLeod, Ryan (2018) – McLeod played a real strong two way game. He was dynamic with the puck on his stick and was a one-man zone exit and entry. He used his high-end speed to blow by defenders and also showed the ability to stick handle around and elude players trying to pressure him. In the offensive zone, he used a quick burst to beat the goaltender to the other side of the net and bury one on a wraparound. He also showed the ability to adapt on the fly as he accepted a pass in his feet at full speed and then put his stick through his legs to get a good shot off. Everything he did was with great pace. Defensively, he was relentless after the puck. He forced a turnover by closing quickly on the forecheck and pickpocketing the puck before an outlet could be made. He was always back to help out defensively and was on his man like a shadow. He showed good instincts sniffing out danger and preventing chances before they came about and he collected a couple big rebounds before Barrie players were able to pounce on them.

Final Score: Mississauga Steelheads: 7 – Barrie Colts: 4

Seattle Thunderbirds at Kelowna Rockets, February 23rd, 2018

KEL #26 LW – Kindree, Liam (2018) – Appears fully up to speed after a long absence and needing a few games regaining his timing and get back into game shape. Given an opportunity on the powerplay to work from the half board, was taking passes and using his feet effectively to dart toward middle ice and either look for a shot or move the puck quickly across the ice. Ended up with a primary assist on the powerplay by darting in feeding and opened defending at the point, good move to look off the defender and buy a split second of time.

KEL #6 RD – Korczak, Kaeden (2019) – A calm and collected game he looks very poised in most viewings but tonight he was a really steady rock on the back end and ended up chipping in with a goal on the powerplay. In recent viewings he's been the single defender on the second powerplay unit and does a good job of moving pucks quickly and making intelligent decisions but more recently he's been utilizing his laterally movement more and working east/west along the line. He took a pass and made a quick move to just enough to get it past a shot blockers and beat the goalie clean through a little bit of traffic. Icetime and defensive situation play continues to increase and other than losing his man and giving up inside position on the opening goal of the game his positioning was really steady.

SEA #22 LW – Hamaliuk, Dillon (2019) – Easily one of Seattle's best players in this game as he finished with a goal and 2 assists, on his goal he snuck behind the defense and tapped a puck in the open net after his linemate wrapped around the net and fed the puck through the crease, he did a good job of watching the play develop and timing his net drive to get open. Both his set ups were secondary assists his one on the opening goal was the best, he drew in a defender and made a nice button hook play to feed the point for a shot that was tipped in. Hamaliuk did a good job of imposing his will on others, he's strong and uses his strength well to hold position and knock opponents off pucks; players seem to bounce off him as he absorbs hits really well. Skating needs some work still but he still managed to get in a lay hits on the forecheck as the F1 into the play but he did seem to slow down when he carried puck for more than a few strides. Had no problem jumping in scrums and sticking up for his teammates.

SEA #24 LD – Lee, Jake (2018) – Lots of ice-time for the rookie defender who's light on his feet and quick with his edge work, his pivots are very smooth and his ability to move with the puck is a strong especially when he was coming out of the zone. Appeared stronger and did a good job of buying time by pivoting players on to his back and using his reach to keep pucks away; good puck protector. Had a few miscues with the puck one which he turned it over behind the net that led to a goal, needed to be a little better with the puck and at times move it up the ice quicker.

Final Score: Kelowna Rockets: 5 – Seattle Thunderbirds: 4

Regina Pats at Saskatoon Blades, February 23, 2018

Blades –

SAS #73 G Maier, Nolan (2019) – came up big at the start of the game where he looked focused and ready to play after cutting off his angels aggressively and stopping two scoring chances, this helped decrease the Pats initial momentum to start the game. Had an aggressive butterfly save on Steel that he controlled the rebound on in the first-half of the second, his transitional butterfly was looking quick on the save. Didn't have much chance on the first goal he let in on the powerplay, showed plus extension on the save attempt as he kicked out the pad on blocker but couldn't get there in time. Had a difficult third period where he let in 5 goals but all of them were high-percentage chances. Despite blowing a big lead and letting in 6 goals, Maier flashed some potential today

SAS #8 RD Bafaro, Seth (2018) – had a transitional rush in the neutral zone where he showed some elusiveness before making a smart chip pass off the boards, showed that he was up to the task against Steel in a one-on-one situation where he had good spacing before using his stick to deflect the Pats shooting attempt, taking away a scoring chance, scored off a seeing-eye shot at the point after he recognized that the Pats goalie was screened, fantastic end-to-end rush where he generated a lot of speed before making a pass at the top of the left circle that was labelled for a teammate who just missed it near the goal-line. In the third, he had a shot from the point that was deflected in my Wouters, his shots got through heavy traffic today, he showed some transitional ability, but he had some difficulty against larger opponents in his own-end on the forecheck

SAS #17 LC Florchuk, Eric (2018) – had a good game while showing chemistry with Dach and Farren. Both Dach and Florchuk are pass first players which led well to a good amount of cycling between the two of them, hemming the Pats top-lines in their own end for much of the opening frame, he scored in the slot with a quick wrist-shot that went short-side after receiving a feed from Dach

SAS #27 RC Michael Farren (2018) – played with a lot of energy and displayed an active motor that complimented a line featuring Dach and Florchuk which was that the best line on the Blades, nice stop-up at the line during a powerplay in the third that helped generate a good scoring chance that went off the bar, made a nice move in the neutral zone which helped evade a check and helped his team enter the offensive-end

SAS #44 RC/LW Wouters, Chase (2018) – centered the top-line to start the game, had a well-timed fake at the left circle which re-opened his passing lanes on the powerplay, he fed a pass down near the goal-line that almost resulted in a scoring chance, later in the opening frame he drove down the left wing and showed a combination of plus edges and vision, threading a pass across the slot, great block in the high-slot on the penalty-kill to start the second, on the same kill he had a great forecheck which led to a scoring chance after winning a board battle and passing it back to the point to kill extra time, tipped home Bafero's point shot in the slot, he was good today, setting up his teammates and playing his heavy and fast paced style of game

SAS #77 RC Dach, Kirby (2019) – scored the opening goal for the Blades after driving towards the front of the net and firing a quick wrist-shot that went under Wasserman's pad, he showed an excellent cycle game, using his frame to absorb contact and showed a high-degree of skill that allowed him to control possession for extended time, had a nice pass to Florchuk for the third goal of the game

Pats –

REG #35 G Jacob Wasserman (2018) – let in the first goal of the game on the first shot of the game but came up big on the 5-on-3 powerplay after moving laterally through the crease and absorbing a one-timer in his butterfly. Takes up an enormous amount of the net in his reverse V-H and showed fluid movement when pushing off when in his butterfly. Had a difficult opening period after allowing 3 goals, the second shot needed to be stopped but he couldn't track it through bodies, though the third was a well-placed shot in a prime scoring area. Had a great save in the first half of the second where he pushed out of his reverse-VH and took the top part of the net away with his shoulder on a hard shot from the slot area, came out to play the puck but threw a cross crease pass directly to Ramsay for an empty netter. Made up for the earlier misplay by having a tremendous sequence early in the third by making a butterfly save then he pushed over and fully extended taking the bottom of the net away resulting in a great rebound save, he then saved his best for last as he scrambled back into the net and pushed across the crease, taking away the net with his left-pad and glove-hand, it was the best save of the game and was the momentum shifter for the Pats to mount their impressive comeback win

REG #24 LC Koby Morrisseau (2019) – scored the 2nd Pats goal after rushing down the ice during a transitional breakout and putting himself in good position to receive a pass from Oskanen, he needed little time to bury it over the Blades netminder who was sprawled out while trying to get across the crease

REG #29 F Logan Nijhoff (2019) – had a good sequence midway though the first where he collected a puck below the goal-line and found room along the point to get a seeing-eye shot through traffic, helped support his team in the defensive-end during a backcheck where he grabbed a loose puck and helped transition it up the ice

REG #20 LW/RW Emil Oskanen (2018+) – Oskanen used his size and length to create a take-away in the neutral zone before making a clean zone-entry, made a good body fake angling himself towards the net before turning his hips and making a nice pass across the slot area resulting in the second goal of the game

Final Score 7-5 Pats

Regina Pats at Moose Jaw Warriors, February 24th, 2018

REG#20 Oksanen, Emil (2018) – Emil struggled to find the offensive side of him game, even against the short handed defense of Moose Jaw. Had some turnovers exiting his own zone. He did not stand out in any aspect throughout the game. Second power play unit.

REG#33 Paddock, Max (2018) – Max had another strong game in the absence of Kubic. The first goal I feel he should have stopped. Wrist shot from the half wall and was beaten five hole. However, Paddock gave the Pats an opportunity to come back making some big saves in the third period. Stopped 23 of 26 shots.

MJW#4 Woo, Jett (2018) – Jett was out of the lineup serving the second game of a three game suspension.

MJW#8 Almeida, Justin (2018) – Scored his 34th of the season on the power play. He snuck behind the Pats D and received a great pass from Kale Clague sending him on a partial break. He beat the defender and went backhand top shelf. Excellent speed entering the offensive zone forced the defense to be on their heels all night. Played big minutes in all situations.

MJW#15 Peckford, Ryan (2018) – Peckford played on the third line tonight. His line mates and him created problems for the Pats in the offensive zone all night. His fore-check and pressure caused multiple turnovers and lead to controlled cycle play and zone time. They didn't fine the score sheet but were arguably the top line for Moose Jaw. Peckford played second unit power play.

Luela HF vs. Mora IK, March 1st, 2018

LHF #3 RHD Lundkvist, Nils (2018) - Moves well in the defensive zone, using his skating and smart passes to escape pressure. Lundkvist displayed one of his best attributes in this game - the breakout pass. 9 out of 10 times, the pass was tape to tape and play moved immediately to the neutral zone. On one occasion, a nice breakout pass was followed up by a breakaway pass that resulted in the second Lulea goal by penalty shot. Lundkvist threw a big open ice hit which allowed a teammate to strip the puck. He joined the rush and guided the puck all the way to the goal line and passed back toward the crease, but Lulea players were too far away. He joined a rush in the first period but left his partner hanging for a 2-on-1, forcing the goalie to make a great save. The rebound bounced over a stick or it would've been a wide open cage. Any other time he joined the rush, there was a forward back to cover him.

LHF #10 RW Emanuelsson, Einar (2018*) - Emanuelsson displayed a few puck skills today, creatively moving the puck around Mora defender Gormley with a combination of puck skill and body position. On the same play he also lost the puck behind the net. His strongest asset appears to be a very smooth skating style, he moves very well around the ice.

LHF #37 C Lundestrom, Isac (2018) - Solid work in the defensive zone throughout the game, but was outmatched physically in the first period. He was knocked off the puck a few times while trying to protect it. When helping out defensively, he showed clean breakout passes. Lundestrom created a turnover deep in the defensive zone in the third period, dangerously dangled around a forechecker right beside the net and got the puck up the ice; this puck possession led to Lulea's second goal a few seconds later. He possesses a decent top speed, which he used once in this game to blow by both Mora defenders, coming close to setting up a goal.

LHF #39 LHD Sjalin, Pontus (MIN 2014) - Sjalin played a fairly quiet game, which suited the team just fine in a 3-0 win. He read a developing play well in the first period, joining the rush early and catching Mora sleeping. Stood up a couple Mora forwards at the defending blue line, which turned the puck over and play went right back into the offensive zone.

LHF #96 LW Kovacs, Robin (NYR 2015) - Was strong in front of the net on the power play, not afraid to push or shove before and after the whistle. He also showed off a few creative passes early in the game. Kovacs held onto the puck way too long in the defensive zone in the first period while being hounded by a Mora player instead of utilizing an easy pass back to Lundkvist. He skated to the boards and tried to get the puck to Lundkvist way too late, and it would have been a brutal giveaway had the puck not skipped. Attempted one cross-ice pass to a teammate the was well behind.

MIK #97 C Kase, David (PHI 2015) - Kase was mostly noticeable on the power play. Quick passing on the power play opened up a lane for a cross-ice pass back to him, but even with plenty of time to load up a shot, he directed it right into the goalie's crest. Outside of his power play time, I did not see anything notable from Kase.

Hudson vs Fond du Lac Springs, March 1st, 2018

HUD #20 LD Halverson, Jordon (2018) –Halverson has good size and strength and showed flashes of playing a reliable puck moving game from the back end. Where he got into trouble is when he tried to do too much in key areas of the ice and committed some turnovers because of it. On one breakout sequence he passed on an opportunity to move the puck up ice, instead trying to stick handle around two players at his own blue line with no support that resulted in a breakaway that his goalie was able to bail him out on. Halverson showed physicality and compete along the walls, coming close to getting called for some roughing penalties on a couple puck battles. Halverson didn't' show a lot of dynamic puck skills but has a quick shot with good velocity from the point and did a decent job of making sure his shots got through.

Notre Dame Academy vs Verona HS, March 1st, 2018

VER #16 RW Baker, Brockton (2019) – Baker was the best player on the ice for either team in this game. He won a lot of races to loose pucks in all areas of the ice, scored 2 goals for his team, in doing so displayed good offensive instincts, getting himself into scoring areas and did a good job finding open ice. Baker doesn't have impressive size but he has explosive skating and showed his hands can keep up with his feet with the puck on his stick. Showed the ability to get the puck off his tape quickly and accurately. His older brother, Tarek Baker was a late Bloomer and is having a very successful freshman campaign and U. of Wisconsin, Brockton seems to be following a similar trend. Brockton is expected to be drafted into the USHL this spring in the Phase 2 draft.

VER #13 LW McCormick, Mason (2019) – McCormick was a physical force in this game. Mason possesses impressive size and decent skating mobility but the knock on his game is he doesn't play to his size. That was not the case in this game; he used his body well along the wall and in puck battles, was physical against the opposition and drove hard to the net both with and without the puck.

ND #20 LD Conrad, Jacob (2020) – Conrad looked to have solid edgework and a powerful skating. Not a big kid listed at 5'9" but was strong on his skates and didn't get handled in front of the net or in the corners against bigger players. Conrad moved the puck out of his own end effectively and made some good reads with some passes from the point on the Power Play that just missed connecting for goals or the goalie made terrific saves on the shot.

ND #13 RW Poshak, Brendan (2020) – Showed a high compete level and the ability to play an up-tempo game in transition. Poshak had some very good offensive zone entries and his line was difficult to handle for most of the night and had a fair share of good scoring chances. Had 1 Assist on his team's only goal early in the 3rd period. When Verona started to get some momentum, Poshak's line would come out and be able to flip the momentum regularly.

ND #6 LD Laatsch, Daniel (2020) – Laatsch did not play in this game.

Eau Claire Memorial vs West Salem HS, March 1st, 2018

WS #11 LC Gorniak, Jack (2018) – Aside from a few shifts early in the game as well as scoring a goal in the 3rd on a breakaway with the game almost out of reach, Jack was not very good in this game. Gorniak didn't use his speed very well. He tended to attempt to pullup with the puck and try to stick handle through defenders rather than gaining the edge and driving the net. He didn't make a lot of attempts to gain middle ice in the offensive zone and as a result played a very perimeter game. West Salem was overmatched depth wise in this game and it showed as Eau Claire was able to shut down Gorniak' s line and dictate the game using their depth.

ECM #32 RF Olson, Brenden (2019) – Olson dominated in this game, registering 2 goals and 2 assists in this game. Olson made plays on nearly every shift using his speed and ability to read the play and react quicker than anyone else on the ice. Showed good vision in the offensive zone, threading passes through open lanes as well as getting his stick or body in open lanes to receive passes in scoring areas.

Saskatoon Blades at Moose Jaw Warriors, March 3rd, 2018

SAS#17 Florchuk, Eric (2018) – Eric struggled to get anything going offensively all night. Tried to use his size but never created anything. I was disappointed in his game tonight. Played second power play and penalty kill units.

SAS#44 Wouters, Chase (2018) – Chase is fitting into his new leadership role great. Wearing the A, and leading by example every shift tonight. His compete level is second to none. Even though he was a minus 2, Defensively very strong. Especially in the faceoff circle and on the penalty. Blocked multiple shots. First penalty kill and power play units.

SAS#77 Dach, Kirby (2019) – I know the high-end skill is there but it wasn't on display tonight. Looked slow and fatigued at times. Was leaned on heavily to create offensive but couldn't get it done playing against Moose Jaw's top D pair. Forced passes trying to exit his zone. First power play unit.

MJW#4 Woo, Jett (2018) – Started the game very strong with a big hit to set the tone, but followed it up by throwing the puck up the middle right to a Blades player for a scoring chance. Had multiple turnovers early in the game. Finished the game very strong defensively. Used his strength and position to get the puck out his own zone. Second power play and penalty kill time.

MJW#8 Almeida, Justin (2018) – Another strong game from Justin. Had a goal and assist. Scored a on a great wrist shot from the slot. He passed up on a great scoring opportunely while on a partial breakaway. Looked for the pass when I would have liked to see him use his shot. Continued to impress on the penalty kill. Gap control and active stick in lanes. First power play and penalty kill.

MJW#15 Peckford, Ryan (2018) – Much of the same tonight from Peckford. Nothing flashy, See past reports. Second power play unit.

Spokane Chiefs at Kelowna Rockets, March 3rd, 2018

SPK #24 RD – Smith, Ty (2018) – The top pair all situation defender for Spokane who played a really high amount of time on the ice, he kept his energy level up which showed how good his level of fitness is; rarely looked tired. Had a couple early gaffs with the puck turning it over in his own zone, tried to make a reverse play behind the net and wasn't paying attention to who was behind him and back peddled under pressure and lost control of the puck however he settled down and managed the puck better the rest of the game. Smith was a high event player which is typical based on how much he played, most breakouts and powerplay movement go through him, his lateral play was on display as he was moving quite fluidly along the offensive blueline, he incredibly deceptive and was consistently getting his shots pass the high blocker and giving his teammates a change around the net. His goal was scored off the rush on a nice give and go where he dish it off darted between 2 defenders and presented his stick for a nice tip, great use of his speed here. Had a knack for making players miss on hits, he moved out of the way last minute on a few hits a couple of which were to make a play with the puck he was consistently slippery.

SPK #29 C – Zummack, Eli (2018) – Played a mobile game and is always roaming as part of the rotation, worked his way from he half wall to the net front and was rarely static in doing so, played a bit sneaky showing off his skills to find the soft coverage. Picked up a nice primary assist on a zone entry as he gain the line and started to drive the net dropping a pass back to the defender and distracted the goalie with a screen for his teammate to beat him. Skated well with the puck and had no fear to work through bodies and lead the rush through the neutral zone, his puck skills are shifty and he moves it well around defending sticks. He was digging well along the boards below the goal line and did a good job physically against bigger players, he's a great part of the Spokane penalty kill getting into lanes to block shots, used his speed to close quickly on shooters and played really aggressive to the points.

SPK #18 LD – Kral, Filip (2018) – Playing smart throughout this game made several quick efficient outlet passes that looked routine for him, the played calms down as soon as he gather pucks in his own zone. Knows his move before he gathered the puck and turned the play up ice in an impressive manner. Excellent passing accuracy in all situations, working the point on the second powerplay unit he keys in as set man mostly feed the forwards down low, didn't see him send a single pass off the mark in this viewing and showed a strong ability to move laterally along the line to keep puck in.

KEL #26 RW – Kindree, Liam (2018) – Most puck touches he's seen in a while because to begin this game he was on the first line, looked a little off in his puck handling and had a tough time getting through the defense to the net. His speed was top notch both in top end and acceleration; he gets back up the ice quickly and paid good attention to defensive assignments. Did a good job of getting to the net without the puck and causing some goalie annoyances and screens. Was a good physical presence and through a couple really strong hits against the boards, eventually shifted lower down the lineup to more of that checking role instead of his original scoring opportunity.

KEL #1 G – Porter, James (2018) – Up and down game for Porter as he let in 3 goals on 27 shots but made a few excellent saves, showed off his quick glove hand and snapped a few pucks quickly out of the air. Looked calm and stayed in good position most of the night, was compact and not flailing as he sometimes does. Made a couple of saves and showed some confidence to direct shots to the corner or to a defender on purpose. Let in one bad goal (something he does often in viewings) from well below the circles on a poor angle, was caught cheating to the middle and opened up off the post.

KEL #6 RD – Korczak, Kaeden (2019) – Not many stand out plays for him tonight but he was shifted up to the to pairing with Foote, calmed his game down and was fading back each time his partner pinched to protected the defensive end exhibiting a great example of his hockey IQ. Started in all zones and played a ton of minutes, its very clear the coaching staff appreciate his game lately and adding more and more responsibility to his game.

Final Score: Spokane Chiefs: 4 – Kelowna Rockets: 2

Eau Claire Memorial vs Hudson, March 4th, 2018

HUD #20 LD Halverson, Jordon (2018) –Halverson was solid in all areas of his game. He defended well all over the ice, showed an active stick, sound stick position and had some good shot blocks on the Penalty Kill. Halverson showed good creativity with the puck in the offensive end, executing a nice slap pass to a teammate at the side of the net that nearly connected for a goal. Made a quick move to catch the puck off the glass keep in the puck in the zone in which his team eventually scored on the play.

HUD #11 LC Hanson, Peyton (2020) –Showed good size and explosive skating ability. Showed good offensive instincts, was able to be on and around the puck a ton in this game. Hanson was sound in the faceoff circle, winning a number of draws cleanly. Showed good skill and strength to stickhandle between two defenders as he entered the offensive zone and drove the net, resulting in his team scoring on a delayed penalty call. Showed a plus backhand shot from the slot. Hanson showed good effort on the back check, tying up the opponents stick and negating a scoring chance on one sequence. Hanson is a late 01' Birth date so it will be interested to see where he goes in the Phase 2 USHL Draft after coming off a solid sophomore campaign for Hudson.

Halifax Mooseheads vs Rimouski Océanic, March 6th, 2018

HFX #11 LW Zadina, Filip (2018): Strong game for Zadina, who finished the game with 3 points. He set the tone early on, with a goal on his first shift. He's a smart player, and I like how he's quick to move pucks to his teammate on the ice. He has decent speed, but always has a small burst that he will use to create quick separation when he sees an opportunity for himself in the offensive zone. He worked hard away from the puck, and his puck-protection was solid as well.

HFX #14 LD McIsaac, Jared (2018): Very impressed with McIsaac's ability to skate pucks out of trouble tonight. His footwork and strides are impressive, and he didn't shy away to jump in the play. I saw him skate the puck out of his zone often tonight. His passing game was decent; his passes are crisp but lacked a bit accuracy. On the point in the offensive zone, he had some issues in terms of getting his shot blocked, as Rimouski did a good job blocking shots all night.

HFX #19 C Groulx, Benoit-Olivier (2018): Had a tough time staying out of the penalty box tonight, with 4 minor penalties. He worked hard at both ends of the ice; I liked his effort on the backcheck on a couple of sequences.

Offensively, it was a quiet night. There were some chances near the net. After getting out of the penalty box after his 4 penalties, he made a nice short pass to Durandeau, who scored on the breakaway. However, his skating didn't stand out and his offensive skills didn't stand out either.

HFX #20 RD Barron, Justin (2020): The youngest player on the Mooseheads was playing with some great poise tonight; Barron saw some significant ice time and was a regular on the power play. In the first period, he established more of his shutdown role, playing really well twice one-on-one while facing Alexis Lafrenière. In the 2nd period, he started making more plays with the puck and moving his feet more in the offensive zone. He made some good passes and showed good vision in the offensive zone.

HFX #50 C/W Lavoie, Raphaël (2019): Lavoie used his long reach well tonight, manoeuvring with the puck in the offensive zone. His puck-protection was good; once again, he used his size and reach to his advantage. In one rush, I saw him keep possession of the puck with one hand on his stick to control the puck while using his other arm to push away defenders coming to challenge him, which was a really special play. Skating is still a work-in-progress with him, but he has made some good strides this year in that department. Today, he played on the wing with Groulx and Fortier.

HFX #67 LW Parent, Xavier (2019): Parent started the game with a great first shift, making a high-IQ play: a no-look pass from behind the net on his backhand to set up Zadina for the 1st goal of the game. Parent had a good first period where he showed a lot of energy and hustle. He disappeared a bit in the 2nd period, but came back with a strong 3rd period. His compete level was good; he went to the net and was a bit of an agitator at times.

HFX #1 G Gravel, Alexis (2018): Gravel was moving well from post to post. His footwork was fluid in his crease. He fought the puck a lot in this game, seeming to stabilize his rebound-control in the 3rd period but for the first two periods, it was a struggle. He had a tendency to be overly aggressive with his pokecheck, also finding himself out of position when he would miss, and when the play would go behind the net, he would appear lost in his crease. Credit to him for fighting and finding his game in the 3rd period.

RIM #11 LW Lafrenière, Alexis (2020): Halifax did a great job containing him in this game at 5-on-5. He had 2-3 scoring chances in this game at best. He was overmatched physically in some battles along the boards, but was quick to push the puck to his teammates with his long reach instead of losing the battle completely. He thinks the game really well; even in games such as this one where he didn't shine, he made some smart little plays. His skating is decent, but he has worked hard to keep improving his bursts of speed - it showed in a couple of sequences today.

RIM #17 LW Zavgordoniy, Dmitry (2018): Not a good viewing for Zavgorodniy, who started the game playing too soft and avoiding hits. He didn't create much offense today, and was not really a factor in the game. His speed for his size is not good enough; he lacks some good explosiveness in his stride.

RIM #92 G Ellis, Colten (2019): In the first half of the first period, he was fighting the puck hard, but eventually found his game and was solid the rest of the time. His rebound-control was good, as he didn't give up many of them and was, as always, very calm and poised in his net. Rimouski lost the game, but it was not his fault, and he was better than Gravel tonight.

Mankato East Cougars vs Mahtomedi Zephyrs, March 7th, 2018

MAH #9 LW Dulak, Nikolai (2020) – Despite being a tad undersized, Dulak played a heavy, up tempo style of play in this game. Showed good compete and willingness to go to the hard areas and use physicality to win puck battles. Showed good offensive instincts in finding the open areas of the ice in the offensive zone and get to the scoring areas. Showed good strength on his skates in making a power move down the slot to the net to help create his teams 4th goal by drawing defenders to him. Dulak registered 2 assists in this game and was impressive in all areas.

ME #22 LW Leffrig, Layten (2020) – Liffrig is a big body, listed at 6'2" and used his size extremely well both with the puck and in puck battles being physical and moving opponents off pucks. Leffrig played a solid 200 foot game, staying on the right side of pucks in his own zone. Leffrig didn't register any points in this game but was able to dominate for stretches with the puck and showed good hands and footwork in traffic, able to stick handle and protect the puck and get it to scoring areas. With his line pressing to take the lead late in the 3rd period and controlling possession in the offensive zone, Leffrig took a bad 5 minute checking from behind major penalty that Mahtomedi scored twice on and Mankato East lost 4-2.

Monticello Moose vs Hermantown Hawks, March 7th, 2018

HMN #27 RW Biondi, Blake (2020) – The UMD commit dominated this game from start to finish and was in on all 4 Hermantown goals, registering 3 goals and an Assist. Biondi showed excellent scoring touch, scoring three goals in different ways. His first goal, showing good compete in front and was able to out muscle defender for position and get his stick on a loose puck and jam the puck past the goalie. On his 2nd goal he showed the ability to get the puck off his stick quickly as a loose puck found his tape in front and Biondi fired a quick shot into the top shelf and his 3rd on a nice deflection on a shot from the point. Biondi didn't display a real explosive skating stride or elite top speed but didn't have any issue getting to loose pucks or keeping up with the pace. Biondi looked to have the skills and hockey sense to be a high pick in this spring's USHL Phase 1 Draft.

Vancouver Giants at Kelowna Rockets, March 7th, 2018

VAN #13 C – Popowich, Tyler (2018) - Playing the roles of 3rd line center as more of a checker in what would be one of the deeper Vancouver lineups viewed this season. Taking a lot of defensive zone draws and using his big body on the board to create an effective cycle game, but his defensive positioning is a little suspect and he kept trying to cheat up to the blueline. Picked a primary assist after grabbing a puck along the board and making a nice look pass through a double team. Took a couple bad penalties this game and seemingly went from being effective in the first period to becoming a non-factor the rest of the game.

VAN #41 RD – Kannok-Leipert, Alex (2018) – Started with a minimal role in this game however ended up getting a little more icetime toward the latter stages of the game, getting a quite a few defensive zone starts and generating a few shots on goal. Scored a nice goal off the rush, used his speed to join the forward group driving right down the middle of the ice and burying a rebound off a shot that was kicked back into the slot; a great show of his speed and willingness to join the attack. As pre usual Kannok-Leipert is great at battling in front of the net and was doing a great job tying up sticks and making it difficult for forward to tip pucks or pounce on second chance opportunities.

VAN #30 G – Tendeck, David (2018) – Played solid throughout this game giving up only 3 goals on a flurry of shots in what was a high tempo game, two of which were on the powerplay and one was a 5 on 3 and the other was an unlucky bounce off the glass that went up in the air and off his back. He looked big tonight and tracked the puck well, he was letting a few rebounds out but did a good job stopping secondary chances. Over committed on a few shots and slid out of position a little far past the post but was lucky not to give anything on these plays.

VAN #44 LD – Byram, Bowen (2019) – Aggressive decision making tonight with some timely pinches and a knack for driving the net looking to create offense. Played point man on the second powerplay unit using his quick decision making and accurate passing ability to take command of his unit and keep the puck moving forcing penalty killers to adjust frequently. Really strong player on zone exits and in the transition game, mixed his breakouts up between quick passes and using his feet well, has no issue grabbing the puck and pushing the play up ice and doing so impressively a couple times in this game. Overall a strong possession game (especially in 3 on 3 overtime) and defensively he closed quickly when attackers entered the zone on his side always making sure to finish those plays physically.

KEL #1 G – Porter, James (2018) – Flexibility was on display in this game, showed a great ability to stretch the full length of the net quickly and cover the entire lower part of the net. Made a couple great second chance saves but they were a product of him giving up a few too many dangerous rebounds. Made one really impressive glove save, darted toward the top of the crease to cut down an open shooter in the slot and snapped it out of the air with impressive quickness and had a second aggressive save off the shaft of his stick. Would have like to see him save the overtime winner, had a clean look at it and got a piece of it but it fluttered over him, squeezed his body and looked in an awkward position.

KEL #6 – Korczak, Kaeden (2019) – Looked really mobile on the blueline tonight working the line both forward and reverse to create space for plays. Stepped into the zone a couple times to draw in defenders and with pass the puck off or creating a shot on net for himself, jumped into the rush a little more often that usual looking for a scoring play. Games continues to grow, did turn a couple of pucks over in his own end one especially poor play trying to exit the zone with a pass up the wall that immediately was fed to the slot for a scoring chance; normally would look a little tentative after his mistakes but kept trying to make plays.

Final Score: Vancouver Giants: 4 – Kelowna Rockets: 3 – OT

Lakeville North Panthers vs Edina Hornets, March 8th, 2018

ED #22 L/RW Jungles, Jett (2018) – 2 Goals and 2 assists in this game and his line was dominating the entire game. Jungles displayed high end puck skills in this game. Jungles finished 2 setups from Sammy Walker for his 2 goals and executed an excellent one-touch pass through the slot to the backdoor to setup and tap in goal. Jungles showed the ability to visualize passing lanes and thread passes through tight seams to teammates and stretch out the offensive zone on a lot of offensive zone possessions.

ED #17 LD Brinkman, Ben (2019) – Even with all the talent on display on the Edina squad in this game, Brinkman was the best player on the ice on almost every shift. Brinkman made a couple excellent defensive plays against the rush using excellent body and stick position to strip the player of the puck and then had great explosiveness to turn and get separation from fore-checkers and move the play up ice. Showed the ability to rush the puck up ice and good skill with the puck to navigate through the neutral zone and have clean offensive zone entries. Brinkman displays a low, heavy shot from the point that he gets off his tape quickly. Did a good job finding a lane and threading a pass down to the backdoor for an easy goal on the Power Play. Brinkman was able to control the game with the puck on his stick and showed all the makings of a high end prospect for the 2019 NHL Draft.

ED #20 RD Vorlicky, Mike (2018) –Vorlicky played a reliable defensive game from the back end. Showed good straight line speed to come off the bench in a bad change to get back and break up a partial breakaway for Lakeville. Displayed some good puck skills on some rushes up the ice and made sound decisions with the puck in some tight areas in his own zone. Used his body well on puck retrievals against on coming forwards to slow their progress and gain position on the fore-checker without drawing a penalty. Made things difficult for opposing forwards in front of his net. Defended his goaltender and cleared the crease before and after whistles.

ED #23 LW Koumontzis, Demetrios (2018) – Koumontzis played the role of work horse for his line in this game. Despite not being the biggest player, Koumontzis displayed a strong base and was able to win possession for his team. Koumontzis was first to be in on the fore-check for most of the night and was able to throw some big hits and create some turnovers as a result. Displayed good poise with the puck down low and was able to find the open man after gaining possession. Koumontzis showed decent agility and footwork and his strong on his skates, however his straight line skating and explosiveness need to improve in order to make as big of an impact at the upper levels going forward.

ED #2 RD Boltmann, Jake (2020) – Played a pretty physical stay at home style in this game and supported his d-partner well. Boltmann had a nice finish along the wall against the player, using good stick and body position to force the player to the outside and finish the check along the wall and turn the puck up ice.

LVN #25 RC Griffin, Shane (2019) – While his team was pretty overwhelmed for most of the night, Griffin showed good compete until the end of the game. Scored a beautiful goal in the 2nd period by showing good jump in the neutral zone with the puck, going wide on the Edina Defender and getting a quick shot off and beating the goalie on the short side. Giffin has good size and showed flashes of good puck possession skills down low but just didn't have enough around him to create much for scoring chances. Griffin is undrafted to the USHL as of now and Victoria drafted him in 2016 I the 8th Round so it wouldn't be surprising to see him in the WHL next season.

St. Michael Albertville Knights vs Duluth East Greyhounds, March 8th, 2018

DE #22 RC Donovan, Ryder (2019) – Donavan was a bit snake bit in this game but still registered 2 assists and displayed his Power Forward game on a number of occasions. Donovan displayed another gear with the puck in the neutral zone and was able to get defenseman to turn early and gain the edge in a number of situations, just missing on one drive and shot to the net. Donavan was able to gain middle ice with the puck and open up space for his wingers in other areas of the slot.

DE #5 RW Worth, Garret (2018+) – Worth had a hat trick in this game and was the beneficiary of the open space his centerman Donovan was able to create. Worth scored on a great shot off the rush where he used the defender as a screen, showed good hockey sense to find a soft area at the back door where the puck popped on his tape for a tap in goal as well as deflecting a point shot on his 3rd goal of the game. Worth isn't the biggest player but he showed the willingness to compete in all areas of the ice and showed a good understanding of the offensive zone and got himself into scoring positions well. Worth is Undrafted in the USHL but coming off the season and playoffs he just had, it's hard to imagine a USHL team not taking him early on in the Phase 2 draft this spring.

DE #25 RD Lamaster, Luke (2018) –Did some good work clearing in front of his goalie, especially on the penalty kill where he was able to box out and tie up his opponent to avoid a wide open scoring chance. Lamaster showed the ability to stretch the ice both with his passing and skating but made some rushed decisions and passes with the puck when he had time to survey the ice, that resulted in icings or passes being intercepted. Showed the ability to make quick plays at the offensive blue line, either to keep pucks in the zone or make quick moves to the net. Showed good hands and footwork at the point to get around the challenging player and skate the puck down the wall.

DE #28 LF Anderson, Logan (2020) – Anderson showed the ability to get his shot off in stride as he was hit with a pass at the blue line skated in and quickly fired a shot that beat the goalie on the stick side. Anderson showed good poise and vision in the offensive end on a couple pullup plays where he was able to find teammates coming into the zone with speed. Anderson's showed decent skating mechanics in his stride but needs to get stronger and add some explosiveness as he was beat to some loose pucks despite having a stride or two advantage.

Hill Murray School Pioneers vs Minnetonka Skippers, March 8th, 2018

HM #9 LC Helgeson, Ben (2018) – Helgeson wasn't noticeable for much of the beginning of this game as his team spent a lot of the first period on their heels. Has good size and displayed good skating explosiveness off the jump but made a few risky plays with the puck in an effort to trying to turn the tide that resulted in turnovers and opportunities going the other way. Has good velocity on his release and got some quick shots off in traffic later in the game. Passed up a side door jam play to attempt to feed a teammate across the crease at the back door that didn't connect.

HM #19 Oberle, Brett (2019) – Displayed some elusiveness with the puck and made some solid plays when under pressure to exit the zone but had a couple defensive lapses in his own end where he failed to clear or tie up his man in front.

HM #11 RF Pierre, Nick (2021) – His young age and inexperience showed a bit in this game as he struggled with the speed and having limited time and space. Pierre had a good shift in the 2nd period on the fore-check where he showed his speed to pressure the defenseman and force a turnover that resulted in some offensive zone time and a scoring chance for his team. Pierre showed offensive instincts on his team's first goal to drive hard to the net and draw defender to him that created time and space for teammate to come down from the point and score.

MIN #8 RC Loheit, Luke (2018) – Loheit showed good compete level all over the ice, especially on the Penalty kill where he was effective at challenging plays without losing position and blocking shots as well as winning draws in his own end. Scored a Power Play goal in the 1st by out muscle the Hill Murray defenseman in front of the net and get his stick available for a pass from below the goal line that he was able to get past the goaltender. Wasn't a flashy game for Loheit but he did a lot of the little things you would expect from an older player to help his team win.

MIN #2 LD Docter, Grant (2019) – Docter was a key factor in the result of this game. His skating agility and puck skills allowed him to control the pace of the game. Grant had a number of crisp outlets where he was able to find his teammates with speed and gain zones using his skating ability. Despite only being listed at 5'11" Docter showed his strength along with wall and in front of the net, the combination of quick hands and strength allowed him to strip pucks and make clean zone exits. Docter had 3 assists in this game, one of which coming when he gathered the puck off the near boards and in one motion zipped a pass across the slot to the back door on the tape for a tap in goal. Docter looked to be a high prospect for this year's USHL Phase 2 Draft in this game.

MIN #9 RC Brink, Bobby (2019) – Brink scored 2 goals in this game, one coming shorthanded. Brink did a good job of finding open ice as well as creating space for himself in the offensive zone. Showed good 200 foot effort and good play away from the puck, tracking back into the play and picking up the late guy coming into his defensive zone. Made some high risk plays in the neutral zone and coming out of his own end that likely won't turn out as well at the next levels but got away with them in this game.

Duluth East Greyhounds vs Edina Hornets, March 9th, 2018

DE #22 RC Donovan, Ryder (2019) – Tallying two assists in this game, Donovan was able to control possession below the faceoff dots against a big a talented Edina Defensive core. He used his big frame and long reach extremely well to protect the puck along the boards and showed some elusiveness to escape from the boards and get the puck to the slot. Donovan wasn't physical in the sense of throwing big hits to knock guys off pucks but often in battles he would initiate contact just enough to gain the separation he needed to make a play. Donovan was also impressive in his 200 foot game, going up against Edina's top line; Ryder was able to neutralize the speedy Sammy Walker in this game. The goals and points may not show it but Ryder Donovan has been one of the more dominate players in this tournament through two games!

DE #25 RD Lamaster, Luke (2018) – First thing that came to mind when watching Lamaster in this game was maturity. Lamaster looked confident and calm under pressure with the puck; he showed the ability to rush the puck or join the rush up ice and picked his spots well to do so. Lamaster had good size and showed excellent footwork and defensive posture and did a good job picking his spots when to challenge plays in the neutral zone against a highly skilled and fast Edina team.

Centennial Cougars vs Minnetonka Skippers, March 9th, 2018

MIN #3 RD Luedke, Josh (2019) – Luedke is an undersized defenseman but showcased his hockey smarts and ability to affect the game at both ends of the ice. Luedke showed good effort to get back to the play the break up a 2 on 1 against and then joined the rush on the ensuing play to create an odd man rush going the other way. Josh took a few risks at the offensive blue line that were ill advised but they worked out and didn't result in chances against. Luedke had 2 goals in this game, both as a result of jumping into the play on the rush or coming down from his point position and getting available for a pass.

MIN #9 RC Brink, Bobby (2019) – Brink was dominate in this game, his ability to play at a quick pace and make quick decisions was on display all night. Brink showed the willingness to go to the hard areas and take or give a hit to make a play; on my races to loose pucks he would initiate contact to generate separation. His ability to read and anticipate the play was impressive, as a result he had a couple shorthanded opportunities, and including one early in the 3rd period that he scored on that broke the 2-2 tie. Brink showed a high motor and high compete level and was engaged throughout the game.

MIN #34 RW Lagerback, Teddy (2019) – Lagerback has a big, strong frame and was effective along the walls and in front of the opponents net. Showed high end puck skills on one play, stick handling around defender entering the offensive zone and threading a pass across the slot to Bobby Brink for a Power Play goal in the first period. Lagerback displayed a power forward, heavy style of play with good puck skills in traffic. Skating explosiveness is lacking a bit at this stage but showed quick feet and good edges and mobility.

Mississauga Steelheads at Barrie Colts, March 22nd, 2018

BAR #2 D Tucker, Tyler (2018) – Tucker played a strong defensive game. He had good gap control in the neutral zone and forced dump-ins more often than not. When Steelheads attacked him with the puck, he used a good stick to steer them wide before sealing them off with along the wall. He showed the ability to line players up while landing a couple heavy hits in open ice. His decision making for when to check could still use work, though. On one play he stepped up and missed a hit, which led to a 2-on-1 and a good chance for Owen Tippett.

BAR #61 LW Suzuki, Ryan (2019) – Suzuki's strong passing skills were on display in this game. Though he did not register a point, he did create some chances. He did a nice job of leading teammates with passes into space where they'd be in better position to attack. He also drew a penalty on a nice give-and-go play. He wasn't able to get much on his shots when the puck came to him in dangerous areas.

BAR #72 Allensen, Nathan (2019) – He was a little sloppy with the puck in this game. He looked like he had some jitters with it on his stick, particularly early on, and wasn't able to cleanly make routine outlet passes. He was worked over in the cycle a couple times and also got beat clean on an inside-out move which led to a Grade A opportunity in the slot for the Steelheads. It wasn't his best night.

MISS #1 G Ingham, Jacob (2018) – Ingham allowed a weak goal early on where it hit him directly in the arm but he was unable to get enough of it and it trickled in. He really settled in after that. He showed good movement going post-to-post to make quality stops. His rebound control was mostly good and he did a nice job of resetting and squaring up when there was a second chance opportunity available.

MISS #7 LW Little, Michael (2018) – He bobbled some pucks in the neutral zone and did not look confident making plays. It felt like he was trying to get rid of the puck as soon as possible and he forced passes that weren't there as a result. He did win some battles along the wall to get pucks to Ryan McLeod and Owen Tippett but he didn't show much offensive ability at all.

MISS #91 C McLeod, Ryan (2018) – McLeod was very dynamic with the puck on his stick. He did a lot of the heavy lifting in terms of driving play up ice. He showed great burst while flying through neutral zone and showed the stickhandling ability, and edgework, to elude challenging players with relative ease. On one rush he worked his way around two or three Colts, gained the line, and hit an open teammate driving towards the net for a great chance. He consistently closed quickly on puck carriers and forced some rushed passes. While killing a penalty a play like that led to Michael McLeod intercepting a pass and the two of them taking off and connecting on a 2-on-1 short-handed goal. McLeod taking a goalie interference penalty while driving to the net was probably the lone negative for him in terms of results but I liked to see that aggressiveness.

Final Score: Mississauga Steelheads: 6 – Barrie Colts: 2

Tri City Americans at Kelowna Rockets, March 22nd, 2018

KEL #24 C – Topping, Kyle (2018) – One of the few Kelowna players to bring their best effort tonight, able to work his way into the slot for chances and crashing the crease on what was a stingy defense in a playoff game, played relentless in his pursuit of scoring chances. Created a few odd many rushes by reading plays in the neutral zone and stepping up to intercept pass from the defense just couldn't finishes himself or have his line mates do so. Playing against a mobile and quick defense his line was able to transition pucks well through the neutral zone and gain an entry, something difficult for the rest of team on the night.

KEL #29 LW – Foote, Nolan (2019) – Fighting the puck tonight and unable to get his powerful shot off in time, when quick defenders were closing on him. At his best when he's a one-touch type of handlers and looked to be trying to hard and his team was more and more frustrated. It was the clear that Tri-Cities game plan was to put as much pressure on him as possible and force Foote into plenty of turnovers, it worked and he was visibly frustrated by the end of the game.

KEL #6 RD – Korczak, Kaeden (2019) – Looked out matched by a couple of the bigger forwards from the opposition and ended up getting hemmed into his ow zone on several occasions. Role was reduced from more recent viewings as he was allotted no powerplay time and very little ok the penalty kill. Not the type of player to usually roam for a big hit but tried to step up his physical game with mixed results, missed his timing on a few attempts and took himself out of defensive position.

TC #4 LD – Kalinichenko, Roman (2018) – Was one of the few defenders that rotated in with the big 3 on Tri-Cities backend. When he was on the ice he looked quick in all aspects of the game, keeping pace with his quick partners and even showing his ability to join the rush or transition pucks with his feet. Uses his head a lot and was constantly checking his surroundings, his speed was allowing him to cut down guys on the rush and close quickly on puck carriers. Battled hard along the boards and used his reach and body to be physical and grind down Kelowna's forwards.

Final Score: Tri-City Americans: 5 – Kelowna Rockets: 0

Final Score TC 5 KEL 0

Prince Albert Raiders at Moose Jaw Warriors, March 23rd, 2018

PA#24 Fonstad, Cole (2018) – Fonstad had an outstanding game offensively. Scored 2 amazing goals to lead Prince Albert to victory. The first he walked in over the blue line coming in two on two, then cut across the middle and snapped a wrist shot top corner. The second showed of his great hands. He came in one on one and went inside out then back in on Josh Brook, crossing him up then beating the goalie under the arm far side. First power play unit.

MJW#4 Woo, Jett (2018) – Very strong defensive play all night. Played the shut down roll against PA's top forwards. Used his strength and body position multiple times to protect the puck and skate it out of his zone. Had a great end-to-end rush to set up a scoring chance. Showed off his speed and acceleration on the back check to break up a potential breakaway.

MJW#8 Almeida, Justin (2018) – Nerves seemed to get the best of almeida tonight. Struggled to get anything going offensively. The physical play of Price Albert seemed to get him off his game. Still one of the fastest players on the ice. First power play and second penalty kill units.

MJW#15 Peckford, Ryan (2018) – Peckford saw third line minutes and was on a line with two grinders. So, it was a tough situation for Peckford to generate scoring chances since he isn't suited for that checking roll. Made some poor plays along his half wall trying to be too cute with the puck. Second power play unit.

Tri-City Americans at Kelowna Rockets, March 24th, 2018

KEL #24 C – Topping, Kyle (2018) - 3 point night for Topping and much better effort for his line in general than game 1. Helped open the scoring on the powerplay working the puck from behind the goal line to the point for a secondary assist. His goal was a great move after entering the zone making a quick pivot faking a pass back and firing a no look shot; his moved shifted the goalie and had him completely fooled. Screened his own goaltender on shot from a bad angle in a poor attempt at making at block. Was good offensively and poor defensively, missed to many attempts to stick check and was collapsing around his goalie instead of defending passing lanes and attacking puck carries.

KEL #26 RW – Kindree, Liam (2018) – Made one really impressive move when he won a puck battle for 2 opponents and slipped their check quickly darting off the wall and centering it to a open defending for an impressive assist. Defensively was out matched by the larger forwards and ended up on the ice for several goals, was losing inside position too often and allowing his man to make plays, looked completely over matched going top line on top line.

KEL #6 - RD Korczak, Kaeden (2019) – Scored a goal on end to end rush from a bit of a poor angle but the play was still strong, skated hard and dumped the puck in at the blueline and going hard after it and grabbing a bounce straight off the boards and finishing short side. Consistently the member of his defensive pair to be leading the rush up ice and joining the forwards letting his partner take more if the defensive role and stay back. Lost inside position on both goals he was on the ice for and looked over matched physically by the larger Tri-City forwards that were consistently crashing the net.

KEL #29 – LW Foote, Nolan (2019) – A 2 point night for Foote but his goal was pretty impressive, he read a clearing attempt quite well picking off the pass at the offensive blueline took a few strides in and snapped and powerful wrist shot on net showing off his high quality release, however his skating looked sloppy charging in with the puck. Did a have a good battle level and a physically presence, was aggressive with his hits and strong on his board battles, especially in the offensive zone.

TC #34 – RW Mutala, Sasha (2019) – Didn't play much in this game but was noticeable with his speed on a few of his shifts carrying the puck. Did a good job of squeezing the puck up the wall but getting to loose pucks first and either chipping it out of the zone or carrying it out before he can get checked. Made a great back check play to pick a puck clean off a forwards stick and kill a high quality scoring chance.

Final Score: Tri-City Americans: 9 – Kelowna Rockets: 7

Prince Albert Raiders at Moose Jaw Warriors, March 31st, 2018

PA#24 Fonstad, Cole (2018) – Cole continued to impress. He was arguably the best player on the ice. His calm and controlled play really stood out. Every time he carried the puck into the offensive zone with ease, and created multiple scoring chances. He did take a bad-tripping penalty in the offensive zone. First power play unit.

MJW#4 Woo, Jett (2018) – Moose Jaw's best defenseman tonight. Defensively he was strong and unmatched. He controlled the puck every time he was on the ice. Offensively he passed up on a shot opportunity that he needed to take. First penalty kill unit and some power play time.

MJW#8 Almeida, Justin (2018) – Justin had the loan goal for MJ. A nice sap shot from the middle of the slot. He was the third star of the game but I don't think he deserved it. Other than the goal he did little throughout the game. However all of Moose Jaw struggled. First power play and second penalty kill units.

MJW#15 Peckford, Ryan (2018) – Started off the game on the top line for MJ, but they didn't produce anything. He lost multiple races for pucks. Peckfords compete level wasn't at the same point as PA's. Made poor decisions along the wall with the puck which resulted in turnovers. Second power play unit.

Kingston Frontenacs at Barrie Colts, April 4th, 2018

BAR #2 D Tucker, Tyler (2018) – Tucker was very aggressive defensively. He stayed on top of puck carriers and didn't back off as Kingston forwards made their way through the neutral zone. They had very few clean entries against him as a result. Tucker was also aggressive at the opposing blue line as he regularly stepped up and used a good stick to poke the puck away and Kingston to reset with their breakouts. He wasn't shy about activating from the point if he saw an open lane to get a good shot off but he missed the net entirely on his best two or three chances. His defensive game was better than his offensive game.

BAR #14 RW Svechnikov, Andrei (2018) – He smartly used the give-and-go to create some space, and speed, for himself when Kingston defenders pressed up on him. He showed the ability to accept passes without breaking stride. His passes were crisp and on target regardless of the distance. On one play, he made a firm one-touch pass rink-wide to lead a teammate into the offensive zone with speed. When he decided to keep the puck for himself he was dangerous, as always. He was able to get a step on defenders and drive to the net to create chances in tight. Even when defenders kept up with him, he powered his way through contact and get to where he wanted to go. He only managed to tally one point but it wasn't due to a lack of created chances, be it for himself or his linemates.

BAR #61 LW Suzuki, Ryan (2019) – Suzuki played one of the best games I've seen from him all year. His passing, in particular, was exceptional. He seemingly created chances every time he touched the ice. He had passes lined up before the puck even got to him and always seemed to be a step ahead of the play. He routinely led teammates into open pockets of space in the slot area, which led to several excellent chances. Suzuki showed great vision hitting a teammate backdoor for a tap-in from the half-wall on the power play. He wasn't great at creating his own shot with the puck but he did do a good job of getting himself open without it. His one-time goal was scored that way. Though he's small in stature, he won his share of puck battles and didn't hesitate to get involved along the boards.

BAR #72 Allensen, Nathan (2019) – Allensen made some accurate passes while breaking out of the defensive zone and didn't hesitate to put his skating ability to use and rush the puck up ice if space was given to him. His play without it was sketchy at times. He misplayed a pop up and the puck got by him for a Kingston chance. He was also burned by the Fronts depth guys and took a penalty trying to get back in the play, which Kingston ended up capitalizing on.

KGN #17 RW Pringle, Justin (2018) – Pringle didn't get a ton of ice but made the most of what he did get. He was in the right place at the right time to bang in a rebound goal. He also drew a penalty on a net drive. He didn't showcase the puck skills needed to get around defenders or create his own shot but he worked hard, stuck to what he is capable of doing (playing a north-south game) and was rewarded accordingly.

Final Score: Barrie Colts: 6 – Kingston Frontenacs: 5 – OT

Acadie-Bathurst Titan vs Sherbrooke Phoenix, April 10th, 2018

AB #29 LD Ivan, Michal (2018): Solid and not flashy game from Ivan tonight. He played with Galipeau at even strength and was a regular on the PK unit. He's good one on one and was aggressive on the puck carrier.

AB #53 RD Dobson, Noah (2018): Okay game from Dobson, he got hit hard in the 3rd period but was okay after, looked like a head shot. He played on the first power play unit with Galipeau , he was not involved a lot as Galipeau was playing like the real PP QB on that unit moving pucks and taking shot on net. Very cool under pressure, good puck poise but didn't played with a lot of urgency out there. Bathurst outplayed Sherbrooke during the game and Dobson didn't need to be a difference maker in this one.

AB #71 RW Ducharme, Justin (2018): He did some good work on the PK, he used his speed well. He created couples of turnovers including one that lead to the 4-0 goal. Good puck pursuit, his skating and footwork is excellent. On the PK he has a quick stick that helped him stole pucks from opponents. He was not very noticeable at even strength and no power play time.

SHE #29 LW Poulin, Samuel (2019): In the offensive zone his shooting selection was poor, his shot was often blocked and rush some of his play selection. He played on the top line and had good ice time on both the PP and PK unit. His puck protection was good, had some good shifts holding on the puck for a long time in the offensive zone. Speed is okay.

SHE #32 RD Joncas, Alexandre (2019): He hurt his one of his leg in period 1 and looked somewhat slow after retrieving pucks after the rest of the game. Not big but he's strong and competes hard. He was pinned often deep in his zone and had some long shifts. He played on the PK unit but no PP time for him.

SHE #72 LD Bellamy, Jaxon (2019): He was slow retrieving pucks in the first period, didn't looked very confident in the first period in his own zone. He tried to play some physical game in his own zone. He looked lost in his zone in some sequences and saw limited ice time in period two and three.

CREDITS

Once again this year I'm very pleased with the work ethic from our team of people at HockeyProspect.com. I want to thank all our scouts for all their hours spent in the rinks, and also for the time spent on their computers writing reports. We also thank Kathy Kocur for her assistance with photography and translation efforts. This year I even put my 11 year old daughter to work, she helped edit the font styles for all the 2019 & 2020 player profiles. She asked me if she would be in the credits so now you know why I mentioned her.

From our long time scouts like Jerome Berube, to rookies like Brad Allen, it takes everyone to put this monster book together every year. Jerome is my right hand man and also a friend. I can't thank him enough for his time and effort.

I hope you enjoy our 2018 version of our NHL Draft Black Book

Thanks to all these hard workers:

Jerome Berube	Scott McDougall
Mike Mackley –	Andy Levangie
Justin Sproule	Dan Markewich
Russ Bitely	Anthony Lenting
Dusten Braaksma	Anton Wallsten –
Ron Berman –	Andreas Eklund
Brad Allen –	William Hogberg
Cameron MacEachern	

Kathy Kocur – Photographer, Translations, editing etc…

Alyssa Edwards -Little tasks that I hate doing

Mark Edwards

© 2018 HockeyProspect.com